Serial Film S...

1

Serial Film Stars

A Biographical Dictionary, 1912–1956

BUCK RAINEY

Volume 1

(Abbreviations; Preface;
Art Acord–E.K. Lincoln)

McFarland & Company, Inc., Publishers
Jefferson, North Carolina, and London

ALSO BY BUCK RAINEY
AND FROM MCFARLAND

The Strong Silent Type:
Over 100 Screen Cowboys, 1903–1930 (2004)

Serials and Series:
A World Filmography, 1912–1956 (1999)

Western Gunslingers in Fact and on Film:
Hollywood's Famous Lawmen and Outlaws (1997)

The Reel Cowboy:
Essays on the Myth in Movies and Literature (1996)

Sweethearts of the Sage:
Biographies and Filmographies of 258 Actresses
Appearing in Western Movies (1992)

The present work is a reprint of the illustrated case bound one volume edition of Serial Film Stars: A Biographical Dictionary, 1912–1956, *first published in 2005 by McFarland.*

Volume 1

LIBRARY OF CONGRESS CATALOGUING-IN-PUBLICATION DATA

Rainey, Buck.
Serial film stars : a biographical dictionary, 1912–1956 / Buck Rainey.
p.   cm.
Includes bibliographical references and index.

2 volume set—
ISBN 978-0-7864-7529-2
softcover : acid free paper ∞

1. Motion picture actors and actresses—United States—Biography—Dictionaries.
2. Motion picture serials—United States.   I. Title.
PN1998.2.R35   2013   791.4302'8'092273—dc22   2004022964

BRITISH LIBRARY CATALOGUING DATA ARE AVAILABLE

On the cover: Charles Middleton as Ming the Merciless in the *Flash Gordon* serials;
(upper inset) Dick Purcell slugs Ken Terrell (*Captain America*, Republic 1944); (lower
inset) Sammy Baugh cuffs Jack Ingram (*King of the Texas Rangers*, Republic 1941)

Manufactured in the United States of America

McFarland & Company, Inc., Publishers
Box 611, Jefferson, North Carolina 28640
www.mcfarlandpub.com

Contents

• Volume 1 •

v

• Volume 2 •

Abbreviations

Preface

Recently I was reading the Holy Bible in preparation for participating in a Sunday School discussion of the Book of Ecclesiastes. As I read Chapter Three, verses 1–2 ("To everything there is a season, a time for every purpose under heaven, a time to be born, and a time to die; a time to plant, and a time to pluck what is planted"), my mind got sidetracked onto motion picture serials (forgive me, Lord) and how the serial genre pretty well fulfilled that scripture.

The serial was born in 1912. *What Happened to Mary?* is credited with being the first of all screened "continued-next-week" stories. The Edison company produced it with the cooperation of *The Ladies' World*, in which the stories were published concurrently with their screening. This arrangement increased both circulation for the magazine and theater attendance. The series opened the floodgates to over 500 American serials and series spanning 44 years.

In 1914, Selig released *The Adventures of Kathlyn*, the longest photoplay that had been released up to that time. The first episode was three reels in length followed by 12 chapters of two reels in length. Each chapter left the heroine, played by Kathlyn Williams, in some dangerous predicament designed to lure the audience back to see how she would extricate herself in the next chapter. The sensational vogue of this serial attracted the attention of other film manufacturers. The indefatigable Thanhouser Company soon produced *The Million Dollar Mystery* (1914) in 23 two-reel chapters. Pathé started grinding out *The Perils of Pauline* (1914) with Pearl White at about the same time. Both were winners.

By starring a beautiful heroine instead of a hero, Pathé uncovered a gold mine. Pearl took the movies by storm and leaped to stardom, going on to do a string of goose-flesh serials that crowded theaters to the aisles for each segment of her thrillers and brought her a salary of $10,000 per week.

But Pearl was not alone in the thrills-a-minute world of ridiculous plots, weird disguises, hair-raising escapes, hidden treasures, diabolic scientific devices, wild animals, depraved men, runaway trains, claustrophobic horrors and the endless procession of knock-down, drag-out fights. Also rising to prominence were Grace Cunard, Marie Walcamp, Neva Gerber, Louise Lorraine, Eileen Sedgwick, Ruth Roland, Juanita Hansen, Allene Ray and others.

Women were the glittering stars in a large number of the early serials, but before long eminence shifted to their male counterparts. William Duncan, for example, became so popular that he could also command a salary of $10,000 a week. Also stirring up a whirlwind of enthusiasm among serial devotees were William Desmond, Ben Wilson, Walter Miller, Francis Ford, Charles Hutchison, Jack Dougherty and Eddie Polo.

The sound era had its own serial royalty, and reverence was heaped upon such continued-next-week idols as Buster Crabbe, Clayton Moore, Ralph Byrd, Herman Brix, Buck Jones, Tom Tyler, Jean Rogers, Lucile Browne, Kane Richmond,

Frances Gifford, Kay Aldridge, Linda Stirling and Phyllis Coates. In their own fantasy world, they reigned supreme as the kings and queens of thrills.

Throughout the 30s and 40s, serials were staple ingredients for weekend showings, especially in the smaller towns of the south and southwest. The serials etched indelible impressions on the minds of millions of youngsters, impressions that would remain vivid decades after having seen the films. *The Lone Ranger, Flash Gordon, The Wolf Dog, Ace Drummond, Dick Tracy, Gordon of Ghost City, The Phantom Empire, The Lost City, The Shadow, Undersea Kingdoms*—fans still get goosebumps at the recollection of the serials that contributed much to childhood's pleasure.

The serial died a slow death. For the last six years of its existence, it was beset with escalating production costs, dwindling markets, television competition, rising sophistication, etc. But, as the scripture says, "a time to pluck what is planted." Hollywood today is "plucking" techniques, production know-how, story ideas and you-name-it from the serials. Flash Gordon, Superman, Batman, Dick Tracy, the Lone Ranger, Zorro and other serial heroes have had multi-million dollar films built around them. We enjoy today many innovations that serials pioneered.

But as to this book. I have given nutshell information on your favorites of yesteryear. Birth and death, life before and after the movies, major films and whatever data I could include. Now you can know whatever happened to your favorite serial actor, the serials that he or she played in and other things of interest. Here in this one book will be found over 440 performers who milked the serial for what it was worth.

No one book could possibly cover *all* the actors and actresses who worked in serials from 1912 to 1956. But I have endeavored to include as many players as possible who appeared in principal roles. Of course, information on some players was not readily available, particularly those who labored in the silent era. However, I believe the reader will concede that I have covered the major stars—and then some! I have included a number of character actors who made watching the Saturday cliffhangers so much fun. Some of them made as many as 50 or more serials, and most of them actually piled up more screen time than the stars who made only one, two or three serials, for example Tom London, George Chesebro, Bud Osborne and Frank Ellis. The ladies have not been overlooked; nearly 200 to them are included in the book. Certainly I would have liked to include another 50 or more actors and actresses, but book length had to be considered (although my publisher probably thinks I never considered it!).

I hope that my efforts will culminate in many hours of pleasure for the serial lover who merely wishes to recall old serials and serial personnel that he has seen. For me, it has been a labor of love which has added a wealth of data and knowledge on a genre which I thought I was an authority on already.

ART ACORD

In the book *The Hollywood Posse*, Diana Serra Cary describes Art Acord as "The cowboys' cowboy" and says that, even above his friend Hoot Gibson, Art was considered by his peers as the greatest rodeo champ who ever lived. She says that Acord had the typical gunslinger's stance; he had "packed a gun so long he stood slanchways; he was "solidly built as a brick wall, with the typical cowboy's squared eyelids (from squinting into the sun), a long face, pistol-butt nose, and sharply defined jawline."

His passion for excitement led to rodeo competition. A topnotch cowboy, he was an excellent bronc rider and the winner of several championships in bull-dogging and roping.

Artemus Ward Acord was born on April 17, 1890, in what today is known as Glenwood, in Sevier County, Utah. He was part Ute Indian and grew to manhood as a rather carefree, uneducated cowpuncher. His rodeo success led to work in the Stanley-Atkinson Wild West Show as a trick roper, bulldogger and bronc buster. While in New York with the show he was approached by Adam Kessel, who was in the process of organizing the Bison Film Company. The year was 1909. Art accepted Kessel's offer of work as a stuntman, double and rider and was off to California where he was put to work in the one- and two-reelers then in vogue.

Art met and married actress Edythe Sterling in 1913. Two years later, Kriterion Films co-starred them in several two-reelers. *When the Fiddler Came to Big Horn* was typical of the fast action (and little romancing) content of these quickly dashed-off short sagebrushers.

American Films signed Art in 1915 and starred him in a string of two- and three-reelers, often with Nita Davis or Dixie Straton filling the soubrette role. While these rough-and-tumble sagas were so much tripe,

the films were strung together with such good and swiftly moving continuity as to take on deserved interest.

In 1916 Art signed with Fox to make pictures in their New Jersey studio, but the promised stardom never materialized; instead, he was kept busy doing stunts in Theda Bara films. Finally, however, he was rewarded with a co-starring role with Gladys Coburn in *The Battle of Life*, a melodrama of the New York slums. He also appeared in the Broadway plays *Nearly a Lad* and *The Pretty Mrs. Smith*.

Things were not going well in his personal life; he was divorced by Edythe Sterling. Art took it hard. Quite despondent, he became belligerent and turned to the bottle to drown his sorrows.

In 1917 Art joined the Army and saw action in the battle of Verdun. He was awarded the French Croix de Guerre for bravery. Art returned home an authentic hero in 1919 after 18 months of military service.

Trying matrimony again, Art married minor actress Edna Nores, subsequently signing a contract to make Westerns for Universal. Career-wise it was a good decision; marriage-wise, it wasn't. Edna soon divorced Art, naming Universal serial heroine Louise Lorraine, age 16, as co-respondent. Art married Louise but this marriage, too, ended in divorce around 1928.

Art completed a number of two-reelers in 1919–20 under the direction of B. Reeves Eason. Then Universal put him into the film that made a real star of him. The film was *The Moon Riders* ('20), an 18-chapter serial that was never forgotten by Art's fans. In the story, he chases after a treasure owned by a lost race of mysterious Indians. Naturally there were rogues who also wanted the treasure. The serial was one of the most popular chapter plays turned out by any studio in the silent era.

Universal had not expected the stupendous success that *The Moon Riders* enjoyed; movie patrons clamored for another Acord serial. The studio readied a second film scripted by Ford Beebe and titled *The White Horseman*. It proved to be as popular as *The Moon Rider*. The story involved a mountain whose inner caverns were once inhabited by a race of Indians extinct except for two who return to open the mountain once again and reclaim the treasures therein. Art was looked upon as sort of a reincarnation of a white horseman who, centuries earlier (according to Indian legend), befriended the tribe and protected it against its enemies.

With *Winners of the West* (1921) Universal started a program to cash in on historical names and combine fictional characters with historical personages in semi-fictional stories. In this one, Burton C. Law plays Capt. John C. Fremont, while Art is cast as Arthur Standish, a young frontiersman. Trying to "stay with a good thing," the scriptwriters again had Art seeking a lost treasure and fighting for possession of the map indicating its whereabouts. Naturally, he managed to find a girl along the way in the person of Myrtle Lind and kept her safe from a multitude of dangers.

In the Days of Buffalo Bill (1922) deviated from the lost treasure theme to concentrate on the building of the transcontinental railway. Art stayed busy saving Dorothy Woods from both renegade whites and Sioux Indians, and protecting the railroad crews as they sought to lay track.

Art had as his co-star in *The Oregon Trail* (1923) serial queen Louise Lorraine, his wife in real life. Ed Laemmle once again directed Art, this time in a story of an independent trapper fighting an unscrupulous syndicate in the vast Oregon territory. It was Art's last serial.

Beginning in 1924, Art headed up five-reel features, making two for Sameth; 17 for Universal; four for Truart; six for Davis; and one for Hollywood Enterprises.

The group of programmers Art made for Universal were known as "Blue Streak" Westerns and were designed to display his prowess as a trick rider and featuring him in plenty of daredevil stunt work. All were profitable and this period (1925–27) may be said to represent the peak of the cowboy star's career. It soon went into a steady but inexorable decline.

Universal was fed up with Art's drinking and fighting by 1928 and would not pick up his option. Not only was he a victim of alcoholism but he had turned to excessive gambling and drugs. Things went really bad for Art in 1929. He was arrested for transporting bootleg whiskey and again on a robbery charge. He extricated himself from these troubles and went south into Mexico for personal appearances. Later he was involved in mining ventures.

On January 4, 1937, Art Acord died, suddenly, violently, alone, and with few friends to mourn his passing. He died under mysterious circumstances on the second floor of the Chichuahua Hotel in Mexico. Some say he died from a knifing; others, from cyanide poison; others, alcohol poisoning. But whatever the cause, Art Acord died a broken, pathetic man stripped of his glory and his manhood.

But, regardless, Art's serial record lives on — five pulsating 18-chapter sagas, as well as his many features and shorts. He remains one of the silent era's most popular Western and serial stars.

Serials

1920

The Moon Riders. Univ., [18 Chapters] D: B. Reeves Eason, Albert Russell; SP: George Hively, Albert Russell, Theodore Wharton; S: Albert Russell, George Hively, William Piggott, Theodore Wharton, Karl Coolidge; LP: Art Acord, Mildred Moore, Charles Newton, George Field, Tote DuCrow.

1921

The White Horseman. Univ., [18 Chapters] D: Albert Russell; S/SP: Albert Russell, Ford Beebe; LP: Art Acord, Eva Forrestor, Beatrice Dominguez, Duke R. Lee.

Winners of the West. Univ., [18 Chapters] D: Ed Laemmle; S/SP: Robert Dillon, Ford Beebe; LP: Art Acord, Myrtle Lind, Burton C. Law, Percy Pembroke, Burt Wilson, Jim Corey.

1922

In the Days of Buffalo Bill. Univ., [18 Chapters] D: Edward Laemmle; S/SP: Robert Dillon; LP: Art Acord, Dorothy Woods, Duke R. Lee, Ruth Royce, George A. Williams, Jay Morley.

1923

The Oregon Trail. Univ., [18 Chapters] D: Edward Laemmle; S: Robert Dillon; SP: Anthony Coldeway, Douglas Bronston, Jefferson Moffitt; LP: Art Acord, Louise Lorraine, Ruth Royce, Duke R. Lee, Jim Corey, Burton C. Law.

JANE ADAMS

Western heroine Jane (Poni) Adams, born in Texas but raised in California, began life as Betty Jane Bierce. At Beverly Hills High School she studied drama and violin. Upon graduation she received a scholarship to the Pasadena Playhouse, where she studied for four years. She gained practical experience through the plays put on by the Playhouse and acted with a number of other performers destined for Hollywood fame.

Jane met and fell in love with a young Navy ensign and married him shortly before this country entered World War II. But, married less than a year, her husband was killed in action. Of necessity Jane became a model for the Harry Conover Agency in New York. When *Esquire* magazine published a full-page layout of her, she was asked to come to Hollywood for a screen test. The result was a Universal contract.

Jane's first Western was *Code of the Lawless* ('45) starring Kirby Grant. This was followed by *Trail to Vengeance* ('45), *Gunman's Code* ('46), *Lawless Breed* ('46) and *Rustlers' Roundup* ('46), all starring Grant. Also at Universal she had a good role in *House of Dracula* ('45) as a lab assistant with a disfigurement. In 1946's *The Brute Man* (made by Universal but released by PRC), she played a blind girl opposite Tom Neal. Other Universal films in which she played are *This Love of Ours* ('45), *Lady on a Train* ('45), *Salome, Where She Danced* ('45), *The Runaround* ('46) and *Smooth as Silk* ('46).

In *Lost City of the Jungle* ('46) Jane has the female lead opposite Russell Hayden. Meteorium 245, a defense against the atomic bomb, is sought by a power-mad Englishman, but thwarting his plans to rule the world is a United Peace Foundation investigator, a scientist's daughter and a Pendrang tribesman. The search for the rare substance takes all the principals to the lost city of the jungle, where the two leading villains wind up with the chest containing the 245, only to be blown to smithereens when the substance explodes during their getaway in a plane.

Jane made no films in '47 or '48 but in 1949 she was back on screen in the Columbia serial *Batman and Robin* ('49), playing a commercial photographer who aids Batman and Robin in their hunt for a hooded figure known as "The Wizard," who desires to acquire the powerful explosive X-90.

At Monogram Jane appeared in a couple of Bowery Boys films, three Johnny Mack Brown prairie dusters, and one Western with Jimmy Wakely and one with Duncan Renaldo. In 1951 she made *Street Bandits* with Robert Clarke. Afterwards she switched her film activity to television.

Jane married her second husband, Lt. Tom Turnage, about 1946, thus accounting for her screen absence in '47 and '48. When he was recalled for the Korean War, she returned for the '49–'50 films, but when he came home she moved with him from one base to another. He finally retired as a major general and the couple took up residence in Southern California where Turnage recently passed away.

They have two children and several grandchildren.

Serials

1946

Lost City of the Jungle. Univ., [13 Chapters] D: Ray Taylor and Lewis D. Collins; SP: Joseph F. Poland, Paul Huston, Tom Gibson; LP: Russell Hayden, Jane Adams, Lionel Atwill, Keye Luke, Helen Bennett, John Eldredge.

1949

Batman and Robin. Col., 1949 [15 Chapters] D: Spencer G. Bennet; SP: George H. Plymp-

Left to right: George Lynn, Dick Curtis, Jane Adams and John Eldredge in *Lost City of the Jungle* (Universal, 1946).

ton, Joseph F. Poland, Royal K. Cole; P: Sam Katzman; Cam: Ira H. Morgan; Mus: Mischa Bakaleinikoff; LP: Robert Lowery, Johnny Duncan, Jane Adams, Lyle Talbot, Ralph Graves.

KATHRYN ADAMS

Kathryn Adams was a pretty girl who was in films from 1939 to 1942, and one film with husband Hugh Beaumont in 1946. One of her earliest films was RKO's *The Hunchback of Notre Dame* ('39) in which she had a minor role. In fact, most of her roles were minor ones, although she had the female lead in *Black Diamonds* ('41) opposite Richard Arlen and Andy Devine.

Also in 1941 she appeared in *Arizona Cyclone*, *Bury Me Not on the Lone Prairie*, and *Rawhide Rangers*, in each case being billed fourth behind Johnny Mack Brown, Fuzzy Knight and Nell O'Day.

Kathryn's role in *Junior G-Men of the Air* ('42) was an unbilled one, but in *Sky Raiders* ('41) she has the heroine's role as Mary Blake, Capt. Robert Dayton's (Donald

Woods) attractive secretary. The story revolves about a foreign agent's attempts to steal the plans for a fast pursuit plane and a new, improved bombsite.

Adams was a recent guest at the Memphis Film Festival.

Serials

1941

Sky Raiders. Univ., 1941 [12 Chapters] D: Ford Beebe, Ray Taylor; SP: Clarence Upson Young,

Paul Huston; S: Eliot Gibbons; AP: Henry MacRae; LP: Billy Halop, Donald Woods, Robert Armstrong, Kathryn Adams, Eduardo Ciannelli.

1942

Junior G-Men of the Air. Univ., [12 Chapters] D: Ray Taylor, Lewis D. Collins; LP: Billy Halop, Gene Reynolds, Lionel Atwill, Frank Albertson, Huntz Hall.

TED ADAMS

Ted Adams nearly always played a badman throughout his 25-year career. During the 1930s and 1940s Ted found himself well-established among the leading screen villains in Westerns and serials. He was equally at home as an outlaw leader or as a bandit henchman. He never smiled. Possibly taking a cue from Fred Kohler, he often resorted to a sneer when things were not going his way.

Ted could switch from Western to gangster-type heavies with ease, as can be seen in *The Fighting Marines* ('35), *The Mysterious Pilot* ('37), or *Holt of the Secret Service* ('41). but his career was built on B-Westerns and when they ceased to be made, his career was over.

Adams worked with many Western leading men in the '30s and '40s. Bob Steele was the most frequent opponent followed by Johnny Mack Brown and Tim McCoy. Many pleasant hours were spent at Saturday matinees watching Ted get bested by the white-hat hero. For most, Ted Adams was a nameless face. They never knew his name though seeing him frequently on the screen battling their heroes. What they did know was that he

was a member of the B-Western fraternity and that meant that he was okay.

Serials

1935

The Fighting Marines. Mascot, [12 Chapters] D: B. Reeves Eason, Joseph Kane; SP: Barney Sarecky, Sherman Lowe; Supv.: Barney Sarecky; S: Ray Trampe, Wallace MacDonald, Maurice Geraghty; P: Nat Levine; Mus: Arthur Kay; LP: Grant Withers, Adrian Morris, Ann Rutherford, Robert Warwick, Robert Frazer.

1936

Custer's Last Stand. S&S, [15 Chapters] D: Elmer Clifton; SP: George Durlam, Eddy Graneman, William Lively; P: George M. Merrick; Supv: Louis Weiss; Cam: Bert Longnecker; Mus: Hal Chasnolf; LP: Rex Lease, William Farnum, Reed Howes, Jack Mulhall, Lona Andre, George Chesebro, Dorothy Gulliver, Helen Gibson.

1937

The Mysterious Pilot. Col., [15 Chapters] D: Spencer G. Bennet; S: William Byron Mowery; P: Jack Fier, Louis Weiss; Cam: Edward Linden, Herman Schoop; Mus: Abe Meyer; LP: Fred Hawks, Dorothy Sebastian, Rex Lease, Guy Bates Post, Kenneth Harlan, Yakima Canutt, Frank Lackteen.

1938

The Lone Ranger. Rep., [15 Chapters] D: William Witney, John English; SP: Barry Shipman, George W. Yates, Franklyn Adreon, Ronald Davidson, Lois Elby; S: Fran Striker; Supv.: Robert Beche; Cam: William Nobles; Mus: Alberto Colombo; LP: Lee Powell, Chief Thundercloud, Herman Brix, Lynn Roberts, Lane Chandler, Wally Wales, Stanley Andrews, George Letz (Montgomery).

1941

Riders of Death Valley. Univ., [15 Chapters] D: Ray Taylor, Ford Beebe; S: Oliver Drake; SP: Sherman Lowe, Basil Dickey, George Plympton, Jack Connell; P: Henry MacRae; Cam: Jerone Ash, William Sickner; Mus: Charles Previn; LP: Dick Foran, Buck Jones, Charles Bickford, Leo Carrillo, Jeanne Kelly, Monte Blue, Lon Chaney, Jr., Noah Beery, Jr.

Holt of the Secret Service. Col, [15 Chapters] D: James W. Horne; SP: Basil Dickey, George H. Plympton, Wyndham Gittens; Cam: James S. Brown, Jr.; Mus: Lee Zahler; P: Larry Darmour; LP: Jack Holt, Evelyn Brent, Tristram Coffin, Montague Shaw, John ward, Ted Adams.

1943

Daredevils of the West. Rep., [12 Chapters] D: John English; SP: Ronald Davidson, Basil Dickey, William Lively, Joseph O'Donnell, Joseph Poland; Cam: Bud Thackery; Mus: Mort Glickman; LP: Allan Lane, Kay Aldridge, Eddie Acuff, William Haade, Robert Frazer, Ted Adams, George J. Lewis.

1945

Jungle Raiders. Col., [15 Chapters] D: Lesley Selander; SP: Ande Lamb, George H. Plympton; P: Sam Katzman; Cam: Ira H. Morgan; Mus: Lee Zahler; LP: Kane Richmond, Eddie Quillan, Veda Ann Borg, Carol Hughes, Janet Shaw, John Elliott, Jack Ingram.

1947

Son of Zorro. Rep., [13 Chapters] D: Spencer G. Bennet, Fred C. Brannon; SP: Franklyn Adreon, Basil Dickey, Jesse Duffy, Sol Shor; AP: Ronald Davidson; Cam: Bud Thackery; Mus: Mort Glickman; LP: George Turner, Peggy Stewart, Roy Barcroft, Edward Cassidy, Ernie Adams, Stanley Price, Edmund Cobb.

The Vigilante. Col., [15 Chapters] D: Wallace Fox; SP: George H. Plympton, Lewis Clay, Arthur Hoerl; P: Sam Katzman; Cam: Ira H. Morgan; Mus: Mischa Bakaleinikoff; LP: Ralph Byrd, Ramsay Ames, Lyle Talbot, George Offerman, Robert Barron, George Chesebro.

1948

Dangers of the Canadian Mounted. Rep., [12 Chapters] D: Fred Brannon, Yakima Canutt; SP: Franklyn Adreon, Basil Dickey, Sol Shor, Robert C. Walker; Cam: John MacBurnie; Mus: Mort Glickman; LP: Jim Bannon, Virginia Belmont, Anthony Warde, Dorothy Granger, Bill Van Sickel, Ken Terrell.

1949

King of the Rocket Men. Rep., [12 Chapters] D: Fred C. Brannon; SP: Sol Shor, Royal Cole, William Lively; Cam: Ellis W. Carter; Mus: Stanley Wilson; LP: Tris Coffin, Mae Clarke, Don Haggerty, House Peters, Jr., James Craven, I. Stanford Jolley.

FRANK ALBERTSON

Frank Albertson was born on February 2, 1909, in Fergus Falls, Minnesota. He entered films in 1922 as a prop boy and developed into a light leading man of "B" programmers and later a character player in scores of Hollywood productions.

His first of two serials was *The Lost Special* ('32). Two college athletes and two young ladies solve the disappearance of the Golden Special, a train carrying gold from the Golconda mines.

The second serial, made ten years later, was *Junior G-Men of the Air* ('42). The Dead End Kids (Billy Halop, Huntz Hall, Gabriel Dell and Bernard Punsley) pretty much dominate the action. The boys help FBI agent Frank Albertson who has been assigned to break up a Japanese spy ring that is trying to steal the plans for a new airplane muffler invented by Halop's brother. The spy ring is headed by Lionel Atwill and is known as the Black Dragonflies. Halop and Albertson personally capture Atwill and bring the sabotage ring to justice.

Albertson acted in scores of films in his career beginning in 1928 and ending with his death at age 55 in Santa Monica, California, in 1964. His last film was *Johnny Cool* ('63) featuring Elizabeth Montgomery, Henry Silva, Sammy Davis, Jr., and Wanda Hendrix.

Frank Albertson (left), Bill Elliott and Anita Louise in *Personal Maid's Secret* (Warner Bros., 1938).

Serials

1932

The Lost Special. Univ., [12 Chapters] D: Henry MacRae; S: Arthur Conan Doyle; SP: Ella O'Neill, George Plympton, Basil Dickey, George Morgan; LP: Frank Albertson, Cecilia Parker, Caryl Lincoln, Francis Ford, Ernie Nevers.

1942

Junior G-Men of the Air. Univ., [12 Chapters] D: Ray Taylor, Lewis D. Collins; SP: Paul Huston, George H. Plympton, Griffin Jay; AP: Henry MacRae; LP: Billy Halop, Gene Reynolds, Lionel Atwill, Frank Albertson, Huntz Hall, Richard Lane, Gabriel Dell.

KAY ALDRIDGE

Kay Aldridge, a striking, full-breasted Powers model, starred in three of the most exciting serials ever produced by Republic. A popular cover girl whose old-fashioned beauty and honey-colored hair may have reminded senior filmgoers of Pearl White, she appeared on the cover of *Redbook* a dozen or more times and on the covers of *Life, Look, Ladies' Home Journal, Colliers, Country Gentleman, Modern Romances* and other magazines.

Upon seeing Kay in the September 5, 1938, issue of *Life*, David O. Selznick screen-tested her for both the Scarlett O'Hara and Melanie roles in *Gone with the Wind*. Kay demonstrated that she had more than her share of Southern charm, though she lost the coveted roles to Vivien Leigh and Olivia de Havilland.

Kay was born in Tallahassee, Florida, on July 9, 1917, one of five children being reared by a widowed mother and some great-aunts who lived in a remote section of Virginia near Tappahannock in an old house (built in 1690) named Bladensfield. The book *The Children of Bladensfield* (1978) was written by Kay and one of the aunts. Kay grew up in this very poor-but-proud rural part of Virginia.

After graduation from high school, Kay went to Baltimore and took a secretarial job.

A cousin showed Kay's picture to John Robert Powers of the famed modeling agency. He liked what he saw and invited her to become one of his models. She became one of the highest-paid models in the country. In 1937 she was selected as one of the ten most photographed girls in the world and, as a result of this honor, was brought to Hollywood with the nine other models to appear in the United Artists movie, *Vogues of 1938*. As soon as *Vogues* was completed, Kay was offered a part in *Rosalie*, a film being produced by MGM and co-starring Nelson Eddy and Eleanor Powell.

In 1939 Kay and her close friend, model Georgia Carrol (who became Mrs. Kay Kyser) were selected by *Redbook* magazine, Saks Fifth Avenue and Matson Shipping Lines to travel for a "Cover Girls See the World" series of articles for *Redbook*. The two girls eventually wound up in Hollywood where they did the layout for the article "Magazine Cover Girls Look at the Stars" and made the rounds of the various studios. Kay was spotted by Twentieth Century-Fox, given a screen test and signed to a studio contract.

Kay's first film under this contract was *Hotel for Women*, which introduced Linda Darnell in her film debut. Kay plays the other woman in the life of James Ellison. Kay then made ten others at Fox.

Kay Aldridge, Clayton Moore (hands up) and Tris Coffin (by tree) in *Perils of Nyoka* (Republic, 1942).

In *Here I Am a Stranger* ('39) she plays the other woman in the life of Richard Greene, a young college man who helps rehabilitate his down-and-out father. In *Free, Blonde, and 21* ('39), a comedy-melodrama sequel to *Hotel for Women*, she is one of the residents in a New York City hotel for girls. In *Shooting High* ('40) Kay plays the part of an actress involved in the filming of a Western adventure on the scene of the actual event. The star is Gene Autry (on loan from Republic) who tries to settle a feud between his family and Marjorie Weaver's folks.

Girl in 313 ('40) is a mystery drama starring Kent Taylor and Florence Rice. Kay is an attractive and capable link in the jewel ring headed by Taylor. In *Sailor's Lady* ('40) she is the girlfriend of one of the sailors in this comedy about sailors, their girls and a stowaway baby. Nancy Kelly and Jon Hall headed the cast. Kay shares honors with Jane Withers and Kent Taylor in *Girl from Avenue*

A ('40), a story about a playwright who takes in a child of the street to study her.

In *Yesterday's Heroes* ('40) Kay is the other woman in a story about a medical student who becomes a college football hero, deserts his childhood sweetheart, marries a celebrity-hunting widow and then finds his world torn asunder. *Down Argentine Way* ('40) presents Kay as an acquaintance of Betty Grable in a musical comedy in which a New York heiress (Grable) falls in love with a visiting South American cowboy (Don Ameche) and follows him to Argentina, where songs, dances and horse races ensue. In *Golden Hoofs* ('41), a story of harness racing, Kay plays the fiancée of "Buddy" Rogers. Jane Withers, a trainer, inveigles her new boss, Rogers, not to sell off the trotters. And in *Dead Men Tell* ('41), her last Fox feature, she and her bridegroom board a treasure-hunting ship for a honeymoon trip, but the ship never leaves the dock due to two murders by an unknown assailant dressed in a pirate's outfit. Eventually Charlie Chan (Sidney Toler) solves everything.

After Fox failed to pick up her option, Kay became a freelancer. At Warner Brothers she and five other girls (including Marguerite Chapman) make up the Navy Blues Sextet in the musical comedy *Navy Blues* ('41), about a couple of gambling sailors (Jack Oakie and Jack Haley) who try to keep an ace gunner on their ship until after the gunnery trials. Ann Sheridan also starred. The Sextet make an encore appearance in *You're in the Army Now* ('41), a slapstick comedy about two vacuum cleaner salesmen (Jimmy Durante and Phil Silvers) who unwittingly become soldiers in Uncle Sam's Army. The Sextet performs during a U.S.O. show. At Paramount, Kay is one of the many showgirls in *Louisiana Purchase* ('41), Irving Berlin's musical comedy about an attempt to frame a senator from Louisiana. Bob Hope's filibuster scene in Congress has come to be considered a classic.

When Kay was informed by her agent that Republic was searching for a new serial star, she set her sights on the part in the hope that it would finally break the cover girl mold in which she was cast. However, she had no idea what a serial was, having never seen any. Both William Witney, director, and Herbert J. Yates, Republic president, were captivated by Kay's verve and warmth and her claim that she wanted to be more than just glamorous set-dressing. She got the part.

Republic's wrangling with author Edgar Rice Burroughs had dogged their serial *Jungle Girl* ('41). Thus the studio made efforts to distance *Perils of Nyoka* ('42) from the former serial. Frances Gifford had been a smash hit as Nyoka in the first serial but was unavailable for the second as she was under contract to another studio. Besides, using her again could lead to more trouble with Burroughs. Yates decided to use a different girl to avoid copyright disputes with Burroughs. Although Burroughs owned the title "Jungle Girl," Republic owned the name Nyoka. Republic changed the surname of Nyoka from Meredith to Gordon; the location from the

Sianbula Swamps to the exotic, desert wastelands of Central Africa; and Nyoka's costume to a dreadfully designed, one-piece safari number of a very unflattering length and material. Thus, Kay lost a little glamour as well as some of Gifford's eroticism.

It is ironic that Kay Aldridge should attain cinema immortality with her serial performances, which she herself thought of as trivial. Dozens of more competent and charismatic starlets around her would disappear into Hollywood oblivion, while Kay's performances in cliffhangers survived all their "starring" efforts and studio publicity campaigns. In Bill Feret's *Lure of the Tropix*, he says that Kay brought to her portrayal of Nyoka Gordon a conviction and heroism that gave the character a larger-than-life credibility. When she was booming orders to her tribe of Bedouins, galloping on horseback or slugging it out with the bad guys, it never looked ludicrous or unreal. Kay's Nyoka was a far more physical protagonist than Frances Gifford's. Not since Pearl White had a serial heroine taken part in all the action, whether it involved a fistfight with a man or combat with a gorilla. It should be noted, however, that David Sharpe deserves credit for the really rough stuff in that he doubled Kay. He had done the same for Frances Gifford in *Jungle Girl*.

Even though the budget on *Perils of Nyoka* was less than that for *Jungle Girl*, it appears more elaborate and imaginative than its predecessor. Many of the cliffhangers were placed in elaborate and imaginative settings, with powerfully directed, furious action, extremely effective lighting and quick cutting to liven the pace. The story is a good one.

After *Perils of Nyoka*, Aldridge moved on to *Daredevils of the West* ('43), directed by John English. She shared billing with Allan Lane. They were hailed as their Majesties, the King and Queen of Serials. Some writers have hailed this serial as the greatest Western serial of all time. This writer would not praise it that much, but it was a good chapterplay, making up in fast-moving action what it lacked in story content. Aldridge and

Lane were pitted against a frontier speculator who tried to keep a fledgling stagecoach line from spanning the unopened Comanche Strip. Theater goers were subjected to the usual unimaginable Western cliffhangers.

Aldridge's third and final serial for Republic was *Haunted Harbor* ('44). Adapted from the Dayle Douglas book, the production was a 15-chapter jungle-horror-mystery-sea story that incorporated all the cliff hanging tricks Republic could muster, including a rigged sea monster that rose from the depths of a lagoon, emitting great roaring sounds, keeping the native population in a continual state of fright. Gold bullion on a sunken yacht was the fatal fascination for the villain Kane (Roy Barcroft), and he set out to prove there was nothing he wouldn't do to gain it.

Writer William Cline in his book *In the Nick of Time*, writes:

> Perhaps the most quickly remembered serial heroine of all for that trait of guileless wholesomeness was Kay Aldridge, the second Nyoka. In all three of her featured cliffhanger roles for Republic she projected the image of the deserving young daughter of a kidnapped or murdered pioneer or man of science struggling valiantly against all odds to continue his work. With her clean-cut, symmetrical beauty and round, imploring eyes, she enlisted without much difficulty the full cooperation of heroes Clayton Moore, Allan Lane and Kane Richmond in *Perils of Nyoka*, *Daredevils of the West* and *Haunted Harbor*. Although in only three films, the lovely Powers model closely trails Linda Stirling for the imaginary honor of being Republic's "Serial Queen."

In 1945 Kay married Arthur Cameron, a Los Angeles businessman, and settled down to become a full-fledged wife and mother. She and Mr. Cameron became the parents of four children. The first child, Melissa, was born on November 8, 1945. Then came Arthur, December 27, 1946; Scott, October 24, 1949; and Carey, January 12, 1953. After nine years of married life, the Camerons were separated and divorced a couple of years later. Cameron died in 1967.

In 1956 Kay met and married Richard Derby Tucker, an artist and writer. They lived in Hollywood for a number of years but moved to Camden, Maine, to a home on Penobscot Bay. After Tucker died, Kay married Harry Naslund, an old friend and building contractor.

Kay Aldridge suffered a heart attack in Camden and died at the age of 77 in 1995.

Serials

1942

Perils of Nyoka. Rep., [15 Chapters] D: William Witney; SP: Ronald Davidson, Norman S. Hall, William Lively, Joseph Poland, Joseph O'Donnell; AP: W. J. O'Sullivan; Cam: Reggie Lanning; Mus: Mort Glickman; LP: Kay Aldridge, Clayton Moore, William Benedict Lorna Gray, Charles Middleton, Tristram Coffin.

1943

Daredevils of the West. Rep., [12 Chapters] D: John English; SP: Ronald Davidson, Basil Dickey, William Lively, Joseph O'Donnell, Joseph Poland; AP: W. J. O'Sullivan; Cam: Bud Thackery; Mus: Mort Glickman; LP: Kay Aldridge, Allan Lane, Eddie Acuff, William Haade, Robert Frazer, Stanley Andrews, Ted Adams.

1944

Haunted Harbor. Rep., [15 Chapters] D: Spencer Bennet, Wallace Grissell; SP: Royal Cole, Basil Dickey, Jesse Duffy, Grant Nelson, Joseph Poland; S: Dayle Douglas; AP: Ronald Davidson; Cam: Bud Thackery; Mus: Joseph Dubin; LP: Kane Richmond, Kay Aldridge, Roy Barcroft, Clancy Cooper, Marshall Reed, Oscar O'Shea, Forrest Taylor, Hal Taliaferro.

BEN ALEXANDER

Ben Alexander starred in the Rayart serial *Scotty of the Scouts* ('26) when only 15 years old. In the story, a valuable historic document is stolen from the national museum and Scotty takes charge and pursues the quarry with a tenacity remarkable for one so young. Now and again his scout friends rally to his aid. It is not unlike *Scouts to the Rescue* ('39) starring young Jackie Cooper.

Evidently Rayart liked Ben for the next year he was featured in *Fighting for Fame* ('27). Frank Manning (Eddie Fetherston), a newspaper reporter, exposes a harbor ring and obtains further information that will implicate the controller of the waterfront interests. The controller plants a spy in the newspaper office and plots to get Manning out of the way. Manning is aided by Mary Aynsworth (Hazel Dean), a secretary, and Danny Ryan (Ben Alexander), a printer's devil.

Ben Alexander was born Nicholas Benton Alexander on May 26, 1911, in Goldfield, Nevada. He was a popular child actor from age four (his first directors were Cecil B. DeMille and D. W. Griffith). He later played juveniles and eventually supporting parts in sound films. His better films include *The Lit-tle American* ('17), *Penrod and Sam* ('23), *Pampered Youth* ('25), *All Quiet on the Western Front* ('30), *Tom Brown of Culver* ('32), *Annapolis Farewell* ('35), *Hearts in Bondage* ('36), *Convict's Code* ('39), *Dragnet* ('54) and *Man in the Shadow* ('57).

In the '30s Alexander was well known as a radio announcer and in the '50s he reemerged from obscurity as Jack Webb's patrol partner in TV's *Dragnet* series. He later starred in *Felony Squad*. Ben died in 1969 from natural causes in Westchester, California. He was 58.

Serials

1926

Scotty of the Scouts. Rayart, [10 Chapters] D: Duke Worne; LP: Ben Alexander, Paddy O'Flynn, Mary Jane Irving, Ben Hall, Frank Baker, Edna May Cooper, Albert J. Smith.

1927

Fighting for Fame. Rayart, [10 Chapters] D: Duke Worne; SP: George Pyper; LP: Ben Alexander, Hazel Dean, Eddie Fetherston.

RICHARD (DICK) ALEXANDER

Richard was born in Dallas, Texas, in 1902. After finishing school he worked as a bank clerk and lived at home with his family. About 1920 he decided to move to California, as some members of the family lived there. He got a job as a clerk in a bank, but after a short time he moved to New York and later Chicago. However, he loved California

John Carroll as Zorro and Dick Alexander in *Zorro Rides Again* (Republic, 1937).

best and returned there. He lived with his grandmother and went back to work as a bank clerk.

About 1924, Richard started working in the movie industry as an extra. He did very well and kept busy as an extra.

Richard's beginning as an actor was *Leopard Lady* ('24), a Pathé film in which he plays Hector, the lion tamer. He was billed sixth in a cast headed by Jacqueline Logan. After that his career was on the way up. *All Quiet on the Western Front* ('30) was one of his favorite films. In it he is "Westhus," a soldier. Other films in which he was credited were *The Sin Sister* ('29), *The Viking* ('29), *The Big Broadcast of 1936* ('35) and *Modern Times* ('36). In the latter film he plays a prisoner and has the opportunity to work with Charlie Chaplin, which gave him a thrill. He occasionally used his bulk to play slightly deranged characters.

Although he would continue to play in non–Westerns, Westerns and serials became his bread and butter. Dick worked with such stars as Buck Jones, Tim McCoy, Johnny Mack Brown, Tom Mix, Rod Cameron, Jack Randall, Russell Hayden and John Wayne. He nearly always played the rogue with limited brain power. His Western output included *Lone Star Rangers* ('30), *Law and Order* ('32), *The Sunset Trail* ('32), *One Man Law* ('32), *Texas Badman* ('32), *The Fighting Code* ('33), *Drift Fence* ('36), *Wild Brian Kent* ('36), *Where the West Begins* ('38), *Gunsmoke Mesa* ('44) and *Boss of Boomtown* ('44).

Richard acted in 16 serials and had very good roles in some of them, but it is as Prince Baron in *Flash Gordon* ('36) and *Flash Gordon's Trip to Mars* ('38) that he is best remembered by serial buffs. His role was a sympathetic one. He usually played bullies such as El Lobo in *Zorro Rides Again* ('37), Thorg in *S O S Coast Guard* ('37), Ivan in *The Fighting Marines* ('35), Olaf in *The*

Clutching Hand ('36) and Gorth in *Trader Tom of the China Seas*. Dick's last role was in *Give the Little Lady a Big Hand* ('71). His health forced him to retire.

In 1926 he married Frances Smith and they lived together in wedded bliss for 58 years, until her death in 1984. Dick died on August 9, 1989, of pulmonary edema at the Motion Picture & Television Hospital in Woodland Hills, California, where he had been a resident since 1976. He was 86 years old. He left no survivors.

Serials

1934

The Law of the Wild. Mascot, [12 Chapters] D: Armand Schaefer, B. Reeves Eason; LP: Bob Custer, Rex (horse), Rin-Tin-Tin, Jr. (dog), Lucile Browne, Richard Cramer, Ben Turpin.

1935

The Fighting Marines. Mascot, [12 Chapters] D: B. Reeves Eason, Joseph Kane; LP: Grant Withers, Adrian Morris, Ann Rutherford, Robert Warwick, George J. Lewis.

The Miracle Rider. Mascot, [15 Chapters] D: Armand Schaefer, B. Reeves Eason; LP: Tom Mix, Joan Gale, Charles Middleton, Jason Robards, Sr., Robert Kortman.

1936

The Clutching Hand. S & S, [15 Chapters] D: Albert Herman; LP: Jack Mulhall, Ruth Mix, Marion Shilling, Rex Lease.

Flash Gordon. Univ., [13 Chapters] D: Frederick Stephani; LP: Buster Crabbe, Jean Rogers, Charles Middleton, Priscilla Lawson, Richard Alexander.

1937

Jungle Menace. Col., [15 Chapters] D: George Melford, Harry Fraser; LP: Frank Buck, Esther Ralston, John St. Polis, Reginald Denny, Charlotte Henry, Duncan Renaldo.

S O S Coast Guard. Rep., [12 Chapters] D: William Witney, Alan James; LP: Ralph Byrd, Bela Lugosi, Maxine Doyle, Richard Alexander, Herbert Rawlinson.

Zorro Rides Again. Rep., [12 Chapters] D: William Witney, John English; LP: John Carroll, Helen Christian, Duncan Renaldo, Noah Beery, Sr., Yakima Canutt, Richard Alexander.

1938

Flash Gordon's Trip to Mars. Univ., [15 Chapters] D: Ford Beebe, Robert Hill; LP: Buster Crabbe, Jean Rogers, Charles Middleton, Frank Shannon, Beatrice Roberts, Donald Kerr.

1939

The Oregon Trail. Univ., [15 Chapters] D: Ford Beebe, Saul A. Goodkind; LP: Johnny Mack Brown, Louise Stanley, Fuzzy Knight, Bill Cody, Jr., Forrest Taylor.

1941

Sea Raiders. Univ., [12 Chapters] D: Ford Beebe, John Rawlins; LP: Billy Halop, Bernard Punsley, William Hall, Gabriel Dell.

Riders of Death Valley. Univ., [15 Chapters] D: Ray Taylor, Ford Beebe; LP: Dick Foran, Buck Jones, Leo Carrillo, Charles Bickford, Lon Chaney, Jr.

1945

The Royal Mounted Rides Again. Univ., [13 Chapters] D: Ray Taylor, Lewis D. Collins; LP: George Dolenz, Bill Kennedy, Daun Kennedy, Paul E. Burns.

1947

Jesse James Rides Again. Rep., [13 Chapters] D: Fred C. Brannon, Thomas Carr; LP: Clayton Moore, Linda Stirling, Roy Barcroft, Tris Coffin, John Compton.

1954

Trader Tom of the China Seas. Rep., [12 Chapters] D: Franklyn Adreon; LP: Harry Lauter, Aline Towne, Lyle Talbot, Robert Shayne.

1955

King of the Carnival. Rep., [12 Chapters] D: Franklyn Adreon; LP: Harry Lauter, Fran Bennett, Keith Richards, Robert Shayne, Rick Vallin.

KIRK ALYN

Kirk Alyn, the movies' first Superman, came to Hollywood from a career of stage work in the East, including musicals. He began life as John Feggo, Jr., in Oxford, New Jersey, on October 8, 1910. He was a Broadway chorus boy and vaudeville performer before entering films.

A shy, retiring lad, his entry into the world of entertainment was unplanned. He was enrolled in Columbia University in New York City in 1928 and expected to enter the journalism field. Then he became interested in dancing and musical comedy. After appearing in his first stage play as an extra, he was convinced that musical comedy was for him. In *Girl Crazy* ('30) he was a member of the chorus. In 1931 he appeared in *Of Thee I Sing*, a hit musical running for two years. Other plays followed. Whenever show jobs dried up, he hit the vaudeville trail, at one time touring with comedians Ole Olsen and Chick Johnson for a year in *Hellzapoppin*. He even became one-half of the dance team billed as Nadine and Kirk while employed by the Tommy Dorsey Orchestra. Between other assignments, Kirk appeared in short films made in New York, helped *Portia* face life on the radio and appeared in several musical revues with Imogene Coca and Billy de Wolfe.

In 1942 Kirk was vacationing in California. At a party he met singer-comedienne Virginia O'Brien. After a brief courtship, Kirk and Virginia married. Kirk decided to remain in California and try his luck with the Hollywood studios. He had no trouble in getting acting jobs and appeared in supporting roles in *You Were Never Lovelier* ('42), *Lucky Jordan* ('42), *My Sister Eileen* ('42), *Destroyer* ('43), *Pistol Packin' Mama* ('43), *Mystery Broadcast* ('43), *The Man from the Rio Grande* ('43), *A Guy Named Joe* ('43), *The Girl Who Dared* ('44), *Four Jills in a Jeep* ('44), *Once Upon a Time* ('44), *Forty Thieves* ('44) and *Call of the Rockies* ('44).

In 1944, Alyn joined the Maritime Service and spent nearly all of the next 18 months stationed on Catalina Island, off the California coast. After the war he resumed his acting career, getting his first serial co-starring role in Republic's *Daughter of Don Q* ('46). Daughter of the title was Adrian Booth, formerly known by the name Lorna Gray. As Dolores Quantaro, daughter of Zorro's son, Adrian played a detective in a large modern city out to wreck the criminal plans of villains Manning (LeRoy Mason) and Donovan (Roy Barcroft). Manning is out to kill the descendants of an early-day Spanish land grant settler. Success in this endeavor will leave only himself to inherit a large fortune. Dolores, also a descendant, and reporter Cliff Roberts (Alyn) uncover the plot and proceed to warn the descendants of Don Quantaro. Manning is ultimately exposed as the chief villain.

Producer Sam Katzman was given the assignment of bringing comic book hero Superman to the screen. He cast as "the man of steel" young Alyn, who resembled as much as anyone the handsome Superman, and who possessed the coy wit expected of his alter ego, Clark Kent. *Superman* ('48) followed with relative fidelity the comic book origin of Superman. The planet Krypton is doomed. Superman's father, a scientist, has developed an experimental rocketship and is able to put young Superman in it and blast it off just before Krypton explodes. The baby Superman is found in the crashed rocketship by an old couple who raise him as their own son. The youngster grows up to value truth and justice and vows to use his super powers to combat evil. As Clark Kent, he leaves home to seek employment in Metropolis. He goes to work for *The Daily Planet* as a reporter. Noel Neill plays reporter Lois Lane, Tommy Bond (bully in the Our Gang comedies) is cub reporter Jimmy Olson and Pierre Warkin

Kirk Alyn and Noel Neill in *Superman* (Columbia, 1948).

plays *Daily Planet* editor Perry White. The story involves a number of sinister underworld figures led by the beautiful but cunning Spider Lady (Carol Forman). With the help of a criminal scientist (Charles Quigley), she threatens the destruction of Metropolis with a disintegrator weapon called a reducer ray, which in the end destroys her.

Columbia had a number of technical problems to solve in bringing this comic book character to the screen—foremost, how to make him fly. But another non-technical problem faced the writers. One of the most important factors for a serial hero is the fact that he can get the audience worried about his life being in constant peril. In this respect

Superman was his own worst enemy. His super invulnerability made it very difficult for an audience to worry about his safety. Even his alter-ego of Clark Kent never raised a goose pimple when he was in danger. Underneath the civilian trappings and glasses, it was still Superman. But solve the problem he did.

Alyn's third serial, *Federal Agents vs. Underworld, Inc.* ('49), was made by Republic. Federal agent Dave Worth's (Alyn) assignment is to find Prof. Clayton, who has vanished after discovering the famous Golden Hands of Kurigal, key to a great fortune. Nila (Carol Forman), an international thief and one of the founders of Underworld, Inc., is responsible for Clayton's disappearance. She has one of the hands and with her minions is ruthlessly murdering anyone in her way as she seeks the second hand.

What with the blockbuster success of *Superman*, a sequel was almost assured. Luckily Alyn, Neill, Bond and Watkin were available to reprise their original roles. Columbia's new serial, *Atom Man vs. Superman* ('50), was far more gimmicky and gadget-prone than *Superman*, but the small budget showed in the cheapness of the production.

The film pits Superman against Luthor (Lyle Talbot), a criminal genius who, in his quest to impose his will on the city of Metropolis, devises an arsenal of scientific weapons, including Kryptonite, the one substance known to be deadly to Superman. Eventually Luthor's clever schemes are thwarted by Superman. Alyn claimed that being typecast as Superman hurt his acting career and was somewhat bitter for a while. But in his later years, after attending several film festivals and seeing the fans' admiration of him, he changed his mind about the role.

It was back to Republic for his fifth cliffhanger, *Radar Patrol vs. Spy King* ('50). It concerns a dangerous sabotage ring whose aim is the destruction of radar defense systems that protect the U.S. against invasion from enemy planes. The sinister head of the ring is Baroda (John Merton). Aiding him is a female accomplice, Nitra (Eve Whitney). The saboteurs kidnap Joan Hughes, (Jean Dean), a radar scientist in charge of the installation of the radar system at Keystone Station, the particular target of Baroda and his gang. Radar Defense Bureau operator Chris Calvert (Alyn) is able to rescue Joan and thwart the activities of the saboteurs until they are finally put out of commission for good.

After completing the second Superman film, Kirk was typecast as the Man of Steel and found it difficult to obtain acting roles. He has small supporting roles in *Bridge of Vengeance* ('49), *Gambling House* ('50), and *When Worlds Collide* ('51). He was about ready to head back to New York and the stage when Columbia decided to star him in yet another serial—*Blackhawk* ('52), based on the comic strip. Blackhawk (Alyn) is the leader of an international brotherhood sworn to combat the forces of tyranny throughout the world. Foreign agent Laska (Carol Forman), working for an unidentified boss known only as the Leader, plants one of her men in the organization and manages to steal a deadly electronic ray. Blackhawk battles spies and saboteurs until finally Laska is trapped in the secret office of the Leader. She is denouncing him for his efforts to destroy her as the Blackhawks enter the room. Laska kills the Leader, a double for Defense Council member Case (Michael Fox), but is herself captured.

Alyn left Hollywood to return to the New York stage in the early 1950s. He appeared in various Broadway productions and made numerous commercials. He became a popular figure on the nostalgia circuit in the 1970s, appearing at conventions and on college campuses. He authored a book of memories, *A Job for Superman*, which he published himself. He and Noel Neill were given small roles as the young Lois Lane's parents on a train in *Superman, the Movie* ('78) starring Christopher Reeve. Alyn also played a small role in Fred Olen Ray's horror film *Scalps* ('83).

Alyn had been in poor health for several years prior to his death on March 14, 1999. He died in a hospital near Houston from a combination of dementia and Alzheimer's.

Serials

1946

Daughter of Don Q. Rep., [12 Chapters] D: Spender Bennet, Fred Brannon; SP: Albert De Mond, Basil Dickey, Jesse Duffy, Lynn Perkins; AP: Ronald Davidson; Cam: Bud Thackery; Mus: Raoul Kraushaar; LP: Adrian Booth, Kirk Alyn, LeRoy Mason, Roy Barcroft, Claire Meade, Eddie Parker.

1948

Superman. Col., [15 Chapters] D: Spencer G. Bennet, Thomas Carr; P: Sam Katzman; Cam: Ira H. Morgan; Mus: Mischa Bakaleinikoff; SP: Arthur Hoerl, Lewis Clay, Royal Cole; Adapt: George Plympton, Joseph F. Poland; LP: Kirk Alyn, Noel Neill, Tommy Bond, Pierre Watkin, Carol Forman, George Meeker.

1949

Federal Agents vs. Underworld, Inc. Rep., [12 Chapters] D: Fred C. Brannon; SP: Royal K. Cole, Basil Dickey, William Lively, Sol Shor; AP: Franklyn Adreon; Cam: John MacBurnie; Mus: Stanley Wilson; LP: Kirk Alyn, Roy Bar-

croft, Rosemary LaPlanche, Carol Forman, James Dale.

1950

Atom Man vs. Superman. Col., [15 Chapters] D: Spencer G. Bennet; P: Sam Katzman; SP: George Plympton, Joseph F. Poland, David Mathews; Cam: Ira H. Morgan; Mus: Mischa Bakaleinikoff; LP: Kirk Alyn, Noel Neill, Lyle Talbot, Tommy Bond, Pierre Watkin, Jack Ingram.

Radar Patrol vs. Spy King. Rep., [12 Chapters] D: Fred C. Brannon; SP: Royal Cole, William Lively, Sol Shor; AP: Franklyn Adreon; Cam: Ellis W. Carter; Mus: Stanley Wilson; LP: Kirk Alyn, Jean Dale, Anthony Warde, George J. Lewis, Eve Whitney, John Merton.

1952

Blackhawk. Col., [15 Chapters] D: Spencer G. Bennet; Fred F. Sears; SP: George H. Plympton, Royal K. Cole, Sherman L. Lowe; P: Sam Katzman; Cam: William Whitley; Mus: Mischa Bakaleinikoff; LP: Kirk Alyn, Carol Forman, John Crawford, Michael Fox, Don C. Harvey, Rick Vallin.

RAMSAY AMES

Ramsay "Body Beautiful" Ames was born in New York City on March 30, 1924, and christened Rita Rebecca Phillips. Her mother was Spanish and her father English, which helped to account for Ramsay's unusual coloring—hazel-green eyes, auburn hair and tawny complexion.

Educated at Edgewood Park, Briarcliff Manor, in New York, she revealed an early flair for dramatics, dancing and swimming. After graduation, she enrolled in the Walter Hillhouse School of Dancing.

Come the New York World's Fair and Ramsay landed her first job, modeling at a

fashion show for Eastman Kodak. By the time the fair ended, she had definitely made up her mind to be a professional dancer. Spurning two offers to continue modeling, she went to Miami Beach where she became one-half of a dance team at the Royal Palms.

Ramsay learned to play the bongo drums, the nanigo, the claves and other tropic percussion instruments, and as she learned she evolved her own routine, torrid, primitive voodoo dances that seemed newly sprung from the heart of the jungle.

By the time she had Florida nitery patrons in the palm of her hand, she had se-

Ramsay Ames and Clayton Moore in *G-Men Never Forget* (Republic, 1948).

made two serials for Republic and one for Columbia. In *The Black Widow* ('47) she has a minor part as Dr. Curry. Principal female roles went to Carol Forman and Virginia Lindley. Republic did better by her in *G-Men Never Forget* ('47), in which she plays opposite Clayton Moore. As Sgt. Frances Blake, she and Moore, as Ted O'Hara, strive to thwart escaped convict Murkland's (Roy Barcroft) protective insurance racket. And in the Columbia chapterplay *The Vigilante* ('47) she plays a rodeo queen saved from death innumerable times by Gregg Sanders (Ralph Byrd), secretly "The Vigilante," undercover agent out to stop gang leader X-1 (Lyle Talbot) from acquiring a string of pearls called the "100 Tears of Blood." The pearls, which have a mysterious origin, are concealed in the hooves of five stallions belonging to George Pierce's (Talbot) ranch guests.

lected other worlds to conquer, returning to New York where the Gypsy Carmen Amaya whetted the town's interest in fiery solo dances. Ramsay organized her own rhumba band, worked with Xavier Cugat and achieved enough attention to be sought out by movie scouts. She traveled west, going to work the day after her arrival in Hollywood in Columbia's *Two Señoritas from Chicago* ('42) starring Joan Davis and Jinx Falkenberg, following which she was signed by Universal. Some of her roles were as the exotic favorite of the caliph in *Ali Baba and the Forty Thieves* ('44), a college girl who turns out to be the reincarnation of an Egyptian princess in *The Mummy's Ghost* ('44), an alluring movie queen who finds eventual come-uppance in *Hat Check Honey* ('44) and the indiscreet wife whose loveliness overpowered her husband's best friend in *Calling Dr. Death* ('43).

After she became a freelancer, Ramsay

Ames never achieved much success as a leading lady and gave up her career in Bs with *Philo Vance Returns* ('47). However, she returned to the screen in *Alexander the Great* ('56) and again in *The Running Man* and *The Rampage* (both '63).

Around 1966 Ramsay married playwright Dale Wasserman of *Man of La Mancha* fame and lived the good life with a villa on the Costa del Sol in Spain and other residences in London and New York. However, wedded bliss came to an end on February 20, 1980, when a final divorce decree came through after 14 years of marriage. She died a few years ago.

Serials

1947

The Vigilante. Col., [15 Chapters] D: Wallace Fox; SP: George H. Plympton, Lewis Clay, Arthur Hoerl; P: Sam Katzman; Cam: Ira H. Morgan; Mus: Mischa Bakaleinikoff; LP: Ralph Byrd, Ramsay Ames, Lyle Talbot, George Offerman, Jr., Robert Barron, George Chesebro, Hugh Prosser, Jack Ingram.

The Black Widow. Rep., [13 Chapters] D: Spencer Bennet and Fred C. Brannon; SP: Franklyn Adreon, Basil Dickey, Jesse Duffy, Sol Shor; AP: Mike Frankovich; Cam: John MacBurnie; Mus: Mort Glickman; LP: Carol Forman, Bruce Edwards, Virginia Lindley, Anthony Warde, Ramsay Ames, I. Stanford Jolley, Ernie Adams.

G-Men Never Forget. Rep., [12 Chapters] D: Fred Brannon and Yakima Canutt; AP: Mike Frankovich; SP: Franklyn Adreon, Basil Dickey, Jesse Duffy, Sol Shor; Cam: John MacBurnie; Mus: Mort Glickman; LP: Clayton Moore, Ramsay Ames, Roy Barcroft, Drew Allen, Edmund Cobb, Tom Steele.

CLAIRE ANDERSON

Claire Anderson was a Sennett beauty who first made films at Triangle in 1918. She died in 1964 at age 68 in Venice, California. Although biographical information is unavailable, we do have a record of her film appearances.

In *The Answer* ('18) Claire plays Goldie Shepherd, whose fondness for luxuries causes her husband to donate his estate to English charities and return to America. Guido Garcia, who had been Goldie's suitor, learns of her marriage and murders her. As a refugee in *Crown Jewels* ('18) she is instrumental in safeguarding the crown jewels of a European nation threatened by revolution. She plays the wife of Roy Stewart in *The Fly God* ('18). He is convicted of murder by a vengeful sheriff.

In *The Grey Parosol* ('18), Claire hides the formula for an inexpensive substitute for coal in the handle of her parosol. German agents try to steal it but in the end she outwits them and delivers the formula to U.S. government officials.

Mlle Paulette ('18) is a comedy in which Claire portrays a vaudeville star and Wallace MacDonald is a Broadway playboy who falls in love with her. In *The Mask* ('18) Claire is a country girl who inherits a fortune, but soon realizes that money can't buy happiness. In *The Girl in Number 29* Claire participates in a trick to restore playwright Frank Mayo's interest in life and winds up marrying him. *The Rider of the Law* ('19) stars Harry Carey and Claire as a dance hall girl who sets outlaws free because Harry has refused her advances.

Claire is an American girl imprisoned by the rajah of a province with intention of adding her to his harem in the thriller *The Palace of Darkened Windows* ('20). She is rescued by an American who has fallen in love with her. In *The Path She Chose* ('20) Claire is the wastrel sister of Anne Cornwall, whom Anne rescues from her lot as a scrubwoman. In *The Servent in the House* ('20) Jean Hersholt effects a reconciliation among the members of a vicar's family. Claire is the sister of quarreling brothers.

Claire's first film in 1921 was *The Road Demon* opposite Tom Mix. *When We Were Twenty-One* is a comedy-drama in which Claire marries H. B. Warner. Claire inherits from her deceased father in *Who Am I?* ('21). She gambles to pay off a debt to George Periolat until one of her victims tries to commit suicide and she realizes the wrong she is doing. Periolat is unmasked as a cheater. She decides to marry Niles Welch, an associate.

In *The Yellow Stain* ('22), Claire is involved with John Barrymore in a story of a young lawyer winning his case in spite of the shenanigans of the town's most feared citizen. In *The Clean Up* ('23) Claire, Herbert Rawlinson's society fiancée, abandons him when he supposedly is left only one dollar in his grandfather's will. In *The Meddler* ('25) Claire jilts William Desmond when he fails to provide her with the romance and adventure she craved. He goes west to prove himself and becomes a bandit called the Meddler. He meets Dolores Rousse and falls in love with her, proves his innocence and stays

in the west, while Claire marries a retired army officer.

The Meddler was Claire's last film. What she did after that is not known to the author.

It was in 1920 that she made the serial *The Fatal Sign* for Arrow Pictures. Harry Carter had the male lead. The number of chapters was either 14 or 15. Plot is unknown.

Serial

1920

The Fatal Sign. Arrow, [14 or 15 Chapters] D: Stuart Paton; LP: Claire Anderson, Harry Carter, Joseph W. Girard, Boyd Irwin, Leo Maloney.

LONA ANDRE

Lona Andre made more publicity stills than she did movies. She came to Hollywood as a result of the "Panther Woman" contest conducted by Paramount. She didn't win but she got a Paramount contract and posed for lots of fan magazine leg art. In 1932 she was selected as one of 15 Wampas Baby Stars by the Western Association of Motion Picture Advertisers, an organization of Hollywood publicists. ("Wampas" is the acronym concocted from the name of the organization.) The annual selection of young ladies expected to achieve stardom, with the attendant publicity, enhanced the prestige of press agents within the movie industry.

Lona never achieved the stardom expected of her, but she did act in a number of Paramount films as a supporting player: *The Mysterious Rider* ('33, Kent Taylor), *The Woman Accused* ('33, Nancy Carroll), *Pick Up* ('33, Sylvia Sidney), *College Humor* ('33, Bing Crosby), *International House* ('33, W. C. Fields), *Her Bodyguard* ('33, Edmund Lowe),

Take a Chance ('33, James Dunn), *Come On Marines* ('34, Richard Arlen), and *Murder at the Vanities* ('34, Victor McLaglen).

Her option was not picked up in 1934 and she became a freelancer, appearing in *School for Girls* ('34, Liberty, Paul Kelly), *Two Heads on a Pillow* ('34, Liberty, Neil Hamilton), *The Merry Widow* ('34, MGM, Jeanette MacDonald), *By Your Leave* ('34, Radio, Frank Morgan), *One Run Elmer* ('35, Educational, Buster Keaton), *Under the Pampas Moon* ('35, Fox, Warner Baxter), *Happiness C.O.D.* ('35, Chesterfield, Maude Eburne), *The Timid Young Man* ('35, Educational, Buster Keaton), *Skybound* ('35, Puritan, Eddie Nugent), *Lucky Terror* ('36, Diversion, Hoot Gibson), *Three on a Limb* ('36, Educational, Buster Keaton) and *Our Relations* ('36, MGM, Stan Laurel and Oliver Hardy).

In 1936 Andre appeared as Belle Meade in the Stage and Screen serial *Custer's Last Stand*. A sacred medicine arrow is lost during one of the skirmishes between red men

Lona Andre and Donald Barry in *Ghost Valley Raiders* (Republic, 1940).

and whites and is recovered by Major Trent, who is unaware that it carries the secret of the location of an Indian cavern of gold. Knowing about the arrow, renegade Tom Blade seeks to steal it. To achieve this purpose, he finds it necessary to keep hostilities going. Scout Kit Cardigan suspects Blade and fights to prevent all-out war, but the stage is set for Custer's Last Stand.

Lona continued playing leads and supporting parts for several years, including the soubrette in *Trailing Trouble* ('37, GN, Ken Maynard), *The Great Hospital Mystery* ('37, TCF, Jane Darwell), *Death in the Air* ('37, Puritan, John Carroll), *Ghost Valley Raiders* ('40, Republic, Don Barry), *The Sunset Strip Case* ('41, GN, Sally Rand), *Pardon My Sarong* ('42, Univ., Bud Abbott and Lou Costello) and *Confessions of a Vice Baron* ('43, Real Life Dramas, Constance Worth).

Lona was born Laura Anderson on March 2, 1915, in Nashville, Tennessee. For four days she was married to actor Edward Norris. She retired in 1943 to become a Hollywood businesswoman.

Serial

1936

Custer's Last Stand. S&S, [15 Chapters] D: Elmer Clifton; SP: George A. Durlam, Eddy Graneman, William Lively; P: George M. Merrick; Spv: Louis Weiss; Cam: Bert Longenecker; Mus: Hal Chasnoff; LP: Rex Lease, Reed Howes, William Farnum, Jack Mulhall, Lona Andre, Ruth Mix, Bobby Nelson, William Desmond, Nancy Caswell, Helen Gibson, Dorothy Gulliver.

STANLEY ANDREWS

Character actor Stanley Andrews, the Old Ranger on TV's *Death Valley Days* for many years, had a show business career that spanned a half century in movies, radio and television. He died at age 77 on June 23, 1969, in Magnolia Gardens Convalescent Hospital in Granada Hills, California. Burial was at Glenhaven Memorial Park. Two nephews survived.

Though he is most closely linked to Westerns, a review of 262 of his films reveals only 75 (29 percent) are Westerns. Of his seven serials, five are Westerns. The one he is most remembered for is *The Lone Ranger* ('38) in which he portrays outlaw Mark Smith who, in his assumed role of Commissioner Jeffries, lusts to be dictator of all Texas. In the final chapter, the villains are routed and the Lone Ranger and Jeffries fall over a precipice seemingly locked in a death grip. Only the Lone Ranger survives. In the remaining serials, Andrews only has minor

parts easily forgotten. Andrews played good guys and bad guys with equal relish.

Andrews can be seen in the following Westerns. In some he has a pretty good part; in others, one must be diligent to spot him: *Wanderer of the Wasteland* ('36), *Drift Fence* ('36), *The Texas Rangers* ('36), *Bad Man of Brimstone* ('37), *The Plainsman* ('37), *Forbidden Valley* ('38), *The Mysterious Rider* ('38), *Prairie Moon* ('38), *Stablemates* ('38), *Union Pacific* ('39), *Geronimo* ('40), *The Mark of Zorro* ('40), *The Westerner* ('40), *In Old Colorado* ('41), *The Yukon Patrol* ('42), *In Old Oklahoma* ('43), *The Ox-Bow Incident* ('43), *Tucson Raiders* ('44), *Vigilantes of Dodge City* ('44), *The Daltons Ride Again* ('45), *Trail of Vengeance* ('45), *Bad Bascomb* ('46), *God's Country* ('46), *The Virginian* ('46), *Smoky* ('46), *California* ('47), *The Fabulous Texan* ('46), *King of the Wild Horses* ('47), *Robin Hood of Texas* ('47), *Trail Street* ('47), *Last of the Wild Horses* ('48), *The Man from Colorado* ('48), *The Man from Texas* ('48), *Panhandle* ('48), *The Paleface* ('48), *The Return of Wildfire* ('48), *Northwest Stampede* ('48), *Brimstone* ('49), *Brothers in the Saddle* ('49), *The Doolins of Oklahoma* ('49), *Roughshod* ('49), *The Last Bandit* ('49), *Trail of the Yukon* ('49), *The Valiant Hombre* ('49), *Across the Badlands* ('50), *The Arizona Cowboy* ('50), *Colt .45* ('50), *Mule Train* ('50), *The Nevadan* ('50), *Outcast of Black Mesa* ('50), *Rock Island Trail* ('50), *Salt Lake Raiders* ('50), *Short Grass* ('50), *Streets of Ghost Town* ('50), *Trigger, Jr.* ('50), *Two Flags West* ('50), *Mexicali Stars* ('50), *West of Wyoming* ('50), *Stage to Tucson* ('51), *Vengeance Valley* ('51), *Al Jennings of Oklahoma* ('51), *Saddle Legion* ('51) *Waco* ('52), *Man from the Black Hills* ('51), *Kansas Territory* ('52), *Carson City* ('52), *Woman of the North Country* ('52), *Fargo* ('52), *Montana Belle* ('52), *Border River* ('53), *El Paso Stampede* ('53), *Dawn at Socorro* ('54), *The Three Outlaws* ('56) and *Frontier Gambler* ('56).

Serials

1935

The Call of the Savage. Univ., [12 Chapters] D: Lewis Friedlander [Lew Landers]; S: Otis Adelbert Kline; SP: Nate Gazert, George Plympton, Basil Dickey; LP: Noah Beery, Jr., Dorothy Short, Harry Woods, Walter Miller, Grace Cunard, Bryant Washburn.

1938

The Lone Ranger. Rep., [15 Chapters] D: William Witney, John English; SP: Barry Shipman, George W. Yates, Franklyn Adreon, Ronald Davidson, Lois Eby; Spv: Robert Beche; AP: Sol. C. Siegel; Cam: William Nobles; Mus: Alberto Colombo; LP: Lee Powell, Lynne Roberts, Chief Thundercloud, Herman Brix, Stanley Andrews, Lane Chandler, Hal Taliaferro, George Cleveland.

1939

The Green Hornet. Univ., [13 Chapters] D: Ford Beebe, Ray Taylor; SP: George Plympton, Basil Dickey, Morrison C. Wood, Lyonel Margolies; AP: Henry MacRae; Cam: William Sickner; LP: Gordon Jones, Anne Nagel, Keye Luke, Wade Boteler, Philip Trent, Walter McGrail, Anne Gwynne.

1940

King of the Royal Mounted. Rep., [12 Chapters] D: William Witney, John English; SP: Franklyn Adreon, Norman S. Hall, Joseph Poland, Barney A. Sarecky, Sol Shor; AP: Hiram S. Brown, Jr.; Cam: William Nobles; Mus: Cy Feuer; LP: Allan Lane, Robert Strange, Robert Kellard, Lita Conway, Herbert Rawlinson, Stanley Andrews.

1943

Daredevils of the West. Rep., [12 Chapters] D: John English; SP: Ronald Davidson, Basil Dickey, William Lively, Joseph O'Donnell, Joseph Poland; AP: W. J. O'Sullivan; Cam: Bud Thackery; Mus: Mort Glickman; LP: Allan Lane, Kay Aldridge, Eddie Acuff, William Haade, Ted Adams, Stanley Andrews, George J. Lewis

Adventures of Frank and Jesse James. Rep., 1948 [13 Chapters] D: Fred Brannon, Yakima Canutt; SP: Franklyn Adreon, Basil Dickey, Sol Shor; AP: Franklyn Adreon; Cam: John MacBurnie; Mus: Morton Scott; LP: Clayton Moore, Steve Darrell, Noel Neill, George J. Lewis, Stanley Andrews, Tom Steele.

Canadian Mounties vs. Atomic Invaders. Rep., 1953 [12 Chapters] D/AP: Franklyn Adreon; SP: Ronald Davidson; Cam: John MacBurnie; Mus: Stanley Wilson; LP: Bill Henry, Susan Morrow, Arthur Space, Pierre Watkin, Stanley Andrews, Mike Ragan.

ARMIDA

Armida acted in one serial only, *Congo Bill* ('48), in the role of the tribal girl Zalea. It was a minor role that normally would not justify her inclusion in this book. However, the author likes her; thus, has taken this means of paying tribute to her for the fine little actress that she was. One might think of her as a more subdued Lupe Velez, although Armida could also be fiery.

Her first film, made in Mexico, was *La Mexicana* ('29). *Fiesta* ('41) was made by Hal Roach and released through United Artists. Anne Ayars and George Negrete headed the cast with Armida and Antonio Morena and Guadalajara Trio featured. *The Girl from Monterey* ('43) features Armida as a cantina singer fired for refusing to serve a customer at his table. One thing leads to another. Action centers around the boxing ring. Edgar Kennedy, Jack La Rue and Veda Ann Borg support.

PRC's *Machine Gun Mama* ('48), a slapstick comedy, features Armida as the daughter of a carnival owner who aids El Brendel and Wallace Ford in their efforts to get rid of an elephant. *Jungle Goddess* ('48) features Armida as a jungle girl in support of George Reeves and Wanda McKay.

Armida was born in Sonora, Mexico. Other than that statistic, the author has found no biographical information on her. Other films include *General Crook* ('29), *Show of Shows* ('29), *Wings of Adventure* ('30), *Border Romance* ('30), *La Conga Nights* ('40), *South of Tahita* ('40) and *Melody Parade* ('43).

Serial

1948

Congo Bill. Col., [15 Chapters] D: Spencer G. Bennet, Thomas Carr; SP: George H. Plympton, Lewis Clay, Arthur Hoerl; P: Sam Katzman; LP: Don McGuire, Cleo Moore, I. Stanford Jolley, Jack Ingram, Leonard Penn, Armida, Charles King.

ROBERT ARMSTRONG

Robert Armstrong will forever be remembered as Carl Denham, intrepid movie director, in RKO's *King Kong*, and he played the same character in the sequel *The Son of Kong* ('33). Sixteen years later he would play basically the same character under a different name in RKO's *Mighty Joe Young* ('49). So he was closely associated with apes.

Another close association was Armstrong and prizefighting. In the play *Is Zat So?* ('26) Armstrong played a not-so-bright lightweight boxing champ. He later directed a road company of the play as well as the London production.

Pathé signed Armstrong to a term contract and put him into *The Main Event* ('27) in which he again plays a prizefighter. Other boxing films in which he played were *Celebrity* ('28), *Be Yourself* ('30), *Dumbbells in Ermine* ('30), *The Tip-Off* ('31), *Iron Man* ('31) and *Unmarried* ('39).

Armstrong was born on November 20, 1890, in Saginaw, Michigan. The family moved to Seattle, Washington, while Robert was still a youth and he graduated from high school there, going on to the University of Washington where he studied law and got involved in dramatics. When World War I broke out, Robert joined the infantry as a buck private, but he was discharged as a first lieutenant.

Pursuing an acting career, he spent two years in stock in North Carolina and followed with a part in the national company of *The Man Who Came Back*. All told he spent ten years in vaudeville and on the legitimate stage before making his screen debut in 1927's *The Main Event*. He soon became one of Hollywood's busiest character actors, appearing mostly in action pictures and usually cast in the role of a good tough guy, on either side of the law, both in leads and supporting parts.

A few of Armstrong's films, excluding the "ape" and "boxing" pictures already mentioned, are *The Most Dangerous Game* ('32), *Above the Clouds* ('33), *G-Men* ('35), *The Ex-Mrs. Bradford* ('36), *Mystery Man* ('37), *Call a Messenger* ('39), *Citadel of Crime* ('41), *Baby Face Morgan* ('42), *Belle of the Yukon* ('44), *Blood on the Sun* ('45), *Criminal Court* ('46), *The Fugitive* ('47), *The Paleface* ('48), *The Crime Doctor's Diary* ('49) and *Las Vegas Shakedown* ('55). As is apparent from these titles, a majority of his films were action-oriented.

Armstrong's first of four serials, all made for Universal, was *Sky Raiders* ('41), in which he shared honors with Donald Woods and Billy Halop. He played Lt. Ed Corey. Woods is famed aviator Bob Dayton, the target of enemy agents who want plans for a new type of fighter plane and a bombsight which his company has developed. Billy Halop is Tim Bryant, a member of the Air Youth of America, who is hired by Dayton to do experimental work.

In 1942, Armstrong appeared in his second serial, *Gang Busters*. Detectives find that a gang of terrorists is made up of criminals officially listed in police files as dead. Detectives Kent Taylor and Armstrong are assigned to run down the League of Murdered Men. Ralph Morgan, the ringleader, has a death-simulating drug and a anti-death treatment he uses to recruit gang members. The detectives are aided by Irene Hervey, a news photographer and girlfriend of Taylor.

Adventures of the Flying Cadets ('43) was Armstrong's third serial. Johnny Downs, Bobby Jordan, Ward Wood and Billy Benedict are air cadets suspected of a series of murders masterminded by the Black Hangman (Armstrong), actually an engineer who, as a member of an exploring expedition, locates lost helium deposits in Africa. To keep the location a secret, he kills all the expedition members except Selmer Jackson and his daughter Jennifer Holt, whom he imprisons.

Robert Armstrong (with revolver) and Richard Davies in *Gang Busters* (Universal, 1942).

The cadets, believing Armstrong to be a friend, fly with him to Africa to try and clear their names of murder charges; he leads them into a Nazi trap. In the final showdown, Armstrong is exposed as the Black Hangman and the cadets are given their wings.

Armstrong returned to Universal for one last serial, *The Royal Mounted Rides Again* ('45). Two Canadian Mounties investigate the murder of a mine operator by an outlaw gang attempting to gain possession of rich gold mines. A number of other killings occur before the operator of the Yukon Palace (Armstrong) is discovered to be the leader of the outlaws.

In 1947, Armstrong played a police sergeant in John Ford's *The Fugitive*, starring Henry Fonda and Dolores Del Rio; and he is a police lieutenant in Republic's *The Streets of San Francisco* ('49). A few other films followed, including Gene Autry's *Sons of New Mexico*

('50), but Robert chose to retire in 1957, subsequently coming out of retirement for one last film, *For Those Who Think Young* ('64).

Robert Armstrong died at the age of 82 at the Santa Monica Hospital on April 20, 1973.

Serials

1941

Sky Raiders. Univ., [12 Chapters] D: Ford Beebe, Ray Taylor; SP: Clarence Upson Young, Paul Huston; S: Eliot Gibbons; AP: Henry MacRae; LP: Donald Woods, Billy Halop, Robert Armstrong, Kathryn Adams, Eduardo Ciannelli.

1942

Gang Busters. Univ., [13 Chapters] D: Ray Taylor, Noel Smith; AP: Ford Beebe; SP:

Morgan B. Cox, Al Martin, Vin Martin, George H. Plympton; Cam: William Sickner, John Boyle; LP: Kent Taylor, Irene Hervey, Robert Armstrong, Ralph Morgan, Richard Davies.

1943

Adventures of the Flying Cadets. Univ., [13 Chapters] D: Ray Taylor, Lewis D. Collins; SP: Morgan B. Cox, George H. Plympton, Paul Huston; AP: Henry MacRae; Cam: William Sickner; Mus: Hans J. Salter; LP: Johnny Downs, Bobby Jordan, Jennifer Holt, Eduardo Ciannelli, Robert Armstrong.

1945

The Royal Mounted Rides Again. Univ., [13 Chapters] D: Ray Taylor, Lewis D. Collins; SP: Joseph O'Donnell, Tom Gibson, Harold C. Wire; P: Morgan Cox; LP: George Dolenz, Bill Kennedy, Daun Kennedy, Paul E. Burns, Milburn Stone, Robert Armstrong, Addison Richards.

JEAN ARTHUR

Jean Arthur was born Gladys Georgianne Green in New York City on October 17, 1908. Her father was a photographer, her mother a homemaker. Jean was the youngest of four children, her three brothers being considerably older than she. Much of Jean's schooling was in the Washington Heights section of New York City and her childhood was pretty much a normal one.

Thoughts of becoming a dancer or language teacher were discarded when a photographer dissuaded her from pursuing those dreams. She became his model on a part-time basis and soon was modeling full-time for Howard Chandler Christy and other illustrators. A Fox talent scout noticed her and arranged a screen test, which resulted in a contract and her debut in *Cameo Kirby* ('23) with John Gilbert. Her name was changed to Jean Arthur. One can only wonder how the shy, sensitive Miss Arthur could survive working under irracible John Ford, although, strangely enough, her shy complex was more evident as the years progressed than in the beginning of her career when she worked in horse operas, custard pie comedies and garden-variety dramas.

Jean got some of her training as a co-median in the vehicles of Wally Wales (Hal Taliaferro), Buffalo Bill, Jr. [Jay Wilsey], and Franklyn Farnum. All had a flair for comedy and quite often the script provided for humorous byplay between hero and heroine.

Arthur's only serial was *The Masked Menace* ('27), one of Pathé's least popular releases. Jean depicts a heroine with a vein of obstinate courage in the face of the impossible, which might refer as much to the script as to perils within the film. That it provided moderately satisfying entertainment was due solely to Arthur and co-star Larry Kent, who tried valiantly to achieve believability in a film having little production finesse. Apparently director Arch B. Heath's concentration was on other things. Plot situations were generally unlikely and unconvincing and the serial dragged in spots, though only 10 chapters in length. It didn't come anywhere close to measuring up to the standards usually necessary to display the rooster trademark.

Jean was building credits as a comedienne during the late '20s with films such as *Horse Shoes* ('27) and *Flying Luck* ('27), both with Monty Banks for Pathé release, and *The Poor Nut* ('27), a First National film starring Jack Mulhall.

Bob Custer and Jean Arthur in *A Man of Nerve* (FBO, 1925).

Paramount signed Jean in '28 and put her in better pictures. And it was that same year that she married a photographer named Julian Anker—for all of one day! Twenty-four hours after the ceremony, she was having the marriage annulled on the grounds that she was unaware her Paramount contract forbade her marrying.

In 1929, Miss Arthur was selected as a Wampas Baby Star by Western Associated Motion Picture Advertisers, sponsors of the popular annual event. Her film roles were varied, and she attained a modicum of recognition in *The Saturday Night Kid* ('29) and *The Green Murder Case* ('29) starring Clara Bow and William Powell, respectively. Most of her films still qualified as programmers—for instance, *The Mysterious Dr. Fu*

Manchu ('29), *The Return of Dr. Fu Manchu* ('30) and *The Gang Buster* ('31). Her only Westerns of the period were *Stairs of Sand* ('29) with Wallace Beery and *The Silver Horde* ('30), in a secondary role to Evelyn Brent and Joel McCrea.

The petite, squeaky-voiced actress adapted easily enough to sound, but her career seemed to be going nowhere, and she was thought to be through when her contract with Paramount expired in 1930. Arthur decided to return to New York to pursue her career via the stage. Her Broadway debut was in *Foreign Affairs* with Dorothy Gish in 1932. Later she appeared with Claude Rains in *The Man Who Reclaimed His Head* ('35). While in New York she married Frank Ross, Jr., an entertainer who later became a movie producer. In the next two years she appeared in *Twenty-five Dollars an Hour*, *The Curtain Rises* and *The Bride of Torozko* in addition to summer stock.

In 1934, Jean signed with Columbia after playing heroine to Jack Holt in *Whirlpool* ('34). Later that year she again provided the love interest in a Holt melodrama called *The Defense Rests* ('34). Another programmer followed and then John Ford used her in *The Whole Town's Talking* ('35), a comedy-melodrama with Arthur as a hard-boiled secretary who helps Edward G. Robinson, a timid clerk who is taken for a notorious gangster, to thwart the gang and become a hero. The picture was a hit and Arthur triumphed personally. It was the turning point in her career. No longer would she be cast in saccharine ingenue roles not worthy of her talents.

Arthur's popularity soon zoomed with the release of *Public Hero Number One* ('35), *Diamond Jim* ('35) and *If You Could Cook* ('35). Space does not allow a discussion of all of Jean Arthur's hit movies of the '30s and '40s, but mention must be made of the three Frank Capra films: *Mr. Deeds Goes to Town* ('36), a comedy classic co-starring Gary Cooper, *You Can't Take It with You* ('38), which won an Oscar as best picture, and *Mr. Smith Goes to Washington* ('39), a contender as Best Picture of 1939. Arthur topped all previous successes in her respective roles as a sob sister, an uninhibited working girl and a worldly-wise secretary displaying a grand sense of comedy and a charming personality. Jean could be both soft and tough, something that appealed to audiences. Her memorable Westerns were *The Plainsman* ('37), co-starring Gary Cooper, *Arizona* ('40), co-starring William Holden, and *Shane* ('53) co-starring Alan Ladd.

A divorce from Frank Ross was granted Arthur in 1949. In 1966 she starred in her own television series, *The Jean Arthur Show*.

Arthur was plagued with stage and camera fright for most of her career. Frank Capra recalled, "When the cameras stopped, she'd run to her dressing room, lock herself in, and cry. When called for another scene she could come out looking like a mop, walk aimlessly around muttering a torrent of non-sequitur excuses for not being ready. And it wasn't an act. Those were not butterflies in her stomach. They were wasps. But push that neurotic girl forcibly, but gently, in front of a camera and turn on the lights—and that whining mop would magically blossom into a warm, lovely, poised and confident actress."

In 1973, Jean was an artist in residence at the North Carolina School of the Arts in Winston-Salem. She loved painting and animals. She long worked for more humane treatment of animals and was a great pet fancier.

Arthur lived in Carmel, California, for many years and until her dying day remained aloof to fans, reporters and photographers and seldom signed autographs or answered mail. She never got over her shyness.

Jean Arthur died at age 89 in 1991 from heart failure following a paralyzing stroke.

Serial

1927

The Masked Menace. Pathé, 1927 [10 Chapters] D: Arch B. Heath; SP: Paul Fairfax Fuller; S: Clarence Budington Kelland; LP: Larry Kent, Jean Arthur, Tom Holding, Laura Alberta, John F. Hamilton.

GERTRUDE ASTOR

Gertrude Astor was one of the most popular leading ladies in Universal silents and was under contract there from 1914 until 1925. She continued her career, in supporting roles, for another 35 years. She was a stage actress in stock from age 13. On screen she typically played vampy roles, often as the calculating "other woman." She was quite popular among fans and enjoyed the reputation of being one of Hollywood's most elegant and best-dressed women. John Ford liked her and used her in a number of his films.

Gertrude was born November 9, 1887, in Lakewood, Ohio. She died on her birthday, November 9, 1977. A veteran of several hundred films, she liked *Uncle Tom's Cabin* ('27) best of her many roles.

In 1975, Universal honored her with a luncheon. Present to salute her were numerous directors for whom she had worked, including George Cukor, Allan Dwan and Henry Hathaway. Accepting a bouquet of roses, she brought listeners to tears by saying, "I am very proud. I thought life was over and I should just crawl in a corner and die. I have no family. I haven't a soul on earth to enjoy this with, but I'm going to do plenty of that."

Gertrude never starred in a serial but she added her talent to seven. The first was *The Gray Ghost* ('17), a 16-chapter cliffhanger made during World War I. It starred Harry Carter and Priscilla Dean. The next year she supported Marie Walcamp in the popular *The Lion's Claws* ('18). *The Lion Man* ('19) followed, supporting Kathleen O'Connor and Jack Perrin. In 1924 she supported Jack Dempsey and Esther Ralston in the ten-episode *Fight and Win* (usually labeled a series rather than a serial). *The Fatal Warning* ('29), *Finger Prints* ('31) and *Tailspin Tommy* ('34) were her other serials.

Astor retired from acting after a bit role in John Ford's *The Man Who Shot Liberty Valance* ('62).

Serials

1917

The Gray Ghost. Univ., [16 Chapters] D/SP: Stuart Paton; S: Arthur Somers Roche; LP: Harry Carter, Priscilla Dean, Emory Johnson, Eddie Polo, Gertrude Astor, Wilton Tayler.

1918

The Lion's Claws. Univ., [18 Chapters] D: Jacques Jaccard, Harry Harvey; SP: W. B. Pearson, Jacques Jaccard; S: W. B. Pearson; LP: Marie Walcamp, Roy Hanford, Neal Hart, Frank Lanning, Thomas Lingham, Gertrude Astor.

1919

The Lion Man. Univ., [18 Chapters] D: Albert Russell, Jack Wells; SP: Karl Coolidge; S: Randall Parrish; LP: Kathleen O'Connor, Jack Perrin, Mark Wright, J. Barney Sherry, Gertrude Astor.

1924

Fight and Win. Univ., [10 Episodes] D: Erle Kenton, Jesse Robbins; LP: Jack Dempsey, Esther Ralston, Hayden Stevenson, Edgar Kennedy.

1929

The Fatal Warning. Mascot, [10 Chapters] D: Richard Thorpe; P: Nat Levine; LP: Helene Costello, Ralph Graves, George Periolat, Boris Karloff, Phillip Smalley, Gertrude Astor.

1931

Finger Prints. Univ., [10 Chapters] D: Ray Taylor; SP: George Morgan, George H. Plympton, Basil Dickey; S: Arthur B. Reeve; LP: Kenneth Harlan, Edna Murphy, Gayne Whitman, Gertrude Astor.

1934

Tailspin Tommy. Univ., [12 Chapters] D: Louis Friedlander [Lew Landers]; SP: Norman S. Hall, Vin Moore, Basil Dickey, Ella O'Neill; LP: Maurice Murphy, Noah Beery, Jr., Patricia Farr, Walter Miller, Grant Withers, Gertrude Astor.

HOOPER ATCHLEY

Little is known about Hooper Atchley. He was born in Tennessee in 1889, was roughly six feet in height, and had brown hair and dark brown eyes. He graduated from Knoxville High School and attended the University of Tennessee. He was married to Violet Mahor, a non-professional.

Atchley spent approximately 20 years on the stage and entered films about 1931. The author has found 177 film credits for him, though he probably was in other films as an unbilled player. His better roles were in "B" Westerns of the '30s and early '40s. They are *Arizona Terror* ('31, Ken Maynard); *Branded Men* ('31, Ken Maynard); *Clearing the Range* ('31, Hoot Gibson); *Near Trails End* ('31, Bob Steele); *Sundown Trail* ('31, Tom Keene); *Fighting for Justice* ('32, Tim McCoy); *Gold* ('32, Jack Hoxie); *The Local Bad Man* ('32, Hoot Gibson); *The Spirit of the West* ('32, Hoot Gibson); *The Dude Bandit* ('33, Hoot Gibson); *Gun Justice* ('33, Ken Maynard); *Scarlet River* ('33, Tom Keene); *Drum Taps* ('33, Ken Maynard); *The Prescott Kid* ('34, Tim McCoy); *The Westerner* ('34, Tim McCoy); *The New Frontier* ('35, John Wayne); *The Outlaw Deputy* ('35, Tim McCoy); *The Sagebrush Troubador* ('35, Gene Autry); *Roarin' Lead* ('36, Three Mesquiteers); *The Plainsman* ('37, Gary Cooper); *The Old Barn Dance* ('38, Gene Autry); *Mountain Rhythm* ('39, Gene Autry); *Saga of Death Valley* ('39, Roy Rogers); *The Gay Caballero* ('40, Cesar Romero); *Arizona Terrors* ('42, Donald Barry); *In Old California* ('42, John Wayne); *The Omaha Trail* ('42, James Craig); *The Black Hills Express* ('43, Donald Barry) and *In Old Oklahoma* ('43, John Wayne).

Atchley made four films each with Ken Maynard, Hoot Gibson and Tim McCoy. He had principal roles in these films, so they were probably his best work. He offered a believable performance, whatever his role; however, his role seldom changed. He was the gang leader and could lay on the menace thickly enough.

Left to right: Hooper Atchley, Hoot Gibson, Doris Hill and Al Bridge in *The Spirit of the West* (Allied Artists, 1932).

Atchley's roles in the nine serials he graced were not principal ones, but they contributed to the overall excitement generated by these "continued-next-week" sagas.

Atchley committed suicide in Hollywood in 1943. No other details are available to the author. Several films he played in were not released until 1944.

Atchley always did justice to his assignment, be it large or be it small.

Serials

1933

The Three Musketeers. Mascot, [12 Chapters] D: Armand Schaefer, Colbert Clark; LP: Jack Mulhall, Raymond Hatton, Francis X. Bushman, Jr., John Wayne, Ruth Hall.

1934

Mystery Mountain. Mascot, [12 Chapters] D: B. Reeves Eason, Otto Brower; LP: Ken Maynard, Verna Hillie, Syd Saylor, Edward Earle, Lynton Brent, Lafe McKee.

The Adventures of Rex and Rinty. Mascot, [12 Chapters] D: B. Reeves Eason, Ford Beebe; LP: Rex (horse), Rin-Tin-Tin, Jr. (dog), Kane Richmond, Norma Taylor, Mischa Auer, Harry Woods.

1936

Ace Drummond. Univ., [13 Chapters] D: Ford Beebe, Cliff Smith; LP: John King, Jean Rogers, Noah Beery, Jr., Guy Bates Post, Arthur Loft.

1938

Flash Gordon's Trip to Mars. Univ., [15 Chapters] D: Ford Beebe, Robert Hill; LP: Buster

Crabbe, Jean Rogers, Charles Middleton, Frank Shannon, Beatrice Roberts.

1940

Adventures of Red Ryder. Rep., [12 Chapters] D: William Witney, John English; LP: Donald Barry, Noah Beery, Sr., Tommy Cook, Vivian Coe, Maude Pierce Allen.

1941

Dick Tracy vs. Crime, Inc. Rep., [15 Chapters] D: William Witney, John English; LP:

Ralph Byrd, Jan Wiley, John Davidson, Ralph Morgan, Kenneth Harlan.

King of the Texas Rangers. Rep., [12 Chapters] D: William Witney, John English; LP: Slingin' Sammy Baugh, Neil Hamilton, Pauline Moore, Duncan Renaldo.

1943

G-Men vs. The Black Dragon. Rep., [15 Chapters] D: William Witney; LP: Rod Cameron, Constance Worth, George J. Lewis, Nino Pipitone, Noel Cravat.

LIONEL ATWILL

Lionel Atwill, smooth as any villain ever in the movies, was at his evil best in films such as *Mystery of the Wax Museum* ('33) in which he becomes a proficient sculptor of new wax facades on the lifeless bodies of his many victims. This role provided Atwill with his definitive horror film role as Henry Jarrod, who became a scarred madman after his business was deliberately torched and his face disfigured in the fire. In *The Vampire Bat* ('33), Atwill is a deranged scientist in a primitive European village who domesticates bats, using them in a hoax to cover up his actual experiments (kidnapping villagers and draining them of their blood). *Murders in the Zoo* ('33) has Atwill murdering his wife's lovers in outlandish fashion; in *Son of Frankenstein* ('39), Atwill is a gendarme handicapped by a wooden arm.

The Hound of the Baskervilles ('39), one of the best of all Sherlock Holmes mystery films, has Atwill as James Mortimer, a red herring at eerie Baskerville Hall. In *Man Made Monster* ('41), Atwill plays Dr. Rigas, an electrobiologist who experiments on Lon Chaney, Jr., gradually building his tolerance to charges of electricity. Chaney is turned into a monster who goes to the electric chair

for a murder Rigas caused him to commit. The execution voltage does not kill Chaney and he escapes to take revenge on the doctor. In 1942, Atwill played Dr. Bohmer in *The Ghost of Frankenstein*. Betraying Dr. Frankenstein, Bohmer puts the brain of Ygor into the body of the Monster.

Atwill was an actor of considerable ability and this more than once permitted him to rise above a banal script and make something worthwhile out of the films in which he performed.

Lionel Atwill was born in Croydon, England, on March 1, 1885. His affluent origin permitted attendance at Mercer's School in London and a succession of private tutors. Although he studied architecture, he did not enter that profession but, instead, launched upon a theatrical career in 1904, appearing in plays by Ibsen, Shaw and Pinero. His success in Britain led to an invitation to tour Australia with a theatrical company from 1910 to 1912. Lily Langtry coaxed the British actor into a journey to America in 1915 and three years later he became Nazimova's leading man in *A Doll's House*. This was followed by Broadway runs with the actress in *The Wild Duck* and *Hedda Gabler*. That same year

(1918) he also made his film debut in *Eve's Daughter* and he would continue to make an occasional film, although he preferred the stage to the medium of the silent movie.

During the 1920s he became one of the top leading men of the stage, both on Broadway and in touring companies. In 1931 he was working on broadway in *The Silent Witness*; a Fox scout saw him and he was brought to Hollywood the next year to repeat his role on film. He never went back to the stage. He became a master actor of the macabre; as a result, he devoted much of the latter stages of his career to the weird, the ghastly, the morbid and the supernatural.

Atwill's personal life did not flow along as smoothly as his film career. He was married four times, and the second of his wives was the former wife of Gen. Douglas MacArthur. The actor's son was killed in 1941 while serving with the Royal Air Force. In 1940, Atwill was arrested for showing pornographic films and allegedly allowing orgies in his home. The jury found insufficient evidence to convict, but the next year he was indicted for perjury. Pleading guilty, he received five years' probation.

In *Junior G-Men of the Air* ('42), Atwill plays the Baron, head of a Japanese spy ring known as the Black Dragonflies. When the ring attempts to steal the plans for a new airplane muffler, the inventor's brother Ace (Billy Halop) and his buddies assist FBI agent Jerry Markham (Frank Albertson) in bringing the ring to justice. Although Atwill would not have considered playing in a serial earlier in his career, by now he was taking what roles he could get.

Captain America ('44), another serial, finds Atwill as Dr. Maldor, angry because he feels he was cheated out of fame and wealth that was rightfully his. Calling himself "The Scarab," he eliminates the former members of an archaeological group by means of a poison known as "The Purple Death." He also steals plans for a dynamic vibrator that has great destructive power, a newly invented life-restoring machine and the map to a Mayan treasure. Captain America (Dick Purcell) and his assistant Gail Richards (Lorna Gray) brings Maldor and his hoodlums to justice.

Atwill, as Alex Morel, is secretly leader of an outlaw gang pretending to be Confederate soldiers in *Raiders of Ghost City* ('44), and he has ties to Prussian spies. His identity is eventually discovered by Capt. Clark, who, with the help of his friend Idaho (Joe Sawyer), rounds up the raiders and spies.

Atwill's last film was *Lost City of the Jungle* ('46), in which he plays a power-mad Englishman after Meteorium 245, a defense against the atomic bomb. He completed about half the serial before succumbing to pneumonia on April 22, 1946. His double, George Sorel, finished the film for him.

Serials

1942

Junior G-Men of the Air. Univ., [12 Chapters] D: Ray Taylor, Lewis D. Collins; SP: Paul Huston, George H. Plympton, Griffin Jay; AP: Henry MacRae; LP: Billy Halop, Gene Reynolds, Lionel Atwill, Frank Albertson, Richard Lane, Huntz Hall.

1944

Captain America. Rep., [15 Chapters] D: John English, Elmer Clifton; SP: Royal Cole, Ronald Davidson, Basil Dickey, Jesse Duffy, Harry Fraser, Grant Nelson, Joseph F. Poland; AP: W. J. O'Sullivan; Cam: John MacBurnie; Mus: Mort Glickman; LP: Dick Purcell, Lorna Gray, Lionel Atwill, Charles Trowbridge, Russell Hicks.

Raiders of Ghost City. Univ., [13 Chapters] D: Ray Taylor, Lewis D. Collins; SP: Luci Ward, Morgan Cox; P: Morgan Cox, Ray Taylor; LP: Dennis Moore, Wanda McKay, Lionel Atwill, Joe Sawyer, Regis Toomey, Eddy Waller.

1946

Lost City of the Jungle. Univ., [13 Chapters] D: Ray Taylor, Lewis D. Collins; SP: Joseph F. Poland, Paul Huston, Tom Gibson; LP: Russell Hayden, Jane Adams, Lionel Atwill, Keye Luke, Helen Bennett, Dick Curtis.

MISCHA AUER

In his only serial role, *Tarzan the Fearless* ('33), a 15-chapter cliffhanger, Mischa Auer, mostly remembered as a comedian, played High Priest Eltar. A condensed 55-minute feature version was released later.

Auer was born Mischa Ounskowski on November 17, 1905, in Saint Petersburg, Russia. He was brought to the U.S. in 1920 by his maternal grandfather, violinist Leopold Auer. After attending New York's Ethical Culture School, Mischa turned to the theater. He was appearing in the play *Magda* on Broadway when director Frank Tuttle offered him a part in the film *Something Always Happens* ('28). For several years he appeared in small parts, mostly as a villain. Then came *My Man Godfrey* ('36), for which he was nominated for an Oscar.

Comedies of the '30s and '40s wouldn't have been the same without this frenetic, pole-thin, language-mangling, bug-eyed, sad-faced Russian. A few of his many films: *Drums of Jeopardy* ('31), *Midnight Patrol* ('32), *Girl Without a Room* ('33), *Wharf Angel* ('34), *Lives of a Bengal Lancer* ('35), *The Crusades* ('35), *Clive of India* ('35), *House of a Thousand Candles* ('36), *Three Smart Girls* ('37), *You Can't Take It with You* ('38), *Destry Rides Again* ('39), *Seven Sinners* ('40), *Flame of New Orleans* ('41), *Hellzapoppin* ('41), *Up in Mabel's Room* ('44), *Brewster's Millions* ('45), *Sentimental Journey* ('46), *A Dog, a Mouse, and a Sputnik* ('60) and *The Christmas That Almost Wasn't* ('65).

Auer appeared in some 60 American films before settling in Europe, where he played many more. France and Italy were favored countries. His last film made shortly before his death was *Arrivederci Baby!*

Mischa Auer died in 1967 from a heart attack in Rome, Italy.

Serial

1933

Tarzan the Fearless. Principal, [15 Chapters] D: Robert F. Hill; SP: Basil Dickey, George Plympton, Walter Anthony; Spv.: William Lora Wright; P: Sol Lesser; Cam: Harry Neuman, Joe Brotherton; LP: Buster Crabbe, Jacqueline Wells [Diana Duval/Julie Bishop], Philo McCullough, Mischa Auer, Matthew Betz.

VIVIAN AUSTIN (COE)

Vivian Irene Coe, leading lady to Donald Barry in *Adventures of Red Ryder* ('40), was born in the film city on February 23, 1923. A very pretty girl, Vivian won two dozen beauty contests before becoming an actress. All thoughts of attending college were dismissed when Warner Brothers signed her to a contract. She appeared in *Hollywood Hotel* ('37), *The Goldwyn Follies* ('38), *Brother Rat* ('38), *The Adventures of Robin Hood* ('38) and *Eternally Yours* ('39).

She was a member of "The Earl Carroll Vanities" in '38 and '39 and in 1940 Republic signed her to play in the Barry serial.

There wasn't much for her to do except decorate the scenery, and she did that quite well.

As a result of her winning so many beauty contests, she was selected to play opposite Buddy Ebsen in *Good Night Ladies*, a stage show which opened in San Francisco. A Universal talent scout spotted her and she was signed to a Universal contract. From this point on she used the last name "Austin," since she had married a man named Glenn Austin. For several years she was kept busy in a succession of "B" features.

In 1946 she began a two-year association with Eagle-Lion Films, where she appeared in *Born to Speed, Philo Vance's Gamble, Philo Vance Returns, Stepchild* and *T-Men*.

In 1955, while still living in Bel-Air with her husband Glenn Austin, Vivian helped Jane Russell found the Los Angeles chapter of WAIF. When she moved to Palm Springs in 1957, she started a local chapter of WAIF and was president for eight years. Then she organized a local auxiliary of Children's Home Society. After her husband's death, Vivian married her doctor, Kenneth A. Grow, an ophthalmologist. Vivian founded the Braille Auxiliary of the Desert and was president for six years.

Vivian enjoyed her volunteer work and derived a great amount of satisfaction from helping others. Writer Michael Fitzgerald reported in *Serial Report* that Vivian had many eye surgeries in the past after being blind for many years and had one eye removed and a glass eye implanted.

Vivian's only daughter, Angela, is a registered nurse and has made Vivian a grandmother.

Serial

1940

Adventures of Red Ryder. Rep., [12 Chapters] D: William Witney, John English; AP: Hiram S. Brown, Jr.; SP: Franklyn Adreon, Ronald Davidson, Norman S. Hall, Barney Sarecky, Sol Shor; Cam: William Nobles; Mus: Cy Feuer; LP: Donald Barry, Tommy Cook, Noah Beery, Sr., Maude Pierce Allen, Vivian Coe, Harry Worth, William Farnum.

GENE AUTRY

Gene Autry was one of the most popular singing stars of all time, as his record sales show. He was the biggest thing in cowboy movies for much of the period from 1935 to 1953, though Roy Rogers fans might disagree with the statement. Gene was awarded the first gold record ever for his recording of "That Silver-Haired Daddy of Mine" (over ten million records sold), and will always be identified with such songs as "Back in the Saddle Again" (his theme), "Tumbling Tumbleweeds" and "Rudolph, the Red-Nosed Reindeer" (one of the all-time top selling records).

Autry was the first Western star to become a Top Ten box office favorite and is the only entertainer to have five stars on the Hollywood Walk of Fame (for records, radio, movies, television and live theatrical-rodeo appearances).

Orvon Gene Autry was born on September 29, 1907, in the little town of Tioga, Texas, but the family shortly thereafter moved into Oklahoma, settling in the Tishomingo area. He quit school at an early age to take a job as a railroad telegraph operator. With a lot of idle time on his hands, he bought an $8 guitar and learned to play it to amuse himself during the long nights between messages. One night Will Rogers dropped in to send a telegram, heard Gene singing and advised him to try for a career in radio. Taking the advice, Gene headed for New York but once there was unable to get a radio job. But back in Oklahoma he secured a spot on Station KVOO in Tulsa and was billed "Oklahoma's Yodeling Cowboy."

Once again trying his luck in New York, Gene took along a song he had co-written with a friend. The song, "That Silver-Haired Daddy of Mine," landed him a contract with Columbia Records and a place on the National Barn Dance Broadcast from Chicago. The year was 1928.

In 1932, Gene met Ina Mae Spivey, the niece of Jimmy Long who had co-written "That Silver-Haired Daddy of Mine." She was boarding with the Longs while she attended teachers' college in Springfield, Missouri. After a courtship of several months, they were married on April 1, 1932.

Gene met fellow performer Smiley Burnette on the National Barn Dance. When Nat Levine, president of Mascot Pictures, beckoned, both Gene and Smiley responded. Levine signed Gene (at $100 a week) and Smiley (at $75 a week) with the intention of having them as musical backup for Ken Maynard, who had introduced music in his films, and who technically was the first singing cowboy. Gene and Smiley had to learn to ride, and Tracey Lane took on the job of teaching them. Cowboy star Reb Russell also pitched in to help.

Gene and Smiley had non-speaking bit parts in the Maynard serial *Mystery Mountain* ('34). Then came *In Old Santa Fe* ('34) with Gene and Smiley providing the musical interlude in what many consider to be Maynard's finest film. When Maynard balked at doing another serial for Levine, the producer decided to gamble on Autry and cast him in

Faye McKenzie and Gene Autry.

the lead of *The Phantom Empire* ('35), a 12-chapter cliffhanger still being shown ten years later. Burnette also had a part in the film but the real backup for Gene were the kid actors Frankie Darro and Betsy King Ross. The film was the first major sci-fi serial produced in the sound era and was considered very futuristic for its time. The story was a wild one, its incongruity of ingredients unbelievable, yet this bizarre bit of weekly make-believe clicked. Not only did audiences like the fantasy story, they also liked the guitar-plucking young hero with the friendly, natural, honest manner and pleasant, nasal-twang voice. Physically he wasn't much to write home about, and the histrionic abilities he demonstrated could easily have been the outcome of a three-day stint in a high school senior play. But his enthralling personality attracted a considerable coterie of fans.

Unquestionably there was a charisma

Gene Autry (center) with Smiley Burnette, Noah Beery, Sr., and Luana Walters in *Mexicali Rose* (Republic, 1939).

about Gene Autry. Any doubts on the subject were dispelled with the fantastic success of his first starring feature, *Tumbling Tumbleweeds* ('35), a $75,000 investment that quickly grossed over $500,000.

By 1936, Gene ranked third in popularity among cowboy stars. From 1937 through 1942 he was America's favorite cowboy, and in 1940 he was the fourth most popular movie star in the world, ranking behind Mickey Rooney, Spencer Tracy and Clark Gable. His fan mail averaged 80,000 letters a month. He slipped to sixth rank in 1941 and seventh rank in 1942, the year he went into military service. His records sold in the millions.

Gene went on to star in 89 features—57 for Republic, one for Fox and 31 for Columbia. Every film he made was guaranteed to provide wholesome entertainment for eager audiences, and all accrued fat bundles of loot for the studios. The Autry phenomenon was in motion. Setting a high standard for programmer Westerns were such films as *The Big Show* ('36), *Gold Mine in the Sky* ('38), *Mexicali Rose* ('39), *South of the Border* ('39), *Melody Ranch* ('40), *Down Mexico Way* ('40), *Sierra Sue* ('41), *The Last Roundup* ('47), *The Strawberry Roan* ('48), *Whirlwind* ('51), *Barbed Wire* ('52) and *Last of the Pony Riders* ('53).

Gene entered the U.S. Air Force in 1942. After three years in the service, he returned to find that Republic had been giving Roy Rogers the big push as King of the Cowboys; Gene made five films for Republic to finish out his contract and then headed for greener pastures. He formed his own company to make his films for Columbia release.

Gene lasted to the very end of the "B" era, voluntarily withdrawing from the production of theatrical films when it seemed they would no longer be profitable; instead he devoted himself to television, starring in 91 half-hour Westerns. In addition he produced 76 episodes of *The Range Rider* (Jock Mahoney, Dick Jones), 39 episodes of *Death Valley Days* (Stanley Andrews as the Old Ranger), 80 episodes of *Annie Oakley* (Gail Davis), 40 episodes of *Buffalo Bill, Jr.* (Dick Jones), and 26 episodes of *The Adventures of Champion* (Jim Bannon, Champion).

Gene invested in hotels, TV stations, oil, cattle, real estate, merchandising, baseball, etc. At the time of his death he had assets worth well over $100,000,000.

Gene Autry passed away on October 2, 1998.

Serials

1934

Mystery Mountain. Mascot, [12 Chapters] D: B. Reeves Eason, Otto Brower; LP: Ken Maynard, Tarzan (horse), Verna Hillie, Edward Earle, Syd Saylor.

1935

The Phantom Empire. Mascot, [12 Chapters] D: Otto Brower, B. Reeves Eason; S: Wallace MacDonald, Gerald Geraghty, Hy Freedman, Maurice Geraghty; SP: Armand Schaefer, John Rathmell; Spv.: Armand Schaefer; P: Nat Levine; LP: Gene Autry, Smiley Burnette, Frankie Darro, Betsy King Ross, Wheeler Oakman.

KING BAGGOT

Coming to the movies from the stage, King Baggot was one of the first American film performers to be publicized by name, and he quickly developed into a popular star of silent adventure dramas. Virile and handsome, he appeared in an estimated 250 shorts and feature films, then turned to directing dozens of films, most of which have deteriorated with the passage of time.

Baggot was an actor in a St. Louis stock company who finally made it to Broadway, only to leave the stage in 1909 to become one of the "flicker folk" in an era when motion picture actors were considered even less respectable than those who toured the country in traveling stock companies. King Baggot joined Carl Laemmle's IMP (Independent Motion Picture Co.) that year to begin a career that would last until only a few months before his death in 1948.

During the following decade he earned the reputation of "the most photographed man in the world." Although he was usually cast as the handsome leading man, in one picture, *Shadows*, he played the ten principal characters, which included roles as a Chinese servant, a German innkeeper, a betrayed girl, a prostitute, jailer, merchant, an old man and a policeman.

Most of Baggot's success was attributed to his versatility as an actor. Among the pictures in which he starred were *The Scarlet Letter* ('11), *Dr. Jekyll and Mr. Hyde* ('13), *Ivanhoe* ('13), *Absinthe* ('14), *Across the Atlantic* ('14), *The Corsican Brothers* ('15) and the serials, *The Eagle's Eye* ('18) and *The Hawk's Trail* ('18).

Irving Thalberg engaged Baggot as a director for Universal when the actor got a little old for playing leading man roles. Baggot sat behind the Kleig lights directing the great stars of the time. Probably his most out-

Buck Jones and King Baggot (right) in *Hello Trouble* (Columbia, 1932).

standing directorial success was William S. Hart's drama of the Oklahoma land rush, *Tumbleweeds* ('25), but he turned out creditable program pictures into the sound era.

Both of the serials in which he starred were made in 1918. In *The Eagle's Eye*, Harrison Grant (Baggot), president of the Criminology Club, and secret service agent Dixie Mason (Marguerite Snow) combat the furtive, no uniforms armies whose weapons are spying, sabotage, bomb-planting, murder, incendiarism and a hundred forms of insidious and demoralizing propaganda as they take on the Kaiser's spies in the U.S. during World War I.

In *The Hawk's Trail*, Baggot is seen as Stanton Steele, a noted criminologist hired by Claire Drake (Rhea Mitchell) to investigate a mysterious burglary. "Iron" Dugan

(Harry Lorraine), a master criminal, poses as the uncle of Jean (Grace Darmond) and Claire in an effort to obtain their fortunes. Each attempt to do away with the sisters is thwarted by Steele. Finally Dugan is exposed.

Baggot's wife of 18 years divorced him in 1930. The stock market crash of 1929 took most of his money. He went back to work as an actor, playing many character roles in his later years with all the gusto of a big-time star. He even worked as an extra.

He lived in the Aberdeen Hotel, Venice, where he became seriously ill a few days prior to his death, which came as a result of a stroke. Surviving was his son, Robert King Baggott of West Los Angeles.

King Baggot, 69, died July 11, 1948. His death brought an end to a notable career.

Serials

1918

The Eagle's Eye. Wharton/Amer., [20 Chapters] D: George A. Lessey, Wellington Playter; S: William J. Flynn; SP: Courtney Ryler Cooper; LP: King Baggot, Marguerite Snow, Bertram Marburgh, William N. Bailey.

1920

The Hawk's Trail. Burston, [15 Chapters] D: W. S. Van Dyke; S: Nan Blair; SP: John B. Clymer, Louis and George Burston; Spv: Louis Burston; LP: King Baggot, Rhea Mitchell, Grace Darmond, Harry Lorraine, Fred Windermere.

1934

The Red Rider. Univ., [15 Chapters] D: Louis Friedlander [Lew Landers]; LP: Buck Jones, Grant Withers, Marion Shilling, Walter Miller, Richard Cramer.

Tailspin Tommy. Univ., [12 Chapters] D: Louis Friedlander [Lew Landers]; LP: Maurice Murphy, Noah Beery, Jr., Patricia Farr, Walter Miller, Grant Withers.

1935

The Call of the Savage. Univ., [12 Chapters] D: Louis Friedlander [Lew Landers]; LP: Noah Beery, Jr., Dorothy Short, Harry Woods, Walter Miller, Bryant Washburn.

1936

The Adventures of Frank Merriwell. Univ., [12 Chapters] D: Cliff Smith; LP: Don Briggs, Jean Rogers, John King, Carla Laemmle, Al Bridge.

LEAH BAIRD

In her only serial, *Wolves of Kultur* ('18), Leah Baird appeared in the principal role. Charles Hutchison was the hero; Sheldon Lewis, the villain. The film was produced by Western Photoplays, with release through Pathé.

Baird was born in 1887 and from an early age acted on stage. At age 21 she appeared with Douglas Fairbanks on Broadway in *The Gentleman from Mississippi* (1908–10). She entered films with Vitagraph in 1911 or 1912. Some of her American films, typically domestic melodramas, were produced lavishly in Europe by her husband, Arthur Beck.

Baird's talents also extended to writing screenplays. In addition to acting in the following films, Baird wrote the screenplays and often the story as well: *Don't Doubt Your Wife* ('22), *When the Devil Drives* ('22), *When Husbands Deceive* ('22), *Is Divorce a Failure?* ('22), *The Destroying Angel* ('23), *The Miracle Makers* ('23) and *The Unnamed* ('25).

When she retired from acting, she continued writing screenplays: *Barriers Burned Away* ('25), *The Primrose Path* ('25), *The Shadow of the Law* ('26), *Devil's Island* ('26), *The False Alarm* ('26), *Spangles* ('26), *Stolen Pleasures* ('27) and *The Return of Boston Blackie* ('27).

Wolves of Kultur ('18) was Baird's only serial. The story is set in World War I days. An unnamed foreign power poses a serious threat to American interests. The film is replete with spies, sabotage, traitors, stolen inventions and cliffhanger endings.

Leah Baird died at age 88 from anemia after a long illness.

Serial

1918

Wolves of Kultur. Pathé, 1918 D: Joseph A. Golden; LP: Leah Baird, Charles Hutchison, Sheldon Lewis, Betty Howe.

WILLIAM BAKEWELL

William Bakewell began his film career at age 17 in 1925 as an extra. He had just graduated from the Harvard Military Academy in Los Angeles. His initial film appearance is believed to have been in *A Regular Fellow* ('25). Other walk-ons and bit parts followed; the parts soon got larger. *Old Ironsides* ('26) and *West Point* ('27) got the attention of both critics and the movie going public.

A few of his most noteworthy films include *The Iron Mask* ('29), *Hot Stuff* ('29), *All Quiet on the Western Front* ('30), *You Can't Buy Everything* ('34), *The Sea Spoilers* ('36), *Trapped by G-Men* ('37) and *King of the Turf* ('39).

In 1936, Bakewell appeared on the Broadway stage in *The Night of January 16th* but, preferring motion pictures to the stage, he returned to Hollywood as soon as the play closed.

Jungle Menace ('37) was Columbia's first serial and starred Frank Buck, the "Bring-'em-Back-Alive" adventurer. For a first effort at serial-making, it wasn't bad. In fact, it was better than many later Columbia serials. Bakewell played a plantation owner in the Asian jungles of Malay whose rubber shipments are being attacked by a band of river pirates led by LeRoy Mason and Sasha Seimel. Frank Buck joins Bakewell in hunting down the pirates, being helped in their attempts by police inspector Robert Warwick. Charlotte Henry plays Bakewell's girl-friend, Duncan Renaldo is a crooked nightclub owner, Reginald Denny is the plantation foreman and Esther Ralston plays Charlotte's aunt.

Bakewell appeared in Republic's *King of the Mounties* ('42), but his role was a minor one. The story dealt with Nazi agents in Canada bombing key targets with a mystery plane called the Phantom. When they are threatened with identification of the plane by a new type of plane detector, they go all out to acquire the detector. The inventor is killed. His daughter carries on his work with the aid of Sgt. King (Allan Lane).

Bakewell joined the Army in 1942. At first a buck private, he was recommended for Officer Candidate School and became a second lieutenant. Most of his military time was spent Stateside. Once out of the service in 1946 he starred in the Columbia serial *Hop Harrigan* ('46). The serial was adapted from a Mutual Network radio program and also from the cartoon strip by Jon Blummer that ran during the 1940s in *All American Comics*. Hop operates a small airfield, from which he becomes involved with many airborne mysteries. John Merton is Dr. Tabor, an eccentric scientist who invents a powerful motor which he claims to be better than even those powered by atomic energy. A mysterious villain called the Chief Pilot seeks the motor. Dr. Tabor manages to escape the Chief Pilot, but not with a sound mind. He plans to destroy the world with his super power unit,

Jennifer Holt, Sumner Getchell and William Bakewell (right) in *Hop Harrigan* (Columbia, 1946).

and it is up to Harrigan to stop him. Jennifer Holt is the heroine who helps Harrigan corral the evil ones. She and Bakewell were married in 1947. They were divorced in 1951.

Radar Men from the Moon ('52) was the fourth and last serial for Bakewell. He plays an associate of Commander Cody (George Wallace). Retik (Roy Barcroft), leader of a race of moon men, attempts to soften Earth's defenses to prepare for an invasion. When the Earth experiences a series of mysterious explosions, Commander Cody and his aide are called on to investigate.

For a number of years, Bakewell was involved in real estate selling for the Jack Hupp Real Estate Agency. His income from this activity far exceeded his income from acting. He also owned property in Fontana and Carmel which he managed.

Bakewell was born on May 2, 1908, in Los Angeles and died from leukemia on April 15, 1993.

Serials

1937

Jungle Menace. Col., [15 Chapters] D: George Mulford, Harry Fraser; SP: George Rosener, Sherman L. Lowe, Harry Hoyt, George Melford; S: George M. Merrick, Arthur Hoerl, Dallas Fitzgerald, Gordon Griffith; P: Jack Fier, Louis Weiss; Cam: Edward Linden, Herman Schoff; Mus: Abe Meyer; LP: Frank Buck, Esther Ralston, John St. Polis, William Bakewell, Reginald Denny, Duncan Renaldo, Charlotte Henry.

1942

King of the Mounties. Rep., [12 Chapters] D: William Witney: AP: W. J. O'Sullivan; SP: Taylor Caven, Ronald Davidson, William Lively, Joseph O'Donnell, Joseph Poland; Cam: Bud Thackery; Mus: Mort Glickman; LP: Allan Lane, Peggy Drake, Gilbert Emery, William Bakewell, Russell Hicks.

1946

Hop Harrigan. Col., [15 Chapters] D: Derwin Abrahams; P: Sam Katzman; SP: George H. Plympton, Ande Lamb; Cam: Ira H. Morgan; Mus: Lee Zahler; LP: William Bakewell, Jennifer Holt, Robert "Buzz" Henry, Sumner Getchell, Emmett Vogan, Claire James, John Merton, Wheeler Oakman.

1952

Radar Men from the Moon. Rep., [12 Chapters] D: Fred C. Brannon; SP: Ronald Davidson; AP: Franklyn Adreon; Cam: John MacBurnie; Mus: Stanley Wilson; LP: George Wallace, Aline Towne, Roy Barcroft, William Bakewell, Clayton Moore, Peter Brocco, Tom Steele.

JIM BANNON

Jim Bannon was the last of the "Red Ryders," outliving the three other Ryders (Donald Barry, Bill Elliott and Allan Lane). He was born in Kansas City, Missouri, on April 9, 1917. He attended Redemptorist Parochial School in Kansas City and was taught by the Sisters of St. Joseph. He went to both high school and college at a Jesuit institution in Kansas City, Rockhurst, graduating in 1937 with a degree in English.

He started a radio career after graduation, working for a small station in Kansas City, Kansas. In short order he was announcing at KMOX, a CBS outlet in St. Louis. Again on the move, he got a job at KFI in Los Angeles, the local NBC outlet. He had announcing jobs on *The Chase and Sanborn Hour*, the number one program in the ratings, and Joe Penner's show.

Jim married actress Bea Benaderet in August 1938. Their first child, Jack, arrived in June or July 1940. In March 1947, a daughter, Margaret Benaderet Bannon was born.

Jim Bannon and Marin Sais in *Cowboy and the Prizefighter* (Eagle-Lion, 1949).

Jim went under a seven-year contract to Columbia and had to bow out of his radio commitments. At the time he was doing the announcing on *I Love a Mystery*, *The Great Gildersleeve*, *The Rudy Vallee Show*, *Cavalcade of America*, *Walter Winchell's Jergen Journal*, *Stars Over Hollywood* and *Those We Love*. He was able to hang onto *Those We Love* and *Winchell's Jergen Journal* because they were Sunday shows. Later he announced Texaco's *The Eddie Bracken Show*, also a Sunday program.

Jim's first film was probably a supporting role in William Boyd's *Riders of the Deadline* ('43). His first starrer was *The Missing Juror* ('44) with Janis Carter. Three other films followed in the *I Love a Mystery* series before Harry Cohn dumped the series. However, Bannon stayed on for a year or so doing whatever came along.

By 1947 Bannon was getting kind of fed up and asked for his release. As a freelancer he starred in the Republic serial *Dangers of the Canadian Mounted* ('48). In the story, a gang ostensibly headed by Anthony Warde, but masterminded by a mystery figure called the Chief (Dorothy Granger), is searching for riches left by Genghis Khan's treasure-hunting in the thirteenth century. The gang tries to stop the territory from being opened up to homesteaders, with the result that Capt. Royal (Bannon) of the Mounties is called in to apprehend those guilty of attacks on the road builders. The search for the suspected fortune leads to the Cave of a Thousand Tunnels, then back to a Chinese junk and a chest. In the final showdown in Skagway Kate's boarding house, diamonds are discovered and Skagway Kate is revealed to be the Chief and is arrested.

When Bannon found out that Harry and Jerry Thomas had formed a company called Equity Pictures and were going to make Red Ryder films in Cinecolor for Eagle-Lion release, he dyed his hair red, wore worn Levis, an ordinary denim shirt and a hat that had a few miles on it, went for an interview and got the job. There were only four of the series filmed because of an in-company conflict. Completed were *Ride, Ryder, Ride* ('49), *Roll, Thunder, Roll* ('49), *The Fighting Redhead* ('49) and *The Cowboy and the Prizefighter* ('50).

Bannon's horse Thunder was the same one Lash LaRue had used as Black Diamonds, which was the same one Allan Lane had ridden as Black Jack and Thunder, which was the same one Bill Elliott used as Thunder. The horse's real name was Black Jack. He did get around! Bannon continued in a variety of things. He could be seen in support of Whip Wilson in the early '50s, as the male lead in the TV series *Adventures of Champion* in '55–'56 and as a supporting player in both Western and non–Western features.

Bea Benaderet and Bannon were divorced in 1950. In 1960 he married Barbara Cork, a beautiful girl 23 years his junior. They had three children, Lee, Robyn, and Pepi. Barbara was a model at Marshall Fields in Dallas. Blessed with a vivacious personality, she was the perfect mate for Jim. Theirs was a happy marriage.

Jim Bannon died in Ojal, California, on July 28, 1984.

Serial

1948

Dangers of the Canadian Mounted. Rep., [12 Chapters] D: Fred Brannon, Yakima Canutt; SP: Franklyn Adreon, Basil Dickey, Sol Shor, Robert C. Walker; Cam: John MacBurnie; Mus: Mort Glickman; LP: Jim Bannon, Virginia Belmont, Anthony Warde, Dorothy Granger, Bill Van Sickel, I. Stanford Jolley, Dale Van Sickel.

JOAN BARCLAY

Joan Barclay was one of the better known "B" Western heroines, making approximately 25 Westerns and working opposite Cowboys Rex Bell, Tim Holt, Tom Tyler, Hoot Gibson, Kermit Maynard, Ken Maynard, Bob Steele, John King, Tim McCoy, Bob Baker, The Three Mesquiteers, Jack Luden, Tex Fletcher and Buster Crabbe. She was at home in that world where everybody galloped around the sagebrush in a literal blur, taking potshots at each other, choreographing new brawl routines, breaking a few softened props and indulging in some unbelievably asinine dialogue. She was as real and as down-to-earth as a geranium in a garden of exotic flowers.

Joan was born in Minneapolis, Minnesota, on August 31, 1920. It is assumed that her real name was Geraine Geear, since that is the name under which she first made a screen appearance as a child. She had red hair and hazel eyes, stood 5'4" tall and weighed around 120 pounds during her screen career. She needed little makeup because of her naturally fine complexion.

Because she was a frail child, Joan's parents did not send her to public schools; she received her entire education through pri-

Left to right: Earle Dwire, Bob Steele, Joan Barclay and William Farnum in *The Kid Ranger* (Republic, 1936).

vate tutoring. She outgrew her childhood frailties and by the time she was 16 years old was well established as a photographer's and artist's model. Her face was used in advertising everything from beer and bread to baby buggies. She also adorned the covers of national magazines, and these helped open the gates of Hollywood for her. It was in 1936 that Bradshaw Crandall, well-known artist, painted her for a *Cosmopolitan* cover. That resulted in her being signed for the female lead in her first Western, *Ridin' On*, starring Tom Tyler.

Joan was a good ingenue in low-budget thrillers. Even though films such as *Prison Shadows* ('36), *Island Captives* ('37), *Sky Racket* ('37), *Amateur Crook* ('37) and *Million Dollar Racket* ('37) might have been extremely crude, they were entertaining and filled the bottom half of a dual program adequately. Her Victory pictures were similar to the Lonestar Westerns featuring John Wayne. One could criticize the Wayne Westerns from now to Doomsday as an embarrassment to all concerned, but the people who really count, the ticket-buying public, thoroughly enjoyed them regardless of what reviewers or Wayne himself thought. The same is true of the Barclay melodramas; they provided pleasurable escape for an hour, and no one seems to have wanted their money back.

Her two serials were also made for Sam Katzman's Victory Pictures. In *Shadow of Chinatown* ('37) she plays a journalist who, along with Herman Brix (Bruce Bennett), tries to stop the nefarious activities of Bela Lugosi and Luana Walters in San Francisco's Chinatown. In *Blake of Scotland Yard* ('37) she is the inventor of a death ray that a munitions maker tries to steal with the help of a mystery figure, the Scorpion. Ralph Byrd stars as the hero and Herbert Rawlinson is Blake of Scotland Yard.

In late 1941 or early 1942 Joan signed a long-term contract with RKO. Her last cred-

ited film seems to have been *The Shanghai Cobra* ('45).

Serials

1936

Shadow of Chinatown. Victory, [15 Chapters] D: Robert Hill; SP: Isador Bernstein, Basil Dickey; S: Rock Hawkey; Spv.: Sam Katzman; Cam.: Bill Hyer; LP: Bela Lugosi, Herman Brix, Joan Barclay, Luana Walters, Charles King, Forrest Taylor.

1937

Blake of Scotland Yard. Victory, [15 Chapters] D: Bob Hill; S: Rock Hawkey; Spv.: Robert Stillman; SP: Basil Dickey, William Buchanan; Cam: Bill Hyer; P: Sam Katzman; LP: Ralph Byrd, Herbert Rawlinson, Joan Barclay, Lloyd Hughes, Dickie Jones, Lucille Lund, Nick Stuart.

ROY BARCROFT

If a poll was taken of serial buffs, Roy Barcroft would have to get the nod as the undisputed "King of the Heavies." His villainous portrayals throughout the years in many Republic serials are legendary to the serial buff.

Roy Barcroft was born Howard Ravenscroft on September 7, 1902, in Crab Orchard, Nebraska, the youngest of seven children born into a sharecropper family. He was only 12 when his father died; three years later, he lied his way into the Army and quickly found himself in combat in France during World War I. He re-enlisted in 1923 and was stationed for three years in Hawaii, where he learned to play the saxophone and clarinet.

Leaving the Army in 1926, he played with various bands in the Chicago area until the stock market crash of 1929, at which time he packed his wife Vera, a child and his saxophone into a Model A Ford Roadster and headed west for California. There he became a salesman of various products. A friend urged him to try out for a neighborhood church play. He wound up with the lead role and the acting bug bit.

He had an unbilled bit in Greta Garbo's *Mata Hari* ('31) and Pola Negri's *A Woman Commands* ('32) as a result of belonging to an American Legion post which was frequently called upon to supply soldiers for bit parts in the studios around Culver City. There may have been other unbilled roles. It was 1937 when Roy "took the bull by the horns" and set about becoming a full-time actor.

Roy received bigger and better roles until he became the chief villain in many films. Without doubt, he became one of the greatest serial and "B" Western villains of all time. He was to the 1940s what Charles King and George Chesebro were to the 1930s. In late 1942 he signed an exclusive contract with Republic and for ten years (1943–53) appeared only in Republic pictures. In his career he is credited with appearing in 19 Republic serials, eight Universal serials and three Columbia serials. In features he menaced at least 30 cowboy stars, among them Allan Lane (49), Roy Rogers (18), Bill Elliott (16), Monte Hale (13), Rex Allen (10) and William Boyd (8).

Roy's most memorable portrayal in a serial was as Captain Mephisto, an eighteenth-century pirate, in *Manhunt of Mystery Island* ('45). This was followed closely by the title role in *The Purple Monster Strikes* ('45). In *G-Men Never Forget* ('47), he all but stole the film from Clayton Moore when he (Roy) played both the heavy and police commissioner in a dual role. In *Federal Agents vs. Underworld, Inc.* ('49) he was aided by voluptuous Carol Forman in his nefarious crimes. He again gave Clayton Moore a hard time in *Ghost of Zorro* ('49). In *Radar Men from the Moon* ('52) he had an interesting role as Retik, leader of a group of aliens on the Moon, plotting to conquer the Earth.

After his Republic contract ended, Roy worked in many big-budget features, a sampling being *Montana Belle* (Jane Russell, '52); *Rogue Cop* (Robert Taylor, '54); *Oklahoma* (Gordon MacRae, '55); *The Last Hunt* (Robert Taylor, '56); *Band of Angels* (Clark Gable, '57); *The Way West* (Kirk Douglas, '67); *Bandolero* (James Stewart, '68) and *Monte Walsh* (Lee Marvin, '70).

He could be seen in such television shows as *The Wild Wild West, Man from Cochise, The Lone Ranger, Zane Grey Theatre, Maverick, Cowboy G-Men, Wanted Dead or Alive, Iron Horse, Johnny Ringo, Have Gun Will Travel, Death Valley Days, Gunslinger, Tale of Wells Fargo, Frontier Circus, Empire, Superman, The Virginian, Lawman, Western Start Theatre, Frontier Doctor, Annie Oakley, The Andy Griffith Show, Hennessey, Circus Boy* and *National Velvet*.

Roy Barcroft died of Cancer on November 28, 1969, at the Motion Picture Country House in Woodland Hills, California.

Serials

1936

Flash Gordon. Univ., [13 Chapters] D: Frederick Staphani; LP: Buster Crabbe, Jean Rogers, Charles Middleton, Frank Shannon, Dick Alexander.

1937

Dick Tracy. Rep., [15 Chapters] D: Ray Taylor, Alan James; LP: Ralph Byrd, Kay Hughes, Smiley Burnette, Lee Van Atta, John Picorri.

S O S Coast Guard. Rep., [12 Chapters] D: William Witney, Alan James; LP: Ralph Byrd, Bela Lugosi, Maxine Doyle, Dick Alexander, Herbert Rawlinson.

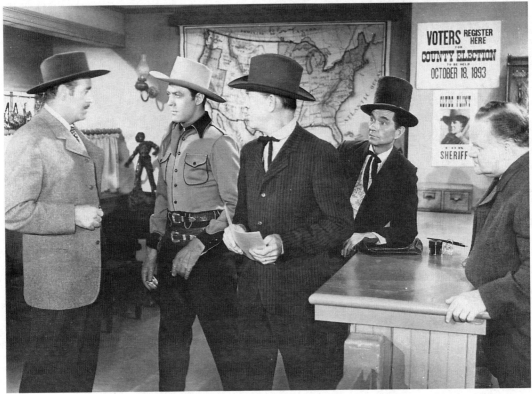

Left to right: Roy Barcroft, Allan Lane, Tom London, Earle Hodgins and an unidentified actor in *The Topeka Terror* (Republic, 1945).

1938

Flaming Frontiers. Univ., [13 Chapters] D: Ray Taylor, Alan James; LP: Johnny Mack Brown, Eleanor Hansen, Ralph Bowman (John Archer), James Blaine.

1939

Daredevils of the Red Circle. Rep., [12 Chapters] D: William Witney, John English; LP: Charles Quigley, Herman Brix, David Sharpe, Carole Landis.

The Oregon Trail. Univ., [15 Chapters] D: Ford Beebe, Saul A. Goodkind; LP: Johnny Mack Brown, Louise Stanley, Fuzzy Knight, Bill Cody, Jr.

The Phantom Creeps. Univ., [12 Chapters] D: Ford Beebe, Saul A. Goodkind; LP: Bela Lugosi, Robert Kent, Dorothy Arnold, Regis Toomey, Eddie Acuff.

1940

Flash Gordon Conquers the Universe. Univ., [12 Chapters] D: Ford Beebe, Ray Taylor; LP: Buster Crabbe, Carol Hughes, Charles Middleton, Anne Gwynne, Roland Drew, Lee Powell.

The Green Hornet Strikes Again. Univ., [15 Chapters] LP: Warren Hull, Keye Luke, Wade Boteler, Anne Nagel, Pierre Watkin, Eddie Acuff.

Deadwood Dick. Co., [15 Chapters] D: James W. Horne; LP: Don Douglas, Lorna Gray, Lane Chandler, Charles King, Marin Sais, Jack Ingram.

1941

King of the Texas Rangers. Rep., [12 Chapters] D: William Witney, John English; LP: Slingin' Sammy Baugh, Neil Hamilton, Pauline Moore, Duncan Renaldo, Herbert Rawlinson, Charles Trowbridge.

Riders of Death Valley. Univ., [15 Chapters] D: Ray Taylor, Ford Beebe; LP: Dick Foran, Buck Jones, Leo Carrillo, Charles Bickford, Jeanne Kelly (Jean Brooks).

White Eagle. Col., [15 Chapters] D: James W. Horne; LP: Buck Jones, Raymond Hatton, Dorothy Fay, James Craven, Jack Ingram, Charles King.

Sky Raiders. Univ., [12 Chapters] D: Ford Beebe, Ray Taylor; LP: Donald Woods, Billy Halop, Robert Armstrong, Kathryn Adams, Eduardo Ciannelli.

1942

The Valley of Vanishing Men. Col., [15 Chapters] D: Spencer G. Bennet; SP: Harry Fraser, Lewis Clay, George Gray; P: Larry Darmour; Mus: Lee Zahler; Cam: James S. Brown, Jr.; LP: Bill Elliott, Slim Summerville, Carmen Morales, Kenneth MacDonald, Jack Ingram, George Chesebro, Roy Barcroft.

1943

The Masked Marvel. Rep., [12 Chapters] D: Spencer Bennet; SP: Royal Cole, Ronald Davidson, Basil Dickey, Jesse Duffy, Grant Nelson, George H. Plympton, Joseph Poland; AP: W. J. O'Sullivan; Cam: Reggie Lanning; Mus: Mort Glickman; LP: William Forrest, Louise Currie, Johnny Arthur, David Bacon, Tom Steele, Rod Bacon, Roy Barcroft.

1944

Haunted Harbor. Rep., [15 Chapters] D: Spencer Bennet, Wallace Grissell; SP: Royal Cole, Basil Dickey, Jesse Duffy, Grant Nelson, Joseph Poland; S: Dayle Douglas; AP: Ronald Davidson; Cam: Bud Thackery; Mus: Joseph Dubin; LP: Kane Richmond, Kay Aldridge, Roy Barcroft, Clancy Cooper, Marshall Reed, Hal Taliaferro.

1945

Manhunt of Mystery Island. Rep., [15 Chapters] D: Spencer Bennet, Yakima Canutt, Wallace A. Grissell; SP: Albert DeMond, Basil Dickey, Jesse Duffy, Alan James, Grant Nelson, Joseph Poland; AP: Ronald Davidson; Cam: Bud Thackery; Mus: Richard Cherwin; LP: Linda Stirling, Roy Barcroft, Richard Bailey, Kenne Duncan, Jack Ingram, Forrest Taylor, Forbes Murray.

The Purple Monster Strikes. Rep., [15 Chapters] D: Spencer Bennet, Fred Brannon; SP: Royal Cole, Albert DeMond, Basil Dickey, Lynn Perkins, Joseph Poland, Barney Sarecky; AP: Bud Thackery; Mus: Richard Cherwin; LP: Linda Stirling, Dennis Moore, Roy Barcroft, James Craven, Bud Geary, Mary Moore.

1946

The Phantom Rider. Rep., [12 Chapters] D: Spencer Bennet, Fred Brannon; SP: Albert DeMond, Basil Dickey, Jesse Duffy, Lynn Perkins, Barney Sarecky; AP: Ronald Davidson; Cam: Bud Thackery; Mus: Richard Cherwin; LP: Robert Kent, Peggy Stewart, LeRoy Mason, George J. Lewis, Hal Taliaferro, Tom London, Chief Thundercloud, Roy Barcroft.

1947

Son of Zorro. Rep., [13 Chapters] D: Spencer Bennet, Fred Brannon; SP: Franklyn Adreon, Basil Dickey, Jesse Duffy, Sol Shor; AP: Ronald Davidson; Cam: Bud Thackery; Mus: Mort Glickman; LP: George Turner, Peggy Stewart, Roy Barcroft, Edward Cassidy, Ernie Adams, Stanley Price, Charles King.

Jesse James Rides Again. Rep., [13 Chapters] D: Fred C. Brannon, Thomas Carr; SP: Franklyn Adreon, Basil Dickey, Jesse Duffy, Sol Shor; AP: Mike Frankovich; Cam: John MacBurnie; Mus: Mort Glickman; LP: Clayton Moore, Linda Stirling, Roy Barcroft, John Compton, Tris Coffin, Tom London, Edmund Cobb.

G-Men Never Forget. Rep., [12 Chapters] D: Fred C. Brannon, Yakima Canutt; AP: Mike Frankovich; SP: Franklyn Adreon, Basil Dickey, Jesse Duffy, Sol Shor; Cam: John MacBurnie; Mus: Mort Glickman; LP: Clayton Moore, Ramsay Ames, Roy Barcroft, Drew Allen, Edmund Cobb, Tom Steele, Dale Van Sickel, Ken Terrell.

1949

Federal Agents vs. Underworld, Inc. Rep., [12 Chapters] D: Fred C. Brannon; SP: Royal K. Cole, Basil Dickey, William Lively, Sol Shor; P: Franklyn Adreon; Cam: John MacBurnie; Mus: Stanley Wilson; LP: Kirk Alyn, Roy Barcroft, Rosemary La Planche, Carol Forman, James Dale, Bruce Edwards, James Craven, Tris Coffin, Jack O'Shea.

Ghost of Zorro. Rep., [12 Chapters] D: Fred C. Brannon; SP: Royal Cole, William Lively, Sol Shor; AP: Franklyn Adreon; Cam: John MacBurnie; Mus: Stanley Wilson; LP: Clayton Moore, Pamela Blake, Roy Barcroft, George J. Lewis, I. Stanford Jolley, Gene Roth, Steve Clark.

1950

The James Brothers of Missouri. Rep., [12 Chapters] D: Fred C. Brannon; SP: Royal Cole, William Lively, Sol Shor; AP: Franklyn Adreon; Cam: Ellis W. Carter; Mus: Stanley Wilson; LP: Keith Richards, Robert Bice, Noel Neill, Roy Barcroft, Patricia Knox, Edmund Cobb, Lane Bradford.

1951

Don Daredevil Rides Again. Rep., [12 Chapters] D: Fred C. Brannon; SP: Ronald Davidson; AP: Franklyn Adreon; Cam: Ellis W. Carter; Mus: Stanley Wilson; LP: Ken Curtis, Aline Towne, Roy Barcroft, Lane Bradford, Robert Einer, John Cason, Lee Phelps.

1952

Radar Men from the Moon. Rep., [12 Chapters] D: Fred C. Brannon; SP: Ronald Davidson; AP: Franklyn Adreon; Cam: John MacBurnie; Mus: Stanley Wilson; LP: George Wallace, Aline Towne, Roy Barcroft, William Bakewell, Clayton Moore, Peter Brocco.

1954

Man with the Steel Whip. Rep., [12 Chapters] D: Franklyn Adreon; SP: Ronald Davidson; AP: Franklyn Adreon; Mus: R. Dale Butts; LP: Richard Simmons, Barbara Bestar, Dale Van Sickel, Mauritz Hugo, Roy Barcroft, Edmund Cobb, I. Stanford Jolley.

TREVOR BARDETTE

Trevor Bardette was born in Nashville, Arkansas, on November 19, 1902. Educated at the University of Oregon and Northwestern University, he majored in engineering. After an apprenticeship on stage in New York, Bardette entered films in 1936.

As a character actor, Trevor played in numerous films, mostly action pictures, usually as a villain and quite often the top henchman. His films include *White Bondage* ('37), *They Won't Forget* ('37), *Jezebel* ('38), *Valley of the Giants* ('38), *The Oklahoma Kid* ('39), *Stand Up and Fight* ('39), *Abe Lincoln in Illinois* ('40), *Dark Command* ('40), *The Grapes of Wrath* ('40), *Three Faces West* ('40), *Virginia City* ('40), *Wagons Westward* ('40), *Bad Men of Missouri* ('41), *Apache Trail* ('42), *The Moon Is Down* ('43), *Tampico* ('44), *A Thousand and One Nights* ('45), *Dragonwyck* ('46), *Song of India* ('47), *Ramrod* ('47), *The Gallant Legion* ('48), *The Paleface* ('48), *Unconquered* ('48), *The Doolins of Oklahoma* ('49), *Hellfire* ('49), *The Texas Rangers* ('51), *Lone Star* ('52), *The Desert Song* ('53), *Destry* ('54), *The Man from Bitter Ridge* ('56), *The Rack* ('56), *The Hard Man* ('57), *The Mating Game* ('59), *Papa's Delicate Condition* ('63), *The Raiders* ('64) and *Mackenna's Gold* ('69).

Bardette is probably best remembered for his dual role portrayal of French trapper Arthur Mitchell and Pegleg, a one-legged Napoleon who envisages setting up a Western empire with himself as its dictator. The serial was *Overland with Kit Carson* ('39), the second best Western chapterplay produced by Columbia. A great supporting cast helped make this Bill Elliott starrer what it was.

Bardette's role in *Jungle Girl* ('41) is likewise a dual one, but one twin brother is dispensed with in the first chapter. Dr. Meredith, friend of a savage tribe, brings up his daughter, Nyoka, in the jungles of Africa, *a la* Tarzan. His criminal twin brother learns that the doctor has access to a hoard of diamonds and is determined to steal them. Due to his standing in the tribal village, Dr. Meredith has possession of an amulet which entitles him to enter the caves of Nakross, where the diamonds are housed. The doctor uses the diamonds to purchase medical supplies. His evil brother has the doctor killed, assumes his identity and enters into an alliance with the village's evil witch doctor. Nyoka is fooled for awhile, not realizing that her "father" is actually her uncle. Jack Stanton (Tom Neal) and Curly Rogers (Eddie Acuff), American pilots, come to the aid of Nyoka and a young tribal boy, Kimbu (Tommy Cook), and the four eventually defeat the jungle criminals, both white and black.

In *The Secret Code* ('42), Bardette plays the part of Jensen, leader of a ring of enemy sabotage agents, while in *Winners of the West* ('40) he is part of the gang opposing construction of Hartford Transcontinental Railroad through Hell's Gate Pass.

Trevor Bardette died in 1977 at age 75.

Serials

1939

Overland with Kit Carson. Col., [15 Chapters] D: Sam Nelson, Norman Deming; SP: Joseph F. Poland, Morgan B. Cox, Ned Dandy; P: Jack Fier; Cam: Benjamin Kline, George Meehan; Mus: Lee Zahler; LP: Bill Elliott, Iris Meredith, Trevor Bardette, Richard Fiske, Bobby Clark.

1940

Winners of the West. Univ., [13 Chapters] D: Ford Beebe, Ray Taylor. LP: Dick Foran, Anne Nagel, James Craig, Tom Fadden, Charles Stevens.

1941

Jungle Girl. Rep., [15 Chapters] D: William Witney, John English; SP: Ronald Davidson, Norman S. Hall, William Lively, Joseph O'-Donnell, Joseph F. Poland, Alfred Batson; AP: Hiram S. Brown, Jr.; Mus: Cy Feuer; Cam: Reggie Lanning; LP: Frances Gifford, Tom Neal, Eddie Acuff, Trevor Bardette, Gerald Mohr, Frank Lackteen.

1942

The Secret Code. Col., [15 Chapters] D: Spencer G. Bennet; SP: Basil Dickey, Leighton Brill, Robert Beche; P: Larry Darmour; Cam: James S. Brown, Jr.; Mus: Lee Zahler; LP: Paul Kelly, Anne Nagel, Clancy Cooper, Trevor Bardette, Robert O. Davis, Gregory Gay.

DONALD (RED) BARRY

On January 11, 1912, there was born in a poorer section of Houston, Texas, a little boy who was named Donald Michael Barry De Acosta. That baby later went by the names Donald Barry and Don (Red) Barry. Apparently his parents either died or abandoned the baby. His maternal grandmother took him in and provided as best she could for him. Barry grew up in a tough neighborhood and learned to take care of himself. He attended the Texas School of Mines and was elected to the Texas All-Stars ('29). The athletically trim Barry came with the Texas football team to California to compete against a Southern California all-star contingent.

Quite taken with California and Hollywood, Barry returned the following year intent upon becoming an actor. With more "brass" than a government mule and with an incalculable ego, he persevered. The going was a little tough at first. He took a job on a trade paper, *Daily Variety*, while waiting for his big break to come along. Through friendship with Mickey Rooney he got the role of Mickey's brother in the film *Boys Town* ('38). When it finally came time to shoot a scene in which he appeared with Spencer Tracy, he froze up and couldn't talk. He was replaced over noon break and Edward Norris assumed the role.

An opportunity arose to appear in the roadshow production of *Tobacco Road*. Barry bluffed his way into the role of "Dude," and he took to it like a duck to water. The role netted him such splendid notices that RKO hired him for a small role in *Night Waitress* ('36), his first screen appearance. Other small roles followed, including three *Dr. Kildare* films at MGM. Impressed by his acting, Republic used him in *Wyoming Outlaw* ('39), a Three Mesquiteers film starring John Wayne, Ray Corrigan and Raymond Hatton, subsequent to which he was signed to a ten-year Republic contract. In his next two films he supported Roy Rogers: *Saga of Death Valley* ('39) and *Days of Jesse James* ('40).

Then came the film that would make him a star, the serial *Adventures of Red Ryder* ('40). Picking Barry for the role of Red Ryder was a most unusual bit of casting. The comic-strip Ryder was tall and slender, as good heroes are expected to be. Don was short and inclined to be a bit on the heavy side. In no way did he even remotely resemble the favorite of millions of comic-strip fans.

A blue-eyed redhead, Donald was 5'8½" tall and tipped the scale at 170 pounds. Not exactly handsome, but good-looking in a sense of the word, Don had the appearance of an outlaw written all over his face. When the situation became tense and Don clenched his

In *Frontier Vengeance* (Republic, 1949).

lips together tightly, he looked for all the world like a shifty scoundrel whose determination would see him through any rough spots. The realism of casting Barry as the underdog on whom all suspicion fell was heightened by this appearance. Such a script proved to be Barry's forte. He performed equally well as hero or villain and was one of the few B Western stars who came across convincingly while masquerading as an outlaw.

William Farnum (left), Tommy Cook and Donald Barry in *Adventures of Red Ryder* (Republic, 1940).

After 12 successive weeks, Barry's identification with the Red Ryder character was so strong, and the serial so popular, the studio christened him thereafter with a new middle name, "Red." The name stuck in spite of Barry's later attempts to abandon it.

Following the serial, Don was starred in a series of 29 Western features and was named as one of the Top Ten Money-Making Western Stars in the *Motion Picture Herald* polls of 1942, 1943 and 1944. Wanting to broaden his dramatic talents, he accepted the lead in Republic's *Remember Pearl Harbor* ('42). Other non–Westerns in which he starred included *The Traitor Within* ('42), *West Side Kid* ('43), *My Buddy* ('44) and *The Purple Heart* ('44).

Barry was 4F as result of a polo injury and rejected for military service during World War II. He did what he could and that was entertain the service men at the front in the South Pacific arena.

In 1945, Don stepped out of his B-West-ern series as Don (Red) Barry and concentrated on dramatic films or A-Westerns as Donald Barry. *The Chicago Kid* ('45), *Madonna of the Desert* ('48), *Train to Alcatraz* ('48) and *Ringside* ('49) were completed in the late 1940s.

In 1949–50 Barry starred in nine features for Lippert Films, six of which were Westerns. He virtually ended his B oater career with *Jesse James' Women* ('54), a United Artists release of an independently produced Western directed by Barry. But as a character actor he would appear in many fine films during the next 25 years.

Barry had a second career in television. He worked in at least 37 series that the author is aware of and on some of these he worked more than once. They include *Sugarfoot, Gunsmoke, Have Gun, Will Travel, Maverick, F Troop, Frontier Circus, The Wild Wild West, The Virginian, Lawman, SurfSide Six* and *Police Woman.*

Barry was married to actress Peggy

Stewart in the early 1940s, but they were divorced on April 11, 1944. Miss Stewart testified that Barry had a bad temper and sometimes stayed out all night without explanation. Stewart got custody of their five-month-old son Michael.

Throughout his career Barry was quite a ladies man, dating some of the film capitol's leading beauties. Joan Crawford, Linda Darnell, Ann Sheridan, Susan Hayward...the list goes on. In 1956 he made headlines when he and Hayward were caught together early one morning at his home by his girlfriend, Jil Jarmyn.

By 1980 Barry was separated from his wife, the former Barbara Patin, the mother of their two daughters, Christina, 15, and Deborah, 10. On the evening of July 17, 1980, LAPD officers came to Barry's home to settle a violent quarrel between Barry and his estranged wife. As the officers were leaving, Barry appeared on the front porch with a .38 caliber pistol. They urged him to drop the weapon but he put the gun to his head and fired a single shot. He was rushed to Riverside Hospital but was dead on arrival. Newspaper accounts indicated he may have been drinking that evening.

What you saw of Don (Red) Barry was what you got and what he was. His screen personification was basically his private one. He was one of the more talented cowboy actors to emerge from the B-Western era, but he was never really happy being known as only a cowboy. He proved his versatility. However, it is *Adventures of Red Ryder* and his B-Westerns that he will be remembered for.

Serial

1940

Adventures of Red Ryder. Rep., [12 Chapters] D: William Witney, John English; AP: Hiram S. Brown; SP: Franklyn Adreon, Ronald Davidson, Barney Sarecky, Norman S. Hall, Sol Shor; Cam: William Nobles; Mus: Cy Feuer; LP: Donald Barry, Tommy Cook, Noah Beery, Sr., Maude Pierce Allen, Vivian Coe, Hal Taliaferro, Harry Worth, Robert Kortman, William Farnum.

WILLIAM BARRYMORE

William Barrymore was the star of *The Mansion of Mystery* ('27), an indie serial produced by Capital in ten chapters. It received limited distribution to third-rate theaters on a states-right market setup and was not booked into larger, better theaters. There are no known prints of it in existence today.

Who was William Barrymore? He acted under three names. As Boris Bullock he was in eight Westerns from 1920 to 1927 as a villain or supporting player. As Kit Carson he starred in seven Westerns during the same period. As William Barrymore he was in a number of films, including the above-mentioned serial.

Barrymore was born in Russia on August 17, 1899. He moved to the U.S. in 1920 after serving a hitch in the Russian Army cavalry.

Barrymore dropped out of films with the advent of talkies because of his heavy Russian accent. From 1933 to 1953 he was a deputy in the Los Angelous sheriff's office. He founded the Mira Mesa Village Players in 1977 and was a member of the Toastmasters and Kiwanis clubs in Oceanside.

The actor died in the Veterans Administration Hospital in San Diego, which would seem to imply that he served in the U.S. military forces. He was survived by his wife, three sons, one daughter, two stepchildren and six grandchildren. Cause of death was respiratory failure brought on by pseudomonas pneumonia and chronic obstructive pulmonary disease.

Serial

1927

The Mansion of Mystery. Capital, [10 Chapters] D: Robert J. Horner; LP: William Barrymore, Teddy Reeves, Fred Church, Jack Richardson, Kalla Pasha, Earl Gunn.

JEANNE BATES

Tom Tyler (left), Frank Shannon and Jeanne Bates in *The Phantom* (Columbia, 1943).

Jeanne Bates played the fiancée of Tom Tyler in Columbia's *The Phantom* ('43), a good serial equal to Tyler's *Adventures of Captain Marvel* ('41). Unfortunately, Jeanne's comeliness was covered up but she still looked beautiful.

Jeanne's best roles apart from the serial were as the female lead in *The Chance of a Lifetime* ('43) with Chester Morris; *The Racket Man* ('43) with Tom Neal and Hugh Beaumont; *Sergeant Mike* ('44) with Larry Parks; *Sundown Valley* ('44) with Charles Starrett; and *The Mask of Diijon* ('46). She had the second femme lead in *The Soul of a Monster* ('44) with Rose Hobart and *The Black Parachute* ('44) with Ona Munson.

Jeanne has been active in movies and television right up to the present date.

Left to right: **Kenneth MacDonald, Tom Tyler, Frank Shannon and Jeanne Bates in *The Phantom* (Columbia, 1943).**

Serial

1943

The Phantom. Col., [15 Chapters] D: B. Reeves Eason; P: Rudolph C. Flathow; Mus: Lee Zahler; Cam: James S. Brown, Jr.; SP: Morgan B. Cox, Victor McLeod, Sherman Lowe, Leslie J. Swabacker; LP: Tom Tyler, Jeanne Bates, Kenneth MacDonald, Frank Shannon, Ace (dog), Guy Kingsford, Joe Devlin, Ernie Adams, George Chesebro.

SLINGIN' SAMMY BAUGH

It was in February 1941 that Slingin' Sammy Baugh, the greatest all-around football player who ever played the game, signed a Republic contract to star in the serial *King of the Texas Rangers* at a salary of $1,000 a week with five weeks guaranteed. The serial was filmed in June and July at a cost of roughly $140,000.

Sammy Baugh was born on March 17, 1914, near Temple, Texas, and lived there

Sammy Baugh (left) and Monte Blue in *King of the Texas Rangers* (Republic, 1941).

through his first year of high school. Sammy's father, who worked for the Santa Fe Railroad, moved the family to Sweetwater, Texas, when his job demanded he do so. Upon graduation, Baugh went to Texas Christian University in Fort Worth on a scholarship allowing him to play football, baseball and basketball. He burst into national sports prominence as a sophomore, leading the Texas Christian University Horned Frogs against the Southern Methodist Mustangs in a game for the Southwestern Conference title, the mythical national championship and a Rose Bowl invitation.

Baugh was a legend in Texas when he left to join the NFL Washington Redskins with a contract for the highest salary ever paid a professional football player at that time. Upon his retirement 15 years later, he had long prior been acknowledged as one of

the greatest passers of all time in addition to being one of the best all-around players to ever step on a gridiron. Although he had a brush with minor league baseball, playing shortstop for the St. Louis Cardinals in 1938, Sammy was destined to become a football legend. Also, in 1938, after his first season with the Redskins, Sam married his high school sweetheart, Edmonia Smith, and went on to raise five children.

After his retirement from active playing in 1952, Baugh entered the coaching ranks and has served as head coach, assistant or special assignment for (among others) Hardin-Simmons University, the Houston Oilers, the Detroit Lions and the New York Jets (when they were called the Titans). But coaching developed into a full time, year-round profession and Baugh was forced to choose between devoting all his time coaching or his ranch. No contest. He returned

Sammy Baugh (left) and Jack Ingram in *King of the Texas Rangers* (Republic, 1941).

home to Texas. And "home" is the nearly 8,000-acre Double Mountain he has owned since 1940 and where he has raised his three children: Todd, a lawyer in Montana; David, a coach in Texas; and daughter Frances, who attends Texas Tech University.

King of the Texas Rangers ('41) proved to be a popular serial set in a modern time. Saboteurs try to destroy Texas oil fields to disrupt the war effort. Sgt. Tom King, out to avenge his father's murder, combines forces with Pedro Garcia of the Mexican Rurales to hunt down the foreign agents and their American cohorts, receiving ample help and encouragement from Sally Crane, not only his sweetheart but a first-rate newspaperwoman as well.

Serial

1941

King of the Texas Rangers. Rep., [12 Chapters] D: William Witney, John English; SP: Ronald Davidson, Norman S. Hall, William Lively, Joseph Poland, Joseph O'Donnell; AP: Hiram S. Brown, Jr.; Mus: Cy Feuer; Cam: Reggie Lanning; LP: Slingin' Sammy Baugh, Pauline Moore, Duncan Renaldo, Neil Hamilton, Charles Trowbridge, Herbert Rawlinson.

CLYDE BEATTY

"FORTY MAGNIFICENT, MON-STROUS, MENACING MAN-EATERS MIRACULOUSLY MINGLED," the signs used to say. That was in the '30s, when "circus" was a word with magic, when kids impatiently waited through the year until the big tent went up again. And what they waited for most was the instant when a trim, 5'6" man, dressed in spotless white shirt and breeches with soft leather belt, bounded into the spotlight of the center ring and doffed his pith helmet. Then, whip in his right hand, a steel reinforced chair plus blank-loaded pistol in his left, he would summon the first ferocious cat into the cage.

That was Clyde Beatty, king of the beasts, the greatest animal trainer in the world.

Clyde Raymond Beatty was born near Chillicothe, Ohio, on June 10, 1903. His childhood was normal except for an over-zealous passion for animals. He loved them all. When he was about 15 years old, he ran away from home to join a traveling circus in order to be near the animals. His father soon appeared, however, and it was back to school. With schooling behind him, he launched his career in 1921 with Gollmer Bros. Circus. At first he cleaned out cages and fed the animals. Later he was asked to be an assistant in a polar bear act.

Time passed. Now a full-fledged trainer, he presented an act with tigers, lions and leopards, almost immediately becoming known for absolute fearlessness in the cage and with a knack of making various species of wild animals work with one another. In addition to Gollmer Bros., Beatty also traveled with the John Robinson Circus and Hagenback-Wallace Shows with an act of 20 wild animals, then nearly lost his life when a 600-pound lion attacked him. He was hospitalized for five weeks.

Beatty co-authored a book entitled *The Big Cage* which was well-received. The book did well in the marketplace and film rights were bought by Universal. *The Big Cage* ('33) starred Beatty with Anita Page, Andy Devine, Wallace Ford, Raymond Hatton and Mickey Rooney. In the story, Ford, animal trainer, has lost his nerve. He is in love with trapeze artist Anita Page and regains his courage when he sees that his sweetheart is in real danger. Beatty and his cage full of 40 wild cats had to adjust to strange new working conditions, including glaring lights and cameras. But they rose to the challenge; the animal segments were spectacular and the film was popular, turning a sizable profit.

Nat Levine, president of Mascot Pictures, aware of the popularity of the Beatty feature, decided that a jungle serial starring Beatty would be popular. Beatty was signed for a 12-chapter serial titled *The Lost Jungle* ('34). A review in the *New York Times* (June 8, 1934) reads:

> With superb indifferences for his personal safety, Clyde Beatty in *The Lost Jungle* comes to grips with a scenario that makes his lions and tigers look like over-fed house cats. There are shipwrecks, a dirigible crash, buried treasure, a mutinous crew, a lost civilization, a treacherous assistant and an island loaded with savage fauna. Mr. Beatty, traveling under his own name, takes everything in stride, although his histrionic manner is a shade too reticent. As the Frank Merriwell of the big top, the shy lover, the scourge of the black-hearted, the one-man jungle safari, he puts on a good show... . it all has a synthetic look, but the lions and tigers are real, and Mr. Beatty knows his business. The children will sit through it twice.

Republic released its first serial in 1936, *Darkest Africa*, in 15 chapters. Beatty again starred under his own name. Supporting him were Manuel King, billed as "The World's

In *Ring of Fear* (Warner Bros., 1954).

Youngest Animal Trainer," Elaine Shepard, Lucien Prival, Ray Bernard (Corrigan), Wheeler Oakman and Naba. In it, he meets Baru, a jungle boy who has come to the outland for assistance. Baru's sister Valerie, Goddess of Joba, a city in unexplored Africa, is being held captive. Beatty agrees to help Baru rescue the girl. With the aid of an ape, Bonga, Baru's protector, they manage to get back to Joba after many thrilling and breathtaking encounters with lions, savages and Bat-Men.

Once in Joba, they run up against Dagna, the high priest, who tries to prevent them from leaving. Aiding Dagna are Durkin and Craddock, rival animal traders. At the climax of the excitement-packed chapterplay, Valerie is about to sacrifice herself in a death leap from Pinnacle Rock so that Clyde and her brother may be released from Dagna's clutches. She is saved in a surprise act and Valerie, Clyde and Baru manage to escape from Joba in the nick of time — just before the city is engulfed in an earthquake.

Beatty married Ernestine Pegg in 1926 and was divorced in 1931. On September 16, 1933, he married circus aerialist Harriet Evans. The second Mrs. Beatty announced that she would like to perform on the ground, and before she realized what was taking place, Clyde had started her on a path which would lead her to becoming "The World's Greatest Female Wild Animal Trainer." Together they appeared in a Pete Smith Specialty short film *Cat College* ('40).

Several different radio serials were based on Beatty's real-life adventures. One, *The Clyde Beatty Show*, debuted over the Mutual network on December 11, 1950, with dramatizations of real-life incidents of the animal trainer. Beatty narrated the program and participated in the enactments.

By June 10, 1963, when he reached his sixtieth birthday, Beatty had given over 30,000 performances, had travelled over 1,000,000 miles in the process and had played to 40,000,000 people, including post-season engagements in the U.S. and abroad. His schedule called for 14 performances a week but the records show many weeks when special Saturday and Sunday morning performances for children brought the total to 16 shows a week. He played to some of the largest crowds in the history of show business. The biggest was at the Nebraska State Fair where he had an audience of 103,000.

During his long career as a performer, Beatty trained almost 1,000 lions, about the same number of tigers and a much smaller contingent of other members of the big-cat family, including 60 leopards and 25 jaguars and pumas. Eventually he settled down to being a lion-and-tiger man exclusively.

In 1950 Beatty married the former Jane Abel. Evidently the Beatty-Evans marriage had ended either in divorce or in her death.

In 1941, Beatty authored a second book, *Jungle Performers*, and in 1965 he turned out a third book, *Facing the Big Cats*. He joined Frank Buck on the screen in 1949 for *Africa Screams* with Abbott and Costello. In 1954, Beatty made a return to films in *Ring of Fear*, in which he was seen as himself.

In July 1964, Beatty underwent surgery for stomach cancer. Despite severe pain and a great loss of weight, he resumed his career in April of the following year. Beatty made his last personal appearance at Salisbury, Maryland, on May 26, 1965. He then returned to his home in Ventura, California, where he died on July 19, 1965, at the age of 62.

Beatty was survived by his wife Jane, a son, Clyde Jr., 13, and a daughter by a former marriage, Mrs. Joyce Ferguson of Peru, Indiana. Services for Beatty were held in the Church of the Hills in Forest Lawn Memorial Park.

Left to right: unidentified actor, Wheeler Oakman, Clyde Beatty and Edward LeSaint in *The Lost Jungle* (Mascot, 1934).

Serials

1934

The Lost Jungle. Mascot, [12 Chapters] D: Armand Schaefer, David Howard; SP: Armand Schaefer, Barney Sarecky, David Howard, Wyndham Gittens; S: Al Martin, Sherman Lowe; P: Nat Levine; Cam: Alvin Wyckoff, William Nobles; Mus: Hal Chasnoff; LP: Clyde Beatty, Cecilia Parker, Syd Saylor, Warner Richmond, Wheeler Oakman, Maston Williams, Jim Corey.

1936

Darkest Africa. Rep., [15 Chapters] D: B. Reeves Eason, Joseph Kane; SP: John Rathmell,

Tracy Knight; Spv: Barney Sarecky; S: John Rathmell, Tracy Knight; Cam: William Nobles, Edgar Lyons; P: Nat Levine; LP: Clyde Beatty, Manuel King, Elaine Shepard, Lucien Prival, Ray Benard (Corrigan), Wheeler Oakman.

NOAH BEERY

In the days of the silent screen, no one could play the wicked, horrible, bloodthirsty villain in quite the same way as Noah Beery, Sr. One would just hate him on the screen, but off-screen there was never a sweeter soul. He shared this quality of gentility with Boris Karloff, another on-screen repulsive person, but off-screen a man who liked to putter in his flower bed. Noah portrayed so many despicable characters that it is extremely difficult to pick out one particular role as his best. He was the villain's villain. He gave the impression that the only fun to be gained out of life had to be obtained by cheating, lying, raping or just plain skull-duggery.

Noah Beery first saw the light of day in Kansas City on January 17, 1884. There were three brothers: William C., the oldest; Noah, the second; and Wallace, the youngest. The two younger brothers became famous screen actors. In the early days when they were striving for supremacy as bad men of the screen, there was some rivalry. In later years they forgot all this competition and were very close.

Noah is said to have first smelled greasepaint when he was a peanut vendor in a circus. Perhaps. What is known for sure is that at age 16 he headed for Broadway with just enough money for railroad fare and with two revolvers stuck in his belt. He pawned the weapons to buy food a few days after arriving in the Big Apple. He was able to get a job as a singer in vaudeville. Later he appeared with the headline teams of Cohan & Harris and Klaw & Erlanger before beginning an association with H. B. Harris, who helped him become a stage success. While working in a play about 1910, Noah met his wife-to-be, Marguerite Abbot. She, too, was in the play. They had two sons, the oldest dying young and Noah, Jr., surviving when the family moved to Southern California on a doctor's recommendation.

Noah and Marguerite had a very happy marriage until she died in 1935. Noah entered films in late 1915 and soon began his rise to fame and fortune as a "heavy." He appeared in more than 100 silent and sound pictures. His greatest success was in silent pictures, whereas in sound films he faded into "B" films. He was a big man, which was an asset to his appearance as a villain. He was 6'1½" tall and weighed anywhere from 225 to 235 pounds. He gave the appearance of a much larger man.

In the 1920s, Noah played a cruel renegade in a series of Zane Grey Westerns and a cheerfully lecherous scoundrel in the DeMille production *The Coming of Amos* ('25) in which, having tricked a White Russian princess into marriage, he is determined to exercise his rights. Kidnapping his bride, he takes her to his island fortress and, leading her to the bedroom, tells her, "Come, my dear, our nest is ready!" Outraged by the suggestion, his bride refuses, whereupon the resourceful Beery locks her in a cellar prepared for such emergencies, turns sundry locks and floodgates and gradually fills the cellar with sea water. A further title tells her: "My last wife changed her mind down here!" Fortunately, Rod La Rocque arrives in time to save her.

Beery enjoyed such roles to the hilt, but subtler villainy was well within his range. His

Sgt. Lajaune in the silent *Beau Geste* ('26) was a fine characterization of a man who was a sadist and a killer, and yet at the same time a brilliant strategist and a courageous soldier. However, Beery seldom strayed so far from lecherous situations.

Among his best silent vehicles were *The White Man's Law* ('18), *Believe Me Xantippe* ('18), *The Mark of Zorro* ('20), *The Sea Wolf* ('20), *The Sagebrusher* ('20), *The Fighting Shepherdess* ('20), *The Call of the North* ('21), *Tillie* ('22), *The Spoilers* ('23), *Wanderer of the Wasteland* ('24), *North of '36* ('24), *The Thundering Herd* ('25) and *Love in the Desert* ('29).

Noah was a specialist in playing black-hearted villains and he seemed particularly capable in Western films. When Paramount filmed the features based on Zane Grey novels, he was constantly on hand to threaten the hero. In spite of his menacing roles, Noah rose to full-fledged stardom and became known as the "villain's villain."

In the sound era, Noah acted in a number of Westerns which never failed to thrill the front-row kids. He easily made the transition to sound films for he possessed a deep, resonant voice that suited him perfectly. During the early 1930s, Paramount decided to revive the Zane Grey Westerns by making a new series of talking versions starring such stalwarts as Randolph Scott and Richard Dix. (RKO and 20th Century-Fox also joined in with a few features that had George O'Brien, Tom Keene and Smith Ballew in the lead.) Meanwhile, Noah was welcomed back into the fold playing the same roles he had done in the silent series and continuing his foul deeds with even more zest. Substantial amounts of stock footage was lifted from the old silent films and inserted into the sound films.

Beery's Westerns of the 1930s and 1940s follow: *Riders of the Purple Sage* (Fox, '31, George O'Brien), *Cornered* (Col., '32, Tim McCoy), *The Big Stampede* (WB, '32, John Wayne), *The Thundering Herd* (Par., '33, Jack Holt), *Sunset Pass* (Par., '33, Randolph Scott), *Man of the Forest* (Par., '33, Randolph Scott), *To the Last Man* (Par., '33 Randolph

Noah Beery, Sr., in *A Little Bit of Heaven* (Universal, 1940).

Scott), *The Trail Beyond* (Mon., '34, John Wayne), *The Bad Man of Brimstone* (MGM, '37, Wallace Beery), *Panamint's Bad Man* (TCF, '38, Smith Ballew), *Mexicali Rose* (Rep., '39, Gene Autry), *Pioneers of the West* (Rep., '40, Robert Livingston), *The Tulsa Kid* (Rep., '40, Donald Barry), *A Missouri Outlaw* (Rep., '41, Donald Barry), *Outlaws of Pine Ridge* (Rep., '42 Donald Barry), *The Devil's Trail* (Col., '42, Bill Elliott, Tex Ritter), *Pardon My Gun* (Col., '42, Charles Starrett) and *Carson City Cyclone* (Rep., '43, Donald Barry).

Noah Beery made five serials. In *The Devil Horse* ('32) he is head of an outlaw gang that stops at nothing to gain possession of the Devil Horse, leader of a wild horse pack in which a wild boy is reared. Beery's plot is to recapture the horse that had once been a great race horse and present it as a new discovery.

In *Fighting with Kit Carson* ('33) Johnny Mack Brown (Carson) is employed to escort a caravan carrying a large quantity

Noah Beery, Sr. (left), and Tom Keene in *Sunset Pass* (Paramount, 1933).

of gold destined for army posts in California. Unscrupulous men attempt to steal the gold by causing the murder of an Indian chief and placing the blame on Carson and his party, thus setting the Indians on the warpath. Beery played the outlaws' leader.

In *Zorro Rides Again* ('37), John Carroll (Zorro/James Vega) comes to the aid of the California-Yucatan Railroad when it is threatened by a gang of outlaws ostensibly headed by Dick Alexander (El Lobo) but secretly masterminded by Beery (Marsden), supposedly an upstanding citizen.

In *Adventures of Red Ryder* ('40), Donald Barry's (Red Ryder) father is killed by a gang headed by Beery and Harry Worth, who wish to gain control of all the land in the territory through which they know a railroad is to be built. Donald vows vengeance and with the help of Tommy Cook (Little Beaver) and his other friends he rids the territory of badmen.

In *Overland Mail* ('42), Lon Chaney, Jr., Don Terry and Noah Beery, Jr., investigate a breakdown of U.S. mail delivery in the La Paz country. They discover that the attacks on Overland Company are not Indian attacks but are led by gunmen disguised as Indians. In tracking down the renegades, the friends learn that Beery, Sr., is causing the trouble because he wants to take over the mail delivery franchise owned by Helen Parrish's father. His gang overpowered, Sr. is killed trying to make a getaway.

Noah was a mustachioed blackguard of the old school, a swaggering scoundrel who loved villainy for its own sake, and who had not a single redeeming feature — except possibly a sense of humor.

Some of his best opportunities to display beastliness came in the Zane Grey Westerns, for example, *Man of the Forest* ('33). There is a classic moment in which, finally tired of playing the noble protector of the heroine (Verna Hillie), Noah determines to, as the expression goes, "have his way with her." His mistress tries to reason with him by calling on his loyalty. "I've been with you for 20 years," she tells him piteously. "Well, you needn't count the last 19 of 'em!" growls Noah before stalking out in search of Hillie.

Noah's last film was a part in his brother Wallace's *This Man's Navy* in 1945. He died suddenly of a heart attack on April 1, 1946. Wally said his brother had been in great spirits, for he was just home from a year on Broadway, where he had made a great success as Boss Tweed in the stage hit *Up in Central Park*.

The two brothers, with Wallace's daughter Carol Ann, were scheduled to appear on a Lux radio broadcast the evening of Noah's death. As an old trouper, Wally carried out the tradition that the show must go on by appearing on schedule with Carol Ann.

Serials

1932

The Devil Horse. Mascot, [12 Chapters] D: Otto Brower; 2nd Unit D: Yakima Canutt; SP: George Morgan, Barney Sarecky, George H. Plympton, Wyndham Gittens; P: Nat Levine; Cam: Ernest Miller, Carl Webster; LP: Harry Carey, Noah Beery, Sr., Frankie Darro, Greta Granstedt, Al Bridge, Apache (horse), Yakima Canutt, Jack Mower.

1933

Fighting with Kit Carson. Mascot, [12 Chapters] D: Armand Schaefer, Colbert Clark; SP: J. F. Natteford, Barney Sarecky, Colbert Clark, Wyndham Gittens; P: Nat Levine; LP: Johnny Mack Brown, Betsy King Ross, Noah Beery, Sr., Noah Beery, Jr., Tully Marshall, Robert Warwick.

1937

Zorro Rides Again. Rep., [12 Chapters] D: William Witney, John English; SP: Barry Shipman, Franklyn Adreon, Morgan Cox, John Rathmell, Ronald Davidson; AP: Sol C. Siegel; Cam: William Nobles; Mus: Alberto Colombo; LP: John Carroll, Helen Christian, Duncan Renaldo, Noah Beery, Sr., Dick Alexander, Reed Howes, Yakima Canutt, Jack Ingram.

1940

Adventures of Red Ryder. Rep., [12 Chapters] D: William Witney, John English; AP: Hiram S. Brown, Jr.; SP: Franklyn Adreon, Ronald Davidson, Norman S. Hall, Barney Sarecky, Sol Shor; Cam: William Nobles; Mus: Cy Feuer; LP: Donald Barry, Noah Beery, Sr., Tommy Cook, Vivian Coe, Maude Pierce Allen, Hal Taliaferro.

1942

Overland Mail. Univ., [15 Chapters] D: Ford Beebe, John Rawlins; S: Paul Huston; P: Henry MacRae; LP: Lon Chaney, Jr., Don Terry, Noah Beery, Jr., Noah Beery, Sr., Helen Parrish, Tom Chatterton, Bob Baker.

NOAH BEERY, JR.

Noah Beery, Jr., son of Noah Beery, Sr., and nephew of Wallace Beery, was born August 10, either 1913 or 1915, in New York City. His education was received in Hollywood High School and Harvard Military Academy between stock company appearances with his father. Young Noah was ill for several months as a youngster, so when doctors advised his parents to move to a milder climate, they left for Southern California

Noah Beery, Jr. (left), and Walter Miller in *Stormy* (Universal, 1935).

where Noah, Jr., subsequently spent the rest of his life.

Noah, Jr., made his screen debut as a child in the silent classic *The Mark of Zorro* ('20) with his father and Douglas Fairbanks. He had a few other parts during the late silent era but mostly he grew up as normally as possible for son of an increasingly successful actor. Away from school he was raised on his parents' San Fernando Valley ranch, thus providing him the opportunity to learn to ride at an early age.

Shortly before Noah, Jr., graduated from high school, a talent scout noticed him and arranged for a screen test. He was signed by Universal. His first film was the serial *Heroes of the West*, which depicts the laying of a hundred miles of track for the first transcontinental line in 1867 when the Indians were on the warpath, the Pony Express was in its glory period and wagon trains wended

their way across the plains. In the story, William Desmond is responsible for laying track but has been plagued by bad luck and accidents which have left him far behind schedule. Now he is in danger of losing his contract. Noah and Diane Duval (a.k.a. Jacqueline Wells/Julie Bishop) are his children and they help troubleshooter Onslow Stevens defeat the opposition headed by Philo McCullough, Harry Tenbrook and Frank Lackteen. Noah Beery, Jr., gave the casual, easygoing performance that characterized his entire career.

Noah established an image early on of portraying the brother of the girl or friend of the leading man. His philosophy was, "If you want to keep busy, don't be a romeo." He therefore built a career playing sidekicks, first in movies and later in television. His serials totaled ten — eight for Universal and two for Mascot. *Heroes of the West* has al-

Russell Hayden (left), Anita Louise and Noah Beery, Jr., in *Two in a Taxi* (Columbia, 1941).

ready been mentioned. The remaining nine are

• *The Jungle Mystery* ('32): Competing expeditions vie for buried ivory hidden in Africa by a slave trader, long dead.

• *The Three Musketeers* ('33): Three Legionnaires and an American aviator become involved in thwarting the attempts of a mysterious leader of a desert tribe cult that is attempting to wipe out the Foreign Legion.

• *Fighting with Kit Carson* ('33): Kit Carson is employed to escort a caravan carrying a large quantity of gold destined for army posts in California. Unscrupulous men attempt to steal the gold by murdering Chief Dark Eagle and placing the blame on Carson, thus setting the Indians on the warpath.

• *Tailspin Tommy* ('34): Two gangsters try every means possible to gain control of Three Point Airlines, but are foiled by Tailspin Tommy and his friends.

• *Tailspin Tommy in the Great Air Mystery* ('35): Tailspin Tommy and pal Skeeter are hired to survey oil properties and blaze a pipeline from the air. They are opposed by a villainous American in cahoots with the agent of a Central American country.

• *The Call of the Savage* ('35): Beery as "Jan of the Jungle" defeats evil doctors who vow to steal a formula for curing infantile paralysis.

• *Ace Drummond* ('36): A mysterious criminal known as "The Dragon" is determined to stop the Mongolian link needed to complete a globe-circling airplane service. Ace Drummond (John King) agrees to investigate, as well as to help Peggy Trainor (Jean Rogers) search for her lost father and a hidden mountain containing enormous quantities of jade.

• *Riders of Death Valley* ('41): The Riders of Death Valley, a vigilante group, seeks to protect miners against outlaws who hope to take over all the mines in the Panamint District. Beery is "Smokey," a member of the Riders of Death Valley under the leadership of Dick Foran.

• *Overland Mail* ('42): Three agents of the Overlander Company, which has a contract to carry the U.S. mail, investigate attacks on the Overland Company.

A few of Noah Beery, Jr.'s, features are: *The Road Back* ('37); *Forbidden Valley* ('38); *Only Angels Have Wings* ('39); *Of Mice and Men* ('40); *The Carson City Kid* ('40); *Twenty-Mule Team* ('40); *Sergeant York* ('41); *Tennessee Johnson* '42); *Dudes Are Pretty People* ('42); *Gung Ho!* ('43); *Corvette K-325* ('43); *Frontier Badman* ('43); *Follow the Boys* ('44); *Under Western Skies* ('45); *The Daltons Ride Again* ('45); *Crimson Canary* ('45); *Red River* ('48); *Indian Agent* ('48); *The Doolins of Oklahoma* ('49); *The Savage Horde* ('50); *The Last Outpost* ('51); *The Texas Rangers* ('51); *The Cimarron Kid* ('51); *The Will Rogers Story* ('52); *Wings of the Hawk* ('53); *The Black Dakotas* ('54); *Yellow Tomahawk* ('54); *White Feather* ('55); *Jubal* ('56); *The Fastest Gun Alive* ('56); *Spirit of St. Louis* ('57); *Decision at Sundown* ('57); *Escort West* ('59); *Guns of the Timberland* ('60); *Inherit the Wind* ('60); *7 Faces of Dr. Lao* ('64); *Incident at Phantom Hill* ('66); *Heaven with a Gun* ('69); *Cockeyed Cowboys of Calico County* ('69); *Little Fauss and Big Halsey* ('70); *The Petty Story* ('72); *Walking Tall* ('73); *Waltz Across Texas* ('73); *The Spikes Gang* ('74) and *The Best Little Whorehouse in Texas* ('83).

Television work eventually became a staple for Noah. He was a regular in the following TV series: *Riverboat* ('59–'61); *Circus Boy* ('56–'58); *Hondo* ('67); *Doc Elliott* ('74); *The Rockford Files* ('74–80); *The Quest* ('82) and *The Yellow Rose*)'83–84).

In addition to television series, Noah appeared in the following telefilms: *Journey to Shiloh* ('68); *The Alpha Caper* ('73); *Sidekicks* ('74); *Savages* ('74); *Frances Gary Powers: The True Story of the U.S. Spy Incident* ('76); and *The Capture of Grizzly Adams* ('81).

Noah married Maxine Jones, daughter of Buck Jones, in 1940. They had three children, Muffett, Melissa and Bucklind. Noah and Maxine were divorced in 1966 and he married again, to a non-professional, in 1969.

Noah suffered a stroke in the mid–80s from which he never fully recovered. In his later years he enjoyed life collecting Western literature and artifacts and gained a small reputation as a Western artist. He died on his ranch about 80 miles north of Los Angeles on November 1, 1994. Cause of death was bleeding in the brain following surgery.

Noah is remembered today for his portrayal of Rocky, father of James Garner, on *The Rockford Files*. He was nominated twice for an Emmy award. But serial lovers will always remember him for his serial performances.

Serials

1932

Heroes of the West. Univ., [12 Chapters] D: Ray Taylor; SP: George H. Plympton, Basil Dickey, Joe Roach, Ella O'Neill; Cam: John Hickson; LP: Noah Beery, Jr., Diane Duval [a.k.a. Jacqueline Wells/Julie Bishop], Onslow Stevens, William Desmond, Philo McCullough, Harry Tenbrook.

The Jungle Mystery. Univ., [12 Chapters] D: Ray Taylor; SP: George H. Plympton, Basil Dickey, George Mason; S: Talbot Mundy; AP: Henry MacRae; Adapt: Ella O'Neill; LP: Tom Tyler, Cecilia Parker, William Desmond, Noah Beery, Jr., Philo McCullough, Carmelita Geraghty.

1933

The Three Musketeers. Mascot, [12 Chapters] D: Armand Schaefer, Colbert Clark; SP: Norman Hall, Colbert Clark, Ben Cohn, Wyndham Gittens; S: Alexander Dumas; P: Nat Levine; LP: Jack Mulhall, Raymond Hatton, Francis X. Bushman, Jr., John Wayne, Ruth Hall, Lon Chaney, Jr., Noah Beery, Jr., Hooper Atchley.

Fighting with Kit Carson. Mascot, [12 Chapters] D: Armand Schaefer, Colbert Clark; SP: J. F. Natteford, Barney Sarecky, Colbert Clark, Wyndham Gittens; P: Nat Levine; LP: Johnny Mack Brown, Betsy King Ross, Noah Beery, Jr., Tully Marshall, Edmund Breese, Edward Hearn.

1934

Tailspin Tommy. Univ., [12 Chapters] D: Louis Friedlander [Lew Landers]; SP: Norman S. Hall, Vin Moore, Basil Dickey, Ella O'Neill; LP: Maurice Murphy, Noah Beery, Jr., Patricia Farr, Walter Miller, Grant Withers, John Davidson, Edmund Cobb.

1935

Tailspin Tommy in the Great Air Mystery. Univ., [12 Chapters] D: Ray Taylor; SP: Ray Cannon, Ella O'Neill, Basil Dickey, Robert Herschon, George H. Plympton; LP: Clark Williams, Jean Rogers, Noah Beery, Jr., Bryant Washburn, Helen Brown, Inez Alvarado.

The Call of the Savage. Univ., [12 Chapters] D: Lewis Friedlander [Lew Landers]; S: Otis Adelbert Kline; SP: Nate Gazert, George H. Plympton, Basil Dickey; LP: Noah Beery, Jr., Dorothy Short, Harry Woods, Walter Miller, Bryant Washburn, Viva Tattersall.

1936

Ace Drummond. Univ., [13 Chapters] D: Ford Beebe, Cliff Smith; SP: Wyndham Gittens, Norman S. Hall, Ray Trampe; AP: Barney A. Sarecky, Ben Koenig; LP: John King, Jean Rogers, Noah Beery, Jr., Guy Bates Post, Chester Gan, Arthur Loft, Jackie Morrow.

1941

Riders of Death Valley. Univ., [15 chapters] D: Ray Taylor, Ford Beebe; S: Oliver Drake; SP: Sharman Lowe, Basil Dickey, George H. Plympton, Jack Connell; P: Henry MacRae; Cam: Jerome Ash, William Sickner; Mus: Charles Previn; LP: Dick Foran, Buck Jones, Charles Bickford, Leo Carrillo, Jeanne Kelly [Jean Brooks], Lon Chaney, Jr., Noah Beery, Jr., Glenn Strange.

1942

Overland Mail. Univ., [15 Chapters] D: Ford Beebe, John Rawlins; P: Henry MacRae; SP: Paul Huston; LP: Lon Chaney, Jr., Don Terry, Noah Beery, Jr., Helen Parrish, Noah Beery, Sr., Bob Baker.

MADGE BELLAMY

Madge Bellamy was a Texas gal, born Margaret Philpott in Hillsboro on June 30, 1900. Her father was a professor of English at Texas A&M University; her mother, a concert pianist. At 16, Madge starred on Broadway as the premier ballerina in *The Love Mill* and at 17 starred in the play *Dear Brutus*. A long succession of plays followed.

Madge entered films in 1921 and by the end of the year was definitely a star. *The Call of the North* ('21) with Jack Holt was perhaps her best film. She projected as a beautiful and desirable woman caught in a bitter conflict between her father, played by Noah Beery, Sr., and hero Jack Holt. Two years later she was back in the Canadian woods, this time as a runaway from abusive stepfather Noah Beery, Sr. Though she falls in love with Cullen Landis, it is Oscar, the elephant, that provides most of the heroics as he helps his mistress avoid the clutches of Beery. The film was *Soul of the Beast* ('23).

It was in '24 that Madge made her finest film, the 12-reel Fox super–Western, *The Iron Horse*. It was directed by John Ford and George O'Brien co-starred. In '27 she ap-

Buck Jones and Madge Bellamy in *Gordon of Ghost City* (Universal, 1933).

peared in *Coleen*, a comedy-drama set in Ireland with a horse racing theme. It was a big box office hit. In 1928 she co-starred with Johnny Mack Brown in *Soft Living* and *The Play Girl*, made prior to Brown's emergence as a Western star.

Bellamy made only a handful of films in the sound era, and of these the two best are *White Zombie* ('32) and the serial *Gordon of Ghost City* ('33). The former has Madge as John Harron's wife, carried off by Bela Lugosi to his castle (Lugosi has placed her in a death-like trance). In the latter film, Buck Jones is hired to stop cattle rustling on the ranch of William Desmond, but soon finds himself hunting in Ghost City. There he meets Bel-

lamy, who enlists his help in protecting her grandfather's secret gold strike underneath one of the stores in the town. Walter Miller, foreman of the Desmond ranch and leader of the outlaws, uses Ghost City as a gang hideout. A mystery man with a gun makes it rough for both Buck and the outlaws, but Buck is able to defeat the outlaws, capture the leader, unravel the mystery of the grizzly old gunman and win himself a bride.

Madge retired in the early '30s, moving to her Riverside, California, ranch. Later came a move to Ontario, Canada. There she wrote three novels and some plays. She came out of screen retirement in 1945 to make the Cinecolor film *Northwest Trail* for Action Pictures starring Bob Steele and Joan Woodbury. It was her last screen appearance. As a screen personality, she projected sweet innocence and good breeding.

Madge Bellamy died at the age of 89 at San Antonio Community Hospital in Upland, California.

Serial

1933

Gordon of Ghost City. Univ., [12 Chapters] D: Ray Taylor; SP: Ella O'Neill, Basil Dickey, George Plympton, Harry O. Hoyt, Het Mannheim; S: Peter B. Kyne; P: Henry MacRae; LP: Buck Jones, Madge Bellamy, Walter Miller, William Desmond, Hugh Enfield, Francis Ford, Tom Ricketts, Edmund Cobb, Dick Rush.

VIRGINIA BELMONT

Virginia Belmont served as catalyst for Jimmy Wakely's outbursts of song, romantic inclinations and "Justice must be served" demeanor in three Monogram oaters (*Oklahoma Blues, The Rangers Ride, Courtin' Trouble*), as well as fulfilling the necessary ingenue role in a couple of prairie dusters with Johnny Mack Brown (*Prairie Express, Overland Trails*) and one with William Boyd (*Silent Conflict*). She also supported Robert Mitchum and Anne Jeffreys in RKO's *Nevada* ('44).

Virginia did yeoman service in the Republic cliffhanger *Dangers of the Canadian Mounted* ('48). Jim Bannon has the lead in this story about gold seekers and their attempt to keep the territory from being opened up to settlers.

Belmont seemed to have some potential, but nothing panned out for her and she quietly disappeared into the ranks of extras. Her other films include *The Falcon in Hollywood* ('44), *Girl Rush* ('44), *Betrayal from the East* ('45), *The Enchanted Cottage* ('45), *George White's Scandals* ('45), *Having Wonderful Crime* ('45), *Johnny Angel* ('45), *Pan-Americana* ('45), *Sing Your Way Home* ('45), *What a Blonde* ('45), *Ding Dong Williams*

Left to right: Charles King, Virginia Belmont, unidentified player, Jimmy Wakely, I. Stanford Jolley and Frank LaRue in *Oklahoma Blues* (Monogram, 1946).

('46), *The Kid from Brooklyn* ('46), *Sweet Genevieve* ('47) and *Joe Palooka in Fighting Mad* ('48).

Serial

1948

Dangers of the Canadian Mounted. Rep., [12 Chapters] D: Fred Brannon, Yakima Canutt; SP: Franklyn Adreon, Basil Dickey, Sol Shor, Robert C. Walker; Cam: John MacBurnie; Mus: Mort Glickman; LP: Jim Bannon, Virginia Belmont, Anthony Warde, Dorothy Granger, Dale Van Sickel, Tom Steele, I. Stanford Jolley, Ken Terrell, Robert Wilke, Marshall Reed.

WILLIAM (BILLY) BENEDICT

Perhaps character actor William Benedict is best known as Whitey in the first 24 Bowery Boys films (1946–50). Earlier he played Skinny in some of the low-budget East Side Kids films about the exploits of a tough gang of New York youngsters. And then there were the Little Tough Guys, and later Dead End Kids and Little Tough Guys in serials and features. Membership in these gangs changed often and it was a challenge to remember where an actor belonged.

William Benedict was born in Haskell, Oklahoma, on April 16, 1917. He was a newsboy, a plumber's assistant, bank clerk, day laborer and a few other menial jobs before becoming an actor in the mid–30s. His ambition in high school was to become a dancer and he took dancing lessons in Tulsa. However, the family moved to California in 1934 during the Depression and lived very close to the original Fox studio, so it was easy for Billy to drop in to their casting office to see if he could get a job. He so impressed the casting director that he soon cast Billy in many acting bits, including two with humorist Will Rogers (*Doubting Thomas* and *Steamboat 'Round the Bend*, both '36). From that time on, he was seldom idle for lack of work.

Billy was featured in seven serials, three from Universal, three from Republic and one from Columbia. *Adventures of Captain Marvel* ('41) was the most popular serial in which he appeared, with *Perils of Nyoka* ('42) a close second.

Billy worked in both "A" and "B" features and never seemed to grow up. In his late twenties and early thirties, he continued to be seen mostly as a precocious adolescent.

Westerns in which Benedict had a supporting role included *Man of Conquest* ('39), *Melody Ranch* ('40), *Jesse James at Bay* ('41), *Heart of the Golden West* ('42), *The Valley of Hunted Men* ('42), *Home in Wyomin'* ('42), *The Ox-Bow Incident* ('43), *Last Train from Gun Hill* ('59) and *The Hallelujah Trail* ('65).

On television Benedict had roles on *The Blue Knight, Bonanza, the Next Generation, Cheyenne, Jim Bowie, Wild Bill Hickok, Tales of Wells Fargo, The Rifleman, Branded, Gunsmoke, Hondo, The Guns of Will Sonnett, Alias Smith and Jones* and *Petticoat Junction*.

William (Billy) Benedict, 82, died November 25, 2001, of complications from open heart surgery at Cedars-Sinai Hospital.

Serials

1937

Tim Tyler's Luck. Univ., [12 Chapters] D: Ford Beebe, Wyndham Gittens; SP: Wyndham Gittens, Norman S. Hall, Roy Trampe; LP: Frankie Thomas, Frances Robinson, Norman Willis, Jack Mulhall, Al Shean, William Benedict.

1940

Adventures of Red Ryder. Rep., [12 Chapters] D: William Witney, John English; LP: Donald Barry, Noah Beery, Sr., Tommy Cook, Maude Pierce Allen, Hal Taliaferro, Harry Worth.

1941

Adventures of Captain Marvel. Rep., [12 Chapters] D: William Witney, John English; AP: Hiram S. Brown, Jr.; SP: Ronald Davidson, Norman S. Hall, Arch B. Heath, Joseph Poland, Sol Shor; Cam: William Nobles; Mus: Cy Feuer; LP: Tom Tyler, Frank Coghlan, Jr., William Benedict, Louise Currie, Harry Worth, Robert Strange.

1942

Perils of Nyoka. Rep., [15 Chapters] D: William Witney; SP: Ronald Davidson, Norman S. Hall, William Lively, Joseph Poland, Joseph O'Donnell; AP: W. J. O'Sullivan; Cam: Reggie Lanning; Mus: Mort Glickman; LP: Kay Aldridge, Clayton Moore, William Benedict, Lorna Gray, Charles Middleton, Tris Coffin, Forbes Murray, Robert Strange.

Junior G-Men of the Air. Univ., [12 Chapters] D: Ray Taylor, Lewis D. Collins; SP: Paul Huston, George H. Plympton, Griffin Jay; AP: Henry MacRae; LP: Billy Halop, Gene Reynolds, Lionel Atwill, Frank Albertson, Richard Lane, Huntz Hall, Gabriel Dell, William Benedict, Frankie Darro.

1943

Adventures of the Flying Cadets. Univ., [13 Chapters] D: Ray Taylor, Lewis D. Collins; SP: Morgan B. Cox, George H. Plympton, Paul Huston; AP: Henry MacRae; Cam: William Sickner; Mus: Hans J. Salter; LP: Johnny Downs, Bobby Jordan, Jennifer Holt, Eduardo Ciannelli, William Benedict, Ward Wood.

1945

Brenda Starr, Reporter. Col., [13 Chapters] D: Wallace Fox; SP: Ande Lamb, George H. Plympton; P: Sam Katzman; Cam: Ira H. Morgan; Mus: Edward Kay; LP: Joan Woodbury, Kane Richmond, Syd Saylor, Joe Devlin, Wheeler Oakman, Jack Ingram, William Benedict, Anthony Warde.

CONSTANCE BENNETT

Constance Bennett is best remembered today as the blonde, beautiful and very funny ghost who, with her co-star Cary Grant, pulled off numerous pranks in the delightful comedies *Topper* ('37) and *Topper Takes a Trip* ('39).

Constance Campbell Bennett was born in New York City on October 22, 1905, the eldest of stage actor Richard Bennett's three daughters. (Joan Bennett also became a star and Barbara had a short film career.) Apart from a bit role at age 12 in a film starring her father, she made her screen debut at age 17 and soon developed into a popular leading lady of Hollywood silents. A brilliant sophisticated comedienne, she was a major star in films for a very long time, and in the early '30s was said to be the highest paid actress in the world.

Constance was educated at private

schools in New York and Paris. Impulsive and determined, she wed at 16, but the marriage was soon annulled. Since she was so popular, her sleek page-boy haircut was a much imitated trademark. In most of her romantic comedies she played a kind of worldly-wise flapper, with an attractive, husky voice and a wonderful air of slight disdain and amusement. Her first major role was in George Fitzmaurice's *Cyntherea* ('24). That same year she was billed third in the Pathé serial *Into the Net* ('24), a story of murder and kidnapping. The action is brisk, the plot quite complicated, but clearly presented. The action swings from one melodramatic peak to another.

Constance was exceptional in *The Goose Woman* ('25) and *Sally, Irene and Mary* ('25), but she dropped out of movies and eloped with a millionaire steamship-railroad heir and became an active member of the swinging international set. She returned to the screen in 1929 at an enormous salary after divorcing her husband and re-established herself as a leading star in talkies.

Her voice and natural delivery of wisecracking lines became valuable assets in her specialty, the sophisticated comedy, but she also had her share of leads in sentimental melodramas and unabashed tearjerkers. From 1941 to 1944 she was married to actor Gilbert Roland. Her career begun to lose momentum in the '40s; in the early '50s, she left films for the stage, mostly on the road. She also ventured into business with Constance Bennett Cosmetics. She ended her career in excellent form, portraying Lana Turner's mother in *Madame X* ('66).

Constance Bennett died of a cerebral hemorrhage shortly after completing *Madame X*. The last of her five husbands was at her bedside at death.

The best of her films include *Cytherea* ('24); *This Thing Called Love* ('29); *Three Faces East* ('30); *What Price Hollywood?* ('32); *Two Against the World* ('32); *Bed of Roses* ('33); *The Affairs of Cellini* ('34); *After Office Hours* ('35); *Ladies in Love* ('36); *Topper* ('37); *Merrily We Live* ('38); *Topper Takes a Trip* ('39); *Tail Spin* ('39); *Two-Faced Woman* ('41); *Angel on the Amazon* ('48); *It Should Happen to You* ('54); and *Madame X* ('66).

Serial

1924

Into the Net. Pathé, [10 Chapters] D: George B. Seitz; SP: Frank Leon Smith; S: Richard E. Enright; LP: Edna Murphy, Jack Mulhall, Constance Bennett, Bradley Barker, Frank Lackteen, Frances Landau, Paul Porter, Tom Goodwin, Harry Semels.

CARLYLE BLACKWELL

Carlyle Blackwell was enrolled at Cornell University when he decided that acting rather than engineering was what he wanted to do; therefore, over his father's objections, he dropped out of the university.

In Denver he joined the Elitch's Stock Company; a year later he signed with the Keith-Proctor Stock Company. After playing a number of juvenile roles, he made the jump to Broadway. It wasn't long before his thoughts turned to the infant motion picture industry. Trusting that his decision was the right one, he abandoned the stage and joined the Vitagraph Company at its Flatbush studio. He was seen in numerous one- and two-reel films for eight months, but still playing juvenile roles.

Induced by a larger salary and better

roles, Blackwell joined Kalem in 1911 and for three years played a variety of roles. Still, Blackwell was not satisfied. He wanted more control, better scripts and the producer's share of the film revenue. Accordingly he set up his own film company and arranged for his films to be released through International Film Service. Though he made several films, the "one man" organization turned out to be too much for Blackwell.

From 1915 to 1922, Blackwell worked for World and Paramount and was one of the first actors to draw a weekly salary of $2,000. In 1922 he chose to move to England and there he functioned as an actor, director and producer for 14 years at London's Gainsborough Films.

His first wife was a Chicago girl named Ruth Hartman whom he met while playing on the legitimate stage and by whom he had two children. He had four more wives, the last being a former secretary.

It is estimated that Blackwell was in 200 to 300 films, including *Uncle Tom's Cabin* ('09); *The Indian Uprising at Santa Fe* ('12); *The Ocean Waife* ('14); *The Secret Orchard* ('15); *His Royal Highness* ('18); *The Virgin Queen* ('20); *Bulldog Drummond* ('23); *The Beloved Vagabond* ('23); *She* ('25); and *The Hound of the Baskervilles* ('31).

Blackwell was born January 20, 1884 (sources disagree), in Troy, Pennsylvania. He died in Miami Beach, Florida, in 1955.

He was quite popular in his time and could have advanced further as an actor had he pushed himself. But he yearned only to give a good performance. Superstardom never appealed to him.

Blackwell has been credited as the man who gave Alfred Hitchcock his chance to direct in England.

Carlyle Blackwell made only one serial. It was made in France while he was living abroad.

Serial

1924

Les Deux Gosses. France-Cinematographs, [8 Chapters] D: Louis Mercanton; LP: Gabriel Signoret, Edouard Mathe, Carlyle Blackwell, Yvette Guilbert.

MONTE BLUE

Gerard Monte Blue was born January 11, 1887, in Indianapolis, Indiana, the son of a railroader. His father was killed in a head-on collision when Monte was eight years old. There were four boys and Mrs. Blue, herself in ill health, could not feed and clothe a family of five. The two younger boys were admitted to the Soldiers and Sailors Orphans Home in Knightstown, Indiana. There Monte lived for several years, playing in the band and on the football team. He grew fast, eventually reaching a height of 6'3" and weighing 185 pounds.

When he left the home as a young teenager, he decided to follow his father's trade as a railroader; but he, too, was in a wreck that put him in the hospital for 18 months. Upon his discharge he became a steel worker, coal miner, cowboy, lumberman, sailor, stuntman and eventually an extra in D. W. Griffith's *The Birth of a Nation* ('15). He gradually got better roles and by 1921 was a star, appearing with Gloria Swanson in Cecil B. DeMille's *The Affairs of Anatol* ('21) and D. W. Griffith's *Orphans of the Storm* ('21) with Dorothy and Lillian Gish. Many consider this his best film.

In 1923, Blue signed a contract with

Top: Leila Hyams and Monte Blue in *The Brute* (Warner Bros., 1927). *Bottom:* In *King of the Texas Rangers* (Republic, 1941).

Warner Bros. and starred in 35 films in eight years, playing tough romantic leads. He became world-famous with wide-ranging roles.

Also in 1923, Monte divorced his first wife, Gladys Erma Blue, and that same year married actress Tove Danor. He was 36, she was 19. Tove had been an extra in *Orphans of the Storm* and was a model for famed illustrator Harrison Fisher. The Blue-Danor union produced two children, Barbara and Richard Monte.

After a hectic 1929 in which he made six films, Monte and Tove took a world cruise. While they were gone, the stock market crashed. His investments had failed. He was broke. He was no longer in demand as a leading man. In fact, he was no longer in demand, period. But after a time he managed to get steady work in Westerns and serials. He worked with Ken Maynard, Gene Autry, Roy Rogers, Buster Crabbe, Randolph Scott, Dick Foran and others.

In 1918, Monte played in his first serial, *Hands Up*, starring Ruth Roland. His next six chapterplays were made over the period 1936–41. All of these were sound serials. Three of the six were Westerns.

Monte once again became a contract player in 1942. This time, however, he would be working as a supporting player, not the star. But he had some good roles occasionally, among them *Key Largo* ('48), *Homicide* ('49) and *Dallas* ('50). Blue plays a sheriff in each of these films.

Tove died in 1956. Three years later, Monte married portrait artist Betty Jean Munson. In his later years, Monte was very active in the Masons and did ad-

Monte Blue (center), Edna Murphy and an unidentified player in *The Greyhound Limited* (Warner Bros., 1929).

vance work for the Shrine Circus, as well as for the Hamid-Morton Circus. It was while doing work for this latter circus that he collapsed in his Milwaukee hotel room and died from a heart attack on February 18, 1963. His last film is believed to be *Apache* ('54), in which Monte plays the part of Geronimo.

Serials

1918

Hands Up. Astra/Pathé, [15 Chapters] D: James W. Horne; SP: Jack Cunningham, Gilson Willets; S: Gilson Willets; LP: Ruth Roland, George Chesebro, George Larkin, Easter Walters, William A. Carroll, Monte Blue.

1936

Undersea Kingdom. Rep., [12 Chapters] D: B. Reeves Eason, Joseph Kane; SP: John Rathmell, Maurice Geraghty, Oliver Drake; S: Tracy Knight, John Rathmell; Spv.: Barney Sarecky; Cam: William Nobles, Edgar Lyons; Mus: Harry Grey; P: Nat Levine; LP: Ray Corrigan, Lois Wilde, Monte Blue, William Farnum, Lee Van Atta, Raymond Hatton, Smiley Burnette.

1937

Secret Agent X-9. Univ., [12 Chapters]: D: Ford Beebe, Cliff Smith; SP: Wyndham Gittens, Norman S. Hall, Ray Trampe, Leslie Charteris; P: Henry MacRae; LP: Scott Kolk, Jean Rogers, Henry Hunter, Henry Brandon, David Oliver, Larry Blake, Monte Blue.

1938

Hawk of the Wilderness. Rep., [12 Chapters] D: William Witney, John English; SP: Barry Shipman, Rex Taylor, Norman S. Hall; S: William L. Chester; AP: Robert Beche; Cam: William Nobles; Mus: William Lava; LP: Herman Brix, Ray Mala, Monte Blue, Jill Martin, Noble Johnson, William Royle.

The Great Adventures of Wild Bill Hickok. Col., [15 Chapters] D: Mack V. Wright, Sam Nelson; SP: George Rosener, Charles A. Powell, G. A. Durlan, Dallas Fitzgerald, Tom Gibson; AP: Harry Webb; P: Jack Fier; Cam: George Meehan, Benjamin Kline; Mus: Abe Meyer; LP: Bill Elliott, Carole Wayne, Frankie Darro, Monte Blue, Dick Jones, Sammy McKim, Kermit Maynard.

1941

Riders of Death Valley. Univ., [15 Chapters] D: Ray Taylor, Ford Beebe; S: Oliver Drake; SP: Sherman Lowe, Basil Dickey, George Plympton, Jack Connell; P: Henry MacRae; Cam: Jerome Ash, William Sickner; Mus: Charles Previn; LP: Dick Foran, Buck Jones, Leo Carrillo, Charles Bickford, Monte Blue, Lon Chaney, Jr., Glenn Strange, Guinn Williams, Jeanne Kelly [Jean Brooks].

King of the Texas Rangers. Rep., [12 Chapters] D: William Witney, John English; SP: Ronald Davidson, Norman S. Hall, William Lively, Joseph Poland, Joseph O'Donnell; AP: Hiram S. Brown, Jr.; Cam: Reggie Lanning; Mus: Cy Feuer; LP: Slingin' Sammy Baugh, Pauline Moore, Neil Hamilton, Duncan Renaldo, Herbert Rawlinson, Monte Blue, Stanley Blystone, Roy Barcroft, Kermit Maynard.

STANLEY BLYSTONE

On July 16, 1956, William Stanley Blystone, rugged character actor who nearly always played a "heavy," collapsed and died on a Hollywood street corner at Cahuenga Blvd. and Waring Avenue. He was pronounced dead, apparently from a heart attack, on arrival at Hollywood Receiving Hospital. He was dressed in full cowboy regalia for a part in a *Wyatt Earp* television film near the Desilu Studio. He was 61 years of age.

The actor was a brother of the late John G. Blystone, motion picture director, and Jasper Blystone, former assistant director. He was married to actress Alma Tell in 1932. The couple had no children. Alma and Jasper survived him.

An obituary in the *Los Angeles Examiner* stated that he began his career in 1915. Possibly he did, but his credits in *The AFI Catalog* begin in 1924 with *Excitement* and *Darwin Was Right.* In the latter film, a farce, he was billed third in the cast. He had one credit in each of '25, '27 and '28 with none in '26. It is likely that he was playing non-credited roles through the '20s. In 1930 he had supporting roles in *The Fighting Legion, Parade of the West* and *Young Eagles* and hit his stride in talking pictures.

Blystone appeared in over 300 films, including 20 serials. One need not see him on screen to identify him. That sonorous voice was not to be mistaken for anyone else's. Like George Chesebro, his voice was his giveaway. On screen, he was one tough hombre.

Serials

1933

The Wolf Dog. Mascot, [12 Chapters] D: Colbert Clark, Harry Fraser; LP: Frankie Darro, Rin-Tin-Tin, Jr., George J. Lewis, Boots Mallory, Fred Kohler, Henry B. Walthall, Tom London, George Magrill, Yakima Canutt.

1934

Burn 'Em Up Barnes. Mascot, [12 Chapters] D: Colbert Clark, Armand Schaefer; LP: Jack

Mulhall, Frankie Darro, Lola Lane, Julian Rivero, Jason Robards, Edwin Maxwell, Al Bridge, Stanley Blystone, Robert Kortman.

1935

The Phantom Empire. Mascot, [12 Chapters] D: Otto Brower, B. Reeves Eason; LP: Gene Autry, Smiley Burnette, Frankie Darro, Betsy King Ross, Dorothy Christie, Wheeler Oakman, Edward Peil, Sr., Charles K. French, Stanley Blystone, John Davidson.

The Fighting Marines. Mascot, [12 Chapters] D: B. Reeves Eason, Joseph Kane; LP: Grant Withers, Adrian Morris, Ann Rutherford, Robert Warwick, George J. Lewis, Pat O'Malley, Robert Frazer, Tom London.

1936

Ace Drummond. Univ., [13 Chapters] D: Ford Beebe, Cliff Smith; LP: John King, Jean Rogers, Noah Beery, Jr., Guy Bates Post, Arthur Loft, Chester Gan, James B. Leong, Robert Warwick, Stanley Blystone, Selmer Jackson.

The Vigilantes Are Coming. Rep., [12 Chapters] D: Mack V. Wright, Ray Taylor; LP: Robert Livingston, Kay Hughes, Guinn Williams, Raymond Hatton, Fred Kohler, William Desmond, Ray Corrigan, Robert Kortman, John Merton.

1937

Tim Tyler's Luck. Univ., [12 Chapters] D: Ford Beebe, Wyndham Gittens; LP: Frankie Thomas, Frances Robinson, Norman Willis, Jack Mulhall, Al Shean, Earle Douglas, Anthony Warde, Billy Benedict, Stanley Blystone, Al Bridge.

1939

The Lone Ranger Rides Again. Rep., [15 Chapters] D: William Witney, John English; LP: Robert Livingston, Chief Thundercloud, Duncan Renaldo, Jinx Falken, Robert Dunn, J. Farrell MacDonald, Rex Lease, William Gould, Carleton Young, Stanley Blystone, Eddie Dean.

1941

Sea Raiders. Univ., [12 Chapters] D: Ford Beebe, John Rawlins; LP: Billy Halop, Huntz Hall, Gabriel Dell, Bernard Punsley, Hally Chester, William Hall.

King of the Texas Rangers. Rep., [12 Chapters] D: William Witney, John English; LP: Slingin' Sammy Baugh, Pauline Moore, Neil Hamilton, Duncan Renaldo, Charles Trowbridge, Herbert Rawlinson, Monte Blue, Kermit Maynard, Stanley Blystone.

Holt of the Secret Service. Col., [15 Chapters] D: James W. Horne; LP: Jack Holt, Evelyn Brent, Montague Shaw, Tristram Coffin, John Ward, Ted Adams, George Chesebro, Stanley Blystone, Ray Parsons, Joe McQuinn.

1942

Gang Busters. Univ., [13 Chapters] D: Ray Taylor, Noel Smith; LP: Kent Taylor, Irene Hervey, Ralph Morgan, Robert Armstrong, Richard Davies.

1943

Don Winslow of the Coast Guard. Univ., [13 Chapters] D: Ford Beebe, Ray Taylor; LP: Don Terry, Walter Sande, Elyse Knox, Nestor Paiva, Lionel Royce.

1946

King of the Forrest Rangers. Rep., [12 Chapters] D: Spencer G. Bennet, Fred C. Brannon; LP: Larry Thompson, Helen Talbot, Stuart Hamblen, Anthony Warde, LeRoy Mason, Tom London, Robert Wilke, Buddy Roosevelt.

1947

The Sea Hound. Col., [15 Chapters] D: Walter B. Eason, Mack Wright; LP: Buster Crabbe, James Lloyd, Pamela Blake, Ralph Hodges, Spencer Chan, Hugh Prosser, Robert Barron, Rick Vallin, Milton Kibbee, Jack Ingram, Stanley Blystone.

Brick Bradford. Col., [15 Chapters] D: Spencer G. Bennet; LP: Kane Richmond, Rick Vallin, Linda Johnson, Pierre Watkin, Charles Qujigley, Jack Ingram, Charles King, John Merton, Leonard Penn, Wheeler Oakman.

1949

Ghost of Zorro. Rep., [12 Chapters] D: Fred C. Brannon; LP: Clayton Moore, Pamela Blake, Roy Barcroft, George J. Lewis, I. Stanford Jolley.

Adventures of Sir Galahad. Col., [15 Chapters] D: Spencer G. Bennet; LP: George Reeves, Charles King, William Fawcett, Lois Hall, Marjorie Stapp.

1950

Atom Man vs. Superman. Col., [15 Chapters] D: Spencer G. Bennet; LP: Kirk Alyn, Noel Neill, Lyle Talbot, Tommy Bond, Pierre Watkin, Jack Ingram, Rusty Wescoatt, Terry Frost, Stanley Blystone, William Fawcett.

Desperados of the West. Rep., [12 Chapters] D: Fred C. Brannon; LP: Richard Powers [Tom Keene], Judy Clark, Roy Barcroft, I. Stanford Jolley, Lee Phelps, Lee Roberts, Edmund Cobb, Dennis Moore, George Chesebro, Bud Osborne.

TRUE BOARDMAN

True Boardman was a two-fisted, good-looking star of early Kalem action features and serials. When Kalem made *The Hazards of Helen* ('14) in 119 episodes, it seems that everybody who someday would be "somebody" had a part in it. It made stars of Helen Holmes and Helen Gibson, but in addition the casts included Leo Maloney, Hart (Jack) Hoxie, Anna Q. Nilsson, Hoot Gibson and True Boardman, all of whom rose to prominence.

Boardman appeared in *The Barnstormers* (1915) playing the lead actor in a theatrical troupe. He was listed fifth in the cast, headed by Myrtle Tonnehill and William H. West. In another '15 film, *The Pitfall*, he is the hero district attorney who loves Marin Sais and saves her from being killed by her husband, Tom Santschi.

Kalem produced the serial *Stingaree* ('15) with Boardman as wealthy Irving Randolph. He is falsely denounced as a deliberate murderer by his greedy brother when Randolph, during a rifle-shooting contest, accidentally kills a man with whom he has had an altercation. Fleeing to Australia, Randolph becomes known as the bandit Stingaree. He is aided in his Robin Hood–like adventures by his friend Howie (Paul Hurst) and his sweetheart Ethel (Marin Sais).

In *The Social Pirates* ('16), Marin Sais (Mona) and Ollie Kirby (Mary) work as a team in exposing social injustices and bringing criminals to justice in a series of unrelated episodes. Boardman heads the supporting cast. This is not a cliffhanger serial. Except for the two leading ladies, roles change from one episode to another. Each episode is complete in itself.

The Girl from Frisco ('16) was filmed in 25 episodes and starred Marin Sais as Barbara Brent, True Boardman as Congressman Wallace and Frank Jonasson as Ace Brent. Western cowgirl Barbara Brent aids the cause of justice in the Old West, often aided by her rancher father, Ace Brent, and her fiancée, Congressman John Wallace. Each episode tells a complete story, but with the three continuing principal characters. The episodes are similar to serial chapters in that there is action — action — and more action!

In *The Further Adventures of Stingaree* ('17) Irving Randolph/Stingaree (Boardman) receives word from his lawyers that an appraisal of his family estate shows that his entire fortune has been squandered by his deceased brother while he (Irving) was absent in Australia. He realizes that as a penniless man he cannot marry his fiancée, Ethel Porter (Marin Sais). His old friend Howie (Paul Hurst) crosses the ocean to warn him that government officers are on his trail with a warrant for his arrest. Howie persuades Irving to return to Australia with him, thus setting off a whole new series of adventures in the Australian back country. Naturally, Ethel follows him Down Under.

At Universal in 1918 in *Dangers Within*, Boardman played a dishonest plant manager who plots to ruin the owner by faking a smallpox epidemic. Hero and heroine were William Carroll and Zoe Rae. In *The Doctor and the Woman* ('18) with Mildred Harris, Boardman plays a doctor whose career has been ruined by a jealous nurse. In *Molly, Go Get 'Em* ('18), he is a dishonest count who is repulsed by Margarita Fischer, who loves Jack Mowery.

In *Tarzan of the Apes* ('18), Boardman plays Lord Greystoke, father of Tarzan (Elmo Lincoln). Produced by National Pictures, many of the jungle scenes were shot in Louisiana and Brazil. The E. & R. jungle studios in Los Angeles was used for scenes with lions. Enid Markey plays Jane Porter and Kathleen Kirkham plays Lady Greystoke, Tarzan's mother.

Boardman plays Broncho Harrigan in *The Terror of the Range* ('19), the shortest serial ever released by Pathé. Betty Compson and George Larkin have the leads. A U.S. government agent clashes with a mysterious bandit wearing a wolf's head whenever he leads his marauders down a bloodthirsty trail of murder and looting.

Boardman's career was cut short by his early death in 1918. He was married to actress Virginia True Boardman, who filled key character roles, often as a mother, in many Hollywood films of the '20s and '30s. She had a supporting role in the serial *King of the Jungle* ('27). In addition to many features, she played the mother of Shirley Temple in a series of shorts which began the moppet's career.

Boardman's son True Boardman, Jr., was a scriptwriter in the early '40s.

Serials

1914

The Hazards of Helen. Kalem, [119 Episodes] D: J. P. McGowan, James Davis; S: W. Scott Darling; LP: Helen Holmes, Helen Gibson, Robyn Adair, Ethel Clisbee, Tom Trent, G. A. Williams, Hoot Gibson, Leo Maloney, True Boardman, Hart (Jack) Hoxie, Anna Q. Nilsson, George Routh, Pearl Anibus.

1915

Stingaree. Kalem, [12 Chapters] P/D/SP: James W. Horne; S: E. W. Horning; LP: True Boardman, Marin Sais, Paul Hurst, Thomas Lingham, James W. Horne, Lucius Brady, Frank Jonasson, William Brunton, Ollie Kirby, Edward Clisbee, Hoot Gibson.

1916

The Social Pirates. Kalem, [15 Episodes] D: James W. Horne; LP: Marin Sais, Ollie Kirby, True Boardman, Frank Jonasson, Paul Hurst, Jess Arnold, Thomas Lingham, Edward Clisbee, Priscilla Dean, E. Forrest Taylor, Barney Furey.

The Girl from Frisco. Kalem, [25 Episodes] D: James W. Horne; S: Robert Welles Ritchie; LP: Marin Sais, True Boardman, Frank Jonasson, Ronald Bradbury, Edward Clisbee, Hart (Jack) Hoxie, Barney Furey, E. Forrest Taylor.

1917

The Further Adventures of Stingaree. Kalem, [15 Chapters] D: Paul Hurst; SP: Joseph F. Poland; S: E. W. Hornung; LP: True Boardman, Marin Sais, Paul Hurst, Frank Jonasson, Ollie Kirby, Thomas Lingham, Edward Clisbee, Hal Clements, Edythe Sterling, Barney Furey.

1919

The Terror of the Range. Pathé, [7 Chapters] D: Stuart Paton; S: W. A. S. Douglas; SP: Lucien Hubbard; LP: Betty Compson, George Larkin, H. P. Carpenter, Fred M. Malatesta, Ora Carew, True Boardman, Billy Quinn, Alice Saunders, Wally McNamera.

JOE BONOMO

As a stuntman, Joe Bonomo crashed, smashed and slashed his way through film after film. He was a professional strongman and daredevil whose muscular physique and

Joe Bonomo and Louise Lorraine

derring-do helped get him started as a movie star in the days of silent movies. During his career as a stuntman, Joe was exposed to every filmable calamity the screenwriters could come up with.

Bonomo starred in *Perils of the Wild* ('25), *The Great Circus Mystery* ('28) and *The Chinatown Mystery* ('28), plus supporting roles in 16 other serials. He isn't always recognizable; for instance, he was inside a gorilla suit for *King of the Kongo* ('29); in *Hurricane Hutch* ('21) and *The Eagle's Talons* ('23), he doubles the stars and it was not meant for theater-goers to recognize him.

The unbelievable feats of Bonomo ranged from diving off high cliffs into bodies of water and jumping a motorcycle off a pier onto a passing ferryboat to fighting on the wings of bi-planes and driving automobiles across railroad crossings just in time to avoid being scattered over the surrounding countryside. He became known as the "Hercules of the Screen" and was recognized as one of the strongest men in the world.

As a youth he was frail and other boys mistreated him. He determined to build himself into a perfect physique. In 1921 the *New York Daily News* sponsored a "Modern Apollo" contest to find the man whose physique measured nearest to those of Apollo. Over 5,000 applicants were viewed by the judges. Joe won hands down. His prize consisted of $1,000 and a film contract, albeit for ten weeks only.

In his first film, *A Light in the Dark* ('22), he doubled for Lon Chaney, Sr., which led to his going to Hollywood to repeat this task for Chaney's *The Hunchback of Notre Dame* ('23). His big break came when Universal signed him to a seven-year contract with a starting salary of $150 a week.

Joe was cast in the Pete Morrison two-reel Westerns where he learned to ride, and where he doubled most of the Western stars of the day. Fred Thompson was among his closest friends. Joe starred in the two-reeler *The College Cowboy* ('24), but most of his starring vehicles were serials.

Joe was an all-around athlete. Back during his school days, he won letters in football, swimming, basketball, wrestling, hockey and track. His dad did not approve of athletics; he wanted Joe to spend his hours studying for some profession. Therefore he enrolled Joe at the Military Academy, thinking that Joe wouldn't have time for sports, but rather that he would concentrate on developing his mind. Learning of Joe's involvement in sports, his parents withdrew him from the Academy and enrolled him in Erasmus Hall High School. Here it was the same story. Anything to develop the body and make him stronger was far more important than "book learning." He dropped out of high school at the end of the junior year.

Joe married Ethel Newman, a statuesque blonde dancer whom he met while judging a dance contest (yes, he was a dancer too). He competed against Arthur Murray, George Raft, Ricardo Cortez and others to win many cups for ballroom dancing, for he was extremely graceful despite his size.

Joe and Ethel had a daughter, Joan, who in turn made Joe the grandfather of two boys, Ricky and Ronnie.

The advent of talking films marked the eclipse of Bonomo's film career. He returned to New York and became a manufacturer of physical fitness products and published books and magazines on health and fitness. In 1977 the Museum of Modern Art paid a special tribute to him, screening the only surviving print of the 1925 film *The Great Circus Mystery*. Bonomo starred in the film as "Sandow the Strongman" and was billed as the World's strongest human.

One of the books he published was his autobiography, *The Strongman*. In its 352 pages are 450 photos and much interesting text. The book effectively gets across Bonomo's folksy personality and well reflects earlier decades when show business had a more madcap nature.

Joe Bonomo died on March 28, 1978, from a kidney ailment and pneumonia in Hollywood Presbyterian Hospital, Los Angeles. His widow, Ethel Bonomo, age 92, died April 26, 1995, in Culver City, California.

Serials

1921

Hurricane Hutch. Pathé, [15 Chapters] D: George B. Seitz; LP: Charles Hutchison, Lucy Fox, Warner Oland, Diana Deer, Ann Hastings, Harry Semels. [Spencer G. Bennet, George B. Seitz and Joe Bonomo all doubled Hutchison.]

1923

The Eagle's Talons. Univ., [15 Chapters] D: Duke Worne; LP: Ann Little, Fred Thomson, Al Wilson, Herbert Fortier, Joseph W. Girard, Edith Stayart.

Beasts of Paradise. Univ., [15 Chapters] D: William Craft; SP/S: Val Cleveland; LP: William Desmond, Eileen Sedgwick, William Gould, Ruth Royce, Joe Bonomo, Margaret Morris.

1924

The Iron Man. Univ., [15 Chapters] D: Jay Marchant; S/SP: Arthur Henry Gooden, William Wyler; LP: Lucien Albertini, Margaret Morris, Joe Bonomo, Jack Daugherty, Lola Todd.

Wolves of the North. Univ., [10 Chapters] D: William Duncan; SP: Frank H. Clark; S: Katherene and Robert Pinkerton; LP: William Duncan, Edith Johnson, Joseph W. Girard, Clark Comstock, Esther Ralston, Harry Woods, Frank Rice, Joe Bonomo, Melvina Polo.

1925

Perils of the Wild. Univ., [15 Chapters] D: Francis Ford; S: Johann David Wyss; SP: Isadore Bernstein, William Lord Wright; LP: Joe Bonomo, Margaret Quimby, Jack Mower, Alfred Allen, Eva Gordon, Jack Murphy.

The Great Circus Mystery. Univ., [15 Chapters] D: Jay Marchant; SP: Leigh Jacobson; Cont: George Morgan; S: Isadore Bernstein, William Lord Wright; LP: Joe Bonomo, Louise Lorraine, Robert J. Graves, Robert Seiter, Carmen Phillips, Slim Cole.

1927

The Golden Stallion. Mascot, [10 Chapters] D: Harry Webb; P: Nat Levine; S/SP: Karl Kru-

sada, William Lester; LP: Maurice "Lefty" Flynn, Molly Malone, Joe Bonomo, Tom London, Burr McIntosh, Joseph Swickard.

Heroes of the Wild. Mascot, [10 Chapters] D: Harry Webb; S/SP: Karl Krusada, Harry Webb; P: Nat Levine; LP: Jack Hoxie, Josephine Hill, Joe Bonomo, White Fury (horse), Linda Laredo, Helen Gibson, Tornado (dog).

1928

The Chinatown Mystery. Syn., [10 Chapters] D: J. P. McGowan; S: Francis Ford; P: Trem Carr; LP: Joe Bonomo, Ruth Hiatt, Paul Malvern, Francis Ford, Sheldon Lewis, Paul Panzer.

1929

King of the Kongo. Mascot, [10 Chapters] D: Richard Thorpe; SP: Harry Drago; P: Nat Levine; LP: Jacqueline Logan, Walter Miller, Richard Tucker, Larry Steers, Boris Karloff, Joe Bonomo.

1930

The Lone Defender. Mascot, [10 Chapters] D: Richard Thorne; P: Nat Levine; LP: Rin-Tin-Tin, Sr., Walter Miller, June Marlowe, Buzz Barton, Josef Swickard, Lee Shumway.

1931

Battling with Buffalo Bill. Univ., [12 Chapters] D: Tom Tyler, Rex Bell, Lucile Browne, Francis Ford, William Desmond.

Heroes of the Flames. Univ., [12 Chapters] D: Robert F. Hill; LP: Tim McCoy, Marion Shockley, William Gould, Grace Cunard, Bobby Nelson, Gayne Whitman, Beulah Hutton, Joe Bonomo, Bud Osborne.

The Sign of the Wolf. Met, [10 Chapters] D: Forrest Sheldon, Harry S. Webb; S/SP: Betty Burbridge, Karl Krusada; P: Harry S. Webb; Cam: William Nobles, Herbert Kilpatrick; LP: Rex Lease, Virginia Brown Faire, Joe Bonomo, Jack Mower, Al Ferguson.

The Phantom of the West. Mascot, [10 Chapters] D: Ross Lederman; LP: Tom Tyler, Dorothy Gulliver, William Desmond, Tom Santschi, Tom Dugan, Joe Bonomo.

The Vanishing Legion. Mascot, [12 Chapters] D: B. Reeves Eason; LP: Harry Carey, Edwina

Booth, Rex (horse), Frankie Darro, Philo Mc-Cullough.

1932

The Lost Special. Univ., [12 Chapters] D: Henry MacRae; LP: Frank Albertson, Cecilia Parker, Caryl Lincoln, Ernie Nevers, Francis Ford.

The Last Frontier. RKO, [12 Chapters] D: Spencer G. Bennet, Thomas L. Story; SP: George Plympton, Robert F. Hill; S: Courtney R. Cooper; LP: Creighton Chaney [Lon Chaney, Jr.], Dorothy Gulliver, Mary Jo Desmond, Francis X. Bushman, Jr., Joe Bonomo.

VEDA ANN BORG

Veda Ann Borg (her real name) was born January 11, either 1915 or 1919 in West Roxbury, Massachusetts. Her father, Gottfried Borg, was a painter and decorator who had immigrated from Sweden. Her mother (née Minna Noble) was a secretary before her marriage.

One summer Veda traveled to Sweden with her father for a visit. While she was abroad, a friend mailed her photograph to Paramount's Casting Office as a joke. But when Veda returned home, she found a letter from Paramount inviting her to come in for an interview. Her lanky good looks and slight lisp got her a screen test and a contract.

Her first film was *Three Cheers for Love* ('36), a minor musical in which she played a cheating wife. For some reason Paramount didn't take up her option and she was hired by Warner Brothers. She appeared in small roles for two years. In 1939 she was making her first big movie, *One More Tomorrow* (and getting the publicity treatment that Ann Sheridan later received), when she was nearly killed in an auto accident.

When she went through the windshield of actor Dick Purcell's roadster in a head-on collision the night of August 7, 1939, the broken glass sheared her features away and replaced one of Hollywood's most beautiful faces with a mass of raw flesh. She was slashed beyond recognition, and most of her nose

was cut off. Purcell and the other driver were not hurt as badly.

It was feared that Veda would not live, but she did. She was put in touch with Dr. Josif Ginsberg, a famed plastic surgeon. There was a piece of glass in her left eye, and it was feared she would lose her sight. The doctor fixed her eye and then went to work on her face. She spent eight months in the hospital, was swathed in bandages for months, and endured ten operations. The doctor removed a piece of her rib to build up a new nose; for cartilage he took pieces of her earlobes.

Warner Brothers footed the bill for her enormous hospital expenses. But, her face rebuilt, Veda was dropped when her contract expired. Though the surgeon had done a magnificent job in reconstructing her features, the studio thought she would not photograph well. Thus, Veda, who a year before had been the subject of a big Warners buildup, which was promoting her as another Garbo, was suddenly out on the street looking for work.

Between operations on her face, Larry Darmour offered her the female lead opposite Victor Jory in Columbia's *The Shadow* ('39), first of the two serials for which continued-next-week fans fondly remember her. Thus, Veda Ann Borg, the actress who literally lost her face in an automobile wreck, became a movie star again after a long, uphill

Bob Steele and Veda Ann Borg in *Marked Trails* (Monogram, 1945).

climb from near death. It was thrilling chapterplay, and the Saturday matinee audiences readily accepted Veda, who worked hard at all the stunting and swashbuckling. But although the cameraman did what he could to hide the scars, she didn't photograph well. More surgery and a few insignificant parts followed. Then Gregory Ratoff gave her the part of Akim Tamiroff's mistress in *The Corsican Brothers* ('41), a turning point in her career, and saw to it that special care was taken in lighting her. Because Virginia Grey was ill and could not accept the part, Veda played the blonde gun moll in MGM's *The Penalty* ('41), boosting her career still further. As Edward Arnold's mistress, Veda received better reviews than anyone else in the cast.

In 1942, Veda married a wealthy playboy named Paul Herrick, but the marriage was short-lived, reports having it that the break came because Veda would not abandon her career to live the quiet, domestic life.

The Penalty established a new image for Veda. In *Honky Tonk* ('41) she was a raucous lady barber. Director Gregory Ratoff gave her important roles in *Two Yanks in Trinidad* ('42) and *Something to Shout About* ('43) and the song "Be My Little Bumblebee" in *Irish Eyes Are Smiling* ('44). Her role as a burlesque queen in the musical helped convince Hollywood that Veda was just as beautiful as she had been before the shattering accident. Betty Grable requested her for her best friend in *Mother Wore Tights* ('47).

Veda gave a sprightly performance as Vivian Blaine's showgirl buddy in Goldwyn's *Guys and Dolls* ('55) and an outstanding one as an ex-drinker waitress in a brief scene with Susan Hayward in *I'll Cry Tomorrow*

William Elliott (left), Veda Ann Borg and Carleton Young in *Bitter Creek* (Allied Artists, 1954).

('55). She practically stole the film in *Big Jim McLain* ('52) with John Wayne.

Western buffs will remember her in *The Law Comes to Texas* ('36), *Melody Ranch* ('40), *Marked Trails* ('45), *Rider from Tucson* ('50), *The Kangaroo Kid* ('50), *Bitter Creek* ('54), *Frontier Gambler* ('56) and *Naked Gun* ('56). Certainly serial aficionados will recall her fondly as Cora in Columbia's *Jungle Raiders* ('45). But it is for a multitude of "B" programmers that she is best remembered. As a tough, wise-cracking blonde in whodunits and minor melodramas, she endeared herself to a loyal following.

Veda Ann married Andrew McLaglen, son of Victor McLaglen, in May of 1946. A son was born to them in 1954, a few months after the couple separated. They divorced in June 1957, after three years of court battles. She retained custody of Andrew, Jr.

Veda was a stock performer on TV's *The Abbott and Costello Show* and could be seen in many other television shows.

Her screen appearances tapered off during the 1950s. Her last film was *The Alamo* ('60) in which she played a dramatic role as Blind Nell. Thereafter she retired. In 1970 she learned that she had cancer and underwent treatments, to no avail. She died on August 16, 1973, and was cremated. Her elderly mother was placed in a nursing home, and her son went to live with his father.

Veda Ann Borg was at her best playing women of strong character, not necessarily of high morals.

Serials

1940

The Shadow. Col., [15 Chapters] D: James W. Horne; SP: Joseph Poland, Ned Dandy, Joseph O'Donnell; P: Larry Darmour; Cam: James S. Brown, Jr.; Mus: Lee Zahler; LP: Victor Jory, Veda Ann Borg, Robert Moore, Robert Fiske,

Jack Ingram, Edward Piel, Sr., J. Paul Jones, Charles King.

1945

Jungle Raiders. Col., [15 Chapters] D: Lesley Selander; SP: Ande Lamb, George H. Plympton; P: Sam Katzman: Cam: Ira H. Morgan; Mus: Lee Zahler; LP: Kane Richmond, Eddie Quillan, Veda Ann Borg, Carol Hughes, Janet Shaw, Charles King, John Elliott, I. Stanford Jolley, Jack Ingram.

HOBART BOSWORTH

Hobart Van Zandt Bosworth was born August 11, 1867, in Marietta, Ohio. Either because he didn't get along with his parents, or out of an overwhelming desire for adventure, he ran away from home was he was only 12. He went to sea as a cabin boy on a Merchant Marine ship. Although he was illiterate, he had a strong desire to learn and set about educating himself during the three years at sea.

In San Francisco he boxed, wrestled and did odd jobs. At 18 years of age he was taking parts with the McKee Rankin Stock Company. He later became a member of the Augustin Daly Stock Company in New York City and stayed with that firm for ten years, playing roles in *Marta of the Lowlands*, *Ghosts*, *Mary of Magdala* and *Tess of D'Urbervilles*. When he was around 30 his doctors informed him that he had tuberculosis and that there was no cure for it.

Bosworth packed up and left for Arizona, where he lived in the open reading and studying the classics and Shakespearean drama. The tuberculosis went away but doctors warned him against the Eastern winters. He decided to look over California, and what he saw he liked. He soon became director of a company that achieved a national reputation for the excellence of its productions.

Francis Boggs, Selig Pictures director, talked Bosworth into giving motion pictures a whirl. The year was 1908. No legitimate stage actor was acting before a camera. This was only three years after *The Great Train Robbery* ushered in "story" films. Movie actors were considered second-rate performers. It was a challenge and Bosworth couldn't resist a challenge. His first film was probably *The Spirit of '76* ('08), a one-reeler featuring Betty Harte and Tom Santschi.

Many of Bosworth's films for Selig between 1908 and 1913 were outdoor adventure stories, mostly Westerns and sea stories. He directed and wrote scripts in addition to acting. Bosworth's leaving to form his own company was a blow to Selig. He had a chance to buy the rights to the Jack London stories. His first film was *The Sea Wolf* ('13). Most historians consider it the first multiple-reel picture produced in the United States. He later wrote a treatment of *The Sea Wolf* and appeared in vaudeville with it in 1918–19.

Bosworth made one feature film in 1918, *Border Legion*; went into vaudeville; and bounced back to make five features in 1920. Bosworth Productions produced two pictures in 1921: *Blind Hearts* and *The Sea Lion*. He then turned to freelancing and only made films with the major companies from 1921 to 1930 with the exception of two films he made for Principal and the Christie Company. Bosworth appeared in 59 films in the period 1921–30.

In the sound era Bosworth was active until 1942. His last film was *Sin Town* ('42). He had principal roles in the serials *The Last of the Mohicans* ('32) and *The Secret of Treasure Island* ('38).

Bosworth died in 1943 from pneumonia in Glendale, California, at age 76.

Serials

1932

The Last of the Mohicans. Mascot, [12 Chapters] D: B. Reeves Eason, Ford Beebe; SP: Colbert Clark, John F. Natteford, Ford Beebe, Wyndham Gittens; S: James Fenimore Cooper; P: Nat Levine; Cam: Ernest Miller, Jack Young; LP: Harry Carey, Hobart Bosworth, Frank Coghlan, Jr., Edwina Booth, Lucile Browne, Walter Miller, Robert Kortman, Yakima Canutt.

1938

The Secret of Treasure Island. Col., [15 Chapters] D: Elmer Clifton; L. Ron Hubbard; AP: Louis Weiss; P: Jack Fier; Cam: Edward Linden, Herman Schopp; Mus: Abe Meyer; LP: Don Terry, Gwen Gaze, Grant Withers, Hobart Bosworth, William Farnum, Walter Miller, Dave O'Brien, Yakima Canutt.

WILLIAM (STAGE) BOYD

The Lost City ('35), a much-maligned Krellberg serial, has been rebuked by the majority of writers who have commented on the film. It has been labelled one of the worst serials ever made by "serial experts." Suffice it to say this writer does not rank it nearly so low, *but*— it is not likely to appear on anyone's "top ten." In spite of its many production faults, it was mighty enjoyable to this writer and other ten-year-old boys in 1935. An introduction to the serial's main character follows.

Unknown to anyone in the outside world, there exists below the base of a mountain in deepest Africa a fabulous ancient city made out of metal. In a great laboratory known as the control room, filled with humming, sparking electrical machinery, we see a dark-haired, middle-aged man clad entirely in white satin, his tunic emblazoned with many futuristic symbols and devices and his great blazing eyes giving mute evidence of both his tremendous strength of personality and the madness lurking within. He is Zolok, a leader of the Lost City, master of electricity, and author of the great storms of unprecedented size and ferocity causing earthquakes, floods and hurricanes throughout the world.

Dr. Zolok was portrayed by William

(Stage) Boyd — and behind the name, a story. William Boyd was a New York stage actor who infrequently appeared in movies. In 1930 he could be seen in the latest filming of Rex Beach's classic *The Spoilers*, starring Gary Cooper as Roy Glenister and Boyd as Alec McNamara, with Kay Johnson as Helen Chester and Betty Compson as Cherry Malotte.

The other William Boyd, who became the screen Hopalong Cassidy in 1935, was a popular star who could be seen in a number of films in 1931. Two actors with the same name was not a good thing, as one William Boyd found out. In February 1931, Los Angeles newspapers ran a story in which William Boyd, Walter Catlett and Pat O'Brien were arrested in a raid by Hollywood police on a party in Boyd's home. The raiders reported found more than a score of fashionably dressed men and women drinking and gambling in the house and seized gambling paraphernalia, liquor and a sensational (porno?) motion picture film.

"Big Bill" was reported to have put up a stiff battle with the raiding police and to have socked one of the policemen. Boyd, who formerly was well-known in pictures, had returned only recently to Hollywood under new contracts after several years on the New York stage. He was divorced from Dora Boyd, New York actress, in 1930. Papers mistakenly ran a picture of the better-known Boyd to accompany the story. It destroyed his career, even though the newspapers ran a retraction. It was because he couldn't find work that William (Hopalong) Boyd jumped at the chance to star in a Western series, never mind the fact that he could not ride. Henceforth "Big Bill" added the "Stage" to his name to differentiate himself from the other Boyd.

William (Stage) Boyd made the following sound films: *The False Madonna* ('31), *Gun Smoke* ('31), *State's Attorney* ('32), *The House on 56th Street* ('33), *Trans-Atlantic Merry-Go-Round* ('34) and *Night Life of the Gods* ('35). *The Lost City* ('35) may have been his last film.

Boyd died on March 20, 1935. Principal causes of death were gastric hemorrhage and intestinal hemorrhage with contributory causes of cirrhosis of the liver, stomach ulcers and alcoholism.

Boyd was born December 18, 1889, in New York City. At death he was 45 years, three months and two days of age, according to his death certificate.

The Lost City is now available on video tape. A feature version of the serial was released as *City of Lost Men*.

Serial

1935

The Lost City. Krellberg, [12 Chapters] D: Harry Revier; SP: Perley Poore Sheehan, Eddy Graneman, Leon D'Usseau; S: Zelma Carroll; P: Sherman S. Krelberg; Cam: Edward Linden, Roland Price; LP: William (Stage) Boyd, Kane Richmond, Claudia Dell, Joseph Swickard, George F. Hayes, William Bletcher, Eddie Fetherston, Jerry Frank, Sam Baker, Gino Corrado.

HENRY BRANDON

Four serials were made even better by the presence of Henry Brandon in them. In the first, *Jungle Jim* ('37), Grant Withers starred in the title role and Henry Brandon played "Cobra" with demonic fury. The serial was based on King Features' newspaper strip, written and drawn by Alex Raymond, better known for his creation *Flash Gordon*.

In *Secret Agent X-9* ('37), Brandon plays a well-known criminal who turns out to be the thief who has stolen the crown jewels of Belgravia.

Brandon essays the role of Capt. Lasca, one of the band of gangsters who threaten to take over the world, in *Buck Rogers* ('39). As Killer Kane's right hand man, he makes things rough for Buck Rogers.

In *Drums of Fu Manchu* ('40), Brandon plays the insidious Oriental mastermind with extreme relish, gloating over his every new method of inflicting horrible death. Manchu wants to bring about a revolution in central Asia. At his command are creatures slightly less than human. These "Dacoits" are zombie products of Manchu's own sinister surgery. It was a role really relished by Brandon. For many, the epitome of villainous arrogance in serials was Brandon's portrayal of the infamous Fu Manchu. The result was one of the studio's better chapterplays which, oddly enough, relied more on plot development than the usual destructive brawls that became Republic's trademark. In 1943, *Drums of Fu Manchu* was re-edited into a compact feature length film, complete in itself.

Henry Brandon was born Henry Kleinbach in Berlin, Germany, in 1912, and came to the U.S. as a baby. He studied at the Pasadena Playhouse for several years and was acting in the play *The Drunkard* when Hal Roach offered him the villain role opposite Stan Laurel and Oliver Hardy in *Babes in Toyland* ('34). Other good roles followed: *The Trail of the Lonesome Pine* ('36), *The Garden of Allah* ('36), *Island Captives* ('37), *Beau Geste* ('39) and *Dark Streets of Cairo* ('40).

Brandon served in the Armed Forces during World War II and upon his discharge continued his movie career. Some of his later pictures are *Joan of Arc* ('48), *Garzan's Magic Fountain* ('49), *Vera Cruz* ('54), *Comanche* ('56), *The Searchers* ('56), *Captain Sinbad* ('63) and *When the North Wind Blows* ('74), the only feature film in which he starred. Un-

Top: In *The Searchers* (Warner Bros., 1956). *Bottom:* Brandon (left) and William Royle in *Drums of Fu Manchu* (Republic, 1940).

doubtedly he will be most remembered for his role of "Chief Scar" in *The Searchers* and Fu Manchu in *Drums of Fu Manchu*.

Brandon's film work was interspersed with stage work, which included *Medea, The Taming of the Shrew, The Lady's Not for Burning, Arsenic and Old Lace* and *Macbeth*.

On February 15, 1990, Henry Brandon died of an apparent heart attack while asleep in his home in Hollywood.

Serials

1937

Jungle Jim. Univ., [12 Chapters] D: Ford Beebe, Cliff Smith; AP: Henry MacRae; SP: Wyndham Gittens, Norman S. Hall, Ray Trampe; LP: Grant Withers, Betty Jane Rhodes, Raymond Hatton, Henry Brandon, Evelyn Brent, Bryant Washburn, Al Bridge.

Secret Agent X-9. Univ., [12 Chapters] D: Ford Beebe, Cliff Smith; SP: Wyndham Gittens,

Norman S. Hall, Ray Trampe, Leslie Charteris; AP: Henry MacRae; LP: Scott Kolk, Jean Rogers, Henry Hunter, David Oliver, Larry Blake, Henry Brandon, Monte Blue, Lon Chaney, Jr.

1939

Buck Rogers. Univ., [12 Chapters] D: Ford Beebe, Saul A. Goodkind; SP: Norman S. Hall, Ray Trampe; AP: Barney Sarecky; Cam: Jerry Ash; LP: Buster Crabbe, Constance Moore, Jackie Moran, Jack Mulhall, Anthony Warde, Henry Brandon, C. Montague Shaw.

1940

Drums of Fu Manchu. Rep., [15 Chapters] D: William Witney, John English; SP: Franklyn Adreon, Morgan Cox, Ronald Davidson, Norman S. Hall, Barney Sarecky, Sol Shor; AP: Hiram S. Brown, Jr.; Cam: William Nobles; Mus: Cy Feuer; LP: Henry Brandon, William Royle, Gloria Franklin, Tom Chatterton, Robert Kellard, Luana Walters.

EVELYN BRENT

Evelyn Brent's first screen appearance was in *A Gentleman from Mississippi* ('14), made at the World Films Studio in Fort Lee, New Jersey, when she was 15 years of age. By 1916 she was playing leads. Among her early roles, she played the feminine lead opposite John Barrymore in *Raffles, the Amateur Cracksman* ('17). She starred in several British pictures of the early '20s and, upon returning to Hollywood in 1922, soon rose to prominence in silents, notably as the star of Josef von Sternberg's *Underworld* ('27) in which she is "Feathers McCoy," hard as nails and soft as feathers. Her second von Sternberg film was *The Last Command* ('27), playing a revolutionary whose fate is sealed when she allows a Czarist general to escape. In *The*

Dragnet ('27), her third and last film under director von Sternberg, she is the perfect moll, a role she was to play over and over. But she could play many roles and did, with gusto.

Evelyn was born Mary Elizabeth Riggs on October 20, 1899, in Tampa, Florida, the illegitimate baby of a 13-year-old Syracuse, New York, girl. The mother died while Evelyn was still an infant. Evelyn's grandmother took care of her for years; then she, too, died, leaving Evelyn on her own at the age of 14.

Brent was a femme fatale, although more fatal to herself than to the men in her life. Like Barbara Stanwyck, who brought a neurotic edge to the same type of roles, Brent paid her dues and owed the world nothing.

Happy endings were not her thing and innocence was not her forte.

In 1922 she was named a Wampas Baby Star and began to hit her stride in fast-moving programmers at Fox. In *The Plunderer* ('24) she plays the Lily, owner of the mining town saloon. It was the "heart of gold" kind of film for which she became famous. But she could also play the sweet girl from the East, as in *The Desert Outlaw* ('24) with Buck Jones. Typical of her tough gal roles was *Lady Robinhood* ('25), in which she plays a masked bandit, Catalina, who avenges injustice, aids the poor and plots a revolution.

In 1926 she went to work for Paramount, and the quality of her pictures improved as a result of larger budgets. She continued to thrill audiences with her hard-as-nails roles, relieved occasionally by portrayals of conventional

Jack Holt and Evelyn Brent in *Holt of the Secret Service* (Columbia, 1941).

heroines. Her sultry good looks were put to best use in "vampy" or gang moll roles. She made a smooth transition to talking films, but her roles and her films gradually diminished in quality and importance until her retirement in 1948.

During the 1930s Evelyn worked freelance at RKO, Paramount, Majestic, Warner Bros., Invincible, Liberty, Republic, Imperial, Columbia, Universal, Metropolitan and Monogram. By 1934 her career had fizzled and jobs were scarce, so when vaudeville beckoned, Evelyn toured the country with her own show for two years.

Her Westerns and serials of the 1930s were *Home on the Range* ('35), *Song of the Trail* ('36), *Hopalong Cassidy Returns* ('36),

Sudden Bill Dorn ('37), *Jungle Jim* ('37) and *The Law West of Tombstone* ('38). She also appeared in low-budget thrillers such as *Daughter of the Tong* ('39), a program filler about Chinese aliens and smuggling. Film fare of this sort ensured her popularity with neighborhood audiences.

During the 1940s, Evelyn was a dependable supporting player at various studios. Her major film of the decade was the Columbia serial *Holt of the Secret Service*, a hard-fighting action story about two undercover agents and a counterfeit operation being set up through illicit gambling outlets. She also played in Westerns with William Boyd, Johnny Mack Brown and Gilbert Roland and appeared in *Charlie Chan* and

Bowery Boys films. Her last screen appearance was in 1950.

After a brief period as an agent, Evelyn drifted out of the film world altogether and lived a quiet life in Westwood Village, spending some time in the Motion Picture Country Home.

Her marriages were to B. F. Fineman, a producer, in 1926 (and a divorce in 1928); Harry Edwards, director-producer, in 1928 (divorce in the late 1930s); Harry Fox, a showman of sorts, late 1930s or early 1940s until his death in 1959.

Evelyn Brent died on June 4, 1975, of a heart attack in her home. She was 75.

Serials

1937

Jungle Jim. Univ., [12 Chapters] D: Ford Beebe, Cliff Smith; SP: Wyndham Gittens, Norman S. Hall, Ray Trampe; AP: Henry MacRae; LP: Grant Withers, Betty Jane Rhodes, Raymond Hatton, Henry Brandon, Evelyn Brent, Alan Bridge.

1941

Holt of the Secret Service. Col., 1941 [15 Chapters] D: James W. Horne; SP: Basil Dickey, George H. Plympton, Wyndham Gittens; Cam: James Brown, Jr.; Mus: Lee Zahler; P: Larry Darmour; LP: Jack Holt, Evelyn Brent, Tris Coffin, Montague Shaw, John ward, George Chesebro, Ted Adams, Edward Hearn.

GEORGE BRENT

The popular leading man of movies was born George Brendon Nolan on March 3, 1904, in Shannonsbridge, Ireland. At age 11 he came to the U.S. to stay with relatives after the death of his parents. When he was 18, he returned to Ireland where he worked at the Abbey Players, appearing in bit parts and walk-ons. Because of his subversive activities during the Irish Rebellion, he was forced to flee the country aboard a freighter bound for Canada. There he joined a stock company with which he toured Canada for two years. Following his Canadian experience, he went to New York and began his American career with a stage company in the Bronx.

In 1925 Brent toured the country in *Abie's Irish Rose.* With the proceeds from this endeavor, he opened his own theater in Pawtucket, but the venture failed. He tried another in Florida and broke even. Back in New York he appeared in a number of Broadway productions in the late '20s. At this time he

George Brent (left), Robert Kortman and Rin-Tin-Tin in *The Lightning Warrior* (Mascot, 1931).

married a young actress he remembered only as "Molly."

In 1930 he was in a play, *Love, Honor and Betray* that got the attention of movie-makers. He was promised a test for the lead in *The Man Who Came Back* ('30) and he went to Hollywood. When he got there, he found Charles Farrell had been given the role. However, he landed a job at Fox. He has been quoted as saying, "I was a stooge for Charlie Chan and Rin-Tin-Tin."

In 1931 Brent went blind. An operation on his eyes was successful but he was unable to work for several months while he stayed at his sister's home in New York.

Back in Hollywood, he made a test at Warner Bros. and was signed to a seven-year contract. His first film there was *The Rich Are Always with Us* ('32) starring Ruth Chatterton, who liked him so much she married him. He soon became established as one of Hollywood's most dependable leading men.

He projected restrained virility opposite screen idols Greta Garbo, Ginger Rogers, Barbara Stanwyck, Myrna Loy, Olivia de Havilland and especially Bette Davis, with whom he appeared in 11 Warner Bros. films of the late '30s and early '40s. He made four films with Ruth Chatterton, but their marriage was dissolved after a couple of years. He made six films with Kay Francis and five with Barbara Stanwyck.

Author Fred Watkins writes in *Film Fan Monthly* (No. 136, 1972): "He was a professional. Directors liked him, his leading ladies found it easy to work with him. And he remains the most durable leading man at Warner Bros. He was congenial, attractive, and he could memorize 25 pages of dialogue in an hour."

Brent was a ladies' man and his studio made the most of it. He dressed impeccably, spoke beautifully and had an air that suggested he would stand only for so much non-

George Brent (left) and Tim Holt in *Gold Is Where You Find It* (Warner Bros., 1938).

sense. The quality was a good foil to the antics of his leading ladies.

Brent retired from the screen in the early '50s to run a horse-breeding ranch, but gave it up after a few years. In the mid–50s he co-starred in one of the first hour-long filmed television shows, *Wire Service*, alternating every third week with Mercedes McCambridge and Dane Clark. The series lasted only 39 weeks.

Brent was married to Helen Campbell, a non-professional, early in his career; to actress Constance Worth in 1937; and to actress Ann Sheridan in 1942–43. His last marriage, to artist Jane Michael in 1947, produced two daughters and a son. Brent made his home in exclusive Rancho Santa Fe.

George Brent died from emphysema in Solana Beach, California, in 1979 at age 75.

Brent's only serial, *Lightning Warrior*, was made very early in his career for Nat Levine's serial factory. The story has "The Wolfman" and his followers attempting to drive whites out of a mining district. Also, young Jimmy Carter (Frankie Darro) must be prevented from taking possession of his murdered father's mine. Unknown to the settlers, there is a rich vein of gold beneath many of the claims in the district. Alan Scott (Brent), brother of a murdered lawman, aids Jimmy, as does the dog Rinty and Dianne (Georgia Hale), adopted daughter of the sheriff. Rin-Tin-Tin was the star and his name appeared above the title. It was his last film.

Serial

1932

The Lightning Warrior. Mascot, [12 Chapters] D: Armand Schaefer, Ben Kline; SP: Wyndham Gittens, Ford Beebe, Colbert Clark; P: Nat Levine; Spv: Wyndham Gittens; Mus: Lee Zahler; Cam: Ernest Miller, William Nobles, Tom Galligan; LP: Rin-Tin-Tin, Frankie Darro, Georgia Hale, George Brent, Pat O'Malley, Theodore Lorch, Robert Kortman, Lafe McKee.

ALAN (AL) BRIDGE

Alan (Al) Bridge was a competent actor who played despicable, unsavory characters with aplomb. Although he worked primarily in "B" Westerns, he was versatile enough to play supporting parts in non–Westerns, both "A" features and "B" features. He can be compared with Harry Woods or Roy Barcroft, who essayed similar roles.

The author has been unable to find any biographical information on him, which is a surprise since he made nearly 500 film appearances between 1931 and 1951.

Serials and features were more enjoyable, more spine-tingling affairs for his participation in them. He died in Los Angeles in 1957 at age 66.

Serials

1932

The Hurricane Express. Mascot, [12 Chapters] D: Armand Schaefer, J. P. McGowan; LP: John Wayne, Shirley Grey, Tully Marshall, J. Farrell MacDonald.

The Devil Horse. Mascot, [12 Chapters] LP: Harry Carey, Noah Beery, Jr., Greta Granstedt, Noah Beery, Sr., Al Bridge, Jack Mower.

1933

Fighting with Kit Carson. Mascot, [12 Chapters] D: Colbert Clark, Armand Schaefer; LP: Johnny Mack Brown, Betsy King Ross, Noah Beery, Jr., Noah Beery, Sr.

1934

Burn 'Em Up Barnes. Mascot, [12 Chapters] D: Colbert Clark, Armand Schaefer; LP: Jack Mulhall, Frankie Darro, Lola Lane, Julian Rivero, Edwin Maxwell.

Mystery Mountain. Mascot, [12 Chapters] D: B. Reeves Eason, Otto Brower; LP: Ken Maynard, Verna Hillie, Syd Saylor, Edward Earle, Al Bridge, Lafe McKee, Bob Kortman.

1935

The Adventures of Rex and Rinty. Mascot, [11 Chapters] D: B. Reeves Eason, Ford Beebe; LP: Rex, Tin-Tin-Tin, Jr., Kane Richmond, Norma

Noah Beery, Sr., and Al Bridge (right) in *Fighting with Kit Carson* (Mascot, 1933).

Taylor, Mischa Auer, Wheeler Oakman, Charles King, Edmund Cobb.

1936

Adventures of Frank Merriwell. Univ., [12 Chapters] D: Cliff Smith; LP: Don Briggs, Jean Rogers, John King, Carla Laemmle, Summer Getchell.

Ace Drummond. Univ., [13 Chapters] D: Ford Beebe, Cliff Smith; LP: John King, Jean Rogers, Noah Beery, Jr., Guy Bates Post, Chester Gan, Arthur Loft, Jackie Morrow, Edmund Cobb, Lon Chaney, Jr., Robert Warwick, Selmer Jackson.

1937

Wild West Days. Univ., [13 Chapters] D: Ford Beebe, Cliff Smith; LP: Johnny Mack Brown, Lynn Gilbert, Robert Kortman, George Shelley, Frank Yaconelli.

Jungle Jim. Univ., [12 Chapters] D: Ford Beebe, Cliff Smith; LP: Grant Withers, Betty Jane Rhodes, Raymond Hatton, Henry Brandon, Evelyn Brent, Al Bridge.

Tim Tyler's Luck. Univ., [12 Chapters] D: Ford Beebe, Wyndham Gittens; LP: Frankie Thomas, Frances Robinson, Al Shean, Norman Willis, Stanley Blystone, Alan Bridge, Earle Douglas, Edward Hearn.

1938

Flaming Frontiers. Univ., [15 Chapters] D: Ray Taylor, Alan James; LP: Johnny Mack Brown, Eleanor Hansen, John Archer, Charles Middleton, Al Bridge.

The Great Adventures of Wild Bill Hickok. Col., [15 Chapters] D: Mack V. Wright, Sam Nelson; LP: Bill Elliott, Carole Wayne, Frankie Darro, Monte Blue, Dickie Jones, Sammy McKim, Hal Taliaferro, Reed Hadley, Earle Hodgins, Robert Fiske.

1940

Winners of the West. Univ., [13 Chapters] D: Ford Beebe, Ray Taylor; LP: Dick Foran, Anne Nagel, James Craig, Tom Fadden, Harry Woods, Charles Stevens.

LLOYD BRIDGES

Lloyd Bridges needs little introduction to frequent movie addicts, as he was involved in moviemaking for 60 years! Earlier on, he had a brief stint on Broadway (in the late '30s and early '40s) but Columbia signed him in 1941. During his four years at Columbia, he appeared in 25 low-budget films. Being tall, blonde and rugged, he was used frequently in Westerns, especially those starring Charles Starrett.

Among his Columbia releases are *Two Latins from Manhattan* ('41), *Alias Boston Blackie* ('42), *Shut My Big Mouth* ('42), *West of Tombstone* ('42), *Riders of the Northland* ('42), *Talk of the Town* ('42) and *Passport to Suez* ('43).

Bridges began freelancing in 1945. His roles and films improved, including many lead parts in "B" films and important support roles in "A" pictures, such as his role as the calculating deputy sheriff in *High Noon* ('52). Other good Bridges films are *Ramrod* ('47), *Little Big Horn* ('51), *Plymouth Adventure* ('52), *Apache Woman* ('55), *Wichita* ('55), *Around the World Under the Sea* ('66), *Lost Flight* ('71), *Running Wild* ('73), *Airplane* ('80), *Behind the Iron Mask* ('85), *Blown Away* ('94) and *The War at Home* ('96).

Bridges is best remembered for his role as Mike Nelson in the television series *Sea Hunt* (1957–61). Other series included *The Lloyd Bridges Show*, consisting of varied stories, and *Joe Forrester*, about a cop.

Bridges was born January 15, 1913, in San Seandro, California. His collegiate education was received at U.C.L.A. His marriage to Dorothy Simpson produced three sons, two of whom, Beau and Jeff, are film personalities in their own right.

Bridges made only one serial, *Secret Agent X-9* (Universal, 1945). In the story, X-9, with agents from Austria and China, battles the Japanese Black Dragon Intelligence Service headed by Japan's top female spy, Nabura. The Japanese wish to steal a secret formula for synthetic fuel and are operating from a base on Shadow Island, off the coast of China. The island is privately owned by gangster Lucky Kamber as a neutral hideout for fugitives on the lam. X-9, trying to stop Axis agents from learning the secret of 722, an explosive formula that created an excellent aviation gas substitute when mixed with distilled water, found himself up to his neck in plot twists involving Kamber, the Japanese agents, a mysterious man known only on notes as "The Man with the Secret" and a plot to send a double for an explosives expert to the U.S. to steal the 722 formula.

Lloyd Bridges died at age 85 in 1998 at his Los Angeles home.

Serial

1945

Secret Agent X-9. Univ., [13 Chapters] D: Ray Taylor, Lewis D. Collins; SP: Joseph O'Donnell, Patricia Harper; S: Joseph O'Donnell, Harold C. Wire; LP: Lloyd Bridges, Keye Luke, Jan Wiley, Victoria Horne, Samuel S. Hinds, Cy Kendall, Edmund Cobb, George Lynn.

HERMAN BRIX/ BRUCE BENNETT

Few serial devotees would contest the statement that Herman Brix/Bruce Bennett was one of the sound era's most outstanding serial heroes, ranking right up there with the likes of Buster Crabbe, Ralph Byrd, Clayton Moore, Kane Richmond, Walter Miller, Buck Jones, Tom Tyler and Ben Wilson. He appeared in six serials.

The New Adventures of Tarzan ('35) was co-produced by Burroughs-Tarzan Productions and the Dearholt-Stout-Cohen Company and filmed on location in Guatemala and at the Selig Zoo in Los Angeles. The story has Tarzan traveling to Guatemala in search of his friend, D'Arnat, a French explorer captured by the half-human inhabitants of an ancient Mayan ruins. Tarzan is followed by the Martling Expedition seeking the Green Goddess, a sacred monolith containing a fortune in gems as well as the secret of a powerful explosive. A group of rebel revolutionaries also want the explosive formula, as does the Guatemalan Secret Service.

The serial was unique in that the first chapter was 45 minutes in length. A 75-minute feature (later cut to 61 minutes), with the same title, was also released. Then, in 1938, a 72-minute feature, *Tarzan and the Green Goddess*, comprised of outtakes from the serial and added material, was released.

Although plagued with production and health problems through the lengthy filming, the final product was not bad for an indie serial. Brix made an ideal Tarzan. He played the role of Tarzan as a literate hero in keeping with Burroughs' novels.

The cast was rather amateurish and nearly all technical niceties left much to be desired, and yet the film had an inestimable fascination for mid–1930s audiences living humdrum lives in the lean years of recovery following the worst economic depression in the nation's history. The film's crudeness was apparent, but also apparent was its escapist charm. And it was released at a time when jungle serials were popular in the action houses. Released in a four-year period were *Tarzan the Fearless* ('33), *The Lost Jungle* ('34), *Young Eagles* ('34), *The Call of the Savage* ('35), *The Lost City* ('35), *Darkest Africa* ('36), *Jungle Jim* ('37), *Jungle Menace* ('37) and *Tim Tyler's Luck* ('37). The jungle definitely had an appeal for episodic thrills fans.

Brix's second serial outing was also for a minor outfit — Sam Katzman's Victory Pictures. This time around, the production quality was somewhat better. The cast was a good one, with Bela Lugosi in the lead role and, in addition to Brix, such players as Joan Barclay, Luana Walters, Charles King, John Elliott and Forrest Taylor. The film was *Shadow of Chinatown* ('36), brought to the screen by director Robert F. Hill. It was also released as a theatrical film titled *Yellow Phantom* ('36).

In the story, Sonya Rokoff (Walters), a Eurasian, is a West Coast representative of a European importing company. She is instructed by her superiors to close San Francisco's Chinatown to tourists because Chinese competition has become too great. She enlists the help of Victor Poten (Lugosi), also a Eurasian, but unknown to her, a crazed scientist. Assigned by her newspaper to investigate the strange happenings in Chinatown is reporter Joan Whiting (Barclay). She enlists the help of novelist Martin Andrews (Brix).

Long out of circulation and once feared lost, the complete serial is now available on video cassette.

Brix's move to Republic for his next four serials was a fortuitous one, for the studio, an outgrowth of Mascot, specialized in serials and Westerns and had assembled personnel who were proficient in this unique type of film fare. His first cliffhanger for the Valley studio was *The Lone Ranger* ('38), one of the most popular and lavishly produced of Republic serials. Five lawmen fight lawlessness in the Old West in the post–Civil War era. One of the five is the unidentified Lone Ranger. With his Indian companion Tonto, the Lone Ranger leads the forces of justice against outlaw Mark Smith, who, in his assumed role of finance commissioner Jeffries, lusts to become dictator of all Texas. One by one the rangers are killed until only Allan King (Lee Powell), the Lone Ranger, remains.

Brix, George Letz (Montgomery), Lane Chandler and Hal Taliaferro (Wally Wales) played the rangers gradually killed off, with Brix the last one to die. A theatrical feature, *Hi-Yo Silver* ('40), was released with added footage of Raymond Hatton and Dickie Moore. Powell and Brix were immediately cast in another serial, *The Fighting Devil Dogs* ('38), with William Witney

Top to bottom: George Letz (Montgomery), Lee Powell, Herman Brix (Bruce Bennett), Hal Taliaferro (Wally Wales), Lane Chandler in *The Lone Ranger* (Republic, 1938).

and John English again at the directorial helm. In the story, a mysterious villain calling himself "The Lightning" invents an artificial thunderbolt weapon capable of discharging huge amounts of electricity from his superplane, "The Wing." Two marine lieutenants are assigned to track down the criminal and put a stop to his terror. A group of scientists is organized to develop a counter measure to the Lightning's device, but it becomes obvious that one of their number is the Lightning himself. But which one?

It was a popular serial and a good role for Brix, even though the limelight was shared with Powell. Two theatrical features were extracted from the serial—*Fighting Devil Dogs* ('43) and *Torpedo of Doom* ('66).

In his next effort, the spotlight was strictly on Brix as he essayed a Tarzan-like role as Kioga in *Hawk of the Wilderness* ('38). Infant survivor of a shipwreck, Kioga grows to manhood in Tarzan-like fashion on an unknown Pacific island populated by a lost tribe. An expedition arrives looking for survivors, bringing evil men as well as good, and when it is discovered that rare gems abound on the island, the crooks show their true colors. Kioga uses all of his cunning and strength to save his friends, thwart the scoundrels and appease the superstitious tribespeople.

Brix's athletic prowess is more than adequately demonstrated as he romps through what is essentially a Tarzan film.

Brix's last serial was *Daredevils of the Red Circle* ('39). Like his three previous Republic serials, this, too, was directed by the winning team of Witney and English. The story was a modern one with a carnival background. Convict 39013 (Charles Middleton) escapes from a penitentiary after 15 years of imprisonment and engages in a campaign of vengeance against his former partner, Granville (Miles Mander), who was responsible for his conviction as an embezzler. Kidnapping Granville, Convict 39013 assumes Granville's identity and sets about to wreck his enterprises. The Daredevils of the Red Circle, employed at a Granville amusement pier, become involved when the small brother of one of them is killed and the pier destroyed. They align themselves with Granville's granddaughter in a fight against 39013, receiving help from the Red Circle, a mysterious personage. Brix, Dave Sharpe and Charles Quigley shared hero honors, while Carole Landis provided the feminine pulchritude.

To sports fans, Brix will be remembered as a 6'2" All-American tackle for the University of Washington and Olympic shotput record-holder for four years. Brix was born in Tacoma, Washington, on May 19, 1906, and enjoyed a rugged childhood in the northwest, working for his father, who was a lumberman. He trained at Douglas Fairbanks, Sr.'s, quarters while preparing for the 1928 Olympics. His acquaintance with Fairbanks led him into the acting profession. Totally without acting experience, Brix started at the bottom. He didn't remain an extra long; he stood out in any crowd. He soon found himself playing small parts, which, from picture to picture, grew in size.

While working in a football picture at Paramount, he suffered a severe accident when an over-enthusiastic actor indulged in a particularly heavy flying tackle. Four months in recuperation from a broken shoulder followed for Brix, then a period of screen idleness. Forgetting motion pictures for the time being, he held, in succession, jobs as a stock and bond salesman, logger, oil well driller, insurance salesman, bill collector, saw mill foreman, athletic coach, maitre d' and brakeman. All of these experiences contributed to his understanding of the screen roles he later received.

While filming the Tarzan serial in Guatemala, he was struck by a tropical ailment that was to trouble him for years and keep him out of World War II.

Following the Tarzan stint came a number of independent films for Victory Pictures and the serials previously mentioned. At this juncture he signed with Columbia and underwent the name change to Bruce Bennett.

After four years at Columbia, he requested his release to accept better offers. Warner Bros. tempted him with a seven-year contract and a prospect of stardom. Thereafter, especially after tackling the role of Joan Crawford's husband in *Mildred Pierce* ('45), he found himself playing the virile hero in a succession of drawing room dramas, opposite such glamour queens as Ann Sheridan, Jane Wyman, Ida Lupino and others.

In 1948 he secured his release from Warner Bros. and decided to freelance. He won roles in several good films and went on to work extensively in television.

Bennett married the former Jeanette Braddock in early 1933. They have two children, Christine, born June 4, 1944, and Christopher, born May 13, 1947.

Off-screen, Bennett enjoys woodworking and cabinet making, golfing and horseback riding. For years he was a successful business executive in the building and redecorating field. He has completed his autobiography and, at age 94, has appeared at a film festival.

Serials

1935

The New Adventures of Tarzan. Burroughs-Stout, [12 Chapters] D: Edward Kull, W. F. McGaugh; SP: Charles F. Royal; S: Edgar Rice Burroughs; LP: Herman Brix, Ula Holt, Frank Baker, Dale Walsh, Harry Ernest, Don Costello, Merrill McCormick, Jack Mower, Earl Dwire, Ashton Dearholt.

1936

Shadow of Chinatown. Victory, [15 Chapters] D: Robert Hill; SP: Isadore Bernstein, Basil Dickey; S: Rock Hawkey; Spv: Sam Katzman; Cam: Bill Hyer; LP: Bela Lugosi, Herman Brix, Joan Barclay, Luana Walters, Charles King, Maurice Liu.

1937

Blake of Scotland Yard. Victory, [15 Chapters] D: Bob Hill; LP: Ralph Byrd, Joan Barclay, Herbert Rawlinson, Lloyd Hughes, Dickie Jones, Herman Brix (bit).

1938

The Lone Ranger. Rep., [15 Chapters] D: William Witney, John English; SP: Barry Shipman, George W. Yates, Franklyn Adreon, Ronald Davidson, Lois Eby; Spv: Robert Beche; AP: Sol C. Siegel; Cam: William Nobles; Mus: Alberto Colombo; LP: Lee Powell, Chief Thundercloud, Herman Brix, Lynne Roberts, Lane Chandler, Hal Taliaferro, Stanley Andrews.

The Fighting Devil Dogs. Rep., [12 Chapters] D: William Witney, John English; SP: Barry Shipman, Franklyn Adreon, Ronald Davidson, Sol Shor; Cam: William Nobles; Mus: Alberto Colombo; LP: Lee Powell, Herman Brix, Eleanor Stewart, Montagu Love, Hugh Sothern.

Hawk of the Wilderness. Rep., [12 Chapters] D: William Witney, John English; SP: Barry Shipman; LP: Herman Brix, Ray Mala, Monte Blue, Jill Martin, Noble Johnson.

1939

Daredevils of the Red Circle. Rep., [12 Chapters] D: William Witney, John English; SP: Barry Shipman, Franklyn Adreon, Rex Taylor, Ronald Davidson, Sol Shor; AP: Robert Beche; Cam: William Nobles; Mus: William Lava; LP: Charles Quigley, Herman Brix, David Sharpe, Carole Landis, Miles Mander, Charles Middleton.

JOHNNY MACK BROWN

Johnny Mack Brown was one of the most enduring of cowboy stars. His record as a Western hero is an impressive one, the actor having starred in 121 of the 127 Westerns in which he appeared. Added to this illustrious record are another 40 films in

In *Ragtime Cowboy Joe* (Universal, 1940).

which Johnny appeared as a dramatic actor, many of them for MGM.

Brown was born in Dothan, Alabama, on September 1, 1904, and he always retained traces of a Southern drawl. As a football hero at the University of Alabama, Johnny caught two spine-tingling touchdown passes in the New Year's Day Rose Bowl game of '26 to lead his team to a 20–19 victory over the University of Washington. Football accolades continued to echo for years following that triumph. In addition to being elected to the Football Hall of Fame, Brown was the first to be so honored in the Alabama Sports Hall of Fame.

Brown became an assistant coach at Alabama upon his graduation and was in California for the Rose Bowl on New Year's Day, 1927. An actor friend, George Faucett, arranged for a screen test for Johnny at MGM, Paramount and 20th Century-Fox. MGM came through first with a contract,

which led to small parts in several features. He quickly rose to prominent parts as leading man to some of Hollywood's most beautiful actresses. One of his most successful silent features was *Our Dancing Daughters* ('28), which boosted his stock as a leading man and which made a star of Joan Crawford.

Brown's star was on the rise. Subsequently Brown made films with Jeanette Loff (*Annapolis*), Norma Shearer (*A Lady of Chance*), Greta Garbo (*A Woman of Affairs* and *The Single Standard*), Mary Pickford (*Coquette*), Leila Hyams (*Hurricane*), Sally O'Neill (*Jazz Heaven*) and Mary Nolan (*Undertow*).

MGM co-starred him once more with Joan Crawford in *Montana Moon* ('30), a comedy Western and an all-talking picture. Next came his most famous film —*Billy the Kid* ('30), directed by King Vidor and co-starring Wallace Beery. It was filmed in

Jean Harlow and Johnny Mack Brown in *The Secret Six* (MGM, 1931).

Metro's widescreen 70mm process on location in and around Gallup, New Mexico. Coached by William S. Hart, Brown turned in a memorable performance as the Kid. It remained his most publicized film.

The Great Meadow ('31) was a less auspicious semi–Western, followed by *The Secret Six* ('31), an early gangster film featuring, in addition to Brown, Clark Gable, Wallace Beery, Jean Harlow, Lewis Stone, Marjorie Rambeau, Ralph Bellamy and John Miljan. Brown and Gable were teamed as racket-busting newspaper reporters.

Leaving MGM in '31, Brown freelanced for awhile, co-starring in *The Lost Flight* ('31) at First National, a story of World War I pilots, and *Lasca of the Rio Grande* ('31) at Universal. In the latter film Brown is a Texas Ranger, Leo Carrillo is the badman and Dorothy Burgess is Lasca, a dance hall girl

loved by both men. Although Brown would later make many formula Westerns for Universal, this one was a non-series film. At Paramount he made *70,000 Witnesses* ('32), a football picture. Monogram used Brown in *Flames* ('32) a full decade before the studio hired him to carry on in the place of Buck Jones following the latter's 1942 death in the Coconut Grove holocaust in Boston. *Malay Nights* ('32), a film much sought after by collectors, was made for Mayfair, a Gower Gulch independent studio. Featured with Brown in this offbeat story was Raymond Hatton, his future sidekick in a long-running Monogram series.

Nat Levine, a master at making serials, hired Brown to star in the 12-episode *Fighting with Kit Carson* for Mascot release in '33. Brown was well accepted by Saturday matinee crowds in this, his first serial undertak-

Left to right: Raymond Hatton, Johnny Mack Brown, Christine McIntyre and Dennis Moore in *West of the Rio Grande* (Monogram, 1944).

ing. As usual with Mascot productions, a tremendous cast of competent supporting players pitched in to keep the excitement high and the action pace furious.

Continuing to freelance and not yet typed as a cowboy actor, Brown then worked for First National, Chesterfield, Fox, Tower, Paramount, Showmen and Columbia in assorted non–Westerns. As a society dude, he courts Mae West in *Belle of the Nineties* ('34). In *Son of a Sailor* ('33) Brown shares humorous antics with Joe E. Brown, Thelma Todd and Frank McHugh, and in *Cross Streets* ('34) he is an alcoholic who makes his own murder appear to be a suicide to save the reputation of the man whose daughter and wife he loves. *Three on a Honeymoon* ('34) is noteworthy because it features both Brown and Charles Starrett, another great Western ace, in a love story with a seafaring background. Brown was a football player once

again in *St. Louis Woman* ('34); *Marrying Widows* ('34) has him portraying an opportunist who marries for money only to find out his wife has none; and in *Against the Law* ('34) Johnny is an ambulance driver in love with Sally Blane.

When Universal hired Johnny to star in his second Western serial, *Rustlers of Red Dog* ('35), the die was cast. He was on his way to becoming one of Western filmdom's greatest stars. Raymond Hatton plays his sidekick in the film, while Joyce Compton provides the feminine charm.

Brown could have continued as a dramatic actor but, convinced by his experiences that he was cut out for outdoor films, he signed a contract with A. W. Haeckle for a series of Westerns to be released by Supreme Pictures. The series did so well at the box office that Haeckle renewed Brown's contract and produced a second series of eight films, which were released by the newly organized Republic Pictures.

Brown was no slouch as an actor, rider or fighter. His Westerns were full of brawls and hard riding, and built around stories allowing him to display his acting talents as well as perform feats of agility with convincing realism.

Universal again picked Johnny for a starring role in a serial, his third. This time it was *Wild West Days* ('37), directed by veteran Cliff Smith, formerly director of Pete Morrison and Tom Mix Westerns. Robert Kortman, nearly always a villain, played the hero's pal for a change.

Brown teamed with John Wayne in Paramount's *Born to the West* ('37), a non-series special. He also supported Joel McCrea in *Wells Fargo* ('37). Cast as a Confederate officer in love with Frances Dee, Brown is killed trying to capture a gold train, leaving McCrea to get the girl (actually his wife in real life).

Universal put Brown under contract in '38 and proceeded to cast him as the star of two more serials, *Flaming Frontiers* ('38) and *The Oregon Trail* ('39). After this he would appear only in features for the remainder of his career. His first feature Western at Universal was *Desperate Trails* ('39). He was supported by funnyman Fuzzy Knight and singing cowboy Bob Baker, who had just completed his own series of Westerns. Baker would also support Brown in *Oklahoma Frontier* ('39), *Chip of the Flying U* ('39), *West of Carson City* ('40), *Riders of Pasco Basin* ('40) and *Badman from Red Butte* ('40). But after these features, Baker was dropped and Brown and Knight would go it alone for another 15 before being joined by Tex Ritter for a final seven features.

The Brown Universal features were excellently made films, far above the typical horse opera in production values. They boasted fine musical scores, running inserts, competent editing, believable scripts, good photography, location filming and direction by professionals Ray Taylor, Ford Beebe and Joseph H. Lewis.

Brown easily moved into *Motion Pic-ture Herald*'s "Big 10" of Western films, remaining there until the demise of the series Western a decade later.

In '43 he signed with Monogram as a replacement for Buck Jones. Raymond Hatton, who had appeared with Jones in the popular "Rough Riders" series, retained his identity as "Sandy Hopkins" and stayed on to ride to greater fame with Brown, the two stars making 45 slam-bang shoot-'em-ups between '43 and '49. The first in the Brown Monograms series was *The Ghost Rider* ('43), in which Brown portrayed Nevada Jack McKenzie, a character he continued to portray until '46, when he and Hatton abandoned the roles of McKenzie and Hopkins, respectively, to play assorted roles. The team of Brown and Hatton was a popular one during the World War II years. Audiences could always count on plenty of action and a generous number of familiar faces in each film — nameless faces to many, but, to real Western fans, the faces had names (Charles King, Tristram Coffin, Jack Mulhall, George Chesebro, etc.). The Brown Westerns provided buffs with a truly enjoyable hour of entertainment. Saturday night was something to look forward to when one could throw the kids in the back seat of the family car and take off to the bijou to see one of Brown's films, coupled with a chapter of an equally exciting cliffhanger.

By 1950 Johnny was showing his age and putting on weight, yet his films were still profitable. Beginning with *West of Wyoming* ('50), Johnny made the remainder of his films without the aid of a comedy sidekick, something few cowboy stars ever did. He made 12 series Westerns during 1950–51 and one special, *Short Grass* ('50), an Allied Artists film with Rod Cameron. *Canyon Ambush* ('52), released by Monogram on October 12, 1952, was Johnny's last starring Western. With its release, Monogram stopped production on the series. Television, mounting production costs and a shrinking market made B-Westerns on a series basis a thing of the past. Johnny had lasted almost to the end of the "B" era.

Johnny served as host of a swanky Hollywood restaurant for a while and made several appearances on television over the years. He also traveled with Royal American shows and made numerous personal appearances. When declining health overtook him, he was content to spend his last years quietly with his wife, the former Cornelia Foster, in their apartment at the posh Park La Brea Towers in Los Angeles. His three daughters and one son were all grown and going about their own lives. Like William Boyd, Johnny wanted his fans to remember him as he had appeared in the movies. For that reason, he was reluctant to attend any of the Western film festivals.

And so, on November 14, 1974, Johnny Mack Brown, victor in a thousand screen fights, lost his fight for life, a victim of a kidney ailment. He was 70 years old.

Serials

1933

Fighting with Kit Carson. Mascot, [12 Chapters] D: Armand Schaefer, Colbert Clark; SP: J. F. Natteford, Barney Sarecky, Colbert Clark, Wyndham Gittens; P: Nat Levine; LP: Johnny Mack Brown, Betsy King Ross, Noah Beery, Jr., Noah Beery, Sr., Tully Marshall.

1935

Rustlers of Red Dog. Univ., [12 Chapters] D: Louis Friedlander [Lew Landers]; SP: George H. Plympton, Basil Dickey, Ella O'Neill, Nate Gatzert, Vim Moore; S: Nathanial Eddy; LP: Johnny Mack Brown, Joyce Compton, Walter Miller, Raymond Hatton, Harry Woods, Lafe McKee.

1937

Wild West Days. Univ., [13 Chapters] D: Ford Beebe, Cliff Smith; S: W. R. Burnett; SP: Wyndham Gittens, Norman S. Hall, Ray Trampe; P: Ben Koenig, Henry MacRae; LP: Johnny Mack Brown, Lynn Gilbert, Robert Kortman, George Shelley, Frank Yaconelli, Frank McGlynn, Jr.

1938

Flaming Frontiers. Univ., [15 Chapters] D: Ray Taylor, Alan James; S: Peter B. Kyne; SP: Wyndham Gittens, George Plympton, Basil Dickey, Paul Perez; P: Henry MacRae; LP: Johnny Mack Brown, Eleanor Hansen, Ralph Bowman [John Archer], Charles Middleton, Charles Stevens, Chief Thundercloud, Al Bridge.

1939

The Oregon Trail. Univ., [15 Chapters] D: Ford Beebe, Saul A. Goodkind; SP: Edmund Kelso, George H. Plympton, Basil Dickey, W. W. Watson; P: Henry MacRae; LP: Johnny Mack Brown, Louise Stanley, Fuzzy Knight, Bill Cody, Jr., Forrest Taylor, James Blaine, Frank Ellis, Helen Gibson, Horace Murphy.

TOM BROWN

Tom Brown came by acting naturally. His father was a vaudevillian, his mother a musical comedy star. He was born Thomas Edward Brown, Jr., in New York City in 1913. He attended a Professional Children's School in New York and performed on stage from infancy. He was nine when he reached Broadway and ten when he made his screen debut. He is best remembered as a clean-cut boy-next-door in Hollywood talkies of the 1930s. Appealingly baby-faced, he became typecast as a cadet, collegian or kid brother of hero or heroine in numerous high- and low-budget films.

In his only cliffhanger, Tom essays the title role in *The Adventures of Smilin' Jack*

Tom Brown (front left), Marjorie Lord and players in *Adventures of Smilin' Jack* (Universal, 1943).

('43). It is set prior to the start of World War II on the island of Mandon, the scene of a life-and-death espionage struggle. The Chinese and Americans, having secured the friendship of the local people, confront the evil designs of the Japanese and Germans who dominate the island. Fortunately the Germans and Japanese are at loggerheads, thus allowing Jack and his friends more time to maneuver.

The films of Tom Brown include *The Hoosier Schoolmaster* ('24); *The Lady Lies* ('29); *The Famous Ferguson Case* ('32); *Central Airport* ('33); *Anne of Green Gables* ('34); *Judge Priest* ('34); *Annapolis Farewell* ('35); *Rose Bowl* ('36); *Navy Blue and Gold* ('37); *Ex-Champ* ('39); *Oh, Johnny, How You Can Love* ('40); *Margie* ('40); *Hello Annapolis* ('42); *House on 92nd Street* ('45); *Buck Privates Come Home* ('47); *Ringside* ('49); *Fireman, Save My Child* ('54); *The Choppers* ('62) and many others.

In World War II, Brown was a paratrooper; he was recalled for action in the Korean War. Out of this conflict he emerged a lieutenant colonel. He was no longer the clean-cut young collegian and attempted to shed this image by playing heavies. He also could be seen on television in *Gunsmoke* as rancher Ed O'Connor, who sometimes served as a catalyst for mischief but could usually be counted on for level-headed wisdom at the showdown. And on ABC's daytime serial *General Hospital*, he was the loudmouthed, sometimes coarse Al Weeks.

Brown was married and divorced from three wives. His first marriage, in 1937, ended in divorce in 1939. By a later wife, Tom had two sons and a daughter.

Tom Brown died in 1990 at age 75 in the Motion Picture Hospital at Woodland Hills, California.

Serial

1943

The Adventures of Smilin' Jack. Univ., [13 Chapters] D: Ray Taylor, Lewis D. Collins; SP: Morgan B. Cox; Cam: William Sickner; LP: Tom Brown, Edgar Barrier, Marjorie Lord, Rose Hobart, Turhan Bey, Keye Luke.

LUCILE BROWNE

Lucile Browne was a pretty blonde who played with the kind of wide-eyed trusting innocence that her roles demanded. She was often called upon to register adoration while the hero did his manly thing — or worse yet, sang! That's a thankless assignment at best. She could show the whites of her eyes (and what beautiful eyes they were!) in tight places, romance in a subdued manner, withstand the harshness of the elements in which she worked, and fill the screen with her exquisite charm. Her genteel beauty and repressed manner served her well in those halcyon years.

Edwina Booth and Lucile Browne (right) in *The Last of the Mohicans* (Mascot, 1932).

Lucile added her considerable charms to the overall enjoyment of '30s movies, as she scored heavily in both horse operas and serials. And the decade was a gold mine for those movie patrons who hankered for Westerns and serials as their basic film fare. Add in a sack of popcorn, a Coke and a Three Stooges comedy and one could experience Heaven on earth.

Lucile was a Tennessee girl from Memphis, where she was born in 1907. After her public school education there and at National Park Seminary in Washington, D.C., she studied dramatics in Memphis and did modeling both in New York and Chicago. In the latter city she joined a stock company and played juveniles for six months before going into a major play with Richard Bennett. In 1930 she was signed by Fox.

Danger Island ('31) was Lucile's first serial. In the story, her father dies after telling her of a rich radium deposit on an African island. Walter Miller and Beulah Hutton, faking friendship for Browne, accompany her to the island with the objective of stealing the riches for themselves. Capt. Kenneth Harlan falls in love with Lucile and protects her, even when she believes him to be a scoundrel.

Viewing *Danger Island* ('31) today, it would probably seem ridiculous and crude. But judging a film in the context of 70 years of subsequent technical progress is not fair to the vintage product. Audiences of 1931 found this story of adventure on an African island quite palatable.

In *Battling with Buffalo Bill* ('31), Tom Tyler and Rex Bell oppose gambler Francis Ford and his minions, who are out to seize the gold claims in Hard Rock. Ford incites the Indians to attack the townspeople and also gets himself the job of sheriff in a rigged election, but Tyler and Bell are able to expose him, destroy his gang and bring peace to the territory once again.

The Airmail Mystery ('32) introduces airplanes into the West for added excitement. The Black Hawk, a mystery figure, plans to steal gold being shipped from a Western mine by airmail plane. Pilot James Flavin,

Brown and her brother Al Wilson see that the gold gets through and that the Black Hawk (Wheeler Oakman) will never again cause anyone trouble. Ray Taylor was able to elicit good performances from his principals, though the storyline could easily be summarized on a postage stamp.

In her fourth serial Lucile shared honors with Edwina Booth as one of the Monroe sisters in Mascot's adaptation of James Fenimore Cooper's *The Last of the Mohicans* ('32). Harry Carey plays Hawkeye, Hobart Bosworth is Chingachgook, Robert Kortman is the evil Huron chief Magua and Walter Miller is Major Duncan Heywood (on the side of righteousness for a change).

A romance developed between Lucile and co-star James Flavin which culminated in marriage in Tijuana, Mexico, on September 17, 1933. James Dunn served as best man and Lona Andre was maid of honor.

Mascot was sufficiently impressed with Lucile that she was signed for two more chapterplays. First was *Mystery Squadron* ('33). A mystery squadron, led by an unidentified figure calling himself the Black Ace, repeatedly attacks a huge dam construction project that threatens a secret gold mine. Two stunt pilots, Bob Steele and "Big Boy" Williams, are hired by Lafe McKee, owner of the construction firm, to protect the dam site. Jack Mulhall, foreman of the project and a friend of the two pilots, is revealed as the Black Ace and plunges to his death in the final chapter after an air fight with his erstwhile buddies.

In Lucile's sixth and final serial, *The Law of the Wild* ('34), Rex, a wild horse tamed by young rancher Bob Custer, is stolen by an employee, Dick Alexander. Later, while searching for Rex, Custer meets Lucile and her father, a racehorse owner. At the track, Custer's horse is entered in a race and wins. In a dispute over the winnings, Alexander is killed by a co-conspirator and the blame shifted to Custer. Rex, Rinty, Custer and Lucile survive numerous ordeals before justice is served and horse and master legally reunited. Lucile rides Rex in the sweepstakes in the final showdown.

The Browne-Flavin union was a happy one and lasted until Flavin's death just two weeks prior to her own death on May 10, 1976, at age 69. She died in Lexington, Kentucky, and was survived by her son, Capt. William Flavin, U.S. Army.

Serials

1931

Danger Island. Univ., [12 Chapters] D: Ray Taylor; SP: Basil Dickey, Ella O'Neill; S: Henry MacRae; LP: Kenneth Harlan, Lucile Browne, Walter Miller, W. L. Thorne.

Battling with Buffalo Bill. Univ., [12 Chapters] D: Ray Taylor; SP: George Plympton, Ella O'Neill; P/S: Henry MacRae; LP: Tom Tyler, Rex Bell, Lucile Browne, Francis Ford, William Desmond, Yakima Canutt.

1932

The Airmail Mystery. Univ., [12 Chapters] D: Ray Taylor; SP: Basil Dickey, George Plympton, George Morgan; S: Ella O'Neill; LP: James Flavin, Lucile Browne, Wheeler Oakman, Al Wilson.

The Last of the Mohicans. Mascot, [12 Chapters] D: B. Reeves Eason, Ford Beebe; SP: Colbert Clark, John F. Natteford, Ford Beebe, Wyndham Gittens; P: Nat Levine; Cam: Ernest Miller, Jack Young; LP: Harry Carey, Hobart Bosworth, Frank Coghlan, Jr., Edwina Booth, Lucile Browne.

1933

Mystery Squadron. Mascot, [12 Chapters] D: Colbert Clark, David Howard; SP: Barney Sarecky, Colbert Clark, David Howard, Wyndham Gittens; S: Sherman Lowe, Al Martin; P: Nat Levine; LP: Bob Steele, "Big Boy" Williams, Lucile Browne, Jack Mulhall, Robert Kortman, J. Carrol Naish, Lafe McKee.

1934

The Law of the Wild. Mascot, [12 Chapters] D: Armand Schaefer, B. Reeves Eason; S: Ford Beebe, John Rathmall, Al Martin; P: Nat Levine; SP: Sherman Lowe, B. Reeves Eason; P: Nat Levine; LP: Bob Custer, Rin-Tin-Tin, Jr., Lucile Browne, Ben Turpin, Richard Cramer.

FRANK BUCK

Frank Buck, animal entrepreneur extraordinaire, intrepid explorer and film producer, is probably "the most glorified Boy Scout of the Golden Years." *Bring 'Em Back Alive* ('30), the title of Buck's first and best-known book, became an appendage to Buck's name, a title bestowed upon him by his admiring public for his great exploits in the field of animal hunting and (although they may be unaware of this) for his great skill in publicizing these exploits. There have been animal hunters before, but none whose name echoes through the length and breadth of the land like Frank Buck's. Thousands of small boys vicariously experienced the numerous hair-raising, blood-curdling adventures he unfolded for them in his books and motion pictures.

Frank Buck was born in a wagon yard in Gainsville, Texas, on March 17, 1884, the son of Howard O. and Ada (Sites) Buck. He lived in the wagon yard (which his father owned) for five years. Then the family moved to Dallas, Texas, a small town of 35,000 inhabitants. Buck did not like school and his education ended at the end of the seventh grade. The one subject that fascinated him was geography.

Young Buck chopped cotton and roped and branded cattle on various Texas ranches

Unidentified player, Charlotte Henry and Frank Buck (right) in *Jungle Menace* (Columbia, 1937).

at 75 cents a day. In '19 he accompanied a load of cattle to Chicago. There he got a job as a bellhop at the fashionable Virginia Hotel and met Amy Leslie (real name: Lily West), a prominent Chicago drama critic and former actress. They were married. For a period of several years the couple lived in Chicago, where Buck was general assistant to the head of the Western Vaudeville Managers Association and later western representative of the *New York Telegraph*. He started an aviary at his Chicago home and once again began to read books on animals.

His marriage ended in divorce. In 1911, with the proceeds of $3,000 won in a card game, Buck sailed for Bahia, Brazil, where he purchased a quantity of birds. Back in New York, the zoos and bird dealers snapped them up and Buck made a large profit. Successive expeditions to South America followed.

After journeying to Singapore, where he penetrated the jungles and caught his first python, Buck's fame as an explorer spread. On one occasion, he delivered to the city of Dallas a zoo complete with 500 specimens of birds, animals and reptiles. He also began to gain a reputation as a showman.

It was at the suggestion of the late Floyd Gibbons, war correspondent, that Buck, in conjunction with Edward Anthony, wrote *Bring 'Em Back Alive*, published in 1930. The book went into many editions and became a best-seller. Buck followed it with *Wild Cargo*, with the same collaborator, the next year. In 1933, Anthony sued Buck for part of the profits of *Bring 'Em Back Alive*; almost all of Buck's subsequent books were written with another collaborator, his good friend Ferrin Fraser. In 1935 both *Fang and Claws* and *Tim Thompson in the Jungle* were published. Two years later came *On Jungle Trails* and, in 1939, *Animals Are Like That!* (with Carol

Weld). His autobiography *All in a Lifetime* (with Fraser) appeared in 1941.

In 1937, Buck starred in Columbia's first serial, *Jungle Menace* ('37).* The serial was a good one considering that it was Columbia's first. A murderous gang attempts to acquire a rubber plantation in Asia through murder and sabotage. Adventurer Frank Hardy vows to find out who is behind the plot and why, and is especially determined when his plantation owner friend is killed and the man's daughter endangered. Adding to the mysterious events is a powerful stalking Tiger Man who mysteriously appears from out of the jungle to aid the bloodthirsty rubber thieves.

For many years Buck pursued his calling, beset by many adventures. Some were in the line of duty, such as knocking out an orangutan in a fair fight with his fists, trapping the only authentic man-eating tiger ever to be exhibited in the United States, and capturing a leopard that had escaped from its cage on a trans-oceanic passenger steamer.

At the end of 25 years, an investment of a considerable sum collapsed and he was virtually penniless. At this time he fell in love with a girl named Muriel Riley, but he was unable to marry her because of his poverty-stricken condition. His friends, however, lent him $6,000, with which he was able to recoup his fortunes and marry the lady. They had one daughter, Barbara Muriel.

In 25 years as a gatherer of alive animals, Buck collected 49 elephants, 60 tigers, 63 assorted leopards, 20 hyenas, 20 tapirs, 52 orangutans, 100 gibbon apes, over 5,000 monkeys, 120 Asiatic antelope and deer, nine anoas or pigmy water buffalo, one pair of seladang (Malayan guar), five babirussa, rarest of wild swine, two African cape buffalo, 18 African antelope, two giraffes, 40 wild goats and sheep, 11 camels, 40 kangaroos and wallabies, five Indian rhinoceroses, 60 bears, 90 large pythons, ten king cobras, over 100 smaller snakes, 25 giant monitor lizards, 15 crocodiles, more than 500 small mammals of different species, and more than 100,000 birds, ranging all the way from the big ostrich-like cassowaries of the Panpan Islands down to Australian finches as small as hummingbirds. Add to this record his seven books, numerous articles and five motion pictures. His favorite among his books is not *Bring 'Em Back Alive* but *On Jungle Trails*, a story-textbook that was used in schools all over the United States.

Frank Buck died of a lung ailment at the Hermann Hospital in Houston, Texas, on March 25, 1950, at age 66.

Serial

1937

Jungle Menace. Col., [15 Chapters] D: George Melford, Harry Fraser; S: George M. Merrick, Arthur Hoerl, Dallas Fitzgerald, Gordon Griffith; SP: George Rosener, Sherman L. Lowe, Harry Hoyt, George Melford; P: Jack Fier, Louis Weiss; Cam: Edward Linden, Herman Schopp; Mus: Abe Meyer; LP: Frank Buck, Esther Ralston, John St. Polis, Reginald Denny, Charlotte Henry, Sash Siemel, Willie Fung, LeRoy Mason.

BILLY BURKE

Gloria's Romance ('16) was a 20-chapter serial that started out to be a novel in the magazine style. It ended as a disastrous enterprise despite the fact that Billie Burke was

---

Also that year he joined the Ringling Bros. and Barnum & Bailey Circus and exhibited his animals at the Chicago Fair. He later displayed them at the New York World's Fair.

an extremely popular actress—so popular that she was paid $10,000 a week for 14 weeks ($140,000). Total production costs ran to $640,000, making it the most expensive serial ever made—and it was a loser. The public rejected its "high browism," having grown accustomed to action thrillers. Few theaters booked all 20 chapters. The story reads like a soap opera.

Mary William Ethelbert Appleton Burke was born August 7, 1885, in Washington, D.C., the only child of William (Billy) Burke, a singing clown in the Barnum and Bailey Circus who also toured with his own music hall act, and Blanche Hodkinson Burke, a Treasury worker. The baby was given the nickname "Billie" and it was as Billie Burke that she acted both on the stage and in films. In 1893 the family moved to London, where she was schooled. Vacations were often spent following her father's music hall act all over the world.

Those readers old enough to remember Billie Burke probably think of her as the addle-pated, scatterbrained, twittery, jittery, skittish, fluttery, irresponsible older lady whose lack of logic induced despair in the rest of the cast and hilarity in the audience. *The New Statesman* magazine commenting on *Topper Takes a Trip* ('39) enthused: "Here I must pay tribute to Billie Burke, who excels all her previous studies in good-natured imbecility, her every word proceeding from a wonderfully complete inner vacuum."

Billie made her debut as a singer in 1899 when she was only 14. By 1907 she was a popular stage actress in England. That year she was brought to New York City to co-star with John Drew in *My Wife*. A delicate beauty of piquant personality, she soon was the toast of Broadway. In 1913 she met Florenz Ziegfeld at a New Year's Eve party at the Astor Hotel. The following year, on April 10, 1914, the two eloped and were married in a Hoboken, New Jersey, parsonage.

In 1916, Billie embarked on a silent film career. She was paid the unbelievable sum of

Right: **In *Gloria's Romance* (Kleine, 1916).**

$300,000 by Thomas H. Ince to star in *Peggy* ('16).

Billie's only child, Patricia, was born on October 23, 1916. In 1917, Billie signed a long-term contract with Paramount-Artcraft and made 14 films for the studio during the years 1917–21, also managing to star in five Broadway plays. She then returned to the stage full time.

Flo Ziegfeld was broke by 1930. Poor investments, gambling, stage flops, extramarital affairs, and the 1929 stock market crash had left him penniless. He died of heart failure on July 22, 1932. Billie had returned to the screen to help him out of debt. After his death, she continued working. By 1933 she was being cast in the comedic character roles for which she is best remembered today.

Billie wrote her autobiography, *With a Feather on My Nose* (1948), and an advice book for women, *With Powder on My Nose*

(1959). Her last film was *Pepe* (1960), in which she played a cameo role.

Burke died on May 14, 1970. Undoubtedly, her favorite role was as Glinda the Good Witch of the East in *The Wizard of Oz* (1939).

Readers wanting more information on Burke will find Eve Golden's article "Billie Burke: That Charming Mrs. Ziegfeld" in *Films of the Golden Age*, Spring, 1996, one of the best.

Serial

1916

Gloria's Romance. Kleine, [20 Chapters] D: Walter Edwin; S: Mr. and Mrs. Rupert Hughes; P: Randolph Film Company; LP: Billie Burke, David Powell, William Roselle, Frank Belcher, William T. Carleton.

FRANCIS X. BUSHMAN

Francis Xavier Bushman was born January 10, 1883, in Baltimore, Maryland, the ninth of ten children. His theatrical career began with stock companies in the East, and he made his Broadway debut in 1907 in *Queen of the Moulin Rouge*. His acting career was preceded, or accompanied, by work as a clerk, wrestler, boxer, weight lifter, bicyclist and sculptor's model. He claimed to have worked at 37 occupations.

In 1902, 19-year-old Francis married Josephine Fladune and by 1909 they had five children.

Bushman joined the Essanay Company in Chicago in April 1911. His first film, a one-reeler, was *His Friend's Wife*, released on June 6, 1911. He was a handsome man of sturdy physique and was the object of unprecedented adulation among cinema audiences of the pre–20s. His popularity reached a peak

when he joined Metro soon after its formation in 1915. He was rushed from one set to the other, playing hundreds of dashing romantic roles.

At the same time, Bushman became the first great off-screen exhibitionist. He gave $100 tips to busboys and ordered lavender cigarettes to match his lavender boudoir and his lavender Rolls-Royce. There was a time when he rolled along the streets in the largest automobile in the world, a custom-built Mormon guaranteed to do 110 miles an hour. All the exposed metal parts were gold-plated. Appropriately it was painted royal purple and his name, Francis X. Bushman, was lettered on it in gold. Five Great Danes followed him wherever he went. It was written, though no doubt an exaggeration, that he had 300 Danes on his 280-acre estate, Bushmanor, outside of Baltimore.

In 1915, a national poll elected him King of the Movies. At the peak of his amazing vogue, he employed eight or more secretaries to answer the 7,000 letters a week from lovesick women. He earned over $1,000,000 a year (and no income tax). He lived like a king and spent money like a Congressional committee. He became a legend as the "handsomest man in the world."

His hit films included *One Wonderful Night* ('14), *Graustark* ('15), *Pennington's Choice* ('15) and *Romeo and Juliet* ('16).

Louis B. Mayer desired to get into the production of movies. Previously he had primarily been in the release and distribution end of the business. He made arrangements for finances and distribution and signed Bushman and Beverly Bayne as stars of an 18-chapter serial, *The Great Secret* ('17). In spite of the popularity of Bushman and Bayne, the serial did not achieve popular success. Many theaters stopped showing the serial chapters before the eighteenth chapter was reached. Bushman's public image was hurt.

But what hurt even more was the discovery by the public that Bushman was a married man with five children. His marriage had always been kept a secret so as not to destroy his "attainability." It was written into his contract that the fact must be kept a secret. But when he sued Josephine for divorce in order to marry Bayne, Josephine yelled loud and clear to the press that Bushman had beaten her and the children on many occasions during their marriage. Overnight his glittering house of celluloid cards tumbled. The worshippers who had mobbed him were even more frenzied in their rush to desert him. Within two weeks, one secretary was enough to handle the few tear-stained letters still trickling in.

Bushman and Bayne were married on July 29, 1915. A son was born to them on June 9, 1919.

After several non-productive years, Bushman got a chance to portray the Roman Messala, Ramon Novarro's rival, in *Ben Hur* ('26). His career faded away after that, due in part to blacklisting by Louis B. Mayer, who

blamed him for the failure of *The Great Secret* and because he thought Bushman outshined Novarro, whom Mayer was promoting.

Although he had given his greatest performance as Messala, Bushman found no more opportunities to work. Presently he vanished. The abyss into which the movie great fall, once they begin to slide, swallowed him. The 1929 stock market crash cuffed the screen's most outstanding Humpty-Dumpty around still more. His fortune was gone. He filed a bankruptcy petition that showed him more than $100,000 in debt.

Beverly Bayne divorced him in 1925. In 1932 he married Norma Emily Atkins, who remained his wife until her death on February 4, 1956. On August 15, 1956, he married Iva Millicent Richardson, who survived him.

From 1929 to 1966 Bushman appeared in a few movies, but in none of them did he have a big part. He played Bernard M. Baruck, the financier, in *Wilson* ('43), King Saul in *David and Bathsheba* ('51) and Moses in *The Story of Mankind* ('57). Other films were *Hollywood Boulevard* ('36), the serial *Dick Tracy* ('37), *The Bad and the Beautiful* ('52), *Apache Country* ('52), *Sabrina* ('54), *The Phantom Planet* ('62) and his last, *The Ghost in the Invisible Bikini* ('66).

Bushman was not down for the count. He bounced back, making a financial comeback in radio soap operas and later television. He was said to have had more than 2,500 bit parts in radio alone before he began getting television work.

Francis X. Bushman suffered a stroke on the morning of August 23, 1966, before leaving his Pacific Palisades home for a day of filming. He died shortly afterwards. He was 81.

Serials

1917

The Great Secret. Metro, 1917 [18 Chapters] D: William Christy Cabanne; S: Fred de Gresac; LP: Francis X. Bushman, Beverly Bayne, Fred R. Stanton, Ed Connelly, Tom Blake, Helen Dunbar, Neva Gerber, Charles Ripley, Art Ortego.

1937

Dick Tracy. Rep., [15 Chapters] D: Ray Taylor, Alan James; LP: Ralph Byrd, Kay Hughes, Smiley Burnette, Lee Van Atta, John Picorri, Carleton Young, Francis X. Bushman.

FRANCIS X. BUSHMAN, JR. /RALPH E. BUSHMAN

Ralph E. Bushman was born May 1, 1903, to Francis X. Bushman, Sr., and Josephine Fladune. On screen Ralph traded on his father's name by adopting the name Francis X. Bushman, Jr. Later in his career he reverted to his real name.

Bushman began his screen career in the silent era in romantic roles but his athletic ability and his great strength brought him in demand for parts in which his physical strength attributes could better be used.

Bushman, Jr., was big, no doubt about that. He was more than six feet tall, usually weighing in the neighborhood of 200 pounds.

In his first serial *The Scarlet Arrow* ('28), Bushman is Capt. Bob North of the Northwest Mounted Police, combating fur thieves and the crooked saloon owner who wants the other half of a map showing where gold can be found. Unbeknownst to her, the

heroine (Hazel Keener) has the missing half of the map.

In *The Galloping Ghost* (a 1931 Mascot all-talking serial), Red Grange is wrongly accused of accepting a bribe and is dismissed from Clay College. He maintains his silence to protect his buddy (Bushman).

In *Spell of the Circus* (1931), Bushman is headliner of the wild west concert. Tom London is chief villain. London tries to force Alberta to marry him in order that he might wind up owning the circus. Alberta loves Bushman. All ends well.

In *The Last Frontier* ('32), Bushman is involved in an attempt to drive settlers off of land where gold is located.

In *The Three Musketeers* ('33), Jack Mulhall, Raymond Hatton and Francis Bushman are Legionnaires rescued from desert rebels. The four become involved in thwart-

Left to right: Francis X. Bushman, Jr., unidentified player, Claude Peyton, Yakima Canutt and Lon Chaney, Jr., in *The Last Frontier* (RKO, 1932).

ing the attempts of the mysterious leader of a desert tribal cult that is attempting to wipe out the Foreign Legion. The serial's cast is a good one, with several former stars in support.

Bushman's initial credited role was in *It's a Great Life* ('20) at which time he would have been only 17. Other features followed until 1943, after which he had no film credits. In most of the features he was a supporting player. He died on April 16, 1978, in Los Angeles from respiratory failure.

Serials

1928

The Scarlet Arrow. Univ., [10 Chapters] D: Ray Taylor; SP: Arthur Henry Gooden; S:

Frank Howard Clark; LP: Francis X. Bushman, Jr., Hazel Keener, Edmund Cobb, Al Ferguson, Clark Comstock.

1931

The Galloping Ghost. Mascot, [12 Chapters] D: B. Reeves Eason; AD: Armand Schaeffer; P: Nat Levine; LP: Harold (Red) Grange, Dorothy Gulliver, Walter Miller, Gwen Lee, Francis X. Bushman, Jr.

Spell of the Circus. Univ., [10 Chapters] D: Robert F. Hill; S/SP: Ian McClosky Heath; LP: Francis X. Bushman, Jr., Alberta Vaughn, Tom London, Walter Shumway, Charles Murphy.

1932

The Last Frontier. RKO, [12 Chapters] D: Spencer G. Bennet, Thomas L. Story; SP: George Plympton, Robert F. Hill; S: Courtney Riley

Cooper; Spv: Fred J. McConnell; LP: Creighton Chaney [Lon Chaney, Jr.], Dorothy Gulliver, Mary Jo Desmond, Francis X. Bushman, Jr.

1933

The Three Musketeers. Mascot, [12 Chapters] D: Armand Schaeffer, Colbert Clark; SP: Nor-man Hall, Colbert Clark, Ben Cohn, Wyndham Gittens; P: Nat Levine; Cam: Ernest Miller, Tom Galligan; Mus: Lee Zahler; LP: Jack Mulhall, John Wayne, Raymond Hatton, Francis X. Bushman, Jr., Ruth Hall.

RALPH BYRD

Ralph Byrd, known to most Saturday matinee audiences as Dick Tracy, died from cancer in the Veterans Hospital in Sawtell, California, on August 18, 1952. He was just 43 years old. He was survived by his actress wife Virginia Carroll and his daughter, Carroll, age 13.

Byrd had been in films for 18 years and had just recently completed 39 episodes of the television series *Dick Tracy* (1950–51); there were plans to produce 39 more episodes.

Byrd appeared in nearly 50 films before going into the armed forces in World War II. He served with the U.S. Army Signal Corps

Kay Hughes and Ralph Byrd in *Dick Tracy* (Republic, 1937).

for two years and taught demolition at Camp Crowder, Missouri. He was discharged in April 1946 with the rank of Technical Sergeant.

In addition to the highly popular Dick Tracy serials for Republic, Byrd also starred in the cliffhangers *SOS Coast Guard* (Rep., '37), *Blake of Scotland Yard* (Victory, '37) and *The Vigilante* (Col., '47). Thus, on the basis of the seven chapterplays, he rates as one of the sound era's most prolific and popular serial heroes. Back in 1935 he had a supporting role in Mascot's *The Adventures of Rex and Rinty*, which featured Kane Richmond, Rex (horse) and Rin-Tin-Tin, Jr.

Byrd was born in Dayton, Ohio, on April 22, 1919. He was a four-letter athlete at Steele High School in Dayton and he played in school dramatic productions as well.

As a small boy and on up into young manhood, Byrd was an enthusiastic Boy Scout. He became an Eagle Scout and eventually earned 37 merit badges. Then he became a scoutmaster and finally a District Commissioner by the time he was 21 years old.

Byrd was also soloist in a Dayton church choir; the choir training led to amateur musical comedy and local radio work. These in turn won him his first professional job with the Albright Players, a local stock company which toured the Midwest. Byrd accompanied the company on tour, remaining with them for over a year. Subsequently he tried his hand at singing with a band, which brought him to Hollywood in 1934. Here he did radio work and studied at the Hollywood Little Theatre. Eventually a talent scout saw him and arranged to get him his first movie assignment.

Hundreds of actors tried out for the role which gave Byrd his real start, that of the square-jawed paragon of sleuths, *Dick Tracy* ('37). The fact that he was over six feet tall, handsome, debonair and square-shouldered helped in winning the Tracy role, but more importantly was his acting ability, which also won him a long term contract with 20th Century–Fox.

Four Dick Tracy serials for Republic

made him a name and gave him a following with the action fans, but it was a comparatively insignificant role, that of Al Bennett in *A Yank in the R.A.F.* ('41), which brought a change in his career. Studio executives were so struck by this performance that they made immediate inquiries as to who this actor was and whence he came. Likewise, Alexander Korda had been impressed by Byrd and wanted him for the role of "Durga" in *The Jungle Book* ('42). Byrd won both this role and the 20th Century–Fox contract, which was more than justified by Byrd's first performance under its terms. As the minister in *Moontide* ('42), Byrd had the privilege of marrying Jean Gabin and Ida Lupino.

His next and most difficult role came in *Ten Gentlemen from West Point* ('42), in which he was required to play a tough nineteenth century soldier. The role demanded a mixture of comedy and straightforward rough and tumble, which brought him high praise from director Henry Hathaway.

Byrd lived on a small ranch in the San Fernando Valley and raised rabbits, chickens and turkeys and did a little painting and carpentry work as hobbies. He loved horses and dogs and always had one or two. And he swam, played ping pong, tennis, badminton, gin rummy and poker.

He was quite interested in poetry and music and had a collection of several thousand records of symphony and modern American music. He also had a collection of over 350 pipes. His favorite mode of entertaining was at outdoor barbecue parties. A cook, he was noted around Hollywood for his particular brand of Swiss steak.

Brief comments are given here for Byrd's serials:

The Adventures of Rex and Rinty ('35) is the story of Rex, a "God Horse" to the natives of Sujan, a primitive island. He is stolen by three American crooks and sold to Crawford, a wealthy ranch owner in the U.S., who attempts to train him as a polo pony. Rex escapes and teams up with Rin-Tin-Tin, Jr. They roam the range together and outwit their tormentors, with the help of Frank Bradley (Kane Richmond). Bradley is able to

Ralph Byrd and Jan Wiley in *Dick Tracy vs. Crime, Inc.* (Republic, 1941).

take them back to Sujan. Crawford follows but Bradley, Rex and Rinty are able to put an end to Crawford's activities. Byrd has only a small role.

SOS Coast Guard ('37) is an exciting, action-packed adventure of sabotage and danger. When mad munitions expert Boroff (Bela Lugosi) decides to sell his deadly disintegrating gas to a sinister foreign power, it's up to Lt. Terry Kent (Ralph Byrd) to "save the day." But stopping Bela Lugosi is never easy, especially when he's playing a devious and brilliant scientist. From mid-ocean to the deepest mine shaft, Boroff eludes capture amid a series of hair-raising episodes, until he and Kent meet at sea for a final confrontation that will determine the fate of the world.

Blake of Scotland Yard ('37). A foreign munitions maker offers a small fortune to a mysterious hooded criminal known as the Scorpion, who wears a claw-like apparatus on his right hand. In return, the Scorpion must steal a death ray machine invented by Jerry Sheechan (Byrd) and Hope Mason (Joan Barclay), niece of Sir James Blake, formerly an inspector with Scotland Yard. Blake has invested heavily in the machine. A struggle for possession of the powerful weapon ensues. This serial was also released in feature form.

Dick Tracy ('37) turned out to be a more popular and profitable serial than even Republic had hoped for. Casting Byrd in the chief role was a stroke of luck for the studio. Audiences liked Byrd's portrayal of the famous comic-strip detective who, in this story, tenaciously seeks to discover the identity of "the Lame One," bring an end to the terrorist activities of the Spider Gang, and find his brother, Gordon, who has been kidnapped. Unknown to Tracy, his brother

(Carleton Young) has become a pawn to the Lame One through an operation performed by Moloch (John Picorri), the Lame One's lieutenant. Tracy must not only contend with ordinary hoodlums but also with such scientific apparatus as a disintegrating machine located aboard "The Wing," the Lame One's super-modern aircraft.

The tremendous success of *Dick Tracy* convinced Republic hierarchy that a follow-up serial should be made. The result was *Dick Tracy Returns* ('38), which likewise received kudos from serial fans and registered a nice profit for Republic. It is generally regarded as one of the finest serials to come out of Hollywood. The story revolves around Pa Stark (Charles Middleton) and his five criminal sons who are holding America in a grip of terror. Tracy is assigned to apprehend the gang. One by one the Starks are killed in the act of committing crimes, with Pa the last to die as he attempts to escape in an airplane. Byrd won new fame as the imperturbable Tracy.

Believing that the adventures of Dick Tracy could be milked a third time, Republic produced *Dick Tracy's G-Men* ('39). Nicholas Zaroff (Irving Pichel), master spy and the world's most hated man, is sentenced to die in the gas chamber of a California prison. By using a secret drug which does not permit the gas to enter the lungs, Zaroff cheats death and his body is revived by his minions. Dick Tracy, the government's ace investigator, is assigned the task of tracking and bringing Zaroff to justice. Swearing revenge on Tracy, Zaroff resumes his diabolical spy and crime activities, with Tracy, again played by Byrd, in hot pursuit.

Republic set an unbroken record with its release of *Dick Tracy vs. Crime, Inc.* ('41). No other fictional character had been serialized as many times, and with the same actor playing the part. This time Dick Tracy's genius and luck are taxed to the limit as he endeavors to capture and learn the identity of "The Ghost," a master criminal determined to destroy the city to avenge the death of his brother. The Ghost, so called because he can make himself invisible, is actually a member of an anti-crime council. Because Tracy suspects that a council member is the Ghost, he is ultimately able to bring about the downfall of the insidious criminal. The same high production standards prevailed for this film as had existed for the preceding three.

In his only serial for Columbia, Byrd plays *The Vigilante* ('47), an undercover agent for the government who is really Greg Sanders, a Western movie star. An assignment takes him to the ranch of wealthy George Pierce (Lyle Talbot), secretly gang leader "X-1," who is after a string of pearls called "100 Tears of Blood." The pearls have been concealed in the hooves of five stallions (if you can believe it!) belonging to Pierce's guests. Pierce stops at nothing in his efforts to secure the cursed pearls, but the Vigilante is victorious and Pierce is killed in a final showdown. Prince Amil (Robert Barron), one of the guests, destroys the pearls with acid to prevent the curse of the pearls from hurting others. The serial did not measure up to his Republic offerings, but was nevertheless entertaining.

Serials

1935

The Adventures of Rex and Rinty. Mascot, [12 Chapters] D: B. Reeves Eason, Ford Beebe; SP: John Rathman, Barney Sarecky; P: Nat Levine; S: B. Reeves Eason, Ray Trampe, Maurice Geraghty; Cam: William Nobles; LP: Rex, Rin-Tin-Tin, Jr., Kane Richmond, Norma Taylor, Mischa Auer, Harry Woods.

1937

SOS Coast Guard. Rep., [12 Chapters] D: William Witney, Alan James; SP: Barry Shipman, Franklyn Adreon; S: Morgan Cox, Ronald Davidson; Cam: William Nobles; AP: Sol C. Siegel; Mus: Raoul Kraushaar; LP: Ralph Byrd, Bela Lugosi, Maxine Doyle, Richard Alexander, Herbert Rawlinson, John Picorri, George Chesebro.

Dick Tracy. Rep., [15 Chapters] D: Ray Taylor, Alan James; SP: Barry Shipman; S: Norman Cox, George Morgan; AP: J. Laurence Wickland; P: Nat Levine; Cam: William Nobles, Edgar Lyons; Mus: Harry Grey; LP: Ralph Byrd, Kay Hughes, Smiley Burnette, Lee Van Atta, John Picorri, Carleton Young.

Blake of Scotland Yard. Victory, [15 Chapters] D: Bob Hill; S: Rock Hawkey; Spv: Robert Stillman; Cam: Bill Hyer; P: Sam Katzman; LP: Ralph Byrd, Herbert Rawlinson, Joan Barclay, Lloyd Hughes, Dickie Jones, Herman Brix.

1938

Dick Tracy Returns. Rep., [15 Chapters] D: William Witney, John English; SP: Barry Shipman, Franklyn Adreon, Ronald Davidson, Rex Taylor, Sol Shor; AP: Robert Beche; Cam: William Nobles; LP: Ralph Byrd, Lynne Roberts, Charles Middleton, Jerry Tucker, David Sharpe.

1939

Dick Tracy's G-Men. Rep., [15 Chapters] D: William Witney, John English; AP: R. Beche; SP: Barry Shipman, Franklyn Adreon, Rex Tay-

lor, Ronald Davidson, Sol Shor; Cam: William Nobles; Mus: William Lava; LP: Ralph Byrd, Phylis Isley [Jennifer Jones], Irving Pichel, Ted Pearson, Walter Miller.

1941

Dick Tracy vs. Crime, Inc. Rep., [15 Chapters] D: William Witney, John English; SP: Ronald Davidson, Norman S. Hall, William Lively, Joseph O'Donnell, Joseph Poland; AP: W. J. O'Sullivan; Cam: Reggie Lanning; Mus: Cy Feuer; LP: Ralph Byrd, Jan Wiley, John Davidson, Ralph Morgan, Jack Mulhall, Robert Fiske.

1947

The Vigilante. Col., [15 Chapters] D: Wallace Fox; SP: George H. Plympton, Lewis Clay, Arthur Hoerl; P: Sam Katzman; Cam: Ira H. Morgan; Mus: Mischa Bakaleinikoff; LP: Ralph Byrd, Ramsay Ames, Lyle Talbot, George Offerman, Jr., Robert Barron, George Chesebro, Jack Ingram.

ROD CAMERON

Born Roderick Cox on December 7, 1910, in Calgary, Alberta, Canada, this future cowboy ace worked as a construction laborer and sandhog on the Holland Tunnel in New York. In the 1930s he moved to Los Angeles to work on tunnels for the Metropolitan Water District, later working at various jobs.

Rod broke into pictures as a stunt double. A bit in the Bette Davis starrer *The Old Maid* ('39) wound up on the cutting room floor, but Paramount thought he had potential and signed him. For three years Rod played assorted bits and small parts in Paramount films, even appearing in the Hopalong Cassidy Western *Stagecoach War* ('40) in a very small role. But the parts got bigger and he did some creditable things while at

the studio—films such as *The Forest Rangers* ('42), *The Fleet's In* ('42) and *Wake Island* ('42).

When his option came up, with no raise offered, Rod left the studio to freelance, being picked up by Republic for the starring role of "Rex Bennett," American agent, in the now-famous serials *G-Men vs. the Black Dragon* and *Secret Service in Darkest Africa*, filmed in 1943. The latter was the third most costly of all Republic serials, exceeded only slightly by *Captain America* ('44) and *The Lone Ranger Rides Again* ('39). Both of the Cameron serials were highly popular with the Saturday matinee audience. As a result, Rod's per picture salary was boosted.

G-Men vs. the Black Dragon had Cameron

in the only continuing non–comic strip role in Republic's serial output, Rex Bennett of the Secret Service. Crammed with action, *Black Dragon* was one of the many '40s adventures that moved like a runaway express train, with fights, chases and cliffhangers popping up at the drop of a hat. Battling with Cameron against the sinister Black Dragon were Constance Worth (an excellent choice) as a British agent and Roland Got as a member of the Chinese Secret Service. The master spy was Nino Pippitone, while henchmen included George J. Lewis and Noel Cravat. Here the villains were truly hissable with none of them above shooting, killing, strangling and stabbing.

Secret Service in Darkest Africa ('43) had Bennett pop up in Casablanca to stop Axis agents led by a German baron (played with thorough nastiness by Lionel Royce), an exact double for a Moslem leader whose place he has taken while keeping the real

official chained up in a secret dungeon. Joan Marsh and Duncan Renaldo joined Cameron on the side of democracy while Kurt Kreuger and Frederic Brunn were Royce's chief aides. Almost every chapter had two or three super-brawls interspersed in the action while the screenplay gave audiences additional ideas as to what kind of s.o.b.s the Nazis were.

These two serials perhaps helped move Rod up to leading man status. He was picked up by Universal and had fairly good roles in the studio's *Honeymoon Lodge* ('43) and United Artists' *The Kansan* ('43) before being signed to a long-term contract by Universal after his performance in *Gung Ho* ('43) in which he played "Tedrow," the hillbilly. It was shortly after this appearance that MGM borrowed him to play in support of Greer Garson in *Mrs. Parkington* ('44), for which he received good notices.

Realizing that Rod would probably make good prairie fodder, Universal cast him as the lead in a series of six B-Western thrillers produced by Oliver Drake. Fuzzy Knight provided the comic interludes, while Ray Whitley and his Bar-6 cowboys supplied the musical segments. Vivian Austin (two films), Jennifer Holt (three films) and Marjorie Clements (one film) filled the necessary femme roles. Lewis Collins directed two entries and the other four were captained by Ray Taylor, Wallace Fox, Howard Bretherton and Lambert Hillyer respectively. In the first film, *Boss of Boomtown* ('44), Rod shares the spotlight with Tom Tyler, and they seemed to complement each other adroitly. But the remaining five films (*Trigger Trail, Riders of the Santa Fe, The Old Texas Trail, Beyond the Pecos* and *Renegades of the Rio Grande*) featured as second banana Eddie Dew, a far less exciting personality than Tyler.

Universal executives believed that Rod was ready for the big time and henceforth he worked in "A" productions. He co-starred with Yvonne DeCarlo in *Frontier Gal* ('45) and *Salome, Where She Danced* ('45), and they were reunited in *River Lady* ('48). *Pirates of Monterey* co-starred Rod with Maria Montez. Upon completion of *Pirates*, Rod

Jennifer Holt and Rod Cameron in *Beyond the Pecos* (Universal, 1945).

was given nothing to do for eight months, as the studio was going through a reorganization shuffle, and no story was made ready for him. Finally he asked for and was given his release, at which point he became a freelance artist. The titles of his better films are *Belle Starr's Daughter* ('48), *Panhandle* ('48), *The Plunderers* ('48), *Brimstone* ('49), *Dakota Lil* ('50), *Short Grass* ('50), *Stage to Tucson* ('51), *Fort Osage* ('52), *The Jungle* ('52), *Ride the Man Down* ('53), *Hell's Outpost* ('54), *Yaqui Drums* ('56), and *Spoilers of the Forest* ('57).

Rod was one of the first motion picture stars to enter television, starring in three half-hour syndicated series made by Revue Productions and distributed by MCA-TV. *City Detective* was filmed from 1953 through 1955 and had Rod playing the part of Lt. Bart Grant of the New York City Police Department. *State Trooper* found him in Nevada as Rod Blake, chief of the Nevada State Troopers. Produced from 1957 to 1959, this series

was the most popular of Rod's three; according to Rod, a total of 140 segments were filmed. The third and least popular of the trio was *Coronado 9*, filmed in 1959. Cameron played Dan Adams, a retired naval officer turned private investigator.

For over 20 years Cameron guest starred in various television plays on such programs as *Pepsi Cola Playhouse, Studio 57, Fireside Theatre, The Loretta Young Show, Star Stage, Crossroads, Laramie, Tales of Wells Fargo, Burke's Law, Perry Mason, Bob Hope Chrysler Theatre, Bonanza, Iron Horse, Alias Smith and Jones, Adam 12* and *Hondo*.

Rod's last feature film, *Love and the Midnight Auto Supply*, was made in 1978. He eventually retired and he and his wife took up residence in Georgia so that he could be near his son, a baseball player.

His death on December 31, 1983, was a shock to his legion of fans.

Serials

1943

G-Men vs. the Black Dragon. Rep., [15 Chapters] D: William Witney; SP: Ronald Davidson, William Lively, Joseph O'Donnell, Joseph Poland; Cam: Bud Thackery; Mus: Mort Glickman; LP: Rod Cameron, Constance Worth, Roland Got, George J. Lewis, Nino Pipitone, Noel Cravat, Maxine Doyle.

Secret Service in Darkest Africa. Rep., [15 Chapters] D: Spencer Bennet; SP: Roy Cole, Basil Dickey, Jesse Duffy, Ronald Davidson, Joseph O'Donnell, Joseph Poland; Cam: William Bradford; Mus: Mort Glickman; AP: W. J. O'Sullivan; LP: Rod Cameron, Joan Marsh, Duncan Renaldo, Lionel Royce, Kurt Kreuger, Frederic Brunn, Kurt Katch.

YAKIMA CANUTT

Yak was born Enos Edward Canutt on a ranch near Colfax, Washington, on November 29, 1896. He got his nickname at the Pendleton, Oregon, rodeo in 1914 when he was participating in the bronc riding event. Some cowboys from Yakima were also appearing in the rodeo, a newspaper photo showing Yak was captioned "the cowboy from Yakima" and it became his moniker thereafter.

Yak came to California after the rodeo season of 1919, when the cowboys were getting up to $7.50 a day for doing fights, riding and acting. Work was easy to find. He did some riding and stunting in a few Westerns that year. He had won the title of "World's All-Around Cowboy" at the Pendleton Round-up in 1917 and traveled the rodeo circuit all the way to the old Madison Square Garden with fantastic success. He again won the title "World's All-Around Cowboy" in 1919, 1920 and 1923. He might have also earned the title in 1918 except that he was serving his country on a minesweeper in the Navy in World War I. Yak's income from rodeoing reached as high as $30,000 a year in a time before income taxes and inflated dollars. He was awarded the Police Gazette cowboy championship Belt in 1917, 1918, 1919, 1921 and 1923. In 1923 he was also awarded the Roosevelt Trophy.

While still holding the title of "World's All-Around Cowboy," Yak gradually drifted into the acting end of the movie business as well as increasing the amount of stunt work he accepted. After all, two paychecks were better than one, in Yak's opinion. Two of his early roles as a principal supporting player were in the Neal Hart Westerns *The Heart of a Texan* (Steiner, '22) and *The Forbidden Range* ('Steiner, '23). In '24 he appeared in the serials *Days of '49* (Arrow) starring Neva Gerber and Edmund Cobb and *The Riddle Rider* (Universal) starring William Desmond. Also, he supported Dick Hatton in *Sell 'Em Cowboy* (Arrow '24) and became a Western lead for Ben Wilson Productions, a company releasing primarily through Arrow Film Corporation. Yak supported Wilson, himself a star as well as a producer-director, in *The Desert Hawk* ('24).

Ridin' Mad ('24) was possibly Yak's first starring Western for Ben Wilson Productions. It was followed in short order by *Branded a Bandit* ('24). The film gave Yak ample opportunity to display his bag of athletic tricks as he eludes a sheriff's posse and eventually clears himself of a murder charge by bringing in the guilty man.

Canutt played second lead to Dick Hatton in *The Cactus Cure* for Ben Wilson Pro-

Bob Reeves and Yakima Canutt (right) in *Canyon Hawks* (Big 4, 1930).

ductions in '25 and starred in eight horse operas for the same firm (*The Human Tornado, Ridin' Comet, Romance and Rustlers, Scar Hannon, The Strange Rider, A Two-Fisted Sheriff, White Thunder* and *Wolves of the Road*). Considered the best of this series were *The Human Tornado* and *Scar Hannon*, both released by FBO. The former involves a strongbox, Yak's arrest for stealing it, the dishonesty of Yak's brother and several killings. All ends well as Yak is exonerated, recovers some of the inheritance his brother cheated him out of, and settles down with his sweetheart. In the latter film Yak is called "Scar" because of a disfigurement of his face, rectified by an operation midway through the film (a result of saving the life of a young lady who later introduces him to her father, a surgeon). Scar ultimately recovers a ranch that had been stolen from his father and marries the girl whose life he saved.

In *White Thunder*, released by FBO, Yak plays a Zorro-type role, perhaps inspired by Douglas Fairbanks' *Zorro* and *Don Q, Son of Zorro*. He portrays a sissy dude returned home from college following his father's murder. A feud is going on between sheepmen and ranchers. Soon after he returns, a white-robed rider appears in town, fighting for the rights of the oppressed sheepmen. Ultimately, the sissy is revealed as the masked rider.

The two most memorable of Yak's films of 1926 were *The Devil Horse* and *The Fighting Stallion*, the first produced by Hal Roach and distributed by Pathé, the second released by Goodwill Pictures. Rex, the famous movie stallion, plays the title role in *The Devil Horse*, with Yak cast as a young Indian-hater whose parents were the victims of a redskin attack on a wagon train. He manages to save the fort from an Indian massacre. A slightly higher budget and distribution by Pathé enhanced this film considerably. With limited distribution through Goodwill, *The Fighting Stallion* was of less importance but a good Canutt film, and one containing some good horse scenes.

Canutt continued grinding out low-budget Westerns for the next several years, films strong on action but weak in most other respects. He failed to achieve stardom in the sense that Mix, Jones, Maynard, Gibson or Thomson did. He remained in the third echelon of cowboy stars (the second echelon was comprised of such cowboys as Tom Tyler, Bill Cody, Jack Perrin, etc.). This was partially due to his inept acting, but more importantly because his films were made for the independent market. And too, he was bucking the greatest aggregation of talent in the Western genre's history, as there must have been at least 30 active cowboys at the time.

Best remembered of Canutt's films of 1928 is *The Vanishing West*, an early Mascot serial in which he shared top honors with Jack Daugherty, Leo Maloney, Jack Perrin, William Fairbanks, Eileen Sedgwick, Fred Church and Helen Gibson — truly an all-star cast. He was destined to become a permanent fixture at Mascot as actor-stuntman on serials characterized by fast action, novel stories, daring rescues, masked villains, thrills a-plenty and a crisis every minute. Small budgets and high quality somehow became merged in the Mascot serial offerings, due mainly to professionals like Canutt who knew how to get the job done right and on time. Leading men would come and go, but the stock company of players and technicians employed by Nat Levine kept the Mascot product in demand and the little studio survived until, merging with Monogram and Consolidated Film Laboratories, it became Republic Studios in 1935.

Canyon Hawks (National 1930), distributed by Big 4 Film Corporation, was the last starring Western of Canutt and was a sound film. Yakima slipped comfortably into supporting roles and concentrated on doubling for just about everyone in a film that was involved in a scene where a good stunt-man was needed. He also had principal parts in a number of Western features and serials and stunted in even a greater number of films. In features, he doubled just about everyone from Gene Autry to Carleton Young, while at the same time continuing to act before the camera. At Lonestar (a division of Monogram), Yak played principal roles, nearly always as head honcho of the outlaws, in a marvelously entertaining series of oaters that somehow have managed to retain their appeal over the years, in spite of being cheap quickie (three- or four-day) productions. Certainly John Wayne and Yakima were the two ingredients that lent magic to these films, but there was able support by veterans George F. (Gabby) Hayes, Buffalo Bill, Jr. (Jay Wilsey), and Charles King. And not to be overlooked was direction by Robert N. Bradbury, the father of Bob Steele and one of the best directors of low-budget Westerns at the time.

Canutt appeared as actor/stuntman in 19 of the John Wayne Westerns filmed between 1933 and 1937: *The Telegraph Trail, Sagebrush Trail, West of the Divide, Lucky Texan, Blue Steel, The Man from Utah, Randy Rides Alone, The Star Packer, 'Neath the Arizona Skies, Lawless Frontier, Paradise Canyon, The Dawn Rider, Westward Ho, The Lone Trail, New Frontier, Lawless Range, King of the Pecos, Winds of the Wasteland* and *The Oregon Trail.*

Canutt was a dastardly badman and it was pure ecstasy to see Wayne give him his just deserts in the final reel. Little did we know as kids that when we were cheering Wayne in his hair-raising leaps from a balcony onto his horse, in slugfests and in other rough-and-tumble action, that we were cheering Yak dressed as Wayne, who would switch back to his villain clothes in order that we might hiss him and whistle and cheer at his demise in the end.

When Republic began its long-running Three Mesquiteers series in 1937, Yak was often called upon to supply villainy. He again got the chance to work with his pal Wayne in *Wyoming Outlaw, Santa Fe Stampede* and *Overland Stage Riders*, as Wayne temporarily

Rex Lease and Yakima Canutt (right) in *Pals of the Range* (Superior, 1935).

replaced Robert Livingston. Canutt gave solid performances in the Three Mesquiteers sagas *Ghost Town Gold, Roaring Lead, Riders of the Whistling Skull, Hit the Saddle, Gunsmoke Ranch, Range Defenders, Heart of the Rockies, Kansas Terrors* and *Cowboys from Texas.*

Canutt continued to act in various Republic Westerns in the '40s but devoted most of his time to stunting. After suffering a mishap on a Roy Rogers film in 1945, which left him with two broken ankles, Yak began to train other stuntmen and to direct stunting sequences for Republic, gradually reducing his own stunting efforts. At 50, his bones were a little more brittle, his timing a little less exact than when he romped across the prairie in the '20s. He finally became a director at Republic and, when the studio

closed down in the mid–50s, Canutt continued his career as a second unit director at the big studios (Warner Brothers, Walt Disney, MGM, 20th Century-Fox). He earned as much on some films as he did for years of B-Western work.

Yakima Canutt is a fellow whose achievements are both legendary and unbelievable. Yak was one of the most respected men in the film colony, having professionalized the field of stunting. He developed most of the techniques now used universally in the shooting of outdoor action scenes and, with John Wayne as an adept pupil, mastered the technique of staging screen fights that were not only believable, but literally works of art.

In his last few years, Yak attended film festivals and was amazed at his reception. Fans literally mobbed him for autographs and questions. He was awarded a special Oscar in 1966 for helping to create the stuntmen's profession and for developing safety devices used by stuntmen everywhere.

Yakima Canutt died from cardiac arrest on May 24, 1986, at the age of 90 years in the North Hollywood Medical Center.

Serials

1919

Lightning Bryce. National, [15 Chapters] D: Paul Hurst; LP: Jack Hoxie, Ann Little, Paul Hurst, Jill Woodward, Noble Johnson, Yakima Canutt.

1924

The Riddle Rider. Univ., [15 Chapters] D: William Craft; LP: William Desmond, Eileen Sedgwick, Helen Holmes, Claude Payton, Yakima Canutt.

Days of '49. Arrow, [15 Chapters] D: Jacques Jaccard, Jay Marchant; LP: Neva Gerber, Edmund Cobb, Charles Brinley, Wilbur McGaugh.

1926

The Mystery Box. Davis, [10 Chapters] D: Alvin J. Neitz; LP: Ben Wilson, Neva Gerber, Lafe McKee, Robert Walker.

1928

The Vanishing West. Mascot, [10 Chapters] D: Richard Thorpe; LP: Jack Perrin, Eileen Sedgwick, Jack Daugherty, Leo Maloney, Yakima Canutt.

1931

The Lightning Warrior. Mascot, [12 Chapters] D: Armand Schaefer; LP: Rin-Tin-Tin, Frankie Darro, Georgia Hale, George Brent.

Battling with Buffalo Bill. Univ., [12 Chapters] D: Ray Taylor; LP: Tom Tyler, Rex Bell, Lucile Browne, Francis Ford, William Desmond, Yakima Canutt.

The Vanishing Legion. Mascot, [12 Chapters] D: B. Reeves Eason; LP: Harry Carey, Edwina Booth, Rex [horse], Frankie Darro, Philo McCullough.

1932

The Last Frontier. RKO, [12 Chapters] D: Spencer G. Bennet, Thomas L. Story; LP: Creighton Chaney [Lon Chaney, Jr.], Dorothy Gulliver, Mary Jo Desmond, Francis X. Bushman, Jr.

The Last of the Mohicans. Mascot, [12 Chapters] D: B. Reeves Eason, Ford Beebe; LP: Harry Carey, Hobart Bosworth, Frank Coghlan, Jr., Walter Miller.

The Devil Horse. Mascot, [12 Chapters] D: Otto Brower; LP: Harry Carey, Noah Beery, Sr., Frankie Darro, Greta Granstedt, Apache [horse], Al Bridge.

1933

The Wolf Dog. Mascot, [12 Chapters] D: Colbert Clark, Harry Fraser; LP: Frankie Darro, Rin-Tin-Tin, Jr., George J. Lewis, Boots Mallory.

The Three Musketeers. Mascot, [12 Chapters] D: Armand Schaefer, Colbert Clark; LP: Jack Mulhall, Raymond Hatton, Francis X. Bushman, Jr., Ruth Hall, John Wayne, Creighton Chaney [Lon Chaney, Jr.], Hooper Atchley, Robert Frazer.

Fighting with Kit Carson. Mascot, [12 Chapters] D: Armand Schaefer, Colbert Clark; LP: Johnny Mack Brown, Betsy King Ross, Noah Beery, Jr.

1936

The Vigilantes Are Coming. Republic, [12 Chapters] D: Mack V. Wright, Ray Taylor; LP: Robert Livingston, Kay Hughes, "Big Boy" Williams, Raymond Hatton.

The Clutching Hand. S & S, [15 Chapters] D: Albert Herman; LP: Jack Mulhall, Ruth Mix, Marion Shilling, Rex Lease, William Farnum, Yakima Canutt.

The Black Coin. S & S, [15 Chapters] D: Albert Herman; LP: Ralph Graves, Dave O'Brien, Ruth Mix, Constance Bergan, Robert Frazer, Bryant Washburn.

Shadow of Chinatown. Victory, [15 Chapters] D: Robert Hill; LP: Bela Lugosi, Herman Brix [Bruce Bennett], Joan Barclay, Luana Walters, Charles King.

1937

Zorro Rides Again. Rep., [12 Chapters] D: William Witney, John English; LP: John Carroll, Helen Christian, Duncan Renaldo, Noah Beery, Sr. (There is disagreement as to whether Canutt doubled Carroll.)

The Painted Stallion. Rep., [12 Chapters] D: William Witney, Alan James, Ray Taylor; LP: Ray Corrigan, Hoot Gibson, Jack Perrin, Hal Taliaferro [Wally Wales], Julia Thayer, Duncan Renaldo.

S O S Coast Guard. Rep., [12 Chapters] D: William Witney, Alan James; LP: Bela Lugosi, Ralph Byrd, Maxine Doyle, Dick Alexander, George Chesebro.

The Mysterious Pilot. Col., [15 Chapters] D: Spencer G. Bennet; LP: Frank Hawks, Dorothy Sebastian, Rex Lease, Guy Bates Post, Kenneth Harlan, Yakima Canutt.

1938

The Secret of Treasure Island. Col., [15 Chapters] D: Elmer Clifton; LP: Don Terry, Gwen Gaze, Grant Withers, Hobart Bosworth, William Farnum.

The Lone Ranger. Rep., [15 Chapters] D: William Witney, John English; LP: Lee Powell, Chief Thundercloud, Lynne Roberts, Herman Brix, Lane Chandler, Hal Taliaferro, Stanley Andrews, George Cleveland, John Merton, George Letz [Montgomery].

Dick Tracy Returns. Rep., [15 Chapters] D: William Witney, John English; LP: Ralph Byrd, Lynne Roberts, Charles Middleton, Jerry Tucker, David Sharpe.

1939

Daredevils of the Red Circle. Rep., [12 Chapters] D: William Witney, John English; LP: Charles Quigley, Herman Brix, David Sharpe, Carole Landis.

Zorro's Fighting Legion. Rep., [12 Chapters] D: William Witney, John English; LP: Reed Hadley, Sheila Darcy, William Carson, Leander de Cordova.

1940

Mysterious Doctor Satan. Rep., [15 Chapters] D: William Witney, John English; LP: Eduardo Ciannelli, Robert Wilcox, Ella Neal, William Newell.

Deadwood Dick. Col., [15 Chapters] D: James W. Horne; LP: Don Douglas, Lorna Gray [Adrian Booth], Lane Chandler, Marin Sais, Charles King.

1941

White Eagle. Col., [15 Chapters] D: James W. Horne; LP: Buck Jones, Raymond Hatton, Dorothy Fay, James Craven, Jack Ingram, Charles King.

Jungle Girl. Rep., [15 Chapters] D: William Witney, John English; LP: Frances Gifford, Tom Neal, Eddie Acuff, Gerald Mohr, Trevor Bardette.

1942

Perils of Nyoka. Rep., [15 Chapters] D: William Witney; LP: Kay Aldridge, Clayton Moore, William Benedict, Lorna Gray [Adrian Booth], Charles Middleton.

Spy Smasher. Rep., [12 Chapters] D: William Witney; LP: Kane Richmond, Marguerite Chapman, Sam Flint, Hans Schumm, Tris Coffin, Tom Steele, Tom London.

JUNE CAPRICE

June Caprice was born in 1899 in Arlington, Virginia. Her career dated from 1916 when she starred in her film debut, *Caprice of the Mountains*. In the story she is a mountaineer's daughter, forced by her father into a shotgun wedding with a New York playboy. Her husband took her back to New York, where she found life unendurable. She returns to the mountains. Her husband comes to realize that he loves her, hightails it to the mountains and, finding her, promises that they will never go back to New York.

In *Little Miss Happiness* ('16) she pretends to be the mother of a newborn baby born to Zena Keefe, who is having marital difficulties. The reason for the deception is never made crystal clear. Harry Hilliard, June's sweetheart, stands by her, risking the condemnation of the community. All ends well when Zena and husband Leo Kennedy are reconciled and take back the baby. June and Harry wed. *The Ragged Princess* ('16) finds June running away from an orphanage and putting on boys' clothing in order to get work on a farm. Love blossoms with a farmhand and she turns out to be the owner of the farm.

The Mischief Maker ('16) is a comedy-drama in which June is expelled from boarding school after modeling for a sculptor whose nude statue looks like June, who only posed for the head. In *A Modern Cinderella* ('17) she jumps into shark-infested waters to test the sincerity of the man who proposed to her.

Miss U.S.A. ('17) is a war drama in which June captures a spy. In *A Child of the Wild* ('17) June loves a teacher whose sister she mistakes to be his wife. June is a foundling in *Every Girl's Dream* ('17), ending up married to a king. The discovery of a precious jewel in the heel of a shoe in *A Small Town Girl* ('17) propels June into hide-and-seek situations with a band of thieves.

Other features starring June are *Patsy* ('17), *The Sunshine Maid* ('17), *Unknown 274* ('17), *Blue-Eyed Mary* ('18), *The Heart of Romance* ('18), *Miss Innocence* ('18), *A Damsel in Distress* ('19), *The Love Cheat* ('19), *Oh, Boy!* ('19), *In Walked Mary* ('20) and *Rogues and Romance* ('29).

June was the star of every picture she was in, never having to work her way to stardom, and she never became a character actress because she quit while she was still headlining films. She portrayed youthful in-

nocence in the style of Mary Pickford. Her pictures were clean, wholesome fun to watch.

In the serial *The Sky Ranger* ('21), the story hinges on the existence of a powerful light invented by the heroine's father. June portrayed the female lead. Crooks conspire to obtain the light. Weird effects are introduced through the person of a mysterious man who appears in a plane and becomes one of the conspirators. George B. Seitz directed and played the male lead. Frank Leon Smith wrote the story. The film was originally titled *The Man Who Stole the Moon*.

June was married to actor-director Harry Millarde. She died in 1936.

Serial

1921

The Sky Ranger. [15 Chapters] D: George B. Seitz; SP: Frank Leon Smith; P: George B. Seitz; LP: June Caprice, George B. Seitz, Harry Semels, Frank Redman, Joe Cuny, Peggy Shanor, Charles Revada, Spencer G. Bennet, Thomas Goodwin.

HARRY CAREY

Harry Carey was one of the greatest of the great movie cowboys. No less than John Wayne rated him Number One. He was a perennial favorite who made moviegoing such a great adventure decades ago.

Harry did not grow up a cowboy. He was born in the Bronx, New York, on January 16, 1878, the son of a New York City judge. In due time he was attending New York University with the intention of becoming a lawyer, but a severe case of pneumonia forced him to temporarily withdraw from the university. His father sent him to the Montana ranch of a friend to convalesce. Harry whiled away his time during recuperation by writing a play which he called *Montana*.

He was so taken with his writing effort that he decided to put his play on the stage. His father and friends financed the venture. It was successful enough that Harry toured the eastern part of the U.S. for nearly three years (1908–10). All thoughts of a career in law were abandoned; although he did graduate from NYU, he never took the New York bar exam.

A second melodrama from the Carey pen, *The Heart of Alaska*, soon folded. Needing work and now definitely intent on an acting career, he applied for and was accepted by Biograph Studios in New York City and was soon part of the stock company of famed director D. W. Griffith that consisted of Lillian and Dorothy Gish, Mae Marsh, Mary Pickford, Owen Moore, Lionel Barrymore, Blanche Sweet, Henry Walthall and Walter Miller.

Bill Sharkey's Last Game ('11) is reputed to be his first film of importance. A two-reeler, it was filmed on Staten Island. Harry remained active for Griffith for the next several years and went with him when Griffith transferred his operation to the West Coast in 1913.

Carey alternated between Western and melodramas from 1912 to 1915. In 1915 he signed with Universal at $150 a week and was soon cast as a Western lead in two-reelers directed by John Ford. In 1915 Carey starred in 17 of the 20 chapters comprising the serial *Graft*, written by 15 authors, each handling a chapter in their own manner. The next author would take up the story where the previous author had stopped. Hobart Henley starred as the young attorney in the first three chapters but was replaced by Carey.

In 1917, Carey began his series of feature Westerns directed by Ford. They proved a winning combination, making a total of 25 films together, often co-scripting. Some of the titles are *The Secret Man* ('17), *A Marked Man* ('17), *Bucking Broadway* ('17), *Phantom Riders* ('18), *Hell Bent* ('18), *Roped* ('19), *The Outcast of Poker Flats* ('19), *Marked Men* ('19) (Ford's first version of *Three Godfathers*), and *Desperate Trails* ('21).

In most of his Western features he played a character called "Cheyenne Harry," just as G. M. Anderson consistently played the character "Broncho Billy."

Often likened to Will Rogers, Carey had personal charm that somehow struck a responsive chord in his audience and people warmed to him. That wrinkled face, those kindly eyes and the boyishly innocent smile got to people. Too, his characters were always a little more human, more flexible than those of William S. Hart. Last and by no means least, Harry Carey was a better actor than Hart.

When Carey left Universal in 1922, the Western was in a state of flux. Hart's popularity was waning and Tom Mix was rapidly nailing down "King of the Cowboys" honors with his flashy, action-packed flickers. Universal boss Carl Laemmle was so impressed by the reception that Hoot Gibson received by movie patrons that he decided not to re-

Harry Carey (left) and Tom Tyler in *Powdersmoke Range* (RKO, 1935).

hire Carey but put his money into the production of Gibson Westerns. The public seemed to want straightforward, non-realistic, action-packed range dramas, and Fred Thomson and Ken Maynard would soon capture the fancy of Saturday matinee crowds with their acrobatics.

Carey made several Westerns for R-C Pictures (releasing through FBO) in 1922–23, shortly before Fred Thomson became FBO's big moneymaker. In spite of the trend away from realism and strong plots, Harry's Westerns remained unusually popular, more so with adults than with kids. In 1922 he was 44 years old, hardly a young man. Neither was he handsome. But he was a solid performer and his pictures were good, and people — even kids who wanted nothing but fights, riding and stunts—came to love his craggy, weatherbeaten features, the wry grin, the smiling eyes and his taciturn characteri-

zations. His austere visage was ideally suited to Westerns and somehow, even back in the '20s, it was kind of nice to see ladies treated as if they were only a little less divine than angels. Carey always treated his heroines with the greatest of respect, usually loving them in silence, and often riding away, heartbroken from a feeling of unworthiness to make his love known to the fair maiden.

Following the R-C/FBO series, Harry signed with Hunt Stromberg for a series to be released through PDC (Producers' Distributing Corporation). Upon completion of the first series, Carey contracted for and completed a second series of excellent Westerns. Both series have been rated by Western film historians as among the finest Westerns of the period.

Carey left Stromberg after completion of his second series hoping that with a different company, he could overtake Mix,

Thomson, Jones and Gibson in popularity. In 1926 he signed with Pathé, one of the finest producers of silent Westerns, and remained with them until the discontinuance of most Western series in 1928 due to technical problems associated with shooting outdoor sound films.

Harry's last silent Western was MGM's *The Trail of '98*, a non-programmer Western directed by Clarence Brown and featuring Dolores Del Rio. Luckily for Carey, MGM followed up by choosing him to star in their major sound film *Trader Horn*, filmed partly in Africa and considered one of the classics of all time.

Nat Levine of Mascot Pictures, who specialized in serial productions, sought to capitalize on the new popularity of Carey and the publicity generated by *Trader Horn* by hiring Carey for the lead role in *The Vanishing Legion* ('31), which proved to be a popular serial, making several times its cost in revenue.

Carey was contracted for two more serials for 1932, to be paid $10,000 for each. The first was *Last of the Mohicans*, featuring Edwina Booth. Carey played the part of "Hawkeye" in this adaptation of the James

Fenimore Cooper novel. As was characteristic of all Mascot serials, action was maximized, dialogue minimized, and it is generally rated as one of the best of Mascot serials.

The Devil Horse was released in November 1932 by Mascot. Noah Beery and Frankie Darro furnished the principal support for Harry in this slam-bang Western serial. That same year Harry co-starred with Walter Huston in one of the better Westerns of the early '30s, *Law and Order*. Harry's performance as Doc Holliday still stands today as one of the better portrayals of the gambler-dentist-gunfighter.

Cavalier of the West ('31), *Without Honors* ('32), *Night Rider* ('32) and *Border Devils* ('32) were Carey features produced by the Weiss-Artcraft organization.

In 1935 Harry starred in RKO's *Powdersmoke Range*, billed as "The Barnum and Bailey of Westerns" in which Carey had the principal role as Tucson Smith in an all-star cast. Thirteen current or former cowboy stars were featured in the cast. Hoot Gibson was Stony Brooke and "Big Boy" Williams was Lullaby Joslin in this first and best of the Three Mesquiteers films.

In 1936 Carey and Gibson teamed again in RKO's *The Last Outlaw*. It represented Carey at his best. John Ford helped to script the film.

Rustler's Paradise, Wagon Trail, Wild Mustang, Ghost Town, Aces Wild and *Last of the Clintons* were Carey Westerns made in 1935 for the independent market.

In 1938 Harry starred in his last slam-bang shoot-'em-up programmer Western, although it, too, was in the "special" category, certainly no formula film. Carey also co-starred with John Wayne and Betty Field in Paramount's *The Shepherd of the Hills* ('41). This beautifully photographed film contained an excellent performance by Carey as the beloved stranger.

Carey turned character actor in the remainder of his career, turning in good performances in *The Prisoner of Shark Island* ('36), *Kid Galahad* ('37), *Border Cafe* ('37), *Port of Missing Girls* ('38), *Mr. Smith Goes to Washington* ('39), *My Son Is Guilty* ('40),

Parachute Battalion ('41), *Sundown* ('41), *The Spoilers* ('42), *Air Force* ('43), *Happy Land* ('43), *China's Little Devils* ('44), *Duel in the Sun* ('46), *Angel and the Badman* ('47), *Sea of Grass* ('47) and *Red River* ('48).

Harry Carey died on September 21, 1947. Cause of death was cancer of the lungs aggravated by a black widow spider bite. His ashes are in the Carey mausoleum at Woodlawn, New York. Just about all of Hollywood was at his funeral.

Serials

1915

Graft. Univ., [20 Chapters] D: Richard Stanton, George A. Lessey; SP: Walter Woods, Hugh Weir, Joe Brandt; S: *The Crack O' Doom*, a selection of short stories by Zane Grey, Irwin Cobb, Frederick Isham, Nina Wilcox Putnam, James Oppenheim, Louis Joseph Vance, A. M. Williamson, Joe Mitchell Chappie, Leroy Scott, George Bronson Howard, Wallace Irwin, Rupert Hughes, Mrs. Woodrow Wilson, Reginald Wright Kauffman, James Francis Dwyer, Anna Katharine Green; LP: Harry Carey, Robert Henley, Jane Novak, Richard Stanton, Nanine

Wright, Mina Cunard, Eddie Polo, Rex De Rosselli.

1931

The Vanishing Legion. Mascot, [12 Chapters] D: B. Reeves Eason; S: Wyndham Gittens, Ford Beebe, Helmer Bergman; P: Nat Levine; Cam: Benjamin Kline, Ernest Miller; LP: Harry Carey, Edwina Booth, Rex (horse), Frankie Darro, Philo McCullough, William Desmond, Lafe McKee, Pete Morrison.

1932

Last of the Mohicans. Mascot, [12 Chapters] D: B. Reeves Eason, Ford Beebe; SP: Colbert Clark, John Francis Natteford, Ford Beebe, Wyndham Gittens; S: James Fenimore Cooper; P: Nat Levine; Cam: Ernest Miller, Jack Young; LP: Harry Carey, Hobart Bosworth, Frank Coghlan, Jr., Edwina Booth, Lucile Browne, Walter Miller, Robert Kortman.

The Devil Horse. Mascot, [12 Chapters] D: Otto Brower; 2nd Unit D: Yakima Canutt; SP: George Morgan, Barney Sarecky, George Plympton, Wyndham Gittens; P: Nat Levine; Cam: Ernest Miller, Carl Webster, Victor Schurich; LP: Harry Carey, Noah Beery, Sr., Frankie Darro, Greta Granstedt, Apache [horse], Al Bridge, Jack Mower.

JEAN CARMEN/ JULIA THAYER

Jean Carmen (her real name) was born in Portland, Oregon, on April 17 — the year is her secret.

Her one claim to serial immortality is *The Painted Stallion* ('37) in which she plays "The Rider," a mystery figure appearing on horseback at moments when Ray Corrigan, Hoot Gibson or Jack Perrin were in danger. For no apparent reason, she was billed as

Julia Thayer, although in several feature Westerns she was billed as Jean Carmen.

According to Carmen she was in show business nearly all her life, beginning as a child performer at the age of five. She had film work in England, Germany, Switzerland, Mexico and Italy (unverified). As a writer she worked with George S. Kaufman, wrote screenplays with Andrea Scott and wrote and produced with John Croydon, a London producer.

Carmen wrote, produced, directed and starred in *The Pawn*, filmed in Italy with her son Guy in a prominent role. Evidently Jean was married to a man named Dillow at some time, but she does not talk about that.

She was a circus trick rider for one sea-

Jean Carmen in *Kiss and Make Up* (Paramount, 1934).

son, and appeared as a dancer in "Midnight Follies" in London. She claims to have had parts in three British pictures and to have been in Kaufman's *Stage Door*.

Her film credits include *Kiss and Make Up* ('34), *Young and Beautiful* ('34), *Born to Battle* ('35), *The Arizona Gunfighter* ('37), *Gunsmoke Ranch* ('37), *Paroled from the Big House* ('38), *Wolves of the Sea* ('38), *The Sunset Strip Case* ('38), *Crashing Thru* ('39), *Four Girls in White* ('38) and *In Old Montana* ('39).

Jean Carmen was effective enough in her Westerns, but she preferred non–Westerns. She will be remembered, however, for the sagebrush sagas she made in the years 1935–39 and for the mystery girl rider she portrayed in *The Painted Stallion*.

Serial

1937

The Painted Stallion. Rep., [12 Chapters] D: William Witney, Alan James, Ray Taylor; SP: Barry Shipman, Winston Miller; AP: J. Laurence Wickland; LP: Ray Corrigan, Hoot Gibson, Jack Perrin, LeRoy Mason, Duncan Renaldo, Sammy McKim, Hal Taliaferro.

LEO CARRILLO

Los Angeles, California, was the birthplace of Leo Carrillo, the man who would become known as "Mr. California." The date was August 6, 1880.

Serial addicts will have no trouble in naming the one serial Leo acted in — Universal's highly touted million-dollar super serial *Riders of Death Valley* ('41) starring Dick Foran, Buck Jones, Charles Bickford and Leo. Comedy was supplied by Leo as

"Pancho" and "Big Boy" Williams as "Borax Bill." The "Riders" were a band of vigilantes organized to protect the miners against raiders. The Riders set out to break up a fake protection league that is trying to gain control of the big mining claims. His character Pancho would again be used by Carrillo as he played Pancho, the sidekick of TV's *Cisco Kid*.

A graduate of St. Vincent of Loyola,

Carrillo was a newsman and cartoonist before becoming a dialect comedian in vaudeville (experience which served him well in his movie/TV roles). He was on the legitimate stage before entering movies around 1929. He also toured with stock companies.

At first a male lead, Leo later provided comedy as an amiable Latin. A few of his many movies are *Lasca of the Rio Grande* ('31), *Girl of the Rio* ('32), *Viva Villa* ('34), *The Gay Desperado* ('36), *The Girl and the Gambler* ('39), *Twenty-Mule Team* ('40), *Lillian Russell* ('40), *Wyoming* ('40) *Sin Town* ('41), *Barnacle Bill* ('41), *Horror Island* ('41), *American Empire* ('42), *Gypsy Wildcat* ('44), *Mexicana* ('45), *Crime Incorporated* ('45), *The Fugitive* ('47) and *The Girl from San Lorenzo* ('50).

Carrillo became known as "Mr. California" as he traveled the world as the state's official ambassador of good will. For a number of years he served as the Grand Marshal of the annual Rose Parade in Pasadena. His civic activities included serving on the California Beaches and Parks Commission. He helped to bring about the Los Angeles Olivera Street Complex, the Los Angeles Arboretum and the Anza-Borrego Desert State Park. He also helped the State of California acquire the Hearst Castle at San Simeon. He was a friend of William Randolph Hearst and his family.

Carrillo's death came in 1961 at the Mexican style ranch house in Santa Monica where he lived with his daughter. Cause of death was cancer.

Serial

1941

Riders of Death Valley. Univ., [15 Chapters] D: Ray Taylor, Ford Beebe; SP: Sherman Lowe, Basil Dickey, George Plympton, Jack Connell; S: Oliver Drake; P: Henry MacRae; LP: Dick Foran, Buck Jones, Charles Bickford, Leo Carrillo, "Big Boy" Williams, Lon Chaney, Jr., Jeanne Kelly [Jean Brooks].

JOHN CARROLL

In *Zorro Rides Again* '37), John Carroll played James Vega, supposedly a spineless, rich wastrel. But as Zorro he comes to the aid of the California-Yucatan Railroad when it is threatened by a gang of outlaws ostensibly headed by El Lobo (Dick Alexander), but secretly masterminded by Marsden (Noah Beery), to outward appearances an upstanding citizen.

Much of the action content involving Zorro featured a stuntman behind the mask. However, Carroll was an inimitable actor deserving of the kudos he received by serial aficionados.

Carroll was well known in Hollywood as a boisterous, loquacious young man who bluffed his way into an RKO contract and whose panache was outlandish and eyebrow-raising. Though he was considered talentless in some quarters, he proved he could act in *Only Angels Have Wings* ('39) and *A Letter for Evie* ('45). Other credits include *Wyoming* ('47), *The Fabulous Texan* ('47), *Fiesta* ('47), *Belle Le Grande* ('51), *The Farmer Takes a Wife* ('53) and *Decision at Sundown* ('57). Considered by some to be Carroll's worst picture was Monogram's *Rose of the Rio Grande* ('38) in which he co-starred with Movita.

Carroll lived high, wide and handsome, but lucky for him he had bought 800 San Fernando Valley acres in the old days when land

Leo Carrillo and Jeanne Kelly (Jean Brooks) in *Riders of Death Valley* (Universal, 1941).

was cheap. When the land boom came to the Valley in the '50s he became a millionaire through manipulation and speculation in real estate. He retired to Bayway Isles in St. Petersburg with his wife Lucille Ryman, formerly Head of Talent at MGM. Retirement soon palled. Fishing and golf weren't enough. He built a shrimp boat and a thriving business in shrimping. Other business ventures followed.

Fate took him back into the movie business as a producer. His first film production was *Ride in a Pink Car*; others followed.

John Carroll's real name was Julian Lafay. He was born in New Orleans on July 17, 1905. He ran away from home in his early teens and after a number of jobs—steel worker, merchant seaman, etc.—he wound up in Hollywood as a stuntman in the early '30s.

Carroll died from leukemia at age 71 in Hollywood.

Serial

1937

Zorro Rides Again. Rep., [12 Chapters] D: William Witney, John English; SP: Barry Shipman, John Rathmell, Franklyn Adreon, Ronald Davidson, Morgan B. Cox; AP: Sol C. Siegel; LP: John Carroll, Helen Christian, Reed Howes, Richard Alexander, Noah Beery, Robert Kortman, Tom London, Roger Williams.

VIRGINIA CARROLL

She did the best she could with the hand fate dealt her. She might be found second or third in a cast listing, or she might not be listed at all. Such was the range of her parts.

Virginia Elizabeth Carroll was born in Los Angeles on December 2, 1913. She was working as a model at a department store when she was spotted by an RKO scout and signed at $75 a week. Her first role, an uncredited one, was as a sports model in *Roberta* ('35) starring Ginger Rogers, Irene Dunne and Fred Astaire. Next came *George White's 1935 Scandals* with Alice Faye, Jimmy Durante and a whole host of known players. Virginia was uncredited as a dancer.

Virginia had the femme lead in *A Tenderfoot Goes West* ('36, Jack LaRue); *Oklahoma Terror* ('39, Jack Randall); *The Phantom Cowboy* ('41, Donald Barry); *Prairie Gunsmoke* ('42, Bill Elliott, Tex Ritter); *Raiders of the West* ('42, Lee Powell, Art Davis, Bill Boyd); and *Triggerman* ('47, Johnny Mack Brown). She had supporting roles in many others.

Virginia had small roles in *The Toast of New York* ('37, Cary Grant); *Waterloo Bridge* ('40, Vivien Leigh); *Pot o' Gold* ('41, James Stewart); *Lake Placid Serenade* ('44, Vera Hruba Ralston); *So Goes My Love* ('46, Myrna Loy); *Smash Up — the Story of a Woman* ('47, Susan Hayward) and *That's My Gal* ('47, Lynne Roberts).

Virginia met Ralph Byrd in 1935 at a little theater in Beverly Hills, where they were doing a play together. They wed in 1936. Their daughter, Carroll, was born in 1940.

Virginia appeared in seven serials, though not in a leading role. In *Dick Tracy* ('38) she was a stewardess; *Mysterious Doctor Satan* ('40), a nurse; *G-Men vs. the Black Dragon* ('43), a nurse; *The Crimson Ghost* ('46), a nurse; *Daughter of Don Q* ('46), "Rosa Peralta"; *The Black Widow* ('47), "Ann Curry"; and *Superman* ('48), "Mrs. Kent."

In *Prairie Gunsmoke* (Columbia, 1942).

Byrd died in 1952 from cancer at the Veterans Hospital in Sawtell, California. It has been erroneously reported that he died from a heart attack while waiting in a car for his wife to finish grocery shopping. That is quite a twist on the truth!

From 1957 until his death in 1969 (also from cancer), Virginia was married to Lloyd McLean, a cameraman at 20th Century-Fox.

Serials

1938

Dick Tracy Returns. Rep., [15 Chapters] D: William Witney, John English; LP: Ralph Byrd,

Lynne Roberts, Charles Middleton, Jerry Tucker, Lee Ford, Tom Steele, John Merton, Virginia Carroll.

1940

Mysterious Doctor Satan. Rep., [15 Chapters] D: William Witney, John English; LP: Eduardo Ciannelli, Robert Wilcox, Ella Neal, William Newell, C. Montague Shaw, Jack Mulhall, Virginia Carroll.

1943

G-Men vs. the Black Dragon. Rep., [15 Chapters] D: William Witney; LP: Rod Cameron, Constance Worth, Roland Got, Nino Pipitone, George J. Lewis, Maxine Doyle, Hooper Atchley, Virginia Carroll.

1946

The Crimson Ghost. Rep., [12 Chapters] D: William Witney, Fred C. Brannon; LP: Charles Quigley, Linda Stirling, Clayton Moore, I. Stanford Jolley, Kenne Duncan, Forrest Taylor, Virginia Carroll, Sam Flint, Rex Lease.

Daughter of Don Q. Rep., [12 Chapters] D: Spencer G. Bennet, Fred C. Brannon; LP: Kirk Alyn, Adrian Booth, LeRoy Mason, Roy Barcroft, Claire Meade, Kernan Cripps.

1947

The Black Widow. Rep., [13 Chapters] D: Spencer G. Bennet, Fred C. Brannon; LP: Carol Forman, Bruce Edwards, Virginia Lindley, Anthony Warde, I. Stanford Jolley, Virginia Carroll, Tom Steele.

1948

Superman. Col., [15 Chapters] D: Spencer G. Bennet, Thomas Carr; LP: Kirk Alyn, Noel Neill, Tommy Bond, Pierre Watkin, Carol Forman, Jack Ingram, Charles King, Charles Quigley, Virginia Carroll.

HARRY CARTER

The author has found no biographical information on Harry Carter, which is surprising since he starred or was featured in several serials and was quite active in feature films.

Carter successfully menaced Ella Hall in *The Master Key* ('14), the earliest credit found for him. He went on to play heroes and heavies in the early silent days.

In *The Gray Ghost* ('17), Carter played the title role of a master criminal given over to the planning and execution of the wholesale looting of a jewelry house in broad daylight. It took 16 chapters to bring this audacious thief and his gang to justice.

Serials

1914

The Master Key. Univ., [15 Chapters] D: Robert Leonard; SP: Colder Johnson; S: John Fleming Wilson; Spv.: Otis Turner; LP: Robert Leonard, Ella Hall, Harry Carter, Jean Hathaway, Alfred Hickman, Wilbur Higby.

1915

The New Adventures of Terrance O'Rourke. Univ., [3 Chapters] D: Jacques Jaccard, J. Warren Kerrigan; SP: Walter Woods, McGrew Willis; S: Louis Joseph Vance; LP: J. Warren Kerrigan, Lois Wilson, Harry Carter, Maude George.

1917

The Gray Ghost. Univ., [16 Chapters] D/SP:

Stuart Paton; S: Arthur Somers Roche; LP: Harry carter, Priscilla Dean, Emory Johnson, Eddie Polo.

1918

Lure of the Circus. Univ., [18 Chapters] D: J. P. McGowan; S: William Wing; SP: Hope Loring; LP: Eddie Polo, Eileen Sedgwick, Harry Carter, Molly Malone.

1920

The Fatal Sign. Arrow, [15 Chapters] D: Stuart Paton; SP: Bertram Millhauser; LP: Claire Anderson, Harry Carter, Leo Maloney, Joseph Girard, Boyd Irwin.

1921

The Hope Diamond Mystery. Kosmik, [15 Chapters] D: Stuart Paton; SP: Charles Goddard, John B. Clymer; P: George Kleine; Cam: William Thornley; LP: Harry Carter, Grace Darmond, George Chesebro, Boris Karloff, Carmen Phillips.

1923

The Steel Trail. Univ., [15 Chapters] D: William Duncan; S/SP: George Plympton, Karl Coolidge, Paul M. Bryan; LP: William Duncan, Edith Johnson, Harry Carter, Harry Woods, Ralph McCullough, John Cossar, Albert J. Smith.

1924

The Fast Express. Univ., [15 Chapters] D: William Duncan; LP: William Duncan, Edith Johnson, Edward Cecil, Eva Gorden, Harry Carter (bit).

EDWARD CASSIDY

Edward Cassidy played in 210 feature films and 19 serials from 1935 through 1956. He usually played villains but sometimes played sheriffs, ranchers, bankers or other sterling characters. Only about 16 percent of his features were non–Westerns.

Cassidy was not the dog heavy who participates in an impromptu brouhaha at the drop of an insult; rather, he was usually a smooth-talking fourflusher attempting to get what he wanted through deception.

Serials

1936

Robinson Crusoe of Clipper Island. Rep., [14 Chapters] D: Mack V. Wright, Ray Taylor; LP: Ray Mala, Rex (horse), Buck (dog), Mamo Clark, Herbert Rawlinson.

1937

S O S Coast Guard. Rep., [12 Chapters] D: William Witney, Alan James; LP: Ralph Byrd, Bela Lugosi, Maxine Doyle, Dick Alexander, George Chesebro.

1938

Flaming Frontiers. Univ., [15 Chapters] D: Ray Taylor, Alan James; LP: Johnny Mack Brown, Eleanor Hansen, Ralph Bowman [John Archer], Charles Middleton.

The Secret of Treasure Island. Col., [15 Chapters] D: Elmer Clifton; LP: Don Terry, Gwen Gaze, Grant Withers, Hobart Bosworth, William Farnum, Walter Miller.

The Fighting Devil Dogs. Rep., [12 Chapters] D: William Witney, John English; LP: Lee Powell, Herman Brix [Bruce Bennett], Eleanor Stewart, Forrest Taylor, John Picorri, Carleton Young.

Edward Cassidy (left), Tex Ritter and Hank Worden in *Hittin' the Trail* (Grand National, 1937).

1939

The Green Hornet. Univ., [13 Chapters] D: Ford Beebe, Ray Taylor; LP: Gordon Jones, Anne Nagel, Keye Luke, Wade Boteler, Philip Trent.

Dick Tracy's G-Men. Rep., [15 Chapters] D: William Witney, John English; LP: Ralph Byrd, Irving Pichel, Phylis Isley [Jennifer Jones], Ted Pearson, Walter Miller.

1940

Winners of the West. Univ., [13 Chapters] D: Ford Beebe, Ray Taylor; LP: Dick Foran, Anne Nagel, James Craig, Tom Fadden, Harry Woods, Charles Stevens.

Deadwood Dick. Col., [15 chapters] D: James W. Horne; LP: Don Douglas, Lorna Gray, Lane chandler, Harry Harvey, Charles King, Edward Cassidy.

Mysterious Doctor Satan. Rep., [15 Chapters] D: William Witney, John English; LP: Eduardo Ciannelli, Robert Wilcox, Ella Neal, William Newell, Jack Mulhall.

Adventures of Red Ryder. Rep., [12 Chapters] D: William Witney, John english; Donald Barry, Noah Beery, Sr., Noah Beery, Jr., Vivian Coe, Hal Taliaferro, Harry Worth, William Farnum, Robert Kortman, Carleton Young.

1941

King of the Texas Rangers. Rep., [12 Chapters] D: William Witney, John English; LP: Slingin' Sammy Baugh, Neil Hamilton, Pauline Moore, Duncan Renaldo, Herbert Rawlinson, Charles Trowbridge, Stanley Blystone, Kermit Maynard, Roy Barcroft.

Adventures of Captain Marvel. Rep., [12 Chapters] D: William Witney, John English; LP: Tom Tyler, Louise Currie, Frank Coghlan, Jr., Billy Benedict, Robert Strange, Harry Worth, Bryant Washburn, John Davidson, Jack Mulhall.

1943

Daredevils of the West. Rep., [12 Chapters] D: John English; LP: Allan Lane, Kay Aldridge, Eddie Acuff, William Haade, Robert Frazer, Ted Adams.

1944

Captain America. Rep., [15 Chapters] D: John English, Elmer Clifton; LP: Dick Purcell, Lorna Gray, Lionel Atwill, Charles Trowbridge, Russell Hicks.

1945

Manhunt of Mystery Island. Rep., [15 Chapters] D: Spencer Bennet, Yakima Canutt, Wallace A. Grissell; LP: Linda Stirling, Roy Barcroft, Richard Bailey, Kenneth Duncan, Forrest Taylor.

1947

Jesse James Rides Again. Rep., [13 Chapters] D: Fred C. Brannon, Thomas Carr; LP: Clayton Moore, Linda Stirling, Roy Barcroft, John Compton, Tristram Coffin, Tom London, Edmund Cobb.

Son of Zorro. Rep., [13 Chapters] D: Spencer Bennet, Fred C. Brannon; LP: George Turner, Peggy Stewart, Roy Barcroft, Edward Cassidy, Ernie Adams, Stanley Price.

1948

Superman. Col., [15 Chapters] D: Spencer Bennet, Thomas Carr; LP: Kirk Alyn, Noel Neill, Tommy Bond, Pierre Watkin, Carol Forman.

LANE CHANDLER

Lane Chandler — a familiar face, an unknown name — was born Robert C. Oakes on June 4, 1899. His Certificate of Death, filed with the California Department of Public Health, states that he was born in South Dakota, though most sources give Walsh County, North Dakota, as the place of birth.

His father raised horses, and the family later moved to Montana. From there Chandler made his way to Los Angeles, but only after enduring numerous hardships. He drove a freight-carrying wagon in the Yellowstone region, worked as a ranger in the park, had numerous menial jobs, and once in Los Angeles worked as a mechanic in a garage while spending his off-duty hours trying to get a foot inside a studio door. Ultimately he was successful and was signed by Paramount as a contract player. Thinking that he had the potential of being an important star, the studio briefly billed him equally with Gary Cooper, who was just getting his start in pictures.

Chandler's first lead was in *Open Range* ('27), based on a story by Zane Grey. The leading lady, Betty Bronson, had achieved stardom as *Peter Pan* in 1924. Villainy was in the capable hands of Fred Kohler.

Following *Open Range*, Paramount cast him opposite two of its biggest stars, Esther Ralston (*Love and Learn*) and Clara Bow (*Red Hair*). He had good roles in *Legion of the Condemned* ('28) and *The First Kiss* ('28), both of which starred Gary Cooper, a friend with whom Chandler would work often in the coming years. He appeared to good advantage in *The Big Killing* ('28) starring Wallace Beery and Raymond Hatton. Another good film for Chandler was *The Studio Murder Mystery* ('29) with Fredric March and Doris Hill.

During an economy move, Chandler was dropped by Paramount, as the studio had too many leading men.

Chandler made one film at MGM with Greta Garbo, *The Single Standard* ('29),

Left to right: **Hal Taliaferro (Wally Wales), Herman Brix (Bruce Bennett), George Letz (George Montgomery), Chief Thundercloud (in back), Lyn Roberts, Lane Chandler and Lee Powell in *The Lone Ranger* (Republic, 1938).**

which also featured Johnny Mack Brown. At Warner Brothers he had the male lead in *Rough Waters* ('30), a vehicle for the great canine star, Rin-Tin-Tin. Lane's only starring serial, *The Lightning Express* ('30), co-starred Louise Lorraine, Greta Granstedt and Al Ferguson.

Chandler starred in two cheaply made Westerns for independent producers, *Beyond the Law* ('30) and *Firebrand Jordan* ('30). In 1931 he began an association with producer Willis Kent that resulted in his starring in eight low-budget Westerns: *The Hurricane Horseman* ('31), *The Reckless Rider* ('31), *The Cheyenne Cyclone* ('32), *Wyoming Whirlwind* ('32), *Texas Tornado* ('34), *Battling Buckaroo* ('34), *Lawless Valley* ('35), and *Guns for Hire* ('35).

In 1939 he received top billing for the last time when he appeared as Davy Crockett in *Heroes of the Alamo*, a Sunset produc-

tion that was later picked up by Columbia for national release.

Chandler became an excellent character actor and played supporting roles in many features ranging from Poverty Row to the major studios. Cecil B. DeMille liked him and used him in ten major productions.

Of his many serial appearances, fans remember him best for *The Lone Ranger* ('38) in which he played "Dick Forrest," one of the five men suspected of being the Ranger.

Over the years he supported John Wayne, Rex Bell, Bob Allen, Harry Carey, Ray Corrigan, Roy Rogers, William Boyd, Charles Starrett, Jack Hoxie, Buster Crabbe, Joel McCrea, Rod Cameron, Tim Holt, Gene Autry, Jack Perrin, Jack Holt and others.

A few of the major productions in which he appeared as a supporting player were *Wells Fargo* ('37), *Angels with Dirty Faces* ('38), *Too Hot to Handle* ('38), *Jezebel*

Lane Chandler and Raven in *Lawless Valley* (Kent, 1932).

('38, *North West Mounted Police* ('40), *I Wanted Wings* ('41), *Sergeant York* ('41), *The Pride of the Yankees* ('42), *Reap the Wild Wind* ('42), *The Story of Dr. Wassell* ('44), *Casanova Brown* ('44), *Duel in the Sun* ('46), *Unconquered* ('47), *Red River* ('48), *Samson and Delilah* ('49) and *The Greatest Show on Earth* ('52).

Lane Chandler may not have been a star but he endeared himself to action fans for his many contributions to such film fare.

Serials

1930

The Lightning Express. Univ., [10 Chapters] D: Henry MacRae; LP: Lane Chandler, Louise Lorraine, Greta Granstedt, Al Ferguson, J. Gordon Russell, John Oscar.

1932

The Devil Horse. Mascot, [12 Chapters] D: Yakima Canutt; LP: Harry Carey, Noah Beery, Sr., Frankie Darro, Greta Granstedt, Apache (horse).

1933

The Wolf Dog. Mascot, [12 Chapters] D: Colbert Clark, Harry Fraser; LP: Frankie Darro, Rin-Tin-Tin, Jr., George J. Lewis, Boots Mallory, Henry B. Walthall.

Fighting with Kit Carson. Mascot, [12 Chapters] D: Armand Schaefer, Colbert Clark; LP: Johnny Mack Brown, Betsy King Ross, Noah Beery, Sr., Noah Beery, Jr., Tully Marshall.

1936

Undersea Kingdom. Rep., [12 Chapters] D: B. Reeves Eason, Joseph Kane; LP: Ray Corrigan,

Lois Wilde, Monte Blue, William Farnum, Lee Van Atta, Raymond Hatton.

The Black Coin. Stage & Screen, [15 Chapters] D: Albert Herman; LP: Ralph Graves, Dave O'Brien, Ruth Mix, Constance Bergen, Matthew Betz, Clara Kimball Young.

1938

Flash Gordon's Trip to Mars. Univ., [15 Chapters] D: Ford Beebe, Robert Hill; LP: Buster Crabbe, Jean Rogers, Charles Middleton, Frank Shannon, Beatrice Roberts.

The Spider's Web. Col., [15 Chapters] D: Ray Taylor, James W. Horne; LP: Warren Hull, Iris Meredith, Richard Fiske, Kenne Duncan, Forbes Murray.

The Lone Ranger. Rep., [15 Chapters] D: William Witney, John English; LP: Lee Powell, Chief Thundercloud, Lynne Roberts, Herman Brix, Lane Chandler, Hal Taliaferro, George Letz [Montgomery], William Farnum, Stanley Andrews, John Merton.

Red Barry. Univ., [13 Chapters] D: Ford Beebe, Alan James; LP: Buster Crabbe, Frances Robinson, Wade Boteler, Philip Ahn, Edna Sedgwick.

Hawk of the Wilderness. Rep., [12 Chapters] D: William Witney, John English; LP: Herman Brix, Ray Mala, Monte Blue, Jill Martin, Noble Johnson, William Royle.

1939

The Green Hornet. Univ., [13 Chapters] D: Ford Beebe, Ray Taylor; LP: Gordon Jones, Anne Nagel, Keye Luke, Wade Boteler, Philip Trent.

1940

Junior G-Men. Univ., [12 Chapters] D: Ford Beebe, John Rawlins; LP: Billy Halop, Huntz Hall, Gabriel Dell, Bernard Punsley, Philip Terry, Roger Daniele.

Flash Gordon Conquers the Universe. Univ., [12 Chapters] D: Ford Beebe, Ray Taylor; LP: Buster Crabbe, Carol Hughes, Charles Middleton, Anne Gwynne, Frank Shannon.

Deadwood Dick. Col., [15 Chapters] D: James W. Horne; LP: Don Douglas, Lorna Gray, Lane Chandler, Marin Sais, Harry Harvey, Jack Ingram, Charles King.

1941

The Spider Returns. Col., [15 Chapters] D: James W. Horne; LP: Warren Hull, Mary Ainslee, Kenne Duncan, Dave O'Brien, Joe Girard, Corbit Harris.

Don Winslow of the Navy. Univ., [12 Chapters] D: Ford Beebe, Ray Taylor; LP: Don Terry, Walter Sande, Wade Boteler, John Litel, Anne Nagel, Claire Dodd.

1942

The Valley of Vanishing Men. Col., [15 Chapters] D: Spencer G. Bennet; LP: Bill Elliott, Slim Summerville, Jack Ingram, Kenneth MacDonald, Carmen Morales.

1945

Manhunt of Mystery Island. Rep., [15 Chapters] D: Spencer G. Bennet, Yakima Canutt, Wallace Grissell; LP: Linda Stirling, Roy Barcroft, Richard Bailey, Kenne Duncan, Forrest Taylor.

The Royal Mounted Rides Again. Univ., [13 Chapters] D: Ray Taylor, Lewis D. Collins; LP: George Dolenz, Bill Kennedy, Duan Kennedy, Paul E. Burns, Milburn Stone.

LON CHANEY, JR.

Creighton Tull Chaney was said to have been stillborn on February 10, 1906, near Oklahoma City and was made to breathe after being dunked in the icy waters of a lake outside the cabin where he was born.

When his parents separated, young

Creighton went with his father who at that time was appearing in vaudeville. In 1913 the senior Chaney was able to join Universal and Creighton was able to attend Hollywood High School. Since Senior did not want his son to follow in his footsteps, Creighton attended trade school after graduation from high school and became a plumber. He was married in 1928 and the couple had two sons, Lon and Ronald.

Lon Chaney, Sr., died in 1930 and, when the Depression overtook the country, Creighton, forgetting the plumbing trade, was able to become a contract player at RKO Radio Pictures in 1932. Lon was 24 when his dad died and at that time had already gained an enviable reputation in the field of amateur athletics as a wrestler, tennis buff and swimmer. He received roles on the value of his physical capabilities rather than his acting skills. He had a small role in Mascot's *The Galloping Ghost* ('31) starring Red Grange. At RKO his first role was as a supporting actor in *Bird of Paradise* ('32), a South Seas melodrama starring Joel McCrea and Dolores Del Rio.

His next film was as star of the serial *The Last Frontier* ('32), the only serial ever released by RKO Radio. Lon was being billed as Creighton Chaney. Basically a Zorro figure, Tom Kirby (Chaney) effects the Black Ghost disguise with a Mexican accent, a mustache, pointed and slanted sideburns, a head bandanna and a mask. It would be ten years before he again had the starring role in a serial but from 1932 to 1942 he had supporting roles in the chapterplays *The Three Muskeeters* ('33), *Undersea Kingdom* ('36), *Ace Drummond* ('36), *Secret Agent X-9* ('37) and *Riders of Death Valley* ('41) before taking on the starring role in Universal's *Overland Mail* ('42).

His non-starring serial characters were usually nefarious ones, for his tall, rugged physique, brutish, offbeat handsomeness and somewhat harsh voice made him a better menace than hero.

At RKO he appeared in *Lucky Devils* ('32), *Scarlet River* ('33) and *Son of the Border* ('34). He continued his somewhat stilted

Lon Chaney, Jr., in *Too Many Blondes* (Universal, 1941).

career as villain-gangster sidekick in films such as *The Shadow of Silk Lennox* ('35) and *Scream in the Night* ('35) and in 1935 he was billed as Lon Chaney, Jr.

In 1937, Chaney began a long association with 20th Century-Fox, appearing in 30 films spread over two years. His big break came in 1939 when he co-starred with Burgess Meredith in John Steinbeck's *Of Mice and Men*. He received critical acclaim for his performance as the dim-witted, lumbering Lennie, his portrayal packed with strength, dignity and pathos.

Lon gave a most dramatic performance as Akhoba, the scarred warrior leader of the rock people in *One Million B.C.* (1940). Following its success, Universal signed him to a long-term contract. *Man Made Monster* ('41) was his first of many horror films. He plays a carnival worker who withstands a huge amount of electricity in a bus accident. After a few more films, Lon was cast as Lawrence Talbot in *The Wolf Man* ('41), a box office hit that catapulted him into a place among the studio's most popular stars. Horror films became his forte. In *Frankenstein Meets the Wolf Man* ('43) he reprised the role of the hairy creature, as he did in *House of Frankenstein* (1944), *House of Dracula* ('45) and *Abbott and Costello Meet Frankenstein* ('48).

In *Son of Dracula* ('43) he was a Lugosi-inspired Count Alucard. *The Mummy's Ghost* ('44) and *The Mummy's Curse* ('44) were popular enough but his portrayals never properly utilized his acting skills and lacked the depth found in the Lennie character. Lon was often saddled with Lennie-type roles.

In 1943, Lon began the somewhat dubious series based on the Inner Sanctum radio show, appearing as both hero and villain as the series progressed. The series consisted of *Calling Dr. Death* ('43), *Dead Man's Eyes* ('44), *Weird Woman* ('44), *Strange Confession* ('45), *The Frozen Ghost* ('45) and *Pillow of Death* ('45). In this low-budget but highly profitable series, Chaney was cast in other than monster roles.

In his later years, Lon drifted into productions with minimal budgets and results. His later films included *Captain China* ('49), *The Bushwackers* ('51), *Only the Valiant* ('51), *High Noon* ('52), *The Black Castle* ('52), *Jivaro* ('54), *Casanova's Big Night* ('54), *Manfish* ('56), *The Black Sleep* ('56), *Indestructible Man* ('56), *Pardners* ('56), *Cyclops* ('57), *The Defiant Ones* ('58), *Money, Women and Guns* ('58), *The Alligator People* ('59), *Rebellion in Cuba* ('61), *The Haunted Palace* ('63), *Law of the Lawless* ('64), *Stage to Thunder Rock* ('64), *Black Spurs* ('65), *Town Tamer* ('65), *Johnny Reno* ('66), *Apache Uprising* ('66), *Dr. Terror's Gallery of Horrors* ('66), *Welcome to Hard Times* ('67), *Buckskin* ('68), and *The Female Bunch* ('71).

He was also a regular on two TV series. Chaney was an alcoholic and suffered from throat cancer. He was planning to return to films as well as go on a stage tour, but he fell ill and, after days of what his friends called "agony," finally died on July 12, 1973.

Serials

1931

The Galloping Ghost. Mascot, [12 Chapters] D: B. Reeves Eason; LP: Harold (Red) Grange, Dorothy Gulliver, Walter Miller, Gwen Lee, Francis X. Bushman, Jr.

1932

The Last Frontier. RKO, [12 Chapters] D: Spencer G. Bennet, Thomas L. Storey; SP: George Plympton, Robert F. Hill; S: Courtney Riley Cooper; Spv: Fred J. McConnell; LP: Creighton [Lon] Chaney, Dorothy Gulliver, Francis X. Bushman, Jr., Mary Jo Desmond, Joe Bonomo, William Desmond, LeRoy Mason, Yakima Canutt, Judith Barrie, Slim Cole.

1933

The Three Musketeers. Mascot, [12 Chapters] D: Armand Schaefer, Colbert Clark; SP: Norman Hall, Colbert Clark, Ben Cohn, Wyndham Gittens; P: Nat Levine; Cam: Ernest Miller, Tom Galligan; Mus: Lee Zahler; LP: Jack Mulhall, Raymond Hatton, Francis X. Bushman, Jr., John Wayne, Ruth Hall, Creighton [Lon] Chaney.

1936

Ace Drummond. Univ., [13 Chapters] D: Ford Beebe, Cliff Smith; LP: John King, Jean Rogers, Noah Beery, Jr., Guy Bates Post, Arthur Loft, Creighton [Lon] Chaney.

Undersea Kingdom. Rep., [12 Chapters] D: B. Reeves Eason, Joseph Kane; SP: John Rathmall, Maurice Geraghty, Oliver Drake; S: Tracy Knight, John Rathmell; Spv.: Barney Sarecky; Cam: William Nobles, Edgar Lyons; Mus: Harry Grey; P: Nat Levine; LP: Ray Corrigan, Lois Wilde, Monte Blue, William Farnum, Lee Van Atta, Raymond Hatton, Lon Chaney, Jr., Smiley Burnette.

1937

Secret Agent X-9. Univ., [12 Chapters] D: Ford Beebe, Cliff Smith; SP: Wyndham Gittens, Norman S. Hall, Ray Trampe, Leslie Charteris; AP: Henry MacRae; LP: Scott Kolk, Jean Rogers, Henry Hunter, David Oliver, Lon Chaney, Jr., Larry Blake.

1941

Riders of Death Valley. Univ., [15 Chapters] D: Ray Taylor, Ford Beebe; S: Oliver Drake; SP: Sherman Lowe, Basil Dickey, George Plympton, Jack Connell; P: Henry MacRae; Cam: Jerome Ash, William Sickner; Mus: Charles Previn; LP: Dick Foran, Buck Jones, Charles Bickford, Jeanne Kelly [Jean Brooks], Monte Blue, Lon Chaney, Jr., Glenn Strange.

1942

Overland Mail. Univ., [15 Chapters] D: Ford Beebe, John Rawlins; S: Johnston McCulley; SP: Paul Huston; P: Henry MacRae; LP: Lon Chaney, Jr., Don Terry, Noah Beery, Jr., Helen Parrish, Tom Chatterton, Bob Baker.

MARGUERITE CHAPMAN

Marguerite Chapman was born on March 9, 1920, in Chatham, New York. She began her working career not as an actress, but as a typist and switchboard operator in White Plains, New York. She also worked as a dental assistant and in a department store. Her dreams of becoming a movie star became a reality soon after the day she was selected as a John Powers model. She graced the covers of various magazines, catching the attention of a Warner Brothers talent scout who invited her to be in movies.

Her first role was not in a Warner Brothers film but in the 20th Century-Fox film *On Their Own* ('40), the last of the popular Jones family series. Another Fox release was *Charlie Chan at the Wax Museum* ('40). She appeared in RKO's *A Girl, a Guy, and a Gob* ('41). Then came three Warner Bros. films. *Navy Blues* ('41) was the first and it featured the Navy Blues Sextette, of which Marguerite was a member. The Sextette went on an extensive promotional tour beginning in Honolulu and ending in New York City. The Sextette was also featured in *You're in the Army Now* ('42). Her third Warners' film was *The Body Disappears* ('41).

It was in 1942 that Marguerite went to Republic to play in the serial *Spy Smasher* as the sweetheart of the hero, Kane Richmond.

Columbia boss Harry Cohn offered her a long-term contract which she accepted and for the next several years she appeared in 21 Columbia features, advancing from supporting roles in programmers to starring roles in big budget features. When she left Columbia in 1948, she made films at RKO, Universal, Monogram, Lippert and Fox.

During the 1950s, Marguerite was one of the foremost dramatic actresses on television, appearing in starring roles on most of the Hollywood-based network anthology series, acting four times on CBS's *Climax* and three times on NBC's *Lux Video Theatre*. In 1955–56 she was the weekly spokeslady for De Soto automobiles. She appeared on such television shows as *Richard Diamond, Marcus Welby, M.D., Hawaii Five-O, Laramie, The Millionaire, Studio One, Rawhide, Perry Mason, The Ann Sothern Show, The Eve Arden Show, Police Story* and *Barnaby Jones*. She appeared on stage in two plays, one in 1957 and one in 1960, receiving rave reviews in both.

On the personal front, Marguerite married attorney G. Bentley Ryan in 1948 but the marriage was short-lived; they divorced in 1951 after a year's separation. Socially, Marguerite was one of the most popular personalities on the Hollywood nightclub scene. After many romances she wed J. Richard Bremerkamp, an assistant director in television

Marguerite Chapman and Kane Richmond in *Spy Smasher* (Republic, 1942).

in 1964. They were divorced in 1974; thereafter, Marguerite remained single, became a Hollywood realtor and pursued her interest in painting.

For what it's worth, the author liked *Parachute Nurse* ('42), *One Dangerous Night* ('43), *Destroyer* ('43), *Counter-attack* ('45), *Relentless* ('48), *Coroner Creek* ('48) and *Kansas Raiders* ('50).

Marguerite died at Providence St. Joseph Medical Center at age 81.

Serial

1942

Spy Smasher. Rep. [12 Chapters] D: William Witney; SP: Ronald Davidson, Norman S. Hall, Joseph Poland, William Lively, Joseph O'Donnell; AP: W. J. O'Sullivan; Cam: Reggie Lanning; Mus: Mort Glickman; LP: Kane Richmond, Marguerite Chapman, Sam Flint, Hans Schumm, Tristram Coffin, Franco Corsaro.

TOM CHATTERTON

Tom Chatterton was born in Geneva, New York, February 12, 1881. Early on he went on the stage and for 13 years he traveled over the country. It was during these years

Juanita Hansen (left), Tom Chatterton and an unidentified player in *The Secret of the Submarine* (American, 1916).

that he made up his mind to get into some work where he could have a home. The first step was motion pictures—N.Y.C.P. Company, then Universal and finally American, where he was both star and director. As such, he was in *The Cactus Blossom* ('15), *The Quagmire* ('16), *The Ranger of Lonesome Gulch* ('16), *Silent Selby* ('16) and *Two Bits* ('16).

By 1917 he had a 500-acre ranch on the Sacramento River, one of the most fertile portions of the blossomy state of California.

Although he was in several serials, his one starring serial appearance was *The Secret of the Submarine* ('16) as hero opposite Juanita Hansen. In it, Dr. Ralph Burke, scientist and inventor, perfects an apparatus enabling submarines to remain underwater indefinitely without relying wholly upon their supply of compressed air. Dr. Burke is killed and various individuals and govern-

ments attempt to gain the secret of the doctor's invention. Lt. Hope (Chatterton) and Cleo (Hansen), the doctor's daughter, with whom Hope has fallen in love, strive to get the secret for the U.S. Navy.

Chatterton remained an actor until the beginning of World War II, by which time he was working as a character actor. He died in Los Angeles on August 17, 1952.

Serials

1916

The Secret of the Submarine. Amer., [15 chapters] D: George L. Sargent; SP: C. C. Hoadley, William Parker; S: Russell E. Smith; LP: Juanita Hansen, Tom Chatterton, George Clancy, Lamar Johnstone, George Webb.

1938

Hawk of the Wilderness. Rep., [12 Chapters] D: William Witney, John English; LP: Herman Brix, Ray Mala, Monte Blue, Jill Martin, Noble Johnson.

1940

Flash Gordon Conquers the Universe. Univ., [12 Chapters] D: Ford Beebe, Ray Taylor; LP: Buster Crabbe, Carol Hughes, Charles Middleton, Frank Shannon.

Drums of Fu Manchu. Rep., [15 chapters] D: William Witney, John English; LP: Henry Brandon, William Royle, Gloria Franklin, Robert Kellard.

1942

Overland Mail. Univ., [15 Chapters] D: Ford Beebe, John Rawlins; LP: Don Terry, Lon Chaney, Jr., Noah Beery, Jr., Helen Parrish, Noah Beery, Sr.

1944

Zorro's Black Whip. Rep., [12 Chapters] D: Spencer Bennet, Wallace Grissell; LP: Linda Stirling, George J. Lewis, Lucien Littlefield, Francis McDonald.

Captain America. Rep., [15 Chapters] D: John English, Elmer Clifton; LP: Dick Purcell, Lorna Gray [Adrian Booth], Lionel Atwill, Charles Trowbridge.

1947

Jesse James Rides Again. Rep., [13 Chapters] D: Fred C. Brannon, Thomas Carr; LP: Clayton Moore, Linda Stirling, Roy Barcroft, Tris Coffin, John Compton.

GEORGE CHESEBRO

George Chesebro's villains ranged from the "brains heavy" (seldom) to the "action heavy" (frequently) to the "dog heavy" (most often). He took a back seat only to Bob Kortman in the leering and sneering department and was second to none when it came to volume — he came in talking loud and went out the same way.

Chesebro was born in Minneapolis, Minnesota, on July 29, 1888. He toured the Orient with a musical show for two years before hitting Hollywood around 1915. At first he was a leading man. In the serial *Hands Up* ('18) he played opposite serial queen Ruth Roland. During production he entered the U.S. Army and was replaced by George Larkin for the remainder of the production. In *The Lost City* ('20) he plays opposite Juanita Hansen in a hair-raising story of adventure in Africa, a lost city of whites and a white princess. In *The Hope Diamond Mystery* ('21) he is billed behind Harry Carter and Grace Darmond, but in *The Diamond Queen* ('21) he is the hero coming to the rescue of Eileen Sedgwick. He also appeared in a variety of other films and was the star of several Northwest Mounted Police adventures released by the Clark-Cornelius Corporation.

With the coming of sound, Chesebro became a character actor and stayed with movies for nearly 40 years. He became a fixture in Westerns and serials and the call for "dirty work" volunteers never had to be issued more than once if Chesebro was in the cast. The hero could wear him to a frazzle and send him off with his tail between his legs, but one thing you could count on from old George — he would still be issuing threats at full volume on his exit.

Not only did Chesebro's scraggly face qualify him as a movie badman, but his voice perfectly matched his scowling expression, making him ideal to continue his career upon the arrival of sound movies.

Chesebro worked with practically every Western star active in the 1930s and 1940s. He appeared in at least 32 serials. There may have been others.

Chesebro died on May 28, 1959, at the age of 70 in Hermosa Beach, California. Cause of death was arteriosclerosis.

Serials

1918

Hands Up. Pathé, [15 Chapters] D: James W. Horne; SP: Jack Cunningham; S: Gilson Willets; LP: Ruth Roland, George Chesebro, George Larkin.

1920

The Lost City. WB, [15 Chapters] D: E. A. Martin; P: William N. Selig; LP: Juanita Hansen, George Chesebro, Frank Clark, Irene Wallace.

1921

The Hope Diamond Mystery. Kosmik, [15 Chapters] D: Stuart Paton; LP: Harry Carter, Grace Darmond, George Chesebro, Boris Karloff, Carmen Phillips.

The Diamond Queen. Univ., [18 Chapters] D: Ed Kull; LP: Eileen Sedgwick, George Chesebro, Frank Clark, Burton Wilson, Alfred Fisher.

1928

The Chinatown Mystery. Sun., [10 Chapters] D: J. P. McGowan; LP: Joe Bonomo, Ruth Hiatt, Paul Malvern, Francis Ford, Paul Panzer.

1934

Mystery Mountain. Mascot, [12 Chapters] D: B. Reeves Eason, Otto Brower; LP: Ken Maynard, Verna Hillie, Syd Sayler, Edward Earle, Lafe McKee.

The Law of the Wild. Mascot, [12 Chapters] D: Armand Schaefer, B. Reeves Eason; LP: Bob Custer, Rex, Rin-Tin-Tin, Jr., Lucile Browne, Richard Cramer.

1935

Queen of the Jungle. Screen Attractions, [12 Chapters] D: Robert Hill; LP: Reed Howes, Mary Kornman, George Chesebro, Lafe McKee.

The Miracle Rider. Mascot, [15 Chapters] D: Armand Schaefer, Reeves Eason; LP: Tom Mix, Charles Middleton, Joan Gale, Jason Robards, Robert Kortman.

1936

Robinson Crusoe of Clipper Island. Rep., [14 chapters] D: Mack V. Wright, Ray Taylor; LP: Ray Mala, Rex, Mamo Clark, Herbert Rawlinson, Buck (dog).

Custer's Last Stand. S & S, [15 Chapters] D: Elmer Clifton; LP: Rex Lease, William Farnum, Jack Mulhall, Reed Howes, Lona Andre, Dorothy Gulliver, Ruth Mix.

1937

S O S Coast Guard. Rep., [12 Chapters] D: William Witney, Alan James; LP: Ralph Byrd,

Bela Lugosi, Maxine Doyle, Richard Alexander, George Chesebro.

1938

The Great Adventures of Wild Bill Hickok. Col., [15 Chapters] D: Mack Wright, Sam Nelson; LP: Bill Elliot, Carole Wayne, Frankie Darro, Monte Blue.

1939

Daredevils of the Red Circle. Rep., [12 Chapters] D: William Witney, John English; LP: Charles Quigley, Herman Brix, David Sharpe, Carole Landis.

Flying G-Men. Col., [15 Chapters] D: Ray Taylor, James W. Horne; LP: Robert Paige, Richard Fiske, James Craig, Lorna Gray [Adrian Booth], Don Beddoe.

Mandrake the Magician. Col., [12 Chapters] D: Sam Nelson, Norman Deming; LP: Warren Hull, Doris Weston, Al Kikume, Rex Downing, Edward Earle.

1941

Holt of the Secret Service. Col., [15 Chapters] D: James W. Horne; LP: Jack Holt, Evelyn Brent, Tris Coffin, C. Montague Shaw, John Ward, George Chesebro.

White Eagle. Col., [15 Chapters] D: James W. Horne; LP: Buck Jones, Raymond Hatton, Dorothy Fay, James Craven, Jack Ingram, Charles King, John Merton.

1942

Perils of the Royal Mounted. Col., [15 Chapters] D: James W. Horne; LP: Nell O'Day, Robert Stevens, Herbert Rawlinson, Kenneth MacDonald, John Elliott.

The Valley of Vanishing Men. Col., [15 Chapters] D: Spencer G. Bennet; LP: Bill Eliott, Slim Summerville, Carmen Morales, Kenneth MacDonald, Jack Ingram.

1943

The Phantom. Col., [15 Chapters] D: B. Reeves Eason; LP: Tom Tyler, Jeanne Bates, Kenneth MacDonald, Frank Shannon, Ace (dog), Guy Kingsford.

Batman. Col., [15 Chapters] D: Lambert Hillyer; LP: Lewis Wilson, Douglas Croft, J.

Carrol Naish, Shirley Patterson, William C. Austin, George Chesebro.

1945

Secret Agent X-9. Univ., [13 Chapters] D: Ray Taylor, Lewis D. Collins; LP: Lloyd Bridges, Keye Luke, Jan Wiley, Victoria Horne, Samuel S. Hinds.

Federal Operator 99. Rep., [12 Chapters] D: Spencer Bennet, Wallace Grissell; LP: Martin Lamont, Helen Talbot, George J. Lewis, Lorna Gray, Hal Taliaferro.

The Purple Monster Strikes. Rep., [15 Chapters] D: Spencer Bennet, Fred Brannon; LP: Linda Stirling, Dennis Moore, Roy Barcroft, James Craven.

1946

The Phantom Rider. Rep., [12 Chapters] D: Spencer G. Bennet, Fred Brannon; LP: robert Kent, Peggy Stewart, LeRoy Mason, George J. Lewis, Kenne Duncan.

Daughter of Don Q. Rep., [12 Chapters] D: Spencer G. Bennet, Fred Brannon; LP: Adrian Booth, Kirk Alyn, LeRoy Mason, Roy Barcroft, I. Stanford Jolley.

1947

The Vigilante. Col., [15 Chapters] D: Wallace Fox; LP: Ralph Byrd, Ramsay Ames, Lyle Talbot, George Chesebro, George Offerman, Edmund Cobb, Robert Barron.

Jesse James Rides Again. Rep., [13 Chapters] D: Fred C. Brannon, Thomas Carr; LP: Clayton Moore, Linda Stirling, Roy Barcroft, John Compton, Tris Coffin.

The Black Widow. Rep., [13 Chapters] D: Spencer Bennet, Fred C. Brannon; LP: Carol Forman, Bruce Edwards, Virginia Lindley, Ramsay Ames, Anthony Warde.

Son of Zorro. Rep., [13 Chapters] D: Spencer Bennet, Fred C. Brannon; LP: George Turner, Peggy Stewart, Roy Barcroft, Edward Cassidy, George Chesebro.

1949

Ghost of Zorro. Rep., [12 Chapters] D: Fred C. Brannon; LP: Clayton Moore, Pamela Blake, Roy Barcroft, George J. Lewis, I. Stanford Jolley.

1950

Desperadoes of the West. Rep., [12 Chapters] D: Fred C. Brannon; LP: Richard Powers [Tom Keene], Judy Clark, Roy Barcroft, I. Stanford Jolley, Lee Roberts.

DOROTHY CHRISTY

Dorothy Christy was a two-serial woman, but it was in her role of Queen Tika of Murania in *Phantom Empire* ('35) that she achieved serial immortality. Her demise in Chapter 12 as the victim of a death ray is a scene not to be forgotten by serial enthusiasts. Previously she had supported Walter Miller and Nora Lane in the Mascot chapterplay *King of the Wild* ('30). As Mrs. La Salle, Dorothy agrees to help two conspirators, Boris Karloff and Tom Santschi, obtain the whereabouts of a diamond mine from Carroll Nye. She later is mysteriously shot and killed. It takes Walter Miller and Nora Lane to unravel things.

Christy was born on May 26, 1906, in Reading, Pennsylvania. In *Playboy of Paris* ('30) she portrays Berengere, a French gold digger who fights with Frances Dee for the love of Maurice Chevalier. The film was also produced in a French-language version, *Le Petit Cafe.* She also had a good part in *Extravagance* ('30) as a friend of June Collyer who becomes disillusioned and commits suicide as result of her adultery. June Collyer is shocked into reconciling with husband Lloyd Hughes.

Christy worked through the '30s and '40s as character player. Her other films included *Gold Dust Gertie* ('31), *Parlor, Bedroom, and Bath* ('32), *Union Depot* ('32), *Sons of the Desert* ('34), *Bright Eyes* ('34), *Love Birds* ('34), *The Daring Young Man* ('35), *Slave Ship* ('37), *Submarine Patrol* ('38), *East Side of Heaven* ('39), *Rough Riders Round-Up* ('39), *City of Chance* ('40), *Man from Cheyenne* ('42), *Junior Miss* ('45), *Fighting Back* ('48), and *The Fountainhead* ('49).

Serials

1931

King of the Wild. Mascot, [12 Chapters] D: B. Reeves Eason, Richard Thorpe; P: Nat Levine; S/SP: Wyndham Gittens, Ford Beebe; Cam: Bob Kline, Edward Kull; Mus: Lee Zahler; LP: Walter Miller, Nora Lane, Dorothy Christy, Boris Karloff, Thomas Santschi, Victor Potel, Mischa Auer, Arthur McLaglen.

1935

Phantom Empire. Mascot, [12 Chapters] D: B. Reeves Eason; S: Wallace MacDonald, Gerald Geraghty, Hy Freedman; SP: John Rathmell, Armand Schaefer; Spv.: Armand Schaefer; P: Nat Levine; Cam: Ernest Miller, William Nobles; Mus: Lee Zahler; LP: Gene Autry, Frankie Darro, Betsy King Ross, Dorothy Christy, Wheeler Oakman, Charles K. French, Smiley Burnette, Wally Wales, William Moore, Buffalo Bill, Jr., Fred Burns.

EDUARDO CIANNELLI

Eduardo (also, Edward) Ciannelli took top billing in Republic's *Mysterious Doctor Satan* ('40). His Satan was more businesslike than bizarre. Yet, the actor created a villain who projected an understated yet total menace comparable to that of Henry Brandon in the earlier *Drums of Fu Manchu* ('40). Eduardo, billed "Edward" in this one picture, was a talented performer who became stereotyped as the Continental villain, the epitome of motion picture serial villainy.

Ciannelli's performance was probably the key to acceptance of the serial. If you believed Doctor Satan, the rest followed. And he brought it off. His calm, self-assured performance left little doubt as to Satan's ability to carry out his criminal endeavors.

In 1942 he played Felix Lynx in Universal's 12-chapter *Sky Raiders*. As the agent of a foreign power, he is out to steal the plans for a new type of fighter plane and a bombsight that famed aviator Bob Dayton (Donald Woods) has developed. The serial is entertaining but failed to "grab" the audience as had the earlier Republic serial.

In 1943 Ciannelli portrayed Nazi agent Karl Von Heiger in the serial *Adventures of the Flying Cadets*. Four young Cadets are suspected in a series of murders and set about proving their innocence.

Ciannelli studied to be a doctor but never practiced. Instead he trained for the opera at schools in Italy, France and Russia. After singing in opera in Europe, he emigrated to the U.S. after World War I. He was hired as a stage manager of the play *Broadway* and later had a singing role in the musical comedy *Lady Billy*. He also had a role in the operetta *Rose Marie*. Other roles followed.

Motion pictures beckoned and he made his film debut in *Reunion in Vienna* ('33). Most of his roles were menacing ones but occasionally he played men of good character, as in *The Lost Moment* ('47) and *California*

('47). Other Ciannelli films included: *Crime Lawyer* ('37), *The Angels Wash Their Faces* ('39), *Gunga Din* ('39), *Strange Cargo* ('40) *Zanzibar* ('40), *Cairo* ('42), *The Mask of Dimitrios* ('44), *Incendiary Blonde* ('45), *Gilda* ('46), *Seven Keys to Baldpate* ('47), *Prince of Foxes* ('49), *The People Against O'Hara* ('51), *Love Slaves of the Amazons* ('57), *The Visit* ('64), *The Brotherhood* ('68), *Mackenna's Gold* ('69) and *The Secret of Santa Vittoria* ('69).

Eduardo married Alma Wolfe in 1918 and had twin sons, Eduardo, Jr., and Lewis. Mrs Ciannelli died in 1968. Eduardo died in Rome on October 8, 1969, at age 80.

Serials

1940

Mysterious Doctor Satan. Rep., [15 Chapters] D: William Witney, John English; SP: Franklyn Adreon, Ronald Davidson, Norman S. Hall, Joseph Poland, Sol Shor; Mus: Cy Feuer; LP: Eduardo Ciannelli, Robert Wilcox, Ella Neal, William Newell, Dorothy Herbert, Charles Trowbridge, Lynton Brent.

1942

Sky Raiders. Univ., [12 Chapters] D: Ford Beebe, Ray Taylor; SP: Clarence Upson Young, Paul Huston; S: Eliot Gibbons; AP: Henry MacRae; LP: Donald Woods, Billy Halop, Robert Armstrong, Kathryn Adams, Eduardo Ciannelli, Reed Hadley, Jacqueline Dalya.

1943

Adventures of the Flying Cadets. Univ., [13 Chapters] D: Ray Taylor, Lewis D. Collins; SP: Morgan B. Cox, George H. Plympton, Paul Huston; AP: Henry MacRae; Mus: Everett Carter, Milton Rosen; Cam: William Sickner; LP: Johnny Downs, Bobby Jordon, Jennifer Holt, Ward Wood, Eduardo Ciannelli, Billy Benedict.

Ella Hall and Eduardo Ciannelli in *Mysterious Doctor Satan* (Republic, 1940).

ETHLYNE CLAIR

Ethlyne Clair, a beautiful young brunette, was born in Talladega, Alabama, in 1904 and raised in Atlanta, Georgia. Her father was Edward Williams, inventor of the ten-key adding machine. She attended Brenan College in Georgia, Woodbury Hall in Atlanta and the National Academy of Fine and Applied Arts in Washington, D.C., where she studied art.

Her brother, an actor, invited her to New York and promised to help her get a start as an actress. She accepted his invitation and he kept his promise. It wasn't long before the 16-year-old Ethlyne had a bit in first Na-

tional's *Sundra* ('24). Other small parts followed and these led to a contract to co-star as Mrs. Newlywed in the series *The Newlyweds and Their Baby* (1927–28) which Stern Brothers released through Universal. Syd Saylor was Mr. Newlywed. There were 32 of these two-reel comedies made. In addition, she worked in 13 or more episodes of the *Mike and Ike* ('1927–29) series starring Charles King (yep, *that* Charles King!) and Charles Dorety.

When she wasn't busy making comedies, she was used in Westerns. She made three with Hoot Gibson, two with Jack Perrin and two with Tom Tyler. Her first serial was *The Vanishing Rider* ('28) starring William Desmond. It proved popular. After leaving Universal, she co-starred with Walter Miller in Pathé's *Queen of the Northwoods* ('29), an equally popular cliffhanger.

Ethlyne retired in the early 1930s when she married Ern Westmore, one of the famous make-up brothers. Her first marriage was to a producer who drove her to Mexico and forced her to wed at gunpoint. She was later divorced from Westmore and married Merle Frost. She signed with Warner Brothers in 1929 but, according to Ethlyne, Darryl Zanuck short-circuited her career when she rejected his romantic advances.

Ethlyne Clair died February 27, 1996, at a Tarzana, California hospital of respiratory failure after ulcer surgery.

Serials

1928

The Vanishing Rider. Univ., [10 Chapters] D: Ray Taylor; SP: George H. Plympton, Val Cleveland; LP: William Desmond, Ethlyne Clair, Nelson McDowell, Bud Osborne, Boris Karloff.

1929

Queen of the Northwoods. Pathé, [10 Chapters] D: Spencer G. Bennet, Thomas L. Storey; SP: George Arthur Gray; LP: Walter Miller, Ethlyne Clair, Tom London, Frank Lackteen, Edward Cecil, George Magrill.

ELLEN CLANCY/ JANET SHAW

Ellen Clancy was born in Beatrice, Nebraska, on January 23, 1919. She began her career in films in the early 1930s, billed as Ellen Clancy from 1935 to mid–1938, and then as Janet Shaw.

She was featured in such films as *She Married Her Boss* ('35), *Alcatraz Island* ('37), *Jezebel* ('38), *King of the Underworld* ('39), *Waterloo Bridge* ('40), *The Mummy's Tomb* ('42), *Night Monster* ('42), *Shadow of a Doubt* ('43), *Ladies Courageous* ('44), *The Scarlet Clue* ('45), *House of Horrors* ('46), *Nocturne* ('46) and *They Won't Believe Me* ('47).

Western buffs remember her opposite Dick Foran in *Prairie Thunder* ('37); Tex Ritter in *Arizona Trail* ('43); and Jim Newill and Dave O'Brien in *Bad Men of Thunder Gap* ('43).

Left to right: Ellen Clancy (Janet Shaw), Kane Richmond, Eddie Quillan, Charles King and Jack Ingram in ***Jungle Raiders*** (Columbia, 1945).

In the Columbia cliffhanger *Jungle Raiders* ('45), Janet is the heroine looking for her father in the wilds of Africa. Kane Richmond is also looking for his father who has been kidnapped by Charles King to extract from him information about a treasure map. Kane and Janet team up in an attempt to rescue their dads. Zara (Carol Hughes), Priestess of the Hidden City, allies herself with Charles King's group, and in combating this double-barreled threat, Kane and Janet survive a number of deadly obstacles, including a landslide in the Valley of Sounds, a crocodile-infested swamp, the Fire Test and the Dagger Pit. Eventually the two are reunited with their fathers and prepare to return to civilization.

In *The Scarlet Horseman* ('46), Janet is a supporting player. She plays Elsie Halliday, daughter of a prominent senator who is taken captive by agents of Zero Quick (Edward M. Howard), who is supplying guns to the Comanches in preparation for a major Indian uprising. As the uprising begins, two government agents arrive to help quell the rampaging Indians. One of them (Paul Guilfoyle) assumes the identity of the Scarlet Horseman, the legendary champion of the Comanches whose leadership they have always followed. The agents discover that wives and daughters of influential Texas senators have been kidnapped by a mysterious traitor known only as Matosca. The captives are being held hostage as part of the traitor's scheme to pressure the senators into supporting the partitioning of Texas. In the final showdown, Carla Marquette (Virginia Christine) is revealed to be the diabolical Matosca and Elsie is rescued just as she was about to be shot by Matosca.

Janet Shaw died at age 82, in Beatrice, Nebraska, on October 15, 2001, after a long battle with Alzheimer's disease.

Serials

1945

Jungle Raiders. Col., [15 Chapters] D: Lesley Selander; SP: Ande Lamb, George H. Plympton; P: Sam Katzman; Cam: Ira H. Morgan; Mus: Lee Zahler; LP: Kane Richmond, Eddie

Quillan, Veda Ann Borg, Carol Hughes, Janet Shaw, John Elliott, Charles King, Jack Ingram, I. Stanford Jolley, Ernie Adams.

1946

The Scarlet Horseman. Col., [13 Chapters] D: Ray Taylor, Lewis D. Collins; SP: Joseph O'-Donnel, Patricia Harper, Tom Gibson; P: Morgan Cox; LP: Peter Cookson, Paul Guilfoyle, Victoria Horne, Virginia Christine, Janet Shaw, Jack Ingram, Edmund Cobb, Cy Kendall, Hal Taliaferro, William Desmond, Jack Rockwell.

LEONARD CLAPHAM/ TOM LONDON

Leonard Clapham [Tom London] was born in Louisville, Kentucky, on August 24, 1882. (The years 1883, 1889, and 1893 have been reported by some authors, but this writer is almost certain that Clapham's birth year was 1882.)

Clapham is said to have appeared in the first Western film, *The Great Train Robbery* ('05). Maybe. The writer has viewed the film several times but cannot verify his appearance therein.

After completing his schooling, Clapham worked at about any job that came his way. He is known to have worked as a salesman in both New York and Chicago. In Chicago he met Col. William Selig, who hired him as a prop man. When Selig moved his operation to California, Clapham went along. He got to appear in many of the one- and two-reel films being churned out by Selig and also by G. M. (Bronco Billy) Anderson.

Clapham met a fellow Kentuckian, J. M. Kerrigan, who was instrumental in Clapham's getting a job at Universal. There he

played anything from extra to minor roles, but soon was given more challenging roles. In 1916 he appeared in *Liberty, a Daughter of the U.S.A.* a 20-chapter serial with Marie Walcamp. It has the distinction of being the very first Western serial; also in '16 he played in *The Purple Mask*, a Universal serial starring Grace Cunard and Francis Ford.

Clapham gradually worked his way up the career ladder. He had a fairly good role in *The Lion's Claws* ('18) and *The Lion Man* ('19). He supported Hoot Gibson in a series of two-reel Westerns and Eddie Polo in *King of the Circus* ('20).

In 1920–21 Universal featured Clapham in ten two-reel films in which he portrays an indefatigable Northwest Mounted Policeman. Virginia Brown Faire was his leading lady in these films.

In 1922, Leonard co-starred with Ann Little in the Arrow serial *Nan of the North*. In '22, '23 and '24 he worked often with Leo Maloney and Roy Stewart. Toward the end of '24 he realized his headliner roles were behind him and changed his name to Tom London, becoming one of the best character actors in Westerns and serials. In the late '20s, '30s and the early '40s, Tom was usually cast as an outlaw but after signing a term contract with Republic in '43 he was often seen as a sheriff and other men who respected the law. He even took out his false teeth and played comic sidekick to Sunset Carson.

When the production of B-Westerns and serials decreased in the late '40s and early '50s, Tom became a character actor in television series as well as in feature films. He worked frequently in *The Gene Autry Show*, *The Roy Rogers Show*, *The Range Rider*, *Adventures of Kit Carson*, *The Cisco Kid*, *Annie Oakley*, *Wyatt Earp*, *The Texan* and others.

Writer Ken Law (*The Big Reel*, January 15, 1987, #152) has written: "Tom London was a tall, lithe of limb, wiry looking man of the outdoors, possessing good masculine features and clear grey-blue eyes. He did not stay attached to any one film company. He kept moving around, keeping always active and in demand. Like Ol' Man River, he just kept moving along."

Writer Frank Dolven (*The Big Reel*, #262, March 1996) writes: "London easily made the transition to the 'talkies,' and his proven talent was well received by both the little independent studios and the majors during the rest of his career. He had a fine screen presence and the reasons for his popularity were many. First, he was a very likable man with an enormous amount of natural warmth and friendliness. He didn't have to work at getting along with anyone ... it was instinctive. The director and co-stars liked London because he was punctual, patient, and genuinely enjoyed his work. He was a fine actor, a common man in the best sense of the word, uncomplicated, stable and definitely 'one of the guys.'"

Tom London died on December 5, 1963.

Serials

1916

The Purple Mask. Univ., [16 Chapters] D: Francis Ford; SP: Grace Cunard, Francis Ford;

LP: Grace Cunard, Francis Ford, Joan Hatchaway, Peter Gerald.

Liberty (A Daughter of the U.S.A.). Univ., [20 Chapters] D: Jacques Jaccard, Henry MacRae; LP: Marie Walcamp, Jack Holt, Eddie Polo, G. Raymond Nye.

1918

The Lion's Claws. Univ., [18 Chapters] D: Jacques Jaccard, Harry Harvey; LP: Marie Walcamp, Roy Hanford, Neal Hart, Frank Lanning, Thomas Lingham.

1919

The Lion Man. Univ., [18 Chapters] D: Albert Russell, Jack Wells; LP: Kathleen O'Connor, Jack Perrin, Mack Wright, J. Barney Sherry, Gertrude Astor.

1922

Nan of the North. Arrow, [15 Chapters] D: Duke Worne; S/SP: Karl Coolidge; P: Ben Wilson; LP: Ann Little, Leonard Clapham, Joseph W. Girard, Hal Wilson, Edith Stayart, Howard Crampton, J. Morris Foster.

1923

The Social Buccaneer. Univ., [10 Chapters] D: Robert F. Hill; LP: Jack Mulhall, Margaret Livingston, William Welsh, Harry T. DeVere.

1926

Snowed In. Pathé, [10 Chapters] D: Spencer G. Bennet; SP: Frank Leon Smith; LP: Allene Ray, Walter Miller, Frank Austin, Leonard Clapham.

The Spider Net. Tenneck/Goodwill, [? Chapters] D: Hans Tirsler; LP: Eileen Sedgwick, Lightning (dog), Robert Walker, Tom London.

1927

Return of the Riddle Rider. Univ., [10 Chapters] D: Robert Hill, Jay Marchant; LP: William Desmond, Lola Todd, Scotty Mattrow, Tom London, Norbett Myles.

The Golden Stallion. Mascot, [10 Chapters] D: Harry Webb; LP: Maurice (Lefty) Flynn, Joe Bonomo, Molly Malone, Tom London.

1928

The Mystery Rider. Univ., [10 Chapters] D: Jack Nelson; LP: William Desmond, Derelys Perdue, Tom London, Bud Osborne, Walter Shumway, Syd Saylor.

The Yellow Cameo. Pathé, [10 Chapters] D: Spencer G. Bennet; LP: Allene Ray, Edward Hearn, Noble Johnson, Tom London, Cyclone (dog), Harry Semels.

1929

Queen of the Northwoods. Pathé, [10 Chapters] D: Spencer G. Bennet, Thomas Storey; LP: Walter Miller, Ethlyne Claire, Tom London, Frank Lackteen.

1931

The Galloping Ghost. Mascot, [12 Chapters] D: Reeves Eason; LP: Harold (Red) Grange, Dorothy Gulliver, Walter Miller, Gwen Lee, Tom London.

Spell of the Circus. Univ., [10 Chapters] D: Robert F. Hill; LP: Francis X. Bushman, Jr., Alberta Vaughn, Tom London, Walter Shumway, Bobby Nelson.

1932

The Lost Special. Univ., [12 Chapters] D: Henry MacRae; LP: Frank Albertson, Cecilia Parker, Caryl Lincoln, Ernie Nevers, Francis Ford, Joe Bonomo.

1933

The Phantom of the Air. Univ., [12 Chapters] D: Ray Taylor; LP: Tom Tyler, Gloria Shea, LeRoy Mason, Hugh Enfield [Craig Reynolds].

Gordon of Ghost City. Univ., [12 Chapters] D: Ray Taylor; LP: Buck Jones, Madge Bellamy, Walter Miller, Hugh Enfield [Craig Reynolds], Tom London.

The Whispering Shadow. Mascot, [12 Chapters] D: Albert Herman, Colbert Clark; LP: Bela Lugosi, Henry B. Walthall, Viva Tattersall, Malcolm McGregory.

Clancy of the Mounted. Univ., [12 Chapters] D: Ray Taylor; LP: Tom Tyler, Jacqueline Wells, William Desmond, Rosalie Roy, Tom London, Francis Ford.

The Wolf Dog. Mascot, [12 Chapters] D: Colbert Clark, Harry Fraser; LP: Rin-Tin-Tin, Jr., George J. Lewis, Frankie Darro, Boots Mallory, Henry Walthall.

1934

Burn 'Em Up Barnes. Mascot, [12 Chapters] D: Colbert Clark, Armand Schaefer; LP: Jack Mulhall, Frankie Darro, Lola Lane, Julian Rivero, Edwin Maxwell.

Mystery Mountain. Mascot, [12 Chapters] D: B. Reeves Eason, Otto Brower; LP: Ken Maynard, Verna Hillie, Syd Saylor, Edward Earle, Lafe McKee.

The Vanishing Shadow. Univ., [12 Chapters] D: Louis Friedlander [Lew Landers]; LP: Ada Ince, Onslow Stevens, Walter Miller, William Desmond, James Durkin.

1935

The Fighting Marines. Mascot, [12 Chapters] D: B. Reeves Eason, Joseph Kane; LP: Grant Withers, Adrian Morris, Ann Rutherford, Robert Warwick.

The Miracle Rider. Mascot, [15 Chapters] D: Armand Schaefer, B. Reeves Eason; LP: Tom Mix, Joan Gale, Charles Middleton, Jason Robards, Sr., Wally Wales.

The Roaring West. Univ., [15 Chapters] D: Ray Taylor; LP: Buck Jones, Muriel Evans, Walter Miller, Frank McGlynn, Sr., Harlan Knight, Tom London.

1936

The Clutching Hand. Stage & Screen, [15 Chapters] D: Albert Herman; LP: Jack Mulhall, Ruth Mix, Marion Shilling, Rex Lease, William Farnum.

The Phantom Rider. Univ., [15 Chapters] D: Ray Taylor; LP: Buck Jones, Maria Shelton, Diana Gibson, Harry Woods, Frank LaRue, George Cooper.

1937

Radio Patrol. Univ., [12 Chapters] D: Ford Beebe, Cliff Smith; LP: Grant Withers, Catherine (Kay) Hughes, Mickey Rentschier, Adrian Morris.

The Mysterious Pilot. Col., [15 Chapters] D: Spencer G. Bennet; LP: Frank Hawks, Dorothy Sebastian, Rex Lease, Guy Bates Post, Kenneth Harlan.

Jungle Menace. Col., [15 Chapters] D: George Melford, Harry Fraser; LP: Frank Buck, Esther Ralston, John St. Polis, Reginald Denny.

Zorro Rides Again. Rep., [12 Chapters] D: William Witney, John English; LP: John Carroll, Helen Christian, Duncan Renaldo, Noah Beery, Sr.

1938

The Lone Ranger. Rep., [15 Chapters] D: William Witney, John English; LP: Lee Powell, Chief Thundercloud, Herman Brix, Lynne Roberts, Stanley Andrews.

The Great Adventures of Wild Bill Hickok. Col., [15 Chapters] D: Mack V. Wright, Sam Nelson; LP: Bill Elliott, Carole Wayne, Frankie Darro, Monte Blue.

The Fighting Devil Dogs. Rep., [12 Chapters] D: William Witney, John English; LP: Lee Powell, Herman Brix, Eleanor Stewart, Montagu Love, Hugh Sothern.

The Spider's Web. Col., [15 Chapters] D: Ray Taylor, James W. Horne; LP: Warren Hull, Irish Meredith, Richard Fiske, Kenneth Duncan, Forbes Murray.

1940

Deadwood Dick. Col., [15 Chapters] D: James W. Horne; LP: Donald Douglas, Lorna Gray [Adrian Booth], Lane Chandler, Marin Sais, Charles King.

Junior G-Men. Univ., [12 Chapters] D: Ford Beebe, John Rawlins; LP: Billy Halop, Huntz Hall, Gabriel Dell, Bernard Punsley, Philip Terry, Roger Daniels.

Winners of the West. Univ., [13 Chapters] D: Ford Beebe, Ray Taylor; LP: Dick Foran, Anne Nagel, James Craig, Tom Fadden, Charles Stevens, Harry Woods.

1942

The Valley of Vanishing Men. Col., [15 Chapters] D: Spencer G. Bennet; LP: Bill Elliott, Slim Summerville, Carmen Morales, Kenneth MacDonald.

Perils of the Royal Mounted. Col., [15 Chapters] D: James W. Horne; LP: Nell O'Day, Robert Stevens [Kellard], Herbert Rawlinson, Kenneth MacDonald.

Spy Smasher. Rep., [12 Chapters] D: William Witney; LP: Kane Richmond, Marguerite Chapman, Sam Flint, Hans Schumm, Tristram Coffin, Franco Corsaro.

1943

Batman. Col., [15 Chapters] D: Lambert Hillyer; LP: Lewis Wilson, Douglas Croft, J. Carrol Naish, Shirley Patterson, William C. Austin, Charles Wilson.

Daredevils of the West. Rep., [12 Chapters] D: John English; LP: Allan Lane, Kay Aldridge, Eddie Acuff, William Haade, Robert Frazer, Ted Adams.

The Masked Marvel. Rep., [12 Chapters] D: Spencer Bennet; LP: William Forrest, Tom Steele, Louise Currie, Johnny Arthur, David Bacon.

1944

Zorro's Black Whip. Rep., [12 Chapters] D: Spencer G. Bennet, Wallace Grissell; LP: Linda Stirling, George J. Lewis, Lucien Littlefield, Francis McDonald.

The Tiger Woman. Rep., [12 Chapters] D: Spencer G. Bennet, Wallace Grissell; LP: Linda Stirling, George J. Lewis.

1945

Federal Operator 99. Rep., [12 Chapters] D: Spencer G. Bennet, Yakima Canutt, Wallace A. Grissell; LP: Marten Lamont, Helen Talbot, Lorna Gray [Adrian Booth], George J. Lewis.

1946

King of the Forrest Rangers. Rep., [12 Chapters] D: Spencer G. Bennet, Fred Brannon; LP: Larry Thompson, Helen Talbot, Stuart Hamblen, LeRoy Mason.

The Phantom Rider. Rep., [12 Chapters] D: Spencer G. Bennet, Fred Brannon; LP: Robert Kent, Peggy Stewart, LeRoy Mason, George J. Lewis, Hal Taliaferro.

1947

Jesse James Rides Again. Rep., [13 Chapters] D: Fred C. Brannon, Thomas Carr; LP: Clay-ton Moore, Linda Stirling, Roy Barcroft, Tristram Coffin.

Son of Zorro. Rep., [13 Chapters] D: Spencer G. Bennet, Fred C. Brannon; LP: George Turner, Peggy Stewart, Roy Barcroft, Edward Cassidy.

1950

Cody of the Pony Express. Col., [15 Chapters] D: Spencer G. Bennet; LP: Jock Mahoney, Dickie Moore, Peggy Stewart, William Fawcett, Tom London.

King of the Carnival. Rep., [12 Chapters] D: Franklyn Adreon; LP: Harry Lauter, Fran Bennett, Keith Richards, Robert Shayne, Rick Vallin, Gregory Gay.

MAE CLARKE

Mae Clarke, born Violet Mary Klotz, began life in Philadelphia, Pennsylvania, in 1910. Her father was a theater organist; as a result, Mae got to see a lot of free movies. The family moved to Atlantic City when she was small and it was there that she went to school. She studied dancing at Dawson's Dancing School and started out as a cabaret dancer at age 16. Two years later she began playing supporting roles in stage dramas and musicals such as *Sitting Pretty* ('24), *Gay Paree* ('25), *The Noose* ('26) (which ran for 197 performances) and *Manhattan Mary* ('27) (lasting 265 performances). After a vaudeville tour, Fox brought her to Hollywood to star in *Big Time* ('29).

Mae was a successful and popular leading lady for several years. Perhaps her most recognizable role was as Henry Frankenstein's fiancée in *Frankenstein* ('31). She was a gangster's moll in *Public Enemy* ('31) and achieved some sort of immortality when James Cagney pushed a grapefruit in her face in one of two scenes she had in the film. Among nostalgic cinema buffs, she is most closely identified with this film.

At Universal, Mae starred in *Waterloo Bridge* ('31), a big hit. In *The Front Page* ('31) she gives a good performance as the pathetic prostitute Molly Malloy. In *Impatient Maiden* ('32) she was in love with ambulance driver Lew Ayres, and was again with him in *Night World* ('32), in which she plays a hoofer. She was a tough reporter in *Final Edition* ('34), and so it went. Reunited with James Cagney in *Lady Killer* ('33), she was dragged out of bed by her hair, pulled across the floor and pushed down a corridor. In a later film, *Great Guy* ('36), she was Cagney's sweetheart.

After 1934, Mae's career quickly declined and she was reduced to playing supporting roles. Through the 1940s, 1950s and

1960s she was mostly seen in bit parts. Her Western credits are *Wild Brian Kent* ('36), *Gun Runner* ('49), *Horizons West* ('52), *Wichita* ('55), *The Desperados Are in Town* ('56) and *A Big Hand for the Little Lady* ('66).

Mae was married three times. The first husband was Fannie Brice's brother, Lew. The date was either late 1926 or early 1930s. When that marriage ended, she married Capt. Stevens Bancroft, a China Clipper pilot, in 1937. That marriage was dissolved and she married Capt. Herbert Langdon in 1946. By 1953 she was again single.

In her later years she was a resident of the Motion Picture Country Home in Woodland Hills. It was there that she died from cancer at age 81 in 1992.

Tris Coffin and Mae Clarke in *King of the Rocket Men* (Republic, 1949).

Serial

1949

King of the Rocket Men. Rep., [12 Chapters] D: Fred C. Brannon; SP: Royal Cole, William Lively, Sol Shor; Cam: Elis W. Carter; Mus: Stanley Wilson; LP: Tristram Coffin, Mae Clarke, Don Haggerty, House Peters, Jr., James Craven.

MARGUERITE CLAYTON

Salt Lake City was Marguerite's birthplace and the year was 1891. She was educated at St. Mary's Academy in Salt Lake City and had a stage career in Chicago and New York before entering movies in 1909. Her first film of record was *A Mexican's*

Gratitude ('09) playing opposite G. M. ("Broncho Billy") Anderson. Marguerite and Broncho Billy made innumerable crude Westerns together in the period 1909–15, and Marguerite was often as visible as the heroine. The stories were frequently made up as they went along. Marguerite made 70 or more Westerns with Broncho Billy — quite a record!

In 1916–17 Essanay cast her in various roles that helped her career. She freelanced beginning in 1918. From December 23, 1916, to April 7, 1917, Marguerite co-starred with Sydney Ainsworth in the series *Is Marriage Sacred?* It is believed that each episode (16) tells a complete story and that the continuing cast play different roles in each episode.

Bride 13 ('20) was a 15-chapter serial made by Fox, one of its few episodic films (this was their first). It had to do with Tripoli pirates kidnapping 13 wealthy brides for ransom and the navy's attempt to rescue them. One might call the subject matter a variation on *Ali Baba and the Forty Thieves*. It's a tale of intrigue, adventure, romance, thrills and stunts galore. Improbable? Decidedly. But what's the difference? One is looking at hokum in a serial and not at reality. The un-

lucky brides are held in a castle guarded by bestial blacks.

Go Get 'Em Hutch ('22), made for Pathé, was better for four reasons: (1) a story by Frank Leon Smith; (2) direction by George Seitz; (3) Charles Hutchison as co-star; and (4) the Pathé technical touch that spelled superiority in the silent era.

Clayton continued to work in films through 1928, at which time she retired from the screen. Details of her personal life thereafter are sketchy. In her movie days she stood 5'4", weighed 120, and had a fair complexion, blond hair and blue eyes. She died under the name of Mrs. Marguerite Bertrandias on December 20, 1960, nearly 60 years after starting her career. The death of "The Broncho Billy Girl" failed to make any of the trade papers, once again underscoring the fact that fame is indeed ephemeral.

Serials

1920

Bride 13. Fox, [15 Chapters] D: Richard Stanton; SP: Edward Sedgwick, Thomas P. Fallen; S:

Edward Sedgwick; LP: Marguerite Clayton, John O'Brien, William Laurence, Lynten Chambers, Justine Holland, Dorothy Langley.

1922

Go Get 'Em Hutch. Pathé, [15 Chapters]

D: George B. Seitz; S/SP: Frank Leon Smith; P: George B. Seitz; LP: Charles Hutchison, Marguerite Clayton, Richard R. Neill, Frank Hagney, Pearl Shepard, Joe Cuny.

RUTH CLIFFORD

Ruth Clifford was born on Friday, February 16, 1900, in Pawtucket, Rhode Island. There she attended elementary school. At age 11, after her mother's death, Ruth and her sister were placed in St. Mary's Seminary on Narragansett Bay where they lived for three years. At age 15, they came to California to live with an aunt who had been on the stage. Ruth visited Universal Studios many times and one day director Henry MacRae asked her if she would like to play a scene the next day. She did such a good job that Universal gave her a three-year contract.

Actually, her first film role was a bit in *Birth of Our Savior* ('14), a ten-minute short produced by the Edison Company and released in December 1914. Back then she was on her way to Fordham High School in New York when she got a one-day job playing an angel sent to warn Joseph to flee with his wife and the infant Jesus to Egypt.

Ruth was featured in well over 20 of Universal's Bluebird Productions. Also, she had a principal role in the series *Timothy Dobbs, That's Me* ('16), a combination of comedy and action. Each episode was entirely independent of the others. After her contract was completed, Ruth was signed to do four films in New York and Florida by Charles Frohman Company.

One of the Frohman films was the 15-chapter serial *The Invisible Ray* ('20). The story begins with a young mineralogist scouring the rocky countryside of Persia and accidentally exposing a strange new sub-stance which seems to possess an unusual ray power that can have a fatal effect on humans. He hurriedly secures samples of the rock and places them in a sealed lead box. Two keys are required to open the box. One is placed around the neck of his infant daughter and the other sent to Prof. Stone, a famous mineralogist. Thinking himself dying, the explorer sends his daughter back to England to live with a relative. However, blunders are made and she winds up in a foundling home.

The years pass and she grew to womanhood, still retaining the key around her neck (and now played by Clifford). A chance meeting occurs with Prof. Stone, who informs her that she is the lost daughter of his friend and also relates the story behind the key she wears. She also meets Jack Stone, son of the professor, and the two fall in love. Clifford is kidnapped by a gang known as the Crime Creators and the action begins.

Returning to California, Ruth married James Cornelius, president of Beverly Hills Realty Board and builder of the First National Bank in Beverly Hills and many of the beautiful homes there. They had one son, James Cornelius, Jr. Ruth took a six-year vacation to devote herself to her family. The marriage hit the skids in August 1934 when Ruth sued for divorce on grounds of infidelity with a Miss Marian Elder in a cottage at Seal Beach on August 14. She also charged him with "persistent association with other women."

Ruth appeared in such silent films as *A*

Kentucky Cinderella ('17), *The Cabaret Girl* ('18), *The Kaiser, the Beast of Berlin* ('18), *The Millionaire Pirate* ('19) and *Abraham Lincoln* ('24), in which she played Ann Rutledge.

In the sound era she became a character actress and had roles in many films including those of John Ford: *Wagonmaster, The Searchers, Drums Along the Mohawk, She Wore a Yellow Ribbon, My Darling Clementine*, etc.

She appeared in these stage plays: *This Thing Called Love, Private Lives, One Way Ticket, Juno and the Paycock, Hogan's Goat, White Headed Boy* and *Claudio*. Ruth also did nine commercials for the BBC and local television.

Ruth could be seen in the features *Stand Up and Cheer* ('34), *Dante's Inferno* ('35), *Hollywood Boulevard* ('36), *Sailor's Lady* ('40), *Along the Rio Grande* ('41), *The Keys of the Kingdom* ('44), *Luck of the Irish* ('48) and *Father was a Fullback* ('49).

In the '50s, Ruth worked in television and had running parts on *Highway Patrol* with Broderick Crawford and *I Led Three Lives* with Richard Carlson.

The *Los Angeles Herald-Express* reported on December 17, 1953, that Ruth had been secretly married to E. H. Hobden since August of that year. The author has found no other reference to this marriage. There was no identification of Hobden. What is known for sure is that she came to the Motion Picture and Television Country House in October 1987. There she died on November 30, 1998.

Serial

1920

The Invisible Ray. Frohman, [15 Chapters] D: Henry A. Pollard, Jack Sherrill; SP: Guy McConnell; LP: Jack Sherrill, Ruth Clifford, Sidney Bracey, Carrine Uzzell, Edith Forrest.

PHYLLIS COATES

Phyllis Coates was a pretty, blue-eyed redhead who came to Hollywood as a dancer. She was born in Wichita Falls, Texas, on January 15, 1927. She was educated in her native Texas in Catholic schools at Abilene and Stanton and in Odessa, Texas High School.

She first wanted to be a great dancer. Her first professional work was done soon after her arrival in Hollywood when she appeared in the famed Ken Murray's "Blackouts" at the El Capitan Theatre. Later she was a featured dancer at the Florentine Gardens.

As soon as Richard A. Bare, a Warner Bros. director, saw her, she was offered a screen contract at that studio, where she remained for more than a year. She regularly appeared as the wife of George O'Hanlon in the *Joe McDoakes* series of one-reel comedies. She took the role in 1948 and stayed through 1953.

Like any other star, Phyllis Coates (real name: Gypsie Ann Stell) was neither wholly unique nor wholly representative. Her range of abilities was greater than that possessed by most serial and Western heroines, she was strikingly beautiful, and she was athletic enough to cope with the rigors of action films.

Coates became the screen's last serial queen when she appeared in *Panther Girl of the Kongo* (Rep. 1955). Dressed in Frances Gifford's outfit, she battled gigantic claw monsters created by a villainous scientist. The use of this type of monster was no doubt an attempt to cash in on the science fiction films becoming popular at that time.

Phyllis Coates and Jock Mahoney in *Gunfighters of the Northwest* (Columbia, 1953).

In *Panther Girl* Phyllis received top billing over her leading man, Myron Healey. Only three serial actresses in Republic's 20-year history had been so billed — Frances Gifford in *Jungle Girl* ('41), Kay Aldridge in *Perils of Nyoka* ('42) and Adrian Booth in *Daughter of Don Q* ('46). Not even Linda Stirling in *The Tiger Woman* ('44) received top billing distinction. Possibly Republic had hoped to create in Phyllis a serial queen on the order of Pearl White, but it was a little late for that. The studio made only one more serial. In fact, only three serials were released after *Panther Girl of the Kongo*, one by Republic and two by Columbia. That was it — the end of an era and the end of the line for what had been a profitable and popular film genre.

Certainly Phyllis was a great choice for the last-ditch effort to inject life into the cliffhanger film, for she was attractive and she could act. But the production values of the film were just not there to back her up. Both Phyllis and Myron Healey did their best, but their abilities could only go so far in overcoming the inadequacies of the low-budget, poorly scripted, stock-footage–padded film.

Phyllis had received second billing to Clayton Moore in an earlier serial, also set in Africa. In *Jungle Drums of Africa* ('53) she had played the daughter of a medical missionary carrying on in her father's place after his death. She befriended Moore and his partner, who were prospecting for uranium, and they were all in constant peril from those who wanted the uranium for themselves and from the witch doctor who hated Phyllis. This serial, too, had been interesting enough to the juvenile audience, but the product itself was becoming impotent by this time.

Between the two Republic cliffhangers, Phyllis had played the heroine in one of Columbia's last chapterplays, *Gunfighters of the Northwest* ('54), but the Columbia product was even shoddier than Republic's and did nothing to sustain or promote interest in the genre. It was unfortunate that such an attractive and talented girl could not have been

discovered and promoted five or ten years earlier. She had what it took to become a real serial star.

In her Westerns she was believable, although she sometimes got bogged down in pedestrian screenplays. Her heroine was often the strong, self-sufficient type, but less brassy than Dale Evans' heroine.

Phyllis had a successful television career. Her best-remembered characterization is that of Lois Lane on the *Superman* series before Noel Neill took over. Coates had a sexy chemistry with Reeves in the 1951 film *Superman and the Mole Men* and the syndicated TV series which ran from 1952 to 1957. She left *Superman* after the first 26 episodes to work on other television pilots. During the summer season of 1954 she was featured as the girlfriend of Paul Gilbert on *The Duke*, a series about a retired prizefighter. Her talent was also utilized in such television shows as *Jewelers Showcase*, *G. E. Theatre*, *Death Valley Days*, *Perry Mason*, *The Untouchables*, *Rawhide*, *Gunslinger*, *Hennesey* and *Black Saddle*.

Phyllis Coates retired from acting in 1961.

Serials

1953

Jungle Drums of Africa. Rep., [12 Chapters] D: Fred C. Brannon; SP: Ronald Davidson; AP: Franklyn Adreon; Cam: John MacBurnie; LP: Clayton Moore, Phyllis Coates, Johnny Spencer, Roy Glenn, Tom Steele, Henry Rowland.

Gunfighters of the Northwest. Col., [15 Chapters] D: Spencer G. Bennet, Charles S. Gould; SP: George H. Plympton, Royal Cole, Arthur Hoel; P: Sam Katzman; Cam: William Whitley; Mus: Mischa Bakaleinikoff; LP: Jock Mahoney, Clayton Moore, Phyllis Coates, Don Harvey, Rodd Redwing, Lyle Talbot.

1955

Panther Girl of the Kongo. Rep., [12 Chapters] D: Franklyn Adreon; SP: Ronald Davidson; AP: Franklyn Adreon; Cam: Bud Thackery; Mus: R. Dale Butts; LP: Phyllis Coates, Myron Healey, Arthur Space, John Daheim, Mike Ragan, Roy Glenn, Morris Buchanan, Ramsay Hill, Charles Sullivan.

EDMUND COBB

Edmund Cobb has the distinction of appearing in more serials than any other actor. His first, *The Adventures of Kathlyn* ('14); his last, 40 years later, *Man with the Steel Whip* ('54).

Edmund Fessenden Cobb was born on June 23, 1892, in Albuquerque, the grandson of Edmund Gibson Ross, former editor of *The Kansas Tribune*, United States Senator 1866–71 and governor of the Territory of New Mexico in 1885. In 1889 Ross became a lawyer. Little is known about Edmund's parents, but it is believed they operated a photography studio.

Edmund's formative years were spent partially in town and partially on a nearby ranch where he learned riding, roping and other cowboy skills.

It was expected that Edmund, like his grandfather, would go into politics, and his early formal education was somewhat oriented toward such a career. Ed loved his grandfather and acquiesced to his wishes but, with the death of his grandfather in 1907, Cobb lost all interest in politics. He turned to the local theatrical groups in Albuquerque. When the St. Louis Picture Company came to Albuquerque in 1910 for some location shooting, Edmund got work in the film. He was only 18. A couple of years later, he went to Hollywood where he got work as a rider and stuntman, and in 1913 a part in Selig's *The Adventures of Kathlyn*. Prior to that he had a few bit roles, one of which was in *The Pueblo Legend* ('12). In 1913 he worked in Westerns filmed around Las Vegas.

In 1914 he was with the Colorado Film Company making movies in the Canon City–Colorado Springs region. He had the lead with Grace McHugh in *Across the Border* ('14). In 1915 he was employed at Essanay in a number of non–Western films and in 1916 was featured in the serial *The Strange Case of Mary Page* starring Henry B. Walthall and Edna Mayo. Throughout 1916, Cobb worked in Essanay films.

The author has found only one credit for Edmund in 1917, two in '18 and none in '19. Probably he was working in non–credited bits or perhaps he was in the military service during this time. At any rate, in '20 he starred in *The Desert Scorpion* and *Wolves of the Street*, both for Arrow. In 1921 he was featured in *Finders Keepers* and *Out of the Depths* for Pioneer/Art-O-Graf. By 1923 he was starring in the Universal two-reelers *Face to Face*, *Dropped from the Clouds* and *No Tenderfoot*, and in the feature Westerns *The Sting of the Scorpion* (Arrow), *At Devil's Gorge* (Arrow), *Battling Bates* (Arrow), and *Riders of the Range* (Truart). In 1924 he starred in Arrow's *Western Yesterdays*, *Western Feuds*, *Blasted Hopes*, *Range Blood* and the serial *Days of '49* with Neva Gerber.

In mid–'24 Cobb signed with Universal to star in western two-reelers, making close to 60 of them. As an example of the entertainment that Cobb offered in his Mustang two-reelers, let's take *Pawns and Queens*. As the title indicates, the characters in this Western are like those in a game of chess. Cobb, a wandering cowpuncher, gets a job at a ranch, learns that the foreman is a member of a noted gang, forces him to take him to headquarters where he finds that the leader has imprisoned a cattle buyer and taken his place. Cobb gives chase, holds the bandit and his henchmen until the sheriff arrives and of course wins the girl. The story is a variation of familiar Western formulas, and there are no surprises, but plenty of action.

In his third serial, *Fighting with Buffalo Bill* (Univ. '25), Cobb supported Wallace MacDonald and Elsa Benham. He made five features in 1927–28 with the dog star Dynamite, and another serial, *A Fatal Reckoning* ('29).

Beginning in the sound era, Edmund slipped quietly into character roles and supported most of the sound era cowboys from Gene Autry to "Big Boy" Williams. The author has counted 260 credits, exclusive of serials. Seventy-four of the 260 films were non–Westerns. There is no telling how many more films there were in which he did not get screen credit.

Cobb's last films were *Requiem for a Gunfighter* ('65) and *Johnny Reno* ('66). He also worked in television in his later years.

Some writers have criticized Cobb's acting as inferior. It depended on the script and director. Take *Arizona Bad Man* (Kent '35). Cobb walked away with acting honors. He generally held his own in the acting department, otherwise his career would not have carried him through six decades.

Edmund Cobb died from a heart attack on August 15, 1974, at Woodland Hills, California. He had been in poor health for several years.

Serials

1914

The Adventures of Kathlyn. Selig, [13 Chapters] D: F. J. Grandon; LP: Kathlyn Williams, Charles Clary, Thomas Santschi, William Carpenter.

1916

The Strange Case of Mary Page. Ess., [15 Chapters] D: J. Charles Haydon; LP: Henry B. Walthall, Edna Mayo, Sydney Ainsworth, Harry Dunkinson.

1924

Days of '49. Arrow, [15 Chapters] D: Jacques Jaccard, Jay Marchant; LP: Neva Gerber, Edmund Cobb, Charles Brinley, Yakima Canutt, Ruth Royce.

1926

Fighting with Buffalo Bill. Univ., [10 Chapters] D: Ray Taylor; LP: Wallace MacDonald, Elsa Benham, Edmund Cobb, Robert E. Homans.

1928

The Scarlet Arrow. Univ., [10 Chapters] D: Ray Taylor; LP: Francis X. Bushman, Jr., Hazel Keener, Edmund Cobb, Al Ferguson.

A Final Reckoning. Univ., [12 Chapters] D: Ray Taylor; LP: Newton House, Louise Lorraine, Jay Wilsey, Edmund Cobb, Frank Clark.

1930

The Indians Are Coming. Univ., [12 Chapters] D: Henry MacRae; LP: Tim McCoy, Allene Ray, Charles Roy, Edmund Cobb.

1931

The Sign of the Wolf. Met., [10 Chapters] D: Forrest Sheldon, Harry S. Webb; LP: Rex Lease, Virginia Brown Faire, Joe Bonomo, Jack Mower.

Heroes of the Flames. Univ., [12 Chapters] D:

Robert F. Hill; LP: Tim McCoy, Marion Shockley, William Gould, Grace Cunard, Edmund Cobb.

Battling with Buffalo Bill. Univ., [12 Chapters] D: Ray Taylor; LP: Tom Tyler, Rex Bell, Lucile Browne, Francis Ford, Edmund Cobb.

1932

The Lost Special. Univ., [12 Chapters] D: Henry MacRae; LP: Frank Albertson, Cecilia Parker, Caryl Lincoln, Ernie Nevers.

Heroes of the West. Univ., [12 Chapters] D: Ray Taylor; LP: Noah Beery, Jr., Diane Duval (Julie Bishop/Jacqueline Wells), Onslow Stevens, William Desmond.

1933

Gordon of Ghost City. Univ., [12 Chapters] D: Ray Taylor; LP: Buck Jones, Madge Bellamy, Walter Miller, William Desmond, Francis Ford, Edmund Cobb.

The Phantom of the Air. Univ., [12 Chapters] D: Ray Taylor; LP: Tom Tyler, Gloria Shea, LeRoy Mason, Hugh Enfield, Edmund Cobb.

Clancy of the Mounted. Univ., [12 Chapters] D: Ray Taylor; LP: Tom Tyler, Jacqueline Wells, William Desmond, Rosalie Roy, Francis Ford, Edmund Cobb.

1934

Pirate Treasure. Univ., [12 Chapters] D: Ray Taylor; LP: Richard Talmadge, Lucille Lund, Walter Miller, Pat O'Malley.

The Red Rider. Univ., [15 Chapters] D: Louis Friedlander [Lew Landers]; LP: Buck Jones, Grant Withers, Marion Shilling, Walter Miller, Edmund Cobb.

The Vanishing Shadow. Univ., [12 Chapters] D: Louis Friedlander [Lew Landers]; LP: Onslow Stevens, Ada Ince, Walter Miller, James Durkin.

Mystery Mountain. Mascot, [12 Chapters] D: B. Reeves Eason, Otto Brower; LP: Ken Maynard, Verna Hillie, Syd Saylor, Edward Earle, Edmund Cobb.

The Law of the Wild. Mascot, [12 Chapters] D: Armand Schaefer, B. Reeves Eason; LP: Bob Custer, Rex (horse), Rin-Tin-Tin, Jr. (dog), Ben Turpin, Lucile Browne.

1935

Rustlers of Red Dog. Univ., [12 Chapters] D: Louis Friedlander [Lew Landers]; LP: Johnny Mack Brown, Joyce Compton, Walter Miller, Raymond Hatton.

The Roaring West. Univ., [15 Chapters] D: Ray Taylor; LP: Buck Jones, Muriel Evans, Walter Miller, Frank McGlynn, Sr., Edmund Cobb.

The Miracle Rider. Mascot, [15 Chapters] D: Armand Schaefer, B. Reeves Eason; LP: Tom Mix, Charles Middleton, Joan Gale, Jason Robards, Robert Kortman.

The Adventures of Rex and Rinty. Mascot, [12 Chapters] D: B. Reeves Eason, Ford Beebe; LP: Rex, Rin-Tin-Tin, Jr., Kane Richmond, Norma Taylor.

1936

Robinson Crusoe of Clipper Island. Rep., [14 Chapters] D: Mack V. Wright, Ray Taylor; LP: Ray Mala, Rex (horse), Buck (dog), Mamo Clark, Herbert Rawlinson.

Ace Drummond. Univ., [13 Chapters] D: Ford Beebe, Cliff Smith; LP: John King, Jean Rogers, Noah Beery, Jr., Guy Bates Post, Edmund Cobb.

Darkest Africa. Rep., [15 Chapters] D: B.

Reeves Eason, Joseph Kane; LP: Clyde Beatty, Manuel King, Elaine Sheppard, Lucien Prival.

The Adventures of Frank Merriwell. Univ., [12 Chapters] D: Cliff Smith; LP: Don Briggs, Jean Rogers, John King, Carla Laemmle.

1937

Zorro Rides Again. Rep., [12 Chapters] D: William Witney, John English; LP: John Carroll, Helen Christian, Duncan Renaldo, Noah Beery, Sr., Dick Alexander.

1938

The Lone Ranger. Rep., [15 Chapters] D: William Witney, John English; LP: Lee Powell, Chief Thundercloud, Lynne Roberts, Herman Brix, Stanley Andrews.

The Spider's Web. Col., [15 Chapters] D: Ray Taylor, James W. Horne; LP: Warren Hull, Iris Meredith, Richard Fiske, Kenneth Duncan.

The Great Adventures of Wild Bill Hickok. Col., [15 Chapters] D: Mack V. Wright, Sam Nelson; LP: Bill Elliott, Carole Wayne, Frankie Darro, Monte Blue.

1939

Dick Tracy's G-Men. Rep., [15 Chapters] D: William Witney, John English; LP: Ralph Byrd, Phylis Isley [Jennifer Jones], Irving Pichel, Ted Pearson, Walter Miller.

Zorro's Fighting Legion. Rep., [12 Chapters] D: William Witney, John English; LP: Reed Hadley, Sheila Darcy, William Corson, Leander de Cordova.

Daredevils of the Red Circle. Rep., [12 Chapters] D: William Witney, John English; LP: Charles Quigley, Herman Brix, David Sharpe, Carole Landis.

1940

Winners of the West. Univ., [13 Chapters] D: Ford Beebe, Ray Taylor; LP: Dick Foran, Anne Nagle, James Craig, Tom Fadden.

Deadwood Dick. Col., [15 Chapters] D: James W. Horne; LP: Don Douglas, Lorna Gray, Lane Chandler, Marin Sais, Charles King.

1941

Riders of Death Valley. Univ., [15 Chapters] D: Ray Taylor, Ford Beebe; LP: Dick Foran, Buck Jones, Leo Carrillo, Charles Bickford, Lon Chaney, Jr.

White Eagle. Col., [15 Chapters] D: James W. Horne; LP: Buck Jones, Dorothy Fay, Raymond Hatton, James Craven, Charles King, John Merton, Roy Barcroft.

Dick Tracy vs. Crime, Inc. Rep., [15 Chapters] D: William Witney, John English; LP: Ralph Byrd, Jan Wiley, John Davidson, Ralph Morgan, Michael Owen.

1942

Overland Mail. Univ., [15 Chapters] D: Ford Beebe, John Rawlins; LP: Lon Chaney, Jr., Don Terry, Noah Beery, Jr., Helen Parrish, Noah Beery, Sr., Tom Chatterton.

1943

Daredevils of the West. Rep., [12 Chapters] D: John English; LP: Allan Lane, Kay Aldridge, Eddie Acuff, William Haade, Robert Frazer, George J. Lewis.

The Phantom. Col., [15 Chapters] D: B. Reeves Eason; LP: Tom Tyler, Jeanne Bates, Kenneth MacDonald, Frank Shannon, Ernie Adams.

G-Men vs. the Black Dragon. Rep., [15 Chapters] D: William Witney; LP: Rod Cameron, Constance Worth, Roland Got, Nino Pipitone, Edmund Cobb.

1944

Raiders of Ghost City. Univ., [13 Chapters] D: Ray Taylor, Lewis Collins; LP: Dennis Moore, Wanda McKay, Lionel Atwill, Joe Sawyer, Edmund Cobb.

1945

Jungle Queen. Univ., [13 Chapters] D: Ray Taylor, Lewis D. Collins; LP: Edward Norris, Lois Collier, Eddie Quillan, Douglas Dumbrille.

Secret Agent X-9. Univ., [13 Chapters] D: Ray Taylor, Lewis D. Collins; LP: Lloyd Bridges, Keye Luke, Jan Wiley, Victoria Horne.

Federal Operator 99. Rep., [12 Chapters] D: Spencer Bennet, Yakima Canutt, Wallace A. Grissell; LP: Marten Lamont, Helen Talbot, George J. Lewis, Lorna Gray.

1946

The Scarlet Horseman. Univ., [13 Chapters] D: Ray Taylor, Lewis D. Collins; LP: Peter Cookson, Paul Guilfoyle, Virginia Horne, Virginia Christine.

1947

G-Men Never Forget. Rep., [12 Chapters] D: Fred Brannon, Yakima Canutt; LP: Clayton Moore, Ramsay Ames, Roy Barcroft, Drew Allen.

Jesse James Rides Again. Rep., [13 Chapters] D: Fred C. Brannon, Thomas Carr; LP: Clayton Moore, Linda Stirling, Roy Barcroft, Tristram Coffin, Edmund Cobb.

Son of Zorro. Rep., [13 Chapters] D: Spencer Bennet, Fred Brannon; LP: George Turner, Peggy Stewart, Roy Barcroft, Edward Cassidy, Edmund Cobb.

The Vigilante. Col., [15 Chapters] D: Wallace Fox; LP: Ralph Byrd, Lyle Talbot, Ramsay Ames, George Offerman.

1948

Tex Granger. Col., [15 Chapters] D: Derwin Abrahams; LP: Robert Kellard [Stevens], Peggy Stewart, Smith Ballew, Jack Ingram, Buzz Henry.

1950

The James Brothers of Missouri. Rep., [12 Chapters] D: Fred C. Brannon; LP: Keith Richards, Robert Bice, Noel Neill, Roy Barcroft.

Desperados of the West. Rep., [12 Chapters] D: Fred C. Brannon; LP: Richard Powers [Tom Keene], Roy Barcroft, I. Stanford, Jolley, Lee Roberts.

1951

Government Agents vs. Phantom Legion. Rep., [12 Chapters] D: Fred C. Brannon; LP: Walter Reed, Mary Ellen Kay, Dick Curtis, John Pickard.

1953

Canadian Mounties vs. Atomic Invaders. Rep., [12 Chapters] D: Franklyn Adreon; LP: Bill Henry, Susan Morrow, Arthur Space, Dale Van Sickel.

The Great Adventures of Captain Kidd. Col., [15 Chapters] D: Derwin Abbe, Charles S. Gould; LP: Richard Crane, David Bruce, John Crawford, George Wallace.

1954

Man with the Steel Whip. Rep., [12 Chapters] D: Franklyn Adreon; LP: Richard Simmons, Barbara Bestar, Dale Van Sickel, Mauritz Hugo.

IRON EYES CODY

It has been claimed that Iron Eyes Cody was born an Italian; be that as it may, he claimed to be a Cherokee Indian born in 1916 in Oklahoma and from an early age performed with Wild West shows and circuses. As early as 1929 he traveled with the Buck Jones Wild West show. In later years he became famous as the Indian shedding a tear over the destruction of the environment in TV ecology spots and print advertising.

His screen career dates from the late '20s. He portrayed Indians in B Westerns and in 15 serials. In three other serials he portrayed jungle tribesmen. In addition to B Westerns he has appeared in such A productions as: *North West Mounted Police* ('40), *Unconquered* ('47), *The Paleface* ('48), *Blood on the Moon* ('48), *Broken Arrow* ('50), *Nevada Smith* ('69), *El Condor* ('70), *A Man Called Horse* ('70) and *Hearts of the West* ('75).

Cody has worked hard on behalf of the American Indians. He was on the board of directors of the Los Angeles Indian Center, the Southwest Museum and the Los Angeles

Library Association. He served as vice-president of the Little Big Horn Indian Association, was a life member of the Verdugo Council of the Boy Scouts of America, and was Grand Marshal of Indian pow wows nationwide.

His wife of many years was Ga Yehwas, a Seneca Indian, a descendant of General Ely S. Parker, the first commissioner of Indian Affairs. They had two sons, also active in Indian affairs.

Iron Eyes was a guest at numerous film festivals and was always a hit with the festival crowds. He died in 1991 at age 84.

Serials

1933

Fighting with Kit Carson. Mascot, [12 Chapters] D: Armand Schaefer, Colbert Clark; LP: Johnny Mack Brown, Betsy King Ross, Noah Beery, Sr., Noah Beery, Jr., Tully Marshall.

1934

The Return of Chandu. Principal, [12 Chapters] D: Ray Taylor; LP: Bela Lugosi, Maria Alba, Clara Kimball Young, Peggy Montgomery, Lucien Prival.

1936

Rustlers of Red Dog. Univ., [15 Chapters] D: Louis Friedlander [Lew Landers]; LP: Johnny Mack Brown, Joyce Compton, Walter Miller, Raymond Hatton, Harry Woods.

The Phantom Rider. Univ., [15 Chapters] D: Ray Taylor; LP: Buck Jones, Maria Shelton, Diana Gibson, Harry Woods, George Cooper, Charles King.

Custer's Last Stand. S & S, [15 Chapters] D: Elmer Clifton; LP: Rex Lease, Dorothy Gulliver, William Farnum, Reed Howes, Jack Mulhall, George Chesebro.

1937

Wild West Days. Univ., [13 Chapters] D: Ford Beebe, Cliff Smith; LP: Johnny Mack Brown, Lynn Gilbert, Robert Kortman, George Shelley,

Frank Yaconelli, Al Bridge, Joe Girard, William Royle, Chief Thundercloud, Iron Eyes Cody.

1938

Hawk of the Wilderness. Rep., [12 Chapters] D: William Witney, John English; LP: Herman Brix [Bruce Bennett[, Ray Mala, Monte Blue, Jill Martin, Noble Johnson.

The Great Adventures of Wild Bill Hickok. Col., [15 Chapters] D: Mack V. Wright, Sam Nelson; LP: Gordon [Bill] Elliott, Carole Wayne, Frankie Darro, Monte Blue, Dickie Jones, Sammy McKim, Kermit Maynard.

Flaming Frontiers. Univ., [15 Chapters] D: Ray Taylor, Alan James; LP: Johnny Mack Brown, Eleanor Hansen, Ralph Bowman [John Archer], Charles Middleton, Charles Stevens, Charles King, Horace Murphy, Iron Eyes Cody, William Royle.

The Lone Ranger. Rep., [15 Chapters] D: William Witney, John English; LP: Lee Powell, Chief Thundercloud, Herman Brix [Bruce Bennett], Lynne Roberts, Hal Taliaferro [Wally Wales], Lane Chandler, Stanley Andrews, John Merton.

1939

The Oregon Trail. Univ., [15 Chapters] D: Ford Beebe, Saul A. Goodkind; LP: Johnny Mack Brown, Louise Stanley, Fuzzy Knight, Bill Cody, Jr., Forrest Taylor, Edward LeSaint, Roy Barcroft, Lane Chandler, Charles Stevens.

Overland with Kit Carson. Col., [15 Chapters] D: Sam Nelson, Norman Deming; LP: Bill Elliott, Iris Meredith, Trevor Bardette, Richard Fiske, Bobby Clark.

1940

Winners of the West. Univ., [13 Chapters] D: Ford Beebe, Ray Taylor; LP: Dick Foran, Anne Nagel, James Craig, Tom Fadden, Charles Stevens.

1941

King of the Texas Rangers. Rep., [12 Chapters] D: William Witney, John English; LP: Slingin' Sammy Baugh, Pauline Moore, Duncan Renaldo, Neil Hamilton, Monte Blue.

Iron Eyes Cody (left) and Roy Rogers in *North of the Great Divide* (Republic, 1950).

1942

Perils of Nyoka. Rep., [15 Chapters] D: William Witney; LP: Kay Aldridge, Clayton Moore, William Benedict, Lorna Gray, Charles Middleton.

Perils of the Royal Mounted. Col., [15 Chapters] D: James W. Horne; LP: Nell O'Day, Robert Stevens [Kellard], Herbert Rawlinson, Kenneth MacDonald, George Chesebro.

The Valley of Vanishing Men. Col., [15 Chapters] D: Spencer Bennet; LP: Bill Elliott, Slim Summerville, Carmen Morales, Kenneth MacDonald, Jack Ingram.

1944

Black Arrow. Col., [15 Chapters] D: Lew Landers; LP: Robert Scott, Adele Jergens, Kenneth MacDonald, Robert Williams, Charles Middleton.

TRISTRAM COFFIN

Tristram Coffin was nearly everyone's favorite bad man in Westerns and serials. But we also think of him as a hero as he portrayed the dashing Jeff King in *King of the*

Rocket Men, the famed Republic serial of 1949.

Coffin began his serial appearances in 1939 in *Dick Tracy's G-Men*. The white-haired actor was seen in *Mysterious Dr. Satan* in 1940. Running over to Columbia in 1941, he appeared in *Holt of the Secret Service*; running back to Republic in '42, he was a baddie in the war time thriller *Spy Smasher*. Also in '42, Tris did *Perils of Nyoka* and in '47 joined the cast of *Jesse James Rides Again*. In 1948 he was spotted in *Federal Agents vs. Underworld, Inc.*

In 1949's *Rocketmen* he played his first "hero" role. *Radar Patrol vs. Spy King* opposite Kirk Alyn came along in 1950 and a stint with Buster Crabbe in *Pirates of the High Seas* over at Columbia in 1950 completed his serial career.

Coffin's best-known sustaining role was when he played Capt. Tom Rynning in *26 Men*, a true tale of a handful of Texas Rangers types trying to maintain law and order in Arizona at the turn of the century. In fact, there were only 26 of them because the Arizona Territory couldn't afford any more. The TV series ran 78 episodes (1957–59).

Born and raised in a rugged silver mining community high in the Utah Wasatch Mountains, Tris was forced to journey each day to Salt Lake City for his grade and high schooling. For the love of mimicry, he became interested in a resident stock company. He traveled the stock circuits throughout the Northwest and ended with a degree in speech from the University of Washington. A scholarship to Leland Powers in Boston brought about his second phase of experience. He taught at this school while forging ahead as a news analyst and sportscaster. A Hollywood talent scout heard him broadcast, liked Tris' Western accent and persuaded him to come to California.

During the next several decades Tris played in close to 300 Westerns, serials and television shows, plus many other dramatic roles. His films include: *Queen of the Yukon* ('39), *Arizona Bound* ('41), *The Corpse Vanishes* ('42), *The Crime Smasher* ('43), *The In-visible Informer* ('46), *The Baron of Arizona* ('49), *Short Grass* ('50), *Combat Squad* ('53), *Fireman, Save My Child* ('54), *Creature with the Atom Brain* ('55), *The Night the World Exploded* ('57), *Last Stagecoach West* ('60), *Good Neighbor Sam* ('64) and *Zebra in the Kitchen* ('65).

Coffin did a lot of television work, including *Wyatt Earp*, *Judge Roy Bean*, *The Lone Ranger*, *Cisco Kid*, *Kit Carson*, *Wild Bill Hickok*, *The Bob Cummings Show*, *My Little Margie*, *The Loretta Young Show*, *Favorite Story*, *I Love Lucy*, *Climax*, *Lux Video Theatre* and *Hallmark Hall of Fame*.

Coffin died in March 1990. He was 80 years old.

Serials

1939

The Green Hornet. Univ., [13 Chapters] D: Ford Beebe, Ray Taylor; LP: Gordon Jones, Anne Nagel, Keye Luke, Wade Boteler, Philip Trent, John Kelly.

Dick Tracy's G-Men. Rep., [15 Chapters] D: William Witney, John English; LP: Ralph Byrd, Irving Pichel, Phylis Isley [Jennifer Jones], Ted Pearson.

1940

Mysterious Doctor Satan. Rep., [15 Chapters] D: William Witney, John English; LP: Eduardo Ciannelli, Robert Wilcox, Ella Neal, William Newell.

1941

Holt of the Secret Service. Col., [15 Chapters] D: James W. Horne; LP: Jack Holt, Evelyn Brent, Montague Shaw, Tristram Coffin, George Chesebro.

1942

Spy Smasher. Rep., [12 Chapters] D: William Witney; LP: Kane Richmond, Marguerite Chapman, Sam Flint, Tristram Coffin, Hans Schumm.

Perils of Nyoka. Rep., [15 Chapters] D: William Witney; LP: Kay Aldridge, Clayton Moore,

William Benedict, Lorna Gray, Tristram Coffin, Charles Middleton.

1947

Jesse James Rides Again. Rep., [13 Chapters] D: Fred C. Brannon, Thomas Carr; LP: Clayton Moore, Linda Stirling, Roy Barcroft, Tristram Coffin, John Compton.

1949

King of the Rocket Men. Rep., [12 Chapters] D: Fred C. Brannon; SP: Royal Cole, William Lively, Sol Shor; AP: Franklyn Adreon; Cam: Ellis W. Carter; Mus: Stanley Wilson; LP: Tristram Coffin, Mae Clarke, Don Haggerty, House Peters, Jr., I. Stanford Jolley, James Craven, Ted Adams.

Bruce Gentry. Col., [15 Chapters] D: Spencer G. Bennet, Thomas Carr; LP: Tom Neal, Judy Clark, Ralph Hodges, Forrest Taylor.

Federal Agents vs. Underworld, Inc. Rep., [12 Chapters] D: Fred C. Brannon; LP: Kirk Alyn, Rosemary LaPlanche, Roy Barcroft, Carol Forman, James Dale.

1950

Radar Patrol vs. Spy King. Rep., [12 Chapters] D: Fred C. Brannon; LP: Kirk Alyn, Jean Dean, Anthony Warde, George J. Lewis, Eve Whitney, John Merton.

Pirates of the High Seas. Col., [15 Chapters] D: Spencer G. Bennet, Thomas Carr; LP: Buster Crabbe, Lois Hall, Tommy Farrell, Tristram Coffin, Gene Roth, Stanley Price.

FRANK COGHLAN, JR.

Born Frank Coghlan, Jr., on March 15, 1916, in New Haven, Connecticut, the young freckle-faced kid moved with his family to California in 1919. A baby when he first appeared in films, he began his rise to fame with a brief appearance in a Tom Santschi Western in 1920. At age four he played Leatrice Joy's son in *The Poverty of Riches* ('21). He was a member of the original *Our Gang* comedy cast and soon was in demand in feature films with many of the big stars of the screen.

Realart Pictures featured Junior in its comedy hit *Bobbed Hair*. The following year he played the young son of David Butler in *Cause for Divorce*. He was the "Ross Kid" in *The Darling of New York*, a 1923 Universal picture starring Baby Peggy Montgomery.

With experience the young actor received more important roles. Cecil B. De-

Mille was so impressed with the youngster's progress that he signed him to a five-year contract. Two movies in which Coghlan played were *Whispering Smith* with H. B. Warner and *The Last Frontier*, in which he was cast behind William Boyd as the wagonmaster. He was a Boy Scout in *The Road to Yesterday*, with Boyd again featured. He was also a scout in his other 1925 appearance, MGM's *The Great Love*. *The Skyrocket* ('25) and *Mike* ('26) followed. With the advent of talking pictures, Coghlan played supporting roles in numerous features, including *Penrod and Sam* ('31), *Union Depot* ('31), *Charlie Chan at the Race Track* ('36), *Service De Luxe* ('38), *Meet Dr. Christian* ('38), *Gone with the Wind* ('39) and *Henry Aldrich for President* ('41).

In *Last of the Mohicans* ('32), Mascot's 12-chapter serial, Coghlan was billed third as Uncas. In this filmed version of the famed novel, Hawkeye, his friends and the last two surviving Mohicans fight their mortal enemy, the treacherous Huron chief Magua (Robert Kortman). A cast of veteran players and direction by competent directors produced a serial that was entertaining from beginning to end.

Scouts to the Rescue ('39) was a serial starring Jackie Cooper. Coghlan was one of the scouts involved in the search for counterfeiters after the scouts rescue a G-man from a plane crash in the wilds and find a large sum of counterfeit money. As things turn out, the father of one of the scouts is implicated in the counterfeiting and is arrested by the G-man only to escape. The scouts attempt to prove the man innocent, but in the process are imperiled by a gang of marauding Indians.

Coghlan seems destined to always be remembered as Billy Batson in the serial *Adventures of Captain Marvel* ('41), one of the most popular serials of the sound era. In the story, the Malcolm Expedition searched in a remote section of Siam for the lost secret of the Scorpion, a powerful weapon controlled by focusing the highly polished lenses. Bill Batson is the only member of the group who did not enter a forbidden chamber inside an underground tomb. When a volcanic eruption causes part of the tomb to collapse, Shazam, the tomb's guardian, appears because Billy had heeded the warning not to enter the tomb. Shazam endows Billy with the magic power to transform himself into Captain Marvel. The scientists discover the Scorpion, the lenses are divided among them and they return home to the U.S. However, a gang whose masked leader calls himself the Scorpion finally succeeds in stealing the various lenses and activating the powerful Scorpion machine. But Captain Marvel thwarts the Scorpion's destructive plans, unmasks him and destroys the deadly instrument.

Coghlan was a Navy Pilot in World War II and retired in 1965 as a lieutenant commander after serving 23 years. Back in Hollywood he had a small part in *The Sand Pebbles*, and was soon appearing in television programs and commercials. He could be seen in Curtis Mathes commercials for a long time.

Coghlan has five children by his first wife, who died in the mid–1970s. Subsequently he married a widow who also had five children.

Junior Coghlan is given an especially warm reception at film festivals, where he is deluged with questions about Captain Marvel.

Serials

1932

The Last of the Mohicans. Mascot, [12 Chapters] D: D. Reeves Eason, Ford Beebe; SP: Colbert Clark, John F. Natteford, Ford Beebe, Wyndham Gittens; P: Nat Levine; Cam: Ernest Miller, Jack Young; LP: Harry Carey, Hobart Bosworth, Frank Coghlan, Jr., Edwina Booth, Lucile Browne, Walter Miller.

1939

Scouts to the Rescue. Univ., [12 Chapters] D: Ray Taylor, Alan James; SP: Wyndham Gittens, George Plympton, Basil Dickens, Joseph Poland; S: Irving Crump; LP: Jackie Cooper, Vondell Darr, Edwin Stanley, Bill Cody, Jr., David Durand, William Ruhl, Frank Coghlan, Jr.

1941

Adventures of Captain Marvel. Rep., [12 Chapters] D: William Witney, John English; SP: Ronald Davidson, Norman S. Hall, Arch B. Heath, Joseph Poland, Sol Shor; AP: Hiram S. Brown, Jr.; Cam: William Nobles; Mus: Cy Feuer; LP: Tom Tyler, Frank Coghlan, Jr., William Benedict, Louise Currie, Robert Strange, Harry Worth.

LOIS COLLIER

Lois Collier, 80, died October 27, 1999, following a bout with Alzheimer's at the Motion Picture Hospital in Woodland Hills, California. She was born Madelyn Earle Jones in Sally, South Carolina, on March 21, 1922. Beautiful, auburn-haired, petite with a dynamite figure, she came to Hollywood following a school contest in 1935.

It was Lois's voice that led her from the obscurity of a small South Carolina town to the bright lights of the cinema's capital, but the other elements of her personality — her big blue eyes, her cameo profile, her slim graceful body and her unusual talent for acting — kept her there for nearly 15 years.

Lois' first appearance before the cameras was in 1938 as a bit player in *Desperate Adventure.* Her next three years were spent going to school, having her teeth straightened, doing radio work and taking some lessons from a drama coach. She adopted the name Lois Collier after playing a character with that name in a radio show.

In 1941–42 Lois filled the heroine's role in seven of Republic's Three Mesquiteers program oaters starring Bob Steele, Tom Tyler and Rufe Davis, handling her horse admirably. Although these films will never be known for climactic battles or for the emotions radiated by the principals, they are nevertheless fondly remembered by Western aficionados. Slickly made "Bs," they entertained those audiences who lived from one Saturday to the next awaiting the heroes of the range to beat the stuffing out of the dastardly scalawags who would mistreat a horse, defile the school marm or sell firewater to the redskins.

Lois was doing well in radio and made frequent appearances on *Lux Radio Theater* and some short engagements in stage leads. A memorable performance was that of "Eileen" in Irving Berlin's *This Is the Army.* In fact, it was that part which led to her contract with Universal. The studio overlooked a real bet when they cast her in mostly non-singing parts. She invariably got good reviews and it is regrettable that neither Universal or Republic really promoted her as they should have. *Ladies Courageous* ('44), in which she played an aviatrix, aptly demonstrated her acting ability. She had a great deal to offer the screen, but she never got a chance at the meaty roles that would have escalated her career. She did, however, register pleasantly as the love interest.

Some of her Universal films were *She's for Me* ('43), *Cobra Woman* ('44), *Weird Woman* ('44), *Jungle Woman* ('44), *The Naughty Nineties* ('45), *The Crimson Canary* ('45), *The Cat Creeps* ('46), *Wild Beauty* ('46) and *Slave Girl* ('47).

In 1945 Lois appeared in Universal's chapterplay *Jungle Queen*, portraying white huntress Pamela Courtney, the "real" heroine of the serial. The 13-episode melodrama featured budding star Ruth Roman as Lothel, mysterious queen of the jungle. Known to the natives as the White Butterfly, Lothel darted in and out of the leafy shadows in a bare-midriff chiffon ensemble (not terribly primeval for a jungle queen). She commandeered the local fauna and was seemingly impervious to flames.

After a modicum of success as a contract player at Universal from 1943 to 1950, Lois returned to Republic as feminine lead in the cliffhanger *Flying Disc Man from Mars* ('51), playing Helen Hall, secretary to Walter Reed, the hero who combats an intruder from outer space who has designs on the Earth. She did exceedingly well with a role that allowed her little opportunity to emote.

Lois may not have had an opportunity for many striking and powerful characterizations, and the critical contingent was prone to write her off along with most other cliffhanger and Western ingenues, but she was an accomplished actress with a charm decidedly her own. One can hardly say that her influence in the Western and serial genres

was monumental, but she was positively stunning — an elfin creature who presented a most enchanting effect and injected a little vitality into the bloodstream of most males.

Lois teamed up with Kent Taylor in the *Boston Blackie* television series. Production started in 1950 and continued for four years. And it is for her role as Mary in this series that she is remembered by many TV fans unfamiliar with her big-screen career.

Lois was awarded "The Billboard Award for Outstanding Achievement in TV Films," voted by the TV Film Industry, as the best actress on a non-network mystery series for the *Boston Blackie* season of 1953–54.

Lois was married to a young Hollywood bank official in the early 1940s, but the couple found their careers were not compatible and they divorced in 1944. In 1957 she married a very successful Los Angeles attorney. Over the years they traveled extensively. She was a happily married woman with diverse interests and the health and money to pursue them.

Serials

1945

Jungle Queen. Univ., [13 Chapters] D: Ray Taylor, Lewis D. Collins; SP: George H. Plympton, Ande Lamb, Morgan B. Cox; LP: Douglas Dumbrille, Edward Norris, Eddie Quillan, Ruth Roman, Lois Collier, Tala Birell, Clarence Muse.

1951

Flying Disc Man from Mars. Rep., [12 Chapters] D: Fred C. Brannon; SP: Ronald Davidson; LP: Walter Reed, Lois Collier, Gregory Gay, James Craven, Harry Lauter, Richard Irving, Sandy Sanders.

GOLDIE COLWELL

Goldie Colwell played "Pundita" in *The Adventures of Kathlyn* ('13), the first cliffhanger serial. She also played opposite Tom Mix in 26 known Westerns. There may have been others, for information is lacking as to the identity of the heroine in a number of Mix's early endeavors.

Goldie apparently went to work for Selig in 1912; the earliest of her credits the author has found is *Betty Fools Dear Old Dad* ('12), a one-reeler. In December 1912 she appeared with Dorothy Davenport in *Our Lady of the Pearls*, also a one-reeler, as were nearly all of her Selig films.

During 1914–15 Goldie worked mostly with Tom Mix in *The Real Thing in Cowboys, The Way of the Redman, The Mexican, Jimmy Hayes and Muriel, Why the Sheriff Is a Bachelor, The Telltale Knife, The Ranger's Romance, The Sheriff's Reward, The Scapegoat, The Rival Stage Lines, Saved by a Watch, The Man from the East, A Militant School Ma'am, Cactus Jake Heart-Breaker, Harold's Bad Man, Cactus Jim's Shopgirl, Forked Trails, Roping a Bride, Slim Higgins, The Stagecoach Driver and the Girl, Sagebrush Tom* and others.

In 1915 Goldie joined the Min A organization and appeared in about 14 segments of the "Jerry" comedy series featuring George Ovey, made from 1915 to 1917. About half of the films were released through Cub. She made a couple of jungle thrillers for Bison in 1916, *The Jungle Hero* and *Under the Lion's Paw*. Both films featured Rex De Rosselli and Colin Chase. Two other films were made with Tom Mix, the five-reelers *In the Days of Daring* ('16) and *The Heart of Texas Ryan* ('17).

In 1918 Goldie made *Code of the Yukon* (Select) with Tom Santschi, but no other credits for that year have been found.

There was one film credit for her in 1919, Triangle's *The Railroader* with Santschi. Goldie simply disappeared in 1919, never to be heard of again by movie fans. She deserves special recognition for pioneering the trails later to be ridden by hundreds of beautiful young ladies providing the inspiration for all the male heroics. Goldie's radiant simplicity served her well in the crude, quickly made hay burners of her day.

Serial

1913

The Adventures of Kathlyn. Selig, [13 Chapters] D: F. J. Grandon; SP: Gilson Willets; S: Harold MacGrath; LP: Kathlyn Williams, Charles Clary, Thomas Santschi, Lafe McKee, Edmund Cobb.

BETTY COMPSON

Betty Compson was born Eleanor Luicime Compson on March 18, 1897, in Beaver, Utah. The daughter of a mining engineer, she started out in vaudeville at 15, billed as "The Vagabond Violinist." A stunning blonde, she broke into films in 1915 as the heroine of Al Christie's comedy shorts. She appeared in about 60 of these during the next three years. Betty was paid $40 a week. In mid–1918 Betty was fired by Christie for refusing to make a personal appearance. Mack Sennett had offered her $150 a week to leave Christie, but she had turned him down when she found that he wanted her services off the set as well as on.

The Miracle Man ('19) made stars of Betty Compson, Tom Meighan and Lon Chaney and is still the best-remembered film Compson ever made. Her career was floundering when George Tucker saw her in an old Christie comedy and chose her for the tough babe in *The Miracle Man*. Thereafter her name shined in electric lights, and she became one of the most popular stars of the 1920s.

Before she hit the big time, however, she did not have a job. After several months without work, and with the bills mounting, Betty landed a job with Pathé as heroine of the seven-chapter serial *The Terror of the Range* ('19), long lost and forgotten except for a dwindling few historians and buffs who find pleasure in the study of Hollywood's primitive years. Betty was the love interest, of course, and George Larkin a government agent out to round up the mysterious outlaw who always wore a wolf's head when he and his raiders swept down on unsuspecting ranchers.

Before his death, George Tucker directed Betty in *Ladies Must Live* ('21) and negotiated a $2500-a-week contract for her with Paramount under which she also had her own production company and a share of the profits her features generated.

Betty's last two pictures for Paramount under her contract were *The Woman with Four Faces* ('23) and *The Rustle of Silk* ('23), both successful and dramatically challenging. At her option time, Paramount wanted to keep her on at $2500 a week without raising her to the $3000 she should have gotten. Hurt that her work was not thought deserving of a raise, she left to accept a three-picture deal in England. Alfred Hitchcock was assistant director on all three films. Betty

stayed around to make a fourth film, got homesick and returned to Hollywood, where she again was contracted to Paramount as a result of her English successes.

Betty's first film under her new contract was *The Stranger* ('24). *The Enemy Sex* ('24) was an even better film for Betty, who received the role after James Cruze insisted on her for the part of Dodo Baxter, a chorus girl with a heart. In the next year she appeared in a number of Paramount's big productions, ending with *The Pony Express* ('25), directed by Cruze and released shortly before he and Betty were married on October 25, 1925. She left Paramount to appear in a series of less than blockbuster movies for various studios, finally being relegated to female leads in Poverty Row quickies.

In 1928 Betty's luck changed and she landed several good roles, the first opposite Jack Holt in *Courtmartial* for Columbia. However, the more important films were Paramount's *The Docks of New York* and First National's *The Barker*. In *The Docks of New York* Betty plays Sadie, a waterfront tramp who attempts suicide but is saved by George Bancroft, who marries her while he is drunk, leaves her, then returns after a series of mishaps when he realizes he loves her. Opposite Milton Sills in *The Barker* Betty is Carrie, a hula dancer. She was nominated for Best Actress of 1928 but lost out to Mary Pickford, who won for her *Coquette*. Added laurels came her way with the release of *Scarlet Seas* ('29) and *Weary River* ('29), both opposite Richard Barthelmess, both for First National, and both with sound effects and music scores. Of nine features made in 1930, the most important was *The Spoilers* ('30) in which she played the faro-dealing Cherry Malotte opposite Gary Cooper.

Her marriage to James Cruze was terminated on May 20, 1930. Returning to Hollywood, she was embroiled in legal and tax problems left over from her marriage. Producer Irving Weinberg came to her aid and helped her to resolve them. The two fell in love and were married on December 13, 1933. During the Depression she took out her fiddle and went on the vaudeville circuit with

Fanchon and Marco for about a year, appearing as star of *A Night at the Cocoanut Grove.*

Betty was soon divorced and she had to take whatever screen work she could get. She made her name as a major star of melodramas during the silent era and as a leading lady and support player of better house programs during the 1930s.

During World War II days she toured with two plays, *This Thing Called Love* and *Smilin' Through.* She married again, to a sailor named Jack Gall. Together they organized a business called Ashtrays Unlimited, which proved to be profitable. After her husband's death in 1962, Betty continued its management.

During the 1940s Betty made only a few scattered film appearances. She died on April 18, 1974 in Glendale, California.

Serial

1919

The Terror of the Range. Pathé, [7 Chapters] D: Stuart Paton; SP: Lucien Hubbard; LP: Betty

Compson, George Larkin, Horace Carpenter, Fred M. Malatesta, Ota Carew, True Boardman.

JOYCE COMPTON

Joyce Compton, effervescent and resilient, entered films in 1925 as a result of a beauty contest. She was born in Lexington, Kentucky, but her family moved around. Much of her youth was spent in Oklahoma and Texas. She attended Oklahoma University before the family moved permanently to Hollywood. Her first role was as an extra in Paramount's *The Golden Bed* ('25). She was 18 (born in 1907 as Eleanor Hunt).

Other early films in which she played were *Sally* ('25) with Colleen Moore, *What Fools Men* ('25) with Lewis Stone and *Broadway Lady* with Evelyn Brent. In 1926 she was

chosen to be a Wampas Baby Star. Among 12 others who were chosen were Dolores Costello, Janet Gaynor, Fay Wray and Joan Crawford.

In a career lasting nearly 30 years she appeared in over 130 features and numerous two-reel comedies. She occasionally was in leads, but most often was cast as a bubbling dumb blonde. Other silent features were *Syncopating Sue* ('26) with Corrine Griffith, *Ankles Preferred* ('27) with Madge Bellamy, *The Border Cavalier* ('27) with Fred Humes, *Soft Living* (28) with Johnny Mack Brown, *The Wild Party* ('29) with Clara Bow, *Dan-*

gerous Curves ('29) with Clara Bow, *Salute* ('29) with George O'Brien and *The Sky Hawk* ('29) with Helen Chandler.

Joyce fared much better in talkies, where her Southern drawl was used to advantage in one dizzy role after another.

Mack Sennett hired her in 1933 for a series of two-reel comedies in which she co-starred with Walter Catlett, Franklin Pangborn and Grady Sutton. She found the work tiring and the atmosphere haphazard. Although her Sennett period established her as a comedienne, it was the co-star who usually got the laughs. Mainly she was a foil for such comics as Clark & McCullough or Charlie Chase. Joyce was the bird-brained blonde on TV's *Abbott and Costello Show, Pete and Gladys* and many features.

Joyce was not a Western player, though she appeared in one feature each with Johnny Mack Brown and Tim McCoy, and was the heroine in Universal's *Rustlers of Red Dog* ('35), a ripsnortin' chapterplay starring Brown. In the story, Jack (Brown), Deacon (Walter Miller) and Laramie (Raymond Hatton) protect a wagon train carrying a huge amount of gold. Bandits are determined to steal the gold. Renegade Indians likewise cause the trio much trouble. Jack is persuaded to accept the job as town marshall of Nugget and is able to kill Rocky (Harry Woods), leader of the gang, in a shootout during an attempted looting of the town.

In the mid–1930s Joyce drew up plans for a Tudor-style farmhouse in Benedict Hills, where she lived with her parents, to whom she was devoted. Joyce was an only child. The three of them did much of the work on their own. When the author contacted her in 1979, she was doing all her own gardening, trimming trees, planting fruit

Joyce Compton in *Swing Out the Blues* (Columbia, 1944).

trees, fixing hanging plants, making a strawberry bed — plus preparing orange marmalade and fig jam and baking homemade bread. Other than that, she was just sitting around deteriorating!

Joyce devoted many hours to part-time nursing, church work and her painting.

Joyce Compton died at age 90 in Los Angeles in 1997. She never married. Her last film was *Girl in the Woods* (Republic, 1958).

Serial

1935

Rustlers of Red Dog. Univ., [12 Chapters] D: Louis Friedlander [Lew Landers]; S: Nathanial Eddy; SP: George Plympton, Basil Dickey, Ella O'Neill, Nate Gatzert, Vin Moore; LP: Johnny Mack Brown, Joyce Compton, Walter Miller, Raymond Hatton, Harry Woods, Charles K. French.

TOMMY COOK

Tommy Cook's best-remembered roles are Little Beaver in *Adventures of Red Ryder* (Rep., 1940) and Kimba in *Jungle Girl* (Rep., 1941). Later Tommy played Little Beaver on the ABC radio series which starred Reed Hadley as Red. He was particularly active in radio where he played in over 2500 programs. Two of his most famous portrayals were as Alexander Bumstead in the CBS *Blondie* series and Junior in NBC's *The Life of Riley*.

As a young man, he appeared in *The Vicious Years*, which won him the coveted Photoplay Award for outstanding performance in 1949. He also led the cast in *Teenage Crime Wave* and *Michael O'Halloran*. As a supporting player he was in *Cry of the City* with Victor Mature, *Tarzan and the Leopard Woman* with Johnny Weissmuller, *American Guerrilla in the Philippines* with Tyrone Power, *Mohawk* with Scott Brady, *The Battle of Apache Pass* with John Lund and *Night Passage* with James Stewart.

Cook also performed in many television series, including *The Untouchables*, *Fireside Theatre*, *Climax*, *Streets of San Francisco*, *Dragnet*, *Zane Grey Theatre*, *Celebrity Playhouse*, *Perry Mason*, *Have Gun Will Travel*, *The Rifleman*, *M Squad*, *Richard Diamond Detective* and *Broken Arrow*.

In addition to on screen roles, Cook was in plays at the Pasadena Playhouse, the La Jolla Playhouse and the Circle Arts Theatre. Television commercials and voice-overs have also been on his agenda.

As one of California's best-known tennis pros, his occupation aside from acting is arranging and promoting celebrity tennis tournaments—that and producing concert appearances for music stars. Combining his show biz know-how with his favorite sport, he has become tennis' leading TV promoter, tournament producer, pro-celebrity innovator and master of ceremonies.

Serials

1940

Adventures of Red Ryder. Rep., [12 Chapters] D: William Witney, John English; AP: Hiram

William Farnum and Tommy Cook (right) in *Adventures of the Red Ryder* (Republic, 1940).

S. Brown, Jr.; SP: Franklyn Adreon, Ronald Davidson, Norman S. Hall, Barney Sarecky, Sol Shor; Cam: William Nobles; Mus: Cy Feuer; LP: Donald Barry, Tommy Cook, Maude Pierce Allen, Vivian Coe, Harry Worth, Noah Beery, Sr.

1941

Jungle Girl. Rep., [15 Chapters] D: William Witney, John English; SP: Ronald Davidson, Norman S. Hall, William Lively, Joseph O'-Donnell, Joseph F. Poland, Alfred Batson; AP: Hiram S. Brown, Jr.; LP: Frances Gifford, Tom Neal, Trevor Bardette, Gerald Mohr, Tommy Cook, Frank Lackteen, Robert Barron, Bud Geary.

JACKIE COOPER

Jackie Cooper is a show business veteran, having been an actor or director since he was three years old. He was born John Cooper, Jr., on September 15, 1921, in Los Angeles. He began appearing in Bobby Clark and Lloyd Hamilton comedies at three and later appeared in eight of the Our Gang comedies. He was nominated for an Academy Award as best actor of 1930 for his performance in *Skippy*, and was one of the most popular child stars of the 1930s.

At MGM he was teamed with Wallace Beery in three successful films—*The Champ* ('31), *The Bowery* ('33) and *Treasure Island* ('34). They were real tearjerkers, as well as moneymakers. *O'Shaughnessy's Boy* ('35) was another Beery-Cooper–co-starring film effort that paid off handsomely for the studio.

Other memorable films of the '30s were *Peck's Bad Boy* ('34), *Boy of the Streets* ('37), *Gangster's Boy* ('38) and *Streets of New York* ('39).

Cooper's career was starting to decline by 1939 when he accepted the role of Bruce Scott in Universal's *Scouts to the Rescue*. *Scouts* had lush scenery—the Sierra Nevada mountains near Sonora, California—to make plausible the absurdity that a lost branch of Inca Indians (savages) could exist undetected, in 1939, in the High Sierra. Scott (Cooper), leader of Martinsville Troop Number One, and his pack set off in search of lost treasure, using a map provided by Tenderfoot Skeets Scanlon (Bill Cody, Jr.). The map leads them to Ghost Town and the "treasure" turns out to be a large cache of counterfeit $20 bills, plus the copper plates used to print them. Joining the scouts in Chapter Two is G-man Hal Marvin (William Ruhl), who helps them do battle with the Indians, but also a ring of counterfeiters (which includes Jason Robards and Ralph Dunn).

Cooper served in the military during World War II and upon his discharge attempted a comeback in films, then tried summer stock and Broadway, later touring with the national company of *Mister Roberts* as Ensign Pulver. He finally launched a highly successful career on TV, starring in the series *The People's Choice* and *Hennessey* and becoming a director and executive producer. In 1972 he made his debut as film director with *Stand Up and Be Counted*.

His postwar films include *Where Are Your Children?* ('44), *Stork Bites Man* ('47), *Kilroy Was Here* ('47), *French Leave* ('48), *Everything's Ducky* ('61), *The Love Machine* ('71), *Chosen Survivors* ('74) and *Superman* ('78).

Jackie Cooper (left), Eddie Bracken and unidentified girls in *Life with Henry* (Paramount, 1940).

Serial

1939

Scouts to the Rescue. Univ., [12 Chapters] D: Ray Taylor, Alan James; SP: Wyndham Gittens, George Plympton, Basil Dickey, Joseph Poland; S: Irving Crump; LP: Jackie Cooper, Vondell Darr, Edwin Stanley, William Ruhl, Bill Cody, Jr., Frank Coghlan, Jr., Jason Robards, David Durand.

JAMES J. CORBETT

James John "Gentleman Jim" Corbett was born in San Francisco on September 1, 1866. While working in a San Francisco bank, he joined the Olympic Club, where he be-

came an expert amateur boxer. He entered the professional ring in 1886 and won a number of minor fights.

On June 5, 1889, in a 28-round bout on

a barge in San Francisco Bay, he defeated heavyweight Joe Choynski. A month later he did it again. The following year he vanquished Jake Kilrain in New Orleans and Dominick McCaffrey in Brooklyn.

On May 21, 1891, Corbett fought Peter Jackson to a draw in a bout lasting 61 rounds. In a match held in New Orleans on September 7, 1892, the first title bout fought under the Marquess of Queensberry rules, he won decisively in 21 rounds over John L. Sullivan. Corbett defended his title successfully against Charles Mitchell (1893), Peter Courtney (1894) and other contenders but on March 17, 1897, he was defeated at Carson City, Nevada, when Robert Fitzsimmons knocked him out in the fourteenth round.

In an attempt to regain the title, Corbett was defeated by Jeffries in 23 rounds (May 11, 1900) and in ten rounds on August 14, 1903. He retired and turned to the stage. After appearing in vaudeville and plays, he acted in motion pictures and in radio. His autobiography, *The Roar of the Crowd*, was published in 1925.

Corbett starred in the Universal serial *The Midnight Man* ('19), which was less than spectacular in spite of the former heavyweight champion of the world in the lead. It was more melodrama that an action epic and Corbett was not an accomplished actor.

Corbett died in 1933 at age 65 from cancer of the liver in Bayside, New York.

Serial

1919

The Midnight Man. Univ., [18 Chapters] D: James W. Horne; SP: Harvey Gates; S: James W. Horne, Frank Howard Clarke; LP: James J. Corbett, Kathleen O'Connor, Joseph W. Girard, Frank Jonasson, Joseph Singleton, Noble Johnson, Sam Polo, Ann Forrest.

RAY CORRIGAN

Ray Corrigan was born Ray Benard, son of a grand opera singer, on February 14, 1902, in Milwaukee, Wisconsin, but was brought up in Denver, attending North Denver High School. While studying and experimenting with electricity and electronics, Ray worked with a furniture company. However, a few years later he opened his own electronics shop, turning out some 21 inventions for which he held patents. One of these inventions was an electrical blood circulator that has been widely used in hospitals for a number of years.

When his electronics business failed, he turned to physical education as a way to make a living. He opened a physical culture school and went on to become a popular male model.

Ray's interests also included dramatics. He joined the Benham Stock Company and then the Hollywood Community Theatre, where he acted in a series of six plays. Having developed a system for physical culture, it was a short and logical step to stunting and thence to bit parts in the movies.

One of his early jobs was doubling Johnny Weissmuller. When you saw Tarzan swinging from limb to limb, it was probably Corrigan and not Weissmuller.

Corrigan was at MGM three and a half years, appearing in a number of uncredited roles. He landed a speaking part in 1934 when he played Apollo in *Night Life of the Gods*. There followed roles in *Dante's Inferno* (Fox), *Mutiny on the Bounty* (MGM), *The Singing Vagabond* (Rep.), *Romance in the Rain* (Univ.), *She* (RKO) and *Darkest Africa*, Republic's first cliffhanger. Clyde Beatty starred. He had a featured role in *The Leathernecks Have Landed* ('36) and got an even greater break when he was given the lead in *Undersea Kingdom* ('36), a 12-chapter actioner directed by B. Reeves Eason and Joseph Kane. This early Republic serial was a spinoff of the old Mascot serials and was an indication of things to come from Republic as it began its rise to leadership among the serial studios. It was another serial to take advantage of the popularity of science fiction begun by the success of the Universal serial *Flash Gordon*. The story of *Undersea Kingdom* was a mixture of science fiction and mythology, based upon the legend of the "lost continent of Atlantis."

Replete with spectacle and action, *Undersea Kingdom* was a popular success and made a star of former stuntman "Crash" Corrigan (billed under his name). He soon went on to more fame as Tucson Smith, one of the Three Mesquiteers, in the highly successful Republic Western film series.

That same year, 1936, Crash appeared in the exciting Republic serial *The Vigilantes Are Coming*, a forerunner to the great Zorro serials Republic would later produce. It starred Robert Livingston, whom Crash would later team up with in the Mesquiteers series.

The serial takes place during the 1840s in California, which has been "invaded" by Russian Cossacks imported by Gen. Jason Burr (Fred Kohler), who is after the rich oil fields belonging to Bob's father. Bob returns to California to find his father and brother murdered and the land taken. Donning a black mask and outfit, he becomes the mysterious Eagle. With the help of Capt. Fremont (Corrigan), the Eagle ends the plot to establish a foreign empire in America.

In 1936 Republic began their long-running Three Mesquiteers series. Ray became a member and appeared in the first 24 films from 1936 to 1939. The last eight films (1938–39) were made with John Wayne replacing Robert Livingston, who moved up to non–Westerns. Later, when Livingston returned to the series replacing Wayne, Ray (who didn't get along with Livingston, and also didn't like Wayne) opted to leave the series when his demands for a raise were rejected.

Wayne's exit also marked Corrigan's departure from the series. He took Max Terhune with him for a series tagged "The Range Busters" at Monogram, where singer-actor John King was added as the third member. The series began in 1940, with Corrigan appearing in the first 16 films (1940–42) and the last four (1943). The series was a popular one although not up to Republic's slick standards.

In 1937, Corrigan bought 17,000 Simi Valley acres which had been used as a dump for $15,000 and spent five years cleaning up the property. He built what became known as Corriganville, a site for countless film locations for Hollywood producers and a popular tourist attraction. In 1965, Crash sold the property to Bob Hope for $2,800,000, after a divorce, a heart attack and the impending development of the Simi Valley Freeway over part of his land.

After the Range Busters series ended, Corrigan appeared in supporting roles in *She's for Me* ('43), *Renegade Girl* ('46), *Trail of Robin Hood* ('50), *Apache Ambush* ('55) and *Domino Kid* ('57). He also played small

roles in the serials *Adventures of Sir Galahad* ('47) and *The Great Adventures of Captain Kidd* ('53).

During the post–Range Busters era, Corrigan supplemented his income by donning a gorilla suit and portraying giant simians in various low-grade features. Corrigan's ape was not exactly accurate by actual anthropological standards, but who cared? His ape looked scary as hell on the screen.

In the Columbia chapterplay *The Monster and the Ape* ('45), Corrigan plays Thor, the ape. At best, this 15-episode serial is schlock entertainment.

In *White Pongo* Corrigan actually plays two parts: his usual dark gorilla plus the title character, a white gorilla thought to be the missing link. Besides boasting two gorillas, the film also sports a number of alternate titles, including *Blond Gorilla*, and *Congo Pongo* while in England it was retitled *Adventure Unlimited* and in Italy it became *La Sfida de King Kong* (Challenge of King Kong). Other films featuring Corrigan are *Zamba* ('49), *Killer Ape* ('53), *Zombies of Mora Tau* ('57) and his last screen appearance, *It! The Terror from Beyond Space* ('58).

Ray (Crash) Corrigan died from a heart attack in Brookings, Oregon, on August 10, 1976. He was buried at Inglewood, California. Surviving were his wife, a son and a daughter.

Serials

1936

Darkest Africa. Rep., [15 Chapters] D: B. Reeves Eason, Joseph Kane; P: Nat Levine; LP: Clyde Beatty, Manuel King, Elaine Sheppard, Lucien Prival, Wheeler Oakman, Edmund Cobb, Ray Corrigan.

The Vigilantes Are Coming. Rep., [12 Chapters] D: Mack V. Wright, Ray Taylor; SP: John Rathmell, Maurice Geraghty, Winston Miller; S: Maurice Geraghty, Leslie Swabacker; Cam: William Nobles, Edgar Lyons; Mus: Harry Grey;

P: Nat Levine; LP: Robert Livingston, Kay Hughes, Robert Warwick, Fred Kohler, William Farnum, "Big Boy" Williams, Ray Corrigan, Raymond Hatton.

Undersea Kingdom. Rep., [12 Chapters] D: B. Reeves Eason, Joseph Kane; S: Tracy Knight, John Rathmell; SP: John Rathmell, Maurice Geraghty, Oliver Drake; Cam: William Nobles, Edgar Lyons; Mus: Harry Grey; Spv: Barney Sarecky; LP: Ray Corrigan, Lois Wilde, Monte Blue, William Farnum, Lee Van Atta, Lon Chaney, Jr., Raymond Hatton, Lane Chandler.

1937

The Painted Stallion. Rep., [12 Chapters] D: William Witney, Alan James, Ray Taylor; SP: Barry Shipman, Winston Miller; AP: J. Laurence Wickland; Cam: William Nobles, Edgar Lyons; Mus: Raoul Kraushaar; LP: Ray Corrigan, Hoot Gibson, Jack Perrin, Hal Taliaferro [Wally Wales], Duncan Renaldo, Julia Thayer, LeRoy Mason, Sammy McKim, Yakima Canutt, Charles King.

1945

The Monster and the Ape. Col., [15 Chapters] D: Howard Bretherton; LP: Robert Lowery, George Macready, Ralph Morgan, Carole Mathews, Willie Best, Ray Corrigan.

1949

Adventures of Sir Galahad. Col., [15 Chapters] D: Spencer G. Bennet; LP: George Reeves, Charles King, William Fawcett, Hugh Prosser, Lois Hall, Ray Corrigan.

1953

The Great Adventures of Captain Kidd. Col., [15 Chapters] D: Derwin Abbe, Charles S. Gould; LP: Richard Crane, David Bruce, John Crawford, George Wallace, Lee Roberts, Paul Newlan, Ray Corrigan.

HELENE COSTELLO

Helen Costello simply added an "e" to her first name to get her screen name. As the daughter of Maurice Costello, she was born June 21, 1903, in New York City. Along with her sister Dolores, two years her junior, she began appearing as a child in Vitagraph films starring their father. She had the luxury of attending private schools, modeling in New York and dancing with her sister in the 1924 *George White Scandals.* She returned to films and for a short while rivaled her sister's popularity. However, her career waned and shortly after the advent of sound she disappeared from the screen, except for a bit part in a 1935 film. At one time (1930–32) she was married to director-actor Lowell Sherman.

Helene Costello died from a combination of pneumonia, tuberculosis and narcotics in Los Angeles in 1957 at age 53. Her sister outlived her by 20 years.

Serial

1929

The Fatal Warning. Mascot, [10 Chapters] D: Richard Thorpe; P: Nat Levine; LP: Helene Costello, Ralph Graves, George Periolat, Phillips Smalley, Boris Karloff, Gertrude Astor, Lloyd Whitlock.

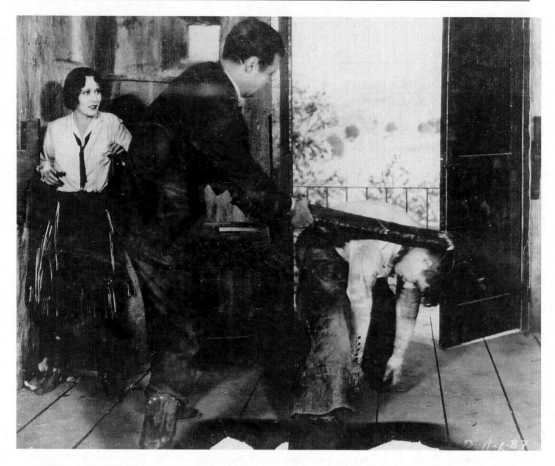

Helene Costello (left), unidentified player and Tom Mix in *The Broncho Twister* (Fox, 1926).

MAURICE COSTELLO

Maurice George Washington Costello was born in 1877 in Pittsburgh, Pennsylvania. A Broadway matinee idol for 15 years, he was among the first important American stage actors to turn to the screen. At first with Edison, he moved to Vitagraph in 1908 where he spent seven years. Costello's biggest hit at Vitagraph was *A Tale of Two Cities* ('11).

In the following films Costello directed as well as starred in *Cupid versus Women's Rights* ('11), *Extremities* ('13), *The Ambassador's Disappearance* ('13), *Matrimonial Maneuvers* ('13), *The Sale of a Heart* ('13), *Mr. Barnes of New York* (co-dir., '14), *The Mysterious Lodger* (co-dir., '14), *The Moonstone of Fez* (co-dir., '14), *The Plot* (co-dir., '14), *The Man Who Couldn't Beat God* (co-dir. '15). His co-director was Robert Gaillord.

The serial *The Crimson Stain Mystery* ('16) starred Costello as a reporter on his father's paper. He sees a murder being committed and leaps into the room through a window, but is too late to save the victim; he sees the glint of the murderer's eye, and knows him for the Crimson Stain. The Crimson Stain is head of a band of desperate criminals, made so by a drug discovered by Dr. Montrose; the doctor expected this drug would elevate the mental and moral plane of the human race, but instead it has only bred a band of criminals. The reporter's father criticizes the police for their failure to run down the criminals, and is murdered while a guest of Dr. Montrose.

Costello switched to character roles in the mid–20s and gave support to Frank Clarke, noted aviator, in the Pathé serial *Eagle of the Night* ('28). The serial was built around Clarke's airplane thrills.

Costello appeared in only a few sound films. He was in *Hollywood Boulevard* ('36), *A Little Bit of Heaven* ('40), and *Lady from Louisiana* ('41) and possibly others.

He had two daughters, Dolores and Helen, both of whom became actresses of note. He died in 1950.

Serials

1916

The Crimson Satin Mystery. Consolidated/Metro, [16 Chapters] D: T. Hayes Hunter; S: Albert Payson Terhune; LP: Maurice Costello, Ethel Grandin, Thomas J. McGrane, Olga Olonova, William Cavanaugh.

1928

Eagle of the Night. Pathé, [10 Chapters] D: Jimmie Fulton; S/SP: Paul Cruger; LP: Frank Clarke, Shirley Palmer, Earle Metcalf, Maurice Costello, Joseph Swickard, Max Hawley.

MARGUERITE COURTOT

Marguerite Courtot, the actress with auburn hair that looked like molten gold in the sunlight, was born Marguerite Gabrielle Courtot in Summit, New Jersey, of French parentage on August 20, 1897. She learned to dance at the insistence of her mother. Marguerite danced and posed until she was 12, at which time she was sent abroad to Lausanne, Switzerland, to be educated in a convent.

In June 1912, during summer vacation, her mother permitted Marguerite to work as an extra in the Kalem Studio in Cliffside, New Jersey. In a few short months this eager young lady was doing leads, and at 16 she was one of the hottest properties on the lot. She played her first lead at 15, in *The War Correspondent* ('13). Raised in the studio, she became a favorite there. Hers was a demure prettiness, and her manners were ladylike.

Despite her youthfulness (her chief charm) and her fascinating facility in comedy, Marguerite preferred strong plays of emotional and problematic tendency. However, she loved real comedies too. One of her favorite comedy films was *The Adventure of Briarcliff* ('15), made with Tom Moore, her most frequent leading man in her early career. They made nearly a score of films together at Kalem, mostly adventure-drama, with *The Barefoot Boy* ('14) considered by Marguerite as one of her finest pieces of work. *The First Commandment* ('15), *The Secret Room* ('15) and *The Black Ring* ('15) also stand out as among the best.

Prior to teaming with Moore, Marguerite played the demanding role of Zoe in *The Octaroon* ('13) when she was only 15 years old. She followed with successes in *A Celebrated Case* ('14) and *The Green Rose* ('14). By late 1915, Tom Moore had ceased to be Marguerite's leading man, and it was Richard Purdom who provided the heroics as she charmed her way through the 16 one-reel episodes of *The Ventures of Marguerite* ('15). It was hardly a serial in the sense of the suspenseful, action-packed chapterplays of the 1930s and '40s; it was more like a series of unconnected short stories.

Marguerite left Kalem with some reluctance to make two films for Gaumont (*The Dead Alive* and *Feathertop*) and two films for Famous Players–Lasky (*Rolling Stones* and *The Kiss*). All four of these feature-length films were made in 1916.

During World War I there was a recruiting office for the Marines in Weehawken, her home town, and Marguerite helped out there. When the sergeant who did the desk work was ordered to France, Marguerite volunteered to take his place. It took all her time, so she had to drop her studio work. Then she made tours and sold war savings stamps. Few men could resist their patriotic duty when confronted by this lovely lady. She even adopted a group of Midwestern soldiers and wrote them all once a week while they were abroad. Her wartime work kept her away from the screen for about a year.

Courtot's first postwar movies were *The Perfect Lover* ('19) and *Teeth of the Tiger* ('19). Then came the film that started her on the road to serial immortality, *Bound and Gagged* ('19). George B. Seitz co-starred and directed and Frank Leon Smith did the scenario. The serial was successful, and the trio followed up with *Pirate Gold* ('22), also a comedy melodrama in ten chapters. In *Velvet Fingers* ('20), the length was extended to 15 chapters, and Seitz also took over the writing in addition to directing and co-starring. Marguerite's last serial outing was as one of the three principals (along with Juanita Hansen and Warner Oland) in *The Yellow Arm* ('21), a moneymaking thriller with an Oriental flavor.

On September 25, 1922, after a year in production, *Down to the Sea in Ships* ('22) premiered at the Olympia Theatre in New Bedford, Massachusetts. Long at 12 reels, it was filmed on the open sea and in New Bedford. During production, Marguerite and co-star Raymond McKee fell in love, and they were married not long afterward. A few films followed for Marguerite, but she soon gave up her career to devote more time to being Mrs. Raymond McKee. The McKees were married for over 50 years. Theirs was one of Hollywood's more successful marriages.

Marguerite Courtot died May 28, 1986, and Raymond McKee died October 3, 1984, at Long Beach, California.

Serials

1915

The Ventures of Marguerite. Kalem, [16 Chapters] D: Hamilton Smith, John E. Macklin, Robert Ellis; LP: Marguerite Courtot, Richard Purdon, E. T. Roseman, Paul Sherman, Bradley Barker.

1919

Bound and Gagged. Pathé, [10 Chapters] D: George B. Seitz; SP/S: Frank Leon Smith; LP: Marguerite Courtot, George B. Seitz, Nellie Burt, Harry Semels, Frank Redman.

1920

Pirate Gold. Pathé, [10 Chapters] D: George B. Seitz; SP: Bertram Millhauser; S: Frank Leon Smith; LP: Marguerite Courtot, George B. Seitz, Frank Redman, Harry Semels, Harry Stone, William Burt, Joe Cuny.

Velvet Fingers. Pathé, [15 Chapters] D: Bertram Millhauser; P: George B. Seitz; SP: James Hamilton; LP: George B. Seitz, Marguerite

Courtot, Harry Semels, Lucille Lennox, Frank Redman, Tommy Carr.

1921

The Yellow Arm. Pathé, [15 Chapters] D: Bertram Millhauser; P: George B. Seitz; SP: James Hamilton; LP: Juanita Hansen, Warner Oland, Marguerite Courtot, Stephen Carr, William N. Bailey, Tom Keith, Al Franklyn.

LARRY (BUSTER) CRABBE

Larry (Buster) Crabbe was the most gifted, the best-known, the longest lasting, the best-looking, the best actor and the best "built" (his chest measured four inches more than Johnny Weissmuller) of Olympic winners to try their luck in Hollywood. Paramount signed him to a seven-year contract.

After a couple bit roles, Paramount starred him in *King of the Jungle* ('33) as Kaspa, the Lion Man. *Time* magazine noted: "From the neck down Crabbe easily equals Weissmuller as an attraction to female audiences; from the neck up he is a vast improvement." Shortly afterward Buster had his try as Tarzan, the Ape Man in *Tarzan the Fearless* ('33), a 12-chapter serial produced by Sol Lesser for his Principal Productions. (It was also released in a condensed 85-minute version.)

The story has Tarzan (Crabbe) aiding Mary Brooks (Jacqueline Wells) and Bob Hall (Edward Woods) in the search for Mary's father, a prisoner of the people of Zor, god of the Emerald Fingers. Mary's guide Jeff (Philo McCullough) wants Mary and secretly seeks a lost treasure. The followers of Zor further complicate the situation by trying to kill everyone. However,

Tarzan triumphs and, though he speaks no English, wins Mary as his mate.

Crabbe set 16 world and American swimming records, won 35 national championships and, in 1932, won the Gold Medal for the U.S. Olympic swimming team for the 400-meter freestyle. Thus his nickname, "Buster."

Between 1933 and 1937, Paramount put Buster into ten above-par Zane Grey Westerns. They also loaned him out to other studios during this period, as well as casting him in a variety of non–Westerns.

It was in 1936 that Universal produced the serial *Flash Gordon* and Buster was loaned by Paramount to essay the title role. It has been claimed that *Flash Gordon* was both the most expensive and the most popular sound serial ever made. In 1937 it earned more money than any films produced by the studio that year.

Several features were constructed from the serial: *Rocketship*, *Perils from the Planet Mongo*, *Spaceship to the Unknown*, *Space Soldiers* and *Atomic Rocketship*. Buster gained cinema immortality for his role of Flash Gordon.

Universal wisely borrowed him again for their *Flash Gordon's Trip to Mars* ('38). That was also edited into features *Mars Attacks the*

Buster Crabbe and Jean Rogers in *Flash Gordon* (Universal, 1936).

World and *The Deadly Ray from Mars*. *Look* magazine serialized the serial in three issues commencing with the March 19, 1938 issue.

Universal followed up by starring Buster in the serial *Red Barry* ('38), based on King Features' comic strip character, and in 1939 he was back to sci-fi as *Buck Rogers*, a 12-chapter serial also released as a feature, *Planet Outlaws*. In 1940 he starred in the final space odyssey serial, *Flash Gordon Conquers the Universe*. The feature version title was *Space Soldiers Conquer the Universe*.

Paramount had continued to use Buster in many of its "B" features, but after *Million Dollar Legs* ('39) with Betty Grable he was free of the Paramount contract. He had been averaging five to six features a year.

In 1941, PRC signed Crabbe to star in the *Billy the Kid* series being vacated by Bob Steele, who went to Republic as one of the Three Mesquiteers. With Al (Fuzzy) St. John co-starring as Fuzzy Q. Jones, Buster made nearly 40 of these low-budget oaters for the bottom-of-the-barrel studio. However, they were often made entertaining to the true aficionado by the use of top "heavies" such as Charles King (21 films), Kermit Maynard (17 films), Slim Whitaker, Karl Hackett, George Chesebro, Reed Howes, Frank Ellis, Steven Clark, Kenne Duncan, etc. Buster finally quit because of the overall shoddiness of the films. While at PRC he had made several non–Westerns: *Jungle Man* ('41), *Jungle Siren* ('42), *Queen of Broadway* ('43), *Nabonga* ('44) and *The Contender* ('44).

In 1940, Buster captured the men's professional three-mile swimming event held in Los Angeles. He also appeared in Billy Rose's Aquacade at the New York World's Fair and later formed Buster Crabbe's Aquacade and toured the U.S. and Europe for five years.

In 1951, Buster had his own WOR-TV program on which he showed and commented on his old PRC Westerns. He also had a radio exercise show and a Saturday radio program, *Luncheon with Buster Crabbe.*

Crabbe, his son Cuffy and Fuzzy Knight filmed the TV series *Captain Gallant of the Foreign Legion* (1955–57) in Morocco and Italy. Sixty-five episodes were made.

Buster starred in the Columbia serials *The Sea Hound* ('47), *Pirates of the High Seas* ('50) and *King of the Congo* ('52), making a total of nine serials and giving him the unofficial title of "King of the Sound Serials."

In 1972 Buster co-starred with Ina Balin in the Western comedy *The Comeback Trail.* It was never released due to Buster's insistence that some sex scenes be deleted. The producers would not comply, so the film still resides in the lab. At one time he was athletic director for a resort in the Catskill Mountains and he became involved in the swimming pool business. He also authored a book on physical fitness entitled *Energetics* ('70).

On the personal front, Buster was born Clarence Linden Crabbe on February 7, 1908, in Oakland, California. The family moved to Hawaii when he was an infant. He attended Puna Hou High School where he became a star athlete, winning 16 letters in football, baseball, track and swimming. He attended for one year the University of Hawaii, adding boxing to his sports achievements. He then transferred to the University of Southern California to continue his pre-law education. He earned a spot on the U.S. Olympic swimming team in the 1932 Olympics held in Los Angeles. Talent scouts at Paramount took notice of him, signed him and gave him a role in *Island of Lost Souls* ('32) starring Charles Laughton. He also doubled for Joel McCrea in *The Most Dangerous Game* ('32).

Buster married in 1933 and he and wife Adah had three children — Susan, Caren and Cullen (called "Cuffy"). Caren died of anorexia, a form of starvation created by an emotional stress that robs one of any desire to eat.

Buster received another gold medal in 1981. This time it was for his effort in promoting better health and fitness for older persons; the President's Council on Physical Fitness and Sports gave the award.

On April 23, 1983, Buster died from a heart attack at his home in Scottsdale, Arizona. He was one of the last of the great serial stars and B-Western stars.

Serials

1933

Tarzan the Fearless. Principal, [12 Chapters] D: Robert F. Hill; SP: Basil Dickey, George H. Plympton, Walter Anthony; P: Sol Lesser; Cam: Harry Newman, Joe Grotherton; Spv.: William Lora Wright; LP: Buster Crabbe, Jacqueline Wells [Julie Bishop], E. Alyn Warren, Edward Woods, Philo McCullough, Mischa Auer, Frank Lackteen.

Left to right: Frank Shannon, Dick Alexander, Jean Rogers, Buster Crabbe and Donald Kerr in *Flash Gordon's Trip to Mars* (Universal, 1938).

1935

Red Barry. Univ., [13 Chapters] D: Ford Beebe, Alan James; SP: Norman Hall, Ray Trampe; LP: Buster Crabbe, Frances Robinson, Wade Boteler, Edna Sedgwick, Philip Ahn, Frank Lackteen, Wheeler Oakman.

1936

Flash Gordon. Univ., [13 Chapters] D: Frederick Stephani; SP: George H. Plympton, Frederick Stephani, Basil Dickey, Ella O'Neill; P: Henry MacRae; Cam: Jerry Ash, Richard Freyer; LP: Buster Crabbe, Jean Rogers, Charles Middleton, Frank Shannon, Priscilla Lawson, Richard Alexander.

1938

Flash Gordon's Trip to Mars. Univ., [15 Chapters] D: Ford Beebe, Robert F. Hill; S/SP: Wyn-

dham Gittens, Norman S. Hall, Ray Trampe, Herbert Dalmas; LP: Buster Crabbe, Jean Rogers, Frank Shannon, Charles Middleton, Beatrice Roberts, Donald Kerr, Richard Alexander, C. Montague Shaw, Wheeler Oakman, Kane Richmond.

1939

Buck Rogers. Univ., [12 Chapters] D: Ford Beebe, Saul A. Goodkind; SP: Barney Sarecky; S/SP: Norman S. Hall, Ray Trampe; Cam: Jerry Ash; LP: Buster Crabbe, Constance Moore, Jackie Moran, Jack Mulhall, Anthony Warde, Henry Brandon.

1940

Flash Gordon Conquers the Universe. Univ., [12 Chapters] D: Ford Beebe, Ray Taylor; SP: George H. Plympton, Basil Dickey, Barry Shipment; P: Henry MacRae; Cam: Jerry Ash; LP: Buster Crabbe, Carol Hughes, Charles Middleton, Anne Gwynne, Frank Shannon, Roland Drew.

1947

The Sea Hound. Col., [15 Chapters] D: Water B. Eason, Mack V. Wright; P: Sam Katzman; SP: George H. Plympton, Lewis Clay, Arthur Hoerl; Cam: Ira H. Morgan; Mus: Mischa Bakaleinikoff; LP: Buster Crabbe, Pamela Blake, James Lloyd, Ralph Hodges, Spencer Chan, Robert Barron.

1950

Pirates of the High Seas. Col., [15 Chapters] D: Spencer G. Bennet, Thomas Carr; SP: George H. Plympton, Joseph Poland, David Mathews, Charles R. Condon; P: Sam Katzman; Cam: Ira H. Morgan; Mus: Mischa Bakaleinikoff; LP: Buster Crabbe, Lois Hall, Tommy Farrell, Gene Roth, Tristram Coffin, Lee Roberts.

1952

King of the Congo. Col., [15 Chapters] D: Spencer G. Bennet, Wallace A. Grissell; SP: George H. Plympton, Royal K. Cole, Arthur Hoerl; Cam: William Whitley; P: Sam Katzman; Mus: Mischa Bakaleinikoff; LP: Buster Crabbe, Gloria Dea, Leonard Penn, Jack Ingram, Rusty Wescoatt, Nick Stuart, Rick Vallin.

JAMES CRAIG

James Craig was born James Henry Meador, February 4, 1912, in Nashville, Tennessee. His father was a contractor. James graduated from Rice Institute, where he excelled at football and tennis.

While working for General Motors in Houston, Craig traveled to Hollywood during his vacation, thinking that maybe he could crash the movies. He got an appointment with an agent who advised him to go back home, get into a little theater production, work on his diction and come back the next year. He took the advice and did return to Hollywood, where he got an audition with Paramount executives. They liked what they saw and heard (his Southern drawl) and signed him to a contract.

Paramount featured him in *Thunder Trail* ('37) with Gilbert Roland, *Born to the West* ('37) with John Wayne and Johnny Mack Brown and *Pride of the West* ('37) with William Boyd. In 1938 he spent part of the year working in the New York play *Missouri Legend.* Switching to Columbia, he appeared in *The Man They Could Not Hang* ('39), *Taming of the West* ('39), *Overland with Kit Carson* ('39), the Bill Elliott serial, and was one of the principals in the serial *Flying G-Men* ('39). In 1940 he was third-ranked in the Universal serial *Winners of the West* starring Dick Foran.

He was given his best acting opportunity when he portrayed a Faustian character torn between the satanic "Mr Scratch" (Walter Huston) and orator Daniel Webster (Edward Arnold) in *All That Money Can Buy* ('41), an adaptation of Stephen Vincent Benet's story "The Devil and Daniel Webster."

Darkly handsome and bearing a strong resemblance to Clark Gable, Craig was recruited by MGM as the superstar's replacement during World War II. However, he appeared mostly in routine programmers or as a supporting player in larger-budgeted films.

His other films include *The Human Comedy* ('43), *Kismet* ('44), *Marriage Is a Private Affair* ('44), *She Went to the Races* ('45),

Boys Ranch ('46), *Dark Delusion* ('47), *Northwest Stampede* ('48), *Side Street* ('50), *Drums in the Deep South* ('51), *Hurricane Smith* ('52), *Fort Vengeance* ('53), *Massacre* ('56), *The Cyclops* ('57), *Four Fast Guns* ('60), *Fort Utah* ('67), *Bigfoot* ('70) and *The Doomsday Machine* ('73).

Craig married starlet Mary Ray in 1939 and they had three children but the marriage ended in divorce. In 1959 he married actress Jil Jarmyn. It didn't last long. His third marriage was to Sumie Jassi but it, too, was doomed. There may have been a marriage to Jane Valentine, but the author cannot confirm it. In 1963 he remarried his first wife and, so far as the author knows, it "took."

He drank heavily. At one time he managed race horses, a building company and a liquor store. When acting offers dried up, he would work as a realtor. At one point he acted in the TV series *Hannibal Cobb*. He also worked in commercials and finally returned to selling real estate again.

James Craig died in 1985 at age 73 in Santa Ana, California. Cause of death was lung cancer.

Serials

1939

Overland with Kit Carson. Col., [15 Chapters] D: Sam Nelson, Norman Deming; SP: Joseph F. Poland, Morgan B. Cox,; P: Jack Fier; Cam: Benjamin Kline, George Meehan; Mus: Lee Zahler; LP: Bill Elliott, Iris Meredith, Trevor Bardette, Richard Fiske, Bobby Clark, James Craig, Dick Curtis, Kenneth MacDonald, Hal Taliaferro.

Flying G-Men. Col., [15 Chapters] D: Ray Taylor, James W. Horne; SP: Robert E. Kent, Basil Dickey, Sherman Lowe; P: Jack Fier; Cam: Benjamin Kline, John Stumar; Mus: Lee Zahler; LP: Robert Paige, Robert Fiske, James Craig, Lorna Gray [Adrian Booth], Don Beddoe, Dick Curtis, Forbes Murray, Ann Doran, Nestor Paiva.

1940

Winners of the West. Univ., [13 Chapters] D: Ford Beebe, Ray Taylor; SP: Basil Dickey, George H. Plympton, Charles R. Condon; P: Henry MacRae; Cam: Jerome Ash, William Sickner, John Hickson; LP: Dick Foran, Anne Nagel, James Craig, Tom Fadden, Charles Stevens, Trevor Bardette, Harry Woods.

RICHARD CRANE

Richard Crane was born in Newcastle, Indiana, on June 6, 1918. He appeared in three serials. In the first, Universal's *Don Winslow of the Coast Guard* ('43), Richard has a small role as a pilot. Don Winslow (Don Terry) and his pal Red (Walter Sande), on loan to the Coast Guard, battle the Scorpion and his Nazi and Japanese aides.

In the second serial, Columbia's *Mysterious Island* ('51), Crane has the main role as Capt. Harding. Marshall Reed, Karen Randle, Ralph Hodges and Hugh Prosser head up the support. By 1951 the often maligned

Columbia was producing serials on a par with, or better than those from Republic. However, cost-cutting was obvious as Sam Katzman strived to bring the film in under budget. The story is about several Yankee prisoners escaping a Confederate prison in a balloon and days later finding themselves marooned on a deserted (they thought!) island. Here they encounter two men and a girl from Mercury who are seeking a mysterious and rare metal to be used in making an explosive capable of destroying the Earth. The Yanks also encounter hostile locals, pirates and Captain Nemo, who aids them because of his desire to stop Mercurian Rura. There were few dull moments as various plot twists were unveiled.

Crane also has the lead in *The Great Adventures of Captain Kidd* (Col., '53). In the story Captain Kidd (John Crawford) is not the villain he is made out to be, but the victim of false propaganda put out by one of his crew, who teams up with pirate captain Culliford (Marshall Reed) to pin their crimes on Kidd. Although two British naval officers believe in him and plead his case, Kidd goes to the gallows after helping the British fleet destroy the pirates' stronghold. The two officers, Richard Dale (Richard Crane) and Alan Duncan (David Bruce), leave England bound for America firmly believing that Kidd was the greatest man who ever sailed the sea. The cast boasted six men who once starred in serials: John Hart, George Wallace, Ray Corrigan, Lyle Talbot, Myron Healey and Edmund Cobb.

Crane was in scores of movies and many television series. He was briefly popular among the bobby-soxer crowd. At the time of his death, March 2, 1969, he was president of Film Trend Productions. He was 51 when felled by a heart attack.

Serials

1943

Don Winslow of the Coast Guard. Univ., [13 Chapters] D: Ford Beebe, Ray Taylor; SP: George H. Plympton, Paul Huston, Griffin Jay; Mus: H. J. Salter; AP: Henry MacRae; LP: Don Terry, Walter Sande, Elyse Knox, Nestor Paiva, Henry Victor, Stanley Blystone, Rex Lease, Richard Crane, Charles Wagenheim.

1951

Mysterious Island. Col., [15 Chapters] D: Spencer G. Bennet; SP: Lewis Clay, Royal K. Cole, George H. Plympton; S: Jules Verne; P: Sam Katzman; Cam: Faye Browne; Mus: Mischa Bakaleinikoff; LP: Richard Crane, Karen Randle, Marshall Reed, Ralph Hodges, Gene Roth, Hugh Prosser, Terry Frost.

1953

The Great Adventures of Captain Kidd. Col., [15 Chapters] D: Derwin Abbe, Charles S. Gould; SP: George H. Plympton, Arthur Hoerl; P: Sam Katzman; Cam: William Whitley; Mus: Mischa Bakaleinikoff; LP: Richard Crane, David Bruce, John Crawford, George Wallace, Lee Roberts, John Hart, Lyle Talbot, Myron Healey, Charles King, Ray Corrigan, Paul Newlan, Willetta Smith.

JAMES CRUZE

James Cruze is better known as a director than as an actor. One film that comes to mind when his name is mentioned is *The Covered Wagon* ('23), a meticulously reconstructed Western that influenced not only future Westerns but also historic epics and documentary films. It would take millions of dollars to make the film today. His *Hollywood* of the same year, an unusual fantasy film, contained bold references to the "Fatty" Arbuckle scandal that was rocking Hollywood at the time.

Contemporary critics were even more impressed with Cruze's surrealistic *Beggar on Horseback* ('25), an inventive expressionist film. Made the same year was another successful Western, *The Pony Express* ('25).

Cruze began directing in 1918 and on most of the films after 1923 he also produced. One film that he both produced and directed was *Old Ironsides* ('26). It was an attempt at historic reconstruction, but neither the public nor critics appreciated it. A few of the films he both directed and produced are *Ruggles of Red Gap* ('23), *Merton of the Movies* ('24), *The Enemy Sex* ('24), *The City That Never Sleeps* ('24), *The Goose Hangs High* ('25), *Mannequin* ('26), *The City Gone Wild* ('27), *Excess Baggage* ('28), *She Got What She Wanted* ('31) and *Washington Merry-Go-Round* ('32).

James Cruze was born on March 27, 1884, in Ogden, Utah, the son of a Morman family of Danish descent. He worked as a fisherman in the Bering Strait to pay his way through drama school. By age 16 he was an actor, appearing in medicine shows, road shows and stock. In 1906 he became a member of the famed Belasco company and appeared frequently on Broadway.

In 1908 he joined the Thanhauser Company and starred in many of its productions, including two serials. In 1916 he moved on to Lasky, still as an actor, and in 1918 made his directorial debut. Some of the films he appeared in as an actor are *She* ('11), *Dr. Jekyll and Mr. Hyde* ('11), *The Arab's Bride* ('11), *Whom God Hath Joined* ('12), *The Dove in the Eagle's Nest* ('13), *The Legend of Provence* ('13), *Joseph in the Land of Egypt* ('14), *Cardinal Richelieu's Ward* ('14), *The Roaring Road* ('19) and *Valley of the Giants* ('19).

Cruze's first serial was *The Million Dollar Mystery* ('14). The story employs the well-proved formula of a pretty, persecuted heroine with enemies more powerful than her friends — at least until the climax — and embellished with a thrill or more for each of the 23 chapters. Cruze played Jim Norton, a newspaper reporter in love with heroine Florence Hargreave (Florence La Badie). Marguerite Snow was Countess Olga, in cahoots

with the thieves. An extremely popular serial, it grossed almost $1.5 million on an investment of $125,000. This serial is given credit for starting the craze for masked conspirators.

Cruze's second serial was *Zudora (The Twenty Million Dollar Mystery)* (1914). In this sequel to *The Million Dollar Mystery*, a cache of money sets off the rapidly moving series of events as Zudora (Marguerite Snow), the heroine, and her newspaper reporter boyfriend (James Cruze) try to unravel the mystery and elude death at every turn. With the tenth chapter, the title was changed to *The Twenty Million Dollar Mystery*.*

James Cruze died from a heart ailment at age 58 in 1942. He married and divorced actresses Marguerite Snow and Betty Compson.

Serials

1914

The Million Dollar Mystery. Thanhauser, [23 Chapters] D: Howell Hansell; S: Harold McGrath; SP: Lloyd Lonergan; LP: Florence La Badie, James Cruze, Margaret Snow, Frank Farrington, Sidney Bracey.

Zudora (The Twenty Million Dollar Mystery). Thanhouser, [20 Chapters] D: Howell Hansell; SP: Lloyd Lonergan, F. W. Doughty; S: Daniel Carson Goodman, Harold McGrath; LP: Margaret Snow, James Cruze, Harry Benham, Sidney Bracey, Frank Farrington.

1919

The Demon Shadow. Arrow, [10 Chapters]. This is a re-release and re-edited (to 10 chapters) *Zudora (The Twenty Million Dollar Mystery.*

---

*The Demon Shadow *(Arrow 1919)* was a re-release of the 1914 Thanhouser serial entitled Zudora or The Twenty Million Dollar Mystery. *The length was cut to ten chapters.*

GRACE CUNARD

Grace Cunard, whose real name was Harriet Mildred Jeffries, was one of the early serial queens. *Lucille Love, Girl of Mystery* ('14), a 15-chapter Universal serial, had Grace playing the heroine menaced by villain Francis Ford, who pursues her around the world in an attempt to steal a valuable map from her. The film hit the market just ahead of Pearl White's *The Perils of Pauline* ('14). Tremendously successful, it prompted Universal czar Carl Laemmle to commit his studio wholeheartedly to the production of serials. In the next 32 years, Universal would make 139 serials.

At the age of 13, Grace persuaded her mother to let her go on the road with a stock company. In the next two or three years she gained knowledge of the stage in plays with Eddie Foy and other professionals of the day. Around 1910 Grace received an invitation to enter the movies, which were not socially acceptable at that time. However, she decided to give the "flickers" a try. *The Duke's Plan* ('10) may have been her first. In 1912 she met Francis Ford (real name Frank Feeney). Francis was both director and actor and anything else necessary to get a film made. Grace had a flair for writing and the two found they had much in common. They formed a partnership with Ford as director-actor and Grace as writer-actress.

After they joined Universal, things begin to pick up for them. The couple co-starred in, directed and wrote a series of historical films, Westerns and melodramas that included *Custer's Last Raid* ('12), *The Battle of Bull Run* ('13), *Texas Kelly at Bay* ('13), *The She Wolf* ('13), *The Belle of Yorktown* ('13), *The Bride of Mystery* ('14), *The Mysterious Leopard Lady* ('14) and *Washington at Valley Forge* ('14). Grace portrayed characters from tomboy to queen in her long series of Universal shorts with Ford, but it was serials that immortalized her. *The Broken Coin* ('15) was one of the most sensational and thrilling films produced up to that time, and its success made movie history. Ford directed and Grace wrote the scenario based on an Emerson Hough story. *The Adventures of Peg o' the Ring* ('16) was another popular serial directed and written by Francis and Grace, who also played the lead roles.

More short films followed, and then the serial *The Purple Mask* ('16), in which Grace is a lady Robin Hood who leaves a purple mask as her sign after each robbery. Ford is the detective bent on capturing her. Cost of production ran high and returns were disappointing. Laemmle made an attempt to break up the Ford-Cunard partnership. Grace was put into some five-reel features. In 1919 she was cast opposite Elmo Lincoln in *Elmo, the Mighty*. Her work in this serial plus acting in and writing the long succession of shorter films exhausted her physically and emotionally. When she was unable to do the sequel *Elmo, the Fearless* ('20), Louise Lorraine replaced her.

When Grace was able to face the grind again, she worked in the independent market. She even appeared once more with Francis Ford, in a cheap production called *The Woman of Mystery* ('22).

Grace worked again for Universal, appearing in several serials and features, but as a featured player, not as a star.

In 1928 Syndicate made *The Chinatown Mystery*. Appearing in the serial as principals were Joe Bonomo, Ruth Hiatt and Francis Ford, while Grace Cunard, Rosemary Theby, Peggy O'Day and Helen Gibson ably supported. It was the last time Ford and Cunard worked together.

Grace wed stuntman Jack Shannon in 1925 and the marriage was a lasting one. Although she worked until the early 1940s, mostly at Universal, her roles were small. Her last good part was in *Last Man on Earth*

('24), a science fiction comedy in which she was a gangster out to collect from the all-female government a ransom for the only male survivor on Earth.

Grace Cunard was born on April 8, 1903, in Columbus, Ohio. She died on January 19, 1967, at the Motion Picture Country Home after a long bout with cancer. She was survived by her husband Jack Shannon and her sister, former actress Mina Cunard.

Serials

1914

Lucille Love, Girl of Mystery. Univ., [15 Chapters] D: Francis Ford; SP: Grace Cunard, Francis Ford; S: James Keeley; Spv.: Otis Turner; LP: Grace Cunard, Francis Ford, Harry Schumm, Ernest Shields, E. M. Kelly.

1915

The Broken Coin. Univ., [22 Chapters] D: Francis Ford: SP: Grace Cunard; S: Emerson Hough; P: Francis Ford; LP: Francis Ford,

Grace Cunard, Harry Schumm, John Ford, Jack Holt, Eddie Polo, Mina Cunard, Ernest Shields.

1916

The Purple Mask. Univ., [16 Chapters] D: Francis Ford; SP: Grace Cunard, Francis Ford; LP: Grace Cunard, Francis Ford, Joan Hathaway, Peter Gerald, Jerry Ash, John Duff.

The Adventures of Peg o' the Ring. Univ., [15 Chapters] D: Francis Ford, Jacques Jaccard; SP: Grace Cunard; LP: Grace Cunard, Francis Ford, Peter Gerald, Raymond Nye, Charles Munn, Jean Hathaway.

1919

Elmo, the Mighty. Univ., [18 Chapters] D: Henry MacRae; S: Joe Brandt, William E. Wing; LP: Elmo Lincoln, Grace Cunard, Fred Starr, Virginia Craft, Bob Reeves, Ivor McFadden, Madge Hunt, Chai Hong.

1926

The Winking Idol. Univ., [10 Chapters] D: Francis Ford; SP: Arthur Henry Golden, George Morgan; S: Charles E. Van Loan; LP: William Desmond, Eileen Sedgwick, Jack Richardson, Grace Cunard, Monavana, Dorothy Gulliver.

Strings of Steel. Univ., [10 Chapters] D: Henry MacRae; LP: William Desmond, Eileen Sedgwick, Albert J. Smith, Arthur Morrison, Dorothy Gulliver.

Fighting with Buffalo Bill. Univ., [10 Chapters] D: Ray Taylor; LP: Wallace MacDonald, Elsa Benham, Edmund Cobb, Robert E. Homans, Cuyler Supplee.

1927

Return of the Riddle Rider. Univ., [10 Chapters] D: Robert Hill, Jay Marchant; LP: William Desmond, Lola Todd, Scotty Mattraw, Norbett Myles, Tom London.

Blake of Scotland Yard. Univ., [12 Chapters] D: Robert F. Hill; LP: Hayden Stevenson, Gloria Grey, Herbert Prior, Monte Montague, Grace Cunard.

1928

Haunted Island. Univ., [10 Chapters] D: Robert F. Hill; LP: Jack Daugherty, Helen Fos-

KITTY PLANS TO FIND THE
SECRET TORTURE CHAMBERS

B.C. No. 11

Grace Cunard in *The Broken Coin* (Universal, 1915).

ter, Carl Miller, Al Ferguson, John T. Prince, Wilbur Mack.

The Chinatown Mystery. Syn., [10 Chapters] D: J. P. McGowan; LP: Joe Bonomo, Ruth Hiatt, Paul Malvern, Francis Ford, Paul Panzer, Grace Cunard, Peggy O'Day, Rosemary Theby, George Chesebro, Sheldon Lewis, Ernest Shields.

1929

The Ace of Scotland Yard. Univ., [10 Chapters] D: Ray Taylor; LP: Crauford Kent, Florence Allen, Herbert Prior, Monte Montague, Grace Cunard, Albert Prisco.

1931

Heroes of the Flames. Univ., [12 Chapters] D: Robert F. Hill; SP: George H. Plympton, George Morgan, Basil Dickey; LP: Tim McCoy, Marion Shockley, William Gould, Grace Cunard, Bobby Nelson, Gayne Whitman.

1932

Heroes of the West. Univ., [12 Chapters] D: Ray Taylor; LP: Noah Beery, Jr., Diane Duval, Onslow Stevens, William Desmond, Martha Mattox, Grace Cunard.

1935

Rustlers of Red Dog. Univ., [12 Chapters] D: Louis Friedlander [Lew Landers]; LP: Johnny Mack Brown, Joyce Compton, Walter Miller, Raymond Hatton, Harry Woods.

The Call of the Savage. Univ., [12 Chapters] D: Lewis Friedlander [Lew Landers]; LP: Noah Beery, Jr., Dorothy Short, Harry Woods, Walter Miller, Bryant Washburn.

1940

Winners of the West. Univ., [13 Chapters] D: Ford Beebe, Ray Taylor; LP: Dick Foran, Anne Nagel, James Craig, Tom Fadden, Charles Stevens, Trevor Bardette.

1942

Gang Busters. Univ., [13 Chapters] D: Ray Taylor, Noel Smith; LP: Kent Taylor, Irene Hervey, Ralph Morgan, Robert Armstrong, Joseph Crehan.

1943

Adventures of Smilin' Jack. Univ., [13 Chapters] Ray Taylor, Lew Collins; LP: Tom Brown, Marjorie Lord, Sidney Toler, Edgar Barrier, Rose Hobart.

PAULINE CURLEY

Pauline Curley was entertaining the public since she was three years of age. She was born in Holyoke, Massachusetts, where she attended the public schools and, when school was not in session, appeared in child parts of the plays produced by a local stock company. At the age of eight she was a regular member of the Jay Packard Stock Company. For several years she played with them, appearing in such well-known vehicles as *Uncle Tom's Cabin* and *Little Lord Fauntleroy.*

Then came the call of the movies. For a year she appeared in the films made by Imp, Reliance and Rame Film Companies. Then back to the footlights; for two seasons, she appeared in a sketch titled *A Daddy by Express.* With the close of the vaudeville engagement, she returned to picture work under the Famous Players Management. She appeared in *The Straight Road* with Florence Reed; in the production *Polygamy* she was a hit as Rhoda. She later appeared in Fox and Triangle pictures and starred in Herbert Brenon's *The Fall of the Romanoffs* ('17).

She also played in *The Dancing Doll* ('15) with Vivian Wessell, *Life Without Soul* ('15) with Percy Stand, *The Man Beneath* ('19) with Sessue Hayakawa and *The Solitary Sin* ('19) with Jack Mulhall. Probably her best role was opposite Douglas Fairbanks in *Bound in Morocco* ('18), a Famous Players–Lasky film.

In 1920 she played opposite Antonio Moreno in *The Invisible Hand*, a 15-chapter serial from Vitagraph. After making a hopeless fight against a band of criminals headed by Iron Hand (Brinsley Shaw), the Secret Service decides to call in John Sharpe (Moreno), famous analytical detective, to help them. Sharpe accepts the job and immediately puts his powers to work and discovers the clerk in the Secret Service office is a traitor. Burnett (Jay Morley), head of the Secret Service, sends a famous woman agent (Pauline Curley) to help Sharpe. With the aid of some captured papers she joins the Crime Trust and palms herself off to Iron Hand as a crook. Thus begins 15 chapters of daring and deviltry, courage and cunning, roguishness and romance.

Pauline also appeared in *Hands Off* ('21) with Tom Mix; *Judge Her Not* ('21) with Jack Livingston; *The Vengeance Trail* ('21), *Shackles of Fear* ('24) and *The Trail of Vengeance* ('24) with Al Ferguson; *The Prairie Mystery* ('22) with Bud Osborne; *Border Law* ('22), *Smoked Out* ('23), *Double Cinched* ('23) and *Lost, Strayed or Stolen* ('23), all four with Leo Maloney; *The Laffin' Fool* ('27), *Thunderbolt's Tracks* ('27), *Code of the Range* ('27) and *West of the Rainbow's End* ('26), all four with Jack Perrin; *Prince of the Saddle* ('26) and *Two-Fisted Buckaroo* ('26), both with Fred Church (Montana Bill); and the following with Kit Carson: *His Greatest Battle* ('25), *Ridin' Wild* ('25), *Cowboy Courage* ('25), *Walloping Kid* ('26), *Twin Six O'Brien* ('26), *Pony Express Rider* ('26) and *The Millionaire Orphan* ('26).

No doubt there were other films in which she appeared, but in the third-rate films with Al Ferguson, Kit Carson, Bud Osborne and Fred Church, there was no way her career would be advanced. The films played the small neighborhood theaters in small towns, primarily in the South. One film that did reach first-rate theaters was *Power*, a Pathé release with William Boyd, Joan Bennett, Jacqueline Logan and Carole Lombard. Pauline had too much feminine competition.

Though Pauline was on the Hollywood scene for a dozen years or more, she never made much of a splash, and by 1929 her career as a leading woman was at an end.

The second of Pauline's serials was *The Veiled Mystery* ('20). The plot was an old one. Abe Sawyer (Henry A. Ballows) is guardian of Ralph Moore's sweetheart, Ruth Sawyer (Pauline Curley). He wishes to do away with Moore (Antonio Moreno) in order to keep control of Ruth's fortune. Ethel Seymour (Nenette de Courey) is Ruth's devoted friend. Scriptwriters led audiences to believe that the Veiled Mystery was a woman, but Abe Sawyer turned out to be the criminal.

Pauline got trapped in Westerns made on shoestring budgets by small independents. Had she been able to become affiliated with Universal, Fox, Pathé or other majors, her story might have had a happier ending. She was married to cinematographer Kenneth Peach (who died in '88). She retired in 1929 to rear her family.

Pauline died December 16, 2001, in Santa Monica, California. She was 97.

Serials

1920

The Invisible Hand. Vit., [15 Chapters] D: William J. Bowman; S: Albert E. Smith, C. T. Brady; SP: Graham Baker; LP: Antonio Moreno,

Pauline Curley, Brinsley Shaw, Jay Morley, Sam Polo, George Mellcrest, Gordon Sackville.

The Veiled Mystery. Vit., [15 Chapters] D: F. J. Frandon, Webster Cullison, William J. Bowman; S: Albert Smith, Cleveland Moffett; SP: Graham Baker; LP: Antonio Moreno, Pauline Curley, H. A. Barrows, Nenette de Courey, W. L. Rogers, George Cooper, Valera Olivo, W. S. Smith.

LOUISE CURRIE

Louise Currie was one ingenue who didn't disappear into the woodwork following her movie career. During her movie years, Louise supplemented her income by working as an interior decorator, a field she was in for many years as head of Louise Currie Interiors of Los Angeles.

Married to businessman John Good, who operated John Good Imports, she traveled extensively with her husband. For years

Louise Currie and Gene Autry in *Stardust on the Sage* (Republic, 1942).

they owned a yacht and sailed the Mediterranean each summer. No, she was not the typical ex–B-Western ingenue out looking for a job once the Westerns dried up in the early 1950s.

Currie's modest claim to fame is founded on two better-than-average serials. As Betty Wallace, Currie achieved a small degree of film immortality in Republic's highly successful, pioneering fantasy *Adventures of Captain Marvel* ('41), which starred Tom Tyler as the world's mightiest mortal as portrayed in Whiz Comics. The film is rated by many serial devotees as Republic's best chapterplay. Superb special effects by the Lydecker brothers, unusually good casting, a well-written script, good direction and excellent stunt work (particularly by Dave Sharpe) got results.

Currie's identification with the genre was strengthened by the release of *The Masked Marvel* ('43), which contained thrills and great stunt work by Tom Steel in the title role. Though not as well produced as *Adventures of Captain Marvel*, the film gave Currie a far better part.

Currie was born in Oklahoma City, the daughter of a bank president. She attended schools in Washington, D.C., and Bronxville, New York, before entering Sarah Lawrence College. There she became interested in films and was invited by Max Reinhardt, discoverer of many famous stars, to join his Hollywood drama workshop. She stayed for two years, starring in many of the shows he produced. Then she was signed by agent Sue

Caroll, who got her the heroine role in Columbia's Charles Starrett vehicle *The Pinto Kid* ('41). Other Westerns followed with Tim Holt, Bob Steele, Kirby Grant, Gene Autry and Eddie Dean. *Gun Town* ('46) gave Currie her finest acting opportunity in Westerns, and it remains her favorite film. She plays a mannish Calamity Jane–type character, with much cracking of a bullwhip.

In the early 1950s, she left the screen to concentrate her efforts entirely on decorating and designing. Currie and Good had two sons, one daughter and six grandchildren. After Good's death in 1998, Curried married Col. Grover Asmus, widower of Donna Reed.

Serials

1941

The Adventures of Captain Marvel. Rep., [12 Chapters] D: William Witney, John English; SP: Ronald Davidson, Norman S. Hall, Arch B. Heath, Joseph Poland, Sol Shor; AP: Hiram S. Brown, Jr.; Cam: William Nobles; Mus: Cy Feuer; LP: Tom Tyler, Frank Coghlan, Jr., William Benedict, Louise Currie, Robert Strange, Harry Worth, Gerald Mohr.

1943

The Masked Marvel. Univ., [12 Chapters] D: Spencer Bennet; SP: Royal Cole, Ronald Davidson, Basil Dickey, Jesse Duffy, Grant Nelson, George H. Plympton, Joseph Poland; AP: W. J. O'Sullivan; Cam: Reggie Lanning; Mus: Mort Glickman; LP: William Forrest, Louise Currie, Johnny Arthur, David Bacon, Rod Bacon, Tom Steele, Gayne Whitman, Howard Hickman.

DICK CURTIS

Dick Curtis, the baddie with the sardonic smile and who looked too mean to be real, was born on May 13, 1902, in Newport, Kentucky. His real name was Richard D. Dye. Both parents were professionals. He was educated in Los Angeles and started in pictures as an extra in D. W. Griffith's *The Unpardonable Sin* (1918). Very little is known of his work in silent pictures but he did have some stage experience in New York and in touring road companies and he worked in stock in such cities as Patterson and Bayonne, New Jersey, and Springfield, Massachusetts.

A big man (6'3" and weighing over 200 pounds) with brown hair and blue eyes, Curtis first began to attract attention as a "heavy" in the outdoor action films starring Kermit Maynard for Ambassador. These led to better parts in the Tim McCoy Westerns then being made by Puritan and in the Johnny Mack Brown series that A. W. Hackel was producing for his Supreme Pictures. Shortly thereafter, Curtis joined Columbia Pictures as a contract player. He played minor roles in major productions (such as *You Can't Take It with You*, 1938) and a variety of parts in various second features. He was also in a number of two-reel comedies with the Three Stooges and several serials. *Terry and the Pirates* ('40) was one of the better cliffhangers and Curtis had his best serial role as the archvillain "Fang," a piratical half-caste warlord who dominated and terrorized the Asiatic wilds.

But the majority of his films for Columbia were Westerns, and he was the perennial villain in most of the early (and best) Charles Starrett pictures. He would also occasionally menace the up-and-coming Bill Elliott. Later, as a freelance actor, Curtis played

Bill Elliott and Dick Curtis (right) in *Pioneers of the Frontier* (Columbia, 1942).

minor roles at MGM, Paramount and PRC. Some of these were uncredited roles that were little more than bit parts. But he also had good featured roles in Westerns with Johnny Mack Brown (Universal), Wallace Beery (MGM) and the Dave O'Brien–Jim Newill team (PRC). Republic used him to good advantage in the films of Roy Rogers, Allan Lane, Monte Blue and Bill Elliott (who had moved over from Columbia). Toward the end of his career, Curtis returned to Columbia for several features, more two-reelers with the Three Stooges and another serial, *Roar of the Iron Horse* ('51).

Dick Curtis died on January 3, 1952.

Serials

1935

The Miracle Rider. Mascot, [15 Chapters] D: Armand Schaefer, B. Reeves Eason; LP: Tom Mix, Joan Gale, Charles Middleton, Jason Robards, Sr., Robert Kortman.

1937

Blake of Scotland Yard. Victory, [15 Chapters] D: Bob Hill; LP: Ralph Byrd, Herbert Rawlinson, Joan Barclay, Lloyd Hughes.

1938

The Spider's Web. Col., [15 Chapters] D: James W. Horne; LP: Warren Hull, Iris Meredith, Richard Fiske, Kenne Duncan, Forbes Murray, Donald Douglas, Marc Lawrence, Edward J. LeSaint, Edward Earle, John Tyrrell.

1939

Overland with Kit Carson. Col., [15 Chapters] D: Sam Nelson, Norman Deming; LP: Bill Elliott, Iris Meredith, Trevor Bardette, Richard Fiske, Bobby Clark.

Mandrake, the Magician. Col., [12 Chapters] D: Sam Nelson, Norman Deming; LP: Warren Hull, Doris Weston, Al Kikume, Rex Downing, Edward Earle, Dick Curtis.

Flying G-Men. Col., [15 Chapters] D: Ray Taylor, James W. Horne; LP: Robert Paige, Lorna Gray [Adrian Booth], Richard Fiske, James Craig, Don Beddoe.

1940

Terry and the Pirates. Col., [15 Chapters] D: James W. Horne; LP: William Tracy, Granville Owens, Joyce Bryant, Allen Jung, Dick Curtis.

1941

Sea Raiders. Univ., [12 Chapters] D: Ford Beebe, John Rawlins; LP: Billy Halop, Huntz Hall, Hally Chester, William Hall, Marcia Ralston, Joe Recht.

1943

Batman. Col., [15 Chapters] D: Lambert Hillyer; LP: Lewis Wilson, Douglas Croft, J. Carrol Naish, Shirley Patterson, Charles Middleton, Charles Wilson, Robert Fiske.

The Phantom. Col., [15 Chapters] D: B. Reeves Eason; LP: Tom Tyler, Jeanne Bates, Kenneth MacDonald, Frank Shannon, Ace (dog), Guy Kingsford, Joe Devlin.

1944

Mystery of the River Boat. Univ., [13 Chapters] D: Ray Taylor, Lewis D. Collins; LP: Robert Lowery, Eddie Quillan, Marion Martin, Marjorie Clements, Lyle Talbot, Mantan Moreland, Dick Curtis.

1945

The Master Key. Univ., [13 Chapters] D: Ray Taylor, Lewis D. Collins; LP: Milburn Stone, Jan Wiley, Dennis Moore, Sarah Padden, Russell Hicks, Addison Richards, Byron Foulger.

1946

Lost City of the Jungle. Univ., [13 Chapters] D: Ray Taylor, Lewis D. Collins; LP: Russell Hayden, Jane Adams, Lionel Atwill, Keye Luke, Helen Bennett.

1951

Government Agents vs. Phantom Legion. Rep., [12 Chapters] D: Fred C. Brannon; LP: Walter Reed, Mary Ellen Kay, Dick Curtis, John Pickard, Pierce Lyden.

Roar of the Iron Horse. Col., [15 Chapters] D: Spencer G. Bennett, Thomas Carr; LP: Jock Mahoney, Virginia Herrick, William Faucett, Hal Landon.

KEN CURTIS

Most folks probably remember Ken Curtis as "Festus" on television's *Gunsmoke.* It would come as a surprise to learn that he had been a singing cowboy in a low-budget series of Columbia Westerns. Not only that, but he had been vocalist with the Shep Fields Orchestra and the Tommy Dorsey Band.

Ken was born on July 12, 1916. His real name was Curtis Gates. He attended Colorado University.

After military service in World War II, Ken joined the Sons of the Pioneers. He sang with them on several soundtracks. Ken took up his acting career and appeared in *Rio Grande* ('50), *Mister Roberts* ('55), *The Searchers* ('56), *The Wings of Eagles* ('57), *The Last Hurrah* ('58), *The Horse Soldiers* ('59), *The Alamo* ('60), *Two Rode Together* ('61), *Cheyenne Autumn* ('64), *Pony Express Rider* ('76) and *Conagher* ('91).

In Republic's *Don Daredevil rides Again* ('51), Curtis (as Lee Hadley) dons the mask of Don Daredevil to battle Douglas Stratton (Roy Barcroft) who, under a forged Spanish

Ken Curtis and Aline Towne in *Don Daredevil Rides Again* (Republic, 1951).

land grant, is trying to claim title to valuable ranchland owned in part by Lee's cousin, Patricia (Aline Towne). Supposedly a tenderfoot Easterner, Lee homesteads the Doyle Ranch and encourages ranchers to stand pat against Stratton's night riders and his crooked sheriff co-conspirator (I. Stanford Jolley). The serial wasn't much to brag about — just a typical Republic Western with plenty of fighting and unspectacular cliffhangers.

Starting in 1963, Curtis played Marshal Dillon's whiskered sidekick Festus. He died at age 74 in Fresno, California, in 1991.

Serial

1951

Don Daredevil Rides Again. Rep., [12 Chapters] D: Fred C. Brannon; SP: Ronald Davidson; Cam: Ellis W. Carter; Mus: Stanley Wilson; LP: Ken Curtis, Aline Towne, Roy Barcroft, Lane Bradford, John Cason.

BOB CUSTER

Bob Custer (real name Raymond Anthony Glenn) was born October 18, 1898. The seventh and last child of John and Mary Glenn, he had four sisters and two brothers.

Victoria Vinton, Bob Custer (center) and Roger Williams in *Vengeance of Rannah* (Reliable, 1936).

His father was a stone mason before going into the grocery business. Being Catholic, the Glenns sent their children to parochial schools. Bob attended public high school and the University of Kentucky, majoring in civil engineering.

In 1920 he made his first trip to Hollywood, got homesick and returned home for a couple of years. Then, with a friend who had a car, he made the trip to California in about five weeks. The only paved roads then were around the big cities. They traveled mostly on dirt roads.

Bob wanted to get into the movies and played extras for a couple months before landing the lead in a Western series produced by Jesse Goldburg's Independent Pictures Corporation and distributed by FBO. His screen debut came in 1924 with the film *Trigger Fingers*. It was followed in quick succession by *Flashing Spurs*, *The Bloodhound*, *Galloping Vengeance*, *A Man of Nerve* and 17 other hayburners.

In his book *Winners of the West*, Kalton Lahue has this to say about Custer: "[H]e couldn't act to save his life, his on-screen performances were stiff and awkward, his physical appearance changed markedly during his career, he was not photogenic and his later pictures were as bad as his acting. Custer's stern, relentless visage never changed its expression; he marched through film after film like a wooden soldier. Occasionally, he showed a gleam of his acting range by cracking a half-smile."

Yet Custer was popular. Like Jack Perrin, Custer was a comfortable hero in that he was completely predictable. There was never any doubt that he would win out in the end and even the seemingly insurmountable odds he usually faced could not shake the audience's confidence — Bob Custer *would win*.

Bob's weekly paycheck was $100 the first year, $200 the second year and $300 the third. After completing 21 films, Custer left Goldberg and formed his own Bob Custer Productions, grinding out *The Fighting Hombre* ('27), *Galloping Thunder* ('27) and *Terror of the Bar X* ('27). For whatever reason, only those three films were made. But Bob didn't slow up. For Chadwick Pictures he made three non–Westerns using his real name of Raymond Glenn—*Ladies at Ease*, *Return of Boston Blackie* and *Temptations of a Shop Girl*.

Bob married Ann Cudahy in Hollywood; her father was John Cudahy, son of the wealthy Omaha meat packer. They had one son, Raymond, Jr. The couple pooled their wealth and built a 15-room home. Then came the Depression and Custer, like so many, lost a fortune. He also lost a wife.

In 1928, Bob signed with Syndicate Pictures for a Western series and 21 pictures were made in 1928–31. When the Syndicate series ended, Bob made four films for Big 4 Productions, a small independent firm. After that series ended Bob was unable to get a job until Mascot hired him to play the lead (although a horse and a dog were billed over him) in the serial *Law of the Wild* ('34). Custer is a young rancher who has tamed a wild horse (Rex). The horse is stolen by an employee and entered in a race, which he wins. Custer has met Lucile Browne and her father while searching for Rex. At the track, Rex's winnings are argued over by two thugs, one kills the other and the blame is put on Custer. Custer, Rex, Rin-Tin-Tin, Jr., Browne and Ben Turpin survive numerous ordeals before horse and master are reunited.

In 1936, Custer was hired by Reliable Pictures to star in three Westerns. After those, he couldn't find work. He returned to engineering, starting a construction business in the San Fernando Valley. Heart problems left him 4-F for World War II service and he worked shipyards in the Los Angeles area. After the war, he became city inspector for Los Angeles, street superintendent in Redondo Beach and building inspector for the cities of Newport Beach and El Segundo.

In 1948, at the age of 50, he married Mildred Bowers, age 25. She idolized him. He retired in 1968 and on December 28, 1974, while walking his dog near his Redondo Beach apartment, Custer had a fatal heart attack.

Serial

1934

Law of the Wild. Mascot, [12 Chapters] D: Armand Schaefer, B. Reeves Eason; S: Ford Beebe, John Rathmall, Al Martin; SP: Sherman Lowe, B. Reeves Eason; P: Nat Levine; LP: Rex, Rin-Tin-Tin, Jr., Ben Turpin, Bob Custer, Lucile Browne, Richard Cramer, Ernie Adams, Edmund Cobb, Dick Alexander.

SHEILA DARCY

Sheila Darcy began her screen career in 1937 in the film *Wells Fargo* and appeared in at least 15 other films in 1938, including *Men with Wings, Thanks for the Memory, Bluebeard's Eighth Wife* and *Arrest Bulldog Drummond*. In 1939 she was in *Hotel Imperial, The Man in the Iron Mask, South of the Border, Union Pacific* and other feature films.

Her first serial, and her best-remembered role, was *Zorro's Fighting Legion* ('39) in which she plays Volita. It was the best of all the Zorro serials. In her second serial, *Terry and the Pirates* ('40), she plays the Dragon Lady. In 1941 she appeared in *Blossoms in the Dust, Honky Tonk, Jungle Man, Raiders of the Desert, Tumble Down Ranch in Arizona* and more.

Sheila was married to actor Preston Foster, by whom she had a daughter, Stephanie. After the death of Preston in 1970, Sheila retired to San Diego where she owned an interest in a marina. In the 1950s she, Preston, and daughter had a musical act with which they barnstormed the country, at fairs, auto shows, and auditoriums several months of each year. She died in 2004.

Serials

1939

Zorro's Fighting Legion. Rep., [12 Chapters] D: William Witney, John English; SP: Ronald Davidson, Franklyn Adreon, Morgan Cox, Sol Shor, Barney Sarecky; AP: Hiram S. Brown, Jr.; Cam: Reggie Lanning; Mus: William Lava; LP: Reed Hadley, Sheila Darcy, William Corson, Leander de Cordova, C. Montague Shaw.

1940

Terry and the Pirates. Col., [15 Chapters] D: James W. Horne; LP: William Tracy, Granville Owens, Joyce Bryant, Allen Jung, Sheila Darcy.

GRACE DARMOND

Grace Darmond's personality was quintessentially feminine by traditional standards. In the early 1920s she was the type of girl whom a man would instinctively choose to be his wife. Dependent and trustful, she lacked the touch of hardness which can in some degree become associated with the woman who makes her own way in the world. Timidity, sensitivity, shyness have traditionally been admirable qualities in a woman — not only admirable but lovable as well. And Grace Darmond had all these qualities.

Grace was born in Toronto, Canada, in 1898. Her father was a concert violinist. After his death, she and her mother went to Chicago where she appeared on the stage in *Editha's Burglar.* Col. Selig of the Selig Company met her and asked her to play in his films. Her first picture was a comedy, *When the Clock Went Wrong* ('14). After about a year with Selig, she went to Astra Film Corporation, releasing through Pathé, to star in *The Shielding Shadow* ('16), a suspenseful serial about a mantle of invisibility. Its 15 chapters were written by George Seitz.

By 1918, Grace was a star at Vitagraph, playing an assortment of roles. *The Gulf Between* ('18) should also be mentioned as it was produced by the Technicolor Motion Picture Company. Miss Darmond had the distinction of being the first actress to star in a Technicolor film. In 1919 she worked for several studios. But two big features of that year were for Paramount: *The Valley of the Giants* ('19) opposite Wallace Reid and *Behind the Door* ('19) as female lead with Hobart Bosworth.

Grace played one of two female leads opposite King Baggot in Burston's serial thriller *The Hawk's Trail* ('20). That same year she played again with Hobart Bosworth in Paramount's *Below the Surface*. But her career never really shifted into high gear, and she was soon back in the serial genre with *The Hope Diamond Mystery* ('21) for Kosmik and *A Dangerous Adventure* ('22) for Warner Brothers. She drifted into vamp roles and was often the "other woman" in love triangles, until she decided she had had enough of filmmaking and quit the business with the advent of talkies.

On January 22, 1928, Grace married Randolph P. Jennings, wealthy theater owner and mining operator of Beverly Hills and Mexico City. But in December 1935 she won an uncontested divorce on grounds that her husband had cursed and criticized her in the presence of guests and servants. Several suits followed but the millionaire ex-husband won each time.

We have no knowledge of Grace's activities from 1928 until her death at age 65 on October 7, 1963. She had been undergoing treatment for a lung ailment at the Motion Picture Country Hospital, although she died at her home. The actress left instructions that her body be donated to the University of Southern California Medical School.

Serials

1916

The Shielding Shadow. Astra/Pathé, [15 Chapters] D: Louis Gasnier, Donald McKenzie; SP:

George B. Seitz; S: Randall Parrish; LP: Grace Darmond, Ralph Kellard, Leon Barry, Madeline Traverse, Frankie Mann.

1920

The Hawks' Trail. Burston, [15 Chapters] D: W. S. Van Dyke; SP: John B. Clymer, Louis and George Burston; S: Nan Blair; Spv.: Louis Burston; LP: King Baggot, Rhea Mitchell, Grace Darmond, Harry Lorraine.

1921

The Hope Diamond Mystery. Kosmik, [15 Chapters] D: Stuart Paton; SP: Charles Goddard, John P. Clymer; P: George Kleine; Cam: William Thornley; S: May Yohe; LP: Harry Carter, Grace Darmond, George Chesebro, Boris Karloff.

1922

A Dangerous Adventure. Warner Bros., [15 Chapters] D: Sam Warner, Jack L. Warner; SP: Sam Warner; S: Frances Guihan; P: William N. Selig; LP: Grace Darmond, Philo McCullough, Jack Richardson, Robert Agnew, Derelys Perdue.

FRANKIE DARRO

Frankie Darro practically made a career at playing jockeys, not only in horse racing films but in such "A" films as *Broadway Bill* ('34), *Saratoga* ('37), *Salty O'Rourke* ('45) and *Riding High* ('50).

Darro was born Frank Johnson in Chicago, Illinois, on December 22, 1917. His parents were aerialists with Sells Brothers Circus. When Mrs. Johnson became ill (a nervous breakdown) while the circus was in Long Beach, the Johnsons left the circus and settled in Hollywood, where Mr. Johnson obtained work as a stuntman. Through his friendship with Producer Ralph Ince, Frankie was able to get small roles in movies. His first was *Judgment of the Storm* ('23) with Wallace Beery. For a time during the 1920s, Frankie was under contract to FBO and supported Tom Tyler in a series of Westerns.

Darro continued playing child roles throughout the silent era. In the 1930s he often played tough kids of the Depression, then played leads in low-budget Monogram action programmers. Because of his small frame, he also portrayed many pint-size punks. Gradually he drifted into bit parts and finally stuntwork. For years he played an old lady on *The Red Skelton Show*.

Darro played in six Mascot serials in the early 1930s and these assured him a place in the hearts of serial devotees.

In *The Vanishing Legion* ('31) he plays young Jimmy Williams, a friend to Rex, King of the Wild Horses. His father is falsely accused of murder and Jimmy and Rex help him escape both the law and the Vanishing Legion, an outlaw gang that wants him dead so they can take over his land. The leader of the Vanishing Legion is "the Voice," so named because his instructions to the gang come via telephone or wireless. Happy Hardigan (Harry Carey) becomes involved in helping Jimmy when the Vanishing Legion tries to stop Hardigan from delivering equipment to an oil company that the Voice wishes to buy out cheap.

In *The Lightning Warrior* ('31), Frankie shares honors with Rin-Tin-Tin (Sr.), Georgia Hale and George Brent in his first major role. The Wolf Man, a mysterious outlaw, and his Indian followers attempt to drive the whites out of a mining district and to prevent young Jimmy Carter (Darro) from taking possession of his murdered father's mine. Alan Scott (Brent), brother to a murdered lawman, aids Jimmy, as does the dog Rinty and Dianne (Hale), adopted daughter of the sheriff.

In *The Devil Horse* ('32), an outlaw (Noah Beery) and his gang stop at nothing to gain possession of the Devil Horse (Apache), leader of a wild horse pack in which a wild boy (Darro) is reared. The villain's plot is to recapture the horse that had once been a great race horse and present it as a new "discovery," but they are frustrated by the presence of the wild boy, who protects the Devil Horse and in turn is protected by him. When the gang kills a forest ranger, the ranger's brother (Harry Carey) vows vengeance and becomes a friend of the Wild Boy and the Devil Horse in tracking down the outlaw leader. It is the steed that has the final revenge.

In *The Wolf Dog* ('33), Bob Whitlock (George J. Lewis) invents an electric ray that can destroy ships at a distance of several miles. Norman Bryan (Hale Hamilton), general manager of the Courtney Steamship Lines, plans to steal it. Bob becomes friends with a young boy, Frank, and his dog Pal. All three are involved in a desperate struggle to stay alive and protect the invention until it can be turned over to the government.

In *Burn 'Em Up Barnes* ('34), Jack Mulhall plays the title role. As a race driver, Barnes comes to the aid of Marjorie Temple (Lola Lane), owner of a financially troubled bus line and a seemingly worthless piece of property that, unknown to her, has rich oil deposits. Barnes adopts a homeless boy who develops into a first-rate newsreel cameraman. Because of film taken by the boy, Barnes is cleared of any implication in a murder and the gangsters are brought to justice.

In *Phantom Empire* ('35), Darro and Betsy King Ross are friends of Gene Autry, part-owner of Radio Ranch, from which he broadcast a popular radio show designed to bring guests flocking to the dude ranch. Crooked scientists know of valuable minerals on the land and desire to close down the ranch. Trailing some night riders, Autry finds his way into the subterranean kingdom of Murania, ruled over by Queen Tika (Dorothy Christie), there to do battle with the Muranians and to experience the wiz-

ardry of an advanced civilization before it is destroyed by an awesome death ray that literally melts Murania. The crooked scientists above ground are subdued and Radio Ranch is saved. This futuristic film is filled with robots, strange weapons and television sets, death rays and flame guns and was exceedingly popular, thoroughly captivating rural audiences of the 1930s. Universal was thus encouraged to make *Flash Gordon* ('36) and Republic *Undersea Kingdom* ('36) a short time later.

Darro was in three more serials—two for Columbia and one for Universal. These were made after he had reached adulthood, and his roles were not as appealing as when he was a boy. Of the three roles, perhaps "Creeper" in *Chick Carter, Detective* ('46) is the most interesting.

Darro married a girl by the name of Betty Marie on March 16, 1943, but they were divorced in 1952. The judge ordered Frankie to pay $50 a month for the support of his six-year-old daughter, Darlene. His second wife, Aloha Wray, died in 1968 (one source says "by suicide"). For the last 25 years of his life he was married to Dorothy Carroll. They were together on Christmas night, December 25, 1976, visiting friends in Huntington Beach when he had a fatal heart attack.

Rex Lease and Frankie Darro (right) in *Moulders of Men* (FBO, 1927).

Serials

1931

The Vanishing Legion. Mascot, [12 Chapters] D: B. Reeves Eason; SP: Wyndham Gittens, Ford Beebe, Helmer Bergman; P: Nat Levine; Cam: Benjamin Kline, Ernest Miller, J. Novak; LP: Harry Carey, Edwina Booth, Rex (horse), Frankie Darro, Philo McCullough.

The Lightning Warrior. Mascot, [12 Chapters] D: Armand Schaefer,

Benjamin Kline; SP: Wyndham Gittens, Ford Beebe, Colbert Clark; Spv.: Wyndham Gittens; Cam: Ernest Miller, William Nobles, Tom Galligan; Mus: Lee Zahler; P: Nat Levine; LP: Rin-Tin-Tin, Sr., Frankie Darro, Georgia Hale, George Brent, Pat O'Malley, Theodore Lorch.

1932

The Devil Horse. Mascot, [12 Chapters] D: Otto Brower, Yakima Canutt; SP: George Morgan, Barney Sarecky, George Plympton, Wyndham Gittens; Cam: Ernest Miller, Carl Webster, Victor Schurich; P: Nat Levine; LP: Harry Carey, Frankie Darro, Noah Beery, Sr., Greta Granstedt, Apache (horse), Al Bridge.

1933

The Wolf Dog. Mascot, [12 Chapters] D: Colbert Clark, Harry Fraser; SP: Al Martin, Colbert Clark, Wyndham Gittens; S: Barney Sarecky, Sherman Lowe; P: Nat Levine; Cam: Herry Neumann, William Nobles, Tom Galligan; Spv.: Victor Zobel; P: Nat Levine; LP: George J. Lewis, Frankie Darro, Rin-Tin-Tin, Jr., Boots Mallory, Henry B. Walthall.

1934

Burn 'Em Up Barnes. Mascot, [12 Chapters] D: Colbert Clark, Armand Schaefer; SP: Al Martin, Armand Schaefer, Barney Sarecky, Sherman Lowe; S: John Rathmell, Colbert Clark; P: Nat Levine; LP: Jack Mulhall, Frankie Darro, Lola Lane, Julian Rivero, Jason Robards.

1935

Phantom Empire. Mascot, [12 Chapters] D: Otto Brower, B. Reeves Eason; S: Wallace MacDonald, Gerald Geraghty, Hy Freedman; SP: John Rathmell, Armand Schaefer; Spv.: Armand Schaefer; P: Nat Levine; Cam: Ernest Miller, William Nobles; Mus: Lee Zahler; LP: Gene Autry, Smiley Burnette, Frankie Darro, Betsy King Ross, Dorothy Christie, Wheeler Oakman.

1938

The Great Adventures of Wild Bill Hickok. Col., [15 Chapters] D: Mack V. Wright, Sam Nelson; SP: George Rosener, Charles A. Powell, G. A. Durlan, Dallas Fitzgerald, Tom Gibson; AP: Harry Webb; P: Jack Fier; Mus: Abe Meyer; Cam: George Meehan, Benjamin Kline; LP: Bill Elliott, Carole Wayne, Frankie Darro, Monte Blue, Dickie Jones, Sammy McKim.

1942

Junior G-Men of the Air. Univ., [12 Chapters] D: Ray Taylor, Lewis D. Collins; LP: Billy Halop, Gene Reynolds, Lionel Atwill, Frank Albertson.

1946

Chick Carter, Detective. Col., [15 Chapters] D: Derwin Abrahams; LP: Lyle Talbot, Douglas Fowley, Julie Gibson, Pamela Blake, Eddie Acuff, Frankie Darro.

JOHN DAVIDSON

John Davidson was born in New York City on Christmas Day, December 25, 1886. He died at age 81 in Los Angeles, January 15, 1968, from heart failure. Outside of these dates, we know very little about John Davidson, the person.

But we know him as the evil-eyed character actor of innumerable Hollywood silent and sound features and 13 serials, usually in suave roles, often as a menacing foreigner. In shaved widow's peak or turban, he set a sinister standard for Saturday serial villains of the '30s and '40s; made his evil hollow-cheeked presence felt in *Perils of Pauline* ('34) as Dr. Bashan; *Tailspin Tommy* ('34) as Tiger Taggart; *Burn 'Em Up Barnes* ('34) as Chase;

Call of the Savage ('35) as Samu; *Jungle Menace* ('37) as Dr. Coleman; *Fighting Devil Dogs* ('38) as Lin Wing; *King of the Royal Mounted* ('40) as Dr. Shelton; *Adventures of Captain Marvel* ('41) as Tal Chotali; *Dick Tracy vs. Crime, Inc.* ('41) as Lucifer; *Perils of Nyoka* ('42) as Lhoba; *Secret Service in Darkest Africa* ('43) as Sheik; *Captain America* ('44) as Gruber; and *The Purple Monster Strikes* ('45) as the Emperor of Mars.

Davidson was also quite active in features beginning in 1915. His films include *The Danger Signal* ('15), *Under Two Flags* ('22), *Monsieur Beaucaire* ('24), *The 13th Chair* ('29), *Queen of the Night Clubs* ('29), *Arsene Lupin* ('32), *The Scarlet Express* ('34), *A Shot in the Dark* ('35), *The Last Days of Pompeii* ('35), *A Tale of Two Cities* ('35), *Mr. Moto Takes a Vacation* ('38), *The Devil Bat* ('41), *Charlie Chan and the Chinese Cat* ('44), *Sentimental Journey* ('46), *Daisy Kenyon* ('47), and *Slattery's Hurricane* ('49). He died in 1968 at 81.

Serials

1934

Perils of Pauline. Univ., [12 Chapters] D: Ray Taylor; LP: Evalyn Knapp, Robert Allen, James Durkin, John Davidson.

Tailspin Tommy. Univ., [12 Chapters] D: Louis Friedlander [Lew Landers]; LP: Maurice Murphy, Noah Beery, Jr., Patricia Farr, Walter Miller, Grant Withers.

Burn 'Em Up Barnes. Mascot, [12 Chapters] D: Colbert Clark, Armand Schaefer; LP: Jack Mulhall, Frankie Darro, Lola Lane, Julian Rivero, Edwin Maxwell.

1935

The Call of the Savage. Univ., [12 Chapters] D: Lewis Friedlander [Lew Landers]; LP: Noah Beery, Jr., Dorothy Short, Harry Woods, Walter Miller, Frederic Mackaye, Grace Cunard, King Baggot.

1937

Jungle Menace. Col., [15 Chapters] D: George Melford, Harry Fraser; LP: Frank Buck, Esther Ralston, John St. Polis, Reginald Denny, Duncan Renaldo.

1938

The Fighting Devil Dogs. Rep., [12 Chapters] D: William Witney, John English; LP: Lee Powell, Herman Brix, Eleanor Stewart, Montagu Love, Hugh Sothern.

1940

King of the Royal Mounted. Rep., [12 Chapters] D: William Witney, John English; LP: Allan Lane, Robert Strange, Robert Kellard, Lita Conway, Herbert Rawlinson.

1941

Dick Tracy vs. Crime, Inc. Rep., [15 Chapters] D: William Witney, John English; LP: Ralph Byrd, Jan Wiley, John Davidson, Ralph Morgan, Michael Owen, Kenneth Harlan.

Adventures of Captain Marvel. Rep., [12 Chapters] D: William Witney, John English; LP: Tom Tyler, Frank Coghlan, Jr., William Benedict, Louise Currie, Robert Strange, Harry Worth, John Davidson, Bryant Washburn.

1942

Perils of Nyoka. Rep., [15 Chapters] D: William Witney; LP: Kay Aldridge, Clayton Moore, William Benedict, Lorna Gray [Adrian Booth], Charles Middleton, Tris Coffin, George J. Lewis, John Davidson.

1943

Secret Service in Darkest Africa. Rep., [15 Chapters] D: Spencer Bennet; LP: Rod Cameron, Joan Marsh, Duncan Renaldo, Lionel Royce, Kurt Kreuger.

1944

Captain America. Rep., [15 Chapters] D: John English, Elmer Clifton; LP: Dick Purcell, Lorna Gray [Adrian Booth], Lionel Atwill, Charles Trowbridge, George J. Lewis, John Davidson, LeRoy Mason, Stanley Price, Jay Novello.

1945

The Purple Monster Strikes. Rep., [15 Chapters] D: Spencer Bennet, Fred Brannon; LP: Linda Stirling, Dennis Moore, James Craven, Roy Barcroft, Bud Geary, Mary Moore, George Carleton.

PRISCILLA DEAN

Priscilla Dean, "the wildcat of the screen," grew up in the theatrical profession, being the daughter of the well-known actress May Preston Dean. At age four Priscilla appeared with the famed Joseph Jefferson, emitting gurgles and cries in *Rip Van Winkle*. And with James A. Hearne she was in the plays *Shore Acres* and *Hearts of Oak*.

Born in New York City on November 25, 1896, she accompanied her parents and performed in their stock company until age ten, when she entered a convent school. At age 14 she was back on the stage. D. W. Griffith saw her in a specialty dance at the Follies Bergere in New York and she was enticed to work in his pictures made at the Bi-

ograph Studio in the Bronx. One of her first assignments was as an extra at $3 a day in a hit called *New York Hat* starring Mary Pickford. There followed a string of other Griffith successes in which the New York–born teen performed, but always in the shadow of big name stars.

It wasn't long before Priscilla began dreaming of Hollywood. Her big chance came when she was asked to join a small company, formed in New York by friends of Norma Talmadge. The dream became a nightmare. Shortly after invading Hollywood, the company folded and Priscilla found herself without a job and without any money. As luck would have it, she had a

chance to enter a local beauty contest sponsored by auto dealers. She won the contest and Universal offered her a job. She soon became established as the principal soubrette in the Eddie Lyons–Lee Moran comedy series.

She made her leap to stardom in features as a result of her popularity generated by her heroine's role in the 16-chapter serial *The Gray Ghost*. Harry Carter portrayed the Gray Ghost, a jewel thief. He and his gang loot a jewelry store in broad daylight, taking a necklace worth $2,000,000 that was intended as a wedding present for Lady Gwendolyn (Gertrude Astor). A series of thrilling cops-and-robbers chases ensues, as the Gray Ghost also steals money intended to pay for the necklace from the bank and frames the banker's son for murder. Priscilla played "Morn Light," and so impressed studio bigwigs and cinemagoers that she was elevated to features. She subsequently starred in many Universal silent dramas.

Her first big role was in *The Wildcat of Paris* ('18). The role typecast her as a slick feline actress who could use her dark brown eyes to advantage, without a cold stare or a flirtatious wink. The film was billed on theater marquees as "The Amazing Melodrama De Luxe Featuring the Amazing Actress Priscilla Dean." Overnight she became a box office attraction, a star who could pick her co-stars and her scripts. She had electrified the moviegoers of the day. She was irresistible and irrepressible in her vivacity and gay spirits. She soon was making $10,000 a week.

In *Under Two Flags* ('22) Priscilla plays Cigarette vivaciously as a flirt — as sort of an up-to-date Mohammedan flapper. It was a French Foreign Legion melodrama. Claudette Colbert recreated the role in the sound version.

While filming *The Virgin of Stamboul* ('20), she fell in love with co-star Wheeler Oakman and married him. They would later divorce. In 1925 Priscilla spent five months making personal appearances at over 200 theaters and many universities. She was received warmly.

Priscilla Dean's other films include *The Wicked Darling* ('19) and *Outside the Law* ('21) both with Lon Chaney, *Reputation* ('21), an unusual departure from her slick feline characterizations, *Conflict* ('21), *The Flame of Life* ('23), *The White Tiger* ('23), *Drifting* ('23), *The Crimson Runner* ('25), *West of Broadway* ('26), *Birds of Prey* ('27), *Jewels of Desire* ('27) and *Behind Stone Walls* ('32).

In 1928 she met and married a famous flyer, Lt. Leslie Arnold of the U.S. Army Air Corps. Upon his discharge, Arnold, then a colonel, joined Eastern Airlines as vice-president and moved east where he and Dean took up residence in the suburbs of Tenafly, New Jersey. Later they moved to Leonia. There Priscilla joined the Volunteer Ambulance Corps. During World War II she worked as a volunteer Red Cross worker. After her husband's death she lived alone in Leonia for four decades, traveled extensively and devoted many hours a week to various causes.

Priscilla Dean died in Leonia, New Jersey, on December 27, 1988, at the age of 91.

Serial

1917

The Gray Ghost. Univ., [16 Chapters] D/SP: Stuart Paton; S: Arthur Somers Roche; LP: Harry Carter, Priscilla Dean, Emory Johnson, Eddie Polo, Gypsy Hart, Wilton Taylor, Gertrude Astor, Lew Short, Francis McDonald.

CLAUDIA DELL

Claudia Dell had the feminine lead in *The Lost City* ('35), the Krellberg serial starring William (Stage) Boyd and Kane Richmond. Although most writers deplore this film, this writer found it most entertaining, both in 1935 at first viewing and in recent years when a video tape of the film was acquired. Granted, it was a cheap production but therein lies its charm. Having viewed most of Republic's cliffhangers wherein the actors chew up the scenery in one fight after another, this serial is a refreshing departure.

Claudia Dell Smith was born in San Antonio, Texas, on January 10, 1909, and received her education in both San Antonio and Mexico City schools. She went to New York City to visit her aunt, vaudeville's Claudia Coleman. Aunt Claudia suggested that she try the stage; Claudia didn't have to try very hard. Ziegfeld looked at that beautiful blonde with the showgirl figure and put her in the Follies. She had nothing to do but be ornamental in the revue, and she never took being a Ziegfeld beauty seriously. Her chance to use that thrilling voice came later, when she was sent to London to play Marilyn Miller's role in *Rosalie*. She modestly insisted it was luck which made her a movie star. Luck, without a single bow to such potent factors as a thrilling voice, graceful figure, bewitching smile, charm and beauty. While abroad she played the lead in the musical comedy *Merry Mary*.

Sweet Kitty Bellairs ('30) was Claudia's movie debut, and in no less than the starring role, supported by Walter Pidgeon and Ernest Torrence. In her next outing, *Big Boy* ('30), she played opposite Al Jolson but had little chance with Jolson hogging the spotlight throughout the film.

Warners put her into comedies with Joe E. Brown and Olsen and Johnson. After that the studio did not renew her contract and Claudia was relegated to "B" films. It is quite probable that Claudia is remembered best for *The Lost City* ('35), the much-maligned Krellberg serial. Ray Kinnard in *Fifty Years of Serial Thrills* writes of Dell's performance:

The leading lady is a real liability; blonde Claudia Dell emotes in a bug-eyed, hand-fluttering manner (literally bugging her eyes and fluttering her hands in the opening credits, her frantic actions underscored by Lee Zahler's primitive, hyperactive music), and her atrocious performance emerges as the film's single most laughable aspect ... she is clad in unattractive costumes and directed in such a ridiculous style that her efforts are comical.

In contrast, a *Variety* review of *A Bride for Henry* ('37) says of Miss Dell, "Claudia Dell as the prime jealousy-arouser shows up better than other cast members, her acting easily tops others in perception and projection."

Certainly Claudia's Western heroine roles are not imbued with emotional complexity and intensity, but she puts warm vigor into them and gives even, persuasive performances. Personally, the writer has always enjoyed *Ghost Patrol* ('36) with its elements of science fiction and mystery. Claudia plays Natalie Brent, pretty imperiled daughter of a professor who has invented a death ray capable of downing aircraft. And watching her in Ken Maynard's *Boots of Destiny* ('37) causes one to wonder why she was not utilized more in Western programmers.

Claudia was divorced in 1931 from Philip G. Offin, stage producer. On December 29, 1934, she married Edwin S. Silton, theatrical agent in Los Angeles, and separated from him on September 1, 1941. His gambling was her primary complaint. In granting the divorce on April 22, 1943, the judge made this discerning observation: "Gamblers will take all the money you've got and the pink slip on your car. The next time you marry get a man who doesn't know there are 52 cards in a deck."

In December 1947 she married Daniel Emmet, retired chewing gum magnate.

Some of her other film credits are *Confessions of a Co-Ed* ('31), *Destry Rides Again* ('32), *The Midnight Warning* ('32), *Cleopatra* ('34), *Trail's End* ('35), *Yellow Cargo* ('36), *Algiers* ('38), *The Mad Empress* ('39), *Black Magic* ('44), *Call of the Jungle* ('44) and *A Sporting Chance* ('45).

Claudia was born January 10, 1909, and died in September 1977 at age 68.

Serial

1935

The Lost City. Krellberg, 1935 [12 Chapters] D: Harry Revier; SP: Perley Poore Sheehan, Eddie Graneman, Leon D'Usseau; S: Zelma Corroll, George M. Merrick, Robert Dillon; P: Sherman S. Krellberg; Mus: Lee Zahler; Cam: Ronald Price, Ed Linden; LP: Kane Richmond, William (Stage) Boyd, Claudia Dell, Josef Swickard, George F. Hayes, Eddie Fetherston, Sam Baker, Milburn Morante.

JACK DEMPSEY

Jack Dempsey was born William Harrison Dempsey in Manassa, Colorado, on June 25, 1895. He won the heavyweight boxing championship in 1919 by defeating Jess Willard. He successfully defended the title against G. Carpentier in 1921; against Tom Gibbons in 1923; and again Luis Firpo in 1923. He lost the title to Gene Tunney in 1926 and a year later Tunney defeated him again. Dempsey lost a decision to King Levinsky in 1932. Although he did not serve in the military during World War I, he served as a physical training officer in World War II.

Dempsey, known as the "Manassa Mauler," won additional fans as the star of

several silents. He died in 1983 at age 87 following several years of declining health. He had arthritis in both hips and had to walk with a cane. He lived in a plush New York apartment in the East 50s with his wife of many years. His landmark restaurant on Broadway was closed in 1974 when Jack refused to pay a hefty rent increase.

In 1920, Pathé capitalized on his boxing fame by starring him in the serial *Daredevil Jack.* He may not have been much of an actor, but that really didn't matter much. He had Josie Sedgwick as his leading lady to help carry the film. In the story she is given a bracelet by her dying father. It was believed

Daredevil Jack lobby card (Pathé, 1920).

that when this bracelet was joined to another bracelet that it would give the location of a lake of oil. The second bracelet is in the hands of a gang leader. A second gang enters the picture and Jack fights to protect Josie while at the same time endeavoring to prove his father's innocence of trumped-up charges that sent him to prison.

Universal produced the serial *Fight and Win* in 1924. Dempsey was still world heavyweight champion. The story has Jack coming out of retirement to regain the heavyweight title. Later he inherits an orphanage. He has to fight several more bouts to raise money for the orphanage and there are those who wish him to lose his fights. He discovers that he is in love with Esther Ralston and she with him. They marry and have two children to add to the orphanage bunch.

Jack played himself in *Requiem for a Heavyweight* ('62) and can also be seen in *The Prizefighter and the Lady* ('33) and *Off Limits* ('53).

Serials

1920

Daredevil Jack. Pathé, [15 Chapters] D: W. S. Van Dyke; SP: Jack Cunnigan; S: Frederic Chapin, Harry Hoyt; P: Robert Brunton; LP: Jack Dempsey, Josie Sedgwick, Herschel Mayall, Albert Cody, Ruth Langston.

1924

Fight and Win. Univ., [19 Chapters] D: Erle C. Kenton, Jesse Robbins; LP: Jack Dempsey, Esther Ralston, Hayden Stevenson, Carmelita Geraghty.

WILLIAM DESMOND

William Desmond was truly a man for his time, achieving enormous success, first as a stage actor during the years 1905–15, and then as a motion picture star in the years 1915–29. As a principal supporting player during the 30s and early 40s, he had few equals. His name is a revered one among those film buffs whose memories and taste run to Westerns and cliffhanger action films.

Although pressbooks and studio publicity had him born in Dublin, Ireland, other sources have him born in Horseheads, New York, on January 23, 1878. After his graduation from high school, he toured as a gymnast and boxer, but little is known of his activities until he hit California in 1905 and decided to pursue a lifelong dream to be a stage actor.

Oliver Morosco gave Desmond his first opportunity to tread the boards at the time

that Burbank in Los Angeles and the Alcazar in San Francisco became famous for the number of celebrities they developed.

While in stock, Desmond proved one of the most energetic students who ever strove to attain success. He practiced incessantly. Eventually he starred in the greatest plays of the modern age, with dashes of Shakespeare thrown in. One of the earliest was *Quo Vadis*. Others were *The Bird of Paradise* and *Ben Hur*. Later, as a Broadway star, he zoomed to fame as star of *The Halfbreed*, *Romeo and Juliet* and *Under the Bear Flag*.

Around 1911, Desmond married Lillian Lampson and in 1912 went to Australia, where his stage success extended his stay to two years. While there, Mrs. Desmond received injuries in an accident which caused her death in 1917. Upon returning to the U.S., Desmond continued his stage success with roles in *Merchant of Venice*, *If I Were King* and *Law of the Land*.

By 1915, famous stage performers were being lured to the infant film industry by large salary offers. Triangle in particular was courting the Broadway celebrities and Desmond succumbed to the chance at emoting before the camera. (William S. Hart was another stage actor that Triangle recruited.) Before signing with Triangle, however, Desmond was featured in *As the Years Go By* and *Peer Gynt* for the Morosco Company and *The Majesty of the Law* ('15) for Bosworth Company. Then he signed with Triangle and became a celebrated cinema star in melodramas such as *Peggy* ('16), *Bullets and Brown Eyes* ('16), *The Payment* ('16) and *A Gamble in Souls* ('16). During the next several years he starred in many special productions with Ince, Goldwyn, Pathé and other producers. Being of the virile, athletic type, action appealed to him and it was only natural that producers put him into outdoor roles. Some of his feature successes were *Sea Panther*

Desmond with daughter Mary Joana.

('18), *Bare-Fisted Gallagher* ('19), *Dangerous Waters* ('19) and *A Sagebrush Hamlet* ('19).

In 1919, Desmond married Mary Mc-Ivor, an actress who had gotten her start at Triangle. He was 41, his bride 18. The mar-riage lasted and the Desmonds had two daughters.

Bill continued churning out fine film performances in the early 20s. But with the release of *Perils of the Yukon* ('22) and the

William Desmond (left) and Yakima Canutt on the Universal backlot.

signing of a Universal contract, Desmond became almost exclusively a Western and serial star, and it was at Universal in the years 1922–28 that he reached the pinnacle of his successes as a virile, no-nonsense hero.

Desmond is a Northwest Mountie in *McGuire of the Mounted* ('23) and a miner

whose claim has been jumped in *Shadows of the North* ('23). *The Breathless Moment* ('24) finds him a reformed crook while *Big Timber* ('24) is a story of rival lumber bosses in the Northwest. *The Measure of a Man* ('24), too, is set in the Northwest with Desmond playing a recovering Bowery drunk pretending to be a minister in a logging camp where he finds love and reforms the settlement. *The Sunset Trail* ('24), much in the vein of several Buck Jones films, finds Desmond as a hobo cowboy with a heart of gold who befriends a girl and a young boy and wins her love while helping her to obtain title to a gold mine discovered by her late dad. *Barriers of the Law* ('25) was a good melodrama in which Desmond plays a reserve officer out to arrest those bootlegging whiskey on the waterfront. Helen Holmes was the girl involved with the criminals and J. P. McGowan the chief bootlegger. *Duped* ('25) also featured Holmes and McGowan and dealt with mining operations and an honest man's attempts to prevent injustice and to protect a beautiful girl's interests.

Desmond is known first as "God Damn O'Day" then as "Good Deed O'Day" in *Straight Through* ('25), a Western in which he portrays a devil-may-care cowpoke who matures into responsible manhood when he decides to reform. In *The Burning Trail* ('25) he is an ex-prizefighter who goes west after an opponent dies following a beating in the ring. He manages to head off a cattlemen-sheepmen war and also finds romance.

Helen Holmes and J. P. McGowan team with Desmond again in *Outwitted* ('25), a melodrama which has the actor playing a treasury agent, Helen the daughter of his boss and McGowan as the crook who has vowed to kill him.

Blood and Steel ('25) reunites Holmes and Desmond in a Western railroad yarn, the type of film enormously popular in the 20s and, of course, the type that provided Helen with her fame and fortune. Helen is the railroad magnate's daughter, Desmond the man hired to see that a line is completed on time. Villains and runaway trains provide lots of excitement for the two stalwarts of virtue. In *The Meddler* ('25), Desmond is a New Yorker who goes west to prove himself after being jilted by a girl; to prove his courage, he becomes a highwayman who robs and then returns the spoils to the victims later. Ultimately he saves a girl from real bandits, wins her love and forgiveness by all.

In *Ridin' Pretty* ('25), Desmond is a happy-go-lucky cowboy who inherits a fortune but must live under certain restrictions in San Francisco for a year to claim it. There's excitement aplenty as his cousin plots to keep him from obtaining the inheritance and enlists the aid of a pretty girl in disqualifying Desmond. Speeding trains, cars, and motorcycles provide for a fast finish as Desmond triumphs. Love goes astray in *Tongues of Scandal* ('27) as Desmond portrays a governor whose wife thinks him responsible for her sister's suicide. In *Red Clay* ('27) he is an Indian hero of World War I who is a victim of prejudice by the man whose life he saved in the trenches, and in *No Defense* ('29) he is a weakling who causes problems for his sister and father and for hero Monte Blue.

Desmond starred in 11 serials during the silent era. In his first, *Perils of the Yukon* ('22), he was seriously injured in a 50 foot jump off a cliff into an icy river. Thereafter he used stuntmen for the dangerous stunts. In the sound era he had supporting roles in 34 serials and he also supported Western stars Bill Cody, Ken Maynard, Tom Mix, Wally Wales, Rex Lease, Harry Carey, Tom Tyler, Dick Foran, Noah Beery, Jr., Ted Wells, Buster Crabbe, Bob Steele, Tex Ritter, Lee Powell, Charles Starrett, Johnny Mack Brown and Rod Cameron. When not working in films, he often appeared in stage shows.

Desmond was in ill health the last four years of his life. A two-year siege of asthma resulted in the heart condition he lived with the last year of his life. The veteran actor was taken to Cedars of Labanon Hospital by his daughter, Mrs. Robert Robertson, and it was there he died from a respiratory ailment on November 3, 1949. He was 71.

Serials

1922

Perils of the Yukon. Univ., [15 Chapters] D: Perry Vekroff, Jay Marchant, J. P. McGowan; S/SP: George Morgan, George H. Plympton; LP: William Desmond, Laura La Plante, Fred

Stanton, Ruth Royce, Clark Comstock, Mack V. Wright.

1923

Beasts of Paradise. Univ., [15 Chapters] D: William Craft; S/SP: Val Cleveland; LP: William Desmond, Eileen Sedgwick, Ruth Royce, William H. Gould, Joe Bonomo.

Around the World in Eighteen Days. Univ., [12 Chapters] D: B. Reeves Eason, Robert F. Hill; SP: George Bronson, Frank Howard Clark; S: Robert Dillon; LP: William Desmond, Laura La Plante, William P. Du Vall, Wade Boteler, Percy Challinger, William J. Welsh.

The Phantom Fortune. Univ., [12 Chapters] D: Robert F. Hill; S/SP: Anthony W. Coldeway, George Hively; LP: William Desmond, Esther Ralston, Lewis Sargent, George Webb, Harry De Vere, Albert Hart, George Nichols, Pat Harmon.

1924

The Riddle Rider. Univ., [15 Chapters] D: William Craft; SP/S: William Wing, Arthur H. Gooden, George Pyper; LP: William Desmond, Eileen Sedgwick, Helen Holmes, Claude Payton, William H. Gould.

1925

The Ace of Spades. Univ., [15 Chapters] D: Henry MacRae; SP: Isadore Bernstein, William Lord Wright; LP: William Desmond, Mary McAllister, Albert J. Smith, William A. Steele, Cathleen Calhoun.

1926

Strings of Steel. Univ., [10 Chapters] D: Henry MacRae; SP: Phillip D. Horn, Oscar Lund; LP: William Desmond, Eileen Sedgwick, Albert J. Smith, Arthur Morrison, Grace Cunard.

The Winking Idol. Univ., [10 Chapters] D: Francis Ford; SP: Arthur Henry Gooden, George Morgan; S: Charles E. Van Loan; LP: William Desmond, Eileen Sedgwick, Jack Richardson, Grace Cunard, Les Sailor [Syd Saylor], Dorothy Gulliver Monavana.

1928

The Vanishing Rider. Univ., [10 Chapters] D: Ray Taylor; S: Val Cleveland; SP: George

Plympton; LP: William Desmond, Ethlyne Claire, Nelson McDowell, Bud Osborne, Boris Karloff.

The Mystery Rider. Univ., [10 Chapters] D: Jack Nelson; S: George Morgan; LP: William Desmond, Derelys Perdue, Tom London, Bud Osborne, Walter Shumway.

1930

The Lone Defender. Mascot, [12 Chapters] D: Richard Thorpe; LP: Walter Miller, Rin-Tin-Tin, June Marlowe, Buzz Barton.

1931

Battling with Buffalo Bill. Univ., [12 Chapters] D: Ray Taylor; LP: Tom Tyler, Rex Bell, Lucile Browne, Francis Ford, William Desmond, Yakima Canutt.

The Lightning Warrior. Mascot, [12 Chapters] D: Armand Schaefer, Benjamin Kline; LP: Rin-Tin-Tin, Frankie Darro, Georgia Hale, George Brent, Pat O'Malley.

The Phantom of the West. Mascot, [10 chapters] D: Ross Lederman; LP: Tom Tyler, Dorothy Gulliver, William Desmond, Tom Santschi, Tom Dugan.

The Vanishing Legion. Mascot, [12 Chapters] D: B. Reeves Eason; LP: Harry Carey, Edwina Booth, Rex (horse), Frankie Darro, Philo McCullough, Lafe McKee.

The Last Frontier. RKO, [12 Chapters] D: Spencer G. Bennet, Thomas L. Story; LP: Creighton Chaney [Lon Chaney, Jr.], Dorothy Gulliver, Mary Jo Desmond, Francis X. Bushman, Jr.

1932

The Jungle Mystery. Univ., [12 Chapters] D: Ray Taylor; LP: Tom Tyler, Cecilia Parker, William Desmond, Philo McCullough, Noah Beery, Jr.

Heroes of the West. Univ., [12 Chapters] D: Ray Taylor; LP: Noah Beery, Jr., Diane Duval [a.k.a. Jacqueline Wells and Julie Bishop], Onslow Stevens, William Desmond, Philo McCullough, Frank Lackteen, Martha Mattox.

1933

Gordon of Ghost City. Univ., [12 Chapters] D: Ray Taylor; LP: Buck Jones, Madge Bellamy,

Walter Miller, William Desmond, Hugh Enfield [Craig Reynolds], Edmund Cobb, Dick Rush, William Steele, Tom Rickett.

Clancy of the Mounted. Univ., [12 Chapters] D: Ray Taylor; LP: Tom Tyler, Jacqueline Wells, William Desmond, Rosalie Roy, Francis Ford, Earl McCarthy.

The Three Musketeers. Mascot, [12 Chapters] D: Armand Schaefer, Colbert Clark; LP: Jack Mulhall, Raymond Hatton, Francis X. Bushman, Jr., John Wayne, Ruth Hall, Creighton Chaney [Lon Chaney, Jr.], William Desmond, Hooper Atchley, Noah Beery, Jr.

The Phantom of the Air. Univ., [12 Chapters] D: Ray Taylor; LP: Tom Tyler, Gloria Shea, LeRoy Mason, Hugh Enfield [Craig Reynolds], William Desmond.

1934

The Red Rider. Univ., [15 Chapters] D: Louis Friedlander [Lew Landers]; LP: Buck Jones, Grant Withers, Marion Shilling, Walter Miller, Richard Cramer, William Desmond.

Pirate Treasure. Univ., [12 Chapters] D: Ray Taylor; LP: Richard Talmadge, Lucille Lund, Walter Miller, Pat O'Malley, Philo McCullough, Beulah Hutton.

Perils of Pauline. Univ., [12 Chapters] D: Ray Taylor; LP: Evalyn Knapp, Robert Allen, James Durkin, John Davidson, Frank Lackteen.

Tailspin Tommy. Univ., [12 Chapters] D: Louis Friedlander [Lew Landers]; LP: Maurice Murphy, Noah Beery, Jr., Patricia Farr, Walter Miller, Edmund Cobb, John Davidson.

1935

Tailspin Tommy in the Great Air Mystery. Univ., [12 Chapters] D: Ray Taylor; LP: Clark Williams, Jean Rogers, Noah Beery, Jr., Bryant Washburn, Helen Brown.

The Call of the Savage. Univ., [12 Chapters] D: Louis Friedlander [Lew Landers]; LP: Noah Beery, Jr., Dorothy Short, Harry Woods, Walter Miller, Bryant Washburn.

Rustlers of Red Dog. Univ., [12 Chapters] D: Louis Friedlander [Lew Landers]; LP: Johnny Mack Brown, Joyce Compton, Walter Miller, Raymond Hatton, Harry Woods, Edmund Cobb.

The Roaring West. Univ., [15 Chapters] D:

Ray Taylor; LP: Buck Jones, Muriel Evans, Walter Miller, Frank McGlynn, Harlan Knight, William Desmond, Eole Galli.

1936

The Vigilantes Are Coming. Rep., [12 Chapters] D: Mack V. Wright, Ray Taylor; LP: Robert Livingston, Kay Hughes, Guinn Williams, Raymond Hatton, Fred Kohler, Robert Warwick, Robert Kortman, William Desmond, William Farnum, Yakima Canutt.

The Black Coin. S&S, [15 Chapters] D: Albert Herman; LP: Ralph Graves, Ruth Mix, Dave O'Brien, Constance Bergen, Robert Frazer, Clara Kimball Young.

The Adventures of Frank Merrill. Univ., [12 Chapters] D: Cliff Smith; LP: Don Briggs, Jean Rogers, John King, Carla Laemmle, Summer Getchell, Al Bridge.

Flash Gordon. Univ., [13 Chapters] D: Frederick Stephani; LP: Buster Crabbe, Jean Rogers, Frank Shannon, Charles Middleton, Richard Alexander, Priscilla Lawson, Theodore Lorch, William Desmond, John Lipson.

Custer's Last Stand. S&S, [15 Chapters] D: Elmer Clifton; LP: Rex Lease, Lona Andre, William Farnum, Dorothy Gulliver, Ruth Mix, Bobby Nelson, William Desmond.

The Clutching Hand. S&S, [15 Chapters] D: Albert Herman; LP: Jack Mulhall, Ruth Mix, Marion Shilling, Rex Lease, William Farnum, Reed Howes, Robert Frazer.

1939

The Oregon Trail. Univ., [15 Chapters] D: Ford Beebe, Saul A. Goodkind; LP: Johnny Mack Brown, Louise Stanley, Fuzzy Knight, Bill Cody, Jr., Forrest Taylor, James Blaine, Charles King, Roy Barcroft, William Desmond.

1940

Junior G-Men. Univ., [12 Chapters] D: Ford Beebe, John Rawlins; LP: Billy Halop, Huntz Hall, Gabriel Dell, Bernard Punsley, Phillip Terry, Roger Daniels.

Winners of the West. Univ., [13 Chapters] D: Ford Beebe, Ray Taylor; LP: Dick Foran, Anne Nagel, James Craig, Tom Fadden, Charles Stevens, Harry Woods, William Desmond, Roy Barcroft, Edmund Cobb.

1941

Sky Raiders. Univ., [12 Chapters] D: Ford Beebe, Ray Taylor; LP: Donald Woods, Billy Halop, Robert Armstrong, Kathryn Adams, Edwardo Ciannelli, Reed Hadley.

1942

Gang Busters. Univ., [13 Chapters] D: Ray Taylor, Noel Smith; LP: Kent Taylor, Irene Hervey, Ralph Morgan, Robert Armstrong, Joseph Crehan, Richard Davies.

Overland Mail. Univ., [15 Chapters] D: Ford Beebe, John Rawlins; LP: Lon Chaney, Jr., Noah Beery, Jr., Don Terry, Helen Parrish, Noah Beery, Sr., Bob Baker, Tom Chatterton, Charles Stevens, Robert Barron.

Junior G-Men of the Air. Univ., [12 Chapters] D: Ray Taylor, Lewis D. Collins; LP: Billy Halop, Gene Reynolds, Lionel Atwill, Frank Albertson, Richard Lane, Gabriel Dell, Frankie Darro, Harry Cording.

1946

The Scarlet Horseman. Univ., [13 Chapters] D: Ray Taylor, Lewis D. Collins; LP: Peter Cookson, Paul Guilfoyle, Victoria Horne, Virginia Christine, Janet Shaw, Hal Taliaferro, Cy Kendall, Ernie Adams, William Desmond.

ANN DORAN

Ann Doran was one of the screen's most distinguished character actresses. She was born in Amarillo, Texas, in 1911. Her father was a lieutenant in the cavalry. Her mother was a soubrette with the Albert Taylor Stock Company when she married. There were two years in 1922–23 when the family lived in Los Angeles and during this time Mrs. Doran (Rose Allen) became leading lady to Bobby Vernon and Larry Semon, comedians.

Ann finished high school in San Bernardino and attended UCLA for a year. When her father died, she had to quit school to go to work. Following a small part in *Zoo in Budapest* ('33), she became Virginia Bruce's stand-in for two years. After struggling for a while, she got a stock contract at $75 a week at Columbia, where she played the girl in a lot of comedies with the Three Stooges, Charlie Chase, Harry Langdon and Andy Clyde. She played a "fallen girl" so well in *Penitentiary* ('38) that she continued playing streetwalkers in a number of subsequent films. Frank Capra used her in most of his films.

She was under contract to Paramount in the '40s for four years and played a wide variety of roles. Ann was not a beauty, so she often played the girlfriend of the heroine and similar parts. In only one Western, *Rio Grande* ('39), opposite Charles Starrett, did she play the lead heroine. In her next 14 Westerns, scattered over a number of years, she played strong character roles in non-series films of the caliber of *Calamity Jane and Sam Bass* ('49), *Tomahawk* ('51), *War Paint* ('53), *The Badlanders* ('58), *Smoky* ('66) and *The Macahans* ('76).

Doran was quite active on the Screen Actors Guild Board of Directors for more than 20 years and served as the longtime co-chairperson of SAG's senior performers committee.

Her unique talents were as effective and appreciated in open air sagas as in heavy drama, and directors and fellow actors enjoyed working with a real pro. She appeared in over 1,000 films and TV dramas. She had continuing roles in four TV series.

Ann Doran never married. She died at the age of 89 after a series of strokes in Carmichael, California.

Serials

1938

The Spider's Web. Col., [15 Chapters] D: Ray Taylor, James W. Horne; LP: Warren Hull, Iris Meredith, Richard Fiske, Kenne Duncan, Forbes Murray.

1939

The Green Hornet. Univ. [13 Chapters] D: Ford Feebe, Ray Taylor; LP: Gordon Jones, Anne Nagel, Keye Luke, Wade Boteler, Philip Trent, Anne Gwynne.

Flying G-Men. Col., [15 Chapters] D: Ray Taylor, James W. Horne; LP: Robert Paige, Richard Fiske, James Craig, Lorna Grey [Adrian Booth].

JACK DOUGHERTY

Jack Dougherty was number two man to William Desmond as Universal's serial kings during the 1920s. He began his movie career in 1921 after appearing in stage productions for a time.

Jack was born Virgil A. Dougherty in

Bowling Green, Missouri, on November 16, 1895. It is possible that he served in the military during World War I. Since he is known to have attended Paris University, it is conceivable that he may have been mustered out of the service at the end of the War and stayed in France to study awhile.

His early film roles were as a romantic lead. As such, he could have been quickly forgotten, as the competition was great — Douglas Fairbanks, John Gilbert, John Barrymore, Rudolph Valentino, Francis X. Bushman, etc. Dougherty was not in a class with these boys.

In '21, Dougherty played with Alice Lake in *The Greater Claim* and with Gladys Wallace in *Second Hand Rose*, and in 1922 he played with Neva Gerber in *Impulse*, and with Ann Little in *Chain Lightning*. In 1923 he was in the supporting cast of *Money! Money! Money!* starring Katherine MacDonald.

Serial queen Ruth Roland picked him to second her in *Haunted Valley* ('23), a Pathé serial that scored high at the box office. From that time on he was a serial and Western star. He made seven serials at Universal from '24 to '28. He also starred in a series of two-reelers: *The Love Roundup*, *True Gold*, *Linsome Luck*, *Forgettin' the Law* and *Damned*.

In 1924 Dougherty supported Italian daredevil Lucien Albertini in *The Iron Man*. In 1925 he supported William Desmond in *The Burning Trail* and *The Meddler*; also, he starred in the feature *The Runaway Express*. That same year he had the lead in the serials *The Fighting Ranger* and *The Scarlet Streak*. In 1926 he starred in *The Radio Detective* and in between serials he appeared in non–Western feature-length films. In 1927 he starred in *The Trail of the Tiger* and *The Fire Fighters* and supported Gary Cooper in Paramount's *Arizona Bound*. He also had a role in Eddie Cantor's *Special Delivery*.

Dougherty's last serial for Universal was *Haunted Island* ('28). He then joined an all-star lineup in Mascot's *The Vanishing West* ('28). In addition to these cliffhangers, Dougherty also made *Into No Man's Land* with Tom Santschi and *Gypsy of the North* with lovely Georgia Hale.

His final silent picture was *Body Punch* ('29) in which he played a prizefighter. No more credits for Dougherty can be found until 1937 when he supported Gene Autry in *Yodelin' Kid from Pine Ridge*. On May 16, 1938, Jack Dougherty committed suicide by carbon monoxide. Barbara LaMarr and Virginia Brown Faire had each been married to Jack at one time. However, he was single at the end. He was only 42.

Dougherty had a good career while it lasted, but fame is indeed ephemeral, and so the masses forget as they are caught up in the adoration of new screen personalities.

Serials

1923

Haunted Valley. Pathé, [15 Chapters] D: George Marshall; SP: Frank Leon Smith; LP: Ruth Roland, Jack Dougherty, Larry Steers, Eulalie Jensen, Aaron Edwards.

1925

The Iron Man. Univ., [15 Chapters] D: Jay Marchant; S/SP: Arthur Henry Gooden, William E. Wing; LP: Lucien Albertini, Margaret Morris, Lola Todd, Joe Bonomo, Jack Dougherty.

The Fighting Ranger. Univ., [18 Chapters] D: Jay Marchant; S: F. J. McConnell, George W. Pyper; LP: Jack Dougherty, Eileen Sedgwick, Al Wilson, Bud Osborne, William Welch.

The Scarlet Streak. Univ., [10 Chapters] D: Henry MacRae; S: Leigh Jacobson; LP: Jack Dougherty, Lola Todd, John Elliott, Albert J. Smith, Virginia Ainsworth, Monte Montague.

1926

The Radio Detective. Univ., [10 Chapters] D: William Crinley, William Craft; SP: Karl Krusada; S: Arthur B. Reeve; LP: Jack Dougherty, Margaret Quimby, John T. Prince, Wallace Baldwin, Jack Mower.

1927

The Trail of the Tiger. Univ., [10 Chapters] D: Henry MacRae; SP: Karl Krusada, Leigh Jacobson; S: Courtney Ryley Cooper; LP: Jack

Dougherty, Frances Teague, Jack Mower, John Webb Dillon, Charles Murphy.

The Fire Fighters. Univ., [10 Chapters] D: Jacques Jaccard; S: John A. Moroso; LP: Jack Dougherty, Helen Ferguson, Florence Allen, Robert Irwin.

1928

Haunted Island. Univ., [10 Chapters] D: Robert F. Hill; S: Frank R. Adams; SP: George

Morgan, Karl Krusada; LP: Jack Dougherty, Helen Foster, Carl Miller, Al Ferguson, Grace Cunard, John T. Prince.

The Vanishing West. Mascot, [10 Chapters] D: Richard Thorpe; SP: Wyndham Gittens; P: Nat Levine; S: Karl Krusada, William Lester; LP: Jack Perrin, Eileen Sedgwick, Jack Dougherty, Yakima Canutt, Leo Maloney.

DONALD DOUGLAS

Donald Douglas was only 40 when he died in 1945 from complications following an appendectomy in Los Angeles. He had been a prolific actor during the '30s and '40s.

He was primarily a character actor and was not a Western player. It was, therefore, a strange bit of casting when he was given the lead in Columbia's *Deadwood Dick.* As Dick

Don Douglas and Lorna Gray (Adrian Booth) in *Deadwood Dick* (Columbia, 1940).

Stanley, publisher of the Dakota Pioneer Press, he sees a new organization of the territory's outlaw gangs, seemingly in opposition to statehood. Reporter Frank Butler learns that a grotesque master criminal known as the Skull seeks to create an outlaw empire and gain control of the mineral-rich land. Butler is murdered and Hickok, called in by Anne Butler, is murdered by Jack McCall. Stanley adopts the disguise of Deadwood Dick to battle the outlaw forces, while remaining an eager (but cautious) supporter of statehood, especially after it becomes apparent that some member of the Statehood for Dakota Committee must be the Skull.

Douglas does a commendable job in this Western but it did not lead to better things and he slipped back into character roles. In 1938 he had been billed sixth in the cast of *The Spider's Web*. His last nine films, released in 1945 and '46 were *Club Havana*, *Grissly's Millions*, *Murder My Sweet*, *A Royal Scandal*, *Tarzan and the Amazons*, *Tokyo Rose*, *Gilda*, *The Strange Mr. Gregory* and *The Truth About Women*.

Serials

1938

The Spider's Web. Col., [15 Chapters] D: Ray Taylor, James W. Horne; LP: Warren Hull, Irish Meredith, Richard Fiske, Kenneth Duncan, Forbes Murray, Donald Douglas.

1940

Deadwood Dick. Col., [15 Chapters] D: James W. Horne; SP: Wyndham Gittens, Morgan Cox, George Morgan, John Cutting; P: Larry Darmour; LP: Don Douglas, Lorna Gray [Adrian Booth], Lane Chandler, Marin Sais, Harry Harvey, Charles King, Edward Cassidy, Robert Fiske, Edmund Cobb, Tom London.

JOHNNY DOWNS

Johnny Downs is remembered as star of B-musicals made back in the early 1940s. He actually got his start in movies by playing for two years in the *Our Gang* comedies. He also appeared in several features and in 1926 toured in a vaudeville act on the RKO circuit in "Our Gang Kids." He later did singles and worked on the Broadway stage with Jimmy Durante and Lupe Velez in *Strike Me Pink*. Other stage appearances followed and at the age of 21 he returned to Hollywood and a Paramount contract. He was seen in film after film as a singing–tap dancing young musician who was never a threat to Fred Astaire, Gene Kelly or Bing Crosby. But his modest musicals, often seen on double-feature bills, were entertaining enough.

When the cycle of B-movie musicals petered out in the mid–40s he turned to Broadway again and there starred in *Are You with It?* and *Hold It*. Back in Hollywood, he hosted an afternoon local TV show. He also did nightclub shows.

In 1954, Johnny signed on for a new children's program, *The Magic Key*, for KOGO-TV in Coronado. The show lasted 17 years.

In 1943, Johnny took time from musicals to co-star in Universal's *Adventures of the Flying Cadets*. As air cadets, Johnny, Billy Benedict, Ward Wood and Bobby Jordan had the whole serial to clear themselves for murders masterminded by the Black Hangman, a mysterious individual pretending to be a Nazi agent. In reality he is Arthur Galt (Robert Armstrong), an engineer who, as a member of an exploring expedition, locates lost helium deposits in Africa. To keep the location a secret, he kills all the expedition members except Prof. Mason (Selmer Jackson) and his daughter Andre (Jennifer Holt), whom he imprisons. The cadets, believing Galt a friend, fly with him to Africa to try and clear their names. All ends well as Galt is exposed as the Black Hangman. Eduardo Ciannelli was also featured as a rotten Gestapo agent.

Johnny and his wife June had five children (four daughters and one son). He was well liked in Coronado and was quite active in worthwhile events.

Downs, born in 1913, died in his Coronado home from cancer at the age of 80.

Serial

1943

Adventures of the Flying Cadets. Univ., [13 Chapters] D: Ray Taylor, Lewis D. Collins; SP: Morgan B. Cox, George H. Plympton, Paul Huston; AP: Henry MacRae; Cam: William Sickner; Mus: H. J. Salter; LP: Johnny Downs, Bobby Jordan, Jennifer Holt, Robert Armstrong, Regis Toomey, Ward Wood, Billy Benedict.

MAXINE DOYLE

Maxine Doyle was a charming young actress at Warners in the early 1930s, introduced in William Powell's *The Key*. Following that film, she had the feminine lead in Joe E. Brown's *Six Day Bike Rider* ('34) and the ingenue role in *Babbit* ('34). Leaving Warners, she became a freelancer, working mostly at the small independent studios. Some of her films follow: *She Made Her Bed* ('34), *Student Tour* ('34), *Condemned to Live* ('35), *Rio Grande Romance* ('36), *Come On Cowboys!* ('37), *Fury Below* ('38), *Raiders of Sunset Pass* ('43), *Beneath Western Skies* ('44), *San Fernando Valley* ('44) and *Throw a Saddle on a Star* ('46).

In 1937's *SOS Coast Guard*, Maxine had the femme role of newspaper woman Jean Norman who, along with Coast Guardsman Terry Kent (Ralph Byrd), attempts to thwart Boroff (Bela Lugosi) in his plans to manufacture a deadly gas. Ten years later, Maxine has a small part in *The Black Widow* as a fortune teller.

Somewhere along the way Maxine married serial director William Witney (who helmed *SOS Coast Guard*) and was still married to him when she died in Studio City, California, from cancer in 1973. She was 58.

Serials

1937

SOS Coast Guard. Rep., [12 Chapters] D: William Witney, Alan James; SP: Barry Shipman, Franklyn Adreon; S: Morgan Cox, Ronald Davidson; AP: Sol C. Siegel; Cam: William Nobles; Mus: Raoul Kraushaar; LP: Ralph Byrd, Bela Lugosi, Maxine Doyle, Richard Alexander, Herbert Rawlinson, George Chesebro, Roy Barcroft.

1947

The Black Widow. Rep., [13 Chapters] D: Spencer Bennet, Fred C. Brannon; LP: Carol Forman, Bruce Edwards, Virginia Lindley, Anthony Warde, Ramsay Ames, I. Stanford Jolley, Tom Steele, Maxine Doyle, Frank Lackteen.

Maxine Doyle, Russell Gleason (center) and Rex Lease in *Fury Below* (Mercader, 1938).

KENNE DUNCAN

To Western and serial audiences of the 1930s, 1940s and 1950s, Kenne Duncan was a familiar figure, usually playing an associate of the chief badman. He appeared in 26 serials and scores of B-Westerns featuring most of the cowboy stars of the period (Tim McCoy, Tex Ritter, James Newill, Jack Randall, Bob Steele, Tom Keene, The Three Mesquiteers, The Range Busters, George Houston, Tim Holt, Donald Barry, Bob Livingston, Bill Elliott, Rocky Lane, Roy Rogers,

Sunset Carson, Monte Hale, Buck Jones, Johnny Mack Brown, Jimmy Wakely, Gene Autry, George Montgomery, Whip Wilson, Rod Cameron, John Wayne, Dave O'Brien, Hoot Gibson, John King, Ray Corrigan, Buster Crabbe and Charles Starrett).

Kenne hailed from Chatham, Ontario, Canada, where he was born on February 17, 1902. (That is the date on his death certificate. Most writers have used the date 1906.) His real name was Kenneth Duncan Mac-

Left to right: Richard Fiske, Iris Meredith, Warren Hull and Kenneth Duncan in *The Spider's Web* (Columbia, 1938).

Lahlin. His post–high school education was received at St. Andrews College (Toronto) and the Royal School of Infantry (Wolseley Barracks, London, Ontario) as well as business school. Before entering upon a movie career, Kenne worked as an accountant. He is said to have been a professional jockey for a while. Probably so, for he bred, raised and rode race horses during his acting days.

After limited stage experience, Kenne was able to break into movies in 1928 in the silent serial *The Police Reporter.* Only seven of his 26 serials were Westerns, but a large proportion of the features he worked in were B-Westerns. Some of the non–Westerns were *Derelict* ('31), *Racetrack Racketeer* ('36), *Cross My Heart* ('36), *Buck Privates* ('41), *Radar Secret Service* ('50), *The Astounding She-Monster* ('58) and *Night of the Ghouls* ('59). Kenne starred in the feature *Tokaido Road*

('54) while touring Japan in the 1950s. The author has no information on this film but he has seen a photo of Kenne riding Emperor Hiroheto's white horse.

When television came in, the B-Westerns bit the dust. Kenne worked in such TV series as *The Lone Ranger, Sergeant Preston, Gene Autry, Annie Oakley, The Cisco Kid* and *Wild Bill Hickok.*

Kenne never married. When not working in films, he went on personal appearance jaunts, raised race horses, dabbled in oil leases and whatever else he could make a buck at. He was a serious, frugal, introverted man, but he would "open up" with close friends.

Kenne Duncan died on February 7, 1972, at age 69. Cause of death was acute barbiturate intoxication and ingestion of overdose. The coroner listed his death as a suicide.

Serials

1928

The Police Reporter. Artclass, [10 Chapters] D: Jack Nelson; LP: Walter Miller, Eugenia Gilbert, William A. Lowery, Kenne Duncan, Robert Belcher.

1936

The Clutching Hand. S&S, [15 Chapters] D: Albert Harman; LP: Jack Mulhall, Ruth Mix, Marion Shilling, Rex Lease, William Farnum, Yakima Canutt, Reed Howes.

1938

Flash Gordon's Trip to Mars. Univ., [15 Chapters] D: Ford Beebe, Robert Hill; LP: Buster Crabbe, Jean Rogers, Charles Middleton, Frank Shannon.

The Great Adventures of Wild Bill Hickok. Col., [15 Chapters] D: Mack V. Wright, Sam Nelson; LP: Bill Elliott, Carole Wayne, Frankie Darro, Monte Blue, Reed Hadley, Sammy McKim, Kermit Maynard, Roscoe Ates.

The Spider's Web. Col., [15 Chapters] D: Ray Taylor, James W. Horne; LP: Warren Hull, Iris

Meredith, Richard Fiske, Kenne Duncan, Forbes Murray.

1939

Buck Rogers. Univ., [12 Chapters] D: Ford Beebe, Saul A. Goodkind; LP: Buster Crabbe, Constance Moore, Jackie Moran, Jack Mulhall, Anthony Warde.

1940

The Green Archer. Col., [15 Chapters] D: James W. Horne; LP: Victor Jory, Iris Meredith, James Craven, Robert Fiske, Kenne Duncan.

Deadwood Dick. Col., [15 Chapters] D: James W. Horne; LP: Don Douglas, Lorna Gray [Adrian Booth], Lane Chandler, Marin Sais, Charles King.

1941

The Spider Returns. Col., [15 Chapters] D: James W. Horne; LP: Warren Hull, Mary Ainslee, Dave O'Brien, Joe Girard.

Adventures of Captain Marvel. Rep., [12 Chapters] D: William Witney, John English; LP: Frank Coghlan, Jr., Billy Benedict, Louise Currie, Robert Strange, Harry Worth, John Davidson, Bryant Washburn.

White Eagle. Col., [15 Chapters] D: James W. Horne; LP: Buck Jones, Raymond Hatton, Dorothy Fay, Jack Ingram, Chief Yowlachie, Charles King, John Merton, Edward Hearn, Edmund Cobb.

King of the Texas Rangers. Rep., [12 Chapters] D: William Witney, John English; LP: Slingin' Sammy Baugh, Neil Hamilton, Pauline Moore, Duncan Renaldo.

1942

The Valley of Vanishing Men. Col., [15 Chapters] D: Spencer G. Bennet; LP: Bill Elliott, Slim Summerville, Carmen Morales, Kenneth MacDonald, Jack Ingram.

The Secret Code. Col., [15 Chapters] D: Spencer G. Bennet; LP: Paul Kelly, Robert O. Davis, Gregory Gay, Eddie Parker, Jacqueline Dalya.

Perils of Nyoka. Rep., [15 Chapters] D: William Witney; LP: Kay Aldridge, Clayton Moore, William Benedict, Lorna Gray [Adrian Booth], Charles Middleton, Tris Coffin, George J. Lewis.

1943

Batman. Col., [15 Chapters] D: Lambert Hillyer; LP: Lewis Wilson, Douglas Croft, J. Carrol Naish, Shirley Patterson, William C. Austin, Charles Middleton.

Daredevils of the West. Rep., [12 Chapters] D: John English; LP: Allan Lane, Kay Aldridge, Eddie Acuff, William Haade, Robert Frazer, Ted Adams, George J. Lewis.

1944

The Tiger Woman. Rep., [12 Chapters] D: Spencer Bennet, Wallace Grissell; LP: Linda Stirling, Allan Lane, Duncan Renaldo, George J. Lewis.

Haunted Harbor. Rep., [15 Chapters] D: Spencer Bennet, Wallace Grissell; LP: Kane Richmond, Kay Aldridge, Roy Barcroft, Clancy Cooper.

Captain America. Rep., [15 Chapters] D: John English, Elmer Clifton; LP: Dick Purcell, Lorna Gray [Adrian Booth], Lionel Atwill, Charles Trowbridge, George J. Lewis, John Davidson, LeRoy Mason, Kenne Duncan.

1945

The Purple Monster Strikes. Rep., [15 Chapters] D: Spencer Bennet, Fred Brannon; LP: Linda Stirling, Dennis Moore, Roy Barcroft, James Craven.

Manhunt of Mystery Island. Rep., [15 Chapters] D: Spencer Bennet, Yakima Canutt, Wallace Grissell; LP: Linda Stirling, Roy Barcroft, Richard Bailey, Forrest Taylor.

1946

The Phantom Rider. Rep., [12 Chapters] D: Spencer Bennet, Fred Brannon; LP: Robert Kent, Peggy Stewart, LeRoy Mason, George J. Lewis, Hal Taliaferro.

The Crimson Ghost. Rep., [12 Chapters] D: William Witney, Fred C. Brannon; LP: Charles Quigley, Linda Stirling, Clayton Moore, I. Stanford Jolley.

1953

Canadian Mounties vs. Atomic Invaders. Rep., [12 Chapters] D: Franklyn Adreon; LP: Bill Henry, Susan Morrow, Arthur Space, Dale Van Sickel.

1955

Adventures of Captain Africa. Col., [15 Chapters] D: Spencer Bennet; LP: John Hart, Rick Vallin, Ben Welden, June Howard.

WILLIAM DUNCAN

A five-foot-ten-inch Irish-Scotsman born in 1880, William Duncan came to the United States at the age of ten. He attended the University of Pennsylvania and, while working his way through college, he still found time to make records on the cinder-path and in field events. He played football, baseball and other major sports and was a crack swimmer and water polo player.

After graduation he became associated with Sandow, the famous strongman, and for several seasons he toured the country with him. Duncan's versatility led him to repertory work, and he again toured the country, this time with the Forepaugh Stock Company, finally managing, writing and starring in his own productions. He signed with the Selig Polyscope Company about 1910 and was put to work making one-reel Westerns.

During the years 1910–15, Duncan starred in scores of short films. He was prolific and innovative as an actor-director-writer, and the Western genre owes much to Duncan for creating many of its classic situations and technical procedures. As a path-

William Duncan (right) and unidentified player in *Playing It Wild* (Vitagraph, 1923).

finder he blazed a trail, followed first by Mix and later by every cowboy in the business.

In 1915, Duncan switched to Vitagraph. There he appeared in countless short films, mostly outdoor adventures, and both directed and acted in serials. It was 1917 when Duncan hit the big time by starring in *The Fighting Trail*, a story revolving about a secret mine which contains munitions materials of great interest to German agents. Carol Holloway had the femme lead. A second serial, *Vengeance and the Woman* ('17), followed; it, too, featured Holloway as the love interest.

Beginning with *A Fight for Millions* ('18), third in the series of Duncan serials, Edith Johnson became his screen heroine and co-starred with him in eight subsequent chapterplays. Duncan became so popular as a serial star that in 1919 Vitagraph tore up

his contract and rewrote it to call for six serials budgeted at $1,500,000 with Duncan to receive an average salary of $10,000 a week for directing and starring in two serials a year. Four more serials were made by the team for Vitagraph. They were surefire box office, and their bloodthirsty, adventurous and artificial thrills never ceased to satisfy serial patrons of the 1920s. Duncan and Johnson also starred in seven features, all directed by Duncan.

When Vitagraph decided to discontinue serial production, Duncan and Johnson moved to Universal under an arrangement similar to the one Bill had enjoyed at Vitagraph. However, Bill was not happy with all the red tape at Universal. After making three serials, he decided that he could get along nicely without Carl Laemmle as boss.

Duncan and Johnson had married while

at Vitagraph and at this point were quite wealthy. They decided to retire. In the 1930s, just to have something to do, Duncan appeared in a few features, most notably Hopalong Cassidy Westerns where he played Buck Peters, Hoppy's boss.

Duncan died on February 8, 1961.

Serials

1917

The Fighting Trail. Vit., [15 Chapters] D: William Duncan; SP: S. Stuart Blackton, Cyrus Townsend Brady; LP: William Duncan, Carol Holloway, George Holt, Joe Ryan, Fred Burns, Townsend Brady.

Vengeance and the Woman. Vit., [15 Chapters] D: William Duncan; S: Albert E. Smith, Cyrus Townsend Brady; SP: Garfield Thompson, Edward J. Montague; LP: William Duncan, Carol Holloway, George Holt, Tex Allen, Vincent Howard, Fred Burns.

1918

A Fight for Millions. Vit., [15 Chapters] D: William Duncan; SP: Graham Baker; S: Albert E. Smith, Cyrus Townsend Brady; LP: William Duncan, Edith Johnson, Joe Ryan, Willie Calles, Leo Maloney, Jack Hoxie, William McCall.

1919

Smashing Barriers. Vit., [15 Chapters] D: William Duncan; SP: Graham Baker, R. Cecil Smith; S: Albert E. Smith, Cyrus T. Brady; LP: William Duncan, Edith Johnson, Walter Rodgers, William McCall, George Stanley.

Man of Might. Vit., [15 Chapters] D: William Duncan; SP: C. Graham Baker; S: Albert E. Smith, Cyrus Townsend Brady; LP: William Duncan, Edith Johnson, Joe Ryan, Walter Rodgers, Otto Lederer.

1920

The Silent Avenger. Vit., [15 Chapters] D: William Duncan; S: Albert E. Smith, Cleveland Moffett; SP: C. Graham Baker, William B. Courtney; LP: William Duncan, Edith John-

son, Jack Richardson, Virginia Nightingale, Ernest Shields.

1921

Fighting Fate. Vit., [15 Chapters] D: William Duncan; SP: Graham Baker, William B. Courtney; S: Albert E. Smith, Arthur F. Hankins; LP: William Duncan, Edith Johnson, Ford West, George Stanley, William McCall, Frank Weed.

1923

The Steel Trail. Univ., [15 Chapters] D: William Duncan; S/SP: George Plympton, Karl Coolidge, Paul M. Bryan; LP: William Duncan, Edith Johnson, Harry Carter, Harry Woods, Ralph McCullough.

1924

The Fast Express. Univ., [15 Chapters] D: William Duncan; SP: Frank H. Clark, Paul Bryan; S: Courtney Ryler Cooper; LP: William Duncan, Edith Johnson, Edward Cecil, Eve Gordon, Harry Woods.

Wolves of the North. Univ., [10 Chapters] D: William Duncan; SP: Frank H. Clark; S: Katherene and Robert Pinkerton; LP: William Duncan, Edith Johnson, Joseph W. Girard, Clark Comstock, Esther Ralston, Harry Woods.

BRUCE EDWARDS

Bruce Edwards was born Edward Lester Smith on October 6, 1911, in Los Angeles. His father was killed in World War I and he was raised by his mother. Biographical information is mostly lacking, but as an adult he had a car dealership in Los Angeles and married a girl named Virginia Andrews. When a potential customer turned out to be a studio talent scout, Edwards accepted the invitation to take a screen test.

Selling the car dealership, Bruce opened a boys' summer camp on Catalina. Following his screen career, he became a successful photographer who wrote columns for the *Daily Pilot/News-Press* and the Balboa Bay Club's *Bay Window.*

Edwards was a longtime resident of Newport Beach. He died September 20, 2003, in Thousand Oaks, California.

Edwards is best remembered as the hero of *The Black Widow* ('47). He also had a lesser part in *Federal Agents vs. Underworld, Inc.* ('49). He entered movies in 1941. His films are many but include *Sun Valley Serenade* ('41), *Bombardier* ('43), *The Falcon in Danger* ('43), *Seven Miles from Alcatraz* ('43), *Government Girl* ('44), *First Yank into Tokyo* ('45), *West of the Pecos* ('45), *Queen of the Amazons* ('47), *The Denver Kid* ('48), *The Great Plane Robbery* ('50) and *Sands of Iwo Jima* ('50).

Serials

1947

The Black Widow. Rep., [15 Chapters] D: Spencer Bennet, Fred C. Brannon; SP: Franklyn Adreon, Basil Dickey, Jesse Duffy, Sol Shor; AP: Mike Frankovich; Cam: John MacBurnie; Mus: Mort Glickman; LP:

1949

Federal Agents vs. Underworld, Inc. Rep., [12 Chapters] D: Fred C. Brannon; SP: Royal K. Cole, Basil Dickey, William Lively, Sol Shor; AP: Franklyn Adreon; Cam: John MacBurnie; Mus: Stanley Wilson; LP: Kirk Alyn, Rosemary LaPlanche, Carol Forman, Roy Barcroft, Bruce Edwards, James Craven, Tristram Coffin.

Bruce Gentry. Col., [15 Chapters] D: Spencer G. Bennet, Thomas Carr; SP: George Plympton, Joseph F. Poland, Lewis Clay; P: Sam Katzman; Cam: Ira H. Morgan; Mus: Mischa Bakaleinikoff; LP: Tom Neal, Judy Clark, Ralph Hodges, Forrest Taylor, Tom Steele, Jack Ingram, Eddie Parker, Hugh Prosser.

WILLIAM (BILL) ELLIOTT

Screendom's "Wild Bill" was born Gordon Nance on October 16, 1903, near Pattonsburg, Missouri. The family later moved to Kansas City where Gordon's father was employed at the Kansas City stockyards. Gordon spent his spare time hanging around the stockyards with the cowboys. He learned the arts of riding, roping, bulldogging and bronc busting from the best teachers, the cowboys themselves. He took top place in the American Royal Horse and Livestock Show at the age of 16. During his six-year tenure as a rodeo cowboy, he also managed to graduate from high school and attend Rockingham College.

At age 22 Gordon was in Hollywood and soon joined the Pasadena Community Playhouse. He began appearing in bit parts in silent films, one of the first being *The Plastic Age* ('25) starring Clara Bow. With a name change to Gordon Elliott, he made 90 (!) films prior to *The Great Adventures of Wild Bill Hickok* ('38), only seven of which were Westerns—three with Dick Foran, and one each with Gene Autry, Buffalo Bill, Jr., Tom Mix and Smith Ballew. Early on Elliott was signed by Warner Brothers and appeared in approximately 50 films for that studio and on loanout.

Elliott was dropped by Warner Brothers in 1937 and he bounced around from studio to studio until Columbia signed him for *The Great Adventures of Wild Bill Hickok*. He had had a rather undistinguished career from the mid–20s until he was selected to headline the serial. His success in the role established him as a Western star and gave him a new name. He was "Wild Bill," "Bill" and "William" in subsequent features.

The serial was one of Columbia's best and was a smash at the box office, due in part to the expert direction of Mack V. Wright and Sam Nelson. (The directorial reins of Columbia chapterplays had not yet been taken over by James Horne, who was responsible for some of Columbia's later serial travesties.) In the story, Wild Bill Hickok is made the marshal of Abilene, a wild, almost lawless frontier town. The entire area is terrorized by a band of marauders called the Phantom Raiders. Hickok's first job is to keep the Chisholm Trail open for Texas ranchers sending their herds north. The Phantom Raiders try to keep the cattle and the railroad from reaching Abilene by stirring up the Indians against the wagon train and cattle drive and also attacking it several times. But at each turn they are foiled by Hickok, who is finally able to expose the leader of the Raiders and end the reign of terror of the Phantom Raiders.

Gordon Elliott became Bill Elliott and

Columbia starred him in eight features which were released through '38 and '39, the first of which was *In Early Arizona* ('38).

A second Elliott serial, *Overland with Kit Carson*, was released in '39. It, too, was a whopping success. A mysterious outlaw known as Pegleg dreams of an empire in the vast, rich wilderness west of the Mississippi. Lt. Brent (Richard Fiske) is sent from Washington to persuade Kit Carson (Elliott) to help break up Pegleg's gang, the Black Raiders. After many hair-raising adventures, Carson tricks Pegleg into giving away his identity. In the struggle that follows, the outlaw slips and is trampled to death by his black stallion "Midnight."

A second series of eight features starring Elliott were filmed by Columbia. The first film in the new series was titled *The Return of Wild Bill* ('40). Thereafter Elliott would be known as "Wild Bill." In six of the

Iris Meredith and Bill Elliott in *The Son of Davy Crockett* (Columbia, 1941).

eight features he portrayed Wild Bill Hickok.

In a third series of eight features he was co-starred with Tex Ritter. Elliott reprised the roll of Wild Bill Hickok in six of the films, and it is this third series that is considered the best.

To round out his contract with Columbia, Elliott starred in *The Valley of Vanishing Men* ('42), widely considered the best of his three serials. Cowpoke Bill Tolliver (Elliott) searches for his father, a prospector, in New Mexico and discovers that an outlaw has joined forces with an ousted European general to enslave Mexican patriots to work in a gold mine. Also planned is a rebellion against Benito Juarez and the government of Mexico. In a final showdown, Bill and American forces are joined by Mexican forces to defeat the outlaws. Bill and his father are reunited. Old slapstick comedian Slim Summerville is surprisingly good as Bill's sidekick.

Elliott signed with Republic in 1943 and was starred in a series of eight Westerns with George (Gabby) Hayes and Anne Jeffreys. He used his own name. First in the series was *Calling Wild Bill Elliott* ('44). Republic next cast Elliott as Red Rider in a series of 16 Westerns with Bobby Blake as Little Beaver. Elliott was then moved up to "A" productions with *In Old Sacramento* ('46) being the first and *The Showdown* ('50) the ninth.

Between 1951 and 1954, Monogram starred Elliott in 11 A-minus productions. He then was starred in five non–Western detective features before his movie career ended in 1957 with the release of *Footsteps in the Night.*

Back in 1950, Bill did a pilot for a proposed television series that didn't sell. However, it was released to TV as *Marshal of Trail City*.

Elliott died of cancer on November 26, 1965. Surviving was Dolly Moore, his second wife, and Barbara, a daughter by his first marriage which ended in divorce after 33 years. Miss Moore, a model, had two children from a previous marriage.

When Wild Bill Elliott put his hands on his six-guns and warily said, "I'm a peaceable man, but ...," all screen villains had best make for the nearest exit. Kids would whoop, holler, and whistle in anticipation of the action to follow.

Elliott's cowboy career was a successful one. His fans were legion.

Serials

1938

The Great Adventures of Wild Bill Hickok. Col., [15 Chapters] D: Mack V. Wright, Sam Nelson; SP: George Rosener, Charles A. Powell, G. A. Durlan, Dallas Fitzgerald, Tom Gibson; AP: Harry Webb; P: Jack Fier; Cam: George Meehan, Benjamin Kline; Mus: Abe Meyer; LP: Gordon (Bill) Elliott, Carol Wayne, Frankie Darro, Monte Blue, Sammy McKim, Kermit Maynard, Reed Hadley.

1939

Overland with Kit Carson. Col., [15 Chapters] D: Sam Nelson, Norman Deming; SP: Joseph Poland, Morgan B. Cox, Ned Dandy; P: Jack Fier; Cam: Benjamin Kline, George Meehan; Mus: Lee Zahler; LP: Bill Elliott, Iris Meredith, Trevor Bardette, Richard Fiske, Bobby Clark, LeRoy Mason.

1942

The Valley of Vanishing Men. Col., [15 Chapters] D: Spencer G. Bennet; SP: Harry Fraser, Lewis Clay, George Gray; P: Larry Darmour; Cam: James S. Brown, Jr.; Mus: Lee Zahler; LP: Bill Elliott, Slim Summerville, Kenneth MacDonald, Carmen Morales, Jack Ingram, George Chesebro, Tom London, John Shay.

FRANK ELLIS

Frank Birney Ellis was born in Oklahoma Territory on February 29, 1897. His life is a blank page except for nearly 250 Westerns and 36 serials that he worked in. His first credited performance was in *King's Creek Law*, a Leo Maloney Western. From there he went on to work in the films of 50 or more Hollywood cowboys. His name was not known to many, but his sour-faced image was familiar to two generations of moviegoers. He could quickly be identified by noting his paunch and droopy mustache. He never played the lead rogue but was always one of the gang members who took orders from a higher-up blackguard. On-screen he was a son of a bitch who thought nothing of bushwhacking unsuspecting law-abiding citizens. He tended to come across as a "non-thinking" buffoon. And so it was in film after film after film. In 1941, Ellis appeared in 35 (probably more) Westerns; in 1942, the number was close to 30. He continued working in films until the early '50s.

Serials

1920

Elmo, the Fearless. Univ., [18 Chapters] D: J.P. McGowan; LP: Elmo Lincoln, Louise Lorraine, William Chapman, Roy Watson, Frank Ellis.

1926

The Range Fighter. Davis, [10 Chapters] D: Clifford S. Elfelt; LP: Ken Maynard, Dorothy Devore, George Nicholas, J. P. McGowan, Sheldon Lewis.

1927

Whispering Smith Rides. Univ., [10 Chapters] D: Ray Taylor; LP: Wallace MacDonald, Rose Blossom, J. P. McGowan, Clark Comstock, Henry Herbert.

1933

Fighting with Kit Carson. Mascot, [12 Chapters] D: Armand Schaefer, Colbert Clark; LP: Johnny Mack Brown, Betsy King Ross, Noah Beery, Sr., Noah Beery, Jr., Tully Marshall.

1934

The Red Rider. Univ., [15 Chapters] D: Louis Friedlander; LP: Buck Jones, Grant Withers, Marion Shilling, Walter Miller, Richard Cramer.

1935

The Miracle Rider. Mascot, [15 Chapters] D: Armand Schaefer, B. Reeves Eason; LP: Tom Mix, Charles Middleton, Joan Gale, Jason Robards, Sr., Charles King.

Phantom Empire. Mascot, [12 Chapters] D: Otto Brower, B. Reeves Eason; LP: Gene Autry, Frankie Darro, Betsy King Ross, Dorothy Christie, Wheeler Oakman.

1936

The Vigilantes Are Coming. Rep., [12 Chapters] D: Mack V. Wright, Ray Taylor; LP: Robert Livingston, Kay Hughes, Guinn Williams, Raymond Hatton, Fred Kohler, William Desmond.

Robinson Crusoe of Clipper Island. Rep., [14 Chapters] D: Mack V. Wright, Ray Taylor; LP: Ray Mala, Mamo Clark, Herbert Rawlinson, Rex (horse), Buck (dog).

1937

Zorro Rides Again. Rep., [12 Chapters] D: Wm. Witney, John English; LP: John Carroll, Helen Christian, Duncan Renaldo, Noah Beery, Sr.

Wild West Days. Univ., [13 Chapters] D: Ford Beebe, Cliff Smith; LP: Johnny Mack Brown, Lynn Gilbert, Robert Kortman, George Shelley, Frank Yaconelli.

S O S Coast Guard. Rep., [12 Chapters] D: William Witney and Alan James; LP: Ralph Byrd, Bela Lugosi, Maxine Doyle, Richard Alexander, George Chesebro.

1938

The Lone Ranger. Rep., [15 Chapters] D: Wm. Witney, John English; LP: Lee Powell, Chief Thundercloud, Hal Taliaferro, Herman Brix, Lane Chandler, Stanley Andrews, Lynne Roberts.

The Great Adventures of Wild Bill Hickok. Col., [15 Chapters] D: Mack V. Wright and Sam Nelson; LP: Bill Elliott, Carole Wayne, Frankie Darro, Monte Blue, Dickie Jones.

Flaming Frontiers. Univ., [15 Chapters] D: Ray Taylor and Alan James; LP: Johnny Mack Brown, Eleanor Hansen, Ralph Bowman [John Archer], James Blaine, Charles Middleton.

1939

The Oregon Trail. Univ., [15 Chapters] D: Ford Beebe, Saul Goodkind; LP: Johnny Mach Brown, Louise Stanley, Fuzzy Knight, Bill Cody, Jr., Forrest Taylor.

The Lone Ranger Rides Again. Rep., [15 Chapters] D: William Witney, John English; LP: Robert Livingston, Chief Thundercloud, Duncan Renaldo, Jinx Falken, Ralph Dunn.

Zorro's Fighting Legion. Rep., [12 Chapters] D: Wm. Witney, John English; LP: Reed Hadley, Sheila Darcy, William Corson, Leander de Cordova, C. Montague Shaw.

1940

Drums of Fu Manchu. Rep., [15 Chapters] D: Wm. Witney, John English; LP: Henry Brandon, William Royle, John Merton, Gloria Franklin, Luana Walters.

Mysterious Doctor Satan. Rep., [15 Chapters] D: Wm. Witney, John English; LP: Eduardo Ciannelli, Robert Wilcox, Ella Neal, William Newell, C. Montague Shaw.

Winners of the West. Univ., [13 Chapters] D: Ford Beebe, Ray Taylor; LP: Dick Foran, Anne Nagle, James Craig, Tom Fadden.

1942

The Valley of Vanishing Men. Col., [15 Chapters] D: Spencer G. Bennet; LP: Bill Elliott, Slim Summerville, Carmen Morales, Kenneth MacDonald.

1946

Son of the Guardsman. Col., [15 Chapters] D: Derwin Abrahams; LP: Robert Shaw, Duan Kennedy, Hugh Prosser, Robert (Buzz) Henry, Jim Diehl.

1947

The Vigilante. Col., [15 Chapters] D: Mack V. Wright, Ray Taylor; LP: Ralph Byrd, Ramsay Ames, Lyle Talbot, George Offerman, Robert Barron.

Brick Bradford. Col., [15 Chapters] D: Spencer G. Bennet; LP: Kane Richmond, Rick Vallin, Linda Johnson, Pierre Watkin, Charles Quigley.

Son of Zorro. Rep., [13 Chapters] D: Spencer Bennet, Fred Brannon; LP: George Turner, Peggy Stewart, Roy Barcroft, Edward Cassidy.

1948

Adventures of Frank and Jesse James. Rep., [13 Chapters] D: Fred Brannon, Yakima Canutt; LP: Clayton Moore, Noel Neill, George J. Lewis, Stanley Andrews.

Superman. Col., [15 Chapters] D: Spencer Bennet, Thomas Carr; LP: Kirk Alyn, Noel Neill, Tommy Bond, Pierre Watkin, Carol Forman.

1949

Ghost of Zorro. Rep., [12 Chapters] D: Fred Brannon; LP: Clayton Moore, Pamela Blake, George J. Lewis, Roy Barcroft, Gene Roth.

1950

Cody of the Pony Express. Col., [15 Chapters] D: Spencer Bennet; LP: Jock Mahoney, Dickie, Moore, Peggy Stewart, William Fawcett, Tom London.

1951

Mysterious Island. Col., [15 Chapters] D: Spencer Bennet; LP: Richard Crane, Marshall Reed, Karen Randle, Ralph Hodges, Gene Roth.

Roar of the Iron Horse. Col., [15 Chapters] D: Spencer Bennet, Thomas Carr; LP: Jock Mahoney, Virginia Herrick, William Fawcett, Hal Landon, Jack Ingram.

1952

Blackhawk. Col., [15 Chapters] D: Spencer Bennet, Fred F. Sears; LP: Kirk Alyn, Carol Forman, John Crawford, Michael Fox, Don C. Harvey.

Son of Geronimo. Col., [15 Chapters] D: Spencer Bennet; LP: Clayton Moore, Rodd Redwing, Tommy Farrell, Eileen Rowe, Bud Osborne.

King of the Congo. Col., [15 Chapters] D: Spencer Bennet, Walter Grissell; LP: Buster Crabbe, Gloria Dea, Leonard Penn, Jack Ingram, Rusty Wescoatt.

HUGH ENFIELD/ CRAIG REYNOLDS

Hugh Enfield was born in Anaheim, California, on July 15, 1907. After training at the Pasadena Playhouse, work with stock companies and a stint in vaudeville, he made his film debut in 1929 with Mary Pickford in *Coquette*, after which he returned to the stage.

Making his way back to films in 1933, he played supporting roles in *Gordon of Ghost City* starring Buck Jones and *The Phantom of the Air* starring Tom Tyler. Work in *Cross County Cruise*, *I'll Tell the World* and *Love Birds* followed.

Enfield was signed to a three-year contract by Warner Brothers in 1935 and appeared in *Ceiling Zero, The Case of the Lucky Legs, Brides Are Like That, Times Square Playboy, Treachery Rides the Range, Sons O' Guns, Smart Blonde, Jailbreak, Slim, The Great O'Malley, Penrod and Sam* and others.

Reynolds began freelancing in 1938, trying for better luck elsewhere. It was not to be, although he found roles in *House of Mystery, Female Fugitive, I Am a Criminal, Mystery of Mr. Wong, Navy Secrets,* et al.

After ten months of duty in Iceland, Craig was returned to the States for officer candidate training. He emerged as a second lieutenant and was sent to Guadalcanal, where he was severely injured when a Japanese shell exploded near him. He spent months in the Corona Naval Hospital in San Diego, and while he was there he married actress Barbara Pepper in 1943.

Craig was promoted to the rank of captain and awarded two presidential citations and a Purple Heart. Returned to civilian life, he found few roles. There were only ten minor ones from 1944 to 1948: *Nevada* ('44), *Divorce* ('45), *The Lost Weekend* ('45), *The Strange Affair of Uncle Harry* ('45), *Just Before Dawn* ('46), *My Dog Shep* ('46), *Queen of Burlesque* ('46), *The Fabulous Texan* ('47), *Stork Bites Man* ('47) and *The Man from Colorado* ('48).

During the last two years of his life, he drove a taxi for the Yellow Cab Company. On October 22, 1949, he died as a result of a traffic accident. He left behind his wife Barbara and twin sons Dennis and Johnny. Craig was only 42.

Serials

1933

Gordon of Ghost City. Univ. D: Ray Taylor; SP: Ella O'Neill, Basil Dickey, George Plympton, Harry O. Hoyt, Het Mannheim; S: Peter B. Kyne; P: Henry McRae; C: Buck Jones, Madge Bellamy, Walter Miller, Hugh Enfield, William Desmond, Tom Rockett, Francis Ford, Edmund Cobb, Dick Rush, William Steele, Bob Kerrick, Ethan Laidlaw, Jim Corey, Bud Osborne, Tom London, Silver.

The Phantom of the Air. Univ. D: Ray Taylor; SP: Basil Dickey, George Plympton; S: Ella O'Neill; C: Tom Tyler, Gloria Shea, LeRoy Mason, Hugh Enfield, William Desmond, Sidney Bracey, Walter Brennan, Nennie Cramer, Cecil Kellog, Tom London, Edmund Cobb, Wheeler Oakman, Bud Osborne.

1934

Perils of Pauline. Univ. D: Ray Taylor; SP: Ella O'Neill, Basil Dickey, George Plympton, Jack Foley; S: Ella O'Neill, Charles W. Goddard; C: Evelyn Knapp, Robert Allen, James Durkin, John Davidson, Sonny Ray, Frank Lackteen, Pat O'Malley, William Desmond, Adolph Muller, Josef Swickard.

MURIEL EVANS

The blonde, blue-eyed actress (of Norwegian descent) hailed from Minneapolis, Minnesota, where she was born Muriel Adele Evanson on July 20, 1911. After making her film debut in *Mademoiselle Modiste* ('26) and appearing in several two-reel comedies, she returned to school to complete her education.

In 1929, at age 18, she married playboy Michael Cudahy of the rich meatpacking family. This union lasted about two years, one of which was spent living in France.

Back in Hollywood, Muriel studied dancing under Marge Champion's father and was signed by Hal Roach/MGM as featured

Muriel Evans and Buck Jones in *Boss of Lonely Valley* (Universal, 1937).

player in the comedies of Charley Chase. She made nine comedies with him, two with Laurel and Hardy and one with Ben Blue.

Later came the Westerns and independents such as *19 Laps to Go* ('36), *Missing Girls* ('36) and *House of Secrets* ('36). She has held a special place in the hearts of Buck Jones fans for she played opposite the beloved cowboy ace seven times—*The Throwback* ('35), *The Roaring West* ('35), *Silver Spurs* ('36), *Boss Rider of Gun Creek* ('36), *Smoke Tree Range* ('37), *Law for Tombstone* ('37) and *Boss of Lonely Valley* ('37). *The Roaring West*, a serial, allowed fans to see her with Buck for 15 consecutive weeks! "Oh, the thrill of it all," as William S. Hart might say. In the mid–30s, when "B" Westerns were in their heyday, there wasn't anything more exciting to a young boy, unless it was the circus, than seeing Buck Jones thrillers, and

Muriel Evans was the romantic interest in some of the best of them. The chemistry between Jones and Evans was good, and fans easily picked up on it. Other cowboys were not slighted by Miss Evans, however. She graced three Hopalong Cassidy Westerns, and John Wayne and Tex Ritter each fell victim to her charms in two sagebrushers. Cowboys Rex Lease and Tim Holt got to work with her in non–Westerns.

In the late '30s or very early '40s, Muriel married Marshall R. Worcester, theatrical agent, broker and scion of a prominent New York family. They moved to Washington, D.C., thus ending her Hollywood career. Her last film was *Roll, Wagons, Roll* ('40) starring Tex Ritter. However, during her ten-year stay in the capital city she was actively involved in show business. She had four or five radio shows of her own and was star of *Hol-*

lywood Reporter, Washington's only TV show at that time.

The Worchesters eventually moved back to California, but Muriel never resumed an acting career. Mr. Worcester died of a heart attack in 1971. Muriel lived in quiet retirement in Tarzana, California.

Muriel Evans quietly passed away October 26, 2001, of colon cancer at the Motion Picture Home in Woodland Hills, California. She was 90.

Serial

1935

The Roaring West. Univ., [15 Chapters] D: Ray Taylor; S: Edward Earl Repp; SP: George Plympton, Nate Gatzert, Ella O'Neill, Basil Dickey, Robert Rothafel; LP: Buck Jones, Muriel Evans, Frank McGlynn, Sr., Harlan Knight, William Desmond, Charles King.

VIRGINIA BROWN FAIRE

Born in Brooklyn in 1904, Virginia made a number of very brief film appearances in New York and Fort Lee productions before winning the 1919 Motion Picture Classic "Fame and Fortune" contest, sponsored by Brewster Publications. This brought her to California and a Universal contract. Her name was changed from Virginia La Buna to Virginia Brown Faire.

She portrayed the impetuous, loyal yet warm and yielding heroine many times over — to the delight of the humble trade who went faithfully to see her pictures for 15 years. She spent little time writhing about in sexy, provocative poses, nor was she the demure romantic. Rather, she was an accomplished actress with a wistful charm who easily became the epitome of the genteel, strong-willed, persevering frontier woman. There was a spontaneous sexuality about her that was enhanced by the camera, and she was apt to attract any pair of eyes.

Virginia made one exciting film after another, appearing opposite cowboys William Desmond, Hoot Gibson, Harry Carey, Reed Howes, Buck Jones, Ken Maynard, Rex Lease, Wallace MacDonald, Jack Perrin, Tom Tyler and John Wayne.

Virginia had poise, dignity, and a patrician beauty, which might have been enough for horse opera lovers, but she also was an extremely able actress when she had the opportunity. As Tinker Bell, she revived children's wavering belief in fairies in *Peter Pan*

('24), an all-time classic film. In 1923 she was selected as a Wampas Baby Star, and she proved she was worthy of the honor in several good films.

Sign of the Wolf ('31), her only serial, was a "north-westerner" made for Metro-

politan, an independent company. Rex Lease co-starred, and support was provided by a galaxy of old time "B" favorites. For a cheaply made early sound serial, it wasn't at all bad. The story unwinds swiftly, the cast plays well enough, and naturally there are plenty of guns displayed and heaps of slugs tossed around. A dog figures prominently in all the excitement.

Virginia was married to Jack Daugherty in the early 1930s but was later divorced and married director-producer Duke Worne. After his death, she married a third time. Her last known film part was as a leading lady to Tom Tyler in *Tracy Rides* ('35). Shortly before, she had performed with John Wayne in *West of the Divide* ('34) and with Jack Perrin in *Rainbow Riders* ('34).

Virginia died in 1976, 41 years after she retired from the screen.

Serial

The Sign of the Wolf. Metropolitan, 1931 [10 Chapters] D: Forrest Sheldon, Harry S. Webb; SP: Betty Burbridge, Bennett Cohen; LP: Rex Lease, Virginia Brown Faire, Joe Bonomo, Jack Mower, Al Ferguson, Josephine Hill, King (a dog), Edmund Cobb.

FRANKLYN FARNUM

Smiling Franklyn Farnum, the silent screen cowboy with the infectious grin, was, contrary to popular belief at the time, no relation to two actor brothers—Dustin and William, established stars of the stage and screen. He just borrowed their last name. After all, William Smith didn't quite conjure up an image of a hard-riding, fast-shooting son of the sagebrush.

Franklyn was born in Boston on June 5 in the year 1878, if he was 83 in 1961 as re-

ported in obituaries. While still a young lad, he was invited to join the choir of a local church and began to take voice lessons under the choirmaster. Franklyn had a talent for dancing and singing as well as inborn histrionic ability. These talents, coupled with an exceptional voice, led to his becoming a leading man for the Nixon-zimmerman organization which sent out road companies, and which had theaters in New York and Philadelphia. He performed in light opera and musical comedy on Broadway before descending on Hollywood in 1914 or '15.

On stage, Franklyn played leading roles in *The Belle of New York*, *Madame Sherry*, *The Dollar Princess*, *The Only Girl* and other productions. The transition to motion pictures was fairly easy for Franklyn and he made his first film, *Love Never Dies* ('16), for Universal.

Farnum switched primarily to Westerns, although he had never ridden a horse until coming to Hollywood. His career was mostly undistinguished. He appeared at home in the Western environment, became a good horseman and had an infectious grin that was worked into the titles of two of his films, *The Fighting Grin* ('18) and *Smilin' Jim* ('18).

In 1920, Farnum signed with Canyon Pictures to make 26 two-reel Westerns and one serial. These compact little Westerns projected him into the Western limelight. Prints and titles of most have long since vanished. However, four of the films have survived—*The Two Doyles* ('20–21), *the Desert Rat* ('20–21), *When Pals Fall Out* ('20–21) and *Uphill Climb*. Buck Jones supported Farnum in the last three films.

Vanishing Trails ('20) was considered one of the best serials of its time. Produced by film pioneer William Selig, it was a complicated story that started in the home of an Eastern multi-millionaire who is mysteriously murdered. The serial then takes the viewer to the land of Vanishing Trails out west. Farnum is "Silent Joe" and Mary Anderson is the prairie nymph. Shot in a modern (1920) setting, enveloped in an aura of mystery, featuring the manifestations of a crazy scientist and the appearance of a masked rider, *Vanishing Trails* could have been the forerunner of the wild serials made by Nat Levine during the Mascot days (*Mystery Mountain*, *The Miracle Rider*, *The Phantom Empire*).

Farnum replaced Bruce Gordon as male star of *Battling Brewester* in 1924. Helen Holmes had the female lead. It possibly was a Western, but perhaps not. This is another serial that did not survive.

Farnum married beautiful Alma Rubens on June 14, 1918, but were divorced within a year. Farnum remarried in 1921 to a nonprofessional named Edith (last name unknown). This marriage lasted until Edith's death in 1959 and produced a daughter, Mrs. Geraldine Rose, with whom Farnum was living at the time of his death.

A former president of the Screen Extras Guild and a member of the Screen Actors Guild, he was honored on his eightieth birthday with a lifetime membership in the Extras Guild.

It has been estimated that he appeared in over 1,000 films, an enviable record indeed. And if he appeared in only half that number of films, it would still be an enviable record.

Franklyn Farnum died from cancer on July 4, 1961, at the Motion Picture Country Hospital in Woodland Hills, California. He was survived by his daughter and three grandchildren.

Serials

1920

Vanishing Trails. Canyon, [15 Chapters] D: Leon de la Mothe; LP: Franklyn Farnum, Mary Anderson, Duke R. Lee, L. M. Wells, Harry Lonsdale, Vester Pegg.

1924

Battling Brewester. Rayart, [15 Chapters] P/D: Dell Henderson; SP: Robert Dillon; Spv.: Robert Dillon; LP: Franklyn Farnum, Helen Holmes, Leon Holmes.

1931

Battling with Buffalo Bill. Univ., [12 Chapters] D: Ray Taylor; LP: Tom Tyler, Rex Bell, Lucile Browne, Francis Ford.

1936

Custer's Last Stand. S&S, [15 Chapters] D: Elmer Clifton; LP: Rex Lease, William Farnum, Reed Howes, Jack Mulhall, George Chesebro, Dorothy Gulliver.

The Clutching Hand. S&S, [15 Chapters] D: Albert Herman; LP: Jack Mulhall, Ruth Mix, Marion Shilling, Rex Lease, Reed Howes, Franklyn Farnum.

1940

The Green Archer. Col., [15 Chapters] D: James W. Horne; LP: Victory Jory, Iris Meredith, James Craven, Robert Fiske, Dorothy Fay, Forrest Taylor.

The Shadow. Col., [15 Chapters] D: James W. Horne; LP: Victor Jory, Veda Ann Borg, Robert Moore, Robert Fiske, J. Paul Jones, Jack Ingram, Frank LaRue.

Deadwood Dick. Col., [15 Chapters] D: James W. Horne; LP: Don Douglas, Lorna Gray [Adrian Booth], Lane Chandler, Marin Sais, Charles King.

1941

Holt of the Secret Service. Col., [15 Chapters] D: James W. Horne; LP: Jack Holt, Evelyn Brent, Montague Shaw, Tristram Coffin, Franklyn Farnum.

1942

Captain Midnight. Col., [15 Chapters] D: James W. Horne; LP: Dave O'Brien, Dorothy

Short, James Craven, Sam Edwards, Franklyn Farnum, Luana Walters.

The Secret Code. Col. [15 Chapters] D: Spencer Bennet; LP: Paul Kelly, Anne Nagel, Clancy Cooper, Trevor Bardette, Robert O. Davis.

WILLIAM FARNUM

William Farnum was made a star by his very first film, Selig's *The Spoilers* (1914), the first of a number of films based on the book by Rex Beach. The knock-down, drag-out fight between he and Thomas Santschi stands as one of the most realistic ever filmed. The actors agreed to not pull any punches; consequently, each antagonist was beaten to a pulp and took off for a week to recover. Notwithstanding its crudeness, *The Spoilers* is one of the most spectacular productions of the early silent era.

William Farnum was born in 1876 in Boston, but grew up in Bucksport, Maine. He toured vaudeville in an athletic act with his brother Dustin, who became a star in 1914 in Cecil B. DeMille's *The Squaw Man*. Both brothers became stage actors while still in their teens and remained close throughout their lives.

William Farnum switched to Fox in 1915 and made six features that year. He would remain with Fox through 1923. Of interest to action fans were *Fighting Blood* ('16), *The Man from Bitter Roots* ('16), *At the End of the Trail* ('16), *The Conqueror* ('17), *When*

Don Terry and William Farnum (right) in *Secret of Treasure Island* (Columbia, 1938).

a Man Sees Red ('17), *True Blue* ('18), *Riders of the Purple Sage* ('18), *The Rainbow Trail* ('18), *The Jungle Trail* ('19), *The Last of the Duanes* ('19), *The Lone Star Ranger* ('20), *Drag Harlan* ('20), *Moonshine Valley* ('22), *The Gunfighter* ('23) and *Brass Commandments* ('23). Critics and the public alike praised *The Sign of the Cross* ('14), *Les Misérables* ('17), *A Tale of Two Cities* ('17) and *If I Were King* ('20).

At the peak of his career (1919–23), Farnum was earning $10,000 a week, 52 weeks a year. Like a lot of stars, then and now, who hit the big time and think the influx of money will go on indefinitely, he bought an estate in the Hollywood Hills, *two* town houses in New York City and a $450,000 place in Maine. Expensive cars, fine clothes, a domestic staff and generous amounts of money given to down-on-their-luck actors amounted to thousands of dollars a year.

While filming *The Man Who Fights Alone* ('24) at Paramount, Bill was seriously injured, to the extent that it was 1930 before he faced cameras again. For six years (1934–40) he appeared on the stage in *The Buccaneer*, *Julius Caesar* and *Macbeth*. The crash of 1929 cost him over $2 million, with the result that he was reduced to near poverty. At age 55, only supporting roles came his way. He supported Norma Talmadge and Conrad Nagel in *Du Barry, Woman of Passion* ('30); William Boyd and Helen Twelvetrees in *The Painted Desert* ('31); and Will Rogers and Myrna Loy in *A Connecticut Yankee* ('31). He and Thomas Santschi were reunited in *Ten Nights in a Barroom* ('31). He had good roles in the "B" productions *The Drifter* ('32) with

Noah Beery, Sr., *Law of the Sea* ('32) with Rex Bell, *Flashing Guns* ('33) with Tom Mix, *Happy Landing* ('34) with Noah Beery, Sr., *The Scarlet Letter* ('34) with Colleen Moore and *School for Girls* ('34) with Paul Kelly. In the big-budget features *The Count of Monte Cristo* ('34) with Robert Donat and *The Crusades* ('35) with Loretta Young, he had smaller parts.

Beginning in 1935, Farnum found a home in "B" Westerns and serials, while still appearing in such "A" features as *Maid of Salem* ('37), *If I Were King* ('38), *Kit Carson* ('40), *The Corsican Brothers* ('41), *Tennessee Johnson* ('42), *Samson and Delilah* ('49) and *Lone Star* ('52). His last film was *Jack and the Beanstalk* ('52) with Bud Abbott and Lou Costello.

Farnum often played the part of a priest, as in *The Vigilantes Are Coming* ('36) and *South of the Border* ('39). Seldom if ever, did he portray a bad man. It must have been sickening to realize that he was just a "B" Western supporting player when he remembered the glory days when he was at the top of his profession, making over a thousand dollars a day whether he worked or not. But Farnum did not live in the past. He was humble, friendly and worked hard to please.

Farnum was featured in one serial in 1933, four in 1936, two in 1938 and one in 1940. He perhaps is best remembered for these cliffhangers. He died in Los Angeles from cancer in 1953 at the age of 73.

Serials

1933

Fighting with Kit Carson. Mascot, [12 Chapters] D: Armand Schaefer, Colbert Clark; LP: Johnny Mack Brown, Betsy King Ross, Noah Beery, Sr., Noah Beery, Jr.

1936

Custer's Last Stand. S&S, [15 Chapters] D: Elmer Clifton; LP: Rex Lease, William Farnum, Reed Howes, George Chesebro, Jack Mulhall, Lona Andre.

The Clutching Hand. S&S, [15 Chapters] D: Albert Herman; LP: Jack Mulhall, Ruth Mix, Marion Shilling, Rex Lease, Yakima Canutt, William Farnum, William Desmond.

The Vigilantes Are Coming. Rep., [12 Chapters] D: Mack V. Wright, Ray Taylor; LP: Robert Livingston, Kay Hughes, Guinn Williams, Raymond Hatton, Fred Kohler.

Undersea Kingdom. Rep., [12 Chapters] D: B. Reeves Eason, Joseph Kane; LP: Ray Corrigan, Lois Wilde, Monte Blue, William Farnum, Raymond Hatton, Lon Chaney, Jr.

1938

The Lone Ranger. Rep., [15 Chapters] D: William Witney, John English; LP: Lee Powell, Chief Thundercloud, Lynne Roberts, Herman Brix [Bruce Bennett], Wally Wales [Hal Taliaferro], George Letz [George Montgomery], Stanley Andrews.

The Secret of Treasure Island. Col., [15 Chapters] D: Elmer Clifton; LP: Don Terry, Gwen Gaze, Grant Withers, William Farnum, Hobart Bosworth, Yakima Canutt.

1940

Adventures of Red Ryder. Rep., [12 Chapters] D: William Witney, John English; LP: Donald Barry, Noah Beery, Sr., Tommy Cook, Vivian Coe, Hal Taliaferro.

PATRICIA FARR

Patricia Farr is remembered for her role as Betty Lou Barnes in Universal's *Tailspin Tommy* ('34). Although the airplanes are laughable today, it was an exciting thriller in 1934. In the story, Tommy Tompkins (Maurice Murphy) is chosen by pilot Milt Howe (Grant Withers) of Three Point Airline to fly with him in a race against time for a mail contract. Thanks to Tommy, Milt wins the race. But, in the process, he earns the enmity of Tiger Taggart (John Davidson), who wants Three Points to fail. Tommy becomes a Three Points pilot himself and battles Taggart's aerial pirates. In the end, Tommy sees to it that Taggart and his henchmen are brought to justice. He wins a movie contract for himself and his sweetheart, Betty Lou.

Patricia's career extended from 1931 through 1938. We find no credits for her after that. In 1931 she had a minor role in a Richard Arlen political drama (*The Secret Call*). In show business drama *What Price Hollywood?* ('32) with Constance Bennett, she has a minor role. In *Metropolitan* ('35) starring Lawrence Tibbett, she can be seen as a chorus girl. She co-starred with Reginald Denny in Chesterfield's *The Lady in Scarlet* ('35), playing secretary to Denny. The two solve a murder and locate missing bonds.

Lady Luck (Chesterfield '36) was a good film for Patricia. She plays a manicurist and a movie star wannabe who holds a winning ticket for a race won by champion race horse "Lady Luck." Things get complicated for her when a slimy sportsman is found shot to death, the murder weapon in the hand of the starlet. A sharp reporter (William Bakewell) tries to figure out who the real killer is. It is a great little whodunit and Patricia shows up well. She has the leading role in *All-American Sweetheart* (Col. '37) as a girl who manipulates events to cause Scott Kolk to accept a rowing team scholarship. Also in the cast are serial favorites Edmund Cobb, Donald Barry and Iris Meredith.

In *Criminals of the Air* (Col. '37), she plays Mamie, a waitress who helps break up a smuggling ring. Billed over her were Charles Quigley, Rosalind Keith and Rita Hayworth; in *Girls Can Play* (Col. '37) a softball racketeering story, she is "Peanuts" O'Malley. At Republic she got the starring role in *Lady Behave* ('38), playing a girl who gets drunk and marries a man she didn't know, when in fact she is already married.

Patricia dropped out of sight in '38.

Serial

1934

Tailspin Tommy. Univ., 1934 [12 Chapters] D: Louis Friedlander [Lew Landers]; SP: Norman S. Hall, Vin Moore, Basil Dickey, Ella O'Neill; LP: Maurice Murphy, Noah Beery, Jr., Patricia Farr, Grant Withers, John Davidson, Edmund Cobb, Al Ferguson, Bryant Washburn, Slim Whitaker, Bud Osborne, King Baggot.

DOROTHY FAY

Dorothy Fay was leading lady to Buck Jones in *The Stranger from Arizona* ('38), *Law of the Texan* ('38) and the Columbia serial *White Eagle* ('41), the story of Indian brave White Eagle, a Pony Express rider who defends the Indians who have been blamed for murders committed by a gang of white men headed by Bart Darnell (James Craven) and Gregory Cantro (Jack Ingram). White Eagle rescues Janet (Dorothy Fay) and her brother, who have been kidnapped. In the end, White Eagle discovers that he is not an Indian and therefore can make his love known to Janet. The serial used much stock footage from the feature *White Eagle* ('32), but was a popular serial.

Dorothy played opposite George Houston in *Frontier Scout* ('38); Bob Baker in *Prairie Justice* ('38); Tex Ritter in *Song of the Buckaroo* ('38), *Rollin' Westward* ('39), *Sundown on the Prairie* ('39) and *Rainbow Over the Range* ('40); and Bill Elliott in *North From the Lone Star* ('41).

The daughter of a Prescott, Arizona, doctor, Dorothy was born Dorothy Fay Southworth on April 4, 1915. She grew up in Prescott but spent her last year of high school in Los Angeles. After attending the University of Southern California, she studied acting at the Royal Academy of Dramatic Art in London and the Pasadena Playhouse.

Dorothy had a featured role in the serial *The Green Archer* ('40) starring Victor Jory and had bit parts in *The Philadelphia Story* ('40) and *Lady Be Good* ('41).

Dorothy married Tex Ritter in '41 and retired from acting to raise a family. Dorothy and Tex had two sons. John became a television star in such series as *Three's Company*; Tom followed a legal career and has been active in Tennessee politics.

Dorothy Ritter died on November 5, 2003, at the Motion Picture and Television Home and Hospital in Woodland Hills, California, at the age of 88. She had a stroke in 1987 and had lived at the retirement home since 1989. Her death came less than two months after that of John, who died September 11, 2003, from an aortic dissection. Her husband, Tex Ritter, died in 1974 at age 68.

She was survived by son Tom and four grandchildren.

Serials

1940

The Green Archer. Col., 1940 [15 Chapters] D: James W. Horne; SP: Morgan B. Cox, John Cutting, Jesse A. Duffy, James W. Horne; S: Edgar Wallace; P: Larry Darmour; Cam: James S. Brown, Jr.; Mus: Lee Zahler; LP: Victor Jory, Iris Meredith, James Craven, Robert Fiske, Dorothy Fay, Forrest Taylor, Jack Ingram, Charles King, Kenne Duncan, Franklyn Farnum, Eddie Polo.

1941

White Eagle. Col., 1941 [15 Chapters] D: James W. Horne; S: Fred Myton; SP: Arch Heath, Morgan B. Cos, John Cutting, Lawrence Taylor; P: Larry Darmour; Cam: James S. Brown, Jr.; Mus: Lee Zahler; LP: Buck Jones, Dorothy Fay, Raymond Hatton, Yakima Canutt, George Chesebro, Jack Ingram, Charles King, Roy Barcroft, Edmund Cobb, Edward Hearn.

AL FERGUSON

Al Ferguson's first film of record was *Lone Star* ('16), an American Film starring William Russell. Also that year he was in American's *The Voice of Love* ('16) starring Winifred Greenwood. Almost from the beginning, Ferguson played treacherous knaves. His first of 42 serials was *The Lost City* ('20), a Warner Bros. film starring Juanita Hansen and George Chesebro. Ferguson is sixth in the cast.

Three other jungle sagas featured Ferguson as a principal player. In *Miracles of the Jungle* ('20) he portrays Brian, "The Red Fox," the enemy of Ben Hagerty and Wilbur Higby, secret service men sent on assignment to Africa. Seven years later, in *Tarzan, the Mighty* ('28), we find him as Black John, a beachcomber who dominates a jungle village inhabited by descendants of pirates. He conducts a ceremony with incantations to set the evil spirits against Tarzan and the apes, who have raided his cattle. Mary and Bob, sister-and-brother castaways, are living among the tribe. Black John determines to make Mary his wife. Tarzan fights to keep him from doing so. When Tarzan's uncle arrives looking for the family heir, Black John passes himself off as the lost relative.

In *Tarzan, the Tiger* ('29), Ferguson is Werper, posing as a friendly scientist. He kidnaps Jane and sells her into white slavery after Tarzan receives a blow on the head, leaving him confused for most of the serial. In the end, however, Ferguson is defeated, Tarzan gets his memory back and the jewels of Opar are saved.

In *Officer 444* ('26), *Haunted Island* ('28), *The Scarlet Arrow* ('28), *Pirates of Panama* ('29), *The Lightning Express* ('30), *The Mystery Trooper* ('31) and *The Sign of the Wolf* ('31) Ferguson had good roles, but in other serials after 1931 he could be counted on as a repugnant criminal or a member of the outlaw contingent.

In Westerns Ferguson was nearly always a "dog heavy" taking orders from a superior. His face was familiar but few people knew his name. He appeared in over 200 films during his career, a big majority of them Westerns. Here are a few more of his credits: *Mile-a-Minute Kendall* ('18), *High Gear Jeffrey* ('21), *The Trail of Vengeance* ('24), *Tentacles of the North* ('26), *The Saddle King* ('29), *Red Fork Range* ('31), *Escape from Devil's Island* ('35), *Dangerous Waters* ('36), *North of the Rio Grande* ('37), *In Early Arizona* ('38), *Saddle Mountain Roundup* ('41), *Jackass Mail* ('42), *Arizona Whirlwind* ('44), *The Virginian* ('46), *The Fabulous Texan* ('48), *The Fighting O'Flynn* ('49), *Dallas* ('50) and *Union Station* ('50).

Ferguson was a truculent rogue who would fight when forced into it, but who preferred to shoot his prey from ambush. He was a member of the unofficial Gower Gulch gang — those cowboys who hung around there each day, just down the block from Columbia, awaiting a call from one of the studios for riders or bit players. He and his fellow reprehensible, shifty and unsavory outlaws always succumbed to the good guys, but they would be back next week ready to dish out more mayhem. They made Saturday matinees a thrilling experience for the young at heart.

Ferguson died in 1971 at age 83 in Los Angeles.

Serials

1920

The Lost City. WB, [15 Chapters] D: E. A. Martin; LP: Juanita Hansen, Frank Clark, George Chesebro, Hector Dion, Irene Wallace, Al Ferguson.

1921

Miracles of the Jungle. WB, [15 Chapters] D: E. A. Martin, James Conway; LP: Ben Hagerty, Wilbur Higby, Al Ferguson, Frederic Peters, Irene Wallace.

1926

Officer 444. Davis/Goodwill, [10 Chapters] D: Francis Ford; LP: Neva Gerber, Ben Wilson, Ruth Royce, Al Ferguson, Jack Mower, Lafe McKee, Phil Ford.

1928

Tarzan, the Mighty. Univ., [15 Chapters] D: Jack Nelson, Ray Taylor; LP: Frank Merrill, Natalie Kingston, Bobby Nelson, Al Ferguson.

Haunted Island. Univ., [10 Chapters] D: Robert F. Hill; LP: Jack Daugherty, Helen Foster, Carl Miller, Al Ferguson, Grace Cunard.

The Scarlet Arrow. Univ., [10 Chapters] D: Ray Taylor; LP: Francis X. Bushman, Jr., Hazel Keener, Edmund Cobb, Al Ferguson, Aileen Gooden.

1929

Tarzan, the Tiger. Univ., [15 Chapters] D: Henry MacRae; LP: Frank Merrill, Natalie Kingston, Al Ferguson, Mademoiselle Kitnou, Sheldon Lewis.

Pirates of Panama. Univ., [12 Chapters] D: Ray Taylor; LP: Jay Wilsey, Al Ferguson, Natalie Kingston, George Ovey, Mary Sutton.

1930

The Lightning Express. Univ., [10 Chapters] D: Henry MacRae; LP: Lane Chandler, Louise Lorraine, Al Ferguson, Greta Granstedt, J. Gordon Russell.

1931

The Mystery Trooper. Syn., [10 Chapters] D: Stuart Paton; LP: Robert Frazer, Buzz Barton, Blanche Mehaffey, Al Ferguson, Charles King.

The Sign of the Wolf. Metropolitan, [10 Chapters] D: Forrest Sheldon, Harry S. Webb; LP: Rex Lease, Virginia Brown Faire, Joe Bonomo, Jack Mower, Al Ferguson.

1932

The Lost Special. Univ., [12 Chapters] D: Henry MacRae; LP: Frank Albertson, Cecilia Parker, Caryl Lincoln, Ernie Nevers.

The Airmail Mystery. Univ., [12 Chapters] D: Ray Taylor; LP: Lucille Browne, James Flavin, Wheeler Oakman, Al Wilson, Nelson McDowell, Water Brennan.

The Hurricane Express. Mascot, [12 Chapters] D: Armand Schaefer, J. P. McGowan; LP: John Wayne, Shirley Grey, Conway Tearle, Tully Marshall.

1933

Clancy of the Mounted. Univ., [12 Chapters] D: Ray Taylor; LP: Tom Tyler, Jacqueline Wells [Julie Bishop], William Desmond, Rosalie Roy, Francis Ford.

The Three Muskeeters. Mascot, [12 Chapters] D: Armand Schaefer, Colbert Clark; LP: Jack Mulhall, Raymond Hatton, Francis X. Bushman, Jr., John Wayne.

1934

The Red Rider. Univ., [15 Chapters] D: Louis Friedlander [Lew Landers]; LP: Buck Jones, Marion Shilling, Walter Miller, Margaret LaMarr, Richard Cramer, Charles French.

Pirate Treasure. Univ., [12 Chapters] D: Ray Taylor; LP: Richard Talmadge, Lucille Lund, Walter Miller, Pat O'Malley, William Desmond, William E. Thorne.

The Vanishing Shadow. Univ., [12 Chapters] D: Louis Friedlander [Lew Landers]; LP: Onslow Stevens, Ada Ince, Walter Miller, James Durkin, William Desmond, Richard Cramer.

1935

The Call of the Savage. Univ., [12 Chapters] D: Louis Friedlander [Lew Landers]; LP: Noah Beery, Jr., Dorothy Short, Harry Woods, Walter Miller, Frederic Mackaye.

Rustlers of Red Dog. Univ., [12 Chapters] D: Louis Friedlander [Lew Landers]; LP: Johnny Mack Brown, Joyce Compton, Walter Miller, Raymond Hatton, Harry Woods.

1936

The Adventures of Frank Merriwell. Univ., [12 Chapters] D: Cliff Smith; LP: Don Briggs, Jean Rogers, John King, Carla Laemmle, Al Bridge, Summer Getchell.

Flash Gordon. Univ., [13 Chapters] D: Frederick Stephani; LP: Larry (Buster) Crabbe, Jean Rogers, Charles Middleton, Frank Shannon, Priscilla Lawson.

1937

Dick Tracy. Rep., [15 Chapters] D: Ray Taylor, Alan James; LP: Ralph Byrd, Kay Hughes, Smiley Burnette, Lee Van Atta, John Picorri, Carleton Young.

1938

The Spider's Web. Col., [15 Chapters] D: Ray Taylor, James W. Horne; LP: Warren Hull, Iris Meredith, Richard Fiske, Kenneth Duncan, Forbes Murray.

1940

Deadwood Dick. Col., [15 Chapters] D: James W. Horne; LP: Don Douglas, Lorna Gray [Adrian Booth], Marin Sais, Charles King, Lane Chandler, Harry Harvey.

1941

White Eagle. Col., [15 Chapters] D: James W. Horne; LP: Buck Jones, Raymond Hatton, Dorothy Fay, James Craven, Jack Ingram, Charles King, Chief Yowlachie.

1942

Captain Midnight. Col., [15 Chapters] D: James W. Horne; LP: Dave O'Brien, Dorothy

Short, James Craven, Sam Edwards, Guy Wilkerson, Bryant Washburn.

Perils of the Royal Mounted. Col., [15 Chapters] D: James W. Horne; LP: Nell O'Day, Robert Stevens [Kellard], Herbert Rawlinson, Kenneth MacDonald, John Elliott.

1944

Captain America. Rep., [15 Chapters] D: John English, Elmer Clifton; LP: Dick Purcell, Lorna Gray [Adrian Booth], Lionel Atwill, Charles Trowbridge.

The Tiger Woman. Rep., [12 Chapters] D: Spencer Bennet, Wallace Grissell; LP: Linda Stirling, Allan Lane, Duncan Renaldo, George J. Lewis.

1946

Son of the Guardsman. Col., [15 Chapters] D: Derwin Abrahams; LP: Robert Shaw, Duan Kennedy, Robert (Buzz) Henry, Jim Diehl, Hugh Prosser, Leonard Penn.

1947

Brick Bradford. Col., [15 Chapters] D: Spencer G. Bennet; LP: Kane Richmond, Rick Vallin, Linda Johnson, Pierre Watkin, Charles Quigley, Jack Ingram.

Son of Zorro. Rep., [13 Chapters] D: Spencer Bennet, Fred C. Brannon; LP: George Turner, Peggy Stewart, Roy Barcroft, Edward Cassidy, Jim Diehl, Charles King.

1948

Tex Granger. Col., [15 Chapters] D: Derwin Abrahams; LP: Robert Kellard, Peggy Stewart, Buzz Henry, Smith Ballew, Jack Ingram, Charles Whitaker, Duke (dog).

1949

Adventures of Sir Galahad. Col., [15 Chapters] D: Spencer G. Bennet; LP: George Reeves, Charles King, William Fawcett, Pat Barton, Hugh Prosser, Lois Hall.

1950

The James Brothers of Missouri. Rep., [12 Chapters] D: Fred C. Brannon; LP: Keith

Richards, Robert Bice, Noel Neill, Roy Barcroft, Marshall Reed, Lee Roberts.

1954

Riding with Buffalo Bill. Col., [15 Chapters] D: Spencer G. Bennet; LP: Marshall Reed, Rick Vallin, Joanne Rio, Shirley Whitney, Jack Ingram, Lee Roberts. Al Ferguson.

1956

Blazing the Overland Trail. Col., [15 Chapters] D: Spencer G. Bennet; LP: Lee Roberts, Dennis Moore, Norma Brooks, Gregg Barton, Don C. Harvey, Reed Howes.

Perils of the Wilderness. Col., [15 Chapters] D: Spencer G. Bennet; LP: Dennis Moore, Richard Emory, Eve Anderson [Evelyn Finley], Kenneth MacDonald, Rick Vallin.

HELEN FERGUSON

Helen Ferguson was among the first crop of Wampas Baby Stars in 1922, at which time she had been in the movies for about eight years. She is thought to have started in films in Chicago in 1914, with the Essanay Studios when she was 13. She was born July 23, 1901, in Decatur, Illinois.

Her career might be dismissed as inconsequential, were it not for the fact that she was leading lady in three good serials and a handful of action features opposite the big guns of the celluloid range.

During her career she played the fetching soubrette opposite Harry Carey, Lefty Flynn, Richard Talmadge, Hobart Bosworth, Bryant Washburn, Frank Mayo and E. K. Lincoln, but it was in the films of Buck Jones and William Russell, Fox stars at the time, that she made her biggest mark in features. She married Russell in 1925, but he died in 1929. In 1930 she married banker Richard L. Hargreaves. They were together until his death from a heart attack in 1941. She never remarried.

There wasn't any particular distinguishing traits about Helen as an actress, but the roles she had really didn't call for any great thespian talent. Nor was she beautiful, although she was attractive enough to get by. There was nothing about her that really stood head-and-shoulders above the competition.

In the first of her serials, she plays op-

posite Jack Mulhall. Pathé's *Wild West* ('25), filmed on the 101 Ranch in Oklahoma, was about a stranded tent show and required a lot of circus paraphernalia, trained animals and wide open spaces. Pathé was on location in Oklahoma for three months.

Casey of the Coast Guard ('26) was also a Pathé serial built around a routine sea yarn about the Coast Guard's attempts to stamp out smuggling, contraband and illegal aliens.

The Fire Fighter ('27) was another average quality serial put out by Universal with Jack Daugherty as firefighter Cap Fallen and Helen as the love of his life.

Among Helen's best features was *Challenge of the Law* ('20), a well-built drama of the Canadian Northwest that starred William Russell. *Burning Daylight* ('20) was another good film for Helen, as was *Just Pals* ('20) starring Buck Jones. In the Harry Carey starrer *The Freeze-Out* ('21), directed by John Ford, she was the schoolmarm for whom Carey cleans up a sin-ridden town. In *Double Dealing* ('23), one of Hoot Gibson's few non–Westerns, Helen is a servant girl who wins his love and helps him to outmaneuver crooks who seek to take his valuable land. In *The Isle of Hope* ('23) she plays a captain's daughter stranded on a Desert Isle with Richard Talmadge, who is searching for buried treasure.

Helen gave up the movies in 1929 to become a stage actress. She appeared in the legitimate theater for four years with only modest success. In 1933 she became a full-time publicist and for the next 34 years she was a powerhouse in Hollywood. Her reputation was that of a perceptive, hard-driving, result-getting force amid the Hollywood tinsel, fiercely protecting her brood against any intruder — even the press.

In 1967 she retired to Palm Desert. In late 1976 she moved to Clearwater, Florida, suffering from a circulatory disorder. On March 14, 1977, she died there at the age of 76.

Serials

1925

Wild West. Pathé, [10 Chapters] D: Robert F. Hill; SP: J. F. Natteford; LP: Jack Mulhall, Helen Ferguson, Ed Burns, Fred Burns, Eddie Phillips, Larry Steers.

1926

Casey of the Coast Guard. Pathé, [10 Chapters] D: Will Nigh; SP: Lewis Allen Browne; P: Schuyler E. Grey; LP: George O'Hara, Helen Ferguson, J. Barney Sherry, Jean Jarvis, Coit Albertson.

1927

The Fire Fighters. Univ., [10 Chapters] D: Jacques Jaccard; S: John A. Moroso; LP: Jack Daugherty, Helen Ferguson, Florence Allen, Robert Irwin, Milt Brown.

ELINOR FIELD

Elinor Field's screen credits covered the years 1920–23. In 1920 she had supporting roles in *The Blue Moon*, *The Kentucky Colonel* and *Once to Every Woman*. The films were easily forgettable. She was the leading lady in *Hearts and Masks* ('20) with Francis McDonald and Lloyd Bacon supporting. In 1921 she was leading lady to David Butler in *Girls Don't Gamble*.

Also in 1921, Elinor had the heroine role opposite Joe Ryan in the Vitagraph serial *The Purple Riders*. Sheriff Joe Ryan and Elinor are sweethearts. Elinor's brother has been accused of murdering their father. Ryan is committed to proving his innocence. The "Purple Rider" bandits are led by the mysterious Purple Shadow. The sheriff finally unravels the mystery of the Purple Riders and captures Myers — the Purple Shadow, the dead man's partner.

In 1922, Elinor was the *Jungle Goddess* in the serial of the same name. The serial tells of an American who returns to Africa in search of a childhood friend.

Col. William Selig began the American movie serial in 1913 with *The Adventures of Kathlyn*, the story of a girl who journeyed to India in search of her missing father. Selig maintained a zoo of wild animals and featured them in any number of jungle epics. Publicity for *Jungle Goddess* stated that 470 of the beasts were used. The serial begins with a balloon disaster in which a little girl falls from the sky and is considered by the tribespeople to be a goddess. She is actually Betty Castleton, the daughter of an English lord. Many years after the mishap, her childhood playmate Ralph Deane (Trueman Van Dyke) goes to Africa to look for her, and the two, once reunited, experience hair-raising adventures before reaching civilization. The picture was well-received in 1922 and reissued in 1929. A great deal of footage from the serial was used in the 1935 serial *Queen of the Jungle*, and some moments in *The Lost City* ('35) match existing *Goddess* film and stills. With its scenes still being watched today as stock footage in other movies, it must be one of the most widely viewed of the silent serials. The serial was produced on a rather lavish scale and contained many elaborate sets.

In 1923, Field appeared in four Westerns. *Blinky* starred Hoot Gibson with Esther Ralston and Field supporting. *Don Quickshot of the Rio Grande* stars Jack Hoxie with Field as the heroine. She also plays the heroine in Hoxie's *The Red Warning* and Hoot Gibson's *Single Handed*. Apparently 1923 was the last year she worked in films.

Serials

1921

The Purple Riders. Vit., [15 Chapters] D: William Bertram; SP: William B. Courtney, Colder Johnstone, Graham Baker; S: Albert E. Smith, Cleveland Moffett; LP: Joe Ryan, Elinor Field, Joseph Rickson, Maude Emory, Ernest Shields.

1922

Jungle Goddess. Export-Import, [15 Chapters] D: James Conway; SP: Frank Dazey, Agnes Johnston; P: William N. Selig; LP: Elinor Field, Truman Van Dyke, Marie Pavis, L. M. Wells, Lafe McKee, Vonda Phelps, Olin Francis.

EVELYN FINLEY

Evelyn Finley has been seen many times in many places, cinematically speaking, without being recognized — even when the viewer was a Western buff familiar with Evelyn's roles as heroine to Monogram's saddle aces in the early 1940s. The reason is that she was primarily a stuntwoman and double, temporarily replacing the leading ladies (and sometimes men) in innumerable films when some sort of action was involved that might endanger the ingenue or which she was not capable of executing.

Evelyn was born in Douglas, Arizona, right on the border. Her dad, who had a ranch out about seven miles from Douglas, had a small herd of registered Holstein dairy cattle. Evelyn spent hours each day riding horses from the time she could toddle down to the barn and get a hired hand to saddle a horse for her. Several moves later, the Finleys were settled in Albuquerque. It was here she attended junior high, high school and college. Although she excelled in athletics, music was her first love. She was in the high school band and orchestra, the university band and orchestra and the Albuquerque Civic Symphony, playing alto horn, French horn, marimbas and solos (and conducting in the absence of the conductor).

When Paramount came to Albuquerque shooting *The Texas Rangers* ('36), director King Vidor noticed her and she was hired as stand-in and double for Jean Parker. A year later, when a Paramount group came to Santa Fe to shoot *The Light That Failed*, Evelyn was hired as a rider, made up like a man, and led the charge into the enemy.

Evelyn decided to migrate to Hollywood and try to really get into the movie business. There she landed the leading lady role in Tex Ritter's *Arizona Frontier* ('40). She was featured in 11 sagebrushers as heroine — one with Ritter, one with Tom Keene, three with the Range Busters, two with

Buster Crabbe and three with Johnny Mack Brown.

In 1956, director Spencer Bennet needed a blonde who could act, drive a team and ride well for a Columbia serial called *Perils of the Wilderness*. He chose Evelyn, put a wig on her and starred her under the name of Eve Anderson in the 15-chapter outdoor drama. Evelyn hoped that, under a new name, producers and directors would see her as an actress, and not as Evelyn Finley, horsewoman. Lee Roberts had a minor role in the serial and he married Evelyn several months later. The marriage lasted about six years.

From 1940 into the '70s, Evelyn stayed busy, doubling leading ladies in both Westerns and dramas, in both "B" and "A" features. Sometimes she played bit parts, as in *Across the Wide Missouri* ('51), *Plymouth Adventure* ('52), *Westward the Women* ('52), *The Diamond Queen* ('53) and *Silverado* ('85), her last film appearance.

On February 17, 1979, she married again, but the marriage was short-lived. Undaunted by this personal disappointment, she continued to work and was apparently happy in her many activities. She easily made the transition to television, working in various Western teleseries.

It was heart failure that took this courageous cowgirl in the end. She died of a heart attack while shopping in Big Bear City, California, on the evening of April 7, 1989. She was 73. A son and daughter survived her.

Serial

1956

Perils of the Wilderness. Col., [15 Chapters] D: Spencer Bennet; P: Sam Katzman; SP: George H. Plympton; LP: Dennis Moore, Richard Emory, Eve Anderson, Kenneth MacDonald, Rick Vallin, Don C. Harvey, Terry Frost, Rex Lease.

RICHARD FISKE

Richard Fiske appeared as a principal player in four Columbia serials and as a supporting player in a number of features and comedy shorts. In *The Spider's Web* ('38) he plays Jackson, a confidante of Warren Hull, who plays "The Spider." In *Flying G-Men* ('39) he is Bart Davis, one of four flying G-men charged with the responsibility of running down a gang of saboteurs. *Overland with Kit Carson* ('39) finds him playing Lt. David Brent, who fights alongside Kit Carson to defeat "Pegleg" (Trevor Bardette) and his gang. His role as Brady was a minor one in *Perils of the Royal Mounted* ('42).

Fiske supported the Three Stooges in five comedy shorts. Probably his best-remembered role was as the sergeant who tries to make soldiers out of the Stooges in *All the World's a Stooge* ('41). He also appeared in comedies with Buster Keaton, Andy Clyde and Charley Chase.

In features he could be seen in *Blondie* ('39), *Blondie Meets the Boss* ('39), *Five Little Peppers at Home* ('40), *The Stranger from Texas* ('40), *The Son of Davey Crockett* ('41), *The Lone Wolf Takes a Chance* ('41), *The Major and the Minor* ('42) and *Valley of the Sun* ('42).

Iris Meredith, Bill Elliott and Richard Fiske (right) in *Overland with Kit Carson* (Columbia, 1939).

Fiske's real name was Thomas Richard Potts, born in Shelton, Washington, on November 20, 1915. His great-aunt, his grandmother and a cousin were all stage actors. He attended the university of Washington and while there decided he wanted to be a movie actor. Hearing that Columbia was seeking an unknown to star in *Golden Boy* ('39), he travelled to Hollywood via bicycle and freight car. He didn't get the role he auditioned for but Columbia did put him under contract.

Fiske was one of the first Hollywood actors to volunteer for service. He joined the army in 1942. We are indebted to writer Bill Cappello for tracking down the facts behind the question, "What ever happened to Richard Fiske?" Fiske, under his real name, was killed in action in LeCroix, France, on August 10, 1944. At the time of his death, he had attained the rank of First Lieutenant and was a member of the 9th Infantry, 2nd Division. He had been awarded the Bronze Star Medal for gallantry in combat, the Oak Leaf Cluster (given because Fiske had earned more than one Bronze Star) and the Purple Heart. He is buried in the Brittany American Military Cemetery at St. James, France.

Serials

1938

The Spider's Web. Col., [15 Chapters] D: Ray Taylor, James W. Horne; LP: Warren Hull, Iris Meredith, Richard Fiske, Kenneth Duncan, Forbes Murray, Marc Lawrence, Charles Wilson, John Tyrrell.

1939

Flying G-Men. Col., [15 Chapters] D: Ray Taylor, James W. Horne; LP: Robert Paige, Richard Fiske, James Craig, Lorna Gray [Adrian Booth], Don Beddoe, Dick Curtis, Tom Steele, Ann Doran, George Chesebro, Nestor Paiva.

Overland with Kit Carson. Col., [15 Chapters] D: Sam Nelson, Norman Deming; LP: Bill Elliott, Iris Meredith, Trevor Bardette, Richard Fiske, Bobby Clark, LeRoy Mason, James Craig, Kenneth MacDonald.

1942

Perils of the Royal Mounted. Col., [15 Chapters] D: James W. Horne; LP: Nell O'Day, Robert Stevens [Kellard], Herbert Rawlinson, Kenneth MacDonald, Richard Fiske, John Elliott, Rick Vallin, George Chesebro, Charles King.

JAMES FLAVIN

James Flavin was born May 14, 1906, in Portland, Maine. After going through rigorous training at West Point, he graduated and then chose, not a military career, but the acting profession. After appearing with several stock companies, he entered films in the early 1930s. As a character actor he specialized in playing tough cops, crack marine sergeants and Mounties. He had a natural adaptability to a uniform, probably the result of his West Point training.

In a career beginning in 1932 and lasting until 1967, Flavin appeared in scores of features and moved very quickly from leading man roles to substantial character parts because of his very distinct projection of maturity and experience — qualities so much required for credibility in those parts.

In 1932 Flavin could be seen in Universal's *McKenna of the Mounted* starring Buck Jones and in his own starring role in *The Airmail Mystery*, Universal's first airplane serial. In the story, the Black Hawk (Wheeler Oakman) plans to steal gold being shipped from a Western mine by airmail. Pilot Bob Lee (Flavin) and Mary Ross (Lucile Browne) and her brother Jimmy (Al Wilson) see that the gold gets through.

Author William C. Cline (*In the Nick of Time*, McFarland, 1984) wrote, "The dogfights depicted in Howard Hughes' *Hell's Angels* left an indelible impression on the minds of moviegoers, and for years to follow served as the only image many people had of this strange new mode of travel. Outside of their potential as war machines, most were conscious of the airplane's usefulness only as an aerial racer or in its growing role as a carrier of mail. Consequently, most stories involving planes and aviators were about speed contests and getting the mail through."

The action in *The Airmail Mystery* ('32) was very good for that time and it helped set the pattern for the other airplane serials and features to follow. Co-starring with Flavin was Lucile Browne, and romance ("real," not "reel") blossomed during production. The two performers married shortly after completing the serial.

A sampling of Flavin's many films follows: *King Kong* ('33), *G-Men* ('35), *West Point of the Air* ('35), *The Buccaneer* ('38), *Mr. Wong in Chinatown* ('39), *The Great Profile* ('40), *Belle Starr* ('41), *Ten Gentlemen*

from West Point ('42), *Air Force* ('43), *Corvette K-225* ('43), *Anchors Aweigh* ('45), *The Big Sleep* ('46), *Nora Prentiss* ('47), *Mighty Joe Young* ('49), *Prison Warden* ('49), *Oh, Susanna* ('51), *Here Come the Marines* ('52), *The Naked Street* ('55), *Francis in the Haunted House* ('56), *Wild Is the Wind* ('57), *Johnny Rocco* ('58) and *In Cold Blood* ('67).

In 1969, Flavin appeared on Broadway in *The Front Page* and just before his death completed the TV special *The Francis Gary Powers Story*, in which he portrayed President Eisenhower.

James Flavin died in 1976. His wife Lucile Browne also died in 1976, two weeks after he did.

Serial

1932

The Airmail Mystery. Univ., [12 Chapters] D: Ray Taylor; S: Ella O'Neill; SP: Basil Dickey, George H. Plympton, George Morgan; LP: James Flavin, Lucile Browne, Wheeler Oakman, Frank S. Hagney, Walter Brennan, Al Wilson.

DICK FORAN

Dick Foran was born June 18, 1910, in Flemington, New Jersey, and was christened John Nicholas Foran. (In some of his films he is billed *Nick* Foran but Warner Bros. changed it to *Dick*.) He received his primary school education in Flemington and then went to Mercersberg Academy and Hunn School to prepare himself for entrance into Princeton University. The rugged actor weighed around 195 pounds, was six feet three and had distinctively curly red hair. His father was New Jersey senator Arthur F. Foran.

At Princeton, Foran majored in geology and played tackle on the football team. He also won letters in baseball, lacrosse and ice hockey.

While at Princeton, Foran twice used his summer vacation to work as an able seaman on freighters plying sea routes to and from the West Indies and South America. Other summers were spent performing in musicals and stock shows.

After graduation from Princeton, he went to work for the Pennsylvania Railroad as a special investigator. One of his assignments took him to Hollywood, where he met Lew Brown, co-owner of a musical comedy producing company. Foran was persuaded to make a screen test. The result was a job at Twentieth Century-Fox. His first film was *Stand Up and Cheer* ('34). It was followed by *Gentlemen Are Born* ('34) and *Shipmates Forever* ('35).

Moving over to Warner Bros., he soon became established as the singing hero of a string of low-budget Westerns. He played leads in many of the studio's minor dramatic features, second leads and supporting roles in major productions. Foran completed 37 features at the Burbank studio. These included *The Petrified Forest*, *Black Legion*, *Moonlight on the Prairie*, *Song of the Saddle*, *Cherokee Strip*, *The Sisters*, *Four Daughters*, *Four Wives*, *The Fighting 69th*, *Four Mothers*, *Blazing Sixes*, *Daughters Courageous* and *Treachery Rides the Range*.

Late in 1938 Foran signed with Universal, where he appeared in *I Stole a Million*, *The House of the Seven Gables*, *My Little Chickadee*, *The Mummy's Hand*, *The Mummy's Tomb*, *Abbott and Costello in the Navy*, *Ride 'Em Cowboy*, *Private Buckaroo* and *Keep 'Em Flying*.

In 1940 Foran starred in *Winners of the*

West, a good Universal Western even though the script was hardly an original one. It was an action-packed tale about the building of the transcontinental railroad and of the interference of the Indians. King Carter, self-styled ruler of the land through which the railroad will pass, plans to block the railroad. He hires Snakeye, a renegade half-breed, to lead the Indians on raids against the construction camps.

In 1941 Universal released *Riders of Death Valley*, billed as the "Million Dollar Super Serial." The serial boasted Dick Foran, Buck Jones, Charles Bickford, Leo Carrillo, Noah Beery, Jr., Lon Chaney, Jr., Jean Brooks, Jack Rockwell, Dick Alexander and other familiar Western players. The Riders were a group of vigilantes seeking to protect California gold miners from claim jumpers and confidence men.

Foran spent several months in 1943–44 appearing on Broadway in *A Connecticut Yankee in King Arthur's Court* and toured in the roadshow production *The Rain Maker*.

In 1948 for director John Ford he played Sgt. Quincannon in *Fort Apache* and sang the sweet, simple "Genevieve." Other films were *El Paso*, *Treasure of Ruby Hills*, *Chicago Confidential*, *The Fearmakers*, *Thundering Jets*, *The Atomic Submarine*, *The Big Night*, *Donovan's Reef* and *Taggart*.

Foran was quite active in television, appearing one or more times on many series.

Foran was married three times. In 1937 he married socialite Ruth Piper Hollingsworth, who had recently won her divorce from William Hollingsworth, a multi-millionaire. The marriage produced two sons but ended in 1941. In 1942 he married Carole Gallagher, an aspiring actress. Two years and one son later, the couple divorced. In 1951 Dick married Susanne Rosser, a minor actress. Although she filed several suits against him, they were apparently still married when he died on August 10, 1979, at age 69. Dick was in Kaiser Permanente Hospital for a blood disorder.

Dick had a fourth son, Thomas, presumably by Susanne.

Serials

1940

Winners of the West. Univ., 1940 [13 Chapters] D: Ford Beebe, Ray Taylor; P: Henry MacRae; SP: George H. Plympton, Basil Dickey, Charles R. Condon; Cam: Jerome Ash, William Sickner, John Hickson; LP: Dick Foran, Anne Nagel, James Craig, Tom Fadden, Charles Stevens.

1941

Riders of Death Valley. Univ., [15 Chapters] D: Ray Taylor, Ford Beebe; S: Oliver Drake; SP: Sherman Lowe, Basil Dickey, George H. Plympton, Jack Connell; P: Henry MacRae; Cam: Jerome Ash, William Sickner; Mus: Charles Previn; LP: Dick Foran, Buck Jones, Leo Carrillo, Charles Bickford, Lon Chaney, Jr., Noah Beery, Jr., Monte Blue, Jean Brooks.

FRANCIS FORD

Francis O'Fearna was born in Portland, Maine, on August 14, 1881 or 1882. He adopted the name "Ford" when he became an actor. Today he is forgotten, or at most a footnote for the lovable, taciturn, grizzly-bearded, amiable coonskin drunks he played as a character actor in his later years.

As a young man, Francis joined the Army during the Spanish-American War but didn't get any further than Chicamauga. Back home he tried several menial jobs before joining the Amelia Bingham Stock Company. However, this job did not offer him much opportunity to act. He joined a road show playing *The Final Settlement* and other plays. There followed a long period of stock in various towns and a vaudeville sketch entitled "The Fall of 64." Tiring of the road grind, he quit and was at liberty when someone from the Centaur Company spotted him cleaning gas lamps on the streets of New York. He was offered $2 a day to fall off ladders in the movies. His first role was as a drummer boy. He left Centaur for the Nestor Company and then worked briefly for Edison.

It was 1909 when Francis joined the Melies Company and traveled with a troupe to San Antonio, where the studio turned out one-reel Westerns weekly. Ford first came to prominence as a wounded Confederate sol-dier coming home to a ruined Vicksburg in *Under the Stars and Bars* ('10). He played Davy Crockett in *The Immortal Alamo* ('11), the last production of the Melies Company to be made in Texas. Ford continued to direct with Melies in California for a while but was directing and acting in Bison Company Westerns in 1912.

Hustler Thomas Ince talked his way into heading up Bison productions on a trial basis when preferred candidates became unavailable. Ford's directorial contributions were concealed by Ince's habit of claiming credit for the work of others. William S. Hart and Ince clashed over this very thing a few years later. There appears to have been friction between Ince and Ford from the beginning. When actress Grace Cunard was fired for preferring Ford's direction to that of Ince, Ford jumped at the chance to work at Universal and took Grace with him. In collaboration with Cunard (writer, leading lady and occasional assistant director), Ford produced approximately 80 films plus four serials from 1913 to 1916. It was one of the best partnerships in movie history. Ford and Cunard were the hardest-working and fastest directors on the Universal lot.

Lucille Love, the Girl of Mystery ('14) was the first Ford-Cunard serial. Its success was awesome. Their second serial, *The Bro-*

ken Coin ('15), was even more popular and it was extended from 15 to 22 chapters. Fifteen hundred newspapers carried novelized stories of the serial week-by-week. One of Ford's biggest pictures was *The Campbell's Are Coming* ('15), a four-reel film which reportedly used 7,000 extras. Jack Holt, John Ford and Duke Worne had small parts and Ford and Cunard headed the cast.

Peg o' the Ring ('16), the third serial, was a circus film which did not do as well as expected. And the fourth serial, *The Purple Mask* ('16), was an expensive failure. After eight more one- and two-reelers, three of which were made after leaving Universal, the team of Ford and Cunard broke up. Ford had married actress Elsie Van Name around 1910. They later separated and Elsie sued for divorce in 1916. The judge threw the suit out of court and in 1917 they were reconciled. Cunard married Joe Moore, a cowboy actor, that year. Ford and wife Elsie had three sons—Phillip, Robert and William. In 1935, Ford married a woman by the name of Mary Anderson. Either Elsie had passed away or the Fords had split.

Ford starred in and directed three more silent serials in partnership with Louis Burston. Elsie wrote the stories. He played a supporting role in six more silent serials and in seven talking serials.

Francis Ford died on September 6, 1953 after a long illness. He was 71. He was survived by three brothers, the widow, two sisters and three sons.

Serials

1914

Lucille Love, Girl of Mystery. Univ., [15 Chapters] D: Francis Ford; SP: Grace Cunard, Francis Ford; S: James Leeley; Spv.: Otis Turner; LP: Grace Cunard, Francis Ford, Harry Schumm, Ernest Shields.

1915

The Broken Coin. Univ., [22 Chapters] D/P: Francis Ford; SP: Grace Cunard; S: Emerson Hough; LP: Grace Cunard, Francis Ford, Harry Schumm, Reese Gardiner, Jack Holt, John Ford.

1916

The Adventures of Peg o' the Ring. Univ., [15 Chapters] D: Francis Ford, Jacques Jaccard; SP: Grace Cunard; LP: Grace Cunard, Francis Ford, Peter Gerald, G. Raymond Nye, John Ford.

The Purple Mask. Univ., [16 Chapters] D: Francis Ford; SP: Grace Cunard, Francis Ford; LP: Grace Cunard, Francis Ford, Joan Hathaway, Peter Gerald, Jerry Ash.

1918

The Silent Mystery. Burston, [15 Chapters] D: Francis Ford; S/SP: Elsie Van Name; P: Louis Burston; LP: Francis Ford, Mae Gaston, Rosemary Theby, Jerry Ash, Elsie Van Name.

1919

The Mystery of 13. Burston, [15 Chapters] D: Francis Ford; SP: John B. Clymer; S: Elsie Van Name; P: Louis Burston; LP: Francis Ford, Peter Gerald, Rosemary Theby, Mark Fenton.

1921

The Great Reward. Burston, [15 Chapters] D: Francis Ford; SP: Elsie Van Name; Cam: Jerome Ash; P: Francis Ford; LP: Francis Ford, Ella Hall, Carl Gerard, Mark Fenton, Valerio Olivo, Phil Ford.

1923

Haunted Valley. Pathé, [15 Chapters] D: George Marshall; LP: Ruth Roland, Jack Daugherty, Larry Steers, Eulalie Jensen, Aaron Edwards, Francis Ford.

The Fighting Skipper. Arrow, [15 Chapters] D: Francis Ford; LP: Peggy O'Day, Jack Perrin, Bill White, Francis Ford, Steve Murphy.

1926

Officer 444. Davis, 1926 [10 Chapters] D: Ben Wilson; LP: Neva Gerber, Ben Wilson, Ruth Royce, Al Ferguson, Lafe McKee, Jack Mower, Phil Ford, Francis Ford, Harry McDonald, Arthur Beckel.

The Power God. Davis/Goodwell, [15 Chapters] D: Ben Wilson, Francis Ford; LP: Ben Wilson, Neva Gerber, Lafe McKee, Allan Garcia, Ruth Royce, William H. Turner, Allan Garcia, Francis Ford, Nelson McDowell, Catherine Kent.

1928

The Chinatown Mystery. Syn., [10 Chapters] D: J. P. McGowan; S: Francis Ford; P: Trem Carr; LP: Joe Bonomo, Ruth Hiatt, Paul Malvern, Francis Ford.

1930

The Jade Box. Univ., [10 Chapters] D: Ray Taylor; LP: Jack Perrin, Louise Lorraine, Monroe Salisbury, Francis Ford, Wilbur Mack.

The Indians Are Coming. Univ., [12 Chapters] D: Henry MacRae; LP: Tim McCoy, Allene Ray, Charles Roy, Edmund Cobb, Francis Ford, Dynamite (dog).

1931

Battling with Buffalo Bill. Univ., [12 Chapters] D: Ray Taylor; LP: Tom Tyler, Rex Bell, Lucile Browne, William Desmond, Francis Ford, Yakima Canutt, Chief Thundercloud, Bud Osborne, Edmund Cobb.

1932

The Lost Special. Univ., [12 Chapters] D: Henry MacRae; LP: Frank Albertson, Cecial Parker, Caryl Lincoln, Ernie Nevers, Francis Ford, Frank Glendon.

Heroes of the West. Univ., [12 Chapters] D: Ray Taylor; LP: Noah Beery, Jr., Diane Duval [Julie Bishop], Onslow Stevens, William Desmond, Francis Ford.

1933

Gordon of Ghost City. Univ., [12 Chapters] D: Ray Taylor; LP: Buck Jones, Madge Bellamy, Walter Miller, Hugh Enfield, William Desmond, Francis Ford.

Clancy of the Mounted. Univ., [12 Chapters] D: Ray Taylor; LP: Tom Tyler, Jacqueline Wells [Julie Bishop], William Desmond, Rosalie Roy, Francis Ford.

1942

King of the Mounties. Rep., [12 Chapters] D: William Witney; LP: Allan Lane, Peggy Drake, Gilbert Emory, Russell Hicks, George Irving, William Vaughn, Francis Ford.

CAROL FORMAN

Carol Forman endeared herself to serial lovers although she never played the heroine in distress. She did it by playing the villainess, striving to do away with the hero and heroine who dared to thwart her fiendish plans. Fu Manchu had nothing on this cunning, deadly, mysterious female. Her bewitching beauty was capable of luring men's souls to the abyss of doom by the light of her wanton eyes, or of lifting their spirits with a companionable twinkling smile. Villainy was her forte. Her sexy, seductive screen persona registered well with audiences, and her talent made it all believable as she achieved serial immortality in the unforgettable roles of "The Black Widow," "Lasca," "The Spider Lady," "Nila" and "Queen Khana." Though she was a titillating (she was voted by serial fans at the time as "the girl with the prettiest rear end in serials"), personable young woman off-screen, and quite unlike the mean women she played, she made a career of being nasty both in serials and features. Television sometimes gave her a reprieve from her dastardly activities, but not often.

Carol (real name: Carolyn Sawls) was born in Epes, Alabama, on June 9. The author's best guess as to the year is 1930, since she appeared in *From This Day Forward* ('46) at age 16. She was raised in Livingston, Alabama. She stood 5'6", had brown eyes and dark brown hair (in later years she dyed it red). She went to Hollywood immediately after graduation from high school and was appearing in a play put on by the Penthouse

Theatre Guild of Pasadena where RKO scouts saw her. Shortly afterwards she was signed to a contract. She quickly fell into the "bad girl" roles for which she became known.

After a year at RKO, Carol became a freelance for the remainder of her career. When a powerful producer insisted that she take the "casting couch" route to retain her RKO contract, the "good girl" ingrained in her surfaced quickly. Carol lost her contract.

Carol turned down more serials than she made, much to her regret later. Her agent thought more serials would hurt her career, as serials were frowned on by the major studios. She could have become a major serial queen had she continued.

Early in her career she married Robert Forman, a man 20 to 25 years her senior. Forman's Air Force career kept him apart from Carol, whose own career ambitions kept her in California, and so the marriage ultimately ended. Carol was later married for six months to a writer and drama critic. It was a marriage on the rebound and a mistake for Carol. Her third and last marriage was to William Dennis, an associate director with Russell Hayden Productions. Dennis had three daughters by a former marriage. When the mother abandoned the children, Carol took them in and raised them as her own, giving up her career for "instant motherhood." For many years the family lived in Texas, then came back to California about 1977 where Dennis had a fatal heart attack.

On February 11, 1984, she was honored by the Hollywood Appreciation Society at the Masquers Club in Hollywood, and in June 1984 she appeared as a guest at the famed Memphis Film Festival.

Carol Forman passed away on July 9, 1997. She had been ill for some time and refused to see anyone but the closest of family and friends during her illness. As the sultry siren of the serials, she will not soon be forgotten by serial lovers. In real life she was a delightfully charming woman, the antithesis of her screen personality.

Serials

1947

The Black Widow. Rep., [13 Chapters] D: Spencer Bennet, Fred C. Brannon; SP: Franklyn Adreon, Basil Dickey, Jesse Duffy, Sol Shor; AP: Mike Frankovich; Cam: John MacBurnie; Mus: Mort Glickman; LP: Carol Forman, Bruce Edwards, Virginia Lindley, Anthony Warde, Ramsay Ames, I. Stanford Jolley.

Brick Bradford. Col., [15 Chapters] D: Spencer Bennet; SP: George H. Plympton, Arthur Hoerl, Lewis Clay; P: Sam Katzman; LP: Kane Richmond, Rick Vallin, Linda Johnson, Pierre Watkin, Carol Forman, Charles Quigley.

1948

Superman. Col., [15 Chapters] D: Spencer Bennet, Thomas Carr; SP: Arthur Hoerl, Lewis Clay, Royal K. Cole; Adapt: George H. Plympton, Joseph F. Poland; Cam: Ira Morgan; Mus: Mischa Bakaleinikoff; LP: Kirk Alyn, Noel Neill, Tommy Bond, Pierre Watkin, Carol Forman, Charles King, Charles Quigley.

1949

Federal Agents vs. Underworld, Inc. Rep., [12 Chapters] D: Fred C.Brannon; SP: Royal K. Cole, Basil Dickey, William Lively, Sol Shor; AP: Franklyn Adreon; Cam: John MacBurnie; Mus: Stanley Wilson; LP: Kirk Alyn, Rosemary LaPlanche, Roy Barcroft, Carol Forman, Bruce Edwards, Tris Coffin, Dave Sharpe.

1952

Blackhawk. Col., [15 Chapters] D: Spencer Bennet,Fred F. Sears, Sherman Lowe; P: Sam Katzman; Cam: William Whitley; Mus: Mischa Bakaleinikoff; LP: Kirk Alyn, Carol Forman, John Crawford, Michael Fox, Don C. Harvey, Rick Vallin, Larry Stewart.

WILLIAM FORREST

William Forrest made a lot of movies in his long career, which started with *The Amazing Mr. Williams* ('39) and ended sometime after 1970.

From the serial addict's viewpoint, Forrest made one important film, Republic's *The Masked Marvel* ('43). In it he plays Martin Crane, insurance executive in league with Sakima, Japanese agent who is sabotaging war industries. The Masked Marvel, whose identity is unknown, leads the fight against Sakima. Though given no screen credit, it is Tom Steele behind the mask.

A sampling of Forrest's credits: *The Lone Wolf Takes a Chance* ('41), *So Proudly We Hail!* ('43), *The Fighting Seabees* ('44), *The Caribbean Mystery* ('45), *The Corpse Came C.O.D.* ('47), *Trapped by Boston Blackie* ('48), *The Girl from Jones Beach* ('49), *I'll See You in My Dreams* ('51), *The Will Rogers Story* ('52), *A Man Called Peter* ('55), *Good Neighbor Sam* ('64) and *Texas Across the River* ('66).

Serial

1943

The Masked Marvel. Rep., [12 Chapters] D: Spencer Bennet; SP: Royal Cole, Ronald Davidson, Basil Dickey, Jesse Duffy, Grant Nelson, George H. Plympton, Joseph Poland; Cam: Reggie Lanning; Mus: Mort Glickman; AP: W. J. O'Sullivan; LP: William Forrest, Louise Currie, Johnny Arthur, David Bacon, Tom Steele, Rod Bacon, Anthony Warde, Kenneth Harlan, Richard Clarke, Bill Healy.

HELEN FOSTER

Helen Foster was born in Independence, Kansas, on May 23, 1907, and educated in Kansas City and at finishing schools in Florida. She entered movies in 1924 and, long after her starring days were over, continued to work as an extra — not necessarily because she needed the money, but simply because she loved to be part of the movies.

Helen played opposite cowboys Buddy Roosevelt, Jack Perrin, Buffalo Bill, Jr., Rex Bell, Fred Thomson, Bob Steele and Hoot Gibson, so she had a pretty good exposure to Western audiences, who found no fault with her. Hindsight would indicate that her career could have lasted longer had she stayed among the silver sage. She might could have done more in serials, too, if her work in Universal's *Haunted Island* ('28) is any indication. She registered well as the sweet, young soubrette in need of protection by the strong, stalwart hero on the white charger, and she should have had a longer career as a prairie maiden.

In 1929 Helen was selected as a Wampas Baby Star. Though she never skyrocketed to fame, she did make some good non–Westerns during her brief fling at stardom in "B" films. Mrs. Wallace Reid used her as the lead in both versions of *The Road to Ruin* ('28, '34) and Rayart and Universal cast her as leading lady in some low-budget melodramas. Later films include *Parachute Nurse* ('42), *Swing Out the Blues* ('44), *Call Northside 777* ('48), *Good Sam* ('48) and *When My Baby Smiles at Me* ('48).

Serial

1928

Haunted Island. Univ., [10 Chapters] D: Robert F. Hill; SP: George Morgan, Karl Krusada; S: Frank R. Adams; LP: Jack Daugherty, Helen Foster, Carl Miller, Al Ferguson, Grace Cunard.

DOUGLAS FOWLEY

Like so many other film and television actors and actresses, Douglas Fowley spent his last days at the Motion Picture and TV Hospital in Woodland Hills, California, there to recall the days that were …

Doug was born Daniel Vincent Fowley in the Bronx, New York, on May 30, 1911. Little is known of his childhood or when and why he became an actor. Evidently he was an aggressive, ebullient youth. His indefatigable efforts got him stage work and a popular nightclub act.

Moving to Los Angeles, Fowley got his first screen job in Spencer Tracy's *The Mad Game* ('33), and for the next four decades he was a Hollywood character actor seldom out of work.

In his one serial, *Chick Carter, Detective* ('46), he plays Rusty Farrell, newspaper reporter who aids Lyle Talbot's Chick Carter investigate the disappearance of a valuable diamond.

A sampling of his films: *Big Brown Eyes* ('36), *One Mile from Heaven* ('37), *Mr. Moto's Gamble* ('38), *Submarine Patrol* ('38), *Dodge City* ('39), *Charlie Chan at Treasure Island* ('39), *Stand By for Action* ('42), *The Glass Alibi* ('46), *The Hucksters* ('47), *Docks of New Orleans* ('48), *Flaxy Martin* ('49), *Armored Car Robbery* ('50), *The Woman is Dangerous* ('52), *A Slight Case of Larceny* ('53), *Rock Pretty Baby* ('56), *Kelly and Me* ('47),

Miracle of the White Stallions ('63), *Barabbas* ('64), *The Good Guys and the Bad Guys* ('69), *Walking Tall* ('73), *Homebodies* ('74), *The White Buffalo* ('77) and *The North Avenue Irregulars* ('79).

On television Fowley played Doc Holliday on the series *The Life and Legend of Wyatt Earp* ('55–61; on *Pistols 'n Petticoats* (1966–67) he played Andrew Hanks, father of Ann Sheridan's character, for 26 episodes. He also appeared on the following Western TV series: *Rin-Tin-Tin, Cheyenne, Death Valley Days, Gunsmoke, Guns of Will Sonnett, Iron Horse, Laredo, The Texan, Trackdown, Wanted Dead or Alive, The Virginian, Bonanza, Daniel Boone, The Quest* and *Kung Fu*.

Fowley's death, from natural causes, came in 1998 at age 86. He had been ill for some time.

Serial

1946

Chick Carter, Detective. Col., [15 Chapters] D: Derwin Abrahams; P: Sam Katzman; Cam: Ira Morgan; Mus: Lee Zahler; LP: Lyle Talbot, Douglas Fowley, Julie Gibson, Pamela Blake, Eddie Acuff, Charles King, Jack Ingram, Frankie Darro.

LUCY FOX

Lucy Fox was Charles Hutchison's leading lady in the Pathé serial *Hurricane Hutch* ('21), dealing with a paper mill, a mortgage and the struggle to obtain a lost formula for

making paper from seaweed. It was fast-moving with many thrills and stunts—as expected in a Hutchison film.

Speed ('22) was the last Pathé serial that

Hutchison would make. As "Speed" Stansbury, Hutchison was accused of taking money from a bank and attempted murder. The man who could prove his alibi had fled to South America; he was a tool of the man responsible for placing Speed in a false light. A chase to bring him back involves Speed in all sorts of hair's-breadth escapes and adventure. By his side again is his girlfriend, Lucy.

In the films *The Money Maniac* ('21), *My Old Kentucky Home* ('22), *Sonny* ('22), *What Fools Men Are* ('22), *Toilers of the Sea* ('23), *The Lone Wolf* ('24), *Miami* ('24) and *The Wise Virgin* ('24), Lucy usually ranks third, fourth or fifth in the cast.

There her trail seems to end.

Serials

1921

Hurricane Hutch. Pathé, [15 Chapters] D: George B. Seitz; S: Charles Hutchison; LP: Charles Hutchison, Lucy Fox, Warner Oland, Diana Day, Joe Bonomo, Spencer Bennet, George Seitz, Frank Redman.

1922

Speed. Pathé, [15 Chapters] D: George B. Seitz; S: Charles Hutchison; SP: Bertram Millhauser; LP: Charles Hutchison, Lucy Fox, John Webb Dillon, Harry Semels, Cecile Bonnel.

ROBERT FRAZER

Robert Frazer (his real name) was born on June 29, 1890, although some references say 1891. The place of his birth was Worcester, Massachusetts. Most readers will not have had the opportunity of seeing the silent films in which he played the lead. He became a stage actor at an early age with small barnstorming repertory companies. He is reputed to have played 400 roles, including 100 roles as Christ. From 1912 until 1921 he combined both stage and screen acting. His silent features included *Robin Hood* ('12), *Rob Roy* ('13), *The Holy City* ('13), *The Feast of Life* ('16), *Partners of the Sunset* ('22), *Jazzmania* ('23), *Men* ('24), *The Foolish Virgin* ('24), *The White Desert* ('25), *Desert Gold* ('26), *The City* ('26), *Black Butterflies* ('27), *City of Purple Dreams* ('28), *Sioux Blood* ('29) and *Frozen Justice* ('29).

Frazer was a brilliant man. In private life he was an inventor and held patents for a helicopter, a talking machine and a gas range. He was also an expert photographer and knew more about radios than anyone in Hollywood. He was a chemist and painted in oils. When sound came to motion pictures, Frazer became a character actor working mostly for independents such as Chesterfield, Invincible, Imperial, Syndicate, Mayfair, Mascot, Ambassador, Majestic, Monogram, Frueler and Republic.

Frazer's sound films included: *Ten Nights in a Barroom* ('31), *The Rainbow Trail* ('32), *White Zombie* ('32), *The Vampire Bat* ('33), *The Trail Beyond* ('34), *Trails of the Wild* ('35), *Black Aces* ('37), *Daughter of the Tong* ('39), *One Man's Law* ('40), *Gunman From Bodie* ('41), *Wagon Tracks West* ('43), *Law Men* ('44) and *Forty Thieves* ('44), his last film.

Frazer died on August 17, 1944, in Los Angeles after a lingering illness. His wife, Mildred Bright, whom he married about 1913, survived him. In Westerns, Frazer was usually the clean-cut villain who had underlings do his dirty work. One expected him to be a crooked lawyer, banker or upstanding citizen. He was a favorite villain in serials.

Robert Frazer (left) and Buck Jones in *Gunman from Bodie* (Monogram, 1941).

Serials

1929

King of the Kongo. Mascot, [10 Chapters] D: Richard Thorpe; LP: Walter Miller, Jacqueline Logan, Richard Tucker, Boris Karloff, Larry Steers.

1931

The Mystery Trooper. Syn., [10 Chapters] D: Stuart Paton; SP: Karl Krusada; S: Flora Douglas; P: Harry Webb, Flora Douglas; Cam: William Nobles, Edward Kull; LP: Robert Frazer, Buzz Barton, Blanche Mehaffey, Al Ferguson.

1933

The Three Musketeers. Mascot, [12 Chapters] D: Armand Schaeffer, Colbert Clark; LP: Jack Mulhall, Raymond Hatton, Francis X. Bushman, Jr., John Wayne, Ruth Hall, Creighton Chaney [Lon Chaney, Jr.[, Robert Frazer, Noah Beery, Jr.

1935

The Miracle Rider. Mascot, [15 Chapters] D: Armand Schaefer, B. Reeves Eason; LP: Tom Mix, Charles Middleton, Joan Gale, Jason Robards, Sr., Robert Kortman, Robert Frazer, Edward Hearn, Tom London, Charles King.

The Fighting Marines. Mascot, [12 Chapters] D: B. Reeves Eason, Joseph Kane; LP: Grant Withers, Adrian Morris, Ann Rutherford, Robert Warwick, Robert Frazer, George J. Lewis, Dick Alexander, Tom London, Victor Potel.

1936

The Black Coin. S&S, [15 Chapters] D: Albert Herman; LP: Ralph Graves, Ruth Mix, Dave O'Brien, Constance Bergen, Matthew Betz, Robert Frazer.

1941

Dick Tracy vs. Crime, Inc. Rep., [15 Chapters] D: William Witney, John English; LP: Ralph Byrd, Jan Wiley, John Davidson, Ralph Morgan, Robert Frazer, Hooper Atchley, Anthony Warde, Walter Miller, John James.

1943

Daredevils of the West. Rep., [12 Chapters] D: John English; LP: Allan Lane, Kay Aldridge, Eddie Acuff, William Haade, Robert Frazer, Ted Adams.

1944

The Tiger Woman. Rep., [12 Chapters] D: Spencer G. Bennet, Wallace Grissell; LP: Allan Lane, Linda Stirling, Duncan Renaldo, George J. Lewis, LeRoy Mason, Robert Frazer, Crane Whitley.

Captain America. Rep., [15 Chapters] D: John English, Elmer Clifton; LP: Dick Purcell, Lorna Gray [Adrian Booth], Lionel Atwill, Charles Trowbridge, Robert Frazer, Russell Hicks, LeRoy Mason, Jay Novello.

TERRY FROST

Terry Frost was a competent "one-take" character actor who appeared in about 150 films and over 200 television shows. His face was familiar to those growing up in the 1940s but few knew his name. As kids we were concentrating on the hero beating the stuffing out of him. A loquacious man off-screen, with a penchant for the bottle, he would, at the drop of a hat, recite poetry or tell a story that enthralled his audience.

Terry was raised in Bemidji, Minnesota. His father was a lumberjack and bootlegger who died when Terry was 15 years old. His mother worked as a seamstress to support he and a sister. An older brother had already left home. As Terry neared his seventeenth birthday, he took off to make his fortune. After riding the rails for two days and nights, he found himself in Butte, Montana, broke and hungry. Since he had delivered papers to whorehouses as a youth, he sought work in a whorehouse reciting poetry. That's right! Reciting poetry, which had been a love of his always. In Spokane, Seattle, Portland, Minneapolis and Los Angeles, he did the same thing. There was no shortage of bawdy houses and this "occupation" occupied him for two years.

He eventually got work in a stock company and met a dancer who was working in an act at a theater. She became his wife and they got into vaudeville, ultimately arriving in Hollywood and a screen career. It was a happy marriage and they had two daughters.

Terry did 16 serials, all of them for either Republic or Columbia. Once he retired he hit the convention trail, becoming a favorite guest star, always ready with a story and a handshake.

Terry Frost died from heart failure in 1993 at age 86.

Serials

1941

Dick Tracy vs. Crime, Inc. Rep., [15 Chapters] D: William Witney, John English; LP: Ralph Byrd, Jan Wiley, John Davidson, Ralph Morgan, Michael Owen.

1943

Batman. Col., [15 Chapters] D: Lambert Hillyer; LP: Lewis Wilson, Douglas Croft, J. Carrol Naish, Shirley Patterson, William C. Austin, Charles Wilson.

1944

Captain America. Rep., [15 Chapters] D: John English, Elmer Clifton; LP: Dick Purcell, Lorna Gray [Adrian Booth], Lionel Atwill, Charles Trowbridge.

1947

The Vigilante. Col., [15 Chapters] D: Wallace Fox; LP: Ralph Byrd, Ramsay Ames, Lyle Talbot, George Offerman, Robert Barron, George Chesebro.

1948

Superman. Col., [15 Chapters] D: Spencer G. Bennet, Thomas Carr; LP: Kirk Alyn, Noel Neill, Tommy Bond, Pierre Watkin, Carol Forman, George Meeker.

Tex Granger. Col., [15 Chapters] D: Derwin Abrahams; LP: Robert Kellard [Stevens], Peggy Stewart, Buzz Henry, Smith Ballew, Jack Ingram, Terry Frost.

1949

Bruce Gentry. Col., [15 Chapters] D: Spencer G. Bennet, Thomas Carr; LP: Tom Neal, Judy Clark, Ralph Hodges, Forrest Taylor, Hugh Prosser, Jack Ingram.

1950

Atom Man vs. Superman. Col., [15 Chapters] D: Spencer G. Bennet; LP: Kirk Alyn, Noel Neill, Lyle Talbot, Tommy Bond, Pierre Watkin, Jack Ingram.

Pirates of the High Seas. Col., [15 Chapters] D: Spencer G. Bennet, Thomas Carr; LP: Buster Crabbe, Lois Hall, Tommy Farrell, Gene Roth, Tristram Coffin.

1951

Government Agents vs. Phantom Legion. Rep., [12 Chapters] D: Fred C. Brannon; LP: Walter Reed, Mary Ellen Kay, Dick Curtis, John Pickard, Pierce Lyden.

1952

Blackhawk. Col., [15 Chapters] D: Spencer G. Bennet, Fred F. Sears; LP: Kirk Alyn, Carol Forman, John Crawford, Michael Fox, Don C. Harvey, Rick Vallin.

1953

Gunfighters of the Northwest. Col., [15 Chapters] Spencer G. Bennet, Charles S. Gould; LP: Jock Mahoney, Clayton Moore, Phyllis Coates, Don C. Harvey.

1954

Riding with Buffalo Bill. Col., [15 Chapters] D: Spencer G. Bennet; LP: Marshall Reed, Rick Vallin, Joanne Rio, Shirley Whitney, Jack Ingram.

1955

King of the Carnival. Rep., [12 Chapters] D: Franklyn Adreon; LP: Harry Lauter, Fran Bennett, Keith Richards, Robert Shayne, Rick Vallin, Gregory Gay.

Adventures of Captain America. Col., [15 Chapters] D: Spencer G. Bennet; LP: John Hart, Rick Vallin, Ben Welden, June Howard, Terry Frost, Lee Roberts.

1956

Perils of the Wilderness. Col., [15 Chapters] D: Spencer G. Bennet; LP: Dennis Moore, Richard Emory, Eve Anderson [Evelyn Finley], Kenneth MacDonald.

MARY FULLER

Film historians are prone to credit Mary Claire Fuller as the serial genre's first exponent and to *What Happened to Mary?* ('12) as either the first serial or, if not that, at least the forerunner of the serial *per se*. Cliffhanger endings were two or three years away, but *What Happened to Mary?* had many of the other characteristics later identified with serials, chief of which was a multitude of thrills in each episode.

Mary Fuller was born into a well-to-do Washington, D.C., family on October 5, 1888. Her father was a lawyer. Her entrance into motion pictures had not been the result of planning and preparation. She was a member of a theatrical troupe that broke up in New York. She thought of motion pictures and passed a fearful tryout at the Vitagraph studio. She was put to work in one-reelers, the first of record being *Leah the Forsaken* ('08) with Maurice Costello. After perhaps a dozen films for Vitagraph, Mary transferred her talents to Edison and made a long series of split- and one-reelers, often with Marc McDermott as leading man. She joined Edison in 1909 and remained there, one of screenland's most popular stars, until 1914. Some of the film titles were *Lochivar* ('09), *Hansel and Gretel* ('09), *The Luck of Roaring Camp* ('10), *Frankenstein* ('10), *The House of the Seven Gables* ('10), *The Star Spangled Banner* ('11), *Three Musketeers* ('11), *Mr. Pickwick's Predicament* ('12), *Mary Stuart* ('13) and *The Viking Queen* ('14). It was during these years that she made *What Happened to Mary?*, *Who Will Marry Mary?* ('13) and *The Active Life of Dolly of the Dailies* ('14).

Tired from overwork and disappointed when Edison failed to promote the *Dolly* series, Mary left Edison to accept a lucrative film contract from Universal in the spring of 1914. She was featured in two- and three-reelers. Matt Moore and Charles Ogle were often cast in her films.

Mary's first five-reeler was *Under Southern Skies* ('15), which featured Charles Ogle, Milton Sills and Paul Panzer. Other five-reelers were *The Huntress of Men* ('16), *Thrown to the Lions* ('16), *The Long Trail* ('16) and *Public be Damned* ('17).

Mary was known as temperamental, intense, emotional and even poetic. She was a shy, retiring person, but respected by those who worked with her. She dropped out of sight in 1917. Her whereabouts became a mystery that many fans and journalists sought to unravel, without success. But in 1924 an enterprising *Photoplay* magazine writer spent three months searching for her. He finally found Mary living in seclusion with her mother in Washington, D.C. We are indebted to author Billy Doyle (*The Ultimate Directory of the Silent Screen Performers*, Scarecrow Press, 1995) for the rest of the story.

A failed romance with a married opera singer, whose wife refused to divorce him, caused Mary to have a complete nervous collapse. Under the care of her mother, Mary spent her days playing her piano and painting. By the mid–20s, the wealth she had accumulated as an actress had been depleted and she emerged from her seclusion in 1926 to try for a film comeback. For the next three years she tried unsuccessfully to re-enter films. Producers showed no interest in the once famous star. Her only recourse was to return to her mother's home, intensely depressed over her financial situation. The death of her mother in 1940 brought on another breakdown and for the next six years her oldest sister cared for her until her mental deterioration necessitated her being placed in St. Elizabeth Hospital on July 1, 1947. There she remained for the next 25 years until she died on December 9, 1973. The hospital, apparently unable to locate any family members, buried the former star in an unmarked grave in the Congressional Cemetery. There were no obituaries for the former actress; she had long been forgotten by her public and actor friends. She was 85 years old when she died from massive pulmonary embolism.

Serials

1912

What Happened to Mary? Edison, [12 Chapters] D: Walter Edwin, J. Searle Dawley; LP: Mary Fuller, Bliss Milford, Marc MacDermott, Charles Ogle.

1913

Who Will Marry Mary? Edison, [6 Chapters] D: Walter Edwin; SP: Ida Damon; LP: Mary Fuller, Ben Wilson, Richard Tucker, Harry Beaumont.

1914

The Active Life of Dolly of the Dailies. Edison, [12 Chapters] D: Walter Edwin; S: Acton Davies; LP: Mary Fuller, Yale Boss, Charles Ogle, Harry Beaumont, Gladys Hulette, Richard Neil, William H. West, Edwin Clark.

GWEN GAZE

Gwen Gaze had the female lead in Columbia's *The Secret of Treasure Island* ('38), surrounded by he-men Don Terry, Grant Withers, Yakima Canutt, Hobart Bosworth, William Farnum, Walter Miller and Dave O'Brien. In such company it is understandable that she didn't get the spotlight. But it was a routine cliffhanger that afforded her reasonable opportunities to roll her eyes and scream.

Gwen also had the leading lady role in *Bar 20 Justice* ('38), *Partners of the Plains* ('38), *West of Pinto Basin* ('40), *Wrangler's Roost* ('41), *Underground Rustlers* ('41) and *Two-Fisted Justice* ('43), and bits in *I Cover the War* ('37), *Women in War* ('40), *Dr. Jekyll and Mr. Hyde* ('41), and *Thumbs Up* ('43).

Serial

1938

The Secret of Treasure Island. Col., 1938 [15 Chapters] D: Elmer Clifton; S: L. Ron Hubbard; P: Jack Fier; Cam: Edward Linden, Herman Schopp; SP: George Rosener, Elmer Clifton, George Merick; Mus: Abe Meyer; LP: Don Terry, Gwen Gaze, Grant Withers, Hobart Bosworth, William Farnum, Dave O'Brien, Walter Miller, Yakima Canutt, Clara Kimball Young.

Walter Miller and Gwen Gaze in *The Secret of Treasure Island* (Columbia, 1938).

CARMELITA GERAGHTY

Very little is known about Carmelita Geraghty, a black-haired beauty who had good roles in such films as *Brand of Cowardice* ('25) as a rancher's beautiful daughter; *Geared to Go* ('24), a taxi cab war story; *High Speed* ('24) as a bank president's daughter in love with a handsome athlete; *Cyclone Cavalier* ('25) as Latin American beauty loved by Reed Howes; *The Last Rail* ('27) as heroine to Tom Mix; *The Slaver* ('27) with Pat O'Malley, an adventure story along the African coast; *Fighting Thru* ('30) as Quennie, a saloon girl swindler who tries to vamp Ken Maynard; *Men Without Law* ('30) as Juanita, to whom Buck Jones is attracted; *The Texas Ranger* ('31) as a ranch owner turned outlaw loved by Buck Jones; and *The Phantom of Santa Fe* ('36) as Lola, a cantina girl. She supported Clara Bow, Corinne Griffith, Joan Bennett, Earle Williams, and other stars, but never got the chance to rise above that level.

Carmelita was born March 22, 1901, in Rushville, Indiana, the daughter of screenwriter Tom Geraghty. She was educated in New York and at Hollywood High School. She was a continuity clerk when director George Fitzmaurice urged her to give up holding the script on the set in favor of playing a part in *To Have and To Hold* ('22). Since her father did not wish her to become an actress, she used a fictitious name while working as an extra until she got a start. Carmelita was good at sexy, sultry roles and was usually cast as a Latin type.

One of Carmelita's best roles was in *The Pleasure Gordon* ('25), filmed in Germany by a British company, and directed by Alfred Hitchcock. Virginia Valli co-starred. It was a strange story that challenged the two actresses and Hitchcock himself.

Carmelita retired from the screen in 1935 after her marriage to Carey Wilson, a film writer and producer at MGM. When he died, she turned her hobby of painting into a profession, working successfully in a style reminiscent of French impressionism. In 1966 she died of a heart attack in New York while en route to her Los Angeles home, after a Paris exhibition of her paintings. She was buried in Hollywood and was survived by a brother, a sister and a stepson.

Serial

1932

The Jungle Mystery. Univ., [12 Chapters] D: Ray Taylor; SP: George H. Plympton, Basil Dickey, George Mason; S: Talbot Mundy; AP: Henry MacRae; LP: Tom Tyler, Cecilia Parker, William Desmond, Philo McCullough, Carmelita Geraghty, Noah Beery, Jr., Sam Baker, Frank Lackteen, Peggy Watts.

NEVA GERBER

Neva Gerber, co-star of 12 serials and a support in one, ranks second only to Allene Ray (16 serials) in the number of chapterplays acted in.* Thus Neva is one of the four top serial actresses of all time; yet, she is one of the least known. For years aficionados asked "Whatever became of Neva Gerber?" Her mysterious background was cloaked in secrecy by the studios and fan magazines alike. For years film historians searched for her origins.

Genevieve Dolores Gerber was born in Chicago, Illinois, on December 8, 1891 (studio publicity departments stated April 3, 1894), the daughter of Samuel N. Gerber, son of a prosperous landholder, cattleman and horse breeder, and Minnie Pulman, daughter of a carpenter. When her parents split, Neva was taken to Los Angeles by her mother and put in the care of the good nuns of the College of the Immaculate Heart.

By 1912 Neva was appearing in one-reel films made by Kalem. On July 22, 1913, the actress married film actor Arthur Millett. The couple separated in 1914 with their divorce finalized in 1920. She became engaged to director William Desmond Taylor in 1915. However, the delay in getting her divorce from Millett (and the director's murder in 1922!) nixed any marriage. Also in 1915, Neva joined the American Film company, where she made a series of predominantly comic films with Webster Campbell.

*Louise Lorraine and Ruth Rowland each made 12 serials, but had no supporting roles. Pearl White and Eileen Sedgwick each made 11 cliffhangers.

Neva Gerber and Jack Perrin in *The Santa Fe Trail* (Arrow, 1923).

In late 1916, Neva appeared in her first serial, *The Great Secret* (released in 1917). It was a small part in support of Francis X. Bushman and Beverly Bayne. Her fortunes rose when she joined Universal. There she made three three-reelers directed by Ben Wilson before co-starring with him in *The Voice on the Wire* ('17), the first of nine serials that she made opposite him. (Their careers were closely linked for the next dozen years.) It was an auspicious beginning — well-made, suspenseful, a good story and, most important, release by Universal, which guaranteed wide exposure.

During the World War I era, Neva was also appearing in features and shorts. Harry Carey evidently liked her as a heroine, for she played opposite him in four Westerns.

Having left Universal in mid–1919, Neva and Wilson made the serial *Trail of the Oc-*

topus ('19) for Hallmark Pictures. It was unusual in that Chapter Six was five reels in length. *The Screaming Shadow* ('20), also for Hallmark, followed shortly.

In 1920, Wilson and Gerber made *The Branded Four* for Select, with an unusual story by George Pyper and Hope Loring. After a couple of adventure features for Berwilla, the two did a serial titled *The Mysterious Pearl* ('21) for Photoplay Serials. After a couple more features, Neva co-starred with Jack Perrin in Arrow's *The Santa Fe Trail* ('23), then made *In the Days of '49* ('24) with Edmund Cobb. Both were undistinguished Western serials. Subsequently she made a series of features for Wild West Films, released by Arrow. Most were with Dick Hatton. The features were cheapies shown in the independent market in second-rate houses.

Neva was reunited with Wilson in a series of Western features for the J. Charles Davis Distributing Company, with Wilson directing as well as acting. These little gems were a notch above the Gerber-Hatton films, though still inexpensive oaters. Their work at Davis culminated in three Gerber-Wilson serials. The first, *The Mystery Box* ('25), was a Western of average quality. The second, *The Power God* ('25), proved to be a good one. The story revolved around a machine that could generate electric power without consuming fuel. Their third cliffhanger, *Officer 444* ('26), was released by Goodwill Pictures after Davis went out of business. Goodwill also took over distribution of *The Power God*. Neither cliffhanger got many bookings, as Goodwill was a small outfit with a poor distribution setup. It was unfortunate that the Davis serials met such an inglorious end, for they were not bad and Neva deserved more recognition for her serial work.

One of the best Western features released by Goodwill in its short history was *The Fighting Stallion* ('26), starring Yakima Canutt and Gerber. Wilson and Gerber had not yet walked the last mile as a screen team. Seven Westerns were made for release by Rayart, namely *Baited Trap*, *The Sheriff's Girl*, *Wolves of the Desert*, *West of the Law*, *The Mystery Brand*, *A Yellow Streak*, *Riders of the West* and *The Range Riders*. All were released during 1926–27.

After several other features, Neva appeared in her last serial, directed by Wilson and co-starring Wally Wales. Neva was billed as Jean Dolores and it was titled *The Voice from the Sky* ('30). It was never copyrighted, never reviewed and evidently had few playdates.

Neva married three times more. She never had any children and she died broke and forgotten on January 2, 1974. She was buried by the state of California as a pauper.

More information appears in Billy Doyle's "Whatever Became of Neva Gerber?" *Classic Images*, No. 284, February 1999; Edward J. Russo and Curtis R. Mann's "Neva Gerber — The Girl from Argenta" *Classic Images*, February 2001; and Buck Rainey's *Those Fabulous Serial Heroines*, Scarecrow Press, 1990.

Serials

1917

The Great Secret. Metro, [18 Chapters] D/P/SP: William Christy Cabanne; LP: Francis X. Bushman, Beverly Bayne, Fred Stanton, Ed Connelly, Neva Gerber.

The Voice on the Wire. Univ., [15 Chapters] D: Stuart Paton; SP: J. Grubb Alexander; S: Eustace Hale Ball; LP: Ben Wilson, Neva Gerber, Joseph W. Girard, Francis McDonald, Ingsley Benedict, Hoot Gibson.

The Mystery Ship. Univ., [18 Chapters] D: Harry Harvey, Francis Ford; S: William Parker, Elaine Pearson; SP: Milton Moore; LP: Neva Gerber, Ben Wilson, Duke Worne, Nigel De Brulier, Neal Hart, Elsie Jane Wilson, Kingsley Benedict.

1919

The Trail of the Octopus. Hallmark, [15 Chapters] D: Duke Worne; S: J. Grubb Alexander; LP: Ben Wilson, Neva Gerber, Howard Crampton, Marie Pavis, William Carroll, William Dyer.

1920

The Screaming Shadow. Hallmark, [15 Chapters] D: Duke Worne, Ben Wilson; S: J. Grubb Alexander, Harvey Gates; P: Frank G. Hall; LP: Ben Wilson, Neva Gerber, Frances Terry, Howard Crampton, Joseph Girard.

The Branded Four. Select, [15 Chapters] D: Duke Worne; S/SP: Hope Loring, George W. Pyper; Spv.: Ben Wilson; LP: Ben Wilson, Neva Gerber, Joseph Girard, William Dyer, Ashton Dearholt, William Carroll, Pansy Porter.

1921

The Mysterious Pearl. Berwilla, [15 Chapters] D: Ben Wilson, Duke Worne; SP: J. Grubb Alexander, Harvey Gates; P: Ben Wilson; LP: Ben Wilson, Neva Gerber, Joseph W. Girard, William Carroll, Ashton Dearholt, Charles King.

1923

The Santa Fe Trail. Arrow, [15 Chapters] D: Ashton Dearholt, Robert Dillon; S/SP: Ben Wilson; P: Neva Gerber; LP: Jack Perrin, Neva Gerber, Elias Bullock, Wilbur McGaugh, Clark Coffey.

1924

Days of '49. Arrow, [15 Chapters] D: Jacques Jaccard, Jay Marchant; S: Karl Coolidge; LP: Neva Gerber, Edmund Cobb, Charles Brinley, Wilbur McGaugh.

1926

The Mystery Box. David/Vital, [10 Chapters] D: Ben Wilson; LP: Ben Wilson, Neva Gerber, Lafe McKee, Robert Walker, Charles Brinley.

The Power God. Davis/Goodwell, [15 Chapters] D: Ben Wilson, Francis Ford; S: Rex Taylor, Harry Haven; P: Ben Wilson; LP: Ben Wilson, Neva Gerber, Lafe McKee, Ruth Royce, Allan Garcia, Francis Ford, Nelson McDowell.

Officer 444. Davis/Goodwell, [10 Chapters] D/SP: Francis Ford; LP: Ben Wilson, Neva Gerber, Ruth Royce, Al Ferguson, Lafe McKee, Jack Mower.

1930

The Voice from the Sky. G.Y.B., [10 Chapters] D/P: Ben Wilson; S: Robert Dillon; Cam: William Nobles; LP: Wally Wales [Hal Taliaferro], Jean Dolores [Neva Gerber], Robert Walker, J. P. Lockney, Al Haskell, Cliff Lyons.

HELEN GIBSON

Born Rose Helen Wenger to Swiss-German parents, Helen Gibson first saw the light of the day on August 27, 1893 (?), in Cleveland, Ohio. The first 17 years of her life were normal for the times, with the usual schooling and then work in a cigar factory. In 1909 she saw her first Wild West show and caught the fever to hit the sawdust trail. When the Miller Brothers 101 Ranch Show opened in St. Louis in April 1910, Helen was one of the equestriennes. The show closed in Venice, California in 1911, leaving the riders unemployed, and Thomas Ince signed them all to work in his pictures.

So it was that Helen entered the world of make-believe. Paid $8 a week, she rode her horse daily from Venice to Topanga Canyon, where the films were being shot. This work led to a $15-a-week job with Kalem, where she worked with Ruth Roland and Mona Darkfeather. The year 1913 found her doing extra work at Selig while drawing $50 a week from Kalem. She continued to ride professionally, switching to rodeo performances as a way to supplement her income.

At Pendleton, Oregon, she met Hoot Gibson, who had won the all-around championship belt in 1912. They started working rodeos together, and that led to marriage in late 1913 or early 1914. Helen Holmes, who had been starring in the *Hazards of Helen* series at Kalem, bowed out of the series for health reasons. Gibson replaced her and completed 71 episodes, bringing the series to an end.

Helen completed a second series titled *A Daughter of Daring* ('17) and moved on to Universal, where she made two-reel railroad sagas at $150 a week.

In 1920 Helen signed with Capital Film Company at $300 a week to continue making two-reel railroad sagas (*Border Watch Dogs, The Broken Brake, The Broken Trestle, Clutch of the Law, The Danger Signal, The Daring Daughter, Flirting with Terror, Ghost of the Canyon, The Golden Star Bandits, The Overland Express, The Payroll Pirates, Trail*

Helen Gibson in *Captured Alive* (Universal, 1918).

of the Rails, *Winning the Franchise* and *Wires Down*). These were all filmed and released in 1920. The company ceased operations later that year and Helen was picked up by Associated Photoplays in 1921 for starring roles in *No Man's Woman* and *The Wolverine*, both five-reelers. Helen sunk a lot of her own money in the making of *No Man's Woman* and went bankrupt in the process. However, *The Wolverine* was good enough that she was put on the payroll at $450 a week to make further films. None materialized because Helen was hospitalized with a burst appendix and peritonitis. Things went downhill thereafter. An independent producer lured her to make a five-reeler but folded without paying her. Helen wound up back in the hospital as a result of some rough riding she did in the film. She had to sell everything she had to pay the bills.

Out of the hospital, she hit the personal appearance trail in conjunction with the showings of *No Man's Woman* and *The Wolverine*. And in 1924 she contracted with Ringling Brothers–Barnum & Bailey Circus to appear in its Wild West Concert. This employment lasted three seasons. In late 1926 she worked the Keith vaudeville circuit with a Hopi Indian act. In 1927, she returned to Hollywood to double other women stars and to do bit parts.

In 1930, she married Clifton Johnson, a retired Navy chief gunner's mate. (The marriage with Hoot Gibson had long since ended.) John was called back to active duty in 1940. Helen continued doing extra parts in movies. After the war, the Johnsons bought a home in Panorama City, where Helen suffered a stroke in 1957. It did not keep her down, however, and she continued doing extra work in movies and television. Helen's last movie of record was *The Man Who Shot*

Liberty Valance ('62). She retired on a $120 monthly motion picture industry pension. She passed away at age 85 from a heart attack in Roseburg, Oregon, in 1977.

Serials

1914

The Hazard of Helen. Kalem, [119 episodes; Gibson starred in the last 71 episodes] D: J. P. McGowan, James Davis; S: W. Scott Darling; LP: Helen Holmes, Helen Gibson, Robyn Adair, Ethel Clisbee, Leo Maloney, Hoot Gibson.

1917

A Daughter of Daring. Kalem, [11 episodes] D: Walter Morton, Scott Sidney, James Davis; SP: Edward Matlock; LP: Helen Gibson, G. A. Williams, George Routh, R. Ryan, Jack Hoxie.

1927

Heroes of the Wild. Mascot, [10 Chapters] D: Harry Webb; LP: Jack Hoxie, Josephine Hill, Joe Bonomo, White Fury (horse), Helen Gibson, Linda Loredo.

1928

The Vanishing West. Mascot, [10 Chapters] D: Richard Thorpe; LP: Jack Perrin, Eileen Sedgwick, Jack Daugherty, Yakima Canutt, Helen Gibson.

The Chinatown Mystery. Syn., [10 Chapters] D: J. P. McGowan; LP: Joe Bonomo, Ruth Hiatt, Paul Malvern, Francis Ford, Helen Gibson.

1938

Flaming Frontiers. Univ., [15 Chapters] D: Ray Taylor, Alan James; LP: Johnny Mack Brown, Eleanor Hansen, Ralph Bowman [John Archer], Charles Middleton.

HOOT GIBSON

Perhaps more than any other cowboy in the history of the movies, Hoot Gibson was the truest son of the West of them all. Born in Tekamah, Nebraska, in 1892. his first job was as a cowboy — the real kind that drifts from ranch to ranch in state after state. It was a rough life and a very lonely one. It's also a life in which most waking hours were in the saddle, and Hoot became famous among his peers for being one of the most daring riders in the West.

As early as 1907, Hoot had been a performer with the Miller Brothers 101 Ranch Show. Prior to winning the world's championship at Pendleton in 1912, he spent a year or two touring with the Dick Stanley-Bud Atkinson Wild West Show as bronc rider and bulldogger.

In 1914 or '15 Hoot was enticed to Uni-

versal Studios. He was soon working in the Harry Carey Westerns and was just getting his career in gear when patriotism engulfed him. He joined the Army, serving throughout World War I in the Tank Corps in France. Back at Universal, he supported Pete Morrison in a group of two-reelers and then was given his own series of two-reelers.

He wasn't as serious and heavy as William S. Hart, nor as high, wide and fancy as Tom Mix. Oh, he could fight it out with the best of them, as anyone who remembers his pictures can tell you. And he could probably outride all of them. Like Mix, he discovered his greatest audiences were kids and took great care in selecting his scripts, emphasizing high scruples and morality and the good life that a hero should lead.

His movies, done mostly at Universal,

did follow a kind of Western drama formula. But they had a unique kind of humor that was missing in most Westerns. And the humor was due mostly to the character of Hoot. The real Gibson was, in a way, the forerunner of the fictional character Destry, a role he never got to play. Certainly he had more cowboy skills and derring-do. But the irony and the humor of the original Destry were very much a part of Gibson.

His characterizations of the cowboy were a little more believable than those of the other fellows. He dared to be human and found a profitable niche in the hearts of Western fandom. He was the first cowboy to emphasize comedy, with himself as the clowning, fumbling, all-thumbs hero who seldom wore a gun and often got knocked on his butt by the heavies.

Beginning in 1921, Hoot was upped to feature Westerns. Sixty-eight Hoot Gibson features were made through 1930, ending with *The Concentratin' Kid*. So profitable had been Hoot's pictures that he was paid around $14,000 a week during his peak years 1924–30. Budgets ran as high as $100,000.

By the time the '30s rolled around, Hoot was winding up his career. He'd become interested in many other things besides movies. Planes had become a consuming hobby, and he was known for a while as "the flying cowboy."

Carl Laemmle did not renew Hoot's contract in 1931 because he was running scared about the feasibility and profitability of sound Westerns. Consequently, Hoot signed for a series with Allied Pictures, making 11 low-budget (but entertaining) Westerns. Three films for First Division followed, then a couple of excellent Westerns for RKO. In 1936 and '37 he made five oaters for Diversion Pictures and had a featured role in the Republic serial *The Painted Stallion* ('37). After that, it was the sawdust arena and odds-and-ends for Hoot.

During the years 1937–39, Hoot headlined several circuses. After making and spending a fortune during his years as a superstar, he needed work to keep the wolf from the door.

Early on Gibson was married to Helen Gibson. In 1922 he married Helen Johnson. They had a daughter, Hoot's only child. In 1930 Helen was granted a divorce and half of Hoot's property. He then married actress Sally Eilers who, in turn, divorced him. In 1942 Hoot married rodeo performer Dorothy Dunstan, who was with him through hard times and a long illness until his death on August 23, 1962, from cancer. He died broke, humble and at peace with God.

Serials

1914

The Hazards of Helen. Kalem, [119 episodes] D: J. P. McGowan, James Davis; LP: Helen Holmes, Helen Gibson, Robyn Adair, Ethel Clisbee, G. A. Williams, Hoot Gibson, Jack Hoxie. [Hoot was featured prominently in Episode No. 26, *The Wild Engine*, in Episode No. 33, *In Danger's Path*, in Episode No. 83, *Treasure Train*, and in several other episodes.]

1917

The Voice on the Wire. Univ., [15 chapters] D:

John Elliott and Hoot Gibson (right) in *Sunset Range* (First Division, 1935).

Stuart Paton; SP: J. Grubb Alexander; S: Eustace Hale Ball; LP: Neva Gerber, Ben Wilson, Francis McDonald, Ernest Shields, Joseph Girard, Frank Tokonaga, Howard Crampton, Hoot Gibson.

1918

A Woman in the Web. Vit., [15 Chapters] D: David Smith, Paul Hurst; SP: Albert E. Smith, Cyrus Townsend Brady; LP: Hedda Nova, J. Frank Glendon, Robert Bradbury, Otto Led-erer, Chet Bryan, Hoot Gibson, Patricia Palmer, George Kuwa.

1937

The Painted Stallion. Rep., [12 Chapters] D: William Witney, Alan James, Ray Taylor, SP: Barry Shipman, Winston Miller; S: Morgan Cox, Ronald Davidson; LP: Ray Corrigan, Hoot Gibson, Jack Perrin, Sammy McKim, Hal Taliaferro, Yakima Canutt, Duncan Renaldo, Julia Thayer.

FRANCES GIFFORD

Frances Gifford's claim to screen immortality was achieved on loanout from Paramount to Republic for a single serial, *Jungle Girl* ('41), a highly lucrative cliffhanger for the San Fernando Valley thrill factory. Ironically, it was not seen by serial aficionados after its initial release period, as the result of an agreement with the Edgar Rice Burroughs estate, until the late 1990s. It is now available on video tape and DVD.

Nonetheless, it was in release long enough to create quite a sensation both with its action and stuntwork and the sensual performance of the title role by Frances Gifford, probably the most beautiful woman ever to hang from a cliff or dash through the jungle astride an elephant. So intense was her allure that even today, 60 years later, her sex appeal comes across.

Jungle Girl was a return to the serial queen concept, with an athletic female assaying the main role and the leading man a secondary one. Republic hit the jackpot when it chose little-known Gifford to play the lead. She was 20, but looked a womanly 25. Besides being stunningly beautiful with her blue eyes and auburn hair, she possessed a fabulous figure, great legs, adequate bosom, was gracefully athletic — and she could act.

Nyoka Meredith, raised in the jungle by her physician father, guarded the treasure trove of diamonds with the Lion Men at the mysterious caves of Nakros in the Lost Land of the Simbula Swamps. Voodoo sacrifices, apes, quicksand, bottomless pits, swamp fires and lion god idols filled each chapter with thrills galore, and plenty of Frances as well.

In their book *The Great Movie Serials*, Jim Harmon and Donald F. Glut wrote: "Nyoka was portrayed by one of the sexiest-looking actresses ever to battle evil on the chapter-play screen, young and dark-haired Frances Gifford. Frances was completely enticing in her tailored, leopard-trimmed jungle minidress and boots. It is not surprising that many fathers, who would otherwise have preferred staying home to listen to Joe DiMaggio going to bat on the radio or to putter around the garden, personally took their children to the theater for 15 consecutive Saturdays to see each installment of *Jungle Girl*."

If the official biography is to be be-

lieved, she was born December 7, 1920, in Long Beach, California. Frances grew into a brilliant child, excelling in school both academically and athletically. In 1936 she won the title "Queen of Long Beach" and got to visit the set of *Come and Get It* at the Goldwyn Studio. There she was noticed by an executive and given a screen test on the spot, followed by a contract. Most of her time was spent in studio acting classes and posing for bathing suit and other cheesecake art. She remained at Goldwyn for six months but got before the camera only once, as a poolside bathing beauty in *Woman Chases Man* ('37). She transferred to RKO, but it was the same old story of being photographed for glamour and fashion stills. Small parts in *New Faces of 1937* ('37), *Stage Door* ('37), *Living on Love* ('37), *Sky Giant* ('38) and *The Big Shot* ('39) comprised her RKO output.

Frances married actor James Dunn on Christmas Day 1938 and temporarily retired. Then in 1939 she had a bit in *Mr. Smith Goes to Washington* ('39) at Columbia and, in 1940, got her first significant part by co-starring with her husband in two quickie films for PRC.

Her marriage was deteriorating and she

had about decided to enroll at UCLA when Walt Disney chose her for the part of a Disney Studio worker in *The Reluctant Dragon* ('41). Paramount executives liked what they saw and put her under contract. In addition to Republic's *Jungle Girl* ('41), Frances did a variety of roles at Paramount, some ten in all. The sagebrush coterie especially liked *Border Vigilantes* ('41), *Tombstone — The Town Too Tough to Die* ('42) and *American Empire* ('42). Her films at Paramount did little to advance her career.

In RKO's *Tarzan Triumphs* ('43), playing Zandra from Polyndra and attired (barely) in a sarong, she was chased by a lion, hunted by cannibals, almost trampled by an elephant and stalked by a wolf — all the while having to evade the pursuit and evil advances of Nazi invaders.

In January, 1943, charging cruelty, she divorced James Dunn. She never remarried.

Following *Tarzan Triumphs*, she joined MGM where she quickly impressed fans and studio alike with her talents in *Our Vines Have Tender Grapes* ('45), *She Went to the Races* ('45), *Little Mister Jim* ('46) and *The Arnelo Affair* ('49).

In 1948 she and Benny Thau, MGM vice-president, were on the way to Lake Arrowhead by car when a bad accident occurred. No one in the two cars was seriously hurt except Frances, who sustained head injuries. The seriousness of those injuries was not known at the time. She seemed to recover. She did not make another until 1950 when she played with Bing Crosby in *Riding*

High ('50). Then there was a three-year lapse before *Sky Commando* ('53), her last film.

By 1958 her head injuries had taken their toll on her and she was admitted to Camarillo State Hospital, a facility specializing in mental disorders. That was the last the public or the press heard of this fine actress for over 25 years.

Frances surfaced in August 1983 when she wrote a letter to *Hollywood Studio Magazine* informing the readers that she was indeed alive and well and living in Pasadena. Colin Briggs, writing in the December 1983 issue of the magazine, reported an interview with Gifford. He wrote that she was involved with many charitable organizations during 1979–1982 in addition to doing volunteer typing for the Pasadena Library.

Frances died in 1994 at age 72 from emphysema in Pasadena.

Serial

1941

Jungle Girl. [15 Chapters] D: William Witney, John English; SP: Ronald Davidson, Norman S. Hall, William Lively, Joseph O'Donnell, Joseph F. Poland, Alfred Batson; Based on Edgar Rice Burroughs' *Jungle Girl*; AP: Hiram S. Brown, Jr.; Cam: Reggie Lanning; Mus: Cy Feuer; LP: Frances Gifford, Tom Neal, Tommy Cook, Eddie Acuff, Trevor Bardette, Gerald Mohr, Frank Lackteen.

EUGENIA GILBERT

Eugenia Gilbert was chosen by Paramount as one of the world's 14 most beautiful women to appear in *The Dressmaker from Paris* ('25). She had already been selected by Rudolph Valentino as the winner of a na-

tional (1923) beauty contest which she had entered as "Miss Los Angeles." She also won a contest for the most beautiful girl in California.

Eugenia was born in East Orange, New

Jersey, and educated at East Orange public schools and at Marlborough Finishing School in Los Angeles. In 1920 she entered films at age 15 through toe dancing in musical comedy productions. Early on, she appeared in Mack Sennett comedies. It was in 1921 that she appeared in her first Western as a supporting player. In 1924 she played the heroine to Jack Hoxie in *The Back Trail.*

Working at various studios she played in films with Earle Williams, Richard Talmadge, Cleo Madison, Adolphe Menjou, Harry Langdon, Shirley Mason, Conrad Nagel and Ben Turpin. In 1926 she became a full-fledged cowgirl with heroine leads in five leather-burners, followed by four in 1927, five in 1928 and one in 1929. The cowboys she gazed up at were Bob Custer, Art Acord, Leo Maloney, Don Coleman, Hoot Gibson, Ken Maynard and Tom Tyler. She seemed suited, emotionally and physically, for the rigors of Western and serial filmmaking, and audiences of these genres readily accepted her as "one of their own."

Eugenia's first of five cliffhangers, *Melting Millions,* was made in 1927. In it she supported Allene Ray and Walter Miller. But she had the feminine lead opposite Miller in *The Police Reporter* ('28) and *The Mysterious Airman* ('28), and co-starred with Cullen Landis in *The Crimson Flash* ('27) and with Frank Merrill in *Perils of the Jungle* ('27).

Eugenia had dark blue eyes, auburn hair, weighed around 120–125 pounds, and stood 5'4½". She was an accomplished singer, dancer, equestrienne and all-around athlete who liked to bike, ride horses and go hunting whenever the opportunity arose.

With the coming of sound, she drifted out of movies, becoming a "lost player." Her last film was *Courtin' Wildcats* ('29) with Hoot Gibson.

Serials

1927

The Crimson Flash. Pathé, 1927 [10 Chapters] D: Arch B. Heath; SP: Paul Fairfax Fuller; S: George Arthur Gray; LP: Cullen Landis, Eugenia Gilbert, Tom Holding, J. Barney Sherry, Walter P. Lewis, Ivan Linow, Mary Gardiner.

Melting Millions. Pathé, [10 Chapters] D: Spencer G. Bennet; S: Joseph Anthony Roach; LP: Allene Ray, Walter Miller, E. H. Calvert, William Norton Bailey, Eugenia Gilbert, Frank Lackteen, John J. Richardson, George Kuwa.

Perils of the Jungle. Artclass, [10 Chapters] D: Jack Nelson; S: H. P. Crist; LP: Eugenia Gilbert, Frank Merrill, Albert J. Smith, Harry Belmore, Bobby Nelson, Milburn Moranti, Will Herman, Walter Macy, Frank Huttee.

1928

The Police Reporter. Artclass, [10 Chapters] D: Jack Nelson; S: Arthur B. Reeve; Spv.: George M. Merrick; LP: Walter Miller, Eugenia Gilbert, William A. Lowery, Robert Belcher, Kenneth Duncan.

The Mysterious Airman. Artclass, [10 Chapters] D: Harry Revier; SP: Arthur B. Reeve; LP: Walter Miller, Eugenia Gilbert, Robert Walker, Eugene Burr, Dorothy Talcott, James A. Fitzgerald, C. H. Allen, Ray Childs, Hugh Blair.

JOSEPH GIRARD

Joseph Girard entered films in the teens and worked through the '20s into the '40s. He was born in 1881 and died in 1949 at age 68. His earliest film credit is *Conscience* ('15); his last, *Heavenly Days* ('44). His other films include: *Thrown to the Lions* ('16), *The Lair of the Wolf* ('17), *The Kaiser, the Beast of Berlin* ('18), *Chain Lightning* ('22), *We're in the Navy Now* ('26), *King of the Rodeo* ('29), *Desert Vengeance* ('31), *The Texas Bad Man* ('32), *The Ivory-Handled Gun* ('35), *Aces and Eights* ('36), *Frontier Scout* ('38) and *Zenobia* ('39).

Girard played in over 100 features plus 22 serials. In the silent serials Girard was usually listed third in the cast credits, behind the hero and heroine, whereas in sound serials his parts were smaller. The same is true of the silent features in which he was a principal player. The decade of the '30s was a busy one for Girard, who was an effective support in Westerns with Ken Maynard, Buck Jones, Tom Mix, Rex Bell, Tex Ritter and other saddle busters.

Girard's roles varied. In *The Voice on the Wire* ('17) he is a scientist seeking revenge; in *The Brass Bullet* ('18) he is the heroine's villainous uncle seeking a hidden gold cache willed to his niece; he is Paul Kazloff, evil scientist, in *The Mysterious Pearl* ('21); in *The Blue Fox* ('21) he portrays Hawk Baxter, intent on stealing the map to a valuable mine

Joseph Girard (left) and Warren Hull in *The Spider Returns* (Columbia, 1941).

in the far North; *Nan of the North* ('22) found him as the head of a gang out to obtain a powerful substance found in a meteorite. He is a crooked investor in *The Eagle's Talons* ('28) and a ship's doctor in *The Secret of Treasure Island* ('35). In *The Green Archer* ('40) he plays a police inspector; in *Deadwood Dick* ('40) he's a judge; in *The Spider Returns* ('41) he is Commissioner Kirk; and in *Captain Midnight* ('42) he plays Major Steele of the military.

Serials

1915

The Voice on the Wire. Univ., [15 Chapters] D: Stuart Paton; SP: J. Grubb Alexander; S: Eustache Hale Ball; LP: Ben Wilson, Neva Gerber, Joseph W. Girard, Francis McDonald, Kingsley Benedict, Nigel De Brulier.

1918

The Brass Bullet. Univ., [18 Chapters] D: Ben Wilson; SP: Walter Woods; S: Frank R. Adams; P: Ben Wilson; LP: Juanita Hansen, Jack Mulhall, Joseph W. Girard, Helen Wright, Charles Hill Mailes.

1919

The Midnight Man. Univ., [18 Chapters] D: James W. Horne; SP: Harvey Gates; S: James W. Horne, Frank Howard Clark; LP: James J. Corbett, Kathleen O'Connor, Joseph W. Girard, Frank Jonasson, Joseph Singleton.

1920

The Screaming Shadow. Hallmark, [15 Chapters] D: Duke Worne, Ben Wilson; S: J. Grubb Alexander; LP: Ben Wilson, Neva Gerber, Frances Terry, Howard Crampton, Joseph Girard, William Dyer, William Carroll.

The Fatal Sign. Arrow, [15 Chapters] D: Stuart Paton; SP: Bertram Millhauser; LP: Claire Anderson, Harry Carter, Leo Maloney, Joseph Girard, Boyd Irwin.

The Branded Four. Select, [15 Chapters] D: Duke Worne; S/SP: Hope Loring, George W. Pyper; LP: Ben Wilson, Neva Gerber, Joseph Girard, Ashton Dearholt, Pansy Porter.

1921

The Mysterious Pearl. Photoplay, [15 Chapters] D: Ben Wilson, Duke Worne; SP: J. Grubb Alexander, Harvey Gates; LP: Ben Wilson, Neva Gerber, Joseph W. Girard, William Carroll, Charles King.

The Blue Fox. Arrow, [15 Chapters] D: Duke Worne; LP: Ann Little, J. Morris Foster, Joseph W. Girard, Charles Mason.

1922

Nan of the North. Arrow, [15 Chapters] D: Duke Worne; S/SP: Karl Coolidge; P: Ben Wilson; LP: Ann Little, Leonard Clapham [Tom London], Joseph W. Girard, Hal Wilson, J. Morris Foster.

Perils of the Yukon. Univ., [15 Chapters] D: Perry Vekroff, Jay Marchant, J. P. McGowan; S/SP: George H. Plympton, George Morgan; LP: William Desmond, Laura LaPlante, Fred Stanton, Fred Kohler, Joseph Girard, Joe McDermott.

1923

The Eagle's Talons. Univ., [15 Chapters] D: Duke Worne; SP: Anthony Coldeway, Jefferson Moffitt, Bertram Milhauser; LP: Ann Little, Fred Thomson, Al Wilson, Herbert Fortier, Joseph Girard, Edith Stayart.

1924

Wolves of the North. Univ., [10 Chapters] D: William Duncan; SP: Frank H. Clark; LP: William Duncan, Edith Johnson, Joseph W. Girard, Clark Comstock, Esther Ralston.

1932

The Hurricane Express. Mascot, [12 Chapters] D: Armand Schaefer, J. P. McGowan; P: Nat Levine; SP: George Morgan, J. P. McGowan; Cam: Ernest Miller, Carl Webster; LP: John Wayne, Shirley Grey, Conway Tearle, Tully Marshall, Joseph Girard.

1936

The Clutching Hand. S & S, [15 Chapters] D: Albert Herman; Spv.: Louis Weiss; SP: Louis D'Usseau, Dallas Fitzgerald; Mus: Lee Zahler; Cam: James Diamond; LP: Jack Mulhall, Ruth

Mix, Marion Shilling, Rex Lease, Robert Frazer.

1937

Wild West Days. Univ., [13 Chapters] D: Ford Beebe, Cliff Smith; LP: Johnny Mack Brown, Lynn Gilbert, Robert Kortman, George Shiller, Frank Yaconelli.

S O S Coast Guard. Rep., [12 Chapters] D: William Witney, Alan James; SP: Barry Shipman, Franklyn Adreon; LP: Ralph Byrd, Bela Lugosi, Maxine Doyle, Richard Alexander, Herbert Rawlinson, George Chesebro.

1938

The Secret of Treasure Island. Col., [15 Chapters] D: Elmer Clifton; SP: George Rosener, Elmer Clifton,George Merrick; P: Jack Fier; Mus: Abe Meyer; Cam: Edward Linden, Herman Schopp; LP: Don Terry, Gwen Gaze, Grant Withers, Hobart Bosworth, Walter Miller, Dave O'Brien, Yakima Canutt, Joseph Girard.

1940

The Green Archer. Col., [15 Chapters] D: James W. Horne; P: Larry Darmour; S: Edgar Wallace; Mus: Lee Zahler; Cam: James S. Brown, Jr.; LP: Victor Jory, Iris Meredith, James Craven, Richard Fiske, Dorothy Fay, Jack Ingram, Joseph Girard, Forrest Taylor.

Deadwood Dick. Col., [15 Chapters] D: James W. Horne; P: Larry darmour; SP: Wyndham Gittens, Morgan B. Cox, George Morgan, John Cutting; LP: Don Douglas, Lorna Gray [Adrian Booth], Lane Chandler, Marin Sais, Harry Harvey, Charles King.

1941

The Spider Returns. Col., [15 Chapters] D: James W. Horne; SP: George H. Plympton, Jesse A. Duffy; P: Larry Darmour; Cam: James S. Brown, Jr.; Mus: Lee Zahler; LP: Warren Hull, Mary Ainslee, Dave O'Brien, Joseph Girard, Kenneth Duncan, Corbet Harris.

1942

Captain Midnight. Col., [15 Chapters] D: James W. Horne; P: Larry Darmour; SP: George H. Plympton, Basil Dickey, Jack Stanley, Wyndham Gittens; LP: Dave O'Brien, Dorothy Short, James Craven, Luana Walters, Guy Wilkerson, Joseph Girard, Bryant Washburn.

BRUCE GORDON

Bruce Gordon was an enigma as well as a serial leading man. The author has found no biographical information on him. Two serials with Ruth Roland, and one each with Allene Ray and Anita Stewart, all made by Pathé, established him as an action hero in the 1920s. He also supported Gladys McConnell and Hugh Allan in two other Pathé serials.

Bruce was active throughout the 1920s in "B" films, sometimes playing the lead, sometimes a lesser role. For whatever reason, he did not make the transition to talking pictures.

Serials

1922

The Timber Queen. Pathé, [15 Chapters] D: Fred Jackson; SP: Beatrice Millhauser; S: Val Cleveland; P: Hal Roach; LP: Ruth Roland, Bruce Gordon, Val Paul, Leo Willis, Frank Lackteen.

1923

Ruth of the Range. Pathé, [15 Chapters] D: Ernest Warde, W. S. Van Dyke, Frank Leon Smith; SP: Frank Leon Smith, Gilson Willets; P: M. C. Levee; LP: Ruth Roland, Bruce Gordon, Ernest C. Warde, Lorimer Johnson.

Pete Morrison (left), an unidentified actress and Bruce Gordon in *Bucking the Truth* (Universal, 1926).

1924

The Fortieth Door. Pathé, [10 Chapters] D: George B. Seitz; SP: Frank Leon Smith; S: Mary Hastings Bradley; Cam: Vernor Walker; P: C. W. Paton; LP: Allene Ray, Bruce Gordon, Frank Lackteen, Anna May Wong, Lillian Gale.

1926

Dog Detective Series. Chesterfield, [12 Episodes] D: Ernest Van Pelt; LP: Fearless (dog), Jack Mower, Bruce Gordon, Grace Cunard.

1927

The Isle of Sunken Gold. Mascot, [10 Chapters] D: Harry Webb; P: Nat Levine; LP: Anita Stewart, Bruce Gordon, Duke Kahanomoku, Evangeline Russell.

1928

The Tiger's Shadow. Pathé, [10 Chapters] D: Spencer G. Bennet; SP: George Gray; LP: Gladys McConnell, Hugh Allan, Frank Lackteen, Edward Cecil, Bruce Gordon.

1929

The Fire Detective. Pathé, [10 Chapters] D: Spencer G. Bennet, Thomas Storey; LP: Gladys McConnell, Hugh Allan, Leo Maloney, Frank Lackteen, Bruce Gordon.

HAROLD (RED) GRANGE

Harold (Red) Grange was born on June 13, 1903, in Forksville, Pennsylvania, the son of a lumberjack. His mother died when Harold was five years old and his father moved with his four youngsters to Wheaton, west of Chicago.

In high school, Harold scored 75 touchdowns and lettered in track, baseball and basketball. At the University of Illinois he raised college football to new levels of excitement with his quicksilver, broken-field running. Even Americans who hadn't cared about the game became aware of who No. 77 was and what he could do.

In 20 games over three seasons at Illinois he scored 31 touchdowns and ran for 3,637 yards. Grantland Rice called him "The Galloping Ghost." Each of these three years at Illinois he was named All-American, then an uncommon feat.

When he signed a contract with the Chicago Bears in 1925 after finishing his senior season with the Illini, the publicity attendant gave professional football a cachet of respectability it had never before enjoyed.

Grange was one of the first college athletes to capitalize on his popularity with off-field endorsements. He had an agent while he was still a student. He announced in the locker room after his final game in 1925 that he was leaving college immediately to turn pro. And within weeks, playing for the Chicago Bears, he became one of the highest paid athletes in America.

Compared to his college days, his pro career was unspectacular, but his presence

Harold Grange (carrying the ball) in *The Galloping Ghost* (Mascot, 1931).

filled stadiums, and he was credited with igniting interest in professional football, which in 1925 was only six years old. The Bears were drawing an average of 6,000 fans when Grange joined the team. In his first game with them, they drew 36,000, at the time the largest crowd to see a pro football game.

In the weeks after he decided to quit school, his agent, C. C. "Cash and Carry" Pyle was raking in money with endorsement contracts for Grange. In one frenzied weekend in New York in December 1925, Grange made $400,000 by playing football and agreeing to endorse a brand of milk (he contended that it helped him become a great running back), sweaters and a cigarette that he said he would smoke if he ever decided to take up smoking.

He played his last football game, a preseason contest, against the New York Giants in 1935. Even after he retired, his impact on the game was so great he was in constant demand for speeches, public appearances and magazine articles.

He became a successful businessman with an insurance company in Chicago. And in the early days of television he was both a football color commentator and a play-by-play announcer.

Grange's pace told on him physically and he suffered a heart attack. When he recovered, he and his wife moved to Miami and several years later to Indian Lake Estates, south of Orlando, Florida.

Grange died of complications from pneumonia in a hospital at Lake Wales, Florida, according to Margaret Grange, his wife of 49 years. His condition was diagnosed as Parkinson's disease a year earlier. He had been hospitalized for several months and on the critical list for a week.

Death came on January 28, 1991. He was 87.

Grange acted in two features and a serial during his football-playing days. Capitalizing on his name, R-C Pictures starred Grange in *One Minute to Play* ('26) opposite Mary McAlliston. Red wants to attend Claxton College but his father insists that he go to Barlow. On the train he meets Sally Rogers. He goes on to Barlow and eventually is persuaded to play football even though he jeopardizes a large grant to the college from his father. His dad is finally won over and, with one minute to play, Red wins the game.

R-C Pictures followed up with *A Racing Romeo* ('27). Red has misadventures along the way but winds up winning the motor sweepstakes against a champion driver, and he also wins back Sally (Jobyna Ralston) after arousing her jealousy by flirting with another girl.

Mascot Pictures wisely hired Grange and put him into the serial *The Galloping Ghost* ('31). Dorothy Gulliver, Francis X. Bushman, Jr., Walter Miller, Gwen Lee and Theodore Lorch headed up the supporting cast. In the story, Red is wrongly accused of accepting a bribe from a gambling ring and dismissed from Clay College. He maintains his silence to protect his friend and teammate, Buddy Courtland (Bushman). Red fails to convince Buddy's sister, Barbara (Gulliver), of his innocence and is accused by the police of killing another teammate. Following up various clues, Red finally ferrets out the leader of the gambling ring and clears himself of all charges.

Serial

1931

The Galloping Ghost. Mascot, [12 Chapters] D: B. Reeves Eason; P: Nat Levine; LP: Harold (Red) Grange, Dorothy Gulliver, Walter Miller, Gwen Lee, Francis X. Bushman, Jr., Theodore Lorch.

GRETA GRANSTEDT

Greta Granstedt, the petite blond-haired, green-eyed actress born Irene Granstedt in Malmo, Sweden, may not have attained exceptional heights as an actress, but neither her career nor her personal life were ever dull — most assuredly, her personal life!

Just who is Greta Granstedt? No doubt the name is unfamiliar to most moviegoers. Action fans may remember her as the feminine lead in Buck Jones' *McKenna of the Mounted* ('32) or as the maiden in distress in the serials *The Lightning Express* ('30) and *The Devil Horse* ('32). In these oaters, she was a nice-looking heroine providing optical relief without being greatly overworked. Usually, though, she played supporting parts rather than essaying the lead role herself. One of her best early performances was her portrayal of the hard-boiled slum girl in *Street Scene* ('31).

Granstedt was three years old when her family came to this country and settled in Kansas. Eventually they moved to Mountain View, California, and from there to San Francisco. In 1922 the fates seemed to decree that life for Greta (or Irene, as she was known then) was not to be commonplace. She was 14 years old and the typical "flapper" of Mountain View. One night she clutched a revolver and stood in the shadows of a little church waiting for her 16-year-old sweetheart who had spurned her and taken another girl to a church social.

Soon the boy came from the church and there was a quarrel followed by a shot. The boy was seriously wounded. Greta was taken to jail in San Jose. If the boy died, she was to be tried for murder. After many weeks, the boy recovered, and Greta was eventually released from jail, the law holding that the shooting was not premeditated. However, the judge ruled that she was to be banished for life from Mountain View.

Two years later she was married to a young man from Redwood City, but the marriage was annulled because she was only 16. Then came a third romance in which she married an artist in the San Francisco Bohemian quarter. When this marriage failed, she gravitated to the stage. She had been stage struck for some time and had even played hookey from school to get a job as usher at the Columbia Theatre in San Francisco. There she took every opportunity to study the acting technique of the stage players who came to the Coast in Broadway successes. She made her debut on stage and screen almost simultaneously.

While appearing in her first Los Angeles play, *From Hell Came a Lady* with Joseph Schildkraut, she was tapped by James Cruze for a role in *Excess Baggage* ('28). Thereafter she worked both on stage and in movies. Stage productions in which she appeared include *The Bad Woman*, *Troupers*, *Hotel Rates*, *House of the Left Hand*, *Wild Birds*, *Bad Babies* and *Ex Mistress*.

While traveling in Europe in 1932 she played the lead in the London stage production of *Clear all Wires*, and during the winter of 1933 she worked as a dancer at the Palm Island Club in Miami. In November 1933 she married Ramon Ramos, a New York musician, in rites performed by New York Mayor John P. O'Brien, with Nancy Carroll and Xavier Cugat acting as witnesses. The marriage ended in divorce 18 months later, at which time she married Marcel Olis, an artist she had met in Florida. At some point this marriage, too, ended, for *The Daily Mirror* of July 24, 1940, carried a story of her filing a suit of divorce from Max DeVega, a scenic artist.

For a number of years Greta continued her stage work, both on Broadway and elsewhere, when not engaged in film work. *Glory's Child*, *Thirsty Soil*, *Sexes and Seven* and *Tomorrow's Harvest* are just a few of her successes.

Some of Granstedt's other films include *Night World* ('32), *Crime Without Passion* ('34), *There Goes My Heart* ('38), *The Beast of Berlin* ('39), *I Escaped from the Gestapo* ('43), *The Gangster* ('47), *Samson and Delilah* ('49), *The Enforcer* ('51), *The Greatest Show on Earth* ('52) and *The Return of Dracula* ('58).

Serials

1930

The Lightning Express. Univ., [10 Chapters] D: Henry MacRae; S: Frank H. Spearman; LP: Lane Chandler, Louise Lorraine, Al Ferguson, Greta Granstedt.

1932

The Devil Horse. Mascot, [12 Chapters] D: Otto Brower, Yakima Canutt; P: Nat Levine; SP: George Morgan, Barney Sarecky, George Plympton, Wyndham Gittens; Cam: Ernest Miller, Carl Webster, Victor Schurich; LP: Harry Carey, Frankie Darro, Greta Granstedt, Noah Beery, Sr., Al Bridge, Jack Mower.

RALPH GRAVES

The flunking of German and physics at a Cleveland High school were directly responsible for Ralph Graves going into pictures. He had been disgusted with high school and finally determined not to carve the career that his father, a wealthy steel manufacturer of Cleveland, had cut out for him. His father wanted him to go to summer school to make up the credits he lost, but Ralph said "nix," got on a train and went to see his uncle in Chicago. He got caught in a jam of motion picture conventioneers at the Coliseum.

It happened that a newspaper woman (Louella Parsons), who was a friend of Ralph's, gave him a letter of recommendation to the Essanay Studio in Chicago, where he was rewarded with extra work at $3 a day. In a month or so he graduated to bits in various pictures at $2 a day more salary, and at length a good part in Mary MacLane's tragedy, *Men Who Have Made Love to Me* ('18).

It was shortly after the Essanay engagement, while he was playing the juvenile lead with Kitty Gordon in *Tinsel* ('18) at the World Studio in Fort Lee, New Jersey, that Maurice Tourneur first hired Graves. The picture was *Sporting Life* ('18) and the part was Graves' first noteworthy one. Then he signed with Universal, where he played with Mae Murray in two dramas of the inner soul, *What Am I Bid?* and *The Scarlet Shadow* ('19).

He returned to the Tourneur fold in *The White Heather* ('19), later going to Paramount to play opposite Vivian Martin. Among his other silent films were *Her Kingdom of Dreams* ('19), *Polly with a Past* ('20), *Dream Street* ('21), *Kindred of the Dust* ('22), *The Extra Girl* ('23), *Blarney* ('26) and *The Kid Sister* ('27).

Graves was signed by Columbia in 1928 and was teamed with Jack Holt and Dorothy Revier in the blockbuster *Submarine* ('28), his first sound film. Graves and Holt were re-teamed in *Flight* ('29), *Hell's Island* ('30), *Vengeance* ('30), *Dirigible* ('31) and *War Correspondent* ('32), all proving to be winners for Columbia. Graves co-starred with Barbara Stanwyck in *Ladies of Leisure* ('30), directed by Frank Capra. Graves also co-starred with Helen Costello in the Mascot serial *The Fatal Warning* ('29). He plays the part of a detective who helps Costello solve

Fay Wray, Ralph Graves (center) and Jack Holt in *Dirigible* (Columbia, 1931).

the mystery of the disappearance of her father, who has been whisked away by unknown assailants.

Swinging over to MGM, he became an assistant to Irving Thalberg and also produced and acted in films. Following Thalberg's death, Graves started to concentrate on writing for the screen as well as continuing to act.

In 1936, Graves was a principal in the Stage & Screen cliffhanger *The Black Coin.* Graves and Ruth Mix are Secret Service agents involved in a smuggling operation and a search for buried gold. Opposing them is the *Clutching Hand* and his repugnant followers. Following this serial, Graves appeared in *Three Texas Steers* ('39), *Eternally Yours* ('39) and *Street of Missing Men* ('39). It would be ten years before he again appeared before a camera.

In 1922, Graves married Marjorie Seaman, who was an extra in the Griffith film *Dream Street*, which starred Graves. They were divorced some time before 1928, for on April 17, 1928, Graves married Virginia Goodwin, a non-professional. The couple had one child, Ralph, Jr. The marriage fell apart and the couple separated on April 22, 1932. On June 28, 1934, Betty Flournoy, a UCLA debutante and actress, became the third Mrs. Graves. Ralph and Betty had two daughters, Betty and Barbara.

In June 1939, both Ralph and Betty filed bankruptcy petitions in Federal Court.

Graves appeared in *Alimony, Amazon Quest* and *Joe Palooka in the Counterpunch* in 1949 and played a supporting role in the serial *Batman and Robin.*

Graves died of a heart attack February 18, 1977, at his home in Santa Barbara. In his later years, he had been active in real estate. Surviving were his wife Betty and his three children.

Serials

1929

The Fatal Warning. Mascot, [10 Chapters] D: Richard Thorpe; P: Nat Levine; LP: Helene Costello, Ralph Graves, George Periolat, Phillips Smalley, Boris Karloff.

1936

The Black Coin. S&S, [15 Chapters] D: Albert Herman; S: George Merrick; SP: Eddy Grane-man, Dallas M. Fitzgerald, Bob Lively, Albert Herman; Spv.: Louis Weiss; Cam: James Diamond; Mus: Lee Zahler; LP: Dave O'Brien, Ralph Graves, Ruth Mix, Matthew Betz, Constance Bergen, Robert Frazer, Snub Pollard.

1949

Batman and Robin. Col., [15 Chapters] D: Spencer G. Bennet; SP: George H. Plympton, Joseph F. Poland, Royal Cole. P: Sam Katzman; Cam: Ira H. Morgan; Mus: Mischa Bakaleini-koff; LP: Robert Lowery, Johnny Duncan, Jane Adams, Lyle Talbot, Ralph Graves, Rick Vallin, House Peters, Jr.

GLORIA GRAY

Gloria Gray's one and only serial was *Blake of Scotland Yard* (1927) for Universal. Hayden Stevenson starred. Her first role of importance, when she was just a girl, was the northwestern adventure drama *The Great Alone* ('22). Impressed by her performance, Selznick starred her in the comedy *Bag and Baggage* ('23) and FBO followed by headlining her in the melodrama *A Girl of the Limberlost.* Thereafter she was featured in a number of comedies, for which she had a flair, and a number of Westerns opposite Lefty Flynn, Edmund Cobb, Fred Humes, Newton House, George Chandler, Bob Curwood and Fred Gilman. The astute Western fan will recognize these cowboys as lower echelon saddle-sitters whose films played the neighborhood theaters on double-bills.

Gloria was born October 23, 1909, in Stockton, California, and educated in Oak-land. In addition to her cinema work, she appeared on the New York stage and in vaudeville for a short time. She retired in 1934 to marry Ramon Romero, a fan magazine writer.

Gloria died on November 22, 1947, in Hollywood following several months illness. She was survived by her husband, daughter, mother and brother.

Serial

1927

Blake of Scotland Yard. Univ., [12 Chapters] D: Robert F. Hill; Adapt: William Lord Wright; LP: Hayden Stevenson, Gloria Gray, Monte Montague, Grace Cunard, Albert Hart.

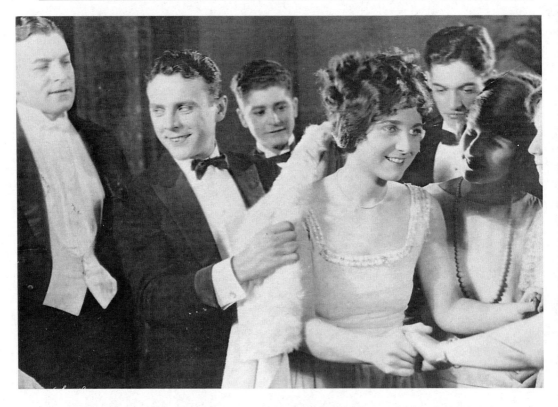

Gloria Gray and unidentified cast members in *Girl of the Limberlost* (FBO, 1924).

LORNA GRAY / ADRIAN BOOTH

Lorna was born Virginia Mae Pound in Grand Rapids, Michigan, on July 26, 1917. [In my book *Those Fabulous Serial Heroines* I erred in reporting her birth year as 1924. She says 1917, and I assume she knows. The year 1921 has been reported by other writers.] Her father was a millinery salesman; her mother, a homemaker.

When the Depression came, the Pound family found themselves in dire circumstances. Business fell off considerably and her father became ill and unable to work for a year. He could not make payments on their home and they lost it in foreclosure. While the parents and her brother went to Saginaw where they had relatives, Lorna was placed with an aunt. Lorna became unhappy living in her aunt's home and left for about a year, singing in small clubs. Saving a little money, she returned home bent on finishing high school. By this time the family was together again, although it was pretty much a hand-to-mouth existence.

Lorna got after-school employment in

a dress shop. While working there, the owner gave her $25 and a new dress to enter the Miss Grand Rapids beauty contest. She won and went on to the Miss Michigan Blossom Queen Festival and was a winner there also. She emerged as "Miss Michigan." That was the first step in a promising histrionic career, but at the time Lorna didn't give it a thought; she wanted to be a writer.

A shortage of funds kept her from going to college, so she took a job as social director at the New Whitcomb Hotel in St. Joseph, Michigan. A guest at the hotel was impressed with her beauty and singing talent and urged her to go to New York to meet producer Ben Yost. She followed this advice and landed a job as singer and mistress of ceremonies with Yost's "Co-Eds."

While the troupe was playing in Cleveland, Ohio, she sang with Roger and his band, who were engaged at the same theater. It was here that she was discovered by a Hollywood talent scout who brought her to the film capital for a screen test. The conclusion was that she "wasn't the type."

The actress was hurt and disillusioned, but for the first time really determined to prove her ability. She made the rounds of the casting offices for weeks and did a few modeling jobs to pay her way. Finally an agent saw her model in a fashion show, signed her and arranged for a test at Columbia.

Lorna was amazed to hear that the test was successful and she soon signed a contract. She was billed as Lorna Gray until mid–1945, when she became Adrian Booth. Her first features were made in late 1938 — two "B" programmers at Columbia and the femme lead in *Red River Range* ('38) on loanout to Republic. This was a Three Mesquiteers film with John Wayne, Ray Corrigan and Max Terhune.

Columbia used her as a foil for the Three Stooges, Andy Clyde, Buster Keaton and Charley Chase in two-reel comedies and as the heroine opposite Charles Starrett in a couple of cowboy flicks. She got a lot of good footage as the daughter of Boris Karloff in *The Man They Could Not Hang* ('39), and she was used advantageously in three Mono-

Lorna Gray in *Flying G-Men* (Columbia, 1939).

gram programmers as the love interest opposite Ralph Byrd and Frank Albertson. Before leaving Columbia, Lorna was featured in two of the studio's routine serials. She played the sister of an aircraft manufacturer who works with the G-Men against a spy ring that is sabotaging American defense industries in *Flying G-Men* ('39). The following year she was the Western heroine who aids a Robin Hood character in his fight against the Skull and his gang in *Deadwood Dick* ('40). It seems that the Skull is trying to prevent law and order from reaching Dakota Territory, which will happen if railroad extension is successful.

In 1942, still known as Lorna Gray, she began her long association with Republic. For the first and only time in cinema history, a serial queen was confronted with a serial villainess. Lorna Gray was the glamorous nemesis Vultura, resplendent in a velvet sarong, emblazoned with a writhing, sequin serpent, and sporting a gold lamé turban. What an arch-fiend she made, almost overshadowing the heroine Kay Aldridge. But

Left to right: unidentified actor, Charles Middleton, Lorna Gray and George J. Lewis, with a reclining Kay Aldridge in *Perils of Nyoka* (Republic, 1942).

Miss Gray was a professional, and she earned her histrionic hisses. As exotic ruler of a band of vicious Arabs who want to obtain the tablets and treasure of Hippocrates, Lorna made an impression on serial audiences. The serial was *Perils of Nyoka.*

Lorna was on the right side of the law as the assistant to Dick Purcell in *Captain America* ('44). As the Scarab, Lionel Atwill is out to kill with his "Purple Death," while also conspiring to steal a life-restoring machine and a Mayan plaque that reveals the location of treasure, and to secure plans for a highly destructive dynamic vibrator. But Lorna and Captain America saw to it that he finally got the hot seat.

In a return to villainy, Lorna portrayed a beautiful adventuress who, along with George J. Lewis, LeRoy Mason and Hal Taliaferro, attempts to steal crown jewels destined for transfer back to Europe in *Federal Operator 99* ('45). But they were foiled by G-men headed by Marten Lamont. Having

learned that crime does not pay, and with the new name of Adrian Booth, she essayed the lead in her final chapterplay, *Daughter of Don Q* ('46), as an heiress under an ancient Spanish land grant. With the aid of Kirk Alyn, she tries to keep another heir from killing all the descendants of Don Quantero. Adrian was now working under a Republic contract and was top-billed.

Adrian made a series of eight Trucolor Westerns with Monte Hale before graduating into "A" Westerns. She met actor David Brian in 1948 and they were married on June 19, 1948, in a garden ceremony performed at the Pacific Palisades home of friends. The couple set up housekeeping in a Monterey-style house on a hillside in Sherman Oaks.

Adrian made *Spoilers of the North* ('47) with Paul Kelly, *Exposed* ('47), with Robert Armstrong, *Lightnin' in the Forest* ('48) and *Hideout* ('49) before working in the "A" features *The Gallant Legion* ('48), *The Plunderers* ('48), *The Last Bandit* ('49), *Brimstone*

('49), *Rock Island Trail* ('50), *Savage Horde* ('50), *Oh Susanna* ('51), *The Sea Hornet* ('51) and *Yellow Fin* ('51).

Republic failed to pick up Adrian's option in 1951. It broke her heart. She had already developed a drinking problem and she drank even more. She didn't realize that Republic was going out of business. A chance meeting with Jane Russell resulted in Adrian agreeing to help Jane organize WAIF, an organization to find homes for orphaned children, both here and abroad. Adrian worked full time for 15 years and Jane has put in over 40 years. One night at Russell's chapel for a Christian group meeting, Adrian gave her heart to Christ. She quit drinking altogether.

David Brian died of cancer on July 15, 1993. He had been ill several years and Adrian was always there to care for him. Adrian ultimately became an ordained minister. Today she is still serving her Creator.

Serials

1939

Flying G-Men. Col., [15 Chapters] D: Ray Taylor, James W. Horne; SP: Basil Dickey, Robert E. Kent, Sherman Lowe; P: Jack Fier; Exec. P: Irving Briskin; LP: Robert Paige, Robert Fiske, James Craig, Lorna Gray, Don Beddoe, Dick Curtis.

1940

Deadwood Dick. Col., [15 Chapters] D: James W. Horne; SP: Wyndham Gittens, Morgan Cox, George Morgan, John Cutting; P: Larry Darmour; LP: Don Douglas, Lorna Gray, Lane

Chandler, Marin Sais, Harry Harvey, Charles King.

1942

Perils of Nyoka. Rep., [15 Chapters] D: William Witney; SP: Ronald Davidson, Norman S. Hall, William Lively, Joseph Poland, Joseph O'Donnell; AP: W. J. O'Sullivan; Cam: Reggie Lanning; Mus: Mort Glickman; LP: Kay Aldridge, Clayton Moore, Lorna Gray, William Benedict, Charles Middleton.

1944

Captain America. Rep., [15 Chapters] D: John English, Elmer Clifton; SP: Harry Fraser, Royal Cole, Ronald Davidson, Basil Dickey, Jesse Duffy, Grant Nelson, Joseph Poland; AP: W. J. O'Sullivan; Cam: John MacBurnie; Mus: Mort Glickman; LP: Dick Purcell, Lorna Gray, Lionel Atwill, Charles Trowbridge, George J. Lewis.

1945

Federal Operator 99. Rep., [12 Chapters] D: Spencer Bennet, Yakima Canutt, Walter A. Grissell; SP: Albert DeMond, Basil Dickey, Jesse Duffy, Joseph Poland; AP: Ronald Davidson; Cam: Bud Thackery; Mus: Richard Cherwin; LP: Marten Lamont, Helen Talbot, George J. Lewis, Lorna Gray, Hal Taliaferro.

1946

Daughter of Don Q. Rep., [12 Chapters] D: Spencer Bennet, Fred Brannon; SP: Albert DeMond, Basil Dickey, Jesse Duffy, Lynn Perkins. AP: Ronald Davidson; Cam: Bud Thackery; Mus: Raoul Kraushaar; LP: Adrian Booth, Kirk Alyn, LeRoy Mason, Roy Barcroft, Claire Meade.

SHIRLEY GREY

Shirley Grey, a 5'6" blonde with lustrous tresses and blue-green eyes, adorned a variety of motion pictures in the early 1930s, including a serial with John Wayne and fast-paced melodramas with Tim McCoy (six films), Jack Holt, Buck Jones (two films),

Lloyd Hughes, Richard Talmadge, Edmund Lowe, Lee Tracy, Charles Starrett, Ralph Bellamy (three films) and Bela Lugosi.

Grey was born Agnes Zetterstrand in Naugatuck, Connecticut, the daughter of a Lutheran minister and the youngest of his seven children. She was of Swedish ancestry. Her dad died when she was eight years old and the Greys moved to Waterbury, where Shirley attended high school. When she was a child, she was forbidden even to walk on a street where there was a theater. But as the influence of her father's memory gradually diminished, Shirley became addicted to the theater. She acted in high school plays and then began to play hookey from school to attend the local theaters.

These youthful indiscretions soon caught up to her. Her mother was apprised — and to the astonishment of all, Shirley's mother declared, "If my daughter prefers the theater to school, by all means let her have the theater." So in her junior year, Shirley was "discovered" in *Stop Thief*. She played in stock in virtually every New England town. Then she went to Oakland in stock.

A bonus which she received for heading the cast of *The Patsy* in an Oakland stock com-

pany started her on the way to success. The play had set a new long-run record and Shirley was to receive an expensive Lincoln automobile as a gift. She asked for the cash instead.

With the money and her own savings, which amounted to about $5,000, she went to Europe for a vacation and returned, determined to become a producer. In Mineola, Long Island, Springfield, Ohio, and Wheeling, West Virginia, she financed her own stock companies and added greatly to her wealth and popularity. She also went on the road in George M. Cohen's play *A Well-Known Woman* and did a revival of *The Tavern*. Later she purchased the stock company in Oakland and closed the one in Mineola. The three companies she retained operated profitably for some time.

Samuel Goldwyn saw a film test of her made in Oakland and wanted a studio test made. Shirley obliged and two weeks later she was in Hollywood to start her screen career. Her first pictures were *The Public Defender* ('31) and *Secret Service* ('31), both with Richard Dix. Then she did a play with Edward Everett Horton, *The Unexpected Husband*. After that came a succession of "B" films in which she had a number of opportunities to reveal her histrionic talent. On the whole she acquitted herself creditably in thrillers with players who had name recognition in the neighborhood and grind theaters. The last credit the author has for her is *The Mystery of the Marie Celeste* ('35), an English-made seagoing chiller with Bela Lugosi. She married her co-star in that film Arthur Margetson, an English actor.

Serial

1932

The Hurricane Express. Mascot, [12 Chapters] D: Armand Schaefer, J. P. McGowan; SP: George Morgan, J. P. McGowan; S: Colbert Clark, Barney Sarecky, Wyndham Gittens; Cam: Ernest Miller, Carl Wester; P: Nat Levine; LP: John Wayne, Shirley Grey, Conway Tearle, Tully Marshall, J. Farrell MacDonald, Al Bridge.

DOROTHY GULLIVER

Dorothy Gulliver was born in Salt Lake City, Utah, on September 6, 1908 (?) and received her education in the public schools there. She was raised in the Mormon faith. At age 15, the petite, hazel-eyed brunette won the title "Miss Salt Lake City" in a "See America First" contest. The local Paramount distributor was ready to send her to Hollywood. But then Dorothy won a beauty and talent contest conducted by Universal, with the prize of a trip to Hollywood, a screen test and a film contract. She appeared in bit roles in a wide variety of films before being cast in the lead in the series *The Collegians*.

For the next five years, the happiest in her professional life, Dorothy was at Universal. She appeared in 48 *Collegians* two-reelers and as a supporting player in *The Winking Idol* ('26) and *Strings of Steel* ('26), two William Desmond-Eileen Sedgwick serials. Her first Western of record was a Jack Hoxie oater called *The Rambling Ranger* ('27). She appeared in subsequent Westerns starring Hoot Gibson, Fred Humes and Rin-Tin-Tin.

In 1928, Dorothy was selected as a Wampas Baby Star, one of 13 young actresses named each year by leading publicists as most likely to reach superstardom.

With the advent of talkies, Dorothy freelanced, making a number of action films. Audiences of the 1930s saw her as the heroine in quickie sagebrushers with Rex Lease, Tim McCoy and Bill Elliott, and she played the leading lady in four serials, three for Nat Levine's Mascot Pictures. In *The Galloping Ghost* ('31), Dorothy played another college sweetheart, this time to Harold (Red) Grange, who is out to clear his name of game-throwing and win reinstatement on the team; in *The Phantom of the West* ('31), she aids Tom Tyler in his search for the murderer of his father; and in *The Shadow of the Eagle* ('32), she risks death with John Wayne to bring the

Eagle to justice and clear her father's name. RKO's only serial, *The Last Frontier* ('32), had Dorothy as the heartthrob of fighting frontier newspaper editor Creighton Chaney (later Lon Chaney, Jr.). Four years later she was one of the principals in the star-studded *Custer's Last Stand* ('36), an independently produced chapterplay from Stage and Screen films.

At the height of her career, Dorothy had a serious accident and was incapacitated for more than a year. This resulted in fewer roles once she returned to work, and she decided to give up her film career. Some years later she did a number of stage plays, including a role in *Face Value* at the Laguna Summer Theatre which won her acclaim as a comedienne. She also appeared in several television shows, but it was not until 1964 that she made her return to films in the John Cassavetes production *Faces* (released in 1968). She played a blowzy, middle-aged woman

Dorothy Gulliver in *The Shadow of the Eagle* (Mascot, 1932).

honest enough to express her attraction for the young hustler she and her friends have picked up in a bar. The role brought her many plaudits. She wanted to re-enter films after *Faces*, but her second husband, Jack Proctor, whom she married in March 1947, never encouraged it, though he was a press agent and probably could have helped her. Proctor died of cancer on August 1, 1976. That year Dorothy did a cameo in *Won Ton Ton, the Dog Who Saved Hollywood*.

About 1993, Dorothy was diagnosed with Alzheimer's disease and her health and memory declined steadily. She passed away on May 23, 1997, in Escondido, California.

Serials

1926

The Winking Idol. Univ., [10 Chapters] D: Francis Ford; LP: William Desmond, Eileen Sedgwick, Jack Richardson, Grace Cunard, Dorothy Gulliver.

String of Steel. Univ., [10 Chapters] D: Henry MacRae; LP: William Desmond, Eileen Sedgwick, Albert J. Smith, Arthur Morrison, Dorothy Gulliver.

1931

The Phantom of the West. Mascot, [10 Chapters] D: Ross Lederman; S: Ford Beebe; P: Nat Levine; Cam: Benjamin Kline; Mus: Lee Zahler; LP: Tom Tyler, Dorothy Gulliver, William Desmond, Tom Santschi, Tom Dugan.

The Galloping Ghost. Mascot, [12 Chapters] D: B. Reeves Eason; P: Nat Levine; LP: Harold (Red) Grange, Dorothy Gulliver, Walter Miller, Gwen Lee, Francis X. Bushman, Jr., Tom Dugan, Tom London.

1932

The Last Frontier. RKO, [12 Chapters] D: Spencer Bennet, Thomas L. Storey; SP: George Plympton, Robert F. Hill; Spv.: Fred J. Mc-

Connell; LP: Creighton Chaney [Lon Chaney, Jr.], Dorothy Gulliver, Mary Joe Desmond, Joe Bonomo, Francis X. Bushman, Jr.

Shadow of the Eagle. Mascot, [12 Chapters] D: Ford Beebe, Colbert Clark, Wyndham Gittens; P: Nat Levine; Mus: Lee Zahler; Cam: Ben Kline, Victor Scheurich; LP: John Wayne, Dorothy Gulliver, Walter Miller, Kenneth Harlan, Edward Hearn.

1936

Custer's Last Stand. S&S [15 Chapters] D: Elmer Clifton; SP: George A. Durlam, Eddy Graneman, William Lively; Spv.: Louis Weiss; Mus: Hal Chasnoff; Cam: Bert Longenecker; LP: Rex Lease, William Farnum, Reed Howes, Lona Andre, Dorothy Gulliver, George Chesebro, Jack Mullhall.

ANNE GWYNNE

Anne Gwynne was signed to a long-term contract by Universal Studios after the shortest interview of its kind on record—approximately one minute! Miss Gwynne was appearing in a Hollywood little theater where she was seen by a Universal executive who was so impressed with her performance that he sent for her the next day. The interview consisted of three questions. No, she never had acted on the stage professionally. No, she had never been in pictures. Yes, she would like to be in pictures. That was it. The executive handed her a contract and she signed it, one of those $50-a-week, six-months-with-option affairs.

There wasn't any waiting for the formality of a screen test. She was assigned immediately to a part in *Unexpected Father* ('39).

Anne's career was helped by a lineless part she played as Edgar Bergen's secretary in a charity short. Her big brown eyes and bathing suit figure were not missed by audiences and the studio was besieged with requests by both sexes to know who she was. During the next several years she became a favorite of Universal's publicity department and was one of their most photographed starlets.

Anne was a cooperative star and worked hard, putting as much effort into her roles as a "B" heroine as many an actress did in "A" films.

Born Marguerite Gwynne Trice in Waco, Texas, on December 10, 1918, the red-haired beauty first drew attention with her dancing and oratory at a San Antonio high school, in a declamation contest for the school district of San Antonio in 1935. Anne won first prize. The following year she moved with her parents to St. Louis, Missouri. She attended Stephens College in Columbia, Missouri, and studied there until 1938 when she was offered her first job—modeling swim suits for a Los Angeles firm, a job ideally suited for the beautiful 5'5", 117–pound, hazel-eyed and titian-haired beauty who was quickly dubbed "Miss TNT" (trim, neat and terrific).

Anne played opposite Buster Crabbe in Universal's 12-chapter serial *Flash Gordon Conquers the Universe* ('40). When Ming the Merciless (Middleton) starts spreading the Plague of the Purple Death, Flash (Crabbe), Dale (Carol Hughes) and Dr. Zarkov (Frank Shannon) head for the planet of Mongo. Joined by Prince Barin (Roland Drew) and Aura (Shirley Deane), they launch an attack on Ming's palace and then take off for Frigia in hopes of mining Polante, an antidote for the Purple Death. Dale and Dr. Zarkov are captured by Thong (Victor Zimmerman), Torch (Don Rowan) and Sonja (Gwynne). Confronted with an electrical death ray, Flash nevertheless manages to rescue Dale and Zarkov before squelching Ming's power-mad dreams by destroying the emperor's stronghold with a solarite explosion.

Anne demonstrated proficiency in portraying both sympathetic and villainous characters, though she was generally cast as a nice girl. She played the feminine lead in "B" Westerns and minor "A's" with a number of different cowboys. Western fans got a chance to drool over her in *Oklahoma Frontier* ('39), in which she played opposite Bob Baker and Johnny Mack Brown. A much better role followed in *Man from Montreal* ('39) with Richard Arlen. She was also effective in horror films and minor musicals, and for over a decade her beauty and talent graced the low-budget films of Universal and other studios specializing in the "B" product.

Anne married attorney and part-time producer Max Gilford on December 30, 1945. The marriage was a long and happy one, terminated by her husband's death in 1965. They had a daughter and a son.

For some time Anne operated a boutique in Westwood, California, and made several forays into TV commercials. After a decade away from the camera, Anne came out of retirement in 1970 to play the mother of Michael Douglas in *Adam at 6 A.M.* ('70). It was her last film.

Her other films include: *Charlie McCarthy, Detective* ('39), *Black Friday* ('40), *The Black Cat* ('41), *Road Agent* ('41), *Ride 'Em Cowboy* ('42), *Frontier Badmen* ('43), *Weird Woman* ('44), *Moon Over Las Vegas* ('44), *House of Frankenstein* ('44), *Fear* ('46), *Dick Tracy Meets Gruesome* ('47), *The Enchanted Valley* ('48), *King of the Bullwhip* ('51), *Phantom of the Jungle* ('55) and *Teenage Monster* ('58).

Gwynne died of complications from a stroke following surgery at the Motion Picture Country Hospital in Woodland Hills, California, on April 1, 2003.

Serials

1940

Flash Gordon Conquers the Universe. Univ., [12 Chapters] D: Ford Beebe, Ray Taylor; SP: George H. Plympton, Basil Dickey, Barry Shipman; AP: Henry MacRae; LP: Buster Crabbe, Carol Hughes, Charles Middleton, Anne Gwynne, Frank Shannon, Lee Powell, Don Rowan, Ray Mala, Lane Chandler, Roy Barcroft.

The Green Hornet. Univ., [13 Chapters] D: Ford Beebe, Ray Taylor; SP: George Plympton, Basil Dickey, Morrison C. Wood, Lyonel Margolies; AP: Henry MacRae; LP: Gordon Jones, Keye Luke, Wade Boteler, Anne Nagel, Philip Trent, Douglas Evans, Anne Gwynne, Cy Kendall, Stanley Andrews.

KARL HACKETT

Karl Hackett died in 1948 at age 55 in Sawtelle, California, after a long illness. The check-shirted outlaw leader appeared in 50 features during the period 1935–1940; 41 of these were B-Westerns. His first film of record was *Bulldog Courage*, starring Tim McCoy and released December 30, 1935. His roles were similar to those played by Ted Adams, I. Stanford Jolley, Harry Woods, Walter Miller, Al Bridge, Robert Fiske, Edward Cassidy, Robert Frazer, LeRoy Mason, Forrest Taylor, Kenneth MacDonald, Wheeler Oakman and other badmen who gave orders for other gang members to carry out.

His last film appearance was in *The Fabulous Texan*, released in November 1947 and starring Bill Elliott. Bob Steele and Tim McCoy top the list of those cowboys he most often worked with. Buster Crabbe also ranks high. Toward the end of his career, Hackett worked mostly for PRC Studios.

Serials

1938

Flaming Frontiers. Univ., [15 Chapters] D: Ray Taylor, Alan James; LP: Johnny Mack Brown, Eleanor Hansen, Ralph Bowman [John Archer], Charles Middleton.

1939

The Green Hornet. Univ., [13 Chapters] D: Ford Beebe, Ray Taylor; LP: Gordon Jones, Anne Nagel, Keye Luke, Wade Boteler, Philip Trent.

The Oregon Trail. Univ., [15 Chapters] D: Ford Beebe, Saul A. Goodkind; LP: Johnny Mack Brown, Louise Stanley, Fuzzy Knight, Bill Cody, Jr., Forrest Taylor, James Blaine, Charles Stevens, Charles King, Karl Hackett, Roy Barcroft.

The Phantom Creeps. Univ., [12 Chapters] D: Ford Beebe, Saul A. Goodkind; LP: Bela Lugosi, Robert Kent, Dorothy Arnold, Regis Toomey, Edward Van Sloan, Charles King, Eddie Acuff, Lee J. Cobb, Roy Barcroft, Karl Hackett.

1940

Deadwood Dick. Col., [15 Chapters] D: James W. Horne; LP: Don Douglas, Lorna Gray [Adrian Booth], Lane Chandler, Marin Sais, Harry Harvey, Charles King, Jack Ingram.

1942

The Valley of Vanishing Men. Col., [15 Chapters] D: Spencer Bennet; LP: Bill Elliott, Slim

In *Six-Gun Trail* (Victory, 1938).

Summerville, Carmen Morales, Kenneth MacDonald, Jack Ingram, Tom London, George Chesebro, Kenneth MacDonald, Julian Rivero, Frank Ellis.

Gang Busters. Univ., [13 Chapters] D: Ray Taylor, Noel Smith; LP: Kent Taylor, Irene Hervey, Ralph Morgan, Robert Armstrong, Richard Davies, Joseph Crehan, George J. Lewis.

1943

Batman. Col., [15 Chapters] D: Lambert Hillyer; LP: Lewis Wilson, Douglas Croft, J. Carrol Naish, Shirley Patterson, William C. Austin, Charles Middleton, Karl Hackett, George Chesebro, Charles Wilson, Stanley Price, Anthony Warde.

REED HADLEY

Tall, handsome Reed Hadley came up through the ranks of stage and radio in the usual manner, but what is unusual is the courage and downright tenacity by which he attained his goal of a movie career — in the face of privations and setbacks.

He traveled as a boy with his father, a wildcat oil driller and their lives was a succession of hard knocks in those days. More ups and downs than a pogo stick.

Petrolia, Texas, claims Hadley as a native son, although the wanderings of Hadley Sr. necessitated Reed's leaving this panhandle town at the tender age of ten. Columbiana, Ohio, was the next home of the Hadley offspring and this time the family remained long enough for Reed to enter high school before packing the trunks for Buffalo, New York.

It was in Buffalo's Bennett High School that Hadley first became interested in dramatics. He was chosen to play the part of a 60-year-old Pennsylvania Dutchman in a play called "Erstwhile Susan."

Graduating from Bennett High School, Hadley entered the University of Buffalo with the intention of studying law, but financial difficulties forced him to withdraw after the first year. The lure of the stage once again exerted its influence on Reed and he became active in the Buffalo Studio Theatre Player's group. During the day he worked in a local department store. He soon resigned his job and, gathering his few belongings, headed for New York. After skirting the brink of starvation for a few weeks, Hadley landed a role in the production of *Hamlet* starring John Gielgud, the English actor. *Hamlet* ran for 32 weeks. When it closed, he cast about for another job. He found one in a New York radio station as an announcer.

He spent much of his time in radio from then on, but in the summers he would take time off to enter summer stock for the experience. He played leading roles in such varied productions as *The Petrified Forest*, *Death Takes a Holiday*, *Petticoat Fever* and *Spring Dance*. When a movie scout heard him in a coast-to-coast radio show and asked him if he wanted a movie chance, Reed jumped at opportunity and flew to Hollywood. By doing so, he tossed overboard a leading role in the Broadway production of John Steinbeck's *Tortilla Flat*.

In Hollywood, Hadley was turned back at the gate. It seemed the scout failed to notify the studio of Hadley's arrival. He returned to radio more determined than ever to make the grade in motion pictures. For a year and a half he was active in radio, taking the part of Red Ryder on the daily 15-minute programs. He also played leading roles on such programs as *Silver Theatre*, *Big Town*, *Cavalcade of America* and others. Eventually the movies noted his ability and he commenced his screen career in 1938 in the features *Female Fugitive*, *Hollywood Stadium Mystery* and *Orphans of the Street*. That same year he played one of the supporting roles in *The Great Adventures of Wild Bill Hickok*, considered Columbia's best serial.

In 1939 he starred in the role for which he is best remembered — Republic's *Zorro's Fighting Legion*. Most Zorro addicts consider this one the best of all the Zorro films. In 1941 Hadley had supporting roles in three serials, *Sea Raiders*, *Adventures of Captain Marvel* and *Sky Raiders*. Some of his feature credits are *Calling Dr. Kildare* ('39), *The Bank Dick* ('40), *Whistling in the Dark* ('41), *Mystery of Marie Roget* ('42), *Roger Touhy — Gangster* ('44), *In the Meantime Darling* ('44), *Diamond Horseshoe* ('45), *Doll Face* ('45), *Captain from Castile* ('47), *Iron Curtain* ('48), *I Shot Jesse James* ('49), *The Baron of Arizona* ('50), *Dallas* ('50), *Young Dillinger* ('65) and *The St. Valentine's Day Massacre* ('66).

Reed Hadley (in mask) fights with Jim Pierce (center) and Charles King in *Zorro's Fighting Legion* (Republic, 1941).

During a four-year stint with 20th Century-Fox, he gave his clear, crisp voice a good workout as narrator for such films as *Guadacanal Diary, Boomerang, 13 Rue Madelaine* and *The House on 92nd Street*.

In the 1950s he played Capt. Braddock, ruthless pursuer of gangsters on TV's *Racket Squad*. He also starred in the '50s TV series *Public Defender*. Hadley married a non-professional, Helen Hampton, in 1940 and they had one child, Dale Sydney.

Reed Hadley died from a heart attack at UCLA Medical Center in 1974. He was 63. His wife and son survived.

Serials

1938

The Great Adventures of Wild Bill Hickok. Col., [15 Chapters] D: Mack V. Wright, Sam Nelson; LP: Bill Elliott, Carole Wayne, Frankie Darro, Monte Blue, Dickie Jones, Sammy McKim, Kermit Maynard, Reed Hadley.

1939

Zorro's Fighting Legion. Rep., [12 Chapters] D: William Witney, John English; SP: Ronald Davidson, Franklyn Adreon, Morgan Cox, Sol Shor, Barney Sarecky; AP: Hiram S. Brown, Jr.; Cam: Reggie Lanning; Mus: William Lava; LP: Reed Hadley, Sheila Darcy, William Corson, Leander De Cordova, C. Montague Shaw, Edmund Cobb, Charles King, John Merton.

1941

Adventures of Captain Marvel. Rep., [12 Chapters] D: William Witney, John English; LP: Tom Tyler, Frank Coghlan, Jr., Louise Currie, Robert Strange, William Benedict, Harry Worth, Bryant Washburn, John Davidson, Reed Hadley.

Sky Raiders. Univ., [12 Chapters] D: Ford Beebe, Ray Taylor; LP: Donald Woods, Billy Halop, Robert Armstrong, Kathryn Adams, Eduardo Ciannelli, Reed Hadley.

Sea Raiders. Univ., [12 Chapters] D: Ford Beebe, John Rawlins; LP: Billy Halop, Huntz Hall, Gabriel Dell, Bernard Punsley, Hally Chester, William Hall, John McGuire, Reed Hadley, Mary Field.

CREIGHTON HALE

Oldtime star Creighton Hale was born Patrick Creighton Hale Fitzgerald in Cork, Ireland, on May 14, 1882. He made his stage debut as an infant with his father's touring stock company and came to the U.S. on a tour with Gertrude Elliott and an Irish troupe in 1913 to appear on Broadway in *The Dawn of Tomorrow*. A dashing, elegant man, he entered films the following year in *The Million Dollar Mystery* ('14), a Thanhouser serial in 23 chapters. His role was a supporting one.

In *Exploits of Elaine* ('14) with Pearl White and Arnold Daly, Hale appears in the first three chapters as newspaper man Walter Jamison. Another actor, Raymond Owens, took over the role in Chapters 4–14. In *The New Exploits of Elaine* ('16), again with White and Daly, Creighton is again Walter Jamison. The three principals continue their respective roles in *The Romance of Elaine* ('15), with Lionel Barrymore appearing as Dr. X, a foreign agent opposing Elaine. Pearl White's name was sufficient to make the film a financial success.

Pearl and Creighton took on new identities in *The Iron Claw* ('16) with Sheldon Lewis as Legar, the Iron Claw. A mystery hero called the Laughing Mask is revealed in the last chapter.

In *The Seven Pearls* ('17), Ilma Bay (Mollie King) and her boyfriend Harry Drake (Hale) must recover pearls taken by Harry from a necklace belonging to a Turkish Sultan, or Ilma will become a member of the Sultan's harem. Ilma's father is held captive pending Ilma's return at the end of six months. Perry Mason (Leon Bary) wants the pearls for himself and hampers the efforts of Ilma and Harry to find them.

In his only other serial, *Custer's Last Stand* ('36), Creighton has only a bit part as Hank.

In 1920 Hale was in *The Idol Dancer* as the lovesick youth, and in *Way Down East* as bespectacled young Prof. Sterling, who watches helplessly as stern Burr McIntosh sends Lillian Gish out into the snow. In *Orphans of the Storm* ('22) he plays with both Lillian and Dorothy Gish and in *Broken Hearts of Broadway* ('23) he plays opposite Colleen Moore. In *The Marriage Circle* ('24) he portrays suave Dr. Muller, who adores married woman Florence Vidor. In *Annie Laurie* ('27) he was back with Lillian Gish, and in *Rose Marie* he is seen with Joan Crawford.

Other silent films included *The Thirteenth Chair* ('19), *Mary of the Movies* ('23), *Three Wise Fools* ('23), *The Bridge of Sighs* ('25), *A Poor Girl's Romance* ('26) and *The Cat and the Canary* ('27).

In the sound era he could be seen as a character actor in such films as *The Masquerader* ('33), *Death from a Distance* ('35), *Hollywood Boulevard* ('36), *The Return of Doctor X* ('39), *Calling Philo Vance* ('40), *Watch on the Rhine* ('43), *The Mysterious Doctor* ('43) and *The Perils of Pauline* ('49), the film biography of Pearl White.

Creighton Hale died August 9, 1965, at age 83 in the Pasadena Actors Home. His death was attributed to natural causes. He was survived by two sons and three grandchildren.

Serials

1914

The Million Dollar Mystery. Thanhouser, [23 Chapters] D: Howell Hansell; SP: Lloyd Lonergan; S: Harold McGrath; LP: Florence La Badie, Marguerite Snow, James Cruze, Frank Farrington, Sidney Bracey, Creighton Hale.

Exploits of Elaine. Pathé, [14 Chapters] D: Louis Gasnier, George B. Seitz; SP: Charles W. Goddard, George B. Seitz; S: Arthur B. Reeve, Bertram Millhauser, Charles L. Goddard; Cam: Joseph Dubray; P: Leopold V. and Theodore W. Wharton; LP: Pearl White, Arnold Daly, Creighton Hale, Sheldon Lewis, Lionel Barrymore, George B. Seitz.

1915

The New Exploits of Elaine. Pathé, [10 Chapters] D: George B. Seitz, Bertram Millhauser; SP: Charles W. Goddard, George B. Seitz, Bertram Millhauser; S: Arthur B. Reeve; P: Leopold V. and Theodore W. Wharton; Cam: Joseph Dubray; LP: Pearl White, Creighton Hale, Arnold Daly, Edwin Arden, M. W. Rale.

The Romance of Elaine. Pathé, [12 Chapters] D: George B. Seitz, Joseph A. Golden, Louis Gasnier; SP: Charles W. Goddard, George B. Seitz, Bertram Millhauser; S: Arthur B. Reeve; LP: Pearl White, Creighton Hale, Arnold Daly, Lionel Barrymore, Bessie E. Wharton, George B. Seitz.

1916

The Iron Claw. Pathé, [20 Chapters] D: Edward Jose, George B. Seitz; SP: George B. Seitz; S: Arthur Stringer; LP: Pearl White, Creighton Hale, Sheldon Lewis, Harry Fraser, J. E. Dunn, Henry G. Sell, Edward Jose, Carey Lee.

1917

The Seven Pearls. Pathé, [15 Chapters] D: Burton L. King, Donald McKenzie; SP: George B. Seitz; S: Charles W. Goddard; LP: Mollie King, Creighton Hale, Leon Bary, John J. Dunn, Henry G. Sell, Floyd Buckley, Walter P. Lewis.

1936

Custer's Last Stand. S&S, [15 Chapters] D: Elmer Clifton; LP: Rex Lease, William Farnum, Reed Howes, Jack Mulhall, Lona Andre, Dorothy Gulliver, Ruth Mix, George Chesebro.

GEORGIA HALE

Georgia Hale was born in 1906 in St. Joseph, Missouri. She was working as an extra on the set of Roy William Neill's *By Divine Right/The Way Men Love* ('24) when she was discovered by then-screenwriter Josef von Sternberg, who made her the star of his first film as a director, *Salvation Hunters* ('25). Later that year, she played her most memorable screen role as the subject of Charlie Chaplin's love and hallucinations in *The Gold Rush*. She was an exceptionally pretty girl, and anyone who has watched *The Gold Rush* is not likely to forget her. Other films included *The Rainmaker* ('26), *The Great Gatsby* ('26), *Man of the Forest* ('26), *The Wheel of Destiny* ('27), *The Rawhide Kid* ('28), *Gypsy of the North* ('28) and *A Trick of Hearts* ('28).

She is remembered by serial lovers for her role in *The Lightning Warrior* ('31). Playing the sheriff's adopted daughter, she helps young Frankie Darro take possession of his murdered father's mine. Also aiding him are George Brent, brother of a murdered lawman, and Rin-Tin-Tin, Sr.

Georgia quit the movies shortly after making this serial. She died in Hollywood in 1985 at age 79.

Serial

1931

The Lightning Warrior. Mascot, [12 Chapters] D: Armand Schaefer, Benjamin Kline; SP: Wyndham Gittens, Ford Beebe, Colbert Clark; P: Nat Levine; Mus: Lee Zahler; Cam: Ernest Miller; LP: George Brent, Georgia Hale, Frankie Darro, Rin-Tin-Tin, Sr., Robert Kortman, Pat O'Malley, Theodore Lorch, Lafe McKee.

ELLA HALL

Ella Hall was born on the 17th of March, in either 1896 or 1897, in New York City. She began her stage career at an early age and was an actress on the legitimate stage for three years. She played in stock companies headed by David Warfield, Isabel Irving, Charlotte Walker, William Elliott, Frank Keenan and other noted stock stars.

Ella made her screen debut for Biograph in 1912 in a film with Mary Pickford. But it was at Universal that she became a star.

She attained stellar roles under the direction of Robert Z. Leonard, with whom she co-starred in the highly successful serial *The Master Key* ('14). A popular item, the film was well-received by avid serial fans. An adventure story of the first order, it was filled with exciting action as two opposing camps sought gold, the location of which was on a map in a sunken ship and the location of the sunken vessel is scratched on a key. Leonard spent his nights writing the scenarios for the entire 30 reels and the entire day was taken up in directing and acting. Many times he worked all night, quitting in time to get ready for the trip to the studio before eight, acting and directing all day and returning to put in another night at preparing scenarios.

Leonard and Hall were co-stars for two years (1913–15) at Universal and ranked as the senior co-stars of the company.

A few of Hall's credits are *The Spy* ('14), *The Silent Command* ('15), *The Charmer* ('17), *The Little Orphan* ('17), *Under the Top* ('19), *The Heart of Lincoln* ('22), *The Flying Dutchman* ('23), *Madam Satan* ('30), and *The Bitter Tea of General Yen* ('33), her last film.

Ella co-starred with Francis Ford in the serial *The Great Reward* ('21), as a beautiful princess whose predicaments cause numerous exciting adventures. Trick photography and double exposure work wherein little figures climb out of glasses, crawl over books, dance upon tables, etc., form an important part of the serial and proved a big attraction to patrons who were unfamiliar with this kind of work.

Hall's marriage to actor-producer Emory Johnson ended in divorce in 1929. She did not remarry. She died at age 85 on September 3, 1982, in Los Angeles and was survived by two daughters and a son.

Serials

1914

The Master Key. Univ., [15 Chapters] D: Robert Z. Leonard; SP: Calder Johnson; S: John Fleming Wilson; Supv.: Otis Turner; LP: Robert Z. Leonard, Ella Hall, Harry Carter, Jean Hathaway, Alfred Hickman, Jack Holt.

1921

The Great Reward. Burstom, [15 Chapters] D: Francis Ford; SP: Elsie Van Name; Cam: Jerome Ash; LP: Francis Ford, Ella Hall, Carl Gerard, Phil Ford, Mark Fenton, Valeria Olivo.

LOIS HALL

Lois Hall has been more active as an actress than most of those fans realize who watched her as a Western heroine opposite Whip Wilson, Charles Starrett, Johnny Mack Brown and Jimmy Wakely in theatrical releases of 1949–51. If those leather burners were all of her work they saw, then they missed a great deal indeed, much of which was in television.

Lois also headed up the cast of *Daughters of the Jungle* ('48), which takes on the characteristics of a serial reduced to 69 minutes, but minus none of the harrowing escapes. And, speaking of serials, she played "The Lady of the Lake" in *Adventures of Sir Galahad* ('49) starring George (Superman) Reeves, and had the female lead opposite Buster Crabbe in *Pirates of the High Seas* ('50). *Duke of Chicago* ('48) found her in the second female lead playing a self-centered society snob; she was one of two female leads in *Slaughter Trail* ('51) and played Carrie's roommate in *Carrie* ('52).

Lois had a number of additional supporting roles in *Love Happy* ('49), *Kill the Umpire* ('50), *Seven Brides for Seven Brothers* ('53), *Hawaii* ('65) and many more.

On television Lois appeared in numerous shows, most of them in the early 1950s. For a year she had the featured role of Beth Holly on *One Man's Family*, an NBC soap opera. She played the female lead in segments of *The Range Rider* series starring Jock Mahoney, *The Cisco Kid* with Duncan Renaldo and in episodes of *Kit Carson*, *Wild Bill Hickok* and *The Lone Ranger*.

Lois was born on August 22, 1926, in Grand Rapids, Minnesota. Her mother was a schoolteacher and her father a businessman. The family moved to Long Beach, California, when Lois was eight years old. Lois attended public schools there and graduated from Wilson High School. From high school she went to the Pasadena Playhouse on a set designer scholarship. There she was noticed by an agent who became her agent until his death in 1955. On stage at the Pasadena Playhouse Lois appeared in *Winterset* ('47), *Mellony Holtspur* ('48), *The Philadelphia Story* ('48) and *The Silver Cord* ('48).

In 1952 Lois married businessman Maurice Willows. For a decade they were away from California serving their Baha'i Faith — three years in the Western desert and seven years in Hawaii, where the actress did public relations for their religion.

Upon returning to Hollywood in the 1970s, Lois resumed her career on a part-time basis.

Serials

1949

Adventures of Sir Galahad. Col., [15 Chapters] D: Spencer G. Bennet; SP: George H. Plympton, Lewis Clay, David Mathews; P: Sam Katzman; Cam: Ira H. Morgan; Mus: Mischa Bakaleinikoff; LP: George Reeves, Charles King, Lois Hall, William Fawcett.

1950

Pirates of the High Seas. Col., [15 Chapters] D: Spencer Bennet, Thomas Carr; SP: Joseph F. Poland, David Mathews, George H. Plympton, Charles R. Condon; P: Sam Katzman; Cam: Ira H. Morgan; Mus: Mischa Bakaleinikoff; LP: Buster Crabbe, Lois Hall, Tommy Farrell, Gene Roth, Tris Coffin.

RUTH HALL

Ruth Hall was an exquisite creature. Ken Maynard and John Wayne thought so, as did Joe E. Brown, Eddie Cantor and other male leads. Her underplayed sexuality was disconcerting. Buster Crabbe, Charles Starrett and Grant Withers had nothing but praise for her.

Ruth was born Ruth Hall Ybanez on December 29, 1912, in either Tampa or Jacksonville, Florida. Her father was a stock broker and her mother was a businesswoman. When *Hell Harbor* ('30) was being shot in Tampa, Mrs. Hall had the job of seeing that the cast and crew were made comfortable. Ruth was on the set observing when a Paramount talent scout noticed her and assured her of a contract if she went to Hollywood. Her mother and grandmother accompanied her west. Ruth worked as an extra for several months while she was being groomed for speaking parts. She posed for a lot of publicity stills during this time.

She received her first speaking role playing a shipboard passenger in the Marx Brothers comedy *Monkey Business* ('31). When Ruth was dropped by Paramount, she was picked up by Warner Brothers. During 1931–32 she appeared in *Local Boy Makes Good* with Joe E. Brown, *Union Depot* with Douglas Fairbanks, Jr., *Miss Pinkerton* with Joan Blondell, *Blessed Event* with Lee Tracy, *Ride Him Cowboy* with John Wayne, *Between Fighting Men* with Ken Maynard, *Gambling Sex* with Grant Withers, *Flaming Guns* with Tom Mix and *One-Way Passage* with William Powell.

In 1933, Ruth had the feminine lead in the Mascot serial *The Three Musketeers*. Jack Mulhall, Francis X. Bushman, Jr., and Raymond Hatton are three Legionnaires rescued by John Wayne from desert rebels, and the four oppose the mysterious leader of a desert tribal cult that is attempting to wipe out the Foreign Legion. Mulhall received top billing.

Ruth co-starred with Charles Starrett in *Return of Casey Jones* ('33) and had a principal role in *Laughing at Life* ('33). In 1934 she played in *Murder on the Campus* with Starrett, *Beloved* with John Boles, *Badge of Honor* with Buster Crabbe and *Meet the Mayor* with Frank Fay.

Ruth married Lee Garmes, an Oscar-winning cinematographer, on September 10, 1933. After a few more films, she gave up her career in order to travel with her husband wherever his job required him to be. Their

Ruth Hall and Ken Maynard in *Between Fighting Men* (World Wide, 1932).

daughter Pamela was born on February 27, 1936. A second daughter, Carole Lee, was born on December 25, 1940. Ruth played in three more films: *Julia Misbehaves* ('48) with Greer Garson, *The I Don't Care Girl* ('52) with Mitzi Gaynor and *The Farmer Takes a Wife* ('53) with Betty Grable.

Lee Garmes died on August 31, 1978, at age 80. Ruth has continued to do church work and to devote much time to her grandchildren and great-grandchildren.

Serial

1933

The Three Musketeers. Mascot, [12 Chapters] D: Armand Schaefer, Colbert Clark; SP: Norman Hall, Colbert Clark, Ben Cohn, Wyndham Gittens; LP: Jack Mulhall, Raymond Hatton, John Wayne, Ruth Hall, Francis X. Bushman, Jr., Creighton Chaney, Hooper Atchley, Noah Beery, Jr., William Desmond, Gordon DeMain.

BILLY HALOP

Going practically from rompers to radio—that was the way Billy Halop began his theatrical career. It all came about when a small radio station adjacent to the private school he attended sent over for some children to appear on a broadcast. He was among those selected, and from that time on he had the acting bug. His lawyer father hoped that Billy might follow in his legal footsteps, but Billy wanted to act and was permitted to enroll in the Professional Children's School.

Billy first appeared on radio as a child singer at age six and four years later had his own show. For five years he starred in a series called *Bobby Benson and His H Bar O Rangers.*

When Sidney Kingsley was looking for a boy to play the leader of a gang of young roughnecks in a play called *Dead End* which he was about to bring to Broadway, he interviewed hundreds of youths. No one satisfied him. Finally he made the rounds of radio stations and that is where he found Billy. After that, it was relatively easy to round up the other five youths needed—Huntz Hall, Leo Gorcey, Gabriel Dell, Bernard Punsley and Bobby Jordan.

Following the close of the play, the kids were brought to Hollywood to appear in the film version. Dubbed "The Dead End Kids," they were a hit with theater audiences and cast in six more films over the next two years: *Crime School* ('38), *Angels with Dirty Faces* ('38), *They Made Me a Criminal* ('39), *Hell's Kitchen* ('39), *The Angels Wash Their Faces* ('39) and *The Dead End Kids on Dress Parade* ('39). Halop was the kids' rebellious leader and Gorcey his wisecracking and jealous rival.

Billy also appeared in *You Can't Get Away with Murder* ('39), *Dust Be My Destiny* ('39), *Tom Brown's School Days* ('40) and *Blues in the Night* ('41) before going to Universal along with the other Dead End Kids.

They continued working together and separately in later years. In the early '40s, the Dead End Kids became the East Side Kids with new recruits.

Halop, Dell, Hall and Punsley starred in three Universal serials. In *Junior G-Men* ('40) Philip Terry (best known as one of Joan Crawford's husbands) was on hand to help the boys cope with a subversive gang known as the Order of the Flaming Torch led by fanatical Cy Kendall. Billy's father, inventor of a new explosive device, is abducted. Billy and his street gang join forces with Kenneth Howell's Junior G-Men in pursuit of Kendall.

Sea Raiders ('41) rambled around with the boys trying to cope with fifth columnists who have stolen a new type of torpedo boat invented by Halop's brother. In tracking down the subversives, the boys end up shanghaied on a whaler and marooned on an island which just happens to be the enemies' headquarters. The heavies included Reed Hadley (as one of the lead saboteurs) and veterans Stanley Blystone, Dick Alexander and Ernie Adams.

Halop's spy-fighting activities weren't over yet as Universal put him in *Sky Raiders* ('41) along with Donald Woods as Capt. Bob Dayton, a famed aviator who becomes the target of the enemy due to a new type of fighter plane his company has made. The heavies were led by Eduardo Ciannelli aided by Jacqueline Dalya and Reed Hadley.

Junior G-Men of the Air ('42) finds the Dead End Kids taking on a Japanese spy ring known as the "Black Dragonflies" led by horror menace Lionel Atwill, in full Japanese makeup, assisted by soon-to-be film heartthrob Turhan Bey. The object of the enemies' intentions was a new airplane muffler invented by Halop's brother. This one had some pretty good moments with the enemy headquarters in a produce farm outside the

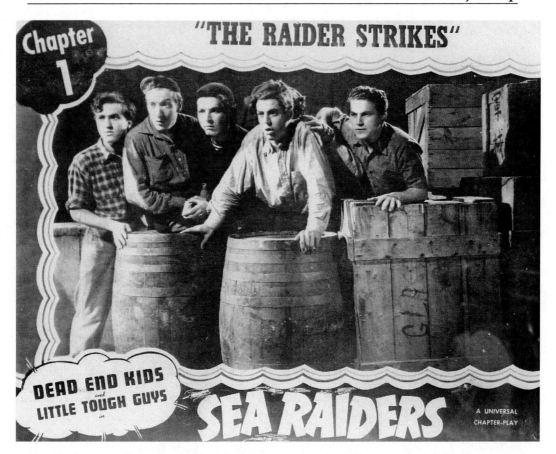

Billy Halop (light shirt, hands on barrels) and the Dead End Kids in *Sea Raiders* (Universal, 1941).

city. Also on the side of law and order was Frank Albertson as the head of the Junior G-Men.

Halop joined the U.S. Army Signal Corps in 1942 and served as an Army sergeant. Back in Hollywood, he found acting jobs scarce. He was no longer a kid. He became an alcoholic but was able to overcome it himself, as brought out in his book *There's No Dead End*.

In 1946 he married New York actress Helen Tupper but they were divorced in 1947 when Billy found out his wife would not cook and did not care to keep house. On St. Valentine Day 1948 he married Barbara Hoon in Palm Springs. The marriage was terminated in 1959. Halop's suit claimed cruelty. There were no children. A third marriage to Suzanne Roe also ended in divorce in 1971. She had suffered from multiple scle-

rosis. Billy trained as a nurse and practiced for five years before dropping out of the profession.

During his career he owned two restaurants at different times, was the head chef at Ted's Rancho in Malibu in 1961, working as an appliance salesman and held other short term jobs. His post–World War II films include *Gas House Kids* ('46), *Dangerous Years* ('47), *Air Strike* ('59), *For Love or Money* ('63), *Move Over Darling* ('63), *A Garden of Cucumbers* ('66), *Mr. Buddwing* ('66) and *Fitzwilly* ('67). On TV he appeared in *Ben Casey*, *Gunsmoke*, *Adam 12* and others and had a continuing role as a cab driver in *All in the Family*.

Halop had two heart attacks and open heart surgery in 1971. He died from a heart attack in his sleep at his Brentwood apartment on November 9, 1976.

Serials

1940

Junior G-Men. Univ., [12 Chapters] D: Ford Beebe, John Rawlins; SP: George H. Plympton, Basil Dickey, Rex Taylor; AP: Henry MacRae; Cam: Jerome Ash; LP: Billy Halop, Huntz Hall, Gabriel Dell, Bernard Punsley, Philip Terry, Roger Daniels, Kenneth Lundy, Cy Kendall, William Hall, William Desmond, Russell Hicks.

1941

Sea Raiders. Univ., [12 Chapters] D: Ford Beebe, John Rawlins; AP: Henry MacRae; SP: Clarence Upson Young, Paul Huston; LP: Billy Halop, Huntz Hall, Gabriel Dell, Bernard Pun-sley, William Hall, John McGuire, Mary Field, Stanley Blystone, Dick Alexander.

Sky Raiders. Univ., [12 Chapters] D: Ray Taylor, Ford Beebe; S: Eliot Gibbons; SP: Clarence Upson Young, Paul Huston; AP: Henry MacRae; LP: Donald Woods, Billy Halop, Robert Armstrong, Kathryn Adams, Eduardo Ciannelli, Reed Hadley, Jacqueline Dalya.

1942

Junior G-Men of the Air. Univ., [12 Chapters] D: Ray Taylor, Lewis D. Collins; SP: George H. Plympton, Paul Huston, Griffin Jay; AP: Henry MacRae; LP: Billy Halop, Gene Reynolds, Lionel Atwill, Frank Albertson, Richard Lane, Huntz Hall, Gabriel Dell, Bernard Punsley, Frankie Darro, Turhan Bey, Billy Benedict.

NEIL HAMILTON

Neil Hamilton, 85 died in Escondido, California, in 1984 from complications from asthma. He will best be remembered for his role of Police Commissioner Gordon in 120 episodes of the popular *Batman* television series filmed at 20th Century-Fox in the '60s.

James Neil Hamilton was born in Lynn, Massachusetts, on September 9, 1899. When he was 17 the family moved to New Haven, Connecticut, and he began working as an extra and bit player in films made in Fort Lee, New Jersey. D. W. Griffith gave him a career boost in *The White Rose* ('23), *Isn't Life Wonderful?* ('24) and *America* ('24).

Hamilton became a major Paramount star in the late '20s. According to Hamilton, he appeared in a total of 265 features, plays of all kinds, and who-knows-how-many TV series. From the mid–30s on, he played character roles.

His films include *Beau Geste* ('26), *The Great Gatsby* ('26), *Ten Modern Commandments* ('27), *The Patriot* ('28), *The Mysterious Dr. Fu Manchu* ('29), *The Return of Dr. Fu Manchu* ('30), *The Dawn Patrol* ('30), *Strangers May Kiss* ('31), *Tarzan the Ape Man* ('32), *Tarzan and His Mate* ('34), *The Little Shepherd of Kingdom Come* ('61), *The Family Jewels* ('65) and *Which Way to the Front?* ('70).

Hamilton's sole serial was Republic's *King of the Texas Rangers* ('41). The serial proved a popular one in spite of Sammy Baugh's lack of acting ability.

Among Hamilton's Broadway appearances, *The Solid Gold Cadillac* was the most successful.

Serial

1941

King of the Texas Rangers. Rep., [12 Chapters] D: William Witney, John English; LP: Slingin' Sammy Baugh, Pauline Moore, Duncan Renaldo, Neil Hamilton, Monte Blue, Kermit Maynard, Charles Trowbridge.

Left to right: Neil Hamilton, Preston Foster and Ralph Byrd in *Army Girl* (Republic, 1938).

JUANITA HANSEN

Juanita Hansen was extremely popular in 1921 and earned nearly $1,500 a week. She enjoyed the "good life," particularly parties, fine clothes and fast cars, and raced her Chalmers speedster down country roads at all hours. The car was so highly geared that it could make 60 in second gear and 90 in third without any trouble at all (except to the police). She was arrested so often that it was a routine event.

Physically worn out from long, hard days before the camera and all-night parties, Hansen turned to the use of cocaine, not realizing the dangers involved. By the time she made *The Yellow Arm* ('21), she was an addict. Pathé had difficulty finishing the film because of her physical condition. The studio dropped her rather than face the bad publicity of having a drug addict as their star attraction. Hansen sought help and went through several "cures" over the years.

She was finally able to secure a part in *The High Hatters* on Broadway in 1928, her addiction apparently behind her. But tragedy struck as scalding water poured over her as she lay unconscious in a tub — she had fainted after turning on the too-hot shower in her New York hotel bathroom. For several weeks, doctors gave her morphine to ease the pain, and once again she became addicted. Most of the $118,000 she received as compensation for the hotel mishap went for hospital bills, lawyers' fees and drugs or drug cures.

Apparently Hansen was cured again in 1934, but by this time she was just a shell. Her spirit was gone, as well as her beauty and wealth. She traveled with carnivals, making her living by lecturing on the evils of drugs. On June 21, 1941, she attempted suicide after being locked out of her room in a cheap hotel. The overdose of sleeping pills failed to kill her.

Portland, Oregon, was her birthplace, if she can be believed. (Some reference sources list Des Moines, Iowa, as her birthplace.) The year of her birth was 1897. At the age of eight, she moved with her parents to Los Angeles and finished high school there. Almost immediately after her graduation, she went before the cameras as a chorus girl and bit player. Her first known credit is *The Love Routh* ('15).

She soon became one of the Mack Sennett bathing beauties. Her best role prior to going with Sennett had been D. W. Griffith's *The Martyrs of the Alamo* ('15). In an attempt to diversify her career, she talked herself in the heroine's role in the war-preparedness serial *The Secret of the Submarine* ('16). Soon she was emoting with Jack Mulhall in *The Brass Bullet* ('18). The popularity of this cliffhanger led to her getting the role of Lurline, a South Seas island girl, in *The Sea Flower* ('18). She was also the love interest opposite William S. Hart in *The Poppy Girl's Husband* ('19) and played Tom Mix's girl in *Rough Riding Romance* ('19). In *A Midnight Romance* ('19) she lost hero Jack Holt to Anita Stewart.

William Selig hired Juanita to star in *The Lost City* ('20), a serial released by Warner Brothers. She ran, jumped, fell, dived, crawled and swam her way through peril after peril. The serial genre was definitely her forte. The popular serial was also released in a feature version, *The Jungle Princess* ('23). Her work convinced Pathé moguls that this graduate of the "Sennett school" was also an actress of the caliber to fill the vacant niche in their serial star department, and they put her into *The Phantom Foe* ('20) and *The Yellow Arm* ('21).

Juanita died from a heart attack on September 26, 1961, in Hollywood. She was 64 and had been working as a train order clerk for the Southern Pacific Railway.

JUANITA HANSEN

Serials

1916

The Secret of the Submarine. Amer., [15 Chapters] D: George Sargent; LP: Juanita Hansen, Tom Chatterton, William Tedmarsh, Lamar Johnstone, George Clancy, George Webb.

1918

The Brass Bullet. Univ., [18 Chapters] D: Ben Wilson; SP: Walter Woods; S: Frank R. Adams; P: Ben Wilson; LP: Juanita Hansen, Jack Mulhall, Charles Hill Mailes, Joseph W. Girard, Helen Wright, Harry Dunkinson, Ashton Dearholt.

1920

The Lost City. Warner Bros., [15 Chapters] D: E. A. Martin; S: Frederic Chapin; P: William N. Selig; LP: Juanita Hansen, George Chesebro, Frank Clark, Hector Dion, Irene Wallace, Al Ferguson, Marjorie Lake, Jack Abraham.

The Phantom Foe. Pathé, [15 Chapters] D: Bertram Millhauser; SP: George B. Seitz; LP: Juanita Hansen, William N. Bailey, Warner Oland, Harry Semels, Wallace McCutcheon, Nina Cassavant, Tom Goodwin, Joe Cuny.

1921

The Yellow Arm. Pathé, [15 Chapters] D: Bertram Millhauser; SP: James Shelley Hamilton; LP: Juanita Hansen, Marguerite Courtot, Warner Oland, Tom Keith, William N. Bailey, Stephen Carr.

KENNETH HARLAN

Kenneth Harlan was born in Boston on July 26, 1895. He was educated in New York schools and from an early age he acted on stage. His mother, Rita Harlan, was a successful actress.

Kenneth had a successful stage career; some of his stage credits were: *Arabian Nights*, *Boys of Company B.*, *The Fortune Hunter* and *Samuran*. He entered movies in 1917. One of his first films was *The Wife He Bought* ('17) with Carmel Myers. They made four more films together: *The Lash of Power* ('17), *My Unmarried Wife* ('18), *The Wine Girl* ('18) and *The Marriage Lie* ('18). Another favorite co-star was Constance Talmadge, with whom he made seven features. Except for the first, *Betsy's Burglar* ('17), made for Triangle, the films were made for Associated First National. In *Dangerous Business* ('20) he is the pipsqueak male secretary who comes back from war a hero and sweeps Constance off her feet. It was followed by *Mama's Affair* ('21), *Lessons in Love* ('21), *Woman's Place* ('21), *Polly of the Follies* ('22) and *The Primite Lover* ('22).

Harlan's major films included *The Hoodlum* ('19, Mary Pickford), *Beautiful and Damned* ('23, Louise Fazenda), *The Virginian* ('23, Florence Vidor), *April Showers* ('23, Colleen Moore), *The Toll of the Sea* ('23, Anna May Wong), *Poisoned Paradise* ('24, Clara Bow), *The Virgin* ('24, Dorothy Revier), *The Butterfly* ('24, Laura La Plante), *On the Stroke of Three* ('24, Madge Bellamy), *The Marriage Whirl* ('25, Corinne Griffith), *The Ranger of the Big Pines* ('25, Helen Costello), *The Fighting Edge* ('26, Patsy Ruth Miller), *Twinkletoes* ('26, Colleen Moore), *Easy Pickings* ('27, Anna Q. Nilsson), *East Side, West Side* ('27, Virginia Valli) and *Cheating Cheaters* ('27, Batty Compson).

It seems that Harlan was a ladies' man, as he had a total of seven wives and as many divorces. Marie Prevost was the best-known. Other wives included Flo Hart, a former Follies dancer, Doris Booth, Emily McLaughlin and Helene Stanton.

Harlan lived a hand-to-mouth existence. He enjoyed expensive clothes, dancing and entertaining. He had exquisite tastes.

Harlan starred in two Universal serials in 1931. He made 12 more serials as a supporting player. In Westerns he was in six with William Boyd, one with Roy Rogers, one with Buck Jones, two with Bill Elliott, one with Tim Holt, two with Johnny Mack Brown, and three with Ken Maynard and Hoot Gibson. Non-Westerns in which he appeared included *Women Men Marry* ('31), *San Francisco* ('36), *China Clipper* ('36), *The Walking Dead* ('36), *Marked Woman* ('37), *The Duke of West Point* ('38) and *Hitler—Dead or Alive* ('43).

Left to right: Kenneth Duncan, Betty Miles, Kenneth Harlan (seated), Jack LaRue, Hoot Gibson and Ken Maynard in *The Law Rides Again* (Monogram, 1943).

Harlan died from an aneurysm in Sacramento in 1967. He was 71 years old.

Serials

1931

Danger Island. Univ., [12 Chapters] D: Ray Taylor; SP: Basil Dickey; S: Henry MacRae, Ella O'Neill; LP: Kenneth Harlan, Lucile Browne, Tom Ricketts, Walter Miller, W. L. Thorne.

Finger Prints. Univ., [10 Chapters] D: Ray Taylor; S: Arthur B. Reeve; SP: George Morgan, George H. Plympton, Basil Dickey; LP: Kenneth Harlan, Edna Murphy, Gayne Whitman, Gertrude Astor.

1932

Shadow of the Eagle. Mascot, [12 Chapters] D: Ford Beebe, Colbert Clark, Wyndham Gittens; LP: John Wayne, Dorothy Gulliver, Walter Miller, Kenneth Harlan, Edward Hearn.

1937

Tim Tyler's Luck. Univ., [12 Chapters] D: Ford Beebe, Wyndham Gittens; LP: Frankie Thomas, Frances Robinson, Norman Willis, Jack Mulhall.

The Mysterious Pilot. Col., [15 Chapters] D: Spencer Gordon Bennet; LP: Frank Hawks, Dorothy Sebastian, Rex Lease, Guy Bates Post.

1939

The Oregon Trail. Univ., [15 Chapters] D: Ford Beebe, Saul A. Goodkind; LP: Johnny Mack Brown, Fuzzy Knight, Bill Cody, Jr., Forrest Taylor, Louise Stanley, James Blaine.

The Green Hornet. Univ., [13 Chapters] D: Ford Beebe, Ray Taylor; LP: Gordon Jones, Anne Nagel, Keye Luke, Wade Boteler, Philip Trent.

Dick Tracy's G-Men. Rep., [15 Chapters] D: William Witney, John English; LP: Ralph Byrd, Irving Pichel, Phylis Isley [Jennifer Jones], Ted Pearson.

1940

Mysterious Doctor Satan. Rep., [15 Chapters] D: William Witney, John English; LP: Eduardo Ciannelli, Robert Wilcox, Ella Neal, William Newell.

Junior G-Men. Univ., [12 Chapters] D: Ford Beebe, John Rawlins; LP: Billy Halop, Henry Hall, Gabriel Dell, Bernard Punsley, Philip Terry.

1941

Dick Tracy vs Crime, Inc. Rep., [15 Chapters] D: William Witney, John English; LP: Ralph Byrd, Jan Wiley, John Davidson, Ralph Morgan.

1943

Daredevils of the West. Rep., [12 Chapters] D: John English; LP: Allan Lane, Kay Aldridge, Eddie Acuff, William Haade, Robert Frazer, Ted Adams, George J. Lewis.

JOHN HART

John Lewis Hart was born in Los Angeles on December 13, 1917, and attended South Pasadena High School. His mother was a drama critic for the *San Marino Tribune*; his father, an accomplished pianist who worked for the California Music Company, sold real estate and grew avocados for the commercial trade.

Tall, athletic and good-looking, John acted on the stage of the renowned Pasadena Playhouse before making his screen debut in *The Buccaneer* ('38), directed by Cecil B. DeMille. His early roles were small: *Prison Farm*, *King of Alcatraz*, *Disbarred*, etc.

With the outbreak of World War II, Hart joined the Army and served for five years in such places as the Philippines, Japan and Okinawa, where he saw action. Attached to the Air Service Command, he produced and directed shows for the military, appeared in training films and did radio programs.

Returning to Hollywood, he signed with Universal and had small roles, usually as a badman, in numerous Westerns. His stunting ability served him well during this period. In 1947 he doubled his friend Jon Hall in Columbia's *The Last of the Redmen*. Producer Sam Katzman saw him and decided

he was right for the lead in *Jack Armstrong* ('47). Following this serial, Hart had minor roles in *Brick Bradford* ('47), *Tex Granger* ('48) and *Pirates of the High Seas* ('50). As a freelancer, Hart worked with a number of B-cowboys— Johnny Mack Brown, Buster Crabbe, Bill Elliott, Jim Bannon and Whip Wilson.

In the early '50s, Hart took the TV role of the Lone Ranger when Clayton Moore was dropped because of a salary dispute. Hart starred in 52 episodes of the series before Moore finally came to terms with the producers and took the role back.

Hart remained busy. He co-starred with Lon Chaney, Jr., in the TV series *Hawkeye and the Last of the Mohicans* ('56–'57). They made 39 episodes, all filmed in Canada. While there, Hart met and married Beryl Braithwaite, a graduate of the Royal Academy in London.

On the film front, Hart appeared as a supporting player in Columbia's *Gunfighters of the Northwest* ('53) and *The Great Adventures of Captain Kidd* ('53), and in 1955 he had the lead role in *Adventures of Captain Africa*, pieced together with much stock footage. It was back to a supporting role in

In *Adventures of Captain Africa* (Columbia, 1955).

Perils of the Wilderness ('56), the last American serial.

Hart continued to work throughout the '60s, '70s and into the '80s. He got over into the horror film genre when he essayed the lead role in *Blackenstein* ('73), also called *Black Frankenstein*, perhaps the ultimate in the black exploitation film craze of the early 1970s. He played a newspaper editor hung early in the big-budgeted *The Legend of the Lone Ranger* ('81) starring Klinton Spilsbury. The film bombed and Spilsbury never made another movie.

Serials

1947

Jack Armstrong. Col., [15 Chapters] D: Wallace Fox; SP: Arthur Hoerl, Lewis Clay, Royal Cole, Leslie Swabacker; P: Sam Katzman; Cam: Ira H. Morgan; Mus: Lee Zahler; LP: John Hart, Rosemary LaPlanche, Joe Brown, Jr., Claire James, Pierre Watkin, Charles Middleton, Jack Ingram, Eddie Parker.

Brick Bradford. Col., [15 Chapters] D: Spencer Bennet; LP: Kane Richmond, Rick Vallin, Linda Johnson, Pierre Watkin, Charles Quigley, John Hart.

1948

Tex Granger. Col., [15 Chapters] D: Derwin Abrahams; LP: Robert Kellard, Peggy Stewart, Buzz Henry, Smith Ballew, I. Stanford Jolley, Jack Ingram.

1950

Pirates of the High Seas. Col., [15 Chapters] D: Spencer Bennet, Thomas Carr; LP: Buster Crabbe, Lois Hall, Tommy Farrell, Gene Roth, Tristram Coffin, Hugh Prosser, Symonia Boniface, John Hart.

1953

The Great Adventures of Captain Kidd. Col., [15 Chapters] D: Derwin Abbe, Charles S. Gould; LP: Richard Crane, David Bruce, John

Crawford, George Wallace, Lee Roberts, Ray Corrigan, Charles King, John Hart.

Gunfighters of the Northwest. Col., [15 Chapters] D: Spencer Bennet, Charles S. Gould; LP: Jock Mahoney, Clayton Moore, Phyllis Coates, Don Harvey, Lyle Talbot, Marshall Reed, Lee Roberts, John Hart.

1955

Adventures of Captain Africa. Col., [15 Chapters] D: Spencer Bennet; P: Sam Katzman; SP:

George Plympton; Cam: Ira H. Morgan; Mus: Mischa Bakaleinikoff; LP: John Hart, Rick Vallin, Ben Welden, June Howard, Bud Osborne.

1956

Perils of the Wilderness. Col., [15 Chapters] D: Spencer Bennet; LP: Dennis Moore, Richard Emory, Eve Anderson [Evelyn Finley], Kenneth MacDonald.

NEAL HART

Only a small handful of film addicts today are aware of the man once known as "America's Pal." This lack of recognition is a sign that, but for the favored few, fame is an ephemeral wisp of acknowledgment in the passage of time.

Neal Hart was born in Richmond, New York, about 1880. At Bucknell University he obtained a degree in engineering, but instead of putting his expensive training to use in a lucrative engineering position, Neal succumbed to wanderlust and drifted westward about 1903. He spent a number of years in Wyoming where he became a good wrangler. In 1907 he became a rider and bulldogger for the famed Miller Brothers 101 Ranch Wild West Show.

From the sawdust arena to the backlots of Hollywood was a logical step, for producers were eager to hire authentic cowboys for stuntwork and riders in the crude Westerns being made at that time. Thus Neal, having left the 101 Show, eked out a living for the next several years as a rider on the payroll of Universal. His talents were eventually recognized. In 1916 he had the distinction of appearing as one of the principals in the first Western serial, *Liberty, A Daughter of the U.S.A.* Marie Walcamp was Liberty; Jack Holt the Texas Rangers captain in love with

her; Neal was Liberty's guardian who, because of gambling losses, was forced to allow Liberty to wed villain G. Raymond Nye. Hart also appeared in *The Lion's Claw* ('18), a Uni-

versal serial again starring Walcamp. Neal was listed tenth in the cast.

In the latter part of 1916, Hart was selected to star in a series of two-reelers which were popular throughout the silent era. Hart attained a huge following in these fast-paced action-oriented range thrillers. In 1917–18 Neal made *Won by Grit* with Lois Wilson, *They Were Four* and *Meet My Wife*, both with Mignon Anderson, and *The Getaway* with Vivian Rich. Other titles were *The Ninth Day*, *Right-of-Way Casey*, *Casey's Border Raid*, *Roped In*, *Border Wolves*, *Desert Ghost*, *Double Suspicion*, *Squarin' It*, *The Raid*, *Bill Brennon's Claim*, *Swede Hearts* and *Trail of No Return*. In the 1918–19 season he starred in *A Knight of Western Land*, *The Deadline*, *Quicksand*, *Out of the Past*, *Man from Montana*, *Sands of the Desert*, *Element of Might*, *Man Getter*, *Heart Beneath*, *The Mission Trail* and *Square Shooter*.

After attaining a modicum of popularity at Universal, where his salary ballooned to around $2,500 a month, Neal struck off on his own as producer-writer-actor-director. His first venture was *When the Desert Smiled* ('19), which was sold to Arrow Film Corporation. Shortly thereafter Neal signed with Capitol, a firm which supplied film product to the independent market. The two-reelers he made were so well-received that Pinnacle signed Neal to do a series of five-reel feature Westerns. The first, *Hell's Oasis*, was released in October 1920; the second, *Skyfire*, in December 1920. *Black Sheep*, *Danger Valley*, *God's Gold* and *The Kingfisher's Roost* followed in 1921.

In late 1921 Hart associated himself with Steiner Productions and made *Tangled Trails* ('21), *Butterfly Range* ('22), *The Heart of a Texan* ('22), *Lure of Gold* ('22), *Rangeland* ('22), *South of Northern Lights* ('22), *Table Top Ranch* ('22), *West of the Pecos* ('22), *Below the Rio Grande* ('23), *The Devil's Bowl* ('23), *The Fighting Strain* ('23), *The Forbidden Range* ('23), *Salty Saunders* ('23), *The Secret of the Pueblo* ('23), *Lawless Men* ('24), *The Left-hand Brand* ('24), *Trucker's Top Hand* ('24), *The Valley of Vanishing Men* ('24) and *The Verdict of the Desert* ('25), the last starring feature Neal made. The declining market for independent Westerns and the growing competition in the Western ranks had taken their toll. In 1926, however, Hart starred in the New-Cal serial *The Scarlet Brand*. For British Canadian Pictures he directed and starred in *North of 49* and *His Destiny* in 1928. It was the end of the trail for Hart. In the 1930s and early 1940s he could occasionally be seen as a bit or extra player. He died in 1949.

Serial

1916

Liberty, A Daughter of the U.S.A. Univ., [20 Chapters] D: Jacques Jaccard and Henry McRae; LP: Jack Holt, Marie Walcamp, Neal Hart, G. Raymond Nye.

1918

The Lion's Claws. Univ., [18 Chapters] D: Harry Harvey and Jacques Jaccard; LP: Neal Hart.

1927

The Scarlet Brand. New-Cal, [10 Chapters] D: Neal Hart; SP: Arthur Henry Gooden; P: William Steiner; LP: Neal Hart, William Quinn, Lucille Irwin, Carmen LaRoux, Henry Britt, William Callen, Tom Wortham.

RAYMOND HATTON

Raymond Hatton was a dedicated professional. He never had but the one occupation — acting; he never considered another occupation. For nearly 55 years he gave of himself for the public — vaudeville, wagon shows, stock companies, circuses, carnivals, films, radio, television.

Hatton was born in the little hamlet of Red Oak, Iowa, on July 7, 1887. When he was ten his doctor-father moved the family to Des Moines. Two years later, Raymond made his debut on the vaudeville stage. Although he was only 12, his parents allowed him to travel the country as an actor in a stock company.

In 1907, 20-year-old Raymond Hatton married 20-year-old actress Frances Roberts. The marriage "took," lasting 64 years. Almost penniless in 1912 in New York City, Raymond found work at the Kalem Studio. From there he went to work for the Biograph Studio, and in 1914 he became associated with Mack Sennett, making one-reel slapstick comedies.

The Hattons moved to California in 1914 and Raymond freelanced at about every studio in Hollywood and vicinity. Early on, Paramount signed him and he was featured in a number of films during the years 1915–23. Following this period he worked for Goldwyn, Mammoth, Universal, Preferred, Warner Brothers and Paramount.

Raymond achieved stardom in 1925 when Paramount co-starred him with Wallace Beery in a comedy series comprised of *Behind the Front* ('26), *We're in the Navy Now* ('26), *Fireman — Save My Child* ('27), *Now We're in the Air* ('27), *Partners in Crime* ('28), *The Big Killing* ('28) and *Wife Savers* ('28).

Raymond was able to work in 25 films directed by Cecil B. DeMille, who liked him and respected his talent. Some of the DeMille films with Hatton are: *The Girl of the Golden West* ('15), *The Warrens of Virginia* ('15),

Chimmie Fadden ('15), *Chimmie Fadden Out West* ('15), *Joan the Woman* ('17), *A Romance of the Redwoods* ('17), *The Whispering Chorus* ('18), *Male and Female* ('19), *The Affairs of Anatol* ('21), *Manslaughter* ('22), *The Squaw Man* ('31), *Reap the Wild Wind* ('42) and *Unconquered* ('47).

As time went along, Raymond gradually slipped over into the Western genre. Some of his non-series Westerns were: *The Virginian* ('23, Kenneth Harlan), *The Thundering Herd* ('25, Jack Holt), *Hell's Heroes* ('29, Charles Bickford), *The Silver Horde* ('31, Joel McCrea), *Law and Order* ('32, Harry Carey), *Vanishing Frontier* ('32, Johnny Mack Brown), *The Fourth Horseman* ('32, Tom Mix), *Cornered* ('32, Tim McCoy), *The Thundering Herd*('33, Randolph Scott), *Wanderer of the Wasteland* ('35, Buster Crabbe), *Bad Men of Brimstone* ('38, Wallace Beery) and *Kit Carson* ('40, Jon Hall).

By 1939 Raymond was working as a sidekick to Roy Rogers and as one of the Three Mesquiteers. In 1941 he switched to Monogram as co-star of the nine-film Rough Riders series with Buck Jones and Tim McCoy. Following Jones' death, Hatton became sidekick to replacement Johnny Mack Brown. The two men made about 45 Western features between 1941 and 1949.

In 1951 he worked for Lippert in support of Russell Hayden and James Ellison in six cheaply made oaters. Semi-retired, Hatton made only a handful of films after 1949. His last Western was *Requiem for a Gunfighter* ('65). His last film appearance was in *In Cold Blood* ('67). During the '60s he could also be seen in various Western television shows.

Raymond's wife of 64 years died of natural causes on October 16, 1971. Raymond was found dead from a heart attack a week later.

Serials

1933

The Three Musketeers. Mascot, [12 Chapters] D: Armand Schaefer, Colbert Clark; SP: Norman Hall, Colbert Clark, Ben Cohn, Wyndham Gittens; P: Nat Levine; LP: Jack Mulhall, Ruth Hall, Raymond Hatton, Francis X. Bushman, Jr., John Wayne, Creighton Chaney [Lon Chaney, Jr.], Hooper Atchley, Noah Beery, Jr., Robert Frazer.

Raymond Hatton in *White Eagle* (Columbia, 1941).

1935

Rustlers of Red Dog. Univ., [12 Chapters] D: Louis Friedlander [Lew Landers]; S: Nathanial Eddy; SP: George Plympton, Basil Dickey, Ella O'Neill, Nate Gatzert, Vin Moore; LP: Johnny Mack Brown, Joyce Compton, Walter Miller, Raymond Hatton, Harry Woods.

1936

The Vigilantes Are Coming. Rep., [12 Chapters] D: Mack V. Wright, Ray Taylor; SP: John Rathmell, Maurice Geraghty, Winston Miller; S: Maurice Geraghty, Leslie Swabacker; Spv.: J. Laurence Wickland; LP: Robert Livingston, Kay Hughes, "Big Boy" Williams, Raymond Hatton, Fred Kohler, Robert Warwick, William Farnum.

Undersea Kingdom. Rep., [12 Chapters] D: B. Reeves Eason, Joseph Kane; SP: John Rathmell, Maurice Geraghty, Oliver Drake; S: Tracy Knight, John Rathmell; Mus: Harry Grey; Cam: William Nobles, Edgar Lyons; Spv.: Barney Sarecky; P: Nat Levine; LP: Ray Corrigan, Lois Wilde, Monte Blue, William Farnum, Booth Howard, Lon Chaney, Jr., Lee Van Atta, C. Montague Shaw, Jack Mulhall.

1941

White Eagle. Col., [15 Chapters] D: James W. Horne; SP: Arch Heath, John Cutting, Morgan B. Cox, Laurence Taylor; P: Larry Darmour; Cam: James S. Brown, Jr., Mus: Lee Zahler; LP: Buck Jones, Raymond Hatton, Dorothy Fay, James Craven, Jack Ingram.

RUSSELL HAYDEN

Russell Hayden was born Pate Lucid on June 12, 1912, in Chico, California. He never aspired to be an actor; however, he found work at Paramount first as a grip, then as a sound recorder, film cutter and assistant cameraman.

In 1937, James Ellison withdrew from the Hopalong Cassidy series in order to pursue bigger and better film roles. Harry (Pop) Sherman, the series' producer, filled the void by signing 25-year-old Hayden. Although Hayden had no acting experience, he worked

Russell Hayden (left) has the drop on Tris Coffin and an unidentified player.

well with William Boyd, George Hayes and Andy Clyde. As Lucky Jenkins, Hayden was high-spirited and prone to starting trouble from which Hoppy would extricate him. And Lucky (Hayden) had an eye for the ladies, too.

Hayden was in 24 Cassidy films at Paramount but, like James Ellison, he wished for a series wherein he would do the heroics and ride off with the girl at the finish.

Columbia hired him to co-star with Charles Starrett in eight horse operas. Then, in 1943, Hayden received his own series with Dub Taylor as comedy relief. He completed eight Westerns in this series, as well as one feature with Tex Ritter at Universal and one solo Western.

After military service in World War II, Hayden returned to filmmaking in 1946. For Screen Guild he did four Northwest Mounted Police films. They were unremarkable even

though filmed in Cinecolor. The films barely qualified as features, as length of the films averaged 45 minutes.

Hayden next produced six shoot-'em-ups with James Ellison co-starred. The supporting casts were the same; the films were all shot at the same time. One nice thing about the series was the supporting casts— Raymond Hatton, Tom Tyler, Fuzzy Knight, Dennis Moore, John Cason, Julie Adams, George J. Lewis and George Chesebro. The films were produced for Lippert films (a name change from Screen Guild) and the titles were *Hostile Country*, *Marshal of Heldorado*, *Colorado Ranger*, *West of the Brazos*, *Fast on the Draw* and *Crooked River*.

In 1951, Hayden appeared in *Texans Never Cry* and *Valley of Fire*, both starring Gene Autry and released by Columbia. He then turned his efforts toward television, starring with Jackie Coogan in the half-hour series *Cowboy G-Men*. Hayden also produced *26 Men* starring Tristram Coffin and *Judge Roy Bean* starring Edgar Buchanan. Hayden made a few appearances in this series.

An early marriage to actress Jan Clayton ended in divorce. In 1946 he married Lillian Porter, a promising 20th Century-Fox actress. The marriage lasted until Hayden's death.

Hayden built Pioneer Town but the lack of water prevented selling lots to homesteaders or investors.

In 1974, Hayden suffered a heart attack and spent weeks in the Eisenhower Hospital in Palm Springs. In his later years his eyesight was failing, which is one reason he stopped appearing in films. He couldn't read the scripts.

Hayden died in 1981 at age 68 in Palm Springs with viral pneumonia. His wife survived.

Serial

1946

Lost City of the Jungle. Univ., [13 Chapters] D: Ray Taylor, Lewis D. Collins; SP: Joseph F. Poland, Paul Huston, Tom Gibson; LP: Russell Hayden, Jane Adams, Lionel Atwill, Keye Luke, Helen Bennett, John Eldredge, Dick Curtis, Ralph Lewis.

MYRON HEALEY

Myron Healey excelled in the role of a hired killer (a role which he liked) in both theatrical and television films. Heroes learned to be wary of his pugnaciousness in the "B" Westerns, and viewers thought of him as one of the gang of badmen who always tried to make life unbearable for the hero or heroine. But his talents extended beyond playing reprehensible rogues.

A 12-chapter serial, *Panther Girl of the Kongo* ('55), revolves around a doctor's attempts to scare people away from a secret diamond mine. He develops a hormone compound which causes ordinary crayfish to become monsters. When Jean Evans (Phyllis Coates), known as the Panther Girl, and big-game hunter Larry Sanders (Healey) arrive in the area, Jean accidentally photographs the Claw Monsters, as the locals call them. The doctor realizes he can't afford to have the photos published, for it would bring on an investigation. Jean and Larry become targets for murder, but outmaneuver their adversaries.

Earlier Healey had played in the serials *Roar of the Iron Horse* ('51) and *The Great Adventures of Captain Kidd* ('53). In those cliffhangers his roles were minor ones.

In 1957 Healey co-starred in Republic's *The Unearthly*, in which he plays an escaped convict who falls in love with Allison Hayes, a girl whom mad surgeon John Carradine plans to use in his gland transplant experiments.

Healey plays John Dillinger in *Guns Don't Argue* ('58), a 92-minute telefilm that recounts the adventures of G-Man Jim Davis and his confreres in battling such infamous underworld figures as Bonnie Parker, Clyde Barrow and Dillinger. In 1962 Healey starred in *Varan the Unbelievable*, a Japanese science-fiction movie. He plays a commander whose experiments unleash a giant prehistoric reptile that destroys a city before being slain. In 1977 he had a major role in *The Incredible Melting Man* as an Army general searching for an astronaut who has returned from Sat-

Mary Ellen Kay and Myron Healey in *Vigilante Terror* (Allied Artists, 1953).

urn as a monster whose flesh is disintegrating (and who desires the flesh of others). Healey had the featured role in *Claws* ('77) as a lawman who is done in by a killer bear. The 1983 telefeature *V* featured the actor as a scientist killed by supposedly friendly aliens. In 1987 he appeared in *Ghost Fever*, a comedy with Sherman Hemsley, and in 1988 he turned up in *Pulse*, concerning a young boy who comes to believe that aliens are communicating with machinery.

Myron Healey was born on June 8, 1923, in Petaluma, California. In the mid–30s he performed as a child singer on radio, gave violin and piano concert recitals as well as dance recitals. He attended junior college in Santa Rosa, California. In 1941 he was able to study under actress Maria Ouspenskaya. He appeared in several plays and also appeared in musicals for the Armed Forces Victory committee.

In 1942 Myron was at MGM in the *Crime Does Not Pay* series. In 1943 he served in the U.S. Air Corps as a navigator and bombardier, twice being awarded the Air Medal. He resumed his career in 1946.

Healey has been exceptionally active in television, appearing on *The Lone Ranger*, *The Gene Autry Show*, *Adventures of Superman*, *Wyatt Earp*, *Bonanza*, *High Chaparral*, *Gunsmoke*, *The Virginian*, *Lassie*, *Adam-12*, *Alfred Hitchcock Presents*, *The Incredible Hulk*, *Men Into Space*, *Land of the Giants*, *Knight Rider* and others.

Serials

1951

Roar of the Iron Horse. Col., [15 Chapters] D: Spencer G. Bennet, Thomas Carr; SP: George H. Plympton, Sherman L. Lowe, Royal K. Cole;

P: Sam Katzman; Cam: Fayte Browne; Mus: Mischa Bakaleinikoff; LP: Jock Mahoney, Virginia Herrick, William Fawcett, Hal Landon, Jack Ingram, Myron Healey, Mickey Simpson.

1953

The Great Adventures of Captain Kidd. Col., [15 Chapters] D: Derwin Abbe, Charles S. Gould; SP: George H. Plympton, Arthur Hoerl; P: Sam Katzman; Cam: William Whitley; Mus: Mischa Bakaleinikoff; LP: Richard Crane, David Bruce, John Crawford, Marshall Reed, John Hart, Charles King, Myron Healey, Ray Corrigan, Edmund Cobb, George Wallace, Terry Frost, Wiletta Smith.

1955

Panther Girl of the Konga. Rep., [12 Chapters] D: Franklyn Adreon; SP: Ronald Davidson; AP: Franklyn Adreon; Cam: Bud Thackery; Mus: R. Dale Butts; LP: Phyllis Coates, Myron Healey, John Daheim, Mike Ragan, Ramsay Hill, James Logan, Fred Graham.

EDWARD HEARN

Guy Edward Hearn was born September 6, 1888, in Dayton, Washington, and his education was completed at Whitman College in Walla Walla. His first theatrical engagement was with the Acme Stock Company in Everett, Washington. Later he was with the Thurlow Bergen Stock Company in Seattle and with Russell and Drew Company in Seattle.

For two seasons Hearn was in vaudeville. Arriving in Los Angeles to play the Pantages House, he was persuaded by friends to try the movies. That he did. His first part was with Hobart Bosworth in *The White Scar* ('15). He then became leading man to Cleo Madison in *Her Defiance* ('16), *A Heart's Crucible* ('16), *Her Bitter Cup* ('16), *Eleanor's Catch* ('16) and *Virginia* ('16).

In 1917 Hearn appeared in *The Lost Express* in support of Helen Holmes and Leo Maloney. That same year he had one of the principal roles in the 21-episode *The American Girl*. He was with the Kalem Company for almost a year. At Pathé, Hearn had the juvenile lead in Jack Dempsey's *Daredevil Jack* ('20) and in 1921 had the male lead opposite Ruth Roland in *The Avenging Arrow*, also at Pathé. He had the lead with Gladys Walton in *All Dolled Up* ('21), with Enid Bennett in *Keeping Up with Lizzie* ('21), with Barbara Bedford in *The Face of the World* ('21) and with Anita Stewart in *Question of Honor* ('22).

Probably his best-remembered film was *The Man Without a Country* ('23), the story of a man sentenced to never see or hear of his country again. He is transferred from one warship to another as the years go by while his sweetheart tries in vain to get him pardoned. Finally, as an old man, he is pardoned by President Lincoln but dies on receiving news of his pardon.

Hearn shared honors with Peter the Great (a dog) in *Sign of the Claw* ('26) and with Ranger (another dog) in *Dog Justice* ('29). In *Winner Take All* ('24) and *The Big Hop* ('28) he supported Buck Jones. In *Hook and Ladder No. 9* (27) Hearn is a fireman who cannot accept the fact that Lucy Beaumont rejected him in favor of fellow fireman Cornelius Keefe.

Hearn's serial career continued in 1928 with a lead in *The Yellow Cameo* and was followed by eighteen other serials, the last being *Dick Tracy vs. Crime, Inc.* ('41). Mascot boss Nat Levine must have liked him, for Hearn acted in nine Mascot cliffhangers.

Edward Hearn died at the age of 74 at

Left to right: Edward Hearn, J. Carrol Naish, Bob Steele and Lucile Browne in *Mystery Squadron* (Mascot, 1933).

the Motion Picture Country Hospital in Woodland Hills, California.

Serials

1917

The American Girl

1920

Daredevil Jack. Pathé, [15 Chapters] D: W. S. Van Dyke; LP: Jack Dempsey, Josie Sedgwich, Herschel Mayall, Edward Hearn, Albert Cody, Frederick Starr.

1921

The Avenging Arrow. Pathé, [15 Chapters] D: W. S. Van Dyke, William Bowman; LP: Ruth

Roland, Edward Hearn, Virginia Ainsworth, S. E. Jennings, William Steele, Frank Lackteen.

1928

The Yellow Cameo. Pathé, [10 Chapters] D: Spencer Bennet; LP: Allene Ray, Edward Hearn, Cyclone (dog), Noble Johnson, Tom London.

1931

The Vanishing Legion. Mascot, [12 Chapters] D: B. Reeves Eason; LP: Harry Carey, Edwina Booth, Rex (horse), Frankie Darro, Philo McCullough.

The Galloping Ghost. Mascot, [12 Chapters] D: Armand Schaeffer; LP: Harold Grange, Dorothy Gulliver, Walter Miller, Gwen Lee.

1932

Shadow of the Eagle. Mascot, [12 Chapters] D: Ford Beebe, Colbert Clark, Wyndham Gittens; LP: John Wayne, Dorothy Gulliver, Walter Miller, Kenneth Harlan.

The Last of the Mohicans. Mascot, [12 Chapters] D: B. Reeves Eason, Ford Beebe; LP: Harry Carey, Hobart Bosworth, Frank Coghlan, Jr., Edwina Booth.

1933

Mystery Squadron. Mascot, [12 Chapters] D: Colbert Clark, David Howard; LP: Bob Steele, "Big Boy" Williams, Lucile Browne, Jack Mulhall, J. Carrol Naish, Robert Kortman, Jack Mower.

Fighting with Kit Carson. Mascot, [12 Chapters] D: Armand Schaeffer, Colbert Clark; LP: Johnny Mack Brown, Betsy King Ross, Noah Beery, Jr., Noah Beery, Sr.

1934

Burn 'Em Up Barnes. Mascot, [12 Chapters] D: Colbert Clark, Armand Schaeffer; LP: Jack Mulhall, Frankie Darro, Lola Lane, Julian Rivero, Jason Robards.

Mystery Mountain. Mascot, [12 Chapters] D: B. Reeves Eason, Otto Brower; LP: Ken Maynard, Verna Hillie, Edward Earle, Syd Saylor, Tarzan (horse).

1935

The Miracle Rider. Mascot, [15 Chapters] D: Armand Schaeffer, B. Reeves Eason; LP: Tom Mix, Joan Gale, Charles Middleton, Jason Robard, Charles King, Wally Wales [Hal Taliaferro], Tom London, Edward Hearn, Jack Rockwell, Robert Kortman, Edmund Cobb.

1938

The Great Adventures of Wild Bill Hickok. Col., [15 Chapters] D: Mack V. Wright, Sam Nelson; LP: Gordon [Bill] Elliott, Carole Wayne, Frankie Darro, Dickie Jones.

The Spider's Web. Col., [15 Chapters] D: Ray Taylor, James W. Horne; LP: Warren Hull, Iris Meredith, Richard Fiske, Kenneth Duncan, Forbes Murray.

Red Barry. Univ., [13 Chapters] D: Ford Beebe, Alan James; LP: Buster Crabbe, Frances Robinson, Wade Boteler, Edna Sedgwick, Philip Ahn, Frank Lackteen.

1939

Dick Tracy's G-Men. Rep., [15 Chapters] D: William Witney, John English; LP: Ralph Byrd, Irving Pichel, Phylis Isley [Jennifer Jones], Ted Pearson, Walter Miller, Kenneth Harlan, George Douglas, Jack Ingram, Edward Hearn, Charles Hutchison, Reed Howes.

1940

Deadwood Dick. Col., [15 Chapters] D: James W. Horne; LP: Donald Douglas, Lorna Gray [Adrian Booth], Lane Chandler, Marin Sais, Harry Harvey, Charles King.

Adventures of Red Ryder. Rep., [12 Chapters] D: William Witney, John English; LP: Donald Barry, Tommy Cook, Maude Pierce Allen, Vivian Coe [Austin], Noah Beery, Sr., William Farnum, Harry Worth, Hal Taliaferro.

1941

White Eagle. Col., [15 Chapters] D: James W. Horne; LP: Buck Jones, Raymond Hatton, Dorothy Fay, James Craven, John Merton, Edward Hearn, Charles King.

Holt of the Secret Service. Col., [15 Chapters] D: James W. Horne; LP: Jack Holt, Evelyn Brent, Tristram Coffin, John Ward, Edward Hearn, George Chesebro.

Dick Tracy vs. Crime, Inc. Rep., [15 Chapters] D: William Witney, John English; LP: Ralph Byrd, Jan Wiley, John Davidson, Ralph Morgan, John Merton, Hooper Atchley, Anthony Warde, Kenneth Hearn, Edward Hearn, Forrest Taylor.

WILLIAM (BILL) HENRY

Bill Henry spent most of his life in the film industry. Born in 1918, he appeared in *Lord Jim* ('26) and other bit roles while attending elementary and high school. In 1934 he was in *The Thin Man* and from there to 1970 acted in a hundred films.

Republic starred Henry in the cliffhanger *Canadian Mounties vs. Atomic Invaders* ('53), made when serial production was shutting down. As Sgt. Don Roberts of the Canadian Mounted Police, Bill is assigned to track down a group of foreign agents who plan to launch guided atomic missiles aimed at key American cities. He is aided by Kay Conway (Susan Morrow), undercover agent for the Canadian government.

Serial

1953

Canadian Mounties vs. Atomic Invaders. Rep., [12 Chapters] D: Franklyn Adreon; SP: Ronald Davidson; Cam: John MacBurnie; Mus: Stanley Wilson; LP: Bill Henry, Susan Morrow, Arthur Space, Dale Van Sickel, Pierre Watkin, Mike Ragan, Stanley Andrews, Harry Lauter, Edmund Cobb.

RUTH HIATT

Ruth Hiatt co-starred in the comedy series "The Smith Family," filmed in 1926–28. There were 23 two-reel episodes starring Ruth, Raymond McKee and Mary Ann Jackson. Mack Sennett produced for Pathé release, and the stories centered around the frustrations of a not-so-typical family. Ruth was pretty, Raymond had a unique comedy talent and Mary Ann touched the heartstrings of audiences. The series was popular.

It is believed that Ruth acted in other two-reelers, but the author does not have information on them.

In 1927, Ruth played opposite Harry Langdon in *His First Flame*, a farce, and opposite Syd Chaplin in *The Missing Link*, another farce. In *Shanghai Rose* ('29), an underworld drama, she supported Irene Rich and William Conklin. In *Her Man* ('30) she had a small role supporting Helen Twelvetrees and Ricardo Cortez.

Ruth played heroine to Ken Maynard in *Sunset Trail* ('32) and to Tom Tyler in *Ridin' Thru* ('34) and had a small role in *Good Dame* ('34) starring Sylvia Sidney and Fredric March. Seven years later she was appearing in Harry Langdon's *Double Trouble* ('41).

The Chinatown Mystery ('28) was a fast-action Syndicate Pictures serial featuring Joe Bonomo and Francis Ford. Ruth had a formula for producing artificial diamonds and the evil "Sphinx" (Ford) was after it. Bonomo was cast as a Secret Service operative who struggles to protect both Ruth and the valuable paper.

Hiatt died at age 88 in 1994 in Montrose, California, from a congestive heart.

Serial

1928

The Chinatown Mystery. Syn., [10 Chapters]
D: J. P. McGowan; LP: Joe Bonomo, Ruth Hiatt,
Francis Ford, George Chesebro, Sheldon Lewis,
Peggy O'Day, Grace Cunard, Helen Gibson,
Rosemary Theby, Al Baffert, Paul Malvern.

JOSEPHINE HILL

Josephine Hill was in four serials, three as a supporting player and one as the female lead. But by no stretch of the imagination could she be thought of as a serial queen. But what about Westerns? There she could claim some sort of fame for the number she made. In the following list the number of films she made with the cowboy is shown in parentheses: Leo Maloney (44), Jack Perrin (15), George Larkin (8), Hoot Gibson (7), Perrin-Gibson (3), Bob Reeves (2), Jack Hoxie (2), Bruce Gordon (2), William Fairbanks (1), Frank Mayo (1), Tom Tyler (1), Lane Chandler (1), Joe Ryan (1), Gareth Hughes (1) and Wally Wales (1). If one merely went by the number of Westerns a girl made, Josephine would be a contender for the title "Queen of the West." Dale Evans, Peggy Stewart, Marjorie Reynolds, Wanda McKay and a slew of other actresses would be left at the starting gate. Dale Evans, for example, made only 29 Westerns.

San Francisco was Josephine's birthplace and the date was October 3, 1902. She began on the stage at the age of four and between stage appearances she attended Hearst Grammar School in San Francisco and Normandie Avenue public schools in Los Angeles. After high school graduation she went to New York, where she appeared in Gus Edwards' Review. She appeared on screen for Edward Lewis, a motion picture producer, followed by a series of comedies at Mitten-thal Studio. Then came a trip to California and a contract with Universal.

In 1922, while working in the Warner Brothers serial *A Dangerous Adventure*, she was clawed by a leopard. That same year she played the female lead in *Night Life in Hollywood*, one of the few non–Westerns she made.

From 1919 through 1921, Hill was under contract to Universal, making light-hearted Western two-reelers with Hoot Gibson and a Northwest series of straightout action opuses with George Larkin.

In 1922 she signed with Malobee, a company formed by Leo Maloney and Ford Beebe, to do a series of two-reel "Range Rider" Westerns. She played the heroine in 23 of the shorts. When the series ended in 1923, she kept right on working with Maloney, but in five- or six-reel features for William Steiner Productions. Josephine made 21 cactus capers with him. She was also playing the love interest in Jack Perrin Westerns for Harry Webb Films—15 of them! The make-believe love on the screen became the real thing off the screen and the two were married. They had a daughter, Patricia, but were divorced in 1937. There her story seems to end, although the author was once told that Hill worked at MGM in some capacity.

Serials

1917

The Voice on the Wire. Univ., [15 Chapters]
D: Stuart Paton; SP: J. Grubb Alexander; S: Eustace Hale Ball; LP: Ben Wilson, Neva Gerber,

Joseph W. Girard, Francis McDonald, Kingsley Benedict, Ernest Shields, Hoot Gibson, Josephine Hill, Nigel De Bruiler.

1922

A Dangerous Adventure. WB, [15 Chapters] D: Sam and Jack L. Warner; SP: Sam Warner; S: Frances Guihan; P: William Selig; LP: Grace Darmond, Philo McCullough, Jack Richardson, Robert Agnew, Derelys Perdue, Rex de Rosselli, Josephine Hill, Mabel Stark.

1927

Heroes of the Wild. Mascot, [10 Chapters] D:

Harry Webb; S/SP: Harry Webb, Karl Krusada; P: Nat Levine: LP: Jack Hoxie, Josephine Hill, Joe Bonomo, Linda Loredo, White Fang (horse), Tornado (dog), Helen Gibson.

1931

Sign of the Wolf. Met., [10 Chapters] D: Forrest Sheldon, Harry S. Webb; S/SP: Betty Burbridge, Karl Krusada, Harry Webb; LP: Rex Lease, Virginia Brown Faire, Joe Bonomo, Jack Mower, Josephine Hill, Al Ferguson, Robert Walker, Edmund Cobb, Jack Perrin, Harry Todd, King (dog).

VERNA HILLIE

Verna Hillie's one claim to serial immortality is *Mystery Mountain*, produced in 1934 by Mascot Pictures and starring Ken Maynard. Anyone having seen the film's 12 chapters is not likely to forget Verna. Although Maynard had a reputation of being cantankerous and a ladies' man, Verna told this writer that she found him to be pleasant and strictly professional during the three weeks the film was in production. *Mystery Mountain* was Mascot's top grosser until surpassed by Tom Mix's *The Miracle Rider* ('35). In the story, a railroad tunnel is to be constructed through Iron Mountain. Only the Rattler knows that the mountain contains a rich gold vein. Ken and his horse Tarzan thwart his nefarious plans.

The multi-talented Hillie was born of Finnish extraction, in Hancock, Michigan, on May 5, 1914. Graduating from high school at age 16, Verna found work as a receptionist for five Detroit attorneys while also studying acting with Jessie Bonstelle. This led to local theater work and a part on the radio drama *Young Widow Brown*, then being broadcast in Detroit. She did some modeling

and industrial films on weekends. This activity led to Hillie's winning a beauty contest and becoming a finalist in the Panther Woman contest being conducted by Paramount. Though she did not win the contest and the chance to play that part in *Island of Lost Souls* ('32), she did receive a Paramount contract. She was brought to Hollywood and won her spurs in *Under the Tonto Rim* ('33), a non-programmer Western starring Stu Erwin, and in *Man of the Forrest* ('33) starring Randolph Scott.

Verna married radio emcee Frank Gill, Jr., on November 18, 1933, and they had two daughters, Pamela and Kelly.

At Paramount, Verna developed Bell's Palsy, which paralyzed one side of her face. The studio let her go. However, she recovered in about two months, and it was during the subsequent year that she freelanced and did the Westerns for which she is fondly remembered. After *House of Mystery* ('34) at Monogram, she had the heroine role in John Wayne's *The Star Packer* ('34) and *The Trail Beyond* ('34). These were made by Monogram but released under the Lone Star logo. For Universal she played small parts but they dried up when Verna repelled the advances of Carl Laemmle, Jr.

Verna next starred with Ralph Forbes in another independent, *Rescue Squad* ('35). With her screen career behind her, Verna started helping her husband with screenplays. She also worked with him as a radio director-writer, and was associated with such radio programs as *Burns and Allen*, *Texaco Comedy Hour*, *Mr. District Attorney* and *Voice of America*. The Gills divorced in 1951.

In 1952 she married Richard Linkroun, who had three daughters himself by a former marriage. He was a vice-president of NBC and directed some of the Jack Benny shows. The marriage lasted 11 years, ending in divorce.

Following the Linkroun divorce she went into hospital administration becoming director of volunteers, nurse recruitment and patient relations at New York Medical College. She kept the job for nine years.

From 1978 to 1983 she was the United States representative for Barbara Cartland, the famed English writer of historical romances. Afterwards she went into business for herself, teaching non-regional speech to corporate executives and lecturing part-time at the New York City YWCA on the topic "How to Project the Image That Gets You What You Want."

Verna suffered from ill health in her last years, enduring a stroke, cataracts and emotional problems. She died on October 3, 1997, at the Carolton Retirement Home in Fairfield, Connecticut. She was 83.

Serial

1934

Mystery Mountain. Mascot, [12 Chapters] D: B. Reeves Eason, Otto Brower; SP: Bennett Cohen, Armand Schaefer; P: Nat Levine; Spv.: Victor Zobel, Armand Schaefer; Cam: Ernest Miller, William Nobles; Mus: Lee Zahler, Abe Meyer; LP: Ken Maynard, Verna Hillie, Syd Saylor, Edward Earle, Lynton Brent, Tarzan (horse).

CAROL HOLLOWAY

Carol Holloway's bright record of adventurous work in four melodramatic serials assured her a niche in the history of that genre, and her several Westerns gave her some claim to recognition in that closely knit film fraternity.

Little is known about this unusually pretty girl. Her eyes contained a sparkling fascination for many — too lovely, too classical, too perfect to be real. She was truly a rare beauty with her curvaceous figure, large blue eyes, dark brown hair, red cheeks (natural — not makeup) and full lips. Her comeliness and sexuality helped her cause as she struggled for the brass ring in the competitive, cutthroat world of motion pictures in the World War I era.

Carol was the daughter of a college professor, of Scottish descent. Born in Williamstown, Massachusetts, and educated in Franklin, Massachusetts, she had a stage career with the Carleton Stock Company and appeared on the New York stage in a production of *Everywoman*. She worked at several studios before joining Vitagraph. Once there she plunged whole-heartedly in the rough-and-tumble of serial production, professing to like the outdoor work.

Carol's first film of record was *A Strange Melody* ('14) for Lubin. After that, she worked mainly for American Film Company before moving on to Vitagraph where her first assignment was the serial *The Fighting Trail* ('17) starring William Duncan. The team of Holloway and Duncan was popular and they made two more features, *Dead Shot Baker* ('17) and *The Tenderfoot* ('17), as well as a second serial, *Vengeance and the Woman* ('17), making for a very busy year. But the team was split up for some reason, with Duncan acquiring Edith Johnson as co-star in his future serials, while Carol was cast opposite Antonio Moreno in the popular serials *The Iron Test* ('18) and *The Perils of Thunder Mountain* ('19). After leaving Vitagraph, Carol worked in several cowboy flicks with Tom Mix and one each with Peter Morrison, Harry Carey, Buck Jones, Hoot Gibson and Tom Tyler, and played good supporting parts in non–Westerns. But with the coming of sound, Carol's career nose-dived into obscurity. She got bit parts and extra work and could be seen as late as 1940 in *Emergency Squad*, the last film credit found for her. Sadly, Carol was just one more example of a heartthrob of Hollywood's youth who was cast aside as the industry grew to maturity.

Serials

1917

The Fighting Trail. Vit., [15 Chapters] D: William Duncan; LP: William Duncan, Carol Holloway, George Holt, Joe Ryan, Walter Rodgers, Fred Burns.

Vengeance and the Woman. Vit., [15 Chapters] D: William Duncan; LP: William Duncan, Carol Holloway, George Holt, Tex Allen, Vincente Howard, Fred Burns.

1918

The Iron Test. Vit., [15 Chapters] D: Robert N. Bradbury, Paul Hurst; S: Albert E. Smith, Cyrus Townsend Brady; LP: Antonio Moreno, Carol Holloway, Barney Furey, Chet Ryan, Jack Hoxie, Frank Jonasson, Charles G. Rich.

1919

The Perils of Thunder Mountain. Vit., [15 Chapters] D: Robert N. Bradbury, W. J. Bauman; S: Albert E. Smith, Cyrus Townsend Brady; LP: Antonio Moreno, Carol Holloway, Kate Price, Jack Waltemeyer, George Stanley, A. D. Regnier, Tote DuCrow.

HELEN HOLMES

Born July 7, 1892, in Louisville, Kentucky, Helen Holmes attended Saint Mary's Convent school in Chicago, where she studied painting at the Art Institute. Because her family was poor, she became a photographer's model in her youth and contributed what she could at home. When the family moved to the Death Valley region of California because of her brother's health, Helen moved with them. Her father had some interest in a California ranch and some Funeral Mountain mines. Because she was the only girl in a 50-mile radius and because help was hard to come by, Helen became adept at ranch life, shooting, riding and roping with real skill.

In 1911, Helen, a buxom girl in her teens, wrote to her friend, Mabel Normand, a Keystone actress, who advised her to come to Hollywood. This she did. She got considerable modeling work and was the subject of the Santa Fe Girl, a railroad poster. Through Mabel she got work in Keystone's *Kings Court* ('12) and *Barney Oldfield's Race for Life* ('13).

Holmes moved over to the Kalem Studio in 1913, where under the direction of J. P. McGowan, whom she later married, she specialized in hair-raising stunts that made her a favorite of millions of silent-era theatergoers. Holmes' favorite stunt was to be tied in front of an onrushing locomotive and being rescued by the hero just a split second before the engine thundered across the tracks.

Holmes' specialties were railroad serials and Western features. She scored a huge success in 1914–15 as the original star of the series *The Hazards of Helen*. She starred in the first 48 episodes of the series before leaving Kalem in 1915. The series continued running successfully through February 1917 (119 episodes) with Helen Gibson in the principal role. When Gibson was unavailable for filming due to illness or the like, her part was quite likely to be played by other actresses (Robyn Adair, Anna Q. Nilsson, or Elsie MacLeod).

After a brief stay at Universal, where she and husband J. P. McGowan made *The Mettle of Jerry McGuire*, *A Desperate Leap* and *When Rogues Fall Out*, Holmes signed with Signal, a subsidiary of Mutual, where she starred in another serial, *The Girl and the Game* ('15). For several years she had a huge following, trailing Pearl White and Ruth Roland for popularity as the screen's "serial queen." Her serials typically had a railroad background and her specialty was chasing bad guys along the top of a moving train and leaping from train to horse or horse to train with both in motion.

The serial *Lass of the Lumberlands* ('16) followed a year later. In 1917, two serials were turned out, *The Railroad Raiders* and *The Lost Express*. Each grossed in excess of $2 million. *Whispering Smith* ('16) and its sequel *Medicine Bend* ('16) were two of Helen's better features. Almost as popular was *Judith of the Cumberlands* ('16), a story of an ancient mountain feud.

The SLK Serial Corporation released *The Fatal Fortune* in 1919. *The Tiger Band*, produced by Holmes and Warner Brothers, was released in 1919, as were several five-reel features. Both serials were states-righted, which meant that a much smaller number of theaters showed the films.

For the next ten years Helen played in a number of Westerns and railroad films, sometimes as star, co-star, or supporting player. *Ghost City* ('21) was one of her better Westerns, and further serial honors were earned with William Desmond in *The Riddle Rider* ('24) and with Franklyn Farnum in *Battling Brewster* ('24). For movie fans, state-righted programmers such as *Duped* ('25), *The Train Wreckers* ('25), *The Open Switch* ('26), *Peril of the Rail* ('26) and *Crossed Sig-*

nals ('26) were enjoyable respites from life's realities.

Some time around 1925, the Holmes-McGowan marriage hit the cacti. Holmes' subsequent marriage to film cowboy–stuntman Lloyd Saunders heralded her retirement from the screen. Her final series had been produced by Morris Schlank's California Studio and marketed by Rayart, one of the more durable independent distributors. Holmes and her husband moved to Sonora to operate a huge ranch into which they plowed much of their savings. Several years of bad luck forced them to give it up, and her husband went back on the rodeo circuit to earn much needed money.

In 1945 Holmes made the papers by becoming a Hollywood animal trainer, specializing in preparing dogs for movie roles. In 1946, Lloyd Saunders died. Holmes was already suffering from a heart condition at the time, and for the next five years her condition deteriorated. She operated a small antiques business until her death on July 8, 1950, from a heart attack. At her bedside when she died was long-time friend, Helen Gibson. Miss Holmes was 58 years old.

Holmes was survived by an adopted daughter, Mrs. Doro McGowan Barone of Redondo Beach, California.

Serials

1914

The Hazards of Helen. Kalem, [119 Episodes] D: J. P. McGowan, James Davis; S: W. Scott Darling; LP: Helen Holmes, Helen Gibson, Robyn Adair, Ethal Clisbee, Tom Trent, G. A. Williams, Hoot Gibson, Hartford [Jack] Hoxie, Leo D. Maloney, True Boardman.

1915

The Girl and the Game. Signal/Mutual, [15 Chapters]. McGowan; S: Frank Hamilton Spearman; P: Samuel S. Hutchinson; LP: Helen Holmes, Leo Maloney, J. P. McGowan, George McDanile.

1916

Lass of the Lumberlands. Signal/Mutual, [15 Chapters] D: J. P. McGowan, Paul Hurst; SP: E. Alexander Powell, Ford Beebe and others; LP: Helen Holmes, Leo Maloney, Thomas Lingham, William J. Chapman.

1917

The Railroad Raiders. Signal/Mutual, [15 Chapters] D: J. P. McGowan; SP: Ford Beebe and others; LP: Helen Holmes, Leo Maloney, William Brunton, William Chapman.

The Lost Express. LP: Helen Holmes.

1919

The Tiger Band. Warner Bros. [15 Chapters] D: Gilbert P. Hamilton; LP: Helen Holmes, Jack Mower, Dwight Crittendon, William Brunton.

The Fatal Fortune. SLK Serial Corp., [15 Chapters] D: Donald McKenzie; SP: Walter Richard Hull; P: Sherman L. Krellberg; LP: Helen Holmes, Jack Levering, Leslie King, Bill Black, Frank Wunderlee.

1924

Battling Brewster. Rayart, [15 Chapters] D/P: Dell Henderson; Spv.: George Blaisdell; SP: Robert Dillon; LP: Franklyn Farnum, Helen

Holmes, Leon Holmes, Robert Walker, Lafe McKee, Emily Barrye.

The Riddle Rider. Univ., [15 Chapters] D: William Craft; SP: William Wing, Arthur H. Gooden, George Pyper; LP: William Desmond, Eileen Sedgwick, Helen Holmes, Claude Payton, William H. Gould, Ben Corbett, Yakima Canutt.

STUART HOLMES

A long nose, mustache and high forehead characterized Stuart Holmes, one of the silent screen's busiest actors. He was born March 10, 1887, in Chicago. A veteran of the stage, he became a screen actor in 1911 in *How Mrs. Murray Saved the Army*. He had the top role in the first Fox venture, 1914's *Life's Shop Window*. Other early starring roles were in *A Daughter of the Gods* ('16) with Arnette Kellerman; *The Scarlet Letter* ('17), based on Nathaniel Hawthorne's novel, with Mary Martin as Hester, a Puritan woman with an illegitimate baby and Holmes as the Reverend Arthur Dimmesdale, her secret lover; *The New Moon* ('19) with Norma Talmadge; *The Prisoner of Zenda* ('22) with Alice Terry and Lewis Stone; *Tess of the D'Urbervilles* ('24), in which Tess (Blanche Sweet) kills her betrayer, Alec D'Urberville (Holmes) and then herself; *The Four Horsemen of the Apocalypse* ('21) with Rudolph Valentino and Alice Terry; and *Passion Fruit* ('21) with Doraldina as Regina and Holmes as Rance, the villain who wants to possess her and her estate.

In the 1920 serial *Trailed by Three*, Holmes is intent on securing pearls brought to the States by Frances Mann to sell so that the proceeds can be used to buy the freedom of South Seas island people who have been enslaved by a cruel pirate. It's a three-way struggle for the pearls.

The serial *The Evil Eye* ('20) stars Benny Leonard, lightweight champion of the world, in a story of a relentless and powerful gang of crooks who are pursuing a million dollars in bonds. A mastermind of the underworld is wheeled about in an invalid chair, burning his "evil eye" into everyone he meets, and blinding those who fall into disfavor with him.

Holmes died in 1981 at age 84 from a ruptured abdominal aorta.

Serials

1920

Trailed by Three. Pathé, [15 Chapters] D: Perry Vekroff; LP: Frances Mann, Stuart Holmes, John Webb Dillon, Wilfred Lytell, William Welsh, Ruby Hoffman, John Wheeler.

The Evil Eye. Hallmark, [15 Chapters] D: J. Gordon Cooper, Wally Van; LP: Benny Leonard, Stuart Holmes, Ruth Dwyer, Maria Shotwell, Marstini, Bernard Randall.

JACK HOLT

The name Jack Holt was synonymous with action and adventure. He was not a great actor and he personally had no pretensions about it. Nevertheless, he was a popular screen player for nearly four decades. He played both heroic and villainous roles with equal aplomb in a career that spanned from the days of silent black-and-white movies made by hand-cranked cameras to the era of sound pictures, full color and power-driven synchronized cameras.

Charles John Holt, Jr. (Jack) was born May 31, 1888, in the rectory of St. James Episcopal Church in the Fordham section of New York City. However, Jack loved the Winchester, Virginia, area and publicly claimed that location as his birthplace.

Holt's adventures began in the spring of 1906 when he was expelled from Virginia Military Institute as the result of a series of practical jokes and pranks that were not appreciated by the school commandant. After a stint of work as a sandhog on the construction of the Hudson River Railroad Tunnel, he went to Alaska where he spent several years as a prospector, a stagecoach driver, a rural mail carrier (horseback in fair weather and dog sled in winter) and a freight packer. In Oregon he worked as a cowhand for a time and wound up in the San Francisco Bay area with a crew of surveyors.

In September 1914, Holt, out of work and nearly broke, hired on as a horse wrangler and extra for the film *Salomy Jane*. When the double for House Peters backed out of a riding stunt (jumping a horse over a dynamited bridge span), Holt took on the stunt for $25 and so his movie career began.

By early 1915 he was working steadily at Universal City as an extra and as a stuntman in fight scenes. In August 1915 he received his first credited role, a cad in *A Cigarette That's All* ('15). During most of the early part of 1916 he was a member of the Grace Cu-

In *Outlaws of the Orient* (Columbia, 1937).

nard-Francis Ford stock item in their action one- and two-reelers, and by the fall of 1916 he was cast as the hero in the first Western serial, *Liberty* ('16).

The serial starred Marie Walcamp as Liberty and Holt as a Texas Ranger captain in love with her. Neal Hart, Roy Stewart and Eddie Polo were featured.

Holt was signed by Paramount in 1917, supporting Sessue Hayakawa in *The Call of the East*, Kathlyn Williams in *The Cost of Hatred*, Hobart Bosworth in *The Inner Shrine*, Margaret Illingyon in *Sacrifice* and Hayakawa and Florence Vidor in *The Secret Game*.

The Little American ('17) directed by Cecil B. DeMille, was the film that launched Holt on the road to stardom. Mary Pickford starred. Clara Kimball Young, Milton Sills and Jack have the leads in *The Claw* ('18), a melodrama set in Africa with Holt cast as a wealthy Englishman and villain extraordinaire.

On the High Seas ('22), a rugged sea adventure with Dorothy Dalton, established the pattern that Holt's non–Westerns would follow for the next 20 years—high adventure seasoned with varying amount of romance, large quantities in the beginning and lesser amounts as Jack grew older in the late 1930s and early 1940s.

Holt was put into a series of Zane Grey Westerns which were to make his name familiar the world over. He would thereafter be considered a Western star. The films—all based on Zane Grey's writings—were *Wanderer of the Wasteland* ('24), *The Thundering Herd* ('25), *The Light of Western Stars* ('25), *Wild Horse Mesa* ('25), *Forlorn River* ('26), *Born to the West* ('26), *The Mysterious Rider* ('27), *The Vanishing Pioneer* ('28), *The Water Hole* ('28), *Avalanche* ('28), *Sunset Pass* ('29) and *The Border Legion* ('30).

Holt became a Columbia star in 1927, signing a long-term contract with the then-minor studio. *Submarine* ('28) was Columbia's first sound film and its most prestigious one to that time. *Flight* ('29) was his second big film at Columbia; *Dirigible* ('31) was his third. These films were successes and Holt was in solid at Columbia. He made a long series of adventure and action pictures. Most of these are generally dismissed as routine programmers but this is precisely where many critics have missed the point. It was the time of the Great Depression and the Holt pictures are purely escapist entertainment and they brought just that to many persons.

Holt was a man of imposing appearance, tall, muscular but trim of build, possessing a strong, handsomely chiseled face and steady brown eyes. For most of his life he wore a neatly trimmed moustache.

Holt was especially popular with the male audience. He was the personification of a "man's man" and a movie fan could escape his worries for a time and go adventuring with Jack Holt.

His last film for Columbia was the serial *Holt of the Secret Service* ('41). Columbia boss Harry Cohn hated Jack and so Jack was assigned to the serial as punishment. Even though cheaply made, it is entertaining for Holt fans. Jack and Evelyn Brent are secret service agents pursuing counterfeiters.

Following the end of his contract with Columbia, Holt was a freelancer. Cohn tried his best to keep Holt from working, but in spite of his black-balling Jack got supporting roles in *Cat People* ('42), *Northwest Rangers* ('42) and *Thunder Birds* ('42).

Among his other talents, Holt had also become an expert judge of horses. At the request of Gen. George C. Marshall, Holt temporarily retired from filmmaking in 1943 to become a buyer of horses for the U.S. Cavalry. He was discharged in 1945 with the rank of major.

John Ford used Holt in *They Were Expendable* ('45); the actor was also seen in *My Pal Trigger* ('46), *The Chase* ('46), *The Treasure of the Sierra Madre* (cameo) ('48), *The Arizona Ranger* ('48), co-starring with son Tim, *Red Desert* ('49), *Task Force* ('49), *The Trail of Robin Hood* ('50), *The Daltons' Women* ('50), *King of the Bullwhip* ('50) and *Across the Wide Missouri* ('51).

Holt died of a heart attack while being admitted to the Veterans Hospital in Santa Monica on January 18, 1951.

Serials

1914

The Master Key. Univ., [15 Chapters] D: Robert Z. Leonard; SP: Calder Johnson; LP: Robert Z. Leonard, Ella Hall, Harry Carter, Jean Hathaway, Alfred Hickman.

1915

The Broken Coin. Univ., [22 Chapters] D: Francis Ford; SP: Grace Cunard; S: Emerson Hough; P: Francis Ford; LP: Francis Ford, Grace Cunard, Harry Schumm, Reese Gardiner, Ernest Shields, W. C. Canfield, Jack Holt, Eddie Polo.

1941

Holt of the Secret Service. Col., [15 Chapters] D: James W. Horne; SP: Basil Dickey, George H. Plympton, Wyndham Gittens; Cam: James S. Brown, Jr.; Mus: Lee Zahler; P: Larry Dar- mour. LP: Jack Holt, Evelyn Brent, Montague Shaw, Tristram Coffin, John Ward, Ted Adams, Edward Hearn, George Chesebro, Stanley Bly- stone.

JENNIFER HOLT

Hollywood was the birthplace of Eliza- beth Marshall Holt, better known as Jennifer. She was born on November 10, 1920, the daughter of Jack Holt and sister of Tim Holt.

The marriage of Jack and wife Margaret was disintegrating and so Jennifer was whisked off to Belgium with her governess to spend two years in a convent in Bruge. She returned from Belgium in 1930 and at- tended Gardner Junction Junior High for one year. It was the last year the Holts would be together as a family living under the same roof. Margaret and her two daughters (she had one by a former marriage) moved for a couple of years to Chile, where Jennifer at- tended American schools.

Back in California in 1934, Jennifer was enrolled in Bishops School and graduated in 1939, at age 19.

Margaret lived in Pacific Palisades dur- ing Jennifer's years at Bishop, and it was to Margaret's house that Jennifer would return during vacations. But she got to see a lot of Jack and Tim, too, usually going to see her

The author, Buck Rainey, and Jennifer Holt, Nashville, Tennessee, 1976.

father on Sundays. Neither Margaret nor Jack ever visited Jennifer at Bishop, for it was a difficult drive in those days.

Jennifer enrolled in Maria Ouspenskaya's drama school and in the summer of 1941 was sent by Maria to work and study with the Peterborough Players in New Hampshire, where she appeared in several plays, the most notable being Thornton Wilder's *Our Town.*

Returning to California in 1941, she got the leading lady part in Paramount's Hopalong Cassidy feature *Stick to Your Guns* ('41). It was the only time she was billed "Jacqueline."

On January 2, 1942, she was signed as a contract player by Universal. She played the leading lady in Johnny Mack Brown's *The Silver Bullet* ('42) and supported Brown and Tex Ritter in a series of seven Westerns: *Deep in the Heart of Texas* ('42), *Little Joe the Wrangler* ('42), *The Old Chisholm Trail* ('42), *Tenting Tonight on the Old Campground* ('43), *Cheyenne Roundup* ('43), *Raiders of the San Joaquin* ('43) and *The Lone Star Trail* ('43).

She also played with Robert Paige in *Cowboy in Manhattan* ('43) and *Get Going* ('43) and with Deanna Durbin in *Hers to Hold* ('43). In the serial *Adventures of the Flying Cadets* ('43), she plays Andre Mason, daughter of Prof. Mason, who heads an expedition into Africa to search for helium deposits. Jennifer ended 1943 by supporting Eddie Dew and Smiley Burnette in *Raiders of Sunset Pass* at Republic and Russell Hayden and Fuzzy Knight in *Frontier Law* at Universal.

During the years 1944–1948 Jennifer played in 28 Westerns, as follows: Eddie Dean, 5; Johnny Mack Brown, 4; Lash Larue, 4; Rod Cameron, 3; Russell Hayden, 3; Tex Ritter, 2; Jimmy Wakely, 2; Dave O'Brien–Jim Newill, 1; Hoot Gibson–Bob Steele, 1; Noah Beery, Jr., 1; Richard Arlen, 1; and Ken Curtis, 1.

Jennifer made industrial films in Chicago and starred in the "Uncle Mistletoe and Aunt Judy" show aired over WENR-TV, Channel 7, Chicago, sponsored by the Marshall Field Company. In 1949 the show won the *TV Guide* award as the best original children's TV show. In 1951 she won the coveted Peabody Award for the best children's show in America. When the show was dropped in the fall of 1950, Jennifer and Johnny Coons went immediately into the "Panhandle Pete and Jennifer" show, initially on ABC and later on NBC.

Jennifer was first married in 1941 and had a succession of marriages after that. In 1975 this author located her in Santa Barbara and she aided him in the preparation of the book *The Fabulous Holts.* She attended several Western film festivals and was warmly received.

During her last years, Jennifer lived in Mexico and then in England, where she died from cancer on September 21, 1997.

Serials

1943

Adventures of the Flying Cadets. Univ., [13 Chapters] D: Ray Taylor, Lewis D. Colllins; SP: Morgan B. Cox, George H. Plympton, Paul Huston; AP: Henry MacRae; Cam: William Sickner; Mus: Everett Carter, Milton Rosen; LP: Johnny Downs, Bobby Jordan, Jennifer Holt, Ward Wood, Eduardo Ciannelli, Billy Benedict, Robert Armstrong, Regis Toomey.

1946

Hop Harrigan. Col., [15 Chapters] D: Derwin Abrahams; SP: George H. Plympton, Ande Lamb; Adapt: Jon Blummer; P: Sam Katzman; Cam: Ira H. Morgan; Mus: Lee Zahler; LP: William Bakewell, Jennifer Holt, Buzz Henry, Sumner Getchell, Claire James, John Merton, Wheeler Oakman.

HARRY HOUDINI

The famed escape artist was born Erich Weiss on March 24, 1874, in Budapest, Hungary, and chose a pseudonym for his professional career. Harry had been a cutter in a clothes factory, which was not a job he wished to pursue for any length of time. It is not known how he learned his "bag of tricks," but learn he did, becoming an accomplished escape artist, lecturer and showman extraordinaire. Harry was not a magician *per se*, but rather he was an escape artist and by 1918 he was becoming world-famous. His stage performances were generally sold out.

Harry had one more challenge — motion pictures. Realizing that he could reach far greater audiences on film than he could in his stage shows, he was enthusiastically receptive to an offer from producer B. A. Rolfe of Octagon Films to star him in a serial. Arthur B. Reeve wrote the story in collaboration with Houdini.

The Master Mystery was released in March 1920. The first of its 15 chapters was three reels in length; the other, two reels. Harry plays Quentin Locke, a Secret Service agent who opposes a ruthless business magnate out to suppress all competition and promote itself. Quentin soon finds himself fighting a metal monster called Q, the automaton, one of the most unlikely villains in cliffhanger history. The automaton could withstand bullets and other weapons. Unknown to Quentin, the metal monster was inhabited by a human. Throughout the serial the "Emissaries of the Automaton" tried their best to kill Quentin but without success. Houdini had an opportunity to display a wide variety of his best tricks.

Jesse Lasky signed Houdini for two Artcraft specials, even though it was apparent that Harry was a poor actor. One might say that he had two expressions—constipation and relief. *The Grim Game* ('19) was released by Paramount-Artcraft in five reels. In the story, Houdini is a newspaper reporter in love with Ann Forrest, the ward of his rich uncle, who opposes the match. A plan is hatched to make Houdini look guilty of the (faked) murder of his uncle, in order to argue against circumstantial evidence. The scheme backfires: The uncle is actually murdered and Houdini is arrested. He then has a series of escapes from handcuffs, chains and a straitjacket, culminating in an airplane collision. Houdini is finally vindicated and reunited with Ann. The film only grossed about $200,000 in world revenues, far less than had been expected.

In *Terror Island* ('20), released by Paramount-Artcraft and directed by James Cruze, Houdini is the inventor of a device for salvaging sunken vessels. His girl Lila Lee acquires his help in rescuing her father from South Seas islanders holding him for ransom. Lee is kidnapped by her guardian and heads out to sea. Houdini follows and saves Lila when she is thrown overboard. Exciting events occur which give Harry a change to demonstrate his magic. This film generated even less revenue than *The Grim Game* and Paramount did not renew his contract.

Houdini left for a six-month tour of Great Britain, where he performed before enthusiastic audiences. His self-esteem renewed, Houdini returned from England and organized the Houdini Film Corporation. He produced and starred in *The Soul of Bronze* ('21), *The Man from Beyond* ('22) and *Haldane of the Secret Service* ('23). The films were not big moneymakers. His inability to loosen up and appear natural on screen accounted in large measure for his failure to master the medium of movies. His personality on the stage sparked an enthusiasm in live audiences that his screen image failed to ignite.

Harry Houdini died in 1926 from peritonitis from a ruptured appendix in Detroit, Michigan. He was 52.

Serial

1920

The Master Mystery. Octagon, [15 Chapters] P: B. A. Rolfe; S/SP: Arthur B. Reeve, Charles A. Logue; LP: Harry Houdini, Marguerite Marsh, Ruth Stonehouse, Floyd Buckley.

REED HOWES

Viewing PRC's *Dead or Alive* ('44), Columbia's *Sante Fe* ('51), Monogram's *Trigger Smith* ('39), PRC's *Billy the Kid in Santa Fe* ('41) or Republic's *Black Hills Express* ('43), one is amazed to realize that the henchman portrayed by Reed Howes in these films is the same man who co-starred with Clara Bow in *Rough House Rosie* ('27) or that, as the model for Arrow Collar dress shirts, he was acclaimed as America's handsomest man on advertisements all over the country.

Reed was born in 1900 in Washington, D.C. After studies at the University of Utah, he attended courses at Harvard. During summer vacations he conducted tours for a travel agency and encountered a lot of silly women who gave him an exaggerated opinion of his good looks. In New York he met Neil Hamilton, an artist's and photographer's model, who showed him the ins and outs of the commercial modeling racket. Reed, Neil and an ex–Annapolis midshipman named Brian Donlevy became collectively The Arrow Collar Man, who simpered or glowered from all the nation's billboards and magazines.

Reed quickly attained stage stardom as leading man to Billie Burke in *Intimate Strangers* and to Peggy Wood in *Artist's Life*. He made his film debut in 1923 and for a decade played dashing romantic heroes (often in action melodramas) opposite some of the screen's most glamorous stars. His popularity declined with the advent of sound.

After leads in a number of low-budget productions he was reduced to supporting roles.

In 1930, Reed starred in one of the last silent serials, *Terry of the Times* (a sound version was also released). A criminal band known as the Mystic Mendicants attempt to keep Terry from inheriting the *Times* by preventing him from fulfilling provisions of his father's will to marry by a certain date. A treacherous (and, as it turns out, fake) brother of publisher Robert McCoy, Terry's uncle, disguises himself as Macy, the paper's publisher, and attempts to block Terry's marriage and his interference with the Mendicants' criminal operations.

In 1935 Reed and co-star Mary Kornman played the leads in the cheaply made *Queen of the Jungle*, a thriller incorporating much footage from the 1922 *Jungle Goddess*. David Worth (Reed) returns to Africa to search for his childhood playmate Joan Lawrence (Mary), who was lost years before when, on an expedition to Africa with their parents, the balloon she was playing in got loose and drifted over the jungle. When it was shot down by tribesmen, Joan became a white priestess to the superstitious tribe and grew up as their queen. Once reunited with David, they attempt to escape from the jungle and the tribespeople who wish to hold her.

Beginning in 1938, Reed appeared almost exclusively in serials and Westerns. However, in his last film, *The Sinister Urge* ('61), he portrays a police inspector who assigns Lt. Matt Carson (Kenne Duncan) and Sgt. Randy Stone (Duke Moore) to bring in the killers of several girls who had posed for pornographic magazines. This obscure exploitation melodrama was the final legitimate theatrical film directed by the "infamous" Edward D. Wood, Jr.

Ill health forced Reed to retire after completion of this film. He died in August 1964 at the Motion Picture Country Hospital. He had no survivors.

Serials

1930

Terry of the Times. Univ., [10 Chapters] D: Henry MacRae; LP: Reed Howes, Lotus Thompson, Sheldon Lewis, John Oscar.

1933

Fighting with Kit Carson. Mascot, [12 Chapters] D: Armand Schaefer, Colbert Clark; LP: Johnny Mack Brown, Betsy King Ross, Noah Beery, Sr., Noah Beery, Jr.

1935

Queen of the Jungle. [12 Chapters] D: Robert Hill; S: Griffin Jay; Spv.: Herman A. Wohl; Cam: William Hyer; Mus: Hal Chasnoff; LP: Reed Howes, Mary Kornman, George Chesebro, Lafe McKee, Dickie Jones.

1936

Flash Gordon. Univ., [13 Chapters] D: Frederick Stephani; LP: Buster Crabbe, Jean Rogers, Charles Middleton, Frank Shannon, Richard Alexander.

Custer's Last Stand. [15 Chapters] D: Elmer Clifton; P: George M. Merrick; SP: George A. Durlam, Eddy Graneman, William Lively; Mus: Hal Chasnoff; Cam: Bert Longnecker; LP: Rex Lease, William Farnum, Reed Howes, Jack Mulhall, Lona Andre, Dorothy Gulliver, George Chesebro.

1937

Zorro Rides Again. Rep., [12 Chapters] D: William Witney, John English; LP: John Carroll, Helen Christin, Duncan Renaldo, Noah Beery, Sr., Richard Alexander.

1938

The Lone Ranger. Rep., [15 Chapters] D: William Witney, John English; LP: Lee Powell, Chief Thundercloud, Lynne Roberts, Herman Brix, Wally Wales [Hal Taliaferro], John Merton, Stanley Andrews.

The Secret of Treasure Island. Col., [15 Chapters] D: Elmer Clifton; LP: Don Terry, Gwen Gaze, Grant Withers, Hobart Bosworth.

Flash Gordon's Trip to Mars. Univ., [15 Chapters] D: Ford Beebe and Robert F. Hill; LP: Buster Crabbe, Jean Rogers, Charles Middleton, Frank Shannon, Beatrice Roberts, Donald Kerr.

The Fighting Devil Dogs. Rep., [12 Chapters] D: William Witney, John English; LP: Lee Powell, Herman Brix, Eleanor Stewart, Montagu Love, Hugh Sothern.

Dick Tracy Returns. Rep., [15 Chapters] D: William Witney, John English; LP: Ralph Byrd, Lynne Roberts, Charles Middleton, Jerry Tucker.

1939

The Phantom Creeps. Univ., [12 Chapters] D: Ford Beebe, Saul A. Goodkind; LP: Bela Lugosi, Robert Kent, Dorothy Arnold, Regis Toomey, Edward Van Sloan.

The Green Hornet. Univ., [13 Chapters] D: Ford Beebe, Ray Taylor; LP: Gordon Jones, Anne Nagel, Keye Luke, Wade Boteler.

Dick Tracy's G-Men. Rep., [15 Chapters] D: William Witney, John English; LP: Ralph Byrd, Irving Pichel, Phylis Isley [Jennifer Jones], Ted Pearson.

Buck Rogers. Univ., [12 Chapters] D: Ford Beebe, Saul A. Goodkind; LP: Buster Crabbe, Constance Moore, Jackie Moran, Jack Mulhall.

Zorro's Fighting Legion. Rep., [12 Chapters] D: William Witney, John English; LP: Reed Hadley, Sheila Darcy, William Corson, Leander de Cordova.

1940

Flash Gordon Conquers the Universe. Univ., [12 Chapters] D: Ford Beebe, Ray Taylor; LP: Buster Crabbe, Carol Hughes, Charles Middleton, Anne Gwynne, Frank Shannon, Roland Drew, Lee Powell.

Adventures of Red Ryder. Rep., [12 Chapters] D: William Witney, John English; LP: Donald Barry, Noah Beery, Sr., Maude Pierce Allen, Vivian Coe [Austin].

1942

The Valley of Vanishing Men. Col., [15 Chapters] D: Spencer G. Bennet; LP: Bill Elliott, Slim Summerville, Carmen Morales, Kenneth MacDonald, Jack Ingram.

1943

Secret Service in Darkest Africa. Rep., [15 Chapters] D: Spencer Bennet; LP: Rod Cameron, Joan Marsh, Duncan Renaldo, Lionel Royce, Kurt Kreuger.

1944

The Great Alaskan Mystery. Univ., [13 Chapters] D: Ray Taylor, Lewis D. Collins; LP: Milburn Stone, Marjorie Weaver, Edgar Kennedy, Samuel S. Hinds, Fuzzy Knight, Joseph Crehan.

The Desert Hawk. Col., [15 Chapters] D: B. Reeves Eason; LP: Gilbert Roland, Mona Maris, Ben Welden, Kenneth MacDonald, Frank Lackteen, Charles Middleton.

1948

Superman. Col., [15 Chapters] D: Spencer Bennet, Thomas Carr; LP: Kirk Alyn, Noel Neill, Tommy Bond, Pierre Watkin, Carol Forman, George Meeker, Jack Ingram.

1956

Blazing the Overland Trail. Col., [15 Chapters] D: Spencer G. Bennet; LP: Lee Roberts, Dennis Moore, Norma Brooks, Gregg Barton, Don C. Harvey, Reed Howes.

JACK HOXIE

Jack Hartford Hoxie was born on January 11, 1888, in Kansas, just a short distance from the Indian Territory, according to a note placed in the family Bible by his mother. The family moved into Indian Territory where Jack's father was a veterinarian; his mother was a full-blood Nez Perce Indian. Hoxie was only five years old when his father was kicked by a stallion and died. His mother remarried. Early on Hoxie took to rodeoing. When his parents sold the Indian Territory ranch and moved to Idaho, Hoxie went along as a full-fledged working cowboy. During this time he married a girl by the name of Pearl Gage. The marriage was a brief one. Tiring of the daily drudgery of cowboy life, Hoxie moved into Boise where he got a job as head packer for the Fort there. His skill and riding ability made him popular in many rodeos as bronc buster and bulldogger.

In 1909, Hoxie signed on with the Dick Stanley Wild West Show. He had met Hazel Panky at the show when it was in Boise and had married her during one of the performances. He and Hazel were off with the show, the first of many Hoxie would work for.

Jobless and stranded in California at the end of the show season, bronc-busting Hoxie overnight became Hartford Hoxie, fledgling motion picture actor. The year was 1911 or '12. With his riding ability it was easy to pick up jobs at various studios as a stuntman, extra and bit player. Gradually he rose to more important roles, one of his most notable early ones being in *The Dumb Girl of Portici* at Universal in 1916. At Kalem he supported Helen Holmes in *The Hazards of Helen* ('14) and various two-reelers.

It was his part in *Blue Blazes Rawden* ('18), a William S. Hart film, that really launched Hoxie as a Western star in the period 1918–27. Other early appearances were in *Man from Nowhere, The Iron Test, Sparks of Flint, Told in the Hills, Valley of the Giants, Nan of Music Mountain* and *Johnny Get Your Gun.*

In his private life, Hoxie was married to five different women. First was to Pearl Gage before he was 21. Next was to Hazel Panky, who bore him two daughters, Ramona and Pearl. The marriage lasted until around 1918 or '19. Hoxie then married Marin Sais, with whom he worked in pictures. He supported her in two series, *The American Girl* and *The Girl from Frisco.* The marriage was a good one in many respects, and she gave Hoxie what polish he might have had, a thin veneer at best. His fourth wife is unknown to this author, but apparently she was the mother of Jack Hoxie, Jr. In 1944 Hoxie married for the fifth and last time. The lady was Bonnie Showwalter and the marriage lasted until Hoxie's death.

In 1919, Hoxie was signed by National Film Company to co-star with Ann Little in *Lightning Bryce,* a 15-chapter cliffhanger well-received by audiences. Hoxie was kept on to star in *Thunderbolt Jack,* another serial. Scoring big again with action fans, Hoxie was signed by Arrow Films for a Western series. He made 13 whirlwind sagebrushers in 1921–22. Hoxie was a mighty man on the horse and in a screen brawl, and his giddyups usually conformed 100 percent to the old-time idea of what a rousing mustanger should be.

In 1922, Hoxie signed with Sunset Productions and made eight Westerns. These films were a cut above the Arrow oaters in quality. Robert North Bradbury (Bob Steele's father) directed most of them.

Hoxie's first film with Universal was *Don Quickshot of the Rio Grande* ('23). He went on to star in about 35 slick oaters for Universal, at a beginning salary of $500 a week. His second contract with Universal called for $1,000 a week.

Something happened between Hoxie and Universal in 1927, the result being that Hoxie tore up his contract. It was like signing his own death warrant. From that day he was washed

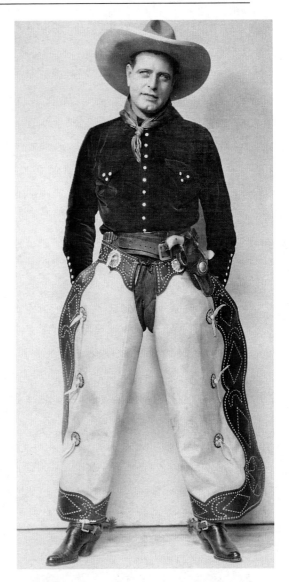

up in the movies. Nat Levine had formed Mascot Pictures about this time and hired Hoxie to head up one of the last silent serials, *Heroes of the Wild* ('27). After that, there were no offers. Studios were gearing for sound.

In 1928, Hoxie toured the country with the Charles Sparks Circus, thrilling audiences with his ability as a trick rider. When Sparks sold his circus, Hoxie joined the Miller Brothers 101 Ranch Show in Oklahoma. Hoxie had a good, fast-moving act and was assisted by the female trick rider, Dixie Starr, his famous mount Scout, his dog Bunkie and a few cowboys.

In 1932–33, Hoxie made his last Western series. It was a cheap group of "quickies" put out by Majestic Pictures that did nothing to bolster his sagging popularity. Audiences were turning to the new breed of cowboys. Hoxie's voice was not very good for sound and he had trouble with the scripts. He could read and write only poorly. He retired permanently from the screen.

Hoxie hit the sawdust trail with the Jack Hoxie Circus in 1937 and 1938. In 1939 he headed up Lewis Brothers Circus. In 1944, after marrying for the fifth time to Bonnie Showwalter, Hoxie joined Mills Brothers Circus and traveled with them for five years. Over the years he traveled with other shows, culminating his circus activity with the Bill Tatum Circus in 1959.

Hoxie lived on his small ranch in Mulberry, Arkansas for a few years until leukemia put a stop to his activities. In the early '60s he moved to Keyes, Oklahoma, to a little place his mother had owned, and it was here he spent his last days quietly, often reminiscing with fans who remembered him and sought him out.

Jack Hoxie died on March 27, 1965, at Elkhart, Kansas, and was buried at Keyes. He was 77 years old.

Serials

1914

The Hazards of Helen. Kalem, [119 Episodes] D: J. P. McGowan, James Davis; LP: Helen Holmes, Helen Gibson, Robyn Adair, Ethel Clisbee, Tom Trent, G. A. Williams, Hoot Gibson, Jack Hoxie, Roy Watson.

1915

The Diamond from the Sky. Amer., [30 Chapters] D: Jacques Jaccard, William Desmond Taylor; LP: Lottie Pickford, Irving Cummings, William Russell, Charlotte Burton.

1916

The Girl from Frisco. Kalem, [16 Chapters] D: James W. Horne; LP: Marin Sais, True Boardman, Frank Johnson, Ronald Bradbury, Josephine West, Edward Clisbee, Hartford Hoxie.

1917

The American Girl. Kalem, [21 Episodes] D: James W. Horne; LP: Marin Sais, Frank Jonasson, Edward Hearn, Edward Clisbee, Hartford Hoxie.

1918

The Iron Test. Vit., [15 Chapters] D: Robert N. Bradbury, Paul C. Hurst; LP: Antonio Moreno, Carol Holloway, Hart Hoxie, Barney Furey, Chet Ryan.

A Fight for Millions. Vit., [15 Chapters] D: William Duncan; LP: William Duncan, Edith Johnson, Joe Ryan, Walter Rodgers, Leo Maloney, Hart Hoxie.

The Bull's Eye. Univ., [18 Chapters] D: James W. Horne; SP: Harvey Gates, Tom Gibson, Frank Clark; LP: Eddie Polo, Vivien Reed, Frank Lanning, Roy Harford, William Welsh, Hal Cody, Walter Coburn, Hartford Hoxie.

1919

Lightning Bryce. National/Arrow, [15 Chapters] D: Paul Hurst; S: Joe Brandt; SP: Harvey Gates; LP: Jack Hoxie, Ann Little, Steve Clemento, Ben Corbett, Paul Hurst, Walter Patterson.

1921

Thunderbolt Jack. Arrow, [15 Chapters] D: Francis Ford or Murdock MacQuarrie; S: Joe Brandt; Spv.: Ben Wilson; LP: Jack Hoxie, Marin Sais, Chris Frank, Alton Stone [Al Hoxie], Edith Stayart.

1927

Heroes of the Wild. Mascot, [10 Chapters] D: Harry Webb; S/SP: Harry Webb, Karl Krusada; P: Nat Levine; LP: Jack Hoxie, Josephine Hill, Joe Bonomo, Tornado (dog), White Fury (horse).

CAROL HUGHES

Carol Hughes is best remembered as Dale Arden in the third Flash Gordon serial, *Flash Gordon Conquers the Universe* ('40). She is also the priestess of the hidden city in Columbia's *Jungle Raiders* ('45) and she has a bit in *Hop Harrigan* ('46), a Columbia serial.

Hughes had the distinction of being Roy Rogers' first leading lady. The film was *Under Western Stars* ('38). She had already impressed audiences in a number of films as a Warner Brothers contract player, and had proven herself a most worthy ingenue in *Renfrew of the Royal Mounted* ('37) with Jim Newill and especially as heartthrob to Gene Autry in *Gold Mine in the Sky* ('38) and *Man from Music Mountain* ('38). At Warners, Hughes had received critics' approval for her performances in two Joe E. Brown comedies, *Polo Joe* ('36) and *Earthworm Tracters* ('36).

Hughes was destined to make two more films with Rogers, *Border Legion* ('40) and *Home in Oklahoma* ('46); one more with Autry, *Under Fiesta Stars* ('41); and one with Tim Holt, *Stagecoach Kid* ('49).

As a contract player at Warners, Hughes could be seen in *The Case of the Velvet Claws* ('36), *Stage Struck* ('36), *Three Men on a Horse* ('36), *Ready Willing and Able* ('37), *Ever Since Eve* ('37) and *Pillow to Post* ('45). For RKO she appeared in *Married and in Love* ('40), *Scattergood Baines* ('41), *The Bachelor and the Bobby-Soxer* ('47) *et al.* and three Gil Lamb two-reel comedies, *Baby Makes Two* ('53), *Fresh Painter* ('53) and *Pardon My Wrench* ('53).

At MGM she played in *The Women* ('39), *I'll Wait for You* ('41), and *Scaramouche* ('52); at Universal she appeared in *The West-land Case* ('37), *She's for Me* ('43), *Weekend Pass* ('44), *The Naughty Nineties* ('45), *The Beautiful Cheat* ('45) and *Girl on the Spot* ('46); at Paramount she was in *Lucky Jordan* ('42); at Monogram she appeared in *Top*

James Newill and Carol Hughes in *Renfrew of the Royal Mounted* (Grand National, 1937).

Sergeant Mulligan ('41), *The Red Dragon* ('46) and *Joe Palooka, Champ* ('46); at PRC she was in *The Miracle Kid* ('41), *Desperate Cargo* ('41) and *My Son the Hero* ('43), and at Columbia she was in *What's Buzzin' Cousin?* ('43).

Hughes was pretty, vivacious and possessed greater acting ability than the ordinary "B" Western ingenue. Unfortunately, though, she was not able to break out of "B" programmers or to even soar to the summits of that film bracket. Her talent was deserving of better film fare than she received.

Hughes married much-older actor Frank Faylen when she was barely out of her teens, but the marriage was a lasting one. She died August 8, 1985, just six days after the death of her husband of 47 years.

Serials

1940

Flash Gordon Conquers the Universe. Univ., [12 Chapters] D: Ford Beebe, Ray Taylor; SP: George H. Plympton, Basil Dickey, Barry Shipman; Cam: Jerry Ash; P: Henry MacRae; LP: Buster Crabbe, Carol Hughes, Charles Middleton, Anne Gwynne, Frank Shannon, Roland Drew.

1945

Jungle Raiders. Col., [15 Chapters] D: Lesley Selander; SP: Ande Lamb, George H. Plympton; P: Sam Katzman; Cam: Ira H. Morgan; Mus: Lee Zahler; LP: Kane Richmond, Eddie Quillan, Veda Ann Borg, Carol Hughes, Janet Shaw.

1946

Hop Harrigan. Col., [15 Chapters] D: Derwin Abrahams; LP: William Bakewell, Jennifer Holt, Robert "Buzz" Henry, Sumner Getchell.

KAY HUGHES

Kay Hughes (born 1914) could have been one of Republic's better heroines had she stayed there longer. But she wasn't employed long enough to build the following enjoyed by Republic heroines such as Linda Stirling, Peggy Stewart, Ruth Terry and Lynne Roberts (Mary Hart).

As the leading lady in two of the studio's popular serials—*The Vigilantes Are Coming* ('36) and *Dick Tracy* ('37)—and two films each with Gene Autry and the Three Mesquiteers, she was off to a good start. Kay made a mistake at this juncture. She wanted to do better things and broke her contract with Republic to go to Universal. Universal changed her name to Catherine and cast her in the serial *Radio Patrol* ('37). She did a few other inconsequential films and retired in 1940 after she married Eric Linden, a still photographer. They had a daughter. Kay made a minor comeback in 1945 at PRC with Buster Crabbe and Dave O'Brien but it wasn't the same and she went back to being a mother to her child. She divorced and remarried in 1947. Husband Number Two died in 1964 and Kay remarried for the third time. After his death, she moved to Desert Hot Springs, California, to be near her sister.

Serials

1936

The Vigilantes Are Coming. Rep., [12 Chapters] D: Mack V. Wright, Ray Taylor; SP: John Rathmell, Maurice Geraghty, Winston Miller; S: Maurice Geraghty, Leslie Swabacker; Cam: William Nobles, Edgar Lyons; Mus: Harry

Grey; P: Nat Levine; LP: Robert Livingston, Kay Hughes, Guinn Williams, Raymond Hatton, Fred Kohler, Robert Warwick, William Farnum.

1937

Dick Tracy. Rep., [15 Chapters] D: Ray Taylor, Alan James; SP: Barry Shipman, Winston Miller; S: Morgan Cox, George Morgan; Cam: William Nobles, Edgar Lyons; Mus: Harry

Grey; LP: Ralph Byrd, Kay Hughes, Smiley Burnette, Lee Van Atta, John Picorri, Carleton Young, Fred Hamilton, Francis X. Bushman.

Radio Patrol. Univ., [12 Chapters] D: Ford Beebe, Cliff Smith; SP: Ray Trampe, Wyndham Gittens, Norman S. Hall; P: Barney Sarecky, Ben Koenig; LP: Grant Withers, Catherine [Kay] Hughes, Mickey Rentschier, Adrian Morris, Max Hoffman, Jr., Frank Lackteen, Leonard Lord, Dick Botiller, Harry Davenport.

WARREN HULL

The actor who played the Spider, Mandrake the Magician and the Green Hornet was born John Warren Hull on January 17, 1903, in Gasport, New York. He graduated from high school in Auburn, New York, and studied at both New York University and the University of Rochester, where he studied voice.

Warren made his professional debut in the chorus of operettas, which led to leading roles in *The Student Prince, My Maryland, Rain or Shine* and *Follow Through,* all on Broadway.

After going to Hollywood where he made his film debut in *Personal Maid's Secret* ('35), he also appeared on radio shows, including the *Maxwell House Showboat* and the Jack Haley show. Later he was co-interviewer on ABC's *Vox Pop.* Following World War II (during which he staged Vox Pop for servicemen at camps and bases in France, Britain, Alaska and Puerto Rico), Hull starred in CBS's *Across the Board* and was emcee for *Cavalcade of Bands* for Dumont ('50).

It was as a master of ceremonies of radio and television that he became most successful. Warren was also a cast member on the variety show *A Couple of Joes* in 1949–50, hosted the Ben Grauer talk show (1950), was host-moderator for the *Crawford*

Warren Hull in *Mandrake the Magician* (Columbia, 1939).

Mystery Theatre drama-quiz in 1951 and hosted the *Who in the World* interview show in 1962.

Hull turned in a most acceptable performance in *The Spider's Web* ('38)—not only as the Spider, but as his alter egos

Richard Wentworth, amateur criminologist, and Blinky McQuade, underworld hood. There is a great deal of action but it does not rely as heavily on fights as do Republic serials. *The Spider's Web* has heavies dropping like flies as the Spider kills no less than two criminals per chapter. It is easily one of the most violent serials as far as mayhem is concerned. It is 15 chapters of explosions, careening automobiles, trap doors, crashing airplanes, poison gas and plain old-fashioned falls off roofs. There are some effective stunts performed by Hull's double, George DeNormand. The Octopus, a grotesque, seemingly crippled criminal genius, threatens a large city and possibly the nation by striking at key industries.

The story of *Mandrake, the Magician* ('39) focuses on a radium energy machine invented by Prof. Houston. The Wasp, master criminal, will do practically anything to possess it, including blowing up a radio station. The Wasp knows it can be used as a weapon of destruction. Learning that Mandrake is returning from Tibet with the formula for a platonite steel alloy needed to perfect the device, the Wasp orders his men to kidnap Houston and steal his prototype model. Thus begins a long struggle between Mandrake and his friends on one side and the Wasp and his criminal band on the other. Hull stars as Mandrake and Al Kikume is his brawny sidekick Lothar, king of an unknown African tribe.

In 1940's *The Green Hornet Strikes Again*, Hull is Britt Reid, crusading newspaper publisher, who again dons his disguise as The Green Hornet to bring to justice a sinister criminal named Grogan and the syndicate he controls. Seeing Hull instead of Gordon Jones (the Hornet in an earlier serial) made *Strikes Again* better than the first, if one is to believe the critics.

Hull repeated his role of the Spider in Columbia's *The Spider Returns* ('41). A group of saboteurs led by a mysterious foreign agent known as the Gargoyle is attempting to neutralize defense projects. Authorities seek the aid of amateur criminologist Richard Wentworth who, unknown to them or the

enemy, sometimes takes on the identity of the Spider. *The Spider Returns* is a less serious serial than *The Spider's Web*. James Horne was noted for some rather hilarious scenes in his serials, but he seems to have outdone himself here.

From 1935 to 1941, Hull made 32 "B" features in addition to the four serials. The features include *Miss Pacific Fleet* ('35), *The Walking Dead* ('36), *Bengel Tiger* ('36), *Fugitive in the Sky* ('37), *Hawaii Calls* ('38), *Smashing the Spy Ring* ('39), *Yukon Flight* ('40) and *Bowery Blitzkreig* ('41).

Hull, who lived in Southbury, Connecticut, died on September 14, 1974, in Waterbury Hospital of congestive heart failure. He was 71. Surviving were his wife, Susan Fossum Hull, three sons, a stepson, two stepdaughters, a sister and 14 grandchildren.

Serials

1938

The Spider's Web. Col., [15 Chapters] D: Ray Taylor, James W. Horne; SP: Robert E. Kent, Basil Dickey, George Plympton, Martin Ramson; Cam: Allen G. Siegler; P: Jack Fier; Mus: Morris Stoloff; LP: Warren Hull, Iris Meredith, Richard Fiske, Kenneth Duncan, Forbes Murray.

1939

Mandrake, the Magician. Col., [12 Chapters] D: Sam Nelson, Norman Deming; SP: Joseph F. Poland, Basil Dickey, Ned Dandy; P: Jack Fier; Cam: Benjamin Kline; Mus: Lee Zahler; LP: Warren Hull, Doris Weston, Al Kikume, Edward Earle, Rex Downing.

1940

The Green Hornet Strikes Again. Univ., [15 Chapters] D: Ford Beebe, John Rawlins; AP: Henry MacRae; LP: Warren Hull, Keye Luke, Wade Boteler, Anne Nagel, Eddie Acuff, Pierre Watkin, Joe Devlin, Al Bridge, Lane Chandler.

1941

The Spider Returns. Col., [15 Chapters] D: James W. Horne; SP: Jesse A. Duffy, George

Plympton; Mus: Lee Zahler; Cam: James S. Brown, Jr.; P: Larry Darmour; LP: Warren Hull, Mary Ainslee, Dave O'Brien, Joseph Girard, Kenneth Duncan, Corbet Harris.

PAUL HURST

Paul Hurst was born in 1888 and reared on the Miller and Lux Ranch in Tulare County, California. A quarter-bred Cherokee Indian, he was mostly self-educated. He worked for a while for utility companies in the Sierras, then moved to San Francisco and sought work with the Alcazar Stock Company. Though he had no acting experience, he was hired. The year was 1907 and he played his first stage role there in *Johnny Comes Marching Home*. For several years thereafter he developed his acting ability as a character actor in various Pacific Coast productions in support of Maude Adams, Lillian Russell, William Collier and other well-known stage performers.

In 1911, Paul entered movies as an actor-director-writer at Kalem. A few of his early acting assignments were in *Redwing and the Paleface* ('12), *Driver of the Deadwood Coach* ('12), *The Big Horn Massacre* ('13), *The Smugglers of Lone Isle* ('14) and *When Thieves Fall Out* ('15).

In 1915, Paul undertook the role of Howie, the "Down Under" friend of Irving Randolph, who flees to Australia when he is falsely accused of murder. There he becomes known as the bandit Stingaree and is aided in his Robin Hood–like adventures by his friend Howie and his sweetheart. The serial was *Stingaree* ('16) and it starred True Boardman and Marin Sais. In 1916, Paul again supported Boardman and Sais. The serial was *The Social Pirates*. That same year Paul could also be seen in *A Lass of the Lumberland* ('16) starring Helen Holmes and Leo Maloney. He also co-directed that serial with J. P. McGowan.

The Further Adventures of Stingaree

('17) was directed by Hurst, who also reprised his role of Howie. Also released in '17 was *The Railroad Raiders* with Hurst in a minor acting role. In *Lightning Bryce* ('19) he both directs and plays the role of Powder Solvang, a pugnacious outlaw leader bent on finding gold deposits which are also sought by hero and heroine, whose fathers had mined it originally.

Hurst also directed the following: *Black Sheep, Shadows of the West* ('21); *The Crow's Nest, The Heart of a Texan, The Kingfisher's Roost, Table Top Ranch* ('22); *Golden Silence* ('23); *The Courageous Coward, The Passing of Wolf Maclean* ('24); *Battling Bunyon, The Demon Rider, The Fighting Cub, The Gold Hunters, The Rattler, The Son of Sontag, A Western Engagement* ('25); *The High Hand, Fighting Ranger, Battling Kid, Law of the Snow Country, Roaring Road, The Midnight Message, Son of a Gun, Shadows of Chinatown* ('26); *The Range Raiders, Rider of the Law* ('27).

Hurst went back to acting in 1927 and again was seen in loathsome, menacing roles. He varied these with occasional character comedy parts and became known as a versatile performer. Much in demand as a freelance player during the first 15 months of the sound era, he only had five days of leisure.

Hurst portrayed a wide variety of characters, easily switching back and forth from comedy to villainy. His most memorable role — that of the Union soldier on the mansion stairwell who is shot by *Gone with the Wind's* Scarlett O'Hara — is etched in the minds of millions of people. Hurst's sound features numbered close to 200, among them *The Secret Six* ('31), *Island of Lost Souls* ('32),

Queen Christina ('34), *Sequoia* ('34), *We Who Are About to Die* ('36), *Slave Ship* ('37), *In Old Chicago* ('38), *Bad Lands* ('39), *The Westerner* ('40), *The Ox-Bow Incident* ('43), *Jack London* ('43), and *Nob Hill* ('45).

In 1949–50 Hurst supported Monte Hale in a series of Republic Westerns, and his career ended in 1953 with a role in *The Sun Shines Bright.*

Hurst learned to fly when airplanes generally were referred to as "crates" and "flying coffins." Bamboo and cheesecloth were among the materials with which they were built. For a time Hurst was part-owner of one of the oldest aviation schools in Los Angeles County.

During World War I, according to Hurst's studio biography, he spent two years with the French Foreign Legion. It has not been verified, so take it with a grain of salt.

His other hobbies were riding and writing, and he was a regular contributor to pulp magazines.

Hurst was found dead on February 27, 1953, in Coldwater Canyon. According to police he had shot himself with a German Luger. There was no suicide note found. A son, daughter and sister survived.

Serials

1915

Stingaree. Kalem, [12 Chapters] D/D/SP: James W. Horne; S: E. W. Hornung; LP: True Boardman, Marin Sais, Paul Hurst, Thomas Lingham, Frank Jonasson.

1916

The Social Pirates. Kalem, [15 Chapters] LP: Marin Sais, Ollie Kirby, True Boardman, Frank Jonasson, Paul Hurst.

A Lass of the Lumberland. Signal/Mutual, [15 Chapters] D: J. P. McGowan, Paul Hurst; LP: Helen Holmes, Leo D. Maloney, Thomas Lingham, William Chapman, Paul Hurst.

1917

The Further Adventures of Stingaree. Kalem, [15 Chapters] D: Paul Hurst; SP: Joseph Poland; S: E. W. Horning; LP: True Boardman, Marin Sais, Paul Hurst, Ollie Kirby, Thomas Lingham, Edythe Sterling, Barney Furey.

The Railroad Raiders. Signal/Mutual, [15 Chapters] D: J. P. McGowan; LP: Helen Holmes, Leo D. Maloney, William Brunton, William Chapman, Thomas Lingham, Paul Hurst.

1919

Lightning Bryce. National/Arrow, [15 Chapters] D: Paul Hurst; LP: Jack Hoxie, Anne Little, Paul Hurst, Jill Woodward, Noble Johnson.

CHARLES HUTCHISON

Charles Hutchison starred in seven serials, six of them Pathé films. In the 1930s and '40s he could be seen (if you didn't bat your eye) in at least six other serials.

So far as is known, Hutchison's first film appearance was in *The Little Angel of Canyon Creek* ('14).

Screen writer Bertram Millhauser, who knew the star, has expressed his opinion of the man: "Hutchison had little personal charm, elicited a minimum of sympathetic interest in his viewers, was not good looking, and was hawk-nosed, joweled, and barrel-chested. He gave the feeling of having no hard core under his muscles. But his brown eyes were clear and bright, and I assume his digestive tract functioned admirably."

Mr. Millhauser's judgment of Hutchison must not have been shared universally or he would never had headlined seven cliff-hangers.

The author has not found any credits for Hutchison for the years 1919–23 except for the serials. But he stayed busy in the remainder of the decade, first as a star, then as a supporting player as the 1920s closed out. His credits included *On Probation* ('24), *Fangs of the Wolf* ('24), *Hutch of the U.S.A.* ('24), *The Law Demands* ('24), *The Hidden Menace* ('25), *The Smoke Eaters* ('26), *Flying High* ('26), *Catch-as-Catch Can* ('27), *Pirates of the Sky* ('27 and *Out with the Tide* ('28).

In the 1930s he was getting bits and un-billed parts, and in the 1940s he was little more than an extra.

Hutchison was a good athlete and he emphasized fast-moving action in his films. It is hard to say what caused the serial addicts to lose interest in him, but personality was a factor.

Serials

1918

Wolves of Kultur. Pathé, [15 Chapters] D: Joseph A. Golden; LP: Leah Baird, Charles Hutchison, Betty Howe, Mary Hull, Edmund Dabby.

1919

The Whirlwind. Allgood, [15 Chapters] D: Joseph A. Golden; LP: Charles Hutchison, Edith Thornton, Richard R. Neill, Ben Walker, Karl Dane.

1921

Hurricane Hutch. Pathé, [15 Chapters] D: George B. Seitz; S: Charles Hutchison; LP: Charles Hutchison, Lucy Fox, Warner Oland, Diana Deer, Ann Hasting, Harry Semels.

Double Adventure. Pathé, [15 Chapters] D: W. S. Van Dyke; S: Jack Cunningham; P: Robert Brunton; LP: Charles Hutchison, Josie Sedgwick, Carl Stockdale, S. E. Jennings.

1922

Speed. Pathé, [15 Chapters] D/P: George B. Seitz; SP: Bertram Millhauser; S: Charles Hutchison; LP: Charles Hutchison, Lucy Fox, John Webb Dillon, Harry Semels, Cecile Bonnel.

Go Get 'Em Hutch. Pathé, [15 Chapters] P/D: George B. Seitz; S: Frank Leon Smith; LP: Charles Hutchison, Margaret Clayton, Richard R. Neill, Frank Hagney, Pearl Shepard.

1926

Lightning Hutch. Arrow, [10 Chapters] D: Charles Hutchison; SP: John Francis Natteford; LP: Charles Hutchison, Edith Thornton, Virginia Pearson, Eddie Phillips, LeRoy Mason.

1939

The Lone Ranger Rides Again. Rep., [15 Chapters] D: William Witney, John English; LP: Robert Livingston, Chief Thundercloud, Duncan Renaldo.

Dick Tracy's G-Men. Rep., [15 Chapters] D: William Witney, John English; LP: Ralph Byrd, Irving Pichel, Phylis Isley [Jennifer Jones], Ted Pearson.

1940

Mysterious Doctor Satan. Rep., [15 Chapters] D: William Witney, John English; LP: Eduardo Ciannelli, Robert Wilcox, Ella Neal, William Newell, Jack Mulhall.

Adventures of Red Ryder. Rep., [12 Chapters] D: William Witney, John English; LP: Donald Barry, Noah Beery, Sr., Tommy Cook, Vivian Coe [Austin].

1943

The Masked Marvel. Rep., [12 Chapters] D: Spencer G. Bennet; LP: William Forrest, Louise Currie, Johnny Arthur, David Bacon, Tom Steele.

1944

Captain America. Rep., [15 Chapters] D: John English, Elmer Clifton; LP: Dick Purcell, Lorna Gray [Adrian Booth], Lionel Atwill, Charles Trowbridge.

JACK INGRAM

Anyone claiming to be a knowledgeable serial buff would most surely be familiar with Jack Ingram, for he worked in at least 48 serials—31 for Columbia, 13 for Republic and four for Universal, and with few exceptions he portrayed indefatigable, straightforward hooligans carrying out the orders of a nefarious leader. As a leading subordinate heavy, he was hard to beat.

Ingram was born John Samuel Ingram in Chicago on November 15, 1902. His boyhood vacations were spent on his uncle's Wisconsin farm, where he learned to ride horses and to love all animals. When his family moved to Dallas, Texas, he went to school there. At age 15, he enlisted and served in the 8th Field Artillery overseas in World War I. Wounded and gassed, he spent two years in a French hospital.

Back home, Ingram registered at the University of Texas to study for a law degree, but love of the performing arts changed his focus. He became a member of a traveling minstrel show. Later he toured with the Mae West stage show, was spotted on Broadway in *Diamond Lil* and signed by Paramount in 1929 as a stuntman.

Arthur Ken Jones (*Western Film Collector*, July 1973) tells of Ingram doing all kinds of stunts with horses and automobiles and driving four-ups and six-ups (teams of horses hitched to a stagecoach), and of a 1936 incident when Ingram was doubling Errol Flynn. As Ingram was doing a leap from a high rock onto a horse and rider, the horse shied just enough for his timing to be off and he broke his arm, wrist and several ribs. It was all in a day's work.

Ingram played in close to 250 features and TV series, not counting the 48 serials. Much of his work was at Republic, but after 1940 he worked primarily for Columbia.

Ingram married Eloise Fullerton, columnist and publicist, in 1944 and the couple bought an old goat ranch off Topanga Canyon Road in Woodland Hills, California, that was being sold by Western stars James Newill and Dave O'Brien. Ingram set about building a Western street set that ultimately consisted of 75 buildings. Many theatrical films and TV shows were partially filmed there.

In the early 1950s Ingram's health declined and he sold the ranch to Four Star Productions. Having bought a 55-foot yacht, berthed at Long Beach Harbor, he sailed up and down the coast and to Catalina, where he and his wife had a summer home. After a while Ingram tired of the sea life and rented his yacht for sea pictures. Ziv used it in their *Sea Hunt* series.

On a fishing trip to Oregon, where he had a cabin, Ingram suffered a heart attack and was hospitalized for a month. Returning to California, he died in Canoga Park from a second heart attack on February 20, 1969. He had been hospitalized since January 1.

Serials

1936

Undersea Kingdom. Rep.., [12 Chapters] D: B. Reeves Eason, Joseph Kane; LP: Ray Corrigan, Lois Wilde, Monte Blue, William Farnum, Boothe Howard.

The Vigilantes Are Coming. Rep., [12 Chapters] D: Mack Wright, Ray Taylor; LP: Robert Livingston, Kay Hughes, Guinn Williams, Raymond Hatton, Fred Kohler.

1937

Dick Tracy. Rep., [15 Chapters] D: Ray Taylor, Alan James; LP: Ralph Byrd, Kay Hughes, Smiley Burnette, Lee Van Atta, Carleton Young, John Picorri.

Jungle Menace. Col., [15 Chapters] D: George

Melford, Harry Fraser; LP: Frank Buck, Esther Ralston, John St. Polis, Reginald Denny, Duncan Renaldo.

SOS Coast Guard. Rep., [12 Chapters] D: William Witney, Alan James; LP: Ralph Byrd, Bela Lugosi, Maxie Doyle, Richard Alexander, Herbert Rawlinson.

Zorro Rides Again. Rep., [12 Chapters] D: William Witney, John English; LP: John Carroll, Helen Christian, Duncan Renaldo, Noah Beery, Sr.

1938

The Lone Ranger. Rep., [15 Chapters] D: William Witney, John English; LP: Lee Powell, Herman Brix, Chief Thundercloud, Wally Wales [Hal Taliaferro], Lane Chandler.

The Fighting Devil Dogs. Rep., [12 Chapters] D: William Witney, John English; LP: Lee Powell, Herman Brix, Eleanor Stewart, Montagu Love, Hugh Sothern.

Dick Tracy Returns. Rep., [15 Chapters] D: William Witney, John English; LP: Ralph Byrd, Lynne Roberts, Charles Middleton, Jerry Tucker, David Sharpe.

1939

Dick Tracy's G-Men. Rep., [15 Chapters] D: Ralph Byrd, Irving Pichel, Phylis Isley [Jennifer Jones], Ted Pearson, Walter Miller, George Douglas, Reed Howes.

1940

Deadwood Dick. Col., [15 Chapters] D: James W. Horne; LP: Don Douglas, Lorna Gray [Adrian Booth], Marin Sais, Harry Harvey, Charles King, Lane Chandler, Robert Fiske.

The Green Archer. Col., [15 Chapters] D: James W. Horne; LP: Victor Jory, Iris Meredith, James Craven, Robert Fiske, Dorothy Fay, Forrest Taylor, Jack Ingram.

The Shadow. Col., [15 Chapters] D: James W. Horne; LP: Victor Jory, Veda Ann Borg, Robert Moore, Robert Fiske, J. Paul Jones, Jack Ingram, Charles King.

Terry and the Pirates. Col., [15 Chapters] D: James W. Horne; LP: William Tracy, Granville Owen, Joyce Bryant, Allen Jung, Victor De Camp, Sheila Darcy.

1941

White Eagle. Col., [15 Chapters] D: James W. Horne; LP: Buck Jones, Raymond Hatton, Dorothy Fay, James Craven, Jack Ingram, Charles King, John Merton.

King of the Texas Rangers. Rep., [12 Chapters] D: William Witney, John English; LP: Slingin' Sammy Baugh, Pauline Moore, Neil Hamilton, Duncan Renaldo, Monte Blue.

1942

Perils of the Royal Mounted. Col., [15 Chapters] D: James W. Horne; LP: Nell O'Day, Robert Stevens [Kellard], Herbert Rawlinson, Kenneth MacDonald, John Elliott.

The Valley of Vanishing Men. Col., [15 Chapters] D: Spencer G. Bennet; LP: Bill Elliott, Slim Summerville, Kenneth MacDonald, Jack Ingram, Carmen Morales.

1943

Batman. Col., [15 Chapters] D: Lambert Hillyer; LP: Lewis Wilson, Douglas Croft, J. Carrol Naish, Shirley Patterson, William C. Austin, Charles Middleton.

1944

The Great Alaskan Mystery. Univ., [13 Chapters] D: Ray Taylor, Lewis D. Collins; LP: Marjorie Weaver, Edgar Kennedy, Samuel S. Hinds, Ralph Morgan, Fuzzy Knight.

Raiders of Ghost City. Univ., [13 Chapters] D: Ray Taylor, Lewis D. Collins; LP: Dennis Moore, Wanda McKay, Lionel Atwill, Joe Sawyer, Regis Toomey, Jack Rockwell.

1945

Federal Operator 99. Rep., [12 Chapters] D: Spencer Bennet, Yakima Canutt, Wallace Grissell; LP: Marten Lamont, Helen Talbot, George J. Lewis, Lorna Gray [Adrian Booth], Hal Taliaferro, Tom London, Jack Ingram, Rex Lease.

Jungle Raiders. Col., [15 Chapters] D: Lesley Selander; LP: Kane Richmond, Veda Ann Borg, Eddie Quillan, Carol Hughes, Janet Shaw, Jack Ingram, John Elliott.

Manhunt of Mystery Island. Rep., [15 Chapters] D: Spencer Bennet, Yakima Canutt, Wallace Grissell; LP: Linda Stirling, Roy Barcroft, Richard Bailey, Kenne Duncan, Forrest Taylor, Forbes Murray, Jack Ingram.

The Monster and the Ape. Col., [15 Chapters] D: Howard Bretherton; LP: Robert Lowery, George Macready, Ralph Morgan, Carole Mathews, Willie Best, Jack Ingram.

Brenda Starr, Reporter. Col., [13 Chapters] D: William Fox; LP: Joan Woodbury, Kane Richmond, Syd Saylor, Joe Devlin, George Meeker, Wheeler Oakman, John Merton.

Who's Guilty? Col., [15 Chapters] D: Howard Bretherton, Wallace Grissell; LP: Robert Kent, Amelita Ward, Tim Ryan, Jayne Hazard, Minerva Urecal, Charles King.

1946

Chick Carter, Detective. Col., [15 Chapters] D: Derwin Abrahams; LP: Lyle Talbot, Douglas Fowley, Julie Gibson, Pamela Blake, Eddie Acuff, Jack Ingram.

Hop Harrigan. Col., [15 Chapters] D: Derwin Abrahams; LP: William Bakewell, Jennifer Holt, Buzz Henry, Sumner Getchell, Emmett Vogan, Clair James.

The Mysterious Mr. M. Univ., [13 Chapters] D: Lewis D. Collins, Vernon Keays; LP: Richard Martin, Pamela Blake, Dennis Moore, Jane Randolph, Danny Morton.

The Scarlet Horseman. Univ., [13 Chapters] D: Ray Taylor, Lewis D. Collins; LP: Peter

Cookson, Paul Guilfoyle, Victoria Horne, Janet Shaw, Virginia Christine.

1947

Brick Bradford. Col., [15 Chapters] D: Spencer G. Bennet; LP: Kane Richmond, Rick Vallin, Linda Johnson, Pierre Watkin, Charles Quigley, Jack Ingram, Charles King.

Jack Armstrong. Col., [15 Chapters] D: Wallace Fox; LP: John Hart, Rosemary LaPlanche, Joe Brown, Jr., Claire James, Pierre Watkin, Charles Middleton.

The Vigilante. Col., [15 Chapters] D: Wallace Fox; LP: Ralph Byrd, Ramsay Ames, Lyle Talbot, George Offerman, Robert Barron, George Chesebro, Jack Ingram.

The Sea Hound. Col., [15 Chapters] D: Walter B. Eason, Mack V. Wright; LP: Buster Crabbe, James Lloyd, Pamela Blake, Ralph Hodges, Spencer Chan, Robert Barron.

1948

Tex Granger. Col., [15 Chapters] D: Derwin Abrahams; LP: Robert Kellard, Peggy Stewart, Buzz Henry, Smith Ballew, Jack Ingram, I. Stanford Jolley, John Hart.

Superman. Col., [15 Chapters] D: Spencer Bennet, Thomas Carr; LP: Kirk Alyn, Noel Neill, Tommy Bond, Pierre Watkin, Carol Forman, George Meeker, Charles Quigley.

Congo Bill. Col., [15 Chapters] D: Spencer Bennet, Thomas Carr; LP: Don McGuire, Cleo Moore, Jack Ingram, I. Stanford Jolley, Leonard Penn, Charles King, Armida.

1949

Bruce Gentry. Col., [15 Chapters] D: Spencer Bennet, Thomas Carr; LP: Tom Neal, Judy Clark, Ralph Hodges, Forrest Taylor, Hugh Prosser, Tristram Coffin.

1950

Atom Man vs. Superman. Col., [15 Chapters] D: Spencer Bennet; LP: Kirk Alyn, Noel Neill, Lyle Talbot, Tommy Bond, Pierre Watkin, Jack Ingram, Stanley Blystone.

Cody of the Pony Express. Col., [15 Chapters] D: Spencer Bennet; LP: Jock Mahoney, Dickie Moore, Peggy Stewart, William Fawcett, Tom London, Jack Ingram.

1951

Captain Video. Col., [15 Chapters] D: Spencer Bennet, Wallace A. Grissell; LP: Judd Holdren, Larry Stewart, George Eldredge, Gene Roth, Don C. Harvey.

Don Daredevil Rides Again. Rep., [12 Chapters] D: Fred C. Brannon; LP: Ken Curtis, Aline Towne, Roy Barcroft, Lane Bradford, I. Stanford Jolley, John Cason.

Roar of the Iron Horse. Col., [15 Chapters] D: spencer Bennet, Thomas Carr; LP: Jock Mahoney, Virginia Herrick, William Fawcett, Jack Ingram, Dick Curtis.

1952

King of the Congo. Col., [15 Chapters] D: Spencer Bennet, Wallace A. Grissell; LP: Buster Crabbe, Gloria Dea, Leonard Penn, Jack Ingram, Rusty Wescoatt.

1954

Riding with Buffalo Bill. Col., [15 Chapters] D: spencer Bennet; LP: Marshall Reed, Rick Vallin, Joanne Rio, Shirley Whitney, Jack Ingram, William Fawcett.

1955

Adventures of Captain Africa. Col., [15 Chapters] D: Spencer Bennet; LP: John Hart, Rick Vallin, Ben Welden, June Howard, Bud Osborne, Lee Roberts.

1956

Perils of the Wilderness. Col., [15 Chapters] D: Spencer Bennet; LP: Dennis Moore, Richard Emory, Eve Anderson [Evelyn Finley], Kenneth MacDonald, Rick Vallin.

ADELE JERGENS

Adele Jergens was born in Brooklyn, New York, on November 28, 1922 (?). She gained some publicity as the winner of the "Miss World's Fairest" contest at New York's 1939 World's Fair.

A former chorine and top model, the buxom silver-blonde beauty decorated a number of Broadway shows and was featured in many Technicolor extravaganzas at Columbia. She played leads or second leads in about 50 films of the 1940s and 1950s, mostly low- to medium-budget productions.

Black Arrow ('44) was her first film. She had little to do except look pretty or scared. As Mary, friend of Black Arrow, she helped him in his struggle to find the killer of the Indian chief he thought was his father.

Her films include *The Prince of Thieves* ('48), *The Treasure of Monte Cristo* ('49), *Side Street* ('50), *Show Boat* ('51), *Abbott and Costello Meet the Invisible Man* ('51), *Aaron Slick from Punkin Creek* ('52), *The Miami Story* ('54), *Strange Lady in Town* ('55) and *Girls in Prison* ('56).

Adele Jergens married actor Glenn Langan in 1954 and gave up her career after 1958. The Langans had one son, Tracy, a successful businessman. Langan died in 1991, Jergens in 2002.

Serial

1944

Black Arrow. Col., 1944 [15 Chapters] D: Lew Landers; SP: Sherman Lowe, Jack Stanley, Leighton Brill, Royal K. Cole; P: Rudolph C. Flothow; Mus: Lee Zahler; Cam: Richard Fryer; LP: Robert Scott, Adele Jergens, Kenneth MacDonald, Robert Williams, Charles Middleton, Martin Garralaga, George J. Lewis, Charles King, I. Stanford Jolley, Harry Harvey.

ARTHUR JOHNSON ·

Arthur Johnson was a fine young stage actor with an extraordinarily handsome, disenchanted face. The son of an Episcopal minister, Arthur ran away from home to join a touring stage company and later played leads in New York productions. D. W. Griffith took notice of him and was impressed to the point of asking him if he would like to play the lead in *The Adventures of Dollie* ('08), Griffith's first film as a director. It was a chance meeting on a New York sidewalk that brought the men together.

Johnson was soon a favorite of film audiences and was probably the first true matinee idol of the American screen. He starred in many of Griffith's early films, often opposite the famous "Biograph Girl," Florence Lawrence. His films include *The Taming of the Shrew* ('08), *The Test of Friendship* ('08), *And a Little Child Shall Lead Them* ('09), *A Drunkard's Reformation* ('09), *In Old California* ('10), *A Romance of the Western Hills* ('10), *The Actress and the Singer* ('11), *The*

Amateur Iceman ('12) and *Annie Rowley's Fortune* ('13).

Johnson was born in 1876 in Davenport, Iowa, and died in 1916. His death was attributed to tuberculosis and alcoholism.

The Beloved Adventurer, his one serial, was comprised of 15 chapters, but each chapter was only one reel in length and was complete in itself. Lord Cecil (Johnson) manipulates people and situations for the betterment of society, finding many a thrill along the way.

Serial

1914

The Beloved Adventurer. Lubin, [15 Chapters] D: Arthur V. Johnson; SP: Emmett Campbell Hall; LP: Arthur V. Johnson, Lottie Brisco, Florence Hackett, Jeanette Hackett, Ruth Bryan, Howard M. Mitchell.

EDITH JOHNSON

Edith Johnson's face was smiling from many media before Hollywood made her a serial queen. She was perhaps the most photographed girl in the world before making her screen debut; her picture appeared in all the leading magazines and on billboards and newspapers. She was the Kodak Girl, employed by the camera company to pose for them. Her photogenic quality was recognized by the Selig Company and she was offered a position as leading lady in the studio's outdoor films after she graduated from Vassar.

For two and a half years Edith made short films such as *Nan's Victory* ('14), *The Van Thornton Diamonds* ('15), *At the Flood Tide* ('15), and *Toll of the Jungle* ('16). *The Cycle of Fate* ('160) and *The Valiants of Virginia* ('16) were five-reelers, and *The Private Banker* ('16) was a three-reeler.

In 1916, Edith switched to Universal, where she made the five-reelers *Behind the Lines* ('16), *The Scarlet Crystal* ('17), *The Scarlet Car* ('17) and *The Fighting Grin* ('18). She made one film for Select in 1918, *The*

Shuttle, in which she shares honors with Constance Talmadge.

These films are mentioned merely to emphasize that Edith Johnson, contrary to popular opinion, was not exclusively a serial star. Nor did she work only with William Duncan, whom she eventually married.

Vitagraph beckoned in 1918 and Edith was cast opposite serial king Duncan in *A Fight for Millions* ('18), an enormously popular serial which Duncan also directed. Edith demonstrated her stamina under the excruciating demands of serial production and won the approval not only of serial audiences but of the rugged Duncan.

In eight serials and eight action features with Duncan, Johnson attained considerable popularity with cliffhanger and adventure audiences. She won new laurels with each release, but her performances were usually overshadowed by the amazing feats of Duncan and, though popular, she never achieved the fame of Ruth Roland, Pearl White or Allene Ray. But she was one of the top dozen serial heroines of the silent era.

The Duncan-Johnson serials were topnotch film entertainment made in a day when the continued-next-week dramas were high in popularity with adult audiences. Duncan received as much as $10,000 a week for his chores as actor-director. However, he was unhappy with the red tape and front office interference imposed on him by Vitagraph and he and his wife moved over to Universal where their last three serials were made. But here he again clashed with the front office, and they retired.

The Duncans had amassed a small fortune so there was no need to face the hazards of serialmaking. After a vaudeville tour, the couple settled down to traveling for fun and enjoying quiet family life with their three children. (Duncan accepted a few roles in the 1930s.) Duncan died on February 7, 1961. Edith lived in Los Angeles until her death on September 5, 1969. Although it had been 45 years since her last serial, she was not forgotten by the press, which paid her due homage for her pioneering film work.

Serials

1918

A Fight for Millions. Vit., [15 Chapters] D: William Duncan; SP: Graham Baker; S: Albert E. Smith, Cyrus Townsend Brady; LP: William Duncan, Edith Johnson, Joe Ryan, Willie Calles, Walter Rodgers, Leo Maloney, Hart [Jack] Hoxie, William McCall.

1919

Man of Might. Vit., [15 Chapters] D: William Duncan; SP: C. Graham Baker; S: Albert E. Smith, Cyrus Townsend Brady; LP: William Duncan, Edith Johnson, Joe Ryan, Walter Rodgers, Willie Calles, Frank Tokanaga, Otto Lederer.

Smashing Barriers. Vit., [15 Chapters] D: William Duncan; SP: Graham Baker, R. Cecil Smith; S: Albert E. Smith, Cyrus Townsend Brady; LP: William Duncan, Edith Johnson, Walter Rodgers, William McCall, George Stanley.

1920

The Silent Avenger. Vit., [15 Chapters] D: William Duncan; S: Albert E. Smith, Cleveland Moffett; SP: C. Graham Baker, William B. Courtney; LP: William Duncan, Edith Johnson, Jack Richardson, Virginia Nightingale, Ernest Shields, Willis L. Robards.

1921

Fighting Fate. Vit., [15 Chapters] D: William Duncan; SP: C. Graham Baker, William B. Courtney; S: Albert E. Smith, Arthur P. Hankins; LP: William Duncan, Edith Johnson, Ford West, George Stanley, Jean Carpenter, Charles Dudley, Will Badger.

1923

The Steel Trail. Univ., [15 Chapters] D: William Duncan; S/SP: George H. Plympton, Karl Coolidge, Paul M. Bryan; LP: William Duncan, Edith Johnson, Harry Carter, Ralph McCullough, Harry Woods, Mabel Randall, John Cossar.

1924

Wolves of the North. Univ., [10 Chapters] D: William Duncan; SP: Frank H. Clark; S: Katherine and Robert Pinkerton; LP: William Duncan, Edith Johnson, Joseph W. Girard, Clark Comstock, Esther Ralston, Harry Woods.

The Fast Express. Univ., [15 Chapters] D: William Duncan; SP: Frank H. Clark, Paul Bryan; S: Courtney Ryley Cooper; LP: William Duncan, Edith Johnson, Edward Cecil, Eva Gordon, Ralph McCullough, Mabel Randall.

I. STANFORD JOLLEY

In I. Stanford Jolley's many Westerns he usually portrayed a sleazy, snake-eyed, slick, sneaky, moustached, contemptible blackguard who schemed and doled out orders to underlings. He was not always the boss heavy; sometimes he was just an ordinary, low-down gang member. And on rare occasions one might find him a law-abiding citizen. But not often.

Jolley was born on October 24, 1900, in Elizabeth, New Jersey, and grew up in nearby Morristown. His father owned a small traveling carnival–circus and later opened four restaurants and an electrical contracting service. However, Jolley was not interested in learning about or managing his father's business affairs.

Jolley met his future wife, Emily Hacker, at a lodge where both were employed for the summer. They fell in love and were married in 1921. He entered show business via vaudeville and in 1926 was acting on Broadway in *Humoresque* starring Vera Gordon. He had to put aside his acting career when his father died, as he was expected to take control of the family's business affairs. Although he didn't like what he was doing, he put his heart and soul into staying solvent. However, the stock market crash of 1929 and the Depression which followed engulfed Jolley in bankruptcy and he lost everything.

Jolley now decided to revive his acting career and headed for Hollywood with his wife, two children and little money in his pocket. In Hollywood, Jolley joined the "Gower Gulch" gang who daily assembled around the corner of Gower and Sunset Blvd., just a few yards from the Columbia lot. It was at this corner that studios in need of riders or extras would come by and pick up the men they required.

There is no record of how many unbilled roles he played, but in 1936 Jolley first received screen credit and speaking parts in Republic's *Ghost Town Gold* and *the Big Show.* He quickly became a member of that stock company of players who dealt misery to the cowboy aces on Saturday afternoons.

His acting was not limited to Westerns, as evidenced by the films *The Fatal Hour* ('40), *Midnight Limited* ('40), *Black Dragons* ('42), *Corregidor* ('43), *Call of the Jungle* ('44), *The Chinese Cat* ('44), *Curtain Call at Cactus Creek* ('50), *The Long Hot Summer* ('58), *Valley of the Dragon* ('61), *The Haunted Palace* ('63) and *Night of the Lepus* ('72).

Half of his 22 serials were Westerns. He easily made the transition to television and played in episodes of *Bonanza, The Cisco Kid, Annie Oakley, Bronco, Daniel Boone, Death Valley Days, The Gene Autry Show, High Chaparral, Fury* and *The Big Valley.*

Jolley was a big hit at Western film festivals and spent hours talking with fans and signing autographs. He died from emphysema on December 5, 1978, at the Motion Picture and TV Hospital in Woodland Hills, California. He was survived by his wife and son Stan, who has made a name for himself as art director, set designer and film director.

Jolley's daughter Sandra, once an Earl Carroll showgirl, was Forrest Tucker's first wife. She was wed to Jack Carson at the time of Jack's death.

Serials

1942

The Valley of Vanishing Men. Col., [15 Chapters] D: Spencer Bennet; LP: Bill Elliott, Slim Summerville, Carmen Morales, Kenneth MacDonald, I. Stanford Jolley, Jack Ingram.

Perils of the Royal Mounted. Col., [15 Chapters] D: James W. Horne; LP: Nell O'Day, Robert Stevens [Kellard], Herbert Rawlinson, I. Stanford Jolley, Kenneth MacDonald, George Chesebro.

1943

Batman. Col., [15 Chapters] D: Lambert Hillyer; LP: Lewis Wilson, Douglas Croft, J. Carrol Naish, Shirley Patterson, I. Stanford Jolley, Robert Fiske.

1944

The Desert Hawk. Col., [15 Chapters] D: B. Reeves Eason; LP: Gilbert Roland, Mona Maris, Kenneth MacDonald, Ben Welden, I. Stanford Jolley, Frank Lackteen, Charles Middleton.

Black Arrow. Col., [15 Chapters] D: Lew Landers; LP: Robert Scott, Adele Jergens, Kenneth MacDonald, Robert Williams, I. Stanford Jolley, George J. Lewis.

1945

Secret Agent X-9. Univ., [13 Chapters] D: Ray Taylor, Lewis D. Collins; LP: Lloyd Bridges, Keye Luke, Jan Wiley, Victoria Horne, I. Stanford Jolley, Samuel S. Hinds, Cy Kendall.

Jungle Raiders. Col., [15 Chapters] D: Lesley Selander; LP: Kane Richmond, Eddie Quillan, Veda Ann Borg, Carol Hughes, Charles King, Jack Ingram.

1946

Son of the Guardsman. Col., [15 Chapters] D: Derwin Abrahams; LP: Robert Shaw, Duan Kennedy, Robert (Buzz) Henry, I. Stanford Jolley, Jim Diehl, Charles King, Wheeler Oakman, John Merton, Hugh Prosser.

The Crimson Ghost. Rep., [12 Chapters] D: William Witney, Fred Brannon; LP: Charles Quigley, Linda Stirling, Clayton Moore, I. Stanford Jolley, Kenne Duncan, Forrest Taylor, Emmet Vogan.

1947

The Black Widow. Rep., [13 Chapters] D: Spencer G. Bennet, Fred C. Brannon; LP: Carol Forman, Bruce Edwards, Virginia Lindley, Anthony Warde, I. Stanford Jolley, Virginia Carroll, Theodore Gottlieb.

1948

Adventures of Frank and Jesse James. Rep., [13 Chapters] D: Fred C. Brannon, Yakima Canutt; LP: Clayton Moore, Steve Darrell, Noel Neill, George J. Lewis, I. Stanford Jolley, Stanley Andrews, Sam Flint.

Congo Bill. Col., [15 Chapters] D: Spencer Bennet, Thomas Carr; LP: Don McGuire, Cleo Moore, Jack Ingram, I. Stanford Jolley, Leonard Penn, Charles King, Armida.

Tex Granger. Col., [15 Chapters] D: Derwin Abrahams; LP: Robert Kellard, Peggy Stewart, Robert (Buzz) Henry, Smith Ballew, I. Stanford Jolley, Jack Ingram, Terry Frost.

Dangers of the Canadian Mounted. Rep., [12 Chapters] D: Fred Brannon, Yakima Canutt; LP: Jim Bannon, Virginia Belmont, Anthony Warde, Dorothy Granger, I. Stanford Jolley, Tom Steele, Dale Van Sickel.

1949

Ghost of Zorro. Rep., [12 Chapters] D: Fred C. Brannon; LP: Clayton Moore, Pamela Blake, Roy Barcroft, George J. Lewis, I. Stanford Jolley, John Crawford.

King of the Rocket Men. Rep., [12 Chapters] D: Fred C. Brannon; LP: Tris Coffin, Mae Clarke, Don Haggerty, House Peters, Jr., I. Stanford Jolley.

1950

Pirates of the High Seas. Col., [15 Chapters] D: Spencer Bennet, Thomas Carr; LP: Buster Crabbe, Lois Hall, Tommy Farrell, Gene Roth, Neyle Morrow, I.Stanford Jolley, Terry Frost, Lee Roberts.

Desperadoes of the West. Rep., [12 Chapters] D: Fred C. Brannon; LP: Richard Powers [Tom Keene], Judy Clark, Roy Barcroft, I. Stanford Jolley, Lee Roberts.

1951

Don Daredevil Rides Again. Rep., [12 Chapters] D: Fred C. Brannon; LP: Ken Curtis, Aline Towne, Roy Barcroft, Lane Bradford, I. Stanford Jolley, John Cason, Lee Phelps.

Captain Video. Col., [15 Chapters] D: Spencer G. Bennet, Wallace Grissell; LP: Judd Holdren, Larry Stewart, George Eldredge, Gene Roth, I. Stanford Jolley, Jack Ingram, William Fawcett, Zon Murray.

1954

Man with the Steel Whip. Rep., [12 Chapters] D: Franklyn Adreon; LP: Richard Simmons, Barbara Bestar, Dale Van Sickel, Mauritz Hugo, I. Stanford Jolley, Roy Barcroft, Edmund Cobb.

1956

Perils of the Wilderness. Col., [15 Chapters] D: Spencer Bennet; LP: Dennis Moore, Richard Emory, Eve Anderson [Evelyn Finley], Kenneth MacDonald, Rick Vallin, John Elliott, I. Stanford Jolley.

BUCK JONES

Buck Jones (real name Charles Frederick Gebhardt) was born on December 12, 1891, in Vincennes, Indiana. He rose from humble beginnings to become a major film personality by the mid–20s.

Born of poor parents who separated and divorced when Buck was a young boy, he mostly raised himself. At age 15 he enlisted in Troop G of the U.S. Cavalry, fought in the Philippines, was wounded and was mustered out of the service in 1909. In 1910 he re-enlisted and rose to the rank of sergeant. Between hitches he briefly worked at the Indianapolis Speedway testing cars and operated his own auto repair garage.

When discharged in 1913 at Texas City, Texas, Jones signed up with the 101 Ranch Wild West Show, rising to become its top bronc buster and, in the off season, working as a cowhand on the 101 Ranch in Oklahoma. While appearing with the show at Madison Square Garden in 1914, he met a young equestrienne named Odille Osborne. The following season both signed with the Julia Allen Wild West Show. On August 11, 1915, they became husband and wife in a center ring ceremony while the show was playing Lima, Ohio.

During the early years of World War I, the couple lived in Chicago where Buck broke horses for Ellworth & McNair, an outfit that purchased horses for the French government. They later barnstormed with their own horses in a one-man, one-woman show, performed in Gollmar Brothers Circus, and became Ringling Brothers Circus performers before settling in Hollywood where both worked as doubles and did stunts in the movies. Their only child, Maxine, was born in February 1918.

Buck was signed to a Fox contract in October 1919 after working in the Tom Mix unit for several months and after being featured in several of Franklyn Farnum's two-reel Westerns for Canyon Pictures. He rapidly became a popular Western lead. By 1918 he was earning $3,000 a week and was one of the most popular Western stars, sharing honors with Tom Mix, Hoot Gibson, Fred Thomson, Ken Maynard, Jack Hoxie, Harry Carey, Tim McCoy and Bob Steele.

The 53 Westerns and eight non–Western films in which Jones starred for Fox were all moneymakers and above-average programmers. He proved his acting ability in John Ford's *Just Pals* ('20) and his flair for comedy was demonstrated in many of his features, though it would be emphasized more in his sound films. Fox made a good product, had a good distribution system and created good publicity for its films. By the end of the decade, Buck Jones was a name known throughout the world where movies were shown.

Leaving Fox over a salary dispute in 1928, Buck starred in the independent production *The Big Hop* ('28) that lost money. Then in 1929 he lost his entire fortune in a Wild West show venture that collapsed when a dishonest employee absconded with the show's receipts after failing to pay (unbeknownst to Buck) accumulated bills. Robbins Brothers Circus signed Jones as their stellar attraction for the two and a half months remaining in the show season. Buck and Odille then returned to Hollywood. Buck avoided bankruptcy by convincing his creditors that he would make good on his debts as soon as possible.

Buck signed with Beverly Productions,

Buck Jones in *White Eagle* (Columbia, 1941).

releasing through Columbia. His salary was $300 a week. To go from $3,000 to $300 must have been a blow to Buck's pride, but he was determined to repay his creditors.

The first of the Beverly productions, *The Lone Rider* ('30), filmed in June and released on July 13, 1930, proved that Jones' voice was ideal for Westerns. It exactly matched his physical appearance and added to his overall charisma. With the filming of *Branded* ('31), Columbia took over the production as well as the distribution of Jones' films. Eighteen other Westerns (plus two non–Westerns) would follow before Jones left Harry Cohn's Gower Gulch fantasy factory.

While still under contract to Columbia for features, Buck signed with Universal to make serials. The first, *Gordon of Ghost City* ('33), is generally regarded the best of the six cliffhangers. Director Ray Taylor injects the maximum of cinematic thrills into this rousing story of a man who defied a desperate band of cattle rustlers in a mysterious ghost city situated over a secret gold mine. Good photography and script, a fine cast and competent editing combine to prove that serials can be as good as feature films.

In *The Red Rider* ('34), Buck's second serial, we find him an outcast sheriff out to prove that a man he has allowed to escape from jail is innocent of murder.

In 1934, Buck signed with Universal to produce and star in a series of feature Westerns. By this time he was the most popular Western star. Buck remained at Universal until 1937. During that time he starred in 22 Westerns and two more serials.

A bitter battle of brain and brawn for the possession of gold claims form the basis for the story of *The Roaring West* ('35). In retrospect the serial may have been draggy and drawn-out, but who was going to think so in 1935? Everyone was too busy just enjoying the sight of Buck and Silver racing across the landscape.

In *The Phantom Rider* ('36), Buck is a government agent sent to the town of Maverick to stop outlawry directed toward Hidden Valley Ranch. Buck becomes the Phantom Rider, wearing a white cape and mask to hide his identity as he seeks to thwart villain Harry Woods and his henchmen.

Declining to sign for another series at Universal, Buck signed with Coronet Pictures releasing through Columbia and made six features.

In the declining months of 1940, Buck received the opportunity to star in a remake of the 1932 *White Eagle*. This time around Columbia was doing it as a 15-chapter serial. It was a rather pedestrian affair, but at least Buck was back in the saddle as a hero in the lead role and his fans could see him for 15 weeks. Buck opposes a gang of renegades who dress like Indians to rob stagecoaches. Everyone did well with a picayune plot.

Riders of Death Valley ('41), touted as "the Million Dollar Serial," was Buck's last film for Universal. (In all he did 36 films for Columbia release and 27 for Universal distribution.) Buck's role as Tombstone was a fairly good one and allowed his comedy talents to be used some, but his role was definitely secondary to Dick Foran.

Buck and Scott R. Dunlap organized a production company to make a series to be called the Rough Riders. Jones, Tim McCoy and Raymond Hatton comprised a trio of retired lawmen who, when trouble brewed, rose to meet the challenge. With the completion of *West of the Law* ('42), Tim McCoy dropped out to re-enlist for active Army service, being awarded the rank of lieutenant colonel.

With the disbanding of the Rough Riders, Monogram decided to star Buck in a series with Raymond Hatton to support him. One picture was made, *Dawn on the Great Divide* ('42).

Buck was on a bond selling trip and promoting his Monogram features when in Boston he was invited by a group of theater owners to attend the Cocoanut Grove night club. It turned out to be the night when death went dancing and claimed nearly 500 lives, the second highest number of deaths by fire in American history. Buck suffered critical burns to the face, mouth and throat. Although taken alive from the inferno, he died on Monday, November 30, 1942.

Serials

1933

Gordon of Ghost City. Univ., [12 Chapters] D: Ray Taylor; SP: Ella O'Neill, Basil Dickey, George Plympton, Harry O. Hoyt, Het Mannheim; S: Peter B. Kyne; LP: Buck Jones, Madge Bellamy, Walter Miller, Hugh Enfield, William Desmond.

1934

The Red Rider. Univ., [15 Chapters] D: Louis Friedlander [Lew Landers]; SP: George Plympton, Vin Moore, Ella O'Neill, George Morgan; S: W. C. Tuttle; P: Henry MacRae; LP: Buck Jones, Grant Withers, Marion Shilling, Walter Miller, Margaret LaMarr.

1935

The Roaring West. Univ., [15 Chapters] D: Ray Taylor; S: Edward Earl Repp; SP: George Plympton, Nate Gatzert, Ella O'Neill, Basil

Dickey, Robert Rothafel; P: Henry MacRae; Cam: William Sicknew, Richard Fryer; LP: Buck Jones, Muriel Evans, Walter Miller, Frank McGlynn, Sr., Harlan Knight, William Desmond.

1936

The Phantom Rider. Univ., [15 Chapters] D: Ray Taylor; S/SP: George Plympton, Basil Dickey, Ella O'Neill, Henry MacRae; Cam: Allen Thompson, John Hickson; P: Henry MacRae; LP: Buck Jones, Maria Shelton, Diana Gibson, Harry Woods, Charles King, George Cooper, Frank LaRue, Eddie Gribbon, Joey Ray.

1941

White Eagle. Col., [15 Chapters] D: James W. Horne; S: Fred Myton; SP: Arch Heath, Morgan B. Cox, John Cutting, Lawrence Taylor; P: Larry Darmour; Cam: James S. Brown, Jr.; Mus: Lee Zahler; LP: Buck Jones, Dorothy Fay, Raymond Hatton, Jack Ingram, Chief Yowlachie, Edmund Cobb, Al Ferguson, Roy Barcroft.

Riders of Death Valley. Univ., [15 Chapters] D: Ray Taylor, Ford Beebe; S: Oliver Drake; SP: Sherman Lowe, Basil Dickey, George Plympton, Jack Connell; P: Henry MacRae; Cam: Jerome Ash, William Sickner; Mus: Charles Previn; LP: Dick Foran, Buck Jones, Leo Carrillo, Charles Bickford, Monte Blue, Guinn Williams.

DICK JONES

Dick (Dickie) Jones was born on February 25, 1927, in Snyder, Texas. He was a rodeo stunt performer from the age of six. By 1934 he was appearing in movies.

He was featured in dozens of films in the '30s, '40s, and '50s with an emphasis on Westerns: *Moonlight on the Prairie* ('35), *Westward Ho* ('35), *Daniel Boone* ('36), *The Land of Fighting Men* ('38), *Destry Rides Again* ('39), *Virginia City* ('40), *The Vanishing Virginian* ('42), *The Strawberry Roan* ('48), *Rocky Mountain* ('50), *Sons of New Mexico* ('50), and *Requiem for a Gunfighter* ('65).

Non-Westerns include *Black Legion* ('37), *Stella Dallas* ('37), *Mr. Smith Goes to Washington* ('39), *Young Mr. Lincoln* ('39), *The Gun for Hire* ('42), *Heaven Can Wait* ('43), *The Adventures of Mark Twain* ('44) and *Battleground* ('50), *Bamboo Prison* ('54). He was the voice of Walt Disney's *Pinocchio* ('40).

On television, Dick starred in 42 episodes of *Buffalo Bill, Jr.* and co-starred with Jock Mahoney in 78 episodes of *The Range Rider.*

Dick and his wife Betty have a working ranch in Salinas, California, and four grown children.

Serials

1935

Queen of the Jungle. Screen Attractions, [12 Chapters] D: Robert Hill; S: Griffin Jay; Mus: Hal Chasnoff; Cam: William Hyer; LP: Reed Howes, Mary Kornman, George Chesebro, Lafe McKee, Eddie Foster, Dickie Jones, William Welsh, Barney Furey.

The Call of the Savage. Univ., [12 Chapters] D: Lewis Friedlander [Lew Landers]; SP: Nate Gazert, George Plympton, Basil Dickey; S: Otis Adelbert Kline; LP: Noah Beery, Jr., Dorothy Short, Harry Woods, Walter Miller, Bryant Washburn, Grace Cunard, Dickie Jones, William Desmond, Wally Wales [Hal Taliaferro], Stanley Andrews.

1936

The Adventures of Frank Merrill. Univ., [12 Chapters] D: Cliff Smith; AP: Henry MacRae;

SP: George Plympton, Maurice Geraghty, Ella O'Neill, Basil Dickey; LP: Don Briggs, Jean Rogers, John King, Carla Laemmle, Sumner Getchell, Al Bridge, Bud Osborne, Edmund Cobb, Dave O'Brien, William Desmond.

1937

Blake of Scotland Yard. Victory, [15 Chapters] D: Bob Hill; SP: Basil Dickey, William Buchanan; Spv.: Robert Stillman; S: Rock Hawkey; Cam: William Hyer; P: Sam Katzman; LP: Ralph Byrd, Joan Barclay, Herbert Rawlinson, Lloyd Hughes, Herman Brix, Dick Curtis, Nick Stewart, Dickie Jones, Jimmy Aubrey.

1938

The Great Adventures of Wild Bill Hickok. Col., [15 Chapters] D: Mack V. Wright, Sam Nelson; SP: George Rosener, Charles A. Powell, G. A. Durlan, Tom Gibson, Dallas Fitzgerald; AP: Harry Webb; P: Jack Fier; Mus: Abe Meyer; LP: Gordon (Bill) Elliott, Carole Wayne, Frankie Darro, Monte Blue, Dickie Jones, Kermit Maynard, Roscoe Ates, Hal Taliaferro, Robert Fiske, Earle Hodgins, Edmund Cobb, Slim Whitaker.

GORDON JONES

Gordon Jones was the muscular football player "Rambling Wreck" in Rosalind Russell's *My Sister Eileen* ('42). After playing dumbbells throughout his career he was a surprising choice to play Britt Reid alias the Green Hornet. However, he pulled it off surprisingly well. But when the second Hornet serial was made, Universal chose Warren Hull to play the masked avenger.

Gordon's film career started in 1931 or '32; some of his films are *Let "Em Have It* ('35), *Night Waitress* ('36), *Out West with the Hardys* ('38), *Pride of the Navy* ('39), *Flying Tigers* ('42), *To the Shore of Tripoli* ('42), *Buffalo Bill* ('44), *The Wistful Widow of Wagon Gap* ('47), *The Untamed Breed* ('48) and *McLintock!* ('63), his last.

In 1950–51 Jones played sidekick to Roy Rogers in *Trigger, Jr.*, *Trail of Robin Hood*, *Sunset in the West*, *North of the Great Divide*, *Heart of the Rockies* and *Spoilers of the Plains*. He died in 1963 at age 52 from a heart attack in Tarzana, California.

Serial

1939

The Green Hornet. Univ., [13 Chapters] D: Ford Beebe, Ray Taylor; SP: George Plympton, Basil Dickey, Morrison C. Wood, Lyonel Margolies; P: Henry MacRae; LP: Gordon Jones, Anne Nagel, Keye Luke, Wade Boteler, Philip Trent, Walter McGrail, John Kelly, Anne Gwynne, Cy Kendall, Selmer Jackson, Gene Rizzi.

VICTOR JORY

Victor Jory was born November 28, 1902, in Dawson City, Yukon Territory, Canada, in the middle of the Alaska gold rush. His father, Edwin Jory, was a prune grower in Salem, Oregon, until the gold fever got into his veins. His mother, Joanne Snyder Jory, was a newspaper writer until Jory took her to Alaska to prospect for gold. They packed over the Chilakoot Pass only a few weeks before Victor was born in a road house.

One might say Victor was brought up in a sleeping bag. His mother did return to civilization long enough to get a divorce, but she returned to Alaska, bought a salted gold mine, tried prospecting again and then bought the road house in which Victor had been born and converted it into a hotel. When Victor was 11, his mother sold the hotel and moved with him to Pasadena, where Victor managed to get through grammar school but was kicked out of Pasadena High School with regularity. The Jorys moved to Victoria and while there Victor won the light heavyweight boxing title of British Columbia. Turning pro, he won eight out of nine bouts, but it was that ninth fight that convinced him he wasn't a fighter. He got beat pretty bad.

Returning to Pasadena, Victor taught a class in boxing at the high school, joined the national guard, won some more boxing and wrestling titles, attended Fullerton College for a year and joined Gilmor Brown's famed Pasadena Playhouse in 1923. He did bits in Pasadena, Vancouver and Hollywood. Bumming his way to Salt Lake City, he worked in stock — doing 120 shows in two seasons. Many plays and stock companies followed. He married his leading lady, actress Jean Inness, on December 23, 1928, in Burns, Wyoming, returning to Denver to play in the Denham Theatre Stock Company's production of *Stella Dallas*. Thereafter Victor and Jean worked together often in plays and summer stock.

Victor's first movie role was a bit in *Renegades* ('30). He had a larger role in *Pride of the Legion* ('33), a Mascot feature starring Barbara Kent, Rin-Tin-Tin, Jr., Glenn Tryon and Sally Blane. He signed a term contract at Fox and was in 11 features in 1933, *The Devil's in Love* and *Smoky* the two better ones. Through the rest of the '30s, Victor played mostly sinister roles. His portrayal of Injun Joe in *The Adventures of Tom Sawyer* ('38) was a memorable one, as was his role of carpetbagger Jonas Wilkerson in *Gone with the Wind* ('39).

In 1940, Jory starred in two Columbia serials. The first was *The Shadow* in which he plays the Shadow, Lamont Cranston and Lin Chang. A well-organized criminal group, headed by an unidentified criminal known as the Black Tiger, menaces the economic life of the city. The serial was a popular one. The choice of Jory for the title role was a perceptive one, as he visually and audibly conveyed the required image of Cranston and the Shadow most credibly. Veda Ann Borg portrayed Margo Lane as a somewhat brash, cynical but completely dedicated ally of the Shadow.

The second serial to star Jory was *The Green Archer* ('40). After having his brother unjustly imprisoned, Abel Bellamy (James Craven) moves into his castle. Other members of the family become inquisitive and hire a detective, Spike Holland (Jory), to inquire into the matter; Abel tries to kill them all (he wants to keep his association with a gang of jewel thieves a secret). His attempts at murder are thwarted by the Green Archer, a masked man who rejects modern weaponry in favor of bow and arrow.

In 1941–43 Jory appeared in seven of the Hopalong Cassidy films starring William Boyd — *Wide Open Town* ('41), *Border Vigi-*

The author, Buck Rainey, and Victor Jory (right).

Tower. He could be seen on *Profiles in Courage* as Thaddeus Stevens, involved in impeachment proceedings against President Andrew Johnson. Jory counted among his many other TV credits *Banacek*, *Mannix*, *Ironside*, *The Virginian*, *Heroes of the Bible*, *Voyage to the Bottom of the Sea*, *Philco Playhouse*, *Studio One*, *Hallmark Hall of Fame*, *Playhouse 90*, *20th Century-Fox Hour*, *Science Fiction Theater*, *The Untouchables*, *Burke's Law*, *I Spy* and *The Alfred Hitchcock Hour*.

Jory starred in the *Manhunt* teleseries as a San Diego detective lieutenant for two seasons in 1958–59 for a total of 78 episodes.

Jory died February 11, 1982, at his Santa Monica apartment of an apparent heart attack. He was survived by his daughter, Jean Anderson, four grandchildren and his son, Jon, artistic director of the Actors Theater in Louisville, Kentucky, a complex that includes one house named the Victor Jory Theater. Victor's wife Jean died on December 27, 1978.

lantes ('41), *Riders of the Timberline* ('41), *Colt Comrades* ('43), *Bar 20* ('43), *Hoppy Serves a Writ* ('43) and *The Leather Burners* ('43).

Over the years Jory starred in many stage productions. He also found time to star in more than 200 radio shows and to record many albums of stories for children, among them "Tubby the Tuba," "Peter Pan," "Peter and the Wolf," "Noah's Ark," "Story of Celeste" and "Paul Bunyon."

Jory's work verged from the top-notch *Gone with the Wind* to what many would call the opposite extreme, such as *Cat Women of the Moon*, a 3-D film released in 1954. He wrote several successful songs ("You Never Miss the Sunshine," "Sunset Trail") and several cowboy ballads.

Television became a gold mine for Jory, who made over 400 appearances. In 1955 he debuted in the teleseries *King's Row* as Dr.

Serials

1940

The Shadow. Col., [15 Chapters] D: James W. Horne; SP: Joseph Poland, Ned Dandy, Joseph O'Donnell; P: Larry Darmour; Cam: James S. Brown, Jr.; Mus: Lee Zahler; LP: Victor Jory, Veda Ann Borg, Robert Moore, Robert Fiske, Jack Ingram, J. Paul Jones, Charles Hamilton, Edward Peil, Sr.

The Green Archer. Col., [15 Chapters] D:

James W. Horne; S: Edgar Wallace; SP: Morgan B. Cox, John Cutting, Jesse A. Duffy; P: Larry Darmour; Cam: James S. Brown, Jr.; Mus: Lee Zahler; LP: Victor Jory, Iris Meredith, James Craven, Robert Fiske, Dorothy Fay, Forrest Taylor, Jack Ingram, Joseph Girard, Kit Guard.

BORIS KARLOFF

Boris Karloff was born William Henry Pratt in Dulwich, South London, England, on November 23, 1887, the youngest of the nine children of a civil servant in the British foreign service. He was educated at Merchant Tailor's School and at London University. His family pressured him to study for the consular service, but having no interest in a diplomatic position, he sailed from Liverpool to Ontario, Canada, in 1907.

An advertisement in a newspaper gave him a chance to join a touring company and it was then he adopted the name of Boris Karloff. For nearly two years he played "the sticks" in melodramas. Often it was a different play every night, sometimes doubling as stage manager. Boris worked for several troupes, perhaps the most distinguished of which was the one which took *The Virginian* to the West. In 1916, during a brief stay in Los Angeles, Boris made his screen debut as an extra in *The Dumb Girl of Portico* starring Anna Pavlov.

Out of work three years later, he returned to Hollywood and began appearing regularly in films in extra and bit parts. His slow, deliberate movements seemed always to create a sense of menace, but he achieved little success in the silent era. He was in 50 or more silent films, ten of them serials. *The Hope Diamond Mystery* ('21), *The Fatal Warning* ('29), *King of the Kongo* ('29) and *King of the Wild* ('30) gave him his best early roles.

It was his role as the Monster in *Frankenstein* ('31) that made him a star; and a star he was to remain for the next 40 years. Although nearly all of his performances were above reproach, the author suggests these as his best: *Frankenstein* (Univ. '32), *The Mummy* (Univ., '32), *The Black Cat* (Univ., '34), *Bride of Frankenstein* (Univ., '35), *The Black Room* (Col., '35), *The Raven* (Univ., '35), *Son of Frankenstein* (Univ., '39), *The Body Snatcher* (REO, '45), *Isle of the Dead* (REO, '45) and *Bedlam* (REO, '46).

In 1941 Karloff returned to the stage in the classic horror-comedy-thriller *Arsenic and Old Lace*. The play ran for three years on Broadway and Karloff also acted in the road tour. It was Karloff's first time on Broadway.

Karloff starred in the British teleseries *Colonel March of Scotland Yard* ('53). Sporting an eye patch for some additional color, the colonel rarely had anything as simple as

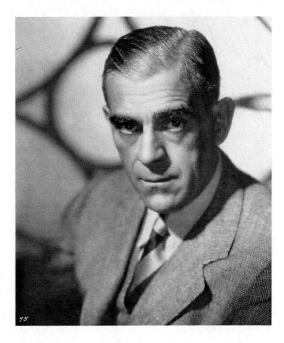

a locked-room mystery to solve. In the one season of 20-odd episodes (telecast at different times over several years), March faced such adversaries as an Abominable Snowman and the Missing Link.

In 1960 he returned to television as the host of the NBC-TV horror anthology series *Thriller*, in which he occasionally appeared.

Karloff joined Jean Arthur in the stage revival of *Peter Pan* in 1950. He played Mr. Darling, father of the children, as well as Captain Hook, the villainous pirate king.

During his latter years his health declined. Because of arthritis, he was forced to rely on a cane and to wear a metal brace on his leg. He died of a respiratory ailment at the King Edward Hospital in Midhurst, Sussex, on February 2, 1969. He was 81 years old.

Serials

1919

The Masked Rider. Arrow, [15 Chapters] D: Audrey C. Kennedy; LP: Harry Myers, Ruth Stonehouse, Paul Panzer, Edna M. Holland, Boris Karloff.

The Lightning Raider. Pathé, [15 Chapters] D: George B. Seitz; LP: Pearl White, Warner Oland, Ruby Hoffman, Boris Karloff.

1921

The Hope Diamond Mystery. Kosmick, [15 Chapters] D: Stuart Paton; LP: Harry Carter, Grace Darmond, George Chesebro, Boris Karloff, Carmen Phillips.

1924

Riders of the Plains. Arrow, [15 Chapters] D: Jacques Jaccard; LP: Jack Perrin, Marilyn Miller, Ruth Royce, Charles Brinley, Boris Karloff.

1925

Perils of the Wild. Univ., [15 Chapters] D: Francis Ford; LP Joe Bonomo, Margaret Quimby, Jack Mower, Alfred Allen, Boris Karloff.

1928

Vultures of the Sea. Mascot, [10 Chapters] D: Richard Thorpe; LP: Johnnie Walker, Shirley Mason, Tom Santschi, Frank Hagney, Boris Karloff.

The Vanishing Rider. Univ., [10 Chapters] D: Ray Taylor; LP: William Desmond, Ethlyne Claire, Bud Osborne, Boris Karloff.

1929

The Fatal Warning. Mascot, [10 Chapters] D: Richard Thorpe; LP: Helene Costello, Ralph Graves, George Periolat, Boris Karloff.

King of the Kong. Mascot, [10 Chapters] D: Richard Thorpe; LP: Walter Miller, Jacqueline Logan, Larry Steers, Boris Karloff.

1930

King of the Wild. Mascot, [12 Chapters] D: Richard Thorpe, B. Reeves Eason; LP: Walter Miller, Nora Lane, Dorothy Christy, Tom Santschi, Boris Karloff.

MARY ELLEN KAY

Mary Ellen Keaggy was born in Boardman, Ohio, on August 29, 1929. She dropped out of high school to sing with a local band in nightclubs and later journeyed west to California to look for work on the stage. Joining one of the theatrical groups, she was seen acting at the Glendale Center Theatre by a talent scout and offered a screen test.

She received a couple of bit roles in 1950, and was handed the feminine lead in Columbia's *Streets of Ghost Town* ('50) starring Charles Starrett. She wasn't called on to do much acting, but she was there for all to see—a lovely 5'2" nymph in an arduous predicament.

After interviewing for a job at Republic, Mary Ellen was signed to a standard player's contract and was put into Rex Allen's *Silver City Bonanza* ('51). She would make five more Westerns with him, as well as three with Allan Lane.

Mary Ellen was billed alongside of Walter Reed in Republic's *Government Agents vs. Phantom Legion* ('51), a mundane 12-chapter serial about hijacking of Interstate Truck Owners' Association trucks. Hal Duncan (Reed) is assigned to track down the culprits stealing critical materials the government is stockpiling. Heading the hijackers is a masked man called "The Voice."

As a freelancer, Mary Ellen essayed the role of the girl in Bill Elliott's *Vigilante Terror* ('53) and Kirby Grant's *Yukon Vengeance* ('54). After that she could be seen in character roles during the '50s (*Voodoo Woman*, '56, *Runaway Daughters*, '56, etc.).

Much of her effort expended in the '50s and '60s was in television. Her network credits include *Cavalcade of America, Schlitz Playhouse, The Lone Ranger, George Burns & Gracie Allen, The Red Skelton Show, I Married Joan* and *The Life of Riley.*

Mary Ellen was married in July 1954 to a cosmetics executive, but the marriage lasted only five years. She married William Ruffalo in 1963 and they were together 30 years, until his death from a heart attack. She has two children, Mary and Bill. With a stiff upper lip she went to work at Troy's Western Heritage Gallery.

Serial

1951

Government Agents vs. Phantom Legion. Rep., [12 Chapters] D: Fred C. Brannon; SP: Ronald Davidson; AP: Franklyn Adreon; Cam: John L. Russell, Jr.; Mus: Stanley Wilson; LP: Walter Reed, Mary Ellen Kay, Dick Curtis, John Picard, Pierce Lyden.

TOM KEENE / RICHARD POWERS

Tom Keene has the distinction of being one of the very few performers to have ever starred in sound films under three names: George Duryea, Tom Keene and Richard Powers. Further, he was one of the most popular Western stars of the 1930s and 1940s and his acting abilities resulted in a most diverse career.

Tom was born George Duryea in New York on December 30, 1897. He was raised by an aunt and uncle after being orphaned at the age of six. After high school he attended Carnegie Tech, then transferred to Columbia University, where he received a degree. After trying his hand at assorted jobs, he joined a stock company and eventually wound up in New York where he hit it big on Broadway. He appeared in *Abie's Irish Rose, White Cargo* and *The Barber Had Two Sons.* A two-year tour with *Abie's Irish Rose* fol-

Tom Keene (left) and Dave Sharpe in *Where Trails Divide* (Monogram, 1937).

lowed with playdates in Europe, New Zealand and Australia. As a result of his success on Broadway, Tom was offered a part in Cecil B. DeMille's *The Godless Girl*, a 1928 Paramount film.

DeMille was so impressed with Tom that he built up his part in the story to that of secondary importance next to Lina Basquette, the star. Tom was still using his real name of George Duryea. *Marked Money* ('28) was another release featuring George. In it he was a Navy flyer who helps an orphan (Junior Coghlan) save his inheritance from crooks. It was followed by his first Western, the Cosmopolitan release *Tide of Empire* ('29) in both silent and music-and-sound-effects versions. George is a young man who wins the love of a girl (Renee Adoree) after saving her from outlaws.

Honky Tonk, Thunder and *In Old Cali-*fornia were other 1929 films. In 1930 he could be seen in *Radio Kisses, Tol'able David* and *Bad Man*. His final film as George Duryea was *Beau Bandit* ('30) in which he was co-starred with Rod LaRocque, Doris Kenyon and Conrad Nagel. When RKO offered him a three-year contract at around $3,000 a picture, he grabbed it.

Now Tom Keene, he starred in 14 more Westerns during the period 1930–33. It was one of the more successful series of the early '30s. Budgets were adequate, stories were superior, casts were competent and photography was excellent.

Upon completion of his RKO series in 1933, Tom went over to Paramount and played one of the principal roles in the Randolph Scott starrer *Sunset Pass* ('33), based on a Zane Grey novel and directed by Henry Hathaway.

In 1934 Keene co-starred in his most dramatic film, *Our Daily Bread*, directed by King Vidor. As a result of his excellent performance, he was given numerous awards from all over the world. The film is now considered a classic.

Keene looked for work in 1935 with very little success in the movie world so again he went back to doing stage work in Los Angeles and New York. He returned to Westerns at Paramount in 1936 co-starring with Buster Crabbe in *Drift Fence* and *Desert Gold*, adaptations of Zane Grey stories.

Keene finally realized that making Westerns was not such a bad way to make a very lucrative living so in 1937 when independent Crescent Films offered him a seven-picture "series" contract, he grabbed it. Tom was back in the saddle with some very interesting and well-produced B-Westerns, on a larger scale than the regular Western programmers. All in all, his Crescent films were enjoyable, and in their concept they were similar to the Tim McCoy historical Westerns at MGM in 1927–28 and the Roy Stewart historical series in the mid–20s at Sunset Productions. With the larger budgets and better distribution provided by MGM, which released the McCoys, the Keene series could have been a much more important one.

Tom did four Westerns for Monogram in 1937–38: *God's Country and the Man, Romance of the Rockies, Where Trails Divide* and *The Painted Trail.*

Tom had been instrumental in working for the formation of the Screen Actors Guild and he was the forty-second member to join the Guild. In 1939 he was elected mayor of Sherman Oaks, California, and this job would keep him off-screen for two years. Also, he put together a troop of entertainers and toured the country for several months in personal appearances.

In mid–41 he was back in the saddle at Monogram for a series of eight films. The first of the Keene oaters was *Wanderers of the West,* followed by *Dynamite Canyon, The Driftin' Kid, Riding the Sunset Trail, Lone Star Law Men, Western Mail, Arizona Roundup* and *Where Trails End* (a rather appropriate title, since it was Keene's last starring feature Western).

In the '40s he began to play character parts, usually under the name of Richard Powers, which he used for the remainder of his career. He was a contract player at RKO, the studio where he achieved Western fame as Tom Keene, for several years in the late '40s and early '50s, appearing in seven Tim Holt Westerns and in dramatic films such as *San Quentin* ('46), *Dick Tracy's Dilemma* ('47), *Seven Keys to Baldpate* ('47), *Crossfire* ('47) and *Berlin Express* ('48). He supported Randolph Scott in *Return of the Bad Men* ('48) and Robert Mitchum in *Blood on the Moon* ('48). In 1950 he starred in the Republic serial *Desperadoes of the West.* It's a puzzle why Republic didn't bill him as Tom Keene, since the name meant something to Western fans, even in 1950, whereas the name Richard Powers did not. The story concerned the attempts of Powers and other ranchers engaged in a cooperative venture, to drill an oil well. I. Stanford Jolley, representing an Eastern firm that wants the oil lease, tries to stop the project. He hires Roy Barcroft and Lee Roberts to prevent the completion of the well. The serial is pretty standard fare and representative of the lowered standards in the last few years of serial production.

In the comedy *Once Upon a Horse* ('58), he reverted to the name Tom Keene. It starred Dan Rowan and Dick Martin and also featured as guest stars old Western stalwarts Robert Livingston, Kermit Maynard and Bob Steele. He also was billed Tom Keene when he made a guest appearance with several other Western stars (Rex Allen, Allan Lane, William Farnum, Kermit Maynard, Monte Hale, Tom Tyler, Ray Corrigan and George Chesebro) in *Trail of Robin Hood* ('50).

Edward D. Wood, Jr., attempted to star Keene in a proposed Western television series to be called *The Adventures of the Tucson Kid* and a pilot for the series, titled "The Crossroads Avenger," was filmed. Tom starred as the Tucson Kid, an insurance investigator in the Old West. Tom Tyler and Lyle Talbot were in the supporting cast. A second episode called "The Crossroads Avenger Returns" was also filmed but the series did not sell. Tom appeared in some other TV shows and for a time he headlined "The Tom Keene Review," a musical-Western-variety stage show which appeared in various theaters in the Southern California area in the mid to late '50s.

Plan 9 from Outer Space was filmed by Ed Wood in 1956 but it was not released until 1959. In this science fiction thriller, Keene got third billing as an Air Force officer who leads the fight to defend the Earth against sinister alien invaders. Over the years the film has taken on a cult following and is often called "The worst film of all time."

Around 1958, Keene drifted out of movies and into the insurance and real estate business. He was once married to Grace Stafford, who later became Mrs. Walter Lantz. Tom remarried, date unknown. Tom died of cancer at the Motion Picture Country Hospital in Woodland Hills on August 5, 1963. His death was hardly noticed by the press. His wife Florence and a stepson survived.

Few will remember George Duryea of Broadway in the '20s or Richard Powers, minor actor of the '40s and '50s. But Tom Keene, Western star of the '30s and early '40s for RKO, Crescent and Monogram will be remembered as one of the cowboy performers who helped to mature the Western and who dished out thrills to accompany the consumption of popcorn, candy and soft drinks on Saturday afternoons in "the days that were ..."

Serial

1950

Desperadoes of the West. Rep., [12 Chapters] D: Fred C. Brannon; SP: Ronald Davidson; AP: Franklyn Adreon; Cam: John MacBurnie; Mus: Stanley Wilson; LP: Richard Powers [Tom Keene], Judy Clark, Roy Barcroft, I. Stanford Jolley, Lee Roberts, Edmund Cobb, Lee Phelps, Dennis Moore, George Chesebro.

HAZEL KEENER

Information on Hazel Keener's personal life is lacking, except that after her movie career she became a minister in the Church of Religious Science. However, we do know about her movies.

The first film credit was *The Married Flapper* ('22) in which she supported Marie Prevost. In *The Brass Bottle* ('23) she supported Harry Myers, and in *Tea — With a Kick* ('23) she played in support of Doris May and Creighton Hale.

The features for which she is best-remembered are the six Westerns she made with up-and-coming cowboy Fred Thomson at FBO in 1924. They are *The Dangerous Coward, The Fighting Sap, Galloping Gal-* lagher, *The Mask of Lopez, North of Nevada* and *The Silent Stranger*. These dusties were well-received and Thomson was rising fast in popularity. Evidently he and Miss Keener hit it off pretty well or she wouldn't have been assigned to his pictures.

Hazel made three other pictures in 1924. She supported Jack Holt and Norma Shearer in *Empty Hands* at Paramount, played heroine to Buffalo Bill, Jr., in *Hard Hitten' Hamilton* and was a principal in *His Forgotten Wife* starring Madge Bellamy and Warner Baxter.

In 1925 Hazel was in *The Freshman* with Harold Lloyd, *Parisian Love* with Clara Bow, *Ports of Call* with Edmund Lowe and *Ten*

Days with Richard Holt. She seems to have made only one picture in 1926, *Vanishing Hoofs* with Wally Wales. In 1927 she played opposite Buck Jones in *Whispering Sage* and had featured roles in *The First Night* with Bert Lytell, *The Gingham Girl* with Lois Wilson and *One Hour of Love* with Jacqueline Logan.

In 1928 Hazel co-starred with Francis X. Bushman, Jr., in Universal's serial *The Scarlet Arrow*. The first chapter gave the serial a rousing send-off. Rodney Masterson (Henry Herbert) manages the North Western Fur Company's local branch and is secret owner of the saloon. With his co-hort Brodsky (Al Ferguson), he is planning to dispose of some of the company's furs. They are also trying to find part of a torn map which will show the way to the gold mine of Masterson's former friend, whose ward Kathleen (Hazel) has been his ward since the mysterious death of her father some years before.

Bob North (Bushman), captain of the North West Mounted Police, visits Masterson's store trying to trace the fur thieves and meets Kathleen. Masterson, realizing that North can endanger his plans, promises Kathleen to Brodsky if he will do away with

North. Later, Kathleen finds a piece of torn map in an old trunk. She is interrupted by Masterson, who demands the map. She escapes and flees, but is caught in a terrible forest fire. Thus, Chapter One gets off to a flying start. Subsequent chapters carried the story forward without a let-up in the action.

Ten years elapse before we find further film credits for her. She had bit parts in *Wells Fargo* ('37) with Joel McCrea and Frances Dee, *Gateway* ('38) with Don Ameche and Arleen Whelan, *I Love You Again* ('49) with William Powell and Myrna Loy, *That Gang of Mine* ('40) with Bobby Jordan and Leo Gorcey, and *Untamed* ('40) with Ray Milland and Patricia Morison.

Serial

1928

The Scarlet Arrow. Univ., [10 Chapters] D: Ray Tailor; SP: Arthur Henry Gooden; S: Frank H. Clark; LP: Francis H. Clark; LP: Francis X. Bushman, Jr., Hazel Keener, Al Ferguson, Edmund Cobb, Aileen Goodwin, Clark Comstock, Henry Herbert.

ROBERT KELLARD / STEVENS

Robert Kellard's destiny was to be an actor. His mother and father were brought up in the atmosphere of the theater, as was Robert. His aunt, Virginia Harned Courtenay, was also a well-known actress.

Robert was born in Los Angeles on April 23, 1915. He graduated from Hollywood High School and Santa Monica Junior College.

While at Hollywood High, Robert got

his first taste of acting. Through David Butler, the director, he worked as an extra in *Connecticut Yankee* ('31). That was the sum total of his experience when he headed back to New York for his real initiation as an actor.

Beulah Bondi was responsible for his first chance to act. The play was *Mother Lode*, in which Miss Bondi appeared with Melvyn Douglas and Helen Gahagan. Virginia Harned coached him for the part. That was in 1934.

Robert Kellard, Luana Walters and Henry Brandon (as Fu Manchu) in *Drums of Fu Manchu* (Republic, 1940).

Bob followed with two more plays, both starring Conway Tearle. Between engagements on Broadway, Robert played in stock in Mineola, Long Island, Wilkes-Barre, Pennsylvania, and Nuangola, Pennsylvania.

While he was appearing in *Hitch Your Wagon to a Star* in 1937, 20th Century-Fox gave him a screen test in the East. Before he heard from them again, however, he was engaged for a part in *Annapolis Salute* ('37), a picture made at the U.S. Naval Academy. He went to Hollywood after that, under contract to Fox. He appeared in a number of Fox films as a bit player, including *The Boy Friend* ('37), *Battle of Broadway* ('38), *Kentucky* ('38), *Josette* ('38) and *Island in the Sky* ('38).

Kellard was one of the four principals in *Drums of Fu Manchu* ('40). As Allan Parker, he aided Sir Dennis Nayland Smith (William Royle) in the fight against Fu Manchu (Henry Brandon). In *King of the Royal Mounted* ('40)

he played Corp. Tom Merrit, Jr., sidekick of Sgt. King (Allan Lane) who had been assigned to capture the murderer of Merrit, Sr., a Canadian inventor. A foreign power has learned that Merrit, Sr.'s, Compound X has certain magnetic properties which would make their mines effective against the British fleet.

Eight years later, Kellard had the lead role in the serial *Tex Granger* ('48). In the story, he purchases a newspaper in Three Buttes where Dancer Carson (I. Stanford Jolley) is operating outside the law. The marshal is actually an outlaw, and one of the badmen (Smith Ballew) is operating more or less independently. Tex occasionally dons a mask to become a mysterious fighter for good and ultimately subdues the criminal element.

In September 1942 Mrs. Beatrice Kellard (known professionally as Bebe LaMonte when she worked as a fashion model in New

York) divorced Kellard. She testified that he would taunt her with sarcastic references to her three previous marriages.

On December 29, 1946, Robert married socialite Jerelyn W. Arthur. In March 1949, Kellard was accused of attempting to smother his wife with a pillow in a divorce action she filed. She testified that he had used her as a punching bag on more than one occasion.

Kellard's career was undistinguished and he faded silently from the screen. He died on January 13, 1981.

Serials

1940

Drums of Fu Manchu. Rep., [15 Chapters] D: William Witney, John English; AP: Hiram S. Brown, Jr.; Cam: William Nobles; Mus: Cy Feuer; SP: Franklyn Adreon, Morgan Cox, Ronald Davidson, Norman Hall, Barney Sarecky, Sol Shor; LP: Henry Brandon, William Royle, Gloria Franklin, Robert Kellard, Luana Walters.

King of the Royal Mounted. Rep., [12 Chapters] D: William Witney, John English; SP: Franklyn Adreon, Norman S. Hall, Joseph Poland, Barney A. Sarecky, Sol Shor; AP: Hiram S. Brown, Jr.; Cam: William Nobles; Mus: Cy Feuer; LP: Allan Lane, Robert Strange, Robert Kellard, Lita Conway, Herbert Rawlinson, Bryant Washburn, Stanley Andrews, Harry Cording.

1948

Tex Granger. Col., [15 Chapters] D: Derwin Abrahams; SP: Arthur Hoerl, Lewis Clay, Harry Fraser, Royal Cole; P: Sam Katzman; Cam: Ira H. Morgan; Mus: Mischa Bakaleinikoff; LP: Robert Kellard, Peggy Stewart, Buzz Henry, Smith Ballew, Jack Ingram, I. Stanford Jolley, Terry Frost, Charles King.

JEANNE KELLY / JEAN BROOKS

Jeanne Kelly (her real name) was born in Houston, Texas, on December 23, 1916. She was taken to Costa Rica as a small child. Her studio biography says her father was a coffee planter. Maybe. What is known for certain is that she attended school there and mastered both Spanish and German, and upon returning to the States she had to learn English.

She became a singing guitarist at the Club Bali, a Latin American nightclub, and at the Waldorf's Sert Room. She was able to secure the position of second lead to Lenor Ulric in Broadway's *Name Your Poison* and to be tested by Twentieth Century-Fox in 1938. They used her in a few minor roles.

Jean did Spanish-language features with Mexican singing star Tito Guizar. Supposedly there are four of these films. Universal signed her in 1940 and she had small roles in *Buck Privates* ('41) and *Meet the Chump* ('41). She then was given the heroine's role in the "million dollar super serial," *Riders of Death Valley* ('41). The production cost is debatable but it did have an all-star cast headed by Dick Foran, Buck Jones and Charles Bickford. In it, a group of vigilantes are organized to protect miners against raiders and confidence men. Jeanne is Mary Morgan, who has been willed a claim on the Lost Aztec mine.

Jeanne played opposite Johnny Mack Brown in *Son of Roaring Dan* ('40), *The Man* from Montana ('41) and *Fighting Bill Fargo* ('42). In *Flash Gordon Conquers the Universe* ('40) Jeanne, as Olga, had the fourth female role, overshadowed by Carol Hughes, Anne Gwynne and Shirley Deane.

These films are the ones remembered by serial and Western aficionados. Her pulchritude was not displayed and her thespian talents held in check.

In 1941 Jeanne joined RKO and changed her name to Jean Brooks (she married director Richard Brooks). In her first film, *The Falcon Strikes Back* ('43), she appears only in the last scene and is unbilled. She fared better in *The Leopard Man* ('43), a Val Lewton production starring Dennis O'Keefe. Jean portrayed a night club singer who makes her entrance one night with a leopard on a leash. The leopard escapes and a number of murders occur in the vicinity. In *The Falcon in Danger* ('43), Brooks helps the Falcon (Tom Conway) solve the murder of her uncle. In Val Lewton's *The Seventh Victim* ('43), as the sister of Kim Hunter, she has been marked for death by a group of Greenwich Village devil worshipers. In *The Falcon and the Coeds* ('43), Brooks becomes owner of an exclusive girls school after dean Barbara Brown is murdered. In her last Val Lewton film, *Youth Runs Wild* ('44), Brooks is a war wife

and mother who starts a day nursery in her backyard to keep kids off the streets of their overcrowded town. *The Falcon in Hollywood* ('44) found Brooks a studio fashion designer; in *The Falcon's Alibi* ('46) she is a mysterious baroness, a red herring who travels with a phony society dowager. In her last film, *The Bamboo Blonde* ('46), she was way down in the cast. Frances Langford starred.

Brooks was later divorced from Richard Brooks — and walked away from Hollywood.

Serials

1940

Flash Gordon Conquers the Universe. Univ., [12 Chapters] D: Ford Beebe, Ray Tailor; LP: Buster Crabbe, Carol Hughes, Charles Middleton, Anne Gwynne, Frank Shannon, Roland Drew, Shirley Deane, Lee Powell, Jeanne Kelly.

1941

Riders of Death Valley. Univ., [15 Chapters] D: Ray Tailor, Ford Beebe; S: Oliver Drake; P: Henry MacRae; LP: Dick Foran, Buck Jones, Charles Bickford, Guinn Williams, Jeanne Kelly, Lon Chaney, Jr., Noah Beery, Jr., Monte Blue.

PAUL KELLY

Paul Kelly was born in Brooklyn, New York, on August 9, 1899. He was a stage actor from age seven and in films from eight. He played child and juvenile roles in many early Vitagraph films.

On Broadway Kelly appeared in *Seventeen* ('18), *Anne of Green Gables* ('19), *Up the Ladder* ('22), *Whispering Wires* ('22), *The Sea Woman* ('25), *9:15 Revue* ('30), *Bad Girl* ('30), *Adam Had Two Sons* ('32), *Beggars Are*

Coming to Town ('45), *Command Decision* ('47) and *The Country Girl* ('50).

Kelly's silent films include *Buddy's Downfall* ('14), *Knights of the Square Table* ('17), *Uncle Sam of Freedom Ridge* ('20), *The Old Oaken Bucket* ('21), *The New Klondike* ('26) and *Slide, Kelly, Slide* ('27).

In the early 1920s Paul met actress Dorothy Mackaye, who was married to a rising musical comedy performer, Ray Raymond. Paul and the Raymonds spent much time together and by 1927 Paul's feelings for Mrs. Raymond had gone far beyond friendship. He and Dorothy realized they were deeply in love. Raymond was an alcoholic and his violent temper would send him into a blinding rage, at which time he would beat Dorothy. On Saturday, April 16, 1927, a fight ensued in which Raymond was severely beaten by Kelly. Raymond was taken to a hospital but on Tuesday morning, April 19, 1927, he died. Paul was arrested and charged with murder. On May 25 a jury found him guilty of manslaughter and he was sentenced to one-to-ten years in San Quentin. Dorothy was likewise sentenced for compounding a felony and being an accessory after the fact in the alleged plot to conceal the true facts involving Raymond's death. On June 30, Dorothy was convicted and, for the benefit of reporters, sang and danced on the boat taking her to San Quentin.

Paul was paroled for excellent behavior on August 2, 1929. Dorothy had been released earlier. They were wed in 1931 and led a quiet life. Their wedded bliss came to an end when Dorothy was killed in an automobile accident on January 5, 1940. Paul was left with two young daughters. He felt remarriage would solve his personal problems. Luckily he met, fell in love with and wed Mardelle Zurcker in 1941.

In the '30s, '40s and '50s, Paul had the lead in scores of "B" films, mostly crime melodramas, and competent supporting roles in major productions.

His films include *School for Girls* ('34), *Silk Hat Kid* ('35), *The Song and Dance Man* ('36), *Parole Racket* ('37), *Navy Blue and Gold* ('37), *Torchy Blane in Panama* ('38), *The Roaring Twenties* ('39), *Queen of the Mob* ('40), *Flying Tigers* ('42), *Dead Man's Eyes* ('44), *The Cat Creeps* ('46), *Fear in the Night* ('47), *Crossfire* ('47), *The File on Thelma Jordon* ('49), *The Painted Hills* ('51), *Springfield Rifle* ('52), *Split Second* ('53), *The High and the Mighty* ('54) and *Storm Center* ('56).

With *The Secret Code* ('42) Columbia tried their hand at straight spy actioners. The serial starred Kelly as a cop who sets out to trap a gang of Axis saboteurs in the guise of the Black Commando. Spencer G. Bennet was at the helm of what many critics thought was one of Columbia's better thrillers.

Paul suffered a heart attack on March 9, 1953, recovered, and went back to work, but he had a fatal heart attack on November 6, 1956.

Serial

1942

The Secret Code. Col., [15 Chapters] D: Spencer G. Bennet; SP: Basil Dickey, Leighton Brill, Robert Beche; P: Larry Darmour; Cam: James S. Brown, Jr.; Mus: Lee Zahler; LP: Paul Kelly, Anne Nagel, Clancy Cooper, Trevor Bardette, Robert O. Davis, Gregory Gay, Jacqueline Dalya.

CY KENDALL

William C. Cline, in his book *In the Nick of Time* (McFarland & Co., 1984), has best described Cy Kendall:

A big, stout, lumbering man, whose first impression of drowsiness was disarmingly deceptive, he portrayed with finesse the sly, crafty, insinuating gang boss who badgered those around him with guile and deceit, praising them with a sarcastic display of oily supercilious charm, while constantly nagging them with a cynical sneer of thinly disguised contempt.

Kendall was very good at what he did. Stabbing, shooting, poisoning, bombing or just plain torture — it was all in the day's work for this cold-eyed criminal, but usually underlings were assigned to these tasks.

Beginning in 1935 Kendall went on to appear in over 125 feature films plus his serial roles. A sampling of his film appearances: *His Night Out* ('35), *The Last Gangster* ('37), *Crime School* ('38), *The Invisible Menace* ('38), *Valley of the Giants* ('38), *The Angels Wash Their Faces* ('39), *Charlie Chan in Honolula* ('39), *Billy the Kid* ('41), *Honky Tonk* ('41), *Alias Boston Blackie* ('42), *The Whistler* ('44), *Lady in the Lake* ('47), *Call Northside 777* ('48) and *Nancy Goes to Reno* ('50).

Kendall contributed tremendously to the image of the top villain in serials. He was so easy to hate that regular serialgoers grew to love him.

Cy Kendall died in 1953 at age 72.

Serials

1939

The Green Hornet. Univ., [13 Chapters] D: Ford Beebe, Ray Tailor; LP: Gordon Jones, Anne Nagel, Keye Luke, Wade Boteler.

1940

Junior G-Men. Univ., [12 Chapters] D: Ford Beebe, John Rawlins; LP: Billy Halop, Huntz Hall, Gabriel Dell, Bernard Punsley, Philip Terry, Roger Daniels.

1945

Secret Agent X-9. Univ., [13 Chapters] D: Ray Tailor, Lewis D. Collins; LP: Lloyd Bridges, Keye Luke, Jan Wiley, Victoria Horne, Samuel S. Hinds, I. Stanford Jolley, Jack Rockwell, Edmund Cobb, Ann Codee, George Chesebro.

Jungle Queen. Univ., [13 Chapters] D: Ray Tailor, Lewis D. Collins; LP: Edward Norris, Lois Collier, Eddie Quillan, Douglas Dumbrille, Ruth Roman.

1946

The Scarlet Horseman. Univ., [13 Chapters] D: Ray Tailor, Lewis D.Collins; LP: Peter Cookson, Paul Guilfoyle, Victoria Horne, Janet Shaw, Jack Ingram, Edmund Cobb, Virginia Christine, Danny Morton, Harold Goodwin, Cy Kendall.

BILL KENNEDY

Bill Kennedy starred in the serial *The Royal Mounted Rides Again* ('45), one of three films (out of a total of 60 or more) in which he appeared in the lead. The serial was a pretty good one, although younger viewers may have found it difficult to follow the story. Sharing the limelight were George Dolenz, Duan Kennedy (no relation), Milburn Stone, Paul E. Burns and Robert Armstrong. Kennedy was also the lead in *Web of Danger* ('45) and *The People's Choice* ('45), both for Republic. But mostly he muddled along in bit parts.

Kennedy was born in Cleveland Heights, Ohio, on June 27, 1908, and grew up there, graduating from Cathedral Latin High School and then attending Assumption College in Windsor, Ontario, for two years. He got a job as an announcer for a radio station in Cleveland, WTAM, and from there he moved to WWJ, the Detroit News in Detroit. In 1942 he relocated to Hollywood, where he worked in radio between acting jobs. But after 14 years of frustration and brushes with poverty, he retired from acting and moved back to Detroit and hosted "Bill Kennedy at the Movies" for 13 years on Channel 9 in Windsor, Ontario (then CKLW-TV, later CBET-TV). He then switched to Detroit's Channel 50 and kept the program going for another 14 years, retiring in 1983. He died at his home in Palm Beach, Florida, on January 27, 1997, after a long battle with emphysema. He was 88. On his program he set a standard for motion picture enjoyment that didn't talk down to viewers or treat them as uninformed idiots.

During his final years in Hollywood, Kennedy played a string of bad guys in early TV Westerns like *The Cisco Kid* and *The Gene Autry Show* as well as in Johnny Mack Brown feature Westerns.

Bill's Westerns were *Sheriff of Medicine Bow*, *Overland Trails*, *Triggerman* and *Law of the West*, all with Johnny Mack Brown; *Trail of the Yukon* with Kirby Grant; *Shadows of the West*, *Gunslingers*, *Canyon Raiders*, *Nevada Badmen* and *Abilene Trail* with Whip Wilson; *Border Outlaws* with Spade Cooley; *Storm Over Wyoming* with Tim Holt; *Silver City Bonanza* with Rex Allen; *I Shot Billy the Kid*, *Train to Tombstone* and *Border Rangers* with Don Barry.

Serial

1945

The Royal Mounted Rides Again. Univ., [13 Chapters] D: Ray Tailor, Lewis D. Collins; SP: Joseph O'Donnell, Tom Gibson, Harold C. Wire; P: Morgan Cox; LP: Bill Kennedy, Duan Kennedy, George Dolenz, Robert Armstrong, Paul E. Burns, Milburn Stone, Addison Richards, Joseph Crehan, Rondo Hatton.

DUAN KENNEDY

Duan Kennedy has been overlooked in all the reference books. Her career was a short one, 1943–47. She worked for REO and Universal in such films as *The Falcon and the Co-eds* ('43), *The Falcon Out West* ('44), *Marine Raiders* ('44), *Mademoiselle Fifi* ('44), *Seven Days Ashore* ('44), *Salome, Where She Danced* ('45), *A Night in Paradise* ('46), *The Thrill of Brazil* ('46) and *Jiggs and Maggie in Society* ('47). In these and other films she was a bit player; her name is usually far down the cast list.

Her two best roles were in *The Royal Mounted Rides Again* ('45) and *Son of the Guardsman* ('46). The first is the better serial; the cast is superior, and the action moves along smoothly. The latter film is enjoyable

and Duan enjoys more screen time, but it is not one of Columbia's better cliffhangers.

Duan failed to make an indelible mark as a heroine and after one film in 1947 there are no more credits for her.

Serials

1945

The Royal Mounted Rides Again. Univ., [13 Chapters] D: Ray Tailor, Lewis D. Collins; SP: Joseph O'Donnell, Tom Gibson, Harold C. Wire; P: Morgan Cox; LP: George Dolenz, Bill Kennedy Duan Kennedy, Paul E. Burns, Milburn Stone, Robert Armstrong, Addison Richards, Tom Fadden, Selmer Jackson, Rondo Hatton.

1946

Son of the Guardsman. Col., [15 Chapters] D: Derwin Abrahams; SP: George H. Plympton, Harry Fraser, Royal Cole, Lewis Clay; P: Sam Katzman; Cam: Ira H. Morgan; Mus: Lee Zahler; AP: Mel DeLay; LP: Robert Shaw, Duan Kennedy, Robert (Buzz) Henry, Jim Diehl, Hugh Prosser, Wheeler Oakman, Al Ferguson.

CRAUFORD KENT

Born in Shepherd's Bush, England, in 1891. Crauford Kent began early to think longingly of the stage as a future for himself. During his early schooling he displayed a wondrous ability in his studies of music and at 12 years of age he made his debut on the concert stage and became one of the country's leading boy sopranos. His schooling was completed at Godolphin College at Hammersmith, where for three years he was master at the piano.

Following college, Kent began a concert tour, singing in both concert and oratorio at nearly all of England's leading auditoriums, and also Scotland, Ireland and France. Then for more than two years he sang arias in the vaudeville halls of England. His first appearance in musical comedy was with a number of the Gilbert & Sullivan revivals, following this with an engagement of *The Geisha Girl*.

Kent took up the art of dancing and came to the U.S. as the juvenile lead in *Our Miss Gibbs*. Later he was three years with *The Pink Lady* and went with that company to London. A subsequent engagement with *Adele* turned out to be his best performance. His first appearance before the camera was in *The Deep Purple* ('15), an instantaneous success. He continued to play film roles until his death, first as a star and later as a supporting player. His films included *The Heart of the Hills* ('16), *Good Gracious, Annabelle* ('19), *The Love Flower* ('20), *Jane Eyre* ('21), *The Eagle's Feather* ('23), *That Model from Paris* ('26), *Seven Keys to Baldpate* ('29), *The House of Rothschild* ('34), *Mutiny on the Bounty* ('35), *The Charge of the Light Brigade* ('36), *Souls at Sea* ('37), *The Adventures of Robin Hood* ('38), *Foreign Correspondent* ('40), *The Dolly Sisters* ('45), *Unconquered* ('47) and *Samson and Delilah* ('49).

A tennis enthusiast for many years, Kent was chairman of the umpires and linesmen committee of the Southern California Tennis Association and was vice-chairman of a similar committee of the U.S. Lawn Tennis Association. In 1952 he received the coveted McGovern Award, given annually to the official who contributes the most to tennis.

Kent starred in the 1929 Universal serial *The Ace of Scotland Yard*, released in both silent and sound versions. The story dealt with the further adventures of Angus Blake, retired agent of Scotland Yard. This time he is opposed by the Queen of Diamonds (Grace Cunard), a female gang leader out to steal his fianceé Lady Diana's (Florence Allen) valuable ring. The acquisition of the famous "love ring" by Lord Blanton (Hubert Prior), Lady Diana's father, worries Blake because his analytical mind senses danger. Prince Darius (Albert Prisco) has taken the vow of his ancestors to recover the ring and the mummified image of an ancient princess of his race (now in Lord Blanton's house), stolen from its resting place in the Gobi Desert.

In 1934 Kent played the minor role of an explorer in Clyde Beatty's serial *The Lost Jungle*.

On May 15, 1953, at his Los Angeles home, Kent awoke at 4 A.M. and collapsed, dying before an ambulance arrived. He left his wife Constance and a brother and nephew in England.

Serials

1929

The Ace of Scotland Yard. Univ., 1929 [10 Chapters] D: Ray Taylor; S/SP: Harold M. Atkinson; LP: Craufurd Kent, Florence Allen, Herbert Prior, Monte Montague, Grace Cunard, Albert Prisco.

1934

The Lost Jungle. Mascot, [12 Chapters] D: Armand Schaefer, David Howard; LP: Clyde Beatty, Cecilia Parker, Syn Saylor, Warner Richmond, Wheeler Oakman.

ROBERT KENT

Robert Kent, whose real name was Douglas Blackley, Jr., was born in Hartford, Connecticut, on December 3, 1908. The family soon moved to Brooklyn, New York, where he went to grammar school and Erasmus Hall High School. He later attended Mount Hermon Prep School in Massachusetts, then Bryant Evening High School in Long Island. He was expelled from each of these schools because he couldn't take the criticism of teachers without answering them back. There was a time during his high school that he boxed as an amateur, bidding fair to make it his regular profession. But after six months of this, he quit after his eye was cut open in a fight.

His father, a Scotch-Canadian wallpaper manufacturer, died when Robert was six. Mrs. Blackley obtained a secretarial position in New York City and it was there that he got a $65-a-month job as a messenger boy at the Seaboard National Bank. This indoor job didn't agree with him, and it was cut short when he developed an illness. Then began a series of outdoor jobs. He worked on a farm in Vermont, labored in a lumberyard and finally shipped out to sea as an able-bodied seaman on the New York–Valparaiso, Chile, and New York–San Francisco runs of the Grace Lines.

From friends he learned that professional modeling furnished an easy living. His rugged physique and handsome face quickly earned him plenty of work. While doing this work, he became acquainted with a little theater group known as the Brooklyn Neighborhood Theater. He obtain a role in the group's production of *King Lear*, in the basement of a Swedenborgian church.

Kent played his first professional role with Lyle Talbot in *The Criminal Code* with the Robert Williams Company in Boston.

In the first of his three serials, *The Phantom Creeps* ('39), Kent was Capt. Bob West of Military Intelligence. Dr. Alan Zorka (Bela Lugosi) has invented a devisualizer belt which renders him invisible, a robot eight feet tall, and a chemical that can put a whole army into suspended animation. West's job was to see that Zorka did not turn his inventions over to a foreign power or use them against the United States.

In his second serial outing, *Who's Guilty* ('45), he is detective Bob Stewart, who tries to find out who is behind the attempts to murder various members of a wealthy family. Eventually he proves that a member thought dead is really alive and that that individual is the mystery Voice.

In his third cliffhanger, *The Phantom Rider* ('46). Kent is Dr. James Sterling, secretly the heroic Phantom Rider. Villain Fred

Carson (LeRoy Mason) uses his official status as the local Indian agent to steal Indian allotment money and, with the aid of the Indian medicine man, directs raiding and robbing activities.

Kent was married to actress Astrid Allwyn. He died at age 46 on May 4, 1955.

Serials

1939

The Phantom Creeps. Univ., [12 Chapters] D: Ford Beebe, Saul A. Goodkind; S: Willis Cooper; SP: George H. Plympton, Basil Dickey, Mildred Barish; LP: Bela Lugosi, Robert Kent, Dorothy Arnold, Regis Toomey, Edward Van Sloan, Eddie Acuff, Charles King, Karl Hackett.

1945

Who's Guilty? Col., [15 Chapters] D: Howard Bretherton, Wallace Grissell; SP: Ande Lamb, George H. Plympton; P: Sam Katzman; Cam: Ira H. Morgan; Mus: Lee Zahler; LP: Robert Kent, Amelita Ward, Tim Ryan, Jayne Hazard, Minerva Urecal, Charles Middleton, Wheeler Oakman, Charles King, Jack Ingram.

1946

The Phantom Rider. Rep., [12 Chapters] D: Spencer Bennet, Fred C. Brannon; SP: Albert DeMond, Basil Dickey, Jesse Duffy, Lynn Perkins, Barney Sarecky; AP: Ronald Davidson; Cam: Bud Thackery; Mus: Richard Charwin; LP: Robert Kent, Peggy Stewart, LeRoy Mason, George J. Lewis, Kenne Duncan, Hal Taliaferro.

DORIS KENYON

Doris Kenyon was born on September 5, 1897, in Syracuse, New York, the daughter of a clergyman-poet. Victor Herbert heard her sing at the Authors Club and gave her a small part in his musical *Princess Pat* ('15). Kenyon appeared on stage in such vehicles as *The Girl in the Limousine* ('19), *The White Villa* ('21) and *The Gift* ('24).

Kenyon made her screen debut at 18 in 1916, appearing in such features as *The Man Who Stood Still* ('16), *The Ocean Waif* ('16), *The Great White Trail* ('17), *The Inn of the Blue Moon* ('18) and *Up the Road with Sallie* ('18).

The serial *The Hidden Hand* ('17) was made when actresses were quite often given the main lead. Such was the case with Kenyon; she was supported by Arline Pretty, Sheldon Lewis and Mahlon Hamilton. In the story two men are murdered, a millionaire named Whitney and his visitor, the grand duke of a foreign country. Before he dies,

Whitney accuses Jack Ramsey (Hamilton) of having inflicted a mortal wound on him in some mysterious way. The grand duke's story, which he states in his dying moments, reveals a series of events dating back to his own country. These events have to do with the birth of a girl known as Doris Whitney, who believes herself to be Whitney's daughter. The villain, "The Hidden Hand," a creature whose right hand is covered by a claw-like mitten, is a master of plastic surgery and a wizard with deadly chemicals and gases. He tries to pass off a confederate (Arline Pretty) as the millionaire's daughter.

Kenyon was quite active during the '20s, playing opposite such stars as Rudolph Valentino, Thomas Meighan, Milton Sills, George Arliss and Lewis Stone. She had principal parts in *Burning Daylight* ('20), *The Conquest of Canaan* ('21), *Shadows of the Sea* ('22), *Lights of Broadway* ('23), *Monsieur Beaucaire* ('24), *The Half-Way Girl* ('25), *The*

In *The Hidden Hand* (Pathé, 1917).

Blonde Saint ('26), *The Valley of the Giants* ('27), *The Hawk's Nest* ('28), *Interference* ('28) and *Beau Bandit* ('30)

During the '30s, Kenyon spent two years in Europe singing and studying. She also began to write magazine articles targeted at middle-age women. Later, during World War II, she sang for the USO quite a bit.

In the '30s she was in *Alexander Hamilton* ('31) as Betsy Hamilton, *Road to Singapore* ('31), *The Man Called Back* ('32), *Voltaire* ('33) as Madame Pompadour, *Counsellor-at-Law* ('33), *Whom the Gods Destroy* ('34) and *The Man in the Iron Mask* ('39) as Queen Anne.

Her first husband was Milton Sills

(1927–30). After he died in '30, she was married briefly to broker Arthur Hopkins and then to Albert Lasker. Her only child, Kenyon Sills, died in 1971 and his son went to live with Kenyon in Beverly Hills. Kenyon was married for 24 years to musicologist Bronislaw Mylnarski, who died in 1971.

Serial

1917

The Hidden Hand. Pathé, [15 Chapters] D: James Vincent; SP: Arthur B. Reese, Charles W. Goddard; LP: Doris Kenyon, Sheldon Lewis, Mahlon Hamilton, Arline Pretty, Henry Sedley.

CHARLES KING

Charles King's name is a revered one among Western and serial aficionados. He appeared in at least 39 serials and over 400 features and shorts. In the silent era he appeared in a lot of comedies, but after 1930 he nearly always played the resident badman in Poverty Row productions. He is credited with appearing as an extra in *The Birth of a Nation* (1914); throughout the 1920s he worked mainly at Universal, where he made 45 films, most of them two-reel comedies. In 1924 he was in the "Telephone Girl" series with Alberta Vaughn. In 1926–27 he co-starred in the "Excuse Makers" and "What Happened to Jane" series, and in 1927–28 he co-starred with Charles Dorety in the popular "Ike and Mike" series.

His earliest serial was *The Mysterious Pearl* (1921); his earliest Western *Hearts of the West* (1925). It was in 1930 that he began his nearly uninterrupted career as a badman in Westerns and serials. He had the physical

requirements to play a villain (a black mustache, heavy eyebrows, a head of jet black hair). His friends called him "Blackie" and he was so named in various films; thus, many moviegoers, especially the small fry, knew him by that name only. He was short and pudgy but a superb fighter as witness his slugfests with Bob Steele, Buster Crabbe, Johnny Mack Brown and Tex Ritter. He weighed around 200 pounds but was exceptionally agile for a man that size. From 1930 to 1945 he was one of the busiest screen heavies in Hollywood.

Everyone liked Charlie. He had a good sense of humor and was an avid practical joker. However, he was his own worst enemy. He loved "the fruit of the vine" and would party and drink to the point where his wife would have to go to the studio on payday and get his check before he squandered all the money. Toward the end of his career, as he put on more pounds, he was featured more in semi-comic roles, especially at PRC; the studio made him look like a buffoon, complete with droopy Snub Pollard–type mustache. He was to one generation what Roy Barcroft was to a later one — the best of the best.

Charles was born Charles Lafayette King, Jr., on February 21, 1895 in Hillsboro, Texas. He disappointed his father when he didn't become a doctor, electing instead to join the acting profession. He had two sons, one of whom was named Charles L. King.

When B-western production ceased in the early 1950s, King moved into TV but his roles were only bits. In his last years he led an almost "skid row" existence. During those years he attempted suicide twice, first by shooting himself with a .22, then by climbing a tree, tying a rope around his neck and a limb and jumping. Either the rope broke or the tree limb did, and Charles broke his leg. He was probably drunk at the time.

Charles King died May 7, 1957, at John Wesley County Hospital, Los Angeles. Cause of death was hepatic coma, with antecedent causes being cirrhosis and chronic alcoholism. His body was cremated.

Today scores of Charles' movies can be viewed on home video; thus, we continue to enjoy his fine work. William Cline in *In the Nick of Time* (McFarland, 1984) writes, "As a cocky, loud-mouthed bully, his penchant was for provoking saloon brawls with the hero (who was earnestly trying to mind his own business) and consequently getting the bejabbers beat out of himself, to the great delight of the audience."

Serials

1921

The Mysterious Pearl. Berwilla, [15 Chapters] D: Ben Wilson, Duke Worne; SP: J. Grubb Alexander, Harvey Gates; P: Ben Wilson; LP: Ben Wilson, Neva Gerber, Joseph W. Girard, William Carroll.

1931

The Mystery Trooper. Syn., [10 Chapters] D: Stuart Paton; SP: Karl Krusada, S: Flora Douglas; P: Harry S. Webb, Flora Douglas; Cam: William Nobles, Edward Kull; LP: Robert Frazer, Blanche Mehaffey, Buzz Barton, Charles King.

1932

The Hurricane Express. Mascot, [12 Chapters] D: Armand Schaefer, J. P. McGowan; SP: George Morgan, J. P. McGowan; S: Colbert Clark, Barney Sarecky, Wyndham Gittons; Cam: Ernest Miller, Carl Webster; P: Nat Levine; LP: John Wayne, Shirley Grey, Conway Tearle, Tully Marshall, J. Farrell MacDonald.

1934

The Law of the Wild. Mascot, [12 Chapters] D: Armand Schaefer, B. Reeves Eason; SP: Sherman Lowe, B. Reeves Eason; S: Ford Beebe, John Rathmall, Al Martin; P: Nat Levine; LP: Bob Custer, Rex (horse), Rin-Tin-Tin, Jr.

(dog), Lucile Browne, Richard Cramer, Ernie Adams.

1935

The Miracle Rider. Mascot, [12 Chapters] D: Armand Schaefer, B. Reeves Eason; SP: John rathmall; S: Barney Sarecky, Wellyn Totman, Gerald and Maurice Geraghty; Cam: Ernest Miller, William Nobles; LP: Tom Mix, Charles Middleton, Joan Gale, Jason Robards, Robert Kortman.

The Roaring West. Univ., (15 Chapters] D: Ray Taylor; SP: George Plympton, Nate Gazert, Ella O'Neill, Basil Dickey, Robert Rothafel; S: Edward Earl Repp; P: Henry MacRae; Cam: William Sicknew, Richard Fryer; LP: Buck Jones, Muriel Evans, Walter Miller, Frank McGlynn, Sr., Harlan Knight, William Desmond.

Adventures of Rex and Rinty. Mascot, [12 Chapters] D: B. Reeves Eason, Ford Beebe; SP: John Rathmell, Barney Sarecky; S: B. Reeves Eason, Ray Trampe, Maurice Geraghty; P: Nat Levine; LP: Rex (horse), Rin-Tin-Tin, Jr., Kane Richmond, Norma Taylor, Mischa Auer, Wheeler Oakman.

1936

The Phantom Rider. Univ., [15 Chapters] D: Ray Taylor; S/SP: George Plympton, Basil Dickey, Ella O'Neill, Henry MacRae; P: Henry MacRae; Cam: Allen Thompson, John Hickson; LP: Buck Jones, Maria Shelton, Diana Gibson, Harry Woods.

Shadows of Chinatown. Victory, [15 Chapters] D: Robert Hill; SP: Isadore Bernstein, Basil Dickey; S: Rock Hawkey; P: Sam Katzman; Cam: Bill Hyer; LP: Bela Lugosi, Herman Brix, Joan Barclay, Luana Walters, Charles King.

1937

The Painted Stallion. Rep., [12 Chapters] D: William Witney, Alan James, Ray Taylor; SP: Barry Shipman, Winston Miller; Cam: William Nobles, Edgar Lyons; AP: J. Laurence Wickland; Mus: Raoul Kraushaar; LP: Ray Corrigan, Hoot Gibson, Hal Taliaferro, Jack Perrin, Duncan Renaldo, LeRoy Mason.

1938

The Lone Ranger. Rep., [15 Chapters] D: William Witney, John English; SP: Barry Shipment, George W. Yates, Franklyn Adreon, Ronald Davidson, Lois Eby; AP: Sol C. Siegel; Mus: Alberto Colombo; Cam: William Nobles; LP: Lee Powell, Chief Thundercloud, Lynne Roberts, Herman Brix, Lane Chandler, Stanley Andrews.

Flaming Frontiers. Univ., [15 Chapters] D: Ray Taylor, Alan James; SP: Wyndham Gittens, George Plympton, Basil Dickey, Paul Perez; S: Peter B. Kyne; P: Henry MacRae; LP: Johnny Mack Brown, Eleanor Hansen, Charles Middleton.

1939

The Oregon Trail. Univ., [15 Chapters] D: Ford Beebe, Saul Goodkind; SP: Edmund Kelso, George Plympton, Basil Dickey, W. W. Watson; P: Henry MacRae; LP: Johnny Mack Brown, Louise Stanley, Fuzzy Knight, Bill Cody, Jr.

Zorro's Fighting Legion. Rep., [12 Chapters] D: William Witney, John English; SP: Ronald Davidson, Franklyn Adreon, Morgan Cox, Sol Shor, Barney Sarecky; AP: Hiram S. Brown, Jr.; Cam: Reggie Lanning; LP: Reed Hadley, Sheila Darcy, William Carson, Leander de Cordova, C. Montague Shaw, Edmund Cobb.

The Phantom Creeps. Univ., [12 Chapters] D: Ford Beebe, Saul A. Goodkind; SP: George H. Plympton, Basil Dickey, Mildred Barish; S: Willis Cooper; LP: Bela Lugosi, Robert Kent, Dorothy Arnold, Regis Toomey, Edward Van Sloan.

1940

The Shadow. Col., [15 Chapters] D: James W. Horne; SP: Joseph Poland, Ned Dandy, Joseph O'Connell; P: Larry Darmour; Cam: James S. Brown, Jr., Mus: Lee Zahler; LP: Victor Jory, Veda Ann Borg, Robert Moore, Robert Fiske, Jack Ingram, Charles King, Jack Perrin.

Terry and the Pirates. Col., [15 Chapters] D: James W. Horne; SP: Mark Layton, George Morgan, Joseph Levering; P: Larry Darmour; Cam: James S. Brown, Jr.; Mus: Lee Zahler; LP: William Tracy, Granville Owen, Joyce Bryant, Sheila Darcy, Allen Jung, Dick Curtis.

The Green Archer. Col., [15 Chapters] D: James W. Horne; SP: Morgan B. Cox, John Cutting, Jesse A. Duffy, James W. Horne; S: Edgar Wallace; Cam: James S. Brown, Jr.; Mus: Lee Zahler; LP: Victor Jory, Iris Meredith, James Craven, Robert Fiske, Dorothy Fay.

1941

The Iron Claw. Col., [15 Chapters] D: James W. Horne; SP: Basil Dickey, George H. Plympton, Jesse A. Duffy, Charles R. Condon, Jack Stanley; S: Arthur Stringer; P: Larry Darmour; Cam: James S. Brown, Jr.; Mus: Lee Zahler; LP: Charles Quigley, Joyce Bryant, Forrest Taylor, Walter Sande, Norman Willis.

White Eagle. Col., [15 Chapters] D: James W. Horne; SP: Arch Heath, Morgan B. Cox, John Cutting, Laurence Taylor; P: Larry Darmour; Cam: James S. Brown, Jr.; Mus: Lee Zahler; LP: Buck Jones, Raymond Hatton, Dorothy Fay, James Craven, Jack Ingram, Charles King.

1942

Perils of the Royal Mounted. Col., [15 Chapters] D: James W. Horne; Basil Dickey, Scott Littleton, Louis Heifetz, James Duffy; P: Larry Darmour; Cam: James S. Brown, Jr.; Mus: Lee Zahler; LP: Nell O'Day, Robert Stevens [Kellard], Herbert Rawlinson, Kenneth MacDonald, John Elliott, Richard Fiske, Kermit Maynard.

1944

Black Arrow. Col., [15 Chapters] D: Lew Landers; SP: Sherman Lowe, Jack Stanley, Leighton Brill, Royal K. Cole; P: Rudolph C. Flothow; Cam: Richard Fryer; Mus: Lee Zahler; LP: Robert Scott, Adele Jergens, Kenneth MacDonald, Charles Middleton, George J. Lewis.

1945

Who's Guilty? Col., [15 Chapters] D: Howard Bretherton, Wallace Grissell; SP: Ande Lamb, George H. Plympton; P: Sam Katzman; Cam: Ira H. Morgan; Mus: Lee Zahler; LP: Robert Kent, Amelita Ward, Tim Ryan, Jayne Hazard, Charles Middleton, Wheeler Oakman.

The Monster and the Ape. Col., [15 Chapters] D: Howard Bretherton; SP: Sherman Lowe, Royal K. Cole; P: Rudolph C. Flothow; Cam: L.

W. O'Donnell; Mus: Lee Zahler; LP: Robert Lowery, Carole Mathews, Ralph Morgan, George Macready.

Jungle Raiders. Col., [15 Chapters] D: Lesley Selander; SP: Ande Lamb, George H. Plympton; P: Sam Katzman; Cam: Ira H. Morgan; Mus: Lee Zahler; LP: Kane Richmond, Eddie Quillan, Veda Ann Borg, Carol Hughes, Janet Shaw, Charles King.

1946

Son of the Guardsman. Col., [15 Chapters] D: Darwin Abrahams; SP: George H. Plympton, Harry Fraser, Royal Cole, Lewis Clay; P: Sam Katzman; Cam: Ira H. Morgan; Mus: Lee Zahler; LP: Robert Shaw, Duan Kennedy, Robert Henry, Jim Diehl, Hugh Prosser.

The Phantom Rider. Rep., [12 Chapters] D: Spencer Bennet, Fred Brannon; SP: Albert De-Mond, Basil Dickey, Jesse Duffy, Lynn Perkins, Barney Sarecky; AP: Ronald Davidson; Mus: Richard Cherwin; Cam: Bud Thackery; LP: Robert Kent, Peggy Stewart, Hal Taliaferro, LeRoy Mason, George J. Lewis, Kenne Duncan.

Chick Carter, Detective. Col., [15 Chapters] D: Derwin Abrahams; SP: George H. Plympton, Harry fraser; P: Sam Katzman; Cam: Ira H. Morgan; Mus: Lee Zahler; LP: Lyle Talbot, Douglas Fowley, Julie Gibson, Pamela Blake, Eddie Acuff.

Hop Harrigan. Col., [15 Chapters] D: Derwin Abrahams; SP: George H. Plympton, Ande Lamb; S: Jon Blummer; P: Sam Katzman; Mus: Lee Zahler, Cam: Ira H. Morgan; LP: William Bakewell, Jennifer Holt, Robert "Buzz" Henry, John Merton, Charles King.

1947

Son of Zorro. Rep., [13 Chapters] D: Spencer G. Bennet, Fred C. Brannon; SP: Franklyn Adreon, Basil Dickey, Jesse Duffy, Sol Shor; AP: Ronald Davidson; Cam: Bud Thackery; Mus: Mort Glickman; LP: George Turner, Peggy Stewart, Roy Barcroft, Edward Cassidy, Ernie Adams, Stanley Price, Charles King, Edmund Cobb.

Brick Bradford. Col., [15 Chapters] D: Spencer G. Bennet; SP: George H. Plympton, Arthur Hoerl, Lewis Clay; P: Sam Katzman; Cam: Ira H. Morgan; Mus. Mischa Bakaleini-

koff; LP: Kane Richmond, Rick Vallin, Linda Johnson, Pierre Watkin, Charles Quigley, Jack Ingram, John Merton, Charles King, Carol Forman.

Jesse James Rides Again. Rep., [13 Chapters] D: Fred C. Brannon, Thomas Carr; SP: Franklyn Adreon, Basil Dickey, Jesse Duffy, Sol Shor; AP: Mike Frankovich; Cam: John MacBurnie; Mus: Mort Glickman; LP: Clayton Moore, Linda Stirling, Roy Barcroft, Tris Coffin, John Compton, Tom London, Edmund Cobb, Holly Bane.

1948

Congo Bill. Col., [15 Chapters] D: Spencer G. Bennet, Thomas Carr; SP: George H. Plympton, Arthur Hoerl, Lewis Clay; P: Sam Katzman; Cam: Ira H. Morgan; Mus: Mischa Bakaleinikoff; LP: Don McGuire, Cleo Moore, Jack Ingram, I. Stanford Jolley, Leonard Penn, Nelson Leigh, Charles King, Armida.

Superman. Col., [15 Chapters] D: Spencer G. Bennet, Thomas Carr; SP: Arthur Hoerl, Lewis Clay, Royal Cole; P: Sam Katzman; Mus: Mischa Bakaleinikoff; Cam: Ira H. Morgan; LP: Kirk Alyn, Noel Neill, Tommy Bond, Pierre Watkin, Carol Forman, George Meeker, Jack Ingram, Herbert Rawlinson.

Tex Granger. Col., [15 Chapters] D: Derwin Abrahams; SP: Arthur Hoerl, Lewis Clay, Harry Fraser, Royal Cole; P: Sam Katzman; Cam: Ira H. Morgan; Mus: Mischa Bakaleinikoff; LP: Robert Kellard [Stevens], Peggy Stewart, Buzz Henry, Smith Ballew, Jack Ingram, I. Stanford Jolley, Charles King.

1949

Bruce Gentry. Col., [15 Chapters] D: Spencer G. Bennet; SP: George H. Plympton, Joseph F. Poland, Lewis Clay; P: Sam Katzman; Cam: Ira H. Morgan; Mus: Mischa Bakaleinikoff; LP: Tom Neal, Judy Clark, Ralph Hodges, Forrest Taylor, Hugh Prosser, Tris Coffin, Jack Ingram, Charles King, Terry Frost.

Adventures of Sir Galahad. Col., [15 Chapters] D: Spencer G. Bennet; SP: George H. Plympton, Lewis Clay, David Mathews; P: Sam Katzman; Cam: Ira H. Morgan; Mus: Mischa Bakaleinikoff; LP: George Reeves, Charles King, William Fawcett, Hugh Prosser, Lois Hall, John Merton.

1950

Atom Man vs. Superman. Col, [15 Chapters] D: Spencer G. Bennet; SP: George H. Plympton, Joseph Poland, David Mathews; Cam: Ira H. Morgan; Mus: Mischa Bakaleinikoff; P: Sam Katzman; LP: Kirk Alyn, Noel Neill, Lyle Talbot, Tommy Bond, Pierre Watkin, Jack Ingram, Charles King.

1953

The Great Adventures of Captain Kidd. Col., [15 Chapters] D: Derwin Abbe, Charles S. Gould; SP: George H. Plympton, Arthur Hoerl; P: Sam Katzman; Cam: William Whitley; Mus: Mischa Bakaleinikoff; LP: Richard Crane, David Bruce, Joan Crawford, George Wallace, Lee Roberts, John Hart, Ray Corrigan.

JOHN (DUSTY) KING

Ben Bernie, the ol' maestro, and Zeppo Marx are responsible for John King's start in the theater. These two famous theatrical personalities took King and pushed him on to success, first in radio work and later in screen endeavors.

Born in Cincinnati, Ohio, July 11, 1909, the only child of Ernest E. Everson, a realtor, and his wife, Ruth (Brumfield) Everson, King got his preparatory education in Cincinnati public schools. He attended the University of Cincinnati night college after high school graduation, studying for a business career.

Out of college, King began earning his daily bread as a checker and stoker at a local grain elevator. Tiring of this job, he became a clerk with a radio concern, a furniture salesman, a chauffeur driving new cars from Detroit to Cincinnati, a candy salesman, a lumberjack in New Mexico and a "hand" on a 30,000 acre Arizona ranch.

In 1930, King returned to his Cincinnati home. By this time his naturally fine baritone voice had been improved greatly because of his habit of singing as he went about his labors on the ranch. Through a friend whom he met in New Mexico, King was given an audition at station WCKY, in Covington, Kentucky. He got the job, which began with a 30-day trial without pay. But King stuck with it because he liked it, and at the end of the month he was working on four commercial programs.

King was chief entertainer on these programs, singing ballads, popular songs and classical numbers. Convinced that his voice was his fortune, King became seriously interested in cultivating his voice and turned to prominent voice teachers for additional instruction.

King stayed with WCKY for eight months. Then he advanced to the position of chief announcer and featured singing star over at station WKRC in Cincinnati. He stayed there four years.

In 1934, Ben Bernie came to Cincinnati; by chance he heard King sing and he was so struck with the young man's ability that he immediately signed King to go on tour with his band. King accepted gladly. Bernie realized the singer was tall, dark and handsome and all that was needed to suit him for a stage or screen career was stage presence. So Bernie gave him that, developing stage poise and confidence in King.

By February 1935, Bernie's band had traveled across the country to Hollywood. There the bandleader told King he was ready for a screen career. King was unwilling to leave the man who had given him so much help, but when Bernie got Zeppo Marx, an agent, to also insist that he go into pictures, King acquiesced.

Universal gave King a screen test and the following day he was signed to the standard player contract.

King appeared with the Ben Bernie Band in Paramount's *Stolen Harmony* ('35) and he was one of the principals in Universal's serial *The Adventures of Frank Merriwell* ('36), also featuring Don Briggs and Jean Rogers. When his dad disappears, Frank Merriwell (Briggs) is called home by his mother, who thinks a mysterious intruder she encountered was after a ring the senior Merriwell entrusted to her. Frank and his college chums (King, Rogers) manage to decipher an inscription on the ring, which leads them to $30,000 in gold nuggets and the imprisoned senior Merriwell. A stranger, later identified as a distant relative, and his gang attempt to steal the money, but are thwarted and captured. Merriwell arrives back at college to lead his team to victory.

King was soon given the lead role in the serial *Ace Drummond* ('36), based on Capt. Eddie Rickenbacker's King Features newspaper strip. A mysterious known as "The Dragon" is determined to stop the Mongolian link needed to complete a globe-circling airplane service. Ace Drummond (King), famed flyer, agrees to investigate. In Asia he seeks not only to learn the identity of the Dragon, but helps Peggy Trainor (Jean Rogers) search for her lost father and a hidden mountain containing enormous quantities of jade. There are quite a few action-packed flying sequences where Ace is placed in serious jeopardy. Although the aerobatics are often impressively handled, our hero too often survives crashes and the like by, well, just surviving — simply walking away from the wreckage with no real explanation.

King was used in routine programmers following *Ace Drummond*. But in 1937 he garnered the main role in *The Road Back*, a story of German soldiers trying to resume their civilian lives after World War I. King shared honors with Slim Summerville, Noah Beery, Jr., Andy Devine and Richard Cromwell.

King also appeared in *Three Smart Girls* ('37), *Charlie Chan in Honolula* ('38), *The Three Musketeers* ('39), *Mr. Moto Takes a Vacation* ('39) and *The Gentleman from Arizona* ('39), a Monogram Cinecolor Western with

John King in *The Road Back* (Universal, 1937).

Joan Barclay and J. Farrell MacDonald. It was King's first Monogram pictures.

Between 1940 and 1943, Monogram released 24 Range Buster B-Westerns with Ray Corrigan, Max Terhune and John King, signed to provide the vocalizing and romancing. The Range Busters were fun to watch; although Corrigan and King did not like each other, they worked well together on screen. King appeared in the first 20 films.

Following the wrap-up of *Haunted Ranch* ('43), King was drafted into the Air Force and spent nearly four years in Special Services in Douglas, Arizona. Discharged, he returned to Hollywood and, not receiving any film offers, wound up back in radio at CBS. Later he bought an NBC station in Douglas, but late in the 1950s family health considerations prompted a move to La Jolla, California, where King owned and operated a waffle house.

King had married in 1940 and the Kings had one daughter, Anne. Mrs. King died several years before King's death on November 11, 1987.

Serials

1936

The Adventures of Frank Merriwell. Univ., [12 Chapters] D: Cliff Smith; SP: George H. Plympton, Maurice Geraghty, Ella O'Neill, Basil Dickey; AP: Henry MacRae; LP: Don Briggs, Jean Rogers, John King, Carla Laemmle, Dick Jones, Al Bridge, Bud Osborne, Edmund Cobb, William Desmond, Al Ferguson.

Ace Drummond. Univ., [13 Chapters] D: Ford Beebe, Cliff Smith; SP: Wyndham Gittens, Norman S. Hall, Ray Trampe; AP: Barney A. Sarecky, Ben Koeing; LP: John King, Jean Rogers, Noah Beery, Jr., Guy Bates Post, Chester Gan.

MOLLIE KING

Mollie King's career was a relatively short one, 1916–22. Her first feature was *A Woman's Power* ('16) with Douglas MacLean, followed by *Fate's Boomerang*, *The Summer Girl* and *All Man*. In 1917 she made *Kick In* with William Courtnay, *Blind Man's Luck* with Earle Foxe and *The On-the-Square-Girl* with L. Robert Lytton. *Human Clay* was made in 1918; *Suspense* was made in 1919; *Greater Than Love* and *Women Men Forget* were both made in 1920; *Suspicious Wives* was made in 1921, and *Her Majesty* was completed in 1922.

Her two serials were both made in 1917. *Mystery of the Double Cross* is an interesting story. It revolves around the efforts of Peter Hale (Leon Bary), a wealthy young man returning to the United States on a transatlantic steamer, to identify a mysterious and beautiful young passenger. During a panic caused by the sighting of a submarine, her dress is torn at the shoulder and he catches a brief look at an unusual mark of a double cross on her arm. Later, at the office of his father's lawyer, he learns that in order to inherit the Hale fortune, he must find and marry the girl of the double cross, who is described as being perfect in mind and body and trained to be his wife. How Hale meets Phillipa Brewster (King) when he is certain she is the one he seeks, how she denies his premise, how he doubts her and seeks to prove that she is really the Girl of the Double Cross, despite her willing engagement to villainous Bridgey Bentley (Ralph Stuart), makes a fast-moving torrent of action and thrills.

In *The Seven Pearls* ('17), Ilma Bay (King) and her boyfriend Harry Drake (Creighton Hale) must recover pearls taken

by Harry from a necklace belonging to a Turkish Sultan, or Ilma will become a member of the Sultan's harem. Ilma's father is held captive pending Ilma's return at the end of six months. Perry Mason (Leon Bary) wants the pearls for himself and hampers the efforts of Ilma and Harry to find them.

Although Mollie headlined the films she was in, they were not great pictures, merely "B" programmers. She died in Fort Lauderdale, Florida, in 1982 from a stroke. She was 86.

Serials

1917

Mystery of the Double Cross. Astra/Pathé, [15 Chapters] D: William Parke; SP: Gilson Willets; S: Jacques Futrelle; LP: Mollie King, Leon Bary, Ralph Stuart, Gladden James, Harry Fraser, Helene Chadwick.

The Seven Pearls. Astra/Pathé, [15 Chapters] D: Burton L. King, Donald McKenzie; SP: George B. Seitz; A: Charles W. Goddard; LP: Mollie King, Creighton Hale, Leon Bary, John J. Dunn, Henry G. Sell, Floyd Buckley.

NATALIE KINGSTON

Natalie Kingston was born in Somona, California (possibly 1905), and convent-educated. She appeared in Broadway musicals before breaking into movies in 1924. Her early picture work was in Mack Sennett comedies starring Harry Langdon (eight films) and Ben Turpin (three films).

Natalie was selected as a Wampas Baby Star in 1927, but she could never seem to get her career off the launching pad. She is known primarily for the two Tarzan serials she made at the end of the silent era. *Tarzan, the Mighty* ('28) starred Frank Merrill as Tarzan and Natalie as Mary Trevor, forerunner of Jane. In *Tarzan, the Tiger* ('29) she became the familiar Jane, with Merrill again as Tarzan. Both Universal serials proved exceedingly popular. Less popular was *Pirates of Panama* ('29), in which she played opposite Jay Wilsey, better known as Buffalo Bill, Jr. Opposing them as they search for the map to a buried treasure was Al Ferguson.

Her 30-chapter swing through the jungle as Tarzan's mate, plus her 12-chapter defiance of the Panamanian pirates, guaranteed her a place in serialdom. Greater and more successful actresses have been forgotten, but Natalie has lived on in that continued-next-week world kept alive by those who choose to relive the happier moments of childhood.

Serials

1928

Tarzan the Mighty. Univ., [15 Chapters] D: Jack Nelson, Ray Taylor; S: Edgar Rice Burroughs; SP: Ian McClosky; LP: Frank Merrill, Natalie Kingston, Al Ferguson, Lorimer Johnson, Tantor (elephant).

1929

Tarzan the Tiger. Univ., [15 Chapters] D: Henry MacRae; SP: Ian McClosky; S: Edgar Rice Burroughs; LP: Frank Merrill, Natalie Kingston, Al Ferguson, Sheldon Lewis, Frank Lanning, Mademoiselle Kithnou.

Pirates of Panama. Univ., [12 Chapters] D: Ray Taylor; SP: Arthur Henry Gooden; S: William MacLeon Raine; LP: Jay Wilsey, Natalie Kingston, Al Ferguson, George Ovey, Mary Sutton, Otto Bibber.

EVALYN KNAPP

Born on June 17, 1908, in Kansas City, Missouri of Swedish-American stock, Evalyn Knapp, sister of Orville Knapp, an orchestra leader, originally wanted to become a newspaper writer. She attended Kansas City High School and Kansas Junior College. Appearing in amateur theatricals in school changed her goal to becoming an actress. Pursuing her thespian ambition, she joined a Kansas City stock company and worked her way up from bits to leads on the stage, landing a role in *Mr. Moneypenny*, a Broadway production of the 1928–29 season.

While in New York City she made a screen test at Vitaphone Studios of Warner Brothers in Brooklyn and was used in several shorts. Her shorts (two-reelers) in 1929–30 were enjoyable to watch and built up Knapp's confidence that she could succeed in sound features. Her Pathé two-reelers were *Big Time Charlie*, *Beach Babies*, *A Smooth Guy*, *Haunted: or, Who Killed the Cat*, *Hard Boiled*

Hampton, *Love, Honor and Oh Baby*, *Keeping Company*, *A Tight Squeeze*, *All Stuck Up*, *Chills and Fever*, *Gentlemen of the Evening* and *Wednesday at the Ritz*.

Knapp went to work for Warner Brothers in 1930. Her career was in high gear when, in June 1931, she suffered a 15-foot fall in the hills near Hollywood Lake. The 22-year-old lost her balance and fell from the upper road encircling the lake to a drive known as the Lower Road, striking a rocky ledge. She suffered a distinct break in her spinal column and two broken ribs, as well as cuts and bruises. Her condition was described as extremely serious. In late August she was regaining the use of her legs after being confined to her bed for two months. Luckily, she recovered completely.

Knapp was a 1932 Wampas Baby Star. In the same class of '32 were Ruth Hall, Boots Mallory, Gloria Stuart, Patricia Ellis, Ginger Rogers, Eleanor Holm, Mary Carlisle and Dorothy Wilson. Not a bad class!

Knapp's first feature role at Warner Brothers was *Maybe It's Love* ('30) starring Joe E. Brown. She then was given the feminine lead in *Sinner's Holiday* ('30) with Grant Withers and *River's End* ('31) with Charles Bickford. Supporting roles followed in *Smart Money* ('31), *Fifty Million Frenchmen* ('31), *Big City Blues* ('32) and *The Strange Love of Molly Louvain* ('32). She played the female lead with Joe E. Brown in *Fireman, Save My Child* ('32). Knapp was released by Warners in 1932.

It is for the programmers she made as a freelancer from 1932 to 1938 that Knapp is best remembered. Some of these are *Night Mayor* (Col. '32, Lee Tracy); *This Sporting Age* (Col. '32, Jack Holt); *Police Car 17* (Col. '33, Tim McCoy); *Corruption* (Imperial '33, Preston Foster); *State Trooper* (Col. '33, Regis Toomey); *His Private Secretary* (Showmens '33, John Wayne); *In Old Santa Fe*

(Mascot '34, Ken Maynard); *A Man's Game* (Col. '34, Tim McCoy); and *Hawaiian Buckaroo* (TCF '38, Smith Ballew).

After 1938 Knapp could get only supporting roles and retired after *Two Weeks to Live* (RKO '43, Lum & Abner).

In 1934, Universal attempted to bring back the serial queen, the dominant figure of the silent serial. After a number of actresses had been tested, Knapp got the assignment. *Perils of Pauline* ('34) did *not* repopularize the serial queen, though it was not the fault of Knapp (the script was faulty). It was, however, an enjoyable cliffhanger, the story having to do with two groups contending for a sacred ivory disk which reveals the formula for an invisible poison gas that destroyed ancient civilizations.

On November 10, 1934, Knapp wed surgeon George A. Snyder in Santa Barbara. After her retirement from the screen in 1943, she remained the wife of Dr. Snyder until his death in the early 1970s.

Knapp passed away on June 10, 1981, in West Hollywood.

Serial

1934

Perils of Pauline. Univ., [12 Chapters] D: Ray Taylor; SP: Ella O'Neill, Basil Dickey, George H. Plympton, Jack Foley; S: Ella O'Neill, Charles W. Goddard; LP: Evalyn Knapp, Craig Reynolds, James Durkin, John Davidson, Frank Lackteen, William Desmond, Pat O'Malley.

ELYSE KNOX

Elyse Knox, the daughter of Frank Knox, Secretary of the Navy under Franklin Roosevelt during World War II, was born on December 14, 1917, in Hartford, Connecticut. She trained as an artist, began her career as a designer for *Vogue* and later worked as a photographer's model. Films beckoned in 1940 and she appeared in small roles in *Free, Blonde and 21* and *Lillian Russell*. In the following decade she played leads and second leads in a variety of films, mainly routine "B" pictures.

Representative films are *Sheriff of Tombstone* ('41, Roy Rogers), *The Mummy's Tomb* ('42, Dick Foran), *Top Sergeant* ('42, Leo Carrillo), *Hay Foot* ('42, Noah Beery, Jr.), *Hit the Ice* ('43, Abbott and Costello), *Moonlight and Cactus* ('44, The Andrews Sisters), *Army Wives* ('44, Rick Vallin) and the Joe Palooka series.

Her one serial, a good one, was *Don Winslow of the Coast Guard* ('43). She played Mercedes Colby, taking over the role played by Claire Dodd in *Don Winslow of the Navy* ('41).

Knox married Michigan's famous halfback football hero, Tom Harmon. It has been a good marriage. Their son Mark Harmon also became an actor.

Serial

1943

Don Winslow of the Coast Guard. Univ., [13 Chapters] D: Ford Beebe, Ray Taylor; SP: George H. Plympton, Paul Huston, Griffin Jay; AP: Henry MacRae; Mus: Hans J. Salter; LP: Don Terry, Walter Sande, Elyse Knox, Nestor Paiva, Lionel Royce, Philip Ahn, Richard Crane, Rex Lease, Stanley Blystone.

MARY KORNMAN

Mary Kornman, daughter of a cameraman and a youthful exponent of economic independence for women, became a wage earner at the age of two. Her first part was with Madeleine Travers in *The Iron Heart* ('20). Hal Roach later organized a troupe of talented youngsters to produce comedies, and she became its leading lady. Her first of 40-plus "Our Gang" shorts was *Young Sherlocks* ('22).

Kornman re-emerged on the screen in 1930, after several years in school, in the series "The Boy Friends," which also featured Mickey Daniels, Grady Sutton, Gertie Messinger and Dave Sharpe. When the series ended in 1932, she became a freelancer,

playing supporting roles in unmemorable films.

In 1935, however, she made three movies that are of interest here. In *The Desert Trail* ('35) and *Smokey Smith* ('35) she was the love interest opposite John Wayne and Bob Steele, respectively. And in the independent serial *Queen of the Jungle* ('35), she had the leading role. Screen Attractions put the latter on the market on a state-right basis. Comparable to *The Lost City* ('35), *Young Eagles* ('34), *The New Adventures of Tarzan* ('35) and other indies of the period, it was cheaply made (built around footage from the 1922 silent *Jungle Goddess*). But it had that indefinable appeal that often surrounded the "lesser" serials. Accustomed to the polish of a Pathé, a Universal, or even a Mascot cliffhanger, one could still be intrigued by a product that even the kids recognized as a cheapie.

Unfortunately, that was about it for Mary Kornman. She married cameraman Leo Tovar in the early '30s, but they were divorced a few years later. She retired from the screen in 1938 to marry animal trainer Ralph McCutcheon, who supplied livestock to the Hollywood studios and who owned a good part of the TV series *Fury* at a later date.

Kornman died of cancer on June 1, 1973. She was 56 years old.

Serials

1935

Queen of the Jungle. Screen Attractions, [12 Chapters] D: Robert Hill; LP: Mary Kornman, Reed Howes, George Chesebro, Lafe McKee, Eddie Foster, Dickie Jones.

ROBERT KORTMAN

The gaunt, skeletal face of Robert Kortman was enough to make one shudder. When he glared or smiled with his unevenly spaced teeth, the small fry gulped and the goosebumps appeared. Who could forget him as Longboat in *The Miracle Rider* ('35), Braken (the Black Ace's pilot) in *Mystery Squadron* ('33), One-Eye Chapin in *Adventures of Red Ryder* ('40), Magua in *The Last of the Mohicans* ('22), Russian Cossack Boris Petroff in *The Vigilantes are Coming* ('36), and Trigger, saddlemate of Johnny Mack Brown in *Wild West Days* ('37)?

Kortman was born in either Brackville, Texas or Philadelphia, Pennsylvania, on December 24, 1887. As an adult he stood six feet in height, weighed about 185 pounds and had light brown hair and dark blue eyes. After spending six years in the U.S. Cavalry, he entered movies in 1911 for the New York Motion Picture Company at Inceville. In the beginning he worked as an extra or was given bit roles, but in 1915 he played in *The Ruse* starring William S. Hart, who evidently liked him for he (Kortman) went on to work with Hart in *Cash Parrish's Pal* ('15), *Double Crossed* ('15), *The Disciple* ('16), *Hell's Hinges* ('16), *The Captive God* ('16), *The Narrow Trail* ('17), *Square Deal Saunderson* ('19) and *Travelin' On* ('22).

Non-Westerns that Kortman played in included *City Streets* ('31, Gary Cooper), *The Criminal Code* ('31, Walter Huston), *Pardon Us* ('31, Laurel & Hardy), *Island of Lost Souls* ('32, Charles Laughton), *The Whispering Shadow* ('33, Bela Lugosi), *Bulldog Drummond Strikes Back* ('34, Ronald Colman), *The Trail of the Lonesome Pine* ('36, Sylvia Sidney), *Spawn of the North* ('38, Henry Fonda), *You Can't Take it with You* ('38, James Stewart), *Along Came Jones* ('45, Gary Cooper), *Two Years Before the Mast* ('46, Alan Ladd), *Blaze of Noon* ('47, William Holden), *The Paleface* ('48, Bob Hope) and *The Big Carnival* ('51, Kirk Douglas).

Cowboys he worked with the most were, in order of frequency, Buck Jones, William S. Hart, Johnny Mack Brown, William Boyd, Ken Maynard, Bob Steele, Donald Barry, Harry Carey, Charles Starrett and Richard Dix.

Actors and directors who worked with him have said that he was a real professional. On screen he scared the hell out of the Saturday matinee front row kids; they would have gasped had they known he was a real softie off-screen.

Kortman died from cancer in Long Beach, California, in 1967 at age 79.

Serials

1919

The Great Radium Mystery. Univ., [18 Chapters] D: Robert Broadwell, Robert F. Hill; LP: Cleo Madison, Eileen Sedgwick, Bob Reeves, Edwin J. Brady, Robert Kortman, Robert Gray.

1930

The Lone Defender. Mascot, [12 Chapters] D: Richard Thorpe; LP: Walter Miller, Rin-Tin-Tin, Jr., June Marlowe, Buzz Barton, Josef Swickard, Robert Kortman, William Desmond, Kermit Maynard, Joe Bonomo.

1931

The Lightning Warrior. Mascot, [12 Chapters] D: Armand Schaefer, Benjamin Kline; P: Nat Levine; LP: Rin-Tin-Tin, Sr., Frankie Darro, Georgia Hale, George Brent, Pat O'-Malley, Robert Kortman, Lafe McKee.

The Vanishing Legion. Mascot, [12 Chapters] D: B. Reeves Eason; P: Nat Levine; LP: Harry Carey, Edwina Booth, Rex (horse), Frankie

Darro, William Desmond, Philo McCullough, Robert Kortman, Edward Hearn.

1932

The Last of the Mohicans. Mascot, [12 Chapters] D: B. Reeves Eason, Ford Beebe; P: Nat Levine; LP: Harry Carey, Hobart Bosworth, Edwina Booth, Lucile Browne, Walter Miller, Robert Kortman, Walter McGrail, Nelson McDowell.

1933

Mystery Squadron. Mascot, [12 Chapters] D: Colbert Clark, David Howard; P: Nat Levine; LP: Bob Steele, Guinn "Big Boy" Williams, Jack Mulhall, Lucile Browne, Robert Kortman, Purnell Pratt, Robert Frazer, Jack Mower.

The Whispering Shadow. Mascot, [12 Chapters] D: Albert Herman, Colbert Clark; P: Nat Levine; LP: Bela Lugosi, Henry B. Walthall, Viva Tattersall, Robert Warwick, Ethel Clayton, Robert Kortman.

1934

Burn 'Em Up Barnes. Mascot, [12 Chapters] D: Colbert Clark, Armand Schaefer; P: Nat Levine; LP: Jack Mulhall, Lola Lane, Frankie Darro, Julian Rivero, Edwin Maxwell, Jason Robards, Sr., Stanley Blystone, Robert Kortman.

1935

The Miracle Rider. Mascot, [15 Chapters] D: Armand Schaefer, B. Reeves Eason; P: Nat Levine; LP: Tom Mix, Joan Gale, Charles Middleton, Robert Kortman, Jason Robards, Sr., Edward Earle, Edmund Cobb, Charles King.

1936

Robinson Crusoe of Clipper Island. Republic, [14 Chapters] D: Mack V. Wright, Ray Taylor; P: Nat Levine; LP: Ray Mala, Rex (horse), Buck (dog), Mamo Clark, Herbert Rawlinson, Selmer Jackson, John Dilson, Robert Kortman, Lloyd Whitlock.

The Clutching Hand. S & S, [15 Chapters] D: Albert Herman; Spv.: Louis Weiss; LP: Jack Mulhall, Ruth Mix, Marion Shilling, Rex Lease, William Farnum, Reed Howes, Yakima Canutt, Slim Whitaker, Tom London, Robert Kortman.

The Vigilantes Are Coming. Rep., [12 Chapters] D: Mack V. Wright, Ray Taylor; P: Nat Levine; LP: Robert Livingston, Kay Hughes, Guinn "Big Boy" Williams, Raymond Hatton, Fred Kohler, Robert Warwick, William Farnum, Robert Kortman.

1937

Wild West Days. Univ., [13 Chapters] D: Ford Beebe, Cliff Smith; LP: Johnny Mack Brown, Lynn Gilbert, Robert Kortman, George Shelley, Frank Yaconelli, Walter Miller, Frank McGlynn, Jr., Charles Stevens.

Secret Agent X-9. Univ., [12 Chapters] D: Ford Beebe, Cliff Smith; LP: Scott Kolk, Jean Rogers, Henry Hunter, David Oliver, Monte Blue, Henry Brandon, Lon Chaney, Jr.

Zorro Rides Again. Rep., [12 Chapters] D: William Witney, John English; LP: John Carroll, Helen Christian, Duncan Renaldo, Noah Beery, Sr., Yakima Canutt, Dick Alexander, Robert Kortman, Reed Howes.

1938

The Fighting Devil Dogs. Rep., [12 Chapters] D: William Witney, John English; AP: Robert Beche; LP: Lee Powell, Herman Brix, Eleanor Stewart, Montagu Love, Hugh Sothern, Sam Flint, Lester Dorr, Forrest Taylor.

The Lone Ranger. Rep., [15 Chapters] D: William Witney, John English; LP: Lee Powell, Chief Thundercloud, Lynne Roberts, Herman Brix, Lane Chandler, Hal Taliaferro, George Montgomery, Stanley Andrews, William Farnum, John Merton.

1939

The Green Hornet. Univ., [13 Chapters] D: Ford Beebe, Ray Taylor; AP: Henry MacRae; LP: Gordon Jones, Anne Nagel, Keye Luke, Wade Boteler, Philip Trent, Walter McGrail, John Kelly.

1940

Adventures of Red Ryder. Rep., [12 Chapters] D: William Witney, John English; LP: Donald Barry, Noah Beery, Sr., Tommy Cook, Vivian Coe, Harry Worth, Hal Taliaferro, William Farnum, Jack Rockwell, Carleton Young.

Winners of the West. Univ., [13 Chapters] D:

Ford Beebe, Ray Taylor; LP: Dick Foran, Anne Nagel, James Craig, Tom Fadden, Charles Stevens, Trevor Bardette, Harry Woods, Roy Barcroft, Robert Kortman.

LAURA LA PLANTE

Hedda Hopper once referred to Laura La Plante as a "cute blond bundle of loveliness." Somebody else said that "as a comedienne she has no equal." The publication *Screenland* went so far as to say she was "the real reason gentlemen prefer blondes," and *Picture Play* said, "She is as real and friendly — as primitive — as a geranium in a garden of exotic flowers."

Laura entered films at 15, playing bit parts in Christie comedies.

Serial-wise she began with *Perils of the Yukon* ('22) starring William Desmond, a love triangle set in early-day Alaska. In it, the daughter of a wealthy Russian trader is loved by both hero Jack Merrill, Sr., and villain Petroff. Laura and the whole company had to undergo many hardships on location in the High Sierras, where they were snowed in for some time. It took about three months to film this adventure story. Laura, the only girl in the company, was expected to do all her stunts without relying on the services of a double. Thus, she had to fall into icy streams and allow herself to be thrown in by others.

A second serial, *Around the World in 18 Days* ('23) was adapted from Jules Verne's *Around the World in 80 Days*. The grandson of Phineas Fogg (Desmond) travels the globe on behalf of an international fuel corporation after the idea is suggested by his daughter Madge (La Plante). She goes with him on the trek, which is accomplished with submarines, speed boats, express trains, airplanes and other modes of transportation. Phineas and Madge circle the globe in search of proxies from the firm's scattered stockholders. They are opposed at every turn by villainous forces, but arrive back home in time to swing an important election.

In 1923, Laura was making about $150 a week. Being selected a Wampas Baby Star started her rise to popularity (and a salary of $3,500 a week). In 1926 she married William Seiter, who had directed several of her light comedies. She continued to work, becoming a bigger star each year. *Show Boat* ('29) started out as a silent but became a part-talkie through dubbing after the film was completed. It ranked with *The Cat and the Canary* ('27) as the most popular of Laura's films.

After divorcing director Seiter in 1932 in Riga, Latvia, she wed producer Irving Asher in Paris, France, on June 19, 1934. For the next eight years they lived in London and then moved to Beverly Hills, and from there to a home in Palm Desert. They had two children, Tony and Jill, both born in England. In the 1940s, Laura appeared on TV several times and in 1957 made her last film, Paramount's *Spring Reunion*, in support of Betty Hutton.

Though she became a big star, Laura never put down her humble beginnings, and often recalled her serial and Western days with affection.

In the 1960s, Laura began spending her days beside her swimming pool at her charming Palm Desert home, where she and her husband enjoyed a relaxed and happy home life.

Laura La Plante was born in 1904 in St. Louis, Missouri. Her death came in 1996 at age 91 at the Motion Picture Country Home and Hospital in Woodland Hills, California.

Serials

1922

Perils of the Yukon. Univ., [15 Chapters] D: Perry Vekroff, Jay Marchant, J. P. McGowan; S/SP: George Morgan, George Plympton; LP: William Desmond, Laura La Plante, Fred Stanton, Joe McDermott, Princess Neela, Ruth Royce.

1923

Around the World in 18 Days. Univ., [12 Chapters] D: B. Reeves Eason, Robert F. Hill; SP: George Bronson Howard, Frank Howard Clark; S: Robert Dillon; LP: William Desmond, Laura La Plante, William P. DuVall, Wade Boteler, William J. Welsh, Percy Challenger, Hamilton Morse.

FRANK LACKTEEN

In the serial *Jungle Girl* ('41), Frank Lackteen was Shamba, the nefarious, crease-faced witch doctor in the horned Viking headdress who yearned to sacrifice Frances Gifford to the gods. Lackteen had been up to no good in serials since 1916, soon after his arrival from his native land (now Lebanon); first a villainous Chinese in *The Yellow Menace* ('16), then in 36 more serial thrillers.

Frank Lackteen's career was a tribute to exotic villainy, spanning nearly five decades. He was born in 1894 in Kubber-Ilias, Asia Minor. His forte was the sinister ethnic. Whether he played an Oriental, or an Arab, a tribesman, or an Indian, they were inevitably malevolent. His thick European accent, which seemed to fit almost any nationality, was always in demand once the silent screen became the talking screen.

In sound serials, Lackteen's savage-eyed, bony visage lured menacingly in Buster Crabbe's *Tarzan the Fearless* (as Abdul), *Perils of Pauline* (as Fang), *The Mysterious Pilot* (as Yoroslaf), and through 34 other chapter-plays. In features he could be seen in *Juarez* ('39), *The Sea Wolf* ('41), *Frontier Gal* ('45), *Man-Eater of Kumaon* ('48), *Three Came to Kill* ('60) and other hair-raisers. His last film was *Requiem for a Gunfighter* ('65).

Lackteen died of cerebral and respiratory illness in Woodland Hills, California, in 1968. He was 73 years old.

Serials

1916

The Yellow Menace. Serial Film Co., [16 Chapters] D: William Kennedy; LP: Edwin Stevens, Florence Malone, Margaret Gale, Armand Cortes, Dave Wall, Marie Treador.

1920

The Veiled Mystery. Vit., [15 Chapters] D: F. J. Grandon, Webster Cullison, William J. Bowman; LP: Antonio Moreno, Pauline Curley, Henry A. Barrows, Nenette de Courey, W. L. Rogers, Frank Lackteen, George Reed.

1921

The Avenging Arrow. Pathé, [15 Chapters] D: w. S. Van Dyke, William Bowman; LP: Ruth Roland, Edward Hearn, Virginia Ainsworth, S. E. Jennings, Frank Lackteen, Vera Sisson.

1922

White Eagle. Pathé, [15 Chapters] D: W. S. Van Dyke, Fred Jackman; LP: Ruth Roland, Earl Metcalfe, Henry Girard, Virginia Ainsworth, Bud Osborne, Frank Lackteen, Gertrude Douglas.

The Timber Queen. Pathé, [15 Chapters] D: Fred Jackson; LP: Ruth Roland, Bruce Gordon, Val Paul, Leo Willis, Frank Lackteen, Al Ferguson, Bull Montana.

1923

Her Dangerous Path. Pathé, [10 Chapters] D: Roy Clements; LP: Edna Murphy, Charles Parrott, Hayford Hobbs, William Moran, Frank Lackteen, Glen Tryon, Hayford Hobbs, William Gillespie.

1924

Leatherstocking. Pathé, [10 Chapters] D: C. W. Patton; LP: Edna Murphy, Harold Miller, Whitehorse, Frank Lackteen, Roy Myers, Tom Tyler, James Pierce.

The Fortieth Door. Pathé, [10 Chapters] D: George B. Seitz; LP: Allene Ray, Bruce Gordon, Frank Lackteen, Anna May Wong, David Dunbar, Lillian Gale.

Into the Net. Pathé, [10 Chapters] D: George B. Seitz; LP: Edna Murphy, Jack Mulhall, Constance Bennett, Bradley Barker, Frank Lackteen, Harry Semels.

1925

Idaho. Pathé, [10 Chapters] D: Robert F. Hill; SP: Frank Leon Smith; S: Theodore Burrell; P: C. W. Patton; LP: Vivian Rich, Mahlon Hamilton, Frederick Vroom, Frank Lackteen, Omar Whitehead, Fred De Silva.

The Green Archer. Pathé, [10 Chapters] D: Spencer G. Bennet; SP: Frank Leon Smith; S: Edgar Wallace; LP: Allene Ray, Walter Miller, Burr McIntosh, Frank Lackteen, Dorothy King, William Randall, Walter P. Lewis.

Sunken Silver. Pathé, [10 Chapters] D: George B. Seitz; SP: Frank Leon Smith; S: Albert Payson Terhune; LP: Allene Ray, Walter Miller, Frank Lackteen, Albert Roccardi, Jean Brunette.

1926

The Spider Net. Goodwell, D: Hans Tirsler; LP: Eileen Sedgwick, Lightning (dog), Robert Walker, Tom London, Frank Lackteen. (A "paste-up" serial made up from several shorts.)

The House Without a Key. Pathé, [10 Chapters] D: Spencer G. Bennet; LP: Allene Ray, Walter Miller, E. H. Calvert, Betty Caldwell, Natalie Warfield, William N. Bailey, Frank Lackteen, Charles West.

1927

The Hawk of the Hills. Pathé, [10 Chapters] D: Spencer G. Bennet; SP: George Arthur Gray; Cam: Edward Snyder, Frank Redman; LP: Allene Ray, Walter Miller, Frank Lackteen, Paul Panzer, Harry Semels, Wally Oettel, Evangeline Russell, Jack Pratt, George Magrill.

Melting Millions. Pathé, [10 Chapters] D: Spencer G. Bennet; LP: Allene Ray, Walter Miller, E. H. Calvert, William Norton Bailey, Eugenia Gilbert, Frank Lackteen, Bob Burns, Ernie Adams.

1928

Mark of the Frog. Pathé, [10 Chapters] D: Arch B. Heath; S: Edgar Wallace; LP: Donald Reed, Margaret Morris, George Harcourt, Frank Lackteen, Tony Hughes.

The Tiger's Shadow. Pathé, [10 Chapters] D: Spencer G. Bennet; S/SP: George Gray; LP: Gladys McConnell, Hugh Allen, Frank Lackteen, Edward Cecil.

1929

The Fire Detective. Pathé, [10 Chapters] D: Spencer G. Bennet, Thomas L. Storey; S: Frank Leon Smith; SP: George Arthur Gray; LP: Gladys McConnell, Hugh Allen, Leo Maloney, John Cossar, Frank Lackteen.

The Black Book. Pathé, [10 Chapters] D: Spencer G. Bennet, Thomas L. Storey; S: Joseph Anthony Roach; LP: Allene Ray, Walter Miller, Frank Lackteen, Edith London, Willie Fung, Paul Panzer.

Queen of the Northwoods. Pathé, [10 Chapters] D: Spencer G. Bennet, Thomas L. Storey; SP: George Arthur Gray; LP: Walter Miller, Ethlyne Claire, Tom London, Frank Lackteen, Edward Cecil.

1932

Heroes of the West. Univ., [12 Chapters] D: Ray Taylor; LP: Noah Beery, Jr., Diane Duval [a.k.a. Jacqueline Wells/Julie Bishop), Onslow Stevens, William Desmond, Martha Mattox.

The Jungle Mystery. Univ., [12 Chapters] D: Ray Taylor; LP: Tom Tyler, Cecilia Parker, William Desmond, Philo McCullough, Noah Beery, Jr., Frank Lackteen.

1933

Clancy of the Mounted. Univ., [12 Chapters] D: Ray Taylor; LP: Tom Tyler, Jacqueline Wells, William Desmond, Rosalie Roy, Francis Ford, Frank Lackteen.

Tarzan the Fearless. Principal, [15 Chapters] D: Robert F. Hill; LP: Buster Crabbe, Jacqueline Wells, E. Alyn Warren, Edward Woods, Philo McCullough, Mischa Auer, Frank Lackteen.

1934

Young Eagles. First Div., [12 Chapters] D: Spencer Bennet, Vin Moore, Edward Laurier; LP: Bobbie Cox, Jim Vance, Carter Dixon, Philo McCullough.

Perils of Pauline. Univ., [12 Chapters] D: Ray Taylor; LP: Evalyn Knapp, Craig Reynolds, James Durkin, John Davidson, Sonny Ray.

1937

The Mysterious Pilot. Col., [15 Chapters] D: Spencer G. Bennet; LP: Frank Hawks, Dorothy Sebastian, Rex Lease, Guy Bates Post, Kenneth Harlan.

Radio Patrol. Univ., [12 Chapters] D: Ford Beebe, Cliff Smith; LP: Grant Withers, Catherine (Kay) Hughes, Mickey Rentschier, Adrian Morris, Max Hoffman, Jr.

1938

The Secret of Treasure Island. Col., [15 Chapters] D: Elmer Clifton; LP: Don Terry, Gwen Gaze, Grant Withers, Hobart Bosworth, William Farnum, Walter Miller, Yakima Canutt.

Red Barry. Univ., [13 Chapters] D: Ford Beebe, Alan James; LP: Buster Crabbe, Frances Robinson, Wade Boteler, Edna Sedgwick, Philip Ahn, Frank Lackteen.

1941

Don Winslow of the Navy. Univ., [12 Chapters] D: Ford Beebe, Ray Taylor; LP: Don Terry, Walter Sande, Wade Boteler, John Litel, Anne Nagel, Samuel S. Hinds.

Jungle Girl. Rep., [15 Chapters] D: William Witney, John English; LP: Frances Gifford, Tom Neal, Trevor Bardette, Gerald Mohr, Eddie Acuff, Frank Lackteen.

1946

The Scarlet Horseman. Univ., [13 Chapters] D: Ray Taylor, Lewis D. Collins; LP: Peter Cookson, Paul Guilfoyle, Victoria Horne, Virginia Christine, Janet Shaw.

Lost City of the Jungle. Univ., [13 Chapters] D: Ray Taylor, Lewis D. Collins; LP: Russell Hayden, Jane Adams, Lionel Atwill, Keye Luke, Helen Bennett.

1947

The Black Widow. Rep., [13 Chapters] D: Spencer G. Bennet, Fred C. Brannon; LP: Carol Forman, Bruce Edwards, Virginia Lindley, Anthony Warde, I. Stanford Jolley, Ernie Adams.

1956

Perils of the Wilderness. Col., [15 Chapters] D: Spencer G. Bennet; LP: Dennis Moore, Richard Emory, Eve Anderson [Evelyn Finley], Kenneth MacDonald, Rick Vallin, John Elliott, Terry Frost, Rex Lease, Pierce Lyden.

CAROLE LANDIS

A shapely blonde, Carole Landis began competing in beauty contests at age 12. At 15 she eloped with a writer, but they separated after only three weeks. She subsequently married and divorced three more times.

Carole was born Frances Lillian Mary Ridste, January 1, 1919, in Fairchild, Wisconsin. She was of half–Norwegian, half–Polish descent and possessed a sensational figure. Her physique prompted one man to describe her as "like a bureau with the top drawer pulled out."

After working as a milliner, waitress and usherette in her hometown, she went to San Francisco where she made her debut at 16 as a singer–hula dancer at a plush night spot. Wanting to be an actress, she quit her job and at 18 arrived in Hollywood, where she found a job in a chorus line that Busby Berkeley was training for Warner Brothers' *Varsity Show* ('37). Executives there cast her in a succession of extra roles, but Republic gave her a chance as the leading lady in *Daredevils of the Red Circle* ('39). In the same year she appeared with Ray Corrigan and John Wayne in *Three Texas Steers* ('39) and with Robert Livingston and Duncan Renaldo in *Cowboys from Texas*. Republic offered her nothing else, but D. W. Griffith saw potential in her and gave her the role opposite Victor Mature in *One Million B.C.* ('40). Clad in a skin that could hardly have warmed a rabbit, she held her own with Mature and prehistoric beasts. Audiences loved her and Twentieth Century-Fox hastened to sign her to a contract.

Moon Over Miami ('40) and *I Wake Up Screaming* ('41) gave her star billing, but her vehicles were seldom better than routine. She was good in *Orchestra Wives* ('42), *Manila Calling* ('42) and *Wintertime* ('43). Carole was scheduled to make *Blood and Sand* opposite Tyrone Power but refused to dye her hair red. She lost the part to Rita Hayworth.

Rita went on to star in *My Gal Sal* ('42), a role originally scheduled for Carole. However, Carole did appear in the film in a supporting role.

Better pictures might have built Carole into a major star but Twentieth Century-Fox did not promote her properly. In 1944 she scored a personal triumph in *Four Jills in a Jeep*. She herself had written the book that inspired the film. She followed with *Having Wonderful Crime* ('45), *It Shouldn't Happen to a Dog* ('46) and *Thieves Holiday* ('46). She demonstrated her gift for humor in *Out of the Blue* ('47) and seemed to have hit her stride as a wistful clown who could handle drama; often second-billed to another actress, but never second-rate; still at the peak of her looks and improving with each performance.

But glamour girls are not smart with men. With four failed marriages behind her, she entered into an illicit relationship with Rex Harrison ("Sexy Rexy") who was married to actress Lilli Palmer. When Harrison decided to break off the affair, Carole couldn't handle the rejection. She had expected Rex to divorce his wife and marry her. She was already despondent about her career and her debts. She cracked. An overdose of sleeping pills and she went to sleep forever. It was July 4, 1948.

Serial

1939

Daredevils of the Red Circle. Rep., 1939 [12 Chapters] D: William Witney, John English; SP: Barry Shipman, Franklyn Adreon, Rex Taylor, Ronald Davidson, Sol Shor; AP: Robert Beche; Cam: William Nobles; Mus: William Lava; LP: Charles Quigley, Herman Brix, David Sharpe, Carole Landis, Miles Mander, Charles Middleton, C. Montague Shaw, George Chesebro, Ben Taggart.

CULLEN LANDIS

James Cullen Landis was born in Nashville, Tennessee, on July 9, 1895. He was educated in the public schools of Nashville and later attended Duncan Preparatory, a private school where he received his tuition in exchange for his stellar ability as athlete, excelling in both football and baseball and leading both teams to numerous championships. He also had two years at a military academy.

While still in school he had a newspaper route, rising promptly at 3 A.M. every morning so that subscribers to *The Nashville American* would have no reasons to complain of their service. The pay was $12 a month. He soon rose to the dignity of a regular position in the circulation department and at age 17 had 12 boys working under him.

Cullen descended on Los Angeles in 1913. Unable to find a position with a newspaper, he finally secured a job driving a jitney bus for three or four months. Ultimately he secured work at Balboa Studio in Long Beach, beginning as a switchboard operator, then a truck driver, then assistant property man and finally assistant director. This job ate into his time, so he decided to take a fling at the assistant cameraman's job. It was more to his liking. When an actor on one of his pictures broke a leg, Cullen was pressed into service, and thus began his long career in films. He continued to get better parts. He completed 52 one-reel comedies at Al Christie Studio and Goldwyn gave him a contract as a juvenile leading man.

Landis' serial career began in 1917 at Paramount opposite Kathleen Clifford in *Who is Number 1?* Camille Arnot sought to ruin the famous inventor Graham Hale by destroying his most beloved possessions one by one, culminating with the loss of his son. Aimee Villon (Kathleen Clifford) loved young Tommy Hale and fought to save the Hale family from the mysterious "Number One," who seemed determined to ruin their happiness. It took until the final chapter to clear it all up, for Camille was, in fact, the estranged wife of Graham Hale, Tommy was his son by another woman, and Aimee was the daughter of Graham and Camille. Under a spell at times, Aimee had really been "Number One" all along and had been stationed with her father for the purpose of avenging her mother. Suffice it to say that Paramount shied away from serial films thereafter.

At the Christie Studio, Cullen was hired to play opposite Billy Rhodes in one-reel comedies. He made 52 of these before 1923. In 1919 he was featured as a young backwoods preacher in *Almost a Husband* for Goldwyn. That same year he portrayed the young gambler in John Ford's adaptation of Bret Harte's *The Outcast of Poker Flat* for Universal. Shortly afterwards Cullen got the part of the Curley Kid in *The Girl from Outside*, taken from the Rex Beach book *The Wag Lady*. When Goldwyn saw the completed film, he gave Cullen a five-year contract.

As a leading man in silents, Cullen appeared in nearly 100 films back in the days when Mary Pickford wore long, golden curls, Charles Chaplin was always dressed in his famous tramp gear and Douglas Fairbanks scaled walls and fought duels all for the love of a lady fair.

In 1927 Cullen starred in his second serial. It was Pathé's *On Guard*, filmed at Fort Benning, Georgia, based on R. F. Glassburn's spy-chasing stories and co-starring Muriel Kingston. Some of the first army tanks were used in the film. It dealt with international spies who desire certain valuable information enough to plant their own men in the U.S. Army.

Cullen's third serial, Pathé's *The Crimson Flash* ('27), co-starred Eugenia Gilbert. A stolen ruby was "The MacGuffin" and a shadowy underworld figure, "The Ghost," provided the mystery element.

In 1927, at the peak of his career, Landis was divorced by his first wife. They had two small daughters. Landis agreed to pay her $350 a month and to place a $20,000 piece of real estate in trust for the two children.

A year later, Landis appeared in the first all-talking movie, *The Lights of New York*, and made personal appearances around the country where the film was shown.

Landis' career did not extend far into the era of sound films. He would not accept less than leading roles, and his films after 1928 are few in number. Frank Mattison directed him in *Little Wild Girl* ('29). This adventure film of the wilderness focussed on the dog Cyclone and featured Lila Lee and Boris Karloff. Syndicate's *The Convicts Code* ('30) was the type of crime melodramas then becoming increasingly popular.

Landis left Hollywood and went to Detroit. General Motors, Ford and Chrysler were beginning to produce industrial films there and he became a film director, his favorite role. In Detroit he married Jane Grenier, daughter of the city's correspondent for *The Saturday Evening Post*.

During World War II Cullen volunteered his service, was taken in as a captain and rose to the rank of major. With the Army Signal Corps he made training and combat films in the South Pacific. After discharge, he directed television films and did some documentaries for the government. In the 1950s, working for the United States Information Agency, he and Jane travelled around the world as he directed films in England, Baghdad, Saigon, Cambodia, Turkey, Afghanistan, Kabul and Manila.

In January 1964, the Landises retired to their summer place at Mullett Lake near Cheboygan, Michigan. Cullen died in 1975 at age 77 in Bloomfield Hills, Michigan.

Serials

1917

Who is Number 1? Paramount, [15 Chapters] D: William Bertram or Frank H. Crane; S: Anna Katherine Green; LP: Kathleen Clifford, Cullen Landis, Gordon Sackville, Neil C. Hardon, Ruth Smith.

1927

On Guard. Pathé, [10 Chapters] D: Arch B. Heath; S: Robert F. Glassburn; LP: Cullen Landis, Muriel Kingston, Louise Du Pre, Walter P. Lewis.

The Crimson Flash. Pathé, [10 Chapters] D: Arch B. Heath; S: George Arthur Gray; LP: Cullen Landis, Eugenia Gilbert, Tom Holding, J. Barney Sherry, Walter P. Lewis.

ALLAN (ROCKY) LANE

Harry Leonard Albershart was born on September 22, 1909, in Mishawaka, Indiana, according to his Indiana birth certificate. Most sources give 1904 as the date.

About the time he finished grammar school, the family moved to Grand Rapids, Michigan, and it was here that he finished high school. Most accounts indicate that upon graduation he headed back to Indiana and enrolled at the University of Notre Dame and that while attending Notre Dame for three years he won letters in football, baseball and basketball.

In his biography of Lane, Ronnie Jones writes, "No proof of Lane's Notre Dame tenure can be found. In corresponding with

Mr. Edward Krause, Director of Athletics at Notre Dame, and in receiving replies from both Mr. Krause and the University's Sports Information Department, again there was a lack of information. Not only was there no record of Lane (Albershart) appearing as a Notre Dame athlete, but also nothing could be found that would confirm Lane's ever having enrolled at Notre Dame."

At some point Lane became interested in acting and joined National Players, a Cincinnati roadshow company. Most sources indicate that it was at this time that the name "Allan Lane" was created. On loan to another roadshow, whose lead player had become quite ill, Lane stepped in and starred in the production *Hit the Deck*. For nearly two years Lane alternated between acting in such productions and in operating a photography business (he had become interested in commercial photography about the time he started acting and had founded his own company). Among his customers were the Ford Motor Company, Lucky Strike cigarettes, Wrigley chewing gun, Camay soap, etc.

In 1929 Lane came to the attention of Winfred Sheehan, Fox Film Company executive producer. Lane was screen-tested and assigned a principal role in that year's *Not Quite Decent*. The film featured Louise Dresser and June Collyer. For his next 14 films, Lane hopped from studio to studio—First National, Fox, MGM, Warner Bros., Educational, Republic, Vitaphone and Mascot.

Lane was dissatisfied with the kind of roles he was given and in 1932 decided to return to New York and stage work. He also planned to re-establish his commercial photography business. Then instead he began what was to be a long and often uphill climb to screen fame. He made no pictures in 1934 or 1935 and only one in 1936, that being *Stowaway*. Reviews were complimentary to Lane. In 1937 he starred in *The Duke Comes Back*, a boxing yarn for Republic, and five films for 20th Century-Fox.

Lane signed with RKO in 1938–39, where he had better roles than at 20th Century-Fox. Still, they were not the action pic-

tures he longed for. The one exception was *The Law West of Tombstone* ('38) starring Harry Carey. Lane enjoyed being in a Western.

In 1940, Lane was signed to play Sgt. King in the Republic serial *King of the Royal Mounted* ('40). This was the kind of role for which he had waited ten years to play. He was right at home in the role of the mountie, fighting international spies in motorboats and airplanes, on horseback and with his fists. Lane had the physical stamina that the rough-and-tough serials required, and his handsome profile and excellent speaking voice served him well. The serial was a box office success country-wide — so much so that Lane again played Sgt. King in the sequel *King of the Mounties* ('42). It also was a popular serial.

Two more serials followed, *Daredevils of the West* ('43) and *The Tiger Woman* ('44). After his success in these four serials, Lane received his own Western series. The first entry was *Silver City Kid* ('44), followed by six others, the best of which was probably *Sheriff of Sundown* ('44).

Wild Bill Elliott, who had been playing Red Ryder, was booted up to "A" Westerns in 1944 and this left a gap in the Red Ryder series. Lane became the new Rider and starred in seven Ryders during 1946–47, culminating with *Marshal of Cripple Creek*.

Republic immediately gave Lane a new series and a new billing — Allan "Rocky" Lane. The first entry was *The Wild Frontier* ('47) with Jack Holt. Eddy Waller, who played the crusty old character Nugget Clark, was Lane's sidekick in these 32 "Rocky" films and kept the comedy to a tolerable level. Lane rode a stallion named Blackjack throughout the 38 film series.

The "Rocky" films were Lane's best. Every one was shot in about seven days, and production values were always good. The series ended with the release of *El Paso Stampede* ('53). Republic was left with one Western star, Rex Allen, and he was dropped the following year. Republic abandoned film production for TV fare.

After the termination of his movie se-

ries, Lane's career hit a downward trend. His attitude towards others in the movie business had left him few friends and he was cold-shouldered by the industry, eventually having to take a job as a car salesman in Los Angeles.

Lane was married twice, to Gladys Leslie and Sheila Ryan. Both marriages ended in divorce.

Lane made personal appearances with Blackjack for a couple of years. He had a few roles on *Gunsmoke* and he made a pilot for a

Allan (Rocky) Lane

Red Ryder TV series, but it failed to impress the sponsors and was dropped. *The Rocky Lane Comics Fanzine* began in 1949 and continued until 1959.

Allan (Rocky) Lane died on October 27, 1973, from a bone marrow disorder at the Motion Picture Country Hospital in Woodland Hills, California. His death went largely unreported by the press. Besides the minister and his mother, Lane's funeral was attended by two friends. His mother was his sole survivor.

Serials

1940

King of the Royal Mounted. Rep., [12 Chapters] D: William Witney, John English; SP: Franklyn Adreon, Norman S. Hall, Joseph Poland, Barney Sarecky, Sol Shor; AP: Hiram S. Brown, Jr.; Cam: William Nobles; Mus: Cy Feuer; LP: Allan Lane, Robert Strange, Robert Kellard, Lita Conway, Herbert Rawlinson.

1942

King of the Mounties. Rep., [12 Chapters] D: William Witney, John English; SP: Ronald Davidson, William Lively, Joseph O'Donnell, Joseph Poland; AP: W. J. O'Sullivan; Cam: Bud Thackery; Mus: Mort Glickman; LP: Allan Lane, Peggy Drake, Gilbert Emery, Russell Hicks, George Irving, Bradley Page.

1943

Daredevils of the West. Rep., [12 Chapters] D: John English; SP: Ronald Davidson, Basil Dickey, William Lively, Joseph O'Donnell, Joseph Poland; AP: W. J. O'Sullivan; Cam: Bud

Thackery; Mus: Mort Glickman; LP: Allan Lane, Kay Aldridge, Eddie Acuff, William Haade, Robert Frazer, Ted Adams.

1944

The Tiger Woman. Rep., [12 Chapters] D: Wallace Grissell; AP: W. J. O'Sullivan; SP: Royal Cole, Ronald Davidson, Basil Dickey, Jesse Duffy, Grant Nelson, Joseph Poland; Cam: Bud Thackery; Mus: Joseph Dubin; LP: Allan Lane, Linda Stirling, Duncan Renaldo, George J. Lewis, LeRoy Mason, Crane Whitley, Kenne Duncan, Stanley Price, Eddie Parker, Ken Terrell.

NORA LANE

Nora Lane was born in Chester, Illinois, and educated in the public schools of St. Louis. Her father was a hotel owner. In her childhood she desired to become an actress, and after finishing her education she joined a stock company at Davenport, Iowa. Later she did some modeling in St. Louis.

On a trip to Hollywood to visit a friend, but with no intention of seeking a film career, she was noticed by a casting director who was impressed by her beauty and unusual charm. He asked her to make a screen test. Reluctantly she agreed. The test was a success and she was induced to play a small role in a picture, "just for the fun of it." Her success was instantaneous and she decided to stick to pictures as a means of a livelihood.

Nora first worked at FBO with Fred Thomson and Tom Tyler before moving with Thomson to Paramount to play Zerelda Mimms, Jesse's girlfriend, in *Jesse James* ('27). She caught the eye of critics and won the hearts of thousands overnight. She possessed an irresistible, vibrant appeal for action fans. Paramount followed up by teaming Thomson and Lane in *The Pioneer Scout* ('28), in which Nora plays a settler's daughter loved by scout Thomson, and *Kit Carson* ('28), with Nora portraying Jaramillo, the beautiful Spanish girl of Taos, New Mexico, who married Kit Carson at the height of his romantic career. Any possibilities of further films with Thomson were shattered by his sudden demise.

Nora added to her laurels with fine performances opposite Jack Holt in *Sunset Pass* ('29), Ken Maynard in *The Lawless Legion* ('29) and George O'Brien in *Masked Emotions* ('29), her last silent film.

Her first talkie was *Sally* ('29), a musical. She played in *King of the Wild* ('30), an early sound serial, made a series of ten Universal shorts under the general title "The Leather Pushers" ('30–31).She appeared in numerous non–Westerns and played opposite Warner Baxter, Tim McCoy, William Boyd and Ken Maynard before drifting into supporting character roles that carried her career into the 1940s.

Serials

1930

King of the Wild. Mascot, [12 Chapters] D: Richard Thorpe, B. Reeves Eason; Mus: Lee Zahler; SP/S: Wyndham Gittens, Ford Beebe; P: Nat Levine; Cam: Bob Kline, Edward Kull; LP: Walter Miller, Nora Lane, Dorothy Christy, Tom Santschi, Boris Karloff.

1930–31

The Leather Pushers. Univ., [10 Episodes—a series rather than a serial] D: Albert Keller; LP: Kane Richmond, Sam Hardy, Sally Blane, Nora Lane, Joan Marsh.

1941

Dick Tracy vs. Crime, Inc. Rep., [15 Chapters] D: William Witney, John English; LP: Ralph Byrd, Jan Wiley, John Davidson, Ralph Morgan.

1943

The Masked Marvel. Rep., [12 Chapters] D: Spencer G. Bennet; LP: Tom Steele, William Forrest, Louise Currie, Johnny Arthur.

ROSEMARY LAPLANCHE

Rosemary LaPlanche, Miss America of 1941, was born in 1923. As Miss America she had little trouble in getting movie offers. Although she appeared in films throughout the 1940s, she made no big impression as an actress and was limited to low-budget films. That fact notwithstanding, Rosemary was in some entertaining films.

The first of her serials was *Jack Armstrong* ('47), adapted from the radio serial *Jack Armstrong, the All-American Boy.* Rosemary plays Betty, niece of Jim Fairfield, head of an aviation company concerned with the development of atomic-powered motors. Vic Hardy, an employee of Fairfield, makes the discovery that cosmic radiation is being used by human agencies. Hardy is subsequently kidnapped and taken to an island far out in the Pacific. Armstrong and friends follow to encounter J. Grood (Charles Middleton), the brains behind a scheme to develop a ray gun which, suspended in outer space, will dominate the Earth and destroy all opposition.

Rosemary's second serial was *Federal Agents vs. Underworld, Inc.* Kirk Alyn stars as a federal agent assigned to find Prof. Clayton, missing after discovering the famous Golden Hands of Kurigal, key to a great fortune. Nila, an international thief and one of the founders of "Underworld, Inc.," has stolen one of the hands and is murdering people ruthlessly in an attempt to track down the second Hand. Carol Forman is Nila; LaPlanche is Laura, friend of Worth.

Rosemary was married for almost three decades to radio emcee-TV producer Harry Koplan, until his death in '73. They had two children.

After retiring from the screen in 1949, Rosemary was a professional painter. She had regular one-woman showings of oils both in Los Angeles and Laguna, and sold over 500 paintings.

Some of her features are *Two Weeks to Live* ('43), *Gildersleeve on Broadway* ('43), *Prairie Chickens* ('43), *Manhattan Serenade* ('43), *Girl Rush* ('44), *Mademoiselle Fifi* ('44), *Zombies on Broadway* ('45), *Strangler of the Swamp* ('46) and *An Old-fashioned Girl* ('49).

Serials

1947

Jack Armstrong. Col., [15 Chapters] D: Wallace Fox; SP: Arthur Hoerl, Royal Cole, Leslie Swabacker; AP: Melville DeLay; Cam: Ira H. Morgan; Mus: Lee Zahler; LP: John Hart, Rosemary LaPlanche, Joe Brown, Jr., Claire James, Pierre Watkin.

1949

Federal Agents vs. Underworld, Inc. Rep., [12 Chapters] D: Fred C. Brannon; SP: Royal K. Cole, Basil Dickey, William Lively, Sol Shor; AP: Franklyn Adreon; Cam: John MacBurnie; Mus: Stanley Wilson; LP: Kirk Alyn, Rosemary LaPlanche, Roy Barcroft, Carol Forman, Bruce Edwards, James Dale.

GEORGE LARKIN

One could say that George Larkin was a physical fitness freak, perhaps on the order of Joe Bonomo, Richard Talmadge, Douglas Fairbanks and Yakima Canutt. He was his own stuntman, performing feats that would cause the aforementioned gentlemen to pause and reflect.

Larkin was born into a family of acrobats in New York City on November 11, 1887. He became a circus performer as a youth, carrying on after his parents were killed in a railroad accident. At 16 he began his theatrical career, appearing for two seasons in vaudeville playing comedy and musical sketches. He became an actor in the Temple Stock Company for a couple of years; after that, in the Proctor Stock Company for 18 months. His diverse background made him a natural for films. Ed Porter of the Edison Company cast him in the one-reelers *The Animated Snowball* and *The Bridge of Sighs* ('08).

Between 1910 and 1912, Larkin appeared in both outdoor and indoor films. Diving off high cliffs, crashing through railway crossing gates in front of speeding trains, falling off the masts of ships into shark-infested waters, hanging off the roofs of skyscrapers, making daring leaps to grasp swinging wires at dizzy heights, swimming through roaring rapids and performing other spectacular stunts was all in a day's work.

In 1913–14 he co-starred with Ruth Roland in 15 or more one-reelers for Kalem. In 1914 he made five films with Cleo Madison plus a serial, Universal's *The Trey O'-Hearts*.

The series *Grant, Police Reporter*, consisting of 29 one-reel episodes, was filmed in 1916–17 with Larkin and Ollie Kirkby. It was a popular Kalem series.

In 1918, Larkin played opposite serial queen Ruth Roland in *Hands Up*, a 15-chapter Pathé serial. Larkin plays a mystery figure who helps Roland keep her ranch, which is desired by her ruthless cousin. *The Tiger's Trail* ('19) gave a big boost to Larkin. The story revolves about Roland's attempts to hang onto her valuable mineral land desired by Hindu tiger worshippers and western cutthroats. Larkin is Johnny-on-the-spot when she needs him. (Evidently Roland liked working with Larkin.) It was an exceptionally popular cliffhanger.

Switching to Arrow for his next serial, Larkin starred in *The Lurking Peril* ('19). During a financial crunch, a young man sells the right to his brain after his death to a fiendish professor who seemingly just can't wait to begin dissecting it. Anne Luther played the heroine.

Speaking of unusual, *The Terror of the Range* ('19) was unusual in that it consisted of only seven chapters. A U.S. government agent clashes with a mysterious bandit wearing a wolf's head whenever he leads his marauders down a bloodthirsty trail of killing and looting. Betty Compson was in the thick of things.

In 1921, Larkin teamed with popular Eileen Sedgwick in Universal's 18-chapter serial *The Terror Trail*, a robust saga of the West. The same year he headlined six two-reel Westerns featuring Josephine Hill, who should be considered queen of the Western based on the number she made.

Larkin married Ollie Kirkby in 1919 and they frequently worked together during the 1920s. He starred in his last silent film, *Midnight Rose*, in 1928 and retired. He had no financial woes. Just for kicks he played bits in a few sound films, including two serials. He died March 27, 1946. His wife survived.

Serials

1914

The Trey O'Hearts. Univ., [15 Chapters] D: Wilfred Lucas, Henry MacRae; SP: Bess Meredyth; S: Louis Joseph Vance; LP: Cleo Madison, George Larkin, Edward Sloman, Tom Walsh, Roy Hanford.

1916–17

Grant, Police Reporter. Kalem, [29 Episodes] D: George Larkin, Robert Ellis, et al.; LP: George Larkin, Ollie Kirkby, Robert Ellis, William McKay, Cyril Courtney.

1918

Hands Up. Astra/Pathé, [15 Chapters] D: James W. Horne; SP: Jack Cunningham; S: Gilson Willets; LP: Ruth Roland, George Chesebro, George Larkin, Easter Walters, Monte Blue.

1919

The Terror of the Range. Pathé, [7 Chapters] D: Stuart Paton; S: W. A. S. Douglas; SP: Lucien Hubbard; LP: Betty Compson, George Larkin, H. P. Carpenter, Fred M. Malatesta, Ora Carew, True Boardman.

The Lurking Peril. Arrow, [15 Chapters] D: George Morgan, Burton King; SP: Lloyd Lonergan, George Larkin; S: Lloyd Lonergan; SP: George Larkin, Anne Luther, William Betchel, Ruth Dwyer, Peggy Shannon.

The Tiger's Trail. Astra/Pathé, [15 Chapters] D: Robert Ellis, Paul Hurst; SP: Arthur B. Reeve, Charles A. Logue; S: Gilson Willets; LP: Ruth Roland, George Larkin, Mark Strong, Harry G. Moody, Fred Kohler.

1921

The Terror Trail. Univ., [18 Chapters] D: Edward Kull; S/SP: Edward Kull, John W. Grey, George H. Plympton; LP: Eileen Sedgwick, George Larkin, Barney Furey, Theodore Brown, Albert J. Smith.

1941

White Eagle. Col., [15 Chapters] D: James W. Horne; LP: Buck Jones, Raymond Hatton, Dorothy Fay.

The Spider Returns. Col., [15 Chapters] D: James W. Horne; LP: Warren Hull, Mary Ainslee, Dave O'Brien, Joe Girard.

HARRY LAUTER

Harry Lauter was born June 19, 1914, in White Plains, New York, and moved to Colorado at a very young age. He lived there several years, later attending high school in San Diego. Summer vacations were spent in Cody, Wyoming, where he became a proficient horseman. His father was an artist, his paternal grandparents circus performers.

Lauter attended the Balboa College of Fine Arts. Just prior to World War II, he did four years of summer stock at Martha's Vineyard.

He was in the military service during hostilities. Upon his discharge he worked in several Broadway shows, and in 1946 was brought to Hollywood by Twentieth Century-Fox. His first film was *Hit Parade of 1946*, in which he had a bit. He drew $175 a week for a year but the studio did not use him in any other movie. Consequently he asked for his release and began working in Westerns, both bit (A) and small (B). He played good guys and bad guys with equal aplomb.

With the advent of television, Lauter worked a lot in network programs as well as in theatrical films. He was under contract to Gene Autry for four or five years, playing not only in Autry features and TV episodes but in Autry's Flying A productions *Anne Oakley, The Range Rider, Buffalo Bill, Jr., Death Valley Days* and others.

In 1953, Lauter became a regular on *Waterfront*, one of television's earliest seagoing adventure series. Preston Foster starred as captain of the tugboat *Cheryl Ann*. Lauter played the skipper's son. The series was syndicated and aired from 1954 to '56. This series was followed by *Tales of the Texas Rangers*, airing from September 1955 to May 1959, first on CBS and later ABC. Lauter played Clay Morgan and Willard Parker played Jace Pearson in the long-running (185 episodes) series.

During his career, when he wasn't pulling a gun from the hip or being knocked about by Gene Autry and other "white hats," Harry was painting, using oils to paint dramatic scenes of the Tetons, the High Sierras and the Rockies. He was married to an artist, Doris Gilbert, who had painted all her life. Together they painted, exhibited and sold their works. They had a studio in Ojai and traveled by trailer to art shows all over the west.

Lauter appeared in four Republic serials including their very last one (*King of the Carnival*). Serials produced in the 1950s didn't have much chance to be anything but bad. Only Columbia and Republic were still producing them, and production costs had been to the bone. An excessive amount of stock footage was incorporated into the serials. Lauter enjoyed making the serials and gave his characters his best shot.

Harry Lauter died of heart failure on October 30, 1990, at his home in Ojai.

Serials

1951

Flying Disc Man from Mars. Rep., [12 Chapters] D: Fred C. Brannon; SP: Ronald Davidson; AP: Franklyn Adreon; Cam: Walter Strenge; Mus: Stanley Wilson; LP: Walter Reed, Lois Collier, Gregory Gay, James Craven, Harry Lauter, Clayton Moore, Tom Steele, Dale Van Sickel.

1953

Canadian Mounties vs. Atomic Invaders. Rep., [12 Chapters] D: Franklyn Adreon; SP: Ronald Davidson; LP: Bill Henry, Susan Morrow, Arthur Space, Dale Van Sickel, Pierre Watkin, Harry Lauter, Edmund Cobb, Stanley Andrews.

1954

Trader Tom of the China Seas. Rep., [12 Chapters] D: Franklyn Adreon; SP: Ronald Davidson; Cam: Bud Thackery; Mus: R. Dale Butts; LP: Harry Lauter, Aline Towne, Lyle Talbot, Robert Shayne, Victor Sen Yung, Fred Graham, Tom Steele, Richard Reeves.

1955

King of the Carnival. Rep., [12 Chapters] D/AP: Franklyn Adreon; SP: Ronald Davidson; Cam: Bud Thackery; Mus: R. Dale Butts; LP: Harry Lauter, Fran Bennett, Keith Richards, Robert Shayne, Rick Vallin, Robert Clarke, Gregory Gay, Lee Roberts.

REX LEASE

Rex Lease was a handsome young man — 5'10", of medium build, green eyes and dark brown hair. He was born in Central City, West Virginia, on February 11, 1903.

His childhood was that of a normal boy, ultimately leading him to Ohio Wesleyan College and study for the ministry. He soon found that acting and writing appealed to him more than the ministry and he gave up his ministerial studies to join a stock company to get needed experience.

Around 1922 he trekked to Hollywood and soon found work as an extra. He liked action dramas and gravitated to them, easily winning recognition by the closely knit fraternity of thrillmakers congregated along Poverty Row and Gower Gulch. He had many small, uncredited roles before finally getting his break at stardom in FBO's *A Woman Who Sinned* ('24) playing an evangelist who aids his mother (who has lived in sin for several years) to gain forgiveness by God and acceptance by her family. Lease's *Chalk Marks* ('24), *Easy Money* ('25), *Before Midnight* ('25) and *The Last Edition* ('25) were aimed at lower billing on double-feature programs.

By 1926 he was getting star billing in some low-budget melodramas and featured billing in others. None were worth writing home about, yet afforded the viewer respite from the world of trouble for an hour or so.

Lease's first real introduction to action fans came as the star of Rayart's ten-chapter serial *Mystery Pilot* ('26). He was finally getting the type of role he had been seeking. The story revolves about a jewel case desired by several parties, one of which is the Mystery Pilot. The case is in the hands of Col. Mark Finlay (Jack McReedy), whose daughter June (Kathryn McGuire) makes the acquaintance of Bob Jones (Lease), a young sailor. After many adventures, the secret of the jewel case is disclosed and a treasure is divided. Rex proved a worthy contender for action ace honors, adapting easily to the fast pace and rough stuff inherent in cliffhanger capers. *The Outlaw Dog* ('27) also gave him a chance to be a true-blue hero type in an outdoor yarn. His dramatic performances improved and MGM signed him as the principal support for Tim McCoy and Joan Crawford in *The Law of the Range* ('28). Lease plays the part of Tim's brother, an outlaw called "The Solitaire Kid." Both he and McCoy are in love with Joan. MGM followed this fine feature with *Riders of the Dark* ('28) with McCoy, Lease and Dorothy Dawn heading

the cast. Both films played the MGM circuit of first-class theaters.

On Poverty Row, Lease continued to build a name for himself with starring roles in *Queen of the Chorus* ('28), *Phantom of the Turf* ('28), *Red Riders of Canada* ('28), *The Speed Classic* ('28) and other titles. His first talkie was Columbia's *The Younger Generation* ('29) and his performance received high praise by reviewers. He soon had a contract with Tiffany Pictures playing romantic leads in the programmers *Sunny Skies* ('30), *Hot Curves* ('30), *Wings of Adventure* ('30) and *Borrowed Wives* ('30). Two of his early Tiffany features stand out above the others. *Troopers Three* ('30) is a comedy-drama about three ham actors who mistakenly enlist in the Army. Lease falls in love with a sergeant's daughter (Dorothy Gulliver) and incurs the wrath of her suitor, Tom London. Lease ultimately proves his manhood and wins the girl. The story of *The Utah Kid* ('30) finds Dorothy Sebastian, a teacher, wandering into Robber's Roost, a gang's stronghold. Lease, a young outlaw, marries her to save her from his rough confederates. Dorothy is loved by Walter Miller, who eventually captures Lease. However, once the sheriff realizes that Dorothy is genuinely in love with Lease, he gallantly steps aside and gives the youth an opportunity to make good.

Two of his more interesting mellers in '31 were *The Monster Walks* and *Chinatown After Dark*, made for Ralph M. Like and released on the states-right market by Action Pictures. Although it failed to live up to its advertising as the most horrifying story ever brought to the screen, *The Monster Walks* was an entertaining escapist film well suited to double-feature showing. The story details the efforts of a rich man's brother to wipe out all possible heirs to the brother's fortune. To carry out his murderous plans he uses a vicious ape and also the half-witted son of his brother's housekeeper. Lease fights to protect his sweetheart, Vera Reynolds, daughter of the deceased rich scientist. For *Chinatown After Dark*, scenarist Betty Burbridge wove a mystery tale in which Rex was a Johnny-on-the-spot hero and Barbara Kent the object of his affections. Depression-era audiences in double-feature houses readily devoured low-budget crime thrillers and horror stories of this sort and their "come-on" catch lines such as "intrigue — mystery — suspense — among sinister shadows — the oriental mask stripped from the underworld warfare of terrorizing bandits — unbelievable revelations — matchless drama — a startling expose of the myriad mysteries of the orient — a dramatic revelation of what goes on in the inner chambers of the denizens of the underworld." No red-blooded boy could turn down such an enticement, even if the film was amateurishly directed, sloppily directed and hampered by bad photography.

Metropolitan starred Lease in *The Sign of the Wolf* ('31), one of the few independent serials produced in the sound era. Virginia Brown Faire, Joe Bonomo, Jack Mower, Edmund Cobb, Josephine Hill and "King," the dog, supported him in this mediocre-to-good film. Although Rex delivered dialogue convincingly and handled action well, the production values were not good and the modest budget provided for the serial was evident throughout.

Lease's first wife was Charlotte Merriam, his second wife Eleanor Hunt. The third marriage (1934) was to a girl named Elsa Roberts. She was engaged to the editor of one of Hollywood's leading trade papers when she suddenly eloped with Lease to Las Vegas. The gentleman didn't appreciate the turn of events and proceeded to blackball the actor. The professional blackballing plus Lease's drinking habit fairly well destroyed his career as a star. For years thereafter, he was able to work only for the independents.

In 1935 Lease got his own Western series for Louis Weiss, releasing through Superior. Production-wise the films were barely average in quality, but Lease went about his chores in a workmanlike manner and the films were rather charming after one became attuned to their defects. One is left with the feeling that Rex had a potential charisma never allowed to blossom.

During the '30s, Lease played second lead to the more popular cowboys in a number of palatable hoss operas. But on occasion he would take over the reins as chief hero, as in *Custer's Last Stand*, his best-remembered Western. Many critics have labeled it a cheap, plodding, generally pedestrian affair, but it did not meet with such criticism by audiences in 1936. Its cast was a strong one and it had that indefinable attraction associated with indie serials. Stage and Screen, the producing company, also featured Lease in the Jack Mulhall serial *The Clutching Hand* that same year. In '37 he starred in Reliable's *The Silver Trail*, Ace's *10 Laps to Go* and Sunset's *Heroes of the Alamo*. Columbia used him as second lead to Frank Hawks in the serial *The Mysterious Pilot* ('37). In '38 he was one of the principals in the carelessly slapped-together quickie *Fury Below*, but it was about all over for Lease as a star. For the next 30 years he played supporting roles in sagebrush and serial opuses, accumulating a second coterie of fans who had not known him as a star in the earlier days. With the demise of the "B" programmers, he moved into television and high-caliber features as a minor player.

Lease seemed to have the qualities necessary for becoming a first-magnitude Western star. But somehow he failed to make the grade — failed to create that magic spark that would excite the Saturday matinee crowds and set him apart from the masses. He was never able to break out of the independent market, although he was a darn good actor.

Throughout his career he continued to write and produced some screenplays and short stories. With actor Kenneth Harlan he wrote and published a cookbook called *What Actors Eat When They Eat*.

Lease married for the fourth time in 1938 and this union, with Isabelle Riehle, lasted until 1952. They had two sons; one was killed in 1965. The other son, Gary, became a doctor of Theology and when last heard from was teaching at the University of California at Santa Cruz. Rex's fifth and last marriage was in the mid–50s to Helen Ince, widow of producer Ralph Ince. It, too, ended in divorce.

Lease's close friends indicated that the

thing which kept him from gaining real stardom was his drinking problem. Producers were afraid to put their trust in him because of it. There was a time when Herbert Yates of Republic, a personal friend of Rex, was about the only studio head who would hire him. Lease was never able to lick the problem and in his final years he became an alcoholic, barely able to get by on the income from his bit roles. On January 3, 1966, he was found dead in his apartment. Doctors listed the cause as coronary artery arteriosclerosis and acute alcoholism.

A happier ending—both career-wise and personal—should have befallen this congenial cowboy who liked people and worked hard at his craft. Although he had personal problems, he was always "Mr. Nice Guy" to associates.

Serials

1926

Mystery Pilot. Rayart, [10 Chapters] D: Harry Moody; LP: Rex Lease, Kathryn McGuire, Jack McReedy, Max Asher, Barney Furey.

1931

The Sign of the Wolf. Met., [10 Chapters] D: Forrest Sheldon, Harry S. Webb; S/SP: Betty Burbridge, Karl Krusada; P: Harry S. Webb; Cam: William Nobles, Herbert Kilpatrick; LP: Rex Lease, Virginia Brown Faire, Joe Bonomo, Jack Mower, Josephine Hill, Al Ferguson.

1936

Custer's Last Stand. S&S, [15 Chapters] D: Elmer Clifton; P: George M. Merrick; SP: George A. Durlam, Eddy Graneman, William Lively; Spv.: Louis Weiss; Cam: Bert Longenecker; Mus: Hal Chasnoff; LP: Rex Lease, Jack Mulhall, William Farnum, Reed Howes, Lona Andre, Dorothy Gulliver, Bobby Nelson, William Desmond, Helen Gibson, Nancy Caswell.

The Clutching Hand. S&S, [15 Chapters] D: Albert Herman; Spv.: Louis Weiss; SP: Louis D'Usseau, Dallas Fitzherald; Adapt: George M.

Merrick, Eddy Graneman; Cam: James Diamond; Mus: Lee Zahler; LP: Jack Mulhall, Ruth Mix, Marion Shilling, Rex Lease, William Farnum.

1937

S O S Coast Guard. Rep., [12 Chapters] D: William Witney, Alan James; LP: Ralph Byrd, Bela Lugosi, Maxine Doyle, Richard Alexander, George Chesebro.

The Mysterious Pilot. Col., [15 Chapters] D: Spencer Bennet; S: William Byron Mowery; P: Jack Fier, Louis Weiss; Cam: Edward Linden, Herman Schoop; Mus; Abe Meyer; LP: Frank Hawks, Dorothy sebastian, Rex Lease, Guy Bates Post, Yakima Canutt.

1939

The Lone Ranger Rides Again. Rep., [15 Chapters] D: William Witney, John English; LP: Robert Livingston, Chief Thundercloud, Jinx Falken, Ralph Dunn, Duncan Renaldo, J. Farrell MacDonald, Rex Lease, Glenn Strange.

1943

Daredevils of the West. Rep., [12 Chapters] D: John English; LP: Allan Lane, Kay Aldridge, Eddie Acuff, William Haade, Robert Frazer, Ted Adams.

Don Winslow of the Coast Guard. Univ., [13 Chapters] D: Ford Beebe, Ray Taylor; LP: Don Terry, Walter Sande, Elyse Knox, Nestor Paiva.

1944

The Tiger Woman. Rep., [12 Chapters] D: Spencer Bennet, Wallace Grissell; LP: Linda Stirling, Allan Lane, Duncan Renaldo, George J. Lewis, LeRoy Mason.

Raiders of Ghost City. Univ., [13 Chapters] D: Ray Taylor, Lewis Collins; LP: Dennis Moore, Wanda McKay, Lionel Atwill, Joe Sawyer.

1945

Federal Operator 99. Rep., [12 Chapters] D: Spencer Bennet, Yakima Canutt, Wallace Grissell; LP: Marten Lamont, Helen Talbot, George J. Lewis, Lorna Gray [Adrian Booth], Hal Taliaferro, Elaine Lange.

1946

The Scarlet Horseman. Univ., [13 Chapters] D: Ray Taylor, Lewis D. Collins; LP: Peter Cookson, Paul Guilfoyle, Virginia Christine, Janet Shaw, Rex Lease.

The Phantom Rider. Rep., [12 Chapters] D: Spencer Bennet, Fred Brannon; LP: Robert Kent, Peggy Stewart, LeRoy Mason, George J. Lewis, Hal Taliaferro, Kenne Duncan, Chief Thundercloud, Rex Lease.

The Crimson Ghost. Rep., [12 Chapters] D: William Witney, John English; LP: Charles Quigley, Linda Stirling, Clayton Moore, I. Stanford Jolley.

King of the Forest Rangers. Rep., [12 Chapters] D: Spencer Bennet, Fred Brannon; LP: Larry Thompson, Helen Talbot, Stuart Hamblen, Anthony Warde, Rex Lease.

1956

Perils of the Wilderness. Col., [15 Chapters] D: Spencer G. Bennet; LP: Dennis Moore, Richard Emory, Eve Anderson [Evelyn Finley], Kenneth MacDonald.

ROBERT Z. LEONARD

Robert Z. Leonard had only one contact with serials. He made his debut as a director with the serial *The Master Key* ('14), and in which he also co-starred with Ella Hall. Hall plays the daughter of Gallon, a prospector who shoots his pard (Harry Carter) so that the gold he has stumbled onto can be his alone. Gallon makes his way to San Francisco and boards a ship, hoping to escape the murder charge which he believes will soon catch up with him. The ship sinks off the Oregon coast, but Gallon makes his way to shore with the key to a chest containing directions to the location of the rich lode of ore.

Many years pass and Gallon is next seen as the semi-prosperous owner of a mediocre mine which he had named "The Master Key." Robert Z. Leonard is brought in to revitalize the mine when the presumed-dead prospector suddenly appears and makes an open bid to obtain the mine from Hall.

Leonard directed scores of silent and sound Hollywood films over a period spanning four decades, working for Universal, Paramount and other studios but especially for MGM. It was as an MGM director that he made his best-known films from the mid-20s through the mid–50s. His specialty was the high-gloss glamour films, and his pictures ranged from soggy melodramas and saccharine romances to lavish musicals.

Films that he directed and produced (or co-produced) include *The Bachelor Father* ('31), *Lovers Courageous* ('32), *Peg o' My Heart* ('33), *The Great Ziegfeld* ('36), *The Firefly* ('37), *Broadway Serenade* ('39), *Stand By for Action* ('42), *The Man from Down Under* ('43), *Week-end at the Waldorf* ('45), *In the Good Old Summertime* ('49) and *The Great Diamond Robbery* ('53).

Leonard was born October 7, 1889 in Chicago. A stage actor from age 14, he acted and sang with the California Light Opera Company before entering films with the Selig Polyscope Company in 1907. He starred in such early silents as *Code of Honor* ('07), *The Courtship of Miles Standish* ('10) and *Robinson Crusoe* ('13).

His first wife was actress Mae Murray; his second, actress Gertrude Olmstead. He died at age 78 of an aneurysm in Beverly Hills.

Serial

1914

The Master Key. Univ., [15 Chapters] D: Robert Z. Leonard; SP: Calder Johnson; S: John Fleming Johnson; Spv.: Otis Turner; LP: Robert Z. Leonard, Ella Hall, Harry Carter, Jean Hathaway, Jack Holt, Alfred Hickman.

GEORGE J. LEWIS

George J. Lewis was born in Guadalajara, Mexico, on December 10, 1904. He stood six feet, had brown hair and eyes, and weighed 165 lbs. The elder Lewis served in the U.S. Army as a commissioned officer. Therefore, the family did not stay in one place long. George attended Coronado High school and participated in all outdoor sports. He also acted in amateur theatrics.

George was discovered by a Universal talent scout and signed to star with Dorothy Gulliver in a series of two-reelers with the overall title "The Collegians" (1924–26). It is believed that Lewis and Gulliver played in all 48 shorts. *Honeymoon Flats* ('29) and *College Love* ('29), features reteaming Lewis and Gulliver, more or less picked up where the shorts ended.

In 1931, George starred in the Spanish-language film *Horizontes Nuevos*, which was the same story as *The Big Trail* ('30) starring John Wayne. Another Spanish-language Lewis-starring film was *El Ultimo De Los Vargas* ('30).

George made his first serial, *The Wolf Dog* ('33), for Mascot, sharing top honors with Rin-Tin-Tin, Jr., and Frankie Darro. He also had a minor part in the serial *The Whispering Shadow* ('33) and a major supporting role in *The Fighting Marines* ('35).

For the next 30 years, George stayed busy. Just a few of his films are *Storm Over the Andes* ('35), *Captain Calamity* ('36), *Back Door to Heaven* ('39), *Outside the Three-Mile Limit* ('40), *The Falcon in Mexico* ('44), *South of the Rio Grande* ('45), *Beauty and the Bandit* ('46), *Docks of New Orleans* ('48), *Silver Trails* ('49), *Fast on the Draw* ('50), *Viva Zapata* ('52), *Desert Legion* ('53), *Saskatchewan* ('54), *Hell on Frisco Bay* ('55) and *The Big Land* ('57).

George played in many television series, among them *The Lone Ranger, Rin-Tin-Tin, Buffalo Bill, Jr., The Range Rider, The Cisco Kid* and *Annie Oakley*.

As he grew older, he essayed roles requiring that he be on the side of justice. One of his best TV roles, a continuing one, was playing Don Alizandro de la Vega, the father of Zorro, on Walt Disney's ABC-TV series *Zorro* 1957–59.

Lewis died on December 8, 1995, in Los Angeles.

Serials

1933

The Whispering Shadow. Mascot, [12 Chapters] D: Albert Herman, Colbert Clark; S/SP: Barney Sarecky, George Morgan, Norman S. Hall, Colbert Clark, Wyndham Gittens; Cam: Ernest Miller, Edgar Lyons; Mus: Abe Meyer; P: Nat Levine; LP: Bela Lugosi, Henry B. Walthall, Viva Tattersall, Roy D'Arcy, Robert Warwick.

The Wolf Dog. Mascot, [12 Chapters] D: Colbert Clark, Harry Frazer; SP: Al Martin, Colbert Clark, Wyndham Gittens; S: Barney Sarecky, Sherman Lowe; P: Nat Levine; LP:

Rin-Tin-Tin, Jr., Frankie Darro, George J. Lewis, Boots Mallory, Henry B. Walthall, Hale Hamilton, Fred Kohler.

The Fighting Marines. Mascot, [12 Chapters] D: B. Reeves Eason, Joseph Kane; SP: Barney Sarecky, Sherman Lowe; Spv.: Barney Sarecky; S: Ray Trampe, Wallace MacDonald, Maurice Geraghty; P: Nat Levine; Mus: Arthur Kay; LP: Grant Withers, Adrian Morris, Ann Rutherford, Robert Warwick, George J. Lewis, Pat O'Malley, Robert Frazer, Victor Potel.

1942

Perils of Nyoka. Rep., [15 Chapters] D: William Witney; SP: Ronald Davidson, Norman S. Hall, William Lively, Joseph Poland, Joseph O'Donnell; Cam: Reggie Lanning; Mus: Mort Glickman; LP: Kay Aldridge, Clayton Moore, William Benedict, Lorna Gray [Adrian Booth], Charles Middleton.

Spy Smasher. Rep., [12 Chapters] D: William Witney; SP: Ronald Davidson, Norman S. Hall, Joseph Poland, William Lively, Joseph O'Donnell; Cam: Reggie Lanning; Mus: Mort Glickman; LP: Kane Richmond, Marguerite Chapman, Sam Flint, Tristram Coffin, Hans Schumm.

Gang Busters. Univ., [13 Chapters] D: Ray Taylor, Noel Smith; SP: Morgan B. Cox, Al Martin, Vin Martin, George H. Plympton; LP: Kent Taylor, Irene Harvey, Ralph Morgan, Robert Armstrong.

1943

G-Men vs. The Black Dragon. Rep., [15 Chapters] D: William Witney; SP: Ronald Davidson, William Lively, Joseph O'Donnell, Joseph Poland; Cam: Bud Thackery; Mus: Mort Glickman; LP: Rod Cameron, Constance Worth, Roland Got, Nino Pipitone, George J. Lewis, Maxine Doyle, Hooper Atchley, Donald Kirke.

Daredevils of the West. Rep., [12 Chapters] D: John English; SP: Ronald Davidson, Bail Dickey, William Lively, Joseph O'Donnell, Joseph Poland; Cam: Bud Thackery; Mus: Mort Glickman; LP: allan Lane, Kay Aldridge, Eddie Acuff, William Haade, Robert Frazer, Ted Adams, George J. Lewis, Jack Rockwell, Stanley Andrews.

The Masked Marvel. Rep., [12 Chapters] D:

Spencer Bennet; SP: Royal Cole, Ronald Davidson, Basil Dickey, Grant Nelson, Jean Duffy, George J. Plympton, Reggie Lanning; LP: William Forrest, Louise Currie, Johnny Arthur, David Bacon, Tom Steele, Rod Bacon, Richard Clarke, Kenneth Harlan, Nora Lane, George J. Lewis.

Secret Service in Darkest Africa. Rep., [15 Chapters] D: Spencer Bennet; SP: Royal Cole, Basil Dickey, Jesse Duffy, Ronald Davidson, Joseph Poland, Joseph O'Donnell; Cam: William Bradford; Mus: Mort Glickman; LP: Rod Cameron, Joan Marsh, Duncan Renaldo, Lionel Royce, Kurt Kreuger, Reed Howes, George J. Lewis.

Batman. Col., [15 Chapters] D: Lambert Hillyer; SP: Victor McLeod, Leslie Swabacker, Harry Fraser; P: Rudolph C. Flothow; Mus: Lee Zahler; LP: Lewis Wilson, Douglas Croft, J. Carrol Naish, Shirley Patterson, William C. Austin, Charles Middleton, Robert Fiske, Karl Hackett.

1944

Haunted Harbor. Rep., [15 Chapters] D: Spencer Bennet, Wallace Grissell; AP: Ronald Davidson; SP: Royal Cole, Basil Dickey, Jesse Duffy, Grant Nelson; LP: Kane Richmond, Kay Aldridge, Roy Barcroft, Clancy Cooper, Marshall Reed.

The Tiger Woman. Rep., [12 Chapters] D: Spencer Bennet, Wallace Grissell; SP: Royal Cole, Ronald Davidson, Basil Dickey, Jesse Duffy, Grant Nelson, Joseph Poland; Cam: Bud Thackery; Mus: Joseph Dubin; LP: Linda Stirling, Allan Lane, Duncan Renaldo, George J. Lewis, LeRoy Mason.

The Desert Hawk. Col., [15 Chapters] D: B. Reeves Eason; SP: Sherman Lowe, Leslie Swabacher, Jack Stanley, Leighton Brill; P: Rudolph C. Flothow; Cam: James S. Brown, Jr.; Mus: Lee Zahler; LP: Gilbert Roland, Mona Maris, Kenneth MacDonald, Frank Lackteen, Jack Ingram, Rick Vallin.

Zorro's Black Whip. Rep., [12 Chapters] D: Spencer Bennet, Wallace Grissell; SP: Basil Dickey, Jesse Duffy, Grant Nelson, Joseph Poland; AP: Ronald Davidson; Cam: Bud Thackery; Mus: Richard Cherwin; AP: Ronald Davidson; 2nd Unit D: Yakima Canutt; LP:

Helen Deverell, George J. Lewis (center), and Tom Tyler in *The Blocked Trail* (Republic, 1943).

Linda Stirling, George J. Lewis, Lucien Littlefield, Francis McDonald, Hal Taliaferro.

Black Arrow. Col., [15 Chapters] D: Lew Landers; SP: Sherman Lowe, Jack Stanley, Leighton Brill, Royal K. Cole; P: Rudolph C. Flothow; Cam: Richard Fryer; Mus: Lee Zahler; LP: Robert Scott, Adele Jergens, Kenneth MacDonald, Charles Middleton, Martin Garralaga, Charles King, George J. Lewis, Robert Williams, Elmo Lincoln.

Captain America. Rep., [15 Chapters] D: John English, Elmer Clifton; SP: Ronald Davidson, Royal Cole, Basil Dickey, Jesse Duffy, Harry Fraser, Grant Nelson, Joseph Poland; AP: W. J. O'Sullivan; Cam: John MacBurnie; Mus: Mort Glickman; LP: Dick Purcell, Orna Gray [Adrian Booth], Lionel Atwill, Charles Trowbridge, George J. Lewis.

1945

Federal Operator 99. Rep., [12 Chapters] D: Spencer Bennet, Yakima Canutt, Wallace Gris-

sell; SP: Albert DeMond, Basil Dickey, Jesse Duffy, Joseph Poland; AP: Ronald Davidson; Cam: Bud Thackery; Mus: Richard Cherwin; LP: Marten Lamont, Helen Talbot, George J. lewis, Lorna Gray [Adrian Booth], Hal Taliaferro.

1946

The Phantom Rider. Rep., [12 Chapters] D: Spencer Bennet, Fred Brannon; SP: Albert DeMond Basil Dickey, Jesse Duffy, Lynn Perkins, Barney Sarecky; Cam: Bud Thackery; AP: Ronald Davidson; Mus: Richard Cherwin; LP: Robert Kent, Peggy Stewart, LeRoy Mason, George J. Lewis, Kenne Duncan.

1948

Adventures of Frank and Jesse James. Rep., [13 Chapters] D: Fred Brannon, Yakima Canutt; SP: Franklyn Adreon, Basil Dickey, Sol Shor; AP: Franklyn Adreon; Cam: John MacBurnie;

Mus: Morton Scott; LP: Clayton Moore, Steve Darrell, Noel Neill, Stanley Andrews, George J. Lewis.

1949

Ghost of Zorro. Rep., [12 Chapters] D: Fred C. Brannon; SP: Royal Cole, William Lively, Sol Shor; AP: Franklyn Adreon; Cam: John MacBurnie; Mus: Stanley Wilson; LP: Clayton Moore, Pamela Blake, Roy Barcroft, George J. Lewis, I. Stanford Jolley, Tom Steele, John Crawford, Steve Clark.

1950

Radar Patrol vs. Spy King. Rep., [12 Chapters] D: Fred C. Brannon; SP: Royal Cole, William Lively, Sol Shor; AP: Franklyn Adreon; Cam: Ellis W. Carter; Mus: Stanley Wilson; LP: Kirk Alyn, Jean Dean, Anthony Warde, George J. Lewis, Eve Whitney, John Merton, Harold Goodwin.

Cody of the Pony Express. Col., [15 Chapters] D: Spencer G. Bennet; SP: David Mathews, Lewis Clay, Charles Condon; S: George H. Plympton, Joseph Poland; Cam: Ira H. Morgan; Mus: Mischa Bakaleinikoff; LP: Jock Mahoney, Dickie Moore, Peggy Stewart, William Fawcett, Tom London, Rick Vallin.

SHELDON LEWIS

Sheldon Lewis has not fared well when the films' master criminals are talked about or written about, even though he sent chills surging through the bodies of those watching *Exploits of Elaine* ('14), *The Iron Claw* ('16), *Dr. Jekyll and Mr. Hyde* ('21), *Orphans of the Storm* ('22) and other serials and features of the silent screen.

Lewis made the transition to talkies without difficulty and continued to be villainously active. He was last seen in *The Cattle Thief* ('36) starring Ken Maynard, with Geneva Mitchell as the object of his affections.

Lewis died in San Gabriel, California, at age 89 in 1958.

Serials

1914

Exploits of Elaine. Pathé, [14 Chapters] D: Louis Gasnier, George B. Seitz; SP: C. W. God-dard, George B. Seitz; P: Theodore and Leopold V. Wharton; S: Arthur B. Reeve, Bertram Millhauser, Charles L. Goddard; Cam: Joseph Dubray; LP: Pearl White, Arnold Daly, Creighton Hale, Sheldon Lewis.

1916

The Iron Claw. Pathé, [20 Chapters] D: Edward Jose, George B. Seitz; SP: George B. Seitz; S: Arthur Stringer; P: Leopold and Theodore Wharton; LP: Pearl White, Creighton Hale, Sheldon Lewis, Harry Fraser, J. E. Dunn.

1917

The Hidden Hand. Pathé, [15 Chapters] D: James Vincent; SP: Arthur B. Reeve, Charles W. Goddard; LP: Doris Kenyon, Sheldon Lewis, Mahlon Hamilton, Arline Pretty.

1918

Wolves of Kultur. Pathé, [15 Chapters] D/SP: Joseph A. Golden; LP: Leah Baird, Charles Hutchison, Sheldon Lewis, Betty Howe, Mary Hull.

1926

Vanishing Millions. Sierra, [15 Chapters] D: Alvin J. Neitz; LP: William Fairbanks, Vivian Rich, Alec B. Francis, Sheldon Lewis, Bull Montana.

Lightning Hutch. Arrow, [10 Chapters] D: Charles Hutchison; SP: John Francis Netteford; LP: Charles Hutchison, Edith Thornton, Virginia Pearson, Eddie Phillips, Sheldon Lewis.

The Range Fighter. Davis, [10 Chapters] D: Clifford S. Elfelt, Paul Hurst, Forrest Sheldon; P: Clifford S. Elfelt; LP: Ken Maynard, Dorothy Devore, George Nichols, J.P. McGowan.

1928

The Chinatown Mystery. Syn., [10 Chapters] D: J. P. McGowan; LP: Joe Bonomo, Ruth Hiatt, Paul Malvern, Francis Ford, Sheldon Lewis.

1929

Tarzan the Tiger. Univ., [15 Chapters] D: Henry MacRae; LP: Frank Merrill, Natalie Kingston, Lillian Worth, Al Ferguson, Sheldon Lewis.

1930

Terry of the Times. Univ., [10 Chapters] D: Henry MacRae; LP: Reed Howes, Lotus Thompson, Sheldon Lewis, John Oscar, William Hayes, Mary Grant, Kingsley Benedict.

E. K. LINCOLN

Elmo K. Lincoln, not to be confused with Elmo (Tarzan) Lincoln, starred in the serial *Jimmy Dale Alias the Grey Seal*, filmed in 16 chapters and released in March 1917 after its release had been held up several months due to legal entanglements. Socially prominent Jimmy Dale (Lincoln) uses three aliases to fight crime: "The Grey Seal" (a safecracker), "Larry the Bat" (underworld figure) and Smarlinghue (a second-rate artist). Aided by a woman of mystery, Dale commits crimes to correct wrongs.

Lincoln's career dates from 1914. That year he made *The Littlest Rebel*, a historical drama, and *A Million Paid* with Anita Stewart. He had no credits in 1915; in 1916 he starred in *The Almighty Dollar* with June Elvidge, a domestic drama; *The Fighting Chance* with Violet Horner, the story of a man's struggle to overcome alcoholism; and *The World Against Him*, in which he is a cowboy in love with June Elvidge. In 1917, Lincoln made *For the Freedom of the World*, a World War I drama with Barbara Castleton. Another war drama was *Lafayette, We Come* ('18) with Dolores Cassinelli. In *The Beloved Traitor* ('18), E. K. wins fame as an artist, marries the wrong woman (Hedda Hopper) and is saved by his true love, Mae Marsh. Violet Horner gets his attention in *The Girl from Alaska* ('18).

Fighting Through ('19) sees Lincoln fighting Mexican kidnappers to free Millicent Fisher; *The Unknown Love* ('19) is a war drama with Dolores Cassinelli; *Virtuous Men* ('19) is a social drama (with Grace Darling as Lincoln's true love and Clara Joel as his seductive former girlfriend), in which saboteurs try to kill him. In Zane Grey's *Desert Gold* ('19), Lincoln is a cowboy and Eileen Percy and Margery Wilson are featured.

The Inner Voice ('20) with Agnes Ayres is a gold field drama; *Devotion* ('21) is a society melodrama with Hazel Dawn. In *The Woman God Changed* ('21), Lincoln is a detective taking Seena Owen back from Tahiti to the States by ship to face murder charges. A violent storm sinks the ship and they are cast ashore on a deserted island (all other passengers perished). During two years on

In *Jimmy Dale vs. the Grey Seal* (Mutual, 1917).

the island, they fall in love. Things end satisfactorily. *The Light in the Dark* ('22), a romantic drama, has Hope Hampton and Lon Chaney in support. *The Woman in Chains* ('23) is an underworld story in which a faithless wife deserts her husband and child to become a cabaret dancer. Martha Mansfield and Mrs. Rudolph Valentino are featured. Lincoln also co-starred with Mansfield in the melodrama *The Little Red Schoolhouse* ('23), dealing with bootleggers operating in the basement of the school where Mansfield teaches. Lincoln is a revenue agent.

Lincoln made *The Right of the Strongest*, a rural melodrama with Helen Ferguson, in 1924. Tom London has a small role. Lincoln's last film *My Neighbor's Wife* ('25), a comedy

with Helen Ferguson, was based on a James Oliver Curwood story. Also in the cast where Tom Santschi, Herbert Rawlinson, William Russell and Mildred Harris. This was Lincoln's last film.

Serial

1917

Jimmy Dale Alias the Grey Seal. Mutual, [16 Chapters] D: Harry Webster; SP: Mildred Considine; S: Frank L. Packard; LP: Elmo K. Lincoln, Edna Hunter, Doris Mitchell, Paul Panzer, Louis Haine, George Pauncefort, Austin Webb, Jules Ferrer, William H. Turner.

Serial Film Stars

2

Serial Film Stars

A Biographical Dictionary, 1912–1956

BUCK RAINEY

Volume 2

*(Elmo Lincoln–Clara Kimball Young;
Bibliography; Index)*

McFarland & Company, Inc., Publishers
Jefferson, North Carolina, and London

Volume

LIBRARY OF CONGRESS CATALOGUING-IN-PUBLICATION DATA

Rainey, Buck.
Serial film stars : a biographical dictionary, 1912–1956 / Buck Rainey.
p.   cm.
Includes bibliographical references and index.

2 volume set—
ISBN 978-0-7864-7529-2
softcover : acid free paper ∞

1. Motion picture actors and actresses—United States—Biography—Dictionaries.
2. Motion picture serials—United States.   I. Title.
PN1998.2.R35   2013   791.4302'8'092273—dc22   2004022964

BRITISH LIBRARY CATALOGUING DATA ARE AVAILABLE

On the cover: Charles Middleton as Ming the Merciless in the *Flash Gordon* serials;
(upper inset) Dick Purcell slugs Ken Terrell (*Captain America*, Republic 1944); (lower
inset) Sammy Baugh cuffs Jack Ingram (*King of the Texas Rangers*, Republic 1941)

Manufactured in the United States of America

McFarland & Company, Inc., Publishers
Box 611, Jefferson, North Carolina 28640
www.mcfarlandpub.com

Contents

• Volume 1 •

• Volume 2 •

Contents

ELMO LINCOLN

Otto Elmo Linkenhelt was born in Rochester, Fulton County, Indiana, on February 6, 1889. In his late teens he left home as a brakeman on a train to try and make a living for himself. He wanted to be a railroad engineer and stuck with railroading for several years.

One day after several years' hard work as a railroad employee, he arrived in California, where he left his job and tried working as a dock hand, sailor and boxer. D. W. Griffith, impressed by Lincoln's splendid physique, invited him to try out for the movies. With his name changed to Elmo Lincoln (a suggestion from Griffith), he began his movie career in bit parts for Biograph, where he remained from 1913 to 1916. He was in *The Battle at Ederbush Gulch, Judith of Bethula* and other Griffith epics. He claimed to have played at least a dozen parts in *Birth of a Nation*, among them White Arm Jim and a Negro "mammy."

In The Babylonian episode of *Intolerance* ('16) he was the mighty man of valor who defended Belshazzar against the troops of Cyrus with tremendous strokes of his sword.

A muscular athlete with the largest chest (52 inches expanded) in Hollywood, Lincoln was chosen by producer Bill Parsons to portray the mighty Tarzan in the first movie production ever made about Edgar Rice Burroughs' popular character. *Tarzan of the Apes* ('18), an eight-reel feature with Enid Markey appearing as Jane Porter, was the stepping stone for Lincoln to stardom.

The Romance of Tarzan ('18) followed less than nine months later. It was shot mainly in California; some of the footage taken in Louisiana during filming of the first feature was incorporated into this feature.

In the Universal serial *Elmo, the Mighty* ('19), Grace Cunard shared the spotlight with Lincoln. *Elmo, the Fearless* ('20) followed with Louise Lorraine as the fetching soubrette. Both of the "Elmo" films were stretched out to 18 chapters.

Lorraine was back with Lincoln in Universal's *The Flaming Disc* ('20), again an 18-chapter affair.

In *The Adventures of Tarzan* ('21), Lincoln and Louise Lorraine kept the jungle humming with wild animals. Much of the action centered on Tarzan's feud with Queen La of Opar (Lillian Worth), whose love he spurned, and his efforts to keep the Bolshevik Rokoff (Frank Whitson) and Clayton (Percy Pembroke), a pretender to Tarzan's title as Lord Greystoke, from reaching Opar.

Lincoln found his career was stuck and that he was unable to find more leading roles, so he left the screen to pursue silver mining in Nevada. Four years later he was back in Hollywood resuming his career in the cheap Rayart serial *King of the Jungle* ('27). In this, his final serial, he plays a white hunter. With his career on a downhill slide, Lincoln retired after making this serial. Years later he returned to Hollywood and appeared in many films as a bit player.

Lincoln died in 1952 from a heart attack while working on a Charles Starrett Western.

Serials

1919

Elmo, the Mighty. Univ., [18 Chapters] D: Henry MacRae; S: Joe Brandt, William E. Wing; LP: Elmo Lincoln, Grace Cunard, Fred Starr, Virginia Craft.

1920

Elmo, the Fearless. Univ., [18 Chapters] D: J. P. McGowan; S: Arthur H. Gooden; LP: Elmo Lincoln, Louise Lorraine, William Chapman, Roy Watson, Frank Ellis.

The Flaming Disc. Univ., [18 Chapters] D: Robert F. Hill; SP: Jerry Ash, Arthur H. Gooden; S: Arthur H. Gooden; LP: Elmo Lincoln, Louise Lorraine, Fay Holderness, Roy Watson, George Williams.

1921

The Adventures of Tarzan. Numa, [15 Chapters] D: Robert F. Hill; SP: Lillian Valentine, Robert F. Hill; LP: Elmo Lincoln, Louise Lorraine, George Momberg, Percy Pembroke, Lillian Worth, Frank Merrill, Joe Martin (ape), Numa (lion).

1927

King of the Jungle. Rayart, [10 Chapters] D: Webster Cullison; LP: Elmo Lincoln, Sally Long, Gordon Standing, George Kotsonaros, Arthur Morrison.

1944

Black Arrow. Col., [15 Chapters] D: Lew Landers; LP: Robert Scott, Adele Jergens, Kenneth MacDonald, Charles Middleton, Elmo Lincoln (bit).

VIRGINIA LINDLEY

Absolutely nothing is known about Virginia Lindley except that she had the second feminine role in *The Black Widow* ('47), a passive one that generated no enthusiasm in the viewing audience. Only one other supporting credit has been found for her among theatrical releases. It is possible that she drifted into early television.

Serial

1947

The Black Widow. Rep., [13 Chapters] D: Spencer Bennet, Fred C. Brannon; SP: Franklyn Adreon, Basil Dickey, Jesse Duffy, Sol Shor; AP: Mike Frankovich; Cam: John MacBurnie; Mus: Mort Glickman; LP: Carol Forman, Bruce Edwards, Virginia Lindley, Anthony Warde, I. Stanford Jolley, Ramsay Ames.

THOMAS (TOM) LINGHAM

Although there is no biographical data on Tom Lingham, excepting his death in 1950 at the Motion Picture Hospital in Woodland Hills, California, the author feels that he should be acknowledged in this serial reference book. He appeared in at least 13 serials over a period of ten years and played in a number of features and two-reelers. More often than not he was the fly in the ointment or chief troublemaker, but he also played lawmen, doting parents, cattlemen and other roles.

The earliest Lingham credit the author has found is *Shannon of the Sixth* ('14), a Marin Sais two-reeler. However, 1915 was a busy one for Lingham. He appeared in the Kalem Studio serials *Stingaree* and *The Girl Detectives* and the two-reelers *The Strangler's Cord, The Closed Door, The Accomplice, The Pitfall, Under Oath, The Vivisectionist, The Man in Irons* and *The Dream Seekers*, all starring Sais.

Lingham also supported Ruth Roland in the 1915 Kalem two-reelers *Affairs of the Deserted House, The Disappearance of Harry Worthington, The Apartment House, The Mystery of the Tea Dansant, Following a Clue* and *Jared Fairfax's Millions.*

In 1916 Lingham supported Marin Sais and Ollie Kirkby in the serial *The Social Pirates.* In *A Lass of the Lumberlands* ('16), a Signal serial, he is billed third behind Helen Holmes and Leo Maloney. He also supported this duo in *Whispering Smith, Medicine Bend, Judith of the Cumberlands, The Diamond Runners* and *The Manager of the B&A.*

In 1917 Lingham supported True Boardman and Marin Sais in *The Further Adventures of Stingaree*, a Kalem serial. In Universal's popular serials *The Lion's Claws* ('18) and *The Red Glove* ('19), Lingham has a major role in support of Marie Walcamp. He is billed third in the 1917 Helen Holmes cliffhangers *The Lost Express* and *The Railroad Raiders.*

Lingham had a principal role in Pathé's *Ruth of the Rockies* ('20) starring Ruth Roland and a lesser role in *The Vanishing Dagger* ('20), a Universal serial starring Eddie Polo. In *The Adventures of Ruth* ('22) he again has a principal role, this time as La Farge, the hound. In his last serial, Rayart's *Trooper 77* ('26), he is a suave villain.

Throughout the '20s, Lingham worked primarily in Westerns with Hoot Gibson (2), Jack Hoxie (4), Harry Carey (1), Tom Tyler (3), Tom Mix (3), Bob Steele (4), Rex Lease (1), Buck Jones (1), Bill Cody (1), Art Acord (1) and Buzz Barton (4). He also appeared in other miscellaneous films.

Serials

1915

Stingaree. Kalem, [12 Chapters] D: James W. Horne; LP: True Boardman, Marin Sais, Paul Hurst, Thomas Lingham, Frank Jonasson, Ollie Kirkby, Hoot Gibson, Edward Clisbee.

The Girl Detectives. Kalem, [14 (?) Chapters] D: James W. Horne; SP: Hamilton Smith *et al.*; LP: Ruth Roland, Cleo Ridgely, Thomas Lingham, Paul Hurst, James Horne, Anna Lingham.

1916

The Social Pirates. Kalem, [15 Chapters] D: James W. Horne; LP: Marin Sais, Ollie Kirkby, True Boardman, Thomas Lingham, Paul Hurst, Priscilla Dean.

The Lass of the Lumberlands. Signal/Mutual, [15 Chapters] D: J. P. McGowan, Paul Hurst; SP: E. Alexander Powell, Ford Beebe *et al.*; LP: Helen Holmes, Leo D. Maloney, Thomas Lingham, William C. Chapman, Paul Hurst.

1917

The Further Adventures of Stingaree. Kalem, [15 Chapters] D: Paul Hurst; LP: True Boardman, Marin Sais, Paul Hurst, Frank Jonasson.

The Lost Express. Signal, [15 Chapters] D: J. P. McGowan; S. Frederick Bennett; SP: J. P. McGowan; LP: Helen Holmes, Leo Maloney, Thomas Lingham, F. O. Whitehead, William Brunton.

The Railroad Raiders. Signal, [15 Chapters] D: J. P. McGowan; SP: Ford Beebe *et al.*; LP: Helen Holmes, Leo Maloney, William Brunton, Thomas Lingham, William Chapman, Paul Hurst.

1918

The Lion's Claws. Univ., [18 Chapters] D: Jacques Jaccard, Harry Harvey; S: W. B. Pearson; SP: W. B. Pearson, Jacques Jaccard; LP: Marie Walcamp, Roy Hanford, Neal Hart, Thomas Lingham, Frank Lanning.

1919

The Red Glove. Univ., [18 Chapters] D: J. P. McGowan; SP: Hope Loring; S: Douglas Grant [Isabel Egenton Ostrander]; LP: Marie Walcamp, Pat O'Malley, Trueman Van Dyke, Thomas Lingham, Evelyn Selbie.

1920

Ruth of the Rockies. Pathé, [15 Chapters] D: George Marshall; S: Johnston McCulley; SP: Frances Guihan; LP: Ruth Roland, Herbert Heyes, Thomas Lingham, Jack Rollens, Fred Burns.

The Vanishing Dagger. Univ., [18 Chapters] D: Ed Kull, Eddie Polo; LP: Eddie Polo, Thelma Percy, G. Normand Hammond, Laura Oakley.

1922

The Adventures of Ruth. Univ., [18 Chapters] D: Robert F. Hill; SP: Emma Bell Clifton; S: Daniel Defoe; LP: Ruth Roland, Herbert Heyes, Thomas Lingham, William Human, Helen Case.

1926

Trooper 77. Rayart, [10 Chapters] D: Duke Worne; LP: Herbert Rawlinson, Hazel Dean, Jimmy Aubrey, Ruth Royce, Thomas Lingham.

ANNA LITTLE

"If nobody else can do the part, give it to Anna Little" is what one director said of this versatile player, who had learned as a girl to ride, shoot, swim and hunt in the wilderness.

She was an athletic girl and an expert horsewoman, well-equipped with vigor and strength to stand the strain of the arduous roles she was called on to play. Producers found her a congenial woman who adapted easily to the movie world of cowboys and horses. However, she liked to play other parts and preferred leads in strong dramas, for which her mature dramatic expression also fitted her. Emotional scenes came naturally to her — she could cry real tears on cue, but sometimes found it hard to smile at the proper time.

Anna Little was born in Sisson, California, on February 1, 1890, and was educated in Chicago and Los Angeles. Until the age of 16, she lived mostly on a ranch at the foot of Mount Shasta. Shortly after finishing her schooling, she joined a stock company in California, making her first stage experience in the chorus of a company in San Francisco.

Anna was a beautiful young woman with dark brown eyes and a luxurious crop of chestnut hair. She was appearing in one-reelers in late 1911, and it is possible that she also worked in films earlier than that. (There are those who believe that she first played with Bronco Billy Anderson at San Rafael for a short time.) Her first bid to fame came during her long engagement with the New York Motion Picture Corp., which handled the output of Bison, Kay-Bee, Rancho and Domino. The NYMPC had a studio at Santa Monica where she played a great variety of parts.

Anne studied the redman thoroughly, and so true were her characterizations that it was difficult to believe that she was a white girl. Her most famous Indian portrayal was that of Naturich in Cecil B. DeMille's *The Squaw Man* ('18). Her sympathetic interpretation of Indians won her the friendship of chiefs, ex-chiefs, subchiefs, braves, squaws and even papooses. Other Indian roles include *A Young Squaw's Bravery* (Bison '11), *Custer's Last Raid* (Bison '12), *The Indian Massacre* (Ince '12) and *The Heart of an Indian* (Bison '13).

Anna was firmly established at Universal by 1914. Among the best-known of her early credits are *The Opened Shutters* ('14), *Called Back* ('14), *Damon and Pythias* ('14),

The Battle at Gettysburgh ('14), *Man Afraid of His Wardrobe* ('15), *Land O'Lizards* ('16), *Nan of Music Mountain* ('17), *Rimrock Jones* ('18) and *The Firecry of France* ('18).

In 1914–15 Anna played opposite Herbert Rawlinson in 23 two- and three-reelers for Universal. Most of the films were directed by William Worthington, who could not resist appearing as actor in many of them. In 1915–16 Anna worked with Tom Chatterton, Jack Richardson and E. Forrest Taylor in a dozen or more two-reelers for Mustang Photoplay. Anna and her co-stars contributed some great teamwork, and the action was entertaining. The stories may have been implausible, but they stepped along so briskly that the lack of probability didn't really bother the viewer.

In 1917–18 Anna dropped the "A" to become simply "Ann." She was signed by Famous Players–Lasky to appear opposite idol Wallace Reed.

The first of her six serials, *The Black Box* ('1x), found her sharing the spotlight with Laura Oakley, with most of the action centered on Herbert Rawlinson as criminologist Sanford Quest. But Anna managed well, as the tempo and hazards of serial production were no more demanding than those of the short Westerns she had been making.

There were more Westerns to come. In a number of mustang Westerns released by Universal and American Mutual, Anna acquired the affectionate title of "The Darling of the Plain," as she proved her versatility in assorted characterizations and her ability as an equestrienne.

In 1919, Ann was lured by National Film Corp. to star with up-and-coming Jack Hoxie in the serial *Lightning Brice* ('19), released by Arrow. It was a success but it could lay no claim to plausibility. Two miners bequeath their respective children a rich secret mine. The daughter of one is made the recipient of a string, the son of the other is given a hunting knife. The mine can be located only by winding the string over the blade — the string carrying the precious information. Naturally villainy enters to complicate matters. Arrow capitalized on Ann's popularity by rushing her in *The Blue Fox* ('21). She portrays the daughter of a white man and an Eskimo girl. She is raised in the U.S. after her father is murdered by the tribe for having taken one of the women in marriage; her mother died of grief. She returns to the northland as a grown woman determined to wreak vengeance on those who destroyed her family. The title of the film was derived from a blue fox skin in the story that holds the key to the location of a rich mine.

Next for Ann came *Nan of the North* ('22). Leonard Clapham (better known as Tom London to those whose memories only reach as far back as the 1930s) was the Canadian Mountie who aids Ann in thwarting the attempts of Joseph Girard and Edith Stayart to obtain the powerful substance "Tilano" from a fallen meteorite.

Ann's exuberant personality and entertaining ways were utilized effectively in Universal's *The Eagle's Talons* ('23), a direct action proposition from start to finish. The film introduced Fred Thomson as the hero. Stunt flyer Al Wilson and strongman Joe Bonomo headed up the supporting cast.

The last of the serials starring Ann Little was *Secret Service Saunders* ('25), undoubtedly the weakest of her serials. It is also the last film credit that the author has found.

Until her death in the spring of 1984, Ann lived in the Los Angeles area and is reported to have been active in Christian Science endeavors for a number of years. She preferred not to talk of her moviemaking days.

Ann Little was 93 at the time of her death.

Serials

1915

The Black Box. Univ., (19 Chapters] D/SP: Otis Turner; S: E. Phillips Oppenheim; LP: Herbert Rawlinson, Anna Little, Laura Oakley, William Worthington, Helen Wright.

1919

Lightning Bryce. National, [15 Chapters] D: Paul Hurst; SP: Harvey Gates; S: Joe Brandt;

LP: Jack Hoxie, Anna Little, Paul Hurst, Jim Woodward, Noble Johnson.

1921

The Blue Fox. Arrow, [15 Chapters] D: Duke Worne; SP: Hope Loring, Joe Brandt; S: Hope Loring; LP: Ann Little, J. Morris Foster, Joseph W. Girard, Charles Mason, Hope Loring.

1922

Nan of the North. Arrow, [15 Chapters] D: Duke Worne; S/SP: Karl Coolidge; P: Ben Wilson; LP: Ann Little, Leonard Clapham [Tom London], Joseph W. Girard, Hal Wilson, Howard Crampton.

1923

The Eagle's Talons. Univ., [15 Chapters] D: Duke Worne; SP: Anthony Coldeway, Jefferson Moffitt, Bertram Millhauser; S: Theodore Wharton, Bertram Millhauser; LP: Ann Little, Fred Thomson, Al Wilson, Joe Bonomo, Albert J. Smith, Roy Tompkins, Jack Fowler, George Magrill.

1925

Secret Service Saunders. Rayart, [15 Chapters] D: Duke Worne; P: Ashton Dearholt [Richard Holt]; SP: Robert Dillon; LP: Richard Holt, Ann Little, Helen Broneau, Ellis Houston.

ROBERT (BOB) LIVINGSTON

It is as Stony Brooke, the character he played 29 times in the "Three Mesquiteers" films, that Robert Livingston's fans will always think of him. The "Mesquiteers" series was among the top Western box office attractions for seven consecutive years, 1937 through 1943.

Nearly all sources report Livingston as born in Quincy, Illinois, on December 8, 1908, yet state that he was 83 at the time of his death in 1988. The arithmetic doesn't pan out. If born in 1908, he would have been only 80 at death. Let's move his birth back to December 1904 and lock it in.

Author Joe Collura writes: "When Bob started acting regularly in Motion Pictures, he tried to conceal his true age for reasons related to his longevity as a romantic leading man."

Livingston was born Robert Randall. He moved with his parents to California when he was 12 and attended high school and college there. His interests during his school days were athletics and journalism. At the completion of his schooling, he went to work as a reporter for a Los Angeles newspaper, but also spent some time as a seaman, lumberjack and cowhand before he became interested in acting.

Bob was doing bit, extra and stunt work in films by the middle of the '20s. In the late '20s he was appearing in a series of comedy shorts at Universal and in early RKO musicals. He had bit parts in the classics *Wings* ('27) and *Frankenstein* ('31).

In the early '30s, Livingston left films for a year or more to train and perform at the prestigious Pasadena Playhouse. When he appeared in the play *Judgment Day* in 1933, he was spotted by Ida Koverman, an MGM talent scout. He was signed and his first role of note was in *Mutiny on the Bounty* ('35).

Left to right: Charles King (on the desk), Frank Ellis, Robert Livingston, Charles Whitaker and Al St. John in ***Raiders of Red Gap*** (PRC, 1943).

Livingston is said to have married a young lady by the name of Dorothy Gee sometime during the late '20s or early '30s; however, the author finds no evidence in the literature of this alleged marriage and can find no information on Gee. It has also been said that Bob was married five times. One of his wives was former actress Margaret Roach, daughter of Hal Roach. They had a son, Addison. Livingston and Roach were married in 1947 and they split in 1951. A later marriage also ended in divorce. So we can account for three wives.

At MGM as a bit player Bob appeared in *The Winning Ticket* ('35), *Baby Face Harrington* ('35), *Murder in the Fleet* ('35), and *Three Godfathers* ('35); bigger parts did not materialize for him there. He left the studio

and signed with the newly formed Republic Pictures in 1936. It was here that he hit paydirt. His first starring role was *The Vigilantes Are Coming* ('36), a serial remake of Rudolph Valentino's earlier epic of 1925. Bob plays Don Loring/the Eagle in a story set in California in 1844. Don Loring's father and brother are killed by Gen. Jason Burr when they discover he is secretly mining gold on their land using kidnapped peons. Don adopts the black mask and cape of the Eagle to bring Burr's gang to account. Posing as a simple-minded organist in the local mission, he is not suspected by Burr and the outlaws of Count Raspinoff and the Russian Cossacks who provide the gang with military muscle in return for gold.

Bob's success in this chapterplay led to

a starring role in the studio's first color film, *The Bold Caballero* ('36), playing the talkies' first Zorro.

Good fortune was still shining on Livingston when he was made one of the stars of a Western series. The series debuted with *The Three Mesquiteers* ('36) with Livingston leading a trio of cowboys as Stony Brooke. This headstrong hero usually got romantically involved with a succession of heroines, and Bob played the role with flair and style. Ray Corrigan and Syd Saylor were co-starred with him but Saylor was replaced in the second and subsequent films by Max Terhune. Bob made 29 features in the series. Ray Corrigan and Max Terhune made 15 films before dropping out with Duncan Renaldo and Raymond Hatton stepping in for seven features. Bob Steele and Rufe Davis then joined Livingston for seven features. After Livingston left the series, it continued with John Wayne and Tom Tyler.

Livingston was booked for bigger things and played leading man in five non–Westerns before tackling the title role in *The Lone Ranger Rides Again* ('39). It was unfortunate that four scriptwriters should offer the Lone Ranger nothing more than a range war to cope with; however, things were kept moving with good stuntwork, superior photography by Edgar Lyons and William Nobles, a rousing William Lava musical score and expert direction by William Witney and John English. Good support was supplied by Duncan Renaldo, Chief Thundercloud, J. Farrell MacDonald, Jinx Falken(berg) and Ralph Dunn. Rex Lease, Buddy Roosevelt, Ted Wells, Eddie Dean, Wheeler Oakman and many more familiar characters also stirred up the dust in this popular serial.

With his Republic contract completed, Bob signed with PRC Studio to replace departing George Houston in the "Lone Rider" series in 1942; he also teamed with Al "Fuzzy" St. John for six popular sagas during 1942–43. Bob starred in one of PRC's best little thrillers, *The Black Raven* ('43) with George Zucco; he was billed under his real name, Robert Randall.

Republic recalled him to co-star with Smiley Burnette in a new series in 1944. Only three films were shot. Bob was back in 1952–53 with supporting roles in four Gene Autry flicks and a couple of Tim Holt Westerns. Bob made a guest appearance in Roy Rogers' all-star lineup in *Bells of Rosarita* ('45); he also had a supporting role in Rogers' *Don't Fence Me In* ('45). His remaining films at Republic during this period included five romantic roles opposite Ruth Terry. *Pistol Packin' Mama* ('43) was a delightful, lower budgeted musical drama that pits feisty Ruth Terry against a slick opportunist. Paired for the first time, Ruth and Bob made four more pictures together.

Following a cameo appearance in Rowan and Martin's Western spoof, *Once Upon a Horse...* ('58) at Universal, Livingston retired from films to devote full time to rearing his young son. To get away from the Hollywood scene, they moved to the Big Bear Lake, where they lived for some time.

Livingston was brought out of retirement in 1974 by his friend Samuel Sherman, president of Independent-International Pictures. Sherman produced three R-rated films featuring Livingston: *Girls for Rent* ('74), *The Naughty Stewardesses* ('75) and *Blazing Stewardesses* ('75).

Livingston was honored in 1987 by the Motion Picture and Television Fund with a "Golden Boot"; he received a standing ovation from the audience of about 1400 Western buffs. The ceremony took place in Los Angeles. Livingston attended the event in a wheelchair.

Bob lived a long life, although not always in the best of health. He suffered seriously and continually from emphysema in his later years.

Livingston's TV credits include episodes *The Cisco Kid*, *The Gene Autry Show*, *The Lone Ranger*, *Wild Bill Hickok* and *Stories of the Century*.

Livingston died at age 83 in Tarzana, California, on March 7, 1988.

Serials

1938

The Vigilantes Are Coming. Rep., [12 Chapters] D: Mack V. Wright, Rex Taylor; SP: John Rathmell, Maurice Geraghty, Winston Miller; S: Maurice Geraghty, Leslie Swabacker; Spv.: J. Laurence Wickland; Cam: William Nobles, Edgar Lyons; Mus: Harry Grey; P: Nat Levine; LP: Robert Livingston, Kay Hughes, Guinn "Big Boy" Williams, Raymond Hatton, Fred Kohler, Robert Warwick, Ray Corrigan.

1939

The Lone Ranger Rides Again. Rep., [15 Chapters] D: William Witney, John English; SP: Franklyn Adreon, Ronald Davidson, Sol Shor, Barry Shipman; AP: Robert Beche; Cam: William Nobles, Edgar Lyons; Mus: Alberto Colombo; LP: Robert Livingston, Chief Thundercloud, Duncan Renaldo, Jinx Falken, Ralph Dunn, Carleton Young, J. Farrell MacDonald.

JACQUELINE LOGAN

Jacqueline Logan was born in Texas on November 30, 1901, the daughter of an architect and a prima donna of the Boston Opera company. She made her stage debut in a 1920 Broadway revival of *Floradora*. She also did a successful stint with the Ziegfeld Follies that same year, and then headed for Hollywood where she starred in many silent films. They include *Molly O* ('21) with Mabel Normand; *Ebb Tide* ('22) with Lila Lee and James Kirkwood; *Java Head* ('23) with Leatrice Joy; *The Light That Failed* ('23) with Percy Marmont; *Salomy Jane* ('23) with George Fawcett; *The Dawn of a Tomorrow* ('24) with David Torrence; *Manhattan* ('24) with Richard Dix; *Peacock Feathers* ('25) with Cullen Landis; *Playing with Souls* ('25) with Mary Astor; *White Mice* ('26) with William Powell; *Out of the Storm* ('26) with Tyrone Power; *The Outsider* ('26) with Lou Tellegen; *The King of Kings* ('27) with H. B. Warner; *The Blood Ship* ('27) with Hobart Bosworth; *Stocks and Blondes* ('28) with Gertrude Astor; and *the Cop* ('28) with William Boyd.

Logan's one serial, *King of the Kongo* ('29), was made by Mascot and included synchronized musical score, sound effects and dialogue. And to top it off, it was a jungle picture complete with lions, a gorilla and a jungle temple. Co-starring with Logan was Walter Miller, a veteran serial star playing as a Secret Service man out to solve the disappearance of his brother, another agent. The only clue he found was a golden trinket which pointed to the possibility of buried treasure near the temple. At a trading post he meets Jacqueline, who is looking for her father; she has a golden trinket identical to the one Miller had found.

Film historian Kalton LaHue (*Continued Next Week*, 1964) writes:

Together they returned to the temple to search further for evidence which might help them, only to find that a band of desperate criminals had occupied it as a headquarters while searching for the same treasure. The mystery was projected to a high degree with the revelation of a man who was being held prisoner in the dungeon of the temple because he refused to disclose the location of the hidden wealth. Their efforts were hampered by a ferocious gorilla which plagued their every move, but by the last episode, the matter had been satisfactorily disposed of.

Thrice married and divorced, Jacqueline Logan died in Melbourne, Florida, in 1983. Obituaries stated that she was 78.

Serial

1929

King of the Kongo. Mascot, [10 Chapters] D: Richard Thorpe; SP: Harry Sinclair Drago; P: Nat Levine; LP: Jacqueline Logan, Walter Miller, Richard Tucker, Larry Steers, Boris Karloff, Harry Todd, Richard Neill, Lafe McKee, Joe Bonomo (gorilla), Robert Frazer, Ruth Davis.

MARJORIE LORD

Marjorie Lord, a vivacious and spirited redhead, was born July 26, 1922, in San Francisco. She was a Broadway actress (*The Old Maid*) before becoming a screen actress in 1937. She was moderately successful in a long list of routine "B" features, among them *Border Cafe* ('37), *Shantytown* ('43), *Sherlock Holmes in Washington* ('43), *Johnny Come Lately* ('43), *Riding High* ('50) and *The Lost Volcano* ('50). In 1958 Marjorie married stage producer Randolph Hale and remained happily married to him until his death in 1974.

A previous marriage to actor John Archer produced two children, Gregg Archer, a businessman, and Anne Archer, a leading lady in movies and television.

Marjorie was popular as the wife of Danny Thomas in the TV sitcom *Make Room for Daddy* (1957–64). She became a popular dinner theater star across the country in *Wait Until Dark, Mary, Mary, How the Other Half Loves*, etc. Her most recent movie role was in *Boy, Did I Get a Wrong Number!* ('66).

Her only serial was Universal's *Adventures of Smilin' Jack* ('43). Tom Brown is Smilin' Jack. The action takes place on the island of Mandon before World War II. The Chinese and Americans, having secured the friendship of the local people, confront the evil Japanese and Germans seeking to dominate the island. Smilin' Jack is spearheading the Sino-American effort to prevent the Axis takeover of the island. Marjorie's performance as Jack's friend is quite acceptable.

Serial

1943

Adventures of Smilin' Jack. Univ., [13 Chapters] D: Ray Taylor, Lew Collins; SP: Morgan B. Cox. Based on the newspaper feature by Zach Mosley; LP: Tom Brown, Marjorie Lord, Sidney Toler, Edgar Barrier, Rose Hobart, Philip Ahn, Turhan Bey, Wheeler Oakman, Keye Luke.

LOUISE LORRAINE

Louise Lorraine's unsophisticated personality, along with her beauty and charm and her unquestionable talent, quickly raised her to the ranks of the professionals. Her acting had spirit and honesty. Her small stature and lack of athletic background did not suit a serial heroine, yet she carried out her roles far better than most women cast into the action arena. And, surprisingly, she enjoyed making serials and Westerns.

As Louise Fortune, Louise gained renown in Century Comedies, co-starring with Chai Hong, "the Chaplin of the Orient."

Louise was born in San Francisco on October 1, 1901. Her father was French, her mother Spanish. Her father died while Louise was still a teenager, leaving her mother with five children to care for. Louise was only 13 or 14 when a man taking orders for photographs called at her home in Encino, near Los Angeles. Louise answered his knock at the door. Flabbergasted by her beauty, the

man told her that she ought to be in pictures, and that he had a friend at the Ince Studio who would like to see her. Sure enough, a studio man showed up the following day and offered her a job. Getting Louise's mother to allow her daughter to work in the movies was a harder task. As a movie career was not exactly smiled upon at that time, especially for a girl, her mother firmly resisted the idea. However, Louise's determination to become a movie actress finally wore down her mother's resistance, and she consented to the film career for her daughter with the condition that she would escort her to the studio each day. As time went by, her mother became convinced that a movie career could be as dignified as any other profession. She finally let Louise alone to continue her work in films.

In 1920, Louise was chosen by Universal to act as the leading lady to Elmo Lincoln in his first serial there, the 18-chapter *Elmo, the Fearless.* Louise's professional name became Louise Lorraine. In the serial, a financial blockbuster, Louise played Jane to Elmo Lincoln's Tarzan. Louise was only 18 at the time. The two played the Apeman and his mate again in *The Adventures of Tarzan* ('21) for Weiss Brothers–Numa Corporation. It was Louise's only non–Universal cliffhanger. *With Stanley in Africa* ('22) kept her on the Dark Continent a while longer, this time as a young newspaper woman aiding George Walsh in his search of Dr. Livingstone.

In *The Flaming Disc* ('20), *The Radio King* ('22) and *The Diamond Master* ('29) she battled gangsters and mad scientists who would turn the inventions of modern science to their own nefarious ends. Elmo Lincoln, Roy Stewart and Hayden Stevenson supported respectively.

In *The Oregon Trail* ('23), Louise was a pioneer woman loved by trapper Art Acord, while in *The Lightning Express* ('30) she was the heroine in a more traditional Western with Lane Chandler as the hero. *A Final Reckoning* ('29), set in Australia, had to do with bother and sister Louise and Newton House finding a gold mine discovered by their father before his death. Jay Wilsey (Buffalo Bill, Jr.) lends a helping hand.

In *The Great Circus Mystery* ('25), Louise provides the love interest for strongman Joe Bonomo in an action- and animal-packed circus thriller. *The Silent Flyer* ('26) had her supporting a canine, Silver Streak, in a dog story with a Western setting produced by Nat Levine in association with California Studios. It was sold to and released by Universal. Like *The Lightning Express*, *The Jade Box* ('30) was released in both silent and sound versions. Louise co-starred with Jack Perrin, with whom she had made fine Western featurettes in the early '20s. She took pride in doing most of the routine dangerous sequences without a double.

In 1922, Louise was selected as a Wampas Baby Star, and in 1925 she began to freelance; her most memorable films continued to be those made at Universal. MGM and First National both used her as leading lady in good non–Westerns, but today these features are little remembered, while "B" films remain vividly etched on aging memories. One of her last films was one of Bob Steele's earliest talkies, *Near the Rainbow's End* ('30), a real blood-and-thunder affair for Tiffany–All Talking Pictures. Louise's voice was quite satisfactory for sound films, but for other reasons she left the screen after making *Beyond the Law* ('30) with Lane Chandler. She had married for a second time in 1929 and wished to devote her full time to making a home for her husband and (later) two babies. It was a happy marriage.

Louise was married to Art Acord from 1925 to 1928. The union ended in 1928. Contributing factors was Art's drinking problem, his womanizing and his constant carousing. Second husband Chester Hubbard died in 1963.

Widowed for many years, Louise lived in Southern California and remained a vivacious, happy person until a lengthy illness befell her, resulting in her death in Sacramento on February 2, 1981. She had only pleasant memories of the movie career that made her a world-wide celebrity during the Roaring Twenties.

Louise was survived by her daughter, two granddaughters, a sister and nephew.

Serials

1920

Elmo, the Fearless. Univ., [18 Chapters] D: J. P. McGowan; S: Arthur Henry Goodson; LP: Elmo Lincoln, Louise Lorraine, William Chapman, Roy Watson.

The Flaming Disc. Univ., [18 Chapters] D: Robert F. Hill; S: Arthur Henry Goodson; LP: Elmo Lincoln, Louise Lorraine, Lee Kohlmar, Roy Watson, George Williams, Lillian Lorraine.

1921

The Adventures of Tarzan. Weiss/Numa, [15 Chapters] D: Robert F. Hill; SP/Adapt: Lillian Valentine, Robert F. Hill; LP: Elmo Lincoln, Louise Lorraine, Percy Pembroke, Lillian Worth, Frank Whitson, Frank Merrill.

1922

With Stanley in Africa. Univ., [18 Chapters] D: William Craft, Ed Kull; S/SP: George H. Plympton; LP: George Walsh, Louise Lorraine, Charles Mason, William Welsh, Gordon Snackville, Jack Mower, Fred Kohler.

The Radio King. Univ., [10 Chapters] D: Robert F. Hill; S/SP: Robert Dillon; LP: Roy Stewart, Louise Lorraine, Al Smith, Sidney Bracy, Slim Whitaker, Clark Comstock.

1923

The Oregon Trail. Univ., [18 Chapters] D: Edward Laemmle; SP: Anthony Coldeway, Douglas Bronston, Jefferson Moffitt; S: Robert Dillon; LP: Art Acord, Louise Lorraine, Ruth Royce, Duke R. Lee, Burton C. Law, Jim Corey.

1925

The Great Circus Mystery. Univ., [18 Chapters] D: Jay Marchant; SP: Leigh Jacobson;

Cont: George Morgan; S: Isadore Bernstein, William Lloyd Wright; LP: Joe Bonomo, Louise Lorraine, Robert J. Graves, Tom London, Carmen Phillips.

1926

The Silent Flyer. Univ., [10 Chapters] D: William Craft; S: George Morgan; LP: Silver Streak (dog), Malcolm MacGregory, Louise Lorraine, Thur Fairfax, Edith Yorke, Hughie Mack.

1929

The Diamond Master. Univ., [10 Chapters] D: Jack Nelson; S: Jacques Futrelle; LP: Hayden Stevenson, Louise Lorraine, Al Hart, Monte Montague, Louis Stern, Walter Maly.

A Final Reckoning. Univ., [12 Chapters] D: Ray Taylor; S: G. A. Henry; SP: Basil Dickey, George Morgan; LP: Newton House, Louise Lorraine, Jay Wilsey [Buffalo Bill, Jr.], Edmund Cobb, Frank Clark.

1930

The Jade Box. Univ., [10 Chapters] D: Ray Taylor; S: Fred Jackson; LP: Jack Perrin, Louise Lorraine, Monroe Salisbury, Francis Ford, Wilbur S. Mack.

The Lightning Express. Univ., [10 Chapters] D: Henry MacRae; S: "Whispering Smith Rides" by Frank H. Spearman; LP: Lane Chandler, Louise Lorraine, Al Ferguson, Greta Granstedt, J. Gordon Russell, Jim Pierce, Robert Kelly.

ROBERT LOWERY

Robert Lowery Hanke was born in 1914 in Kansas City, Missouri. Originally a band vocalist and stage performer, he was the hero of numerous low-budgeted action pictures and played supporting roles in many other films. He was ruggedly handsome, dimpled-chinned and, some say, a look alike for Clark Gable. Twentieth Century-Fox kept him busy from 1937 to 1940 in romantic leads in many pictures. His three marriages included one with actress Jean Parker.

Mystery of the River Boat ('44) was Lowery's first serial. Oil-rich land in the bayou country inspires both greed and murder as the disinherited son of the Duval family tries to gain control of the land. Steve Langtry (Lowery), returning home from college, is framed for a murder and jumps ship to escape. Police later believe in his innocence and solicit his help in rounding up the real criminals, which with the aid of his friends he proceeds to do.

The Monster and the Ape ('45), Lowery's second serial, is at best schlock entertainment. Prof. Ernst (Macready) is actually an enemy spy who plots to steal a robot called Metalogen Man which Prof. Arnold (Ralph Morgan) of the Bainbridge Research Foundation has constructed for Ken Morgan (Lowery), the representative of a large business firm. With the aid of his henchmen and a trained ape named Thor (Corrigan), Ernst plans to abscond with the robot for his own nation, as the electronic man houses a weapon with deadly rays. When Thor tries to kill Ken, Arnold shoots the ape. Ken and girlfriend Babe (Carole Mathews), Prof. Arnold's daughter, destroy Ernst's henchmen in a plan crash. In a showdown between Ernst, Ken and Arnold, the spy falls to his death from a high cliff.

Batman and Robin ('49) was Lowery's third and final serial. A remote control machine is stolen and Police Commissioner Gordon (Lyle Talbot) calls on Batman and Robin to help him recover it. Vicki Vale (Jane Adams), a commercial photographer, becomes involved in the dangerous pursuit.

Batman and Robin clash with the hooded figure known as "the Wizard," who desires to acquire a powerful explosive known as X-90. There are numerous clashes between the two forces before the Wizard is caught and his gang smashed.

Some of Lowery's film credits are *Wake Up and Live* ('37), *Submarine Patrol* ('38), *Drums Along the Mohawk* ('38), *Hollywood Cavalcade* ('39), *Free, Blonde, and Twenty One* ('40), *Charlie Chan's Murder Cruise* ('40), *The Mark of Zorro* ('40), *Private Nurse* ('41), *Criminal Investigator* ('42), *Dawn on the Great Divide* ('42), *Tarzan's Desert Mystery* ('43), *The Navy Way* ('44), *Road to Alcatraz* ('45), *Sensation Hunters* ('46), *I Cover Big Town* ('47), *Highway 13* ('48), *Arson, Inc.* ('49), *The Dalton Gang* ('49), *Gunfire* ('50), *Crosswinds* ('51), *Jalopy* ('53), *Lay the Rifle Down* ('55), *The Parson and the Outlaw* ('57), *Rise and Fall of Legs Diamond* ('60), *When the Girls Take Over* ('65), *The Undertaker and his Pals* ('67) and *The Ballad of Josie* ('69).

Lowery played Big Tim Champion on *Circus Boy* in the NBC-ABC television series. Others in the cast were Mickey Braddock, Noah Beery, Jr., and Guinn Williams. The series was broadcast from 1956 to 1958.

Robert died from a heart attack in Hollywood in 1971. He was 57 years of age.

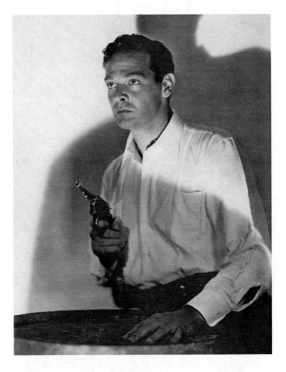

In *They Made Me a Killer* (Paramount, 1946).

Serials

1944

Mystery of the River Boat. Univ., [13 Chapters] D: Ray Taylor, Lewis D. Collins; SP: Maurice Tombragel; S: Ande Lamb; LP: Robert Lowery, Eddie Quillan, Marion Martin, Lyle Talbot, Mantan Moreland.

1945

The Monster and the Ape. Col., [15 Chapters] D: Howard Bretherton; P: Rudolph C. Flothow; SP: Sherman Lowe, Royal K. Cole; Cam: L. W. O'Connell; Mus: Lee Zahler; LP: Robert Lowery, George Macready, Ralph Morgan, Carole Mathews, Willie Best, Jack Ingram, Anthony Warde.

1949

Batman and Robin. Col., [15 Chapters] D: Spencer Bennet; P: Sam Katzman; SP: George Plympton, Joseph F. Poland, Royal K. Cole; Cam: Ira H. Morgan; Mus: Mischa Bakaleinikoff; LP: Robert Lowery, Johnny Duncan, Jane Adams, Lyle Talbot, Ralph Graves, Don C. Harvey, William Fawcett, Rick Vallin.

BELA LUGOSI

"In the course of his lifetime, Bela Lugosi earned hundreds of thousands of dollars. He was however, always in one or two extreme predicaments ... either incalculably wealthy or completely broke. The actor never worried about money. He spent it faster than anyone I have ever known. He lived luxuriously in a stately mansion with lavish furnishings , , , wore elegant clothes and entertained in superlative taste. He owned a priceless stamp collection and his only other hobby, to which he devoted his leisure time, was reading books mainly dealing with scientific subjects and world history."
— Don Marlowe, Bela Lugosi's Manager

Like the character of Count Dracula which made him famous, Bela Lugosi (real name: Bela Ferene Dezo Blaski) was born in Transylvania, Bela in the small Hungarian town of Lugos on October 20, 1882. He made his stage debut in 1900 and in 1903 joined the National Actors' Company, performing in a variety of plays until he joined the Hungarian Theatre in Budapest where he stayed for a season. In 1913 he became a member of Budapest's National Theatre playing romantic leads in plays (*Camille, Romeo and Juliet*,etc.) until he was forced to flee the country for political reasons in 1919. He had made ten or more Hungarian movies under the pseudonym Arisztid Olt beginning in 1917.

In Germany he starred in a number of features now using the name Bela Lugosi. Here he got his first touch of the sinister with a role in F. W. Murnau's film adaptation of *Dr. Jekyll and Mr. Hyde*. In *Der Fluch Der Menscheit* ('20) he portrayed Maelzer, a saboteur; in *Lederstrompf* ('20) he is Chingachgook, the character from James Fenimore Cooper's "Leatherstocking" tales; and in *Der Tanx Auf Dem Volkan* ('21), he played a Parisian aristocrat. It was his last German film.

Lugosi divorced the young wife who fled Hungary with him. Lugosi traveled to America where he joined "The Nest," a company of Hungarian performers. His debut on the American stage came in 1923 opposite Estelle Winwood in *The Red Poppy*. Also in '23 he appeared in his first American film, Fox's *The Silent Command*. Other films followed.

Lugosi got his vampire fangs in 1927, when *Dracula* came to Broadway. He held audiences spellbound through a record 265 performances. Because he radiated such eroticism, critics proclaimed him the new Valentino. He continued to play Dracula for two years in road shows.

Despite his hectic schedule, Bela found time to marry again. Beatrice Weeks was the bride and '24 the year. Bela was an amorous charmer, but the marriage license transformed him into a jealous, paranoid husband who kept constant watch over his property. The marriage lasted two years. But that was longer than his third marriage, which set a record of just four days. It was during this period that he engaged in a tempestuous love affair with silent screen vamp Clara Bow.

When *Dracula* ('31) was issued by Universal, it became the most popular film in the country and made Lugosi an overnight sensation. Women adored him and in the early '30s he vied with Clark Gable for the largest amount of fan mail received. There were glorious days ahead for Lugosi, whose "live for today" credo relished the red-carpet service and first class treatment that came with the title of "star." In 1933 when Bela was 51, Lillian Archer, a 17-year-old, became the fourth Mrs. Lugosi. Bela's career flourished, and he and his bride enjoyed the good life — that is, until 1936, when the horror genre suddenly began to fizzle.

One of his exceptional films was *White Zombie* ('32), one of the eeriest chillers ever made. Lugosi was cast as Murder, a master of voodoo; who turns a girl (Madge Bellamy) into a zombie and controls the man (Robert Frazer) who loves her.

On a much higher budget and for a major studio (Fox), Lugosi played the role of the evil Roxor in *Chandu the Magician* ('32), an adaptation of the popular radio program.

In 1933 Bela starred in a 12-chapter serial for Mascot titled *The Whispering Shadow*, a murder mystery in which he had the red herring role of a magician operating a wax museum. All of the participants are in search of the crown jewels of an Eastern European country. The serial was action-packed, as were all Mascot cliffhangers, but the fight scenes were crude and archaic. The plot gets rather complicated, with one person getting the jewels only to lose them to someone else. The mystery is solved when the seemingly helpless and stupid Sparks (Karl Dane) is revealed to be "The Whispering Shadow."

Next Bela was cast as a mysterious Hindu servant in the Columbia feature *Night of Terror* ('33). In *The Black Cat* ('34) Lugosi plays a prisoner of war who, after his release, goes to the castle of his arch enemy (Boris Karloff) to take revenge on the man for stealing his wife and daughter and causing him to go to prison. It was the first of six appearances with Karloff.

Lugosi returned to Poverty Row to play the title role in the serial *The Return of Chandu* ('34). The story tells of Chandu's attempts to save a beautiful princess (Maria Alba) from agents of the Black Magic Cult of Ubasti from the island of Lemuria. It seems that a princess of royal blood must be sacrificed to bring their dead queen back to life and make them rulers of the world. After a number of adventures and misadventures on the island, Chandu is able to employ a powerful chant which causes the Ubastis' temple to collapse, killing all the bad guys. (Don't laugh, this was exciting stuff in 1934.)

Karloff and Lugosi returned for *The Raven* ('35) and *The Invisible Ray* ('36) at Universal. Then Lugosi signed to star in the Victory serial *Shadow of Chinatown* ('36). In this one, he is an all-out sinister character. Eurasian chemist Victor Poten (Lugosi) conspires with Sonya Rokoff (Luana Walters), West Coast representative of a European importing firm, to get rid of Chinese competition on the West Coast. Writer Martin Andrews (Herman Brix) joins with reporter Joan Whiting (Joan Barclay) to help the Chinese merchants. The serial lacked the polish that Universal or Republic might have given it, but the independents as a whole had an indescribable charm about them that satisfied 1930s audiences. *Shadow of Chinatown* was no exception.

Lugosi got his chance to work in a Republic serial when he was given the co-lead with Ralph Byrd in *S O S Coast Guard* ('37). Bela is an evil inventor named Baroff who, with the aid of giant mute henchman Thorg (Dick Alexander), is attempting to supply a disintegrating gas of his own manufacture to a foreign country.

Lugosi accepted the role of the evil grave robber Ygor in *Son of Frankenstein* ('39), turning in one of his best performances as the grizzled, broken-necked ghoul who befriends Frankenstein's Monster (Karloff).

Making his final serial appearance, Lugosi plays Dr. Alex Zorka, a mad inventor, in Universal's *The Phantom Creeps* ('39). Opposing him is Capt. Bob West (Robert Kent) of the Military Intelligence Department.

One quality role that came Bela's way in '39 was that of Commissar Razinin in *Ninotchka* for MGM. In the '40s he appeared in no less than 25 features. After '48 he did not work again until '52. Nearly all of the seven films he made after that date were worse than poor, culminating with possibly the worst film ever made, *Plan 9 from Outer Space* ('59).

Lugosi began drinking heavily during his long stretches of unemployment. More and more he relied on medically prescribed morphine for a World War I injury and resulting in a duodenal ulcer. Lillian helped to wean him from the drug and, when he was well again, she told him she was leaving. The end of his fourth marriage was the most

Helen Chandler, Bela Lugosi and Dwight Frye in *Dracula* (Universal, 1931).

traumatic event of his long life. After Lillian and 15-year-old Bela, Jr., left, he became a desolate, embittered soul and almost immediately wound up back on drugs.

In 1955, Lugosi had himself committed to a state hospital in California to cure him of drug addiction. After 90 days he was released and pronounced cured.

A fan, Hope Lininger, wrote him every day while he was hospitalized. Lugosi found her when he was discharged and at the end of their first meeting he proposed. Lininger, in her late thirties, agreed to become Mrs. Lugosi No. 5. Hope came home on the evening of August 18, 1956, and found him dead on the bed. He had succumbed to a heart attack. As he stipulated in his will, he was buried in his tuxedo and cape.

Serials

1933

The Whispering Shadow. Mascot, [12 Chapters] D: Albert Herman, Colbert Clark; P: Nat Levine; SP: Barney Sarecky, George Morgan, Norman S. Hall, Colbert Clark, Wyndham Gittens; Cam: Ernest Miller, Edgar Lyons; Mus: Abe Meyer; LP: Bela Lugosi, Henry B. Walthall, Viva Tattersall, Malcom McGregor.

1934

The Return of Chandu. Principal, [12 Chapters] D: Ray Taylor; P: Sol Lesser; SP: Barry Berringer; Spv.: Frank Melford; Mus: Abe Meyer; LP: Bela Lugosi, Maria Alba, Clara Kimball Young, Lucien Prival, Phyllis Ludwig.

1936

Shadow of Chinatown. Victory, [15 Chapters] D: Robert (Bob Hill; S: Rock Hawkey; SP: Isadore Bernstein, Basil Dickey; Spv.: Sam Katzman; Cam: Bill Hyer; LP: Bela Lugosi, Herman Brix [Bruce Bennett], Joan Barclay, Luana Walters, Charles King, Maurice Liu, William Buchanan, Forrest Taylor, James B. Leong.

1937

SOS Coast Guard. Rep., [12 Chapters] D: William Witney, Alan James; SP: Barry Shipman, Franklyn Adreon; S: Morgan Cox, Ronald Davidson; AP: Sol Siegel; Cam: William Nobles; Mus: Raoul Kraushaar; LP: Ralph Byrd, Bela Lugosi, Maxine Doyle, Richard Alexander, Herbert Rawlinson, John Picorri, Lee Ford.

1939

The Phantom Creeps. Univ., [12 Chapters] D: Ford Beebe, Saul A. Goodkind; S: Willis Cooper; SP: George H. Plympton, Basil Dickey, Mildred Barish; LP: Bela Lugosi, Robert Kent, Dorothy Arnold, Regis Toomey, Edward Van Sloan.

KEYE LUKE

Keye Luke was as American as apple pie a la mode, in spite of the fact that he was born in Canton, China, on June 18, 1904, while his parents were vacationing there. He was educated at Washington University in Seattle and entered the film industry as a commercial artist and poster designer. His three brothers and two sisters were born in the U.S.

Luke was a part of the Hollywood scene since his youth. Prior to his acting career, he had been an artist for Fox theaters, an RKO publicity aide and a technical advisor on movies about China (though he never lived in China!).

Luke is best remembered as the No. 1 son of Charlie Chan (eight films with Warner Oland and two with Roland Winters). He made his debut as an actor in Greta Garbo's *The Painted Veil* ('34). He had substantial supporting roles in *The Good Earth* ('37), *Across the Pacific* ('42) and *A Yank on the Burma Road* ('42). The only time he was not steadily occupied as an actor in Hollywood was when he starred on Broadway for three years as Father Wong in the musical *Flower Drum Song* (1958–61) for a total of 601 performances.

Older fans may remember him in MGM's

Dr. Kildare films, while younger viewers may remember him as Master Po in the 1970s series *Kung Fu*.

Luke married Ethel Davis on April 25, 1942. She had two children by a previous marriage. It was a happy, long-lasting union.

Luke landed his first serial assignment in 1939 when Universal cast him as Kato, the Green Hornet's loyal valet in *The Green Hornet* with Gordon Jones in the title role. *The Green Hornet Strikes Again* was released in 1940 with Warren Hull replacing Jones as Britt Reid and the Green Hornet, out to bring to justice a sinister criminal named Grogan (Pierre Watkin) and the syndicate he controls. Luke was back as Kato and Anne Nagel was Lenore Case.

In *Adventures of Smilin' Jack* ('43), Luke portrays Capt. Wing as Smilin' Jack and friends fight German and Japanese operatives for control of the island Manden before World War II.

In *Secret Agent X-9* ('45), U.S. Secret Agent X-9 (Lloyd Bridges) battles the Japanese Black Dragon Intelligence Service headed by Japan's top female spy, Nabura (Victoria Horne). Ah Fong (Luke) and Lynn Moore (Jan Wiley) aid X-9.

As an artist, Luke specialized in black-and-white pen-and-ink drawings and oil paintings. He also did a lot of recording — reading selections from Shakespeare, Keats and others, plus excerpts from art histories.

Luke played in many television shows: *Gunsmoke*, *Perry Mason*, *Falcon Crest*, *Anna and the King*, *Charlie's Angels*, etc.

Death came to Keye Luke in 1991 after a stroke. He was 86.

Serials

1939

The Green Hornet. Univ., [13 Chapters] D: Ford Beebe, Ray Taylor; SP: George Plympton, Basil Dickey, Morrison C. Wood, Lyonel Margolies; AP: Henry MacRae; Cam: William Sickner, Jerry Ash; LP: Gordon Jones, Keye Luke, Anne Nagel, Wade Boteler, Phillip Trent, Anne Gwynne, Cy Kendall.

1940

The Green Hornet Strikes Again. Univ., [13 Chapters] D: Ford Beebe, John Rawlins; AP: Henry MacRae; LP: Warren Hull, Keye Luke, Wade Boteler, Anne Nagel, Eddie Acuff, Pierre Watkin, Joe Devlin.

1943

Adventures of Smilin' Jack. Univ., [12 Chapters] D: Ray Taylor, Lewis D. Collins; LP: Tom Brown, Marjorie Lord, Philip Ahn, Jay Novello, Nigel De Brulier, Edgar Barrier, Keye Luke.

1945

Secret Agent X-9. Univ., [13 Chapters] D: Ray Taylor, Lewis D. Collins; SP: Joseph O'Donnell, Patricia Harper; S: Joseph O'Donnell, Harold C. Wire; LP: Lloyd Bridges, Keye Luke, Jan Wiley, Victoria Horne, Samuel S. Hinds, Cy Kendall, Edmund Cobb.

LUCILLE LUND

Beautiful blonde actress Lucille Lund, 89, died February 16, 2002, at a hospital near her home in Rancho Palos Verdes, California. Suffering back pain, she had received med-ication which may have caused her kidneys and other functions to fail.

Born on June 3, 1912, in Buckley, Washington, Lucille showed interest in performing at an early age, and in high school demonstrated her speaking skills by winning honors in oratorical, dramatic and humorous speaking. After completing a one-year acting course at the American Conservatory of Music and Dramatic Arts in Chicago, she worked for a while in a stock company and then enrolled at Northwestern (Illinois) University majoring in speech.

As the winner of a *College Humor* magazine contest, she got a Universal contract and a chance to work with Boris Karloff and Bela Lugosi in *The Black Cat* ('34). She played Karen, daughter of Lugosi and wife of Karloff.

Also in '34 she played the heroine in the serial *Pirate Treasure*, working with Richard Talmadge, Walter Miller and William Desmond in a story of buried pirate treasure sought by two opposing groups. The serial gave Lucille her greatest exposure. Mention should be made of *Fighting Through* ('34) and *Range Warfare* ('35), made by Kent and starring Reb Russell, and *Timber War* ('35),

made by Ambassador and starring Kermit Maynard. Lucille had the female lead in these range opuses.

Lucille wed Kenneth Higgins in 1937 and they had two daughters. Lucille's career was going nowhere in 1938 and she decided to retire and concentrate on her family.

Serials

1934

Pirate Treasure. Univ., [12 Chapters] D: Ray Taylor; SP: Basil Dickey, Jack Nelson, George Plympton; S: Ella O'Neill; LP: Richard Talmadge, Lucille Lund, Walter Miller, William Desmond, Pat O'Malley, William E. Thorne

1937

Blake of Scotland Yard. Victory, [15 Chapters] D: Bob Hill; SP: Basil Dickey, William Buchanan; S: Rock Hawkey; Spv.: Robert Stillman; Cam: Bill Hyer; P: Sam Katzman.

ANNE LUTHER

Anne Luther played a dual role as twin sisters in the serial *The Great Gamble* ('19). One sister was raised by an adventurer who had taken charge of the child upon the death of her mother. The other sister was raised in wealth and luxury. The story involves an attempt to substitute the poor child for the wealthy one and Charles Hutchison's effort to fathom the mystery surrounding her. It was impossible at times to know which sister Anne was portraying, and therefore the audience often could not tell whether she was for or against the villains.

In *The Lurking Peril* ('19), Phyllis Charlton (Luther) is the girlfriend of Donald Britt (George Larkin). During a financial crunch, Larkin sold the rights to his brain (after his

death) to a fiendish professor who just can't wait to begin dissecting it. Secretly he tries over and over to do away with Donald, often imperiling Phyllis as well.

Luther starred as Anna (for Lubin in 1914's *The Changeling* and others, for Fox in 1916's *The Beast* and others), then starred as Anne in the two popular serials.

Other Luther films include *The Island of Desire* ('17), *Moral Suicide* ('18), *Jungle Trails* ('19), *Woman, Woman* ('19), *Why Women Lie* ('20), *Soul and Body* ('21), *The Woman Who Believed* ('21), *The Truth About Wives* ('23), *The Fatal Plunge* ('24) and *Sinners and Silks* ('24).

Born in 1893, Anne Luther died in Hollywood from a heart condition in 1960 at age 69.

Serials

1919

The Great Gamble. Pathé, [15 Chapters] D/ SP: Joseph A. Golden; LP: Charles Hutchison, Anne Luther, Richard Neill, Billy Moran.

The Lurking Peril. Arrow, [15 Chapters] D: George Morgan, Burton King; SP/S: Lloyd Lonergan; LP: George Larkin, Anne Luther, William Betchel, Ruth Dwyer.

GLADYS MCCONNELL

Gladys McConnell was active in pictures in the 1920s. The exceptionally beautiful actress was born in Oklahoma City on October 22, 1907, and was a graduate of Hollywood High School. She had light blonde hair and blue eyes, stood 5'5" in height, and was a Wampas Baby Star in 1927. She married press agent and Wampas official Archie Hagerman. Either widowed or divorced, she married for the second time in 1932 and retired.

Her one serial was *The Fire Detective* ('29), one of the last serials that Pathé made. A special investigator for the fire department endeavors to uncover the perpetrators of a series of disastrous blazes. Evidence shows that a band of criminals are setting the fires.

Her Western films were *The Flying Horseman* ('26) with Buck Jones; *The Code of Scarlet* ('28), *The Glorious Trail* ('28), *Cheyenne* ('29), and *Parade of the West* ('29), all four with Ken Maynard.

Gladys lived in California until her death on March 4, 1979, at the age of 71.

Serial

1929

The Fire Detective. Pathé, [10 Chapters]

TIM MCCOY

Tim McCoy starred in two serials, 87 features and two shorts. Sixteen of the features were silent Westerns for Metro-Goldwyn-Mayer, two silents for Paramount, two sound serials for Universal, 32 sound features for Columbia, ten for Puritan, six for Victory, six for PRC, 12 for Monogram, one for United Artists, one for RKO and one for Embassay. The shorts were *Injun Talk*, produced by Sinclair Oil Company, and *A Night on the Range*, a one-reel musical short pro-

duced by MGM. McCoy and some cowboys sing around a campfire. Nick Grinde directed both shorts.

Universal's *The Indians Are Coming* ('30), believed to be the first serial to make $1,000,000, was the first all-talking serial. It played first-run theaters as well as the traditional serial outlets. It doesn't hold up too well when viewed today but in 1930 it was a thriller.

When George Woods (Francis Ford)

strikes it rich in Gold Creek, California, he sends his friend Jack Manning (McCoy) to contact his brother Tom (also played by Ford) and niece Mary (Allene Ray) and bring them to join him. At Hillsdale, Jack meets the two and learns that Rance Carter (William McGaugh), who had staked George, is trying to force the girl to marry him. Jack saves her from a runaway wagon and the two fall in love. Jack and Mary head out with a wagon train, as do Carter and his henchman Bull McKee (Bud Osborne). A general uprising against the white invaders menaces both the wagon train and the Gold Creek settlers. Scout Bill Williams (Edmund Cobb) helps George Woods and Jack saves Mary when she is trapped in a prairie fire started by Carter.

When the train is about to be overrun by a huge force of red attackers, Jack sends his dog through with a message, but the dog is wounded. Carter takes advantage of the battle to gun down Tom. The Indians are closing in on the few remaining pioneers when the dog appears with Bill and a posse from Gold Creek.

McCoy's second serial was *Heroes of the Flames* ('31). The entire plot concerned one device: chemical fire extinguisher invented by Bob Darrow (McCoy) on his own time off from the official duties as a fireman. Dan Mitchell (Gayne Whitman) has covetous eyes upon it as well as on June (Marion Shockley). Bob has rescued June and Jackie Madison (Bobby Nelson) from a fire. They are the daughter and son of John Madison (William Gould). In gratitude, he allows Bob to use his laboratory for conducting experiments on the fire extinguisher. Mitchell does everything he can to steal the formula and discredit Bob in the eyes of his benefactors.

McCoy's immaculate grooming and quiet aloofness contradicted the usual image of the rough-and-ready range rider. In roles such as this, Tim performed to perfection.

Heroes of the Flames was not an expensive serial to produce. Newsreel footage and even silent film footage (with necessary sound effects added) was used to excellent advantage.

In *Down Texas Way* (Monarch, 1942).

McCoy vetoed the idea of a third serial. They were difficult to make and were not known as stepping stones to stardom in big-budget features. Tim feared he was on a serial treadmill to oblivion. As much as serials are fondly recalled by many fans, the major studios tended to look down on all personnel employed in serials. Very few serial performers graduated to feature stardom. John Wayne, Rod Cameron and, to a lesser extent, Bill Elliott became feature stars.

McCoy was born in Saganaw, Michigan, on April 10, 1891. After high school he was sent to Saint Ignatius College in Chicago, but he quit and bought a one-way ticket to Wyoming, where he became a working cowboy. In time he was able to buy a spread of his own. As Tim's fortunes grew, so did the size of his ranch.

In World War I, Tim attained the rank of colonel. In 1923 he was serving as adjutant general in Wyoming and was one of only three soldiers who could use the sign language of the Plains Indians. The other two were Gen. Hugh S. Scott and Capt. Philo

Tim McCoy (left), Dorothy Short and Dave O'Brien in *Code of the Cactus* (Victory, 1939).

Clark. When Paramount decided to film *The Covered Wagon* ('23), Tim was asked if he could supply 500 Indians from the western states. Tim agreed to supply the Indians and accompanied them to Hollywood. Paramount then asked him to get up a prologue and appear on the stage at Grauman's Chinese Theatre with the showing of the picture. McCoy's prologue was presented for months and he then appeared at the London Pavilion for almost a year.

After a brief role in Paramount's *The Thundering Herd*, Tim signed with Metro-Goldwyn-Mayer and made 16 frontier-type pictures for that studio in the next three years.

Author Anthony Thomas ("Tim Mc-Coy," *Films in Review*, April 1968) wrote:

An articulate well-spoken man, he performs with a natural dignity, always very much the army officer. His personality and appearance set him apart from more rough-neck contemporaries like Buck Jones, Hoot Gibson, and Ken Maynard. The McCoy Westerns were mostly detective stories on the range, but his image was a distinct one: black shirt, wide-brimmed Stetson worn at a jaunty angle, a large kerchief, and gloves. His pearl-handled pistol and his wide, worked-leather gunbelt with a large Mexican buckle, were worn in all his pictures.

Mention has already been made of the low-budget Westerns he made following his Columbia stint. His last series was the immensely popular "Rough Riders" films. The series could have continued indefinitely had not McCoy re-entered the army as a liaison officer and had not Buck Jones died in the Boston Coconut Grove fire. McCoy served in England, France and Germany. Upon his return to the States, he sold his 5,000-acre ranch near Thermapolis and once made the remark, "Never own anything that eats or needs repainting."

In the early '50s he had a television show in Hollywood. In '51 the show won the PTA's Award for television's most outstanding educational offering. It also won an Emmy for McCoy. In '55 he had a cameo in Mike Todd's *Around the World in 80 Days* and in '57 a cameo in RKO's *Run of the Arrow*. His last screen appearance was in Embassy's *Requiem for a Gunfighter*, playing a circuit-riding judge.

At various times in the '50s and '60s, McCoy traveled with the Al G. Kelly–Miller Brothers Circus, the Carson-Barnes Circus and Tommy Scott's Hollywood Hillbillies, a stage show.

Serials

1930

The Indians Are Coming. Univ., [12 Chapters] D: Henry MacRae; SP: Ford Beebe, George Plympton; S: William F. Cody; LP: Tim McCoy, Allene Ray, Charles Roy, Edmund Cobb, Francis Ford, Bud Osborne, Wilbur McGaugh.

1931

Heroes of the Flames. Univ., [12 Chapters] D: Robert F. Hill; SP: George Morgan, Basil Dickey, George H. Plympton; LP: Tim McCoy, Marion Shockley.

PHILO MCCULLOUGH

A native of San Bernardino, California, McCullough was an original member of the Burbank Stock Company and played in stock for eight years before beginning his motion picture career in 1912. During the silent days he appeared in Fatty Arbuckle comedies and Selig shorts, as well as in the Rin-Tin-Tin series. He was often the villain in Westerns and serials.

Over his long career he worked at one time or another for Selig, Balboa, Kalem, Metro, Pathé, Universal, Ince, Mayflower, Mascot, First National, Principal, First Division, Fox, Warner Brothers, Goldwyn and other studios. After spending four years at Fox and two at First National, he freelanced as an actor for several years before becoming a contract player at Warner Brothers, where he remained for 28 years.

This fine Western heavy, widower of actress Laura Anson (died 1968), played a cameo role in *They Shoot Horses, Don't They?* ('69), his first role in two decades.

McCullough died June 5, 1981, at his home in Burbank. He was 87.

Serials

1915

The Red Circle. Pathé, [14 Chapters] D: Sherwood MacDonald; LP: Ruth Roland, Frank Mayo, Gordon Sackville, Daniel Gilfether, Philo McCullough, Edward Peters.

1916

The Grip of Evil. Pathé, [14 Chapters] D: Sherwood MacDonald; S: Lewis Tracy; LP: Jackie Saunders, Roland Bottomley, Charles Dudley, Gordon Dackville, Philo McCullough.

1917

The Neglected Wife. Pathé, [15 Chapters] D: William Bertram; LP: Ruth Roland, Roland Bottomley, Corinne Grant, Neil C. Hardin, Philo McCullough.

1922

A Dangerous Adventure. WB, [15 Chapters] D: Sam and J. L. Warner; P: William N. Selig; SP: Sam Warner; S: Frances Guihan; S: LP: Grace Darmond, Philo McCullough, Jack Richardson, Derelys Perdue.

Left to right: Philo McCullough, Gordon DeMain, Jack Perrin, Charles Whitaker, Fred Humes and an unidentified actor in *Cactus Kid* (Reliable, 1934).

1926

The Bar-C Mystery. Pathé, [10 Chapters] D: Robert F. Hill; SP: William Sherwood; S: Raymond Spears; LP: Wallace MacDonald, Dorothy Phillips, Ethel Clayton, Philo McCullough.

1931

The Vanishing Legion. Mascot, [12 Chapters] D: B. Reeves Eason; P: Nat Levine; Cam: Benjamin Kline,Ernest Miller, Jo J. Novak; SP: Wyndham Gittens, Ford Beebe; LP: Harry Carey, Edwina Booth, Rex (horse), Frankie Darro, Philo McCullough.

1932

Heroes of the West. Univ., [12 Chapters] D: Ray Taylor; S: Peter B. Kyne; SP: George Plympton, Basil Dickey, Joe Roach; Cam:

John Hickson; LP: Noah Beery, Jr., Diane Duvel [Julie Bishop/Jacqueline Wells], Onslow Stevens, William Desmond, Philo McCullough.

The Jungle Mystery. Univ., [12 Chapters] D: Ray Taylor; SP: George Plympton, Basil Dickey, George Mason; Adapt: Ella O'Neill; AP: Henry MacRae; Cam: John Hickson; LP: Tom Tyler, Cecilia Parker, William Desmond, Philo McCullough, Noah Beery, Jr., Carmelita Geraghy, Sam Baker, James Marcus.

Tarzan the Fearless. Principal, [12 Chapters] D: Robert F. Hill; P: Sol Lesser; SP: Basil Dickey, George Plympton, Walter Anthony; Cam: Harry Newman, Joe Brotherton; LP: Larry (Buster) Crabbe, Jacqueline Wells,E. Alyn Warren, Philo McCullough, Edward Woods, Mischa Auer, Frank Lackteen.

1934

Young Eagles. First Division, [12 Chapters] D: Spencer G. Bennet, Vin Moore, Eduard Laurier; SP: Elizabeth Hayter; S: Harry O. Hoyt; P: George W. Stout; Cam: William C. Hyer, Edward Kull; LP: Bobbie Cox, Jim Vance, Carter Dixon, Philo McCullough, Frank Lackteen.

Pirate Treasure. Univ., [12 Chapters] D: Ray Taylor; SP: Basil Dickey, George Plympton, Jack Nelson; S: Ella O'Neill; LP: Richard Talmadge, Lucille Lund, Walter Miller, Pat O'Malley, Philo McCullough.

Mystery Mountain. Mascot, [12 Chapters] D: B. Reeves Eason, Otto Brower; SP: Bennett Cohen, Armand Schaefer; Cam: William Nobles; Mus: Lee Zahler, Abe Meyer; P: Nat Levine; LP: Ken Maynard, Verna Hillie, Syd Saylor, Edward Earle, Tarzan (horse), Lafe McKee, Jane Corwin, Philo McCullough, Gene Autry.

1936

The Adventures of Frank Merriwell. Univ., [12 Chapters] D: Cliff Smith; AP: Henry MacRae; SP: George Plympton, Maurice Geraghy, Ella O'Neill, Basil Dickey; LP: Don Briggs, Jean Rogers, John King, Carla Laemmle, Philo McCullough, Bud Osborne, Edmund Cobb, William Desmond.

1937

Tim Tyler's Luck. Univ., [12 Chapters] D: Ford Beebe, Wyndham Gittens; SP: Wyndham Gittens, Norman S. Hall, Ray Trampe; LP: Frankie Thomas, Frances Robinson, Norman Willis, Jack Mulhall, Earle Douglas, William Benedict, Philo McCullough.

FRANCIS MCDONALD

Francis McDonald was a fine character actor who made a plethora of films during a 47-year career. He was a stock villain and utility character player who added his talent to hundreds of movies. At one time in his early career he was considered one of the American Screen's most handsome men. He was once married to actress Mae Busch.

His films include *Intolerance* ('16), *The Gates of Doom* ('17), *The Hand at the Window* ('18), *The Divorce Trap* ('19), *Nomads of the North* ('20), *The Call of the North* ('21), *Trooper O'Neill* ('22), *Satan in Sables* ('25), *The Yankee Senor* ('25), *The Wreck* ('27), *The Legion of the Condemned* ('28), *Dangerous Paradise* ('30), *Morocco* ('30), *Honor of the Mounted* ('32), *The Devil Is Driving* ('32), *Terror Trail* ('33), *Voice in the Night* ('34), *Mississippi* ('35), *The Prisoner of Shark Island* ('36), *The Plainsman* ('36), *Robin Hood of El Dorado* ('36), *Parole Racket* ('37), *If I Were King* ('38), *Range War* ('39), *Union Pacific* ('39), *The Carson City Kid* ('40), *The Sea Hawk* ('40), *Green Hell* ('40), *Northwest Mounted Police* ('40), *The Sea Wolf* ('41), *The Kid from Kansas* ('41), *The Girl from Alaska* ('42), *The Kansan* ('43), *Buckskin Frontier* ('43), *Lumberjack* ('44), *Mystery Man* ('44), *South of the Rio Grande* ('45), *The Great Stagecoach Robbery* ('45), *The Catman of Paris* ('46), *Canyon Passage* ('46), *Tangier* 9'46), *My Pal Trigger* ('46), *The Devil's Playground* ('46), *Duel in the Sun* ('47), *The Perils of Pauline* ('47), *Panhandle* ('48), *The Paleface* ('48), *Daughter of the Jungle* ('49), *Samson and Delilah* ('49), *Rim of the Canyon* ('49), *California Passage* ('50), *Rancho Notorious* ('52), *Three Hours to Kill* ('54), *Ten Wanted Men* ('55), *The Ten Commandments* ('56), *The Saga of Hemp Brown* ('58) and *The Big Fisherman* ('59).

In the last two or three decades of his life he was mostly seen as men outside the law, and he played them with conviction. The front row kids hissed him and cheered when he got his comeuppance.

Francis was born in Bowling Green, Kentucky, on August 22, 1891. He died in 1968.

Serials

1917

Perils of the Secret Service. Univ., [9 Episodes] D: George Bronson Howard; LP: Kingsley Benedict, Jay Belasco, M. K. Wilson, Violet Schram.

The Voice on the Wire. Univ., [15 Chapters] D: Stuart Paton; SP: J. Grubb Alexander; S: Eustace Hale Ball; LP: Ben Wilson, Neva Gerber, Joseph W. Girard, Francis McDonald.

The Gray Ghost. Univ., [16 Chapters] D: Stuart Paton; LP: Harry Carter, Priscilla Dean, Emory Johnson, Eddie Polo, Francis McDonald.

1926

The Bar-C Mystery. Pathé, [10 Chapters] D: Robert F. Hill; LP: Wallace MacDonald, Dorothy Phillips, Ethel Clayton, Philo McCullough, Francis McDonald.

1934

Burn 'Em Up Barnes. Mascot, [12 Chapters] D: Colbert Clark, Armand Schaefer; LP: Jack Mulhall, Frankie Darro, Lola Lane, Julian Rivero, Edwin Maxwell, Jason Robards.

1937

Wild West Days. Univ., [13 Chapters] D: Ford Beebe, Cliff Smith; LP: Johnny Mack Brown, Lynn Gilbert, Robert Kortman, George Shelley, Frank Yaconelli.

1944

Zorro's Black Whip. Rep., [12 Chapters] D: Spencer Bennet, Wallace Grissell; SP: Basil Dickey, Jesse Duffy, Grant Nelson, Joseph Poland; AP: Ronald Davidson; Cam: Bud Thackery; Mus: Richard Cherwin; LP: Linda Stirling, George J. Lewis, Lucien Littlefield, Francis McDonald, Hal Taliaferro, John Merton.

Mystery of the River Boat. Univ., [13 Chapters] D: Ray Taylor, Lewis D. Collins; LP: Robert Lowery, Eddie Quillan, Marion Martin, Marjorie Clements, Lyle Talbot.

KENNETH MACDONALD

Kenneth MacDonald, the suave crook with the black mustache, was born Kenneth Dollins on September 8, 1901. He was a child actor at eight on the legitimate stage. His first film was *Slow as Lightning* ('23). His last silent was *Little Buckaroo* with Buzz Barton. In 1931 he had a small role in Jack Holt's *Dirigible.* Much of his work (including all of his serials) was at Columbia, where he menaced Charles Starrett and Bill Elliott. As a top heavy, he could be likened to Harry Woods— both men real pros who made their characters believable.

Mac always wanted to be a director but never attained that goal. According to another veteran heavy, Pierce Lyden, MacDonald refused to do fights or stunts, saying, "Make them double you. They'll have respect for you then as an actor." Pierce said Mac always carried a VIP attache case. "It attracts attention. People ask questions. They notice you."

Serial addicts can be thankful for his work in the nine serials he made, for they were more enjoyable for his having been in them. Likewise, too, the many Westerns and

"B" programmers in which he threatened our heroes.

Kenneth MacDonald died on May 5, 1972. His last film was *40 Guns to Apache Pass* ('67) with Audie Murphy.

Serials

1939

Overland with Kit Carson. Col., [15 Chapters] D: Sam Nelson, Norman Deming; LP: Bill Elliott, Iris Meredith, Trevor Bardette, Richard Fiske, Kenneth MacDonald, Bobby Clark, LeRoy Mason, James Craig, Hal Taliaferro, Dick Curtis.

Mandrake the Magician. Col., [12 Chapters] D: Sam Nelson, Norman Deming; LP: Warren Hull, Doris Weston, Al Kikume, Rex Downing, Kenneth MacDonald.

1942

The Valley of Vanishing Men. Col., [15 Chapters] D: Spencer G. Bennet; LP: Bill Elliott, Slim Summerville, Carmen Morales, Kenneth MacDonald, Jack Ingram, George Chesebro, Tom London.

Perils of the Royal Mounted. Col., [15 Chapters] D: James W. Horne; LP: Nell O'Day, Robert Stevens [Kellard], Herbert Rawlinson, Kenneth MacDonald.

1943

The Phantom. Col., [15 Chapters] D: B. Reeves Eason; LP: Tom Tyler, Jeanne Bates, Kenneth MacDonald, Frank Shannon, Ace (dog), Guy Kingsford, Ernie Adams.

1944

Black Arrow. Col., [15 Chapters] D: Lew Landers; LP: Robert Scott, Adele Jergens, Kenneth MacDonald, Robert Williams, Charles Middleton, George J. Lewis.

The Desert Hawk. Col., [15 Chapters] D: B. Reeves Eason; LP: Gilbert Roland, Mona Maris, Kenneth MacDonald, Ben Welden, Frank Lackteen, I. Stanford Jolley, Charles Middleton, Kermit Maynard, Norman Willis, Reed Howes.

1945

The Monster and the Ape. Col., [15 Chapters] D: Howard Bretherton; LP: Robert Lowery, George Macready, Ralph Morgan, Carole Mathews, Willie Best, Jack Ingram, Kenneth MacDonald, Charles King, John Elliott, Bud Osborne.

1956

Perils of the Wilderness. Col., [15 Chapters] D: Spencer G. Bennet; LP: Dennis Moore, Richard Emory, Eve Anderson [Evelyn Finley], Kenneth MacDonald.

WALLACE MACDONALD

Wallace MacDonald made many pictures in the years 1914 to 1932 but is hardly remembered today as an actor. As a director-producer he is more recognizable. He became a writer for Mascot/Republic in the early '30s and in 1937 turned director-producer of low budget "B" films at Columbia, where he brought to the screen such "B" gems as *Criminals of the Air* ('37), *When G-Men Step In* ('38), *Before I Hang* ('40), *I Was a Prisoner on Devil's Island* ('40), *Parachute Nurse* ('42), *The Redhead from Manhattan* ('43), *The Missing Juror* ('44), *The Devil's Mask* ('46), *When a Girl's Beautiful* ('47), *Port Said* ('48), *Flame of Stamboul* ('51), *El Alamein* ('53), *The Black Dakotas* ('54), *Wyoming Renegades* ('55), *Fury at Gunsight Pass* ('56), *The White Squaw* ('56), *The Phan-*

tom *Stagecoach* ('57), *The Hard Man* ('57), *Return to Warbow* ('58), *Gunman from Laredo* ('58) and more. In all, he produced close to 75 "B" films.

The story is that while a writer at Mascot (forerunner of Republic) he was under anesthesia in a dentist's chair and dreamed up the idea for a science-fiction film, which became Gene Autry's *The Phantom Empire* ('35). Thank goodness he had a toothache.

MacDonald was born in Mulgrave, Nova Scotia, Canada, on May 5, 1891. His father was a postal inspector for the Maritime Provinces and his uncle was a judge of the Supreme Court. A brother was a barrister in Halifax. He began his career on the stage in Vancouver playing the part of Baco White in *The Squaw Man*. While thus employed, he learned the Ute language from an Indian in the company.

His first film work was with Mack Sennett in 1914, in the comedies of Charles Chaplin and Mabel Normand. He appeared in *Tillie's Punctured Romance* ('14) starring Marie Dressler and Chaplin, but one would have to look close to spot him. (He became a film actor because he'd gone broke after opening two Los Angeles theaters with a partner.) His parts grew in size. In 1916, during World War I, he took time out from acting to join the British Army. But he was back in Hollywood in 1918 to resume his career. He built a following appearing in such outstanding films as *The Fighting Shepherdess* ('20), *Maytime* ('23), *The Spoilers* ('23), *The Sea Hawk* ('24), *The Primrose Path* ('25) and *Hell's Four Hundred* ('26).

Wallace made his first serial, *Breaking Through*, in 1921. A young engineer helps a young and pretty girl build a railroad track from a mine in the interior of Alaska to the coast, which she must do to retain title to her property. Members of a gang who wish her to lose this property disrupt the track laying every way they can.

His second serial, *Fighting with Buffalo Bill*, ('26) was made five years later. A crooked lawyer intends to confiscate a gold mine belonging to Doris' (Elsa Benham) father, whom she believes to be dead. Ned

Wheeler (MacDonald) competes with Bart Crosby (Curler Supples), the lawyer's son, for Doris' affections. Doris loves Ned and, with the help of Buffalo Bill (Edmund Cobb), the two manage to uncover the lawyer's plot, thwart it and bring about a reunion with Doris' father.

Pathé starred MacDonald in *The Bar-C Mystery* that same year. A New York girl (Dorothy Phillips) inherits a ranch in the West from a man she does not know. It seems that her benefactor, Nevada (MacDonald), has disappeared into the desert and is presumed dead. When she arrives, a crooked gambler and a dance hall owner try to get control of the ranch because they know there are gold deposits and other minerals on the land. A stranger comes to her rescue and the Bar-C mystery is solved.

MacDonald's fourth and last serial, Universal's *Whispering Smith Rides* ('27), is the story of a western railroad detective's adventures in defending a young woman (Rose Blossom) whose illegal guardian is trying to cheat her and to stop railroad construction. It was remade in 1931 as *The Lightning Express*.

MacDonald was a popular player in his day but after 1927 his career was in decline. He became more involved in writing. In the early '30s he supported Tim McCoy, Ken Maynard, Buck Jones and Johnny Mack Brown in some of their films, typically playing the villain. He also wrote some of the stories. His last acting assignment was in Columbia's *King of the Wild Horses* ('32).

Serials

1921

Breaking Through. Vit., [15 Chapters] D: Robert Ensminger; S/SP: C. Graham Baker; LP: Carmel Myers, Wallace MacDonald, Vincent Howard, Walter Rodgers.

1926

The Bar-C Mystery. Pathé, [10 Chapters] D: Robert F. Hill; SP: William Sherwood; S: Raymond Spears; LP: Wallace MacDonald, Dorothy Phillips, Ethel Clayton, Philo McCullough.

Fighting with Buffalo Bill. Univ., [10 Chapters] D: Ray Taylor; S: William F. Code; LP: Wallace MacDonald, Elsa Benham, Edmund Cobb, Robert E. Homan, Grace Cunard.

1927

Whispering Smith Rides. Univ., [10 Chapters] D: Ray Taylor; SP: Arthur Henry Gooden; S: Frank Hamilton Spearman; LP: Wallace MacDonald, Rose Blossom, J. P. McGowan, Clark Comstock, Willie Fung.

DON MCGUIRE

Screenwriter-director-actor Don McGuire was born on February 28, 1919, in Chicago. A former journalist and press agent, he entered films in 1945 as an actor. He turned screenwriter in 1950 and was a hit-and-run director in the mid–50s. He won a Screenwriter Guild award for his original screenplay which became *Bad Day at Black Rock* ('55); conceived and co-wrote the story that eventually became *Tootsie*; wrote stand-up comedy for Martin and Lewis, Tommy Farrell and others; and wrote and directed *Hennessy* with Jackie Cooper.

As an actor, McGuire appeared in *San Antonio* ('45), *Pride of the Marines* ('46), *Humoresque* ('46), *The Man I Love* ('47), *Possessed* ('47), *Nora Prentiss* ('47), *Whiplash* ('48), *The Fuller Brush Man* ('48), *The Threat* ('49), *Armored Car Robbery* ('50), *Double Dynamite* ('51) and others.

As a screenwriter he penned *Dial 1119* ('50), *Meet Danny Wilson* ('52), *Walking My Baby Back Home* ('53), *Three Ring Circus* ('54) and *Suppose They Gave a War and Nobody Came* ('70).

McGuire played the title role in Columbia's 1948 serial *Congo Bill*. The story re-volves around a circus manager who administers a $500,000 trust fund and tries to keep Congo Bill from finding Ruth Culver, who disappeared as a baby in the African jungles. If she returns within a year, he must relinquish the money and the circus. A letter is given to Congo Bill with instructions to find Ruth and inform her of her inheritance. Rumors persist of a young white queen, Lureena, in the heart of Africa, and Bill leads an expedition to find out if it might be Ruth.

McGuire died April 13, 2000, in Los Angeles of complication from a brief (unspecified) illness.

Serial

1948

Congo Bill. Col., [15 Chapters] D: Spencer G. Bennet, Thomas Carr; P: Sam Katzman; SP: George H. Plympton, Arthur Hoerl, Lewis Clay; Cam: Ira H. Morgan; Mus: Mischa Bakaleinikoff; LP: Don McGuire, Cleo Moore, Armida Jack Ingram, Leonard Penn, I. Stanford Jolley, Charles King, Hugh Prosser.

KATHRYN MCGUIRE

Kathryn was born in Peoria, Illinois, in 1897 and died in 1978. A dancer for several years, she broke into movies as a comedienne, becoming the leading lady to Buster Keaton, Lupino Lane and other silent screen comedians. Her films include *Bucking the Line, The Silent Call, The Shrick of Araby, Flame of Life, Sherlock Jr., The Navigator, The Girl in the Pullman, Lilac Time, The Big Diamond Robbery, Children of the Ritz, The Long Long Trail* and *The Lost Zeppelin*.

She played opposite Rex Lease in the serial *Mystery Pilot* ('26); no prints exist. Hopefully someday a print will be found that can be transferred to tape for the benefit and enjoyment of video serial collectors.

Serial

1926

Mystery Pilot. Rayart, [10 Chapters] D: Harry Moody; LP: Rex Lease, Kathryn McGuire Jack McReedy, Max Asher, Barney Furey.

WANDA MCKAY

Wanda McKay had one of the loveliest figures and faces to be seen in Hollywood in the 1940s and poured a lot of talent into her roles. Film reviewers were nearly always complimentary to her even though they might find fault, and usually did, with the low-budget films in which she appeared. Miss McKay's pulchritude wasn't always enough to raise the sluggish affairs in which she acted, but she was capable of weakening the knees of the West's male population and of a theater's male population.

Wanda was born Dorothy Ellen Quackenbush on June 22, 1923, in Fort Worth, Texas. She attended Fort Worth schools for the first few years of her life and completed high school in Kansas City, Missouri, after her family moved there. After leaving school, Wanda, an extremely beautiful girl with golden brown hair, blue eyes and a captivating smile, modeled and posed for magazine covers. In 1939 she won the title of "Miss American Aviation" in Birmingham, Alabama, in competition with 150 other girls. Jacqueline Cochran, noted woman flyer, suggested that Wanda try for a motion picture career. Taking this advice, Wanda went to New York, obtained an agent and within a few months was signed to a Paramount contract.

After six months of posing for publicity art and playing small parts, McKay decided to do some intensive training for the screen. She enrolled in the Reinhardt Theater in Hollywood where she worked for two years. Next she was associated with the Phoenix Theater in Westwood. Finally she signed a contract with Monogram in 1942. In 1950 she began to do television work and appeared in a number of series, including *The Cisco Kid, The Lone Ranger* and *The Range Rider*.

She made Westerns with Charles Starrett, Russell Hayden, Lee Powell, Art Davis, George Houston, Tex Ritter, Buster Crabbe and William Boyd and appeared in many B horror films—*The Monster Maker, Bowery at Midnight, The Mad Doctor, The Black Raven* and *Voodoo Man.* Her last film was *Roaring City* ('51).

After a 15-year courtship, she was married to songwriter Hoagy Carmichael from 1977 until his death in 1981. Wanda died April 11, 2002, in Los Angeles of cancer.

Serial

1944

Raiders of Ghost City. Univ., [13 Chapters] D: Ray Taylor, Lewis Collins; SP: Luci Ward, Morgan Cox; P: Ray Taylor, Morgan Cox; LP: Dennis Moore, Wanda McKay, Lionel Atwill, Joe Sawyer, Regis Toomey, Eddy Waller.

LAFE MCKEE

Lafayette Stocking McKee, the "grand old man of Westerns," was born in Morrison, Illinois, in January 1872. He stood 5'10" and had blue eyes and white hair. He was married and had a daughter, Lucille, and two sons, Joe and Dick. His chief hobby was fishing.

While still a young man, Lafe joined a traveling vaudeville troupe and eventually became a stock stage actor. In 1912, when motion pictures were still in their infancy, McKee wandered into Hollywood and joined the Selig Polyscope Company as a bit player. The very next year he began his career as a screen father by playing the part in *The Adventures of Kathlyn* ('13), a 13-chapter serial with star Kathlyn Williams as his daughter.

Lafe was a fine actor who, although virtually unknown to the average movie patron or critic, nevertheless conjures up floods of delighted reminiscences from Western enthusiasts. A genuine trouper, he successfully played the field from grizzled military officers to seedy, degenerate barflies.

In the 1920s, McKee was a staple in Western movies, playing a crooked stage coach operator in *Western Grit* ('24) with Lester Cuneo, a Mexican don in *Triple Action* ('25) with Pete Morrison, a millionaire gold miner in *The Bonanza Buckaroo* ('26) with Buffalo Bill, Jr. and a horse breeder in *The Upland Rider* ('28) with Ken Maynard. He appeared in over 100 silent films and nearly 200 talkies, with 43 film credits in 1935 alone.

McKee's versatility helped him stay busy. One of the highlights of his acting career was his role as Col. Burke, commanding officer of Fort Rainee in *End of the Trail* ('32), Tim McCoy's premier Columbia Western. He played the part with the dignity and strength of a West Point graduate. Another notable performance was as the drunk prospector in *Gold* ('32), a Jack Hoxie feature for Majestic Pictures. In 1941, McKee played his final role in the Frank Capra classic *Meet John Doe,* starring Gary Cooper and Barbara Stanwyck. He was convincing as an old man down on his luck.

Lafe McKee retired from acting in 1941 and died in Temple City, California, on August 10, 1959 at the age of 87. He played supporting roles in 32 serials. In the list of serials that follow, only the company, year and stars will be indicated.

Serials

1913

The Adventures of Kathlyn. Selig, (Kathlyn Williams).

1918

The Price of Folly. Pathé, (Ruth Roland).

1922

The Jungle Goddess. Export-Import, (Elinor Field).

1924

Battling Brewster. Rayart, (Franklyn Farnum).

1926

The Mystery Box. Davis, (Ben Wilson, Neva Gerber).

The Power God. Davis, (Ben Wilson, Neva Gerber).

Officer 444. Davis, (Ben Wilson, Neva Gerber).

1928

Vultures of the Sea. Mascot, (Johnnie Walker).

1929

King of the Kongo. Mascot, (Walter Miller, Jacqueline Logan).

1930

King of the Wild. Mascot, (Walter Miller, Nora Lane).

The Indians Are Coming. Univ., (Tim McCoy, Allene Ray).

The Lone Defender. Mascot, (Rin-Tin-Tin, Walter).

1931

The Vanishing Legion. Mascot, (Harry Carey, Edwina Booth).

The Lightning Warrior. Mascot, (Rin-Tin-Tin, Frankie Darro).

1932

Heroes of the West. Univ., (Noah Beery, Jr., Diane Duval [Julie Bishop]).

1933

The Wolf Dog. Mascot, (Frankie Darro, Rin-Tin-Tin, Jr.).

The Whispering Shadow. Mascot, (Bela Lugosi).

Mystery Squadron. Mascot, (Bob Steele, Guinn Williams).

Fighting with Kit Carson. Mascot, (Johnny Mack Brown, Betsy King Ross).

1934

Mystery Mountain. Mascot, (Ken Maynard, Verna Hillie).

The Law of the Wild. Mascot, (Bob Custer, Lucile Browne).

1935

Queen of the Jungle. Screen Attractions, (Reed Howes, Mary Kornman).

The Roaring West. Univ., (Buck Jones, Muriel Evans).

Rustlers of Red Dog. Univ., (Johnny Mack Brown, Joyce Compton).

The Miracle Rider. Mascot, (Tom Mix, Joan Gale).

1936

The Phantom Rider. Univ., (Buck Jones, Maria Shelton).

Custer's Last Stand. Screen & Stage, (Rex Lease, William Farnum).

1937

Wild West Days. Univ., (Johnny Mack Brown, Lynn Gilbert).

The Painted Stallion. Rep., (Ray Corrigan, Hoot Gibson).

1938

The Lone Ranger. Rep., (Robert Livingston, Chief Thundercloud).

1939

The Oregon Trail. Univ., (Johnny Mack Brown, Louise Stanley).

The Lone Ranger Rides Again. Rep., (Robert Livingston, Chief Thundercloud).

SAMMY MCKIM

Young Sammy McKim played in four serials—*The Painted Stallion* ('37), *The Lone Ranger* ('38), *The Great Adventures of Wild Bill Hickok* ('38) and *Dick Tracy's G-Men* ('39). He seems to be best remembered for his role of young Kit Carson in *The Painted Stallion*.

Sammy was born John Samuel McKim on December 20, 1924, in North Vancouver, B.C., Canada. There was an early move to Seattle, Washington, and then on to Los Angeles in the summer of 1935. It was the Depression and the McKims all pitched in to keep food on the table. Sammy, his two brothers and two sisters all became kid actors.

When he was put under contract by Republic, Sammy was paid $50 a week. His first Western was *Hit the Saddle* ('37) with Ray Corrigan, Robert Livingston and Max Terhune.

Sammy graduated from Hollywood High School and then attended art school. He went into the Army as an 18-year-old private in April 1943. He remained in the reserves after the war; when the Korean War broke out, he was commissioned a First Lieutenant in Infantry and was with the First Cavalry Division. He saw battle duty and received the Distinguished Service Cross for action against the enemy on February 12, 1951.

Upon his discharge in 1952, Sammy went to work as an illustrator at 20th Century-Fox, but in December 1954 he became employed as a sketch artist and illustrator at Disney, spending over 30 years with that studio.

Several months after an April 1982 heart attack, Sammy had open-heart surgery. He and his wife Dorothy have two grown sons.

Sammy's Westerns include *Gunsmoke Ranch* ('37), *Heart of the Rockies* ('37), *The Old Wyoming Trail* ('37), *The Trigger Trio* ('37), *Call the Mesquiteers* ('38), *Red River Range* ('38), *New Frontier* ('39), *The Night Riders* ('39), *Rovin' Tumbleweeds* ('39), *The Old Barn Dance* ('38), *Western Caravans* ('39), *Rocky Mountain Rangers* ('40) and *Texas Terrors* ('40).

Among his non–Westerns are *It Happened in Hollywood* ('37), *The Crowd Roars* ('38), *Mr. Smith Goes to Washington* ('39), *Laddie* ('40), *Little Men* ('40), *Men of Boys' Town* ('40), *Pacific Blackout* ('41), *Sergeant York* ('41), *Undercover Maisie* ('47), *Flamingo Road* ('49), *Lonely Hearts Bandits* ('50) and more.

Serials

1937

The Painted Stallion. Rep., [12 Chapters] D: William Witney, Ray Taylor; SP: Barry Shipman, Winston Miller; Cam: William Nobles, Edgar Lyons; Mus: Raoul Kraushaar; LP: Ray Corrigan, Hoot Gibson, Hal Taliaferro, Jack Perrin, Duncan Renaldo, Sammy McKim, LeRoy Mason, Charles King.

1938

The Lone Ranger. Rep., [15 Chapters] D: William Witney, John English; SP: Barry Shipman *et al.*; AP: Sol C. Siegel; Cam: William Nobles; Mus: Alberto Colombo; LP: Lee Powell, Chief Thundercloud, Lynne Roberts, Hal Taliaferro, Herman Brix, George Letz [George Montgomery], Sammy McKim, George Cleveland, John Merton, Stanley Andrews.

The Great Adventures of Wild Bill Hickok. Col., [15 Chapters] D: Mack V. Wright, Sam Nelson; AP: Harry Webb; SP: George Rosener, Charles A. Powell, G. A. Durlan, Dallas Fitzgerald, Tom Gibson; P: Jack Fier; Cam: George Meehan, Benjamin Kline; Mus: Abe

Meyer; LP: Gordon (Bill) Elliott, Carole Wayne, Frankie Darro, Monte Blue, Dickie Jones, Sammy McKim, Kermit Maynard, Reed Hadley, Chief Thundercloud, Alan Bridges, Hal Taliaferro.

1939

Dick Tracy's G-Men. Rep., [15 Chapters] D:

William Witney, John English; SP: Barry Shipman, Franklyn Adreon, Rex Taylor, Ronald Davidson, Sol Shor; Cam: William Nobles; Mus: William Lava; LP: Ralph Byrd, Irving Pichel, Phylis Isley [Jennifer Jones], Ted Pearson, Walter Miller, Jack Ingram, Reed Howes, Edmund Cobb, Sammy McKim, Charles Hutchison.

CLEO MADISON

Cleo Madison was born in Bloomington, Illinois, but soon moved to California. Little is known of her personal life even though she was a popular actress in the World War I era. Around 1910 she presented herself at the stage door of a Santa Barbara theater. She secured work with the company rehearsing for a tour. By the time the company was ready for the road, Cleo had advanced so rapidly that she was given the leading role. Before long she was manager. She continued upon the stage for several years. Ultimately, a company was organized to star her and she played the big vaudeville circuits in such well-known successes as "The Bishop's Carriage," "Paid in Full," "The Great Divide" and "Wildfire."

Back home in 1913 for a vacation, she found a growing art, right in her line, just outside her door. Motion pictures had begun to make quite a noise — in a silent sort of way. Cleo went out to the Universal lot and easily obtained work because of her stage experience. Her first film of record was *His Pal's Request* ('13), believed to be a one-reeler. The Universal serial *The Trey O' Hearts* ('14) starred Cleo and went over big, and she found herself much in demand thereafter. *The Trey O' Hearts* had the usual quota of hair-raising thrills crammed into its 15 chapters, but its real claim to uniqueness was that Cleo played a double role — that of twin sisters, one good, one bad. She measured up to

the challenge admirably. The serial was designed primarily as adult entertainment, not as Saturday matinee fare for the kiddies.

Her next serial assignment was a supporting role in *The Master Key* ('14) with Ella Hall and Robert Leonard. Considered one of Universal's finest serials, the story concerns a rich lode of ore that can only be found by following the directions hidden in an Oriental vase lying at the bottom of the sea in a sunken ship.

The serial *The Great Radium Mystery* ('19) made its chief pitch for acceptance on the basis of Cleo's name, which by then carried some weight with theater audiences. The action content of the 18 chapters is reflected in such episode titles as "The Death Trap," "The Fatal Ride," "The Torture Chamber," "The Tunnel of Doom," "In the Clutches of the Mad Man" and "The Scalding Pit."

Cleo quickly won a place of distinction as an emotional actress, scoring success after success. She had become a triple threat in 1915, turning her talents to directing and producing in addition to acting. Cleo could handle Westerns as well as anything else. In *Dolores, Lady of Sorrows* ('14) she plays a Mexican girl who thwarts the villain's nefarious schemes. *Sealed Orders* ('14) finds her as a nice girl lured to a Western bordello. The film is replete with roof-top chases *a la* Ken Maynard and a fierce gun-fighting episode as Cleo's honor is protected.

Tearjerker melodramas seemed especially suited to Cleo, and she handled them effectively. *To Another Woman* ('16), *The Girl Who Lost* ('17) and *When the Wolf Howls* ('16) were all designed to bring handkerchiefs to the ladies' eyes. Such films were popular in the World War I era, and Cleo worked steadily.

Constant effort brought on a nervous breakdown, which forced her to retire to private life for over a year. But with her health restored, and still possessing the talent and personality which made her a distinctive favorite for so many years, she came back to make several films in 1923 and '24, including *Gold Madness* ('23), an adaptation of the James Oliver Curwood story "The Man from Ten Stroke." Cleo left the screen in 1924. Why, or what she did thereafter, is unknown to the author.

On March 11, 1964, at the age of 81, Cleo suffered a fatal heart attack in Burbank, California, leaving a sister, her closest surviving relative.

The Master Key. Univ., [15 Chapters] D: Robert Leonard; SP: Calder Johnson; LP: Robert Leonard, Ella Hall, Harry Carter, Jean Hathaway, Wilbur Higby, Cleo Madison, Jack Holt, Jim Corey.

Serials

1914

The Trey O' Hearts. Univ., [15 Chapters] D: Wilfred Lucas, Henry MacRae; SP: Bess Meredyth; S: Louis Joseph Vance; LP: Cleo Madison, George Larkin, Edward Sloman, Tom Walsh, Charles Brinley, Doris Pawn, Roy Hanford.

1919

The Great Radium Mystery. Univ., [18 Chapters] D: Robert Broadwell, Robert F. Hill; SP: Frederick Bennett; LP: Cleo Madison, Eileen Sedgwick, Bob Reeves, Edwin J. Brady, Robert Kortman, Jeff Osborne, Gordon McGregor.

JOCK MAHONEY

Jock Mahoney was born Jacques O'Mahoney in Chicago on February 7, 1919, of French and Irish parents. Whether he was billed as Jacques, Jock O, Jack, Joko or Jock, he was a sight to behold performing stunts.

He grew up in Davenport, Iowa, and attended the University of Iowa in its premedicine curriculum. He excelled in swimming, basketball, football and boxing while still keeping up his grades. But the country was caught up in World War II, and he withdrew from the university at the end of his second year and joined the Marines, where he became a fighter pilot and swimming instructor.

At the close of the war, Jock headed for California with the thought that he might get a chance to act; if not, he toyed with the idea of breeding horses for the movies. Instead, he stumbled into a job as stuntman. He found that he was good at it and was soon doubling Errol Flynn and other big stars. His reputation grew. At Columbia he doubled Charles Starrett time and time again in the Durango Kid series. Since the Durango Kid wore a bandanna to hide his face, it was easy for Mahoney to take on the same disguise and do the fights and chases with only the most assiduous viewers noticing the substitution.

By 1946, Mahoney was among the most active stuntmen in Hollywood. Starrett gave him a chance to act in *Fighting Frontiersman* ('46), and in a span of four years he progressed from bit parts to supporting role status. By the end of the series, he was playing the secondary lead.

By the 1950s, Jock shared with Dave Sharpe the reputation as the best stuntmen around. Mahoney was an incredible leaper

and jumper and his services were constantly in demand.

Columbia gave Mahoney the lead in its serial *Cody of the Pony Express* ('50). He is an undercover investigator assigned to bring to justice a band of outlaws secretly headed by attorney Mort Black (George J. Lewis). He is aided by young Bill Cody (Dickie Moore). The outlaws are the minions of an Eastern syndicate that wants to control the territory by acquiring all of its transportation facilities. *Roar of the Iron Horse* ('51) followed with Jock assigned to find out who is sabotaging work on the transcontinental railroad. And in 1954 he co-starred with Clayton Moore in *Gunfighters of the Northwest*. A mysterious villain called "The Leader" is trying to locate a lost gold mine in Indian Territory. He pits the Indians against the Mounties by creating trouble for the Indians and blaming the Mounties. All three serials were made fast and cheap, as the serial genre was on its last legs.

Gene Autry hired Jock to portray *The Range Rider*, which premiered on CBS in the fall of 1952; after its network run of 78 (1952–54) half-hour episodes, it ran in syndication for years. Mahoney went on to star in another weekly TV series titled *Yancy Derringer* ('58) in which he portrayed a roguish riverboat gambler.

In 1960, Jock played the heavy opposite Gordon Scott in Paramount's *Tarzan the Magnificent* and two years later he portrayed the famous jungle king himself in *Tarzan Goes to India* ('62) and *Tarzan's Three Challenges* ('63). These were Jock's favorite roles. While filming in the tropics of Thailand he contracted dengue, pneumonia and amoebic dysentery. It was many months before he could go back to work.

Jock appeared in 50 or more feature films and about 150 television shows (*Kung Fu, Rawhide, The Loretta Young Show, Laramie, Gunslinger*, etc.). In 1975 he suffered a stroke from which he recovered. In 1986 he was honored with a Golden Boot Award for a lifetime of contributions to Western films.

Mahoney died in Bremerton, Washington, on December 14, 1989, from an apparent stroke. He was survived by his wife, a daughter and a son.

Serials

1950

Cody of the Pony Express. Col., [15 Chapters] D: Spencer G. Bennet; P: Sam Katzman; S: George H. Plympton, Joseph F. Poland; SP: David Mathews, Lewis Clay, Charles R. Condon; Cam: Ira H. Morgan; Mus: Mischa Bakaleinikoff; LP: Jock Mahoney, Dickie Moore, Peggy Stewart, William Fawcett, Tom London.

1951

Roar of the Iron Horse. Col., [15 Chapters] D: Spencer G. Bennet, Thomas Carr; SP: George H. Plympton, Sherman Lowe, Royal Cole; P: Sam Katzman; Cam: Fayte Browne; Mus: Mischa Bakaleinikoff; LP: Jock Mahoney, Virginia Herrick, William Fawcett, Hal Landon, Jack Ingram, George Eldredge, Bud Osborne.

Gunfighters of the Northwest. Col., 1953 [15 Chapters] D: Spencer G. Bennet, Charles S. Gould; SP: George H. Plympton, Royal Cole, Arthur Hoel; P: Sam Katzman; Mus: Mischa Bakaleinikoff; Cam: William Whitley; LP: Jock Mahoney, Clayton Moore, Phyllis Coates, Don Harvey, Marshall Reed, Rodd Redwing, Lyle Talbot.

RAY MALA

Ray Mala was born Ray Wise near Candle, Alaska, in 1906. The son of an American trader and his Eskimo wife, he made his living as a hunter and fisherman before enter-

Herman Brix and Ray Mala (right) in *Hawk of the Wilderness* (Republic, 1938).

ing films in 1932. With a rugged physique, he was popular for a decade after starring in 1932's *Igloo* and 1933's *Eskimo*. He had exotic supporting roles in many others. His films include *Last of the Pugans* ('36), *The Jungle Princess* ('36), *Mutiny on the Blackhawk* ('39), *Union Pacific* ('39), *Zanzibar* ('40), *Green Hell* ('40), *North West Mounted Police* ('40), *Girl from God's Country* ('40), *The Devil's Pipeline* ('40), *Hold Back the Dawn* ('41), *Honolulu* ('41), *Girl from Alaska* ('42), *The Mad Doctor of Market Street* ('42), *Son of Fury* ('42), *The Tuttles of Tahiti* ('42) and *Red Snow* ('52).

Republic starred Mala in the serial *Robinson Crusoe of Clipper Island* ('36) at a time when the country was in an economic depression. The serial was good escapist entertainment. Mala is assigned by the management of a corporation to investigate the burning of fuel storage tanks on Clipper Island and the sabotaging of the airship *San Francisco* over the island on its maiden voyage to Australia. A mysterious spy group headed by the unidentified "H.K." has caused both the fire and sabotage. They do not want a refueling station on the island because of a secret fortress and submarine base located there. Princess Melani (Mamo Clark) and two animal friends, Rex, a horse, and Buck, a dog, aid Mala in besting the saboteurs and their human allies.

Republic's *Hawk of the Wilderness* ('38) featured Herman Brix as Kioga and Mala as Kias in a Tarzan-like story. Kioga, infant survivor of a shipwreck, grows to manhood on an unknown Pacific island populated by a lost tribe. When an expedition arrives looking for survivors, it brings evil men as well as good. When it is discovered that rare gems abound on the island, the crooks show their colors. Kioga must use all of his cunning and strength to save his friends, thwart the badmen and appease the superstitious tribespeople.

In *The Great Adventures of Wild Bill Hickok* ('38), Mala has a supporting role as Little Elk in the serial considered by most buffs to be the best of Columbia's chapterplays. Both the budget and production val-

ues were above par for Columbia. Its popularity led to a name change for Gordon Elliott (to Bill Elliott) and his becoming a major Western star.

In Mala's last serial appearance, he played the king's son in *Flash Gordon Conquers the Universe* ('40). The valiant Flash Gordon, Dale Arden and Dr. Zarkov are off again on another adventure against their old foe, Ming the Merciless.

Ray Mala died from a heart attack in Hollywood in 1952. He was 46 years of age.

Serials

1936

Robinson Crusoe of Clipper Island. Rep., [14 Chapters] D: Mack V. Wright, Ray Taylor; S/SP: Morgan Cox, Barry Shipman, Maurice Geraghty; P: Nat Levine; Cam: William Nobles; Mus: Harry Grey; LP: Ray Mala, Rex, Buck, Mamo Clark, John Picorri, John Dilson, George Chesebro.

1938

Hawk of the Wilderness. Rep., [12 Chapters] D: William Witney, John English; S: William L. Chester, Barry Shipman, Ray Taylor, Norman Hall; AP: Robert Beche; Cam: William Nobles; Mus: William Lava; LP: Herman Brix, Ray Mala, Monte Blue, Jill Martin, Noble Johnson, Tom Chatterton, William Royle.

The Great Adventures of Wild Bill Hickok. Col., [15 Chapters] D: Mack V. Wright, Sam Nelson; SP: George Rosener, Charles A. Powell, G. A. Durlan, Dallas Fitzgerald, Tom Gibson; Cam: George Meehan, Benjamin Kline; Mus: Abe Meyer; LP:

1940

Flash Gordon Conquers the Universe. Univ., [12 Chapters] D: Ford Beebe, Ray Taylor; SP: George H. Plympton, Basil dickey, Barry Shipman; P: Henry MacRae; Cam: Jerry Ash; LP: Buster Crabbe, Carol Hughes, Charles Middleton, Anne Gwynne, Frank Shannon, Roland Drew, Shirley Deane, Lee Powell, Ray Mala.

BOOTS MALLORY

Patricia Mallory was born in October 1913. At age 12 she was a banjo player in a girls' band and at 16 a vaudeville dancer. She appeared in Broadway musicals before making her screen debut in 1932. In the following few years she played ingenue leads in a number of minor films. Her second husband was producer William Cagney; her third, actor Herbert Marshall.

In *The Wolf Dog* ('33) she is the friend of Bob Whitlock, who invents an electric ray that can destroy ships at a distance of several miles. Norman Bryan, (Hale Hamilton), general manager of the Courtney Steamship Lines, plans to steal it. Bob becomes friends with a young boy, Frank (Frankie Darro), and his dog (Rin-Tin-Tin, Jr). All three are involved in a desperate struggle to protect the invention until it can be turned over to the government. Mallory is Irene Courtney, who gives solace to the trio of fighters.

Western fans will remember her as the ingenue in *Powdersmoke Range* ('36), the all-star film with a cast headed by Harry Carey, Hoot Gibson, Bob Steele, Tom Tyler and "Big Boy" Williams. It was the first Three Mesquiteers Western.

Her other films include *Handle with Care*, *Humanity*, *Hello Sister!*, *Sing Sing Nights* and *Here's Flash Casey*.

Boots died in Santa Monica, California, at age 45 in 1958.

Serial

1933

The Wolf Dog. Mascot, [12 Chapters] D: Colbert Clark, Harry Fraser; SP: Al Martin, Colbert Clark, Wyndham Gittens; S: Barney Sarecky, Sherman Lowe; P: Nat Levine; Cam: Harry Neumann, William Nobles, Tom Galligan; LP: Frankie Darro, Boots Mallory, George J. Lewis, Fred Kohler, Hale Hamilton, Henry B. Walthall, Sara Padden, Tom London, Rin-Tin-Tin, Jr.

MOLLY MALONE

Molly Malone was many a boy's first experience with unrequited love. She was born in Denver, Colorado, on February 2, 1897, the daughter of a mining engineer. Her education was received in California and South Africa, and she spent a year or more in Mexico with her father when he was working there. She entered movies in 1916 via an introduction by a friend to Cecil B. DeMille.

Her earliest credits are not known but by mid–1917 she was appearing opposite Harry Carey in Universal Westerns. Molly was remarkably tiny, just over five feet tall and proportionately slight. She was undoubtedly pretty, with dark brown hair, deep brown eyes and an expressive face. She took direction well and was one of the first actresses with whom director John Ford worked.

Under Ford's direction and with Harry Carey as star, she made *Straight Shooting* ('176), *A Marked Man* ('17), *Bucking Broadway* ('17), *The Phantom Riders* ('18), *Wild*

Women ('18), *Thieves' Gold* ('18), *The Scarlet Drop* ('18) and *A Woman's Fool* ('18). Both Ford and Carey liked the soft-spoken actress, and all the cowboys on the lot spoke of her tenderly as "Little Molly" and towered protectively over her.

Molly married Forrest Cornett, a minister's son, in 1917. She was 20 and he was 21. It is believed that the marriage was soon dissolved, for Molly listed no husband in her biographical data sheet when going to work for Goldwyn in 1920.

After appearing in a principal role in the Universal serial *Lure of the Circus* ('18), Molly made a series of comedies with Fatty Arbuckle at Paramount. Then she signed with Goldwyn as a stock player.

She had the lead in *It's a Great Life* ('20), adapted from Mary Roberts Rinehart's *Em-*

pire Builders; played opposite Will Rogers in *An Unwilling Hero* ('21); and had major roles in several other important features.

Her climb to stardom was short-lived and she was soon back in Westerns opposite Hoot Gibson, Maurice B. Flynn, Guinn "Big Boy" Williams, Jack Perrin, Buffalo Bill, Jr., and Buddy Roosevelt. She did *Sure Fire* ('21) with Hoot Gibson for John Ford, her ninth Western for the man destined to become one of the greatest Western directors of all time.

In 1927, Molly had the heroine's role in *The Golden Stallion*, Nat Levine's first serial offering from his newly formed Mascot Pictures. The film was a moneymaker and enabled Levine to go ahead with production on other serials.

But apparently it did little for Molly. After playing opposite Billy Sullivan in the comedy *Daring Deeds* ('27), she dropped from the movie scene. No one seems to know much about the last 25 years of her life, but it is known that she died in 1952.

Serials

1918

Lure of the Circus. Univ., [18 Chapters] D: J. P. McGowan; S: William Wing; SP: Hope Loring; LP: Eddie Polo, Eileen Sedgwick, Harry Carter, Molly Malone, Noble Johnson, Frederick Starr.

1927

The Golden Stallion. Mascot, [10 Chapters] D: Harry Webb; S/SP: Karl Krusada, William Lester; LP: Lefty Flynn, Joe Bonomo, Molly Malone, Tom London, Burr McIntosh, White Fury (horse).

LEO D. MALONEY

It is understandable that the name Leo Maloney does not mean much to most serial buffs who have grown to adulthood idolizing the serial and saddle aces of the sound era. Information regarding his pre-movie years is somewhat sketchy. He was born in 1888; sources differ as to his birthplace. Evidently he grew up in California and entered movies around 1912.

In those days it was relatively easy for a good rider to "walk in" and get a job at the makeshift studios, especially if he was also well-built and good-looking. After some work with Nestor he joined the Thomas Ince organization and did duty as an assistant director, writer, actor and stuntman. While serving in the latter capacity, he broke his leg in three places while jumping from a moving stagecoach and almost suffered a serious accident when he failed to disengage himself from the stirrups of his horse in a 60-foot jump into a lake.

At Kalem in 1913 he first came into prominence via the shorts of Helen Holmes and in 1914's *The Hazards of Helen*, the 119-episode series starring Holmes (the first 48 episodes) and Helen Gibson (the remaining 71 episodes). Shortly after completing his work in this historic series of one-reelers, Maloney joined Selig and worked as a principal player in many of the Tom Mix films. In 1915 he renewed his association with Helen Holmes and played opposite her in four railroad serials and a number of shorter railroad films. Railroad thrillers were popular in the early years and Holmes and Maloney packed in audiences to the tune of $2,000,000 or more.

Maloney would become one of the silent era's most popular Western stars. It is regrettable that so much of his work during the years 1912 to 1921 is lost forever to film history. We do know that by 1919 he was starring in Western shorts.

Maloney was a competent screen cowboy who, despite his personal problems (most centered around his penchant for the bottle), took pride in the product with which he was associated. He enjoyed "B" Westerns and tried to make them just a little better than anyone else. He strived for originality and willingly paid scenarist Ford Beebe $1500 a picture when making his Pathé feature Westerns, even though many "formula" scripters were available at one-fourth the price.

Maloney could handle action convincingly and, though not the clown that Hoot Gibson was, could inject humor into his Westerns. His dramatic ability exceeded that of the majority of the Hollywood cowboy contingent. His untimely death cut short a career that probably could have lasted through the 1930s. He died on November 2, 1929, with the official cause of death listed as alcoholic poisoning. Leo had been despondent and drinking heavily because of his difficulty in selling *Overland Bound* ('30), which actually was an above-average Western praised by critics for its story and acting. The problem in marketing had been strictly because of the poor quality of the bootleg sound that Leo had used, and which did not register low tones.

Serials

1914

The Hazards of Helen. Kalem, [119 episodes] D: J. P. McGowan, James Davis; S: W. Scott Darling; LP: Helen Holmes, Helen Gibson, Robyn Adair, Ethel Clisbee, Hoot Gibson, Leo D. Maloney, Jack Hoxie, Anna Q. Nilsson, G. A. Williams.

1915

The Girl and the Game. Signa/Mutual, [15 Chapters] D: J. P. McGowan; S: Frank Hamilton Spearman; P: Samuel S. Hutchinson; LP: Helen Holmes, Leo D. Maloney, George McDaniel, J. H. Farley, William Brunton.

A Lass of the Lumberlands. Signal/Mutual, [15 Chapters] D: J. P. McGowan, Paul Hurst; SP: E. Alexander Powell, Ford Beebe *et al.*; LP: Helen Holmes, Leo D. Maloney, Thomas Lingham, William M. Chapman, Paul Hurst, Katherine Goodrich.

1917

The Railroad Raiders. Signal/Mutual, [15 Chapters] D: J. P. McGowan; SP: Ford Beebe *et al.*; LP: Helen Holmes, Leo D. Maloney, William Brunton, Paul Hurst, Thomas Lingham, William Chapman.

The Lost Express. Signald/Mutual, [15 Chapters] D/SP: J. P. McGowan; S: Frederick Bennett; LP: Helen Holmes, Leo D. Maloney, Thomas Lingham, F. O. Whitehead, Edward Hearn, William Brunton.

1918

A Fight for Millions. Vit., [15 Chapters] D: William Duncan; LP: William Duncan, Edith Johnson, Joe Ryan, Leo D. Maloney, Willie Calles.

1920

The Fatal Sign. Arrow, [15 Chapters] D: Stuart Paton; SP: Bertram Millhauser; LP: Claire Anderson, Harry Carter, Leo D. Maloney, Boyd Irwin.

1928

The Vanishing West. Mascot, [10 Chapters] D: Richard Thorpe; P: Nat Levine; SP: Wyndham Gittens; S: Karl Krusada, William Lester; LP: Jack Perrin, Eileen Sedgwick, Jack Daugherty, Leo D. Maloney, Yakima Canutt, William Fairbanks, Helen Gibson.

1929

The Fire Detective. Pathé, [10 Chapters] D: Spencer G. Bennet, Thomas L. Storey; SP: George Anthony Gray; S: Frank Leon Smith; LP: Gladys McConnell, Leo D. Maloney, Frank Lackteen, John Cossaar, Hugh Allan, Larry Steers, Bruce Gordon.

MONA MARIS

Mona Maris was born Maria Capdevielle in 1903 in Buenos Aires, Argentina. She was convent-educated in France and appeared in several British and German films before embarking in the late '20s upon a Hollywood career that consisted of some leads and many second leads, often as a sultry, exotic type. In the '30s she starred in several Hollywood-made Spanish-language films.

Divorced from director Clarence

Brown, she married a Dutch millionaire in 1960, retired from films and became a resident of Lima, Peru. She liked to travel and could be seen shopping in the most expensive shops in Hollywood, New York or Paris but could also be seen in the less ritzy (hole-in-the-wall) places of the poor.

Her films include *The Little People* (UK '26), *Die Leibei genen* (Ger. '27), *Rutschbahn /Bondage* (Ger. '28), *Marquis d'Ein der Spion der Pompadour/The Spy of Madam de Pompadour* (Ger. '28), *Die Drei Frauen von Urban Hell* (Ger. '28), *Romance of the Rio Grande* ('29), *One Mad Kiss* ('30), *A Devil with Women* ('30), *The Passionate Plumber* ('32), *The Man Called Back* ('32), *Vidua Romantica* ('33), *The Death Kiss* ('33), *El Precio de un Beso* (Mex '33), *White Heat* ('34), *Tres Amores* ('34), *Law of the Tropics* ('41), *Flight from Destiny* ('41), *My Gal Sal* ('41), *Pacific Rendezvous* ('41), *I Married an Angel* ('41), *Tampico* ('44), *The Falcon in Mexico* ('44), *Heartbeat* ('46), *The Avengers* ('50) and *La Mujer de las Camelias* ('Arg. '52).

Serial

1944

The Desert Hawk. Col., [15 Chapters] D: B. Reeves Eason; SP: Sherman Lowe, Leslie Swabocker, Jack Stanley, Leighton Brill; P: Rudolph C. Flothaw; Mus: Lee Zahler; Cam: James S. Brown, Jr.; LP: Gilbert Roland, Mona Maris, Kenneth MacDonald, Frank Lackteen, Ben Welden.

JOAN MARSH

Joan Marsh was born Nancy Ann Rosher in Porterville, California, on July 10, 1913. The daughter of cinematographer Charles Rosher, she made her film debut as a child in Mary Pickford silent films. Billed as Dorothy Rosher, she was featured in *Hearts Aflame* ('15), *The Little Princess* ('17), *How Could You Jean* ('18), *Daddy Long Legs* ('19), *Pollyanna* ('20) and *Thou Art the Man* ('20).

Ten years later she returned to the screen as a platinum blonde. The year was 1930 and henceforth she would be billed as Joan Marsh, playing leads and supporting roles in many Hollywood productions, usually glamorous types. In 1931 she was chosen as a Wampas Baby star, one of 13 young actresses named each year by leading publicists as most likely to reach superstardom.

Her sound films include *All Quiet on the Western Front* ('31), *The King of Jazz* ('31), *Dance, Fools, Dance* ('31), *Maker of Men* ('31), *Shipmates* ('31), *They Called It Sin* ('32), *Rainbow Over Broadway* ('33), *Daring Daughters* ('33), *Anna Karenina* ('35), *Dancing Feet* ('36), *Charlie Chan on Broadway* ('37), *The Lady Objects* ('38), *Fast and Loose* ('39), *Road to Zanziber* ('41) and *Police Bullets* ('43).

In 1943 Joan played United Nations agent Janet Blake in the Republic cliffhanger *Secret Service in Darkest Africa*. Along with French officer Pierre LaSalle (Duncan Renaldo), she aids Rex Bennett (Rod Cameron) in breaking up a Nazi attempt to gain the support of African Arabs during World War II.

Marsh retired from the screen following her 1943 marriage to John D. W. Morrell. She had previously been married to screenwriter Charles Belden. Joan's last film, *Follow the Leader*, was released in 1944. For years she owned and operated Paper Unlimited, a successful stationery business in Los Angeles.

Joan Marsh died in Ojai, California, on August 10, 2000.

Serial

1943

Secret Service in Darkest Africa. Rep., [15 Chapters] D: Spencer Bennet; SP: Royal Cole, Basil Dickey, Jesse Duffy, Ronald Davidson, Joseph O'Donnell, Joseph Poland; P: W. J. O'Sullivan; Cam: William Bradford; Mus: Mort Glickman; LP: Rod Cameron, Joan Marsh, Duncan Renaldo, Lionel Royce, Kurt Kreuger, John Davidson.

MARGUERITE MARSH

Marguerite Marsh had been in movies about five years when she appeared in *The Carter Case* ('19), a.k.a. *The Craig Kennedy Serial*, opposite Herbert Rawlinson. It was a reasonably good serial with Rawlinson playing Kennedy. In the story, Shelby Carter is owner of a big chemical works, whose secret formulas are being stolen and given to his competitors abroad. He is driven by fear from his secret observation tower and killed by the mysterious Avion. His daughter, Anita (Marguerite Marsh), calls in Kennedy to solve the mysteries of his death and the missing formulas. Her life and fortune are imperiled by a band of mysterious evildoers led by Avion.

That same year (1919), Marguerite played opposite Harry Houdini in *The Master Mystery*. Quentin Locke (Houdini), a Secret Service agent, opposes a ruthless business magnate who heads up International Patents, Inc., an organization out to suppress all competition and progress itself. Quentin soon finds himself fighting a metal monster called Q, the Automaton (Floyd Buckley). Unknown to Quentin, the metal monster is inhabited by a human. Throughout the serial the "emissaries of the Automaton" try their best to kill Quentin. Eva (Marguerite Marsh), girlfriend of Quentin, also comes in for danger. Other opponents of Quentin include De Luxe Dora (Ruth Stonehouse).

Marguerite's earliest-known film was *Threads of Destiny* ('14) in which she had a minor role as a nun. Another small role was in *Casey at the Bat* ('16). But in *The Devil's Needle* ('16) she is billed third behind Tully Marshall and Norma Talmadge. In D. W. Griffith's *Intolerance* ('16), Marguerite has a small part as a party guest in the star-studded spectacular.

Marguerite had minor roles in Dorothy Gish's *Little Meena's Romance* ('16) and in *Mr. Goode, the Samaritan* ('16) with De Wolf Hopper. In *The Price of Power* ('16) with Orrin Johnson, she had the co-lead.

Marguerite did not appear in any 1917 films. In 1918, however, she had the starring role in *Conquered Hearts* and co-starred with her sister Mae as a French girl in *Fields of Honor*. She went on to star in *The Eternal Magdaline* ('19), *The Phantom Honeymoon* ('19), *A Royal Democrat* ('19), *Wits Is Wits* ('19) and *Women Men Love* ('20), the last named with William Desmond.

In *The Idol of the North* ('21), Marguerite supported Dorothy Dalton and Edwin August in a story of love in the Canadian Northwest. *Oh Mary Be Careful* ('21) with Madge Kennedy followed. In *Face to Face* ('22) she finds evidence that acquits a condemned man. *Iron to Gold* ('22) was a Western drama in which Marguerite cares for wounded Dustin Farnum, an outlaw who has a grudge against her husband. In *Boomerang* ('22) Marguerite was co-starred with

Lionel Barrymore. This film seems to be her last screen appearance.

Marguerite died in 1925 at age 33 (?) from bronchial pneumonia in New York. Although she helped her sister Mae crash the movies, she never achieved the success that Mae did.

Serials

1919

The Carter Case. Oliver, [15 Chapters] D: Donald MacKenzie; LP: Herbert Rawlinson, Marguerite Marsh, Ethel Grey Terry, Kempton Green, William Pike, Coit Albertson, Joseph Marba, Don Hall, Louie R. Wolheim, Gene Baker.

The Master Mystery. Octagon, [15 Chapters] D: Burton King; LP: Harry Houdini, Marguerite Marsh, Ruth Stonehouse, William Pike, Charles Graham, Edna Britton, Floyd Buckley.

MARION MARTIN

Marion Martin, the statuesque, blue-eyed platinum blond with a high, fully developed bosom and a low voice, was not an actress easily forgotten. At 5'6½", in high heels and elaborate headdresses, the sexy blonde with the plush curves was a knockout! Her role in Universal's serial *Mystery of the River Boat* ('44) was not a showy one but even fully clothed she set male fantasies aglow.

Marion was born on June 7, either 1916 or 1918, in Philadelphia, the daughter of a Bethlehem Steel executive. She was educated in private schools and attended the exclusive Bayonne School in Switzerland until the 1929 stock market crash wiped out the family fortune. Thereafter she went looking for a job. It wasn't long before she was signed for a featured spot in the chorus line of one of Earl Carroll's early stage extravaganzas.

She replaced Gypsy Rose Lee in "Follies of 1933" and was paid $500 weekly to strut across the stage wearing, as one reviewer put it, nothing but a feather and some beads. On May 19, 1936, she opened on Broadway in *New Faces of 1936.* On a Hollywood vacation in 1938 she was signed by Universal. After acting in several comedy shorts, she was cast in *Sinners in Paradise* ('38), receiving good reviews.

Marion was signed as an official model for "Flame-Glo" lipstick and her seductive face was featured prominently in advertisements. To add to her stage image, she fashioned her attractive lips into an alluring "Cupid's Bow" with scarlet lipstick.

By 1940 her career picked up momentum. Best remembered perhaps is *Boom Town* ('40) in which she was a tough dance hall girl who attracts the attention of Clark Gable.

Marion was chased by the Marx Brothers in *Go West* ('40) and appeared with them a second time in *The Big Store* ('41). Film after film followed in which Marion's dramatic and comedy talents were tapped. The majority of the films were "B's" but she was no stranger to big budget films: *Star Spangled Rhythm, They Got Me Covered, Come to the Stable, Lady of Burlesque, Angel on My Shoulder, My Dream Is Yours, Oh, You Beautiful Doll, The Big Street, Irish Eyes Are Smiling, Key to the City* and *State of the Union.*

Marion retired from acting in 195x. Happily married but childless, she became active in Santa Monica society and devoted much of her time to charitable causes.

Marion died on August 13, 1985, and is buried in Holy Cross Cemetery in Culver City.

The author acknowledges Charles Stumpf's detailed account of Martin's life in "Marion Martin: The Blonde Menace," *Classic Images*, July 2000, as an information source for this brief account.

Serial

1944

Mystery of the River Boat. Univ., [13 Chapters] D: Ray Taylor, Lewis Collins; SP: Maurice Tombragel; S: Ande Lamb; LP: Robert Lowery, Eddie Quillan, Marion Martin, Marjorie Clements, Lyle Talbot, Arthur Hohl, Mantan Moreland, Anthony Warde.

LEROY MASON

LeRoy Mason, swarthy, muscular, with curly raven-black hair and a fine set of teeth, seemed a sure bet for stardom, especially after romantic leads with actresses such as Pauline Starke (in 1929's *The Viking*). But instead he became the lithe, slick "big boss" in scores of "B" Westerns and serials.

Mason was born October 15, 1903, at Larimore, North Dakota. In high school he was active in both sports and drama. In the early 1920s he started out for Los Angeles and found work with a stage company. Later he broke into movies at Fox.

In the 1930s and 1940s, Mason appeared in scores of Westerns, menacing Gene Autry, Bob Steele, John Wayne, Bill Elliott, George O'Brien, Tim Holt, Sunset Carson, Allan Lane, Bill Cody, Kermit Maynard, Bob Livingston, Ray Corrigan, Smith Ballew, Bob Baker, Charles Starrett, Donald Barry, Johnny Mack Brown, Monte Hale and others. He could also be seen in non–Westerns. His was a familiar face to those who watch "cliffhangers" and "oaters."

Mason was under contract to Republic when he died from a heart attack on October 13, 1947, while filming *California Firebrand* ('48).

Serials

1926

Lightning Hutch. Arrow, [10 Chapters] D: Charles Hutchison; SP: John Francis Natteford; LP: Charles Hutchison, Edith Thornton, Virginia Pearson, Eddie Phillips, Violet Schram, LeRoy Mason.

193x

The Last Frontier. RKO, [12 Chapters] D: Spencer G. Bennet, Thomas L. Story; SP: George H. Plympton, Robert F. Hill; S: Courtney Riley Cooper; Supv.: Fred J. McConnell; LP: Creighton Chaney [Lon Chaney, Jr.], Dorothy Gulliver, Mary Jo Desmond, Francis X. Bushman, Jr., Joe Bonomo, William Desmond, LeRoy Mason.

1933

The Phantom of the Air. Univ., 1933 [12 Chapters] D: Ray Taylor; SP: Basil Dickey, George H. Plympton; S: Ella O'Neill; LP: Tom Tyler, Gloria Shea, LeRoy Mason, Hugh Enfield [Craig Reynolds], William Davidson, Tom London.

1937

Jungle Menace. Col., 1937 [15 Chapters] D: George Melford, Harry Fraser; S: George M.

Robert Livingston and LeRoy Mason (right) in *Beneath Western Skies* (Republic, 1944).

Merrick, Arthur Hoerl, Dallas Fitzgerald, Gordon Griffith; SP: George Rosener, Sherman L. Lowe, Harry Hoyt [Fraser], George Melford; P: Jack Fier, Louis Weiss; Cam: Edward Linden, Herman Schopp; Mus: Abe Meyer; LP: Frank Buck, Esther Ralston, John St. Polis, Reginald Denny, Charlotte Henry, William Bakewell, LeRoy Mason.

The Painted Stallion. Rep., [12 Chapters] D: William Witney, Alan James, Ray Taylor; AP: J. Laurence Wickland; Cam: Edgar Lyons; Mus: Raoul Kraushaar; LP: Ray Corrigan, Hoot Gibson, Hal Taliaferro, Jack Perrin, Duncan Renaldo, LeRoy Mason, Sammy McKim.

1939

Overland with Kit Carson. Col., [15 Chapters] D: Sam Nelson, Norman Deming; SP: Joseph F. Poland, Morgan B. Cox, Ned Dandy; P: Jack Fier; Cam: Benjamin Kline, George Meehan; LP: Bill Elliott, Iris Meredith, Trevor Bardette, Richard Fiske, Bobby Clark, LeRoy Mason, James Craig.

1944

The Tiger Woman. Rep., [12 Chapters] D: Spencer Bennet, Wallace Grissell; SP: Royal Cole, Ronald Davidson, Basil Dickey, Jesse Duffy, Grant Nelson, Joseph Poland; AP: W. J. O'Sullivan; Cam: Bud Thackery; Mus: Joseph Dubin; LP: Linda Stirling, Allan Lane, Duncan Renaldo, George J. Lewis, LeRoy Mason, Robert Frazer.

Captain America. Rep., [15 Chapters] D: John English, Elmer Clifton; SP: Royal Cole, Ronald Davidson, Basil Dickey, Jesse Duffy, Harry Fraser, Grant Nelson, Joseph Poland; AP: W. J. O'Sullivan; Cam: John MacBurnie; Mus: Mort Glickman; LP: Dick Purcell, Lorna Gray [Adrian Booth], Lionel Atwill, Charles Trowbridge, Russell Hicks, George J. Lewis, LeRoy Mason.

1946

The Phantom Rider. Rep., [12 Chapters] D: Spencer Bennet, Fred Brannon; SP: Albert DeMond, Basil Dickey, Jesse Duffy, Lynn Perkins,

Barney Sarecky; AP: Ronald Davidson; Cam: Bud Thackery; Mus: Richard Charwin; LP: Robert Kent, Peggy Stewart, LeRoy Mason, George J. Lewis, Kenne Duncan, Hal Taliaferro, Chief Thundercloud.

King of the Forest Rangers. Rep., [12 Chapters] D: Spencer G. Bennet, Fred C. Brannon; SP: Albert Demond, Basil Dickey, Jesse Duffy, Lynn Perkins; AP: Ronald Davidson; Cam: Bud Thackery; Mus: Raoul Kraushaar; LP: Larry Thompson, Helen Talbot, Stuart Hamblem, Anthony Warde, LeRoy Mason, Tom London, Robert Wilke.

1947

The Black Widow. Rep., [13 Chapters] D: Spencer Bennet, Fred C. Brannon; SP: Franklyn Adreon, Basil Dickey, Jesse Duffy, Sol Shor; AP: Mike Frankovich; Cam: John MacBurnie; Mus: Mort Glickman; LP: Carol Forman, Bruce Edwards, Virginia Lindley, Anthony Warde, Ramsay Ames, LeRoy Mason, I. Stanford Jolley.

Jesse James Rides Again. Rep., [13 Chapters] D: Fred C. Brannon, Thomas Carr; SP: Franklyn Adreon, Basil Dickey, Jesse Duffy, Sol Shor; Cam: John MacBurnie; Mus: Mort Glickman; LP: Clayton Moore, Linda Stirling, Roy Barcroft, John Compton, Tristram Coffin, Tom London, LeRoy Mason, Edmund Cobb.

SHIRLEY MASON

Shirley Mason was born Leonie Flugrath in Brooklyn, New York, in 1901. Her two sisters, Edna Flugrath and Viola Dana, were also actresses. Shirley began acting on the stage as a child and entered films as a juvenile lead in 1914. She typically played innocent romantic roles. Her films include *Goodbye Bill* ('18), *Girl of My Heart* ('20), *Shirley of the Circus* ('22), *South Sea Love* ('23), *Lord Jim* ('25), *Desert Gold* ('26), *Don Juan's Three Nights* ('26), *Rose of the Tenements* ('26), *Sally in Our Alley* ('27), *Runaway Girls* ('28) and *Anne Against the World* ('29).

Shirley was married to director Sidney Lanfield and with his retirement in 1952 they moved to Palm Springs where they reared their family. But with Lanfield's 1972 death (after four decades of marriage), she moved to Marina Del Rey to be near her sister Viola Dana.

Shirley's only serial was a thrilling one — *Vultures of the Sea* ('28), an early Mascot picture. It is produced more along the lines of a feature picture with each of the chapters almost a story in itself. It is a sea tale having to do with the rough crew aboard a ship. A murder has been committed because loot is hidden aboard. An innocent man is found guilty of the crime and sentenced to hang. His son ships out aboard the ship to clear up the mystery. He falls in love with the ship's girl owner, who has been left in charge of the cruel mate. Attempts are made to do away with the youth and the girl. They have some thrilling experiences, coming through them all safely. The real murderer is discovered and the stolen loot recovered.

The production is exceptional for a serial. There are many remarkable shots in the rigging of the ship and elsewhere. There is action a plenty and Shirley comes through as a real trouper.

Shirley Mason died from cancer at age 78 in 1979.

Serial

1928

Vultures of the Sea. Mascot, 1928 [10 Chap-

ters] D: Richard Thorpe; P: Nat Levine; LP: Johnnie Walker, Shirley Mason, Tom Santschi, Boris Karloff.

CAROLE MATHEWS

Carole Mathews was born Jean Diefel on September 13, 1920, in Montgomery, Illinois. Her entrance into films was under the name Jeanne Francis. She signed with Columbia in 1943 after a short period as an Earl Carroll showgirl. She was at Columbia for a couple of years and then was fired as a result of a run-in with the head hairdresser. She did just as well as a freelancer. Her film credits include *The Girl in the Case* ('44), *She's a Sweetheart* ('45), *The Missing Juror* ('45), *Tahiti Nights* ('45), *A Thousand and One Nights* ('45), *Sing Me a Song of Texas* ('46), *Blazing the Western Trail* ('46), *Outlaws of the Rockies* ('46), *I Love a Mystery* ('46), *Massacre River* ('48), *The Great Gatsby* ('49), *Cry Murder* ('50), *No Man of Her Own* ('50), *The Man with My Face* ('51), *Red Snow* (52), *City of Bad Men* ('53), *Port of Hell* ('54), *Treasure of Ruby Hills* ('55), *Female Fiend* ('59) and *Thirteen Fighting Men* ('60).

In Carole's one serial, *The Monster and the Ape* ('45), she plays Babs Arnold, daughter of the professor (Ralph Morgan) who invents the Metalogen. An evil professor (George Macready) tries to steal the robot and the Metalogen metal from which it is made. Ray Corrigan plays the trained gorilla which makes things difficult for the "good guys."

Carole continued to freelance and in 1958 had a regular role on TV's *The Californians.* She eventually opened her own travel agency. Later she began to raise miniature horses. Carole had a stroke and is on her third pacemaker; also, she has fought cancer and a hip replacement. Although plagued by various illnesses for years, she is now in good health again.

Serial

1945

The Monster and the Ape. Col., [15 Chapters] D: Howard Bretherton; SP: Sherman Lowe, Royal K. Cole; P: Rudolph C. Flothow; Cam: L. W. O'Connell; Mus: Lee Zahler; LP: Robert Lowery, George Macready, Ralph Morgan, Carole Mathews, Willie Best, Ray Corrigan, Jack Ingram, Anthony Warde.

KEN MAYNARD

Ken Maynard was one of the greatest trick riders of all time and one of the great-

est movie cowboys ever to sit a saddle. He was providing horsemanship thrills for Ringling Brothers–Barnum & Bailey Circus audiences when he attracted the attention of director Lynn Reynolds, who was then making Tom Mix features for Fox. He suggested that Maynard make a screen test, which resulted in a Fox contract. He had bit roles in *Brass Commandments* ('23) with *William Farnum* and *Cameo Kirby* ('23) with John Gilbert, and played a principal role in *Somebody Lied* ('23), a two-reeler with Jean Arthur.

Maynard first attracted nationwide attention when he played Paul Revere in Cosmopolitan's *Janice Meredith* ('25). His first job as a cowboy star was for J. Charles Davis, who signed him for eight Westerns, the first of which was *$50,000 Reward* ('26). The Davis features were well-received by avid Western fans.* Following the Davis series, Ken co-starred with Strongheart, the canine competitor of Rin-Tin-Tin, in *North Star* ('26) for Associated Exhibitors. Clark Gable was a supporting player.

First National, recognizing Maynard's box office potential, inked him for a string of higher-budgeted horse operas. From 1926 to 1929 he made 18 Westerns, fabulous produc-

In *Honor of the Range* (Universal, 1934).

tions presenting Ken in some of the most spectacular stunt riding sequences ever filmed. *The Red Raiders* ('27), still available for viewing today, packs more punch than most of the Westerns of that time, with hordes of real Indian extras.

In 1929, Ken signed with Universal and was given his own production unit to make his first "talkies." These were not talkies as we know them today; the sound was recorded on "discs" or "records" that theaters would play on a turntable in conjunction with the showing of the film. Problems of synchronization naturally occurred. Universal also incurred the wrath of exhibitors by selling these Maynard films as "100% Talkies," when in reality they were only *part dialogue* and the rest *music over silent-titled footage*!

From 1930 through 1932, Ken made his first series of 12 *true* talkies for the Tiffany-Stahl Studios. Eight World Wide productions followed in 1932–33.

To Ken goes credit as the first singing cowboy and the first to introduce musical interludes into Westerns. Ken had a pleasant enough voice and was a dandy fiddle player. The music was never allowed to take over the pictures, as in the case of Autry and Rogers, and Ken's singing and playing were usually in a humorous vein rather than a romantic one.

Tarzan had more to do than just run his fetlocks sore. He got a chance to act as well as to push Ken into the arms of the receptive heroine at the finis. *Come on Tarzan* ('32) and *Dynamite Ranch* ('32) were probably the best of this series. But all the entries from both Tiffany and World Wide had good photography, intelligent direction, plenty of thrills and better-than-average sound.

Ken was almost able to write his own ticket once Carl Laemmle realized that sound was going to help rather than kill off the program Westerns. Ken got his own production company at Universal in 1933 and complete control of all facets of production. Budgets approached $100,000 per film. *Strawberry Roan* ('33) stands out as probably the best of the eight films in the 1933–34 series, although *The Fiddlin' Buckaroo* ('33) and *Trail*

Drive ('33) are nearly as good. Ken left Universal when he couldn't get his way in an argument with Laemmle. It was a bad career move.

Nat Levine of Mascot signed Ken for two 1934 pictures, the serial *Mystery Mountain* and the feature *In Old Santa Fe*, which served to introduce Gene Autry and Smiley Burnette to the cinema world. Ken was paid $10,000 a week. The serial was an action-packed chapterplay in which Ken battles for 12 episodes to defeat the deadly masked "Rattler." Lovely Verna Hillie improved the scenery.

After a series of eight oaters for Columbia in 1935–36, four Grand National releases in 1937–38 and four Colony "state righters" in 1939–40, Ken left the screen. *Western Frontier* ('35) stands out as his finest Columbia film. It was a charming film enhanced by Ken's original story and the presence of two lovely ladies, Lucile Browne and Nora Lane.

In 1937, 1938 and 1940, Ken headed up the wild west concert of Cole Brothers Circus. He returned to filmmaking in 1943–44 for Monogram, co-starring with Hoot Gibson in the *Trail Blazers* series. After three films were made, Monogram added Bob Steele to the series. Ken was unhappy over salary and other things and didn't much like Steele and quit after making six entries in the series. Chief Thundercloud took his place.

Maynard's last film was *Harmony Trail* ('44) for a cheapie outfit called Mattox Productions. Surprisingly, the film was not bad and it introduced Ruth Roman to cinemagoers.

Ken made personal appearances with rodeos for a number of years. His last circus appearances were with Biller Brothers and Arthur Brothers circus in 1945.

His last years were tragic ones. His third wife, Bertha, a former Ringling Brothers aerialist to whom he was married for 20 years, died suddenly in 1968. Thereafter Ken lived alone in a trailer in the San Fernando Valley. His drinking and his disposition grew worse. In 1970, director Robert Slatzer gave him a supporting role in *Bigfoot*. The role led nowhere and his health failed. A woman who variously claimed to be his wife, his agent and his daughter took him for whatever he might have had and sold all his personal effects. Finally, unable to care for himself, he was admitted to the Motion Picture Country Hospital on January 18, 1973, for treatment of nutritional deficiency, arthritis and general physical deterioration. He passed away on March 23, 1973, at age 77.

Despite his human failings, Ken Maynard was truly one of the sons of the great West and will always be remembered as a pioneer in the field of Western moviemaking. At his best, Maynard was unmatchable for fast-action thrills, and it is in that capacity that history will remember him.

Serials

1926

The Range Fighter. Davis, 1926 [10 Chapters] D: Clifford S. Elfelt, Paul Hurst, Forrest Sheldon; LP: Ken Maynard, Dorothy Devore, George Nichols, J. P. McGowan, Charles Whitaker, Frank Ellis, Buck Black, Hank Bell, Joseph Swickard.

1934

Mystery Mountain. Mascot, [12 Chapters] D: B. Reeves Eason, Otto Brower; P: Nat Levine; SP: Bennett Cohen, Armand Schaefer; S: Sherman Lowe, Barney Sarecky, B. Reeves Eason; Cam: Ernest Miller, William Nobles; Mus: Lee Zahler, Abe Meyer; LP: Ken Maynard, Verna Hillie, Syd Saylor, Edward Earle, Lynton Brent, Lafe McKee, Al Bridge, Edward Hearn, Carmencita Johnson.

KERMIT MAYNARD

Veteran Western star and stuntman Kermit Maynard was as different from his brother Ken as night is from day. Whereas Ken had a mean disposition when he was drinking (which was often), Kermit never drank and was friendly to all, extending a helping hand to those he could help. With his passing on January 16, 1971, Western buffs lost one of the most friendly and lovable personalities of the B-Western fraternity of movie thrillmakers. His interest in his fans was genuine. His unassuming modesty, courtesy and sense of humor endeared him to fans and colleagues alike.

Kermit was born September 20, 1897, in Vevay, Indiana. The family later moved to Columbus, Indiana, where Kermit attended school. After high school he attended Indiana University with the goal of a law degree. He excelled in football, baseball and track. Leaving the University without a degree, he was accepted into the Hormel Meat Packing management trainee program. He became a claims department assistant and ultimately was promoted to department head.

In 1926 brother Ken, already established in films, urged Kermit to come west. Kermit and wife Edith, married only two years, pulled up stakes and headed for Hollywood. Ken was away on location, so Kermit had to pound the pavement seeking work.

Luck was with him. He had loved horses all his life and had become quite proficient as a horseman and trick rider. Rayart signed him to star in a series of six Westerns in 1927 (billed as Tex Maynard). The films were *Prince of the Plains*, *Driftin' Kid*, *Gun Hand Garrison*, *Riding Luck*, *Wild Born* and *Wanderer of the West*.

After the Rayart series, Kermit returned to stunting in 1928. He also rode the rodeo circuits, doing trick-riding and roping; in 1930 he purchased his beloved dappled-grey horse, Rocky, who stayed with him until its death in 1951.

Kermit doubled many of the cowboys, including George O'Brien, Rex Bell, Tom Tyler, brother Ken and others. Nat Levine, head of Mascot, hired Kermit to work in *The Lightning Warrior* ('31) stunting for George Brent and *Phantom of the West* ('31) doubling for Tom Tyler.

Kermit and Rocky entered the competition for the World Championship for trick riding at Salinas, California, and won the event. Also in 1933 he could be seen with brother Ken in *Drum Taps* ('33), with Jack Hoxie in *Outlaw Justice* ('33), and in a short, *West of Broadway* ('33), with El Brendel.

Kermit then signed with Ambassador for a series of Mounted Police and Western features, mostly shot on location around Kernville. These were among the best B-Westerns made at that time. The series started with *Fighting Trooper* ('34) and ended with *Roaring Six Guns* ('37), a total of 17 films. They had good riding and stunt scenes with Kermit also singing in a few and playing various musical instruments. Declining to accept another contract, Kermit became a stuntman–character actor. Stunting aside, the "character" parts were numerous but gave him few opportunities to exercise his decided acting ability. He worked regularly, especially at PRC and Monogram.

On TV he appeared on shows such as *Lawman*, *Perry Mason*, *Rin-Tin-Tin*, *The Cisco Kid*, *Broken Arrow*, *The Gene Autry Show*, *Tales of Wells Fargo*, *Casey Jones*, *The Lone Ranger* and *Maverick*.

Retiring from the screen, Kermit served on the boards of the Screen Actors Guild and Screen Extras Guild and in 1966 took on an appointment as agent for the latter. He and his wife were happily married for 47 years.

They had a son, William, who was 28 at Kermit's death.

Kermit passed away at his home in North Hollywood in June 1971. He had just stepped out his back door to put the trash and, as he was reentering the house, had the fatal heart attack.

Serials

1930

The Lone Defender. Mascot, [12 Chapters] D: Richard Thorpe; LP: Rin-Tin-Tin, Buzz Barton, Josef Swickard, Walter Miller, June Marlowe, Lee Shumway.

1931

The Phantom of the West. Mascot, [10 Chapters] D: D. Ross Lederman; LP: Tom Tyler, Dorothy Gulliver, William Desmond, Tom Santschi, Tom Dugan, Philo McCullough.

The Lightning Warrior. Mascot, [12 Chapters] D: Armand Schaefer; LP: Rin-Tin-Tin, Frankie Darro, Georgia Hale, George Brent, Pat O'Malley.

1938

The Great Adventures of Wild Bill Hickok. Col., [15 Chapters] D: Mack V. Wright, Sam Nelson; LP: Gordon (Bill) Elliott, Carole Wayne, Frankie Darro, Monte Blue, Kermit Maynard, Sammy McKim, Reed Hadley, Dickie Jones.

1941

King of the Texas Rangers. Rep., [12 Chapters] D: William Witney, John English; LP: Slingin' Sammy Baugh, Neil Hamilton, Pauline Moore, Duncan Renaldo, Kermit Maynard, Charles Trowbridge, Herbert Rawlinson, Roy Barcroft.

1942

Perils of the Royal Mounted. Col., [15 Chapters] D: James W. Horne; LP: Nell O'Day, Robert Stevens [Kellard], Herbert Rawlinson, Kenneth MacDonald, John Elliott, Tom London, Charles King, Rick Vallin, Kermit Maynard.

1944

The Desert Hawk. Col., [15 Chapters] D: B. Reeves Eason; LP: Gilbert Roland, Mona Maris, Ben Welden, Kenneth MacDonald, Frank Lackteen, Charles Middleton.

1945

Jungle Raiders. Col., [15 Chapters] D: Lesley Selander; LP: Kane Richmond, Eddie Quillan, Veda Ann Borg, Carol Hughes, Janet Shaw, Charles King.

1946

Chick Carter, Detective. Col., [15 Chapters] D: Derwin Abrahams; LP: Lyle Talbot, Douglas Fowley, Julie Gibson, Pamela Blake, Eddie Acuff.

1947

The Vigilante. Col., [15 Chapters] D: Wallace Fox; LP: Ralph Byrd, Ramsay Ames, Lyle Talbot, George Offerman, George Chesebro, Edmund Cobb, Robert Barron.

1953

Gunfighters of the Northwest. Col., [15 Chapters] D: Spencer G. Bennet, Charles S. Gould; LP: Jock Mahoney, Clayton Moore, Phyllis Coates, Don Harvey.

1956

Perils of the Wilderness. Col., [15 Chapters] D: Spencer G. Bennet; LP: Dennis Moore, Richard Emory, Eve Anderson [Evelyn Finley], Kenneth MacDonald.

Blazing the Overland Trail. Col., [15 Chapters] D: Spencer Bennet; LP: Lee Roberts, Dennis Moore, Norma Brooks, Gregg Barton, Don C. Harvey, Pierce Lyden.

EDNA MAYO

Edna Mayo co-starred with Henry B. Walthall in the serial *The Strange Case of Mary Page* ('16), produced by Essanay. It was the company's only serial. The story was told in flashback, a rather novel idea at the time. A theatrical magnate is murdered and Mary Page (Mayo), on whom he had forced his attention, is accused. Phil Langdon (Walthall), her suitor, stands by her. A large part of the story concerned the magnate's attempts to force her to marry him. The murder occurred in the first chapter and the solution was held back until the last few minutes of Chapter 15. It was quite different from the cliffhangers of the '30s and '40s. Its appeal was more to adults than to children. Future Western star Edmund Cobb had a supporting role.

Edna's career dates back to 1914. That year she starred in *Aristocracy* as the daughter of a San Francisco railroad magnate (Tyrone Power) engaged to the son of an old, aristocratic New York family. The boy's father refuses to consent to the marriage. Edna goes to Europe and there marries fortune-hunting Prince Emil von Haldenuall (Arthur Hoops), thinking that her former fiancé was engaged to someone else. He wasn't and he showed up in time to keep Prince Emil from raping his wife on their wedding night. Emil is later killed in a quarrel over debts, leaving Edna and her suitor free to marry.

In *The Key to Yesterday* ('14) Edna plays Duska Filson, a socialite. She is loved by Carlyle Blackwell, a Parisian artist who loses his memory. On a trip to South America in a quest to learn his identity, he is wounded and returns to France where he regains his memory and rushes to his dying wife's bedside. There he finds Duska, who sees his grief and leaves.

In *The Quest of the Sacred Jewel* ('14), Edna inherits a priceless jewel that her uncle stole while visiting a sacred temple in Barnipore. Priests follow him to the U.S. and murder him but do not find the diamond. At an engagement party, her fiancé is hypnotized by one of the priests and ordered to obtain the diamond. When Edna sees him taking the jewel, she calls off her engagement, but the case is eventually solved by a famous detective and his office boy. The Hindus return the diamond to the temple and Edna and her fiancé are happily reunited.

In *The Blindness of Virtue* ('15), Effie (Edna) is a naive girl who had not been taught about sex. When she innocently comes to Archie's (Bryant Washburn) room clad only in her kimono, her father enters and accuses Archie, who was comforting her, of impropriety. Effie explains to her mother, who then enlightens the young girl about sexual matters. With the father's consent, Effie and Archie decide to marry.

Edna is Countess Dagmar in *Graustark* ('15) in support of Francis X. Bushman and Beverly Bayne; in *The Warning* ('15) she plays the sister of Henry Kolker, who gradually becomes an alcoholic, but a dream awakens him to what his alcoholism will lead to. Lily Leslie plays his wife.

Edna again has a leading role in *The Chaperon* ('16), which features Eugene O'Brien as the man she loves and Sydney Ainsworth as the count she marries because of her mother's fondness of titles. Unhappy with her European lifestyle, she leaves the count and returns home where she once again meets Jim (O'Brien). Their love blossoms again. Her mother pays off the money-hungry count and he grants Edna a divorce so that she can marry Jim.

The Misleading Lady ('16), a comedy-drama, stars Edna and Henry B. Walthall. At a party, Edna, on a bet, vamps woman-hater Henry, who asks her to marry him. She confesses that her wooing was only a practical joke. Embarrassed and angry, Henry kidnaps her and takes her to his home in the woods. While friends try to rescue her, Edna fights with Henry and hits him over the head with a telephone. When friends burst in, they find her with her arms about her kidnapper. After knocking him out, she realizes that she really does love him.

In *The Return of Eve* ('16), Edna (as Eve) and Eugene O'Brien (as Adam) are brought back to civilization after spending 19 years in a wilderness, "Edan"—put there by an eccentric millionaire. Under terms of his will, Edward Arnold has to bring them back before he can marry Clarice (Leona Ball), who inherits the money he is after. Adam dislikes civilization and returns to the forest. Eve is at first delighted with modern civilization but after Arnold tries to seduce her, she renounces the twentieth century and returns to her "Edan," where she is met by Adam. The couple decide to spend the rest of their lives as far away as possible from the modern world.

Hearts of Love, released at the end of 1918, was a Civil War drama. Gladden James elects to remain loyal to the Union. Edna, his fiancée, supports the South. He is led to believe that she has betrayed him to the Confederates, but she later proves her innocence and he comes to her rescue when a cruel overseer tries to harm her.

Edna's career was a brief one—1914–18. Why she left the screen is not known to this author. She has failed to make the reference books. She had proven that she had acting talent. Maybe marriage was her reason for forsaking the world of glitter.

Serial

1916

The Strange Case of Mary Page. Essanay, [15 Chapters] D: J. Charles Haydon; LP: Edna Mayo, H. B. Walthall, Ernest Cossart, Sydney Ainsworth, Henry Dunkinson, Tom Cummerford, John Cossar, Frank Dayton, Edmund Cobb, Lillian Chester, Frankie Raymond, William Chester, Frances Benedict, Arthur Bates.

BLANCHE MEHAFFEY

Blanche Mehaffey was born in Cincinnati, Ohio, on July 28, 1907. She was educated in private schools, including Mary Lyon Seminary at Swarthmor, Pennsylvania, and Lassell Seminary at Auburndale, Massachusetts, where she specialized in music. She spent one year with the Ziegfeld Follies and then entered films in 1924, when she was picked from the Follies by producer Hal Roach. The titian-haired, blue-eyed beauty stood 5'2" and weighed 110–120 pounds. She was also selected as a Wampas Baby Star in 1924. During her career she changed her name twice in hopes of helping her career. It didn't. The first name change was to Joan Alden; the second, to Janet Morgan. Then she reverted again to Blanche Mehaffey.

Although Blanche achieved a modicum of success in the low-budget films in which she labored, her talent was never fully utilized. An actress is only as good as the creative company she keeps and, unfortunately, she was never in the right company to enable her to break away from the Gower Gulch Poverty Row firms. When given a chance, Blanche could be entertaining as well as ornamental. The writer will always remember her portrayal of Goldie in Tiffany's *Sunrise Trail* ('31) opposite Bob Steele. As the folksy saying goes, "There's been a heap of water flow down the old 'crick' since then," but her haunting portrayal has stuck permanently in the memory bank of one who has filtered hundreds of thousands of movie scenes through his mind in 70 years of movie-watching. To this writer, she will be eternally "Goldie."

In 1932, Blanche married producer Ralph M. Like and appeared in a number of independent pictures. Her last film was *Held for Ransom* ('38), in which she was top-billed. However, the cloudy print and bum recording made the film a severe test on eye and ear, and it gravitated to the lower side of duals in the action houses. Apparently Blanche threw in the towel at that point.

Some of her best work was in her four films with Hoot Gibson, and it is her various Westerns and her only serial, *The Mystery Trooper* ('31), for which she is remembered today.

Blanche Mehaffey died in Los Angeles on March 31, 1968, at age 59.

In *Battling Orioles* (Pathé, 1924).

Serial

1931

The Mystery Trooper. Syn., [10 Chapters] D: Stuart Paton; SP: Karl Krusada; S: Flora Douglas; Cam: William Nobles, Edward Kull; LP: Robert Frazer, Buzz Barton, Blanche Mehaffey, Al Ferguson, Charles King.

IRIS MEREDITH

Iris Meredith, the pride of Columbia when Gallantry rode the range, died at 65 on January 22, 1980. As with most other Western heroines of the 1930s and 1940s, her death was barely noticed by the film colony or newspapers. She had fought a valiant fight against oral cancer for nearly 15 years, giving up part of her tongue, throat and jaw in the struggle. What she didn't give up were her indomitable will to live, her sense of humor and her pleasant disposition. At the Western Film Festival in Nashville, Tennessee, in July 1976, she received a standing ovation when, almost unable to talk, her face disfigured by 14 operations, she walked bravely up to the speaker's dais to accept an award. It was a moving moment both for her and for her coterie of fans.

Iris was a fighter all her life. Born in Sioux City, Iowa, she moved with her parents to Minnesota and then to Eagle Rock, California. Her mother died when Iris was around ten years old; her father when she was 13. Iris went to work to support her two younger sisters and a brother, going to school in the morning and working as a theater cashier in the afternoon and evening. While she was working at Loew's downtown Los Angeles theater for $16.50 a week, a friend of Samuel Goldwyn noticed her good looks and, impressed by her charm, took her to see the producer. A screen test resulted in a role as a showgirl in *Roman Scandals* ('33) and a weekly salary of $125. Iris and her family were able to move into a nice apartment, and the children were able to stay in school while Iris brought home the groceries and paid the rent.

After the Goldwyn picture, Iris got a contract with 20th Century-Fox and, as a member of the Fox stock company, appeared in a number of films as a "scene filler" or member of the chorus line. One of several Shirley Temple features she appeared in was *Stand Up and Cheer* ('34).

Somewhere along the way she was noticed by Harry Cohn, Columbia boss, and started her long association with the Gower Gulch studio. She is closely linked with Charles Starrett by most West aficionados, having made 20 sagebrushers with the handsome prairie idol back in the pre–Durango Kid days. Fans became fond of the duo and of the ritual which brought stranger Starrett to the rescue of lady rancher Meredith as the Sons of the Pioneers crooned from behind every rock and bush.

Iris also played opposite other cowboys, notably Bill Elliott. Columbia's *Overland with Kit Carson* ('39), with Elliott and Meredith as leads, is one of the studio's finer serial efforts and a laudable entry in a genre in which Columbia generally had to take a back seat to Republic, Universal and even Mascot. Location filming was done in Utah, and the final result was a creditable film and a financial success. In two non–Western serials, Iris played opposite Warren Hull in *The Spider's Web* ('38), also an above-average Columbia chapterplay, and *The Green Archer* ('40), a run-of-the-mill offering notable only for the game effort by Victor Jory and Meredith to carry through a poorly scripted story under the inept direction of

In *The Green Archer* (Columbia, 1940).

James Horne (a man often at the helm of Columbia's less memorable serials). However, the film had its moments, and certainly the juvenile trade did not write letters of protest, even if their parents thought the whole thing a little silly.

In 1943, Iris married Abby Berlin, a director who worked at Columbia for many years (responsible for, among other things, many of the *Blondie* films). Later, when television came along, he directed *The Ann Sothern Show* and *The Life of Riley*. Iris retired from the screen, bore a daughter and settled into domestic life. Berlin died in 1965. Iris never remarried. She managed well enough on what they had accumulated and continued to live in the Los Angeles area, raising her daughter and spending much time with her sister and brother.

It was about 1965 that she first contracted cancer, and the remaining years of her life were difficult ones. Between operations she lived as normally as possible and enjoyed herself, deriving much pleasure and comfort from the outings she took with her daughter and son-in-law.

Iris' ethereal charm and attractive, restrained acting style endeared her to sagebrush and serial enthusiasts, many of whom experience a nostalgic twinge at her memory.

Serials

1938

The Spider's Web. Col., [15 Chapters] D: Ray Taylor, James W. Horne; SP: Robert E. Kent, Basil Dickey, George H. Plympton, Martie Ramson; P: Jack Fier; Cam: Allen G. Siegler; Mus: Morris Stoloff; LP: Warren Hull, Iris Meredith, Richard Fiske, Kenne Duncan, Forbes Murray.

1939

Overland with Kit Carson. Col., [15 Chapters] D: Sam Nelson, Norman Deming; P: Jack Fier; SP: Joseph Poland, Morgan B. Cox, Ned Dandy; Cam: Benjamin Kline, George Meehan; Mus: Lee Zahler; LP: Bill Elliott, Iris Meredith, Trevor Bardette, Richard Fiske, Bobby Clark, LeRoy Mason, James Craig.

1940

The Green Archer. Col., [15 Chapters] D: James W. Horne; SP: Morgan B. Cox, John Cutting, Jesse A. Duffy, James W. Horne; S: Edgar Wallace; P: Larry Darmour; Cam: James S. Brown, Jr.; Mus: Lee Zahler; LP: Victor Jory, Irish Meredith, James Craven, Robert Fiske, Dorothy Fay, Jack Ingram.

FRANK MERRILL

Stuntman-actor Frank Merrill was the movies' fifth Tarzan, and one of the best actors to portray Edgar Rice Burroughs' jungle hero. He appeared in *The Adventures of Tarzan* ('21) as an Arab guard and double for Lincoln.

Merrill got his chance to star in a jungle serial in 1927 but it was not a Tarzan picture. The serial, produced by Artclass films, was titled *Perils of the Jungle* ('27). The producers apparently decided on thrills at any cost, and this is where the picture errs, for in some instances story structure, plausibility and restraint suffer occasionally so that action can take center stage. There are wild animals galore, threatening the principals at every other moment. The whole ferocious gamut of the jungle is paraded, from owls to crocodiles. Charging lions are as frequent as fights and rescues, of which there are many. Merrill was more than adequate in his starring role.

In 1928, Universal produced the 15-chapter serial *Tarzan the Mighty*. Joe Bonomo had started out as the star but broke his leg early on and was replaced by his double, Frank Merrill. He proved to be a much better Tarzan than Bonomo. In the story, Mary Trevor (Natalie Kingston) and her young brother (Bobby Nelson) are castaways befriended by Tarzan. Tarzan clashes with Black John (Al Ferguson), the ruler of an African village of pirates' descendants, who passes himself off as the long lost heir of the Greystoke family and attempts to wed Mary. The serial was popular and profitable, so preparations began for a follow-up.

Tarzan the Tiger ('29) had music throughout, dubbed sound effects and non-dialogue use of voices for Tarzan's battle and victory cries, Jane's screams and the shouts of the inhabitants of Opar. The serial involves Tarzan's search for the treasure of Opar. Albert Werper (Al Ferguson) also seeks it, while La desires Tarzan and Achmet Zek wants Jane. This basic situation, complicated by Tarzan's loss of memory in Chapter Three, occupies most of the serial. Surprisingly for a 15-episode serial, there were only seven roles named with the players identified. Chapter endings were adequate, if unspectacular, and the escapes were honest. Jane's screams enhanced their effect, as did the musical score.

Merrill was a physically impressive Tarzan. This helped, as the script had him heaving boulders about, climbing vines hand-over-hand, wrestling lions, hurling men about, grappling with crocodiles, etc. A third serial *Tarzan the Terrible*, announced for Merrill, was not made.

Frank Merrill died in Hollywood in 1966 at age 72. Masonic funeral services were held in Pierce Bros.' Hollywood chapel on July 13. He was survived by his wife and a sister.

Serials

1921

The Adventures of Tarzan. Great Western/ Numa, [15 Chapters] D: Robert F. Hill; SP: Lillian Valentine, Robert F. Hill; LP: Elmo Lincoln, Louise Lorraine, Frank Whitson, Lillian Worth.

1927

Perils of the Jungle. Artclass, [10 Chapters] D: Jack Nelson; S: H. P. Crist; LP: Frank Merrill, Eugenia Gilbert, Albert J. Smith, Henry Belmore, Bobby Nelson, Milburn Morante, Will Herman.

1928

Tarzan the Mighty. Univ., [15 Chapters] D: Jack Nelson, Ray Taylor; SP: Ian McClosky; S: Edgar Rice Burroughs; LP: Frank Merrill, Natalie Kingston, Bobby Nelson, Al Ferguson, Tantor (elephant).

1929

Tarzan the Tiger. Univ., [15 Chapters] D: Henry MacRae; SP: Ian McClosky; S: Edgar Rice Burroughs; LP: Frank Merrill, Natalie Kingston, Lillian Worth, Al Ferguson, Sheldon Lewis, Frank Lanning.

JOHN MERTON

John Merton played the pugnacious, treacherous rogue in innumerable "B" action flicks and in 23 serials for 20 years. Seldom was he a good guy. He was Loki, the number one Dacoit, mindless slave of the insidious Oriental genius in *Drums of Fu Manchu* ('40); in *Hop Harrigan* ('46) he was the eccentric Dr. Tabor; in *Dick Tracy Returns* ('38) he was Champ Stark, meanest of the five sons of Pa Stark; in *Zorro's Fighting Legion* ('39) he was Manuel, one of the town councillors suspected of being the power-mad Don Del Oro; in *Adventures of Sir Galahad* ('49) he was the medieval Saxon king Ulric; in *The Lone Ranger* ('38) he was outlaw chief Jeffries' assistant; in *Brenda Starr,*

Reporter ('45) he was big-city gangster Schultz; in *Son of the Guardsman* ('46) he was an English duke; in *Radar Patrol vs. Spy King* ('50) he was a spy chief; in *Undersea Kingdom* ('36) he is Moloch, one of the Black Robes; in *White Eagle* ('41) he is Romino, gang member, while in *Brick Bradford* ('47) he is Dr. Tymok, missile weapons inventor.

"To many, Merton was the ideal Number Two villain. His ramrod-straight bearing and grim expression lent authority to his role as top man of the gang and intermediary to the Chief. As a matter of fact, when he appeared as 'just one of the boys' in a Western or action feature, it was there he seemed unconvincing for there was the nagging feel-

John Merton (left) and Charles Starrett.

ing in the minds of action fans that he ought to be giving orders instead of taking them. It just seemed natural."

William C. Cline, *In the Nick of Time*, McFarland & Co., 1984, p. 126

Merton was born in 1901. In his first serial, *The Red Rider* ('34), he was billed Mert LaVarre, his full name being John Merton LaVarre. For screen purposes, it was changed shortly thereafter to the familiar John Merton.

Included among Merton's films are *The Eagle's Brood* ('35), *Bar 20 Rides Again* ('35), *Call of the Prairie* ('36), *Aces and Eights* ('36), *Drums of Destiny* ('37), *Federal Bullets* ('37), *Colorado Kid* ('37), *Range Defenders* ('37), *Female Fugitive* ('38), *Two Gun Justice* ('38), *Knight of the Plains* ('38), *Gang Bullets* ('38), *The Renegade Trail* ('39), *Melody Ranch* ('40), *Covered Wagon Days* ('40), *Queen of the Yukon* ('40), *The Trail Blazers* ('40), *Under Fiesta Stars* ('41), *Billy the Kid's Smoking Guns* ('42), *Prairie Pals* ('42), *Girl Rush* ('44), *The Gay Cavalier* ('46), *Cheyenne Takes Over* ('47), *Western Renegades* ('49), *Fence Riders* ('50), *Silver Canyon* ('51), *Blue Canadian Rockies* ('52), *Up in Daisy's Penthouse* ('53) and *Saginaw Trail* ('53).

Merton died from a heart attack on September 19, 1959, in Los Angeles.

Serials

1934

The Red Rider. Univ., [15 Chapters] D: Louis Friedlander [Lew Landers]; LP: Buck Jones, Grant Withers, Marion Shilling, Walter Miller, Richard Cramer, Frank Rice.

1936

Undersea Kingdom. Rep., [12 Chapters] D: B. Reeves Eason, Joseph Kane; LP: Ray Corrigan, Lois Wilde, Monte Blue, William Farnum, Boothe Howard, Lee Van Atta.

1936

The Vigilantes Are Coming. Rep., [12 Chapters] D: Mack V. Wright, Ray Taylor; LP: Robert Livingston, Kay Hughes, Guinn Williams, Raymond Hatton, Fred Kohler.

1938

The Lone Ranger. Rep., [15 Chapters] D: william Witney, John English; LP: Lee Powell, Chief Thundercloud, Lynne Roberts, Herman Brix, Lane Chandler, Wally Wales [Hal Taliaferro].

The Fighting Devil Dogs. Rep., [12 Chapters] D: William Witney, John English; LP: Lee Powell, Herman Brix, Eleanor Stewart, Montagu Love.

Dick Tracy Returns. Rep., [15 Chapters] D: William Witney, John English; LP: Ralph Byrd, Lynne Roberts, Charles Middleton, Jerry Tucker, David Sharpe, Lee Ford.

1939

Daredevils of the Red Circle. Rep., [12 Chapters] D: William Witney, John English; LP: Charles Quigley, Herman Brix, David Sharpe, Carole Landis, Charles Middleton.

Zorro's Fighting Legion. Rep., [12 Chapters] D: William Witney, John English; Reed Hadley, Sheila Darcy, William Corson, Carleton Young, Leander de Cordova.

1940

Drums of Fu Manchu. Rep., [15 Chapters] D: William Witney, John English; LP: Henry Brandon, William Royle, Gloria Franklin, Robert Kellard, Luana Walters.

1941

Dick Tracy vs. Crime, Inc. Rep., [15 Chapters] D: William Witney, John English; LP: Ralph byrd, Jan Wiley, John Davidson, Ralph Morgan, Jack Mulhall.

White Eagle. Col., [15 Chapters] D: James W.

Horne; LP: Buck Jones, Raymond Hatton, Dorothy Fay, Jack Ingram, James Craven, John Merton, Edmund Cobb.

1943

Adventures of the Flying Cadets. Univ., [13 Chapters] D: Ray Taylor, Lewis D. Collins; LP: Johnny Downs, Bobby Jordan, Jennifer Holt, Eduardo Ciannelli, Billy Benedict, Regis Toomey, Robert Armstrong.

1944

Zorro's Black Whip. Rep., [12 Chapters] D: Spencer G. Bennet, Wallace Grissell; LP: Linda Stirling, George J. Lewis, Lucien Littlefield, Francis McDonald, John Merton, Hal Taliaferro, Tom London.

1945

Brenda Starr, Reporter. Col., [13 Chapters] D: William W. Fox; LP: Joan Woodbury, Kane Richmond, Syd Saylor, Joe Devlin, George Meeker, Wheeler Oakman.

Secret Agent X-9. Univ., [13 Chapters] D: Ray Taylor, Lewis D. Collins; LP: Lloyd Bridges, Keye Luke, Jan Wiley, Victoria Horne, Cy Kendall, George Lynn.

The Master Key. Univ., [13 Chapters] D: Ray Taylor, Lewis D. Collins; LP: Jan Wiley, Milburn Stone, Dennis Moore, Sarah Padden, Byron Foulger, Russell Hicks.

Jungle Queen. Univ., [13 Chapters] D: Ray Taylor, Lewis D. Collins; LP: Edward Norris, Lois Collier, Eddie Quillan, Douglas Dumbrille, Ruth Roman, Tala Birell.

1946

Hop Harrigan. Col., [15 Chapters] D: Derwin Abrahams; LP: William Bakewell, Jennifer Holt, Sumner Getchell, Emmett Vogan, John Merton, Wheeler Oakman, Claire James, Buzz Henry.

Son of the Guardsman. Col., [15 Chapters] D: Derwin Abrahams; LP: Robert Shaw, Duan Kennedy, Buzz Henry, Jim Diehl, Hugh Prosser, Leonard Penn, John Merton.

1947

Brick Bradford. Col., [15 Chapters] D: Spencer G. Bennet; LP: Kane Richmond, Linda Johnson, Rick Vallin, Pierre Watkin, Charles Quigley, Jack Ingram, John Merton.

Jack Armstrong. Col., [15 Chapters] D: Wallace Fox; LP: John Hart, Rosemary La Planche, Joe Brown, Jr., Claire James, Pierre Watkin, Charles Middleton.

1949

Adventures of Sir Galahad. Col., [15 Chapters] D: Spencer Bennet; LP: George Reeves,

Charles King, William Fawcett, Hugh Prosser, Lois Hall, Rick Vallin, Pat Barton, John Merton, Ray Corrigan, Nelson Leigh, Don Harvey.

1950

Radar Patrol vs. Spy King. Rep., [12 Chapters] D: Fred C. Brannon; LP: Kirk Alyn, Jean Dean, Anthony Warde, George J. Lewis, Eve Whitney, John Merton.

CHARLES MIDDLETON

Who can forget Charles Middleton's claim to fame as Emperor "Ming the Merciless" in the three Flash Gordon serials—*Flash Gordon* ('36), *Flash Gordon's Trip to Mars* ('38) and *Flash Gordon Conquers the Universe* ('40)? He superbly enacted the role of the demonic ruler of the universe while in gangster films he portrayed vindictive, cold-blooded killers: *Dick Tracy Returns* ('38), *Flaming Frontiers* ('38), *Daredevils of the Red Circle* ('39) and more.

Middleton was born in Elizabethtown, Kentucky, on October 7, 1879. Early on he learned how to handle horses, as his father raised thoroughbreds. As a young man he had a passel of jobs. While working as a rodeo rider at the St. Louis Exposition in 1904, he met his future wife, Leora Spillmeyer, who joined him to produce two plays, *A Texas Wooing* and *An Ocean Wooing*, with which they toured the United States. The couple married in 1910.

Middleton entered movies in 1920 in the serial *$1,000,000 Reward*, but he continued acting in stage productions such as *Konga*, *White Cargo* and *The Virginian*. Movie-wise he appeared in Metro's first talkie, *The Bellamy Trial* ('28). The first film to make Middleton known to B-Western and serial enthusiasts was the Mascot serial *The Miracle Rider* ('35). Middleton portrayed the

evil Zaroff, who had developed an explosive called X-94 that he uses to scare the Ravenhead Indians off land that has huge deposits of oil on it. The same year he appeared as Buck Peters in the first *Hop-a-Long Cassidy* film.

The serial that cinched his recognition was Universal's *Flash Gordon* ('36), based on Alex Raymond's comic strip. This serial—one of the most expensive and most successful ever made—has today taken on the aura of a classic and is still being shown on television and at film festivals. Middleton portrays Ming the Merciless, who endeavors to annihilate Flash Gordon (Buster Crabbe), Dr. Zarkov (Frank Shannon) and possibly Dale Arden on the planet Mongo. A sequel made in 1938 starred the principals of the first serial, but the action takes place on Mars, where Emperor Ming has allied himself with Queen Azura (Beatrice Roberts). In the last chapter Ming is thrown into a disintegrating chamber. So ends Ming, but...

Still trading on the popularity of Flash Gordon, Universal produced a third serial, *Flash Gordon Conquers the Universe* ('40). Buster Crabbe, Charles Middleton and Frank Shannon reprise their roles but Carol Hughes plays Dale Arden, as Jean Rogers was not available at that time.

Middleton was excellent as a foil for the

comedy teams of Laurel and Hardy, the Three Stooges, the Marx Brothers, Wheeler and Woolsey and the comedians W. C. Fields, Joe E. Brown, Harold Lloyd and Eddie Cantor. He was a member of the Masquers Club and the Comedy Club.

Middleton's wife, Leora, died in 1945. His grief was great but, refusing to let it get the best of him, he bounded back by doing a play, *January Thaw* ('46). Also that year he had the title role in PRC's *Strangler of the Swamp*.

Middleton was lucky in his business ventures. He operated several oil wells at a profit and invested in a highly successful gold mine.

In 1949, Middleton entered Torrance Memorial Hospital where he died on April 22. On January 7, 1960, his daughter Leora Middleton Ladd died in Hollywood at the age of 44.

Serials

1920

The $1,000,000 Reward. Grossman, [15 Chapters] D: George A. Lessey; S: Arthur B. Reeve, John W. Grey; LP: Lillian Walker, Coit Albertson, Charles Middleton, George A. Lessey, Joseph Marba.

1935

The Miracle Rider. Mascot, [15 Chapters] D: Armand Schaefer, B. Reeves Eason; S: Barney Sarecky, Wellyn Totman, Gerald and Maurice Geraghty; SP: John Rothmell; Cam: Ernest Miller, William Nobles; P: Nat Levine; LP: Tom Mix, Joan Gale, Charles Middleton, Jason Robards, Sr., Robert Kortman.

1936

Flash Gordon. Univ., [13 Chapters] D: Frederic Stephani; SP: George Plympton, Frederic Stephani, Basil Dickey, Ella O'Neill; P: Henry MacRae; Cam: Jerry Ash, Richard Fryer; LP: Buster Crabbe, Jean Rogers, Charles Middleton, Frank Shannon, Priscilla Lawson, John Lipson, James Pierce, Theodore Lorch.

As Ming the Merciless in the *Flash Gordon* serials.

1938

Flaming Frontiers. Univ., [15 Chapters] D: Ray Taylor, Alan James; SP: Wyndham Gittens, George Plympton, Basil Dickey, Paul Perez; P: Henry MacRae; LP: Johnny Mack Brown, Eleanor Hansen, Ralph Bowman [John Archer], Charles Middleton.

Dick Tracy Returns. Rep., [15 Chapters] D: William Witney, John English; SP: Barry Shipman, Franklyn Adreon, Ronald Davidson, Rex Taylor, Sol Shor; Cam: William Nobles; LP: Ralph Byrd, Lynne Roberts, Charles Middleton, Jerry Tucker, David Sharpe.

Flash Gordon's Trip to Mars. Univ., [15 Chapters] D: Ford Beebe, Robert Hill; S/SP: Wyndham Gittens, Norman S. Hall, Ray Trampe, Herbert Dalmas; LP: Buster Crabbe, Jean Rogers, Charles Middleton, Frank Shannon, Beatrice Roberts, Donald Kerr, Richard Alexander, C. Montague Shaw.

1939

Daredevils of the Red Circle. Rep., [12 Chapters] D: William Witney, John English; SP:

Barry Shipman, Franklyn Adreon, Rex Taylor, Ronald Davidson, Sol Shor; Cam: William Nobles; Mus: William Lava; LP: Charles Quigley, Herman Brix, David Sharpe, Carole Landis, Charles Middleton.

1940

Flash Gordon Conquers the Universe. Univ., [12 Chapters] D: Ford Beebe, Ray Taylor; SP: George H. Plympton, Basil Dickey, Barry Shipman; Cam: Jerry Ash; P: Henry MacRae; LP: Buster Crabbe, Carol Hughes, Charles Middleton, Anne Gwynne, Frank Shannon, Roland Drew, Lee Powell.

1942

Perils of Nyoka. Rep., [15 Chapters] D: William Witney; SP: ronald Davidson, Norman S. Hall, William Lively, Joseph Poland, Joseph O'Donnell; Cam: Reggie Lanning; Mus: Mort Glickman; LP: Kay Aldridge, Clayton Moore, William Benedict, Lorna Gray [Adrian Booth], Charles Middleton, George J. Lewis.

1943

Batman. Col., [15 Chapters] D: Lambert Hillyer; Mus: Lee Zahler; SP: Victor McLeod, Leslie Swabacker, Harry Frazer; LP: Lewis Wilson, Douglas Croft, J. Carrol Naish, Shirley Patterson, Charles Middleton.

1944

Black Arrow. Col., [15 Chapters] D: Lew Landers; SP: Sherman Lowe, Jack Stanley, Leighton Brill, Royal K. Cole; Mus: Lee Zahler; Cam: Richard Fryer; LP: Robert Scott, Adele Jergens, Kenneth MacDonald, Charles Middleton, George J. Lewis, I. Stanford Jolley.

The Desert Hawk. Col., [15 Chapters] D: B. Reeves Eason; Cam: James S. Brown, Jr.; Mus: Lee Zahler; LP: Gilbert Roland, Mona Maris, Ben Welden, Kenneth Macdonald, Frank Lackteen, Charles Middleton.

1945

Who's Guilty? Col., [15 Chapters] D: Howard Bretherton, Wallace Grissell; SP: Ande Lamb, George H. Plympton; Cam: Ira H. Morgan; Mus: Lee Zahler; LP: Robert Kent, Amelita Ward, Tim Ryan, Jayne Hazard, Minerva Urecal, Belle Mitchell.

1947

Jack Armstrong. Col., [15 Chapters] D: Wallace Fox; Cam: Ira H. Morgan; Mus: Lee Zahler; SP: Arthur Hoerl, Lewis Clay, Royal Cole, Leslie Swabacher; LP: John Hart, Rosemary LaPlanche, Joe Brown, Jr., Claire James, Pierre Watkin, Wheeler Oakman, Charles Middleton, Jack Ingram, Eddie Parker.

WALTER MILLER

Walter Corwin Miller was born March 9, 1892, in Dayton, Ohio. His elementary school years were spent in Atlanta, Georgia. Later he attended the Manual Training High School in Brooklyn, New York, and then took up acting by joining the first of several stock companies. He played juvenile leads and leaned toward light comedies. At 18 he was offered leading man roles for the Reliance Motion Picture Company. He accepted and made pictures for Reliance during 1911.

He is also said to have made pictures for the Rex and Edison companies. No record of his films before 1912 has been found.

He was drawn to the attention of director D. W. Griffith in 1912 and was hired, becoming a member of the original Biograph Film Company in New York. He made his debut in *The Informer* ('12) with Mary Pickford. The Lillian Gish–starring *Musketeers of Pig Alley* ('12) found him in company with Griffith's stable of actors— Lillian and Dorothy

Walter Miller and Allene Ray in *House Without a Key* (Pathé, 1926).

Gish, Lionel Barrymore, Harry Carey, Robert Harron, Antonio Moreno, Jack Pickford, Jack Dillon and W. C. Robinson.

Miller made at least 25 films for director Griffith in '12 and '13. His 1912 films, with leading lady listed in parentheses: *Two Daughters of Eve* (Lillian Gish); *So Near, Yet So Far* (Mary Pickford); *A Feud in the Kentucky Hills* (Mary Pickford); *My Baby* (Mary Pickford); *Brutality* (Mae Marsh); *A Cry for Help* (Lillian Gish).

Some of his 1913 films were *Oil and Water* (Blanche Sweet); *Adventure in the Autumn Woods* (Mae Marsh); *Love in an Apartment Hotel* (Mae Marsh); *The Unwelcome Guest* (Mary Pickford); *Near to Earth* (Mae Marsh); *The Perfidy of Mary* (Mae Marsh); *The Wanderer* (Mae Marsh); *The Yaqui Cur* (Mae Marsh); *His Mother's Son* (Mae Marsh);

Death's Marathon (Blanche Sweet); *The Coming of Angelo* (Blanche Sweet); *Two Men of the Desert* (Blanche Sweet); *A Modest Hero* (Lillian Gish and *The Mothering Heart* (Lillian Gish).

In 1914, Miller left Biograph to work for Klaw & Erlinger (five films) and Universal (three films). In 1915 he appeared in three Fox features and in 1916 one Fox feature. From 1917 through 1920 he appeared in 19 films for Metro (four), Trans-Russian (one), Advanced Pictures (one), Vitagraph (three), Artclass (one), Arrow (one), Goldwyn (one), Numa/Goldwyn (one), National/Selznick (one), Salient (one), Robertson Cole (one) and Arrow (two). Primarily he was a supporting player. His better films were *The Tie That Binds* ('21) with Barbara Bedford, *The Bootleggers* ('21) opposite Norma Shearer and

The Return of Tarzan ('21) with Gene Polar. He was appearing in films that mostly were quickies for "here today, gone tomorrow" companies. But fortunes took an upswing when Pathé cast him opposite Allene Ray in the serial *Sunken Silver* ('25). Ray had already appeared in four serials. Ray and Miller co-starred in ten Pathé serials between 1925 and 1929. They had what serial fans liked — youth, vitality, good looks and spontaneous adaptability to the unusual. They proved to have more staying power at the box office than the serial teams of William Duncan-Edith Johnson, Ben Wilson-Neva Gerber and Francis Ford-Grace Cunard.

Sunken Silver was ideal serial material. It was based on Albert Payson Terhune's *Black Caesar's Clan* and concerned a three-cornered struggle for buried treasure in the Florida Everglades. Like all Pathé serials of that period, *Sunken Silver* was in ten chapters.

Miller and Allene Ray were immediately put into *Play Ball* ('25), a baseball serial. It had a somewhat complicated plot hinged on the romance of a millionaire's daughter (Ray) and a rookie baseball player (Miller) who was the son of a senator. It seems that the senator was investigating the business methods of the millionaire, who was being influenced by a villainous count bent on getting funds for a dissident faction in his native land. The title of Chapter 10, "A Home Plate Wedding," indicates the importance of love interest in silent serials. When sound came in, love interest went out — of serials.

The next Ray-Miller chapterplay was one of their greatest hits and one of the finest serials ever made: *The Green Archer* ('25), based on the popular Edgar Wallace novel of that title. The problem of changing the English setting of the book to the U.S.A. was solved by having the villain transfer an English castle, stone by stone, to a site on the Hudson. The "ghost" of the castle (i.e., the Green Archer) supposedly travelled along — a plot gambit later found in *The Ghost Goes West* ('36).

Pathé cast Burr McIntosh as the villain. He was a cruel millionaire who kept a mys-terious prisoner locked up in a cell in the castle. A girl (Ray) living on a neighboring estate was determined to solve the mystery of the prisoner, and a captain of the State Police (Miller) helped her. The mysterious figure of the Green Archer, majestic in flowing robes, appeared at critical moments. His actions never seemed wholly evil nor wholly good. The last chapter explained all.

Ray and Miller's next serial was also a great success. It was concerned with spectacular mail robberies in the High Sierras. The center of the criminal activities was an abandoned hotel far from any town or village. Nevertheless, quite an assortment of people visited it, including a girl (Ray) intent on proving her brother innocent of complicity in the mail robberies and a forest ranger (Miller). From Room 28 the arch-criminal Redfield periodically emerged, masked and dressed in a black Commando suit. The identity of Redfield was withheld. The unmasking in Chapter Ten came as a shock to many.

After *Snowed In*, Pathé produced *The Fighting Marine* ('26) starring heavyweight champion Gene Tunney with Miller the second lead. A reporter seeks to protect an heiress who, under the terms of a will, must reside in a western mining town for six months. Naturally there are those who are determined that the conditions of the will not be met in order that *they* might receive the inheritance.

The next serial for Ray and Miller was *The House Without a Key* ('26). Though based on an Earl Derr Biggers Charlie Chan story, the character of Chan is relegated to the sidelines in this story of a long-ago crime and the enmity between two brothers. Cary Egan (Ray), the daughter of the righteous brother's partner, and John Winterslip, a nephew of the wealthy brother, attempt to recover a stolen treasure chest and to solve the mystery of the ancient crime.

The Melting Millions ('27) was next for Ray and Miller. A girl is adopted as a baby by a bandit. Years later, aided by a hero enam-ored of her and opposed by a band of wealthy criminals, she attempts to gain possession of a fortune that is rightfully hers. In addition to the hero, a mysterious stranger comes to her aid at tense moments. It is the least remembered of the ten Ray-Miller chapterplays.

Pathé next put Ray and Miller into *Hawk of the Hills* ('27). The Hawk, halfbreed leader of a band of Indians and renegade whites, captures Mary Selby, daughter of a miner who has a secret gold mine, hoping to trade her for the secret of the mine's location. Laramie, a government agent, poses as an outlaw and joins the Hawk's gang, quickly becoming Mary's friend and protector.

In their next serial, *Man Without a Face* ('27), Miller played a bank teller sent to the China interior — where a rebellion is in progress— to escort two sisters (Allene Ray and Jeanette Loff) back to Los Angeles to inherit a large fortune. Opposing them at every turn was a black-hooded villain called both "The Man Without a Face" and "The Master."

The ninth serial for Ray and Miller was titled *The Terrible People* ('28), from the book by Edgar Wallace. It opened with a punch scene in which a criminal about to be executed threatens drastic vengeance at the hands of the "Terrible People." Two cloaked figures stalk through the thriller.

Miller next co-starred with Ethlyne Clair in *Queen of the North Woods* ('29). A mysterious villain, calling himself the Wolf-Devil and wielding a strange power over wolf packs, terrorizes the Northwest. He dresses as a wolf, complete with an all-concealing wolf's headpiece to disguise his identity. The Royal Mounted Police are called in to investigate.

The tenth and last serial co-starring Allene Ray and Walter Miller was also the last serial Pathé would produce. *The Black Book* ('29) had Ray as a pretty young girl detective and Miller as a one-time wastrel who becomes her adoring suitor, pitting their wits against a criminal coterie. The mystery involves two black books containing information related to a rich platinum deposit.

Miller co-starred with Jacqueline Logan in Mascot's *King of the Kongo* ('29), a part-talking serial. Secret Service agent Larry Trent (Miller) and Diana Martin (Jacqueline Logan) meet while both are searching for missing relatives in the African jungle. They clash with a band of ivory thieves seeking hidden treasure.

Miller continued working in serials but he switched from hero to villain. He also became boss badman, menacing the likes of Ken Maynard, Buck Jones, Tim McCoy, William Boyd, Allan Lane, George O'Brien, Robert Livingston, Harry Carey and Gene Autry. Some think that he was better as a villain than as a hero. He played in many non–Westerns in a variety of roles.

Miller died in harness: On March 28, 1940, he and another actor agreed to pull no punches in a fight scene in a Gene Autry opus. Two days later he died from a heart attack.

Serials

1925

Sunken Silver. Pathé, [10 Chapters] D: George B. Seitz; SP: Frank Leon Smith; S: Albert Payson Terhune; LP: Allene Ray, Walter Miller, Frank Lackteen, Albert Roccardik, Charlie Fang.

Play Ball. Pathé, [10 Chapters] D: Spencer G. Bennet; SP: Frank Leon Smith; S: John J. McGraw; LP: Allene Ray, Walter Miller, Harry Semels, J. Barney Sherry.

The Green Archer. Pathé, [10 Chapters] D: Spencer G. Bennet; SP: Frank Leon Smith; S: Edgar Wallace; LP: Allene Ray, Walter Miller, Dorothy King, Burr McIntosh, Steven Grattan.

1926

Snowed In. Pathé, [10 Chapters] D: Spencer Bennet; SP: Frank Leon Smith; LP: Allene Ray, Walter Miller, Leonard Clapham [Tom London], Harrison Martell.

The Fighting Marine. Pathé, [10 Chapters] D: Spencer Bennet; S/SP: Frank Leon Smith; LP: Gene Tunney, Walter Miller, Marjorie Day, Virginia Vance, Sherman Ross.

The House Without a Key. Pathé, [10 Chapters] D: Spencer Bennet; SP: Frank Leon Smith;

S: Earl Derr Biggers; LP: Allene Ray, Walter Miller, E. H. Calvert, Betty Caldwell, Frank Lackteen.

1927

Melting Millions. Pathé, [10 Chapters] D: Spencer Bennet; S: Joseph Anthony Roach; LP: Allene Ray, Walter Miller, E. H. Calvert, William Norton Bailey, Eugenia Gilbert.

The Hawk of the Hills. Pathé, [10 Chapters] D: Spencer Bennet; S: George Arthur Gray; LP: Allene Ray, Walter Miller, Frank Lackteen, Paul Panzer, Harry Semels.

The Man Without a Face. Pathé, [10 Chapters] D: Spencer G. Bennet; SP: Joseph Anthony Roach; S: C. W. and Alice M. Williamson; LP: Allene Ray, Walter Miller, E. H. Colvert, Jeanette Loff, Gladden James.

1928

The Police Reporter. Artclass, [10 Chapters] D: Jack Nelson; S: Arthur B. Reeve; Spv.: George M. Merrick; LP: Walter Miller, Eugenia Gilbert, Kenneth Duncan, Robert Belcher.

The Mysterious Airman. Artclass, [10 Chapters] D: Harry Revier; SP: Arthur B. Reeve; Spv.: George M. Merrick; LP: Walter Miller, Eugenia Gilbert, Robert Walker, Eugene Burr.

The Terrible People. Pathé, [10 Chapters] D: Spencer G. Bennet; SP: George Arthur Gray; S: Edgar Wallace; LP: Allene Ray, Walter Miller, Larry Steers, Allan Craven, Wilfred North.

1929

Queen of the Northwoods. Pathé, [10 Chapters] D: Spencer Bennet, Thomas L. Storey; SP: George Arthur Gray; LP: Ethlyne Claire, Tom London, Frank Lackteen, Edward Cecil.

The Black Book. Pathé, [10 Chapters] D: Spencer Bennet, Tom Storey; S: Joseph Anthony Roach; LP: Allene Ray, Walter Miller, Frank Lackteen, Edith London, Willie Fung.

King of the Kongo. Mascot, [10 Chapters] D: Richard Thorpe; SP: Harry Sinclair Drago; P: Nat Levine; LP: Jacqueline Logan, Walter Miller, Richard Tucker, Larry Steers.

1930

The Lone Defender. Mascot, [12 Chapters] D: Richard Thorpe; LP: Rin-Tin-Tin, Walter Miller, June Marlowe, Buzz Barton, Josef Swickard, Lafe McKee, Lee Shumway.

King of the Wild. Mascot, [12 Chapters] D: Richard Thorpe, B. Reeves Eason; P: Nat Levine; S/SP: Wyndham Gittens, Ford Beebe; Cam: Bob Kline, Edward Kull; Mus: Lee Zahler; LP: Walter Miller, Nora Lane, Dorothy Christy, Tom Santschi, Boris Karloff.

1931

Danger Island. Univ., [12 Chapters] D: Ray Taylor; SP: Basil Dickey; S: Henry MacRae; LP: Kenneth Harlan, Lucile Browne, Tom Ricketts, Walter Miller.

The Galloping Ghost. Mascot, [12 Chapters] D: B. Reeves Eason; P: Nat Levine; LP: Harold (Red) Grange, Dorothy Gulliver, Walter Miller, Francis X. Bushman, Jr.

1932

Shadow of the Eagle. Mascot, [12 Chapters] D: Ford Beebe, Colbert Clark, Wyndham Gittens; P: Nat Levine; Cam: Benjamin Kline, Victor Scheurich; Mus: Lee Zahler; John Wayne, Dorothy Gulliver, Walter Miller, Kenneth Harlan, Edward Hearn.

The Last of the Mohicans. Mascot, [12 Chapters] D: B. Reeves Eason, Ford Beebe; SP: Colbert Clark, John Natteford, Ford Beebe, Wyndham Gittens; Cam: Ernest Miller, Jack Long; P: Nat Levine; LP: Harry Carey, Edwina Booth, Hobart Bosworth, Junior Coghlan, Walter Miller, Yakima Canutt, Lucille Browne, Edward Hearn.

1933

Gordon of Ghost City. Univ., [12 Chapters] D: Ray Taylor; S: Peter B. Kyne; SP: Ella O'Neill, Basil Dickey, George Plympton, Harry O. Hoyt, Het Manheim; LP: Buck Jones, Madge Bellamy, Walter Miller, Hugh Enfield, William Desmond.

1934

The Vanishing Shadow. Univ., [12 Chapters] D: Louis Friedlander [Lew Landers]; SP: Het Manheim, Basil Dickey, George Morgan; S: Ella O'Neill; Cam: Richard Fryer; LP: Onslow Stevens, Ada Ince, Walter Miller, James Durkin, William Desmond.

The Red Rider. Univ., [15 Chapters] D: Louis Friedlander [Lew Landers]; SP: George Plympton, Vin Moore, Ella O'Neill, George Morgan; S: W. C. Tuttle; P: Henry MacRae; LP: Buck Jones, Grant Withers, Marion Shilling, Walter Miller, Richard Cramer.

Tailspin Tommy. Univ., [12 Chapters] D: Louis Friedlander [Lew Landers]; SP: Norman S. Hall, Vin Moore, Basil Dickey, Ella O'Neill; LP: Maurice Murphy, Noah Beery, Jr., Patricia Farr, Walter Miller, Grant Withers.

Pirate Treasure. Univ., [12 Chapters] D: Ray Taylor; SP: Basil Dickey, Jack Nelson, George Plympton; S: Ella O'Neill; LP: Richard Talmadge, Lucille Lund, Walter Miller, Pat O'Malley, William Desmond.

1935

The Call of the Savage. Univ., [12 Chapters] D: Lewis Friedlander [Lew Landers]; SP: Nate Gatzert, George Plympton, Basil Dickey; S: Otis Adelbert Kline; LP: Noah Beery, Jr., Dorothy Short, Harry Woods, Walter Miller.

Rustlers of Red Dog. Univ., [12 Chapters] D: Louis Friedlander [Lew Landers]; SP: George Plympton, Basil Dickey, Ella O'Neill, Nate Gatzert, Vin Moore; S: Nathanial Eddy; LP: Johnny Mack Brown, Joyce Compton, Walter Miller, Raymond Hatton, Harry Woods, William Desmond, Lafe McKee, Edmund Cobb.

The Roaring West. Univ., [15 Chapters] D: Ray Taylor; SP: George Plympton, Nate Gatzert, Ella O'Neill, Basil Dickey, Robert Rothafel; P: Henry MacRae; S: Edward Earl Repp; Cam: William Sicknew, Richard Fryer; LP: Buck Jones, Muriel Evans, Walter Miller, Frank McGlynn, Harlan Knight, Tom London, Charles King.

1937

Wild West Days. Univ., [13 Chapters] D: Ford Beebe, Cliff Smith; SP: Wyndham Gittens, Norman S. Hall, Ray Trampe; S: W. R. Burnett; P: Ben Koenig, Henry MacRae; LP: Johnny Mack Brown, Lynn Gilbert, Robert Kortman, George Shelley, Walter Miller.

The Secret of Treasure Island. Col., [15 Chapters] D: Elmer Clifton; SP: George Rosener, Elmer Clifton, George Merrick; LP: Don Terry, Gwen Gaze, Grant Withers, Hobart Bosworth, William Farnum, Walter Miller, Dave O'Brien, Yakima Canutt.

1939

Dick Tracy's G-Men. Rep., [15 Chapters] D: William Witney, John English; SP: Sol Shor, Barry Shipman, Franklyn Adreon, Rex Taylor; AP: Robert Becke; Cam: William Nobles; Mus: William Lava; LP: Ralph Byrd, Irving Pichel, Phylis Isley [Jennifer Jones], Walter Miller, Ted Pearson, Jack Ingram, Bud Geary.

1941

Dick Tracy vs. Crime, Inc. Rep., [15 Chapters] D: William Witney, John English; SP: Ronald Davidson, Norman S. Hall, William Lively, Joseph O'Donnell, Joseph Poland; AP: W. J. O'Sullivan; Cam: Reggie Lanning; Mus: Cy Feuer; LP: Ralph Byrd, Jan Wiley, John Davidson, Ralph Morgan, Michael Owen, Kenneth Harlan, Walter Miller, Robert Frazer, Hooper Atchley, Nora Lane, John Merton, Forrest Taylor.

MARILYN MILLS

Marilyn Mills was a good horsewoman, and this talent was her chief asset rather than her histrionics. She was also the wife of J. Charles Davis. However, she was already an established Western heroine before she married him, and it would be inaccurate to suggest that her career was the result of her husband's influence. Marilyn's riding skills should have made her better known than she was, but all her films were for Poverty Row companies, and she never got the promotion she deserved.

Most of Marilyn's Westerns featured her horses, Beverly and Star, and included a few horse bits to play up Marilyn's riding ability. Sometimes comedy was emphasized; in *The Cactus Cure* ('25) she was the beautiful rancher's daughter kidnapped by Yakima Canutt and hidden in the closet of a haunted house, which led to all kinds of shenanigans as bumbling hero Dick Hatton attempted a rescue. Other films were more starkly realistic, like *Two-Fisted Justice* ('24), which was heavy on illicit love and murder.

Most of Marilyn's feature Westerns were made for Arrow, and in most of them she played opposite minor (and we do mean minor!) cowboy star Dick Hatton. She is known to have made two-reelers but the author has no information on them.

Marilyn co-starred with Jack Perrin in Arrow's 15-chapter thriller *Riders of the Plains*. A good Western in its day, it has long been lost and forgotten in spite of the fact that Perrin and his wonder horse Starlight did some of their best work in it.

Marilyn often doubled other stars, for example Mary Pickford in *Dorothy Vernon of Haddon Hall* ('24). It was Marilyn on her beautifully trained Arabian horse Beverly who leaped over a crumbling wall and slid halfway down a steep hill instead of Mary.

With the coming of sound, Marilyn seems to have faded into the sunset along with the independent companies for which she labored.

Serial

1924

Riders of the Plains. Arrow, [15 Chapters] D: Jacques Jaccard; SP: Karl Coolidge, Jacques Jaccard; LP: Jack Perrin, Marilyn Mills, Ruth Royce, Charles Brinley.

RHEA MITCHELL

Rhea Mitchell is best remembered today for having made six films with William S. Hart and for having been murdered by a houseboy who went into a rage when she upbraided him for an innocuous compliment he paid her. Rhea, a deeply religious woman who neither drank nor smoked, apparently misinterpreted his remark. When she ordered him out of her apartment, he choked her to death with the belt from her own robe.

Mitchell's claim to cinema fame rests primarily on her films with Hart—*In the Sage Brush Country* ('14), *On the Night Stage* ('15), *The Scourge of the Desert* ('15), *Mr. Silent Haskins* ('15), *Tools of Providence* ('15) and *The Money Corral* ('19).

Rhea alternated between feminine leads and supporting parts throughout her career. One distinction she had was starring in the shortest serial on record—*Sequel to the Diamond from the Sky* ('16), in four chapters (also released as an eight-reel feature). Her second serial was *The Hawk's Trail* ('19), in 15 chapters with King Baggot as her leading man.

Other films included *Recreation* ('14), a one-half reeler with Charlie Chaplin; *Don Quixote* ('16) with De Wolf Hopper; *The Release of Dan Forbes* ('16), her fifth film with William Stowell; *The Blindness of Divorce* ('18) with Charles Clary; *The Unexpected* ('18) with Bert Lytell; *The Sleeping Lion* ('19) with Monroe Salisbury; *The Scoffer* ('20) with James Kirkwood; *The Innocent Cheat*

('21) with Roy Stewart; *A Ridin' Romeo* ('21) with Tom Mix; *The Greatest Menace* ('23) with Ann Little; and *Danger Patrol* ('28) with William Russell.

Rhea was born on December 10, 1893, in Oregon and grew up in the Portland area. She was a stage actress prior to entering films in 1913. Her career went into a deep slump toward the end of the silent era and throughout the '30s and '40s she played bit parts, especially at MGM. About 1953 she quit to learn apartment house management. It was on September 16, 1957, while working as a manager, that she was murdered. It was a sad ending for the red-haired beauty who had played opposite such early day stalwarts as Hart, Mix, Russell, Lytell and Baggot.

Serials

1916

Sequel to the Diamond from the Sky. Amer., [4 Chapters] D: Edward Sloman; SP: Terry Ramsaye; LP: Rhea Mitchell, William Russell, Charlotte Burton, William Tedmarsh, Oral Humphrey.

1919

The Hawk's Trail. Burston, [15 Chapters] D: W. S. Van Dyke; SP: Louis and George Burston; S: Nan Blair; LP: King Baggot, Rhea Mitchell, Grace Darmond, Harry Lorraine, Fred Windermere.

RUTH MIX

Ruth Mix, daughter of Tom Mix, was born on an Oklahoma ranch on July 13, 1912. Her childhood was spent learning to ride and becoming very good at it. The rodeo, the circus and the variety stage were a part of her life. She was educated at Maryville College of the Sacred Heart in St. Louis, Missouri. Her mother was Olive Stokes, Tom Mix's third wife. Since Olive and Tom were divorced in 1917, Ruth spent most of her youth with her mother.

In 1926, World Lascelle Productions, a minor company, starred Ruth in *Tex*, supported by Robert McKim and Francelia Billington. The company banked on the name "Mix" drawing ticket buyers. Ruth was only 14 at the time. *Tex* ('26) was followed by *That Girl Oklahoma* ('26), *The Little Boss* ('27) and a minor role in *Four Sons* ('28).

Ruth journeyed to New York in 1928 and was able to land a part in *Earl Carroll's Vanities.* She remained on Broadway nearly three years. In 1930–31 she appeared in vaudeville on the RKO circuit with an act

called "Ruth Mix's Rodeo Revue." It was during this time that she eloped to Yuma, Arizona, with actor Douglas Gilmore and was married before her father could stop it. She was only 17, so Tom got the marriage annulled. Ruth returned to Hollywood and played opposite Wally Wales in *Red Fork Range* ('31). The author finds no credits for her in the years '32, '33 and '34. Possibly she was touring with her own stage show.

In 1935, Ruth concentrated on a movie career. She played opposite Rex Bell in *Fighting Pioneers* ('35), *Gunfire* ('35), *Saddle Aces* ('35) and *The Tonto Kid* ('35) for Resolute Pictures. In 1936 she played the heroine in Hoot Gibson's *The Riding Avenger* for Diversion Pictures. Then came the serials. She was Mrs. George Custer in *Custer's Last Stand* ('36), a 15-chapter serial produced by Stage and Screen Productions. Though an independent, cheaply made serial, it boasted a slew of name actors, for example Creighton Hale (thirteenth in cast), Bobby Nelson (fifteenth) and William Desmond (sixteenth). The story centers around a sacred medicine arrow lost during one of the skirmishes between red men and whites. Major Trent (Joseph Swickard) is unaware it carries the secret of the location of an Indian cavern of gold. Knowing about the arrow, renegade Tom Blade (Reed Howes) seeks to steal it. To achieve this purpose, he keeps hostilities going. Scout Kit Cardigan (Rex Lease) suspects Blade and fights to prevent all-out war, but the stage is set for Custer's Last Stand.

In *The Clutching Hand* ('36), Ruth gets a little more screen time. Her father, a researcher, discovers a formula for the manufacture of synthetic gold. Criminals under the command of "The Clutching Hand" kidnap him. Craig Kennedy (Jack Mulhall) and friends attempt to find the abducted scientist.

In *The Black Coin*, her third Stage and Screen serial, Ruth is a Secret Service agent who, with fellow agent Ralph Graves, is after a smuggling gang headed by The Clutching Hand. Aside from the smuggling operation is the matter of buried gold, the location of which is revealed by a map created by assembling 12 black coins. Dave O'Brien, as an agent of the Caswell Shipping Company, handles most of the action.

She often toured with her father and was in charge of the Tom Mix Circus when it foundered in Texas in 1940. Tom had lost interest and creditors were hounding him. There was nothing Ruth could do to keep the circus afloat.

In 1938, Ruth married John A. Guthrie, a rodeo promoter. The marriage lasted into the early '40s, when she divorced Guthrie to marry William H. Hill, a rancher. Hill died in 1976. He and Ruth had three children (Mrs. Henry Lipe, William Hickman Hill and Gordon Hill). Ruth had lived in Corpus Christi, Texas, since 1954. In later years she worked as a secretary at Reynolds Metal Company and as a saleslady at Lichtensteins until her retirement in 1974. She died on September 21, 1977, after a short illness. She was 65.

Serials

1936

Custer's Last Stand. S & S, [15 Chapters] D: Elmer Clifton; SP: George A. Durlan, Eddy Graneman, William Lively; P: George M. Merrick; Spv.: Louis Weiss; Cam: Bert Longnecker; Mus: Hal Chasnoff; LP: Rex Lease, William Farnum, Jack Mulhall, Lona Andre, Dorothy Gulliver, Ruth Mix, George Chesebro.

The Clutching Hand. S & S, [15 Chapters] D: Albert Herman; Spv.: Louis Weiss; SP: Louis D'Usseau, Dallas Fitzgerald; Adapt:George M. Merrick, Eddy Graneman; Cam: James Diamond; Mus: Lee Zahler; LP: Jack Mulhall, Ruth Mix, Marion Shilling, Rex Lease, William Farnum, Reed Howes.

The Black Coin. S & S, [15 Chapters] D: Albert Herman; S: George M. Merrick; SP: Eddy Graneman, Dallas M. Fitzgerald, Bob Lively, Albert Herman; Spv.: Louis Weiss; Cam: James Diamond; Mus: Lee Zahler; LP: Ralph Graves, Ruth Mix, Dave O'Brien, Constance Bergen, Mathew Betz, Clara Kimball Young, Robert Frazer, Yakima Canutt.

TOM MIX

Tom Mix brought flair to the Western film. Unlike his contemporary William S. Hart, Mix had no interest in the realism of the Old West. His was a romanticized vision, with the cowboy as rural knight, and he built a legend for America not unlike the one that exists for England with King Arthur and his merry men. It was all high action and high morality and lots of showmanship, something Tom Mix came by naturally.

Mix was born in Mix Run, Pennsylvania, on January 6, 1880, and grew up in the scenic hill country around DuBois. When war was declared against Spain in 1898, Tom immediately joined the Army and served out the war in Delaware and Pennsylvania. When he was 22 he married a girl named Grace Allin, deserted the Army and took his bride to the wilds of the Indian Territory. The marriage was soon annulled. A marriage to Kitty Perrine in 1905 lasted a year, and in 1907 he married Olive Stokes.

Ruth Mix was born to Tom and Olive on July 13, 1912. The marriage to Olive ended in divorce in 1917, and in 1918 Tom married actress Victoria Forde. Daughter Thomasina was born on February 12, 1922. The marriage lasted until the end of 1930 when Victoria obtained a divorce on grounds of mental cruelty. In early 1932, Tom married Mabel Ward, an aerialist with the Sells-Floto Circus.

Tom's first job in Indian Territory (now Oklahoma) was teaching others physical fitness. Other jobs included deputy marshall of Dewey and drum major with the Oklahoma Cavalry Band. He was working as a bartender shoving drinks across the mahogany in an Oklahoma City bar when Col. Joe Miller blew into town for a cattlemen's convention in 1905. After a little sipping, chewing and jawing, the irascible colonel hired the 22-year-old intractable kid who envisioned himself a cowboy. For cash wages of $15 a month and room and board, Tom went to work as a wrangler of tenderfeet on the 101 dude ranch and quickly worked his way up to livestock foreman of the vast enterprise. Before long he was winning the respect of professional cowboys such as Bill Pickett, entering rodeos and holding his own with the best of them.

When the Selig Company came looking for a ranch on which to shoot *Ranch Life in the Great Southwest*, Tom volunteered a little spread he and Olive had in the Cherokee Territory. Tom was hired to handle stock and act as safety man, but he asked director Francis Boggs for a chance to be featured in the film. Boggs consented, and Tom was cast in a bronco-busting sequence. His career as a motion picture actor was launched. Based upon his limited exposure as one of the rodeo performers in the Selig short, Tom Mix became a regular with the studio from 1910 to 1918.

Tom rose to stardom in the years 1913–14 in one- and two-reel action flicks which appealed to the multitudes. His strong, handsome figure and virile qualities made him an appealing star. His brand of oater was catching on, although he was still several years away from overtaking the ultra-realist, William S. Hart, in popularity.

In 1917, Tom was induced by William Fox to come to work for the Fox studio, where Tom made his greatest Westerns. He became the most popular cowboy of them all in the early 1920s, and his salary rose to about $20,000 a week! His movies were streamlined and showy, specialized in action for its own sake, and presented a superficial and glamorized picture of the West. He could be counted on for his usual rip-snortin', boisterously harmless bronco-bustin' stunts in every picture, stirring up the Western dust literally and figuratively and injecting a modicum of pep into situations.

Kathleen O'Connor and Tom Mix in *Prairie Trails* (Fox, 1921).

Cupid's Roundup ('18) was the first of eighty full-length features Tom made for Fox. His final feature for the studio was *Painted Post* ('28). Mix literally built the Fox Studio into a major corporation.

After leaving Fox in 1928, Tom made a short series of Westerns for entrepreneur Joseph P. Kennedy, head of FBO, which later became RKO. Hollywood was in turmoil. The studios were endeavoring to cope with sound features and theaters around the world were faced with the necessity of new sound equipment. The FBO series failed to generate much enthusiasm although the Mix name practically assured the profitability of the series. However, the quality of the films did not measure up to the Fox product.

Thus, due to the dismal FBO films, the lack of enthusiasm for talking films, and the Wall Street crash, Tom left Hollywood to become the featured star of the Sells Floto Circus.

Universal signed Tom for a series of sound films in 1932. *The Rider of Death Valley* ('32), the first, had a running time of 78 minutes. His nine talkies proved popular enough, but he was seriously injured during the filming of *Rustler's Roundup* ('32) when his horse Tony, Jr., fell with him, and once again Tom retired from moviemaking. For the next eight years he traveled the sawdust trail, first with the Sam B. Dill Circus and then with his own.

Tom took time to make his last movie in 1935 to raise money to keep his circus on the road. Nat Levin, president of Mascot Pictures, offered him $10,000 a week to star in the 15-chapter serial *The Miracle Rider*. The serial was completed in four weeks. It was Mascot's only 15-chapter serial. The opening chapter was five reels in length. The story revolved around the efforts of Ranger Captain Tom Morgan and Ruth, daughter of a murdered chieftain, to save the Ravenhead Indians from being driven off their land by Zaroff (Charles Middleton). Zaroff and his minions are secretly mining Indian ore, which Zaroff needs to produce the world's deadliest explosive, "X-94."

Upon the failure of his circus in 1938, Tom all but faded from public limelight except for a European personal appearance tour in 1938–39.

Tom Mix was killed in a freak one-car accident a few miles north of Florence, Arizona, on October 12, 1940, as he zipped across the landscape in his custom-built Cord roadster with the same frenzy he used to ride "Old Blue" and "Tony." He was lowered to his final resting place in a tree-shaded grave on a hillside in Forest Lawn Memorial Park in Glendale, in a section known as "Whispering Pines." Five thousand mourners paid their respects.

Serial

1935

The Miracle Rider. Mascot, [15 Chapters] D: B. Reeves Eason, Armand Schaefer; SP: John Rathmell; S: Barney Sarecky, Wellyn Totman, Gerald Geraghty; P: Nat Levine; LP: Tom Mix, Charles Middleton, Joan Gale, Jason Robards, Edward Hearn, Robert Frazer, Wally Wales, Charles King, Tom London.

GERALD MOHR

Gerald Mohr died from a heart attack while in Stockholm, Sweden, in 1968. He was 54 years old. Fans remember him for his very first serial role, Slick Latimer in *Jungle Girl* ('41). Fine, sleek and dark, with a headful of curly hair, he was both an excellent villain and convincing hero, as in *The Lone Wolf in Mexico* and *The Lone Wolf in London* and TV's *Foreign Intrigue*. In *Adventures of Captain Marvel*, he was the voice of the Scorpion.

Among his 50 movies were *Gilda*, *Lady of Burlesque*, *Detective Story*, *Ten Tall Men*, *Murder in Times Square*, *The Eddie Cantor Story*, and *Funny Girl*.

Gerald Mohr and Francis Gifford in *Jungle Girl* (Republic, 1941).

Serials

1941

Jungle Girl. Rep., [15 Chapters] D: William Witney, John English; SP: Ronald Davidson, Norman S. Hall, William Lively, Joseph O'-Donnell, Joseph F. Poland, Alfred Batson; AP: Hiram S. Brown, Jr.; Cam: Reggie Lanning; Mus: Cy Feuer; LP: Frances Gifford, Tom Neal, Gerald Mohr, Trevor Bardette, Eddie Acuff, Frank Lackteen.

Adventures of Captain Marvel. Rep., [112 Chapters] D: William Witney, John English; SP: Ronald Davidson, Norman S. Hall, Arch B. Heath, Joseph Poland, Sol Shor; P: Hiram S. Brown, Jr.; Cam: William Nobles; Mus: Cy Feuer; LP: Tom Tyler, Frank Coghlan, Jr., William Benedict, Louise Currie, Gerald Mohr (voice of the Scorpion).

CLAYTON MOORE

There are middle-aged men who never heard Bruce Beemer as Tonto's "Kemo Sabe" on the radio, nor saw Lee Powell or Robert Livingston riding the great white horse "Silver" on the movie screen. To those fans Clayton Moore will always be the Lone Ranger, and his serials will mean nothing. But to those lucky fans who first saw him as a serial hero, he will always be that, and his television fame will be "frosting on the cake."

— Bill Cline

Clayton Moore, "The Lone Ranger" to the world, was born Jack Carlton Moore on September 14, 1914, on the south side of Chicago, the son of a real estate broker. He embarked on a career in show business with a trapeze act at the Century of Progress Exposition in Chicago in 1934. Following his brief circus stint, during which time he suffered several injuries, he worked for modeling agencies in Chicago and New York. As an all-around athlete, proficient in swimming, diving and gymnastics, the trim, broad-shouldered six-footer cut a handsome and commanding presence.

In 1937, Moore went to Hollywood with the intention of becoming an actor. After many months he was tested by Warner Brothers and given a six-month contract. Nothing happened. Similarly at MGM he was not used except possibly in crowd scenes where warm bodies were needed. But producer Edward Small thought Moore had potential and gave him a speaking part in *The Son of Monte Cristo* ('40). Following were such pictures as *Kit Carson* ('40), *Tuxedo Junction* ('41), *International Lady* ('41), *Outlaws of Pine Ridge* ('42) and *Black Dragons* ('42). At Republic he auditioned for and won the role of Larry Grayson in *Perils of Nyoka* ('42). The serial was a runaway success.

Perils of Nyoka is the story of an archaeological expedition searching for the Tablets of Hippocrates, which contain long-lost Greek medical knowledge, and a young woman trying to find her lost father, who was captured by a tribe of Bedouins. It was marked with action and intrigue. Learning of a great treasure supposedly buried with the Tablets, an evil woman named Vultura (Adrian Booth), high priestess of a vicious Arab tribe, and her chief follower Cassib (Charles Middleton) set out to reach the se-

cret location first. The conflicts between the expedition and the treasure-mad plunderers resulted in what has become a serial classic. The director was one of the best of all time — William Witney.

Unfortunately for his career, Moore spent the next three years as a corporal in the U.S. Air Force.

Back from the war, Clayton played a criminal named Ashe in *The Crimson Ghost* ('46), carrying out the orders of the title character, a mysterious robed villain with a black hood over a huge skull-like mask.

In Republic's *Jesse James Rides Again* ('47), Clayton portrays a reformed outlaw (Jesse) who battles a gang of hooded raiders conducting a reign of terror in Tennessee. Roy Barcroft was the bad guy wanting to secure the oil rights in Peaceful Valley, and might have been successful except for the action of the fugitive outlaw.

In *G-Men Never Forget* ('47), Moore plays F.B.I. agent Ted O'Hara who, with fellow agent Frances Blake (Ramsay Ames), sets out to solve the mystery surrounding a prison break and winds up solving the mystery of a phony commissioner as well.

Adventures of Frank and Jesse James came to the screen in 1948 with Clayton returning for his second and last appearance as Jesse. The first serial lacked a Frank James character, but in *Adventures* Steve Darrell played Jesse's brother. Often a heavy, Darrell served well as the auxiliary lead. His rugged, plain features contrasted with and yet complimented the square-jawed handsomeness of Moore, and they made a good serial team.

On the route to reform from their outlaw past, the brothers intend to compensate their former robbery victims from the proceeds of a gold mine, but first they have to work the mine and strike a paying vein. A villain discovers the vein and tries to stop the mine operation until he can gain control of it.

Moore starred in *Ghost of Zorro* ('49) playing the grandson of the original Zorro and donning grandpa's mask to thwart a villain's schemes. Ken Mason (Moore) had learned from a childhood Indian friend (George J.

Clayton Moore and Kay Aldridge in *Perils of Nyoka* (Republic, 1941).

Lewis) that he was the grandson of the famous crimefighter Zorro. As the masked avenger and his Indian sidekick, they stamp out the efforts of a vicious outlaw sabotaging telegraph service to the west.

Flying Disc Man from Mars ('51) featured Moore in footage taken from *The Crimson Ghost.* The serial is practically a remake of *The Purple Monster Strikes* ('45).

In *Radar Men from the Moon* ('52), Moore plays a villain named Graber who was a lot like his character in *The Crimson Ghost.* He and fellow baddie Bob Stephenson are sent by the rulers of the moon (led by Roy Barcroft) to do away with hero Commando Cody (George Wallace) before he is able to warn the Earth's leaders about a planned invasion by the evil men in control of the moon.

In *Gunfighters of the Northwest* ('53) Moore shared billing with stuntman-actor Jock Mahoney, who was billed as *Jack* Mahoney for his role as a Canadian Mountie. It was the only Columbia serial ever filmed completely on location without a single interior shot.

Moore's last Republic serial was *Jungle Drums of Africa* ('53) opposite lovely Phyllis Coates. As a mining engineer he is sent to Africa to discover and develop potential uranium deposits on the tribal lands of Chief Douanga. The village witch doctor joins forces with the foreign agent. Alan (Moore) and Carol (Coates) are endangered many times before finally emerging victorious.

Moore won the role of the Lone Ranger in the television series of that name. The serial debuted on September 15, 1949, and was the first Western series produced for television. Moore appeared on the series every year except for one season — September 1952 to September 1953, when the producers replaced him with John Hart while contract negotiations were going on with Moore. Hart played the masked man in 56 episodes, whereas Moore wore the mask in 169 episodes of the popular series, which is still being aired via syndication.

In 1956, Warner Brothers filmed *The Lone Ranger* with Moore and Jay "Tonto" Silverheels in their original roles. The film was successful and United Artists followed up with *The Lone Ranger and the Lost City of Gold* ('58). The television series closed down in '57 with 225 episodes having been made.

Moore hit the "personal appearance" trail for the next 20 years. The Wrather Corporation, owners of the rights to the Lone Ranger, obtained a 1979 court order restraining Moore from wearing the Lone Range black mask at paid public appearances. The movie that inspired the lawsuit, *The Legend of the Lone Ranger* ('81), lost $11 million. In 1984 the Wrather Corporation, its Hollywood movie have come and gone, relented, and Moore was given permission to don his full regalia again at promotional appearances. At age 70, the old kemo sabe could wear his real Texas Ranger mask once more.

Clayton Moore died of a heart attack on December 28, 1997. He was pronounced dead at a Los Angeles hospital. Surviving were his daughter, Dawn Gerrity, and his fourth wife, Clarita Petrone. Sally Allen, Moore's wife of 43 years, died in 1986.

Serials

1942

Perils of Nyoka. Rep., [15 Chapters] D: William Witney; SP: Ronald Davidson, Norman S. Hall, William Lively, Joseph Poland, Joseph O'-Donnell; AP: W. J. O'Sullivan; Cam: Reggie Lanning; Mus: Mort Lanning; LP: Kay Aldridge, Clayton Moore, William Benedict, Lorna Gray [Adrian Booth], Charles Middleton.

1946

The Crimson Ghost. Rep., [12 Chapters] D: William Witney, Fred Brannon; SP: Albert De-

Mond, Basil Dickey, Jesse Duffy, Sol Shor; AP: Ronald Davidson; Cam: Bud Thackery; Mus: Mort Glickman; LP: Charles Quigley, Linda Stirling, Clayton Moore, I. Stanford Jolley, Kenne Duncan.

1947

Jesse James Rides Again. Rep., [13 Chapters] D: Fred C. Brannon, Thomas Carr; SP: Franklyn Adreon, Basil Dickey, Jesse Duffy, Sol Shor; AP: Mike Frankovich; Cam: John MacBurnie; Mus: Mort Glickman; LP: Clayton Moore, Linda Stirling, Roy Barcroft, John Compton, Tris Coffin, Tom London, Edmund Cobb, LeRoy Mason.

G-Men Never Forget. Rep., [12 Chapters] D: Fred C. Brannon, Yakima Canutt; SP: Franklyn Adreon, Basil Dickey, Jesse Duffy, Sol Shor; AP: Mike Frankovich; Cam: John MacBurnie; Mus: Mort Glickman; LP: Clayton Moore, Ramsay Ames, Roy Barcroft, Drew Allen, Edmund Cobb.

1948

Adventures of Frank and Jesse James. Rep., [13 Chapters] D: Fred C. Brannon, Yakima Canutt; SP: Franklyn Adreon, Basil Dickey, Sol Shor; AP: Franklyn Adreon; Cam: John MacBurnie; Mus: Morton Scott; LP: Clayton Moore, Steve Darrell, Noel Neill, George J. Lewis, Stanley Andrews.

1949

Ghost of Zorro. Rep., [12 Chapters] D: Fred C. Brannon; SP: Royal Cole, William Lively, Sol Shor; AP: Franklyn Adreon; Cam: John MacBurnie; Mus: Stanley Wilson; LP: Clayton Moore, Pamela Blake, Roy Barcroft, George J. Lewis, I. Stanford Jolley.

1951

Flying Disc Man from Mars. Rep., [12 Chapters] D: Fred C. Brannon; SP: Ronald Davidson; AP: Franklyn Adreon; Cam: Walter Strenge; LP: Walter Reed, Lois Collier, Gregory Gay, James Craven, Harry Lauter, Dale Van Sickel, Clayton Moore.

1952

Radar Men from the Moon. Rep., [12 Chapters] D: Fred C. Brannon; AP: Franklyn Adreon;

SP: Ronald Davidson; Cam: John MacBurnie; Mus: Stanley Wilson; LP: George Wallace, Aline Towne, Roy Barcroft, William Bakewell, Clayton Moore.

Son of Geronimo. Col., [15 Chapters] D: Spencer C. Bennet; SP: George H. Plympton, Royal Cole, Arthur Hoerl; P: Sam Katzman; Cam: William Whitley; Mus: Mischa Bakaleinikoff; LP: Clayton Moore, Rodd Redwing, Tommy Farrell, Eileen Rowe, Bud Osborne.

1953

Jungle Drums of Africa. Rep., [12 Chapters] D: Fred C. Brannon; AP: Franklyn Adreon; SP: Ronald Davidson; LP: Clayton Moore, Phyllis Coates, Johnny Spencer, Roy Glenn, John Cason.

Gunfighters of the Northwest. Col., [15 Chapters] D: Spencer Bennet, Charles S. Gould; SP: George H. Plympton, Royal Cole, Arthur Hoel; P: Sam Katzman; Cam: William Whitley; Mus: Mischa Bakaleinikoff; LP: Jock Mahoney, Clayton Moore, Phyllis Coates, Don Harvey, Marshall Reed, Lyle Talbot, Tom Farrell, John Hart, Lee Roberts.

CONSTANCE MOORE

Born on January 18, 1919, in Sioux City, Iowa, and raised in Dallas, Texas. She had always wanted to sing, and when she was 15 her godfather, who owned a chain of drug stores throughout Texas, sponsored a pair of radio programs for her on the CBS Dallas station. For almost a year she performed for 45 minutes at 7 A.M., attended high school, then rushed back to the station for a 5–5:30 P.M. show. When these programs ran their course, the station hired her to sing with its own band. She also warbled with Ken Meyer's Orchestra at a highway club called the Midway.

During the Texas Centennial in 1936, a talent scout from Universal heard Constance singing at the KRLD studios and offered her a Universal contract. She was relegated to "B" films and minor league "A" pictures. In *Border Wolves* ('38) and *The Last Stand* ('38) she was heroine to cowboy Bob Baker. She played opposite William Lundigan in *State Police* ('38), *Wives Under Suspicion* ('38), *Freshman Year* ('38) and *The Missing Guest* ('38).

Moore was one young actress who made a vivid impression in a single serial. As Wilma Deering in Universal's *Buck Rogers* ('39), her impellingly attractive appeal helped to persuade the time-displaced aviator Buck and his sidekick Buddy to join forces with her and Dr. Huer in their fight against Killer Kane in the 25th century. A singing star of radio and the New York stage, the lovely Miss Moore projected on-screen that necessary quality of the deserving heroine — passive importunity — which could only exude from a demeanor of wholesome honesty. After meeting her, Buck and Buddy were in the game to the bitter end.

Moore teamed with Tom Brown in *Swing that Cheer* ('38), *Ex-Champ* ('39) and *Ma, He's Making Eyes at Me* ('40), and with Johnny Downs in *Laugh It Off* ('39) and *Hawaiian Nights* ('39). With Dennis O'Keefe she made *La Conga Nights* ('40) and *I'm Nobody's Sweetheart Now* ('40).

Argentine Nights ('40) was Moore's last film for Universal. Her agent was successful in getting her signed with Paramount, a more prestigious studio. Her first film there was *Las Vegas Nights* ('41). Her next was *I Wanted Wings* ('41), playing second to newcomer Veronica Lake. *Buy Me that Town*

('41) and *Take a Letter, Darling* ('42) followed.

Constance was married to actor's agent John Maschio. They had a daughter, Mary Constance, in '42. Constance reluctantly took the lead in the Rogers and Hart Broadway musical *By Jupiter* with Ray Bolger. The show and Moore were hits.

Back in Hollywood she appeared in Eddie Cantor's *Show Business* (RKO '44). At Republic she starred in *Atlantic City* ('44). For United Artists she did *Delightfully Dangerous* ('45). There followed a series of films for Republic—*Earl Carroll Vanities* ('45), *Mexicana* ('45), *In Old Sacramento* ('46), *Earl Carroll Sketchbook* ('46) and *Hit Parade of 1947* ('47).

Moore was a regular on two TV series in the 1960s—*The Young Marrieds* and *Window on Main Street*, and she had guest appearances on such shows as *Playhouse 90*, *The Donna Reed Show*, *The Lineup* and *Matinee Theater*.

Constance Moore really had glamour. She was always perfectly groomed, she was accommodating, agreeable, witty, but never wisecracking at the expense of someone else. Rather, she was apt to poke fun at herself.

Serial

1939

Buck Rogers. Univ., [12 Chapters] D: Ford Beebe, Saul A. Goodkind; SP/S: Norman Hall, Ray Trampe; AP: Barney Sarecky; Cam: Jerry Ash; LP: Buster Crabbe, Constance Moore, Jackie Moran, Jack Mulhall, Anthony Warde, Wheeler Oakman.

DENNIS MOORE

Born Dennis Meadows in Fort Worth, Texas, on January 26, 1908, Dennis was a familiar figure to Western and serial buffs of the period 1935–1964. Good-looking, tight-lipped and dark-haired, he was for the most part a loner. However, he was a decidedly personable and likable co-star.

As a young man he appeared on stage and, having an avid interest in aviation, earned his commercial pilot's license. After flying for several years, he was injured in a bad crackup, which grounded him. At this point he became physical director at the Dallas Athletic Club. According to his studio biography, he appeared with Ken Murray in the play *Louder Please* and was thus brought to the attention of Hollywood.

In 1934 he had bit roles in the Universal serials *The Red Rider* and *Tailspin Tommy*, and replaced Jack Perrin in *West on Parade*, one of the "Bud'n Ben" shorts.

Thereafter he changed his billing name from Denny Meadows to Dennis Moore and set out on a climb to stardom with supporting roles in Westerns starring Jack Perrin, Gene Autry, Johnny Mack Brown, John Wayne and other cowboys. He can be compared with Dave O'Brien in that he could be seen as a minor heavy in one film and a principal player in another. Like O'Brien, he had bit roles in a number of non–Westerns.

In 1940, Dennis starred in the Cinecolor short *Wells Fargo Days* (original title: *Man from Tascosa*), not released until 1944 by Warner Brothers. In 1942 he had featured roles in six of the "Lone Rider" series starring first George Houston and then Robert Livingston. In 1943 he replaced John King in the final four entries. A couple of Jimmy Wakely oaters were made in 1944–45 in which Dennis was second banana. Thereafter Moore returned to marking time as a heavy. Some re-

viewers believed that his pleasant screen persona and acting ability put Wakely in the shade and that this may be why he was replaced by wishy-washy John James. Later Moore became drunk and angry at a bar one night over what he thought was Wakely's killing any future starring Westerns Monogram planned for him. He was goaded into action against Wakely by musician Foy Willing, for what reason is not known. Perhaps he was harboring a grudge himself against Wakely. At any rate, Moore visited Wakely's resident on August 29, 1945, and assaulted Jimmy with a knife, cutting him in the head. Jimmy warded off his attack and police were called. Wakely did not file a complaint. Two days later, in Deputy District Attorney Howard Hinshaw's office, Moore and Wakely shook hands and reconciled.

There was a rumor that Moore and Tim Holt had fought over a girl. Moore's hair-trigger temper was well known by those who worked with him.

Dennis had more luck as a serial hero than as a Western feature hero. He received top billing in the Universal serial *Raiders of Ghost City* ('44). The action took place in 1865 and for the period the plot was unusual since it dealt with Persia (German) attempting to seize U.S. gold needed to buy Alaska from Russia. Stock footage was used effectively, but sometimes obviously.

In 1945, Moore went over to Republic and topped the cast in *The Purple Monster Strikes*. However, the serial really belonged to Roy Barcroft, the so-called monster from Mars sent ahead to prepare for an invasion of Earth by the Martian army. Moore was legal counsel for a scientific foundation.

At Universal, Moore was one of the principal players in the serial *The Mysterious Mr. M* ('45). Moore was a federal investigator who, with a colleague, seeks to rescue a submarine inventor kidnapped by a gang headed by the title character.

During the next decade, Moore's screen career was spent playing secondary or bit roles, usually as a villain. He could act as well as his peers, but somehow lacked the special personality which attracted a sustained, loyal following. In 1950 he played in all six of the Lippert oaters starring Russell Hayden and Jimmy Ellison. He was outstanding in Lash LaRue's *King of the Bullwhip* ('51). With television taking over most Americans' viewing habits in the 1950s, Dennis found work in the Gene Autry and Roy Rogers shows, *The Lone Ranger*, *Wild Bill Hickok*, *The Cisco Kid* and others. As the 1960s dawned, Dennis found work in adult Westerns such as *Chey-* enne, *Wyatt Earp*, *Tombstone Territory* and *Bat Masterson*.

Moore starred in *Perils of the Wilderness* ('56) as Laramie, a deputy marshal. It was a 15-chapter serial from Columbia. And in *Blazing the Overland Trail* ('56) he co-starred with Lee Roberts in Columbia's last serial in which they portray an Army scout (Roberts) and an agent of the Pony Express (Moore) battling for law and order against a greedy rancher turned outlaw who has organized a gang which attacks and robs settlers coming into the territory. It was the film industry's last serial. Much stock footage from *White Eagle* and other previously made cliffhangers was used to pad it out to 15 chapters.

Moore appeared in many non–Westerns, among them *China Clipper*, *I'm from Missouri*, *Mutiny in the Big House*, *Bombs Over Burma*, *The Crime Doctor's Courage*, *The Mummy's Curse*, *Fangs of the Wild*, *The Imposter*, *Sing Me a Love Song*, *Bachelor Mother* and *Meet Nero Wolfe*.

Moore died from a heart attack on March 1, 1964. He was survived by his wife, Marilyn, and daughter, Linda.

Serials

1934

The Red Rider. Univ., [15 Chapters] D: Louis Friedlander [Lew Landers]; LP: Buck Jones, Marion Shilling, Grant Withers, Walter Miller.

Tailspin Tommy. Univ., [12 Chapters] D: Louis Friedlander [Lew Landers]; LP: Maurice Murphy, Noah Beery, Jr., Patricia Farr, Walter Miller, Grant Withers.

Raiders of Ghost City. Univ., [13 Chapters] D: Ray Taylor, Louis Collins; SP: Luci Ward, Morgan Cox; P: Morgan Cox, Ray Taylor; LP: Dennis Moore, Wanda McKay, Lionel Atwill, Joe Sawyer, Regis Toomey.

1945

The Master Key. Univ., [13 Chapters] D: Ray Taylor, Lewis D. Collins; SP: Joseph O'Donnell, George H. Plympton, Ande Lamb; S: Jack Natteford, Dwight Babcock; LP: Milburn

Stone, Jan Wiley, Dennis Moore, Sarah Padden, Russell Hicks.

The Purple Monster Strikes. Rep., [15 Chapters] D: Spencer Bennet, Fred C. Brannon; SP: Royal Cole, Albert DeMond, Basil Dickey, Lynn Perkins, Joseph Poland, Barney Sarecky; AP: Bud Thackery; Mus: Richard Cherwin. LP: Linda Stirling, Dennis Moore, Roy Barcroft, James Craven, Bud Geary.

The Mysterious Mr. M. Univ., [13 Chapters] D: Lewis D. Collins, Vernon Keays; SP: Joseph Poland, Paul Huston, Barry Shipment; AP: Joseph O'Donnell; LP: Richard Martin, Pamela Blake, Dennis Moore, Jane Randolph, Danny Morton.

1950

Desperadoes of the West. Rep., [12 Chapters] D: Fred C. Brannon; SP: Ronald Davidson; Cam: John MacBurnie; Mus: Stanley Wilson; LP: Richard Powers [Tom Keene], Judy Clark, Roy Barcroft, I. Stanford Jolley, Lee Phelps.

1956

Perils of the Wilderness. Col., [15 Chapters] D: spencer Bennet; SP: George H. Plympton; P: Sam Katzman; Cam: Ira H. Morgan; Mus: Mischa Bakaleinikoff; LP: Dennis Moore, Richard Emory, Eve Anderson [Evelyn Finley], Kenneth MacDonald, Rick Vallin.

Blazing the Overland Trail. Col., [15 Chapters] D: Spencer Bennet; SP: George H. Plympton; P: Sam Katzman; Cam: Ira H. Morgan; Mus: Mischa Bakaleinikoff; LP: Lee Roberts, Dennis Moore, Norma Brooks, Gregg Barton, Don C. Harvey.

MILDRED MOORE

Mildred Moore's too-brief career seems to have been confined to one- and two-reelers except for her one memorable film — the serial *The Moon Riders* ('20), a Universal offering that was a big moneymaker.

In 1919 Mildred could be seen in one-reel comedies with Eddie Lyons and Lee Moran and in 1920 made a series of two-reel Westerns opposite Hoot Gibson, as well as two with Art Acord.

Her presence and disappearance from the screen were akin to raindrops on the desert — a brief splatter and gone with no trace.

Serial

1920

The Moon Riders. Univ., [18 Chapters] D: B. Reeves Eason, Albert Russell; S: Albert Russell, George Hively, Theodore Wharton, William Piggott, Karl Coolidge; SP: George Hively, Albert Russell, Theodore Wharton; LP: Art Acord, Mildred Moore, Charles Newton, George Field, Tote DeCrow, Beatrice Dominquez.

PAULINE MOORE

Pauline Moore is best remembered today as the heroine to "Slingin' Sammy" Baugh in *King of the Texas Rangers* ('41). It was well-received by serial patrons and today, 60 years later, is available on home video. And she will be remembered as Roy Rogers' leading lady in five films. She also played the heroine in distress in one of the Three Mesquiteers films starring Bob Steele and Robert Livingston.

Though she may be remembered by many aficionados of the Western, Moore's acting career was by no means limited to cowboy flicks. She had a notable career in the late 1930s under contract to Twentieth Century-Fox.

Pauline was born Pauline Joeless Love on June 17, 1914, in either Philadelphia or Harrisburg, Pennsylvania. At the age of four during World War I, she sang and danced as part of Liberty Bond campaigns. She knew miles of poetry and dramatic recitation pieces before she turned ten. She took an early step toward a career before the footlights and Klieg lights as a teenager when she became a finalist in the National Constitution Oratorical Contest in Washington.

Pauline's father was a British engineer who was killed in World War I when she was not quite two. When her mother remarried, Pauline took her stepfather's last name.

Upon graduation from William Penn High School, Pauline (at the insistence of her stepfather) enrolled at Darlington Junior College. However, she dropped out of college to accept an offer from a stock company to play the ingenue in its productions. When the summer stock season ended, Pauline (and her mother, acting as chaperone) headed for Hollywood, where she was given a screen test by Universal and then offered a contract with a three-month option.

Pauline's one film under the contract was a bit as a bridesmaid to Mae Clarke in *Frankenstein* ('31). She was released by the studio at the insistence of her stepfather and returning home, she was inundated with reasons why she should resume her college studies. She refused to go back and, again with her mother as chaperone, traveled to New York City to hunt stage roles.

At the Ziegfeld Theatre she was hired as understudy for June Knight, the show's ingenue, who had emergency surgery. However, Knight returned in time to open the show and Pauline never got to face the audience. After the close of the play, she landed a key role in Earl Carroll's *Murder at the Vanities*. When this play had run its course, Pauline modeled for artists and photographers, appearing on the covers of *Ladies Home Journal*, *McCalls* and *Cosmopolitan*. She also was the model for the popular "Hostess Girl" Coca-Cola tray painting in 1934.

In due time she got a contract with Twentieth Century-Fox and over the next several years worked in *Love Is News* ('37), *Charlie Chan at the Olympics* ('37), *Born Reckless* ('37), *Wild and Woolly* ('37), *Heidi* ('37), *Three Blind Mice* ('38), *Passport Husband* ('38), *Five of a Kind* ('38), *The Arizona Wildcat* ('38), *The Three Musketeers* ('39), *Charlie Chan in Reno* ('39), *Young Mr. Lincoln* ('39), *Charlie Chan at Treasure Island* ('39) and more. For Republic she co-starred in the 12-chapter *King of the Texas Rangers* ('41).

Moore married cartoonist Jefferson Machamer in May 1934. They had two daughters and a son. Pauline left films in 1941 to raise a family, but returned 15 years later to briefly renew her career in *Spoilers of the Forest* ('57) and *The Littlest Hobo* ('58).

On television Pauline appeared on the network shows *Four Star Playhouse*, *Crossroads*, *Studio 57*, *Death Valley Days*, *Readers Digest* and *Medic*. In addition, she made commercials for several products.

Slingin' Sammy Baugh and Pauline Moore in *King of the Texas Rangers* (Republic, 1941).

On August 15, 1960, Pauline's husband died from a heart attack. A year later, she married Dodd Watkins, a minister.

Pauline was a very devout Christian and won recognition as an inspirational speaker and for her devotional poetry, short stories and religious plays. Beginning with "The Seamless Robe" and "Mary's Story," Pauline's original monologues were well received and later published.

Pauline Moore died from Lou Gehrig's Disease (ALS) at her home on December 7, 2001. She was survived by her son and two daughters from her first marriage.

Serial

1941

King of the Texas Rangers. Rep., [12 Chapters] D: William Witney, John English; SP: Ronald Davidson, Norman S. Hall, William Lively, Joseph Poland, Joseph O'Donnell; AP: Hiram S. Brown, Jr.; Cam: Reggie Lanning; Mus: Cy Feuer; LP: "Slingin' Sammy" Baugh, Pauline Moore, Neil Hamilton, Duncan Renaldo, Monte Blue.

ANTONIO MORENO

Antonio Garrido Monteagudo Moreno wisely shortened his name for cinema purposes. The Spanish-born actor, who achieved the immigrant's dream of a million dollar movie career plus marriage to a millionaire wife, was a top box office attraction during the 1920s and early '30s. He co-starred with many of the now-legendary names symbolic of feminine glamour in filmdom. His first film was *The Voice of the Million* ('12), a Universal-Rex release. He was soon working for D. W. Griffith and Biograph. *The House of Discord* ('13) with Blanche Sweet, Lionel Barrymore, Dorothy Gish and Jack Mulhall was one of three films he made in 1913.

In 1914 he co-starred with Norma Talmadge in eight films at Vitagraph. He later moved to Mutual-Reliance to play the part of the Country Lover in the long-running series *Our Mutual Girl* ('14). Back at Vitagraph, Moreno made seven features with Edith Storey.

Other actresses who emoted with Moreno in front of a camera included Constance and Norma Talmadge, Gloria Swanson, Alice Terry, Agnes Ayres, Greta Garbo, Clara Bow, Pauline Starke, Julia Swayne Gordon, Mary Anderson, Helen Chadwick, Irene Castle, Marguerite Snow, Mary Miles Minter, Marion Davies, Estelle Taylor, Renee Adoree, Thelma Todd, Billie Dove, Sally Rand and Lupita Tovar.

Pathé cast the popular Moreno in *The House of Hate* ('18), a popular serial of 20 chapters starring Pearl White. Moreno plays a young scientist in love with fearless, peerless Pearl, daughter of a munitions king. The lovers are hounded by "the Hooded Terror," out to imperil and destroy them, but they foil him at every turn. It was one of the best of the serials in which Moreno's Latin allure lent an exotic touch to the romantic plans of Pearl's exploits and perils. *The House of Hate* put black-haired Anthony on the crest of the serial wave.

During the World War I years, Moreno was one of Vitagraph's two serial heroes. The other was William Duncan who, with his wife Edith Johnson, churned out exciting cliffhangers that the fans devoured. Moreno, however, was almost as popular. He was cast in *The Iron Test* ('18) as a circus acrobat who, with the heroine Carol Holloway, is hounded by "The Red Mask." In *The Perils of Thunder Mountain* ('19), Antonio and Carol Holloway surmount every conceivable hazard as they fight to carry out the provisions of an old prospector's will. In *The Invisible Hand*, ('20) the country is agog over the conspiracies and depredations of a band of crooks led by a cunning and cultured master crook, Iron Hand. Antonio, as the most famous analytic detective in the world, takes on the case.

The Veiled Mystery ('20) was Moreno's final serial (he wished to concentrate on features), though Vitagraph pleaded with him to make more. Pauline Curley was Tony's sweetheart in this last serial. Henry A. Burrows, Pauline's guardian, wishes to do away with Moreno so as to keep control of Pauline's wealth. The script writers led audiences to believe that the Veiled Mystery was a woman. Burrows is revealed as the criminal in the last chapter.

Paramount offered Moreno a term contract as one of its top stars, and it is there that he made *The Trail of the Lonesome Pine* ('23) with Mary Miles Minter, *The Exciters* ('23) with Bebe Daniels, *The Spanish Dancer* ('23) with Pola Negri, *Bluff* ('24) with Agnes Ayres and *Flaming Barriers* ('24) with Jacqueline Logan.

In 1923, at the height of his popularity, Moreno married the former Daisy Confield Danziger, daughter of oil millionaire Charles Canfield and a leader of Los Angeles society. Unfortunately, she was killed ten years later when her car plunged over a 300-foot cliff on

Mulholland Drive. Her chauffeur's back was broken but he survived.

In 1925, Moreno received the top role in *Mare Nostrum*, directed by Rex Ingram and shot against lovely Mediterranean backgrounds. Alice Terry co-starred.

Moreno made the transition to talkies with ease, but not as a leading man. Now it was character roles that came his way in abundance, for his slight accent ruined any hopes of his continuing as a star. But in a way this worked to excellent advantage for the actor, who was well into his forties. (At that age he couldn't hope to conquer the sound screen as he had the silent.) Once producers caught his accent, everyone seemed to remember at the same time that Moreno spoke perfect Spanish. From roughly 1930 to 1935, Hollywood filmed its Spanish versions of movies at the same time that the English versions were made, and during those five years, Moreno was in heavy demand as an actor (and sometime director), tearing from studio to studio and set to set to keep up with filming schedules.

In Mexico he directed the first Mexican sound picture, *Santa* ('32), with Lupita Tovar featured. In 1936 Moreno went to Spain to appear with a young Carmen Amaya in a feature titled *Maria de la O*. When he returned to Hollywood, he was not exactly forgotten, but he was 50 years old. Throughout the '40s and '50s his presence graced a number of films, even though his roles were not leads.

Moreno had amassed sufficient funds to easily carry him through 1936–41, a five-year period in which he totaled but 35 days before the camera. (Once the simultaneous English-Spanish shooting schedules were abandoned, producers forgot that Moreno could act as quickly as they had recalled that he could speak Spanish.) A fling at a real estate development named Moreno Highlands occupied part of his spare time and much of his fortune; it turned out to be a financial disaster that cost him several hundred thousand dollars.

Moreno's last film, never released in the U.S., was *El Senor Faron Y La Cleopatra* ('58). *The Searchers* ('56), in which he is seen as an early Spanish American trader, was his last English film.

A stroke felled the Latin lover on February 15, 1967. He was survived by three stepchildren.

Serials

1918

The House of Hate. Pathé, [20 Chapters] D: George B. Seitz; SP: Bertram Millhauser; S: Arthur B. Reeve, Charles A. Logue; LP: Pearl White, Antonio Moreno, Peggy Shanor, John Webb Dillon.

The Iron Test. Vit., [15 Chapters] D: Robert N. Bradbury, Paul Hurst; SP: Graham Baker; S: Albert E. Smith; LP: Antonio Moreno, Carol Holloway, Barney Fuery, Chet Ryan, Jack Hoxie.

1919

The Perils of Thunder Mountain. Vit., [15 Chapters] D: Robert N. Bradbury, W. J. Bauman; S: Albert E. Smith, Cyrus Townsend Brady; SP: Graham Baker; LP: Antonio Moreno, Carol Holloway, Kate Price, George Stanley.

1920

The Veiled Mystery. Vit., [15 Chapters] D: F. J. Grandon, Webster Cullison, William J. Bowman; SP: Graham Baker; S: Albert E. Smith, Cleveland Moffett; Adapt: William B. Courtney; LP: Antonio Moreno, Pauline Curley, Henry A. Borrows, Nenette de Courey, Walter L. Rogers, George Reed.

The Invisible Hand. Vit., [15 Chapters] D: William J. Bowman, Jack Pierce; S: Cyrus Townsend Brady, Albert E. Smith; SP: C. Graham Baker; LP: Antonio Moreno, Pauline Curley, Jay Morley, Brinsley Shaw.

RALPH MORGAN

Ralph Morgan was a talented character actor who could be counted on to deliver a good performance. For 25 years he applied his talents to many fine features and serials— *Rasputin and the Empress*, *The Magnificent Obsession*, *Night Monster*, *Geronimo*, *I've Been Around*, *Black Market Babies*, *Under Suspicion*, and many more.

Ralph was born Raphael Kuhner Wepperman on July 1, 1882. Naturally, he needed to change his name for the screen. His brother Frank was the more popular of the two brothers.

Along with Charles Starrett, Boris Karloff, Alan Mowbray and others, they founded the Screen Actors Guild in 1933 and Ralph served two terms as its president. He was instrumental in keeping organized crime out of the film industry. Threats on his life did not sway him from his duty.

In 1941, Ralph played the Ghost in *Dick Tracy vs. Crime, Inc.* Dick Tracy's genius and luck are taxed to the limit as he endeavors to capture and learn the identity of the Ghost, a master criminal determined to destroy New York City as revenge for the death of his brothers. The Ghost, so called because he can make himself invisible, is actually a member of an anti-crime council.

In *Gang Busters* ('42), Lt. Kent Taylor and detective Robert Armstrong are assigned to run down the League of Murdered Men. Prof. Mortis (Morgan) is the ringleader. He has a death-simulating drug and an anti-death treatment that he uses to recruit gang members.

In *The Great Alaskan Mystery* ('44), Ralph, as Dr. Miller, an American scientist, invents a machine, the Paratron, that promises to be successful as a defense weapon. A ring of fascists are out to steal it.

In *The Monster and the Ape* ('45), Morgan is again a scientist. This time he invents a robot, the Metalogen, to help humanity, but his assistant (George Macready) has other plans and tries to steal the robot and the Metalogen metal from which it is made. He employs a trained gorilla (Ray Corrigan) to make things difficult for the Metalogen inventor, his assistant (Robert Lowery) and daughter (Carole Mathews).

Serials

1941

Dick Tracy vs. Crime, Inc. Rep., [15 Chapters] D: William Witney, John English; SP: Ronald Davidson, Norman S. Hall, William Lively, Joseph O'Donnell, Joseph Poland; Cam: Reggie Lanning; Mus: Cy Feuer; LP: Ralph Byrd, Jan Wiley, John Davidson, Ralph Morgan, Michael Owen, Jack Mulhall, Hooper Atchley, Walter Miller.

1942

Gang Busters. Univ., [13 Chapters] D: Ray Taylor, Noel Smith; SP: Morgan B. Cox, Al Martin, Vin Martin, George H. Plympton; AP: Ford Beebe; Cam: William Sickner, John Boyle; LP: Kent Taylor, Irene Hervey, Ralph Morgan, Robert Armstrong, Richard Davies, George J. Lewis, Joseph Crehan.

1944

The Great Alaskan Mystery. Univ., [13 Chapters] D: Ray Taylor, Lewis D. Collins; SP: Maurice Tombragel, George H. Plympton; S: Jack Foley; LP: Milburn Stone, Marjorie Weaver, Edgar Kennedy, Samuel S. Hinds, Ralph Morgan, Martin Kosleck, Fuzzy Knight, Harry Cording.

1945

The Monster and the Ape. Col., [15 Chapters] D: Howard Bretherton; SP: Sherman Lowe,

Royal K. Cole; P: Rudolph C. Flothow; Cam: L. W. O'Connell; Mus: Lee Zahler; LP: Robert Lowery, George Macready, Ralph Morgan, Willie Best, Carole Mathews, Jack Ingram, Kenneth MacDonald, Charles King.

MARGARET MORRIS

Margaret Morris was born November 7, 1903, in Minneapolis and was a Wampas Baby Star of 1924. However, the cards were never in her favor.

She made four serials. In the first, *Beasts of Paradise* ('23), she and Ruth Royce played second and third fiddle to Eileen Sedgwick, who had the inside track with William Desmond. In her second serial outing, *The Ghost City* ('23), cowboy Pete Morrison endured 15 thrill-packed chapters protecting her. In *The Iron Man* ('24) she was put through the serial grind again in a non–Western setting ranging from Hollywood to Paris. Her final serial was the ludicrous *Mark of the Frog* ('28).

Margaret's best feature Westerns were probably Paramount's *Wild Horse Mesa* ('25) opposite Jack Holt and *Born to the West* ('26), stories adapted from Zane Grey novels. Her best opportunity for dramatic acting came in *The Magic Garden* ('27), Gene Stratton Porter's love story about an aspiring violinist and a young girl he saves from suicide.

In 1926–27 Margaret appeared with Jack Luden and Kit Guard in 11 two-reel comedies produced by FBO. Her Westerns with Edmund Cobb, H. B. Warner, Pete Morrison and Tom Tyler were pedestrian affairs that did nothing for her career. As a supporting player she appeared in Warner Baxter's *Welcome Home* ('25) and *The Best People* ('25); in Richard Dix's *Womanhandled* ('25); and in Douglas MacLean's *That's My Baby* ('26).

After a few character roles in the '30s she married and retired from the screen, subsequently going into business when her husband died. Margaret died on June 7, 1968.

Serials

1923

Beasts of Paradise. Univ., [15 Chapters] D: William Craft; SP/S: Val Cleveland; LP: William Desmond, William H. Gould, Eileen Sedgwick, Ruth Royce, Margaret Morris, Paul Malvern, Gordon McGregor, Alfred Fisher, Slim Cole.

Ghost City. Univ., [15 Chapters] D: Jay Marchant; SP: Karl Coolidge, George W. Pyper; LP: Pete Morrison, Margaret Morris, Frank Rice, Al Wilson, Lola Todd, Princess Neela, Bud Osborne, Alfred Allen, Valeria Olivo.

1925

The Iron Man. Univ., [15 Chapters] D: Jay Marchant; S/SP: Arthur Henry Gooden, William E. Wing; LP: Lucien Albertini, Margaret Morris, Joe Bonomo, Jack Daugherty, Lola Todd, Jean DeBriac, William Welsh, Rose Dione, Harry Mann.

1928

Mark of the Frog. Pathé, [10 Chapters] D: Arch B. Heath; S: Edgar Wallace; LP: Donald Reed, Margaret Morris, George Harcourt, Gus DeWell, Frank Lackteen, Tony Hughes, Frank B. Miller, Helen Greene, Ed Roseman, Sidney Paston.

JACK MOWER

Jack Mower was born in Honolulu in 1890 and lived there until he finished his schooling at Punohou College. He was in stock for several months and in musical comedy for a couple of years. In early 1916 this big, handsome Hawaiian easily broke into motion pictures with Vitagraph and Selig. He was Pacific Coast champion swimmer for four years. He stood six feet, weighed 180 lbs., was of medium complexion, with brown hair and gray eyes.

Among his films of the teen years were *Miss Jackie of the Navy* ('16), *Miss Jackie of the Army* ('17), *The Square Deal* ('18), *The Mantle of Charity* ('18), *The Beloved Cheater* ('19) and *The Island of Intrigue* ('19).

In '20 Pathé cast him in the serial *The Third Eye*, sharing honors with Eileen Percy and Warner Oland. The title referred to a camera lens which had captured what appeared to be a murder. A struggle then begins between movie star Percy, aided by her sweetheart (Mower), and Oland, leader of a murderous gang.

In 1920, Helen Holmes formed the Holmes Producing Corporation and made a contract with Warner Brothers to star in *The Tiger Band*. Mower was chosen as her leading man. The serial was states-righted and received limited bookings.

Switching to Universal, Jack played a supporting role in *With Stanley in Africa* ('22) starring George Walsh as Stanley in his search for Dr. Livingston. Lorraine played a newspaper woman along for the story.

In the serial *In the Days of Daniel Boone* ('23), Mower is the hero with Eileen Sedgwick as heroine in a story of Boone's (Charles Brinley) attempts to establish a frontier colony despite opposition by Tories and Indians.

In *Ten Scars Make a Man* ('24), Jack proposes to Allene Ray but is told he must acquire ten scars before he can marry her.

Exactly why is not made clear. Both Allene and her sister (Rose Burdict) are threatened with expulsion from school unless they pay the villain a lot of money. Jack tackles and solves the problems the girls are having, exposes the villain and wins the hand of Allene.

The conflict which served as a pivot for the story *Perils of the Wild* ('25) was between Frederic Robinson (Bonomo) and Sir Charles Leicester (Mower) for the love of Emily Montrose (Quimby). Mower proved to be a handsome villain.

The Radio Detective ('26) was next for Mower. He plays the part of Craig Kennedy, friend of hero Jack Daugherty, who bands together with a group of Boy Scouts to help Daugherty foil the criminals who are after the secret of a marvelous invention which would revolutionize the field of radio.

In the much-maligned *Officer 444* ('26), Mower was cast as an Irish cop, sidekick to Officer 444 (Ben Wilson). Neva Gerber was her demure self. Released by Goodwill, the serial never did a great deal of business.

Trail of the Tiger ('27) introduced a mysterious organization called "The Mystic Mountebanks." It had the dual function of looking after the welfare of the heroine (Frances Teague) and attempting to wreak revenge on the villain (Mower), who had double-crossed the organization and wrongly heaped disgrace and shame upon the girl's father. Mower gave an excellent performance as the double-dyed menace. Real circus atmosphere was definitely an asset.

Pirates of the Pines ('28) stars George O'Hara as the owner of a big tract of timberland which is coveted by a rival. The latter sets in motion a conspiracy to ruin O'Hara. Mower was billed third. Henceforth he would act in five sound serials but only in minor parts.

A small independent organization (Westart) produced seven feature Westerns co-starring Al Hart and Mower during the early '20s. Jack usually handled the romance, such as there was, and Al concentrated on the action.

Universal gave Mower his own series of two-reel Westerns in 1923. The last of the nine films was released in 1926. The titles were *The Payroll Thief, Western Skies, The Rustlin' Buster, The Crook Buster, The Gunless Bad Man, Ridin' for Love, The Fire Barrier, Don't Shoot* and *The Pinnacle Rider.*

Some poet once observed, "When the wolf comes in at the door, love flies out of the window," but apparently Mrs. Anne Mower, wife of Jack, found it a bit to the contrary. She was granted a divorce in March 1922 saying they had been happy when Jack's income was only $1,500 annually, but when he got into the $15,000 class it seems the extra zero banished love.

Jack became a character actor with the coming of sound to the movies. He appeared in several hundred films in the next 40 years. The role of a policeman was one he often assumed, but in the four decades he played an abundance of characters. In the '30s he was in 25 or more Westerns, but after that hardly any. Beginning with 1937, he appeared almost exclusively in Warner Brothers films.

Mower died on January 6, 1965, after a long illness and was survived by his wife, son and two daughters.

Serials

1920

The Third Eye. Pathé, [15 Chapters] D: James W. Horne; S: H. H. Van Horne; SP: William Parker; LP: Eileen Percy, Warner Oland, Jack Mower, Olga Grey, Mark Strong.

The Tiger Band. WB, [15 Chapters] D: Gilbert P. Hamilton; LP: Helen Holmes, Jack Mower, Dwight Crittendon, Omar Whitehead, Bert Hadley, Yukio Aoyama.

1922

With Stanley in Africa. Univ., [18 Chapters] D: William Craft, Ed Kull; SP/S: George Plympton;

LP: George Walsh, Louise Lorraine, Charles Mason, William Welsh, Jack Mower, Fred Kohler, Gordon Sackville.

1923

In the Days of Daniel Boone. Univ., [15 Chapters] D: William Craft, Jay Marchant, Frank Messinger; SP: Jefferson Moffitt; S: Paul Bryan, Jefferson; LP: Jack Mower, Eileen Sedgwick, Charles Brinley, Duke R. Lee.

1924

Ten Scars Make a Man. Pathé, [10 Chapters] D: William Parke; S: Phillips Barry; P: C. W. Patton; LP: Allene Ray, Jack Mower, Rose Burdick, Frank Whitman, Larry Steers.

1925

Perils of the Wild. Univ., [15 Chapters] D: Francis Ford; SP: Isadore Bernstein, William Lord Wright; S: Johann David Wyss; LP: Joe Bonomo, Margaret Quimby, Jack Mower, Alfred Allen, Eva Gordon, Jack Murphy, Boris Karloff.

1926

The Radio Detective. Univ., [10 Chapters] D: William Crinley, William Craft; LP: Jack Daugherty, Margaret Quimby, John T. Prince, Wallace Baldwin, Jack Mower.

Officer 444. Davis/Goodwill, [10 Chapters] D: Neva Gerber, Ben Wilson, Ruth Royce, Jack Mower, Al Ferguson.

1927

The Trail of the Tiger. Univ., [10 Chapters] D: Henry MacRae; SP: Karl Krusada, Leigh Jacobson; S: Courtney R. Cooper; LP: Jack Daugherty, Frances Teague, Charles Murphy, William Platt, Jack Mower.

1928

Pirates of the Pines. Goodart, [10 Chapters] D: J. C. Cook; SP: Harry Moody, J. C. Cook; P: Charles Penfield; LP: George O'Hara, Rita Roma, Jack Mower, Robert Middleton, Summer Getchell.

1931

The Sign of the Wolf. Met., [10 Chapters] D: Forrest Sheldon, Harry S. Webb; LP: Rex Lease, Virginia Brown Faire, Joe Bonomo, Jack Mower, Al Ferguson.

1932

The Devil Horse. Mascot, [12 Chapters] D: Otto Brown; LP: Harry Carey, Frankie Darro, Noah Beery, Sr., Greta Granstedt, Apache (horse).

1933

Fighting with Kit Carson. Mascot, [12 Chapters] D: Armand Schaefer; LP: Johnny Mack Brown, Betsy King Ross, Noah Beery, Sr., Noah Beery, Jr.

Mystery Squadron. Mascot, [12 Chapters] D: Colbert Clark, David Howard; LP: Bob Steele, Guinn "Big Boy" Williams, Lucile Browne, Jack Mulhall, Jack Mower, Robert Kortman.

1935

The New Adventures of Tarzan. Burroughs-Dearholt-Stout-Cohen, [12 Chapters] D: Edward Kull, W. F. McGaugh; LP: Herman Brix, Ula Holt, Frank Baker, Dale Walsh, Jack Mower.

JACK MULHALL

Starting in pictures around 1911, Jack Mulhall reputedly was one of the first male stars to earn $1,000 a week. A genial personality was his trademark in silent films and in the early days of the talkies. His personality was dynamic and his charm undeniable. The perfect hero, he could always be depended upon to put the villain in his place, to rescue the heroine at the proper time, and to be kind to children and animals.

Jack was in motion pictures for nearly 50 years, starting with the Edison and Biograph companies in New York and ending with *The Atomic Submarine* in 1959. Old-timers will remember Jack for his wavy black hair, ever-smiling face and his eyes, with their jolly Irish twinkle, which had a fetching way of looking at one with a direct boyish frankness that was guaranteed to make the viewer a friend at once.

Serial buffs reserve a special place in their hearts for Mulhall, for he starred or co-starred in seven cliffhangers and appeared in 12 others. Nineteen serials! Not many action aces can match that record. The seven major Mulhall films will be mentioned now before proceeding with a review of his overall career.

In *The Brass Bullet* ('18), Universal's 18-chapter thriller, Rosalind Joy (Juanita Hansen) is the heiress to a hidden gold cache and is threatened by her uncle, Spring Gilbert (Joseph Girard), who would like to acquire the gold hidden on Pleasure Island for himself. Jack James (Mulhall), a young playwright, is confined in a sanitarium by mistake. He escapes to Pleasure Island, where Rosalind is about to be made the victim of a kidnapping plot. He becomes her protector, while also trying to clear up the problem of his escape from the sanitarium. The film was remade by Universal in 1928 as *Haunted Island.*

The Social Buccaneer ('23) was Jack's next serial outing. Princess Elise (Margaret Livingston), whose throne is threatened, must raise money to prevent undesirables from taking over the country. Young Jack Norton (Mulhall), who enjoys a special position in New York, befriends her and helps her save her country. Working mostly undercover, Jack is, to the outside world, merely a New York playboy without much backbone or serious thought. This front serves him well as pursues his objective of saving the princess and her throne.

Into the Net ('24) opens with the discovery of a murder committed by a famous criminal identified by means of fingerprints. Immediately upon the heels of this event, a wealthy girl is kidnapped, the nineteenth to disappear in a mysterious fashion. Madge Clayton (Constance Bennett), the missing girl, was on her way to the home of a woman who was playing hostess at a card party. Among the guests there was Natalie Van Cleef (Edna Murphy), another wealthy girl. Bob Clayton (Mulhall), Madge's brother, joins police in the search and discovers that a Dr. Vining is connected with the kidnapping. When Dr. Vining escorts Natalie Van Cleef to the opera, Bob thwarts an attempt to kidnap her. Thereafter, she joins forces with Bob and they swing into action to capture the master criminal and to secure the release of the young heiresses who are being held for $1,000,000 ransom.

In *The Three Musketeers* ('33), Legionnaires Clancy (Jack Mulhall), Renard (Raymond Hatton) and Schmidt (Francis X.

Bushman, Jr.) are rescued from desert rebels by Tom Wayne (John Wayne), an American aviator. The four become involved in thwarting the attempts of the mysterious leader of a desert tribal cult that is attempting to wipe out the Foreign Legion. Their task is formidable because El Shaitan, the Devil of the Desert, a human vulture who never shows his face, casts a shadow of evil wherever he and his men move, and the desert is an extremely harsh environment.

Burn 'Em Up Barnes ('34) is one of Mulhall's two most popular serials. Marjorie Temple (Lola Lane), owner of a financially troubled bus line and a seemingly worthless piece of property, is menaced by gangsters intent on getting the oil deposits they know to be on her land. Burn 'Em Up Barnes (Mulhall), a racing driver, comes to her rescue and also adopts a homeless boy, Bobbie (Frankie Darro), who develops into a top-flight newsreel cameraman. Barnes enters into partnership with Marjorie and he and Bobbie take desperate chances to raise money to prevent Marjorie from losing her property. Because of film taken by Bobbie, the gangsters are ultimately brought to justice and Barnes cleared of any implication in a murder.

The Clutching Hand ('36) is the other popular Mulhall serial. Dr. Paul Gironda (Robert Frazer) discovers a formula for the manufacture of synthetic gold. Just before the board of directors of the International Research Foundation arrives at his laboratory to witness his achievement, he is heard screaming in his lab and disappears before help arrives. Walter Jamison (Rex Lease), a newspaper reporter engaged to Gironda's daughter (Marion Shilling), calls in Craig Kennedy (Jack Mulhall) to find the abducted scientist. Directing criminal efforts is the Clutching Hand. Though an independent effort, *The Clutching Hand* is a good serial despite some involved subplots. The action has its spectacular moments, and suspense as to the identity of the Clutching Hand is superbly maintained throughout. The film is based (loosely) on a novel by Arthur B. Reeve and was not specifically created from scratch for action fans, which may be a plus factor. The cast is comprised largely of old reliables, and the film holds its own when compared with the output of the majors of that same period. Its charm is undeniable, and Mulhall is ideally suited as sleuth Kennedy.

It was owning a dress suit that really started Mulhall in motion pictures—that and the fact that Rex Ingram, then a scenario writer at the Edison studio in New York, suggested that Jack try the movies. Jack and Rex had become acquainted at the apartment studio of F. Graham Costes, who was associated with writer Harold Bell Wright. At the time, Jack was playing minor parts in Broadway productions. Following Ingram's advice, Jack appeared one day at the Biograph studio, also located in New York City. "Have you a dress suit?" he was asked. When he nodded in assent, he was told to report that afternoon. And so he made his entry on the screen as a society extra in a film, the title of which is lost in antiquity.

Mulhall was born in Wappinger Falls, New York, on October 7, 1887. He attended St. Mary's School through the eighth grade. When the family moved to Yonkers, New York, Jack completed his secondary education there. He was one of six children born to his middle-class parents. He inherited the comedy spirit from his Irish-Scottish parents and was always clowning and acting for the benefit of his school chums.

Jack started in show business at the age of 14 and loved every minute of it. With his special personality, he never had any trouble selling himself. For a while he worked as a sideshow barker in Passaic, New Jersey, to which the family had moved in 1902. Then there were a couple of years as a singer-dancer with the Molton Stock Company. Vaudeville followed with James K. Hackett in "The Grain of Dust" and as a dancer in Neb Wayburn's "The Producers" for Ziegfeld shows. In 1910 he was working at the Hammerstein Theatre in New York when he received a small inheritance from a relative. He forthwith took off for Europe where he proceeded to live it up until his funds were exhausted, then worked his way back home on a tramp steamer.

In New York, in addition to his stage work, he posed for Charles Dana Gibson, becoming nationally known as "The Gibson Man." Other modeling work followed as a moonlighting activity to supplement his income from stage work.

Jack's first screen role of importance was *The House of Discord* (1913), a Biograph two-reeler. At this time Biograph had in its employ Mary, Lottie and Jack Pickford, Lillian and Dorothy Gish, Harry Carey, Blanche Sweet, James Kirkwood, D. W. Griffith and many other then—or later—famous stars and directors. In January 1914, Mulhall was sent by Biograph to its California studio, and it was there he met actress Laura Bundy. Four months later they were married.

For the next couple of years the couple divided their time between Biograph's California facility and the New York studio. A son, Jack, Jr., was born to them in 1916. Laura is reported to have met a tragic death of undetermined nature two or three years later. In 1921, Jack married Evelyn Xenia Winans, a non-professional. She remained his wife until his death in 1979—a marriage lasting 58 years but producing no children. At one time Jack, Jr., lived in Hawaii where he and his wife were in the business of selling sandals to tourists.

By late 1916, Jack had signed with Universal, remaining there until early 1918. Afterwards he freelanced, appearing in films for Metro, Realart, Fox and others. When he signed with First National, he really hit his stride as a star. In the mid–1920s he and Dorothy Mackaill were teamed as a romantic duo in a number of highly successful films. Jack's salary rose to $3,250 a week.

During the 1920s he bought much of what is now Sherman Oaks in the San Fernando Valley. Throughout the decade his career prospered. Besides his real estate holdings, he had a $65,000 home in Beverly Hills, two $56,000 automobiles, stock investments and cash in the bank. In late 1928 or early '29 he took a trip to Europe with William Randolph Hearst and Marion Davies. They stayed about a year. When they got back, the stock market crash of '29 had hit Jack hard.

Ultimately he lost everything, estimated at $1,000,000. Bouncing back without any hiatus in his film work, Jack easily made the transition to talkies. However, his popularity waned considerably in the early 1930s because of his advancing age. He worked principally as a supporting player and became a favorite of those movie patrons whose aesthetic tastes ran to cliffhangers and "B" melodramas.

The actor's career carried him into radio roles in the late 1930s and onto the stage of Ken Murray's highly popular show "Blackouts" in the 1940s for an eight-year run with Ken, Marie Wilson and the rest of the zany troupe at the El Capitan Theatre. Television showings of his old serials in the early 1950s brought him renewed recognition, and he appeared in a number of TV series, among them *Public Defender*, *Playhouse 90*, *Dragnet*, *Goodyear Theatre* and *77 Sunset Strip*.

In 1956 he bounced up smiling as a greeter in a Sunset Strip restaurant at the age of 68.

In September 1959, Jack became a field representative for the Screen Actors Guild, fronting for 15,000 actors with the various studios, negotiating contracts and salaries. He retained this job for years, retiring in 1974 at age 87. For several years Jack was also a greeter at the famous Masquers Club in Hollywood.

Jack and his wife Evelyn moved into the Motion Picture and Television Country House and Hospital in Woodland Hills, California, in 1977. It was there that he died of intractable congestive heart failure on June 1, 1979, at the age of 91. His wife and son survived. Internment was at Holy Cross Cemetery in Hollywood.

Among his other notable successes were *The Bad Man* ('23), *The Goldfish* ('24), *The Far Cry* ('26), *Orchids and Ermine* ('27), *Lady Be Good* ('28), *Waterfront* ('28) and *Dark Streets* ('29). But Jack Mulhall is likely to be remembered most for *Burn 'Em Up Barnes* and *The Clutching Hand*, the two independent serials resurrected for television and the video tape market.

Serials

1918

The Brass Bullet. Univ., [18 Chapters] D: Ben Wilson; SP: Walter Woods; S: Frank R. Adams; P: Ben Wilson; LP: Juanita Hansen, Jack Mulhall, Joseph W. Girard, Helen Wright, Charles Hill Mailes.

1923

The Social Buccaneer. Univ., [10 Chapters] D: Robert F. Hill; SP: anthony Coldeway; S: Frederic Isham; LP: Jack Mulhall, Margaret Livingston, William Walsh, Harry T. DeVere, Wade Boteler.

1924

Into the Net. Pathé, [10 Chapters] D: George B. Seitz; S: Richard E. Enright; SP: Frank Leon Smith; LP: Edna Murphy, Jack Mulhall, Constance Bennett, Bradley Barker.

1925

Wild West. Pathé, [10 Chapters] D: Robert F. Hill; SP: J. F. Natteford; LP: Jack Mulhall, Helen Ferguson, Ed Burns, Eddie Phillips, Fred Burns.

1933

The Three Musketeers. Mascot, [12 Chapters] D: Armand Schaefer, Colbert Clark; SP: Norman Hall, Colbert Clark, Ben Cohn, Wyndham Gittens; P: Nat Levine; Mus: Lee Zahler; Cam: Ernest Miller, Tom Galligan; LP: Jack Mulhall, Raymond Hatton, Francis X. Bushman, Jr., John Wayne, Ruth Hall, Creighton Chaney [Lon Chaney, Jr.], Hooper Atchley.

Mystery Squadron. Mascot, [12 Chapters] D: Colbert Clark, David Howard; SP: Barney Sarecky, Colbert Clark, David Howard, Wyndham Gittens; P: Nat Levine; S: Sherman Lowe, Al Martin; LP: Bob Steele, Lucile Browne, "Big Boy" Williams, Jack Mulhall, Jack Mower, Robert Kortman, Jack Perrin.

1934

Burn 'Em Up Barnes. Mascot, [12 Chapters] D: Colbert Clark, Armand Schaeffer; SP: Al Martin, Armand Schaefer, Barney Sarecky,

Sherman Lowe; S: Colbert Clark, John Rathmell; P: Nat Levine; LP: Jack Mulhall, Lola Lane, Frankie Darro, Julian Rivero, Jason Robards, Francis McDonald.

1936

Undersea Kingdom. Rep., [12 Chapters] D: B. Reeves Eason, Joseph Kane; SP: John Rathmell, Maurice Geraghty, Oliver Drake; LP: Ray Corrigan, Lois Wilde, Monte Blue, William Farnum, Lon Chaney, Jr., Lee Van Atta, Raymond Hatton, Jack Mulhall.

The Clutching Hand. S&S, [12 Chapters] D: Al Herman; Spv.: Louis Weiss; SP: Louis D'Usseau, Dallas Fitzgerald; Adapt: George M. Merrick, Eddy Graneman; Cam: James Diamond; Mus: Lee Zahler; LP: Jack Mulhall, Rex Lease, Ruth Mix, Yakima Canutt, Reed Howes, Marion Shilling, Mae Busch, Bryant Washburn.

1937

Radio Patrol. Univ., [12 Chapters] D: Ford Beebe, Cliff Smith; LP: Grant Withers, Catherine [Kay] Hughes, Mickey Rentschier, Adrian Morris, Frank Lackteen, Max Hoffman, Jr.

Tim Tyler's Luck. Univ., [12 Chapters] D: Ford Beebe, Wyndham Gittens; SP: Wyndham Gittens, Norman S. Hall, Ray Trampe; LP: Frankie Thomas, Frances Robinson, Norman Willis, Jack Mulhall, Al Shean, Anthony Warde, Earle Douglas.

1938

Flash Gordon's Trip to Mars. Univ., [15 Chapters] D: Ford Beebe, Robert Hill; LP: Buster Crabbe, Jean Rogers, Charles Middleton, Frank Shannon, Beatrice Roberts, Donald Kerr, Dick Alexander, Wheeler Oakman.

1939

Buck Rogers. Univ., [12 Chapters] D: Ford Beebe, Saul A. Goodkind; LP: Buster Crabbe, Constance Moore, Jackie Moran, Jack Mulhall, Anthony Warde, Henry Brandon.

1940

Mysterious Doctor Satan. Rep., [15 Chapters] D: William Witney, John English; P: Hiram S. Brown, Jr.; LP: Eduardo Ciannelli, Robert Wilcox, Ella Neal, William Newell, C. Montague Shaw, Jack Mulhall.

1941

The Spider Returns. Col., [15 Chapters] D: James W. Horne; LP: Warren Hull, Mary Ainslee, Dave O'Brien, Joe Girard, Kenneth Duncan, Corbet Harris, Bryant Washburn.

Adventures of Captain Marvel. Rep., [12 Chapters] D: William Witney, John English; LP: Tom Tyler, Frank Coghlan, Jr., William Benedict, Louise Currie, Robert Strange, Gerald Mohr.

Dick Tracy vs. Crime, Inc. Rep., [15 Chapters] D: William Witney, John English; LP: Ralph Byrd, Jan Wiley, John Davidson, Ralph Morgan, Michael Owen.

1942

Gang Busters. Univ., [xx Chapters] D: Ray Taylor and Noel Smith; LP: Kent Taylor, Irene Hervey, Ralph Morgan, Robert Armstrong, George J. Lewis, Richard Davies, Stanley Blyston.

1952

Blackhawk. Col., [15 Chapters] D: Spencer G. Bennet, Fred F. Sears; LP: Kirk Alyn, Carol Forman, John Crawford, Rick Vallin, Michael F, Don C. Harvey.

EDNA MURPHY

Edna Murphy is better remembered today for the serial *Fantomas* ('20) than for any other of her films. It was a Fox 20-chapter cliffhanger that kept the kids unnerved in that glorious, uncomplicated period following World War I. Tinted sequences, a mystery ship, a haunted hotel, ghostly creatures, fire and water thrills, plenty of fights and other action ingredients made it an above-average endeavor quality-wise. Fantomas (Edward Roseman) was a supercriminal who could disguise himself so that no one recognized him. Offering to give up his life of crime if the police will leave him alone, he becomes enraged when the police reject his offer and vows to terrorize New York, his first act being to kidnap Prof. Harrington (Lionel Adams), father of Ruth Harrington (Edna Murphy). Johnnie Walker is Edna's fiancé and John Willard is the relentless detective Dixon.

Following *Fantomas*, Fox gave Edna the feminine lead in *Dynamite Alley* opposite George Walsh and then co-starred Edna and Johnnie Walker in five 1921 features—*Live Wires*, *Play Square*, *What Love Will Do*, *The Jolt* and *Extra! Extra!* They had made *Over the Hill* together in 1920.

Edna had principal roles in films for Universal before she was cast opposite Hoot Gibson in *The Galloping Kid* ('22) and *Ridin' Wild* ('22). In 1923 Pathé starred her in the serial *Her Dangerous Path*, with Charles Parrott (Charley Chase) her main support. It was a disjointed but interesting chapterplay in which Edna took on the role of a different type of woman in each episode, and pursued the different paths that fate might dictate for such a woman.

Pathé liked Edna and put her into the lead in two more serials: *Leatherstocking* ('24), an adaptation of James Fenimore Cooper's classic novels, and *Into the Net* ('24), a New York City police story that had Jack Mulhall as the hero. Miss Murphy's four serials were definitely her own — she was the principal player. She made one more serial later in her career, for Universal. Titled *Fingerprints* ('31), it concerned smugglers and the Secret Service, with Edna the love object of both good guy Kenneth Harlan and bad guy Gayne Whitman. Feature-wise, she was the girl in *The King of Wild Horses* ('24) starring Rex, the Wonder Horse. She played sec-

ond to Aileen Pringle in *Wildfire* ('25); co-starred with James Kirkwood in *The Police Patrol* ('25); teamed with James Pierce in *Tarzan and the Golden Lion* ('27); with Monte Blue in *The Black Diamond Express* ('27); with Fred Thomson in *The Sunset Legion* ('28); and with Cullen Landis in *A Midnight Adventure* ('28). By 1931 she had slipped into the supporting player category and ended her career with an appearance in the Thelma Todd starrer *Cheating Blondes*.

Edna was born on 106th Street in New York City on November 17, 1899. She was educated at Bay Ridge High School and Manual Training High School in Brooklyn. Before she graduated from high school, Edna was posing for commercial photographers as the pretty girl who wore the latest thing in gowns and hats. This work led to her engagement as a model for Lajaren Hiller. From the Hiller studio she started her screen career, playing the lead with Alice Joyce in *To the Highest Bidder* ('18).

Edna married director Mervyn LeRoy in 1930 and retired. She died on August 3, 1974, in Santa Monica, California.

Serials

1920

Fantomas. Fox, [20 Chapters] D: Edward Sedgwick; SP: Edward Sedgwick, George Eshenfelder; LP: Edward Roseman, Edna Murphy, Johnnie Walker, Henry Armetta, Lionel Adams.

1923

Her Dangerous Path. Pathé, [10 Chapters] D: Roy Clements; SP: Frank Howard Clark; P: Hal Roach; LP: Edna Murphy, Charles Parrott [Charley Chase], Hayford Hobbs, Percy Pembroke, Glen Tryon, Frank Lackteen, Fong Wong.

1924

Leatherstocking. Pathé, [10 Chapters] D: George B. Seitz; P: C. W. Paton; LP: Edna Murphy, Harold Miller, Whitehorse, Frank Lackteen, Lillian Hall, Tom Tyler, James H. Pierce.

Into the Net. Pathé, [10 Chapters] D: George B. Seitz; SP: Frank Leon Smith; S: Richard E. Enright; LP: Edna Murphy, Jack Mulhall, Constance Bennett, Frank Lackteen, Frances Landau, Bradley Baker.

1931

Fingerprints. Univ., [10 Chapters] D: Ray Taylor; S: Arthur B. Reeve; SP: George Morgan, George H. Plympton, Basil Dickey; LP: Kenneth Harlan, Edna Murphy, Gayne Whitman, Gertrude Astor, William Worthington, William Thorne.

CARMEL MYERS

References give Carmel Myers' birthday as April 4, 1899, although she contended that it was later. She was born in San Francisco, the daughter of a rabbi. She started her histrionic career as the singing ingenue lead in *The Magic Melody*, which had a year's run

Carmel Myers and William Russell in *Goodbye Girls* (Fox, 1923).

in New York. She entered films as a protégée of D. W. Griffith and Cecil B. DeMille at Triangle. *Intolerance* ('16) was her first film, but don't look for her when you view the film — she was just an extra.

Among her many films: *Sirens of the Sea* ('17) with Jack Mulhall; *The Wine Girl* ('18) with Rex De Rosselli; *The Little White Savage* ('19) with Harry Hilliard; *The Gilded Dream* ('20) with Tom Chatterton; *The Kiss* ('21) with George Periolat; *The Love Gambler* ('22) with John Gilbert; *The Love Pirate* ('23) with Melbourne MacDowell; *Babbitt* ('24) with Willard Lewis; *Tell It to the Marines* ('26) with Lon Chaney; *Sorrell and Son* ('27) with H. B. Warner; *Prowlers of the Sea* ('28) with Ricardo Cortez; *The Careless Age* ('29) with Douglas Fairbanks, Jr.; *The Ship from Shanghai* ('30) with Conrad Nagel; *Svengali* ('31) with John Barrymore; *Pleasure* ('31) with Conway Tearle; *Nice Women* ('32) with Sidney Fox; and *The Countess of Monte Cristo* ('34) with Fay Wray.

Breaking Through ('21) introduced Carmel to serial audiences. A Vitagraph film, it was a Western story centered about a fight to put through a railroad track from a mine in Alaska to the coast. And yes, if it was not completed by a certain time, Myers would lose her title to the property. The outlaw contingent headed by Vincente Howard try to see that she fails, but young engineer Wallace MacDonald aids her in a successful fight.

Carmel frequently played a vamp, and such actors as John Barrymore, John Gilbert, Douglas Fairbanks, Jr., and Rudolph Valen-

tino made love to her. Her most famous roles were that of Iris in *Ben Hur* ('26) with Ramon Novarro and as the principal female in John Barrymore's version of *Beau Brummel* ('24). She was cast for a leading role in the first all-talking Fox picture, *The Ghost Talks* ('28) with Helen Twelvetrees. Carmel gave up her career after 1934, although she accepted supporting roles in *Lady for a Night* ('42) and *Whistle Stop* ('46).

In New York, Carmel created and for years operated the perfume enterprise Zizani, but when her husband, Al Schwalberg, died, she returned to California. Her family were all there — her son, her two daughters and her grandchildren.

In 1975 she found herself back on a sound stage at MGM. She was playing a supporting role, a murder suspect, in an ABC-TV movie, *The Thin Man*. And she did a cameo role in *Won Ton Ton, the Dog that Saved Hollywood* ('76).

Myers died in 1980 after a heart attack in Los Angeles. She was reported to be 79 years of age.

Serial

1921

Breaking Through. Vit., [15 Chapters] D: Robert Ensminger; S/SP: C. Graham Baker; LP: Carmel Myers, Wallace MacDonald, Vincente Howard.

HARRY MYERS

Harry Myers' motion picture career began in 1908. He started out as a handsome, wavy-haired comic leading man. In 1916–17 he teamed with his wife Rosemary Theby in more than 40 short (one-reel) domestic

comedies. One of his first films was *The Guerrilla* ('08). Other films included *Housekeeping* ('16) (the first in the Theby-Myers series), *A Connecticut Yankee in King Arthur's Court* ('21), *Kisses* ('22), *The Bad Man* ('23),

Fritzi Ridgeway and Harry Myers in *Getting Gertie's Garter* (Metropolitan, 1927).

The Beautiful and the Damned ('23), *The Printer's Devil* ('23), *Behold This Woman* ('24), *Grounds for Divorce* ('25), *Getting Gertie's Garter* ('27), *The Savage Girl* ('32), *Police Call* ('33), *Mississippi* ('35) and *Holly-wood Boulevard* ('36). In *City Lights* ('31) he played Charlie Chaplin's bosom buddy only when drunk.

In the serial *The Masked Rider* ('19) he is the man of the title, but the author has no information on the story. However, on the basis of the chapter titles it must have been an exciting serial. Paul Panzer is "Pancho," chief badman with Boris Karloff playing a subordinate outlaw.

The Adventures of Robinson Crusoe ('22) starred Myers as Crusoe. It is straight from the pages of Defoe's classic. Noble Johnson is "Friday," and Gertrude Olmstead has the female role.

Myers has a supporting role in Syndicate's *The Chinatown Mystery* ('28), but the nature of his role is unknown. Likewise, in *The Spider's Web* ('38) he has a very minor role as a detective.

Myers was born in 1886 either in Philadelphia, Pennsylvania, or New Haven, Connecticut. His death came on December 26, 1938, in Los Angeles. Cause of death was pneumonia.

Serials

1919

The Masked Rider. Arrow, [15 Chapters] P: William Steiner; S/D: Audrey C. Kennedy; LP: Harry Myers, Ruth Stonehouse, Paul Panzer, Edna M. Holland, Marie Treador, Blanche Gillespie, Boris Karloff, Robert Tober.

1922

The Adventures of Robinson Crusoe. Univ., [18 Chapters] D: Robert F. Hill; SP: Emma Bell Clifton; S: Daniel Defoe; LP: Harry Myers, Noble Johnson, Gertrude Olmstead, Percy Pembroke, Aaron Edwards.

1928

The Chinatown Mystery. Syn., [10 Chapters] D: J. P. McGowan; LP: Joe Bonomo, Ruth Hiatt, Paul Malvern, Francis Ford, Paul Panzer, Sheldon Lewis, Helen Gibson.

1938

The Spider's Web. Col., [15 Chapters] D: Ray Taylor, James W. Horne; LP: Warren Hull, Iris Meredith, Richard Fiske, Kenneth Duncan, Forbes Murray, Donald Douglas, Marc Lawrence, Charles Wilson.

ANNE NAGEL

Born Anna Dolan in Boston, Massachusetts, on September 30, 1915, Anne was early encouraged to be a nun. At Notre Dame Academy she began her preparation to enter the church and on a part-time basis worked as a commercial photographer's model in Boston. Anne's stepfather, a technicolor expert, had signed a long-term contract as director at Tiffany-Stahl Studios. Anne became definitely interested in the movies and upon graduation from Notre Dame started to learn the acting business in a Boston stock company. The company was presenting revivals of old plays in the Shubert Theatre, and Anne acquired much valuable experience in portraying the time-tested character roles.

Anne ultimately came to California and acted in the Technicolor short subjects directed by her stepfather. She broke into feature-length productions as a dancer in silent pictures. She stood 5'4" in height, generally weighed around 110 pounds, and had blue eyes and brown hair. She danced in George White Scandals and appeared in niteries before making her sound film bow in *I Loved You Wednesday* ('33).

She quickly won light comedy assignments in such films as *Stand Up and Cheer*

('34), *King of Hockey* ('36), *A Bride for Henry* ('37) and *Should a Girl Marry?* ('39). One of her first major roles was in *Here Comes Carter* ('36), opposite Ross Alexander, whom she married shortly after completing the film. A year later, however, Alexander committed suicide.

Nagel generally provided a passable performance, though she sometimes failed to measure up to possibilities and alternated between leads and supporting roles, mostly in medium and low-budget features.

The Green Hornet ('39) was Anne's first venture into serialdom. Within the limitations of the field and budget, she acquitted herself creditably as the girlfriend of the hero, although a less erratic screenplay would have helped. In the sequel *The Green Hornet Strikes Again* ('40), she repeats her role of Lenore Case and effectively shows the whites of her eyes in tight places. Both serial entries are typical thrillers that move along nicely and are paced with action all the way, but lack any particular originality. They were strictly formula stuff from beginning to end, albeit enjoyable escapist entertainment.

Winners of the West ('40) got Anne into the wild west in one of Universal's slick chapterplays. Action is the attraction, and there are hairbreadth escapes a-plenty and enough cliffhanging to keep fans of the genre white-knuckled throughout almost the entire 13 chapters. Anne projected a naturalness in the cliffhanger environs that was immediately discernible by the audience.

Don Winslow of the Navy ('41), the next serial outing for Nagel, was exciting cinematic escapism, and it went down well with popcorn and Coke. However, Nagel's role was secondary to that of Claire Dodd. Anne projected wholesomeness and beauty, but she fell a little short on screen presence, i.e., the quality of simply being noticed in a scene when she wasn't the focal point of the action. In this particular serial the scriptwriters did not provide her a role that would be forever etched in the audience's minds.

Nagel's last serial, *The Secret Code* ('42), had her playing the reporter girlfriend of the Black Commando, a masked protector of justice. Her air of self-assurance, an indication that she was more than capable of the task at hand, came across much better on the screen in this one.

In features such as *Diamond Frontier* ('40), *Man Made Monster* ('41), *Mutiny in the Arctic* ('41) and *The Dawn Express* ('42), Anne performed well in the lead female role, easily conveying the qualities of attractiveness and vulnerability. However, she was more often cast as a "second banana" to another ingenue.

By 1950, Nagel's career was going nowhere and she left films. It cannot be said that she left an indelible mark on filmdom. She didn't. But thanks to the five serials she made, she is an inseparable element of the total serial tradition and is to be admired for her sheer durability.

Anne Nagel died at age 53 from cancer on July 6, 1966, in Sunray North Convalescent Hospital in Los Angeles following surgery in early June.

Serials

1939

The Green Hornet. Univ., [13 Chapters] D: Ford Beebe, Ray Taylor; SP: George Plympton, Basil Dickey, Morrison C. Wood, Lyonel Margolies; AP: Henry MacRae; LP: Gordon Jones, Anne Nagel, Wade Boteler, Keye Luke, Philip Trent, John Kelly.

1940

Winners of the West. Univ., [13 Chapters] D: Ford Beebe, Ray Taylor; P: Henry MacRae; SP: George Plympton, Basil Dickey, Charles R. Condon; LP: Dick Foran, Anne Nagel, James Craig, Tom Fadden, Harry Woods, William Desmond, Edmund Cobb.

The Green Hornet Strikes Again. Univ., [13 Chapters] D: Ford Beebe, John Rawlins; AP: Henry MacRae; LP: Warren Hull, Keye Luke, Anne Nagel, Wade Boteler, Eddie Acuff, Roy Barcroft, Joe Devlin, Dorothy Lovett, Montague Shaw.

1941

Don Winslow of the Navy. Univ., [12 Chapters] D: Ford Beebe, Ray Taylor; SP: Paul Huston, Griffin Jay; LP: Don Terry, Walter Sande, John Litel, Claire Dodd, Anne Nagel, Samuel S. Hinds, Wade Boteler, Herbert Rawlinson.

1942

The Secret Code. Col., [15 Chapters] D: Spencer G. Bennet; SP: Basil Dickey, Leighton Brill, Robert Beche; P: Larry Darmour; LP: Paul Kelly, Anne Nagel, Clancy Cooper, Trevor Bardette, Robert O. Davis, Gregory Gay, Eddie Parker.

J. CARROL NAISH

J. Carrol Naish, the Irish-American character actor, was famous for his roles as a Chinese, Japanese, Arab, Indian, Italian and Latin American. He was often a villain in his character roles; he could be a gracious, caring person if the role demanded it. Adept at playing various ethnic roles, he probably scored his greatest success on radio in *Life with Luigi*, which also had a brief run on television in the early 1950s. A series about Italian street life, it aired Sundays on network radio for many years. He also was the first to portray Charlie Chan on television (in the late 1950s).

Naish once noted that he had played every national type except his own. He explained, "When the part of an Irishman comes along, nobody ever thinks of me."

Naish spent most of his later years in San Diego studying philosophy and theology, once narrating a movie expressly for the Pope. But his youth and most of his adult life was spent in entertainment.

Naish was born Joseph Patrick Carrol

Naish on January 21, 1897, in New York City. He grew up in the tough Yorkville-Harlem area of turn-of-the-century New York and at age 16 dropped out of school to enlist in the Navy. During World War I he saw action in Europe with the Aviation section of the Army Signal Corps. After his discharge he roamed about Europe, performing various odd jobs and acquiring a working knowledge of several languages. He returned to the U.S. aboard a tramp steamer that dropped him off on the West Coast. He appeared in Hollywood as an extra and stuntman in a few films, then headed for Broadway in 1926 as an understudy with the road company of *The Shanghai Gesture*. He later had parts in a couple of Broadway productions and returned to Hollywood in 1930 as a featured player. He soon became established as a reliable and versatile character actor who specialized in the portrayal of foreigners, particularly Italians and Latins; he never portrayed an Irishman because of his swarthy complexion.

Like Karloff, Lugosi, Chaney, Carra-

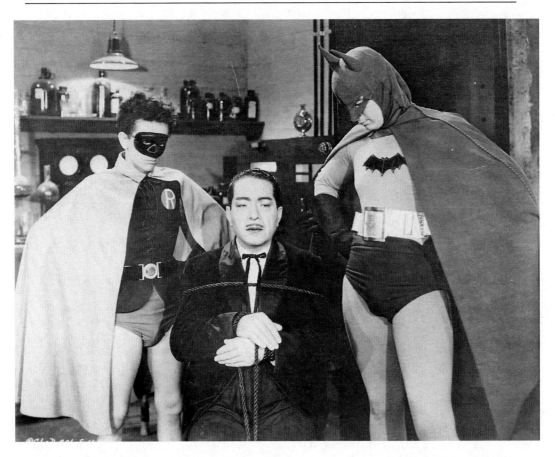

Douglas Croft (Robin), J. Carrol Naish and Lewis Wilson in *Batman* (Columbia, 1943).

dine, Zucco, Lorre, Price and Lee, Naish was a respected performer in the horror film genre. His introduction to horror films was the 1934 Warner Bros. adaptation of Edgar Wallace's *Return of the Terror*, about a madman, the inventor of a futuristic X-ray machine, escaping from a mental institution and stalking several people in an eerie mansion.

In horror films Naish was best when playing sympathetic mutants. This is especially true of his work in *Dr. Renault's Secret* ('42), as a man who was evolved from an ape, and in *House of Frankenstein* ('44), in which he played a hunchback who loved a gypsy girl (Elena Verdugo) who in turn loved the Wolf Man (Lon Chaney, Jr.).

In the 1943 Columbia serial *Batman*, the actor has a field day hamming it up as the evil Oriental spy Dr. Daka, who is trying

to seize control of the U.S. Naish was the true star of the chapterplay. In one scene, Dr. Daka takes delight in feeding the alligators that live beneath the trap door of his secret lair. Naish milked the scene, chortling and rubbing his hands after the alligators consumed all the raw meat he has thrown them. Daka talked to his pets, apologizing for not having any more meat. Then his eyes shifted toward a man under his control standing off to one side. Daka grinned sadistically. But he was interrupted by one of his henchmen, and failed to complete his ghoulish act.

One of Naish's best-liked roles is that of Dr. Igor Markov in the PRC cult classic *The Monster Maker* ('44). Here Naish is so evil he is not even really a mad scientist; he murders a doctor and steals his identity. The plot has Markov falling for a comely young lady (Wanda McKay) but being told by her father (Ralph Morgan), a concert pianist, to leave her alone. To get revenge, Markov and his handyman (Glenn Strange) inject the pianist with a fluid causing him to develop acromegaly and turn into a hideous monster. Markov's nurse (Tala Birell) is jealous of his attentions toward the pianist's daughter and so Markov sets his killer gorilla loose on her. Eventually the nurse turns the tables on the madman and the pianist is given an antidote. *The Monster Maker* is a classic horror movie which is greatly enhanced by Naish's performance as the thoroughly evil Markov.

In *Calling Dr. Death* ('43), Naish plays police Inspector Gregg, who investigates a doctor (Lon Chaney, Jr.) accused of killing his wife. This well-done thriller for director Reginal LeBorg was followed by a lesser feature for the same director, *Jungle Woman* ('44).

In *The Whistler* ('44), Naish is memorable as the job-loving hit man hired by a despondent man (Richard Dix) to kill him, only to have the man change his mind.

In 1960–61 Naish played the part of "Hawkeye" in the TV comedy series *Guestward Ho*.

In *Dracula vs. Frankenstein* ('71), Naish's last movie, he is a wheelchair-bound doctor who runs a sleazy sideshow concession as a front for his experiments in developing a rejuvenation serum from the blood of recently decapitated young girls. The film was the nadir of Naish's otherwise stellar career and a sad cinema finale to one of the movie's greatest character actors.

Naish was twice nominated for an Academy Award—*Sahara* ('43) and *A Medal for Benny* ('45). Other memorable films are *Captain Blood* ('35), *The Charge of the Light Brigade* ('36), *Beau Geste* ('39), *Typhoon* ('40), *Blood and Sand* ('41), *Jackass Mail* ('42), *Gung Ho* ('43), *Behind the Rising Sun* ('43), *Strange Confession* ('45), *Bad Bascomb* ('46), *Joan of Arc* ('48), *Across the Wide Missouri* ('51) and *Violent Saturday* ('55).

Naish died from emphysema at the Scripps Memorial Hospital in 1973 at age 76.

Serial

1933

Mystery Squadron. Mascot, [12 Chapters] D: Colbert Clark, David Howard; SP: Barney Sarecky, Colbert Clark, David Howard, Wyndham Gittens; S: Al Martin, Sherman Lowe; P: Nat Levine; LP: Bob Steele, Guinn "Big Boy" Williams, Lucile Browne, Jack Mulhall, Robert Kortman.

1943

Batman. Col., [15 Chapters] D: Lambert Hillyer; SP: Victor McLeod, Leslie Swabacker, Harry Fraser; P: Rudolph C. Flothow; Mus: Lee Zahler; Narration: Knox Manning; LP: Lewis Wilson, Douglas Croft, J. Carrol Naish, Shirley Patterson, Charles Middleton, George Chesebro.

TOM NEAL

Tom Neal is mostly remembered today, at least by B-film aficionados, for five films: *Jungle Girl* ('41), *Behind the Rising Sun* ('43), *Detour* ('45), *Decoy* ('46) and *Bruce Gentry* ('49).

A muscular, handsome guy who looked great in boxer trunks or military uniforms, he had been groomed for stardom by MGM as another Gable. Instead, his career was made up of little-known B offerings and small bits in A's. They display an agreeable actor inexplicably disregarded by the major studios, and mishandled by the minor ones.

Neal was a very contradictory human being—a man driven by great ambition but somehow held back by his own insecurity, painfully vulnerable and because of that, extremely cruel at times.

He was born in Evanston, Illinois, on January 28, 1914, the son of well-to-do parents. After grade school he was enrolled at Lake Forrest Academy, where he displayed a bad temper; consequently, his parents enrolled him in a military academy. Tom finished high school without further discipline problems. He went on to Northwestern University in Evanston, majoring in mathematics, but a desire for fame caused him to change his focus to dramatics.

After some summer stock in Chicago, he tried New York, landing small parts in *If This Be Treason, Love Is Not Simple, Spring Dance, The Old Maid, Daughters of Atreus* and *Summer Nights*. Then came the road company of *Brother Rat*. He left the company in Florida; he was living with his parents and working as a lifeguard when a Goldwyn talent scout spotted him. He was signed by Goldwyn but was mostly used in non-credit roles. Goldwyn let Neal go after he was rejected for the lead in 1937's *The Hurricane*. He returned to the stage where MGM noticed him and, after a screen test, signed him. For the most part his roles were trivial. However, the parts got better and he was all set to co-star with Clark Gable and Joan Crawford in *Strange Cargo* ('40). But after he supposedly made some crude comments to Crawford, she reported it to Louis B. Mayer and Neal was off the production. After a few small parts, he was dropped by the studio.

Tom tried his luck at RKO and was favorably noticed by the critics for his work in *Courageous Dr. Christian* ('40). It was the turning point in his career. From then on he was never out of work, but that work was mostly in B films.

In 1941 he received the male lead opposite Frances Gifford in *Jungle Girl* ('41), one of Republic's most popular serials. Dr. Meredith (Trevor Bardette), a friend of a savage tribe, brings up his daughter, Nyoka (Gifford), in the jungles of Africa *a la* Tarzan. His twin brother learns that he has access to a hoard of diamonds and is determined to acquire them. He has Dr. Meredith murdered, takes his place and enters into an alliance with the village witch doctor. Jack Stanton (Neal) and Curly Rogers (Eddie Acuff), American pilots, come to the aid of Nyoka (Gifford) and a young boy, Kimbu (Tommy Cook),and the four eventually defeat the jungle criminals under Slick Latimer (Gerald Mohr), both whites and blacks.

Bruce Gentry ('49) starred Neal in the title role with Judy Clark as Juanita Farrell, Ralph Hodges as Frank Farrell and Forrest Taylor as Dr. Alexander Benson. The Gentry character originated in a comic strip where he was one of the successors to Dick Tracy. Neal gave the character a devil-may-care dash and Columbia gave him a topical mystery to solve—the secret of the "flying saucers."

Gentry, famed aviator, clashes with a gang headed by "the Recorder" who has control of a deadly flying disc that endangers the world. Unknown to Gentry, the Recorder is Dr. Benson, the scientist with whom he works. Bruce discovers Benson's double identity and apprehends the criminal gang in time to stop a disc meant for destruction of the Panama Canal.

In 1949, Neal's wife, actress Vicky Lane, obtained a divorce on grounds of mental and physical cruelty, and in 1951 his bloody brawl with Franchot Tone over the affection of buxom, sexy actress Barbara Payton, who was criss-crossing her charms, made more headlines than a Jersey Joe Walcott–Joe Louis championship prizefight. Tone was beaten so badly that he was hospitalized for treatment of a brain concussion and facial injuries.

Neal's career nearly ended as a result of the sordid publicity, also that of Payton, who drifted into alcoholism and prostitution before dying at age 39 in 1967.

Neal wound up in Palm Springs, first as manager of a restaurant and then as self-employed owner of a prosperous gardening business. He wed a local girl, Patricia Fenton, and became father of a robust baby boy. Patricia died of cancer the following year, leaving Tom with a baby on his hands. His sister in Illinois agreed to care for the boy but Tom neglected his business to make frequent trips to see him.

Tom met Gail Bennet at the Palm Springs Tennis Club and they got married in 1961. He was old enough to be her father, and his jealous streak was the cause of many fights. There had been prolonged accusations of infidelity along with excessive drinking. On April 1, 1965, Gail was shot in the head during one of their fights. Tom claimed self-defense. A verdict of involuntary manslaughter was returned November 19, 1965. Neal was sentenced to serve a one- to 15-year prison term. He served six years, winning his parole in December 1973. Eight months later he was found dead in his North Hollywood apartment by his 15-year-old son. Tom died of natural causes.

Serials

1941

Jungle Girl. Rep., [15 Chapters] D: William Witney, John English; SP: Ronald Davidson, Norman S. Hall, William Lively, Joseph O'-Donnell, Joseph F. Poland, Alfred Batson; Cam: Reggie Lanning; Mus: Cy Feuer; LP: Frances Gifford, Tom Neal, Eddie Acuff, Gerald Mohr, Trevor Bardette, Tommy Cook, Frank Lackteen, Bud Geary.

1949

Bruce Gentry. Col., [15 Chapters] D: Spencer G. Bennet, Thomas Carr; SP: George H. Plympton, Joseph F. Poland, Lewis Clay; P: Sam Katzman; Cam: Ira H. Morgan; Mus: Mischa Bakaleinikoff; LP: Tom Neal, Judy Clark, Ralph Hodges, Forrest Taylor, Hugh Prosser, Tristram Coffin, Jack Ingram, Terry Frost.

NOEL NEILL

Noel Neill is most fondly remembered for her portrayal of Lois Lane in two Columbia serials and almost 80 half-hour episodes of the *Adventures of Superman* television series starring George Reeves.

Noel's father, news editor of the *Minneapolis Star-Tribune*, gave her her newspaper training. She earned her first money by writing articles for *Women's Wear Daily*.

Her newspaper career was short-lived. One summer she was spotted at NBC by Bing Crosby, and he signed her to sing at his Del Mar (California) Turf Club. After a season there, the call from Hollywood was inevitable. Signed to a long-term contract by Paramount, Noel made her screen debut in *Henry Aldrich for President* ('41) with Jimmy Lydon and Charles Smith. Other Paramount releases included *The Remarkable Andrew* ('42), *Let's Face It* ('43), *Here Come the Waves* ('45), *The Blue Dahlia* ('46) and *The Greatest Show on Earth* ('52). She had only minor supporting roles in these films.

While under contract to Paramount, she was loaned out to Monogram to do the *High School Hero* series with Freddie Stewart, June Preisser and Frankie Darro.

Noel's introduction to serials came in *Brick Bradford* ('47), a Sam Katzman production for Columbia starring Kane Richmond. Linda Johnson has the female lead; Noel merely flitted in and out of scenes as a minor supporting player. However, Republic picked her up for the female lead in *Adven-*

tures of Frank and Jesse James ('48), which starred Clayton Moore (soon to become the "Heigh-Ho, Silver" crusader) as the infamous Jesse James. Sam Katzman then latched onto her again for the part of Lois Lane in the serial *Superman* ('48), the first live-action motion picture about the comic book hero. Kirk Alyn played Superman and, like Noel, proved to be an excellent choice.

In 1950, Republic used her in another serial about a family of outlaw fame: *The James Brothers of Missouri* ('50). This serial featured Keith Richards and Robert Bice as Jesse and Frank and Noel as the heroine who needed a little help running her stage line.

The Katzman-Columbia *Atom Man vs. Superman* ('50) carried on the adventures of Superman and Lois Lane, as portrayed again by Alyn and Neill, with Tommy Bond and Pierre Watkin once more cast as Jimmy Olson and Perry White.

In 1951, *Superman and the Mole Men* starred George Reeves as the Man of Steel and Phyllis Coates as Lois Lane. The movie, later made into a two-part television episode, served as a pilot of sorts for the *Adventures of Superman* series. Coates appeared in the show for the first two years, then left to make a pilot that never sold.

Noel replaced Coates as Lois Lane in the TV series and appeared in 78 episodes. The series, which ended in 1957, is still being seen 50 years later.

After *Superman* closed down, Neill left the acting profession. However, she and Kirk Alyn made cameo appearances in the 1978 Warner Bros. movie *Superman*, playing the parents of infant Lois Lane in their brief scene. The young Lois spots Superman from the window of a passing train, and Neill tells her to come away from the window. Neill traveled the college lecture circuit in the late 1970s and later settled down to travel, play golf and bridge and just enjoy life.

In 1954, Twentieth Century-Fox cashed in on the popularity of the TV series by releasing five features to theaters, each made up of three edited episodes of the Reeves-Neill TV series.

Serials

1947

Brick Bradford. Col., [15 Chapters] D: Spencer G. Bennet; SP: George Plympton, Arthur Hoerl, Lewis Clay; P: Sam Katzman; LP: Kane Richmond, Rick Vallin, Linda Johnson, Pierre Watkin, Charles Quigley, Jack Ingram, Noel Neill, Charles King, Carol Forman.

1948

Adventures of Frank and Jesse James. Rep., [13 Chapters] D: Fred Brannon, Yakima Canutt; SP: Franklyn Adreon, Sol Shor, Basil Dickey; AP: Franklyn Adreon; LP: Clayton Moore, Steve Darrell, Noel Neill, George J. Lewis, John Crawford, Stanley Andrews, House Peters, Jr.

Superman. Col., [15 Chapters] D: Spencer G. Bennet, Thomas Carr; SP: Arthur Hoerl, Lewis Clay, Royal Cole; P: Sam Katzman; LP: Kirk Alyn, Noel Neill, Tommy Bond, Carol Forman, Pierre Watkin, George Meeker, Jack Ingram, Terry Frost.

1950

The James Brothers of Missouri. Rep., [12 Chapters] D: Fred C. Brannon; SP: Royal Cole,

William Lively, Sol Shor; AP: Franklyn Adreon; LP: Keith Richards, Robert Bice, Noel Neill, Roy Barcroft, Patricia Knox, Lane Bradford.

Atom Man vs. Superman. Col., [15 Chapters] D: Spencer G. Bennet; SP: George H. Plymp-ton, Joseph Poland, David Mathews; P: Sam Katzman; LP: Kirk Alyn, Noel Neill, Lyle Talbot, Tommy Bond, Pierre Watkin, Jack Ingram, Rusty Wescoatt.

BOBBY NELSON

Bobby Nelson, son of director Jack Nelson, starred in 13 two-reel episodes of the Pioneer Kid series for Universal in 1929–30. He was the youngest actor ever to be given his own Western series. It is believed that he was born in 1923. His screen career began in 1926 with appearances in Bob Custer shoot-'em-ups and a couple non–Westerns with Barbara Bedford. He was a good-looking kid who could both ride and act.

In 1927 he was given the part of Kimko in the Artclass serial *Perils of the Jungle.* Made at a time when most Americans had never seen a wild animal (except in circuses and zoos), this cheaply made serial was popular in the South with rural audiences. Intrigue, double crosses and animal jeopardy in the heart of the African jungle prevail, as a father and daughter seek a hidden treasure. A companion seeks to steal the treasure once it is found. When the father becomes ill, he entrusts the treasure map to a young man whom the party had met in Africa and whom the old man trusts. Bobby played a tribal youth and his father directed. In 1945 a feature entitled *The White Gorilla* was composed mainly of stock footage from this serial.

In the Universal serial *Tarzan the Mighty* ('28), Bobby has a principal role as Bobby Trevor, brother of Mary Trevor (Natalie Kingston). They are castaways living among a tribe which is dominated by Black John (Al Ferguson). Tarzan (Frank Merrill) saves Mary from a crocodile and thereafter fights to keep Black John from forcing a marriage on Mary and to free Bobby, held captive by the blackguard.

Bobby began his Pioneer Kid series in 1929, the first film released being *The Boy and the Badman.* Edmund Cobb supported him in a number of the films, the last of which was released on August 9, 1930, after most theaters were already wired for sound.

Bobby's first sound film was *Roaring Ranch* ('30), supporting Hoot Gibson and Sally Eilers. Sound was no problem for the kid and he made 27 films between 1931 and 1937. Westerns predominated. After appearing in the Tom Tyler feature *Two-Fisted Justice* ('30), Bobby was signed to appear with Big Tom in the Western cliffhanger *Battling with Buffalo Bill* ('31). It was followed by two more 1931 serials, *Heroes of the Flames* and *Spell of the Circus.* In the former, Bobby and Marion Shockley are brother and sister who are saved from a fire by Tim McCoy. Their father, William Gould, allows Tim to conduct his experiments on a chemical fire extinguisher in his laboratory. A crook and his henchmen try to steal Tim's formula and discredit him in the eyes of his benefactor. Bobby's role in the latter film is unknown to the author except that he again is named Bobby. Tom London is the malefactor who hopes to gain control of the circus by marrying Alberta Vaughn, the owner's daughter, whose heart belongs to Francis X. Bushman, Jr., headliner of the wild west concert.

Bobby supported these stars from 1932–37: Robert Frazer (1), Hoot Gibson (1), Tim McCoy (1), Buffalo Bill, Jr. (1), Tom Keene

Lucile Browne, Bobby Nelson (center) and Ken Maynard in *King of the Arena* (Universal, 1933).

(1), Ken Maynard (1), John Wayne (1), Richard Talmadge (1), Paul Muni (1), Kane Richmond (1), William Boyd (1), Charles Delaney (1), James Murray (1), Wally Wales (2), Buck Jones (2), Pat Carlyle (1), Johnny Mack Brown (2) and Bob Steele (2). In addition he appeared in *Custer's Last Stand*, his sixth serial, supporting Rex Lease and a host of familiar Western character actors.

Bobby quit the movies in 1937. His last roles were with Bob Steele and Johnny Mack Brown at Republic. There his trail ended. If alive today, he would be the last of the silent Western stars to have survived, and along with Monte Hale the last living members of the Hollywood posse of "B" Westerns.

Serials

1927

Perils of the Jungle. Weiss Bros. Artclass, [10 Chapters] D: Jack Nelson; LP: Eugenia Gilbert, Frank Merrill, Albert J. Smith, Harry Belmore, Bobby Nelson, Milburn Morante.

1928

Tarzan the Mighty. Univ., [15 Chapters] D: Jack Nelson, Ray Taylor; S: Edgar Rice Burroughs; SP: Ian McClosky Heath; LP: Frank Merrill, Natalie Kingston, Bobby Nelson, Al Ferguson, Lorimer Johnson, Tantor (elephant).

1931

Spell of the Circus. Univ., [10 Chapters] D: Robert F. Hill; S/SP: Ian McClosky Heath; LP: Francis X. Bushman, Jr., Alberta Vaughn, Tom London, Walter Shumway, Charles Murphy, Bobby Nelson.

Heroes of the Flames. Univ., [12 Chapters] D: Robert F. Hill; SP: George Morgan, Basil Dickey, George H. Plympton; LP: Tim McCoy, Marion Shockley, William Gould, Grace Cunard, Bobby Nelson, Gayne Whitman, Bruce Cabot, Andy Devine, Edmund Cobb.

Battling with Buffalo Bill. Univ., [12 Chapters] D: Ray Taylor; SP: Ella O'Neill, George H. Plympton; P: Henry MacRae; LP: Tom Tyler, Rex Bell, Lucile Browne, Francis Ford, Bobby Nelson, William Desmond, Jim Thorpe, Chief Thundercloud, Bud Osborne, Yakima Canutt.

1936

Custer's Last Stand. S & S, [15 Chapters] D: Elmer Clifton; SP: George A. Durlam, Eddy Graneman, William Lively; P: George M. Merrick; Spv.: Louis Weiss; Cam: Bert Langenecker; Mus: Hal Chasnoff; LP: Rex Lease, William Farnum, Reed Howes, George Chesebro, Lona Andre, Dorothy Gulliver, Ruth Mix, Bobby Nelson, Jack Mulhall, Ted Adams, Franklyn Farnum.

EDWARD NORRIS

Edward Norris, affectionately known as filmland's baby face gangster by movie aficionados, was born on March 10, 1911, in Philadelphia to socially prominent parents. The young teenager was enrolled in the Culver Military Academy and his father, a doctor, expected the youth to follow in his footsteps. But the 16-year-old dropped out of the Academy in 1927 to marry 18-year-old Virginia Hiller, daughter of a prominent Philadelphia physician.

Norris went to work on a Philadelphia newspaper and Edward Norris, Jr., was born in 1929. The marriage lasted only two and a half years. The child bridegroom went to see his mother (then divorced) in Coronado and, while playing on the beach with his dog, he met director William Wellman, who put him in one scene in *Wings* ('27) with Clara Bow. He then advised Norris to return to the East, get into a stock company and learn his trade. This Norris did. Returning to California in 1933, he got a job in a show called *Doomsday Circus* at the Pasadena Orange Grove Theater. It led to a small role in the classic *Queen Christina* ('33) with Greta Garbo. MGM signed him and, after a promising start as an MGM contractee, his career faltered due to a combination of management, personal problems, professional mistakes and just plain bad luck. However, he kept working. His MGM contract was terminated in 1938, at which time he signed with Fox and was kept busy in 13 features, some of them on loanout to other studios.

On a personal note he married actress Lona Andre — a marriage lasting all of four days! In 1936 he married actress Ann Sheridan. The marriage broke up in 1938 and the divorce followed one year later.

As a result of Pearl Harbor, Norris enlisted in the U.S. Army Air Force. He was assigned to the 7th and later the 14th U.S. Air Force Training Division. He served as a pilot instructor throughout the war, but luckily was able to continue making movies. On July 19, 1942, he married 21-year-old starlet Mickey June Satterlee. In just one month the couple separated and were divorced in September.

In 1945 his film career began looking up when he accepted the leading role in the Universal serial *Jungle Queen*. The studio was impressed with Norris and drew up a long-term contract for him but tore it up when he was blamed for production delays and problems on the set. However, he bounced back with one "B" movie after another. In 1946 he starred in Monogram's noir thriller *Decoy*, which became a classic of the genre. Norris' fifth and final marriage was to B-movie queen Sheila Ryan, whom he married on March 27, 1947. It lasted until 1950.

Norris decided to give up movie making in 1950, as he was tired and disillusioned with Hollywood. He did appear in several television shows, however. Having invested wisely in oceanfront real estate, he had no financial worries. In fact, he purchased an oceanfront house and 5,000 acres in North California. There he retired to enjoy his hobbies. He died in 200x.

Serial

1945

Jungle Queen. Univ., [13 Chapters] D: Ray Taylor, Lewis D.Collins; SP: George H. Plympton, Ande Lamb, Morgan B. Cox; AP: Ray Taylor, Morgan B. Cox; Cam: William Sickner; LP: Edward Norris, Lois Collier, Eddie Quillan, Douglas Dumbrille, Ruth Roman, Clarence Muse, Lumsden Hare, Lester Matthews.

WHEELER OAKMAN

Serial lovers should be familiar with Wheeler Oakman, as he had principal roles in 17 sound serials between 1932 and 1947, and his career dates from 1910 or '11. He was employed at Selig until 1917. There he worked in one-, two- and three-reelers, often in films starring Kathlyn Williams. The best known of these films is *The Spoilers* ('14); others are *The Speck on the Wall* ('14), *Ships of the Flying U* ('14), *The Story of the Blood Red Rose* ('14), *The Rosary* ('15), *Ebb Tide* ('15), *Sweet Alyssum* ('15), *The Carpet from Bagdad* ('15) and *The Brand of Cain* ('16).

There was a time, early on, when Wheeler played leads, but he evolved quickly into the scoundrel so familiar to sound-era audiences. He was to be seen in low-budget Westerns and melodramas.

Wheeler played the heavy in 14 Tim McCoy films. Other Western stars he worked with were Kermit Maynard, Ken Maynard, Tom Mix, Jack Hoxie, Hoot Gibson, Bill Cody, Russell Hayden, Charles Starrett and Buck Jones.

Oakman was divorced by his wife, Francis, in July 1934 on grounds of mental cruelty, which included criticism of her golf playing. Oakman was formerly married to actress Priscilla Dean.

At the time of his death on March 20, 1949, Oakman was working as the assistant manager of a theater in North Hollywood. He was 59 years of age.

Serials

1932

The Air Mail Mystery. Univ., [12 Chapters] D: Ray Taylor; SP: Basil Dickey, George H. Plympton, George Morgan; S: Ella O'Neill; LP: Lucille Browne, James Flavin, Wheeler Oakman, Al Wilson, Nelson McDowell.

1933

The Phantom of the Air. Univ., [12 Chapters] D: Ray Taylor; LP: Tom Tyler, Gloria Shea, LeRoy Mason, Hugh Enfield [Craig Reynolds].

1934

The Lost Jungle. Mascot, [12 Chapters] D: Armand Schaefer, David Howard; LP: Clyde Beatty, Cecilia Parker, Syd Saylor, Warner Richmond, Wheeler Oakman.

1935

Phantom Empire. Mascot, [12 Chapters] D: Otto Brower, B. Reeves Eason; LP: Gene Autry, Frankie Darro, Smiley Burnette, Betsy King Ross, Dorothy Christie.

The Adventures of Rex and Rinty. Mascot, [12 Chapters] D: B. Reeves Eason, Ford Beebe; LP: Rex, Rin-Tin-Tin, Jr., Kane Richmond, Norma Taylor, Mischa Auer, Harry Woods, Wheeler Oakman.

1936

Darkest Africa. Rep., [15 Chapters] D: B. Reeves Eason, Joseph Kane; LP: Clyde Beatty, Manuel King, Elaine Sheppard, Lucien Prival, Ray Corrigan.

1937

Radio Patrol. Univ., [12 Chapters] D: Ford Beebe, Cliff Smith; LP: Grant Withers, Catherine [Kay] Hughes, Mickey Rentschier, Adrian Morris, Wheeler Oakman.

1938

Red Barry. Univ., [13 Chapters] D: Ford Beebe, Alan James; LP: Buster Crabbe, Frances Robinson, Wade Boteler, Edna Sedgwick, Wheeler Oakman.

Flash Gordon's Trip to Mars. Univ., [15 Chapters] D: Ford Beebe, Robert Hill; LP: Buster Crabbe, Jean Rogers, Charles Middleton, Frank Shannon.

1939

The Lone Ranger Rides Again. Rep., [15 Chapters] D: William Witney, John English; LP: Robert Livingston, Chief Thundercloud, Duncan Renaldo, Jinx Falken.

Buck Rogers. Univ., [12 Chapters] D: Ford Beebe, Saul A. Goodkind; LP: Buster Crabbe, Constance Moore, Jackie Moran, Jack Mulhall, Wheeler Oakman.

1943

Adventures of Smilin' Jack. Univ., [13 Chapters] D: Ray Taylor, Lew Collins; LP: Tom Brown, Marjorie Lord, Sidney Toler, Edgar Barrier.

1945

Who's Guilty? Col., [15 Chapters] D: Howard Bretherton, Wallace Grissell; LP: Robert Kent, Amelita Ward, Tim Ryan, Jayne Hazard, Minerva Urecal.

Brenda Starr, Reporter. Col., [13 Chapters] D: William W. Fox; LP: Joan Woodbury, Kane Richmond, Syd Saylor, Joe Devlin, George Meeker.

1946

Son of the Guardsman. Col., [15 Chapters] D: Derwin Abrahams; LP: Robert Shaw, Duan Kennedy, Robert (Buzzy) Henry, Jim Diehl, Hugh Prosser.

Hop Harrigan. Col., [15 Chapters] D: Derwin Abrahams; LP: William Bakewell, Jennifer Holt, Robert (Buzzy) Henry, Sumner Getshell, Wheeler Oakman, Franklyn Farnum.

1947

Brick Bradford. Col., [15 Chapters] D: Spencer Bennet; LP: Kane Richmond, Rick Vallin, Linda Johnson, Pierre Watkin, Wheeler Oakman.

DAVE O'BRIEN

David Poole Fronabarger, known to the movie public as Dave O'Brien, was born in Big Springs, Texas, on May 31, 1912. In 1936 he legally changed his name to David Barclay, but retained Dave O'Brien as a screen name.

Serial and Western viewers were well aware of Dave, who so often appeared in their Saturday matinee film fare. From 1931 to 1937 he had bit or extra roles in many films, and he was also stunting. His presence in Howard Hawks' *Dawn Patrol* ('30) led to a bit in *Flying High* ('31), and that led to *Rasputin and the Empress* ('33). In *Jennie Gerhardt* ('33) he spoke for the first time. He doubled in *The Adventures of Frank Merriwell* ('36) and had the principal role in *The Black Coin* ('36), in which he also did his own stunts.

Dave co-starred with Jim Newill, a singing cowboy, 14 times in the PRC Texas Rangers series and with Tex Ritter eight times in the same series. As a supporting player, he appeared the indicated number of times in the Westerns of the named star: Newill (6), Tex Ritter (6), Bob Steele (3), Ken Maynard (3), Jack Randall (5), Tim McCoy (6), Buster Crabbe (4), John Wayne (2), The Rough Riders (3), Dorothy Page (2), Buzz Henry (1), Chief Thundercloud (1), Buck Jones (1), George Houston (1), Kermit Maynard (1) and Tom Tyler (1).

In between features he worked in the Columbia serial *The Spider's Web* ('38), doubling Warren Hull, and *Secret of Treasure Island* ('38), in which he played Jameson, a policeman, as well as doubling Don Terry and others.

A film he made in '38 about marijuana has gotten considerable publicity. It has been released under varying titles, the best known being *Tell Your Children* ('38) and *Reefer Madness* ('38).

In between films, Dave found time to work as a singer with bands, as a model for magazine ads, in radio (on the *Scattergood Baines* show) and in more stage shows.

Dave's non–Westerns include *Daughter of the Tong* ('39 Evelyn Brent); *Mutiny in the Big House* ('39 Charles Bickford); *Son of the Navy* ('40 Jean Parker); *Boys of the City* ('40 Leo Gorcey); *That Gang of Mine* ('40 Leo Gorcey); *The Devil Bat* ('40 Bela Lugosi); *Flying Wild* ('41 Leo Gorcey); *Murder by Invitation* ('41 Wallace Ford); *Double Trouble* ('41 Harry Langdon); *Prisoner of Japan* ('42 Alan Baxter); *Bowery at Midnight* ('42 Bela Lugosi); *The Yanks Are Coming* ('42 Maxie Rosenbloom); *Salute to the Marines* ('43 Wallace Beery); *Tahiti Nights* ('44 Jinx Falkenberg) and others.

Dave doubled Donald Woods in *Sky Raiders* ('41) and was featured in *The Spider Returns* ('41) as a cohort of the Spider.

In 1942, Dave starred in Columbia's *Captain Midnight*. Playing the heroine was his wife, Dorothy Short, whom he had married in 1936. The serial, adapted from the Mutual network radio series, was popular with the youngsters. He began his association with Pete Smith, ultimately directing and starring in nearly all the Smith *Specialties*; he bought his 60-foot racing sloop, "The White Cloud"; and he contracted with PRC to co-star in the Texas Rangers series. It was a busy year for him.

The Texas Rangers series was extended to 22 films. O'Brien co-starred in all of them. Most writers rate Tex Ritter a better ranger than Newill, who co-starred in the first 14 features. The writer is a Tex Ritter fan but he cannot in good conscience rate Ritter better than Newill. He would call it a draw. The series was profitable enough for PRC to produce it for three years. O'Brien's fine performance in the series has been overlooked by many observers. Likewise, Charles King's appearance in 16 of the films added much to the enjoyment of the features, and he garnered many laughs to boot.

Pete Smith retired in 1955 and O'Brien went to work for Red Skelton as writer, double and sometimes-actor, becoming indispensable to Red. In 1961, Dave received an Emmy award for outstanding writing in comedy. Dave was co-innovator with Skelton of the comedian's "Silent Spot."

Dave's tenure as a Western star was short, but the writer believes he was underrated. Compared to some of the screen cowpokes of his era, he was a better-than-average actor.

Dave's wife divorced him in 1953. The following year he married Nancy Lee Lister, by whom he had three children.

Dave succumbed to a heart attack aboard "The White Cloud" on November 8, 1969. Taken by helicopter to Harbor General Hospital at Torrance, he was dead on arrival. His body was cremated and his ashes scattered at sea. Surviving were his wife and five children (two were by his first wife).

Serials

1936

The Adventures of Frank Merriwell. Univ., [12 Chapters] D: Cliff Smith; SP: George H. Plympton, Maurice Geraghty, Ella O'Neill, Basil Dickey; AP: Henry MacRae; LP: Don Briggs, Jean Rogers, John King, Carla Laemmle, Sumner Getchell, Al Bridge, Dickie Jones, Bud Osborne, Edmund Cobb, Dave O'Brien.

The Black Coin. S&S, [15 Chapters] D: Albert Herman; S: George Merrick; SP: Eddy Graneman, Dallas Fitzgerald, Bob Lively, Albert Herman; Mus: Lee Zahler; Cam: James Diamond; LP: Robert Graves, Ruth Mix, Dave O'Brien, Constance Bergen, Robert Frazer, Snub Pollard, Clara Kimball Young, Josef Swickard, Yakima Canutt.

Dorothy Short and Dave O'Brien in *Captain Midnight* (Columbia, 1942).

1937

The Mysterious Pilot. Col., [15 Chapters] D: Spencer G. Bennet; SP: George M. Merrick; S: William Byron Mowery; P: Jack Fier, Louis Weiss; Cam: Edward Linden; LP: Frank Hawks, Rex Lease, Guy Bates Post, Kenneth Harlan, Clara Kimball Young, Esther Ralston, Yakima Canutt.

1938

The Secret of Treasure Island. Col., [15 Chapters] D: Elmer Clifton; P: Jack Fier; Mus: Abe Meyer; S: L. Ron Hubbard; SP: George Rosener, Elmer Clifton, George Merrick; LP: Don Terry, Gwen Gaze, Grant Withers, Hobart Bosworth, Yakima Canutt, William Farnum, Walter Miller, Dave O'Brien.

1941

Sky Raiders. Univ., [12 Chapters] D: Ford Beebe, Ray Taylor; AP: Henry MacRae; LP: Donald Woods, Billy Halop, Robert Armstrong, Kathryn Adams, Eduardo Ciannelli, Reed Hadley, Jacqueline Dalya, Dave O'Brien [double for Woods].

The Spider Returns. Col., [15 Chapters] D: James W. Horne; SP: Jesse Duffy, George H. Plympton; S: Morgan B. Cox, Lawrence E. Taylor, John Cutting, Harry Fraser; P: Larry Darmour; Cam: James S. Brown, Jr.; Mus: Lee Zahler; LP: Warren Hull, Mary Ainslee, Dave O'Brien, Joseph Girard, Corbet Harris, Bryant Washburn, Charles Miller, Anthony Warde.

1942

Captain Midnight. Col., [15 Chapters] D: James W. Horne; SP: Basil Dickey, George H. Plympton, Jack Stanley, Wyndham Gittens; P: Larry Darmour; Cam: James S. Brown, Jr.; Mus: Lee Zahler; LP: Dave O'Brien, Dorothy Short, James Craven, Sam Edwards, Guy Wilkerson, Bryant Washburn, Luana Walters, Al Ferguson, Joseph Girard, Franklyn Farnum.

KATHLEEN O'CONNOR

Kathleen O'Connor had the feminine lead opposite former heavyweight champion James J. Corbett in *The Midnight Man* ('19). The serial, made to capitalize on the fame of the former boxer, was greeted with mixed emotions. Corbett was not an actor and it showed. However, serial patrons seemed to like Kathleen, who had a winning smile and pleasing on-screen presence.

Also in 1919, Kathleen co-starred with Jack Perrin in *The Lion Man* ('19), adapted from "The Strange Case of Cavandish." Kathleen is a reporter sent by her newspaper to cover a society circus being given by millionaire Frederick Cavandish. Stella sneaks in the exclusive "by invitation" circus posing as one of the female performers. She overhears the nephew of Cavandish plotting with a shady lawyer to kill Cavandish and destroy the new will he had drawn up, disinheriting his nephew. An actress assists them in their plot. A young mining engineer (Jack Perrin) comes to see Cavandish on business and quarrels with him. He is soon accused of killing Cavandish, who had disappeared. Stella and the engineer unite in an effort to recover the will. Assisting them from time to time was a strange being known only as the "Lion Man." The serial was a good one and O'Connor did an admirable job in her role.

In addition, Kathleen played the romantic interest in Sennett two-reel comedies and had secondary roles in *Sunset Jones* ('21), *The Married Flapper* ('22), *Come On Over* ('22), *The Old Homestead* ('22), *Wild Bill Hickok* ('23), *The Trouper* ('22) and *Dark Stairways* ('24). She never headlined a feature, but played second leads to other actresses. She seems to have left the screen in 1924 and her trail ends there.

Blue-eyed, blonde Kathleen was born in Dayton, Ohio, July 7, 1894, and was educated at St. Joseph Convent and Notre Dame Academy in the same city.

Serials

1919

The Midnight Man. Univ., [18 Chapters] D: James W. Horne; SP: Harvey Gates; S: James W. Horne, Frank Howard Clarke; LP: James J. Corbett, Kathleen O'Connor, Joseph W. Girard, Frank Jonasson, Orral Humphery, Sam Polo, Ann Forrest.

The Lion Man. Univ., [18 Chapters] D: Albert Russell, Jack Wells; SP: Karl Coolidge; S: Randall Parrish; LP: Jack Perrin, Kathleen O'Connor, Mack Wright, J. Barney Sherry, Leonard Clapham [Tom London], Gertrude Astor.

NELL O'DAY

Born near Prairie Hill, Texas, at her grandparent's home, Nell O'Day lived in Dallas until she was seven, when the family moved to Los Angeles. Her father, a railroad accountant, died when she was eight and her mother supported the family as a professional photographer. Nell attended schools in Los Angeles and participated in plays and as a dancer in stage shows.

As a student of teacher and choreogra-

In ***Bury Me Not on the Lone Prairie*** (Universal, 1941).

pher Ernest Belcher, she appeared in various stage prologues while attending the professional Children's School. Several years later she teamed up with the Tommy Atkins Sextet: Nell and her six male partners were signed to play a season at the Oriental Theater in Chicago. They were quite successful and soon were signed by John Murray Anderson to play a 28-week tour of the Paramount theaters in an elaborate revue, "Laces and Graces." At the end of this tour, the troupe was signed to appear in the Universal Studio production of *King of Jazz* starring Paul Whiteman and his famous orchestra. When the film was completed, Nell and her partners continued to appear in revues from coast to coast. After a long and successful run in the lavish musical "Fine and Dandy," Nell was signed to a contract by Twentieth Century-Fox.

At Twentieth Century-Fox she made *Smoke Lightning* ('33), a George O'Brien Western in which she had the female lead. She also appeared in a number of Mermaid comedies with Harry Langdon. Though not the lead, Nell had a good part in the play *Many Mansions* starring Alexander Kirkland and directed by Lee Strasberg. In *Flight into China*, Pearl Buck's first play, Nell played a Chinese girl, while in *Fly Away Home* she was the love interest. Andrea King played her young sister. *One for the Money* was a very beautiful and chic revue directed by John Murray Anderson and featuring 14 principals, among them Nell, Grace McDonald, Gene Kelly and Alfred Drake. She also appeared in some of the leading summer stock companies of the Eastern Seaboard.

When Universal was searching for an actress to appear with Johnny Mack Brown in a series of Westerns, Nell won out over a list of a dozen others who had tested for the role.

Perhaps Don Miller in his book *Hollywood Corral* best describes Nell's role:

Filling in, in somewhat peculiar fashion, beginning with *Son of Roaring Dan* ('40) was petite Nell O'Day, as sort of a cowgirl auxiliary. O'Day's function in the series was never properly defined, but she was featured in 13 straight, and always welcomed. She was an expert equestrienne, and shots of her galloping across the flatlands, caught by Universal's camera truck, were exciting in themselves. So were the shots of Brown riding, too—Universal did the best running inserts in the business. But O'Day, although attractive, was seldom if ever considered for the romantic laurels; Brown was invariably given one of the pretty Universal contractees for that purpose alone.

The Brown Westerns elevated Nell to fame in sagebrush circles. Freelancing in 1942, she appeared opposite Tim Holt (in *Pirates of the Prairie*), the Range Busters at Monogram, the Three Mesquiteers at Republic and the Texas Rangers at PRC. For Columbia she co-starred in *Perils of the Royal Mounted* ('42), proving to be far more exciting in the cliffhanger than her male co-star, Robert Stevens.

Most of Nell's fans do not know that she made about 20 industrial films. In one, *The House That Ann Built* (for the Johns Manville Company), Luther Reid was the director, and Beverly Bayne played her mother. Nell played the leading lady opposite Donald Dillaway in two films for General Motors. She was the female lead in all of her many industrials, some of which were feature-length —five, six, even seven reels. Usually the wages paid for leads in the industrials were better than those paid by the Hollywood studios to Western heroines, so Nell was by no means impoverished when she did them. It was good work.

Nell left pictures and Hollywood when she married Larry Williams, an actor. He became ill and was an invalid on and off for many years, with the result that Nell could not work steadily. She worked in television some and was often in radio plays during the times her husband's health would permit. Larry and Nell wrote two original screenplays, one of which was *The Monster Maker*, which featured Ralph Morgan. The other was a suspense mystery originally called *Double Trouble*. Later divorced, Nell married a second time, but this marriage also failed.

In the early 1950s Nell lived abroad—England, Italy, Sicily—writing for various publications. Her play *The Bride of Denmark Hill* was produced by Alfred Esdaile at the Royal Court and Comedy Theaters in London, and later on BBC-TV and on Australian and New Zealand radio and television. She wrote short stories, novelettes and serials for such national magazines as *Redbook*, *This Week*, *Complete Shopper*, *Good Housekeeping*, *Home and Mother* and *Colliers*. This writing led to editorial jobs. After 1974, Nell was mostly self-employed, with a number of clients for whom she did writing and editing.

Nell died January 3, 1989, from cardiac arrest.

Serial

1942

Perils of the Royal Mounted. Col., [15 Chapters] D: James W. Horne; SP: Basil Dickey, Scott Littleton, Louis Heifetz, James A. Duffy; P: Larry Darmour; Cam: James S. Brown, Jr.; Mus: Lee Zahler; LP: Nell O'Day, Robert Stevens [Kellard], Herbert Rawlinson, Kenneth MacDonald, John Elliott, Richard Fiske, Charles King, Kermit Maynard, I. Stanford Jolley, George Chesebro, Rick Vallin.

PEGGY O'DAY

Peggy's greatest claim to fame was co-starring with Jack Perrin in *The Fighting Skipper* ('23), a 15-chapter Arrow serial that gave her many opportunities to display her athletic prowess. The story deals with Peggy's attempts to find a fortune in pearls buried by her father, a sea captain, on a desolate island. As if various cutthroats are not enough frustration, she has a wicked half-sister (also played by Peggy) also out to get the treasure. Perrin assists Skipper (the "good" sister) to gain her rightful inheritance.

Very few, if any, film buffs today react with recognition to mention of Peggy O'Day, the top female stunt rider of the 1920s and heroine of a number of bottom-of-the-barrel independent Westerns. In the early '20s she was working with actors such as Franklyn Farnum, Bill Patton, Guinn Williams, Al Hoxie, Francis Ford, Jack Donovan and Cliff Lyons.

Peggy (real surname: Reis) was born in Youngstown, Ohio, and educated at Poly-technical Junior College and Missouri University. She began her career as a stunt woman with Christy Brothers Studio around 1920. With looks and little talent, it was not hard for an athletic young woman like Peggy to get featured roles in the cheaper Westerns produced for the "indie" market, as it saved penny-pinching producers money when the heroine could ride and do her own stunts. Thus Peggy worked as heroine in her own

right, and did the riding and stunt work for the leads in numerous other films.

While sustaining an injury doing a stunt, Peggy abandoned her career as a performer in the late 1920s and joined Cecil B. DeMille as an assistant film editor. In 1930 she shifted to Metro-Goldwyn-Mayer, where she ultimately took charge of the studio's international department. She retired in 1960 after 30 years with the giant studio, and died in her Santa Monica home on November 26, 1964, after a long illness.

Serials

1920

The Vanishing Dagger. Univ., [18 Chapters] D: Ed Kull, Eddie Polo; LP: Eddie Polo, Thelma Percy, G. Normand Hammond, Laura Oakley, Ruth Royce.

1923

The Fighting Skipper. Arrow, [15 Chapters] D: Francis Ford; LP: Peggy O'Day, Jack Perrin, Francis Ford, Steve Murphy.

1928

The Chinatown Mystery. Syn., [10 Chapters] D: J. P. McGowan; S: Francis Ford; P: Trem Carr; LP: Joe Bonomo, Ruth Hiatt, Paul Malvern, Francis Ford, Paul Panzer, Sheldon Lewis, Harry Myers, Rosemary Theby, Helen Gibson.

GEORGE O'HARA

In 1921, George O'Hara had a bit in *A Small Town Idol.* The next year he co-starred with Noah Beery, Sr., in *The Crossroads of New York*, with Kathleen O'Connor featured.

That same year he co-starred with Shirley Mason in *Shirley at the Circus*.

In 1924, he starred in *Darwin Was Right*, a spoof on evolution, and in *Listen Lester* with Louise Fazenda and Harry Myers. In *The Go-Getters* (1924–25) he was co-starred with Alberta Vaughn in a 12-episode series of railroad thrillers which had a love interest, comedy and pathos woven into it. Alberta is a telegraph operator and O'Hara the railroad fireman who falls in love with her. Each episode was complete in itself.

The Pacemakers ('25) was another series of 12 episodes. A comedy, it paired Vaughn and O'Hara with Kit Guard.

Nineteen twenty-six was a big year for O'Hara. He starred in *Bigger Than Barnum's* with Viola Dane and Ralph Lewis; *The False Alarm* with Dorothy Revier and Ralph Lewis; *Going the Limit* with Sally Long; *Is That Nice?* with Doris Hill; *The Sea Beast*, supporting John Barrymore and Dolores Costello; and *The Timid Terror* with Doris Hill and Rex Lease. In 1927 he starred in *Burnt Fingers* with Eileen Percy and Edna Murphy; *California or Bust* with Helen Foster; *Ladies Beware* with Nola Luxford; and *Yours to Command* with Shirley Palmer.

The first of his two serials was *Casey of the Coast Guard* ('26), produced by Pathé. A gang of crooks, endeavoring to smuggle goods into the United States, plans to kill young Coast Guard officer George Casey, who has been too alert to make their business profitable. The plots of the gang to entrap him or to use his fiancée's father in their work make up the story. *Pirates of the Pines* ('28), the last credit found for O'Hara, was an independent serial made by Sovergin Feature Productions and distributed by Trinity Pictures. A relatively small number of second- and third-rate theaters showed the serial while better theaters stuck with Universal, Columbia, Pathé and Mascot.

O'Hara died of throat cancer at Los Angeles County General Hospital in 1966. Surviving were a sister and a half-brother.

Serials

1926

Casey of the Coast Guard. Pathé, [10 Chapters] D: Will Nigh; P: Schuyler E. Grey; LP: George O'Hara, Helen Ferguson, J. Barney Sherry, Jean Jarvis, Coit Albertson, Robert Craig.

1928

Pirates of the Pines. Sovergin, [10 Chapters] D: J. C. Cook; SP: J. C. Cook, Harry Moody; P: Charles U. Penfield; LP: George O'Hara, Rita Roma, Jack Mower, Robert Middleton, Sumner Getchell, King Zany.

WARNER OLAND

Long before the movie world recognized Warner Oland as the kindly, philosophic, wise detective Charlie Chan, he had earned a reputation as a sleek, unctuous, insidious villain. He was a wicked man par excellence, and his villainies thrilled countless audiences worldwide.

Oland was born Johan Werner Ohlund in Umea, Vesterbotten, Sweden, on October 3, 1880. When he was 13 his father brought the family to America and they settled on a Connecticut farm. After graduation from high school, Warner entered Curry's Dramatic School. His first part to play was Jesus Christ.

Oland made his road debut at $18 per

week. Then for 14 years he devoted himself to the stage. In road shows and stock companies and on Broadway he specialized in Ibsen and Shakespeare.

Performing Shakespeare throughout the country polished his acting considerably. Nazimova recognized his skill and used him in her series of Ibsen plays that rocked the American theater in the winter of 1906. In 1910, Oland portrayed John Bunyon in a one-reel version of *Pilgrim's Progress*, shot at Fort Lee, New Jersey. He is reputed to have supported Theda Bara in *Jewels of the Madonna*, but the author has found no other information on the film. Probably it is another title under which *Sin* ('15) was released. Oland steals bejeweled church relics and then hangs himself. Two other films with Bara followed, *Destruction* ('15) and *The Siren of Seville* ('16), also known as *The Serpent*.

Motion pictures gave Oland opportunity for his first Oriental characterization, that of a Japanese general in the serial *Patria* ('17). The U.S. and Japan had clashed earlier in China, so the heroine was to be victimized by a Japanese villain instead of the usual German. The serial was a big success and Oland soon became celebrated for his Oriental portrayals.

Real fame came to Oland when he played the Chinese villain menacing Pearl White in *The Fatal Ring* ('17), a 20-chapter serial. Pearl, a rich girl, finds life tedious because of her wealth until she acquires a violet diamond. Her father had purchased it after it had been stolen from the Sacred Order of the violet God. A high priestess, her henchmen and Oland attempt to reclaim the diamond.

In 1919, Oland once again supported White, this time in *The Lightning Raider*. As Wu Fang he plotted traps to ensnare harassed Pearl and had audiences on the edges of their seats and screaming. The following year he made *The Third Eye* ('20) and was billed over the hero, Jack Mower. The third eye referred to a movie camera that had captured a murder on a movie set. The film would incriminate Oland as the murderer.

Oland harassed Juanita Hansen in *The Phantom Foe* ('20) and *The Yellow Arm* ('21), both popular serials. His last serial, *Hurricane Hutch* ('21), was filmed partially in England. By this time he was the highest-paid villain in the business.

Oland played heavy roles both as a Caucasian and as an Oriental, appearing in *Don Q* ('25 Douglas Fairbanks); *Riders of the Purple Sage* ('25 Tom Mix); *The Marriage Clause* ('26 Francis X. Bushman); *Tell It to the Marines* ('26 Lon Chaney); *Man of the Forest* ('26 Jack Holt); *When a Man Loves* ('27 John Barrymore); *Don Juan* ('27 John Barrymore); *Flower of the Night* ('25 Pola Negri); *Old San Francisco* ('27 Pola Negri); *The Jazz Singer* ('27 Al Jolson); *Sailor Izzy Murphy* ('27 George Jessel); *Good Time Charlie* ('27 Helene Costello); *Stand and Deliver* ('28 Rod La Rocque); *The Wheel of Chance* ('28 Richard Barthelmess); *Chinatown Nights* ('28 Wallace Beery); *The Studio Murder Mystery* ('29 Doris Hill); *Mysterious Dr. Fu Manchu* ('29 Jean Arthur); *Dangerous Paradise* ('30 Nancy Carroll); *The Vagabond King* ('30 Jeanette MacDonald); *The Return of Dr. Fu Manchu* ('30 Jean Arthur); *Drums of Jeopardy* ('31 June Collyer); *Dishonored* ('31 Marlene Dietrich); *Mandalay* ('34 Kay Francis); *The Painted Veil* ('34 Greta Garbo); *Were Wolf of London* ('35 Valerie Hobson) and *Shanghai* ('35 Loretta Young), plus a few other films.

It was 1931 when Oland tested for the part of Charlie Chan, beating out 18 other actors. The first of the long series of Chan movies, big box office attractions of magnitude in foreign countries far exceeding their popularity in the U.S., was *Charlie Chan Carries On* ('31). The Fox series was well-produced and Oland's unique personality with prophetic phrases endeared him to a loyal public. He became an extremely valuable property for the Fox Corporation. Other titles in the series are:

The Black Camel ('31); *Charlie Chan's Chance* ('32); *Charlie Chan's Greatest Case* ('33); *Charlie Chan's Courage* ('34); *Charlie Chan in London* ('34); *Charlie Chan in Paris* ('35); *Charlie Chan in Egypt* ('35); *Charlie Chan in Shanghai* ('35); *Charlie Chan at the*

Circus ('36); *Charlie Chan's Secret* ('36); *Charlie Chan at the Racetrack* ('36); *Charlie Chan at the Opera* ('36); *Charlie Chan at the Olympics* ('37); *Charlie Chan on Broadway* ('37); *Charlie Chan at Monte Carlo* ('37).

Oland married Edith Schearn, stage actress, on January 17, 1908. The couple separated in 1937 and divorced in 1938. The cause was his drinking problem, according to his wife. Alone in his Beverly Hills home, he drank even more. One afternoon while at Fox working on a new Chan film, Oland went to get a drink of water and never came back. He was suspended by the studio. He was reported confined to his home because of a nervous breakdown. Worry over the separate maintenance suit recently brought by his wife was reported to have caused his condition. Two or three weeks later, in April 1938, Oland sailed for Sweden on a freighter, planning to return in September. While in Sweden, he came down with bronchial pneumonia. Hospitalized in Stockholm, he died on August 6, 1938. He was 57 years old.

Mrs. Oland was unable to get to Sweden before he died.

Serials

1917

Patria. Pathé, [15 Chapters] D: Theodore and Leo Wharton, Jacques Jaccard; SP: J. B. Cly-mer, Louis Joseph Vance, Charles W. Goddard; S: Louis Joseph Vance; LP: Irene Castle, Milton Sills, Warner Oland, Dorothy Green, Wallace Beery.

The Fatal Ring. Pathé, [20 Chapters] D: George B. Seitz; SP: Bertram Millhauser; S: Fred Jackson; LP: Pearl White, Earle Fox, Warner Oland, Ruby Hoffman, Henry G. Sell.

The Lightning Raider. Pathé, [15 Chapters] D: George B. Seitz; SP: George B. Seitz, Bertram Millhauser; LP: Pearl White, Warner Oland, Henry G. Sell, Ruby Hoffman, William Burt.

1920

The Third Eye. Pathé, [15 Chapters] D: James W. Horne; SP: William Parker; S: H. H. Van Loan; LP: Eileen Percy, Warner Oland, Jack Mower, Olga Grey, Mark Strong.

1921

The Yellow Arm. Pathé, [15 Chapters] D: Bertram Millhauser; SP: James Shelley Hamilton; P: George B. Seitz; LP: Juanita Hansen, Warner Oland, Marguerite Courtot, Stephen Carr, William N. Bailey.

Hurricane Hutch. Pathé, [15 Chapters] D: George B. Seitz; S: Charles Hutchison; LP: Charles Hutchison, Lucy Fox, Warner Oland, Diana Deer, Ann Hastings, Spencer Bennet, Joe Bonomo, Thomas C. Good, Frank Redman.

GERTRUDE OLMSTEAD

Gertrude Olmstead was born on November 10, 1904, in Chicago, the daughter of a dentist. Educated in Chicago and LaSalle public schools, she was a beauty contest winner in Chicago shortly after her high school graduation. Gertrude was briefly on the stage before going to Hollywood in 1920 under contract to Universal. Later she would be a Metro contract player.

Gertrude made six Western two-reelers with Hoot Gibson — *Tipped Off* ('20), *The Fighting Fury* ('21), *Driftin' Kid* ('21), *Kickaroo* ('21), *Sweet Revenge* ('21) and *The Loaded Door* ('22).

Gertrude also worked with other cowboys. With Jack Perrin she appeared in *The Phantom Terror* ('22) and *A Blue Jacket's Honor* ('22). With Roy Stewart she made

God's Law ('23), *One of Three* ('23) (Perrin was also in this one), *Better Than Gold* ('23) and *The Guilty Hand* ('23). These films were also two-reelers.

Gertrude appeared in her solo cliff-hanger, *The Adventures of Robinson Crusoe* ('22), with Harry Myers and Noble Johnson. It was a popular serial.

She graduated to the five- or six-reel features and appeared in a long list of films, some of which are: *Ladies to Board* (Fox '24, Tom Mix); *Empty Hands* (Par. '24 Jack Holt); *A Girl of the Limberlost* (FBO '24 Gloria Gray); *California Straight Ahead* (Univ. '25 Reginald Denny); *Cobra* (Par. '25 Rudolph Valentino); *The Boob* (MGM '26 Joan Crawford); *Puppets* (FN '26 Milton Sills); *Hit of the Show* (FBO '28 Joe E. Brown); *Sporting Goods* ('Par. '28 Richard Dix); *The Show of Shows* (WB '29 Frank Fay); and *The Time, the Place, and the Girl* (WB '29 Grant Withers).

Her resilience was proven and she showed true grit in the rough, horsey giddyups that were so popular with rural American audiences, but her talent commanded much better pay in "dude" pictures. She stood 5'2", weighed 115 pounds, had chestnut brown hair and gray-blue eyes. She married director-actor Robert Z. Leonard in 1926 and retired in 1927. She died from cancer on January 18, 1975, in Beverly Hills. Leonard had preceded her in death in 1968.

Serial

1922

The Adventures of Robinson Crusoe. Univ., [18 Chapters] D: Robert F. Hill; SP: Emma Bell Clifton; S: Daniel Defoe; LP: Harry Myers, Noble Johnson, Gertrude Olmstead, Percy Pembroke, Aaron Edwards, Joseph Swickard, Gertrude Claire, Emmet King.

PAT O'MALLEY

Pat O'Malley, not to be confused with bald character comedian J. Pat O'Malley or John P. O'Malley, was born Patrick H. O'-Malley, Jr., on September 3, 1891, in Forest City, Pennsylvania. He entered films with the Edison Company in 1907, and his first film of record was *The Papered Door* ('11).

O'Malley appeared in only one serial, *The Red Glove* ('19) with Marie Walcamp. The story revolves about a gang known as "The Vultures" who terrorize a section of the West and particularly threaten the Blue Chip, owned by Billie (Walcamp), with all parties seeking the riches of the Pool of Lost Souls. The bandits wear masks and headpieces of eagle's wings, and are under the direction of Starr Wiley (Thomas Lingham), agent of an oil company, and his confederate (Leon De La Mothe). A mystery concerning the hero-ine's birth is not explained until the last chapter. O'Malley was replaced by Trueman Van Dyke as leading man in either Chapter 7 or 8, reason unknown.

O'Malley mainly played in romantic melodramas during the 1920s. He co-starred with Agnes Ayres in *Go and Get It* ('20), Jack Kirkwood in *Bob Hampton of Placer* ('21), Claire Windsor in *Brothers Under the Skin* ('22), Pauline Starke in *My Wild Irish Rose* ('22), J. Warren Kerrigan in *The Man from Broadney's* ('23), Marian Nixon in *Spangles* ('26) and many more. A further sampling of his work includes: *The Virginian* ('23), *The Mine with the Iron Door* ('24), *The Fighting American* ('24), *The House of Scandal* ('28), *Alibi* ('29), *The Fall Guy* ('30), *American Madness* ('32), *Mystery of the Wax Museum* ('33), *Crime Doctor* ('34), *The Man on the*

Flying Trapeze ('35), *Hollywood Boulevard* ('36), *Frontier Marshall* ('39), *Captain Caution* ('40), *A Little Bit of Heaven* ('40), *Meet Boston Blackie* ('41), *Over My Dead Body* ('42), *Lassie Come Home* ('43), *The Adventures of Mark Twain* ('44), *Mule Train* ('50) and *Invasion of the Body Snatchers* ('56).

O'Malley died in 1966.

Serial

1919

The Red Glove. Univ., [18 Chapters] D: J. P. McGowan; SP: Hope Loring, Douglas Grant; LP: Marie Walcamp, Pat O'Malley, Trueman Van Dyek, Thomas Lingham, Leon De La Mothe, Alfred Allen, Evelyn Selbie, William Dyer, Leon Kent.

BUD OSBORNE

Bud Osborne seldom adapted a facade of respectability. What you saw is what you got, an uncouth personification of the gang member ready to deliver the *coup de grace* to the hero or heroine. He had one of the most recognizable faces in Western filmdom, and when he appeared in a shoot-'em-up, the front row brigade knew instantly that he was up to no good.

By the mid–1940s, Bud had mended his ways somewhat and he often played stagecoach drivers, sheriffs, and other, more likeable characters. Bud had mastered the art of driving a stage with six or eight up at breakneck speed across the flats and was recognized as the top hand for this endeavor.

Osborne played in 517 films, including 47 serials. There were probably many others, especially in the silent era.

Osborne was born in Knox County, Texas, on July 20, 1884. He was a cowboy from an early age, having grown up on a ranch. He worked as a cowhand on ranches in Texas and the Indian territory before becoming an assistant arena director for the Miller Brothers 101 Ranch Show around 1910. In 1912 he joined the Buffalo Bill Cody's Wild West Show, touring with it throughout the U.S., Canada and Europe.

He appeared in at least one film in 1912. That film was *For the Cause*, a Kay-Bee film starring Harold Lockwood. In 1914 he was in *The Sheep Herder* starring J. Warren Kerrigan.

Bud supported about every Western star in the business. The dozen cowboys he worked with most often, and the number of their films he appeared in are: Johnny Mack Brown (32), Bob Steele (23), Tim McCoy (20), Leo Maloney (18), Tom Tyler (15), Charles Starrett (14), Buck Jones (14), Gene Autry (12), Bill Elliott (12), Neal Hart (12), Jimmy Wakely (11) and Hoot Gibson (11).

Other cowboys he supported are: Robert Livingston (10), John Wayne (9), J. Warren Kerrigan (1), Bill Gettinger (1), Franklyn Farnum (6), Harry Carey (3), Jack Livingston (1), George Larkin (1), Ruth Roland (1), Pete Morrison (1), Jack Perrin (6), Buddy Roosevelt (3), Fred Thomson (2), Cheyenne Bill (1), Jack Daugherty (1), Jack Hoxie (3), Bruce Gordon (1), Boris Bullock (1), George O'Brien (3), Ben Wilson (1), Fred Gilman (1), Fred Humes (1), Dick Carter (1), Bob Custer (8), Don Coleman (1), Edmund Cobb (1), Montana Bill (1), Pawnee Bill, Jr. (6), William Desmond (1), Bob Curwood (2), Yakima Canutt (1), Wally Wales (2), Ted Wells (1), Art Mix (1), Rex Lease (1), Ken Maynard (7), Tom Mix (5), Tom Keene (5), Rex Bell (1), Bill Cody (2), Randolph Scott (4), Buffalo Bill, Jr. (2), Onslow Stevens (1), Bob Allen (4), Buck Coburn (1), Buster Crabbe (9), Dick Foran (9), Noah Beery, Jr. (2), "Big Boy"

Williams (1), Robert Livingston (10), Gary Cooper (1), Buzz Barton (1), Ray Corrigan (9), Tex Ritter (9), Smith Ballew (2), Jack Randall (6), Ricardo Cortez (1), Lee Powell (2), Jack Luden (1), Dennis Moore (5), Roy Rogers (7), Fred Scott (2), Errol Flynn (3), Duncan Renaldo (4), Donald Barry (8), Don Douglas (1), Tim Holt (6), Cesar Romero (1), Sunset Carson (2), Dave O'Brien (8), Eddie Dean (3), Robert Scott (1), Rod Cameron (4), Kirby Grant (1), Lash LaRue (8), Clayton Moore (2), Whip Wilson (5), Russell Hayden (7), James Ellison (7), Jim Bannon (1), Allan Lane (1), Jock Mahoney (2), Rex Allen (2), Guy Madison (1), Stewart Granger (1), Scott Brady (1), James Cagney (1), George Montgomery (1), Glenn Ford (1), John Carpenter (1), John Agar (1), Jack Holt (1), John King (3), Al Wilson (1), Clark Gable (1), Broderick Crawford (1), William Boyd (1), William Bishop (1), Robert Mitchum (1), Dick Powell (1), Spade Cooley (1), James Stewart (1), Ken Curtis (1), Ray Milland (1), Brett King (1), James Newill (1), Raymond McKee (1), Kenneth MacDonald (1), George Chandler (2), Ted Thompson (1), Marie Windsor (1), Allene Ray (1) and Wayne Morris (1).

These numbers should be considered minimal. Osborne may have appeared in films starring these cowboys as an unbilled player that the author failed to find.

The last theatrical credit found for Osborne is Atomic Productions' *Night of the Ghouls* ('59) featuring Kenne Duncan and Tor Johnson. He was active in television Westerns throughout the 1950s and into the early 1960s.

Osborne died at age 79 on February 2, 1964, at the Motion Picture Home and was survived by his wife, son and daughter.

Serials

Because of the large number of serials he was in and the fact that he was only a supporting player, only the title, studio, year and main player will be listed.

1919

The Tiger's Trail. Pathé, Ruth Roland

1920

The Vanishing Dagger. Univ., Eddie Polo.

1922

White Eagle. Pathé, Ruth Roland.

1923

Ghost City. Univ., Pete Morrison.

1924

Way of a Man. Pathé, Allene Ray.

1925

The Fighting Ranger. Univ., Jack Daugherty.

1928

The Mystery Rider. Univ., William Desmond.

1930

The Indians Are Coming. Univ., Tim McCoy.

1931

Battling with Buffalo Bill. Univ., Tom Tyler.
Heroes of the Flames. Univ., Tim McCoy.

1932

Shadow of the Eagle. Mascot, John Wayne.

1933

Gordon of Ghost City. Univ., Buck Jones.
The Phantom of the Air. Univ., Tom Tyler.

1934

The Law of the Wild. Mascot, Bob Custer.
The Red Rider. Univ., Buck Jones.
Tailspin Tommy. Univ., Maurice Murphy.
The Vanishing Shadow. Univ., Onslow Stevens.

1935

Rustlers of Red Dog. Univ., Johnny Mack Brown.

1936

The Adventures of Frank Merriwell. Univ., Don Briggs.

Robinson Crusoe of Clipper Island. Rep., Ray Mala.

The Vigilantes Are Coming. Rep., Robert Livingston.

1937

Wild West Days. Univ., Johnny Mack Brown.

1938

The Fighting Devil Dogs. Rep., Lee Powell.

1940

Deadwood Dick. Col., Don Douglas.
Winners of the West. Univ., Dick Foran.

1941

White Eagle. Col., Buck Jones.
Riders of Death Valley. Univ., Dick Foran.

1943

Batman. Col., Lewis Wilson.

1944

Black Arrow. Col., Robert Scott.

1945

The Monster and the Ape. Col., Robert Lowery.

1947

The Vigilante. Col., Ralph Byrd.

1948

Adventures of Frank and Jesse James. Rep., Clayton Moore.

1950

Desperadoes of the West. Rep., Richard Powers [Tom Keene].

1951

Don Daredevil Rides Again. Rep., Ken Curtis.
Roar of the Iron Horse. Col., Jock Mahoney.

1952

Son of Geronimo. Col., Clayton Moore.

1953

Gunfighters of the Northwest. Col., Jock Mahoney.
The Great Adventures of Captain Kidd. Col., Richard Crane.

1955

Adventures of Captain Africa. Col., John Hart.

1956

Blazing the Overland Trail. Col., Lee Roberts.
Perils of the Wilderness. Col., Dennis Moore.

JEAN PAIGE

Jean Paige's career began in 1917 with *Blind Man's Holiday* and apparently ended in 1924 with *Captain Blood.* During this period she appeared in 18 features and one serial. She usually portrayed a nice girl, as in *Blind Man's Holiday* ('17), *The Indian Summer of Dry Valley Johnson* ('17) and *The Skylight Room* ('17), all three films adapted from the writings of O. Henry.

Jean had the feminine lead in *Hidden Dangers* ('20). Joe Ryan was the male lead and played a character not unlike Dr. Jekyll and Mr. Hyde. When under the influence of a strange disease, his mental capacity is developed at the expense of his moral nature. He becomes a superman without any sense of right or wrong. Jean was the woman he loved.

Serial

1920

Hidden Dangers. VIT., [15 Chapters] D: William Bertram; SP: C. Graham Baker, William C. Courtney; S: Albert E. Smith, Cleveland Moffett; LP: Joe Ryan, Jean Paige, George Stanley, E. J. Denny, Sam Polo, William McCall, Camille Sheeley, Charles Dudley.

ROBERT PAIGE

Columbia's *Flying G-Men* ('39) opened with enemy agents attacking American defense industries from an underground air base on Flame Island, off-shore headquarters of a vast espionage ring. Four government investigators are ordered to deal with the menace. These veteran aviators decide to operate outside the law when necessary to destroy the nation's enemies. A medal is divided among them as their insignia, and one will fly into action against the spies as "The Black Falcon," striking swiftly without prior approval from bureaucratic Washington.

Playing the part of the Falcon was Robert Paige, leading man of 1940s "B" films and minor musicals, mostly for Universal. He was born John Arthur Paige on December 2, 1910. He dropped out of West Point to pursue a career as a radio singer and announcer and began appearing in film shorts in 1931 as David Carlyle. His feature debut was in 1935 and he gradually rose from bits to romantic leads, switching to the screen name Robert Paige when he joined Columbia as a contract player in 1938. He moved to Paramount the following year and to Universal in 1941. He was a Universal stalwart throughout the '40s. After appearing in 61 features he turned to television in the '50s and was a cohort with Bess Myerson on the network game show *The Big Payoff* and was an on-the-air newscaster for local station KABC-TV until 1970.

Later he and his wife, Jo Anne Ludden, whom he had married in '61, formed a business partnership that did sales promotion for TV shows. He also became an executive with a Hollywood public relations firm. Paige died in San Clemente in 1987 at age 76 and was survived by his wife and daughter, Colleen.

Serial

1939

Flying G-Men. Col., [15 Chapters] D: Ray Taylor, James W. Horne; P: Jack Fier; SP: Robert E. Kent, Basil Dickey, Sherman Lowe; LP: Robert Paige, Richard Fiske, James Craig, Lorna Gray [Adrian Booth], Don Beddoe.

PAUL PANZER

Paul Wolfgang Panzerbeiter was born in Wurzburg, Bavaria, of French and German parentage. He was educated at the universities at Wurzburg and Heidelberg and became a lieutenant of artillery in the German army for a while. He made his stage debut in 1899 and played in many musicals and dramatic productions. Paul was a respected actor and singer with the Augustin Daly Company when the flickers were just coming over the peep-show horizon. He had arrived in America in 1900 and immediately turned his talents to the stage.

In 1905, Paul made his debut as a film player in Edison's *Stolen by Gypsies*. It was directed and photographed by Edwin S. Porter. The crude studio was located high up on the roof of an office building on 21st Street between Fourth Avenue and Broadway.

At the suggestion of a girl he knew, he met with Commodore J. Stuart Blackton, head of the burgeoning Vitagraph, about taking a job in moving pictures. The Vitagraph studio was also on the roof of an office building, the Morton Building at Number 116 Nassau Street. The stage was a rough platform measuring 12x15 feet. Here was produced such pictures as *Monsieur Beaucaire*, *Oliver Twist* and comedies of every description — all in single reels.

Four years after entering motion pictures, Paul organized an independent concern known as the Pantograph Corporation. It lasted just six months, and then he was broke. At that point he joined Pathé, which had just organized an American company with a temporary studio in Jersey City. It was here that *The Perils of Pauline* ('14) was made with Panzer playing the crafty villain Koener, who used every devious device to dispatch desperate Pearl White. The die was cast. He became known as the villains' villain in the serials that followed: *Jimmy Dale Alias the Grey Seal* ('17), *The House of Hate* ('18), *The Mystery Mind* ('20), *The Hawk of the Hills* ('27), *The Chinatown Mystery* ('28) and *The Black Book* ('29).

Paul was in numerous features in the '20s and was usually the one audiences hissed. His films included *The Johnstown Flood*, *Under the Red Robe*, *The Best Bad Man*, *Ancient Mariner* and *Sally in Our Alley*.

Just a passable actor, ill-suited to talkies, he was only rarely active in the '30s. However, he was in demand once more, for small roles, when the "Nazi" vogue began: *Beast of Berlin*, *Casablanca*, *Action in the North Atlantic*, *Hotel Berlin* and Betty Hutton's *The Perils of Pauline* ('47). He never acted again.

Paul Panzer, 86, died Saturday, August 17, 1958, after a month's illness at the home of his daughter, Mrs. Coralie Peiffer, in Culver City. Also surviving him was a son, Paul Panzer, Jr., seven grandchildren and two great-grandchildren.

Serials

1914

The Perils of Pauline. Pathé, [20 Chapters] D: Louis Gasnier, Donald MacKenzie; SP: George B. Seitz; S: Charles Goddard; P: Leopold and Theodore Wharton; LP: Pearl White, Crane Wilbur, Paul Panzer, Edward Jose, Francis Carlyle, Clifford Bruce, Donald MacKenzie, Eleanor Woodruff.

1917

Jimmie Dale Alias the Grey Seal. Mutual, [16 Chapters] D: Harry Webster; SP: Mildred Considine; S: Frank L. Packard; LP: Elmo K. Lincoln, Edna Hunter, Doris Mitchell, Paul Panzer, Leslie King, Louis Haine, George Pauncefort.

1918

The House of Hate. Astra/Pathé, [20 Chapters] D: George B. Seitz; SP: Bertram Millhauser; S: Arthur B. Reeve, Charles A. Logue; LP: Pearl White, Antonio Moreno, Peggy Shannor, John Gilmour, John Webb Dillon, Floyd Buckley, Louis Wolheim, Paul Panzer.

1920

The Mystery Mind. Supreme, [15 Chapters] D: William Davis, Fred Sittenham; S/SP: Arthur B. Reeve, John W. Grey; LP: J. Robert Pauline, Peggy Shannor, Paul Panzer, Ed Rogers, Violet MacMillian.

1927

The Hawk of the Hills. Pathé, [10 Chapters] D: Spencer Bennet; S: George Arthur Gray;

Cam: Edward Snyder, Frank Redman; LP: Allene Ray, Walter Miller, Frank Lackteen, Paul Panzer, Harry Semels, Jack Pratt, Chief Yowlachie.

1928

The Chinatown Mystery. Syn., [10 Chapters] D: J. P. McGowan; LP: Joe Bonomo, Ruth Hiatt, Paul Malvern, Francis Ford, Paul Panzer, Sheldon Lewis, Harry Myers, Grace Cunard, Helen Gibson, Peggy O'Day.

1929

The Black Book. Pathé, [10 Chapters] D: Spencer G. Bennet, Tom Storey; LP: Allene Ray, Walter Miller, Frank Lackteen, Edith London, Willie Fung, Marie Mosquini, Paul Panzer, John Webb Dillon.

CECILIA PARKER

Many moviegoers would be surprised to learn that Cecilia Parker had a career before the Hardy Family series, as a Western and serial heroine. She worked with six cowboys in the early '30s, five of whom she had praise for. Want to guess which one she found impossible, coarse and domineering?

Cecilia made *Rainbow Trail* ('32), *The Gay Caballero* ('32), *Mystery Ranch* ('32) and *Hollywood Cowboy* ('37) with George O'Brien; *Tombstone Canyon* ('32), *The Trail Drive* ('33), *Gun Justice* ('33) and *Honor of the Range* ('34) with Ken Maynard; *Riders of Destiny* ('33) with John Wayne; *Unknown Valley* ('33) and *The Man Trailer* ('34) with Buck Jones; *Rainbow Ranch* ('33) and *The Fugitive* ('33) with Rex Bell; and *Roll Along Cowboy* ('37) with Smith Ballew.

In addition to the Westerns, Cecilia played the soubrette in three serials: *Jungle Mystery* (32), *The Lost Special* ('32) and *The Lost Jungle* ('34).

In *Jungle Mystery*, two expeditions vie for tusks of buried ivory hidden in Africa by a slave trader, long dead. The main concern of the Morgan party is not the ivory. The young Morgan boy is somewhere in the jungle and his sister and father are joined by two American hunters in an attempt to find him. A strange jungle creature, an ape-like man, comes to the aid of the Morgan party when the Shillow expedition attempts to murder the Morgans.

In *The Lost Special*, two college athletes and two young ladies solve the disappearance of the Golden Special, a train carrying gold from the Golconda Mines.

In *The Lost Jungle* ('34), Clyde Beatty journeys by dirigible to an uncharted island in the tropic seas in search of his sweetheart and a party of lost explorers. Crashing on the island during a storm, Beatty and a few others survive and Beatty finds his fiancée and her father. The group then sets out to find Prof. Livingston, leader of the exploring expedition. They overcome white gold hunters, hostile tribesmen and fierce beasts to achieve their goal.

Born in Fort Williams, Canada, on April 16, 1914, Parker was the daughter of a British army man. As a child she lived in England, but the family moved to California when she was nine and there she attended high school and the Immaculate Heart Convent. Her ambition was music but there was not money to pay for music lessons. Instead, she became a film extra. While making *High School Girl* ('34) she was spotted by a talent scout and given a screen test which she passed. She made her dramatic debut as Greta Garbo's sister in *The Painted Veil* ('34). Following its completion, Cecilia was loaned out to Paramount for *Here Is My Heart* ('34) and *Enter Madame* ('35). Back at MGM she played the friend of Jeanette MacDonald in *Naughty Marietta* ('35).

In *Ah, Wilderness* ('35) she was paired with Eric Linden, with whom she acted in *Old Hutch* ('36), *Sins of the Children* ('36), *Girl Loves Boy* ('37), *Sweetheart of the Navy* ('37 and *Three Live Ghosts* ('36).

Cecilia was cast as Marian Hardy, daughter of Judge Hardy (Lewis Stone) and sister of Andy Hardy (Mickey Rooney), in 11 of the Hardy Family series made from 1937 to 1942. In 1958 she came out of retirement for *Andy Hardy Comes Home*.

In 1937 Cecilia married actor Robert Baldwin, who co-starred with her in PRC's *Gambling Daughters* ('41). In 1942 she retired to raise a family. They had two sons and a daughter. At one time Cecilia and husband owned and operated a rather sumptuous motel in Ventura County. Later they became real estate agents.

Cecilia Parker died in 1993 at age 79.

Serials

1932

Jungle Mystery. Univ., [12 Chapters] D: Ray Taylor; SP: Ella O'Neal, Basil Dickey, George Plympton, George Morgan; S: Talbot Mundy; LP: Tom Tyler, Cecilia Parker, Noah Beery, Jr., William Desmond, Philo McCullough, Carmelita Geraghty, Frank Lacketeen, Onslow Stevens.

The Lost Special. Univ., [12 Chapters] D: Henry MacRae; SP: Ella O'Neal, George Plympton, Basil Dickey, George Morgan; S: Arthur Conan Doyle; AP: Henry MacRae; LP: Frank Albertson, Cecilia Parker, Ernie Nevers, Caryl Lincoln, Francis Ford, Al Ferguson, Tom London, Edmund Cobb, Frank Glendon.

1934

The Lost Jungle. Mascot, [12 Chapters] D: Armand Schaefer, David Howard; SP: Barney Sarecky, David Howard, Armand Schaefer, Wyndham Gittens; S: Sherman Lowe, Al Marton; LP: Clyde Beatty, Cecilia Parker, Syd Saylor, Warner Richmond, Edward J. LeSaint, Wheeler Oakman, Mickey Rooney, Lloyd Whitlock, Crauford Kent, Wally Wales, Charles Whitaker, Lionel Backus.

HELEN PARRISH

Helen Parrish, a statuesque brunette, will be remembered especially for her *Overland Mail* ('42) role of Barbara Gilbert, a gal fighting to keep her father's mail delivery franchise from being taken over by that old cutthroat, Noah Beery, Sr.

Helen was born on March 12, 1922, in Columbis, Georgia. The daughter of actress Laura Parrish and younger sister of director-to-be Robert Parrish, she entered films at age five, playing Babe Ruth's daughter in *Babe Comes Home* ('27). She followed up this introduction to the camera by playing roles in "Our Gang" and "Smitty" comedies, *His First Command* ('29), *The Big Trail* ('30), *Cimarron* ('31), *The Public Enemy* ('31), *X Marks the Spot* ('32), *When a Fellow Needs a Friend* ('32), *There's Always Tomorrow* ('34), *Straight from the Heart* ('35), *Bride of Frankenstein* ('35), *a Dog of Flanders* ('35) and *Make Way for a Lady* ('36).

Off-screen for the most part during her "awkward age," she reappeared in Deana Durbin's *Mad About Music* ('38). After signing a contract with Universal she appeared in two more Durbin pictures (1939's *Three Smart Girls Grow Up* and *First Love*) and in *Little Tough Guys* ('38) and *Little Tough Guys in Society* ('38).

On loanout, she supported Ann Sheridan and Richard Carlson in *Winter Carnival* ('39) at United Artists and appeared in *You'll Find Out* ('40) with Kay Kyser, Boris Karloff, Bela Lugosi and Peter Lorre at RKO. After that there was a series of entertaining "B" films at Universal with such performers as Leon Errol, Lupe Velez, Dennis O'Keefe,

Rudy Vallee, Ozzie Nelson and Orchestra and Paul Kelly. Freelancing, she played with John Wayne in *In Old California* ('42) and with Roy Rogers in *Sunset Serenade* ('42); then she was back to Universal for *Overland Mail*. She made only three films in 1943, two in 1944 and one in 1945. She had no credits in 1946, but in 1948 she played the heroine in *Quick on the Trigger* with Charles Starrett and *Trouble Makers* with the Bowery Boys. Her last film was *The Wolf Hunters* ('49) with Kirby Grant.

Helen virtually abandoned films for television in 1945. For two years she was hostess on *The Hour Glass*, a show from New York. When the TV industry boomed in California, she returned and appeared with Tom Harmon (covering pro football games) and on a program called *This Is Your Music*.

She made guest appearances on numerous network TV shows and in the '50s was women's editor of *Panorama Pacific*, a pioneer in early morning TV on the West Coast.

In 1942, Helen married film writer Charles Lang. The couple had two children, a boy and a girl. In 1954 she was divorced from Lang. Though the judge exonerated Helen of charges by Lang that she was intimate with musical director Muzzy Marcellino, he awarded the children to Lang.

In 1956 she wed TV producer John Guedel. In 1958 she developed cancer and died at Hollywood Presbyterian Hospital on February 22, 1959. Her husband was at her bedside as she succumbed.

Serial

1942

Overland Mail. Univ., [15 Chapters] D: Ford Beebe, John Rawlins; S: Johnston McCulley; SP: Paul Huston; P: Henry MacRae; LP: Lon Chaney, Jr., Don Terry, Noah Beery, Jr., Helen Parrish, Noah Beery, Sr., Charles Stevens, Bob Baker, Tom Chatterton, William Desmond, Jack Rockwell, Marguerite De La Mothe.

SHIRLEY PATTERSON / SHAWN SMITH

Shirley Patterson was a Canadian by birth. Her father was a druggist in Saskatchewan when she was born in Winnipeg on December 26, 1922. When she was three, the family moved to Los Angeles. Shirley automatically became a U.S. citizen through her parents' action of becoming naturalized citizens.

Although she participated in various sports in Eagle-Rock High School, her specialty was archery. She won the junior archery championship of California, and her wholesome beauty enabled her to earn spending money by modeling at local department stores. This activity projected her into Miss America competition and she became Miss California of 1940. However, she never went to Atlantic City to try for the national title, as her dad objected to her participation.

Shirley's picture made *The Los Angeles Times* as a result of her winning the Miss California title and the archery championship. She got calls from various agents wanting to represent her. Shopping around, she received a contract from Columbia, where she was utilized in "B" films.

The 1943 *Batman* serial is her most memorable film. In it she plays the girlfriend of Batman. Thanks to the 1989 blockbuster movie *Batman*, interest was regenerated in the comic book hero and the old serial once again made money through video sales.

Shirley was a statuesque and sensuous young lady and it is enjoyable to watch her in Westerns with Charles Starrett (4), Eddie Dean (3), Russell Hayden (1), Johnny Mack Brown (1) and Elliott-Ritter (1).

While at Columbia, Shirley met director George Stevens in whose film *The More the Merrier* ('43) she had a small part. He sent her to MGM where she was placed under contract.

She appeared in several MGM features, but her promising career was cut short by marriage to Alfred Smith, Jr., a business executive who objected to her film work. Later, when their son was five or six years old, her husband agreed to a resumption of her career on a part-time basis. It was at this point that her screen name was changed to Shawn Smith. After several small parts in such films as *The French Line* ('54), *The Long Wait* ('54) and *The Silver Chalice* ('55), she co-starred with Jock Mahoney in *The Land Unknown* ('57), a science fiction thriller that also featured Henry Brandon.

Another period of inactivity followed as a result of her leg being fractured in nine places in a skiing accident. She was out of commission for two years.

When her marriage to Smith ended in divorce, Shirley married John Badette, president of FTD (the flowers-by-mail organization) and traveled all over the world with him setting up wire services.

In the mid–1980s Shirley was quite ill, with the result that she had seven abdominal operations. But she recovered and captivated audiences with her beauty and personality at the 1987 Charlotte Film Festival.

Shirley is reported to have died in the 1990s, but no details are available to the writer at this writing.

Serial

1943

Batman. Col., [15 Chapters] D: Lambert Hillyer; SP: Victor McLeod, Leslie Swabacker,

Harry Fraser; P: Rudolph C. Flothow; Mus: Lee Zahler; LP: Lewis Wilson, Douglas Croft, J. Carrol Naish, Shirley Patterson, William C. Austin, Charles Middleton, Robert Fiske, Charles Wilson, George Chesebro.

ADELE PEARCE / PAMELA BLAKE

Adele Pearce (her real name) was born August 6, 1916, in Oakland, California. She was raised by an aunt and uncle after her mother's death when Adele was three years old. Her dad was employed by PG&E in San Francisco.

While in high school, Adele heard that Paramount was conducting a contest to select a young lady for the film *Eight Girls in a Boat* ('33). Adele beat out dozens of girls to get the part of one of the girls. Following the completion of the film, Adele went back to San Francisco where she plunged into the study of dramatics instead of enrolling at the University of California, her initial intent. The acting bug bit her and she joined a Little Theatre group, got dramatic coaching and appeared in radio playlets.

Adele had the feminine lead in *Utah Trail* ('38) starring Tex Ritter at Grand National. When director John Farrow was casting for *Sorority House* ('39), he saw a test film she had done years before and signed her for a prominent role in his film.

Farrow was pleased with Adele's work in *Sorority House* ('39) and used her again in *Full Confession* ('39).

On loanout from RKO, Adele made *The Girl from Rio* ('39) at Monogram and *Wyoming Outlaw* ('39) at Republic. Also, Columbia used her in a couple of their shorts. Then it was back to RKO for four features and two shorts.

Her RKO contract at an end, Adele changed her name to Pamela Blake at the suggestion of Paramount, where she had been picked for *This Gun for Hire* ('42). Metro-Goldwyn-Mayer cast her in *Maisie Gets Her Man* ('42), *The Omaha Trail* ('42), *Swing Shift Maisie* ('42), *Slightly Dangerous* ('43) and *The Immortal Blacksmith* ('43), a one-reeler. Other programmers followed.

Pamela appeared in two serials in 1946. In *Mysterious Mr. M*, two investigators seek to solve the case of the disappearance of a submarine inventor kidnapped by a gang headed by mysterious Mr. M. Pamela is an insurance investigator aiding the two sleuths. In *Chick Carter, Detective*, Pamela is a private eye aiding Lyle Talbot (Chick Carter) in recovering stolen diamonds and bringing the culprits to justice. Douglas Fowley (reporter) and Eddie Acuff (photographer) also aid Talbot.

Pamela's third serial, *The Sea Hound* ('47), has her looking for her father, who is the key to finding gold that went down with a galleon. However, the gold has been removed from the sunken vessel. Her father is the captive of "The Admiral" (Robert Barron), then of the island people. Capt. Silver (Buster Crabbe) is able to reunite father and daughter, obtain the treasure and dispose of the would-be pirates.

Ghost of Zorro ('49) was Pamela's fourth and last serial. Zorro (Clayton Moore) aids Rita White (Pamela), who is trying to carry on the work of the Pioneer Telegraph Company following her father's murder. An outlaw leader, George Crane (Gene Roth), plots to stop the company from extending its telegraph lines in fear that his outlaw empire will be jeopardized.

Throughout the 1940s, Pamela appeared in "B" melodramas, Westerns and serials. She married Bud McTaggart, minor Western supporting player, and divorced him early in the '40s. In January 1943 she wed Air Cadet Mike Stokey (*Pantomime Quiz*). They had two children, Barbara Ann and Michael, Jr., before they were divorced in 1948.

After a few TV segments, she gave up acting, moved to Las Vegas and raised her children there.

Serials

1946

The Mysterious Mr. M. Univ., [13 Chapters] D: Lewis D. Collins, Vernon Keays; SP: Joseph Poland, Paul Huston, Barry Shipman; LP: Richard Martin, Dennis Moore, Jane Randolph, Pamela Blake, Danny Norton, Byron Folger, Joseph Crehan.

Chick Carter, Detective. Col., [15 Chapters] D: Derwin Abrahams; SP: George H. Plympton, Harry Fraser; P: Sam Katzman; Cam: Ira H. Morgan; Mus: Lee Zahler; LP: Lyle Talbot, Douglas Fowley, Julie Gibson, Pamela Blake, Eddie Acuff, Robert Elliott, George Meeker.

1947

The Sea Hound. Col., [15 Chapters] D: Walter B. Eason, Mack Wright; P: Sam Katzman; SP: George H. Plympton, Lewis Clay, Arthur Hoerl; Cam: Ira H. Morgan; Mus: Mischa Bakaleinikoff; LP: Buster Crabbe, Pamela Blake, James Lloyd, Ralph Hodges, Hugh Prosser, Rick Vallin.

1949

Ghost of Zorro. Rep., [12 Chapters] D: Fred C. Brannon; SP: Royal Cole, William Lively, Sol Shor; AP: Franklyn Adreon; Cam: John MacBurnie; Mus: Stanley Wilson; LP: Clayton Moore, Pamela Blake, Roy Barcroft, George J. Lewis, I. Stanford Jolley, Steve Clark.

EILEEN PERCY

Eileen Percy was born on August 1, 1899, in Belfast, Ireland. She came to the U.S. when she was just a kid and attended Catholic schools in New York and Brooklyn. One day a subway rider offered her a small part in the Broadway show *The Bluebird* ('10). This engagement led to *The Arab* ('11) and *Lady of the Slipper* ('12). In 1915 she appeared with Marion Davis in *Stop! Look! Listen!* She began appearing in Ziegfeld roof shows and it was there she was spotted by Douglas Fairbanks and brought to Hollywood. She became his leading lady in *Down to Earth* ('17), *Wild and Wooly* ('17), *Reaching for the Moon* ('17) and *The Man from Painted Post* ('17).

In 1919, she had the femme lead in *Brass Buttons* with William Russell and *In Mizzoura* with Robert Warwick. Her nine films during 1919 also included *Desert Gold* (E. K. Lincoln), *Gold in the Hills* (Robert Warwick) and *Where the West Begins* (William Russell).

Eileen made many movies during the '20s but she never became an important star. Among her films are *The Fast Mail* (Adolphe Menjou), *Pardon My Nerve!* and *Western Speed* (Buck Jones), *The Prisoner* (Herbert Rawlinson), *Within the Law* (Norma Talmadge), *The Cobra* (Rudolph Valentino), *The Unchastened Woman* (Theda Bara), *The Phantom Bullet* (Hoot Gibson), *Race Wild* (Rex Lease), *Twelve Miles Out* (Joan Crawford) and *Telling the World* (William Haines). In the early '30s she made *Temptation* with

Lois Weber, *Sin of Madelon Claudet* with Helen Hayes and her last, *The Cohens and the Kellys in Hollywood.*

Eileen was a friend of William Randolph Hearst and through his influence became the writer of a *Los Angeles Examiner* society column during the '30s. Her marriage to Elric Bush during the '20s ended in divorce about 1930, and she married song writer Harry Ruby in 1936. In the early '70s, Eileen suffered several heart attacks and she died in 1973 at age 72.

Her one serial, *The Third Eye*, was produced by Pathé in 1920. A pretty movie star (Percy) becomes the victim of a murderous gang, the head (Warner Oland) of which has fallen in love with her. He has also marked her as a useful addition to the gang. In his scheme to revenge himself on her for refusing to obey him, he feigns death when she shoots him with a studio revolver. Later it is found that the moving picture camera has recorded the event, leaving the hand that turned the crank a mystery. A struggle then begins between the young woman, aided by her sweetheart (Jack Mower), and the gang leader for possession of the film.

Serial

1920

The Third Eye. Pathé, [15 Chapters] D: James W. Horne; SP: William Parker; S: H. H. Van Loan; LP: Eileen Percy, Warner Oland, Jack Mower, Olga Grey, Mark Strong.

DERELYS PERDUE

A Dangerous Adventure ('21), the Warner Brothers serial starring Grace Darmond, seems to be the first credited role for Derelys Perdue. She may have appeared as an extra before appearing in this film, in which she has a good supporting role. Accidents plagued the production, although Perdue was not involved in any of them. She plays the sister of Darmond and, with her, accompanies their uncle (Jack Richardson) to Africa in quest of a treasure chest he has hidden there. The evil uncle tries to sell Grace to a chieftain in exchange for a caravan. Philo McCullough, in love with Grace, goes to her rescue.

Six years later, the comely Derelys had the lead opposite William Desmond in *The Mystery Rider* ('28). In the story, Walter Shumway finds a method for producing rubber from the sap of the mesquite plant. He is killed by "The Claw" (Tom London), a man with a deformed, clawlike hand, but not before confiding the secret formula to his daughter (Derelys). Her fiancé (William Desmond) is secretly the Mystery Rider, who fights to protect her from the Claw and his gang.

Derelys made only ten features and the two serials from 1921 to 1929, the year she retired from the screen. The features were *The Bishop of the Ozarks* ('23), *Blow Your Own Horn* ('23), *Daytime Wives* ('23), *The Last Man on Earth* ('24), *Untamed Youth* ('24), *Paint and Powder* ('25), *Where the Worst Begins* ('25), *The Gingham Girl* ('27), *Quick Triggers* ('28) and *The Smiling Terror* ('29). Talking pictures, and possibly marriage, probably accounted for her decision to quit the movies, although income might have entered into the decision. She was not making a lot of money.

Serials

1922

A Dangerous Adventure. WB, [15 chapters] D: Sam and J. L. Warner; SP: Frances Guihan; Cam: John W. Boyle *et al.*; P: William N. Selig; LP: Grace Darmond, Philo McCullough, Jack Richardson, Derelys Perdue, Robert Agnew, Mabel Stark, Rex de Roselli, Josephine Hill.

1928

The Mystery Rider. Univ., [10 Chapters] D: Jack Nelson; S: George Morgan; LP: William Desmond, Derelys Perdue, Tom London, Bud Osborn, Walter Shumway, Red Basset, Syd Saylor, Ben Corbett, Slim Lucas, Gus Wadlow.

JACK PERRIN

Born in Three Rivers, Michigan, on July 25, 1896, Jack — whose real name was Lyman Wakefield Perrin — moved with his parents to Hollywood when he was three years old. His father was in real estate and investments. Jack went to grammar school in the Sunset and Alvarada district and received his high school education at Manual Arts High. After graduation, he went to work in the property department at one of the studios, and it was there that he was noticed by the right people; thus, his mode of entry into pictures was exactly like that of John Wayne 12 years later.

Perrin was a prolific cowboy ace in the 1920s and 1930s, turning out oaters at a fast pace and consistently remaining in the second echelon of popular Western and serial stars and at the same time achieving some stature as a dramatic actor. Perrin was undoubtedly one of the most underrated of all Hollywood cowboys.

His first important role was in Triangle's *Toton the Apache* ('17), a six-reeler directed by Frank Borzage. World War I temporarily put a stop to his film activities, and he served in the submarine service throughout the war.

Returning to Hollywood, Jack was given a contract by Universal and cast as a juvenile heavy in the Eddie Polo "Cyclone Smith" two-reelers before he got his first meaty role in Erich von Stroheim's *Blind Husbands* ('19). Then came his big break. He was picked to co-star with Kathleen O'Connor in Universal's 18-chapter serial *The Lion Man* ('19), which dealt with intrigue in a circus where Jack is accused of murder. It was a tasty morsel for the serial-hungry public, with the greatest share of homage going to Jack for his daredevil performance.

Pink Tights ('20) gave Jack a needed push. He made a number of non–Western features such as *The Match-Breaker* ('21), *Partners of the Tide* ('21), *The Torrent* ('21), *The Rage of Paris* ('21), *The Guttersnipe* ('22), *The Dangerous Little Demon* ('22) and *The Trouper* ('22).

It was in the series of two-reelers that Jack made a name for himself. These scrappy little Westerns, constructed with careful technical skill, had a commonsense air of production about them and made up in speed what they lacked in footage. Perrin was emphatically the right man in the right place.

The memorable films for 1923 were the two serials Jack made for Arrow: *The Fighting Skipper* and *Santa Fe Trail*. *The Fighting Skipper* was directed by the old serial champion, Francis Ford, and released on March 1. The plot dealt with Jack helping Peggy O'Day (as Skipper), whose father had amassed a fortune in pearls that he buried on Thunder Island. He remarried and left behind a half-sister, an identical double for Skipper. Shortly after he died, all of the papers proving ownership of the island disappeared. Jack had to assist Skipper to gain possession of her rightful inheritance.

Santa Fe Trail ('23) featured serial queen Neva Gerber as the lovely Sunbonnet Sue whom Jack was forever saving from the clutches of menacing cutthroats. It was a wild and woolly affair.

During the years 1923–26, Jack starred in independent Westerns for Harry Webb (who released through Aywon and Arrow), and also did a series for Morris R. Schlank (releasing through Rayart).

Riders of the Plains ('24), Jack's fourth serial, followed the general formula of successful serial construction with heroism, melodrama, action, villainy, exciting chapter endings and a very mild love angle, with Marilyn Mills playing the garden-fresh sweetheart part.

At Universal where he had started almost a decade before, Jack appeared in both a Northwest Mounted Police series of two-reelers and feature Westerns. The Mountie two-reelers were especially good, and through them he acquired a considerable coterie of fans.

Nat Levine cast Jack as lead player in Mascot's *The Vanishing West* ('28), a zingy Western with Leo Maloney, Jack Daugherty and Yakima Canutt in the cast.

Universal followed up by starring Jack in his sixth serial, *The Jade Box* ('30), released in both silent and sound versions. Jack made the transition to talkies successfully but found work only at the small independents. But work he did, as he and his beautiful white horse Starlight streaked across the plains to the delight of audiences in the hinterlands of America during the early Depression years in cheapie Westerns for such undistinguished studios as Big 4, Cosmos, Robert J. Horner, Atlantic and National. Made for a few thousand dollars and released on the independent market, the films were truly cow-dung products, but Jack and Starlight managed to stand out in these mediocre sagebrushers.

In 1934, Jack teamed up with Ben Corbett in the popular series of "Bud 'n' Ben" three-reelers produced by B. B. Ray for Astor release. Then came a series of feature Westerns for Reliable and Atlantic in 1935–36. But after 1936 it was all downhill. He had a featured role in Republic's *The Painted Stallion* ('37) but his parts got smaller and smaller as the years went by.

His marriage to Josephine Hill ended in divorce around 1937. A daughter, Patricia, was born of this union. In 1943 he married the chief telephone operator at Universal and they remained happily married until his death from a heart attack on December 17, 1967.

Jack Perrin and Starlight ceased riding the range of neighborhood theaters before most readers of this book were born. But his star can still be found on the Walk of Stars on Vine Street, north of Hollywood Boulevard — a fine tribute to one of yesteryear's more interesting saddle aces.

Serials

1919

The Lion Man. Univ., [18 Chapters] D: Albert Russell, Jack Wells; SP: Karl Coolidge; S:

Randall Parrish; LP: Kathleen O'Connor, Jack Perrin, Mack Wright, J. Barney Sherry, Gertrude Astor.

1923

The Fighting Skipper. Arrow, [15 Chapters] D: Francis Ford; LP: Peggy O'Day, Jack Perrin, Bill White, Francis Ford, Steve Murphy.

The Santa Fe Trail. Arrow, [15 Chapters] D: Ashton Dearholt, Robert Dillon; SP: Robert Dillon; S: Ben Wilson; P: Neva Gerber; LP: Jack Perrin, Neva Gerber, James Welsh, Elias Bullock, Wilbur McGaugh.

1924

Riders of the Plains. Arrow, [15 Chapters] D: Jacques Jaccard; SP: Jacques Jaccard, Karl Coolidge; LP: Jack Perrin, Ruth Royce, Charles Brinley, Kingsley Benedict, Running Elk.

1928

The Vanishing West. Mascot, [10 Chapters] D: Richard Thorne; SP: Wyndham Gittens; P: Nat Levine; S: Karl Krusada, William Lester; LP: Jack Perrin, Eileen Sedgwick, Jack Daugherty, Yakima Canutt, Leo Maloney.

1930

The Jade Box. Univ., [10 Chapters] D: Ray Taylor; S: Fred Jackson; LP: Jack Perrin, Louise Lorraine, Monroe Salisbury, Francis Ford, William Mack.

1931

The Sign of the Wolf. Met., [10 Chapters] D: Forrest Sheldon, Harry S. Webb; LP: Rex Lease, Virginia Brown Faire, Joe Bonomo, Jack Mower, Jack Perrin.

1933

The Whispering Shadow. Mascot, [12 Chapters] D: Albert Herman, Colbert Clark; LP: Bela Lugosi, Henry B. Walthall, Viva Tattersall, Malcolm McGregor, Jack Perrin.

Mystery Squadron. Mascot, [12 Chapters] D:

Colbert Clark, David Howard; LP: Bob Steele, Guinn Williams, Lucile Browne, Jack Mulhall, J. Carrol Naish, Robert Kortman, Jack Perrin.

1937

The Painted Stallion. Rep., [12 Chapters] D: William Witney, Alan James, Ray Taylor; SP: Barry Shipman, Winston Miller; P: J. Lawrence Wickland; Cam: William Nobles, Edgar Lyons; Mus: Raoul Kraushaar; LP: Ray Corrigan, Hoot Gibson, Hal Taliaferro, Jack Perrin, Duncan Renaldo, Julia Thayer, Yakima Canutt, Charles King.

1938

The Great Adventures of Wild Bill Hickok. Col., [15 Chapters] D: Mack V. Wright, Sam Nelson: LP: Gordon [Bill] Elliott, Carole Wayne, Frankie Darro, Monte Blue, Dickie Jones, Kermit Maynard, Reed Hadley, Chief Thundercloud.

The Lone Ranger. Rep., [15 Chapters] D: William Witney, John English; LP: Lee Powell, Chief Thundercloud, Lynne Roberts, Wally Wales [Hal Taliaferro], Herman Brix [Bruce Bennett], Lane Chandler, George Letz [George Montgomery].

1940

The Shadow. Col., [15 Chapters] D: James W. Horne; LP: Victor Jory, Veda Ann Borg, Robert Moore, Richard Fiske, J. Paul Jones, Jack Ingram.

1941

The Spider Returns. Col., [15 Chapters] D: James W. Horne; LP: Warren Hull, Mary Ainslee, Dave O'Brien, Joe Girard, Kenne Duncan, Anthony Warde.

1954

Riding with Buffalo Bill. Col., [15 Chapters] D: Spencer G. Bennett; LP: Marshall Reed, Rick Vallin, Joanne Rio, Jack Ingram, Shirley Whitney.

HOUSE PETERS, JR.

House Peters, Jr., was born on January 12, 1916, in New Rochelle, New York. Unlike his father House Peters he never became a star, but he did make a name for himself as a Western character actor. Usually he played one of the "black hats," but in the serial *King of the Rocket Men* ('49) he was the hero's pal. And the hero, Tristram Coffin, was himself playing the role of a good guy, something he seldom did.

House spent a year at Urban Military Academy and graduated from Beverly Hills High School in or about 1934.

In 1935, House had a bit in *Hot Tip* which starred James Gleason and Zasu Pitts. He got small parts in *The Adventures of Frank Merriwell* ('36), *Ace Drummond* ('36) and *Flash Gordon* ('36). His first Western seems to have been *Wells Fargo* ('37), followed by *Public Cowboy No. 1* ('37) starring Gene Autry and *Frontier Pony Express* ('39) starring Roy Rogers.

House was one of the first actors to enlist in the service following the Japanese sneak attack on Pearl Harbor. He spent nearly five years in the Signal Corps in the South Pacific, winding up in the Philippines. It was there he met his wife-to-be, Lucy Pickett, whom he married in 1946. Returning home, he decided to resume his acting career, which had hardly gotten off the ground. But first he enrolled in Ben Bard's Academy of Dramatic Art, under the G.I. Bill.

Beginning in 1948 he became a Western badman. In the years that followed he appeared in more than 45 Westerns and four serials—*Dangers of the Canadian Mounted* ('48), *Adventures of Frank and Jesse James* ('48), *Batman and Robin* ('49) and *King of the Rocket Men* ('49), his best serial role. In addition he appeared in such non–Westerns as *The Red Badge of Courage* ('51), *The Day the Earth Stood Still* ('51), *Red Planet Mars* ('52), *Target Earth* ('54), *The Women of Pit-cairn Island* ('56), *Inside the Mafia* ('59) and *The Big Night* ('60).

House was active in TV Westerns as well as in features, working in the TV series *The Cisco Kid*, *The Lone Ranger*, *The Gene Autry Show*, *The Roy Rogers Show*, *Death Valley Days*, *Buffalo Bill, Jr.*, *The Range Rider*, *Annie Oakley* and *Lassie*.

House retired from acting in 1967. He became a realtor for several years, and he and Lucy traveled widely prior to the discovery of cancer in House's abdominal area. After surgery his health was sufficient that he could attend film festivals. In 2004, he still does.

Serials

1936

The Adventures of Frank Merriwell. Univ., [12 Chapters] D: Cliff Smith; P: Henry MacRae; SP: George H. Plympton, Maurice Geraghty, Ella O'Neill, Basil Dickey; LP: Don Briggs, Jean Rogers, John King, Carla Laemmle, Sumner Getchell, Al Bridge, Bently Hewlett, Dickie Jones, Dave O'Brien, Edmund Cobb.

Flash Gordon. Univ., [13 Chapters] D: Frederick Stephani; SP: George H. Plympton, Ella O'Neill, Frederick Stephani, Basil Dickey; P: Henry MacRae; Cam: Jerry Ash, Richard Fryer; LP: Buster Crabbe, Jean Rogers, Frank Shannon, Charles Middleton, Priscilla Lawson, Richard Alexander, John Lipson, Earl Askam.

Ace Drummond. Univ., [13 Chapters] D: Ford Beebe, Cliff Smith; SP: Wyndham Gittens, Norman S. Hall, Ray Trampe; LP: John King, Jean Rogers, Noah Beery, Jr., Guy Bates Post, Arthur Loft, Chester Gan, Jackie Morrow, James B. Leong.

1948

Adventures of Frank and Jesse James. Rep., [13 Chapters] D: Fred Brannon, Yakima Canutt;

SP: Franklyn Adreon, Basil Dickey, Sol Shor; AP: Franklyn Adreon; Cam: John MacBurnie; Mus: Morton Scott; LP: Clayton Moore, Steve Darrell, Noel Neill, George J. Lewis, Stanley Andrews, John Crawford, Dale Van Sickel, House Peters, Jr., I. Stanford Jolley.

Dangers of the Canadian Mounted. Rep., [12 Chapters] D: Fred Brannon, Yakima Canutt; SP: Franklyn Adreon, Basil Dickey, Sol Shor, Robert C. Walker; Cam: John MacBurnie; Mus: Mort Glickman; LP: Jim Bannon, Virginia Belmont, Anthony Warde, Dorothy Granger, I. Stanford Jolley, Bill Van Sickel, Dale Van Sickel, Tom Steele, Ken Terrell, Ted Adams.

1949

Batman and Robin. Col., [15 Chapters] D: Spencer Bennet; SP: George H. Plympton, Joseph F. Poland, Royal K. Cole; P: Sam Katzman; Cam: Ira H. Morgan; Mus: Mischa Bakaleinikoff; LP: Robert Lowery, Johnny Duncan, Jane Adams, Lyle Talbot, Ralph Graves, Don C. Harvey, William Fawcett, Rick Vallin.

King of the Rocket Men. Rep., [12 Chapters] D: Fred C. Brannon; SP: Royal Cole, William Lively, Sol Shor; AP: Franklyn Adreon; Cam: Ellis W. Carter; LP: Tristram Coffin, Mae Clarke, James Craven, I. Stanford Jolley, House Peters, Jr., Don Haggerty, Douglas Evans.

CARMEN PHILLIPS

Carmen Phillips first appeared on screen in 1915. That year she had supporting roles in *Under the Crescent, The New Adventures of Terrance O'Rourke* and *Lord John's Journal*, each being a short series in which Carmen early on was initiated into "third woman" roles. For example, she is an adventuress in *Forbidden Paths* ('17) who meets death with Sessue Hayakawa, leaving Vivian Martin free to marry the man she loves. In *The Cabaret Girl* ('15) she has a principal role as friend of Ruth Clifford. She is an adulteress in *The Sunset Trail* ('17), also featuring Martin. She had a co-starring role with H. B. Warner in *The Pagan God* ('19), playing Tai Chen, leader of a Chinese rebellion. Margaret De La Motte was featured. Carmen would play a lot of foreign types.

In *Smiles* ('19) she is a spy trailed by Val Paul; she is the "third woman" in *Whitewashed Walls* (William Desmond, Fritzi Brunette); in *The Eater* ('21) she plays a friend of Hoot Gibson and Louise Lorraine; In *Thirty Days* ('23) she is Carlotta, with whom Wallace Reid is innocently friendly. In *Fair Week* ('24) she plays Madame Le Grande, a voluptuous con artist; and in *Six-*

Shootin' Romance ('26), starring Jack Hoxie, she is once more the "other woman."

In 1920 she had one of the supporting roles in *The Hawk's Trail*; in '21 she had a larger role in *The Hope Diamond Mystery*; and in '25 she had a major role in *The Great Circus Mystery*. But in '26 she seems to have called it "quits." There are no film credits for her after that date.

Serials

1915

The New Adventures of Terrance O'Rourke. Univ., [3 Episodes] D: Jacques Jaccard, J. Warren Kerigan; P: Otis Turner; S: Louis Joseph Vance; LP: J. Warren Kerrigan, Lois Wilson, Harry Carter, Maude George, Carmen Phillips, Eddie Polo.

Lord John's Journal. Univ., [5 Episodes] D: Edward J. LeSaint; SP: Harvey Gates; P: Robert Lusk; LP: William Garwood, Stella Razeto, Albert MacQuarrie, Sam Polo, Carmen Phillips, Grace Benham, Eddie Polo.

Under the Crescent. Univ., [6 Episodes] D:

Burton King; SP: Nell Shipman; LP: Ola Humphrey, William Dowlan, Edward Stoman, Helen Wright, Carmen Phillips.

1920

The Hawk's Trail. Burston, [15 Chapters] D: W. S. Van Dyke; S: Nan Blair; Spv.: Louis Burston; LP: King Baggot, Rhea Mitchell, Grace Darmond, Harry Lorraine, Stanton Heck, Carmen Phillips.

1921

The Hope Diamond Mystery. Kosmik, [15 Chapters] D: Stuart Paton; S: May Yoke; P:

George Kleine; LP: Harry Carter, Grace Darmond, George Chesebro, Boris Karloff, Carmen Phillips, William Marion.

1925

The Great Circus Mystery. Univ., [15 Chapters] D: Jay Marchant; SP: Leigh Jacobson, George Morgan; LP: Joe Bonomo, Louise Lorraine, Robert J. Graves, Carmen Phillips, Slim Cole, Eduardo Martini.

DOROTHY PHILLIPS

Born Dorothy Gwendolya Strible in 1892 in Baltimore, this actress was playing leads as early as 1911. Early in her career she was known as "the Kid, Nazimova" for emulating the famous star's style. Her husband, Alan Holubar, often directed her.

Her films include *The Rosary* ('11), *Into the North* ('13), *The Adventure of a Sea-Going Hack* ('15), *Ambition* ('16), *The Debt* ('17), *Broadway Love* ('18), *Mortgaged Wife* ('18), *Destiny* ('19), *The Forfeit* ('19), *Man-Woman-Marriage* ('21), *Hurricane's Gal* ('22), *Slander the Woman* ('23), *Without Mercy* ('25), *The Gay Deceiver* ('26), *The Broken Gate* ('27) and *The Cradle Snatchers* ('27).

Dorothy retired when talkies replaced flicker films, but occasionally did bits in sound films, e.g., *Now I'll Tell* ('34), *The First Baby* ('36), *Thank You, Jeeves* ('36), *Hot Water* ('37), *And One Was Beautiful* ('40), *Boston Blackie Goes Hollywood* ('42), *My Favorite Spy* ('42), *The Cross of Lorraine* ('44), *Mrs. Parkington* ('44), *A Connecticut Yankee in King Arthur's Court* ('49), *The Reckless Moment* ('49), *Father of the Bride* ('50), *Vio-*

lent Saturday ('55) and *The Man Who Shot Liberty Valance* ('62).

Dorothy's only serial was *The Bar-C Mystery* ('26), in which she portrays a New York girl who inherits a ranch in the West from a man she does not know. It seems her benefactor, Nevada (Wallace McDonald), has disappeared into the desert and is presumed dead. When she arrives in town, a crooked gambler and a dance hall owner try to get control of the ranch because they know there is gold and other deposits on the land. A stranger comes to her rescue and the Bar-C mystery is solved.

Serial

1926

The Bar-C Mystery. Pathé, [10 Chapters[D: Robert F. Hill; S: Raymond Spears; LP: Wallace McDonald, Dorothy Phillips, Ethel Clayton, Philo McCullough.

LOTTIE PICKFORD

Lottie Pickford (real name Smith) was the sister of Mary Pickford and Jack Pickford. In curls like her sister Mary's, she starred in the 1915 serial *The Diamond from the Sky*, a 30-chapter cliffhanger. Top-billed, Lottie plays Esther, desired by both William Russell and Irving Cummings. The story dealt with a large diamond handed down in a family for several generations, and desired by two cousins who fight for possession of it.

Lottie also starred in *The House of Bondage* ('14), supported sister Mary in *Fanchon the Cricket* ('15), co-starred with Louise Huff and John Bowers in *The Reward of Patience* ('16), supported Fannie Ward and Harrison Ford in *On the Level* ('17), supported brother Jack in *Mile-a-Minute Kendall* ('18), supported Wallace Reid and Ann Little in *The Man From Funeral Range* ('18), starred in *They Shall Pay* ('21), supported sister Mary in

Dorothy Vernon of Haddon Hall ('24) and had a minor role in Douglas Fairbanks' (Mary's husband) *Don Q, Son of Zorro* ('25). In her last several pictures she was billed Lottie Pickford Forrest, an indication she had married.

Serial

1915

The Diamond from the Sky. American, [30 Chapters] D: Jacques Jaccard, William Desmond Taylor; SP: Roy L. McCardell, Jacques Jaccard; S: Roy L. McCardell; LP: Lottie Pickford, Irving Cummings, William Russell, Charlotte Burton, Orral Humphrey, Roy Stewart, Hartford (Jack) Hoxie, Eugenie Ford.

EDDIE POLO

Born on February 1, 1875, in San Francisco, Eddie Polo was raised and educated in the sawdust ring since the time he was able to toddle. With his parents, sisters and brother he traveled all over Europe and soon became a circus performer himself. When he was six years old he was in Italy with his father's circus. Hurt in a fall, his father decided to distribute his family among other circuses while he went to the U.S. to find work. Eddie was bound as an apprentice to a small circus owner in Europe. Eddie left the show after five years to put on little shows of his own. After about four years of this nomadic life, he stowed away on a cattle boat and made

his way to England. After working and saving his money, he booked passage to the U.S.

Seventeen years of his life were spent under Barnum and Bailey's Big Top, after which he transferred to the Ringling Brothers Circus. Becoming famous as a trapeze artist, he was the first man to catch a fellow acrobat after a triple somersault in the air.

In 1914, Polo was hired by Universal to perform stunts in various films, one of which was *The Campbells Are Coming* ('15). He then was given a small part in the 22-chapter *The Broken Coin* ('15) starring Francis Ford and Grace Cunard. Polo created an impression with his performance, but the sudden sensa-

Inez MacDonald and Eddie Polo in *Do or Die* (Universal, 1921).

tional success rapidly went to Polo's head. He made demands which scenarist Cunard denied and she wrote him out of the production in the twentieth chapter. Directly afterwards he was cast in a small part in Chapter 3 of *Graft* ('15) as punishment for refusing makeup and making demands on *The Broken Coin*. And after *Graft* he was cast in a supporting role in *The Adventures of Peg o' the Ring* ('16) with Ford and Cunard; *Liberty, a Daughter of the U.S.A.* ('16) with Marie Walcamp, Jack Holt and others; and *The Gray Ghost* ('17) with Harry Carter and Priscilla Dean.

In 1918, Polo got his first starring serial role, *The Bull's Eye*. It was followed the same year by *The Lure of the Circus*. Both serials were 18 chapters long. What made Polo such a daring and successful star was not only his iron nerve, but his coordination, strength and athletic ability.

In 1919, Polo starred in ten two-reel Cyclone Smith Westerns, each one a complete story in itself.

The year 1920 was a busy one for Polo. He made two 18-chapter serials, *King of the Circus* and *The Vanishing Dagger*. In 1921, he made six more two-reel Westerns with the overall title *The Return of Cyclone Smith*. *Do or Die* ('21) and *The Secret Four* ('21) were Polo's last serials for Universal. Another had been planned for him, but he was a troublemaker and the studio decided it could do without him.

Wealthy by this time, Polo organized the Star Serial Corporation. The first and only serial made was *Captain Kidd* ('22). By the time it was finished, the company was bankrupt. He made *Dangerous Hour* ('23) and *Prepared to Die* ('23) for Cliff Reid Productions and *The Knock on the Door* ('23) for

Johnnie Walker Productions. While filming *Dangerous Hour* he attempted to jump a horse across a chasm about 450 feet deep and missed. He underwent four surgical operations. It was about a year before he fully recovered. Following his recovery, he organized a revue show and headed for Europe. During his time in Europe, he married for the second time.

Polo made a number of films in Germany, including the two-chapter serial *Die Eule* ('27). Also in '27 he visited South America with a troupe of German actors and was well-received in the principal cities they played.

Polo returned to the States in an effort to find a producer for a film with a circus background. No luck. Returning to Europe, he again could not interest a film company in his idea. He left Europe when the Nazis entered Austria. Hollywood was no longer interested in him. He was old history. The only film parts he could get were bit parts in a few features and serials.

Eddie lived in poverty in a modest hotel in a shabby section of Hollywood in his declining years. He was visiting friends in the Casa D' Amore Restaurant, 1644 Cahuenga Blvd., on the afternoon of June 14, 1961, when he suffered a fatal heart attack. He was survived by his daughter, Mrs. Malvino Polo Romero, and a brother, Sam Polo.

Eddie Polo was 86 years old. He was planning on leaving for Stockholm to begin a movie based on his life story.

Serials

1915

The New Adventures of Terrence O'Rourke. Univ., [?] [series] D: Otis Turner; S: Louis Joseph Vance; SP: Walter Woods, F. McGrew Willis; LP: J. Warren Kerrigan, Lois Wilson, Harry Carter, Maude George, G. Raymond Nye, Fred Church, Carmen Phillips, Eddie Polo.

Lord John's Journal. Univ., [5 Episodes—series] D: Edward J. LeSaint; LP: William Garwood, Stella Razeto, Albert McQuarrie, Sam Polo, Carmen Phillips, Laura Oakley, Jay Belasco, Eddie Polo, Malcolm Blevins.

The Broken Coin. Univ., [22 Chapters] D: Francis Ford; SP: Grace Cunard; S: Emerson Hough; LP: Grace Cunard, Francis Ford, Harry Schumm, Ernest Shields, Reese Gardiner, Jack Holt, John Ford, Eddie Polo.

Graft. Univ., [20 Chapters] D: Richard Stanton, George A. Lessey; LP: Harry Carey, Jane Novak, Hobert Henley, Richard Stanton, Glen White, Eddie Polo.

1916

Liberty, a Daughter of the U.S.A. Univ., [20 Chapters] D/SP: Jacques Jaccard, Henry MacRae; S/P: W. B. Pearson; LP: Marie Walcamp, Jack Holt, Neal Hart, Eddie Polo, G. Raymond Nye.

The Adventures of Peg o' the Ring. Univ., [15 Chapters] D: Francis Ford, Jacques Jaccard; SP: Grace Cunard; LP: Francis Ford, Grace Cunard, Pete Gerald, G. Raymond Nye, Charles Munn, Mark Fenton, John Ford, Jack Duffy, Eddie Polo.

1917

The Gray Ghost. Univ., [16 Chapters] D: Stuart Paton; S: Arthur Somers Roche; LP: Harry Carter, Priscilla Dean, Emory Johnson, Eddie Polo, Gertrude Astor.

Bull's Eye. Univ., [18 Chapters] D: James W. Horne; SP: Harvey Gates, Tom Gibson, Frank H. Clark; LP: Eddie Polo, Vivian Reed, Frank Lanning, Ray Hanford, Noble Johnson.

1918

Lure of the Circus. Univ., [18 Chapters] D: J. P. McGowan; SP: Hope Loring; S: William Wing; LP: Eddie Polo, Eileen Sedgwick, Harry Carter, Molly Malone, Noble Johnson.

1919

Cyclone Smith. Univ., [10 Episodes—series] D: Jacques Jaccard *et al.*; SP: George Hively, Karl Coolidge *et al.*; S: Jacques Jaccard, Marie Walcamp *et al.*; LP: Eddie Polo, Eileen Sedgwick, Kate Meyers, Jack Perrin, Leo Maloney.

1920

King of the Circus. Univ., [18 Chapters] D: J. P. McGowan; SP: Anthony W. Coldeway; LP: Eddie Polo, Corrine Porter, Kittoria Beveridge, Jay Marchant.

The Vanishing Dagger. Univ., [18 Chapters] D: Ed Kull, Eddie Polo; SP: Hope Loring, George W. Pyper; S: Hope Loring, Jacques Jaccard, Milton Moore; LP: Eddie Polo, Thelma Percy, G. Normand Hammond, Laura Oakley, Ray Ripley.

1921

The Return of Cyclone Smith. Univ., [6 Episodes — series] D: Jacques Jaccard; S/SP: George Morgan, Robert Dillon, Anthony W. Coldeway; P: Jacques Jaccard, Jay Marchant; LP: Eddie Polo, Kathleen Myers, Joseph Hazelton, Charles Brimley, Valeria Olivo.

Do or Die. Univ., [18 Chapters] D: J. P. McGowan; S: Anthony W. Coldeway; LP: Eddie Polo, Inez McDonald, Magda Lane, J. P. McGowan, Jay Marchant.

The Secret Four. Univ., [15 Chapters] D: Albert Russell, Perry Vekroff; S/SP: Anthony W. Coldeway; LP: Eddie Polo, Kathleen Myers, Doris Dean, William Welsh, Thelma Daniels.

1922

Captain Kidd. Star, [15 Chapters] D: J. P. McGowan, Burton King; SP: Anthony W. Coldeway, Philip Lonergan; LP: Eddie Polo, Katherine Myers, Sam Polo, Leslie J. Casey, Malvina Polo.

1927

Die Eule. Mana Zach — Munich [2 Chapters] D/S: Eddie Polo; SP: Margarete Schmhal; LP: Eddie Polo, Erich Kaiser-Tilz, Hans Adalbert Von Schlettaw, Dorothy Douglas, Fritz Schnell, Paul Rehkopf.

1940

The Green Archer. Col., [15 Chapters] D: James W. Horne; LP: Victor Jory, Iris Meredith, James Craven, Dorothy Fay, Robert Fiske, Eddie Polo (bit).

1942

Gang Busters. Univ., [13 Chapters] D: Ray Taylor, Noel Smith; LP: Kent Taylor, Irene Hervey, Ralph Morgan, Robert Armstrong, Eddie Polo (bit).

Overland Mail. Univ., [15 Chapters] D: Ford Beebe, John Rawlins; LP: Lon Chaney, Jr., Don Terry, Noah Beery, Jr., Helen Parrish, Noah Beery, Sr., Tom Chatterton, Eddie Polo (bit).

LEE POWELL

Lee Powell, the screen's first Lone Ranger, was born on May 15, 1908, in Long Beach, California. After graduation from high school, he attended the University of Montana, where he excelled in both football and track and was also active in dramatics. Little is known of his early years. Up until 1936 he was content touring with a stock company. Tiring of the constant traveling and low pay, he made his pitch for the movies and was able to get extra or bit parts here and there.

Lee was actually billed in Paramount's *Forlorn River* ('37) starring Buster Crabbe. A year later he was selected by Republic to portray one of the five Rangers in the serial *The Lone Ranger* ('38). In the last chapter he is revealed as the Lone Ranger after the other four Rangers (Lane Chandler, George Montgomery, Herman Brix (Bruce Bennett] and Wally Wales) have been killed. When *The Lone Ranger* was released in 1938, it was a smashing success, and today it ranks with the best serials ever made. Having finally reached stardom, Powell was immediately cast in another Republic serial, *The Fighting Devil Dogs* ('38), sharing top billing with Herman Brix [Bruce Bennett]. This serial is another of Republic's most popular in spite of its overuse of stock footage.

Lee supported Roy Rogers in *Come On Rangers* ('38) but was passed over when Republic cast *The Lone Ranger Rides Again* ('39). Bob Livingston, a favorite of studio head Herbert Yates, was given the assignment. Feeling that the studio was not giving him an opportunity to show what he could do,

Chief Thundercloud and Lee Powell (right) in *The Lone Ranger* (Republic, 1938).

Powell left Republic and signed with Grand National as one member of a trio in what was supposed to be a Western series. Unfortunately, only one film (*Trigger Pals*, 1939) was made before the studio went broke.

With no further film offers, Powell joined Wallace Brothers Circus billed as the original Lone Ranger. His act consisted of wearing a mask, riding a white horse and entering the tent to the cry of "Hi-Yo, Silver."

Lone Ranger, Inc., owners of the rights to the radio program, sued Powell and Wallace Brothers, first in Pennsylvania, then in South Carolina, and finally in North Carolina where the court ruled that Powell could not refer to himself as the Lone Ranger or to use the phrase "Hi-Yo, Silver."

Powell married bareback rider Norma Rogers, daughter of the circus owner, on January 7, 1940. Because of his circus commitment, Powell's only 1940 film appearance was as Roka in *Flash Gordon Conquers the Universe*. In '41 he supported Bill Elliott in *The Return of Daniel Boone* and George Houston in *The Lone Rider Rides On*. He then signed with PRC to co-star in a new series of sagebrushers. His co-stars were Art Davis, who had what it took to star solo but never got the chance, and Bill (Cowboy Rambler) Boyd, a Dallas, Texas, radio performer who couldn't act. The trio were featured in six cheaply made horse operas: *Texas Manhunt* ('42), *Raiders of the West* ('42), *Rolling Down the Great Divide* ('42), *Tumbleweed Trail* ('42), *Along the Sundown Trail* ('43) and *Prairie Pals* ('43).

In mid–1942, Powell joined the Marine Corps and in November of that year was transferred to the South Pacific where he rose to the rank of sergeant and fought at Tarawa and Saipan. He lost his life in the invasion of Tinian on July 20, 1944.

Powell's biggest contribution to motion pictures was that he had been the first actor to portray the Lone Ranger.

Serials

1938

The Lone Ranger. Rep., [15 Chapters] D: William Witney, John English; Spv.: Robert Beche; AP: Sol C. Siegel; SP: Barry Shipman, George W. Yates, Lois Eby, Franklyn Adreon, Ronald Davidson; Cam: William Nobles; Mus: Alberto Colombo; LP: Lee Powell, Chief Thundercloud, Lynne Roberts, Lane Chandler, Stanley Andrews, Hal Taliaferro, George Letz [Montgomery], Herman Brix [Bruce Bennett], George Cleveland, William Farnum, John Merton, Sammy McKim.

The Fighting Devil Dogs. Rep., [12 Chapters] D: William Witney, John English; SP: Barry Shipman, Franklyn Adreon, Ronald Davidson, Sol Shor; AP: Robert Beche; Cam: William Nobles; Mus: Alberto Colombo; LP: Lee Powell, Herman Brix [Bruce Bennett], Eleanor Stewart, Montagu Love, Hugh Sothern, Sam Flint, Forrest Taylor, Tom London, Edmund Cobb.

1940

Flash Gordon Conquers the Universe. Univ., [12 Chapters] D: Ford Beebe, Ray Taylor; LP: Buster Crabbe, Carol Hughes, Charles Middleton, Frank Shannon, Anne Gwynne, Lee Powell.

ARLINE PRETTY

Arline Pretty (her real name) was born in Washington, D.C., on September 5, 1893. After graduating from the public schools and a private finishing school, she joined the Columbia stock company to play ingenue parts and leads for three years. Later she appeared with Charles Hanaford in Shakespearean plays.

Arline made her screen debut in 1913 with a small company based in Tampa, Florida. The film was *Love's Justice* ('13) and the male star was Edwin Carewe. In 1914 she signed with Universal and made 16 two-reelers with King Baggot, the first being *The Old Guard* ('14), the last, *The Millionaire Engineer* ('16).

Arline joined the Vitagraph Company long enough to make a couple of features and the serial *The Secret Kingdom* ('17). The Graustarkian film's location alternated between the mythical kingdom and the American West. Arline was third-billed as Madame Savatz, an evil woman in league with the ambitious Prime Minister Simond, who stops at nothing to gain the throne. Charles Richman is Crown Prince Phillip and Dorothy Kelly is Princess Julia.

Leaving Vitagraph in 1917, Arline played opposite Douglas Fairbanks in *In Again, Out Again* ('17), an Artcraft film featuring Arline as the deputy sheriff's daughter. She kept the hero busy getting into jail so that he could be near her, as her protective father wouldn't allow her outside the jailhouse grounds.

Next she went to Pathé for the third lead in *The Hidden Hand* ('17). Again she is a wicked woman, this time the confederate of the villain, "The Hidden Hand," a creature whose right hand is covered by a claw-like mitten.

Henry G. Sell and Arline Pretty filled the lead roles in *A Woman in Grey* ('20), with capable but unknown actors in the supporting roles. While Sell was best-known at the time for his work with Pearl White in *The Fatal Ring* and *The Lightning Raider* (Pathé serials of 1917–18), Pretty was the real drawing card. The house chosen to represent the Armory estate was as much a star as any of the human actors. Its sliding wall panels, mysterious staircases inside the walls and other trick devices brought into play by the storyline lent themselves well to the eerie feeling sought by the writers, and certainly made access by the villain considerably easier. The end result was a highly enjoyable and most representative example of the silent serial at its very best; writers still had faith in its appeal and future, and audiences shared that faith at the box office by the reappearance week after week to see how the heroine survived.

Arline continued in pictures for many years, but after the coming of sound she worked mainly as an extra at MGM, seldom earning a credit in the cast listing. But in those few years when she was a popular player, she earned and saved enough to provide for herself in leaner times, and did not meet the fate of so many actresses. She enjoyed good health for most of her life and lived to the age of 92, her death occurring in Los Angeles on April 14, 1978. Her survivors were three nieces.

Serials

1917

The Hidden Hand. Pathé, [15 Chapters] D: James Vincent; SP: Arthur B. Reeve, Charles W. Goddard; LP: Doris Kenyon, Sheldon Lewis, Mahlon Hamilton, Arline Pretty.

The Secret Kingdom. Vit., [15 Chapters] D: Theodore Marston, Charles J. Brabin; LP: Charles Richman, Dorothy Kelly, Arline Pretty, William Dunn.

1920

A Woman in Grey. Serico, [15 Chapters] D: James Vincent; S: C. N. and A. M. Williamson; SP: Walter Richard Hall; P: George H. Wiley; LP: Henry G. Sell, Arline Pretty, Fred Jones, James A. Heenan, Ann Brodie, Violet de Bicardi, Jane Mair, Jack Newton, Jack Manning, Adelaine Fitzgallen.

DICK PURCELL

As star of *Captain America* ('44), Richard Gerald Purcell, Jr., billed as Dick Purcell, kept kids whooping it up for 15 successive Saturdays as he went about thwarting the efforts of the minions of "The Scarab" to carry out the dictates of their evil leader. Captain America (who is in reality District Attorney Grant Gardner) is aided by his assistant Gail Richards (Lorna Gray/Adrian Booth). The Scarab is played by Lionel Atwill, and George J. Lewis portrayed Matson, his chief lieutenant.

The serial deviated quite a bit from the comic strip, but young viewers didn't seem to mind. As to be expected from Republic, it was one fight after another and chase after chase. Deserving of credit is stuntman Dale Van Sickel, who doubled Purcell throughout.

Starting with *Ceiling Zero* ('35), Purcell gradually built his career, film after film. He was in 11 programmers in 1936, eight in '37, 12 in '38, five in '39, six in '40, and 22 between '41 and '44.

Purcell was born on August 5, 1905, in Greenwich, Connecticut. He attended Catholic grade school and high school and graduated from Fordham University, where he was active in sports, especially swimming and boxing.

Purcell acted in several plays in New York and it was there that a talent scout from Warner Brothers noticed him and arranged a screen test. He became a Warner Brothers contract player and appeared in all sorts of roles in the years 1936–38. After leaving Warner Brothers, he freelanced "all over town."

A few of his many films are *Brides Are Like That* ('36), *Bullets or Ballots* ('36), *Pub-*

Dick Purcell slugs Ken Terrell in *Captain America* (Republic, 1944).

lic Enemy's Wife ('36), *Navy Blues* ('37), *Reported Missing* ('37), *Wine, Women, and Horses* ('37), *Alcatraz Island* ('38), *Over the Wall* ('38), *Valley of the Giants* ('38, *Garden of the Moon* ('38), *Mystery House* ('38), *Air Devils* ('38), *The Daredevil Drivers* ('38), *Streets of New York* ('39), *Blackwell's Island* ('39), *Heroes in Blue* ('39), *The Bank Dick* ('40), *Outside the Three-Mile Limit* ('40), *New Moon* ('40), *Flight Command* ('40), *King of the Zombies* ('41), *Bullets for O'Hara* ('41), *The Pittsburg Kid* ('41), *No Hands on the Clock* ('41), *Two in a Taxi* ('41), *Torpedo Boat* ('42), *The Phantom Killer* ('42), *I Live on Danger* ('42), *In Old California* ('42), *X Marks the Spot* ('42), *Aerial Gunner* ('43), *High Explosives* ('43), *Reveille for Beverly* ('43), *Mystery of the 13th Guest* ('43), *Timber Queen* ('44), *Trocadero* ('44) and *Farewell My Lovely* ('44).

Purcell married Ethelind Terry, a Ziegfeld Follies girl, in March 1942. The marriage lasted a scant three months. He never remarried.

Purcell was a licensed pilot and active in the Civil Air Patrol. He also enjoyed yachting, a love held in common with Dave O'Brien and Buck Jones.

Leave It to the Irish ('44) was Purcell's last film. In April 1944 he played 18 holes of golf at the Riviera Country Club, and suffered a massive heart attack in the locker room following his game. He was dead when found.

On April 13 a Requiem Mass was held at St. Mary Magdalen Church, followed by interment at the Holy Cross Cemetery and Mausoleum in Culver City, California.

Serials

1938

Red Barry. Univ., [13 Chapters] D: Ford Beebe, Alan James; LP: Buster Crabbe, Frances Robinson, Wade Boteler, Edna Sedgwill, Frank Lackteen, Philip Ahn, Wheeler Oakman, William Gould, Cyril Delevanti.

1944

Captain America. Rep., [15 Chapters] D: John English, Elmer Clifton; SP: Royal Cole, Ronald Davidson, Basil Dickey, Jesse Duffy, Harry Fraser, Grant Nelson, Joseph Poland; AP: W. J. O'Sullivan; LP: Dick Purcell, Lorna Gray [Adrian Booth], Lionel Atwill, Charles Trowbridge, George J. Lewis, Robert Fraser, LeRoy Mason.

CHARLES QUIGLEY

The late Warner Oland was responsible for launching Charles Quigley on a stage and screen career. The two families were neighbors and close friends when Charles was a

Charles Quigley and Joyce Bryant in *The Iron Claw* (Columbia, 1941).

little boy in his home town of New Britain, Connecticut, and the star was always telling the Quigley family that Charles ought to go on the stage.

When young Quigley completed school, he took the advice of Oland and enrolled at the American Academy of Dramatic Arts. Two years after his graduation, David Belasco chose him in the annual selection of the outstanding student of the class and sponsored him in his professional debut as understudy to Ian Keith in the play *The Desert*.

Later he stepped into an important role with Mary and Florence Nash in *Ladies' Virtue*. The following summer he added to his practical experience by playing in stock at Portland, Maine. He returned to New York with the opening of the season to appear in a series of plays, including William A. Brady's *Tin Soldier* (and, incidentally, learned what a phenomenally short time it takes for many Broadway productions to open and close).

Quigley played for a year in *The Road to Rome*, the Robert Sherwood hit, in Chicago and on tour in the Middle West. The next summer he again worked in stock in Rochester, Buffalo and Toronto, appearing with Alice Brady in a number of plays. He went back to Broadway to join Walter Hampden, playing leading and juvenile roles in the great thespian's repertory. He was Christian in Hampden's *Cyrano de Bergerac*.

In the meantime, real love had been blooming along with stage romances in Quigley's career and in 1928 he married Harriet Blue. She was studying at Columbia University and attending the Fagin Drama School where he met her while doing a play there. He appeared with Ethel Barrymore for a year or more in *The Love Duel, Scarlet Sister Mary* and other plays.

Quigley had turned down several previous Hollywood offers when 20th Century-Fox tested him and this time he signed on the dotted line. However, his Hollywood debut was not sensational. He was put in *Charlie Chan's Secret* ('36) and played the juvenile lead in *King of Burlesque* ('36) with Warner Baxter and Alice Faye. He did some

more not-especially-significant parts, but Hollywood still was keeping a close eye on this Broadway newcomer.

Following his stay at 20th Century-Fox he was signed by Columbia. He was Mary Astor's leading man in *Lady from Nowhere* ('36) and in the next two years played romantic leads in numerous Columbia pictures, frequently being teamed with another up-and-coming young player named Rita Cansino (Hayworth).

In 1939, Republic produced its serial *Daredevils of the Red Circle* starring Quigley, Herman Brix [Bruce Bennett] and Dave Sharpe. The part of Gene Townley, professional high diver and all-around athlete (and the apparent brains of the trio), was awarded to Quigley. He made a believable hero, displaying definite acting ability and a winning personality. Sharpe portrayed Burt Knowles, the famous escape artist, and Brix was Tiny Dawson, the strongman of the team. The Red Circle was the label for their sideshow trapeze act.

The fellows become involved with the forces of evil when a deranged escaped convict proceeds to ruin the business and personal life of a former partner. The boys have to rely on their nimble feet, strong physiques and ready fists, whereas the opposition is equipped with all the assorted paraphernalia of serial villains— lethal gas, death-dealing rays, strange gadgets of doom, secret passageways, many henchmen and limitless money.

Quigley broke away from studio contracts and freelanced for a while. Because he was accommodating enough to "stooge" for Evelyn Keyes when she tested for *Gone with the Wind*, he landed a contract with RKO in 1940. Ben Piazza, head of the talent department of the studio, saw the test and signed him. There he played featured and supporting parts in 11 pictures, among them *Men Against the Sky* ('40) with Richard Dix, Edmund Lowe and Kent Taylor. MGM borrowed him for a principal part with Joan Crawford in *A Woman's Face* ('41).

In 1941, Quigley starred in the Columbia chapterplay *The Iron Claw*. In the story, Oliver Benson quarrels with his two brothers over the division of a huge fortune in gold, then is murdered by a mysterious man known as "The Iron Claw."

Newspaper reporter Bob Lane (Quigley) and his pal Jack Strong (Walter Sande) come to the eerie old murder house and find the suspects as numerous as the relatives. These include Anton Benson (Forrest Taylor), older brother of the murdered man; another brother, Roy (Norman Willis), an ex-convict; Benson's nephew, Dr. James Benson (Alex Callam); and Simon Leach (Allen Doone), who is married to Milly, Anton's daughter. Lane discovers all are after Anton's gold and that an outsider, Silk (Charles King), is hanging around conniving with Roy. The only sincere person there is Patricia Benson (Joyce Bryant), Anton's niece. After a series of events, which sees Anton and Simon Leach murdered, Lane succeeds in identifying the Claw and the fiend is shot to death trying to escape.

There are amusing incidents in the serial. Even though the humor is mere slapstick and old-hat gags, there is a general amusing air which brings a share of smiles and chuckles to the viewer who is willing to enjoy a mild send-up of cliffhangers. Even if the humor is discounted, *The Iron Claw* is an action-filled, fast-paced serial with the elements a fan expects mostly present and accounted for. *The Iron Claw* is not one of the great serials, but it is a good one.

Quigley left pictures and Hollywood to take an assistant executive job in a manufacturing firm. He ended his two years sabbatical leave from pictures when a friend, who knew that Paramount was looking for leading men, showed William Meiklejohn, the studio's talent supervisor, a reel of film from one of Charles' little-known pictures. Meiklejohn was so interested that he kept the film to run off the next day for B. G. DeSylvn, Paramount executive producer. After that, Charles was called in for a special screen test. When it was over, he had a Paramount contract and a top spot on the studio's roster of romantic leading men. His first assignment was the masculine starring role in the novel musical *National Barn Dance* ('44).

In 1946, Quigley again headed up the cast of a serial, *The Crimson Ghost*. A counter-atomic device called the Cyclotrode is invented by Prof. Chambers (Kenne Duncan), whose assistant Duncan Richards (Quigley) is a well-known criminologist. Secretly one of Chambers' associates is the Crimson Ghost, who goes all-out to acquire the device, with which he plans to destroy lighting and power systems and paralyze the activities of the police. Richards is assisted by secretary Diana Farnsworth (Linda Stirling).

Quigley appeared in three more serials for Columbia in which he was a supporting player, a comedown for the once-heroic star. Subsequent roles were small, few and far between. He died in Los Angeles in 1964 at age 58 from cirrhosis of the liver.

Serials

1939

Daredevils of the Red Circle. Rep., [12 Chapters] D: William Witney, John English; SP: Barry Shipman, Franklyn Adreon, Rex Taylor, Ronald Davidson, Sol Shor; AP: Robert Beeche; Cam: William Nobles; Mus: William Lava; LP: Charles Quigley, Herman Brix, David Sharpe, Carole Landis, Miles Mander.

1941

The Iron Claw. Col., [15 Chapters] D: James W. Horne; SP: Basil Dickey, George H. Plympton, Jesse A. Duffy, Charles R. Condon, Jack Stanley; S: Arthur Stringer; P: Larry Darmour; Cam: James S. Brown, Jr., Mus: Lee Zahler; LP: Charles Quigley, Joyce Bryant, Forrest Taylor, Walter Sande, Norman Willis, Charles King, Edythe Elliott.

1946

The Crimson Ghost. Rep., [12 Chapters] D: William Witney, Fred C. Brannon; SP: Albert DeMond, Basil Dickey, Jesse Duffy, Sol Shor; AP: Ronald Davidson; Mus: Mort Glickman; Cam: Bud Thackery; LP: Charles Quigley, Linda Stirling, Clayton Moore, I. Stanford Jolley, Forrest Taylor, Sam Flint, Rex Lease, Tom Steele, Virginia Carroll.

1947

Brick Bradford. Col., [15 Chapters] D: Spencer Bennet; SP: George H. Plympton, Arthur Hoerl, Lewis Clay; P: Sam Katzman; Cam: Ira H. Morgan; Mus: Mischa Bakaleinikoff; LP: Kane Richmond, Rick Vallin, Linda Johnson, Pierre Watkin, Charles Quigley, Jack Ingram, John Merton, Charles King, Wheeler Oakman, Carol Forman, John Hart, Noel Neill.

1948

Superman. Col., [15 Chapters] D: Spencer Bennet, Thomas Carr; LP: Kirk Alyn, Noel Neill, Tommy Bond, Pierre Watkin, Carol Forman, Jack Ingram, George Meeker, Charles King, Virginia Carroll, Terry Frost.

1950

Pirates of the High Seas. Col., [15 Chapters] D: Spencer Bennet, Thomas Carr; SP: Joseph Poland, George H. Plympton, Charles R. Condon, David Mathews; LP: Buster Crabbe, Lois Hall, Tommy Farrell, Gene Roth, Tris Coffin, Neyle Morrow, Stanley Price, Hugh Prosser, Lee Roberts, Charles Quigley, John Hart, Terry Frost.

EDDIE QUILLAN

Eddie Quillan was born on March 31, 1907, in Philadelphia. He was on the vaudeville stage with a family act from the age of seven. He entered films in 1926 and appeared in a number of Mack Sennett two-reelers, including *Kitty from Killarney, Pass the Dumplings, The Plumber's Daughter, Puppy Love Time* and others.

Quillan ran the acting gamut — campus hero, light leading man, hero's pal, comedian, supporting player and character parts.

For his role in *Mutiny on the Bounty* (MGM, '35), he received the first Screen Actors Guild Award accorded an actor in a supporting role. For the same portrayal he also won *Box Office* magazine's Blue Ribbon Award. Other memorable roles were in *The Godless Girl* (Pathé, '28), *Made for Each Other* (UA, '39), *Young Mr. Lincoln* (TCF, '39) and *The Grapes of Wrath* (TCF, '40).

Less memorable film roles included *Night Work* ('29), *Geraldine* ('29), *Big Money* ('30), *Girl Crazy* ('32), *The Gridiron Flash* ('34), *London by Night* ('37), *Allegheny Uprising* ('39), *The Flame of New Orleans* ('41), *Flying Blind* ('41), *Here Comes Kelly* ('43), *Dark Mountain* ('44), *The Bounty Killer* ('65), *The Ghost and Mr. Chicken* ('66), *How to Frame a Figg* ('70) and *The Strongest Man in the World* ('75).

Eddie worked in such television series as *The People's Choice, Julia, The James Stewart Show, Columbo, Mannix, Police Story, Perry Mason, I Love Lucy, The Jack Benny Show, Little House on the Prairie, Baretta, Our Miss Brooks, Highway to Heaven, Moonlighting, The A-Team* and *Valentine's Day.*

Quillan was in three serials in the mid–40s. In *Mystery of the River Boat* ('44) he plays the buddy of Robert Lowery, who returns home from college and is framed for a murder. He escapes. Police later believe in his innocence and solicit his help in rounding up the real criminals.

In *Jungle Queen* ('45), the Nazi high command sends agents into the African jungle to stir up the Tongghill tribes against the Allies, but they must reckon with Lothel (Ruth Roman), the mysterious queen of the jungle, who can walk through walls of fire. In times of peril she comes to the aid of three Americans (Edward Norris, Quillan, Lois Collier) who also oppose the Nazis and their leader, a doctor posing as a friendly scientist.

In *Jungle Raiders* ('45), the hero and heroine search for their fathers in the African jungles. Jake Regan (Charles King), owner of a trading post, following up on rumors of a gigantic Arzec treasure, kidnaps Dr. Reed (Budd Buster), one of the parents, hoping to extract information from him about the treasure. When Bob Moore (Kane Richmond) and Ann Reed (Janet Shaw) show up, Regan tries to liquidate them. Meanwhile, Dr. Moore (John Elliott), Bob's father, has aroused the enmity of Zara (Carol Hughes), priestess of the hidden village, who aligns herself with Regan after Dr. Moore cures the chief of a malady. After surviving a number of attempts on their lives, Bob and Ann find their fathers and the bad guys fall victim to one of their own traps. Quillan is Joe, sidekick to the hero.

Quillan never married. He lived with an unmarried sister and his mother until her death in 1969. Three married sisters and two brothers lived nearby.

Quillan died on July 19, 1990.

Serials

1944

Mystery of the River Boat. Univ., [13 Chapters] D: Ray Taylor, Lewis D. Collins; SP: Maurice Tombragel; S: Ande Lamb; LP: Robert Lowery, Eddie Quillan, Lyle Talbot, Marion Martin, Marjorie Clements.

1945

Jungle Queen. Univ., [13 Chapters] D: Ray Taylor, Lewis D. Collins; SP: George H. Plympton, Ande Lamb, Morgan B. Cox; LP: Edward Norris, Lois Collier, Eddie Quillan, Douglass Dumbrille, Ruth Roman, Tala Birell, Clarence Muse, Cy Kendall, Edmund Cobb, John Merton.

Jungle Raiders. Col., [15 Chapters] D: Lesley Selander; SP: Ande Lamb, George H. Plympton; P: Sam Katzman; Cam: Ira H. Morgan; Mus: Lee Zahler; LP: Kane Richmond, Eddie Quillan, Veda Ann Borg, Carol Hughes, Janet Shaw, Jack Ingram.

ESTHER RALSTON

Esther Ralston got her big break in *Peter Pan* ('24) because she epitomized the old-fashioned girl of a bygone era, and yet was only 22 at the time. She was sort of a mid–Victorian throwback, a living portrayal of Jane Eyre, an Amy March of *Little Women* come to life, a living symbol of sweet beauty and grace. And it was because of this particular charm that she was chosen to play a child's conception of a mother, a young person who loves to play with them and to be their companion.

Esther made her stage debut when two years old. She was born in Bar Harbor, Maine, on September 17, 1902. Her parents, May Howard and Henry Walter Ralston, were prominent in a theatrical company known as "The Ralston Family," which toured the country presenting Shakespearean plays to high school and college audiences. Her four brothers also participated in the act. When she was seven, she could recite chapter after chapter from the Bible and entire acts from Shakespearean plays. Esther attended school in a score of states while traveling with her father's company. She performed dramatic scenes from many plays and was billed as "Baby Esther, America's youngest Juliet."

The family settled in California in 1916 or '17 to take advantage of the growing film industry, and Esther was soon employed as an extra while continuing her education. After graduation from Glendale High School, her increasing success eventually broke up the family act for good.

The earliest credit we have for her is Paramount's *Huckleberry Finn* ('19); most of her early films in which she was an extra or bit player are unknown. By 1921 she was playing the heroine in Westerns with such saddle stalwarts as Pete Morrison, Roy Stewart, Ken Maynard, Hoot Gibson and Conway Tearle. In 1923 she won the role as William Desmond's leading lady in the Universal serial *The Phantom Fortune* and in 1924 was billed third behind William Duncan and Edith Johnson in *Wolves of the North*, another thrills-by-the-week release from Universal.

Ralston became, overnight, a major star after playing Mrs. Darling in *Peter Pan*. She was big box office for the next five years and her films and co-stars were legion. She wore $1000 dresses, lived in a mansion, rode in a chauffeur-driven Lincoln town car and enjoyed all the perks of a screen goddess in the golden years of Hollywood, living high, wide and handsome and paying no income tax.

Esther married George Webb, an ex-vaudevillian, in 1925. Her daughter Mary Esther was dubbed the $100,000 baby since that is what it cost Esther in movie contracts to take time out for motherhood. Knowing that her voice was inadequate for sound films, Esther and George put together a vaudeville act and hit the road for 42 consecutive weeks—in miserable tank towns, in theaters whose dressing rooms were not big enough to hold both her and her trunk.

During the grueling 42 weeks, she developed the confidence and voice that enabled her, upon returning to Hollywood, to obtain the leading role opposite Lawrence Tibbett in MGM's *The Prodigal* ('31), playing the part of a smart, sophisticated woman of the world. She earned $3,500 a week in vaudeville, whereas her MGM salary was around $4,000 a week.

She was soon off to England for vaudeville appearances and to make two films, one with Conrad Veidt and one with Basil Rathbone. Upon returning home, MGM gave her a contract and then loaned her out for all her pictures.

By 1937 she was back working in serials, but this time not in a leading capacity. She called it quits in 1941 after appearing in *San Francisco Docks* for Universal. After Webb's death, some time during the 1930s, Esther married a musician, Will Morgan. They were divorced in 1938. In 1939 she married Ted Lloyd, a columnist, and they had two children, a boy, Ted, Jr., and a girl, Judy. It was for this reason that she left the screen for good — to become a full-fledged mother to her youngsters and wife to her husband.

This marriage lasted only until 1954, when the Lloyds were divorced. She then moved to New York, where she reared her children. For ten years she worked in a Long Island department store.

In 1961 she landed the role of Helen Lee in the NBC-TV serial drama *Our Five Daughters* and played in it until its demise. Thereafter, she appeared in summer stock and other television shows for a while. In 1965 she became an actors' agent and worked at it for several years, subsequently becoming a lighting consultant for the Glens Falls, New York, Electrical Supply Company. She worked in that capacity until the mid–70s.

In the summer of 1975 she returned to the stage at Lake George's Towers Hall Playhouse in *Arsenic and Old Lace* for a limited engagement. In 1978, she moved back to California, more or less retired, and spent some time putting the finishing touches on her autobiography, *Some Day We'll Laugh*.

Esther Ralston died in 1994 in Ventura, California, at age 91.

Serials

1923

The Phantom Fortune. Univ., [12 Chapters] D: Robert F. Hill; S/SP: Anthony Coldeway, George Hively; LP: William Desmond, Esther Ralston, Lewis Sargent, Harry DeVere.

1924

Wolves of the North. Univ., [10 Chapters] D: William Duncan; SP: Frank H. Clark; S: Katherine and Robert Pinkerton; LP: William

Duncan, Edith Johnson, Joseph W. Girard, Esther Ralston, Edward Cecil.

Fight and Win. Univ., [10 Episodes] D: Erle C. Kenton, Jesse Robbins; LP: Jack Dempsey, Esther Ralston, Hayden Stevenson, Edgar Kennedy, Carmelita Geraghty.

1937

Jungle Menace. Col., [15 Chapters] D: George Melford, Harry Fraser; SP: George Rosener, Sherman L. Lowe, Harry Hoyt [Fraser], George Melford; P: Jack Fier, Louis Weiss; Mus: Abe Meyer; Cam: Edward Linden, Herman Schoop; LP: Frank Buck, Esther Ralston, Reginald Denny, Charlotte Henry, John St. Polis, Duncan Renaldo.

The Mysterious Pilot. Col., [15 Chapters] D: Spencer G. Bennet; SP: George Rosener, George M. Merrick; LP: Frank Hawks, Dorothy Sebastian, Rex Lease, Guy Bates Post, Kenneth Harlan, Yakima Canutt, Frank Lackteen, Clara Kimball Young, Esther Ralston, Harry Harvey, Ted Adams, Tom London.

JANE RANDOLPH

Jane Randolph, the tall, dark-haired all-American beauty, was born Jane Roermer on October 30, 1919, in Youngstown, Ohio. She is probably remembered best for her role in RKO's *Cat People* ('42) rather than for the serial *The Mysterious Mr. M* ('46) where she was the second (Pamela Blake was first) leading female.

Jane was in *The Curse of the Cat People* ('44) and was active in "B" films until 1948 when she terminated her film career after completing *Abbott and Costello Meet Frankenstein.*

Jane married wealthy Jaime del Amo and moved to Madrid, Spain, where she became a leader in Madrid society.

Her other films include *The Male Animal* ('42), *Highways by Night* ('42), *The Falcon's Brother* ('42), *The Falcon Strikes Back* ('43), *Jealousy* ('45), *A Sporting Chance* ('45), *T-Men* ('48) and *Open Secret* ('48).

Serial

1946

The Mysterious Mr. M. Univ., [13 Chapters] D: Lewis D. Collins, Vernon Keays; SP: Joseph Poland, Paul Huston, Barry Shipman; AP: Morgan B. Cox; LP: Richard Martin, Pamela Blake, Dennis Moore, Jane Randolph, Danny Morton, Byron Foulger, Keith Richards, Beatrice Roberts, Robert Barron, Joseph Hayworth.

HERBERT RAWLINSON

If Herbert Rawlinson's father had not insisted that he become a Canadian farmer, he might never have become an actor. When Rawlinson graduated from school, his father sent him to Canada to learn the intricacies of farming, but young Rawlinson found farm life so dull, he ran away within weeks and joined a traveling circus, as a property man, and thus embarked on a career that eventually led him to the stage and screen.

Born in Brighton, England, on November 15, 1885, the son of a prosperous real estate man, Rawlinson was educated in the English public schools and a private academy in Heywood's Heath. Later he attended the College de St. Servan in Brittany, and had forgotten most of his English by the time he graduated!

His first motion picture job was with his friend Hobart Bosworth in *The Novice* ('11), produced by the Selig Company. Bosworth continued with Selig until he started a company of his own. Rawlinson joined Bosworth, appearing in *The Sea Wolf* ('13), a major film of that year. He later worked in leading roles for Universal in one-, two- and three-reelers. In 1914 he starred in

In *The Black Box* (Universal, 1919).

the six-reel *Damon and Pythias*, which propelled his career forward. The film featured Ann Little and Cleo Madison.

Most of Rawlinson's films through 1914 were one- and two-reelers. His leading ladies included Kathlyn Williams, Betty Harte, Jeanne Pardee, Myrtle Stedman, Ivy Shepard, Bessie Eyton, Lillian Leighton, Jane Keckley, Cleo Madison, Eugenie Besserer, Adele Lane, Victoria Forde, Marguerite Loveridge, Agnes Vernon, Lillian Hayward, Camille Astor and Jean Taylor. Betty Harte and Anna Dodge were the most frequent leading ladies.

In 1915, Rawlinson made his first big splash as the hero of a 15-episode chapterplay, *The Black Box*, in which he plays a variation on the scientific detective theme made popular by Arthur B. Reeve's fictional character, Craig Kennedy.

In 1919, Rawlinson made *The Carter Case* with Marguerite Marsh, this time playing Craig Kennedy, called in by Anita Carver (Marsh) to solve the mystery of the death of her father, whose secret formulas are being stolen and sold to his competitors abroad. Produced by Oliver Films, it lacked the distribution of a major studio.

In 1925–26, Rawlinson starred in one Beacon and two Rayart serials, each in ten chapters. First was *Flame Fighter* ('25), produced by Beacon but released through Rayart. It told the story of fireman Jack Sparks, who squares off against corruption and crooked contractors in the process of proving his innocence of malfeasance.

Phantom Police ('26), a Rayart serial, tells the story of the dangerous work of the New York police force. Rawlinson is a policeman on the lookout for Tracy Downs (Purnell Pratt), suspected of a diamond robbery in Paris. Interestingly, two chimpanzees were also involved in the robbery and their services are requisitioned on behalf of crime detection.

Rayart's *Trooper 77* opens with a man being murdered in a roadhouse; Phil Manning (Duke Worne) imagines that he is the criminal. His desire to escape leads him to join the State Constabulary, in which his brother Steve (Rawlinson) is an inspector. Steve, who is trying to solve the murder, takes to the field as "Trooper 77" and is crossed by Robert Kincaid (Thomas Lingham), a suave villain who, besides planning the murder in question, has been involved in a plot that landed Mary Stanhop's (Hazel Deane) father in jail. Steve and Mary have a series of exciting adventures until the miscreants are finally run to earth.

In feature films (four or more reels in length), Rawlinson's leading ladies were Marie Walcamp, Anna Little, Dorothy Davenport, Neva Gerber, Jean Hathaway, Fritzie Ridgway, Ruth Clifford, Mary MacDonald, Brownie Vernon, Marjorie Rambeau, Blanche Gray, Beatrice Van, Ruby Lafayette, Sally Starr, Mabel Normand, Geraldine Farrar, Billie Burke, Florence Billings, Sylvia Breamer, Catherine Colbert, Leila Valentine, Grace Darmond, Eulalie Jensen, Anita Stewart, Clara Kimball Young, Ethel Clayton, Priscilla Dean, Marjorie Daw, Doris Pawn, Gertrude Olmstead, Virginia Valli, Margaret Campbell, Harriet Hammond, Barbara Bedford, Lillian Rich, Claire Adams, June Elridge, Edna Murphy, Katherine Perry, ZaSu Pitts, Esther Ralston, Beatrice Burnham, Ruth Dwyer, Kathleen Myers, Alice Lake, Carmelita Geraghty, Dorothy Devore, Brenda Lane, Helen Ferguson, Clara Bow, Elaine Hammerstein, Madge Bellamy, Katherine MacDonald, Alma Rubens, Eva Novak, Betty Compson, Wanda Hawley, Gladys Brockwell, Shirley Palmer, Marion Mack and Dorothy Manners.

Rawlinson never starred in any really big pictures, but he always seemed to be in demand and worked steadily in formula ("B") pictures. The Rawlinson image was a familiar sight on the screen almost to the end of the '20s. Among his more popular films were *Come Thru* ('17), *Charge It* ('21), *Prairie Wife* ('25), *The Adventurous Sex* ('25) and *The Bugle Call* ('27).

He made no movies from 1928 to 1933. Another gap in his credits are the years 1945, 1946 (one film), 1947 and 1950. During these years he was appearing on stage or working in radio, where his delightful English voice found a ready market in the golden years of broadcasting. He appeared in more than 100 radio shows and was frequently on *Lux Radio Theatre*.

While often seen as a society dandy in romantic melodramas, he also played police officers, firemen, undercover agents, scientific detectives, cowboys, cavalry officers and a variety of supporting roles.

Rawlinson's first wife was Roberta Arnold, whom he married in the late teens. He divorced her in 1923 on the grounds of desertion. She was an actress who was often on the road or the New York stage. Herbert did not let the grass grow under his feet. He married Lorraine Abigail Long, a society girl, in 1924, but this marriage, too, ended in divorce (in 1947).

Rawlinson collapsed in his apartment at the Hollywood Athletic Club in July 1953 and was rushed to the Motion Picture Hospital in Woodland Hills, where he died on July 13. His physician ascribed the actor's death to lung cancer.

Rawlinson left a son and a daughter. He had just completed a role in an Edward Wood, Jr., film, *Jail Bait*.

Serials

1915

The Black Box. Univ., [15 Chapters] D/SP: Otis Turner; S: E. Phillips Oppenheim; LP: Herbert Rawlinson, Anna Little, Laura Oakley, William Worthington, Helen Wright, Beatrice Van, Frank Lloyd, Duke Worne.

1919

The Carter Case. Oliver, [15 Chapters] D: Donald McKenzie, William W. Grey; SP: Arthur B. Reeve, John W. Grey; LP: Herbert Rawlinson, Margaret Marsh, Ethel Grey Terry, William Pike, Kempton Greene.

1925

The Flame Fighter. Beacon/Rayart, [10 Chapters] D/S: Robert Dillon; LP: Herbert Rawlinson, Brenda Lane, Jerome La Gasse, Edward Fetherstone, Dorothy Donald.

1926

Trooper 77. Rayart, [10 Chapters] D: Duke Worne; S: George W. Pyper; P: W. Ray Johnston; LP: Herbert Rawlinson, Hazel Deane, Jimmy Aubrey, Thomas Lingham, Duke Worne, Ruth Royce.

Phantom Police. Rayart, [10 Chapters] D: Robert Dillon; LP: Herbert Rawlinson, Gloria Joy, Eddie Fetherstone, Purnell Pratt, Dick Gordon, S. G. Wilcox, Jack Fowler, James Gordon, Max and Moritz (chimpanzees).

1936

Robinson Crusoe of Clipper Island. Rep., [14 Chapters] D: Mack V. Wright, Ray Taylor; P: Nat Levine; Cam: William Nobles; Mus: Harry Grey; LP: Ray Mala, Rex, Buck, Mamo Clark, Herbert Rawlinson, William Neill, John Ward, Selmer Jackson, Robert Kortman, George Chesebro, Edmund Cobb, John Picorri.

1937

SOS Coast Guard. Rep., [12 Chapters] D: William Witney, Alan James; SP: Barry Shipman, Franklyn Adreon; S: Morgan Cox, Ronald Davidson; AP: Sol C. Siegel; Cam: William Nobles; LP: Ralph Byrd, Bela Lugosi, Maxine Doyle, Herbert Rawlinson, Dick Alexander, John Picorri, George Chesebro, Roy Barcroft.

Blake of Scotland Yard. Victory, [15 Chapters] D: Robert Hill; P: Sam Katzman; S: Rock Hawkey; Cam: Bill Hyer; SP: Basil Dickey, William Buchanan; LP: Ralph Byrd, Herbert Rawlinson, Joan Barclay, Lloyd Hughes, Lucille Lund, Sam Flint, Nick Stuart, Herman Brix [Bruce Bennett], Gail Newbury.

1940

Flash Gordon Conquers the Universe. Univ., [12 Chapters] D: Ford Beebe, Ray Taylor; LP: Buster Crabbe, Carol Hughes, Charles Middleton, Frank Shannon, Anne Gwynne, Roland Drew, Lee Powell, Ray Mala, Jeanne Kelly [Jean Brooks], Herbert Rawlinson.

King of the Royal Mounted. Rep., [12 Chapters] D: William Witney, John English; LP: Allan Lane, Robert Strange, Robert Kellard,

Lita Conway, Herbert Rawlinson, Bryant Washburn, Stanley Andrews, Richard Simmons, Norman Willis, John Davidson.

1941

King of the Texas Rangers. Rep., [12 Chapters] D: William Witney, John English; LP: Slingin' Sammy Baugh, Neil Hamilton, Pauline Moore, Duncan Renaldo, Charles Trowbridge, Monte Blue, Kermit Maynard, Roy Barcroft, Jack Ingram, Stanley Blystone.

Don Winslow of the Navy. Univ., [12 Chapters] D: Ford Beebe, Ray Taylor; LP: Don Terry, Walter Sande, Wade Boteler, John Litel, Claire Dodd, Anne Nagel, Samuel S. Hinds, Kurt Katch, Robert Barron, Lane Chandler, Herbert Rawlinson.

1942

Perils of the Royal Mounted. Col., [15 Chapters] D: James W. Horne; P: Larry Darmour; LP: Nell O'Day, Robert Stevens [Kellard], Herbert Rawlinson, Kenneth MacDonald, John Elliott, Richard Fiske, Rick Vallin, Charles King, Tom London.

Perils of Nyoka. Rep., [15 Chapters] D: William Witney; LP: Kay Aldridge, Clayton Moore, William Benedict, Lorna Gray [Adrian Booth], Tristram Coffin, Charles Middleton, Forbes Murray, Emil Van Horn, Tom Steele, Herbert Rawlinson.

1943

Daredevils of the West. Rep., [12 Chapters] D: John English; LP: Allan Lane, Kay Aldridge, Eddie Acuff, William Haade, Robert Frazer, Ted Adams, Jack Rockwell, George J. Lewis, Kenneth Harlan, Rex Lease, Chief Thundercloud.

The Masked Marvel. Rep., [12 Chapters] D: Spencer Bennet; LP: Tom Steele, William Forrest, Louise Currie, Johnny Arthur, David Bacon, Rod Bacon, Anthony Warde, Richard Clarke, Roy Barcroft, Bill Healy, Jack O'Shea, Edward Van Sloan, Herbert Rawlinson, George J. Lewis, Lee Roberts.

1948

Superman. Col., [15 Chapters] D: Spencer G. Bennet, Thomas Carr; P: Sam Katzman; LP:

Kirk Alyn, Noel Neill, Tommy Bond, Pierre Watkin, Carol Forman, Charles Quigley, Luana Walters, Virginia Carroll, Jack Ingram, Terry Frost, Herbert Rawlinson, George Meeker.

ALLENE RAY

In 1924, Pathé introduced a new serial star, Allene Ray. She was born in San Antonio, Texas, January 2, 1901. She had blond hair, hazel eyes and was 5'3". She had been educated in San Antonio and Fort Worth, Texas, and was married to Larry Wheeler. Her motion picture debut had been in 1919 for Western Pictures Corporation, a subsidiary of Weiss Brothers–Artclass. Among her pictures for this company had been *The High Card, Tex O'Reilly, Your Friend and Mine, Partners of the Sunset, Honeymoon Ranch* and *West of the Rio Grande*.

With her striking blonde beauty and athletic prowess, ability to project terror convincingly, exceptionally pleasant screen personality, wistful charm and believability in romantic or dramatic interludes, Allene was a natural for the serial world. She took direction well and, unlike Ruth Roland, was most cooperative and friendly to everyone on a set. She was seldom known to use a double, even though she became Pathé's hottest property. Allene was definitely an introvert, but her beguiling ways and sincere charm quickly endeared her to colleagues. One might even say that she was the "Buck Jones of the fairer sex," a laconic and completely professional performer who took pride in her work, appreciated the genre that made her famous and was loved by all who knew her. She conducted herself in a ladylike manner at all times. If anyone in the serial fraternity deserves to be fitted with a nice little niche in the hall of the immortals, it would be Allene Ray, in whom one's childhood idolization was not misplaced.

Way of a Man ('24), a Western, was a good serial beginning for Allene. She obviously was more at home on a horse than was her leading man, Harold Miller, though he was a good thrill maker, and the story was one she was comfortable with. The Pathé luster was in evidence as George Seitz put his players through their paces.

In *The Fortieth Door* ('24), Allene plays a French girl entrapped by Mohammedons headed by a lustful Frank Lackteen, who would make her his wife. Bruce Gordon played the male lead who wins Allene for his own in the end. With Seitz again directing and Frank Leon Smith writing the scenario, the film's success was almost assured. Allene possessed a rare girlish charm that made her immensely popular with all those with whom she came in contact, and this same charm was projected on the screen. Pathé had hit the mother lode once more when they discovered this great lady.

Ten Scars Make a Man ('24) had Allene back in a Western setting and loved by hero Jack Mower, who had to acquire ten scars before he could have her hand in marriage. It was another winner for the increasingly popular golden-haired beauty from Texas.

Allene had yet to hang on to a leading man. In *Galloping Hoofs* ('24), a story revolving about a treasure box and its secret, she has Johnnie Walker as helpmate in overcoming the machinations of those who wanted to steal her inheritance.

In her fifth serial outing, Pathé gave her Walter Miller as a leading man. Walter exuded virility from every pore and was a seasoned performer, having been in the movies since 1912. The film was *Sunken Silver* ('25). Buried treasure in the Florida Everglades was the foundation for all the excitement and

In *Snowed In* (Pathé, 1926).

skullduggery in this one. A hit with serial enthusiasts, the team of Ray and Miller went to bat again in a baseball-oriented story called *Play Ball* ('25). Spencer Gordon Bennet directed this and the eight Ray-Miller cliffhangers to follow, and he proved to be a worthy successor to George Seitz, under whom he had served an apprenticeship. The story involved a romance between a millionaire's daughter (Ray) and a rookie baseball player (Miller).

The Green Archer ('25) was probably the finest and most popular of the Ray-Miller serials, though the plot was a little bizarre. It starts with an English castle being moved, brick by brick, to the U.S., and coming along uninvited is the ghost of the castle. Also, the owner of the castle kept a mysterious prisoner confined in a dungeon. Allene is the neighbor girl whose curiosity gets the better of her, and Miller is a state policeman who helps her unravel the mystery of the ghost and the prisoner.

Snowed In ('26) took Ray and Miller out of doors again as they tried to capture mail robbers in the High Sierras. As customary with serials, the archvillain was hooded and his identity was not revealed until the last episode. Allene played a girl out to prove her brother innocent of complicity in some robberies and Miller was a forest ranger more than happy to assist such a delectable morsel as Miss Ray. Always fetching, Allene seemed even more so this time around, even though she had little opportunity to wear beautiful clothes. Tightly constructed and expertly executed, *Snowed In* showed Pathé's superiority as a serial maker and what could be accomplished on a limited budget by dedicated people.

House Without a Key ('26) was based on a Charlie Chan book by Earl Derr Biggers and adapted to the screen by Frank Leon Smith. It depicted a family feud, a crime supposedly committed some years earlier, and a chest containing information about that crime. The part of Charlie Chan was played down in order to spotlight the Ray-Miller heroics and romance. Without a mystery villain, the serial, though well-done, was not as exciting, at least for the kids, as previous chapterplays had been.

Allene's next outing, *Melting Millions* ('27), at least had a mystery figure, although he was a friend rather than foe. Allene and Miller are again reunited in a story about a young lady who is the rightful heiress of a fortune and her attempts to gain possession of it. An organized band of wealthy criminals commanded by E. H. Calvert try to prevent her from claiming the inheritance, hoping to get it for themselves.

In *Hawk of the Hills* ('27), a return to the West for Allene, she portrays the kidnapped daughter of a miner, while Walter Miller is again her Prince Charming and protector from "The Hawk" (Frank Lackteen) and his band of cutthroats, who are out to find the location of a secret mine that Allene's father and uncle have steadfastly refused to divulge. Miller, at first an outlaw, cannot withstand the allure of Miss Ray, and quickly becomes her champion.

The quality of the Pathé serial, with the exception of the Ray-Miller vehicles, had slipped considerably by 1928, and the rooster trademark was being stamped on products that once would not have met Pathé's standards. But the Ray-Miller outings remained top-notch thrillers that the old rooster, had he a voice in those days, could have really crowed about. Much credit is due Spencer Bennet, as well as Ray and Miller, for the maintenance of quality on mediocre budgets (around $90,000 to $100,000 a picture).

In *The Man Without a Face* ('28), Allene and Jeanette Loff are sisters in China who, after inheriting a fortune back in the States,

are trying to get home with the help of bank emissary Walter Miller. "The Man Without a Face," the mystery figure so essential in serials, was determined that they not succeed. Suspense was high throughout and the serial was popular.

In her second outing of the year, Allene starred in a Western chapterplay titled *The Yellow Cameo* ('28), and with Edward Hearn instead of Miller playing opposite her. The cameo held the secret to a treasure buried somewhere near an old Spanish mission, and the outlaws (headed by Noble Johnson and Tom London) are after it.

Allene and Miller were together again in *The Terrible People* ('28), based on a story by Edgar Wallace. This one boasted two cloaked, intriguing villains—one called "The Professor," head of the terrible people, and one of his henchmen, who dressed in a black robe and displayed hairy, claw-like hands.

Nearly a year went by before Allene and Miller made *The Black Book* ('29), their last film together and the last serial ever made by Pathé. Both stars had used the time off for vaudeville engagements. Rather mediocre when compared to their previous serials, the story is based on the patriotic efforts of a beautiful young girl detective, pitting her wits against a criminal coterie which includes the masterminds of evil in two countries. Her only aides are a faithful Oriental (Willie Fung) and a one-time wastrel (Miller) who pledges his aid to her and wins his own regeneration as love springs, phoenix-like, from the ashes of disaster. The intrigue, mystery and romance revolve about two black books—one useless without the other—that control the destiny of a struggling nation.

Allene made one more serial, *The Indians Are Coming* ('30) with Tim McCoy. Allene's voice was not compatible with the sound recording equipment of that time and she chose to retire after appearing in two or three cheaply made independent features.

Though she was the most popular serial queen created in the '20s, Allene never received more than $500 a week for her labors, Pathé choosing to hold down salaries and use the savings to produce better serials. That she worked as hard and as effectively as she did for so little money is a credit to her, for she literally risked her life numerous times, seldom letting a double take her place and never refusing to do as her director bade.

With all due respect to those two intrepid feminine practitioners of derring-do Pearl White and Ruth Roland, Allene was probably the best serial heroine that has ever graced the genre in either the silent or sound eras. Certainly she was the most prolific, having been co-starred in 16 cliffhangers! And she was one of the most strikingly beautiful queens serial fans ever had the pleasure of drooling over week-by-week and year-by-year. Our hats are off to this underrated ingenue who made a mint of money for Pathé back when serials were respectable film fare and audiences hung precariously as they hissed the villain and shouted encouragement at their idols.

No one seems to know much about the personal life of the movies' most prolific serial heroine. At one time she was married to a man named Larry Wheeler, but beyond that we are in the dark. This we do know—to become enamored of Allene Ray was one of the easiest things a man or boy could do in those halcyon years just before the Great Depression.

Allene Ray died on May 5, 1979, in Temple City, California.

Serials

1924

Way of a Man. Pathé, [10 Chapters] D/SP: George B. Seitz; S: Emerson Hough; LP: Allene Ray, Harold Miller, Bud Osborne, Lillian Gale, Chet Tyan, Chief Whitehorse, Lillian Adreian.

The Fortieth Door. Pathé, [10 Chapters] D: George B. Seitz; SP: Frank Leon Smith; LP: Allene Ray, Bruce Gordon, Anna May Wong, Frank Lackteen, David Dunbar, Frances Mann, Lillian Gale, Bernard Siegel.

Ten Scars Make a Man. Pathé, [10 Chapters] D: William Parke; S: Phillips Barry; P: C. W. Patton; LP: Allene Ray, Jack Mower Rose Bur-

dict, Lillian Gale, Frank Whitson, Larry Steers, Harry Woods, Leon De La Methe.

Galloping Hoofs. Pathé, [10 Chapters] D: George B. Seitz; S: Frank Leon Smith; LP: Allene Ray, Johnnie Walker, J. Barney Sherry, Ernest Hilliard, Armand Cortez, William Nally, George Nardelli, Albert Roccardi.

1925

Sunken Silver. Pathé, [10 Chapters] D: George B. Seitz; SP: Frank Leon Smith; S: Albert Payson Terhune; LP: Allene Ray, Walter Miller, Frank Lackteen, Jean Bronte, Albert Roccardi, Charlie Fang, Frank Wunderlee, Gordon [Spencer] Bennet.

Play Ball. Pathé, [10 Chapters] D: Spencer Bennet; SP: Frank Leon Smith; S: John T. McGraw; LP: Allene Ray, Walter Miller, Harry Semels, J. Barney Sherry, Mary Milnor, Wally Oettel, Franklyn Hanna, Ed Maurelli.

The Green Archer. Pathé, [10 Chapters] D: Spencer G. Bennet; SP: Frank Leon Smith; S: Edgar Wallace; LP: Allene Ray, Walter Miller, Dorothy King, Steven Gratten, Frank Lackteen, Walter P. Lewis, Wally Oettel, Jack Tanner, Tom Cameron, Burr McIntosh.

1926

Snowed In. Pathé, [10 Chapters] D: Spencer G. Bennet; SP: Frank Leon Smith; LP: Allene Ray, Walter Miller, Frank Austin, Leonard Clapham [Tom London], Bert Apling, J. F. McCullough, Ben Walker, Charles West, Harrison Martell.

The House Without a Key. Pathé, [10 Chapters] D: Spencer G. Bennet; SP: Frank Leon Smith; S: Earl Derr Biggers; LP: Allene Ray, Walter Miller, E. H. Calvert, Betty Caldwell, Frank Lackteen, Charles H. West, John Webb Dillon, Natalie Warfield, William Norton Bailey, Jack Pratt, George Kuwa.

1927

Melting Millions. Pathé, [10 Chapters] D: Spencer G. Bennet; S: Joseph Anthony Roach; LP: Allene Ray, Walter Miller, E. H. Calvert, William Norton Bailey, Ann Gladman, Eugenia Gilbert, Richard C. Travers, George Kuwa, Frank Lackteen.

The Hawk of the Hills. Pathé, [10 Chapters]

D: Spencer G. Bennet; S: George Arthur Gray; Cam: Edward Snyder, Frank Redman; LP: Allene Ray, Walter Miller, Frank Lackteen, Paul Panzer, Harry Semels, Wally Oettel, Jack Pratt, John T. Pratt, Chief Whitehorse, Chief Yowlachie.

The Man Without a Face. Pathé, [10 Chapters] D: Spencer G. Bennet; SP: Joseph Anthony Roach; S: C. W. and Alice M. Williamson; LP: Allene Ray, Walter Miller, E. H. Calvert, Jeanette Loff, Gladden James, Kathleen Chambers, Richard R. Neill, Sojin, Toshiye Schioka.

1928

The Yellow Cameo. Pathé, [10 Chapters] D: Spencer G. Bennet; S/SP: George Arthur Gray; LP: Allene Ray, Edward Hearn, Cyclone (dog), Noble Johnson, Tom London, Maurice Klein, Ed Snyder, Frank Redman, Harry Semels.

The Terrible People. Pathé, [10 Chapters] D: Spencer G. Bennet; SP: George Arthur Gray; S:

Edgar Wallace; LP: Allene Ray, Walter Miller, Larry Steers, Allen Craven, Wilfred North, Fred Vroom, Tom Holding, Mary Foy, Alice McCormack.

1929

The Black Book. Pathé, [10 Chapters] D: Spencer G. Bennet, Tom Storey; S: Joseph Anthony Roach; Cam: Edward Snyder; LP: Allene Ray, Walter Miller, Frank Lackteen, Willie Fung, John Webb Dillon, Evan Pearson, Olga Vamma.

1930

The Indians Are Coming. Univ., [12 Chapters] D: Henry MacRae; SP: Ford Beebe, George H. Plympton; S: William F. Cody; P: Henry MacRae; LP: Tim McCoy, Allene Ray, Edmund Cobb, Francis Ford, Dynamite (dog), Bud Osborne, Dick Hatton, Lafe McKee, Bob Reeves, Wilbur McGaugh.

MARSHALL REED

Marshall Reed was born in Englewood, Colorado, in 1917. As a young man he worked as a meter reader, bookkeeper, clerk, horse trainer and addressograph operator. He grew up in Denver and participated in most sports during his high school years. At 17 he studied set and light design at the Denver University Civic Theater. At 18 he and some friends put together a traveling repertory company and toured Colorado and Wyoming for two summers. He went to Hollywood in 1942 and worked at Lockheed in the evenings while spending his days trying to get work at the studios.

His movie career began in 1943 when he appeared briefly in *A Guy Named Joe.* At Monogram he had the role of the kid in *The Texas Kid* ('43) starring Johnny Mack Brown, the cowboy with whom he would

most often be associated. He supported Brown in 30 or more Westerns.

Reed usually played one of the heavies. His serial appearances were as a supporting player. In the beginning they were bits but gradually they became larger: *Son of Geronimo* ('52), *Mysterious Island* ('51), etc. *Ridin' with Buffalo Bill* ('54) capped his career. By this time, however, serial production had ceased at Republic and Universal and Columbia would make only two more. Programmer Westerns were also at death's door. Earlier Reed had lost out on getting the Lone Ranger role—first to Clayton Moore and next to John Hart. He was set to take over the Red Ryder role being vacated by Bill Elliott when Herbert J. Yates, Republic boss, decided at the last minute to give the role to Allan Lane.

Reed had a continuing role as a detective in the TV series *The Lineup* starring Warner Anderson and Tom Tully. He could also be seen in *Commando Cody, Sky Marshall of the Universe* ('54).

Marshall Reed passed away in 1980.

Serials

1944

Zorro's Black Whip. Rep., [12 Chapters] D: Spencer Bennet, Wallace Grissell; LP: Linda Stirling, George J. Lewis, Lucien Littlefield, Francis McDonald.

The Tiger Woman. Rep., [12 Chapters] D: Spencer Bennet, Wallace Grissell; LP: Linda Stirling, Allan Lane, Duncan Renaldo, George J. Lewis, LeRoy Mason.

1946

The Scarlet Horseman. Univ., [13 Chapters] D: Ray Taylor, Lewis D. Collins; LP: Peter Cookson, Paul Guilfoyle, Victoria Horne, Janet Shaw, Edmund Cobb.

1948

Dangers of the Canadian Mounted. Rep., [12 Chapters] D: Fred Brannon, Yakima Canutt; LP: Jim Bannon, Virginia Belmont, Anthony Warde, Dorothy Granger.

1949

Federal Agents vs. Underworld, Inc. Rep., [12 Chapters] D: Fred C.Brannon; LP: Kirk Alyn, Rosemary La Planche, Roy Barcroft, Carol Forman.

Ghost of Zorro. Rep., [12 Chapters] D: Fred C. Brannon; LP: Clayton Moore, Pamela Blake, Roy Barcroft, George J. Lewis, I. Stanford Jolley.

1950

Pirates of the High Seas. Col., [15 Chapters] D: Spencer Bennet, Thomas Carr; LP: Buster Crabbe, Lois Hall, Tommy Farrell, Gene Roth, Tris Coffin.

The James Brothers of Missouri. Rep., [12 Chapters] D: Fred C. Brannon; LP: Keith Richards, Robert Bice, Noel Neill, Roy Barcroft, Patricia Knox.

The Invisible Monster. Rep., [12 Chapters] D: Fred C. Brannon; LP: Richard Webb, Aline Towne, Lane Bradford, Stanley Price, John Crawford, Tom Steele.

1951

Mysterious Island. Col., [15 Chapters] D: Spencer Bennet; LP: Richard Crane, Marshall Reed, Karen Randle, Ralph Hodges, Gene Roth.

1952

Son of Geronimo. Col., [15 Chapters] D: Spencer Bennet; LP: Clayton Moore, Rodd Redwing, Tommy Farrell, Eileen Rowe, Bud Osborne, John Crawford.

Blackhawk. Col., [15 Chapters] D: Spencer Bennet, Fred F. Sears; LP: Kirk Alyn, Carol Forman, John Crawford, Michael Fox, Don C. Harvey, Rick Vallin.

1953

The Great Adventures of Captain Kidd. Col., [15 Chapters] D: Derwin Abbe, Charles S. Gould; LP: Richard Crane, David Bruce, John Crawford, George Wallace, Marshall Reed.

Gunfighters of the Northwest. Col., [15 Chapters] D: Spencer Bennet; LP: Jock Mahoney, Clayton Moore, Phyllis Coates, Don Harvey.

1954

Ridin' with Buffalo Bill. Col., [15 Chapters] D: Spencer Bennet; SP: George H. Plympton; P: Sam Katzman; Cam: Ira H. Morgan; Mus: Mischa Bakaleinikoff; LP: Marshall Reed, Rick Vallin, Joanne Rio, Shirley Whitney, Jack Ingram.

WALTER REED

Film, TV and serial star Walter Reed died of kidney failure in Santa Cruz, California, on August 20, 2001, with his two daughters, Peggy and Kim, and a son, Kirk, at his bedside. He was born Walter Reed Smith in Seattle, Washington, in 1916. His father retired from the Army in 1923 and the family moved to Los Angeles, where Walter got to know a lot of performers. When he was 13 he got his first acting job. The film was *Red Skin* ('29) starring Richard Dix. Reed played an Indian boy. At age 16 he was Joel McCrea's stand-in. When he was 17 he decided that he wanted to go on the stage. He rode the rails to New York, where he managed to get stage jobs in numerous plays and remained in the East doing stock for 68 weeks.

Walter was doing a play in Kennebunkport, Maine, where Joel McCrea saw him and arranged for him to return to Hollywood where he was put under contract by RKO. His first film was *The Mayor of 44th Street* ('42) with George Murphy and Anne Shirley. Approximately 150 films followed through 1969. A sampling: *Bombardier* ('43), *Banjo* ('47), *Return of the Bad Men* ('48), *Fighter Squadron* ('48), *Captain China* ('49), *Tripoli* ('50), *Superman and the Mole Men* ('51), *Submarine Command* ('51), *Target* ('52), *Thunderbirds* ('52), *The Clown* ('52), *Seminole* ('53), *The High and the Mighty* ('54), *The Far Horizons* ('55), *Seven Men from Now* ('55), *Last of the Badmen* ('57), *Slim Carter* ('57), *Westbound* ('58), *The Horse Soldiers* ('59), *Macumba Love* ('60), *How the West was Won* ('62), *Cheyenne Autumn* ('64), *Fort Courageous* ('65), *The Sand Pebbles* ('66), *The Destructors* ('68), *Deadlock* (TV[69) and *The Monk* (TV '69).

Walter went into the Army in 1943 and was discharged in 1945. During the war he toured with dozens of other actors in the army play, *Winged Victory*. Returning to RKO after the war he quickly became a respected character actor.

The number of television appearances of Walter has been estimated by him to be about 400. His television credits include episodes of *Hawaiian Eye, Petticoat Junction, Matinee Theater, Front Row Center, Hennessey, The Deputy, One Step Beyond, Voyage to the Bottom of the Sea, Batman, Lassie, The Virginian, My Three Sons, The Invaders, Family Affair, The Lone Ranger, Hopalong Cassidy, Dragnet, Annie Oakley, Thriller, Cheyenne, Twilight Zone, Bonanza, Buffalo Bill, Jr., Fury, The Adventures of Champion, The Life and Legend of Wyatt Earp, Sergeant Preston of the Yukon, Gunsmoke, The Adventures of Rin Tin Tin, 77 Sunset Strip, Hotel De Paree, Wagon Train, Sky King, Men into Space, World of Giants, Perry Mason, Superman, Buckskin, Lawman, Zane Grey Theater, Maverick, Have Gun — Will Travel* and *Colt 45.*

Walter made two Republic serials in 1951. In *Flying Disc Man from Mars* he plays a young aviator, Kent, operator of a private plane patrol, who shoots down a mysterious aircraft hovering over the factory of scientist Dr. Bryant (James Craven). The aircraft was from the planet Mars and its occupant, Mota (Gregory Gay), is met by Mr. Bryant as he emerged from the wreck. Mota offers to work with Bryant in building atomic-powered planes and bombs if Bryant will help him organize a force to take over Earth and make it a satellite of the Martian dictator. Bryant agrees. Kent and his secretary (Lois Collier) experience many dangerous adventures as they combat the enemy.

In *Government Agents vs. Phantom Legion*, Walter is a government agent, Hal Duncan, assigned to work with the Truck Owners' Association to combat a wave of attacks on highway transportation. This group consists of four individuals played by Pierce

Lyden, George Meeker, Arthur Space and Mauritz Hugo. Mary Ellen Kay was secretary of the board. A mystery villain, "The Voice," directs the attacks for the purpose of stealing the cargos for a foreign power. Hal believes the Voice to be one of the truck owners and in the end has a showdown with Armstrong (Pierce Lyden) — The Voice — who is knocked down and impaled on a piece of broken glass.

At age 49, Walter had a major heart attack and thereafter slowed down on acting and became successful in real estate. He quit pictures in 1969.

Serials

1951

Flying Disc Man from Mars. Rep., [12 Chapters] D: Fred C. Brannon; SP: Ronald Davidson; AP: Franklyn Adreon; Cam: Walter Strenge; Mus: Stanley Wilson; LP: Walter Reed, Lois Collier, Gregory Gay, James Craven, Harry Lauter, Richard Irving, Ken Terrell, Carey Loftin, Sandy Sanders.

Government Agents vs. Phantom Legion. Rep., [12 Chapters] D: Fred C. Brannon; SP: Ronald Davidson; AP: Franklyn Adreon; Cam: John L. Russell, Jr.; Mus: Stanley Wilson; LP: Walter Reed, Mary Ellen Kay, Dick Curtis, John Pickard, Fred Coby, Pierce Lyden, George Meeker, Edmund Cobb, Roy Barcroft.

GEORGE REEVES

George Reeves is best-known as the star of the syndicated *Adventures of Superman* television series. Almost fifty years have passed since the series ended, but it can still be seen on those stations that telecast old series programs.

Reeves was first noticed by the public when he played Brent, one of the Tarleton brothers, in *Gone with the Wind* ('39). Then in 1940 he had roles in *Till We Meet Again, Torrid Zone, Ladies Must Live, Argentine Nights* and *Always a Bride.* In 1941 he appeared in *The Strawberry Blonde, Blood and Sand, Lydia* and *Man at Large.* He was offscreen in 1942 but in 1943 he had a plum role as Claudette Colbert's Army lover in *So Proudly We Hail,* and he worked in a couple of Hopalong Cassidy Westerns.

Other films in which Reeves appeared are *Winged Victory* ('44), *Samson and Delilah* ('49), *Thunder in the Pines* ('49), *The Great Lover* ('49), *The Good Humor Man* ('50), *Superman and the Mole Men* ('51), *Bugles in the Afternoon* ('52), *Rancho Notorious* ('52), *The*

In *Adventures of Sir Galahad* (Columbia, 1949).

Blue Gardenia ('53), *From Here to Eternity* ('53), *Forever Female* ('54) and *Westward Ho the Wagons* ('57).

In 1949, Reeves starred in the Columbia serial *Adventures of Sir Galahad*. It is not one of Columbia's better chapterplays but, to its credit, Charles King has the second lead as Sir Bors, who aids Sir Galahad in his search for the magic sword Excalibur, which makes its possessor invincible. Both George and King did their best with a ridiculous script.

Despondent over being stereotyped as Superman and his failure to advance his career, Reeves committed suicide in 1959.

Serial

1949

Adventures of Sir Galahad. Col., [15 Chapters] D: Spencer G. Bennet; SP: George H. Plympton, Lewis Clay, David Mathews; P: Sam Katzman; Cam: Ira H. Morgan; Mus: Mischa Bakaleinikoff; LP: George Reeves, Charles King, William Fawcett, Pat Barton, Marjorie Stapp, Nelson Leigh, John Merton, Rick Vallin, Ray Corrigan, Al Ferguson, Leonard Penn.

ROBERT (BOB) REEVES

Bob Reeves is one of that coterie of stars whose names once appeared above the titles of Western flicks and who is now forgotten and neglected by film historians and aficionados alike. He was born on January 28, 1892, in or near Marlin, Texas. He was a big man, 6'2" and weighing 200 pounds. He had brown hair and blue eyes and in his starring days was a rather handsome fellow. Bob received his formal education in the Marlin public schools and at Texas A&M University.

Before he entered motion pictures some time after World War I, Bob had been a noted rodeo performer. He probably was in military service during the War, but this is an unverified assumption. In Hollywood he was able to talk to Universal head Carl Laemmle, who was impressed with the young man and agreed to give him a chance at acting. After some extra work he was given a supporting role in Elmo Lincoln's *Elmo, the Mighty* ('19), an 18-chapter serial. Shortly thereafter he co-starred with Cleo Madison and Eileen Sedgwick in the Universal serial *The Great Radium Mystery* ('19). A rather undistinguished

entry in the field, it concerned the disappearance of the heirs to one of the greatest fortunes on earth. In 1920, Reeves starred in several two-reelers for Universal and again lent his support to Elmo Lincoln, this time in the serial *The Flaming Disc*.

During 1921, Reeves starred in a series of two-reelers made by Rogell-Brown Productions operating as Cactus Features and released by Western Pictures Exploitation Company. These films played the hinterland theaters that did not want to pay the higher rental rates for the films of the major stars. There were 13 films in the series. The leading lady was Maryon Aye, and Reeves' horse, Searchlight, was billed as "The Wonder Horse." The films featured a number of sensational rodeo stunts by Reeves and Searchlight. In the United Kingdom these films were released under the overall title "Thrills of the Western Hills" by Page Films Ltd.

In 1922, Reeves was again starring in Universal two-reelers. In the mid–20s he starred in eight features for Larry Wheeler Productions and released through Anchor Film Company. The titles were *Cyclone Bob*,

Desperate Chance, Riding for Life, Ridin' Straight, Ambushed, Iron Fist and *Fighting Luck.*

Reeves soon began to work as a supporting player to other Western stars and continued active well into the sound era. During the last phase of his career he specialized in playing policemen, and it is doubtful that any other actor portrayed as many of them. His parts were only minor ones and sometimes so small that he went uncredited. In the 1930s Reeves apparently was a member of the Ken Maynard stock company for a while, as he was in five Maynard features.

Bob Reeves died of a heart attack in Hollywood on April 2, 1960, at age 68. His passing drew little attention in the film colony. He was probably no better or no worse than many other cowboys, but in a period when the accent was on action rather than acting ability, he was able to supply an adequate amount. He last appeared in *The Parson and the Outlaw* ('57).

Serials

1919

Elmo, the Mighty. Univ., [18 Chapters] D: Henry MacRae; LP: Elmo Lincoln, Grace Cunard, Fred Starr, Virginia Craft, Ivor McFadden, Rex De Rosselli.

The Great Radium Mystery. Univ., [18 Chapters] D: Robert Bradwell, Robert F. Hill; LP: Cleo Madison, Bob Reeves, Eileen Sedgwick, Robert Kortman, Ed Brady, Jeff Osborne, Robert Gray, Gordon McGregor, Fred Hamer.

1920

The Flaming Disc. Univ., [18 Chapters] D: Robert F. Hill; LP: Elmo Lincoln, Louise Lorraine, Fay Holderness, Roy Watson, George Williams, Monte Montague, Lee Kohlmar, Bob Reeves, Lillian Lorraine.

1930

The Lightning Express. Univ., [10 Chapters] D: Henry MacRae; LP: Lane Chandler, Louise

Lorraine, Al Ferguson, Greta Granstedt, J. Gordon Russell, Floyd Criswell, Jim Pierce, Bob Reeves.

The Indians Are Coming. Univ., [12 Chapters] D: Henry MacRae; LP: Tim McCoy, Allene Ray, Edmund Cobb, Francis Ford, Bud Osborne, William McGough, Bob Reeves.

1932

The Airmail Mystery. Univ., [12 Chapters] D: Ray Taylor; LP: Lucile Browne, James Flavin, Frank S. Hagney, Walter Brennan, Cecil Kellogg, Nelson McDowell, Sidney Bracey, Bob Reeves.

1936

The Phantom Rider. Univ., [15 Chapters] D: Ray Taylor; LP: Buck Jones, Marla Shelton, Diana Gibson, Harry Woods, George Cooper, Frank LaRue, Charles King, Bob Reeves, Tom London, Wally Wales [Hal Taliaferro], Frank Ellis.

1937

Dick Tracy. Rep., [15 Chapters] D: Ray Taylor, Alan James; LP: Ralph Byrd, Kay Hughes, Smiley Burnette, Lee Van Atta, John Picorri, Carleton Young.

1947

The Black Widow. Rep., [13 Chapters] D: Spencer G. Bennet, Fred C. Brannon; LP: Carol Forman, Bruce Edwards, Virginia Lindley, Anthony Warde, Ramsay Ames, I. Stanford Jolley, Virginia Carroll, Gene Stutenroth, Bob Reeves.

1950

Desperadoes of the West. Rep., [12 Chapters] D: Fred C. Brannon; LP: Richard Powers [Tom Keene], Judy Clark, Roy Barcroft, I. Stanford Jolley, Lee Roberts, Bud Osborne, Bob Reeves.

1951

Don Daredevil Rides Again. Rep., [12 Chapters] D: Fred C. Brannon; LP: Ken Curtis, Aline Towne, Roy Barcroft, Lane Bradford, I. Stanford Jolley, John Cason.

1952

Canadian Mounties vs. Atomic Invaders. Rep., [12 Chapters] D: Franklyn Adreon; LP: Bill Henry, Susan Morrow, Arthur Space, Dale Van Sickel, Pierre Watkin, Stanley Andrews, Harry Lauter, Edmund Cobb, Hank Patterson, Bob Reeves.

DUNCAN RENALDO

The man who became the Cisco Kid to millions of television viewers during the last half-century was Duncan Renaldo, star of the most Cisco movie features (eight) and the only actor to portray Cisco in the long-running syndicated TV series. *The Cisco Kid* was filmed by Ziv between 1949 and 1956, with Renaldo, in a stroke of forethought and technical savvy, insisting that the 156 episodes be photographed in color even though shown in black-and-white (so that it would still be runnable after color TV came along).

Duncan had a long career in motion pictures, beginning in the silent era, and older action fans are well aware of his several serials and his days as a member of the Three Mesquiteers horse opera series at Republic. Before that, he was the typical Latin lover in many drawing room dramas and outdoor films.

Duncan was born in Valladolid, Spain, on April 23, 1904, the son of Romanian-Spanish parents he never knew. As an orphan he lived with many families, shifted here and there throughout Europe and South America. His education, however, was a good one, obtained in France, Spain and Argentina. Duncan, a good student, displayed early talent in acting, writing, painting, dancing and music.

While living in Argentina, Duncan learned to ride horses, a skill that would come in handy many years later on a range far different from the pampas. While still a boy in years, he joined the Brazilian Merchant Marine and sailed the world for three and a half years. It was in the capacity of a seaman that he reached Baltimore in 1921; there he stayed, finding work mostly as a portrait painter. In 1923 he went to New York as a painter, vaudevillian and designer. This activity led to a small part in a film starring Dorothy Gish. Other small parts followed and in 1924 Duncan was given a plum role opposite Lionel Barrymore and Hope Hampton in Encore's *Fifty-Fifty*. Roles continued to get better for Duncan and in 1928 he appeared in *Marcheta* and *Romany Love*, for which he is given writing and directorial as well as acting credit. He attained added stature as an actor in the 1928 Tiffany-Stahl films *The Devil's Skipper, Clothes Make the Woman, The Naughty Duchess* and *The Gun Runner.*

At FBO, Duncan appeared in his first Western, *Pals of the Prairie* ('29), a silent film with music score and sound effects added. Buzz Barton starred. Duncan purchased the screen rights to Thornton Wilder's *The Bridge of San Luis Rey* shortly after the book was published. MGM wanted very much to film the story. A deal was worked out whereby Duncan swapped his rights to the property to MGM and received a cash consideration, an MGM contract and one of the principal roles in the ten-reel, part-talking extravaganza.

Renaldo's performance was hailed by critics and theater patrons and MGM hastened to capitalize on the young Latin, visualizing another Rudolph Valentino. The result was that he was packed off to Africa with Harry Carey, Edwina Booth, Olive Carey, director W. S. Van Dyke and an MGM technical crew for the filming of *Trader Horn*, the first great outdoor sound film and one destined to become a classic. The production was plagued with troubles from beginning to end; after a year in the wilds of Africa and the exposure of thousands upon thousands of feet of film, the studio still had to shoot some of the footage on the studio backlot. But it was a success and a Depression-hit populace flocked to theaters to live a vicarious adventure in the Dark Continent with an old trader (Carey), his young aid (Renaldo) and a "white princess" (Booth).

The film proved a disaster for Renaldo, however, and in a most unexpected way. His wife, thinking him unfaithful, turned him in to the government for falsifying his passport and hit Edwina Booth with an alienation of affections suit. She lost the suit against Miss Booth but Renaldo lost his freedom, winding up in federal prison on McNeil Island off the coast of Washington for passport perjury. He had claimed Camden, New Jersey, as his birthplace. In actuality, he had never bothered to apply for citizenship or even alien status when he came to the U.S. in 1921. Renaldo was perhaps ill-advised by MGM about the consequences of falsifying passport information but, at any rate, he served nearly two years in the prison before being pardoned by President Roosevelt.

Rather than becoming bitter, Duncan picked up the pieces of his life and continued forward. He was soon back at work before the cameras in *Trapped in Tia Juana*, *Public Stenographer*, *Moonlight Murder*, *Lady Luck*, *Two Minutes to Play*, *Crime Afloat* and *Rebellion*, the latter film casting him with cowboy star Tom Keene and Rita Cansino (Hayworth) in a good historical Western produced by Crescent Pictures. Along about the same time he was teamed with cowboy Rex Lease and Muriel Evans in *10 Laps to Go*, with Duncan playing the suave villain.

In 1937, Renaldo began his long association with serials when he played in Columbia's first chapterplay, *Jungle Menace*. As Armand Rogers, Duncan is a hoodlum nightclub owner in cahoots with the leader of a gang of river pirates (LeRoy Mason), who in the end kills him.

With his next film, Renaldo began his career at Republic. The film was *The Painted Stallion*, starring Ray Corrigan and Hoot Gibson. Again Mason and Renaldo are partners in crime and both wind up quite dead in the end. Many consider *Zorro Rides Again* ('37) Renaldo's best serial role. He plays an elderly servant who is the confidant of Zorro.

Renaldo appeared in several features (among them Roy Rogers' *Rough Riders Roundup* and Gene Autry's *South of the Border*) before hitting the serial trail again as Juan Vasquez, friend of the Lone Ranger, in *The Lone Ranger Rides Again* ('39). Renaldo was featured in the film in an effort to win the Latin American audience. And for the same reason he was co-starred in the Three Mesquiteers series along with Bob Livingston and Raymond Hatton in 1939. His seven features in this series are *The Kansas Terrors*, *Cowboys from Texas*, *Heroes in the Saddle*, *Pioneers of the West*, *Covered Wagon Days*, *Rocky Mountain Rangers* and *Oklahoma Renegades*. Renaldo was replaced by Bob Steele but remained on the Republic payroll, appearing in Gene Autry's *Gaucho Serenade* ('40) and *Down Mexico Way* ('41) and other films.

King of the Texas Rangers ('41), the highly respected cliffhanger starring football hero "Slingin' Sammy" Baugh, featured Duncan as Baugh's co-adventurer Pedro Garcia of the Mexican Rurales.

Duncan was listed eleventh in the serial *King of the Mounties* ('42) but Republic did much better by him in the 15-chapter cliffhanger *Secret Service in Darkest Africa* ('43). Renaldo was second lead to Rod Cameron and was "good guy" Pierre LaSalle, a French officer assigned to aid American undercover agent Rex Bennett, played by Rod Cameron.

From 1942–44 Duncan had good roles in such diverse films as *For Whom the Bell Tolls*, *Mission to Moscow*, *Border Patrol*, *Tiger Fangs*, *Hands Across the Border*, *The Desert Song*, *The Fighting Seabees*, *Call of the South Seas* and *Sheriff of Sundown*.

Renaldo's last serial had him cast as third lead in Republic's *The Tiger Woman* ('44) starring Linda Stirling and Allan Lane. It was a polished, fast-action thriller well-suited as an introduction of Miss Stirling as the new serial queen. Renaldo plays Jose, an oilman in the South American jungle who helps Stirling, leader of a local tribe, and Lane, an American troubleshooter, defeat dishonest, scheming LeRoy Mason (who else!) who is out to keep Lane's company from bringing in an oil well on time.

Duncan was suddenly projected into stardom in 1944 when Monogram decided to produce a series of Cisco Kid Westerns. Renaldo seemed ideally cast as the bandit hero with an eye for the beautiful senoritas. First in these Philip N. Krasne productions was *The Cisco Kid Returns*. It was followed by *In Old New Mexico* and *South of the Rio Grande*. All three films were released in 1945.

Renaldo became involved in wartime exploratory work for the government and relinquished his role to Gilbert Roland, who starred in five Cisco Kid Westerns and carried the series through 1947. By 1948 Duncan was free to resume his movie career and he and Krasne bought the rights to Cisco back from Monogram and produced five Cisco Kid Westerns themselves for United Artists release. Leo Carrillo was chosen to portray Pancho and given equal billing with Renaldo. The films were *The Valiant Hombre* ('49), *The Gay Amigo* ('49), *The Daring Caballero* ('49), *Satan's Cradle* ('49) and *The Girl from San Lorenzo* ('50).

In 1949, Ziv bought the rights to Cisco from Krasne and Renaldo and hired Renaldo and Carrillo to star in a syndicated series of 30-minute Cisco Kid Westerns. Each man received a $500-a-week salary. Production halted in 1956 after 156 episodes and Duncan retired from acting. He made personal appearance tours throughout South America and starred for one season (1967) with the Clyde Beaty Circus.

In his latter years he found time to lecture on college campuses, attend nostalgia conventions and enjoy family and friends.

Duncan Renaldo was a charming, gra-

cious man who will be long remembered for his smooth interpretation of the dashing Cisco Kid and for his ability to make believable — and enjoyable — both the amusing flirtatiousness and the danger-scorning action. Both in his Three Mesquiteers and Cisco Kid series, as well as in other films, Duncan proved an expert in the roughest action and the quickest shooting — and in hand-kissing and heart-stirring.

Duncan Renaldo died at age 76 in Goleta, California, from lung cancer. *Hasta la vista*, Duncan — until we meet again.

Serials

1937

Jungle Menace. Col., [15 Chapters] D: George Melford, Harry Fraser; P: Jack Flier; S: George M. Merrick, Arthur Hoerl, Dallas Fitzgerald, Gordon Griffith; SP: George Rosener, Sherman L. Lowe, Harry Hoyt [Fraser], George Melford; Cam: Edward Linden, Herman Shopp; Mus: Abe Meyer; LP: Frank Buck, Esther Ralston, John St. Polis, Reginald Denny, Charlotte Henry, Duncan Renaldo, LeRoy Mason.

The Painted Stallion. Rep., [12 Chapters] D: William Witney, Alan James, Ray Taylor; SP: Barry Shipman, Winston Miller; P: J. Laurence Wickland; Cam: William Nobles, Edgar Lyons; Mus: Raoul Kraushaar; LP: Ray Corrigan, Hoot Gibson, Hal Taliaferro, Jack Perrin, Duncan Renaldo, LeRoy Mason, Charles King, Julia Thayer, Yakima Canutt.

Zorro Rides Again. Rep., [12 Chapters] D: William Witney, John English; SP: Barry Shipman, Franklyn Adreon, Morgan Cox, John Rathmell, Ronald Davidson; AP: Sol C. Siegel; Cam: William Nobles; Mus: Alberto Colombo; LP: John Carroll, Helen Christian, Duncan Renaldo, Noah Beery, Sr., Yakima Canutt.

1939

The Lone Ranger Rides Again. Rep., [15 Chapters] D: William Witney, John English; SP: Franklyn Adreon, Ronald Davidson, Sol Shor, Barry Shipman; AP: Robert Beche; Cam: William Nobles, Edgar Lyons; Mus: Alberto Colombo; LP: Robert Livingston, Chief Thundercloud, Duncan Renaldo, Jinx Falken, Ralph Dunn, J. Farrell MacDonald, Rex Lease, William Gould, Stanley Blystone.

1941

King of the Texas Rangers. Rep., [12 Chapters] D: William Witney, John English; SP: Ronald Davidson, Norman S. Hall, William Lively, Joseph Poland, Joseph O'Donnell; AP: Hiram S. Brown, Jr.; Cam: Reggie Lanning; Mus: Cy Feuer; LP: Sammy Baugh, Neil Hamilton, Pauline Moore, Duncan Renaldo, Monte Blue.

1942

King of the Mounties. Rep., [12 Chapters] D: William Witney; SP: Joseph Poland, Taylor Caven, Ronald Davidson, William Lively, Joseph O'Donnell; AP: W. J. O'Sullivan; Cam: Bud Thackery; Mus: Mort Glickman; LP: Allan Lane, Peggy Drake, Gilbert Emery, Russell Hicks, George Irving, Duncan Renaldo.

1943

Secret Service in Darkest Africa. Rep., [15 Chapters] D: Spencer Bennet; SP: Royal Cole, Basil Dickey, Jesse Duffy, Ronald Davidson, Joseph O'Donnell, Joseph Poland; AP: W. J. O'Sullivan; Cam: William Bradford; Mus: Mort Glickman; LP: Rod Cameron, Joan Marsh, Duncan Renaldo, Lionel Royce, Kurt Kreuger, Kurt Katch, John Davidson, Fredric Brunn.

1944

The Tiger Woman. Rep., [12 Chapters] D: Spencer Bennet, Wallace Grissell; SP: Royal Cole, Ronald Davidson, Basil Dickey, Jesse Duffy, Grant Nelson, Joseph Poland; AP: W. J. O'Sullivan; Cam: Bud Thackery; Mus: Joseph Dubin; LP: Linda Stirling, Allan Lane, Duncan Renaldo, George J. Lewis, LeRoy Mason, Crane Whitley, Kenne Duncan, Marshall Reed, Robert Frazer.

REX, KING OF WILD HORSES

Mention "King of [the] Wild Horses," "The Devil Horse" or "The Wonder Horse" to those Western film buffs whose memories go back to the years 1924–36 and you are likely to see instant recollection reflected in their eyes. For there was only one horse that fitted these descriptions and wore these titles. His name? *Rex*! He was the only horse up to that time to be starred in his own pictures, with his name above the title. He served no

Top: Rex in *King of the Wild Horses* (Columbia, 1933). *Bottom:* Lobby Card *Law of the Wild* (Mascot, 1934).

cowboy as a faithful companion. Most likely he would send the hero scurrying for cover along with everyone else if he happened to be in a foul mood — which he was about 98 percent of the time.

The stallion was another prototypical animal star and, like many stars, Rex was a thorough bastard off the screen. He was a black bay stallion, a vicious horse that killed two men and injured many wranglers on the set. He was foaled at the Morgan Farms in Texas and as a colt sold to the Colorado State Boys Reformatory, where, perhaps, he suffered from environmental influence. He was abused and publicity has it that one day he went loco, threw his young rider and dragged him to death. Later, when another lad dismounted to drink at a spring, he trampled the youth to death.

Confined for two years to a box stall after the second fatality, the outlaw horse was watered with a hose, fed through a trap door and never touched by man. One day Chick Morrison (brother of Western star Pete Morrison) and a novice trainer, Jack Lindell, discovered him, believed he was intelligent enough for picture work and made arrangements to buy him for Hal Roach, the Hollywood producer. They roped Rex, put hobbles and a halter on him and hauled him off to Hollywood and fame. He was the first horse ever to carry a picture by himself. His wildness and defiance of the world fascinated movie fans. A shot of Rex racing across the floor of a desert valley was worth the price of admission. So was a fight with a mountain lion.

In a letter to the author dated September 25, 1973, Yakima Canutt reminisced about Rex:

> Rex was a Morgan by strain and owned by a state farm of some kind in Colorado. He killed one of his workers or caretakers. Chick Morrison bought him for Hal Roach and then trained him for picture work. His first picture was *The King of Wild Horses* ('24), and I might add one of the best wild horse pictures ever made. In *Lightning Romance* ('24) Rex had a brief part in a Rayart film starring Reed Howes. In *Black Cyclone* ('25)

Rex and Big Boy Williams are featured. During the filming Rex got Big Boy down and cuffed him up a bit. The trainer was able to get him off Big Boy, but after that Big Boy really watched him.

> The next picture Rex did was *The Devil Horse* (do not confuse with the serial of the same title) in which I had the leading role. Big Boy told me to watch that son of a bitch because "He will kill you if he gets a chance." I did a lot of scenes with him and was getting along great until I had an accident with a big flare which blew up and burnt me quite badly. I spent a few days in the hospital and went back to work before I was completely healed up. I think the smell of the medications I was using annoyed him because he turned on me one day and I still have a slight scar on my jaw from his teeth. He got me down and I did quite a job of rolling and kicking him on the head. He was like a bulldog and bit several people.

> I finally rolled over a bank and got to my feet. Even with the trainer working on him with a whip, the bank was all that saved me from being hurt bad. I took the old horse in the training barn and really worked him over and I had no more trouble with him.

> A rancher at Flagstaff, Arizona, bought him and Nat Levine used him in a serial starring Harry Carey. I have forgotten the title of the film. Anyway, that is the one where I swung under his neck and locked my spurs over his withers. Of course we used a bronc to double him in most of the scenes. As I remember, Lee Doyle was the rancher's name that bought Rex. He had a couple of cowhands working for him. He told them that he had been told the old horse was dangerous and to be careful. They got a laugh out of it and one of them told him, "We ain't Hollywood cowboys." Two days later he was in the hospital. The old horse got him down in the corral and fortunately he finally rolled under the corral fence, but he was really badly injured.

One source credits Universal studios as owning him when it produced the films starring Rex, Jack Perrin and Starlight (Perrin's horse) in 1928–29. The films were *Guardians of the Wild* ('28), *The Two Outlaws* ('28), *The Harvest of Hate* ('28), *Hoofbeats of Vengeance*

('29), *Wild Blood* ('29) and *Plunging Hoofs* ('29). A horse by the name of Brownie doubled for Rex in scenes with people, as Rex was ornery, arrogant and, one might say, warped. The only thing the old horse had was a personality. He looked wild and beautiful, but he was an independent, rarely allowing himself to be governed by cues from a handler.

Historian Jon Tuska reports that stock footage from *King of the Wild Horses*, not to be confused with Rex's picture of the same name in 1933, was incorporated by producer Nat Levine into the first chapter of *The Vanishing Legion* ('31), a Mascot serial, because it was so unusual, showing Rex and a painted stallion battling for supremacy of a herd. Levine later used it in Chapter Seven of his Mascot serial *The Devil Horse* (although the horse Apache had the title role and Rex was not featured in the film).* Early in 1930, Rex appeared in *Parade of the West*, another Maynard feature. It was produced in both a silent and sound version.

Rex and Rin-Tin-Tin, Jr., co-starred as themselves in the Mascot serial *The Law of the Wild* ('34) with the human stars being Bob Custer and Lucile Browne. In the story Rex, a wild horse tamed by Sheldon (Custer), a young rancher, is stolen by an employee, Salter (Dick Alexander), who wounds Sheldon in the process. Later, while searching for Rex, Sheldon meets Alice Ingram (Browne) and her father, a race horse owner. At the track, Sheldon's horse is entered in a race and wins. In a dispute over the winnings, Salter is killed by a co-conspirator and the blame put on Sheldon. Rex, Rinty, Sheldon and Alice survive numerous ordeals before justice is served and horse and master reunited, with Alice riding Rex in the sweepstakes in the final showdown.

In *Stormy* ('35), Noah Beery, Jr., plays the title role. He finds Rex as a young colt with his mother, Red Streak, in the desert. Horse owner Mac gives the colt to Stormy but later changes his mind and throws Stormy off the train carrying his horses. Rancher Trin Dorn (J. Farrell MacDonald) hires Stormy to work with his herd of wild horses. Trin's brother Deem (Fred Kohler) wants to sell the herd for their hides. He refuses to let his daughter Kerry (Jean Rogers) associate with Stormy. When Stormy finds out that the train carrying Mac's horses has been wrecked, he searches for Red Streak and her colt. He finds them but Red Streak dies from her injuries. Stormy takes the colt to a secret corral. Kerry discovers his secret and helps Stormy to train the colt, which they name Rex. Rex is later found running with the wild horses and captured by the cowboys. Deem tries to take Rex from Stormy but Kerry and Trin defend Stormy's claim to the horse. Deem's men shoot Trin and leave him in the desert to die. Rex saves him from a rattlesnake and brings Stormy and Kerry to his aid. They later set a fire causing a stampede and Deem is trampled to death. Trin's herd is now safe. Rex is offered his freedom but he chooses to remain with Stormy and Kerry.

In the serial *The Adventures of Rex and Rinty* ('35), Rex is a "God Horse" to the natives of Sujan, a primitive island. He is stolen by three American crooks and sold to Crawford (Harry Woods), a wealthy ranch owner in the U.S.; Crawford attempts to train him as a polo pony. Escaping, Rex teams up with the dog Rinty. They roam the range and together outwit their tormentors with the help of Frank Bradley (Kane Richmond), a rival of Crawford. Bradley ultimately corrals Rex and returns him to Sujan where further attempts to steal him are thwarted. In the end, Rex and Rinty are free and happy as they roam the island together.

In the 1936 Republic serial *Robinson Crusoe of Clipper Island*, Ray Mala is assigned by the management of a corporation to investigate the burning of fuel storage tanks on Clipper Island and the sabotaging of the airship "San Francisco" over the island on its maiden voyage to Australia. A mysterious spy group has caused both the fire and sabotage. They do not want a refueling station on the island because of a secret fortress and submarine base located there. Princess Malani (Mamo Clark) and two animal friends, Rex and Buck (a dog), aid Mala in beating the saboteurs and their native allies.

In Grand National's *King of the Sierras* ('38), Rex is a vicious black beast, a killer. Another stallion, "Whitey," is a horse whose instincts are kind and gentle. One day while Whitey is rescuing his burro friend from a trap, El Diablo, the black stallion, lures the mother-mare away so that the little colt becomes lost. Almost pulled down by wolves, he is rescued by Whitey. The mother is found and they rejoin the other mares. Whitey is concealed when El Diablo, thinking the herd unguarded, approaches with amorous whinnyings, which turn to rage when Whitey rushes out of cover. They engage in a terrific battle, from which Whitey emerges victorious, driving off the black Don Juan. Whitey is played Sheik, Whitey's son by Cappy, mother horse by Thunder, and Peter Pan by Bill. Human actors were Wally Albright, Frank Campeau, Edward Peil and Morgan Brown.

Rex's last film was Monogram's *Gentleman from Arizona* ('39) with John King, J. Farrell MacDonald, Joan Barclay, Craig Reynolds and Nora Lane. Rex saves the old homestead when a rejected lover drugs the father's race horse. Learning of the treachery, Joan seeks out John and convinces him to enter Rex in the race. Rex beats the rejected suitor's (Reynolds) horse to win the race. John is made foreman of the ranch and John and Joan become engaged.

From what information is available, it is a good guess that Rex lived out his last years on the ranch of Lee Doyle near Flagstaff, Arizona. Rex was in a class by himself, a mean horse to the end. Never did he get to where he could be trusted. During his career, he earned more than $100,000.

Serials

1931

The Vanishing Legion. Mascot, [12 Chapters] D: B. Reeves Eason; P: Nat Levine; SP: Wyndham Gittens, Ford Beebe, Helmer Bergman; LP: Harry Carey, Edwina Booth, Rex, King of Wild Horses, Frankie Darro, Philo McCullough, William Desmond.

1934

The Law of the Wild. Mascot, [12 Chapters] D: Armand Schaefer, B. Reeves Eason; P: Nat Levine; SP: Sherman Lowe, B. Reeves Eason; S: Ford Beebe, John Rathmell, Al Martin; LP: Rex, Rin-Tin-Tin, Jr., Bob Custer, Lucile Browne, Richard Cramer.

1935

The Adventures of Rex and Rinty. Mascot, [12 Chapters] D: B. Reeves Eason, Ford Beebe; P: Nat Levine; SP: John Rathmell, Barney Sarecky; S: B. Reeves Eason, Ray Trampe, Maurice Geraghty; LP: Rex, Rin-Tin-Tin, Jr., Kane Richmond, Norma Taylor, Smiley Burnette, Harry Woods, Mischa Auer.

1936

Robinson Crusoe of Clipper Island. Rep., [14 Chapters] D: Mack F. Wright, Ray Taylor; P: Nat Levine; SP/S: Morgan Cox, Barry Shipman, Maurice Geraghty; LP: Ray Mala, Rex, Buck (dog), Mamo Clark, Herbert Rawlinson, William Newell, John Ward, Selmer Jackson, John Picorri, George Chesebro, Robert Kortman.

VIVIAN RICH

Forgotten today, Vivian Rich made a slew of pictures in the pre-talkie era. In the years 1912–16 she was one of American Film Company's most popular actresses, appearing in a wide variety of stories. She was in 17 films with J. Warren Kerrigan, American's Number One male star. Wallace Reid, another popular male star, played opposite her in 11 films.

Other top actors with whom she worked were Sydney Ayres (10), William Garwood (9), Harry Van Meter (21), Jack Richardson (35), Louise Lester (20) and George Periolat (11). These are minimum numbers. One need realize that there are hundreds of one- and two-reelers for which casts are unknown or incomplete.

Once she left American she made feature-length films with William Farnum (Fox '17 *The Price of Silence*); Thomas Santschi (Select '19 *Code of the Yukon*); William Desmond (R-C '19 *The Mints of Hell*); Buck Jones (Fox '20 *The Last Straw*); Philo McCullough (Fox '20 *A World of Folly*); Tom Chatterton (Fox '20 *Would You Forgive*); George Chesebro (Clark-Cornelius '22 *Blind Circumstances*); Dick Hatton (Sanford '23 *Unblazed Trail*); and Matty Mattison (*Shell Shocked Sammy* '23, *The Lone Wagon* '24, and *Mile o' Minute Morgan* '24).

In 1925, Vivian was top billed in Pathé's serial *Idaho*. The following year she co-starred with William Fairbanks in Sierra's *Vanishing Millions* ('26).

In 1928, Vivian appeared in two films for Trinty Pictures—*Must We Marry* and *Old Age Handicap*—as a supporting player, and in 1931 she supported Wally Wales and Virginia Brown Faire in *Hell's Valley* for Big 4. After this sound Western, she married and ended her screen career.

Vivian was born in Philadelphia on May 26, 1893, and appeared on stage prior to her screen debut in 1912 for the Nestor Company, which she soon left to go with American. She was killed in an automobile accident on November 17, 1957. She was 64 years old.

Serials

1925

Idaho. Pathé, [10 Chapters] D: Robert F. Hill; SP: Frank Leon Smith; S: Theodore Burrell; P: C. W. Paton; LP: Vivian Rich, Mahlon Hamilton, Frederick Vroom, Frank Lackteen, Omar Whitehead, Fred De Silva, Lilian Gale.

1926

Vanishing Millions. Sierra, [15 Chapters] D: Alvin J. Neitz; LP: William Fairbanks, Vivian Rich, Alec B. Francis, Sheldon Lewis, Bull Montana, Edward Cecil, William Lowery, J. P. Lockney, George Kotsonaro, Ethel Childers.

KANE RICHMOND

Kane Richmond was one of the sound era's greatest serial stars, headlining six of them and playing a supporting role in one. Nearly all writers agree that *Spy Smasher* ('42) was the best and most popular. Perhaps. This writer is inclined to think differently, but does agree that it was the most popular. The plot revolves around the activities of a Gestapo officer called "The Mask" and his Nazi underlings who attempt to destroy America's economy by whatever means they can, especially by flooding the U.S. with counterfeit money. Spy Smasher and his twin brother thwart the Mask's plan to steal a new bombsight and a weapon capable of melting engines in flight. However, the brother is killed when he takes Spy Smasher's place in an attempt to rescue Eve Corby (Marguerite Chapman). Spy Smasher kills the Mask and other Nazi agents when he runs a motorboat at full speed into the side of a German submarine, jumping to safety before the crash.

Richmond did a superb job of separating his two personalities. The serial benefited by the competent cast, a crack stunt crew headed by daredevil Dave Sharpe, and the direction of William Witney — his first solo job after co-directing 17 of Republic's best serials with John English.

Kane was born Fred W. Bowditch in Minneapolis on December 23, 1906. His connection with movies was made when he went to work as a film booker in Minnesota. His job eventually led him on a Hollywood business trip, and an executive from Universal spotted him. Kane tested for and won the lead in the *Leather Pushers* ('30) series of ten shorts. Kane was 24 years old.

At Artclass, Kane supported Harry Carey in *Cavalier of the West* ('31) and Jack Holt and Boris Karloff in *Behind the Mask* ('32).

Fox extended an offer to Kane to go to India to star in *Devil Tiger* ('33), considered by film buffs to be somewhat of a classic. His leading lady was Marion Burns, whom he later married. Upon his return to the U.S. he

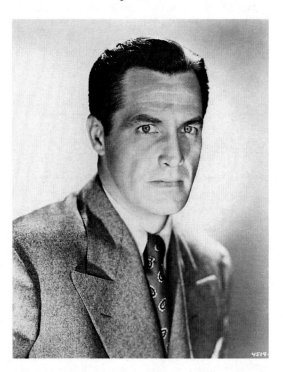

started freelancing. At Columbia he played in *Let's Fall in Love* ('34) with Ann Sothern and *Voice in the Night* ('35), a non–Western with Tim McCoy. For Poverty Row studios Beacon and Peerless he did *I Can't Escape* ('34) and *Circus Shadows* ('35), respectively. At Republic he was in *Forced Landing* ('35), at Mascot *Confidential* ('35), and at Stage & Screen *The Silent Code* ('35).

In the serial *The Lost City* ('35), Richmond played electrical engineer Bruce Gordon, who develops a machine that can trace the cause of world-wide disasters. The source is Magnetic Mountain in Africa, where he and his comrades travel to investigate. Within is a hidden city ruled by a scientific madman, Zolof, the last of the Ligurian race, portrayed by William (Stage) Boyd. Through 12 chapters Richmond battles Boyd, who is bent on unleashing his electrical power in an attempt to conquer the world. The film was independently produced by Sherman S. Krellberg.

Turner and Price (*Forgotten Horrors*, 1981) comment:

> Crude, old-fashioned and over-done, *The Lost City* piles horror upon horror in a manner undreamed of since the days of Pearl White. Its twelve chapters contain enough plot elements and cliffhangers for three times as much film. Members of the cast under direction of old-timer Harry Revier, perform in a wild-eyed manner more suited to silent pictures or Italian opera than to a mid-thirties movie, as one scene after another stretches credulity to the limit. This affront to culture, this paean to *kitsch*, is great entertainment; it keeps the spectator, mouth agape, wondering just what in hell can happen next. There is nary a dull stretch.

Kane made a convincing hero as he struggled against zombie-like giants, a paralyzing gun, drug-induced blindness and a tunnel of electrical current to defeat Zolof. It was a great serial when viewed through the eyes of a ten-year-old boy.

Next for Richmond was Mascot's *The Adventures of Rex and Rinty* ('35). He co-starred with Rex, the Wonder Horse and canine star Rin-Tin-Tin, Jr. Rex, a beautiful black stallion, is stolen from an island where he is looked upon as a god-like horse by the locals. The horsenappers sell Rex to a villainous rancher (Harry Woods) after bringing him to the States. Woods mistreats and beats Rex until he runs away and teams up with a wandering dog, Rinty. Richmond befriends both animals after many hazardous situations. Kane finally returns Rex to his native island. Woods and his accomplices follow him to the island, where more action takes place before a peaceful ending is reached.

What came next for Richmond was a series of action features for Maurice Conn's Majestic Studio; he was teamed with Frankie Darro, a familiar name to serial followers. Their films during 1936 and '37 were *Racing Blood, The Devil Diamond, Headline Crasher, Tough to Handle* and *Anything for a Thrill.* Kane was featured with no fanfare in Universal's *Flash Gordon's Trip to Mars* ('38) playing one of Ming's rocket ship captains who emerges a hero in the final episode.

During the years 1938 to 1944 Richmond was under contract to Twentieth-Century-Fox part of the time but often worked on loanout to other studios. Some of his roles were in *Chicken Wagon Family* ('39), *The Return of the Cisco Kid* ('39), *20,000 Men a Year* ('39), *Tail Spin* ('39), *Knute Rockne, All American* ('40), *Charlie Chan in Panama* ('40), *Sailor's Lady* ('40), *Mountain Music* ('41), *Riders of the Purple Sage* ('41), *Hard Guy* ('41), *Double Cross* ('41), *Great Guns* ('41), *The Bugle Sounds* ('41), *Action in the North Atlantic* ('43), *There's Something About a Soldier* ('43), *Bermuda Mystery* ('44) and *Roger Touhy, Gangster* ('44).

In 1944, Kane made his second and last Republic serial — *Haunted Harbor.* The story concerns Jim Marsden (Richmond), a schooner owner falsely convicted of murder, who escapes and attempts to exonerate himself; concerns himself with helping a doctor and his daughter (Kay Aldridge); fights off villain Roy Barcroft and his gang of henchmen; investigates a sea monster that guards "Haunted Harbor"; to finally clear himself of the murder charge.

In *Brenda Starr, Reporter* ('45), Richmond's principal contribution was getting the main character (Joan Woodbury) out of jam after jam. She was a newspaper reporter and he a police lieutenant.

That same year, Richmond played the lead in the jungle adventure appropriately called *Jungle Raiders.* Cast as Bob Moore, Richmond attempts to rescue his doctor-father who had been captured by that wonderful villain Charles King and his gang. Production-wise, it was superior to *Brenda Starr, Reporter* because it was mostly filmed outside of confining studio "barns." The author found this serial more fun to watch than *Spy Smasher* or his other serials, although *The Lost City* ('35) was highly entertaining too.

Richmond's final serial was *Brick Bradford* ('47), again based on a popular comic strip. Playing the title role, Richmond is asked by the United Nations to protect a missile not yet perfected. Although directed by capable Spencer Bennet, the serial was weak in structure and lacked inspiration. Even Richmond's abilities could not raise it above the ordinary. He is an interstellar gladiator who visits other planets via a "crystal door" that breaks down the body into atoms and propels them through space. He risks deadly acid, being frozen to death and an old-fashioned burning at the stake as he goes about his business of combating Moon people intent on capturing the missile.

Richmond is also fondly remembered for the three Monogram pictures in which he plays "The Shadow." These were *Behind the Mask* ('46), *The Missing Lady* ('46) and *The Shadow Returns* ('46).

Richmond retired from films in 1948 and became part owner and sales manager of a dress manufacturing firm. He died on March 22, 1973, at age 66.

Serials

1930–31

The Leather Pushers. Univ., [series—10 Episodes] D: Albert Kelley; SP: Douglas Doty,

Ralph Cedar, Harry Fraser; P: Stanley Bergerman; LP: Kane Richmond, Sam Hardy, Sally Blane, Nora Lane, Jack White.

1935

The Lost City. Krellberg, [12 Chapters] D: Harry Fraser; SP: Perley Sheehan, Eddie Graneman, Leon D'Usseau; S: Zelma Corroll, George Merick, Robert Dillon; P: Sherman S. Krellberg; Cam: Ronald Price, Ed Linden; Mus: Lee Zahler; LP: Kane Richmond, William (Stage) Boyd, Claudia Dell, Josef Swickard, George Hays.

The Adventures of Rex and Rinty. Mascot, [12 Chapters] D: B. Reeves Eason, Ford Beebe; SP: John Rathmell, Barney Sarecky; S: B. Reeves Eason, Ray Trampe, Maurice Geraghty; P: Nat Levine; Cam: William Nobles; Spv.: Barney Sarecky; LP: Rex, Tin-Tin-Tin, Jr., Kane Richmond, Norma Taylor, Harry Woods.

1938

Flash Gordon's Trip to Mars. Univ., [15 Chapters] D: Ford Beebe, Robert Hill; LP: Buster Crabbe, Jean Rogers, Charles Middleton, Frank Shannon, Beatrice Roberts, Donald Kerr, Wheeler Oakman, C. Montague Shaw.

1942

Spy Smasher. Rep., [12 Chapters] D: William Witney; SP: Ronald Davidson, Norman S. Hall, Joseph Poland, William Lively, Joseph O'Donnell; AP: W. J. O'Sullivan; Cam: Reggie Lanning; Mus: Mort Glickman; LP: Kane Richmond, Marguerite Chapman, Sam Flint, Tristram Coffin, Hans Schumm.

1944

Haunted Harbor. Rep., [15 Chapters] D: Spencer Bennet, Wallace Grissell; SP: Royal Cole, Basil Dickey, Jesse Duffy, Grant Nelson, Joseph Poland; S: Dayle Douglas; AP: Ronald Davidson; Cam: Bud Thackery; Mus: Joseph Dubin; LP: Kane Richmond, Kay Aldridge, Roy Barcroft, Clancy Cooper, Marshall Reed.

1945

Jungle Raiders. Col., [15 Chapters] D: Lesley Selander; SP: Ande Lamb, George H. Plympton; P: Sam Katzman; Cam: Ira H. Morgan; Mus: Lee Zahler; LP: Kane Richmond, Eddie Quillan, Veda Ann Borg, Carol Hughes, Janet Shaw, Charles King, I. Stanford Jolley, John Elliott, Jack Ingram, Ernie Adams.

1947

Brick Bradford. Col., [15 Chapters] D: Spencer Bennet; SP: George H. Plympton, Arthur Hoerl, Lewis Clay; P: Sam Katzman; Cam: Ira H. Morgan; Mus: Mischa Bakaleinikoff; LP: Lane Richmond, Rick Vallin, Linda Johnson, Pierre Watkin. Charles Quigley, Carol Forman, Charles King, Jack Ingram, George Meeker, Terry Frost.

WARNER RICHMOND

Warner Richmond's career dates back to at least 1914 and an unbilled role in *The Man from Home.* Other early credits for Richmond include *The Great Divide* ('15), *Fifty-Fifty* ('16), *The Hero of Submarine D-2* ('16), *Brown of Harvard* ('18), *The Gray Towers Mystery* ('19), in which Richmond is a principal player, and *My Lady's Garter* ('20).

Richmond had a good role in *The Heart of Maryland* ('21), but an even better one in the 1927 remake starring Dolores Costello. He vied with Jason Robards for Maryland's affection. And in another 1921 film, *The Mountain Woman*, with Pearl White, he fights with her father, wounding him.

Warner remained active throughout the

'20s. In *The Challenge* ('22) he is a jealous suitor of Dolores Cassinelli who loses out to Rod La Rocque. In *Isle of Doubt* ('22) he conspires with Dorothy Mackaill to take financial advantage of the man she marries. He stars in *Jan of the Big Snows* ('22) as a young man, inexperienced with women, who falls in love with the young wife of a trapper living in an isolated northern trading post. In *Mark of the Beast* ('23) he is a brutish husband and crook who is killed by his own mother after having attacked his bride in a mountain cabin. In *The Man from Glengarcy* ('23) he is left to settle a blood feud with a rival lumberman. As the father of Dorothy Mackaill in *The Making of O'Malley* ('25) he exposes a bootlegger gang leader but out of love for his fiancée he lets the man go, with the result he is dismissed from the police force. However, he is reinstated later and proclaimed a hero.

Chicago ('27) finds him a district attorney who prosecutes Victor Varconi for theft of money from his lawyer, who has promised to get Varconi's wife, Roxie, acquitted of murder. In *Finger Prints* ('27) he is chief of a gang of mail thieves who is caught and sent to prison, though he does not reveal to the other gang members the location of the loot. The film revolves about the gang's efforts to obtain the secret of the money's location from him. He is a shiftless young Irishman who goes to America to seek his fortune in *Irish Hearts* ('27). May McAvoy and her father follow, as May loves Warner. However, Warner loses his job and takes up with a flapper. May finds happiness with a ship's steward, Jason Robards. Richmond is a district attorney again in *Big News* ('29) with Carole Lombard and Robert Armstrong involved in a murder case.

In *The Apache* ('28), Margaret Livingston falls in love with Richmond, a Paris Apache, and works with him. When an official is mysteriously killed, Richmond is suspected but her former partner is the real murderer. In both *Shadows of the Night* ('28) and *You Can't Beat the Law* ('28) he is leader of a gang of criminals. Still not learning the error of his ways, he again is a thief killed by the gendarmes in *The Redeeming Sin* ('29).

Billy the Kid ('30) was a sound film starring Johnny Mack Brown as Billy and Wallace Beery as Pat Garrett. Warner Richmond played Ballinger, a henchman who kills Tunston (Wyndham Standing), to whom Billy is devoted.

During the '30s and early '40s, Western and serial aficionados came to know Richmond as he menaced serial heroes Don Terry, Clyde Beatty, Grant Withers and cowboys Tex Ritter, Ken Maynard, Johnny Mack Brown, Gene Autry, Bob Steele, William Boyd, Jack Randall, Tom Keene, James Newill and Eddie Dean and cowgirl Dorothy Page.

The author can still recall *Smokey Smith* ('35) which he saw nearly 70 years ago and has not seen since. Richmond's throwing acid in Gabby Hayes' eyes made an impression that stayed with me, though I remember nothing else about the film. Richmond's role as Sharkey in *The Lost Jungle* ('34) is also a memorable one. He always had that Fred Kohler sneer and was adept at playing mongrel characters. One could easily loathe his character.

Warner was injured in 1940 when he fell off of a horse during the making of a Western and was hospitalized several months.

Richmond was born in Racine, Wisconsin, on January 11, 1886. He attended Virginia Military Institute and the University of Virginia, graduating with both B.A. and M.A. degrees.

He died in 1948 at age 62.

Serials

1934

The Lost Jungle. Mascot, [12 Chapters] D: Armand Schaefer, David Howard; P: Nat Levine; LP: Clyde Beatty, Cecilia Parker, Syd Saylor, Warner Richmond, Wheeler Oakman, Maston Williams, Crauford Kent, Edward LeSaint, Lew Meehan.

1935

Phantom Empire. Mascot, [12 Chapters] D: Otto Brower, B.Reeves Eason; SP: John Rathmall, Armand Schaefer; P: Nat Levine; LP: Gene Autry, Frankie Darro, Betsy King Ross, Dorothy Christie, Wheeler Oakman, Charles K. French, Warner Richmond, Smiley Burnette, Wally Wales [Hal Taliaferro].

The Fighting Marines. Mascot, [12 Chapters] D: B. Reeves Eason, Joseph Kane; P: Nat Levine; SP: Barney Sarecky, Sherman Lowe; Spv.: Barney Sarecky; LP: Grant Withers, Ann Rutherford, Adrian Morris, Robert Warwick, Robert Frazer, Warner Richmond, Frank Reicher, Jason Robards, Ted Adams.

1938

The Secret of Treasure Island. Col., [15 Chapters] D: Elmer Clifton; P: Jack Fier; SP: George Rosener, Elmer Clifton, George Merrick; LP: Don Terry, Gwen Gaze, Grant Withers, Hobart Bosworth, William Farnum, Walter Miller, Dave O'Brien, Warner Richmond, Reed Howes.

Flash Gordon's Trip to Mars. Univ., [15 Chapters] D: Ford Beebe, Robert Hill; SP/S: Wyndham Gittens, Norman S. Hall, Ray Trampe, Herbert Dalmas; LP: Larry (Buster) Crabbe, Jean Rogers, Charles Middleton, Frank Shannon, Kane Richmond, Beatrice Roberts, Donald Kerr, Richard Alexander.

1939

The Oregon Trail. Univ., [15 Chapters] D: Ford Beebe,Saul A. Goodkind; P: Henry MacRae; LP: Johnny Mack Brown, Louise Stanley, Fuzzy Knight, Bill Cody, Jr., Forrest Taylor, Edward LeSaint, Charles King, Warner Richmond, Roy Barcroft, Karl Hackett.

CLEO RIDGELY

Cleo Ridgely was an extra in the original *The Spoilers* ('14), but following that she had a much bigger role in *The Invisible Power* ('14). In the story, William H. West uses his powers of mental telepathy to erase Cleo's memory of dance hall owner Paul Hurst, who has lured her away from her family. She was a full-fledged star in 1915 when she made *The Chorus Lady*, a comedy drama in which Cleo is engaged to detective Wallace Reid. When her young sister Marjorie Daw joins the show, things began to sizzle.

In *The Puppet Crown* ('15), Cleo is a villainess, Duchess Sylvia, who gains the throne following an uprising, then orders the arrest of Alexia (Ina Claire), daughter of the deceased king. She is saved by Carlyle Blackwell. Cleo is a kleptomaniac in *Stolen Goods* ('15) and is responsible for Blanche Sweet being sent to prison. She co-stars with Wallace Reid in *The Love Mask* ('16), a California gold rush saga, and in *The Yellow Pawn* ('16), dealing with murder and jealousy.

In *The Golden Chance* ('16), Cleo takes a job as a seamstress when her alcoholic husband won't work, and she falls in love with millionaire Wallace Reid. In *The House with Golden Windows* ('16), Cleo dreams of owning the palatial estate next door. Her husband, Wallace Reid, is only a shepherd. In a dream, she finds that wealth is not all it is cracked up to be, her husband is killed and she is about to be shot when she wakes up in a sweat. She never complains about her station in life again. In *The Selfish Woman* ('16), Cleo and Reid are again married. He is a railroad engineer whose father agrees to pay Cleo $1 million if she will see that his son loses a railroad building job, as he wants his son back in his own firm. Cleo lies to the workmen and they strike. When things get out of hand and violence occurs, she confesses, the men go back to work and she makes up with her husband.

The Victoria Cross ('16) is a historical drama in which Cleo is the courageous wife of Lou Tellegen. In *The Victor of Conscience* ('16) she is a penniless dancer fought over by Tellegen and Elliott Dexter. *Wait for Me* ('20) depicts her as a beautiful siren who tries to lure Lew Cody, but instead causes a man to commit suicide.

In *The Law and the Woman* ('21), a melodrama of passion and murder, Cleo is a villainess. Cleo is a supporting player in *The Sleepwalker* ('22), about a sleepwalker who is misunderstood until, in her sleep, she saves a baby's life. *Forgotten Law* ('22) is a domestic melodrama in which Jack Mulhall, thinking his wife (Cleo) guilty of adultery, changes his will to leave her nothing. Her innocence is established by a murderer in the end. In *Dangerous Pastime* ('22), Cleo co-stars with Lew Cody and Elinor Fair in a story of a young man whose dreams of adventure are wiped out when, in a dream, he is drugged by a previous girlfriend and taken to an isolated cabin. Awakening, he had no further desires for adventure. She has a supporting role in *The Beautiful and Damned* ('22), the story of a couple's reckless, spendthrift ways.

Marie Prevost and Harry Myers starred. And there were other films.

In 1915, Cleo co-starred with Ruth Roland in the *Girl Detective* series. A society girl has a position as a special investigator for the police and works on various cases where her unique talents can help to solve crimes. Each episodes is complete in itself. Roland was star of the first seven episodes, then dropped out to be replaced by Ridgely, who had played a supporting role up to that point.

Cleo Ridgely died in Glendale, California, in 1962 at age 68.

Serial

1915

The Girl Detective. Kalem, [14 or more chapters] D: James W. Horne; SP: Hamilton Smith and others; LP: Ruth Roland, Cleo Ridgely, Thomas Lingham, William H. West, Edward Clisbee, Frank Jonasson, Paul Hurst, James Horne, Robert Gray, Knute Rahman, Anna Lingham, Arthur Shirley.

RIN-TIN-TIN

On the morning of September 15, 1916 (some sources say 1918), Corp. Lee Duncan and Capt. George Bryant left Toul in Lorraine, France, to look for a new field site for the 136th Aero Squadron. In an abandoned German war dog station that had been heavily shelled, in a blasted dugout, Duncan discovered a half-starved mother German Shepherd and five puppies. He was able to bring two of the puppies back to the States but the female contracted pneumonia and died. Duncan named the male Rin-Tin-Tin and took him with him back to California. There he trained the dog.

Rin-Tin-Tin made his film debut in a story attributed to James Oliver Curwood,

The Man from Hell's River (Western Pictures, 1922). He is said to have appeared in three newsreel type shorts in 1922. Warner Brothers took notice of him and entered into a contract with Lee Duncan for the dog's services. Rinty, as he was called, was not docile (he sometimes attacked actors and directors), but he was handsome and very clever, and his rise to stardom was fast. In 1923 he was starred in *Where the North Begins* with Claire Adams. He was an instant hit and Warners planned more films for him. Rinty became so profitable that the studio insured him for $100,000 against death, injury or illness.

In all, Warners made 19 features starring the canine star. They provided a small orchestra for mood music when he worked, paid him $1,000 a week, often served him Chateaubriand steak with all the trimmings, provided him his own production unit, his own valet and chef and a private limousine and chauffeur.

Rinty was called the "mortgage lifter" because of his unfailing commercial success. He was also, surprisingly, rather a good actor. He developed his acting range from film to film until he could go through long and complicated routines without looking to Duncan for direction. He even played a long scene in closeup in the 1925 *The Night Cry*, his eyes moist with emotion and his ears drooping. According to Jack Warner, there was a multiplicity of Rinty dogs in order to protect Warners' investment and to better utilize the various dogs' individual abilities. All the dogs left Warners when Duncan did.

In such '20s hits as *Clash of Wolves* ('25), *A Dog of the Regiment* ('27), *Tracked by the Police* ('27) and *Land of the Silver Fox* ('28), Rinty ran the gamut of emotions as capably as any human star of the period. For several years he provided Warners with its major source of revenue. Accordingly, he was given top billing. He made the fortune of a young writer named Darryl Zanuck, who helped direct the dog's meteoric rise and who went on to become the head of Twentieth Century-Fox. Over the course of his career Rinty earned $5 million for Lee Duncan.

Rinty was the biggest animal movie star of all time and the biggest box office attraction at Warners through the '20s. A superstar he was, receiving around 12,000 fan letters a week. Author Jon Tuska (*The Vanishing Legion*, McFarland, 1982) quotes director D. Ross Lederman:

> Of all the actors I ever worked with in my long career, Rin-Tin-Tin was the most capable. You probably think his trainer, Lee Duncan, always told him what to do. He may have in the beginning. I don't know. But when I worked with him we needed very few retakes and almost no extensive rehearsing. That dog knew just what was expected of him. He would watch Duncan for a signal, if movement was required. He couldn't tell

time. But as for emoting, or playing a scene right, he didn't need any coaching. That's the unusual thing about that dog. He actually seemed to understand the story line well enough to bring off his role better than most of the other actors in the picture. I had more trouble with Tim McCoy and Buck Jones at Columbia that I ever had with Rinty ar Warner's. He was one of the few truly professional actors we had in Hollywood at that time. He just went about his business.

Rinty was signed by Mascot in 1930 after his Warners contract expired. Lee Duncan received $5,000 for the dog's services in the serial *The Lone Defender* ('30) featuring Walter Miller as Ramon, June Marlowe as Dolores and Buzz Barton as Buzz. Rinty plays a dog whose master is killed by Jenkins (Bob Kortman), a member of the Cactus Kid's (Lee Shumway) gang. He aids Ramon, an undercover agent for the Department of Justice, in tracking down the notorious Cactus Kid, who is after the rich mine which has been left to Dolores. Rinty and his friends have harrowing adventures each week. In the action-packed climax, the Cactus Kid and his gang are brought to justice.

Rinty starred in the 1931 serial *The Lightning Warrior* for Mascot. Frankie Darro played Jimmy Carter, whose father is killed by an Indian arrow shot from the riverbank. There are also arrows that whiz through the night with threatening messages. Who is the cloaked and masked Wolf Man? Why are the Kern River residents being driven away? Who killed Rinty's master? Who shot Jimmy's father? It was exciting filmfare at its best. Rinty helps Jimmy uncover the real identity of the Wolf Man, who is in reality the mastermind behind the entire campaign to terrorize the settlers.

Rinty was of very dubious disposition, controllable only by Duncan, for whom he would do anything, and extremely jealous had his master been with other dogs. On August 10, 1932, Rinty and Duncan were romping on their front lawn when Rinty jumped into Duncan's arms. He was dead weight. As Duncan sank to his knees, he attracted the attention of his neighbor, Jean Harlow, who

Rin-Tin-Tin, George Brent and Georgia Hale in *The Lightning Warrior* (Mascot, 1931).

ran over to him. Both cradled the beloved German Shepherd, Jean sobbing her heart out while Duncan wept for a part of himself that also had died. Rin was 16 years old, a real trouper until his end. He is remembered as one of the most loved and greatest of canine actors to have graced the silver screen. He had thrilled and amused the world's millions of motion picture fans and had made Warner Brothers capable of carrying on and achieving great success in the film industry.

Serials

1930

The Lone Defender. Mascot, [12 Chapters] D: Richard Thorpe; SP: William Presley Burt, Harry Fraser, Ben Cohen; P: Nat Levine; LP: Rin-Tin-Tin, Walter Miller, June Marlowe, Buzz Barton, Josef Swickard, Lee Shumway, Frank Lanning, William Desmond, Kermit Maynard, Joe Bonomo, Tom Santschi, Lafe McKee.

1931

The Lightning Warrior. Mascot, [12 Chapters] D: Armand Schaefer, Benjamin H. Kline; SP: Wyndham Gittens, Ford Beebe, Colbert Clark; P: Nat Levine; Cam: Ernest Miller, William Nobles, Tom Galligan; Mus: Lee Zahler; LP: Rin-Tin-Tin, Frankie Darro, George Brent, Georgia Hale, Pat O'Malley, Lafe McKee, Robert Kortman, Yakima Canutt, Kermit Maynard, Cliff Lyons.

RIN-TIN-TIN, JR.

Rin-Tin-Tin, Jr., followed in his father's tracks and achieved a certain stardom, but he could not replace his famous sire. Rinty, Jr., first appeared on screen with Rinty, Sr., in *Hills of Kentucky* ('27). Rinty, Jr., was one of Lee Duncan's stand-ins for the original Rinty. Interestingly, Yakima Canutt considered Junior the better actor — maybe because Rinty, Sr., bit him. At Warner Brothers, Rinty, Sr., had from six to 16 doubles.

In 1933, Rinty, Jr., was in *Pride of the Legion* (aka *The Big Payoff*), an adaptation of a Peter B. Kyne story. Human actors included Barbara Kent, Victor Jory, Sally Blane, J. Farrell MacDonald and Glenn Tryon. Rinty rescues Jory from a river after he had been discharged from the police department for cowardice. In the end, however, Jory regains his place on the force and marries the girl he loves.

Mascot released *The Wolf Dog* in 1933 with Rinty playing the title role and Frankie Darro, George J. Lewis and Boots Mallory supporting. Bob Whitlock (Lewis) invents an electric ray that can destroy ships at a distance of several miles. Norman Bryan (Hale Hamilton), general manager of the Courtney Steamship Lines, plans to steal it. Bob

Kane Richmond and Rinty in *The Adventures of Rex and Rinty* (Mascot, 1935).

Bob Custer and Rin-Tin-Tin, Jr., in *The Law of the Wild* (Mascot, 1934).

becomes friends with a young boy, Frank (Darro), and his dog, Pal (Rinty). All three are involved in a desperate struggle to stay alive and protect the invention until it can be turned over to the government. Frank is the heir to a large fortune and Bryan is secretly trying to rob him of his inheritance.

Rinty was co-starred with Rex, the Wonder Horse, in Mascot's *The Law of the Wild* ('34). Bob Custer and Lucile Browne are the human leads. In the story, Rex and Rinty are pals. Their master (Custer) is falsely accused of murdering a member of Richard Cramer's gang of crooks who have stolen Rex and entered him in a race that he wins. In a dispute over the winnings, Dick Alexander is killed by a co-conspirator and the blame put on Custer. Arrested by sheriff Jack Rockwell, Custer escapes to find his horse and the killer. While searching for Rex Custer meets Lucile Browne who, along with

Rex and Rinty, survive numerous ordeals before justice is served and horse and master are reunited. Lucile rides Rex in the sweepstakes in the final showdown.

Nat Levine thought enough of Rex and Rinty that he starred them in *The Adventures of Rex and Rinty* ('35). Kane Richmond was the human star. Rex is a "god horse" worshipped by the natives of Sujan. He is stolen by three American crooks and sold to Harry Woods, a wealthy ranch owner who attempts to train Rex as a polo pony. Rex escapes and teams up with Rinty and together they outsmart their tormentors with the help of Richmond, who returns Rex and Rinty to Sujan. Woods follows Richmond and his party to Sujan and convinces the people to turn against their "god horse." But Richmond and a loyal priest join forces and rescue Rex just as he is about to be burned as a sacrifice.

In *The Test* (Rel., '35), Rin-Tin-Tin, Jr.,

has the star role. His master is Grant Withers, whose furs are constantly being stolen by Monte Blue or his minions. Withers finds two of Blue's henchmen robbing his trap. In their haste to get away, they drop their bag of furs, which are Grant's furs. Back at the trading post he leaves Rinty to guard the furs while he goes inside to challenge Blue. Rinty is distracted by Nannette, Blue's dog, and he leaves his guardpost to romp in the trees with her.

When Grant finds the furs missing, he scolds Rinty severely. Rinty takes off to recover the stolen furs. He battles twice with Blue and finally outwits him and escapes in a canoe with the furs. Blue and his men are captured by the trappers and master and dog are reunited.

Tough Guy ('35) was an MGM film starring Jackie Cooper. Cooper's father does not like Jackie's dog, Duke. The boy and dog run away, stealing a ride on the back of a truck, unbeknownst to its driver, gang leader Joseph Calleia. When Jackie is discovered, Calleia orders a cohort (Joe) to kill them. Jackie has escaped but is seen hiding on the roof of a building. Joe sees them and shoots, wounding Duke. He then takes the boy and dog with him into the mountains to elude capture. He is nice to Jackie and Duke and tries to send them away, but Jackie prefers Joe's company to his dad's. In the end, Joe is killed trying to keep the gang from killing Jackie, while Duke holds Tony (Ed Pawley) at bay until police arrive.

In *Skull and Crown* (Rel., '35) Bob Franklin (Regis Toomey), a member of the U.S. Customs Patrol on the Mexican border, is joyously preparing for the homecoming of his sister Barbara (Lois January) from a fashionable school. Ed (Jack Mulhall), a brother officer, arrives to tell Bob that Zorro (Jack Mower), a notorious smuggler, has just crossed the line with a contraband cargo. Leaving his dog Rin at the station at the wheel of his car with a note explaining his regrets, Bob hastens with Ed on the trail of Zorro. The contraband truck and its driver are captured, but Zorro escapes afoot.

Barbara arrives, is met by Rin, and they proceed to Bob's cottage to await Bob's arrival. Zorro, passing the cottage, sees the car and determines to have it. He enters the house to obtain the keys. Barbara is ruthlessly killed by Zorro, although valiantly defended by Rin, who is stunned by Zorro's gun. The latter makes his escape with the car.

Incensed at the apparent disloyalty of Rin, whom he had charged with the safekeeping of his sister, Bob turns him out in contempt and anger, unaware that Rin had been subdued by Zorro.

Overcome with grief, and determined to capture the slayer, Bob resigns from the service. Masquerading as a smuggler and a friend of the captured smuggler, he obtains admission to "Skull and Crown," a fashionable resort owned by John Norton (John Elliott), who, together with his daughter Ann (Molly O'Day) are held prisoner there by Zorro and his cohorts, who have commandeered the lodge. Rin, still devoted to Bob, follows his master at a safe distance and also gains entrance, but is captured.

After Bob is unmasked, he is imprisoned to await the arrival of Zorro. Rin escapes and releases Bob as Zorro enters the room. There is a terrific fight, climaxed with the capture of the master smuggler and his gang. Rin and Bob are reunited.

Caryl of the Mountains (Rel., '36) stars Rin-Tin-Tin, Jr., and with Francis X. Bushman, Jr., and Lois Wilde in the principal human roles. Caryl (Wilde) discovers that her employer, Enos Colvin (Robert Walker), is preparing to steal a fortune in negotiable securities from the firm. She circumvents him by stealing them herself, placing them in a package and mailing them to her uncle Jean (Joseph Swickard).

Colvin, discovering the theft, suspects her and traces the packet by studying the blotter, which Caryl used on the envelope. On arrival at Jean's cabin, Colvin instantly stirs the antagonism of Rinty. Colvin demands the securities. Jean refuses, naturally, there is a fierce battle, and the trapper is killed. In a frenzied effort to protect his master, Rinty places himself in range. Colvin fires again and the dog falls back, badly hurt.

Colvin escapes in his powerful car, but without the package, which Jean had hidden with only Rinty as witness.

Sgt. Brad Sheridan (Bushman) of the Mounted Police first learns of trouble when the dog crawls into the barracks, half alive. A warrant is delivered to the barracks for the arrest of Caryl Foray on a charge of embezzlement. Exciting events take place as Rinty, Sgt. Sheridan and Caryl set about proving Colvin guilty of murdering Jean Foray. Rinty reveals the hiding place of the securities and overtakes an escaping Colvin. Caryl and Rinty become the prized possessions of Sgt. Sheridan.

Vengeance of Rannah (Rel., '36) reunites Rinty with Bob Custer. The owner of Twin Oaks Stagecoach is murdered during a $10,000 payroll robbery. Custer goes undercover as an insurance agent to find the killers. He quickly locates the wrecked coach and Pop Warner's body, which Rannah (Rinty) has been guarding. Certain that Rannah can identify the killers, Bob asks Pop's daughter (Victoria Vinton) to hide the dog. The killers hunt for Rannah to kill him. The killers are apprehended with Rannah's help.

In *The Silver Trail* (Rel., '37), Rinty aids Rex Lease in finding the rich silver mine of his murdered friend. Mary Russell's father has been killed and his mine taken over by Triangle Mines, a front for Edward Cassidy and his gang. Rinty and Rex expose Cassidy for what he is.

Death Goes North (Col., '39) finds Rinty playing "King," who helps the Northwest Mounted Police to capture a murderer in a story of skullduggery among rival lumber interests in the Northwest. Edgar Edwards and Sheila Bromley are the human stars.

In *Hollywood Cavalcade* (TCF, '39), Rinty plans Rin-Tin-Tin, Sr., in a lavish film headlined by Alice Faye and Don Ameche. In 1941 he could be seen in *Law of the Wolf*, a Ziehm release featuring Dennis Moore, Luana Walters, Robert Frazer and Tom London.

Serials

1933

The Wolf Dog. Mascot, [12 Chapters] D: Colbert Clark, Harry Fraser; S: Barney Sarecky, Sherman Lowe; Cam: Harry Neumann, William Nobles, Tom Galligan; LP: Rin-Tin-Tin, Jr., George J. Lewis, Frankie Darro, Boots Mallory, Hale Hamilton, Henry B. Walthall, Lafe McKee, Stanley Blystone, Tom London, Fred Kohler.

1935

The Adventures of Rex and Rinty. Mascot, [12 Chapters] D: Ford Beebe, B. Reeves Eason; Spv.: Barney Sarecky; S: V. Reeves Eason, Maurice Geraghty, Ray Trampe; SP: John Rathmell, Barney Sarecky; Cam: William Nobles; LP: Rin-Tin-Tin, Jr., Rex, King of the Wild Horses, Kane Richmond, Norma Taylor, Harry Woods, Mischa Auer, Smiley Burnette, Hooper Atchley, Wheeler Oakman, Jack Rockwell, Charles King.

JASON ROBARDS, SR.

In the sound era, Jason Robards usually played villains, whereas in silent pictures he often played the hero. He was born on December 31, 1892, in Hillsdale, Michigan, and became a prominent actor of the American stage. He became a movie actor in 1921 with the film *The Gilded Lily* in which he plays the country boy in love with Mae Murray, a Broadway cafe hostess. She is also loved by Lowell Sherman, a wealthy man-about-town. She marries Robards, however, and settles down to a quiet country life. Robards begins to drink and encourages his wife to return to her former life, which she does. Collapsing on the dance floor, she is rescued by Sherman, who is then shot at by Robards. Later, at his home, Sherman introduces the girl to his mother as his fiancée.

Stella Maris ('25) is a tearjerker in which two men (Elliott Dexter and Jason Robards) both love Mary Philbin (Stella), a crippled girl. Dexter, separated from his wife, assumes the care of a slavey named Unity Blake when his wife is sent to jail for three years for beating the girl. Dexter declares his love for Stella, who had been healed by a great physician. When Dexter's wife is released from jail, she learns of Dexter's love for Stella and refuses to give him a divorce. Unity, who has fallen in love with Dexter, kills his wife and then turns the gun on herself. Dexter comes to realize that Stella loves Robards and he gives them his blessing.

In *Polly of the Movies* ('27), Robards is in love with Gertrude Short, who desires to become a movie star. When he inherits $25,000, he sinks it into a movie intended as a melodrama. Their picture, however, is a comedy scream and a film mogul pays them well for it. They decide to wed and forget moving pictures.

In *Isle of Lost Ships* ('29), Robards is a prisoner of a detective on board a ship bound from Puerto Rico to New York. Robards and society girl Virginia Valli are attracted to each other. The ship is swept into the Sargasso Sea, a wreckage-cluttered eddy in the central Atlantic, and is stranded amidst an "island" of ships, comprising a colony dominated by Noah Beery, who demands that Virginia marry him. Robards beats him. A mechanic leads Robards, Virginia and the detective to a stranded submarine and they manage to escape. The detective promises to help clear Robards with the law. Robards finds happiness with Valli.

Robards is a hero in *Footloose Widows* ('26), *Casey Jones* ('27), *Streets of Shanghai* ('27) and other silent features, but in talkies he is usually a villain. He can be seen in *Charlie Chan Carries On* ('31), *Docks of San Francisco* ('32), *Dance Hall Hostess* ('33), *The Crusades* ('35), *Damaged Lives* ('37), *The Mad Empress* ('39), *A Game of Death* ('45) and others. He was inactive during the 1950s because of an eye infection; recovered, he appeared on Broadway in '58 in *The Disenchanted* with his namesake son. His last film was *Wild in the Country* ('61).

Jason Robards died in Sherman Oaks, California, of a heart attack in 1963. He was 70 years old. Western addicts will remember him from *White Eagle* ('32), *Range War* ('39), *Wanderer of the Wasteland* ('45), *Thunder Mountain* ('47), *Trail Street* ('47), *Under the Tonto Rim* ('47), *Wild Horse Mesa* ('47), *Guns of Hate* ('48), *Son of God's Country* ('48), *Return of the Bad Men* ('48), *Western Heritage* ('48), *Rimfire* ('49), *South of Death Valley* ('49) and *Riders of the Whispering Pines* ('49).

Serials

1934

Burn 'Em Up Barnes. Mascot, [12 Chapters] D: Colbert Clark, Armand Schaefer; LP: Jack Mulhall, Lola Lane, Frankie Darro, Julian Rivero, Jason Robards.

1935

The Fighting Marines. Mascot, [12 Chapters] D: B. Reeves Eason, Joseph Kane; LP: Grant Withers, Adrian Morris, Ann Rutherford, Robert Warwick, George J. Lewis, Jason Robards.

The Miracle Rider. Mascot, [15 Chapters] D: Armand Schaefer, B. Reeves Eason; LP: Tom Mix, Joan Gale, Charles Middleton, Robert Kortman, Jason Robards, Edward Hearn, Robert Frazer, Ernie Adams, Wally Wales [Hal Taliaferro], Jack Rockwell.

1937

Zorro Rides Again. Rep., [12 Chapters] D: William Witney, John English; LP: John Carroll, Helen Christian, Duncan Renaldo, Noah Beery, Sr., Yakima Canutt, Robert Kortman, Edmund Cobb.

1939

Zorro's Fighting Legion. Rep., [12 Chapters] D: William Witney, John English; LP: Reed Hadley, Sheila Darcy, William Corson, Leander de Cordova, Edmund Cobb.

Scouts to the Rescue. Univ., [12 Chapters] D: Ray Taylor, Alan James; LP: Jackie Cooper, Vondell Darr, Edwin Stanley, William Ruhl, Bill Cody, Jr., Jason Robards, Frank Coghlan, Jr.

BEATRICE ROBERTS

Beatrice Roberts was in a lot of films but perhaps her signature role was as Queen Azura in *Flash Gordon's Trip to Mars* ('38), the sequel to *Flash Gordon* ('36). Roberts relished her role and put her all into it. Flash and his friends rocket to Mars to investigate a ray that is sapping the Earth of nitrogen needed for plant life. There they discover that Emperor Ming is not dead. They also discover and befriend a race of Clay People who had been changed from normal beings to clay by the magic of Azura. A secret rocket subway connects the palace of Azura, in league with Ming, with the dark abode of the Clay

Buster Crabbe, Jean Rogers and Beatrice Roberts (right) in *Flash Gordon* (Universal, 1936).

Men. People walk high above the city supported only by glowing "light bridges" and the enormous Nitron Lamp continued extracting nitrogen from the Earth.

Azura falls in love with Flash but he is not receptive to her advances. In the end, the Clay People are restored to their former human selves by destroying the magical Black and White Sapphires of Azura, the jewels that gave her the power to even vanish and teleport herself. Ming is destroyed (or so we think), and Flash, Dale, Dr. Zarkov and Happy return to Earth.

Beatrice worked throughout the '40s and into the '50s, but most of her roles were bits. She was Varga in *Frankenstein Meets the Wolf Man* ('43); a nurse in *Phantom of the Opera* ('43); a juror in *Jungle Woman* ('44); a secretary in *San Diego, I Love You* ('44) and *Scarlet Street*; a customer in *The Runaround* ('46); Marie in *White Tie and Tails* ('46); Mrs. Weber in *Time Out of Mind* ('47); a manageress in *Ride the Pink Horse* ('47); and Belle in *Family Honeymoon* ('49).

Serial

1938

Flash Gordon's Trip to Mars. Univ., [15 Chapters] D: Ford Beebe, Robert Hill; S/SP: Wyndham Gittens, Norman S. Hall, Ray Trampe, Herbert Dalmas; LP: Buster Crabbe, Jean Rogers, Charles Middleton, Frank Shannon, Beatrice Roberts, Donald Kerr, Richard Alexander, C. Montague Shaw, Wheeler Oakman.

LEE ROBERTS

Lee Roberts' first credited roles were in *Death Valley Rangers* ('43), *The Masked Marvel* ('43) and *Outlaw Trail* ('44). We find no credits for him in 1945, though he may well have played some uncredited roles. From 1946 through 1950 he appeared in 34 features and ten serials.

In 1953 he was in *Kansas Pacific, Cow Country* and *Vigilante Terror*; in '55, *Fort Yuma*; in '56, *Backlash*. There seem to be no further credits for Roberts beyond these.

In the serials his roles were mostly minor, but in his last one, *Blazing the Overland Trail* ('56), he had the lead role of Tom Bridger, Army scout. Unfortunately it was next to the last American serial made. Perhaps if serials and programmer Westerns had continued, Roberts might have made it as a Western lead. We will never know.

Evelyn Finley, his former wife, thought he had potential but that he was not aggressive enough. She did not know what happened to him after 1956. He figuratively fell through the cracks.

Serials

1943

The Masked Marvel. Rep., [12 Chapters] D: Spencer Bennet; LP: Tom Steele, William Forrest, Louise Currie, Johnny Arthur, Rod Bacon, David Bacon.

1950

Pirates of the High Seas. Col., [15 Chapters] D: Spencer Bennet, Thomas Carr; LP: Buster Crabbe, Lois Hall, Tommy Farrell, Gene Roth, Tris Coffin, Hugh Prosser, Lee Roberts, I. Stanford Jolley, John Hart.

Desperados of the West. Rep., [12 Chapters] D: Fred C. Brannon; LP: Richard Powers [Tom Keene], Judy Clark, Roy Barcroft, I. Stanford

Jolley, Lee Phelps, Lee Roberts, Edmund Cobb, Dennis Moore.

The James Brothers of Missouri. Rep., [12 Chapters] D: Fred C. Brannon; LP: Keith Richards, Robert Bice, Noel Neill, Roy Barcroft, Patricia Knox, Edmund Cobb, Lane Bradford, Gene Stutenroth, Lee Roberts, Marshall Reed.

1952

King of the Congo. Col., [15 Chapters] D: Spencer Bennet, Wallace A. Grissell; LP: Buster Crabbe, Gloria Dea, Leonard Penn, Jack Ingram, Rusty Wescoatt, Nick Stuart, Rick Vallin, Lee Roberts, Frank Ellis.

1953

Gunfighters of the Northwest. Col., [15 Chapters] D: Spencer Bennet, Charles S. Gould; LP: Jock Mahoney, Clayton Moore, Phyllis Coates, Don Harvey, Marshall Reed, Lyle Talbot, Rodd Redwing, Lee Roberts, Terry Frost.

The Great Adventures of Captain Kidd. Col., [15 Chapters] D: Derwin Abbe, Charles S. Gould; LP: Richard Crane, David Bruce, John Crawford, George Wallace, Lee Roberts, Nick Stuart, Ray Corrigan, Charles King, Lyle Talbot, Edmund Cobb, Paul Nelan.

1954

Riding with Buffalo Bill. Col., [15 Chapters] D: Spencer Bennet; LP: Marshall Reed, Rick Vallin, Joanne Rio, Shirley Whitney, Jack Ingram, William Fawcett, Gregg Barton, Lee Roberts, Ed Coch.

1955

Adventures of Captain Africa. Col., [15 Chapters] D: Spencer Bennet; LP: John Hart, Rick Vallin, Ben Welden, June Howard, Bud Osborne, Lee Roberts, Paul Marion, Terry Frost.

King of the Carnival. Rep., [12 Chapters] D: Franklyn Adreon; LP: Harry Lauter, Fran Bennett, Keith Richards, Robert Shayne, Rick Vallin, Robert Clarke, Lee Roberts, Terry Frost.

1956

Blazing the Overland Trail. Col., [15 Chapters] D: Spencer Bennet; LP: Lee Roberts, Dennis Moore, Norma Brooks, Gregg Barton, Don C. Harvey.

Perils of the Wilderness. Col., [15 Chapters] D: Spencer Bennet; LP: Dennis Moore, Richard Emory, Eve Anderson [Evelyn Finley], Kenneth MacDonald, Don C. Harvey, Lee Roberts.

LYNNE ROBERTS / MARY HART

Lynne Roberts was one of the prettiest, most charmingly talented, and least appreciated serial and Western actresses. In a melodramatic potboiler she could scream and look as frightened as anyone; in a Western she played her part with all the energy at her command (so much so that she sometimes completely overshadowed her leading man). Yet this able actress was sadly neglected.

Lynne was born in El Paso, Texas, on November 22, 1919. Her family moved to Los Angeles when she was only nine days old. She was enrolled in Lawlor's Professional School when she was four years old and commenced to study dancing and dramatics and to appear in school plays. By the time she was six, she had appeared on the stage and in films. She later went into radio. When she was nine, Lynne and her brother were out on the road in an act. They were moderately successful, but at 12 Lynne was already too mature in appearance to continue in juvenile theatricals.

When she went to work at Republic, it was as Lynn (without the "e") Roberts. The studio changed her name to Mary Hart when she made six Westerns with Roy Rogers (*Billy the Kid Returns, Shine On Harvest Moon, Rough Riders Round-Up, Southward Ho, Frontier Pony Express, In Old Caliente*) and two with the Three Mesquiteers (*Heart of the Rockies, Call the Mesquiteers*).

A change back to Lynn Roberts occurred in late 1938. In both *The Lone Ranger* and *Dick Tracy Returns* she is billed as "Lynn." When she got to 20th Century-Fox it became "Lynne" and remained so for the rest of her career.

Lynne had more talent than most Western and serial heroines, as evidenced by her successful career. Not that she ever became a big star; she didn't. She remained a "B" heroine throughout her career, but an important one.

Her name came to mean something on a marquee. She played in better-than-average programmers, and she was versatile enough to move in and out of Westerns,

mysteries, melodramas and romantic comedies with ease. She stood 5'4½", weighed about 115 pounds, had auburn hair, a lovely complexion and blue eyes.

In addition to the Westerns already mentioned, she played opposite George Montgomery in both *Last of the Duanes* ('41) and *Riders of the Purple Sage* ('41); Cesar Romero in *Ride On Vaquero* ('41) and *Romance of the Rio Grande* ('41); Gene Autry in *Robin Hood of Texas* ('44), *Saddle Pals* ('44), *Sioux City Sue* ('46) and *The Blazing Sun* ('50); Roy Rogers in *Eyes of Texas* ('48); Monte Hale in *The Timber Trail* ('48); Tim Holt in *Dynamite Pass* ('50); Donald Barry in *Madonna of the Desert* ('48); and Kirby Grant in *Call of the Klondike* ('50).

Non-Westerns in which Lynne figured prominently are *Mama Runs Wild* ('38) with Mary Boland; *The Mysterious Miss X* ('39) with Michael Whalen; *My Wife's Relatives* ('39) with James Gleason; *The Bride Wore Crutches* ('41) with Ted North; *Man in the Trunk* ('42) with Raymond Walburn; *Dr. Renault's Secret* ('42) with J. Carrol Naish; *Quiet Please, Murder* ('42) with George Sanders; *The Ghost That Walks Alone* ('44) with Arthur Lake; *The Port of Forty Thieves* ('44) with Richard Powers [Tom Keene]; *Behind City Lights* ('45) with Peter Cookson; *Girls of the Big House* ('45) with Richard Powers [Tom Keene]; *The Phantom Speaks* ('45) with Richard Arlen; *The Chicago Kid* ('45) with Donald Barry; *Pilgrim Lady* ('47) with Warren Douglas; *That's My Gal* ('47) with Donald Barry; *The Magnificent Rogue* ('47) with Warren Douglas; *Secret Service Investigator* ('48) with Lloyd Bridges; *Lightnin' in the Forest* ('48) with Donald Barry; *Sons of Adventure* ('48) with Russell Hayden; *The Great Plane Robbery* ('50) with Tom Conway; *Hunt the Man Down* ('50) with Gig Young; *The Blazing Forest* ('52) with John Payne; and *Port Sinister* ('53) with James Warren.

Despite a good measure of talent and charm, she never hurdled the barrier to big-time stardom and retired from the screen in 1953. In her private life she married William E. Engelbert, Jr., on January 5, 1941. They had a son, William Engelbert III, in April 1942 and were divorced several years later. On September 16, 1944, she married L. J. Gardella, a film producer, thinking that her divorce from Engelbert was final. She was granted a divorce from Gardella on January 11, 1952, on testimony that he made derogatory remarks about her, cursed her continually and threatened her. He had withdrawn an annulment complaint, and did not contest the divorce.

In 1953 she married Hyman B. Samuels, a brassiere manufacturer, and retired at his request. Their daughter, Peri Margaret, was born in 1955. In 1961, Lynne obtained a divorce because her husband made fun of her old movies, called her "dumb" in front of friends and claimed she was a poor actress. In an affidavit she set forth that Samuels had threatened to "wreck her," take the children from her and dispose of an estimated $300,000 in community property. She was awarded custody of her children plus a home in Sherman Oaks.

Lynne was good-natured and popular with everyone with whom she worked. She would laugh at her mistakes and never seemed to get angry or excited. Her leading men found her a delight to work with and praised her acting ability. She never returned to a screen career, to the chagrin of her many fans.

She lived in Sherman Oaks for many years and died there on April 1, 1978. She was survived by her son and daughter.

Serials

1938

The Lone Ranger. Rep., [15 Chapters] D: William Witney, John English; SP: Barry Shipman, George W. Yates, Franklyn Adreon, Ronald Davidson, Lois Eby; AP: Sol C. Siegel; Cam: William Nobles; Mus: Alberto Colombo; Spv.: Robert Beche; LP: Lee Powell, Chief Thundercloud, Herman Brix, Wally Wales [Hal Taliaferro], Lynne Roberts, Lane Chandler, George Letz [Montgomery], Stanley Andrews, George Cleveland, Sammy McKim, Tom London, Yakima Canutt, William Farnum, Jack Rockwell.

Dick Tracy Returns. Rep., [15 Chapters] D: William Witney, John English; SP: Barry Shipman, Ronald Davidson, Franklyn Adreon, Rex Taylor, Sol Shor; AP: Robert Beche; Cam: William Nobles; LP: Ralph Byrd, Lynne Roberts, Charles Middleton, Jerry Tucker, David Sharpe, John Merton, Tom Steele, James Blaine.

FRANCES ROBINSON

Little is known about this actress, even though her career reached into the '60s. She was born in 1916. The first credits we find for her are *A Girl with Ideas* ('37) and *Tim Tyler's Luck* ('37), a Universal serial. In it she plays Lora Graham, on a quest to Africa to find Spider Webb (Norman Willis), who had committed a diamond robbery for which her brother had been framed. Tim Tyler (Frankie Thomas) also takes a ship to Africa to look for his father. In his effort to find a fabulous treasure of ivory, Spider kills Tim's father and takes over his armored jungle cruiser. Tim and Lora team up with Sgt. Gates (Jack Mulhall) to bring the criminal to justice in the gorilla-infested jungle country.

Frances played opposite Larry (Buster) Crabbe in Universal's *Red Barry* ('38) as "Mississippi," a newspaperwoman. Crabbe is the hero of the title. Two million dollars in bonds intended to buy fighter planes for an Oriental nation are stolen, and different factions strive to get them, with detective Barry and "Mississippi" caught in the crossfire.

Frances played Wilda Lanning opposite Noah Beery, Jr., in *Forbidden Valley* ('38). He saves her when she is almost trampled by wild horses and again when she is bitten by a rattlesnake. Fred Kohler steals Noah's wild mustangs that he has rounded up and Frances aids him in recovering them. The two fall in love. She had small parts in other features that year.

In 1939, Frances played heroine to Johnny Mack Brown and Bob Baker in *Desperate Trails*; in addition, she had bit roles in such features as *Big Town Czar*, *Hawaiian Nights*, *Tower of London* and *Society Smugglers*. One of her better roles was as Norman Jameson, a kidnapped girl in *Risky Business* with George Murphy and Dorothea Kent.

Frances was a principal player in *The Lone Wolf Keeps a Date* ('40) starring Warren William; shared the lead with Anita Louise and Roger Pryor in *Glamour for Sale* ('40); played opposite Joe E. Brown in *So You Won't Talk* ('40); and decorated the landscape in *Riders of Pasco Basin* ('40) starring Johnny Mack Brown and Bob Baker.

In 1941 she could be seen opposite Charles Starrett in *Outlaws of the Panhandle* and in supporting roles in *Dr. Jekyll and Mr. Hyde* and *Smiling Through*. Other credits are *Lady in the Dark* ('44), *The Missing Lady* ('46), *Keeper of the Bees* ('47), *Suddenly It's Spring* ('47), *I, Jane Doe* ('48), *Backfire* ('50), *Bedtime Story* ('64), *Kitten with a Whip* ('64), *The Lively Set* ('64) and *The Happiest Millionaire* ('67).

Serials

1937

Tim Tyler's Luck. Univ., [12 Chapters] D: Ford Beebe, Wyndham Gittens; LP: Frankie Thomas, Frances Robinson, Norman Willis, Jack Mulhall, Al Shean, Kenneth Harlan, Anthony Warde, William Benedict, Philo McCullough, Al Bridge.

1938

Red Barry. Univ., [13 Chapters] D: Ford Beebe, Alan James; LP: Larry (Buster) Crabbe, Frances Robinson, Wade Boteler, Edna Sedgwick, Frank Lackteen, Wheeler Oakman, Tom Steele.

JACK ROCKWELL

Ask any ten knowledgeable Western buffs what role comes to mind when Jack Rockwell is mentioned, and it's almost a sure bet that seven of them will say "sheriff." For even though Rockwell often played other roles,* he was the favorite sheriff of perhaps a majority of those who viewed Westerns from week to week.

Rockwell played a no-nonsense lawman in the following films selected at random. They do not represent the total of his lawman roles:

The Train Drive ('33)— Ken Maynard; *The Fiddlin' Buckaroo* ('33)— Ken Maynard; *King of the Arena* ('33)— Ken Maynard; *The Tonto Kid* ('34)— Rex Bell; *The Lawless Fron-*

**A crooked banker in* Guilty Trail *('38) with Bob Baker; a rancher in* Range Defenders *('39) with the Three Mesquiteers and* Prairie Justice *('38) with Bob Baker; an assassin in* Dark Command *('40) with John Wayne; a claim jumper in* Bury Me Not on the Lone Prairie *('41) with Johnny Mack Brown; stage driver in* Young Bill Hickok *('40) with Roy Rogers; a henchman in* Pony Express *('40) with Johnny Mack Brown and* Riders of Death Valley *('41) with Dick Foran.*

Jack Rockwell (left) and Jack Perrin in *Reckless Ranger* (Columbia, 1937).

tier ('34)—John Wayne; *The Law of the Wild* ('34)—Bob Custer; *Bulldog Courage* ('35)—Tim McCoy; *The Roaring West* ('35)—Buck Jones; *The Traitor* ('36)—Tim McCoy; *Heroes of the Range* ('36)—Ken Maynard; *Storm Over Arizona* ('37)—Jack Randall; *The Singing Outlaw* ('38)—Bob Baker; *The Stranger from Texas* ('39)—Charles Starrett; *Bullets for Rustlers* ('40)—Charles Starrett; *Law of the Range* ('41)—Johnny Mack Brown; *Rawhide Rangers* ('41)—Johnny Mack Brown; *Wyoming Wildcat* ('41)—Donald Barry; *The Man from Thunder River* ('43)—Bill Elliott; *The Renegade* ('43)—Buster Crabbe; *The Man from Thunder River* ('43)—Bill Elliott; *Law Men* ('44)—Johnny Mack Brown; *Gunsmoke Mesa* ('44)—Dave O'Brien & James Newill

Rockwell played in 18 (maybe more) serials, but in only two of them did he play a sheriff. Nevertheless, he will always be remembered as "sheriff" Jack Rockwell. His last screen appearance was in *Flashing Guns* ('47), the year of his death.

Serials

1934

The Law of the Wild. Mascot, [12 Chapters] D: B. Reeves "Breezy" Eason and Armand Schaefer; L: Bob Custer, Rex, Rin-Tin-Tin, Jr., Ben Turpin, Lucile Browne, Richard Cramer.

Mystery Mountain. Mascot, [12 Chapters] D: Otto Brower and B. Reeves "Breezy" Eason; L: Ken Maynard, Verna Hillie, Syd Saylor, Edward Earle, Lynton Brent, Lafe McKee.

1935

The Miracle Rider. Mascot, [15 Chapters] D: B. Reeves Eason and Armand Schaefer; L: Tom Mix, Charles Middleton, Joan Gale, Robert Kortman, Jason Robards, Sr., Charles King, Wally Wales [Hal Taliaferro].

The Roaring West. Univ., [15 Chapters] D: Ray Taylor; L: Buck Jones, Muriel Evans, Walter Miller, Frank McGlynn, Sr., Harlan Knight.

Rustlers of Red Dog. Univ., [12 Chapters] D: Lew Landers; L: Johnny Mack Brown, Joyce Compton, Walter Miller, Raymond Hatton, Harry Woods, Jack Rockwell.

The Adventures of Rex and Rinty. Mascot, [12 Chapters] D: Ford Beebe and B. Reeves Eason; L: Rex, Rin-Tin-Tin, Jr., Kane Richmond, Norma Taylor, Mischa Auer.

1938

The Great Adventures of Wild Bill Hickok. Col., [15 Chapters] D: Sam Nelson and Mack V. Wright; L: Gordon [Bill] Elliott, Carole Wayne, Frankie Darro, Monte Blue, Kermit Maynard.

The Lone Ranger. Rep., [15 Chapters] D: John English and William Witney; L: Lee Powell, Chief Thundercloud, Lynn Roberts, Lane Chandler, Hal Taliaferro, Herman Brix [Bruce Bennett], George Letz [Montgomery], Stanley Andrews, John Merton.

1939

Overland with Kit Carson. Col., [15 Chapters] D: Norman Deming and Sam Nelson; L: Bill Elliott, Iris Meredith, Trevor Bardette, Richard Fiske, Bobby Clark, LeRoy Mason.

1940

Adventures of Red Ryder. Rep., [12 Chapters] D: John English and William Witney; L: Donald Barry, Noah Beery, Sr., Tommy Cook, Vivian Coe, Harry Worth.

1941

Riders of Death Valley. Univ., [15 Chapters] D: Ford Beebe and Ray Taylor; L: Dick Foran, Buck Jones, Leo Carrillo, Charles Bickford, Lon Chaney, Jr., Noah Beery, Jr., Glenn Strange.

1942

Overland Mail. Univ., [15 Chapters] D: Ford Beebe and John Rawling; L: Lon chaney, Jr., Don Terry, Noah Beery, Jr., Helen Parrish, Noah Beery, Sr., Bob Baker.

1943

Daredevils of the West. Rep., [12 Chapters] D: John English; L: Allan Lane, Kay Aldridge, Eddie Acuff, William Haade, Robert Frazer, Jack Rockwell.

1944

Raiders of Ghost City. Univ., [13 Chapters] D: Lewis D. Collins and Ray Taylor; L: Dennis Moore, Wanda McKay, Lionel Atwill, Joe Sawyer, Regis Toomey, Eddy Waller.

1945

The Master Key. Univ., [13 Chapters] D: Lewis D. Collins and Ray Taylor; L: Milburn Stone, Jan Wiley, Dennis Moore, Sarah Padden, Russell Hicks.

Secret Agent X-9. Univ., [13 Chapters] D: Lewis D. Collins and Ray Taylor; L: Lloyd Bridges, Keye Luke, Jan Wiley, Victoria Horne, Samuel S. Hinds.

1946

The Scarlet Horseman. Univ., [13 Chapters] D: Lewis D. Collins and Ray Taylor; L: Peter Cookson, Paul Guilfoyle, Victoria Horne, Virginia Christine, Janet Shaw.

The Mysterious Mr. M. Univ., [13 Chapters] D: Lewis D. Collins and Vernon Keays; L: Richard Martin, Pamela Blake, Dennis Moore, Jane Randolph, Danny Morton.

JEAN ROGERS

For all the roles this comely actress appeared in, cinema devotees best remember her portrayals of the enchanting Dale Arden in two of the most profitable and popular sound serials ever produced. Certainly any male with an eye for feminine pulchritude found his heart beating faster and his fantasies running amuck whenever this shimmering moonbeam of perfection appeared on the screen.

Gardenia-white skin with the delicate flush of girlish wholesomeness, crowned by a silken mass of flaxen hair — this was Jean Rogers in the halcyon years of the '30s and '40s. Mark Lamberti, a Roger biographer, described Jean quite aptly when he wrote, "There is an appeal that is not the mystique of legend, nor the grace of an impeccable image on photographic film. There exists that appeal of a sensual nature, the pretty, blonde, girl next door, the American beauty of which dreams are made. Jean Rogers possesses that certain beauty, the prettiness of form and feature, the light blue eyes of an innocent, set beneath sleek, blonde curls that frame a cute, sly smile."

Jean Rogers was born Eleanor Dorothy Lovegren in Belmont, Massachusetts, on March 25, 1916, and got her education in that city. She exhibited a rare natural aptitude for drawing; it was her hope to study art in New York and perhaps abroad. Her artistic talents ran to oil painting, music and charcoal sketching. She was graduated from Belmont High School and intended going to college, but winning a beauty contest changed her plans. The contest was conducted by Charles Rogers as a means of getting new talent for his production *Eight Girls in a Boat* ('33). Jean won first place from a group of 45 candidates and in July 1933 found herself en route to Glamourland — chaperoned, of course, by her mother, Mrs. Ellen Lovegren.

Jean and her mother decided to stay in Hollywood and it wasn't long before Jean was signed by Warners. During the following year she got a lot of dramatic schooling but no screen roles. Offered a second contract by the studio, Jean asked for her release and in May 1935 signed with Universal, which was looking for a young ingenue for the lead in *Stormy* ('35). She got the part without a test.

It is, of course, her six serials for Universal for which she is best known and which established her as the reigning queen of serials in the 1935–40 era.

Jean was a very radiant lead in *Tailspin Tommy in the Great Air Mystery* ('35). It was both brisk and glossy enough to entertain audiences who were not overly demanding. It was a thrilling film in its day, with a mystery plane camouflaged to suggest a great eagle, roaring volcanos, dirigibles, jungle fortresses, wild animals and cannibals.

The Adventures of Frank Merriwell ('36) evolved from a magazine series that ran for nearly 20 years. It's a mixture of college athletics and a treasure hunt hampered by much villainy. As Elsie Belwood, Jean is the nicest thing about the film, though John King and Don Briggs do their chores competently.

It was *Flash Gordon* ('36) that zoomed Jean into almost instant worldwide popularity and, as history has shown, gave her screen immortality. *Flash Gordon* was pure escapist film fare. The cognoscenti and sophisticates might curl a supercilious lip at the childishness of the Alex Raymond characters, but it was just what the doctor ordered, evidently, for a Depression-weary public that yearned for bigger-than-life heroes and cinema fantasy that allowed people to escape for a little while each week the drudgery and hopelessness of their humdrum lives.

Jean's wardrobe was sometimes on the skimpy side. Attractively filling some plunging costumes, Jean showed enough cleavage here and there to tempt male viewers to watch her. She was not, and made no attempt to be, a siren, yet she was all the more appealing for it. Her fragile beauty caused the lechery directed her way to seem all the more sinister. King Vultan stalked her without thought of wedding bells, as brought out in this comment by Raymond Stedman in his book *The Serials* (O.U. Press, 1971):

> Moments after the earth girl is brought to him as a prisoner, Vultan (John Lipson) begins his game by using a pet bear to terrify his prey and force her, trembling, against a wall. Then, ridding the chamber of pets and underlings, he closes in on the nearly hysterical damsel for what clearly is not the kill. The focus at the end of this chapter is not upon the more serious concurrent action— Flash's rocket, about to be blasted from the sky by one of Vultan's ray guns—but upon the predicament of Dale Arden, her slender form pressed against the wall, her midriff sucked in till it will go no farther, her bosom thrust forward to the limit of its dimensions. Shots of the approaching rocket intercut this sequence, each shift to the menaced maiden showing her breathing deeper, ever deeper, until, with Vultan only a few steps away, the

closing titles suspend her agony for another week.

Ace Drummond ('36), based on the newspaper character created by Capt. Eddie Rickenbacker, was produced by Henry MacRae and directed by Ford Beebe and Cliff Smith. Throw in John King, Jean Rogers and Noah Beery, Jr., as the principals, a mystery figure known as "The Dragon," a sinister Russian gang, a Buddhist temple where strange things happen, mysterious electrical wizardry and numerous aerial battles and the result almost assuredly was a great serial for the time. As Ace Drummond, King is out to help Peggy Trainor (Rogers) find her lost father, discover the location of a mountain of jade in Mongolia, and capture the mysterious "Dragon" who has resolved to stop the construction of the Mongolian link necessary in the establishment of a globe-circling airplane service. The serial depended more on a strong plot than continuous action, but the thrills were there.

Secret Agent X-9 ('37), a cops-and-robbers sort of thing, was thoroughly hokey but a reasonably entertaining thriller, though Jean suffers the fate of many cliffhanger and cactus cuties. Because of the always overshadowing hero roles, femmes in these films usually don't get much chance at being anything but "up-gazers" while the big boys emote, which frequently makes the gals not a little ridiculous. The plot of this serial has X-9 (Scott Kolk) assigned to track down the stolen Belgravian crown jewels. Rogers is Shara Graustark, for whom X-9 risks life and limb for 12 chapters.

Flash Gordon's Trip to Mars ('38) is believed by many to be a better serial than the first film, though made for half as much money. This time out, Jean was allowed to keep her natural hair coloring (light brunette) rather than appearing as a full-fledged blonde, as she had in her previous serial outings.

Jean did not appear in the third entry of the Flash Gordon trilogy made in 1940. By that time she had gone to 20th Century-Fox. Later she would sign with MGM.

While at 20th Century-Fox, Jean met Dan Winkler, Myron Selznick's assistant, and they were married. They divorced in 1942. When her contract came up for renewal in 1943, Louis Mayer insisted she not marry — her work had to come first, last and always. Jean and Dan were planning to remarry, so she opted for a family life rather than a film career. She and Winkler married for the second time. She did not make a film in 1944, but did give birth to her daughter, Ellen. In 1945 she made a single film, *Rough, Tough, and Ready* with Chester Morris. In 1946 she played the female lead in a trio of films — one each for Monogram, Paramount and Republic. In 1947 she starred in *Backlash* for 20th Century-Fox; in 1948 she had the lead in *Speed to Spare* for Paramount and *Fighting Back* for 20th Century-Fox. Her last screen appearance was in *The Second Woman* ('51).

By 1960 the Winklers had drifted apart and decided to separate. There was no divorce and no hard feelings. For several years Jean worked as a newspaperwoman. She kept up her painting and sold many of her sketches. Her fans rediscovered her in the '70s and she attended several film festivals.

Jean Rogers passed away following surgery in Sherman Oaks, California, in 1991. She was 74 and had been in ill health several years.

Serials

1935

Tailspin Tommy in the Great Air Mystery. Univ., [12 Chapters] D: Ray Taylor; SP: Ray Cannon, Ella O'Neill, Basil Dickey, Robert Herschon, George Plympton; AP: Henry MacRae; LP: Clark Williams, Jean Rogers, Noah Beery, Jr., Bryant Washburn, Helen Brown, William Desmond.

1936

The Adventures of Frank Merriwell. Univ., [12 Chapters] D: Cliff Smith; SP: George H. Plympton, Maurice Geraghty, Ella O'Neill, Basil Dickey; AP: Henry MacRae; LP: Don Briggs, Jean Rogers, John King, Carla Laemmle, Bentley Hewlett, Dickie Jones, Bud Osborne, William Desmond, Summer Getchell.

Flash Gordon. Univ., [13 Chapters] D: Frederick Stephani; SP: George H. Plympton, Frederick Stephani, Basil Dickey, Ella O'Neill; P: Henry MacRae; Cam: Jerry Ash, Richard Fryer; LP: Larry (Buster) Crabbe, Jean Rogers, Charles Middleton, Frank Shannon, Richard Alexander, Priscilla Lawson, John Lipson, Theodore Lorch, Glenn Strange, William Desmond, Richard Tucker.

Ace Drummond. Univ., [13 Chapters] D: Ford Beebe, Cliff Smith; SP: Wyndham Gittens, Norman S. Hall, Ray Trampe; AP: Barney A. Sarecky, Ben Koenig; LP: John King, Jean Rogers, Noah Beery, Jr., Guy Bates Post, Arthur Loft, Chester Gan, Edmund Cobb, Al Bridge, Stanley Blystone, Hooper Atchley, Lon Chaney, Jr.

1937

Secret Agent X-9. Univ., [12 Chapters] D: Ford Beebe, Cliff Smith; SP: Ray Trampe, Wyndham Gittens, Norman S. Hall, Leslie Charteris; AP: Henry MacRae; LP: Scott Kolk [Colton], Jean Rogers, Henry Hunter, David Oliver, Henry Brandon, Robert Kortman, Lon Chaney, Jr., Robert Dalton, Lynn Gilbert.

1938

Flash Gordon's Trip to Mars. Univ., [15 Chapters] D: Ford Beebe, Robert Hill; S/SP: Wyndham Gittens, Norman S. Hall, Ray Trampe, Herbert Dalmas; LP: Larry (Buster) Crabbe, Jean Rogers, Charles Middleton, Frank Shannon, Beatrice Roberts, Donald Kerr, C. Montague Shaw, Kane Richmond, Wheeler Oakman, Warner Richmond.

GILBERT ROLAND

Luis Antonio Damaso Alonso was born in Chihuahua, Mexico, on December 11, 1905, and was raised in Juarez, Mexico. His father, a former matador, owned a bullring where, at the age of eight, Gilbert sold cushions and distributed programs. When Pancho Villa was rampaging throughout Mexico and his presence became a menace, the Alonso family moved across the border to El Paso to escape his terrorist activities. (He was persecuting those of Spanish blood, and the Alonsos had migrated from Spain.)

Gilbert trained to be a matador, but that desire gave way to an ambition to become a motion picture actor. At around age 15 he hopped a freight train headed for the West Coast and wound up in California with less than $5 in his pocket. In Hollywood he found it wasn't such an easy task to get into the acting profession; to survive, he worked at various jobs (a stevedore, battery plant worker, a lithographer assistant, etc.). When he was able to get inside a studio he was paid $3 a day as an extra, along with fellow extras Clark Gable, Janet Gaynor, Charles Farrell and Richard Arlen.

Eventually Gilbert received a small part in *The Lady Who Lied* ('25). That same year he got a few days' work in Clara Bow's *The Plastic Age* ('26), for which he became Gilbert Roland — a combination of his two favorite performers, John *Gilbert* and Ruth *Roland*. He and Clara carried on a torrid romance for a brief time. He received $50 a week as a stand-in for Ramon Novarro in *The Midshipman* ('25), filmed at Annapolis. He was picked out of a mob scene to double Novarro in a scene in which the star was tossed into the bay.

Gilbert's big chance came when Norma Talmadge selected him to play Armand opposite her in *Camille* ('27). It was Gilbert's first co-starring role. Next came the male lead opposite Mary Astor in *Rose of the Golden West* ('27) and with Talmadge in *The Dove* ('27). Roland was involved in a love affair with Talmadge at this time, even though she was married to producer Joseph Schenck. Gilbert's talkie debut was in Talmadge's first talking venture, a fiasco titled *New York Nights* ('29). Her voice did not register well and after one more film she retired. Gilbert's voice, however, exactly matched his appearance.

Even though the Roland-Talmadge affair ended by 1930, Schenck exacted his retribution by urging other producers not to use him; consequently, Gilbert's career came almost to a halt. He managed to appear in MGM's *Men of the North* ('30) as well as in the Spanish version, *Monsieur Le Fox*, billed as Luis Alonso. In 1931 he starred in the Spanish version of Edwin Carewe's *Resurreccion* for Universal and in Columbia's *Hombres En Su Veda* ('31), the Spanish version of William Beaudine's *Men in Her Life*. In both films he was billed Luis Alonso and had Lupe Velez as co-star.

He was off the screen for over a year. The Latin craze disappeared and Gilbert's roles in the '30s were few and then only in minor roles. Other Spanish-speaking features included *Yo Tu Y Ella* ('33), *Una Viuda Romantica* ('33) and *Julieta Compra Un Hijo* ('35). All three were made by Fox and co-starred Catalina Barcena.

In 1932, Gilbert supported Buster Keaton and Jimmy Durante in *The Passionate Plumber* and was cast as Clara Bow's half-breed lover Moonglow in Fox's *Call Her Savage*. Good fortune smiled on him when he was cast as a South American gigolo in Mae West's hit *She Done Him Wrong* ('33) and when he played with Constance Bennett in *Our Betters* ('33) and *After Tonight* ('33). But, with these exceptions, really good roles avoided him.

In 1934, Gilbert had only one film credit,

Mona Maris and Gilbert Roland.

that being the male lead to Claire Trevor in *Elinor Norton*. In '35 he played with Mona Barrie in *Mystery Woman* and *Ladies Love Danger*. He had no film credits in 1936.

In 1937, Paramount starred Roland in *Thunder Trail*, based on Zane Grey's "Arizona Ames." He received good notices for his playing in the exploitative *Last Train From Madrid* ('37). However he was not swamped with film offers. He supported Don Ameche and Arleen Whelan in *Gateway*, his only film in 1938. The next year Warners featured him as Col. Miguel Lopez, commander of French armies, in *Juarez*, starring Paul Muni and Bette Davis. Columbia cast him in *La Vida Bohemia* ('39).

Roland played Capt. Lopez in the 1940 Errol Flynn swashbuckler *The Sea Hawk*, in which he has a sword duel with Flynn. Warners also gave him the lead in *Gambling on the High Seas* ('40). Also that year RKO featured him in *Isle of Destiny* and Paramount cast him in *Rangers of Fortune*, in which he was one of the title characters.

Roland starred in Republic's *Angels with Broken Wings* and supported Ronald Colman in *Life with Caroline*, both 1941. He had been dating Constance Bennett for some time and they married in 1941. It was his first marriage and her fourth. They had two daughters, Lorinda and Gyl. Gilbert became a U.S. citizen in 1942, made a couple "B" programmers and enlisted in the U.S. Air Force in 1943. He served in Europe and North Africa and attained the rank of Second Lieutenant.

Discharged in 1944, Gilbert went looking for work but found none until Columbia gave him the lead in the serial *The Desert Hawk*. He replaced James Ellison, who was injured during production. He plays twin brothers, one good, the other evil. Kasim, the caliph of Ahad, is kidnapped and almost murdered on the instructions of his evil twin brother, who takes his place on the throne. Later, when Kasim denounces Hasson as an imposter, no one believes him. He assumes the identity of the Desert Hawk to regain his throne and to keep his brother from marrying Azala (Mona Maris), whom the emir of a neighboring country has brought to Ahad to marry Kasim. As the Desert Hawk, Kasim wins Azala's confidence and she helps him expose his brother as a false caliph.

Roland and Bennett were divorced in 1945. Gilbert dated Rita Hayworth and Doris Duke, among numerous beautiful women. He was in no hurry to try marriage again, but in 1955 he met a beautiful socialite from Mexico City named Guillermina Cantu. They wed the same year. It was a good marriage.

Gilbert's only film in 1945 was a supporting role in *Captain Kidd*. In 1946 he made *La Rebellion de Los Fantasmas* for Azteca Films and then was signed by Monogram to star in a Cisco Kid series. He made *The Gay Cavalier*, *South of Monterey* and *Beauty and the Bandit* in 1946 and followed in 1947 with *Ridin' the California Trail*, *Robin Hood of Monterey* and *King of the Bandits*. William K. Everson and George Fenin, in their book *The Western*, comment: "All the Monogram Cisco Kid films with Roland were quite a few notches above the average."

Nick Williams in his article "All the Cisco Kids" in *Filmograph* magazine wrote, "Roland's representation captured more truly the essence of O. Henry's original conception than did the representations of any of Roland's predecessors or followers. His ability to inject pathos into his acting is clearly in evidence in his classic portrayal of the Kid."

Don Miller observed in *Hollywood Corral*, "Everything stopped while Roland would declaim lyrically about the beauty of women, or nature, or both, or some such flowery verbiage. It didn't harm the film because Roland was so adept at dispensing the Latin charm and was so obviously having a good time with his role."

And finally William K. Everson in *A Pictorial History of the Western Film* summed it up: "The Roland Cisco Kids had genuine charm, a quality rarely found in 'B' Westerns, and their polish more than made up for their comparative dearth of action."

In 1949, Roland staged a comeback in the role of Guillermo in Columbia's *We Were Strangers*. The part reestablished him on the screen as the fine actor he was. For the next decade he did not want for work. His films included *The Furies* ('50), *Ten Tall Men* ('51), *Bullfighter and the Lady* ('51), *My Six Convicts* ('52), *The Miracle of Our Lady of Fatima* ('52), *The Bad and the Beautiful* ('52), *Beneath the Twelve-Mile Reef* ('53), *Thunder Bay* ('53), *The French Line* ('54), *The Racers* ('55), *That Lady* ('55), *The Treasure of Pancho Villa* ('55), *Bandido* ('56), *Three Violent People* ('56), *The Midnight Story* ('57) and *The Last of the Fast Guns* ('58).

In the '60s and '70s he appeared in *Guns of the Timberland* ('60), *Samar* ('62), *Cheyenne Autumn* ('64), *The Reward* ('65), *The Poppy Is Also a Flower* ('66), *Catch Me if You Can* ('68), *Johnny Hamlet* ('69), *Between God and the Devil* ('69), *The Christian Licorice Store* ('71), *Running Wild* ('73), *The Black Pearl* ('75), *The Pacific Connection* ('75), *Island in the Stream* ('76) and *Barbarosa* ('81).

Roland died in 1994 from cancer at his home in Beverly Hills. He was 88 years old.

Serial

1944

The Desert Hawk. Col., [15 Chapters] D: B. Reeves Eason; SP: Jack Stanley, Sherman Lowe, Leslie Swabacher, Leighton Brill; P: Rudolph C. Flothow; Cam: James S.Brown, Jr.; Mus: Lee Zahler; LP: Gilbert Roland, Mona Maris, Ben Welden, Kenneth MacDonald, Frank Lackteen, I. Stanford Jolley; George J. Lewis, Charles Middleton, Kermit Maynard, Norman Willis.

RUTH ROLAND

Beautiful and spontaneous, Ruth Roland vied with Pearl White as queen of the serials when screams were silent and guns spoke with smoke. The two actresses were far apart in personality and temperament, although each had approximately ten lush movie years and each starred in about the same number of serials.

Writer Frank Leon Smith, who worked with both, made this comparison:

Both quit with wealth, and both were women of character. And both functioned at a time when movie-makers were individuals. But except for these details, they had nothing in common.

Pearl was a spender, Ruth a saver. Stars accumulate a vast wardrobe — Pearl gave hers away. Ruth disposed of hers with a price tag on each item. Pearl like to live fully as she went along, Ruth lived for the future. Pearl took chances in her films, Ruth was cautious. Pearl was a good mixer at the studio, Ruth was aloof. Pearl had an active sense of humor, Ruth never laughed (she had a lovely smile but no mirth). Pearl was easy to understand, Ruth was like a man driving himself to get to the top.

Ruth was a keen, cool businesswoman who was in movies to make money and who never lost sight of this objective. She shunned Hollywood's much publicized night life. At the studio she had her faithful retinue of cowboys and prop men. But that was it. In many respects, Ruth was a far more exciting performer than Pearl and, unlike Pearl, she was at home in Westerns. Ruth relished making the mustangers with her horse Joker. She was a girl of the outdoors, an expert equestrienne, a strong swimmer, a crack shot with rifle and revolver, and a steady winner in tennis and golf tournaments.

At the same time her screen personality was attractive to audiences, though those who worked with her might have entertained a different image (as was the case with Ken Maynard and Allan Lane).

Most of Pearl White's serials were of the series type. Each episode was complete in itself with a wrap-up at the episode's end and another story in the next chapter. Roland's serials utilized the cliffhanging end to lure patrons back to see how our heroine was saved.

Ruth was born in San Francisco on August 26, 1892 (?). Her mother was a professional singer and her father, a newspaperman, operated the Columbia Theatre in San Francisco. At the age of 3_ years Ruth "went on" in Edward Holdens' *Cinderella* in her father's theater, with her mother also playing a role in the show. Ruth made one of the big hits of the show by her treble warbling of the then-popular ditty "What Could the Poor Girl Do?" From that night on, Ruth was an actress.

After *Cinderella*, Ruth, now firmly established as a child actress, was engaged to play Little Lord Fauntleroy in that famous children's classic. When her mother and father separated, Ruth, under her mother's chaperonage, toured the East for several years in stock and vaudeville as "Baby Ruth." Later she appeared with the Edward Holden Company and in vaudeville's "Broadway Trio." She had a stock engagement with the Morosco Company and was the first child actress to appear in Honolulu, making such a hit that she remained six months playing continuously. Then to San Francisco and a long engagement with the famous Belasco Company at the Alcazar Theatre. David Belasco proclaimed her "the greatest child actress of her time." Most of her 15 years of stock experience was under the Belasco and Morosco companies. She also did the Orpheum Circuit twice.

When her mother died at the age of 27, eight-year-old Ruth went to live with an aunt in Los Angeles and attend school there. At 16 she returned to the theater, now blossomed into an ingenue. Next in the evolution of Ruth came a very successful two-year tour in her own act over the Sullivan-Considine and Majestic vaudeville circuits.

Ruth went to work at Kalem in 1909 making *The Old Soldier's Story*, *The Cardboard Baby* and probably others. We will never know all the titles, but she made a potpourri of nearly 200 one- and two-reel films for Kalem during 1909–15. A sampling of titles:

1910: *Her Indian Mother; An Indian Scout's Revenge*

1911: *Arizona Bill; The Pasadena Peach; The Romance of a Dry Town*

1912: *The Schoolma'm of Stone Gulch; Pulque Pete and the Opera Troupe; Strong Arm Nellie; Death Valley Scotty's Mine; The Beauty Parlor of Stone Gulch*

1913: *The Raiders from Double L Ranch; An Indian Maid's Warning; Hypnotizing Mamie; The Horse that Wouldn't Stay Hitched*

1914: *The Peach at the Beach; The Medicine Show at Stone Gulch; The Joke on Jane; And the Villain Still Pursued Her; Don't Monkey with the Buzz Saw*

1915: *The Love Liar; Following a Clue; Blue Blood and Yellow*

Ruth appeared in Westerns, melodramas and comedies during her tenure at Kalem. John E. Brennan was her most frequent leading man, with George Larkin and Marshall Neilan also appearing in a number of films with her.

In February and March 1915, Ruth starred in seven two-reel films in the *Girl Detective* series, playing a society girl who has a position as a special investigator for the police. Featured in each of the films were Cleo Ridgley and Thomas Lingham. Ridgley took over the top role when Ruth left to join Balboa, which had a releasing arrangement with Pathé. There she starred in twelve three-reel films in the *Who Pays?* series. Henry King and Mollie McConnell were featured. In 1916, Ruth starred in the eight-episode series *The Price of Folly* (aka *Who Wins?*). However, these films were not released until 1918. Frank Mayo was the male lead.

Following a five-reel feature titled *Comrade John* ('15), Ruth made her first true serial, *The Red Circle* ('15), about a wealthy girl cursed with a family taint that caused her to commit crimes against society—a sort of lady Jekyll and Hyde.

Ruth's next serial was *The Neglected Wife* ('17). A love triangle leads to complications, with the heroine cast in the "other woman" role. The serial did little to further Ruth's career. Its dearth of action and story were more typical of a society drama than of a serial thriller.

Switching from Balboa to Astra, a subsidiary of Pathé, Ruth made *Hands Up* ('18), the serial that really put her on the road to serial immortality. There were thrills a-plenty in this story of an Incan tribe and their belief that Ruth, a magazine writer, is their missing princess. During production, leading man George Chesebro entered the U.S. Army; George Larkin replaced him for the remaining chapters.

In 1919, Ruth starred in two tremendously popular cliffhangers. For Astra she

made *The Tiger's Trail*, probably her most popular one, and for her own Ruth Roland Serials Company, releasing through Pathé, she made *The Adventures of Ruth*.

The Tiger's Trail was a semi–Western from the skillful pen of Frank Leon Smith at the insistence of Astra president Louis Gasnier. The original story from which Gilson Willets made the screen adaptation was called "The Long Arm" and was a city melodrama. Smith then changed Willet's scenario into one with a Western flavor. The story revolved about the attempts of Hindu tiger worshippers and Western outlaws to cheat our heroine out of mines that rightfully belonged to her.

The Adventures of Ruth dealt with Ruth's attempts to recover a "peacock fan" which hid a secret affecting her. She carries out the instructions she receives on each of 13 keys handed her by an unknown person, as instructed by her father on his deathbed.

Ruth of the Rockies ('20) concerned a Broadway waitress who flees westward after finding a trunk of diamonds a thief had left unclaimed. The story was from the pen of Johnston E. McCulley. George Marshall directed and Al Hoxie, unbilled, did stunting for Ruth and others in the serial, although Ruth usually used Bob Rose as her stuntman for dangerous sequences, declining to do the really rough stuff. It was all strictly business to Ruth. She saw no need to take a chance if there was no money in it.

In *The Avenging Arrow* ('21), Ruth scampers around Southern California trying to figure out why all her female ancestors were killed on their twenty-first birthday. She also made *White Eagle* and *The Timber Queen* in 1921 for Hal Roach, both serials released through Pathé. *White Eagle* was standard Western stuff with mysterious white riders, deep yawning canyons, wild riders and wilder falls, as opposing factions sought to gain control of an inexhaustible pool of molten gold. But *The Timber Queen* was an excellent cliffhanger with some superb action sequences created by director Fred Jackman. The runaway boxcar episode has remained a serial action classic.

Ruth of the Range ('23) was a mediocre effort with a story concerned with Ruth's attempts to free her father from a gang that wished to steal his formula for making "Fuelite," a substitute for coal. Although the story was pretty much standard serial fare, the action was plentiful. Ruth had begun to be temperamental and unsuccessfully tried to get her leading man, Bruce Gordon, fired. She also had a falling-out with W. S. Van Dyke, the director hired to get the serial going again when production bogged down due to director Ernest Warde emphasizing closeups of Ruth rather than action. Van Dyke finally quit to take another job. To compound problems, Gilson Willets, the scenarist, died during filming with only sketchy notes as to what was to happen next in the story. Frank Leon Smith had to take over and work around existing footage and characters. He wound up as director and Ruth's stuntman, Bob Rose, had to put on a wig and double for her in the last two episodes because Ruth went on vacation!

Ruth made one final serial, *Haunted Valley* ('23), co-starring with Jack Daugherty (whom she also wanted to fire, but couldn't). It had Ruth, the owner of Haunted Valley, borrowing a million dollars from the villain in order to finish a dam. The terms of the loan specified that if she couldn't pay it back in three months, the villain would get Ruth, Lost River Dam and Haunted Valley.

Ruth chose not to renew her Pathé contract. Eleven serials were more than enough for her. Her real estate transactions had made her a millionaires, and she found almost as much satisfaction in being a businesswoman as in facing a camera on Joker. So she sold more real estate, invested in various enterprises, made concert tours and did a lot of vaudeville. She made a couple of inconsequential features in 1925 and played a minor role in an Anna Q. Nilsson vehicle in 1927. In 1929 she married Ben Bard, a theater owner, and it was a happy and lasting marriage. Sound came to the movies and, even though Ruth had no need to work, she could not resist the temptation to try a talkie. The result was *Reno* ('30). Critics panned her "old-fashioned" acting. Ruth hit the road again in 1931 on a nine-month tour in a revue called "Cozy Corner." A picture made in Canada in 1935 called *From Nine to Nine* is practically forgotten.

On September 22, 1937, Ruth Roland died of cancer in Hollywood. She had met an enemy from whom there was no escape. But 80 years after her last serial was made, her status as one of the greatest cliffhanger heroines of all time is as solidly accepted as ever.

Serials

1914–15

"Ham" Series. Kalem, [15 Episodes] D: Marshall Neilan, Chance E. Ward, Rube Miller, Harry Edwards; LP: Lloyd V. Hamilton, Dub Duncan, Marin Sais, Ruth Roland (Episodes 1, 2, 7, 10).

1915

The Girl Detective. Kalem, [14 Episodes] D: James W. Horne; SP: Hamilton Smith et al.; LP: Ruth Roland, Cleo Ridgley, Thomas Lingham, William H. West, Edward Clisbee.

The Red Circle. Balboa/Pathé, [14 Chapters] D: Sherwood MacDonald; SP: Will M. Ritchie, H. M. Horkeimer; LP: Ruth Roland, Frank Mayo, Gordon Sackville, Daniel Gilfether, Mollie McConnell.

1917

The Neglected Wife. Balboa/Pathé, [15 Chapters] D: William Bertram; SP: Joseph Dunn, Will M. Ritchey; S: Mabel Herbert Hurne; LP: Ruth Roland, Roland Bottomley, Corinne Grant, Neil C. Hardin, Philo McCullough.

1918

The Price of Folly. Pathé, [8 three-reel Chapters] S: Will M. Ritchie; LP: Ruth Roland, Frank Mayo, Lafe McKee, Conrad K. Arnold.

Hands Up. Astra/Pathé, [15 Chapters] D: James W. Horne; SP: Jack Cunningham; S: Gilson Willets; LP: Ruth Roland, George Chesebro, George Larkin, Easter Walters.

1919

The Adventures of Ruth. Pathé, [15 Chapters] D: George Marshall, Ruth Roland; SP: Gilson Willets; LP: Ruth Roland, Herbert Heyes, Thomas G. Lingham, George Larkin, William Human, Charles Bennett.

The Tiger's Trail. Astra/Pathé, [15 Chapters] D: Robert Ellis, Paul C. Hurst; SP: Arthur B. Reeve, Charles A. Logue; S: Gilson Willets; LP: Ruth Roland, George Larkin, Mark Strong, Harry G. Moody, George Field, Fred Kohler.

1920

Ruth of the Rockies. Pathé, [15 Chapters] D: George Marshall; S: Johnston McCulley; SP: Frances Guihan; LP: Ruth Roland, Herbert Heyes, Thomas Lingham, Jack Rollens, Fred Burns, Pee Wee Holmes.

1921

The Avenging Arrow. Pathé, [15 Chapters] D: W. S. Van Dyke, William Bowman; SP: Jack Cunningham; S: Arthur Preston Haskins; LP: Ruth Roland, Edward Hearn, Virginia Ainsworth, S. E. Jennings, William Steele, Frank Lackteen.

1922

The Timber Queen. Pathé, [15 Chapters] D: Fred Jackson; SP: Bertram Millhauser; S: Val Cleveland; P: Hal Roach; LP: Ruth Roland, Bruce Gordon, Val Paul, Leo Willis, Frank Lackteen, Bull Montana.

White Eagle. Pathé, [15 Chapters] D: W. S. Van Dyke, Fred Jackman; S/SP: Val Cleveland; Spv.: Hal Roach; P: Ruth Roland; LP: Ruth Roland, Earle Metcalfe, Harry Girard, Virginia Ainsworth, Otto Lederer.

1923

Ruth of the Range. Pathé, [15 Chapters] D: Ernest C. Warde, W. S. Van Dyke, Frank Leon Smith; SP: Frank Leon Smith, Gilson Willets; P: M. C. Levee; LP: Ruth Roland, Bruce Gordon, Ernest C. Warde, Lorimer Johnson.

Haunted Valley. Pathé, [15 Chapters] D: George Marshall; SP: Frank Leon Smith; LP: Ruth Roland, Jack Daugherty, Larry Steers, Eulalie Jensen, Francis Ford.

RUTH ROMAN

Ruth Roman was born on December 22, 1923 or 1924, as Norma Roman in Lynn, Massachusetts, the third daughter of Anthony and Mary Gold Roman. Her father, who worked in carnival concessions and sideshows at New England beach areas, died when Ruth was very young. Her mother was forced to move her family into Boston's West End Tenement District and to do whatever she could to provide for her brood and herself.

Ruth dropped out of high school in her sophomore year to take a job as a movie theater usherette while she worked nights with the New England Repertory Company headquartered on Beacon Hill. For three seasons she did walk-ons and served as a stage hand. She spent one semester at the Bishop Lee Drama School.

When she was 16 she married a boy named Jack Flaxman, who worked in an art store in Boston. They lived with Ruth's family briefly, but the marriage was ill-fated and resulted in separation and divorce six months later.

Ruth first appeared on screen in *Stage Door Canteen* ('43), filmed in New York City. It was a very small part. Traveling to Hollywood on a dime and a prayer in 1944, she landed a role opposite Ken Maynard in *Harmony Trail* (aka *The White Stallion*), his last starring film and one usually overlooked by Ruth's biographers. Small roles followed and in 1945 she portrayed Lothel in Universal's 13-chapter serial *Jungle Queen*. Looking gorgeous in her jungle costume, Ruth, the mysterious leader of the Tongghill tribe, helps Americans Edward Norris and Eddie Quillan defeat Nazi agents sent into the African jungles to stir up the local Tongghill tribes against the British allies. Lothel survives all sorts of perils, even walking through flames unharmed. In the end, Nazi terror is defeated and peace restored to the jungle. Lothel vanishes in a sheet of flame as mysteriously as she had appeared.

Small roles followed until 1949, when she portrayed the title character in *Belle Starr's Daughter*, co-starring with Rod Cameron and George Montgomery. Shortly afterwards she won the role of Kirk Douglas' wife Emma Bryce in Stanley Kramer's *Champion* ('49). On the basis of it and the suspense drama *The Window* ('49), she received a Warner Brothers contract and starred opposite such stars as Gary Cooper (*Dallas* '50), Randolph Scott (*Colt .45* '50) Dane Clark (*Barricade* '50), Eleanor Parker (*Three Secrets* '50), Farley Granger (*Strangers On a Train* '51), Richard Todd (*Lightning Strikes Twice* '51), Steve Cochran (*Tomorrow Is Another Day* '51), Errol Flynn (*Mara Maru* '52) and Barbara Stanwyck (*Blowing Wild* '53).

Roman also appeared in *Beyond the Forest* ('49) with Betty Davis, *Tanganykia* ('54) with Van Heflin, *Down Three Dark Streets* ('54) with Broderick Crawford, *The Far Country* ('55) with James Stewart and *Joe MacBeth* ('55) with Paul Douglas.

Ruth married Mortimer Hall, son of the publisher of *The New York Post*, on December 17, 1950. Her son, Richard Hall, was born in 1953. In April 1955 her marriage to Hall ended in divorce. The following year she married agent Budd Moss. Before marrying Moss, however, Ruth took her three-year-old son on a trip to Europe. Coming home, she and her son were two of the 760 survivors of the collision of the luxury Italian Liner *Andrea Doria* with the Swedish motorship *Stockholm* that claimed 51 lives in July 1956. She divorced Moss in 1958.

Television beckoned in the mid–50s and Ruth over a period of many years appeared in a slew of TV shows: *Police Woman, Fantasy Island, Murder, She Wrote, Story Theatre, Lux Video Theatre, Ford Theatre, Producers Showcase, G. E. Theatre, Climax, Jane*

Wyman Theatre, Mod Squad, Bonanza, The Philadelphia Story, Naked City, The Untouchables, Bus Stop, I Spy, Tarzan, Men from Shiloh, Gunsmoke, Name of the Game, Mission: Impossible, The Girl from U.N.C.L.E., Marcus Welby, M.D., Outcasts, The F.B.I., The Bing Crosby Show, Chrysler Theatre, Dr. Kildare, Burke's Law, Breaking Point, Eleventh Hour, The Greatest Show on Earth, Route 66 and *Sixth Sense*.

Telefeatures included *The Old Man Who Cried Wolf* (ABC 1970, Edward G. Robinson, Diane Baker); *Incident in San Francisco* (ABC 1971, Richard Kiley); *Go Ask Alice* (ABC 1973, Julie Adams, William Shatner); *Punch and Jody* (NBC 1974, Glenn Ford, Pam Griffin); and *The Shadow Riders* (CBS/Columbia-TV 1982, Tom Selleck, Sam Elliott).

In 1986 she became the new face on CBS's *Knots Landing* after separating from her real estate investor husband in Ohio and returning to her longtime home in Laguna Beach.

Ruth Roman died in her sleep at her Laguna Beach home on September 9, 1999.

Serial

1945

Jungle Queen. Univ., [13 Chapters] D: Ray Taylor, Lewis D. Collins; Exec. P: Ben Pivar; AP: Morgan B. Cox, Ray Taylor; Cam: William Sickner; LP: Edward Norris, Lois Collier, Eddie Quillan, Ruth Roman, Douglass Dumbrille.

BETSY KING ROSS

Betsy King Ross, born in 1923, was highly popular for a while in the early '30s. A championship trick rider with a Buster Brown haircut, she played tomboy roles in Westerns with Gene Autry (*Phantom Empire*), Ken Maynard (*In Old Santa Fe*), George O'Brien (*Smoke Lightning*) and Johnny Mack Brown (*Fighting with Kit Carson*).

Betsy dropped out of movies and got a college education at Northwestern, earning a degree and becoming an anthropologist in Mexico. Marriage to engineer David Day took her to a 10,000-acre ranch in Columbia. After her husband's death in a landslide in the Andes, she returned with her son, Rusty, to Los Angeles. She went back to college and earned a Ph.D. and became a medical writer.

As it turned out, little Betsy of Radio Ranch had both perseverance and a brilliant mind. She never returned to films.

Serials

1933

Fighting with Kit Carson. Mascot, [12 Chapters] D: Armand Schaefer, Colbert Clark; SP: Wyndham Gittens, J. F. Natteford, Barney Sarecky, Colbert Clark; P: Nat Levine; LP: Johnny Mack Brown, Betsy King Ross, Noah Beery, Sr., Noah Beery, Jr., Tully Marshall, Edmund Breese, Robert Warwick, Edward Hearn.

1935

Phantom Empire. Mascot, [12 Chapters] D: Otto Brower, B. Reeves Eason; S: Wallace MacDonald, Gerald Geraghty, Hy Freedman; SP: John Rathmell, Armand Schaefer; P: Nat Levine; Cam: Ernest Miller, William Nobles; Mus: Lee Zahler; LP: Gene Autry, Frankie Darro, Betsy King Ross, Dorothy Christie, Wheeler Oakman, Charles K. French, Warner Richmond, Smiley Burnette.

RUTH ROYCE

Ruth Royce was forever the strumpet, out to deceive, seduce, mangle or kill the hero. Self-serving, incorrigible, callous, black-hearted, decadent, wicked and diabolic are adjectives that might be appropriate in describing the characters she portrayed in 11 serials and a score of mostly low-budget Westerns. She was usually a woman of easy virtue with an agenda not to the liking of the decent folks. She played this role in film after film. When she appeared on the screen, viewer knew instantly that she was a "bad egg," just as we knew Charlie King was a disreputable "snake in the grass" when he appeared in a film.

Ruth was born in Cersailles, Missouri, on February 6, 1893, and died on May 7, 1971. Just to say that she was born and died is hardly adequate, yet there seems to be no biographical data on her available.

Early on she was typed as a villainess and never deviated far from that characterization. It is a credit to her talent that parts were written into Westerns to accommodate her particular ability, for it was not customary in "B" Westerns for a woman, other than the heroine, to play a major part. Sometimes there would be a mother involved, but a ruthless, brainy female heading up the lawless element — never! Ruth pioneered the Western bad woman, and her physical appearance (five feet six inches, jet black hair, dark eyes and slightly Oriental-looking features) added to her credibility. Within the definite limitations (she never tried to escape the "bad girl" parts) she was most competent considering the low-budget films in which she labored.

Serials

1920

The Vanishing Dagger. Univ., [18 Chapters] D: Ed Kull, Eddie Polo; SP: Hope Loring, George W. Pyper; S: Hope Loring, Jacques Jaccard, Milton Moore; LP: Eddie Polo, Thelma Percy, G. Normand Hammond, Laura Oakley, Ruth Royce, Thomas Lingham.

1922

Perils of the Yukon. Univ., [15 Chapters] D: Perry Vekeroff, Jay Marchant, J. P. McGowan; S/SP: George Morgan, George Plympton; LP: William Desmond, Laura La Plante, Fred Stanton, Joe McDermott, George A. Williams, Ruth Royce.

In the Days of Buffalo Bill. Univ., [18 Chapters] D: Edward Laemmle; S/SP: Robert Dillon; LP: Art Acord, Dorothy Woods, Duke R. Lee, Ruth Royce, George A. Williams.

1923

Beasts of Paradise. Univ., [15 Chapters] D: William Craft; S/SP: Val Cleveland; LP: William Desmond, Eileen Sedgwick, William H. Gould, Ruth Royce, Joe Bonomo, Margaret Morris.

The Oregon Trail. Univ., [18 Chapters] D: Edward Laemmle; SP: Anthony Coldeway, Douglas Bronston, Jefferson Moffitt; S: Robert Dillon; LP: Art Acord, Louise Lorraine, Ruth Royce, Duke R. Lee, Jim Corey.

In the Days of Daniel Boone. Univ., [15 Chapters] D: William Craft, Jay Marchant, Frank Messinger; SP: Jefferson Moffitt; S: Jefferson Moffitt, Paul Bryan; LP: Jack Mower, Eileen Sedgwick, Charles Brinley, Duke R. Lee, Ruth Royce.

1924

Riders of the Plains. Arrow, [15 Chapters] D: Jacques Jaccard; S: Karl Coolidge, Jacques Jaccard; LP: Jack Perrin, Marilyn Mills, Ruth Royce, Charles Brinley, Boris Karloff.

Days of '49. Arrow, [15 Chapters] D: Jacques Jaccard, Jay Marchant; S: Karl Coolidge; LP: Neva Gerber, Edmund Cobb, Charles Brinley, Wilbur McGaugh, Ruth Royce.

1926

Trooper 77. Rayart, [10 Chapters] D: Duke Worne; S: George W. Pyper; LP: Herbert Rawlinson, Hazel Deane, Ruth Royce, Jimmy Aubrey, Duke Worne.

Officer 444. Davis/Goodwell, [10 Chapters] D/SP: Francis Ford; LP: Neva Gerber, Ben Wilson, Ruth Royce, Al Ferguson, Jack Mower.

The Power God. Davis/Goodwell, [15 Chapters] D: Ben Wilson, Francis Ford; LP: Ben Wilson, Neva Gerber, Lafe McKee, Ruth Royce, Allan Garcia.

ANN RUTHERFORD

Charming Ann Rutherford is remembered by different people for different films. Many fans recall her best as Polly Benedict in the MGM Hardy Family series in which she played Mickey Rooney's girlfriend in 12 entries. Others might think of the three films she did with Red Skelton, *Whistling in the Dark* ('41), *Whistling in Dixie* ('42) and *Whistling in Brooklyn* ('43). Or a good bet would be *Gone with the Wind* ('39) in which she played Careen, the younger sister of Scarlett O'Hara.

But probably Western aficionados will at first recall the four shoot-'em-ups she made with Gene Autry: *Melody Trail* ('35), *The Singing Vagabond* ('35), *Comin' Round the Mountain* ('36) and *Public Cowboy No. 1* ('37). Or the three she did with John Wayne in 1936: *The Lawless Nineties, The Oregon Trail* and *The Lonely Trail.*

Serial devotees are likely to think of *The Fighting Marines* ('35), the Mascot chapterplay that Ann made when she was only 15 years old. In it she portrays Frances Schiller, sister of inventor George J. Lewis, who has created a gyrocompass that will counter the "dead-spot," a lethal magnetic field set up by a mystery figure known as "Tiger Shark," who wishes to keep the Marines from building an air strip on Halfway Island. She is romantically pursued by Corp. Lawrence (Grant Withers) and Sgt. McGowan (Adrian Morris). Ann was a most appealing tidbit, although romance was not played up in the serial. But at the same age she was kissed by Gene Autry, his first and only screen kiss.

After moving to MGM from Republic in 1937, Ann played in many big-budget films there and at 20th Century–Fox, to which she moved in 1942. After World War II she freelanced at various studios, ending her theatrical film career with cameo parts in *They Only Kill Their Masters* ('72) and *Won Ton Ton, the Dog That Saved Hollywood* ('76).

Ann was born in Vancouver, Canada, on November 2, 1920. Under the name John Guilberti, her father sang tenor with the New York Metropolitan and her mother was an ex-silent movie actress, Lucille Mansfield. Ann had an older sister who became a Wampas Baby Star and worked briefly in movies under the name Judith Arlen. When Ann was four, her family moved to San Francisco. When she was in the first grade, she was selected for a part in a stock company production of *Mrs. Wiggs of the Cabbage Patch* with her mother in the lead and traveled with the company on tour.

Over a period of several years she appeared in stage productions of *Little Women, Daddy Long Legs, Jack and the Beanstalk, Peter Pan* and other plays.

When Ann was 11, her parents came to Los Angeles and it was there that she attended junior high school and Los Angeles and Fairfax High Schools. In 1933, Ann secured a role in the radio series "Nancy and Dick and the Spirit of 76" and it led to other radio work. In 1934 she won a role in *Student Tour*, an MGM short featuring Jimmy Durante.

Nat Levine, president of Mascot, saw Ann's picture in the radio section of the newspaper, tested her for a part in *Waterfront Lady* ('35) and she was signed to a long-term contract by Mascot/Republic. Her mother broke Ann's contract by revealing that she was still a minor and Ann switched to MGM where she remained until 1942, appearing in *The Bride Wore Red* ('37), *Of Human Hearts* ('38), *Dramatic School* ('38), *Four Girls in White* ('39), *Pride and Prejudice* ('40), *Wyoming* ('40), *Washington Melodrama* ('41) and *This Time for Keeps* ('42). Counting her loan outs, Ann made 34 films while under contract to MGM.

Louis B. Mayer became angry with Ann when she couldn't report to star in *Seven Sweethearts* ('42) because she contracted measles. He sold her contract to 20th Century-Fox, where Ann had a successful career in films such as *Orchestra Wives* ('42), *Happy Land* ('43) and *Bermuda Mystery* ('44). She married David May, young heir of Los Angeles' famous May Company, in 1942. They adopted a child, Gloria, in 1944. In 1946 they separated and were divorced in 1953. That same year she married producer William Dozier.

In 1949, Ann became Blondie opposite Arthur Lake's Dagwood on the *Blondie* radio series during its last season. As a freelancer she appeared in *Two O'Clock Courage* ('45) with Tom Conway, *Bedside Manner* ('45) with John Carroll, *Murder in the Music Hall* ('46) with Vera Ralston, *The Madonna's Secret* ('46) with Francis Lederer, *Inside Job* ('46) with Preston Foster, *The Secret Life of Walter Mitty* ('47) with Danny Kaye, *Adventures of Don Juan* ('48) with Errol Flynn and *Operation Haylift* ('50) with Bill Williams.

During the '50s and '60s she occasionally appeared on television in *Suspense*,

Robert Montgomery Presents, *The Bob Burns Show*, *The Eddie Bracken Show*, *Perry Mason* and a few others.

Late in life, Ann embarked on a very successful interior design career. She and husband William Dozier were divorced in 1972. He died in 1991.

Serial

1935

The Fighting Marines. Mascot, [12 Chapters] D: B. Reeves Eason, Joseph Kane; SP: Barney Sarecky, Sherman Lowe; S: Wallace MacDonald, Maurice Geraghty, Ray Trampe; P: Nat Levine; Mus: Arthur Kay; LP: Grant Withers, Adrian Morris, Ann Rutherford, Robert Warwick, George J. Lewis, Pat O'Malley, Robert Frazer, Tom London, Frank Reicher, J. Frank Glendon, Victor Potel.

JOE RYAN

Joe Ryan began his motion picture career in 1913. The first credit we find for him is *The Hand of the Law* ('13), a three-reeler made by Colorado Motion Pictures. He continued making Westerns for this company and for Eclair until 1916 when he joined the Selig organization, supporting Tom Mix in his series of one-reelers.

In 1917, he supported William Duncan in a trio of serials—*A Fight for Millions, The Fighting Trail* and *Man of Might*. Impressed with Ryan's performance in these thrillers, Vitagraph gave him the leading role in *Hidden Dangers* ('20), which predated *Dr. Jekyll and Mr. Hyde* ('20) and *The Wolf Man* ('41). As Dr. De Brutel, inventor and scientist, he is infected with a strange disease which, in its irregularly intermittent and recurrent attacks, destroys the balance of his faculties and his nature. When under this "influence," his brain is exalted at the expense of his soul and his mental capacity is developed at the expense of his moral nature. He becomes a superman without any sense of right or wrong. Dr. De Brutel has also overcome certain powers of nature: He has developed a "double X-Ray" through which he is able to pass through solid objects, become invisible, overcome gravitation, etc.

In his "possessed" moments, he entirely loses the identity of his former self, even his face and other physical characteristics. In his normal state he remembers nothing of what he does during his "possessed" condition. When "possessed," however, he recalls what happens in his normal state. Occasionally he can avert this attack by a potent draught. His change from normal to abnormal is generally dependent upon atmospheric conditions. As Dr. De Brutel, he is a respected citizen. In his abnormal state, he is the leader of the Black Circle, a secret organization of men with no moral scruples who indulge in every sort of crime and vice.

Hidden Dangers was a hit serial with the "never miss a Saturday" clientele, and was popular with adults as well.

Ryan got a second opportunity as a serial hero in *The Purple Riders* ('21), in which he portrays Sheriff Dick Ranger, out to chase down the Purple Riders and their bandit leader, the Purple Shadow. Dick's sweetheart is a victim of the gang and her brother is accused of murdering their father. The sheriff finally unravels the mystery of the Purple Riders and captures their leader (Joe Rickson).

Joe was born May 22, 1889, on a ranch in Wyoming. He became a real-life cowboy. On a whim while in Denver, he chucked his Western wear and bought an outfit of fashionable clothes. At an amusement park he won a money prize by riding Dynamite, a bucking steer. He remained with this show for two years. Between seasons he played with a stock company and later organized a company of cowpunchers for a vaudeville act. It was his ability as a rider and dramatic actor that led to his employment as a movie cowboy.

Evidently his popularity declined quickly, for in the 1923 feature *Smashing Barriers* he was listed eighth in the cast. By 1925 his acting career was over and he joined the band of riders hanging out on the corner of Sunset Boulevard and Gower Street near the Columbia studios. This landmark was later made famous as "Gower Gulch," a site where studios needing riders would come to pick up riders. In a way it was comparable to an unemployment office.

Joe Ryan died on December 23, 1944.

Serials

1917

The Fighting Trail. Vit., [15 Chapters] D: William Duncan; SP: J. Stuart Blackton, Cyrus

Townsend Brady; LP: William Duncan, Carol Holloway, George Holt, Joe Ryan, Fred Burns.

1918

A Fight for Millions. Vit., [15 Chapters] D: William Duncan; SP: Graham Baker; S: Albert

E. Smith, Cyrus Townsend Brady; LP: William Duncan, Edith Johnson, Joe Ryan, Willie Calles.

1919

Smashing Barriers. Vit., [15 Chapters] D: William Duncan; SP: Graham Baker, R. Cecil Smith; S: Albert E. Smith, Cyrus T. Brady; LP: William Duncan, Edith Johnson, Walter Rodgers, William McCall, George Stanley, Joe Ryan.

Man of Might. Vit., [15 Chapters] D: William Duncan; SP: C. Graham Baker; S: Albert E. Smith, Cyrus Townsend Brady; LP: William Duncan, Edith Johnson, Joe Ryan, Walter Rodgers, Del Harris.

1920

Hidden Dangers. Vit., [15 Chapters] D: William Bertram; SP: Albert E. Smith, Cleveland Moffett; S: C. Graham Baker, William Courtney; LP: Joe Ryan, Jean Paige, George Stanley, Sam Polo, E. J. Denny.

1921

The Purple Riders. Vit., [15 Chapters] D: William Bertram; SP: William B. Courtney, Calder Johnstone, Graham Baker; S: Albert E. Smith, Cleveland Moffett; LP: Joe Ryan, Elinor Field, Joe Rickson, Maude Emory.

MARIN SAIS

Marin Sais started in pictures in 1910 in the film *Twelfth Night*, a one-reeler released February 2. For the next year and a half she worked at Vitagraph and Bison 101 before joining Kalem, where her first film of record was *How Texas Got Left* ('11). From that point on she appeared in at least 100 films, from one- and two-reelers to five-reel Westerns. She had been pursuing an operatic career in the East when something happened to endanger her voice; therefore, she made a switch to acting. Her first work was in come-

dies, but once employed by Kalem her career took off.

Other early Marin films include *Death Valley Scotty's Mine* ('12), *The Tenderfoot's Troubles* ('12), *The Last Blockhouse* ('13), *The Attack at Rocky Pass* ('13), *The Scheme of Shiftless Sam Smith* ('13), *The Invaders* ('13), *The Big Horn Massacre* ('13), *The Bandit's Child* ('13), *The Death Sign of High Noon* ('14), *The Quicksands* ('14), *The Wolf's Prey* ('15) and *When Things Fall Out* ('15).

In 1915, Marin was cast in *Stingaree*

playing Ethel Porter, estranged sweetheart of Irving Randolph — known in Australia as the bandit Stingaree, a Robin Hood–like character played by True Boardman. A set of unfortunate circumstances caused both principals in the story to leave London at the end of Episode 1 and to appear in Australia in Episode 2, where the story unfolds. Boardman has been falsely accused of murder by his brother, who wants the family fortune, and Boardman has to flee to avoid imprisonment. His flight takes him to the land Down Under and a life as a bandit. His partner in banditry is Howie, played by Paul Hurst, who is instrumental in bringing the two lovers together again.

The Girl from Frisco ('15) was a far better series for Marin. Not only did it run for 25 episodes of two reels each, but Marin was definitely the star and True Boardman, as her fiancé, Congressman John Wallace, the secondary star, a switch from their roles in *Stingaree*. Marin plays Barbara Brent, a girl of the west. Each episode was a complete story, but the characters were continuing.

In the series *The Social Pirates* ('16), Marin shared the stellar honors with Ollie Kirby, and this time True Boardman was the villain of the piece. As in most of her Kalem series, able support was provided by Thomas Lingham, Paul Hurst and Frank Jonasson. Marin and Ollie, as Mona and Mary, respectively, are a slightly embittered pair who vow to put a stop to scoundrels who prey on helpless women by blackmail and other equally deplorable means.

The *American Girl* ('17) series followed for Marin as America was plunged into the first World War. As Madge King she is the central figure in a series of two-reelers of the Old West, all melodramatic and bringing into view much riding and fighting. Frank Jonasson, Edward Hearn, Edward Clisbee, Jack Hoxie, R. E. Bradbury and Knute Rahm supported. Madge, her father, her fiancé and their followers combat Western outlawry in unrelated stories. Though not a serial, it approaches the serial classification because of the serial-like thrills and situations making up each episode and

the fact that it laid the foundation for later cliffhanger-type serials.

In her last series for Kalem, which was about to go belly up, Marin co-starred once more with True Boardman, this time in the 15 episodes of *The Further Adventures of Stingaree* ('17). Irving Randolph, the respected master of Randolph Towers, London, whom the world once knew as Stingaree, the Australian Bushranger, receives notice from his attorneys that an appraisal of his family estate shows that his entire fortune was squandered by his deceased brother while he (Irving) was absent in Australia. He realizes that as a penniless man he cannot marry his fiancée, Ethel Porter. He is surprised by a visit from Howie, his old partner of the Bushranger days, who has crossed the seas to warn Stingaree that government officers are on his trail with a warrant for his arrest. He persuades Stingaree to return to Australia with him, thus setting off a new series of adventures in the Australian back country. Naturally, Ethel follows him Down Under.

With the demise of Kalem, Marin freelanced for several years, her career seemingly in the descent. But in 1920 she played opposite Jack Hoxie in Arrow's *Thunderbolt Jack* and won new laurels as a Western heroine in the popular serial. She also married the big Oklahoma cowboy and rodeo rider who had previously played minor parts in some of her Kalem films. There followed several features with Jack, but when he got a job at Universal she was forced to remain in independent productions. Marin had two daughters by Jack, but the marriage was not a blissful one and the two were divorced about 1925. Marin subsequently worked in several of Jack's Universal Westerns as the "second woman." In the late 1920s she worked only in minor roles, and with the coming of talkies she settled down to character roles.

Marin was a descendent of one of the finest old Spanish families of early California. She was born in 1887 on the Rancho Olompali in Marin County (for which she was named) just across the bay from San Francisco. Her father was a Spaniard, her mother an Englishwoman. Marin stood 5'3" in height, weighed 115–120 pounds, and had brown hair and hazel eyes. She was educated at Notre Dame, San Jose, and Notre Dame, Santa Clara.

Serials

1915

Stingaree. Kalem, [12 Episodes] SP/D: James W. Horne; S: E. W. Hornung; LP: True Boardman, Marin Sais, Paul Hurst, Thomas Lingham.

1916

The Social Pirates. Kalem, [15 Chapters] D: James W. Horne; LP: Marin Sais, Ollie Kirby, True Boardman, Frank Jonasson, Paul Hurst, Tom Lingham, Priscilla Dean, Barney Furey, Robert E. Bradbury.

1917

The Further Adventures of Stingaree. Kalem, [15 Chapters] D: Paul Hurst; S: E. W. Hornung; SP: Joseph F. Poland; LP: True Boardman, Marin Sais, Frank Jonasson, Ollie Kirby, Thomas Lingham, Edward Clisbee, Paul Hurst, Barney Furey, Hal Clements.

The American Girl. Kalem. [21 Chapters] D: James W. Horne; S: Frederick Bechdolt; LP: Marin Sais, Frank Jonasson, Edward Hearn, Edward Clisbee, Jack Hoxie, Ronald Bradbury, Knute Ralman, Robert E. Bradbury, Grace Johnson.

1921

Thunderbolt Jack. Arrow, [15 Chapters] D: Francis Ford (?); Spv.: Ben Wilson; LP: Jack Hoxie, Marin Sais, Chris Frank, Alton Stone [Al Hoxie], Steve Clemento.

1940

Deadwood Dick. Col., [15 Chapters] D: James W. Horne; SP: Wyndham Gittens, Morgan B. Cox, George Morgan, John Cutting; LP: Don Douglas, Lorna Gray [Adrian Booth], Harry Harvey, Marin Sais, Jack Ingram, Charles King, Lane Chandler, Edmund Cobb, Edward Hearn, Kenne Duncan.

The Shadow. Col., [15 Chapters] D: James W. Horne; LP: Victor Jory, Veda Ann Borg, Robert Moore, Robert Fiske, Jack Ingram.

1946

King of the Forest Rangers. Rep., [12 Chapters] D: Spencer G. Bennet, Fred Brannon; LP: Larry Thompson, Helen Talbot, Stuart Hamblen, Anthony Warde, LeRoy Mason, Tom London, Ernie Adams.

1953

Gunfighters of the Northwest. Col., [15 Chapters] D: Spencer G. Bennet, Charles S. Gould; LP: Jock Mahoney, Clayton Moore, Phyllis Coates, Don Harvey.

JACKIE SAUNDERS

Jackie Saunders died in Palm Springs, California, in 1954. Her age has been reported as both 56 and 61 at the time of her death. She is best remembered for the serial *The Grip of Evil* ('16) in which she was co-starred with Roland Bottomley. It followed the adventures of a poor man who inherited a fortune and set out to discover whether humanity was in "the grip of evil." Certain others do not share his social concerns but do have an interest in his money. Ingratitude, jealousy, treachery, murder and criminal carelessness—all are confronted in the hero's search for the answer to the question: "Is humanity in the grip of evil?" The story was not clearly defined from chapter to chapter, and the lack of strong characterizations on the part of the cast detracted from an otherwise interesting possibility.

Her other best-known film was the Fox feature *Drag Harlan* ('20), in which she was William Farnum's leading lady. She was billed as Jacquelin in this film.

The gorgeous dark-blonde star was noted for her perfect nose and limpid gray eyes. She began her career in 1913 with the Balboa Company and appeared in such films as *The Will of the Wisp* ('14), *Pearls of Temptation* ('15), *Rose of the Alley* ('16), *Betty Be Good* ('17), *The Wildcat* ('17), *The Miracle of Love* ('19) and *The Scuttlers* ('20). In the '20s she supported others: Alice Lake in *The Infamous Miss Ravell*, Irene Rich in *Defying Destiny*, Dorothy Davenport Reid in *Broken Laws*, etc.

Serial

1916

The Grip of Evil. Pathé, [15 Chapters] D: W. A. Douglas, Harry Harvey; S: Lewis Tracy; SP: Douglas Bronston; LP: Jackie Saunders, Roland Bottomley, Charles Dudley, Gordon Sackville, Philo McCullough, Gloria Payton, Myrtle Reeves.

EILEEN SEDGWICK

Eileen Sedgwick, the "baby" of the Sedgwick family, was born in Galveston, Texas, in 1899 and grew up there, along with her sister Josie and brother Edward. Her mother and father were stage actors and the family toured the vaudeville circuit billed as "The Five Sedgwicks."

Eileen made her debut in the movies in 1913. Five years later she went to Universal to star in serials, Westerns, features and featurettes. In *Lure of the Circus* ('18), starring Eddie Polo, she was chosen by the studio as a substitute for Molly Malone, a victim of sudden illness. She appeared starting with the fifth episode. In 1919, she was listed third in the cast of *The Great Radium Mystery*, a Western serial in 18 two-reel episodes. Cleo Madison and Bob Reeves were top billed.

Eileen's first opportunity as a star was in *The Diamond Queen* with George Chesebro. It was released by Universal on March 15, 1921. In *The Terror Trail*, another Western serial in 18 two-reel episodes, released on July 8, 1921, she was supported by George Larkin.

Eileen Sedgwick in *The Girl in the Saddle* (Universal, 1921).

In 1920–21, Eileen starred in *The White Rider, Putting it Over, The Heart of Arizona, The Girl in the Saddle, Dream Girl, A Woman's Wit, The Night Attack, A Battle of Wits* and possibly other two-reelers. In 1922–23 she continued making the short Westerns. Included were *False Brand, Judgment, Wolf Pack, Scarred Hands, The Open Wire, The Trail of No Return, Roped and Tied, Dropped from the Clouds* and *When Law Comes to Hades.*

Eileen was the leading lady in several of William Desmond's serials, among them *Beasts of Paradise*, made in 1923. Joe Bonomo was also in the cast and this film was considered by many to be the best work of both Bonomo and Sedgwick. Eileen was second in the cast of *In the Days of Daniel Boone* ('23) starring Jack Mower. Also in '23, she played with Pete Morrison in *Making Good*, a Sanford Western feature. In 1926, she played opposite William Desmond in the serials *Strings of Steel* and *The Winking Idol.*

In 1928, Sedgwick appeared in *The Vanishing West*, a Mascot serial with practically an all-star cast: Leo Maloney, Jack Perrin, Jack Daugherty, Yakima Canutt, Fred Church, Helen Gibson and William Fairbanks. Under the pseudonym of Phalba Morgan, she supported Victor MacLaglen in *A Girl in Every Port* ('28) and with the pseudonym of Greta Yoltz she was seen in *Beautiful but Dumb* ('28) and *Hot Heels* ('28), two features made by Universal with Patsy Ruth Miller as the star. Eileen's last film appearance was with Leo Maloney in *Yellow Contraband* ('28).

With the coming of sound to the movies, Eileen retired. She continued to live in Los Angeles. For many years she and sister Josie lived with their mother, who lived into her nineties. Eileen avoided talking about her movie career. It was something she didn't care to remember. She lived to be 93, dying in Hollywood in 1991.

Serials

1918

Lure of the Circus. Univ., [18 Chapters] D: J. P. McGowan; SP: Hope Loring; S: William Wing; LP: Eddie Polo, Eileen Sedgwick, Harry Carter, Molly Malone, Frederick Starr.

1919

The Great Radium Mystery. Univ., [18 Chapters] D: Robert Broadwell, Robert F. Hill; SP: Frederick Bennett; LP: Cleo Madison, Bob Reeves, Eileen Sedgwick, Edwin J. Brady.

1921

The Diamond Queen. Univ., [18 Chapters] D: Ed Kull; SP: George W. Pyper, Robert F. Roden; S: Jacques Futrelle; LP: Eileen Sedgwick, George Chesebro, Al Smith, Frank Mc Clark, Lew Short, Josephine Scott, Burton Wilson.

The Terror Trail. Univ., [18 Chapters] D: Edward Kull; S/SP: Edward Kull, John W. Grey, George Plympton; LP: Eileen Sedgwick, George Larkin, Theodore Brown, Albert J. Smith, Barney Furey.

1923

In the Days of Daniel Boone. Univ., [15 Chapters] D: William Craft, Jay Marchant, Frank Messinger; SP/S: Jefferson Moffitt, Paul Bryan; LP: Jack Mower, Eileen Sedgwick, Charles Brinley, Duke R. Lee, Ruth Royce.

Beasts of Paradise. Univ., [15 Chapters] D:

William Craft; SP/S: Val Cleveland; LP: William Desmond, Eileen Sedgwick, William N. Gould, Ruth Royce, Margaret Morris, Joe Bonomo, Clark Comstock, Slim Cole.

1925

The Riddle Rider. Univ., [15 Chapters] D: William Craft; SP/S: William Wing, Arthur H. Gooden, George Pyper; LP: William Desmond, Eileen Sedgwick, Helen Holmes, Claude Payton, William H. Gould.

Fighting Ranger. Univ., [18 Chapters] D: Jay Marchant; S/SP: George W. Pyper, F. J. Marchant; LP: Jack Daugherty, Eileen Sedgwick, Al Wilson, Bud Osborn, William Welsh, Charles Avery, Frank Lanning, Slim Cole, Gladys Roy.

1926

Strings of Steel. Univ., [10 Chapters] D: Henry MacRae; SP: Phillip Dutton Horn, Oscar Lund; LP: William Desmond, Eileen Sedgwick, Albert J. Smith, Arthur Morrison, George Ovey, Grace Cunard, Dorothy Gulliver, Ted Duncan.

The Winking Idol. Univ., [10 Chapters] D: Francis Ford; S: Charles E. Van Loan; LP: William Desmond, Eileen Sedgwick, Grace Cunard, Jack Richardson, Dorothy Gulliver, Les Sailor [Syd Saylor], Helen Broneau, Herbert Sutch.

1928

The Vanishing West. Mascot, [10 Chapters] D: Richard Thorpe; SP: Wyndham Gittens; P: Nat Levine; S: Karl Krusada, William Lester; LP: Jack Perrin, Leo Maloney, Yakima Canutt, William Fairbanks, Eileen Sedgwick, Fred Church, Helen Gibson, Harry Lorraine.

JOSIE SEDGWICK

Josie Sedgwick was born in Galveston, Texas, on March 13, 1898, the daughter of stage actors and the sister of Eileen and Edward.

They all appeared in the vaudeville act called "The Five Sedgwicks." She received her education at the Ursuline Convent in Galveston.

Josie Sedgwick and Edward Hearn (hat in hand) in *Daring Days* (Universal, 1925).

Josie was 5'5", had brunette hair, dark blue-gray eyes and weighed around 110 pounds during her movie days.

After a small part in the serial *Lure of the Circus* ('18), Josie's two bids for serial immortality came in the form of *Daredevil Jack* ('20) and *Double Adventure* ('21). Jack Dempsey starred in the first, as a college athlete giving a helping hand to Josie, who is trying to locate a secret oil basin discovered by her father before his death. Josie carried off her assignment in fine style. In *Double Adventure*, Charles Hutchison plays a young reporter determined to put a band of notorious crooks behind bars for stealing Josie's inheritance.

Josie appeared in features beginning in 1917, making nine five-reelers that year. Her features include *The Boss of the Lazy Y* ('17, Roy Stewart), *One Shot Ross* ('17, Roy Stewart), *Indiscreet Corinne* ('17, George Chesebro), *Fighting Back* ('17, William Desmond), *Keith of the Border* ('18, Roy Stewart), *Paying His Debt* ('18, Roy Stewart), *Hell's End* ('18, William Desmond), *Wildlife* ('18, Desmond), *Beyond the Shadows* ('18, Desmond), *Wolves of the Border* ('18, Stewart), *Jubilo* ('19, Will Rogers), *Sunset Sprague* ('20, Buck Jones), *The Duke of Chimney Butte* ('21, Fred Stone), *Daddy* ('23, Jackie Coogan), *The Sunshine Trail* ('23, Douglas MacLean), *The Sawdust Trail* ('24, Hoot Gibson), *Let 'er Buck* ('26, Hoot Gibson), *The Outlaw's Daughter* ('25) and *Son of Oklahoma* ('31, Bob Steele).

Josie was especially popular in the Universal two-reelers she made in the years 1925–26. Some of these were *Montana of the Range*, *Queen of the Roundup*, *The Ropin' Venus*, *A Battle of Wits*, *The Fighting Schoolmarm*, *The Best Man*, *Dynamite's Daughter*,

Queen of the Hills, Miss Robin Hood, Mountain Molly O', Outlaw Love, The Little Warrior and *Jim Hood's Ghost.*

Like her sister Eileen, Josie retired with the coming of sound to film. Most of her work had been at Universal. Although she never equaled the success of Eileen, she nevertheless was a well-known actress in the '20s.

Josie Sedgwick died on April 30, 1973, at age 75 in Santa Monica.

Serials

1918

Lure of the Circus. Univ., [18 Chapters] D: J. P. McGowan; SP: Hope Loring; S: William Wing; LP: Eddie Polo, Eileen Sedgwick, Harry Carter, Molly Malone, Noble Johnson.

1920

Daredevil Jack. Pathé, [15 Chapters] D: W. S. Van Dyke; SP: Jack Cunningham; S: Frederick Chapin, Harry Hoyt; P: Robert Brunton; LP: Jack Dempsey, Josie Sedgwick, Hershall Mayall, Albert Cody, Ruth Langston, Edward Hearn, Carmen Phillips, Noble Johnson, Frank Lanning, Al Kaufman, Bull Montana.

1921

Double Adventure. Pathé, [15 Chapters] D: W. S. Van Dyke; S: Jack Cunningham; P: Robert Brunton; LP: Charles Hutchison, Josie Sedgwick, Carl Stockdale, S. E. Jennings.

GEORGE B. SEITZ

As artist, writer, actor, playwright, director and producer, George B. Seitz had one of the most colorful careers in the entertainment world. Born in Boston on January 3, 1888, and educated there and in Philadelphia, Seitz first worked as a painter, then as a legit actor and a playwright. In 1914 he entered pictures with Pathé, writing, directing and producing the Pearl White serials. He also was one of Pathé's star actors.

At the age of 21 he wrote a play, *The King's Game*, which he left with William A. Brady while he went out on the road with another company. Upon his return he found James K. Hackett starring in the play and a stack of royalties awaiting him. In 1919, he heard of an obscure Tin Pan Alley musician and sent for him to add a score to a musical comedy which Seitz and Alex Aarons produced. The play was *La La Lucille* and the music writer was George Gershwin, who thus made his Broadway debut.

Some of the early films in which Seitz appeared or wrote are *Detective Craig's Coup* ('14), *The Beloved Vagabond* ('15), *The Closing Net* ('15), *Nedra* ('15), *Simon, the Jester* ('15), *The King's Game* ('16), *The Light That Failed* ('16), *The Precious Packet* ('16), *Blind Man's Luck* ('17), *The Hunting of the Hawk* ('17), *The Last of the Carnabys* ('17), *The Naulahka* ('18) and *Rogues and Romance* ('20).

But it is his serials that justify his inclusion in this book. He wrote nine screenplays, directed or co-directed 19 Pathé serials, was a supporting player in five and co-starred in four, three of them with lovely Marguerite Courtot. He also produced four serials. Not a bad record! Seitz virtually dominated the serial field until 1925, when he turned exclusively to features. His silent feature output consisted for the most part of action films, often Westerns. His sound films included much of the same but also a great many lighter in theme, including the Andy Hardy series. He had a reputation for uncompromising professionalism in his work, always completing films on or ahead of schedule and well within the limits of his budget. The effectiveness of some of his work in the thriller genre is quite amazing considering the speed at which he turned out his films.

Seitz was under contract as director at Metro from 1930 to his death, and piloted 13 of the Andy Hardy pictures. *A Family Affair*, his first at Metro, helped make Mickey Rooney a major star, and that picture developed into the Hardy series. Prior to his Metro tenure he had directed for Paramount, Fox, Universal, Metropolitan, PDC, FBO, RKO, Pathé and Columbia.

Among his long list of directorial credits are *Wild Horse Mesa* ('25), *The Vanishing American* ('25), *Desert Gold* ('26), *The Ice Flood* ('26), *The Last Frontier* ('26), *The Tigress* ('27), *Isle of Forgotten Women* ('27), *Court-Martial* ('28), *Black Magic* ('29), *Danger Lights* ('30), *Drums of Jeopardy* ('31), *Sally of the Subway* ('32), *Docks of San Francisco* ('32), *Treason* ('33), *The Fighting Rangers* ('34), *Times Square Lady* ('35), *The Last of the Mohicans* ('36), *My Dear Miss Aldrich* ('37), *Yellow Jack* ('38), *Thunder Afloat* ('39), *Kit Carson* ('40), *A Yank on the Burma Road* ('42) and *Pierre of the Plains* ('42).

Seitz died at the home of his son in Westwood, California, on July 8, 1944. Death was due to a recurrence of a circulatory ailment.

Serials

1914

The Perils of Pauline. Pathé, [20 Chapters] D: Louis Gasnier, Donald McKenzie; S: Charles Goddard; P: Leopold and Theodore Wharton; LP: Pearl White, Crane Wilbur, Paul Panzer, Edward Jose, Francis Carlyle, George B. Seitz, LeRoy Baker.

Exploits of Elaine. Pathé, [14 Chapters] D: Louis Gasnier, George B. Seitz; SP: C. W. Goddard, George B. Seitz; S: Arthur B. Reeve, Bertram Millhauser, Charles L. Goddard; P: Leopold and Theodore Wharton; Cam: Joseph Dubray; LP: Pearl White, Arnold Daly, Creighton Hale, Sheldon Lewis, Lionel Barrymore, George B. Seitz.

1915

The New Exploits of Elaine. Pathé, [10 Chapters] D: George B. Seitz, Bertram Millhauser; SP: Charles W. Goddard, George B. Seitz, Bertram Millhauser; S: Arthur B. Reeve; P: Leopold and Theodore Wharton; Cam: Joseph Dubray; LP: Pearl White, Creighton Hale, Arnold Daly, Edwin Arden, M. W. Rale.

The Romance of Elaine. Pathé, [12 Chapters] D: George B. Seitz, Joseph A. Golden, Louis Gasnier; SP: Charles W. Goddard, George B. Seitz, Bertram Millhauser; S: Arthur P. Reeve; P: Leopold and Theodore Wharton; Cam: Joseph Dubray; LP: Pearl White, Creighton Hale, Arnold Daly, Lionel Barrymore, Bessie E. Wharton, George B. Seitz.

1916

Pearl of the Army. Pathé, [15 Chapters] D: Edward Jose; SP: George B. Seitz; LP: Pearl White, Ralph Kellard, Marie Wayne, Floyd Buckley, W. T. Carleton.

The Iron Claw. Pathé, [20 Chapters] D: Edward Jose, George B. Seitz; S: Arthur Stringer; SP: George B. Seitz; LP: Pearl White, Creighton Hale, Sheldon Lewis, Harry Fraser, J. E. Dunn, Henry G. Sell, Edward Jose, Carey Lee, George B. Seitz.

1917

The Seven Pearls. Pathé, [15 Chapters] D: Burton L. King, Donald McKenzie; SP: George B. Seitz; S: Charles W. Goddard; LP: Mollie King, Creighton Hale, Leon Bary, John J. Dunn, Henry G. Sell, Floyd Buckley, Walter P. Lewis.

1918

The House of Hate. Pathé, [20 Chapters] D: George B. Seitz; S: Arthur B.Reeve,Charles A. Logue; LP: Pearl White, Antonio Moreno, Peggy Shanor, John Gilmour, John Webb Dillon, Floyd Buckley, Paul Panzer, Ruby Hoffman.

1919

The Black Secret. Pathé, [15 Chapters] D: George B. Seitz; SP: Bertram Millhauser; S: Robert W. Chambers; LP: Pearl White, Walter

McGrail, Wallace McCutcheon, Henry Gsell, George B. Seitz.

Bound and Gagged. Pathé, [10 Chapters] D: George B. Seitz; S/SP: Frank Leon Smith; LP: Marguerite Courtot, George B. Seitz, Nellie Burt, Harry Semels.

1920

Velvet Fingers. Pathé, [15 Chapters] D/S: Bertram Millhauser; P: George B. Seitz; SP: James Shelly Hamilton; LP: George B. Seitz, Marguerite Courtot, Harry Semels, Lucille Lennox, Joe Cuny.

Pirate Gold. Pathé, [10 Chapters] D: George B. Seitz; SP: Bertram Millhauser; S: Frank Leon Smith; LP: Marguerite Courtot, George B. Seitz, Frank Redman, William Burt, Harry Semels.

1921

The Sky Ranger. Pathé, [15 Chapters] D/P: George B. Seitz; SP: Frank Leon Smith; LP: George B. Seitz, June Caprice, Harry Semels, Frank Redman, Peggy Shanor.

Hurricane Hutch. Pathé, [15 Chapters] D: George B. Seitz; S: Charles Hutchison; LP: Charles Hutchison, Lucy Fox, Warner Oland, Diana Deer, Harry Semels, George B. Seitz.

1922

Speed. Pathé, [15 Chapters] D: George B. Seitz; SP: Bertram Millhauser; S: Charles Hutchison; LP: Charles Hutchison, Lucy Fox, John Webb Dillon, Harry Semels, Cecile Bonnel, Charles Reveda.

Go Get 'em Hutch. Pathé, [15 Chapters] D/P: George B. Seitz; S: Frank Leon Smith; LP: Charles Hutchison, Marguerite Clayton, Richard R. Neill, Frank Hagney, Joe Cuny, Cecile Bonnell.

1923

Plunder. Pathé, [15 Chapters] D: George B. Seitz; SP: Bertram Millhauser, George B. Seitz; S: Herbert Crooker; LP: Pearl White, Warren Krech [William], Harry Semels, Tom McIntyre, J. Elwood Pool, Wally Oettel, Charles Reveda.

1924

Into the Net. Pathé, [10 Chapters] D: George B. Seitz; SP: Frank Leon Smith; S: Richard E. Enright; LP: Edna Murphy, Jack Mulhall, Constance Bennett, Frank Lackteen, Harry Semels, Bradley Barker, Frances Landau.

Way of a Man. Pathé, [10 Chapters] D/SP: George B. Seitz; S: Emerson Hough; P: C. W. Paton; LP: Allene Ray, Harold Miller, Fred Osborne, Lillian Gale, Whitehorse, Kathryn Appleton, Chet Ryan, Florence Lee.

The Fortieth Door. Pathé, [10 Chapters] D: George B. Seitz; SP: Frank Leon Smith; S: Mary Hastings Bradley; P: C. W. Patton; Cam: Vernon Walker; LP: Allene Ray, Bruce Gordon, Frank Lackteen, Anna May Wong, Whitehorse, David Dunbar, Frankie Mann, Lillian Gale.

Leatherstocking. Pathé, [10 Chapters] D: George B. Seitz; P: C. W. Patton; LP: Edna Murphy, Harold Miller, Whitehorse, Frank Lackteen, Ray Myers, David Dunbar, Tom Tyler, Lillian Hall.

Galloping Hoofs. Pathé, [10 Chapters] D: George B. Seitz; S: Frank Leon Smith; LP: Allene Ray, Johnnie Walker, J. Barney Sherry, Ernest Hilliard, Armand Cortez, William Nally.

1925

Sunken Silver. Pathé, [10 Chapters] D/P: George B. Seitz; SP: Frank Leon Smith; S: Albert Payson Terhune; LP: Allene Ray, Walter Miller, Frank Lackteen, Albert Roccardi, Jean Brunette, Charlie Fang.

FRANK SHANNON

Probably every serial buff knows Frank Shannon as brilliant scientist Dr. Zarkov, builder of the rocketships that enabled Flash Gordon and Dale Arden to rocket into the stratosphere with him three times, there to experience undreamed-of adventures.

Flash Gordon ('36), one of the most expensive and most successful serials ever made, has today taken on the aura of a classic and is still being shown on TV and at film festivals. The planet Mongo is heading toward Earth and the trio of adventurers blast off for that mysterious world. There they do battle with Ming, the Merciless, its cruel dictator.

In *Flash Gordon's Trip to Mars* ('38), the five principals from the first serial are back — Buster Crabbe as Flash Gordon, Jean Rogers as Dale Arden, Shannon as Dr. Zarkov, Charles Middleton as Ming and Richard Alexander as Prince Baron. The earthlings go to Mars in hopes of locating and destroying the mysterious force which is sapping nitrogen from the Earth's atmosphere. They find Ming allied with Queen Azura and for 15 chapters they do battle with Ming's forces until Ming is thrown into a disintegrating chamber. The serial proved to be as popular as its predecessor.

Universal moguls decided that a third Flash Gordon serial would prove profitable, so *Flash Gordon Conquers the Universe* ('40) was filmed with Crabbe, Shannon, Middleton and Carol Hughes in the principal roles. (Jean Rogers was unavailable, thus Hughes played Dale Arden.) Roland Drew took over Richard Alexander's role as Prince Baron. New principals were Anne Gwynne as Sonja, Shirley Deane as Princess Aura, Lee Powell as Roka and Ray Mala as the king's son.

Shannon's role as Dr. Hayden is a minor one in Columbia's *Batman* ('43), but serial buffs were glad to see and hear him again. He got more footage as Prof. Davidson, father of Diana (Jeanne Bates), in *The Phantom* ('43). They are searching Africa for the lost city of Zoloz, reputed to be the source of a vast hidden treasure. The fiancé of Diana is Godfrey Prescott, the Phantom (Tom Tyler). The serial was a good one, comparing favorably with Tyler's *Adventures of Captain Marvel* ('41).

Shannon first came to the screen back in 1921 with a supporting role in *Perjury* starring William Farnum. In his next film, *The Bride's Play* ('22), he plays Sir John Mansfield. Marion Davies starred. In *Boomerang Bill* ('22), he is a police officer; in *Icebound* ('24), a judge; and in *Monsieur Beaucaire* ('24), he plays "Badger," a supporting role to Rudolph Valentino and Bebe Daniels. Ten years later he worked in *Women in the Dark*. Some of his other films are *The Eagle's Brood* ('35), *G-Men* ('35), *The Prisoner of Shark Island* ('36), *The Texas Rangers* ('36), *Black Gold* ('36), *Nancy Steele is Missing!* ('37) and *Off to the Races* ('37). He was McTavish in the Torchy Blane series, playing the part in six films.

Later roles were in *Rulers of the Sea* ('39), *Union Pacific* ('39), *Brigham Young — Frontiersman* ('40), *The Return of Frank James* ('40), *Rage in Heaven* ('41), *Reap the Wild Wind* ('42), *The Iron Major* ('43), *Man Alive* ('45), *Crack-up* ('46) and *A Dangerous Profession* ('49).

In a total of 40 *Flash Gordon* chapters, Shannon thoroughly endeared himself to serial followers. He might play other characters in subsequent films, but his appearance on the screen would often be followed by "There's Dr. Zarkov" from one or more fans in the audience.

Shannon died in 1959 at age 84 in Hollywood.

Serials

1936

Flash Gordon. Univ., [13 Chapters] D: Frederick Stephani; SP: George Plympton, Frederick Stephani, Ella O'Neill; P: Henry MacRae; Cam: Jerry Ash, Richard Fryer; LP: Larry (Buster) Crabbe, Jean Rogers, Charles Middleton, Frank Shannon, Priscilla Lawson, Richard Alexander, George Cleveland, John Lipson, James Pierce, Bull Montana, Glenn Strange.

1938

Flash Gordon's Trip to Mars. Univ., [15 Chapters] D: Ford Beebe, Robert Hill; S/SP: Wyndham Gittens, Norman S. Hall, Ray Trampe,

Herbert Dalmas; LP: Larry (Buster) Crabbe, Jean Rogers, Frank Shannon, Charles Middleton, Beatrice Roberts, Donald Kerr, Richard Alexander, C. Montague Shaw, Hooper Atchley, Wheeler Oakman, Anthony Warde, Lane Chandler, Reed Howes, Kenneth Duncan.

1940

Flash Gordon Conquers the Universe. Univ., [12 Chapters] D: Ford Beebe, Ray Taylor; SP: George H. Plympton, Basil Dickey, Barry Shipman; P: Henry MacRae; Cam: Jerry Ash; LP: Larry (Buster) Crabbe, Carol Hughes, Charles Middleton, Frank Shannon, Roland Drew, Shirley Deane, Lee Powell, Ray Mala, Ben Taggart, Anne Gwynne.

1943

Batman. Col., [15 Chapters] D: Lambert Hillyer; SP: Victor McLeod, Leslie Swabacker, Harry Fraser; P: Rudolph C. Flothow; LP: Lewis Wilson, Douglas Croft, J. Carrol Naish, Shirley Patterson, Charles Middleton, George Chesebro, Frank Shannon, Robert Fiske, George J. Lewis, I. Stanford Jolley, Tom London.

The Phantom. Col., [15 Chapters] D: B. Reeves Eason; SP: Morgan B. Cox, Victor McLeod, Sherman Lowe, Leslie Swabacker; P: Rudolph C. Flothow; Mus: Lee Zahler; Cam: James S. Brown, Jr.; LP: Tom Tyler, Jeanne Bates, Kenneth MacDonald, Frank Shannon, Ace (dog), Guy Kingsford, Ernie Adams, Edmund Cobb, George Chesebro, Joe Devlin, John S. Bagni.

PEGGY SHANOR

Peggy Shanor was a beautiful blonde ingenue who appeared in several serials. She appeared in *The Queen of Hearts* ('18) in support of Virginia Pearson. She was listed fifth in the cast but the nature of her role is unknown. She was also in *The Echo of Youth* ('19), a story of blackmail and young love starring Charles Richman and Leah Baird. And she had a minor role in the domestic drama *The Prodigal Judge* ('22) starring Jean Paige and Maclyn Arbuckle.

Peggy's first serial, *The House of Hate* ('18), starred Pearl White and Antonio Moreno. Peggy played Zelda, a "vamp" cousin of Pearl who loves Antonio and does her best to block his efforts to win Pearl and make secure the House of Walden, celebrated munitions manufacturers. "The Hooded Terror" furnished the necessary spine-tingling mystery as he and his gang set out to destroy the House of Walden.

In Arrow's *The Lurking Peril* ('19), George Larkin sells the right to his brain after his death to a fiendish professor who can't wait to begin dissecting it. He tries everything he can to hasten George's demise. Anne Luther is George's girlfriend and Peggy Shanor has one of the supporting roles.

Peggy co-starred in *The Mystery Mind* ('20), sharing the lead with J. Robert Pauline, a former hypnotist and headline vaudeville artist. A scientific expedition is outfitted to investigate certain native drugs and vegetable poisons along the upper reaches of the Orinoco, where the inhabitants are headhunters, ruled by a priest. There are secret gold deposits on the Orinoco jealously guarded by the headhunters. Intrigue and murder occur as members of the expedition follow their own desires. Peggy faces peril after peril and is in constant danger as the 15 chapters unfold, week by week.

The Sky Ranger ('21) stars June Caprice and George B. Seitz, with Peggy in a supporting role. After a decidedly humorous opening, the plot involves a powerful light which conspirators are seeking to secure.

Nothing else is known to the author about Peggy except that she died in 1935.

Serials

1918

The House of Hate. Pathé, [20 Chapters] D: George B. Seitz; SP: Bertram Millhauser; LP: Pearl White, Antonio Moreno, Peggy Shanor, John Gilmour, John Webb Dillon, Floyd Buckley, Paul Panzer, Helene Chadwick.

1919

The Lurking Peril. Arrow, [15 Chapters] D: George Morgan, Burton King; SP: Lloyd Lonergan, George Larkin; S: Lloyd Lonergan; LP: George Larkin, Anne Luther, William Betchel, Ruth Dyer, John Nicholson, Peggy Shanor.

1920

The Mystery Mind. Supreme, [15 Chapters] D: William Davis, Fred Sittenham; S/SP: Arthur B. Reeve, John W. Grey; LP: J. Robert Pauline, Peggy Shanor, Paul Panzer, Ed Rogers, Violet MacMillian, De Sacia Saville.

1921

The Sky Ranger. Pathé, [15 Chapters] D/P: George B. Seitz; SP: Frank Leon Smith; LP: George B. Seitz, June Caprice, Harry Semels, Frank Redman, Peggy Shanor, Spencer G. Bennet, Joe Cuny.

DAVE SHARPE

Dave Sharpe was one of Hollywood's most respected and requested stuntmen. While competing for the Los Angeles Athletic Club at the Sesquicentennial in Philadelphia in 1926, he won the National A.A.U. tumbling championship and repeated the feat in 1927. He was an all-around stuntman because he could do it all: fights, horse work, car stunts, boxing, wrestling, judo, jujitsu, swordplay. He preferred stunting to acting because it paid much better and there was always work.

Dave primarily worked at Republic after 1938, where he was involved in 25 serials and numerous features. He could perform almost any difficult stunt devised by a director. It was at Republic that he would make his reputation and gain legendary status among professionals and fans alike.

Dave was born in St. Louis, Missouri, in 1910 but grew up in Hollywood where he began motion picture work at a tender age. He appeared in Metro's *Scaramouche* ('23) starring Ramon Novarro and United Artists'

The Thief of Bagdad ('25) starring Douglas Fairbanks, as well as in other films while attending military school in Los Angeles.

In 1929 he got a big break as George O'Brien's brother in Fox's *Masked Emotions*. He was billed fourth in the tale of Chinese smugglers. This role led to Hal Roach hiring him, Mary Kornman and Mickey Daniels for a series of two-reel talkies titled *The Boy Friends*, about the misadventures of three youths.

Sharpe next starred in two outdoor films with Flash, the Wonder Dog, produced by William Berke in 1934 and released by Imperial. *Wild Waters* deals with a group of dam-building grafters who, facing exposure, blow up their own project, placing the blame on innocent Dave. Very cheaply made, most of the footage was shot silent using some early Lee Zahler music as cover-up, and what actual sound recording was done is of extremely poor quality. Despite these shortcomings, however, the film does have one all-important essential and that is action all the way. Sharpe had ample opportunity to demonstrate his formidable stunt talent in this 16-minute film. The other film with Flash is titled *Death Fangs* and has a running time of 14 minutes.

Berke followed with a series called "Young Friends" with Sharpe and his "Boy Friends" co-stars featured. *Adventurous Knights* ('35, Ajax) and *Social Error* ('35, Commodore) were both scripted by Sharpe. *Roaring Roads* ('35, Marcy) was the third film. In 1937, Sharpe supported Herman Brix (Bruce Bennett) in *Two Minutes to Play* (Victory) and Frankie Darro in *Young Dynamite* (Conn). By that time he had started his Western career and would soon be involved in Republic serials.

In 1938, Dave appeared in his first of 30 serials, Republic's *Dick Tracy Returns*. He plays a G-man recruit who is killed early in the proceedings. In 1939 he was a supporting player in *The Lone Ranger Rides Again* and received co-star billing with Charles Quigley and Bruce Bennett in *Daredevils of the Red Circle*, a 12-chapter photoplay. The principals are three college students working at Granville's amusement pier. They become enraged when an escaped convict, played by Charles Middleton, burns the pier. This evil deed results in the death of the young brother of one of the students. The three resolve to bring the criminal to justice. They become "The Daredevils of the Red Circle." Their ally is Blanche (Carole Landis), granddaughter of the real Granville, who has been replaced by the villain. It was a thrill-packed cliffhanger with three stars who would each make their mark in serials. Heroine Carole Landis would also go on to better things.

Veteran producer Ed Finney gave Sharpe perhaps his most impressive leading role of all. This was in Monogram's *Silver Stallion* ('41). Finney himself directed this horse-and-dog drama in which Dave, LeRoy Mason and Chief Thundercloud were pictured as rowdy but lovable horse thieves. Dave was given many chances to exhibit his riding and fighting skills and he also threw in some mighty fancy gunplay to boot!

When Ray Corrigan temporarily left the "Range Buster" trio in a salary dispute in 1942, his place was given to Dave, who rode alongside John King and Max Terhune in four films, *Texas to Bataan*, *Trail Riders*, *Two-Fisted Justice* and *Haunted Ranch*. By the time the last one was filmed, Dave was going into the Air Force (where he attained the rank of captain), so in *Haunted Ranch* the reason for his departure was that he was leaving to join Teddy Roosevelt's Rough Riders. Rex Lease took over in mid-film.

Upon his discharge, Dave resumed his work in front of the cameras. A notable postwar role was in PRC's *Colorado Serenade* ('46). In this adventure, filmed in Cinecolor, Sharpe played a flashy gunman whom star Eddie Dean thought to be a crook until the last reel when he was revealed as an undercover agent. The climax of the film was a terrific fight scene in a saloon with Dave scrambling all over the place, diving from balconies, etc.

In 1941, Sharpe doubled Tom Tyler in the flying sequences of *Adventures of Captain Marvel*, and in 1949 he doubled Tristram Coffin in *King of the Rocket Men*. He became one of the most sought-after artisans in the profession as a double, a ramrod, a second-unit director and personal coach in action techniques for many of the industry's foremost actors.

Of the 31 serials Sharpe worked in, 26 were for Republic. Dave also found steady employment at Republic in Westerns as well. Other films in which Sharpe either acted or stunted include *The Fuller Brush Man* ('48), *The Wild Blue Yonder* ('51), *Desert Legion* ('53), *The Veils of Bagdad* ('53), *The Great Race* ('65) and *Heaven Can Wait* ('78).

While acting in *The Life and Times of Judge Roy Bean* ('72), Sharpe noticed the first signs of Amyotrophic Laterial Sclerosis (Lou Gehrig's Disease), a deteriorating illness which impairs the nervous system and weakens muscles. His last days were spent in the Motion Picture Hospital where he got about in an electric wheelchair. He succumbed to the dreaded disease in 1980. Seventy years old, he had been inducted into the Holly-

In *Silver Stallion* (Monarch, 1941).

wood Stuntmen's Hall of Fame five months before his passing.

Serials

1938

Dick Tracy Returns. Rep., [15 Chapters] D: William Witney, John English; LP: Ralph Byrd, Lynne Roberts, Charles Middleton, Jerry Tucker.

1939

The Lone Ranger Rides Again. Rep., [15 Chapters] D: William Witney, John English; LP: Robert Livingston, Chief Thundercloud, Duncan Renaldo, Jinx Falen.

Daredevils of the Red Circle. Rep., [12 Chapters] D: William Witney, John English; SP:

Barry Shipman, Franklyn Adreon, Rex Taylor, Ronald Davidson, Sol Shor; AP: Robert Beche; Cam: William Nobles; Mus: William Lava; LP: Charles Quigley, Dave Sharpe, Herman Brix [Bruce Bennett], Carole Landis, Ben Taggart, C. Montague Shaw, Fred "Snowflake" Toones, George Chesebro.

Buck Rogers. Univ., [12 Chapters] D: Ford Beebe, Constance Moore, Jackie Moran, Jack Mulhall, Anthony Warde, Wheeler Oakman, Guy Usher, Reed Howes.

1940

Adventures of Red Ryder. Rep., [12 Chapters] D: William Witney, John English; LP: Donald Barry, Noah Beery, Sr., Tommy Cook, Vivian Coe [Austin].

Drums of Fu Manchu. Rep., [15 Chapters] D: William Witney, John English; LP: Henry Brandon, William Royle, John Picorri, Robert

Kellard, Gloria Franklin, Luana Walters, Olaf Hytten, Dwight Frye.

Junior G-Men. Univ., [12 Chapters] D: Ford Beebe, John Rawlins; LP: Billy Halop, Henry Hall, Gabriel Dell, Bernard Punsley, Philip Terry, Cy Kendall.

King of the Royal Mounted. Rep., [12 Chapters] D: William Witney, John English; LP: Allan Lane, Robert Strange, Robert Kellard, Lita Conway, Herbert Rawlinson.

Mysterious Doctor Satan. Rep., [15 Chapters] D: William Witney, John English; LP: Eduardo Ciannelli, Robert Wilcox, William Newell, C. Montague Shaw, Ella Neal.

1941

Dick Tracy vs. Crime, Inc. Rep., [15 Chapters] D: William Witney, John English; LP: Ralph Byrd, Jan Wiley, John Davidson, Ralph Morgan, Michael Owen, Robert Frazer, Robert Fiske, Jack Mulhall, Hooper Atchley, Anthony Warde, John Dilson.

King of the Texas Rangers. Rep., [12 Chapters] D: William Witney, John English; LP: Slingin' Sammy Baugh, Neil Hamilton, Pauline Moore, Duncan Renaldo, Charles Trowbridge, Monte Blue, Kermit Maynard, Jack Ingram, Stanley Blystone.

Adventures of Captain Marvel. Rep., [12 Chapters] D: William Witney, John English; LP: Tom Tyler, Frank Coghlan, Jr., William Benedict, Louise Currie, Harry Worth, Bryant Washburn, Reed Hadley, Jack Mulhall, George Pembroke.

Jungle Girl. Rep., [15 Chapters] D: William Witney, John English; LP: Frances Gifford, Tom Neal, Eddie Acuff, Gerald Mohr, Trevor Bardette, Tommy Cook.

1942

Gang Busters. Univ., [13 Chapters] D: Ray Taylor, Noel Smith; LP: Kent Taylor, Irene Hervey, Ralph Morgan, Robert Armstrong, Joseph Crehan, George J. Lewis, Richard Davies.

Spy Smasher. Rep., [12 Chapters] D: William Witney; LP: Kane Richmond, Marguerite Chapman, Sam Flint, Tris Coffin, Hans Schumm, Franco Corsaro.

Perils of Nyoka. Rep., [15 Chapters] D: William Witney; LP: Kay Aldridge, Clayton Moore,

William Benedict, Lorna Gray [Adrian Booth], Charles Middleton.

King of the Mounties. Rep., [12 Chapters] D: William Witney; LP: Allan Lane, Peggy Drake, Gilbert Emery, Russell Hicks, George Irving, Abner Biberman.

1943

G-Men vs. The Black Dragon. Rep., [15 Chapters] D: William Witney; LP: Rod Cameron, Constance Worth, Roland Got, Nino Pipitone, George J. Lewis.

1946

The Mysterious Mr. M. Univ., [13 Chapters] D: Lewis D. Collins, Vernon Keays; LP: Richard Martin, Pamela Blake, Dennis Moore, Jane Randolph, Danny Norton.

1948

Adventures of Frank and Jesse James. Rep., [13 Chapters] D: Fred Brannon, Yakima Canutt; LP: Clayton Moore, Steve Darrell, Noel Neill, George J. Lewis, Stanley Andrews, John Crawford.

Dangers of the Canadian Mounted. Rep., [12 Chapters] D: Fred Brannon, Yakima Canutt; LP: Jim Bannon, Virginia Belmont, Anthony Warde, Dorothy Granger.

1949

King of the Rocket Men. Rep., [12 Chapters] D: Fred Brannon; LP: Tristram Coffin, Mae Clarke, Don Haggerty, House Peters, Jr., James Craven, I. Stanford Jolley, Ted Adams, Dave Sharpe, Stanley Price.

Federal Agents vs. Underworld, Inc. Rep., [12 Chapters] D: Fred C. Brannon; LP: Kirk Alyn, Rosemary LaPlanche, Roy Barcroft, Carol Forman, Tristram Coffin.

1950

Radar Patrol vs. Spy King. Rep., [12 chapters] D: Fred B. Brannon; LP: Kirk Alyn, Jean Dean, Anthony Warde, George J. Lewis, Eve Whitney, John Merton, Tom Steele, Tristram Coffin, Dale Van Sickel.

The James Brothers of Missouri. Rep., [12 Chapters] D: Fred C. Brannon; LP: Keith Richards, Robert Bice, Noel Neill, Roy Barcroft, Patricia Knox.

The Invisible Monster. Rep., [12 Chapters] D: Fred C. Brannon; LP: Richard Webb, Aline Towne, Lane Bradford, Stanley Price, George Meeker, Tom Steele.

1951

Flying Disc Man From Mars. Rep., [12 Chapters] D: Fred C. Brannon; LP: Walter Reed, Lois Collier, Gregory Gay, James Craven, Harry Lauter, Richard Irving.

Government Agents vs. Phantom Legion. Rep., [12 Chapters] D: Fred C. Brannon; LP: Walter Reed, Mary Ellen Kay, Dick Curtis, John Pickard, Pierce Lyden.

Don Daredevil Rides Again. Rep., [12 Chapters] D: Fred C. Brannon; LP: Ken Curtis, Aline Towne, Roy Barcroft, Lane Bradford, Robert Einer, I. Stanford Jolley.

1952

Blackhawk. Col., [15 Chapters] D: Spencer Bennet, Fred F. Sears; LP: Kirk Alyn, Carol Forman, John Crawford, Michael Fox, Don Harvey, Rick Vallin, Marshall Reed, Larry Stewart.

1953

Canadian Mounties vs. Atomic Invaders. Rep., [12 Chapters] D: Franklyn Adreon; LP: Bill Henry Susan Morrow, Arthur Space, Dale Van Sickel, Pierre Watkin, Harry Lauter, Stanley Andrews.

GLORIA SHEA

Olive Gloria Shea was born May 30, 1913, in New York City and grew to adulthood there. She attended Notre Dame Convent in New York and subsequently did some modeling and radio work at CBS in New York. She was an attractive 5'5" gal with blue eyes and light brown hair who, for thousands of "B" movies fans, made even more enjoyable the watching of *The Dude Bandit* ('33), *The Fiddlin' Buckaroo* ('33), *Smoking Guns* ('34) and *A Demon for Trouble* ('34), leather burners starring popular saddle aces Hoot Gibson, Ken Maynard and Bob Steele. And perhaps her best remembered role (because of its being a serial) was in Universal's *Phantom of the Air* ('33), as Tom Tyler's leading lady.

Non-Westerns in which Gloria played include *Night Mayor* ('32) with Lee Tracy and Evalyn Knapp; *Big City Blues* ('32) with Joan Blondell; *Life Begins* ('32) with Loretta Young; *Women Won't Tell* ('33) with Sarah Padden; *The Eleventh Commandment* ('33) with Marian Marsh; *Strange People* ('33) with Hale Hamilton; *Dance Girl Dance* ('33) with Alan Dinehart; *Big Time or Bust* ('34) with Regis Toomey; *Money Means Nothing* ('34) with Wallace Ford; *We're Rich Again* ('34) with Edna May Oliver; *A Successful Failure* ('34) with Lucile Gleason; *The Oil Raider* ('34) with Buster Crabbe; *Bolero* ('34), with Carole Lombard and George Raft; *Sterling's Aunts* ('34) and *Heartburn* ('34), both two-reelers starring Sterling Holloway; *I Like It That Way* ('34) with Gloria Stuart; *Great God Gold* ('35) with Sidney Blackmer; *Tomorrow's Youth* ('35) with Dickie Moore; *Men of Action* ('35) with Frankie Darro; *One Way Ticket* ('35) with Lloyd Nolan; *Laddie* ('35) with Gloria Stuart; *The Last Days of Pompeii* ('35) with Preston Foster; and *Dangerous Intrigue* ('36) with Ralph Bellamy and Joan Perry.

With her warm-hearted personality she made each of her performances something special, with the result that she is not completely forgotten over 60 years later. She left the screen in 1936. No information is available on her subsequent life, except that it is known that she married and had at least one child, a daughter, who was living in Billings, Montana, in 1978. At that time Gloria, too, was living. The author has been unable to locate either mother or daughter.

In *The Phantom of the Air*, Bob Raymond (Tom Tyler) is hired by Thomas Edmunds to test his new invention, the Contragrav, a device designed to overcome the effects of gravity and thereby revolutionize aviation. Mort Crome, head of a gang of smugglers, would like to get his hands on it. Edmunds has also developed an airplane that he calls "The Phantom," controllable from his underground headquarters. In the end, Crome is killed in an explosion, Edmunds survives and Bob and Mary Edmunds concentrate on romance.

Serial

1933

The Phantom of the Air. Univ., [12 Chapters] D: Ray Taylor; SP: Basil Dickey, George H. Plympton; S: Ella O'Neill; LP: Tom Tyler, Gloria Shea, William Desmond, LeRoy Mason, Hugh Enfield [Craig Reynolds], Walter Brennan.

ELAINE SHEPARD

Elaine Shepard is remembered by serial buffs as Valarie, goddess of the lost African city of Joba, in the serial *Darkest Africa* starring wild animal trainer Clyde Beatty. In the story she is held captive by the high priest Dagna (Lucien Prival), who relies on Valarie's influence with the tribespeople to retain his power. Diamonds are being mined within the city by Dagna, and two crooked animal traders are after the diamonds. Dagna retains a force of bat men to do his bidding. Beatty and Valarie's young brother Baru (Manuel King) come to rescue Valarie. With the aid of Bonga (Ray Corrigan), an ape who is Baru's protector, they manage to get to Joba, but only after encountering wild animals and a tribe of bat men.

Since Dagna relies on Valarie's influence with the native people, he tries to keep her, Beatty and Baru from leaving the city. Aiding Dagna are Durkin (Wheeler Oakman) and Craddock (Edmund Cobb), who are seeking diamonds. Valarie agrees to perform the great sacrifice of leaping from Pinnacle Rock if her brother and Clyde are released from Dagna's clutches. At the last moment, however, Gorn (Edward McWade), her devoted teacher, changes places with her and, wearing her cloak, he makes the leap. Dagna releases Clyde and Baru and they, with Valarie, manage to escape the city just before an earthquake hits. The city is swallowed up.

Elaine had a small part in Gene Autry's *The Singing Vagabond* ('35) and was co-featured with Norman Foster in *I Cover Chinatown* ('36). In '37, she was the leading lady of *The Fighting Texan* (with Kermit Maynard) and *Law of the Ranger* (with Bob Allen) and had a supporting role in *Topper* with Cary Grant. The remainder of her roles could be classified as bits. She was in *The Goldwyn Follies* ('38) with Vera Zorina and Kenny Baker, but one had to look closely to spot her. She also had a bit in *There Goes My Heart* ('38) with Frederic March. There were no recorded credits for her in 1939 and only one—*You Can't Fool Your Wife*—in 1940. Lucille Ball and James Ellison starred in this latter film. Her other credits are *The Falcon in Danger* ('43, Tom Conway), *Seven Days Ashore* ('44, Wally Brown and Alan Carney),

Thirty Seconds Over Tokyo ('44, Spencer Tracy, Van Johnson) and *Ziegfeld Follies* ('46, Fred Astaire).

Elaine turned roving correspondent and published, in addition to her newspaper work, two books. *Forgive Us Our Press Passes* and *The Doom Pussy*, the latter based on her firsthand observations as a war correspondence in Vietnam. She formed her own production company with the intention of bringing the latter story to the screen. The author is unaware of her later activities, but it would seem that journalism was more her calling than acting.

Elaine apparently died September 6, 1998, in New York City.

Serial

1936

Darkest Africa. Rep., [15 Chapters] D: B. Reeves Eason, Joseph Kane; P: Nat Levine; SP: John Rathmell, Barney Sarecky, Ted Parsons; S: John Rathmell, Tracy Knight; Spv.: Barney Sarecky; Cam: William Nobles, Edgar Lyons; LP: Clyde Beatty, Manuel King, Elaine Shepard, Lucien Prival, Ray Benard [Corrigan], Wheeler Oakman, Edmund Cobb.

MARION SHILLING

Born on December 3, 1910, in Denver, Colorado, Marion Helen Schilling (the "c" in her name was dropped for screen billing) was the daughter of a Denver banker who, with a partner, organized a stock company in St. Louis. It was a successful venture and Marion played child and ingenue roles in such productions as *Mrs. Wiggs of the Cabbage Patch*, *Penrod* and *Rebecca of Sunnybrook Farm*.

Marion graduated from high school in St. Louis at 17, signed on for a role in the touring company of *Dracula* and wound up in California. She wanted to attend the University of Southern California and major in journalism, but when MGM tested her and offered a contract, she accepted.

Her first film was *Wise Girls* ('29) with Elliott Nugent. Two other features followed: *Lord Byron of Broadway* ('30), a flop starring Charles Kaley, and Buster Keaton's *Free and Easy* ('30), which returned reasonable profits. Although her option was not picked up, she was immediately signed by Paramount. During six months there she appeared in lots of publicity stills but only one film, *Shadow of the Law* ('30) with William Powell.

In 1931, Marion was selected as a Wampas Baby Star and for several years was spokeswoman for this celebrated group.

As a freelancer, Marion made *The Swellhead* ('30) with James Gleason and *On Your Back* ('30) with Irene Rich before signing with RKO. There she appeared in *Beyond Victory* ('31 William Boyd), *Young Donovan's Kid* ('31 Richard Dix, Jackie Cooper), *The Common Law* ('31 Joel McCrea, Constance Bennett) and *The Sundown Trail* ('31 Tom Keene). She loved making the cowboy flick and when her career became a rudderless ship as a result of her agent's heart attack and slow recovery, she got what parts she could through other agents who split the agent's fee with her disabled agent.

Her other films were *Forgotten Women* (Mon., Rex Bell, '31), *Shop Angel* (Tower, Holmes Herbert, '32), *The County Fair* (Mon., Hobart Bosworth, '32), *A Man's Land* (Allied, Hoot Gibson, '32), *Parisian Romance* (Allied, Gilbert Roland, '32), *Heart Punch* (Mayfair, Lloyd Hughes, '32), *Curtain at Eight* (Majestic, Dorothy Mackaill, '33), *Fighting to Live* (Principal, Reb Russell, '34), *Thunder Over Texas* (Beacon, Guinn Williams, '34), *The*

Westerner (Col., Tim McCoy, '34), *Inside Information* (S&S, Rex Lease, '34), *A Shot in the Dark* (Chesterfield, Charles Starrett, '35), *Stone of Silver Creek* (Univ., Buck Jones, '35), *Keeper of the Bees* (Mon., Neil Hamilton, '35), *Society Fever* (Invincible, Lois Wilson, '35), *Captured in Chinatown* (Superior, Charles Delaney, '35), *Rio Rattler* (Reliable, Tom Tyler, '35), *Gunsmoke on the Guadalupe* (Kent, Buck Coburn, '35), *Gun Play* (Beacon, Guinn Williams, '35), *Blazing Guns* (Kent, Reb Russell, '35), *The Idaho Kid* (Colony, Rex Bell, '36), *Romance Rides the Range* (Spectrum, Fred Scott, '36), and *Cavalcade of the West* (Diversion, Hoot Gibson, '36).

Marion made two serials. The first, Universal's *The Red Rider* ('34), starred Buck Jones. Red Davidson (Buck) attempts to clear his friend Silent Slade (Grant Withers) of murder charges after first relinquishing his job as sheriff because he allowed Slade to escape. Going to work on a ranch near the Mexican border, Red finds his old pal, the man he suspects is the real killer (Walter Miller), and a beautiful girl (Marion). It is unusual for a Western to have two love stories in progress, but besides Buck and Marion, Edmund Cobb woos Margaret LaMarr.

In 1936, Marion appeared in S&S's *The Clutching Hand* with a cast of oldtimers familiar to those who regularly viewed "B" movies. Dr. Paul Gironda (Robert Frazer) discovers a formula for the manufacture of synthetic gold. Just before the board of directors arrive at his lab to witness his achievement, he is heard screaming and disappears before help arrives. Walter Jameson (Rex Lease), a newspaper reporter engaged to Gironda's daughter (Marion), calls in Craig Kennedy (Jack Mulhall) to find the abducted scientist. Directing criminal activities is the Clutching Hand.

Marion attended the 1985 Memphis Film Festival and was amazed at the reception she was given after a 50-year absence from the movie world. Fond memories came flowing back and once again Marion was in a world that had been lost to her for half a century.

In 1932, while filming *Shop Angel*, Marion met a young man named Edward Cook, and after a lengthy courtship they were married in 1937. Thus ended Marion's movie career. The couple spent the first six years of their marriage in Marion Golf Manor, Pennsylvania. Then they moved to Pasadena, California, so that Edward could do graduate work in physics at Cal-Tech. Later there were 20 beautiful years by the sea at Palos Verdes Estates and then a move to Palo Alto. They had two children, a son, Ned, and a daughter, Frances (now deceased). They were a close-knit, devout Christian family.

Today Marion lives alone, Edward having died several years back. At age 93 she still remains upbeat. For the record, she had brown hair and eyes, weighed about 115 pounds and stood 5'4" tall during her screen days.

The author's favorite Shilling films are *The Idaho Kid* ('36) and *The Red Rider* ('34). Admittedly, these and all her films were low-budget programmers, designed to be shown on a double feature basis or as a solo in the hinterlands and nabes. But they entertained that large segment of the public which viewed them. And now, thanks to television and home video, a new audience has come to know her. While heavy dramatics would never be her forte, Marion was often better than her material.

Serials

1934

The Red Rider. Univ., [15 Chapters] D: Louis Friedlander [Lew Landers]; SP: George H. Plympton, Vin Moore, Ella O'Neill, George Morgan; S: W. C. Tuttle; P: Henry MacRae; LP: Buck Jones, Marion Shilling, Grant Withers, Walter Miller, Richard Cramer, Margaret LaMarr, Charles French, Edmund Cobb, J. P. McGowan, William Desmond.

1936

The Clutching Hand. Stage and Screen, [15 Chapters] D: Albert Herman; Spv.: Louis Weiss; SP: Louis D'Usseau, Dallas Fitzgerald; Cam: James Diamond; Mus: Lee Zahler; LP: Jack Mulhall, Marion Shilling, Ruth Mix, Rex Lease, William Farnum, Yakima Canutt, Reed Howes, Bryant Washburn.

MARIAN SHOCKLEY

Marian Shockley is said to have appeared as a leading lady in Al Christie comedies. The author has no record of these. She was Bob Steele's leading lady in *Near the Trail's End* ('31) and had small parts in *Western Limited* ('32) with Estelle Taylor and Edmund Burns and *Elinor Norton* ('34) starring Claire Trevor and Gilbert Roland.

It was 1931 when she played opposite Tim McCoy in the Universal serial *Heroes of the Flames.* Tim, a fireman, rescues Marian and her brother from a fire. Her grateful father allows Tim to use his lab to conduct experiments on a chemical fire extinguisher. A crook and his minions try to steal Tim's in-

vention only to meet with failure. Tim and Marian become romantically involved.

Serial

1931

Heroes of the Flames. Univ., [12 Chapters] D: Robert F. Hill; SP: George Morgan, George H. Plympton, Basil Dickey; LP: Tim McCoy, Marian Shockley, William Gould, Bobby Nelson, Gayne Whitman, Beulah Hutton, Joe Bonomo, Edmund Cobb, Bruce Cabot, Walter Brennan, Andy Devine.

DOROTHY SHORT

Dorothy Short had a (roughly) ten-year movie career. Her first recorded work was in Laurel and Hardy's *Hollywood Party* ('34). It was not an auspicious beginning. She then

had supporting roles in *Student Tour* ('34, Jimmy Durante), *She Married Her Boss* ('35, Claudette Colbert), *More Than a Secretary* ('36, George Brent), *Assassin of Youth* ('37,

Luana Walters) and *Start Cheering* ('38, Jimmy Durante. *Tell Your Children* ('38) featured both Dorothy and her future husband, Dave O'Brien. *Missing Daughters* ('39) had Richard Arlen in the lead. James Stewart played the lead in *Mr. Smith Goes to Washington* ('39) but you have to be vigilant to spot Dorothy. She supported Evelyn Brent and Grant Withers in *Daughter of the Tong* ('39).

It was in Westerns that Dorothy stood out and attracted attention. She was heroine to Tom Tyler in *Brothers of the West* ('38), Tex Ritter in *Where the Buffalo Roam* ('38), William Boyd in *Heart of Arizona* ('38), Jack Randall in *Wild Horse Canyon* ('38), Tim McCoy in *Code of the Cactus* ('39), Dorothy Page in *The Singing Cowgirl* (39), Tim McCoy in *Frontier Crusader* ('40), Ken Maynard in *Phantom Rancher* ('40) and Johnny Mack Brown in *Pony Post* ('40). She adequately handled her assignments in these films.

In 1941, she had a small role in *Aloma of the South Seas* starring Dorothy Lamour and did leading lady chores in *The Lone Rider Fights Back* ('41) with George Houston, *The Phantom Pinto* ('41) with Buzzy Henry and *The Trail of the Silver Spurs* ('41) with the Range Busters (Ray Corrigan, John King, Max Terhune). Her last film of record was

Bullets for Bandits ('42) starring Wild Bill Elliott.

The serial *Captain Midnight* was released that same year. Dorothy plays Joyce Edwards, daughter of inventor John Edwards, who had built a vital range finder. The head of a vast enemy sabotage ring, Ivan Shark (Jack Craven), threatens the security of the U.S. by plotting to steal Edwards' range finder. Capt. Albright (Dave O'Brien), alias Captain Midnight, is called upon to find and stop the saboteurs. In carrying out his assignment he rescues the inventor, his daughter and his superior, all of whom had been made prisoners of Shark. In a final struggle, Shark is electrocuted when he accidently touches a crowbar to live wires.

The marriage of Dave O'Brien and Dorothy ended in divorce.

Serial

1942

Captain Midnight. Col., [15 Chapters] D: James W. Horne; SP: Basil Dickey, George H. Plympton, Jack Stanley, Wyndham Gittens; P: Larry Darmour; Cam: James S. Brown, Jr.; Mus: Lee Zahler; LP: Dave O'Brien, Dorothy Short, James Craven, Sam Edwards, Guy Wilkerson.

MILTON SILLS

Patria ('17) was a 15-chapter "war preparedness" serial pitting Patria (Irene Castle), owner of a large munitions factory, against agents of the Japanese and Mexican governments. She was aided by Capt. Donald Parr (Milton Sills), Secret Service agent. They combat Baron Huroki (Warner Oland), chief of the Japanese Secret Service, and Senor Juan de Lima (George Maharoni) of Mexico, who are plotting the overthrow of

the United States and the acquisition of a huge fortune. This is the serial that President Wilson ordered edited to cut out any names, flags, etc., that identified the invaders. The serial never did pick up the steam to become the hoped-for hit. Several future stars got needed experience as supporting players— Jack Holt, Wallace Beery, Marie Walcamp and Rudolph Valentino.

Sills, one of the most popular of the

early stars, came to the screen in 1914 as star of *The Pit* after a lengthy stage career as a leading man for Belasco, Shubert, Frohman and Brady — all outstanding stage producers. The film launched a career that was to make him well-known to every woman and most of the men in this country. He proved that he was box office material. His rise to screen fame came quickly but unlike other whose star ascended rapidly, his popularity did not fade as the years passed. He found success in a plethora of films. Few silent stars brought as much adventure to the screen as did Sills. *The Honor System* ('17) gave his career an extra boost and he never looked back.

His 84 films included *The Rock* ('16, Alice Brady); *Souls Adrift* ('17, Ethel Clayton); *The Claw* ('18 Clara Kimball Young); *The Savage Woman* ('18, Clara Kimball Young); *The Yellow Ticket* ('18, Fannie Ward); *The Fear Woman* ('19, Pauline Frederick); *Satan, Jr.* ('19, Viola Dana); *Shadows* ('19, Geraldine Farrar); *The Stronger Vow* ('19, Geraldine Farrar); *The Inferior Sex* ('20, Mildred Harris); *At the End of the World* ('21, Betty Compson); *The Great Moment* ('21, Gloria Swanson); *Burning Sands* ('22, Wanda Hawley); *The Isle of Lost Ships* ('23, Anna Q. Nilsson); *The Spoilers* ('23, Anna Q. Nilsson); *The Sea Hawk* ('24, Enid Bennett); *I Want My Man* ('25, Doris Kenyon); *The Making of O'Malley* ('25, Dorothy Mackaill); *Men of Steel* ('26, Doris Kenyon); *The Sea Tiger* ('27, Mary Astor); *The Valley of the Giants* ('27, Doris Kenyon); *The Hawk's Nest* ('28, Doris Kenyon); and *The Sea Wolf* ('30, Jane Keith).

Sills was born in Chicago in 1882 and educated at the University of Chicago. In the movies he portrayed every imaginable role, from comedy to swashbuckler to melodrama to Western. He was particularly effective in swashbucklers (*The Sea Hawk*, *The Sea Wolf*) and other action sagas (*The Spoilers*, *At the End of the World*, *The Knockout*). He worked in Hollywood's most fascinating, glamorous era and acquired a large and fanatically loyal following, especially women.

Sills' marriage to actress Doris Kenyon was a happy one. His death in 1970 from a heart attack while playing tennis closed the book on a long and successful career that had brought him fame the world over.

Serial

1917

Patria. International Film Service, [15 Chapters] D: Theodore and Leo Wharton; S: Louis Joseph Vance; SP: J. B. Clymer, Louis Vance, Charles Goddard; LP: Irene Castle, Milton Sills, Warner Oland, George Maharoni, Allen Murnane, Dorothy Green, Wallace Beery, Jack Holt, Nigel Barrie, Rudolph Valentino, LeRoy Baker, M. W. Rale, George Lessey, Charles Brinley.

RICHARD SIMMONS

Richard Simmons was born in St. Paul, Minnesota, on August 19, 1913, and died January 11, 2003, in a rest home near Oceanside, California, where he had been confined for some time suffering from Alzheimer's. What experiences he had between these two dates could fill a book.

Simmons' childhood and early youth were spent in White Bear Lake, Minnesota. It was here he learned to fly. Following high school graduation, he attended the university of Minnesota, but he did not complete a program there. Instead, he dropped out and rode the rails to California where, after a few menial jobs, he became a radio and band announcer at the famed Palladium Ballroom.

He drifted into films in 1937. Since he had learned fencing while in college, he was able to get the job of doubling Ronald Colman in fencing sequences in *The Prisoner of Zenda* ('37) and played a small part in *A Million to One* ('37).

In 1940, he was Constable Carter in *King of the Royal Mounted*, and in 1941's *King of the Texas Rangers* he was Ranger Red Cameron. Both roles were small. He also appeared in Warner Brothers' *Sergeant York* ('41). When he wasn't making enough money from acting, he became a commercial pilot for Northwest Airlines.

Simmons went under contract to MGM in 1942 and remained with that studio for ten years. Some of his earlier roles were in *Stand By for Action* ('42), *Dr. Gillespie's New Assistant* ('42), *Pilot No. 5* ('42), *Seven Sweethearts* ('42), *The Youngest Profession* ('43) and *Thousands Cheer* ('43).

During World War II, Simmons was a pilot with the Air Transport Command, attaining the rank of Captain. After the war he returned to MGM and appeared in such films as *Love Laughs at Andy Hardy* ('47), *Undercover Maisie* ('47), *Three Daring Daughters* ('48), *Easter Parade* ('48), *On an Island with You* ('48), *A Southern Yankee* ('48), *The Three Musketeers* ('48), *Neptune's Daughter* ('49), *Dial 1119* ('50), *Duchess of Idaho* ('50), *Battle Circus* ('53) *Brigadoon* ('54), *Men of the Fighting Lady* ('54), *Love Me or Leave Me* ('55), *Interrupted Melody* ('55) and *The Scarlet Coat* ('55).

It was in 1954 that Simmons got the lead role in Republic's *Man with the Steel Whip*, playing the part of Jerry Randall and the masked figure El Latigo. Much footage from previous Zorro serials was used to hold down costs. (The studio was phasing out its serial production; only two more would be made.) In the story, rancher Randall tries to head off trouble between Indians and whites by reviving a tribal legend in the form of the masked El Latigo. Mauritz Hugo plays the head villain who wants to stir up trouble with the Indians in order to acquire the gold on their land. By having Simmons wear a black costume like that worn in previous

Zorro serials and *Don Daredevil Rides Again*, it was easy to work in the library footage.

From September 29, 1955, to September 25, 1958, Simmons could be seen as *Sergeant Preston of the Yukon* over CBS-TV on Thursday nights at 7:30. There was a season of reruns during 1963–64 on NBC-TV on Saturdays. He starred for three years in half-hour episodes as Sgt. Frank Preston, who, with his horse Rex and dog Yukon King, brought lawbreakers in the Yukon to justice.

Simmons was active in both radio and television. He often appeared on *The Loretta Young Show* and *Death Valley Days*, as well as *My Little Margie*, *Stories of the Century*, *Leave It to Beaver*, *Black Saddle*, *Rawhide*, *The Munsters*, *Dragnet*, *Perry Mason*, *The Brady Bunch* and the soap opera *The Clear Horizon*. In 1966 he introduced a syndicated, non-fiction series entitled *Adventure Calls*.

On the big screen, Simmons appeared in *Sergeants 3* ('62), *Lassie's Great Adventure* ('63) and *Robin and the 7 Hoods* ('64). A helicopter crash in the mid–60s came close to killing him. His back was broken and both his legs. He was unable to work for nearly three years. He left show business and moved to a mobile home community in Carlsbad, California, where he became the manager until the early 1970s. At that time he returned to Hollywood to make *The Resurrection of Zachary Wheeler* ('71) and the telefeature *Don't Push, I'll Charge When I'm Ready* ('77).

By his first wife, Nora Johnson, he had two sons. Upon the death of Nora, to whom he was married nearly 30 years, he remarried. The traumatic death of his second wife, Mary, in May 2001 is said to have brought on Alzheimer's.

Serials

1940

King of the Royal Mounted. Rep., [12 Chapters] D: William Witney, John English; LP: Allan Lane, Robert Strange, Robert Kellard, Lita Conway, Herbert Rawlinson, Harry Cording, Bryant Washburn, Stanley Andrews, Richard Simmons.

Richard Simmons in *Man with the Steel Whip* (Republic, 1954).

1941

King of the Texas Rangers. Rep., [12 Chapters] D: William Witney, John English; LP: Slingin' Sammy Baugh, Pauline Moore, Neil Hamilton, Duncan Renaldo, Frank Darien, Charles Trowbridge, Monte Blue, Herbert Rawlinson, Richard Simmons.

1954

Man with the Steel Whip. Rep., [12 Chapters] P/D: Franklyn Adreon; SP: Ronald Davidson; Mus: R. Dale Butts; LP: Richard Simmons, Barbara Bestar, Mauritz Hugo, Lane Bradford, Dale Van Sickel, Roy Barcroft, Edmund Cobb, I. Stanford Jolley.

MARGUERITE (PEGGY) SNOW

Although she generally claimed Savannah, Georgia, as her birthplace, Marguerite Snow was born in Salt Lake City. Her father, William G. Snow, was a minstrel comedian for 25 years, half of the team of Snow and West, and he traveled constantly. It simply happened that her mother was in Salt Lake City when Marguerite was born. Almost immediately thereafter they went to Savannah, where they lived several years, her father dying when Marguerite was a baby. After a time, she and her mother went to Denver, where Marguerite spent her childhood.

Marguerite began her theatrical career with a stock company in Denver, later joining James O'Neill in *The Count of Monte Cristo* (1907) and playing with Henry W. Savage in *The College Widow* (1908). In 1909, she made her Broadway debut in the role of Elsa in *The Devil* at the Gordon Theatre. After that came a season in stock work divided between Grand Rapids, Michigan, and Wheeling, West Virginia. In the fall of 1910 she was seen at the Bijou Theatre in New York with Thomas Jefferson in *The Other Fellow.*

Going into pictures was largely accidental. A girlfriend of hers was posing for the Thanhouser Studio and suggested that Marguerite accompany her one day, just to see how motion pictures were made. While watching the work, Mr. Thanhouser asked her if she would like to appear in a picture they were about to film. She indicated she would and was pressed into immediate service in *Baseball and Bloomers.*

She received no end of offers for excellent theatrical engagements, such as the lead in *The Bird of Paradise* and *The Butterfly on the Wheel*, but she resolutely turned them all down, having decided the flickers were for her.

One of the top stars of early films, she appeared in pictures for Thanhouser and Metro. She never made a talking picture. Among her features were *The Star of Bethlehem* ('12) with William Russell, *The Patriot and the Spy* ('15) with James Cruze, *The Silent Vow* ('15) with Francis X.Bushman, *Rosemary* ('15) with Paul Gilmore, *A Corner in Cotton* ('16) with Frank Dayton, *Broadway Jones* ('17) with George M. Cohan, *Lavender and Old Lace* ('21) with Seena Owen, *The Veiled Woman* ('22) with Edward Coxen, *Chalk Marks* ('24) with Ramsey Wallace and *Savages of the Sea* ('25) with Frank Merrill. One of her earliest hits was *Joseph in the Land of Egypt* ('14) with James Cruze as Joseph and Marguerite as Potiphar's wife.

Marguerite's serial *The Million Dollar Mystery* ('14) was released by Thanhouser on June 22, 1914. It was produced in cooperation with the *Chicago Tribune* at a cost of $125,000. It grossed nearly $1,500,000. The story employs the time-tested formula of a pretty, persecuted soubrette with enemies more powerful than friends—at least until the climax—and embellished with a thrill or more for each chapter.

Crooks attempt to steal $1 million belonging to Hargreave (Sidney Bracey) and are aided by Countess Olga (Marguerite), who feigns friendship with Hargreave's daughter, Florence (Florence LaBadie). Jim Norton (James Cruze), a newspaper reporter in love with Florence, is instrumental in keeping the thieves, headed by Braine (Frank Farrington), from obtaining the money or harming Florence.

Thanhouser rushed through a sequel, *Zudora* ('14). A cache of money sets off the rapidly moving events, as Zudora (Marguerite) and her newspaper reporter boyfriend (James Cruze) try to unravel the mystery and elude death at every turn. With the tenth chapter the title was changed to *The Twenty Million Dollar Mystery.* A recut, ten-episode version of *Zudora* appeared in 1919 under the title of *The Demon Shadow* and was states-righted by Arrow Films.

In 1918, Marguerite played opposite King Baggot in the Wharton/American serial, *The Eagle's Eye.* The story dealt with an organization calling itself the Criminology Club. The club convinces the U.S. Secret Service that there are hundreds of German spies loose in the United States and offers its services in unearthing them. Baggot portrays the president of the club and Marguerite is Dixie Mason, a beautiful Secret Service agent dedicated to Baggot and his mission. The serial flopped at the ticket window, as the war was over and the public wanted to forget about it.

Marguerite married James Cruze in

1913, had a daughter by him, and divorced him in 1925, the same year she married Neely Edwards, master of ceremonies of the local *Drunkard* company for 25 years. She underwent a kidney operation in 1957 and complications developed. She died February 17, 1958, at the Motion Picture Country Home and Hospital in Woodland Hills, California. She was 69.

Serials

1914

The Million Dollar Mystery. Than., [23 Chapters] D: Howell Hansell; S: Harold McGrath; SP: Lloyd Lonergan; LP: Florence LaBadie, Marguerite Snow, James Cruze, Frank Farrington, Creighton Hale, Irving Cummings.

Zudora (The Twenty Million Dollar Mystery). Than., [20 Chapters] D: Howell Hansell; SP: Lloyd Lonergan, F. W. Doughty; S: Daniel Carson Goodman, Harold McGrath; LP: Marguerite Snow, James Cruze, Harry Benham, Sidney Bracey, Frank Farrington, Jane Fairbanks, Mary Forbes, Helen Badgley.

1918

The Eagle's Eye. Wharton/American, [20 Chapters] D: George A. Lessey, Wellington Playter; S: William J. Flynn; SP: Courtney Ryley Cooper; LP: King Baggot, Marguerite Snow, Bertram Marburgh, William N. Bailey, Paul Everton, John P. Wade, Fred Jones, Florence Short.

JEAN SOTHERN

Jean Sothern played Louise, the blind orphan, and Theda Bara played Henrieta, another orphan, in Fox's *The Two Orphans* ('15), a hit in its day. The Gish sisters did the remake *Orphans of the Storm* ('21).

In *Dr. Rameau* ('15), Jean played a girl whom Frederick Perry believes to be his daughter. When he finds out that she isn't, he drives her into a storm where she becomes deathly sick. In *Should a Mother Tell?* ('15), Jean was a 16-year-old girl reared in another home because of her father's brutality. In *Whoso Findeth a Wife* ('16), Jean was sold into a marriage by parents for $1 million. In *The Cloud* ('17), a dying man leaves his fortune to Jean, who has been good to him. The man's nephew blackmails Jean with a package of love letters signed by her mother and which hint at sexual misconduct on her (the mother's) part. *Peg o' the Sea* ('18) finds Jean living with her grandfather. She is harassed by a hard-drinking crook. A young inventor saves her from the lecherous scoundrel and they find romance.

It is the 1916 serial *The Mysteries of Myra* that rates Jean a spot in this book. It is the wildest, weirdest serial ever made. The secret Black Order, a cult of powerful magicians who live in an underground city, is involved in thought transference, witchcraft, levitation, and general mysticism and skullduggery. Based largely upon occult phenomena the serial was very dependent on weird camera effects, lighting and superior technical work. Dissolves, double exposures and fades were abundant, as was a two-color treatment in many scenes, intensifying the mood of mysticism. Myra becomes a target of the group because of incriminating evidence which she has. During an experiment with sending out her astral body, an elemental spirit enters her body, leaving her astral self to drift through the netherworlds. The Order captures a woman vampire and puts her on Myra's trail, along with a huge hulking "thought monster." But Dr. Payson Alden (Howard Estabrook), an occult scientist, is able to protect her with a little magic of his own.

Prior to his death, Myra's father had willed his wealth to the group if, by chance, all three daughters should die before reaching 18. The two older girls had committed suicide before attaining 18 and Myra's mother feared for Myra's life, having some inkling of her husband's unnatural connection with the Order. A member of the Black Order was assigned to help Myra die. The remaining chapters found Alden busy keeping Myra alive, against her apparent will, and he ran wild making "thought images" gained by placing photographic plates to her forehead in an attempt to find out what was going on.

All ended well, with the Black Order vanquished and Myra in love with Alden.

Jean's career was cut short by her untimely death in 1924 at age 28.

Serial

1916

The Mysteries of Myra. Pathé, [15 Chapters] D: Theodore and Leo Wharton; LP: Jean Sothern, Howard Estabrook, Allen Murnane, M. W. Rale, Bessie Wharton.

LOUISE STANLEY

Louise Stanley was born Louise Todd Keys in Springfield, Illinois, on January 28, 1915, one of three daughters of insurance executive Alvin S. Keys and Helen Lewis Keys. Her paternal great-grandfather was the brother of Mary Todd Lincoln. As a child she attended private schools, finishing high school several years early. She left Bryn Mawr College at age 17 to visit friends in California, wishing for some relief from the pressure of being pushed too far too fast.

While dining and dancing at the Trocadero, she was approached by director Lewis Milestone, who invited her to Paramount. She began filming the next week in a small part in *Anything Goes* ('36). Her contract was for the standard seven years with six-month options, at a starting salary of $75 a week. She took it to avoid going back to college. Her mother came to Hollywood and established an apartment for her, complete with maid and housekeeper. Her family was wealthy, paid all her expenses and gave her a generous allowance.

A good athlete, Louise trained at one time as a diver for the Olympics. When making Westerns, she performed most of her

own stunts. She only had a double perform for her once, and the double was seriously injured in a cattle stampede scene. Louise finished the scene for her. (Louise had her first horse at the age of five and was an excellent horsewoman.)

Her movie career lasted only about five years. At the age of 22 she left for New York and within five weeks became one of the top three models in the city. She went into several summer stock companies, finally getting to do some good roles.

Louise's Westerns were made with Johnny Mack Brown, Bob Steele, Jack Randall, James Newill and Tex Ritter. Opposite Brown she was the leading lady in *The Oregon Trail* ('39), a Universal serial that maintained production quality despite a heavy use of library footage. *Gun Lords of Stirrup Basin* ('37), opposite Steele, was an excellent part for Louise and remained her favorite role. Her other Westerns were *Lawless Land* ('37, Brown), *Sing, Cowboy, Sing* ('37, Ritter), *Riders of the Rockies* ('37, Ritter), *Thunder in the Desert* ('38, Steele), *Land of Fighting Men* ('38, Randall), *Gunsmoke Trail* ('38, Randall), *Durango Valley Raiders* ('38, Steele),

Gun Packer ('38, Randall), *Yukon Flight* ('40, Newill), *The Cheyenne Kid* ('40, Randall), *Pinto Canyon* ('40, Steele), *Land of the Six Guns* ('40, Randall), *Sky Bandits* ('40, Newill) and *Wells Fargo Days* ('44, Dennis Moore). This latter film was a 20-minute, color Warner Brothers release.

Louise was married three times. Her first husband was Dennis O'Keefe, her second, Jack Randall, and her third, Charles Munn, a Navy pilot. She adopted a boy in 1953. In the 1950s, she bought a 200-year-old farm in Connecticut, set about remodeling the house and barn and raised horses. She owned as many as 20 at one time and raced on parimutuel tracks as one of only ten women licensed to do so in the entire country. She also started making asphalt and selling gravel, even driving a bulldozer and ten-wheel truck herself.

In 1959, Louise moved to Cocoa Beach, Florida, to be near her son. In later years she attended several film festivals, amazed that so many people still remembered her.

Louise died of cancer on December 28, 1982.

Serial

1939

The Oregon Trail. Univ., [15 Chapters] D: Ford Beebe, Saul A. Goodkind; SP: Edmund Kelso, George Plympton, Basil Dickey, W. W. Watson; P: Henry MacRae; LP: Johnny Mack Brown, Louise Stanley, Fuzzy Knight, Bill Cody, Jr., Forrest Taylor, James Blaine, Charles Stevens, Charles King, Edward LeSaint.

BOB STEELE

Bob Steele was born Robert Adrian Bradbury on January 23, 1907, in Portland, Oregon, along with a twin brother, William, to Nieta and Robert Bradbury, a film director. The elder Bradbury starred his sons in 16 one-reel *Adventures of Bill and Bob* shorts which Pathé released during 1921–22.

If we count the 16 shorts, Bob appeared in a minimum of 204 movies: 95 solo starring features, 27 co-starring features, 65 supporting roles and one serial. Bob is said to have worked at Universal as a teenager, but no writer has yet identified the films in which he might have appeared.

Steele's biographer Bob Nareau has uncovered information previously unknown and corrected erroneous information previously accepted as fact. Bob was a little man, standing about 5'5" according to his sister-in-law. He did not graduate from Glendale High School as once assumed; he quit at the end of his junior year to go into acting. Nor did he play football with John Wayne. He and Wayne were friends but Bob was too small to play. He did some amateur boxing, but no professional fighting. The sport in which he excelled was baseball. He was a pretty good pitcher.

During the summer of 1924, Bob worked as a lifeguard at Brookside Park in Pasadena and is credited with saving several lives. He was married three times. On June 10, 1931, he married Louise A. Chessman, a script girl and secretary at both Trem Carr Studios and Paramount. The marriage went sour and they were divorced on February 9, 1935. In August 1935, he married a former schoolmate, Alice Petty Hackley. It seems that this union was another stormy venture that ended around 1938. His third and last wife was Virginia Nash Tatem. This marriage was a lasting one.

When his brother graduated from high school, the two boys put together a comedy act and toured the vaudeville circuit billed as "The Murdock Brothers." But William was soon off to college, while Bob found work at Sunset Productions where his father was directing a series of historical Westerns. Bob was featured in *With Daniel Boone Thru the Wilderness* ('26) starring Roy Stewart, *With Davy Crockett at the Fall of the Alamo* ('26) starring Cullen Landis and *With Sitting Bull at the Spirit Lake Massacre* ('27) starring Bryant Washburn. Bob was billed Bob Bradbury, Jr., in these films. He was sometimes employed at FBO, where he gave a good account of himself in *The College Boob* ('26) starring Lefty Flynn and Jean Arthur.

Beginning with the 1927 season, 20-year-old Bob got his own Western series. His first film, *The Mojave Kid*, was released in September 1927. At this point he adopted the screen name Bob Steele, suggested by Oliver Drake, screenwriter. Thirteen films were made by Bob for FBO release.

In 1929–30, Bob headed up seven Westerns for Syndicate. Two or three had music scores and sound effects; otherwise, they were very similar to the FBO dusties and none stood out perceptibly over the others.

Bob next signed with Tiffany, where he made his first all-talkie Western, *Near the Rainbow's End* ('30), with Louise Lorraine as his leading lady. His voice registered satisfactorily and he seemed at ease on a range suddenly filled with sound. Critics were complimentary in their reviews. Seven more films were completed in this series, including one of his best, *The Sunrise Trail* ('31) with Blanche Mehaffey.

Kalton Lahue (*Winners of the West*, A.S. Barnes, 1970) has written:

> A small man, Steele did not quite measure up to his adversaries in stature, but more than compensated for this lack of height with his ability to project a strong action-adventure characterization; Bob Steele was probably the best scrapper the silent Western ever knew, regardless of size. Fighting with a ferocity larger than life, the boyish hero with the mop of curly hair quickly carved out a

following of fans who were only too happy to applaud his exploits.... In addition to his skill in the manly art of self-defense, he was no slouch at riding and the sight of Bob Steele literally throwing himself on a horse and heading out like a streak was always greeted by a breathless gasp from the audience.

Historian Chuck Anderson (*Classic Images*, January 1981) comments:

> Though small in stature, Battling Bob used his good looks, boxing skills and horsemanship in a starring career that spanned over 20 years from the silent days through the mid-forties. Though most oater stars left much to be desired when reciting dialog, Steele's vocalizing came across quite well and probably aided in extending his career.

Author Don Miller (*Hollywood Corral*, Popular Library, 1976) writes:

> He was immediately recognizable, his intense features topped by the unmistakable mop of curly dark hair. Perhaps his most striking asset, in more ways than one, was a paradoxical one. He was of small stature, yet he could participate in a filmic scrap with the best of them.
> ... What made his task all the more difficult was his lack of size. It was necessary for him to make his audience believe that he could knock about some huge bear of a baddie without getting squashed in the process. That he invariably did so was perhaps his highest achievement in westerns.

Producer Trem Carr took Steele with him to Sono Art-World Wide in 1932. One of the better entries from this Steele series is *Man From Hell's Edges* in which George F. (Gabby) Hayes supported. Author Stormy Weathers, writing in *Classic Images*, writes:

> The six World Wide vehicles were a decided improvement over the Tiffanys. One explanation is that Steele's father directed five of them, and also provided three of the stories and screenplays.... The third entry, *Riders of the Desert* ('32), directed by Bradbury, is notable for the presence of Hayes and Al St. John in supporting roles.
> The one-year association with World

Lucile Browne and Bob Steele in *Mystery Squadron* (Mascot, 1933).

Wide ... might have lasted longer were it not for the organization's declaration of bankruptcy, which brought things to an abrupt halt. The problems of Tiffany and World Wide, despite their more than adequate series with Steele and Maynard, was indicative of what was occurring on poverty row. There were just too many companies, operating on shoestring budgets, churning out too many Westerns.

Still on the move, Bob turned out eight Westerns for Monogram in 1932–33. George Hayes was featured in seven of them. The Steeles had their own distinctive style and were quite pleasant as simple little sagebrushers. There was no pretense of grandeur. Some of the plots were a little zany and incongruous but the films were generally well-photographed, full of thrills and replete with a mild range romance. Sometimes the loca-

tions used were different and interesting and the stories were a notch above the ordinary formula oaters. Robert N. Bradbury directed six of the eight films, and it was apparent that the father and son worked well together. No amount of elaboration could communicate effectively the charisma of the Monogram Steele Westerns. One really had to "live them" to appreciate them to the fullest. Later viewing on TV does not provide the same satisfying feeling that original viewing in the '30s did. They had a charm about them, when viewed on the big screen, that was palpable.

The presence of Doris Hill, Nancy Drexel, Helen Foster, Arletta Duncan and Gertrude Messenger made these Monograms even more enjoyable. Also in 1933, Bob starred in the Mascot serial, *Mystery Squadron*. Led by an unidentified leader calling himself "The Black Act," a mystery squadron repeatedly attacks a huge dam construction project that threatens a secret gold mine. Two stunt pilots, Bob Steele and Guinn (Big Boy) Williams, are hired by Lafe McKee, owner of the construction firm, to protect the dam site. Jack Mulhall, foreman of the project and a friend of the two pilots, is revealed as the Black Ace and plunges to his death in the final chapter after an air fight with the erstwhile heroes.

Steele signed with A. W. Hackel in 1934 and his contract carried through to 1938, during which time he starred in 32 shoot-'em-ups and ranked number 7 in the Motion Picture Herald's Poll of Top Ten Western stars in both 1937 and 1938. Sixteen of the films were released by Supreme and the other 16 by Republic. A number of familiar character actors appeared in these horse operas: Charles King (1), Earl Dwire (11), Steve Clark (12), Jack Rockwell (8), Karl Hackett (9), Ernie Adams (8) and Lew Meehan (7). Leading ladies included Louise Stanley (3), Lois January (3), Marion Weldon (3), Lucile Browne (1), Roberta Gale (2), Margaret Marquis (2), Renee Borden (2), Harley Wood (2), Loraine Hays (Laraine Day) (1), Gloria Shea (1), Gertrude Messinger (1), Jean Carmen (1), Eleanor Stewart (1), Claire Rochelle (1), Beth Marion (1), Mary Kornman (1) and Joan Barclay (1).

In 1935, Steele took a breather from his Supreme series and joined Harry Carey, Hoot Gibson, Guinn Williams and Tom Tyler in "the Barnum & Bailey of Westerns," RKO's *Powdersmoke Range*. Other stars featured in the film were Wally Wales, Buzz Barton, Art Mix, Buddy Roosevelt, William Desmond, Buffalo Bill, Jr., Franklyn Farnum and William Farnum. Boots Mallory did the femme honors.

Don Miller, in *Hollywood Corral*, wrote of the Metropolitan Steeles:

> The Hackel association was terminated at the end of 1937–38. Steele didn't miss a beat and immediately signed for a new series. It was a fall from grace comparatively. Metropolitan Pictures was the company of Harry S. Webb and Bernard B. Ray, who took turns

producing and directing and by this time were excelling in neither function. Their former company had been known as Reliable Pictures, which belied its name, and they had been responsible for Tom Tyler's drop in prestige…. When even the most unassuming Western series was showing signs of improving, the Metropolitan Steeles were a regression to the past, and conceivably could have harmed the future of the most indestructible cowpoke.

This writer saw the Metropolitans through different eyes. It is true they were cheap, but I still found them enjoyable, possibly because they were a regression to the past, but mainly because I was a loyal Steele fan and watching Steele in anything was a thrilling experience.

Steele proved himself an actor in Hal Roach's production of *Of Mice and Men* ('40), his role of Curley receiving wide acclaim from the non-cowboy fraternity. He would later add to his acting credentials with meaty roles in such big-budget melodramas as *The Big Sleep* ('46), *Killer McCoy* ('47) and *The Enforcer* ('51).

Republic's *The Carson City Kid* ('40) featured Steele in the chief villain's role in support of Roy Rogers. Pauline Moore, Hal Taliaferro (Wally Wales) and Noah Beery, Jr., were also featured in this, one of Rogers' better Westerns before they turned into musicals.

Letting no grass grow under his horse, Steele signed with PRC to portray Billy the Kid in a series of action oaters. Al St. John became his sidekick Fuzzy Q. Jones. Although quickly and cheaply made, the six films were fun to watch. You could also count on seeing many of the familiar character people in support. Take for instance Steele's *Billy the Kid's Range War* ('41). It had St. John, Joan Barclay, Rex Lease, Buddy Roosevelt, Charles King, George Chesebro, Carleton Young, Karl Hackett, Ted Adams, Julian Rivero and Steve Clark. What more would one want for a quarter?

Republic hired Steele in the latter part of 1940 to co-star as Tucson Smith with Robert Livingston and Rufe Davis in the popular *Three Mesquiteers* series. Tom Tyler would later replace Livingston and Rufe Davis would be replaced by Jimmie Dodd. Bob co-starred in 20 of the 51 Three Mesquiteers films before the series faded away in 1943. He also played the lead in Republic's non–Western *The Great Train Robbery* ('41) featuring Milburn Stone and Claire Carleton.

Losing no time, Bob jumped into the Monogram *Trail Blazers* series in 1943 to liven it up. Seeing Ken Maynard, Hoot Gibson and Steele together was frosting on the cake. When Maynard dropped out, Chief Thundercloud took his place in two films, and Hoot and Bob co-starred in three other films.

Bob starred in 1945's *Wildfire* and *Northwest Trail* for Action/Lippert films. Both were filmed in Cinecolor. Bob's last series of B-Westerns were made for PRC in 1945–46. Four films were made, the last being *Thunder Town* ('46). Syd Saylor was the comic pal. They were bottom-of-the-barrel sagebrushers.

For the next 25 years, Steele assumed character roles and enhanced the enjoyment of many pictures. Occasionally he appeared in television shows and he had a regular role as Trooper Duffy on *F Troop* in the mid–60s.

Steele died from heart failure on December 21, 1988, after a long illness in Burbank, California.

Serial

1933

Mystery Squadron. Mascot, [12 Chapters] D: Colbert Clark, David Howard; SP: Barney Sarecky, Colbert Clark, David Howard, Wyndham Gittens; S: Al Martin, Sherman Lowe; P: Nat Levine; LP: Bob Steele, Guinn (Big Boy) Williams, Lucile Browne, Jack Mulhall, J. Carrol Naish, Robert Kortman, Jack Mower, Robert Frazer, Wally Wales, Jack Perrin.

TOM STEELE

Tom Steele played in at least 57 serials—48 at Republic, seven at Universal and two at Columbia. There may have been others.

Tom was born Tom Skeoch on June 12, 1909, in Scotland. His father, an engineer, moved his family to New York when Tom was two. Later they moved to San Francisco. It was in 1928 that Tom went down to Los Angeles with the intention of getting film work. He had played polo while attending Stanford University and received encouragement to go to Hollywood because of his background in horse work.

When RKO decided to produce a Western series, Steele was led to believe he would get the starring role, but it went instead to George Duryea (Tom Keene). Steele was bitterly disappointed. He returned to San Francisco and worked for almost a year as a construction worker on the Oakland Bay Bridge project. Finally he quit and returned to Hollywood and almost immediately he landed a stunting job in *Captain Blood* ('35). Thereafter he seldom lacked for a job.

Tom's career reached its peak in 1943 when he played the title role in *The Masked Marvel*, a story written specifically to display his stunting ability—yet he received no screen credit. He played a small character role in addition to his stuntwork behind the mask.

Tom's wide-legged, flat-footed fighting style was easily recognized by fans in more than 50 serials and in Western features where he doubled Bill Elliott and Allan Lane in all

Anthony Warde and Tom Steele (right) in *The Masked Marvel* (Republic, 1943).

their Red Ryder features and also worked in Lane's "Rocky" Lane films—nearly 80 Republic Westerns in all.

Over the next 20 years Tom worked for all of the serial-producing companies, but the bulk of his work was done at Republic where he appeared in the majority of their 66 serials, doubling such well-known stars as Lane, Rod Cameron and Clayton Moore. Doubling for Cameron in *G-Men vs. the Black Dragon* and *Secret Service in Darkest Africa* (both 1943), Tom provided some of the screen's most exciting and memorable fight sequences.

During his long tenure at Republic, he doubled most of the heavies as well as the stars. In recognition of his long and distinguished career, Steele was elected to the Stuntman's Hall of Fame on February 25, 1981. Steele was perhaps the most versatile and hardest worker of all the great Hollywood stuntmen.

Around 1946, Tom became a stunt ramrod, or stunt coordinator as they are called today, at Republic. Coupled with his own stunt performances, he now had to synchronize and stage the maneuvers of others. He hired certain personnel and mapped out from beginning to end how a gag would be done and what precisely was needed to bring it to a safe conclusion.

In more recent years, Steele worked for a variety of filmmakers in films such as *Bullitt* ('68), *Diamonds Are Forever* ('71), *Conquest of the Planet of the Apes* ('72), *The New Centurians* ('72), *Ben* ('72), *Blazing Saddles* ('74), *The Blues Brothers* ('80) and *Last of the Great Survivors* (an '84 TV movie). His television series credits include *The Dukes of Hazzard*, *The Fall Guy*, and *Tales of the Gold Monkey*.

Tom Steele passed away on November 4, 1990.

Serials

1934

The Red Rider. Univ., [15 Chapters] D: Louis Friedlander [Lew Landers]; LP: Buck Jones, Marion Shilling, Grant Withers, Richard Cramer, Margaret LaMarr, Edmund Cobb.

1936

Undersea Kingdom. Rep., [12 Chapters] D: B. Reeves Eason, Joseph Kane; LP: Ray Corrigan, Lois Wilde, Monte Blue, William Farnum, Boothe Howard, Lee Van Atta, Raymond Hatton, Lon Chaney, Jr., Jack Mulhall.

Flash Gordon. Univ., [13 Chapters] D: Frederick Stephani; LP: Larry (Buster) Crabbe, Jean Rogers, Frank Shannon, Charles Middleton, Priscilla Lawson, John Lipson, James Pierce, William Desmond, George Cleveland, Earl Askam, Glenn Strange.

1937

Radio Patrol. Univ., [12 Chapters] D: Ford Beebe, Cliff Smith; LP: Grant Withers, Kay Hughes, Mickey Rentschier, Adrian Morris.

Tim Tyler's Luck. Univ., [12 Chapters] D: Ford Beebe, Wyndham Gittens; LP: Frankie Thomas, Frances Robinson, Norman Willis, Jack Mulhall.

1938

Red Barry. Univ., [13 Chapters] D: Ford Beebe, Alan James; LP: Larry (Buster) Crabbe, Frances Robinson, Wade Boteler, Edna Sedgwick, Philip Ahn, Frank Lackteen, Wheeler Oakman.

Flaming Frontiers. Univ., [15 Chapters] D: Ray Taylor, Alan James; LP: Johnny Mack Brown, Eleanor Hansen, Ralph Bowman [John Archer], Charles Middleton.

The Fighting Devil Dogs. Rep., [12 Chapters] D: William Witney, John English; LP: Lee Powell, Herman Brix, Eleanor Stewart, Montagu Love, Hugh Sothern, Sam Flint, Forrest Taylor, John Picorri, Carleton Young.

Dick Tracy Returns. Rep., [15 Chapters] D: William Witney, John English; LP: Ralph Byrd, Lynne Roberts, Charles Middleton, Jerry Tucker, David Sharpe, Lee Ford, Reed Howes, Tom Steele, John Merton.

1939

Buck Rogers. Univ., [12 Chapters] D: Ford Beebe, Saul A. Goodkind; LP: Larry (Buster) Crabbe, Constance Moore, Jackie Moran, Jack Mulhall, Anthony Warde, Henry Brandon, C. Montague Shaw, Wheeler Oakman, Reed Howes.

Dick Tracy's G-Men. Rep., [15 Chapters] D: William Witney, John English; LP: Ralph Byrd, Irving Pichel, Phylis Isley [Jennifer Jones], Ted Pearson, Walter Miller, Jack Ingram, Edward Cassidy, Charles Hutchison, Budd Buster.

Flying G-Men. Col., [15 Chapters] D: Ray Taylor, James W. Horne; LP: Robert Paige, Richard Fiske, James Craig, Lorna Gray [Adrian Booth], Don Beddoe, Dick Curtis, Ann Doran.

1940

Mysterious Doctor Satan. Rep., [15 Chapters] D: William Witney, John English; LP: Eduardo Ciannelli, Robert Wilcox, Ella Neal, William Newell, C. Montague Shaw, Jack Mulhall, Charles Trowbridge, Kenneth Harlan.

1941

Jungle Girl. Rep., [15 Chapters] D: William Witney, John English; LP: Frances Gifford, Tom Neal, Eddie Acuff, Frank Lackteen, Gerald Mohr, Tommy Cook, Robert Barron, Al Kikume, Yakima Canutt, Bud Geary, Ken Terrell.

1942

Overland Mail. Univ., [15 Chapters] D: Ford Beebe, John Rawlins; LP: Lon Chaney, Jr., Don Terry, Noah Beery, Jr., Helen Parrish, Noah Beery, Sr., Charles Stevens, Bob Baker, Robert Barron, Jack Rockwell, Carleton Young.

Spy Smasher. Rep., [12 Chapters] D: William Witney; LP: Kane Richmond, Marguerite Chapman, Sam Flint, Hans Schumm, Tristram Coffin, Robert O. Davis, Hans Von Morhart, Tom London, Yakima Canutt.

Perils of Nyoka. Rep., [15 Chapters] D: William Witney; LP: Kay Aldridge, Clayton Moore, William Benedict, Lorna Gray [Adrian Booth], Charles Middleton, Tristram Coffin, George J. Lewis, Robert Strange, John Davidson, Kenne Duncan.

King of the Mounties. Rep., [12 Chapters] D:

William Witney; LP: Allan Lane, Peggy Drake, Gilbert Emery, Russell Hicks, George Irving, Abner Biberman, Bradley Page, William Vaughn, Nestor Paiva, William Bakewell.

1943

Daredevils of the West. Rep., [12 Chapters] D: John English; LP: Allan Lane, Kay Aldridge, Eddie Acuff, William Haade, Robert Frazer, Ted Adams, George J. Lewis, Jack Rockwell, Kenne Duncan.

Secret Service in Darkest Africa. Rep., [15 Chapters] D: Spencer Bennet; LP: Rod Cameron, Joan Marsh, Duncan Renaldo, Lionel Royce, Kurt Kreuger, Frederic Brunn, Reed Howes, George J. Lewis.

The Masked Marvel. Rep., [12 Chapters] D: Spencer G. Bennet; LP: Tom Steele, William Forrest, Louise Currie, Johnny Arthur, Rod Bacon, David Bacon.

G-Men vs. the Black Dragon. Rep., [15 Chapters] D: William Witney; LP: Rod Cameron, Constance Worth, Roland Got, Nino Pipitone, George J. Lewis, Noel Cravat, Donald Kirke, Hooper Atchley, John Daheim.

1944

The Tiger Woman. Rep., [12 Chapters] D: Spencer Bennet, Wallace Grissell; LP: Linda Stirling, Allan Lane, Duncan Renaldo, George J. Lewis, LeRoy Mason, Crane Whitley, Robert Frazer, Rico de Montez, Tom Steele, Eddie Parker.

Zorro's Black Whip. Rep., [12 Chapters] D: Spencer Bennet, Wallace Grissell; LP: Linda Stirling, George J. Lewis, Lucien Littlefield, Francis McDonald, Hal Taliaferro, John Merton, Tom London, Tom Chatterton, Tom Steele.

Haunted Harbor. Rep., [15 Chapters] D: Spencer Bennet, Wallace Grissell; LP: Kane Richmond, Kay Aldridge, Roy Barcroft, Clancy Cooper, Marshall Reed, Forrest Taylor, Hal Taliaferro, George J. Lewis.

Captain America. Rep., [15 Chapters] D: John English, Elmer Clifton; LP: Dick Purcell, Lorna Gray [Adrian Booth], Lionel Atwill, Charles Trowbridge, Russell Hicks, George J. Lewis, John Davidson, LeRoy Mason.

1945

The Purple Monster Strikes. Rep., [15 Chapters] D: Spencer Bennet, Fred C. Brannon; LP: Linda Stirling, Dennis Moore, Roy Barcroft, James Craven, Mary Moore, Anthony Warde, John Davidson, Tom Steele, Joe Whitehead.

Manhunt of Mystery Island. Rep., [15 Chapters] D: Spencer Bennet, Yakima Canutt, Wallace A. Grissell; LP: Linda Stirling, Roy Barcroft, Richard Bailey, Kenne Duncan, Forrest Taylor, Lane Chandler, Jack Ingram, Forbes Murray, Russ Vincent.

Federal Operator 99. Rep., [12 Chapters] D: Spencer Bennet, Yakima Canutt, Wallace A. Grissell; LP: Marten Lamont, Helen Talbot, George J. Lewis, Lorna Gray [Adrian Booth], Hal Taliaferro, Maurice Case, Tom London, Jack Ingram.

1946

King of the Forest Rangers. Rep., [12 Chapters] D: Spencer Bennet, Fred C. Brannon; LP: Larry Thompson, Helen Talbot, Stuart Hamblen, Anthony Warde, LeRoy Mason, Tom London, Scott Elliott, Marin Sais, Tom Steele.

Daughter of Don Q. Rep., [12 Chapters] D: Spencer Bennet, Fred C. Brannon; LP: Adrian Booth, Kirk Alyn, LeRoy Mason, Roy Barcroft, Claire Meade, I. Stanford Jolley, Dale Van Sickel, Kernan Cripps, Buddy Roosevelt.

The Crimson Ghost. Rep., [12 Chapters] D: William Witney, Fred C. Brannon; LP: Charles Quigley, Linda Stirling, Clayton Moore, I. Stanford Jolley, Kenne Duncan, Forrest Taylor, Virginia Carroll, Rex Lease, Emmett Vogan.

1947

Jesse James Rides Again. Rep., [13 Chapters] D: Fred C. Brannon, Thomas Carr; LP: Clayton Moore, Linda Stirling, Roy Barcroft, John Compton, Tristram Coffin, Holly Bane, Tom Steele, Tom London, Gene Stutenroth, Dale Van Sickel, Ted Mapes.

The Black Widow. Rep., [13 Chapters] D: Spencer Bennet, Fred C. Brannon; LP: Carol Forman, Bruce Edwards, Virginia Lindley, Anthony Warde, Ramsay Ames, Virginia Carroll, I. Stanford Jolley, Maxine Doyle, George Chesebro, Ernie Adams.

Son of Zorro. Rep., [13 Chapters] D: Spencer

Bennet, Fred C. Brannon; LP: George Turner, Peggy Stewart, Roy Barcroft, Edward Cassidy, Ernie Adams, Charles King, Stanley Price, Edmund Cobb, Newton House, Jack Kirk.

G-Men Never Forget. Rep., [12 Chapters] D: Fred C. Brannon, Yakima Canutt; LP: Clayton Moore, Ramsay Ames, Roy Barcroft, Drew Allen, Edmund Cobb, Tom Steele, Dale Van Sickel, Ken Terrell.

1948

Adventures of Frank and Jesse James. Rep., [13 Chapters] D: Fred C. Brannon, Yakima Canutt; LP: Clayton Moore, Steve Darrell, Noel Neill, George J. Lewis, Stanley Andrews, John Crawford, House Peters, Jr., Tom Steele, Dale Van Sickel.

Dangers of the Canadian Mounted. Rep., [12 Chapters] D: Fred C. Brannon, Yakima Canutt; LP: Jim Bannon, Virginia Belmont, Anthony Warde, Dorothy Granger, Ken Terrell, Tom Steele, Marshall Reed, Holly Bane.

1949

Federal Agents vs. Underworld, Inc. Rep., [12 Chapters] D: Fred C. Brannon; LP: Kirk Alyn, Rosemary LaPlanche, Roy Barcroft, Carol Forman, James Dale, Bruce Edwards, Tristram Coffin, Dale Van Sickel, Marshall Reed.

Ghost of Zorro. Rep., [12 Chapters] D: Fred C. Brannon; LP: Clayton Moore, Pamela Blake, Roy Barcroft, George J. Lewis, Gene Stutenroth, Steve Clark, Dale Van Sickel, Charles King, Tom Steele, Steve Darrell, George Chesebro.

King of the Rocket Men. Rep., [12 Chapters] D: Fred C. Brannon; LP: Tristram Coffin, Mae Clarke, Don Haggerty, House Peters, Jr., James Craven, I. Stanford Jolley.

Bruce Gentry. Col., [15 Chapters] D: Spencer G. Bennet, Thomas Carr; LP: Tom Neal, Judy Clark, Ralph Hodges, Forrest Taylor, Hugh Prosser, Tristram Coffin, Jack Ingram.

1950

Radar Patrol vs. Spy King. Rep., [12 Chapters] D: Fred C. Brannon; LP: Kirk Alyn, Jean Dean, Anthony Warde, George J. Lewis, Eve Whitney, John Merton, Dale Van Sickel, Tristram Coffin, Harold Goodwin.

The James Brothers of Missouri. Rep., [12 Chapters] D: Fred C. Brannon; LP: Keith Richards, Robert Bice, Noel Neill, Roy Barcroft, Patricia Knox, Edmund Cobb, Lane Bradford, Gene Stutenroth, John Hamilton.

The Invisible Monster. Rep., [12 Chapters] D: Fred C. Brannon; LP: Richard Webb, Aline Towne, Lane Bradford, Stanley Price, John Crawford, Tom Steele, Dave Sharpe, George Meeker.

Desperadoes of the West. Rep., [12 Chapters] D: Fred C. Brannon; LP: Richard Powers [Tom Keene], Judy Clark, Roy Barcroft, I. Stanford Jolley, Lee Phelps, Lee Roberts, Edmund Cobb, Bud Osborne, Dennis Moore, Tom Steele.

1951

Don Daredevil Rides Again. Rep., [12 Chapters] D: Fred C. Brannon; LP: Ken Curtis, Aline Towne, Roy Barcroft, Lane Bradford, Robert Einer, John Cason, Tom Steele, I. Stanford Jolley, Hank Patterson.

Flying Disc Man from Mars. Rep., [12 Chapters] D: Fred C. Brannon; LP: Walter Reed, Lois Collier, Gregory Gay, James Craven, Harry Lauter, Richard Irving, Tom Steele, Clayton Moore, Sandy Sanders.

Government Agents vs. Phantom Legion. Rep., [12 Chapters] D: Fred C. Brannon; LP: Walter Reed, Mary Ellen Kay, Dick Curtis, John Pickard, Fred Coby, Pierce Lyden, Edmund Cobb, Eddie Dew, Tom Steele, Dale Van Sickel.

1952

Zombies of the Stratosphere. Rep., [12 Chapters] D: Fred C. Brannon; LP: Judd Holdren, Aline Towne, Wilson Wood, Stanley Waxman, John Crawford, Craig Kelly, Tom Steele, Lane Bradford.

Radar Men from the Moon. Rep., [12 Chapters] D: Fred C. Brannon; LP: George Wallace, Aline Towne, Roy Barcroft, William Bakewell, Clayton Moore, Peter Brocco, Dale Van Sickel.

1953

Canadian Mounties vs. Atomic Invaders. Rep., [12 Chapters] D: Franklyn Adreon; LP: Bill Henry, Susan Morrow, Arthur Space, Dale Van Sickel, Pierce Watkin, Edmund Cobb, Stanley Andrews, Harry Lauter.

Jungle Drums of Africa. Rep., [12 Chapters] D: Fred C. Brannon; LP: Phyllis Coates, Clayton Moore, Johnny Spencer, Roy Glenn, John Cason, Henry Rowland, Tom Steele, Bill Walker, Steve Mitchell, Bill Washington, Robert David, Roy Engel.

1954

Trader Tom of the China Seas. Rep., [12 Chapters] D: Franklyn adreon; LP: Harry Lauter, Aline Towne, Lyle Talbot, Robert Shayne, Fred Graham, Ramsay Hill, Tom Steele, Victor Sen Yung, Robert Bice.

Man with the Steel Whip. Rep., [12 Chapters] D: Franklyn Adreon; LP: Richard Simmons, Barbara Bestar, Dale Van Sickel Mauritz Hugo, Lane Bradford, Edmund Cobb, Roy Barcroft, I. Stanford Jolley, Charles Stevens.

1955

Panther Girl of the Kongo. Rep., [12 Chapters] D: Franklyn Adreon; LP: Phyllis Coates, Myron Healey, Arthur Space, John Daheim, Mike Ragan, Morris Buchanan, Archie Savage, Gene Stutenroth, Ramsay Hill, Tom Steele, Charles Sullivan, Steve Calvert.

King of the Carnival. Rep., [12 Chapters] D: Franklyn Adreon; LP: Harry Lauter, Fran Bennett, Keith Richards, Robert Shayne, Rick Vallin, Gregory Gay, Robert Clarke, Tom Steele.

CHARLES STEVENS

Charles Stevens was a diminutive Apache Indian who was the grandson of Geronimo. Charles was on-screen from *The Birth of the Nation* ('15) to *The Outsider* ('61). In Westerns he nearly always played sneaky, treacherous and abominable redskins who spoke with forked tongues. "Snake Eye" in *Winners of the West* ('40) was a typical Stevens role, but he played in many non–Westerns. Douglas Fairbanks liked him and used him in several of his films.

Stevens played in numerous films over a 45-year career. Some of those features are:

1917: *The Man from Painted Post*; *Wild and Wooly*

1918: *Six-Shooter Andy*

1920: *The Mark of Zorro*; *The Mollycoddle*

1921: *The Three Musketeers*

1924: *The Thief of Bagdad*

1925: *Don Q, Son of Zorro*; *The Vanishing American*

1926: *The Black Pirate*; *Across the Pacific*; *Mantrap*

1927: *The King of Kings*; *Woman's Law*

1928: *The Gaucho*; *Diamond Handcuffs*

1929: *The Iron Mask*; *The Mysterious Dr. Fu Manchu*; *The Virginian*

1930: *The Big Trail*; *Tom Sawyer*

1931: *The Cisco Kid*; *The Conquering Horde*

1932: *Mystery Ranch*; *South of the Rio Grande*; *The Stoker*

1933: *The California Trail*; *Frum Taps*; *Fury of the Jungle*; *Police Call*

1934: *Call of the Coyote*; *Viva Villa*; *Grand Canary*; *The Trumpet Blows*

1935: *The Call of the Wild*; *The Lives of a Bengal Lancer*; *West of the Pecos*

1936: *Aces and Eights*; *The Bold Caballero*; *Robin Hood of El Dorado*; *Three Godfathers*; *Rose of the Rancho*

1937: *The Last Train from Madrid*; *Ebb Tide*; *Fair Warning*

1938: *The Crime of Doctor Hallet*; *The Forbidden Valley*; *Tropic Holiday*; *The Renegade Ranger*; *The Girl and the Gambler*

1939: *The Arizona Wildcat*; *Desperate Trails*; *Frontier Marshal*; *Union Pacific*; *The Real Glory*

1940: *Charlie Chan in Panama*; *Geronimo*; *Kit Carson*; *The Mark of Zorro*; *Wagons Westward*; *South of Karanga*

1941: *The Bad Man; Blood and Sand; Roaring Frontiers*

1942: *Tombstone, the Town Too Tough to Die; Pierre of the Plains; Beyond the Blue Horizon; Halfway to Shanghai*

1944: *Marked Trails; The Mummy's Curse*

1945: *Bad Men of the Border; San Antonio; South of the Rio Grande*

1946: *Border Bandits; My Darling Clementine; Tangier; Masquerade in Mexico*

1947: *Buffalo Bill Rides Again; Calcutta; Sinbad the Sailor; The Exile*

1948: *Belle Starr's Daughter; The Feathered Serpent; Fury at Furnace Creek; Saigon*

1949: *The Cowboy and the Indians; The Walking Hills; Roll Thunder Roll!*

1950: *Ambush; California Passage; Indian Territory; The Savage Horde; Fortunes of Captain Blood; The Showdown; A Ticket to Tomahawk*

1951: *Oh Susanna!; Warpath*

1952: *Smoky Canyon*

1953: *Savage Mutiny; Ride, Vaquero!*

1954: *Jubilee Trail; Killer Leopard*

1955: *The Vanishing American*

1959: *Last Train from Gun Hill*

1960: *Oklahoma Territory*

Charles Stevens died in 1964 at the age of 71.

Serials

1937

Wild West Days. Univ., [13 Chapters] D: Ford Beebe, Cliff Smith; LP: Johnny Mack Brown, Lynn Gilbert, Robert Kortman, George Shelly, Russell Simpson, Frank Yaconelli, Walter Miller, Charles Stevens, Al Bridge, Francis McDonald.

1938

Red Barry. Univ., [13 Chapters] D: Ford Beebe, Alan James; LP: Larry (Buster) Crabbe, Frances Robinson, Wade Boteler, Edna Sedgwick, Philip Ahn, Frank Lackteen, William Gould, Wheeler Oakman, Charles Stevens, Lane Chandler, Stanley Price.

Flaming Frontiers. Univ., [15 Chapters] D: Ray Taylor, Alan James; LP: Johnny Mack Brown, Eleanor Hansen, Ralph Bowman [John Archer], Charles Middleton, Charles Stevens, Chief Thundercloud, William Royle, James Blaine, Charles King.

1939

The Oregon Trail. Univ., [15 Chapters] D: Ford Beebe, Saul A. Goodkind; LP: Johnny Mack Brown, Louise Stanley, Fuzzy Knight, Bill Cody, Jr., Forrest Taylor, Charles Stevens, Charles King, Edward LeSaint, Roy Barcroft, Lafe McKee.

1940

Winners of the West. Univ., [13 Chapters] D: Ford Beebe, Ray Taylor; LP: Dick Foran, Anne Nagel, James Craig, Tom Fadden, Charles Stevens, Harry Woods, Al Bridge, Edmund Cobb, Roy Barcroft, Edward Cassidy, William Desmond.

1942

Overland Mail. Univ., [15 Chapters] D: Ford Beebe, John Rawlins; LP: Lon Chaney, Jr., Don Terry, Helen Parrish, Noah Beery, Jr., Noah Beery, Sr., Bob Baker, Charles Stevens, Tom Chatterton, Jack Rockwell, Carleton Young.

1954

Man with the Steel Whip. Rep., [12 Chapters] D: Franklyn Adreon; LP: Richard Simmons, Barbara Bestar, Dale Van Sickel, Mauritz Hugo, Lane Bradford, Roy Barcroft, I. Stanford Jolley, Edmund Cobb, Tom Steele, Charles Stevens.

ONSLOW STEVENS

Onslow Ford Stevenson, son of the English Actor Houseley Stevenson, was born in Los Angeles on March 3, 1902. He would later shorten his name to Onslow Stevens.

Being the son of an actor, Onslow also took up acting, and at an early age. He made his debut at the Pasadena Playhouse in 1926 and often acted there; he also directed a number of stage productions.

Universal signed Onslow in 1932 and cast him in the serial *Heroes of the West* starring Noah Beery, Jr., and Diana Duval (Julie Bishop). Onslow played engineer Tom Crosby, who helps John Blaine (William Desmond) fulfill his contract to complete a portion of the transcontinental railroad in Wyoming. Also he was cast in four features, one of which was *The Golden West* starring George O'Brien, and he was impressive in *Once in a Lifetime* ('32) starring Jack Oakie. In 1933, he was in seven features. *Peg o' My Heart* opposite Marion Davies and *Counsellor-at-Law* starring John Barrymore were his best, but also good was *Nagana* starring Melvwyn Douglas.

Onslow made ten films in 1934, including the cliffhanger *The Vanishing Shadow*. This time Onslow was the star. As Stanley Stanfield he invents a vest-like apparatus which permits the wearer to vanish, leaving only a shadow. With the aid of Carl Van Dorn (James Durkin), a famed electrical wizard, he determines to bring about the fall of power-crazed, money-mad Wade Barnett (Walter Miller) and his cohort Dorgan (Richard Cramer), who is responsible for the death of Stanfield's father. Gloria Grant (Ada Ince), actually Barnett's daughter, who has rejected her father's methods and adopted an alias, joins forces with Stanfield and Van Doran.

His features in 1934 included *Bombay Mail*, *The Crosby Case*, *Yellow Dust*, *Affairs of a Gentleman* and *I Can't Escape*.

Stevens had a 30-year film career playing mostly supporting roles, and sometimes nasty ones. His talent was never utilized effectively. He was happier when he was treading the boards on Broadway.

A sampling of his better-remembered films are *Under Two Flags* ('36), *Murder with Pictures* ('36), *You Can't Buy Luck* ('37), *Those High Grey Walls* ('39), *The Monster and the Girl* ('41), *Sunset Serenade* ('42), *Idaho* ('43), *House of Dracula* ('45), *O.S.S.* ('46), *The Creeper* ('48), *State Penitentiary* ('50), *Lorna Doone* ('51), *The San Francisco Story* ('52), *The Charge at Feather River* ('53), *Fangs of the Wild* ('54), *Them!* ('54), *Tribute to a Bad Man* ('56), *Kelly and Me* ('57), *Tarawa Beachhead* ('58), *All the Fine Young Cannibals* ('60) and *The Couch* ('62).

Stevens was married and divorced several times. In his later years his health declined, and in 1976 he was admitted as a patient at a Van Nuys, California, convalescent home. He developed pneumonia, which probably would have brought about his death, but on January 5, 1977, he was found severely beaten in his room. An ambulance was summoned but he was dead at the scene. A coroner's jury found that the actor's death came "at the hands of another, other than by accident." The murder was never solved.

Serials

1932

Heroes of the West. Univ., [12 Chapters] D: Ray Taylor; S: Peter B. Kyne; SP: George H. Plympton, Basil Dickey, Joe Roach, Ella O'Neill; LP: Noah Beery, Jr., Diane Duval [Julie Bishop], Onslow Stevens, William Desmond.

1934

The Vanishing Shadow. Univ., [12 Chapters] D: Louis Friedlander [Lew Landers]; S: Ella

O'Neill; SP: Het Manheim, Basil Dickey, George Morgan; Cam: Richard Fryer; LP: On-slow Stevens, Ada Ince, Walter Miller, William Desmond.

ANITA STEWART

The Phantom Sweetheart was played by Anita Stewart, and this film is typical of the dozens in which she co-starred with Earle Williams. Anna M. Stewart was her rightful name, and she used it in many Vitagraph productions until a printer accidentally called her Anita Stewart in a press release, and the name stuck. She was born in Brooklyn on February 7, 1895, and started with the Vitagraph Company as a bit player in 1911; her sister was married to Ralph Ince (brother of Thomas H. Ince), and he persuaded her to enter films.

She starred in Vitagraph productions for six years; among her films were *The Wood Violet* ('12), *The Godmother* ('12), *The Song of the Shell* ('12), *The Wreck* ('13), *Three's a Crowd* ('13), *Shadows of the Past* ('14), *A Million Bid* ('14), *The Girl Philippa* ('16), *My Lady's Slipper* ('16), *The Daring of Diana* ('16), *The Glory of Yolanda* ('17), *The Message of the Mouse* ('17) and *The More Excellent Way* ('17).

By far her most remembered film today is the serial *The Goddess*. The story concerns a modern Joan of Arc, reared on a desert island in the belief that she is a goddess. Upon her escape from the island, Celestia (Anita) meets Tommy Barclay (Earle Williams) and goes about spreading her gospel of love and kindness. (Stewart and Williams were the first-line heartthrob team which was keeping Vitagraph on top at the time.) A hypnotist, Stilleter (Paul Scardon), uses Celestia for his own advantage for a while but in the end his spell is broken when he dies from snake bite, and she sees everything in the proper perspective. She is then free to marry Tommy and return to a happy life on Gull Island.

Good acting and skillful photography raised this serial far and away above its plotline. The story is superior but somewhat lacking in familiar serial action.

Although still under contract to Vitagraph, Anita was lured away by Louis B. Mayer in 1917. Vitagraph took the matter to court, which ruled that for all the days Miss Stewart was "ill," those days would be added onto her Vitagraph contract. This law case is still important today as regards actor-studio contracts. At the time she was #4 at the box office behind the Talmadges and Pickford. She remained an important star until the advent of talkies, when she retired. For a while she headed her own production company with L. B. Mayer as her production executive. She also authored a book, *The Devil's Toy*.

Her later films (1918–28) were *A Midnight Romance*, *Mary Regan*, *Her Kingdom of Dreams*, *The Mind-the-Paint Girl*, *In Old Kentucky*, *The Fighting Shepherdess*, *The Yellow Typhoon*, *Playthings of Destiny*, *The Invisible Fear*, *Sowing the Wind*, *Her Mad Bargain*, *A Question of Honor*, *Rose o' the Sea*, *The Woman He Married*, *The Love Piker*, *The Great White Way*, *The Boomerang*, *Never the Twain Shall Meet*, *The Lodge in the Wilderness*, *Wild Geese* and *Romance of a Rogue*.

In 1927, Anita co-starred with Bruce Gordon in the Mascot serial *The Isle of Sunken Gold*. A sea captain possesses part of a map showing the location of a treasure on a remote island. Traveling there, he finds that the other half of the map is held by a white princess who is practically a prisoner of the local people. Together the captain and the princess battle hostile tribesmen and white mutineers to recover the treasure and to free the princess from enslavement. It was an audience-pleasing cliffhanger.

Earle Williams and Anita Stewart in *The Goddess* (Vitagraph, 1915).

Serials

1915

The Goddess. Vit., [15 Chapters] D: Ralph W. Ince; SP: Gouverneur Morris, Charles W. Goddard; LP: Anita Stewart, Earle Williams, Paul Scardon, Frank Currier, William Dangman, Thomas Brooks, Louise Beaudet, Charles Wellesley.

1927

The Isle of Sunken Gold. Mascot, [10 Chapters] D: Harry Webb; P: Nat Levine; LP: Anita Stewart, Bruce Gordon, Duke Kahanomoku, Evangeline Russell, Curtis McHenry, John Pierce, Vincent Howard, Ammett Wagner, Jay J. Bryan, Alfred Sabota, K. Nambu.

ELEANOR STEWART

Eleanor Stewart attended Northwestern University with another future Western femme, Beth Marion. Their families were friends and when both girls went to Hollywood they shared an apartment for a while. Eleanor's film career came about by winning a talent search contest conducted by MGM. Whisked off to Hollywood, she did well in her screen test and signed a contract with studio head Louis B. Mayer. As a neophyte on the lot she received makeup lessons from Max Factor and attended acting school. Her first movie role was a bit in *Small Town Girl* ('36) starring Janet Gaynor and Robert Taylor.

Her 16 Westerns were made with saddle aces Tex Ritter, Bob Steele, the Three Mesquiteers, Bob Allen, Tom Keene, Jack Luden, Jack Randall and William Boyd. These horse operas endeared her to those who loved leather burners. She was a believable actress and Western aficionados accepted her as one of their own.

Eleanor could also be seen in *Headline Crasher* ('37) with Frankie Darro, *Trapped by G-Men* ('37) with Jack Holt, *Waterloo Bridge* ('40) with Vivien Leigh, *Las Vegas Nights* ('41) with Bert Wheeler, *Louisiana Purchase* ('41) and *Caught in the Draft* ('41), both with Bob Hope, *Men of San Quentin* ('42), in which Eleanor had the leading lady part opposite Anthony Hughes, *Pacific Blackout* ('41) with Robert Preston, *The Great Man's Lady* ('42) with Joel McCrea, *Silver Queen* ('42) with George Brent and *Ziegfeld Follies* ('46) with William Powell.

Eleanor is best-remembered for her role as Janet Warfield in *The Fighting Devil Dogs* ('38), in which a mysterious villain calling himself "The Lightning" invents an artificial thunderbolt weapon capable of discharging huge amounts of electricity from his superplane, "The Wing." Two marine lieutenants are assigned to track down the criminal and put a stop to his terror. A group of scientists is organized to develop a countermeasure to the Lightning's device, but it becomes obvious that one of the members is the Lightning himself.

Eleanor quit films when her daughter Karen was born, but she stayed in the Beverly Hills film colony. Instead of working on camera, she helped stage productions at her daughter's school. She has expressed no regrets about giving up her career. "Filmmaking was just a job; it never became my life," she said. "It was hard work filming hot and dusty scenes and not the glamour the movie magazines made it up to be. The bright lights hurt your eyes and the heavy makeup felt like it would melt your face. To me, it was a job and nothing more."

In 1985, she complete work on her book *Priscilla*, an historical novel in which she concentrates on the Pilgrims' joys and successes rather than their death and hardships. The book was self-published. Eleanor was hoping to interest a film studio in buying the film rights.

For many years Eleanor has lived with her husband, Eugene Jones, in San Diego. Her daughter and granddaughters Heather and Kari live just two doors away. She thinks being a grandma is the best role she has ever had.

Serial

1938

The Fighting Devil Dogs. Rep., [12 Chapters] D: William Witney, John English; SP: Barry Shipman, Franklyn Adreon, Ronald Davidson, Sol Shor; AP: Robert Beche; Cam: William Nobles; Mus: Alberto Colombo; LP: Lee Powell, Herman Brix [Bruce Bennett], Eleanor Stewart, Montagu Love, Hugh Sothern, Sam Flint, John Picorri, Lester Dorr, Carleton Young, Edmund Cobb, Tom London, John Davidson.

PEGGY STEWART

Beauteous Peggy Stewart was luckier than most cowgirls who disappeared over the horizon when the sun set on B-Westerns. She remained active in the entertainment field and has been a favorite at many film festivals. Starting in 1973 she has attended at least one festival each year for the last 30 years.

Peggy was born on June 6, 1923, in West Palm Beach, Florida. Her parents were John O'Rourke and the former Frances McCampbell. A sister, Patricia, who later became Mrs. Wayne Morris, was born to the couple a year earlier. When Peggy was very young, the O'Rourkes divorced, and she and her sister moved with their mother to Chattanooga for a year, then to Brookwood Hills, Georgia, a suburb of Atlanta. It was there that Peggy's mother married John Stewart, a successful attorney, who gave the girls his name. As a result of the marriage, another daughter, Frances, was born.

Peggy attended Atlanta grade schools

and the Marken Professional School. Her summers were spent at a YWCA camp near Tallulah Falls, Georgia, where she and her sister spent hours perfecting their swimming skills. Both became swimmers of Olympic caliber. For two consecutive years Peggy won the Georgia Junior Championship for free-style swimming (1934–35).

When Peggy was 12, Mrs. Stewart took all three girls with her to California to vacation and to attend the wedding of her brother. While there, Peggy enrolled in Neely Dickson's Dramatic School. Two months later, when it was time to return home, she was so much in love with drama school and California that she talked her mother into letting her stay on the condition that her grandmother stay with her.

Peggy and her grandmother stayed at the Alto Nido Apartments. Also living there was character actor Henry O'Neill, who was working in the Western *Wells Fargo* ('37). Henry liked Peggy and, knowing that Paramount was looking for a girl to play Alice McKay, the daughter of Joel McCrea and Frances Dee, he recommended her to director Frank Lloyd. Peggy was tested and got the part.

After completing *Wells Fargo*, Peggy had important roles in four 1938 films: *Little Tough Guys*, *That Certain Age*, *White Banners* and *Little Tough Guys in Society*. *Everybody's Hobby* followed in 1939.

Peggy married actor Donald Barry in 1940 while he was making *Adventures of Red Ryder*. She was only 17. Their marriage lasted four years and produced one son, Michael. During her marriage she made only three films, but when it ended she signed with Republic. For three years Peggy was happy as part of the Republic "family." she made 24 Westerns, seven with Bill Elliott, eight with Sunset Carson, five with Allan Lane, one with Roy Rogers and one with Gene Autry. The other two were the serials *The Phantom Rider* ('46) and *Son of Zorro* ('47).

When Republic scheduled her to appear in another serial, Peggy balked. She didn't like serials, preferring the six-day Westerns. She also had a hankering to play in non–Western "B" pictures like those featuring Adele Mara and Ruth Terry. Republic head Herbert Yates said "no deal"— she was too valuable to the studio in the shoot-'em-ups. She requested her release and received it. As a freelancer, Peggy found it hard to find work in non–Westerns since everyone thought of her as strictly a Western ingenue. She was soon back in sagebrushers opposite Lash LaRue, Whip Wilson, Jim Bannon, Charles Starrett, Bill Elliott and Guy Madison. And even though she had tried to get out of further serials at Republic, she wound up making two at Columbia, each a notch below the Republic standard. *Tex Granger* ('48) was a weak effort featuring Robert Kellard, hardly a convincing cowpoke, while *Cody of the Pony Express* ('50) featured stuntman-turned-actor Jock Mahoney, a believable man of the range, in a far better chapterplay.

After *Six Gun Decision* ('53) Peggy decided to quit movie work for a while to see if she couldn't break out of the Western typecasting. She accepted a job at NBC as assistant casting director and remained in the job for three years, leaving to have her second child, Abigail, by second husband Buck Young. A son, Gregory, arrived in due time, and Peggy interspersed television roles with domestic ones.

Among her television credits are appearances in *Have Gun, Will Travel*, *Wyatt Earp*, *Wild Bill Hickok*, *The Cisco Kid*, *The Range Rider*, *The Virginian*, *The Gene Autry Show*, *Beverly Hills 90210*, *Seinfeld*, *Taxi*, *Daniel Boone*, *Emergency*, *The Roy Rogers Show*, *Hotel de Paree*, *Twilight Zone*, *The Rebel* and *Yancy Derringer*.

A great love of Peggy's is the legitimate theater, in which she has been active over the years. In 1974, she was nominated for an award for best supporting actress by the Los Angeles Drama Critics Circle for her work in *Picnic*. Other plays include *The Great American Family*, *Girls in a Turkish Bath*, *Accidentally Yours*, *John Brown's Body* and *Love and Roses*.

Peggy has been a frequent guest at film festivals in Nashville, Memphis, Charlotte, Atlanta, Los Angeles, Lone Pine and other cities. Fans never tire of her. They always want this spunky lass back for she has a personality that is as welcomely received as a snowcone in Hell in August.

Serials

1946

The Phantom Rider. Rep., [12 Chapters] D: Spencer G. Bennet, Fred C. Brannon; SP: Albert DeMond, Basil Dickey, Jesse Duffy, Lynn Perkins, Barney Sarecky; AP: Ronald Davidson; Cam: Bud Thackery; Mus: Richard Cherwin; LP: Robert Kent, Peggy Stewart, LeRoy Mason, George J. Lewis, Kenne Duncan, Hal Taliaferro, Chief Thundercloud, Rex Lease, Roy Barcroft.

1947

Son of Zorro. Rep., [13 Chapters] D: Spencer G. Bennet, Fred C. Brannon; SP: Franklyn Adreon, Basil Dickey, Jesse Duffy, Sol Shor; AP: Ronald Davidson; Cam: Bud Thackery; Mus: Mort Glickman; LP: George Turner, Peggy Stewart, Roy Barcroft, Edward Cassidy, Ernie Adams, Charles King, Newton House.

1948

Tex Granger. Col., [15 Chapters] D: Derwin Abrahams; SP: Arthur Hoerl, Lewis Clay, Harry Fraser, Royal Cole; P: Sam Katzman; Cam: Ira H. Morgan; Mus: Mischa Bakaleinikoff; LP: Robert Kellard, Peggy Stewart, Buzz Henry, Smith Ballew, Jack Ingram, I. Stanford Jolley, Terry Frost, Charles King, Edmund Cobb, John Hart.

1950

Cody of the Pony Express. Col., [15 Chapters] D: Spencer G. Bennet; SP: David Mathews, Louis Clay, Charles R. Condon; S: George H. Plympton, Joseph F. Poland; P: Sam Katzman; Cam: Ira H. Morgan; Mus: Mischa Bakaleinikoff; LP: Jock Mahoney, Peggy Stewart, Dickie Moore, William Fawcett, Tom London, George J. Lewis, Pierce Lyden, Jack Ingram, Rick Vallin, Frank Ellis.

Peggy Stewart and Gene Autry.

ROY STEWART

Roy Stewart's best-remembered films are the historical Westerns produced by Anthony J. Xydias for Sunset Productions. These were *With Kit Carson Over the Great Divide* ('25), *With Buffalo Bill on the U P Trail* ('26), *With Daniel Boone Thru the Wilderness* ('26) and *With General Custer at Little Big Horn* ('26). These were exceptional films and basically truthful depictions of the frontier stories they espoused to portray.

They have stood up well and are worth viewing today.

Hal Roach used Roy in several films in 1914, casting him opposite Jane Novak and Harold Lloyd in *Just Nuts, The Hungry Actors* and *Into the Light*. At this time Stewart commanded $10 a day as contrasted with $5 for Lloyd.

Stewart appeared in three serials. The first was *The Diamond from the Sky* ('15). He played the part of Blake in the 30-chapter story. One of the big punches of this serial was the fight scene staged by Stewart and star William Russell. The story revolves about a large diamond sought by two cousins who resort to skullduggery to gain possession. Lottie Pickford starred; Stewart's role was a minor one.

In 1916, Universal filmed the first Western serial, *Liberty*, starring Marie Walcamp and Jack Holt, with Stewart and Neal Hart comprising the main support. Liberty's father dies, leaving a vast estate in Mexico and appointing as her guardians Major Winston (Hart) and Jose Leon (L. M. Wells). His will specifies that she is not to marry until she is 21 unless both guardians approve. A rebel leader kidnaps her hoping to finance a revolution with the ransom. Capt. Rutledge of the Texas Rangers (Holt) rescues Liberty (Walcamp) and falls in love with her. Jose Leon blackmails Liberty into marrying his son, Manuel (Bertram Grassby), to prevent exposure of Major Winston (Hart), who had gambled and lost estate funds. Manuel is later killed in the revolution, leaving Liberty free to marry Rutledge. The author is not aware of the role played by Stewart.

Six years later, Stewart was to star in *The Radio King* ('22), filmed in ten chapters. A group of foreign agents, headed by an electrical wizard, plot to steal radio inventions and to overthrow the government. Stewart's job is to see that both the secrets and the inventor are protected. The conflict is fought with the aid of numerous electrical gadgets, including remote-controlled doors which in the end trap the villain and his gang. Louise Lorraine co-starred and her pulchritude was not overlooked by audiences.

Roy really came into prominence when he signed with Triangle as a replacement for William S. Hart, who was going to Paramount. Roy became a major Western star in such films as *The Devil Dogger, The Fugitive, Boss of the Lazy Y, The Medicine Man, The Bond of Fear, The Silent Rider* (all '17), *The Law's Outlaw, Keith of the Border, The Learnin' of Jim Benton, One Shot Ross, Faith Endurin', Cactus Crandall, Wolves of the Border* and *The Fly God* (all '18).

Stewart worked in and out of Westerns. In 1917, he played opposite Lillian Gish in *House Built on Sand*, proving that there was more to his talents than riding a horse and pounding the daylights out of ruffians engaged in egregious violence. Other non–Westerns were *Follow the Girl* ('17) with Ruth Stonehouse, *Come Through* ('17) with Alice Lake, *A Daughter of the Poor* ('17) with Bessie Love and *Red Haired Cupid* ('18) with Peggy Pearce.

Stewart made three above-average Westerns in 1919 for Hodkinson: *The Westerner* with Mildred Manning, *The Sagebrusher* with Marguerite de la Motte and Noah Beery and *The U.P. Trail* with Kathlyn Williams. For Zane Grey Productions he made *Riders of the Dawn* with Claire Adams. He co-starred with Katherine MacDonald in *Beauty Market* ('19) and *Her Social Value* ('21), both made by MacDonald's own company. *The Innocent Cheat* ('21) was a real test of Roy's thespian talents, as he portrayed a man who gradually became a tramp as a result of an unrequited love affair.

Back to Yellow Jacket ('22) is one of the most-often mentioned films of Roy, and equally good were *The Sagebrush Trail* ('22), *One Eighth Apache* ('22) and *The Snowshoe Trail* ('22).

It was in 1922–23 that Roy made two series of two-reel Westerns for Universal. "Timber Tales" presented Roy in seven shorts as a valorous hero fighting for life, love and justice in the great northwest woods country. The second series, "Tales of the Old West," was a more rollicking and vigorous one. Roy agitatedly, and sometimes ferociously, set about to quell the bestial qualities of his fellow man. There were nine films in the series.

Roy's Universal features such as *The Love Brand* ('23) and *Pure Grit* ('23) were more reticent in raw action but his tenacity of purpose was undaunted and he always remained uncompromising — a "stand-patter" for righteousness in a day when morality and noble heroes were respected by movie audiences.

In 1924, Roy and sensuous Bessie Love found romance along the trail to Mexico in First National's *Sundown*, a nine-reeler about a last desperate cattle drive to Mexico by ranchers ousted from the open range by homesteaders. In an off-beat Western, *The Lady From Hell* ('26), Roy is a Scotch officer transplanted to the Western range where he works as a ranch foreman until he is accused of murder. Blanche Sweet co-starred.

In *Sparrows* ('26), Roy was ranked behind Mary Pickford and Gustav von Seyffertitz. In '27, he starred in *The Midnight Watch* with Mary McAllister and *Roaring Fires* with Alice Lake. He was featured in Florence Vidor's *One Woman to Another*. In *Stormy Waters* ('28), he is a sea captain who saves his brother from a barfly, Lola, who has vamped him.

Stewart was an impressive figure, whether slapping leather as a gunfighter or having a tete-a-tete with a comely nymph in her boudoir. His sinewy frame did not lend itself to dancing the Zapateado, and his mere presence in a room seemed to fill it. He was born October 17, 1884, in San Diego. He attended the University of California at Berkeley and graduated with honors.

Deciding on a stage career, he joined a traveling stock company producing *Florodora*, but after a year he longed to settle down, and therefore entered motion pictures.

After 1927 Roy made the transition to featured roles as sound came to the screen and Westerns slipped into disrepute. He was adept at playing different roles with considerable aplomb. In 1929, he was a Viking king in MGM's *The Viking* and a commandant in *In Old Arizona*, the Academy Award winner at Fox. He was in several Westerns with George O'Brien, Tom Mix and Ken Maynard. He was an unbilled player in *King Kong* ('33), a blockbuster film. His last film appearance occurred in the non–Western drama *Zoo in Budapest* ('33) featuring Loretta Young.

Stewart died in Los Angeles of a heart attack in 1933 at age 49.

Serials

1915

The Diamond from the Sky. Amer., [30 Chapters] D: William Desmond Taylor, Jacques Jaccard; S: Roy L. McCardell; LP: Lottie Pickford, Irving Cummings, William Russell, Charlotte Burton, Eugenie Ford, Roy Stewart, W. J. Tedmarsh.

1916

Liberty. Univ., [20 Chapters] D: Jacques Jaccard, Henry MacRae; P/S/SP: Jacques Jaccard; LP: Marie Walcamp, Jack Holt, Neal Hart, G. Raymond Nye, Roy Stewart, Eddie Polo, L. M. Wells, Maude Emory, Bertram Grassby.

1922

The Radio King. Univ., [10 Chapters] D: Robert F. Hill; S/SP: Robert Dillon; LP: Roy Stewart, Louise Lorraine, Al Smith, Sidney Bracey, Clark Comstock, Ernest Butterworth, Jr.

LINDA STIRLING

In 1944, Republic Studio needed a new serial queen: Frances Gifford and Kay Aldridge were unavailable, having flown the coop for more lucrative feeding troughs. She was found in the shapely form of former model Louise Shultz, better known as Linda Stirling. There was a bit of irony in that Linda had never been an outdoor girl and loathed exercise. Dancing had been her entire physical fitness regime. But she rose to the challenge and scored a hit as *The Tiger Woman* ('44), overcoming her terror of horses, snakes and spiders. She was young, healthy and very determined to have a movie career.

Her role called for her to be dressed in a scanty costume supposedly made of tiger skins. However, the wardrobe department could not come up with the necessary tiger skins, so leopard skins were substituted. Her lovely legs were left bare, to the delight of males. Linda looked chic and glamorous in leopard skins and goddess costumes trimmed with feathers. While there was some tree-swinging, *Tiger Woman* has more the aura of a Western about it.

Linda was born on October 11, 1921, in Long Beach, California. She began her acting career at an early age, appearing in amateur productions of the Long Beach Community Players.

Linda graduated from high school when she was 16 and studied at Ben Bard's Academy of Dramatic Art for two years. During this time she became in great demand as a photographer's model, which provided her entree into films. She did *The Powers Girl* ('43) as one of the models. Republic people saw her on a magazine cover and called her in for an audition (she fell off a horse twice but got up laughing) and her life as a serial queen began.

In her next serial, *Zorro's Black Whip* ('44), she had to ride again. Fortunately, be-cause of the mask, her double could do almost all of the riding, so she only fell off her horse once or twice. Heat was the real plague. It was July, with the temperature over 100° in the shade. She had to wear heavy wool pants and shirt, a leather jacket, hat, gloves and a mask most of the time. During takes, reflectors added even more intense heat. She fainted twice from heat prostration.

During World War II, Linda entertained at hospitals and did a U.S.O. tour with Carole Landis after *Powers Girl*. And she had a regular one-night-a-week commitment to the Hollywood Canteen.

Linda married Sloan Nibley, Republic scriptwriter, in 1946. She indicated to the author that it was the third marriage for both of them, but did not give any "who or when" information on the first two.

Unlike many others in the serial and Western genre, Linda radiated intelligence, in a slightly self-conscious way, as she went about overcoming the vicissitudes created by Republic scriptwriters. The *esprit de corps* was never better on a set than when Linda was playing the heroine. She was an actress of transcendent beauty; her largess, vitality and enthusiasm indefatigable.

Next in Linda's march to fame was a devil-and-the-deep-blue-sea adventure called *Manhunt of Mystery Island* ('45) with a weaker male hero in Richard Bailey, but an exceptionally virile villain in Roy Barcroft in his portrayal of Captain Mephisto. It was one of his favorite roles.

Interestingly, Republic had followed parallel courses for both of its popular serial queens, Linda and Kay Aldridge. Both started with a jungle yarn, followed with a Western, then into a sea drama. But whereas Kay bowed out of serial production, and never got into Western features at Republic, Linda continued to carry the Republic banners through three more serials and a number of horse operas. *The Purple Monster Strikes* ('45), her fourth chapterplay, dealt with a hitherto unexplored realm in the Republic serial domain, the depths of outer space. Linda's role as Sheila Layton was more subdued than in her previous outings. Roy Barcroft was the Martian "Purple Monster" and Dennis Moore the hero who, along with Linda, was frequently imperiled during the invasionary assault. In *The Crimson Ghost* ('46), Linda and Charles Quigley battle more earthly creatures who are bent on stealing the Cyclotrode (atom smasher). Clayton Moore, yet several years away from his superhero characterization of the Lone Ranger, plays the Ghost's lieutenant. But in *Jesse James Rides Again* ('47) Clayton is the hero-outlaw in a plot set in the netherworld between fact and fiction that exemplified the true mystique of the legendary bandit. Linda plays Ann Bolton, whose interests he protects. The part was a weak one that did not allow Linda the footage or dramatic scenes that she deserved in her final serial chore.

Fans are apt to remember Linda's ten Western features at Republic, especially *Santa Fe Saddlemates* ('45) in which she played a dance hall girl and sang two songs. Commenting on the Westerns, Linda has said:

> We shot most of the outdoor stuff at Iverson's Ranch, and I still can remember every physical aspect of it — the rocks, the trails, the bushes, everything. I had no skill whatsoever with horses and more than once the crew would find me sprawled in the dust or crumpled in the bushes somewhere after my horse had run away with me.
>
> I remember once Spencer Bennet asked me if I could do a running insert. I said sure, although I had no idea what it was. To my dismay, I found out. [To film a running insert, a camera car moves ahead of the running horse and rider.] My horse took it as a personal challenge to outrun the camera truck, and I went along for the ride, taking in the scenery from every possible angle as I was bounced around from side to side and end to end on that galloping beast. Horses and I never really got on a first-name basis or shared social lives.

In *The Tiger Woman* (Republic, 1944).

While stuntmen did many of the more dangerous scenes in the serials, Miss Stirling had several close calls. Twice she almost drowned filming action scenes in water and once when running from an abandoned building, she put her hand in a black widow spider's web. "I assure you that run was one of my most convincing performances," she laughed.

It was all exhausting work and there were few times to stop and rest. Linda did take advantage of one particular rest period, though. While filming *The Purple Monster Strikes*, she was supposed to be knocked unconscious while a fight raged on a spaceship. She was so tired during the scene she fell asleep on the set floor as the stuntmen fought around her.

Another facet of Linda's career was the stage. In *Decision* ('45), she played a young political liberal who supports her intended father-in-law when he is accused of advancing subversive socialist ideas as a school administrator. In *Angel Face* ('47), she was a wise cracking girl who had been deserted by the man she loved and hides her deep hurt behind a breezy, joking facade. *Russet Mantle* ('48) presented her as a girl who shocks her conventional family by saying outrageous things in a desperate effort to break away from their smug, self-satisfied way of life. In *The Browning Version* ('56), Linda played the evil wife, a subtle, understated role, while in *Ladies in Retirement* ('56) she had a very dramatic lead. In *No Exit* ('57) she played Inez, the lesbian, and in *Country Girl* ('58) she played Georgia Elgin.

Non-Western features in which Linda starred are *The Madonna's Secret* ('46), in which she plays a model whom the artist falls in love with. She was murdered by his mother, who was jealous of any girl he was attracted to. Both *The Invisible Informer* ('46) and *The Invisible Mr. Valentine* ('46) were "B"s of the *Mr. and Mrs. North* type. She and Bill Henry solve the crimes. In *The Pretender* ('47), Linda is a gangster's moll who shoots him because he does her wrong.

Linda left Republic in 1948 to have her first baby, then returned to television in 1952 after her second son was born. She worked in TV until 1961, appearing on such shows as *Mr. District Attorney*, *Dr. Christian*, *The Real McCoys*, *City Detective*, *I Led Three Lives*, *The Joan Blondell Show*, *Heinz 57 Series*, *The Public Defender*, *The Man Behind the Badge*, *The Line Up*, *Cavalcade Theatre*, *The Adventures of Wyatt Earp*, *On Trial*, *The Life of Riley*, *Day in Court*, *Adventures of the Falcon*, *The Bob Hope Show*, *The Joseph Cotten Show*, *Medic*, *Revue Productions*, *Adventures of Kit Carson* and *The Millionaire*.

In 1959 and 1960, Linda attended Los Angeles City College on a parttime basis for self-enrichment. By 1961, she was definitely hooked on college and entered UCLA on a full-time basis, finding the intellectual life enthralling. Before she realized the turn in her life, she had gotten a master's degree and became a teacher of English and drama at Glendale College for 27 years.

Stirling was a very beautiful and gifted actress whose talent was wasted to some extent in the low-budget action opuses at Republic, though serial and Western fans were certainly delighted that fate pushed her in that direction.

Undoubtedly *The Tiger Woman* was her most popular episodic drama and also one of Republic's top moneymakers. She seemed to have that special indescribable charisma that caused audiences to empathize with her.

Linda Stirling died at her home in Studio City, California, after a long battle with cancer. Death came on Sunday, July 20, 1997. She was 75. Her husband Sloan Nibley died in 1990. She was survived by her two sons and a sister.

Serials

1944

The Tiger Woman. Rep., [12 Chapters] D: Spencer Bennet, Wallace Grissell; SP: Royal Cole, Ronald Davidson, Basil Dickey, Jesse Duffy, Grant Nelson, Joseph Poland; Cam: Bud Thackery; Mus: Joseph Dubin; LP: Linda Stirling, Allan Lane, Duncan Renaldo, George J. Lewis, LeRoy Mason, Robert Frazer, Kenne Duncan, Tom Steele, Rico de Montez.

Zorro's Black Whip. Rep., [12 Chapters] D: Spencer Bennet, Wallace Grissell; SP: Basil Dickey, Jesse Duffy, Grant Nelson, Joseph Poland; AP: Ronald Davidson; Cam: Bud Thackery; Mus: Richard Cherwin; 2nd Unit D: Yakima Canutt; LP: Linda Stirling, George J. Lewis, Lucien Littlefield, Francis McDonald, Hal Taliaferro, John Merton, Tom London, Stanley Price.

1945

The Purple Monster Strikes. Rep., [15 Chapters] D: Spencer Bennet, Fred Brannon; SP: Royal Cole, Albert DeMond, Basil Dickey, Lynn Perkins, Joseph Poland, Barney Sarecky; AP: Bud Thackery; Mus: Richard Cherwin; LP: Linda Stirling, Dennis Moore, Roy Barcroft, James Craven, Bud Geary, John Davidson, Kenne Duncan, Monte Hale, Ken Terrell.

Manhunt of Mystery Island. Rep., [15 Chapters] D: Spencer Bennet, Wallace Grissell, Yakima Canutt; SP: Albert DeMond, Basil Dickey, Jesse Duffy, Alan James, Frank Nelson,

Joseph Poland; AP: Ronald Davidson; Cam: Bud Thackery; Mus; Richard Cherwin; LP: Linda Stirling, Roy Barcroft, Richard Bailey, Kenne Duncan, Forrest Taylor, Forbes Murray, Jack Ingram, Lane Chandler.

1946

The Crimson Ghost. Rep., [12 Chapters] D: William Witney, Fred Brannon; AP: Ronald Davidson; SP: Albert DeMond, Basil Dickey, Jesse Duffy, Sol Shor; Cam: Bud Thackery; Mus: Mort Glickman; LP: Charles Quigley, Linda Stirling, Clayton Moore, I. Stanford Jol-

ley, Kenne Duncan, Forrest Taylor, Tom Steele, Emmett Vogan.

1947

Jesse James Rides Again. Rep., [13 Chapters] D: Fred C. Brannon, Thomas Carr; SP: Franklyn Adreon, Basil Dickey, Jesse Duffy, Sol Shor; AP: Mike Frankovich; Cam: John MacBurnie; Mus: Mort Glickman; LP: Clayton Moore, Linda Stirling, Roy Barcroft, John Compton, Tristram Coffin, Tom London, Edmund Cobb, LeRoy Mason.

MILBURN STONE

Veteran character actor Milburn Stone was born July 5, 1904, in Burton, Kansas, and entered films in 1934, although most references say 1936. In 1934, he had a small part in Mascot's *The Fighting Marines*. He was a leading man and supporting player in mainly minor Hollywood films. Before entering films, he toured with stock companies for a decade.

Stone will always be remembered as the kindly, but irascible, warmly human but stubbornly noble Doc Adams in TV's long-running (20 years) Western series *Gunsmoke*, for which he won an Emmy in 1968. He was a principal player on the series for its entire run. Before taking the TV role, he appeared in over 100 features. Included were *China Clipper* ('36), *Federal Bullets* ('37), *Port of Missing Girls* ('38), *Mystery Plane* ('39), *Charlie McCarthy, Detective* ('39), *The Great Plane Robbery* ('40), *The Great Train Robbery* ('41), *Reap the Wild Wind* ('42), *Captive Wild Woman* ('43), *Jungle Woman* ('44), *The Daltons Ride Again* ('45), *The Frozen Ghost* ('45), *The Spider Woman Strikes Back* ('46), *Train to Alcatraz* ('48), *Snow Dog* ('50), *Road Block* ('51), *The Atomic City* ('52), *Pickup on South Street* ('53), *Black Tuesday* ('54), *The*

Private War of Major Benson ('55) and *Drango* ('57).

In the serial *The Great Alaskan Mystery* ('44), Stone joined Ralph Morgan, Marjorie Weaver and Fuzzy Knight to solve the mystery, complete with death-ray and fascists agents led by Samuel S. Hinds, Martin Kosleck and Anthony Warde.

The Master Key ('45) pitted Stone, Jan Wiley and Dennis Moore against fifth columnists led by Addison Richards. A professor develops an Orotron machine that will extract gold from the ocean. Naturally, Nazi agents want it. Aided by a group of street kids, led by a young Al (Lash) LaRue, the web of the F.B.I. tightened on the saboteurs with the unmasking of the Master Key really an unexpected revelation.

In his last chapter play, *The Royal Mounted Rides Again* ('45), Stone played a villain. Two Canadian Mounties (George Dolenz and Bill Kennedy) are assigned to investigate the murder of a mine operator by an outlaw gang attempting to gain possession of rich gold mines. In a series of desperate encounters, Wayne (Kennedy) narrowly escapes death and Taggart (Stone) and a henchman, Bunker (Joseph Haworth), are killed in a gun battle. Another henchman, Grail (George Eldredge), makes a last, futile effort to run the gold "blockade" imposed by Wayne.

The greedy outlaw murders two of his cohorts in an effort to corner the stolen Bailey (Duan Kennedy) gold and is murdered in cold blood by Price (Robert Armstrong), operator of the Yukon Palace. The lawless action establishes Price as the leader of the outlaw gang, and he is placed under custody of the Royal Mounted Police by Capt. Wayne.

Serials

1935

The Fighting Marines. Mascot, [12 Chapters] D: B. Reeves Eason, Joseph Kane; SP: Barney Sarecky, Sherman Lowe; S: Wallace MacDonald, Maurice Geraghty, Ray Tampe; P: Nat Levine; LP: Grant Withers, Adrian Morris, Pat O'Malley, Ann Rutherford, Robert Warwick, George J. Lewis, Robert Frazer, Frank Reicher, Milburn Stone.

1944

The Great Alaskan Mystery. Univ., [13 Chapters] D: Ray Taylor, Lewis D. Collins; SP: Maurice Tombragel, George H. Plympton; S: Jack Foley; LP: Milburn Stone, Marjorie Weaver, Ralph Morgan, Edgar Kennedy, Samuel S. Hinds, Joseph Crehan, Harry Cording, Anthony Warde, Reed Howes, Jack Ingram.

1945

The Royal Mounted Rides Again. Univ., [13 Chapters] D: Ray Taylor, Lewis D. Collins; SP: Joseph O'Donnell, Tom Gibson, Harold C. Wire; P: Morgan Cox; LP: George Dolenz, Bill Kennedy, Duan Kennedy, Paul E. Burns, Milburn Stone, Robert Armstrong, Addison Richards, Danny Morton, Joseph Crehan, Selmer Jackson.

The Master Key. Univ., [13 Chapters] D: Ray Taylor, Lewis D. Collins; S: Jack Natteford, Dwight Babcock; LP: Milburn Stone, Jan Wiley, Dennis Moore, Sarah Padden, Russell Hicks, Addison Richards, Byron Foulger, Maris Wrixon, Lash LaRue, Jack Rockwell, Edmund Cobb, John Merton, Ernie Adams.

P. DEMPSEY TABLER

P. Dempsey Tabler's film accomplishments are not impressive at all. He supported William S. Hart in *The Captive God* and *The Patriot*, William Desmond in *A Gamble in Souls*, Enid Markey in *The Phantom*, Bryant Washburn and Lois Wilson in *Love Insurance*, King Baggot and May Allison in *The Cheater*, Margarite Fisher in *The Gamesters* and Leatrice Joy and David Butler in *Smiling All the Way*.

Tabler played Tarzan in *The Son of Tarzan* ('21), but his Tarzan was a civilized one. In the story, Tarzan's son Jack (Kamuela C. Searle) is kidnapped by Tarzan's enemy, Paubovitch (Eugene Burr), and taken to Africa. Jack manages to escape into the jungle with the help of Akut, the ape. There he encounters Meriem (Monilla Martan), who is being held captive by a band of Arabs. Again with the help of Akut, Jack frees her. Jack (now called Korak) and Meriem grow to adulthood in the jungle and love blossoms between them. They are eventually reunited with Tarzan and Jane (Karla Schram), who show up at their African estate.

During the filming of the last chapter, Kamuela C. Searle was actually killed by an elephant in a freak accident. The chapter was finished using a double. Tabler died in 1953 at age 79 in San Francisco.

Serial

1921

The Son of Tarzan. National, [15 Chapters]
D: Harry Revier; SP: Roy Sommerville; S:
Edgar Rice Burroughs; P: David Howell; LP:
Komuela C. Searle, Manilla Martan, P. Demp-
sey Tabler, Karla Schram, Gordon Griffith, Mae
Giraci, Eugene Burr, Frank Morrell, Ray
Thompson.

HELEN TALBOT

Model Helen Talbot had a brief career at Republic where she acted with Donald Barry, Bill Elliott, Allan Lane and Roy Rogers. The films she appeared in were slick and well-produced, with maximum distribution.

After appearing in several Westerns, she was co-starred with Marten Lamont in the serial *Federal Operator 99* ('45). The audience gets their first glimpse of Helen when she is discovered by Lamont tied up in a closet. She becomes an able ally of Lamont in his 15-chapter struggle to defeat George J. Lewis' villainy.

Throughout the serial, Helen is threatened with death. We see her in a gas chamber; held captive in a runaway laundry basket rolling down the highway; almost shredded in a pulp mill; and nearly sliced up by the whirling blades of a propeller. This latter scene, creatively shot by using a wind machine to simulate the propeller's turbulence and capturing Helen's reactions in a close-up, found itself as one of the opening scenes of a television documentary on Republic serials.

Helen's second serial, *King of the Forest Rangers* ('46), cast her as the owner of a trading post in the north woods. She assists Larry Thompson as the park ranger who battles villains on the trail of a secret treasure map. Shot on location at Big Bear northeast of Los Angeles, the serial gave audiences a nice change of scenery from the all-too-familiar views of Iverson ranch or Corriganville.

Helen left films in 1946, having mar-
ried a serviceman who wanted to attend Notre Dame University. Consequently she moved to Indiana. She had a daughter who has twice (or more) made her a grandmother. Currently single again, she now lives in Northridge, California.

Helen was born in Concordia, Kansas, in 1924. When her mother died about 1937, Helen moved to Westwood Village near the campus of the University of California at Los Angeles. The author assumes that she was probably living with relatives. At any rate,

she started modeling in 1940 and continued until signed by Republic in 1943. While employed by Republic during the war years, she participated in Celebrity caravans to entertain military personnel and to sell war bonds. She also went to the South Pacific, along with Donald Barry, as part of a U.S.O. troupe visiting military installations to bolster the morale of servicemen and women.

Serials

1945

Federal Operator 99. Rep., [12 Chapters] D: Spencer G. Bennet, Yakima Canutt, Wallace A. Grissell; SP: Albert DeMond, Basil Dickey, Jesse Duffy, Joseph Poland; AP: Ronald Davidson; Cam: Bud Thackery; Mus: Richard Cherwin; LP: Marten Lamont, Helen Talbot, George J. Lewis, Lorna Gray [Adrian Booth], Hal Taliaferro, Forrest Taylor, Tom London, Tom Steele, Elaine Lange, Bill Stevens.

1946

King of the Forrest Rangers. Rep., [12 Chapters] D: Spencer G. Bennet, Fred Brannon; SP: Albert DeMond, Basil Dickey, Jesse Duffy, Lynn Perkins; AP: Ronald Davidson; Cam: Bud Thackery; Mus: Raoul Kraushaar; LP: Larry Thompson, Helen Talbot, Stuart Hamblen, Anthony Warde, LeRoy Mason, Tom London, Tom Steele.

LYLE TALBOT

Lyle Talbot did it all — traveling tent shows, repertory companies, dinner theater, off-Broadway productions, Broadway musicals, road shows, radio, television and motion pictures (about 150 of them).

He was born Lysle Henderson on February 8, 1902, to theatrical parents in Brainard, Nebraska. His mother died during his infancy and his grandmother, Mary Talbot, bitter over the death of her daughter, kidnapped the infant, giving him her own surname.

Readers may remember him as Joe Randolph, Ozzie and Harriet Nelson's irritating neighbor on *The Adventures of Ozzie and Harriet* for 11 years and as Bob Cummings' old Army buddy, airline pilot Paul Fonda, the would-be Lothario on *The Bob Cummings Show* for five years while playing in dozens of other television roles.

Lyle (he dropped the "s" from his name) began his show business career at age 17 as a magician's assistant and graduated to magician in traveling tent shows. He later formed his own repertory company, the Lyle Talbot Players.

His first film was a two-reeler, *The Nightingale* (1928), made with Pat O'Brien in Brooklyn at the Warner Brothers studio. But realistically his movie career began in 1932 in William Wellman's *Love Is a Racket*, playing the part of a mobster opposite Frances Dee. The same year he had a supporting role in *Three On a Match* starring Bette Davis and co-starred with Carole Lombard in *No More Orchids*. He went on to support Spencer Tracy in *20,000 Years in Sing Sing* ('33), made *Oil for the Lamps of China* ('35) with Pat O'Brien and scores of other films. He never turned down a job; thus, he appeared in the best and the worst of films. In the late '50s, Lyle earned a measure of undesired notoriety with appearances in a terrible trio of films directed by Edward D. Wood, Jr. *Plan 9 from Outer Space* ('59) won the Golden Turkey Award as the worst movie of all time, and Wood was named the worst director of all time. Two other Wood films in which Talbot played were the classic (of sorts) *Glen or Glenda* ('52), about the life of a transvestite, and *Jail Bait* ('54), a crime melodrama.

In 1935, Lyle risked the wrath of the studios by becoming one of the founding members of the Screen Actors Guild. Charles Starrett and Boris Karloff were two other founding members.

Talbot films include *Murder by an Aristocrat* ('36), *Three Legionaires* ('37), *One Wild Night* ('38), *Forged Passport* ('39), *He Married His Wife* ('40), *Mexican Spitfire's Elephant* ('42), *A Night of Crime* ('43), *The Falcon Out West* ('44), *Dixie Jamboree* ('45), *Gun Town* ('46), *Danger Street* ('47), *The Devil's Cargo* ('48), *Parole, Inc.* ('49), *Abilene Town* ('51), *Montana Incident* ('52), *White Lightning* ('53), *The Steel Cage* ('54), *Jail Busters* ('55), *Guns Don't Argue* ('57), *High School Confidential!* ('58), *City of Fear* ('59) and *Sunrise at Compabello* ('60).

Lyle appeared in nine serials, beginning with *Mystery of the River Boat* ('44) and ending with *Trader Tom of the China Seas* ('54). His favorite was *Atom Man vs. Superman* ('50) in which he portrayed the Man of Steel's arch-enemy (from the comics), Luthor. Wearing a flesh-colored, plastic headpiece to accentuate the character's monomaniacal nature, Talbot made the most of the role: introducing a clever assortment of diabolical gadgets (including man-made Kryptonite, the one substance known to be deadly to Superman) to carry out his fiendish schemes, not the last being the potential destruction of Metropolis by means of a giant torpedo and a fleet of flying saucers.

Talbot was married four times. It was his fourth that "took." He and Margaret were married in Tijuana, Mexico, on June 18, 1948. They had four children — two boys and two girls. Margaret died in 1988 and Lyle moved to San Francisco to be near his children. It was there he died on March 3, 1996, at age 94.

Serials

1944

Mystery of the River Boat. Univ., [13 Chapters] D: Ray Taylor, Lewis D. Collins; SP: Maurice Tombragel; S: Ande Lamb; LP: Robert Lowery, Eddie Quillan, Marion Martin, Marjorie Clements, Lyle Talbot, Arthur Hohl, Mantan Moreland, Jay Novello.

1946

Chick Carter, Detective. Col., [15 Chapters] D: Derwin Abrahams; SP: George H. Plympton, Harry Fraser; P: Sam Katzman; Cam: Ira H. Morgan; Mus: Lee Zahler; LP: Lyle Talbot, Douglas Fowley, Julie Gibson, Pamela Blake, Eddie Acuff, Charles King, Frankie Darro, Ernie Adams, Robert Elliott.

1947

The Vigilante. Col., [15 Chapters] D: Wallace Fox; SP: George H. Plympton, Lewis Clay, Arthur Hoerl; P: Sam Katzman; Cam: Ira H. Morgan; Mus: Mischa Bakaleinikoff; LP: Ralph Byrd, Ramsay Ames, Lyle Talbot, George Offerman, Jr., Robert Barron, George Chesebro, Edmund Cobb, Jack Ingram, Eddie Parker.

1949

Batman and Robin. Col., [15 Chapters] D: Spencer G. Bennet; SP: George H. Plympton, Joseph F. Poland, Royal K. Cole; P: Sam Katzman; Cam: Ira H. Morgan; Mus: Mischa Bakaleinikoff; LP: Robert Lowery, Johnny Duncan, Jane Adams, Lyle Talbot, Ralph Graves, Don C. Harvey, Rick Vallin, House Peters, Jr.

1950

Atom Man vs. Superman. Col., [15 Chapters] D: Spencer G. Bennet; SP: George H. Plympton, Joseph F. Poland, David Mathews; P: Sam Katzman; Cam: Ira H. Morgan; Mus: Mischa Bakaleinikoff; LP: Kirk Alyn, Noel Neill, Lyle Talbot, Tommy Bond, Piere Watkin, Jack Ingram, Don Harvey, Rusty Wescoatt, Terry Frost.

1952

Son of Geronimo. Col., [15 Chapters] D:

Left to right: Anthony Warde, Joe Cates and Lyle Talbot in *Mystery of the River Boat* (Universal, 1944).

Spencer G. Bennet; SP: George H. Plympton, Royal K. Cole, Arthur Hoerl; P: Sam Katzman; Cam: William Whitley; Mus: Mischa Bakaleinikoff; LP: Clayton Moore, Rodd Redwing, Lyle Talbot, John Crawford, Rick Vallin, Frank Ellis.

Gould; SP: George H. Plympton, Arthur Hoerl; P: Sam Katzman; Cam: William Witley; Mus: Mischa Bakaleinikoff; LP: Richard Crane, David Bruce, John Crawford, John Hart, Ray Corrigan, Paul Newlan, Charles King, Bud Osborne, Myron Healey, Edmund Cobb.

1953

Gunfighters of the Northwest. Col., [15 Chapters] D: Spencer G.Bennet, Charles S. Gould; LP: Jock Mahoney, Clayton Moore, Phillis Coates, Don Harvey, Marshall Reed, Rodd Redwing,Tommy Farrell, Chief Yowlachie, John Hart, Bud Osborne.

The Great Adventures of Captain Kidd. Col., [15 Chapters] D: Derwin Abbe, Charles S.

1954

Trader Tom of the China Seas. Rep., [12 Chapters] D: Franklyn Adreon; SP: Ronald Davidson; AP: Franklyn Adreon; Cam: Bud Thackery; Mus: R. Dale Butts; LP: Harry Lauter, Aline Towne, Lyle Talbot,Robert Shayne, Victor Sen Yung, Fred Graham, Dale Van Sickel, John Crawford, Dick Alexander.

HAL TALIAFERRO / WALLY WALES

When Hal Taliaferro undertook the role of Bob Stuart in Republic's *The Lone Ranger* ('38), he was no stranger to horse operas or serials.

He had appeared in at least eight previous serials, including *Voice from the Sky* ('30) in which he had the lead. And just prior to filming *The Lone Ranger*, he had been featured in Republic's *The Painted Stallion* ('37), sharing honors with Ray Corrigan, Hoot Gibson and Jack Perrin. To Hal, serials were sort of silly, and he considered *The Lone Ranger* just another serial to be made and a paycheck to pick up. Certainly there was no thought in his mind that it would someday be considered a serial classic and, as such, a much-written about film. No, to Hal Taliaferro, it was just one more film in a long list of films dating back to 1914 when he started out at Universal in such thrillers as *The New Adventures of Torrence O'Rourke* and *The Adventures of Peg o' the Ring*, the latter a 15-chapter serial with Grace Cunard and Francis Ford in the leading roles.

Hal, whose real name was Floyd T. Alderson, was born November 13, 1895, and raised on his dad's ranch on Hanging Woman Creek in Montana. Taliaferro was his mother's maiden name. As a youth, Hal went on his first roundup in 1908, and from then until 1914 he wrangled horses and punched cows. There was little formal education in store for him.

In 1914, at the age of 19, Alderson set out on his own, heading for Yellowstone Park and a job as a stage driver. Tiring of this job after one season, he made his way to San Francisco to see the World's Fair, subsequently drifting down to Los Angeles some time in 1915. He had no trouble getting a job at Universal as a cowboy extra and bit player,

and it was in these capacities that he worked until he entered the Army in World War I. He served two years in the 91st and Spruce Divisions, his service being all stateside.

After the war, it was back to Hollywood for Floyd, but his parts remained insignificant for several years. However, he did get a chance to work with Tom Mix quite a bit, as well as with Neal Hart and Peter Morrison. At the time, Floyd was billed as Floyd Taliaferro.

In 1925, independent producer Lester F. Scott, Jr., signed Floyd as his third cowboy star, previously having hired Kent Sanderson (Buddy Roosevelt) and Jay Wilsey (Buffalo Bill, Jr.). After someone mentioned that he looked like the Prince of Wales, Floyd T. Alderson, Montana cowboy, became Wally Wales, handsome star of a surprisingly good series of low-budget shoot-'em-ups. Scott's shoestring operation was called Action Pictures, and he produced his features for $10,000 to $15,000 each, taking about a week to shoot a five-reel feature and releasing his product on the states right market. Wally's first film as a Western lead was *Tearin' Loose*; his leading lady, Jean Arthur. In the remainder of the silent era, Wally starred in 20 or more sagebrushers for Scott, with release through first Weiss Brothers' Artclass and then through the prestigious Pathé.

With the advent of sound, Wales kept right on grinding out entertaining Westerns for the cheaper cinema houses. Beginning with a featured role in *Overland Bound* ('29), one of the first sound Westerns (it used sound-on-disc and starred Leo Maloney), Wally remained employed through the early Depression years as a series star for Big 4 and Imperial. He had the distinction of starring in the first all-sound serial, *Voice from the Sky* ('29), now long lost.

Like other lesser cowboys of the '30s, Wally Wales alternated between starring, featured and minor roles. But he remained active and in demand, and that was the name of the game when millions of Americans were standing in breadlines around the nation.

Viewing Wales' Imperial and Big 4 Westerns today leaves one impressed with this fine cowboy, who obviously had much more talent than most of the cowboys of his own or later eras. It was just bad breaks that kept him confined to the independents instead of the major studios that could have promoted him into another Maynard, Jones or O'Brien. For there was a charm, a charisma about Wally Wales that is evident even today in viewing his films of 75 years ago.

In the mid–30s, Wally became a character actor and second lead. He played with them all — the great, near great and the lowly. He was one of the featured stars in RKO's all-star *Powdersmoke Range* ('35). His last starring effort was that same year's *The Way of the West*. Thereafter, he switched entirely to character parts and, in 1936, made the name change to Hal Taliaferro. For several years he continued to receive third, fourth and fifth billing in Westerns starring Bob Allen, Rex Bell, Ken Maynard, Bob Baker, Jack Luden, Charles Starrett, Bill Elliott and others. He quickly became one of the best heavies on the screen, and his face and voice were as welcome to two generations of matinee audiences as a valley of lush, green grass to a hungry buffalo herd.

Throughout the '40s, Wales continued to excel at his brand of villainy. When the series Westerns bit the dust in the early '50s, he left the glamour capital to work for a construction firm in Alaska, returning after a year or two to Montana to work as a cowboy on the ranch of his nephew. Hal Taliaferro was a throwback, retaining the cowboy's pride and preferring to hoist his aching bones into the saddle and ride the trails of the Southwest than to sit at the hitchin' rail spittin' tobacco juice and reminiscing about "the good old days." His trails have not always been downhill and shady; but he never expected them to be. Philosophically, he met life head on and merely shrugged his shoulders at temporary setbacks. For tomorrow was a brand new day, possibly to be as unique or memorable as when he would sit by the creek and watch the Sioux ride by.

Serials

1930

The Voice from the Sky. G.Y.B., [10 Chapters] D/P: Ben Wilson; S: Robert Dillon; Cam: William Nobles; LP: Wally Wales, Jean Dolores [Neva Gerber], Robert Walker, J. P. Lockney.

1933

Mystery Squadron. Mascot, [12 Chapters] D: Colbert Clark, David Howard; SP: Wyndham Gittens (?); LP: Bob Steele, Guinn Williams, Lucile Browne, Jack Mulhall, Robert Kortman, J. Carrol Naish.

1934

The Law of the Wild. Mascot, [12 Chapters] D: Armand Schaefer, B. Reeves Eason; LP: Bob Custer, Rex, Rin-Tin-Tin, Jr., Lucile Browne, Ben Turpin, Richard Cramer, Jack Rockwell, Edmund Cobb, Ernie Adams, George Chesebro.

The Lost Jungle. Mascot, [12 Chapters] D: Armand Schaefer, David Howard; LP: Clyde Beatty, Cecilia Parker, Syd Saylor, Warner Richmond, Wheeler Oakman, Maston Williams, Edward Le Saint, Jim Corey, Max Wagner, Wally Wales.

Mystery Mountain. Mascot, [12 Chapters] D: B. Reeves Eason, Otto Brower; LP: Ken Maynard, Verna Hillie, Edward Earle, Syd Saylor, Edmund Cobb, Lynton Brent, Al Bridge, Edward Hearn, Bob Kortman, Tarzan.

1935

The Call of the Savage. Univ., [12 Chapters] D: Lewis Friedlander [Lew Landers]; LP: Noah Beery, Jr., Dorothy Short, Harry Woods, Walter Miller, Bryant Washburn, John Davidson.

Phantom Empire. Mascot, [12 Chapters] D: Otto Brower, B. Reeves Eason; LP: Gene Autry, Smiley Burnett, Frankie Darro, Betsy King Ross, Dorothy Christy, Wheeler Oakman, Warner Richmond.

The Miracle Rider. Mascot, [15 Chapters] D: Armand Schaefer, B. Reeves Eason; LP: Tom Mix, Joan Gale, Charles Middleton, Jason Robards, Sr., Robert Kortman, Edward Hearn, Robert Frazer, Wally Wales, Pat O'Malley, Ernie Adams.

1937

The Painted Stallion. Rep., [12 Chapters] D: William Witney, Alan James, Ray Taylor; LP: Ray Corrigan, Hoot Gibson, Hal Taliaferro, Jack Perrin, Duncan Renaldo, Julia Thayer [Jean Carmen], Yakima Canutt, Charles King.

1938

The Lone Ranger. Rep., [15 Chapters] D: William Witney, John English; LP: Lee Powell, Chief Thundercloud, Herman Brix, Lynne Roberts, Lane Chandler, Hal Taliaferro, George Letz [Montgomery], Stanley Andrews, John Merton.

The Great Adventures of Wild Bill Hickok. Col., [15 Chapters] D: Mack V. Wright, Sam Nelson; LP: Gordon (Bill) Elliott, Carole Wayne, Frankie Darro, Monte Blue, Kermit Maynard, Dickie Jones, Roscoe Ates, Reed Hadley, George Chesebro.

1939

Overland with Kit Carson. Col., [15 Chapters] D: Sam Nelson, Norman Deming; LP: Bill Elliott, Iris Meredith, Trevor Bardette, Richard Fiske, Bobby Clark, LeRoy Mason, James Craig, Dick Curtis.

1940

Adventures of Red Ryder. Rep., [12 Chapters] D: William Witney, John English; LP: Donald Barry, Noah Beery, Sr., Tommy Cook, Maude Pierce Allen, William Farnum, Robert Kortman, Hal Taliaferro, Vivian Coe, Harry Worth, Carleton Young.

1942

King of the Mounties. Rep., [12 Chapters] D: William Witney; LP: Allan Lane, Peggy Drake, Gilbert Emery, Russell Hicks, George Irving, Duncan Renaldo.

1944

Zorro's Black Whip. Rep., [12 Chapters] D: Spencer G. Bennet, Wallace Grissell; LP: Linda Stirling, George J. Lewis, Lucien Littlefield, Hal Taliaferro, John Merton, Francis McDonald, Tom London, Tom Steele, Tom Chatterton, Si Jenks.

Haunted Harbor. Rep., [15 Chapters] D: Spencer G. Bennet, Wallace Grissell; LP: Kane Richmond, Kay Aldridge, Roy Barcroft, Clancy Cooper, Marshall Reed, George J. Lewis, Kenne Duncan, Forrest Taylor, Hal Taliaferro, Bud Geary.

1945

Federal Operator 99. Rep., [12 Chapters] D: Spencer G. Bennet, Yakima Canutt, Wallace A. Grissell; LP: Marten Lamont, Helen Talbot, George J. Lewis, Lorna Gray [Adrian Booth], Hal Taliaferro, LeRoy Mason, Bill Stevens, Jay Novello.

1946

The Phantom Rider. Rep., 1946 [12 Chapters]
D: Spencer G. Bennet, Fred Brannon; LP:
Robert Kent, Peggy Stewart, LeRoy Mason, Hal
Taliaferro, George J. Lewis, Kenne Duncan,
Rex Lease, Chief Thundercloud, Monte Hale,
John Hamilton, Jack Kirk.

RICHARD TALMADGE

Richard Talmadge's real name was Ricardo Metezzeti and he was born on December 3, 1896, in Munich, Germany of Italian and Swiss parentage. He arrived in Hollywood in the late teens and at first worked strictly as a stuntman. He quite often doubled for Douglas Fairbanks in screen feats when the studio did not want to risk its star being hurt.

But by 1921 Talmadge became an actor himself and throughout the 1920s starred in action-oriented features. With the coming of sound to movies, Talmadge's heavy German accent became a liability. After a few

Richard Talmadge and Lucille Lund in *Pirate Treasure* (Universal, 1934).

sound films he went behind the camera, first as an assistant director and then as a second-unit director. In that capacity he worked on scores of films, including *How the West was Won* ('62), *The 300 Spartans* ('62), *Circus World* ('64), *The Greatest Story Ever Told* ('65), *What's New Pussycat?* ('65), *Hawaii* ('66) and *Casino Royale* ('67).

His silent, starring features included *Wildcat Jordan* ('22, Eugenia Gilbert), *Speed King* ('23, Virginia Warwick), *Laughing at Danger* ('24, Eva Novak), *The Fighting Demon* ('25, Lorraine Eason), *The Night Patrol* ('26, Rose Blossom) and *The Cavalier* ('28, Barbara Bedford).

In 1934, Talmadge had the lead in Universal's *Pirate Treasure*, a serial that kept unsophisticated audiences coming back each week to small town or neighborhood theaters.

Serial

1934

Pirate Treasure. Univ., [12 Chapters] D: Ray Taylor; SP: Basil Dickey, Jack Nelson, George Plympton; S: Ella O'Neill; LP: Richard Talmadge, Lucille Lund, Walter Miller, Pat O'Malley, William Desmond, William E. Thorne.

FORREST TAYLOR

E. Forrest Taylor, born December 29, 1883, in Bloomington, Illinois, was the son of a prominent newspaperman. The family later moved to Texas. Forrest spent several years in the publishing world before becoming an actor. From time to time he would go back to the publishing world for awhile.

Around 1915, Forrest was starring in Selig one- and two-reelers, usually outdoor dramas. He appeared in some jungle films utilizing the Selig Zoo animals.

In 1916, he appeared in Kalem's *The Social Pirates*, a 15-chapter serial, and in the 25-episode series *The Girl from Frisco*.

It wasn't until the 1930s that Taylor became a full-fledged badman in "B" Westerns and serials. *Riders of Destiny* ('34) could be said to be his entry into the shoot-'em-up arena. He opposed John Wayne in that Lonestar feature. Beginning with the one film in 1934 and going to one film in 1954, he appeared in 116 features, 91 of which were Westerns. During this same period he worked in 28 serials. He often was the "brains heavy" but could also carry off the role of the heroine's father, a sheriff or upright citizen.

Among his features are *Between Men* ('35), *Too Much Beef* ('36), *The Mystery of the Hooded Horsemen* ('37), *Black Bandit* ('38), *Riders of Black River* ('39), *The Durango Kid* ('40), *Wrangler's Roost* ('41), *Home in Wyomin'* ('42), *Outlaws of Pine Ridge* ('40), *Silver Spurs* ('43), *Mystery Man* ('44), *Dangerous Intruder* ('45), *Santa Fe Uprising* ('46), *Stagecoach to Denver* ('47), *Buckaroo from Powder River* ('48), *Death Valley Gunfighter* ('49), *Code of the Silver Sage* ('50), *Blazing Bullets* ('51), *Night Riders* ('52), *The Marshal's Daughter* ('53) and *Bitter Creek* ('54).

Taylor also appeared on television in such shows as *Man Without a Gun*, *The Gene Autry Show*, *Wild Bill Hickok* and *The Cisco Kid*.

Forrest Taylor passed away on February 19, 1965, in Garden Grove, California at age 80.

Serials

1916

The Social Pirates. Kalem, [15 Chapters] D: James W. Horne; LP: Marin Sais, Ollie Kirby, True Boardman, Frank Jonasson, Thomas Lingham, Forrest Taylor.

The Girl from Frisco. Kalem, [25 Episodes] D: James W. Horne; LP: Marin Sais, True Boardman, Frank Jonasson, Ronald Bradbury, Edward Clisbee, Forrest Taylor.

1925

Perils of the Wild. Univ., [15 Chapters] D: Francis Ford; LP: Joe Bonomo, Margaret Quimby, Jack Mower, Alfred Allen, Eva Gordon, Jack Murphy, Forrest Taylor.

1936

Shadows of Chinatown. Victory, [15 Chapters] D: Robert Hill; LP: Bela Lugosi, Herman Brix, Joan Barclay, Luana Walters, Mauric Liu, Charles King.

1937

Dick Tracy. Rep., [15 Chapters] D: Ray Taylor, Alan James; LP: Ralph Byrd, Kay Hughes, Smiley Burnette, Lee Van Atta, Carleton Young, Francis X. Bushman.

1938

The Fighting Devil Dogs. Rep., [12 Chapters] D: William Witney, John English; LP: Lee Powell, Herman Brix, Eleanor Stewart, Montagu Love, Hugh Sothern, Sam Flint, Forrest Taylor.

Dick Tracy Returns. Rep., [15 Chapters] D: William Witney, John English; LP: Ralph Byrd, Lynne Roberts, Charles Middleton, Jerry Tucker, David Sharpe, Lee Ford, Reed Howes, Forrest Taylor.

1939

Dick Tracy's G-Men. Rep., [15 Chapters] D: William Witney, John English; LP: Ralph Byrd, Irving Pichel, Phylis Isley [Jennifer Jones], Ted Pearson, Walter Miller, Forrest Taylor, George Doylas, Forrest Taylor.

The Lone Ranger Rides Again. Rep., [15 Chapters] D: William Witney, John English; LP:

Robert Livingston, Chief Thundercloud, Jinx Falken, Duncan Renaldo, Ralph Dunn, J. Farrell MacDonald, Forrest Taylor.

The Oregon Trail. Univ., [15 Chapters] D: Ford Beebe, Saul A. Goodkind; LP: Johnny Mack Brown, Louise Stanley, Fuzzy Knight, Bill Cody, Jr., Forrest Taylor, James Blaine, Charles King.

The Phantom Creeps. Univ., [12 Chapters] D: Ford Beebe, Saul A. Goodkind; LP: Bela Lugosi, Robert Kent, Dorothy Arnold, Regis Toomey, Edward Van Sloan, Forrest Taylor, Eddie Acuff, Charles King.

1940

Terry and the Pirates. Col., [15 Chapters] D: James W. Horne; LP: William Tracy, Granville Owen, Joyce Bryant, Allen Jung, Dick Curtis, Victor De Camp.

The Green Archer. Col., [15 Chapters] D: James W. Horne; LP: Victor Jory, Iris Meredith, James Craven, Robert Fiske, Dorothy Fay, Forrest Taylor, Jack Ingram, Charles King.

1941

Sea Raiders. Univ., [12 Chapters] D: Ford Beebe, John Rawlins; LP: Billy Halop, Huntz Hall, Gabriel Dell, Bernard Punsley, Hally Chester, William Hall.

The Iron Claw. Col., [15 Chapters] D: James W. Horne; LP: Charles Quigley, Joyce Bryant, Forrest Taylor, Walter Sande, Norman Willis, Alex Callam.

King of the Texas Rangers. Rep., [12 Chapters] D: William Witney, John English; LP: Slingin' Sammy Baugh, Pauline Moore, Duncan Renaldo, Neil Hamilton, Monte Blue, Herbert Rawlinson, Forrest Taylor.

Dick Tracy vs. Crime, Inc. Rep., [15 Chapters] D: William Witney, John English; LP: Ralph Byrd, Jan Wiley, John Davidson, Ralph Morgan, Michael Owen, Robert Frazer, Forrest Taylor.

1942

Perils of Nyoka. Rep., [15 Chapters] D: William Witney; LP: Kay Aldridge, Clayton Moore, William Benedict, Lorna Gray [Adrian Booth], Charles Middleton, Tristram Coffin.

Overland Mail. Univ., 1942 [15 Chapters] D:

Ford Beebe, John Rawlins; LP: Lon Chaney, Jr., Noah Beery, Jr., Helen Parrish, Don Terry, Noah Beery, Sr., Bob Baker.

The Valley of Vanishing Men. Col., [15 Chapters] D: Spencer G. Bennet; LP: Bill Elliott, Slim Summerville, Carmen Morales, Kenneth MacDonald, Jack Ingram, Roy Barcroft, Forrest Taylor.

King of the Mounties. Rep., [12 Chapters] D: William Witney; LP: Allan Lane, Peggy Drake, Russell Hicks, Gilbert Emery, George Irving, Bradley Page, Abner Biberman, Nestor Paiva.

1944

Haunted Harbor. Rep., [15 Chapters] D: Spencer G. Bennet, Wallace Grissell; LP: Kane Richmond, Kay Aldridge, Clancy Cooper, Roy Barcroft, Marshall Reed, Forrest Taylor.

Black Arrow. Col., [15 Chapters] D: Lew Landers; LP: Robert Scott, Adele Jergens, Kenneth MacDonald, Robert Williams, Charles Middleton, George J. Lewis, Harry Harvey, Bud Osborne, Charles King, Chief Thundercloud.

1945

Manhunt of Mystery Island. Rep., [15 Chapters] D: Spencer G. Bennet, Wallace A. Grissell; LP: Linda Stirling, Roy Barcroft, Richard Bailey, Kenne Duncan, Forrest Taylor, Forbes Murray.

Federal Operator 99. Rep., [12 Chapters] D: Spencer Bennet, Yakima Canutt, Wall; LP: Marten Lamont, Helen Talbot, George J. Lewis, Lorna Gray [Adrian Booth], Hal Taliaferro, Forrest Taylor, Bill Stevens.

1946

The Crimson Ghost. Rep., [12 Chapters] D: William Witney, Fred Brannon; LP: Charles Quigley, Linda Stirling, Clayton Moore, I. Stanford Jolley, Kenne Duncan, Forrest Taylor.

1947

The Black Widow. Rep., [13 Chapters] D: Spencer G. Bennet, Fred C.Brannon; LP: Carol Forman, Bruce Edwards, Virginia Lindley, Anthony Warde, Ramsay Ames, I. Stanford Jolley, Forrest Taylor, Virginia Carroll, Ernie Adams.

1948

Superman. Col., [15 Chapters] D: Spencer G. Bennet, Thomas Carr; LP: Kirk Alyn, Noel Neill, Tommy Bond, Pierre Watkin, Carol Forman, George Meeker, Jack Ingram.

1949

Bruce Gentry. Col., [15 Chapters] D: Spencer G. Bennet, Thomas Carr; LP: Tom Neal, Judy Clark, Ralph Hodges, Forrest Taylor, Hugh Prosser, Tristram Coffin.

1951

Don Daredevil Rides Again. Rep., [12 Chapters] D: Fred C. Brannon; LP: Ken Curtis, Aline Towne, Roy Barcroft, Lane Bradford, John Cason, Forrest Taylor, I. Stanford Jolley.

1953

The Lost Planet. Col., [15 Chapters] D: Spencer G. Bennet; LP: Judd Holdren, Vivian Mason, Ted Thorpe, Forrest Taylor, Michael Fox, Gene Roth.

KENT TAYLOR

Handsome Kent Taylor began his movie career at Paramount in 1931; 40 years later, he was still an active actor. His real name was Louis William Von Weiss. He was born in Nashua, Iowa, on May 11, 1907. He first appeared in *Road to Reno* ('31) after working at odd jobs until he could get studio work.

Taylor's one serial was *Gang Busters* ('42), in which he was supported by Irene

Hervey, Ralph Morgan, Robert Armstrong and George J. Lewis. As detective Lt. Bill Bannister, he is assigned to run down an unknown gang of terrorists who have spread a net of crime over the city. He and Armstrong, as detective Tim Nolan, project the image of the intelligent hero. They illustrate well the calm, deliberate and analytical skills of the efficient law officers they were supposed to be. Following their investigation closely is Vickie Logan (Hervey), a news photographer in whom Bill is interested romantically. Bill finds that the gang's ringleader is a mysterious Prof. Mortis. His "League of Murdered Men" is made up of criminals who have hanged themselves and officially are listed as dead. Martin has a death-simulating drug and an anti-death treatment that he has used to recruit his gang of criminals. Bill ultimately finds his way into Mortis' underground hideout and the criminal is killed by a subway train as he tries to make his escape.

Taylor is best-known for his syndicated TV series *Boston Blackie* (1951–53) and *The Rough Riders* (1958–59).

In *Boston Blackie*, Taylor plays the criminal-cum-detective with Lois Collier as his lady friend Mary Wesley and Frank Orth as Inspector Faraday. The half-hour series was set in New York rather than Boston. The series was produced by Ziv-TV and directed by Eddie Davis and Sobey Martin.

The Rough Riders was an implausible Western about three Civil War veterans—two Union and one Confederate—who teamed up after the War. Kent plays Capt. Flagg, Jan Merlin was ex–Confederate Lt. Kirby and Peter Whitney was Sgt. Sinclair.

Taylor's films include *If I Had a Million* ('32); *Sunset Pass* ('33); *Mysterious Rider* ('33); *Under the Tonto Rim* ('33), *Death Takes a Holiday* ('34); *David Harum* ('34); *County Chairman* ('35); *Sky Parade* ('36); *Wings Over Honolulu* ('37); *The Jury's Secret* ('38); *The Gracie Allen Murder Case* ('39); *Girl in 313* ('40); *Washington Melodrama* ('41); *Mississippi Gambler* ('42); *Tombstone, the Town Too Tough to Die* ('42); *Halfway to Shanghai* ('43); *Alaska* ('44); *The Daltons Ride Again* ('45); *Tangier* ('46); *The Crimson Key* ('47), *Half Past Midnight* ('48); *The Sickle or the Cross* ('49); *Western Pacific Agent* ('50); *Payment on Demand* ('51); *Playgirl* ('54); *Ghost Town* ('55); *The Phantom from 10,000 Leagues* ('56); *Frontier Gambler* ('56); *Fort Bowie* ('58); *The Purple Hills* ('61); *The Day Mars Invaded Earth* ('63); *Harbor Lights* ('63); *The Crawling Hand* ('64); *Brides of Blood* ('68); *The Mighty Gorga* ('70); and *Brain of Blood* ('71).

The Phantom of Hollywood ('74) was a telefeature about a masked murderer committing murder on the MGM studio lot as he tries to stop its sale, since (unbeknownst to anyone) the place has been his home for many years. Included in the cast were John Ireland, Regis Toomey, Broderick Crawford, Corinne Calvet, Jackie Coogan, Peter Lawford, Billy Halop and Skye Aubrey. With its reliance on the MGM backlot for location, the film turned out to be a joy for movie enthusiasts. Not much favorable could be said for the creaky plotline, but the cast carried it off with finesse, and the use of actual vintage sets made the proceedings atmospheric.

Kent's wife of nearly sixty years was the former Augusta Kulek. They had three children, Kay, Judy and Bill.

Taylor passed away in the Motion Picture County Home and Hospital in Woodland Hill, California, following several heart operations. His death came in 1987; he was 80 years old.

Serial

Gang Busters. Univ., 1942. D: Ray Taylor, Noel Smith; SP: Morgan B. Cox, Al Martin, Vin Martin, George H. Plympton; AP: Ford Beebe, Cam: William Sickner, John Boyle. C: Kent taylor, Irene Hervey, Ralph Morgan, Robert Armstrong, Richard Davies, Joseph Crehan, George J. Lewis, Beatrice Roberts, George Watts, John Gallander, Stanley Blystone, Robert Barron, Grace Cunard, Stanley Price, George Eldredge, William Desmond, Eddie Fetherstone, Eddie Dew, Karl Hackett, Ethan Laidlaw.

Kent Taylor (right) and an unidentified player in *Gang Busters* (Universal, 1942).

DON TERRY

A 15-weeker, Columbia's *Secret of Treasure Island* ('38) is stuffed with fist fighting, gunplay, rough-and-tumble action and enough fright ingredients to keep the kids coming back for each episode. Don Terry, a first class fist swinger, gets into the thick of every struggle in the film and handles the opposition with some backbreaking routines.

Terry was a good choice for the leading role in this chapterplay. If he had continued with his original career instead of turning to motion pictures, he might have been fighting for the world's heavyweight boxing

crown instead of battling the bold, bad villains who beset the hero's pathway toward the happy ending in action thrillers on the screen.

A short time before entering the movies, Terry was battling his way successfully through all fistic competition in the amateur ranks. Promoters spotted him as a potential heavyweight king from the moment he won the heavyweight boxing crown at Harvard University, his alma mater.

Following his graduation, Terry was on his way to appear in a series of amateur ring engagements in Australia when, during a brief visit to Hollywood before embarking from San Francisco, Terry met author Charles Francis Coe, who induced him to take a crack at movies and offered him the lead in *Me, Gangster* ('28), a movie based on Coe's then-current best-selling novel. Terry played the part and it was rated among the ten best performances of the year.

But after two more pictures, Terry got the wanderlust and went to the South Seas with a movie location company. On his return, he went directly to New York and subsequent success on the stage.

Terry was born Donald Prescott Loker on August 8, 1902, in Natick, Massachusetts, where his parents' grocery store was located. From grade school he went to Tennessee Military Academy, but dropped out at 16 to join the Marines. About nine months later he received an honorable disability discharge. He attended Phillips Academy at Andover, Massachusetts, Huntington School in Boston and finally Harvard, where he lettered in football, basketball and baseball. He was a member of the U.S. boxing team to the 1928 Olympics.

In *Don Winslow of the Navy* (Universal, 1942).

Me, Gangster ('28) was followed by roles in *Blindfold* ('28), *The Fugitives* ('29), *The Valiant* ('29), *Untamed* ('29) and *Border Romance* ('30). In 1932 he supported Ken Maynard in *Whistlin' Dan* and then he was off the screen until 1937. That year Columbia signed him for a series of action programmers. Included were *A Fight to the Finish* ('37), *Dangerous Adventure* ('37), *When G-Men Step In* ('38) and *Squadron of Honor* ('38).

Since these actioners proved popular, Columbia next starred him in *The Secret of Treasure Island* ('38). The story covers a hidden treasure search which had gone on for centuries. A newspaper editor has a hankering to find out the secret of the island and dispatches one reporter who never returns, so he puts the job on Terry. A sea captain who owns half a map showing the location of a treasure buried on the island is killed just before he can tell the daughter of his old shipmate about the other half. The daughter, Toni Morrell (Gwen Gaze), happens to be a good friend of reporter Larry Kent (Don Terry) and together they decide to solve the mysteries of the island. She is heir apparent to the treasure.

Larry discovers that the island is ruled by Collins (Walter Miller), who has mined all approaches to it in order to discourage intruders who might interfere with his treasure hunt. Collins is assisted by his henchman Grant Withers. Hobart Bosworth, Yakima Canutt, William Farnum and George Rosener appear prominently in the story, which has many good, suspenseful chapter closes and many attractive episode titles. Not only does Larry round up the gang, he also discovers the treasure and Toni's father.

Terry married Katherine Bogdanovich in 1940. She was the daughter of Martin Bogdanovich, founder of StarKist Foods. They had two daughters, Deborah and Katherine. In 1941, he signed with Universal and in 1942 was cast in the serial *Overland Mail*, sharing honors with Lon Chaney, Jr., and Noah Beery, Sr., and Jr. The story concerned the efforts of the Overland Mail to maintain its franchise and reputation despite the encroachments of a rival line. A marshal and two scouts are assigned to investigate the unusual series of accidents befalling the stagecoaches. Helen Parrish, as the daughter of the Overland owner, provides the romantic interest. Terry plays Buckskin Bill Burke, a trusted frontier scout.

Then came the role that would identify Terry forever, *Don Winslow of the Navy*. As Winslow, commander of the U.S. Navy destroyer 620, Terry is transferred to Naval Intelligence at Pearl Harbor and detailed to investigate the mysterious torpedo sinking of the Corda-Queen in the South Pacific. He and Lt. Red Pennington (Walter Sande) proceed to Tangita, a small island off the main southern trade routes. Rondana Bay is being converted into an auxiliary naval base. Unsuspected by Winslow, the mine which is located at the north tip of Tangita Island is actually a secret submarine base operated by Winslow's old enemy, the spy master known as the Scorpion. The Scorpion's chief agent on the island is Merlin, superintendent of the mine. Only visible as a sinister face on a television screen, the Scorpion, played with nasty relish by Kurt Katch (on the brief occasions when he appeared), would snarl out orders and punish those who bungled their assignments, such as one hapless agent who was ordered to sit in the driver's seat of a human torpedo.

In the serial's action sequences, Terry pilots a mosquito boat in the path of a human torpedo device; dives from a burning automobile into the sea; rams a submarine with a freighter; fights the spies in a dynamited mine kill; gets trapped in a water cell; battles a man-eating shark; is buried alive in a bombing raid; gets locked in a chemical reducing chamber; pilots a fighter plane in a dogfight over the ocean; invades the Scorpion's undersea headquarters; gets caught in a tunnel cave-in; and deliberately signals for a depth bomb attack upon the spy submarine in which he and his friends are captives. Eventually Don succeeds in blowing the whistle on the Scorpion and sealing the lid on his entire operation.

Don Winslow of the Coast Guard ('43)

saw Winslow and his sidekick loaned out by the Navy to help battle sabotage caused by the Scorpion and his fifth columnists. In the first film, the Scorpion's allegiance was unstated, but here it was pretty clear. His chief aides were a Japanese sub commander (Philip Ahn), several Nazi agents, an exotic aide (Tasmia, played by June Duprez, the princess in the Sabu–Conrad Veidt *Thief of Bagdad*) and assorted Fascist and gangster henchmen. For good measure, a squad of Japanese soldiers were thrown in on an off-coast island. Nestor Paiva took over the role of the Scorpion from Kurt Katch and was properly malevolent.

In 1943, after filming *Don Winslow of the Coast Guard* and two feature films for Universal, *Sherlock Holmes in Washington* and *White Savage* with Maria Montez, Don, a U.S. Navy reservist, went on active duty. He was made a lieutenant commander with the amphibious forces in the Pacific. He was later cited for bravery; and after World War II was cited for outstanding service in the Naval Reserves from '45 to '47. After his release from service, his father-in-law purchased his Universal contract and Don entered the family business. In his later years, Don became a noted philanthropist. He enjoyed excellent health until May, 1988, when he suffered a stroke which was soon followed by two more, and he was confined to a wheelchair. On Thursday, October 6, 1988, Don died in an Oceanside hospital at age 86, the result of a massive cerebral hemorrhage suffered the previous day in his home.

On October 13, 1988, after a morning funeral service at St. Mary's Star of the Sea in San Pedro, he was buried in the city's Greenhill Cemetery with full military honors.

Serials

1938

The Secret of Treasure Island. Col., [15 Chapters] D: Elmer Clifton; SP: George Rosener, Elmer Clifton, George Merrick; S: L. Ron Hubbard; AP: Louis Weiss; P: Jack Fier; Cam: Edward Linden, Herman Schopp; Mus: Abe Meyer; LP: Don Terry, Gwen Gaze, Grant Withers, Hobart Bosworth, William Farnum, Yakima Canutt, Walter Miller, Dave O'Brien, Clara Kimball Young, Sandra Karina.

1941

Don Winslow of the Navy. Univ., [12 Chapters] D: Ford Beebe, Ray Taylor; SP: Paul Huston, Griffin Jay, Morgan B. Cox; LP: Don Terry, Walter Sande, Wade Boteler, John Litel, Clare Dodd, Anne Nagel, Samuel S. Hinds, Kurt Katch.

1942

Overland Mail. Univ., [15 Chapters] D: Ford Beebe, John Rawlins; SP: Paul Huston; P: Henry MacRae; LP: Lon Chaney, Jr., Don Terry, Noah Beery, Sr., Noah Beery, Jr., Jack Rockwell, William Desmond, Charles Stevens, Helen Parrish.

1943

Don Winslow of the Coast Guard. Univ., [13 Chapters] D: Ford Beebe, Ray Taylor; SP: George H. Plympton, Paul Huston, Griffin Jay; AP: Henry MacRae; Mus: Hans J. Salter; LP: Don Terry, Walter Sande, Elyse Knox, Philip Ahn, Rex Lease, Richard Crane, Charles Wagenheim.

ROSEMARY THEBY

Rosemary Theby had a career lasting 25 or more years. Yet there is little biographical information on her. In the early years she often essayed the principal feminine role, but by the mid–20s she was playing "the other woman" or downright villainous roles.

Following is a list of the films that she starred in. Her many supporting roles are not reflected here. The co-stars or male leads appear in parentheses:

The Earl of Pawtucket ('15, Lawrence Dorsay); *Boston Blackie's Little Pal* ('18, Bert Lytell); *Love's Payday* ('18, Pete Morrison); *The Midnight Patrol* ('18, Thurston Hall); *Unexpected Places* ('18, Bert Lytell); *Are You Legally Married?* ('19, Lew Cody); *Faith* ('19, Bert Lytell); *Peggy Does Her Darndest* ('19, May Allison); *Tangled Threads* ('19, Bessie Barriscale); *Upstairs and Down* ('19, Olive Thomas); *Kismet* ('20, Otis Skinner); *Rio Grande* ('20, George Stone); *A Splendid Hazard* ('20, Henry B. Walthall); *Unseen Faces* ('20, Sylvia Breamer); *Whispering Devils* ('20), Conway Tearle); *Across the Divide* ('21, Rex Ballard); *Fighting Mad* ('21, William Desmond); *Good Woman* ('21, Hamilton Revelle); *More to be Pitied Than Scorned* ('22, Frank Glendon); *Montmarte Rose* ('29, Marguerite De La Motte); *Midnight Daddies* ('30, Andy Clyde)

Rosemary had good supporting roles in a number of films, one being *A Connecticut Yankee in King Arthur's Court* ('20) in which she played wicked Queen Morgan Le Fay.

Good girls and bad girls— Rosemary could play either, although she leaned toward the naughtiness or damnable roles. She was effective in such roles, for example, *The Silent Mystery* ('18). In Egypt, a jewel of great value is stolen from a mummy by Mrs. Graham (Elsie Van Name). The Priestess Kah (Rosemary) follows Mrs. Graham and her daughter Betty (Mae Gaston) back to the States determined to regain the gem. Strange things begin to happen to all who are associated with the "Eye of the World," as the gem is called. Phil Kelly (Francis Ford) and Betty fight the minions of the priestess throughout the 15 chapters.

In *The Mystery of 13*, Rosemary once

more teams with Francis Ford. A sinister cult of 13 hooded figures oppose the hero and heroine in the pursuit of a lost treasure.

In *The Chinatown Mystery* ('28), Joe Bonomo portrays Joe Masters, a Secret Service agent. Ruth Hiatt possesses the secret formula for producing artificial diamonds and Masters battles evil forces led by the Sphinx, who is determined to have the formula. Theby's role is believed to be that of a villainess.

Rosemary's role in the '30s were mere bits. She was in *Ten Nights in a Barroom* ('31), *The Drunkard* ('35), *San Francisco* ('36), *Make Way for Tomorrow* ('37), *One Million B.C.* ('40) and others.

Serials

1918

The Silent Mystery. Burston, [15 Chapters] D: Francis Ford; P: Louis Burston; S/SP: Elsie Van Name; LP: Francis Ford, Mae Gaston, Rosemary Theby, Jerry Ash, Phil Ford, Elsie Van Name, Valerio Olivo, Hap H. Ward, Pete Gerald.

1919

The Mystery of 13. Burston, [15 Chapters] D: Francis Ford; S: Elsie Van Name; P: Louis Burston; SP: John B. Clymer; LP: Francis Ford, Rosemary Theby, Pete Gerald, Mark Fenton, Ruth Maurice, Doris Dare, Elsie Van Name, Valerio Olivo, Phil Ford.

1928

The Chinatown Mystery. Syn., [10 Chapters] D: J. P. McGowan; S: Francis Ford; P: Trem Carr; LP: Joe Bonomo, Ruth Hiatt, Paul Malvern, Francis Ford, Paul Panzer, Rosemay Theby, Grace Cunard, George Chesebro, Helen Gibson, Peggy O'Day, Paul Malvern, Al Baffert, J. P. McGowan, James Leong.

FRANKIE THOMAS

Frankie Thomas, born on April 9, 1921, grew up in a show business family. He attended the Professional Children's School in New York and from a very early age acted on stage. After several smaller roles, he attained stardom in the play *Wednesday's Child* ('34). RKO brought him to Hollywood to recreate the role in the movie version. For a while he alternated movies and Broadway productions.

Through his agent and Henry MacRae, Universal serial producer, he got the role of Tim Tyler in the chapterplay *Tim Tyler's Luck* ('37). It was a popular jungle thriller, issued at a time when audiences thrilled at this kind of film. Tim (Frankie) is searching for his father, who has disappeared in gorilla country in Africa. At the same time, Lora (Frances Robinson) is seeking Spider Webb (Norman Willis), who had committed a diamond robbery back in the States for which her brother has been framed and imprisoned. Tim and Lora meet and team up against the villainies of a lot of jungle bad men, black and white. Spider Webb kills Tim's father and takes over his armored jungle cruiser to aid him in his quest for a fabulous treasure of ivory. Sgt. Gates (Jack Mulhall) of the Ivory Patrol aids Tim and Lora and the three are able to bring Spider and his cohorts Drake (Anthony Warde) and Lazarre (Earl Douglas) to justice.

Frankie made *Little Tough Guys in Society* ('38) and *Code of the Street* ('39) at Universal and *Boys Town* ('38) at MGM before going under contract to Warners. There he was teamed with Bonita Granville in the Nancy Drew series. They made *Nancy Drew, Detective* ('38), *Nancy Drew, Reporter* ('39), *Nancy Drew — Trouble Shooter* ('39) and *Nancy Drew and the Hidden Staircase* ('39).

The year 1939 was a busy one for Frankie. In addition to the Nancy Drew films, he appeared in *Angels Wash Their Faces, On Dress Parade* and *Invisible Stripes*. In 1941–42 he made *Flying Cadets, One Foot in Heaven, Always in My Heart* and *The Major and the Minor*.

During World War II, Frankie served in the Navy, attaining the rank of lieutenant (j.g.). After his discharge in 1946, he went back East where his parents were working in Broadway shows. Frankie was able to get some stage work himself.

In 1950, Frankie became *Tom Corbett, Space Cadet* on TV in 15-minute, thrice-a-week episodes aired initially on CBS. It later became an ABC program and then was made in 30-minute episodes on NBC and Dumont on Saturday mornings. Overall, it was on the tube for five years.

Frankie became a TV writer following his retirement from acting in 1955, and also became an expert bridge player. He co-authored several books on the subject and published and edited the magazine *Bridge Quarterly* for many years.

Serial

1937

Tim Tyler's Luck. Univ., [12 Chapters] D: Ford Beebe, Wyndham Gittens; SP: Wyndham Gittens, Norman S. Hall, Ray Trampe; LP: Frankie Thomas, Jack Mulhall, Frances Robinson, Anthony Warde, Norman Willis, Al Shean, William Benedict, Earle Douglas, Eddie Parker, Philo McCullough, Al Bridge, Tom Steele.

LOTUS THOMPSON

Lotus Thompson had a brief ride to obscurity playing in about a dozen Westerns and one serial in her six or seven years as a film actress. Her first role of record was in *The Folly of Vanity* ('24) which starred Jack Mulhall and Betty Blythe. Most of her work was at Universal in routine formula Westerns where, if her histrionics didn't attract, her billowing blouse did. But she was adequate as a sagebrush ingenue opposite cowboys Ted Wells, Fred Humes, Tom Tyler, Bob Curwood, Edmund Cobb and Buzz Barton. However, her most memorable film was the serial *Terry of the Times* ('30), released in both silent and sound versions.

In the serial's story, a criminal band known as the Mystic Mendicants attempts to keep Tracy (Reed Howes) from inheriting the *Times* by preventing him from fulfilling a provision of his father's will to marry by a certain date. A treacherous and, as it turns out, fake brother of publisher Robert McCoy, Terry's uncle, disguises himself as Macy (Sheldon Lewis), the paper's publisher, and attempts to block Terry's marriage and his interference with the Mendicants' criminal operations. Lotus played Eileen Parks, Terry's girlfriend.

During the '20s she could be seen in such action flicks as *Flashing Fangs* ('26), *Yellow Back* ('26), *A One Man Game* ('27), *Casey at the Bat* ('27), *Desert Dust* ('27), *The Crimson Canyon* ('28), *The Port of Missing Girls* ('28), *'Neath Western Skies* ('29), *The Phantom Rider* ('29) and *The Freckled Rascal* ('29). Her career as a leading lady ended with the passing of the silent era, but she did continue as a bit player. For example, in *Madam Satan*

('30) she is billed tenth as Eve in the MGM feature starring Kay Johnson and Reginald Denny.

Other films in which she had small roles were *Mutiny on the Bounty* ('35), *Ship Cafe* ('35), *Anthony Adverse* ('36), *The Prince and the Pauper* ('37), *Journey for Margaret* ('42), *National Velvet* ('44), *The Picture of Dorian Gray* ('45) and *The Red Danube* ('49).

Serial

1930

Terry of the Times. Univ., [10 Chapters] D: Henry MacRae; S: Hal Hodes; LP: Reed Howes, Lotus Thompson, Sheldon Lewis, John Oscar, Mary Grant, William Hayes, Norman Thompson, Kingsley Benedict, Taylor Holmes.

FRED THOMSON

Fred Thomson's wife Frances Marion wrote many of his scripts. She had paved the way for his screen debut in 1921 as co-star opposite Mary Pickford in *The Love Light*, which Marion had written. Fred had met Marion when she visited an Army camp in San Diego during World War I. Thomson had enlisted as a chaplain and was then at Camp Kearney. Later he was shipped to France and saw duty in the combat zone.

Upon his return from overseas, Thomson resumed his acquaintance with Marion and that developed into marriage in 1919. In 1921, some studio friends of Marion opened the right doors and launched Fred into pictures. He started at the very top in a film with "America's Sweetheart" Mary Pickford. His performance drew uniform raves and Universal signed him to star in a serial, after which he concentrated on Westerns. In his short but spectacular six-year career, Fred was ranked among the top cowboys of the silent screen.

Fred was born Frederick Clifton Thomson in Pasadena, California, on February 26, 1890, the son of a Presbyterian minister. He earned a bachelor's degree at Occidental College in Los Angeles and went on to attend Princeton Theological Seminary in 1910. He was ordained a Presbyterian minister in 1913 and married classmate Gail Dubois Jepson. After serving as pastor of Hope Chapel in Los Angeles for a year, Fred and Gail moved to Goldfield, Nevada, to assume pastorship of the Presbyterial church there. When his wife succumbed after a short illness in 1916, Fred joined the U.S. Army and was made champlain of the 143rd Field Artillery. By marrying Frances Marion, twice divorced, Fred was forced to give up his ministry.

The Universal serial *The Eagle's Talons* ('23) gave Fred the male lead opposite Ann Little. The story revolved about a gang's attempts to corner the wheat market. In addition to introducing Fred to Saturday matinee audiences, the serial convinced Fred that his desires and forte were for roles of the Western hero type.

His first picture as a Western star was *The Mask of Lopez* (1923), made for Harry Joe Brown on Poverty Row at a cost of $10,000. Fred was an instant hit. His early Westerns were made for an independent, but he soon became associated with FBO, an outgrowth of the Robertson-Cole Company (and later to become RKO-Radio).

Fred was lucky to become associated with both Harry Joe Brown and FBO. Brown was an excellent producer and FBO's Western product was slick and fast-paced, especially written to match the personality, athletic prowess and acting ability of their star.

Fred made 20 films for FBO between 1924 and 1927. It is interesting that Hazel

Keener played the heroine in the first six films (*North of Nevada*, *Galloping Gallagher*, *The Silent Stranger*, *The Dangerous Coward*, *The Fighting Sap* and *Thundering Hoofs*). Brown produced, Albert Rogell directed and Frances Marion wrote the screenplays.

Five Westerns were released in 1925: *That Devil Quemado*, *The Bandit's Baby*, *The Wild Bull's Lair*, *Ridin' the Wind* and *All-Around Frying Pan*. Frances did most of the screenplays; directorial chores varied.

Released in 1926 were *The Tough Guy*, *Hands Across the Border*, *The Two-Gun Man*, *Lone-Hand Saunders* and *A Regular Scout*. The year 1927 saw *Don Mike*, *Silver Comes Through* and *Arizona Nights* released.

These FBO programmers were expertly staged and excellent in all technical aspects. In every picture Silver King was given good scenes in which to demonstrate his superior equine intelligence. Because Thomson's first series was such a hit, he was able to form his own production unit in 1925, with continuing release of the films through FBO. By 1927, he was rapidly overtaking the aging Tom Mix in popularity. He bought an estate in Beverly Hills, reputedly paying in excess of $600,000. Paramount beckoned and Fred left FBO to make bigger-budgeted pictures for the major studio. His contract called for four pictures at a salary of $100,000 each, and he was to have his own production unit.

His first film under the new contract was *Jesse James* ('27). Although a very white-washed account of the bandit, it grossed close to $1.5 million. Critics and public alike, however, came down hard on the film for making heroes of Jesse and Frank James. Fred spared no effort in making *The Pioneer Scout* and *The Sunset Legion* (both '28) and Paramount played up Fred as filmdom's ranking Western star, although Tom Mix fans were ready to argue the point. No Western programmers, these! Yet they fizzled at the box office. So did his last — *Kit Carson* ('28). His career was in deep trouble.

Fred went into a period of depression. He had an operation for gallstones. He was taken ill in December and died on Christmas Day. The cause of death was said to be tetanus, the result of stepping on a rusty nail. He was only 38 years old.

Wally Wales would later ride Silver King in several Westerns.

Serial

1923

The Eagle's Talons. Univ., [15 Chapters] D: Duke Worne; SP: Anthony Coldeway, Jefferson Moffitt, Bertram Millhauser; S. Theodore Wharton, Bertram Millhauser; LP: Fred Thomson, Ann Little, Al Wilson, Herbert Fortier, Roy Tompkins, Joe Bonomo, George Magrill, Albert J. Smith.

CHIEF THUNDERCLOUD

Victor Daniels, better known as Chief Thundercloud, was born in Muskogee, Oklahoma, in 1899. As a young man he worked as a cowboy, miner, boxer and rodeo performer before entering movies in 1928. He appeared in *The Big Trail* ('30), *Battling with Buffalo Bill* ('31), *The Last Frontier* ('32), *Rustlers of Red Dog* ('35), *Custer's Last Stand* ('36), *The Painted Stallion* ('37), *Wild West Days* ('37), *The Great Adventures of Wild Bill Hickok* ('38) and *Flaming Frontiers* ('38) before landing the role that would identify him thereafter.

That role was Tonto, the Lone Ranger's

faithful companion, in both *The Lone Ranger* ('38) and *The Lone Ranger Rides Again* ('39), two of Republic's better Western serials.

In features he could be seen in *Singing Vagabond* ('35), *Rustler's Paradise* ('35), *The Farmer Takes a Wife* ('35), *Ramona* ('36), *The Charge of the Light Brigade* ('36) and *Renfrew of the Royal Mounted* ('37).

In 1939, Paramount cast him in the title role of *Geronimo*; he again portrayed the famed Indian fighter in *I Killed Geronimo* ('50). In '40, he appeared in *Typhoon, Hudson's Bay, Fighting Mad, Wyoming* and *Murder on the Yukon*. In '41, he had a principal role in *Silver Stallion*, and also appeared in *Western Union* and *Young Buffalo Bill*. In '42, he was in *Shut My Big Mouth* and *My Gal Sal*.

In '43, Thundercloud co-starred with Hoot Gibson and Bob Steele in *Outlaw Trail* and *Sonora Stage Coach* and in '44 he could be seen in *The Fighting Seebees* and *Buffalo Bill*. Later features included *Nob Hill* ('45), *Badman's Territory* ('46), *Ride, Ranger, Ride* ('46), *Renegade Girl* ('46), *King of the Stallions* ('46), *Romance of the West* ('47), *Unconquered* ('47), *Blazing Across the Pecos* ('48), *The Beautiful Blonde from Bashful Bend* ('49), *Call of the Forest* ('49), *A Ticket to Tomahawk* ('50), *Indian Scout* ('50), *Colt .45* ('50), *Annie Get Your Gun* ('50), *Tomahawk Trail* ('50), *Last of the Buccaneers* ('51), *Santa Fe* ('51), *Buffalo Bill in Tomahawk Territory* ('52) and *The Halfbreed* ('52).

Other serials in which he played are *The Valley of Vanishing Men* ('42), *Overland Mail* ('42), *Daredevils of the West* ('43), *Raiders of Ghost City* ('44), *Black Arrow* ('44) and *The Phantom Rider* ('46).

Chief Thundercloud died from cancer at age 56 on November 30, 1955. For those old enough to remember, he will always be thought of as the original Tonto.

Serials

1930

The Indians Are Coming. Univ., [12 Chapters] D/P: Henry MacRae; LP: Tim McCoy, Al-lene Ray, Charles Roy, Edmund Cobb, Francis Ford, Bud Osborne, Dick Hatton, Lafe McKee, Chief Thundercloud, Bob Reeves.

1931

Battling with Buffalo Bill. Univ., [12 Chapters] D: Ray Taylor; P: Henry MacRae; LP: Tom Tyler, Rex Bell, Lucile Browne, Francis Ford, William Desmond, Yakima Canutt, Chief Thundercloud.

1932

The Last Frontier. RKO, [12 Chapters] D: Spencer G. Bennet, Thomas L. Story; LP: Creighton Chaney [Lon Chaney, Jr.], Dorothy Gulliver, Mary Jo Desmond, Francis X. Bushman, Jr., Joe Bonomo, Slim Cole, Pete Morrison, Yakima Canutt, Chief Thundercloud, William Desmond, Frank Lackteen.

1935

Rustlers of Red Dog. Univ., [12 Chapters] D: Louis Friedlander [Lew Landers]; LP: Johnny Mack Brown, Joyce Compton, Walter Miller, Raymond Hatton, Harry Woods, Charles K. French, Jack Rockwell, Wally Wales [Hal Taliaferro], Chief Thundercloud, Al Ferguson.

1936

Custer's Last Stand. S & S, [15 Chapters] D: Elmer Clifton; LP: Rex Lease, William Farnum, Reed Howes, Dorothy Gulliver, Lona Andre, Ruth Mix, George Chesebro, Nancy Caswell, Franklyn Farnum, Helen Gibson, Jack Rockwell.

1937

The Painted Stallion. Rep., [12 Chapters] D: William Witney, Alan James, Ray Taylor; LP: Ray Corrigan, Hoot Gibson, Hal Taliaferro, Jack Perrin, LeRoy Mason, Julie Thayer, Sammy McKim, Paul Lopez.

Wild West Days. Univ., [13 Chapters] D: Ford Beebe, Cliff Smith; LP: Johnny Mack Brown, Lynn Gilbert, Robert Kortman, Frank Yaconelli, Walter Miller, Al Bridge, Charles Stevens, Chief Thundercloud.

1938

The Great Adventures of Wild Bill Hickok. Col., [15 Chapters] D: Mack V. Wright, Sam

Nelson; LP: Gordon (Bill) Elliott, Carole Wayne, Frankie Darro, Monte Blue, Dickie Jones, Sammy McKim, Chief Thundercloud.

Flaming Frontiers. Univ., [15 Chapters] D: Ray Taylor, Alan James; LP: Johnny Mack Brown, Eleanor Hansen, Ralph Bowman [John Archer], Charles Middleton, Charles Stevens, Chief Thundercloud.

The Lone Ranger. Rep., [15 Chapters] D: William Witney, John English; LP: Lee Powell, Chief Thundercloud, Lynne Roberts, Herman Brix, Lane Chandler, Hal Taliaferro, Stanley Andrews, George Letz [Montgomery], John Merton, Jack Rockwell.

1939

The Lone Ranger Rides Again. Rep., [15 Chapters] D: William Witney, John English; LP: Robert Livingston, Chief Thundercloud, Duncan Renaldo, Jinx Falken, J. Farrell MacDonald, Rex Lease, William Gould, Eddie Dean.

1942

The Valley of Vanishing Men. Col., [15 Chapters] D: Spencer G. Bennet; LP: Bill Elliott, Slim Summerville, Carmen Morales, Kenneth MacDonald, Jack Ingram, Tom London, I. Stanford Jolley.

Overland Mail. Univ., [15 Chapters] D: Ford Beebe, John Rawlins; LP: Lon Chaney, Jr., Don Terry, Noah Beery, Jr., Helen Parrish, Noah Beery, Sr., Tom Chatterton, Bob Baker, Charles Stevens, Jack Rockwell.

1943

Daredevils of the West. Rep., [12 Chapters] D: John English; LP: Allan Lane, Kay Aldridge, Eddie Acuff, William Haade, Robert Frazer, Ted Adams.

1944

Raiders of Ghost City. Univ., [13 Chapters] D: Ray Taylor, Lewis Collins; LP: Dennis Moore, Wanda McKay, Lionel Atwill, Joe Sawyer, Regis Toomey, Virginia Christine, Eddy Waller, Edmund Cobb, Jack Ingram, Chief Thundercloud.

Black Arrow. Col., [15 Chapters] D: Lew Landers; LP: Robert Scott, Adele Jergens, Kenneth MacDonald, Robert Williams, Charles Middleton.

1946

The Phantom Rider. Rep., [12 Chapters] D: Spencer G. Bennet, Fred Brannon; LP: Robert Kent, Peggy Stewart, LeRoy Mason, George J. Lewis, Kenne Duncan, Hal Taliaferro, Chief Thundercloud.

LOLA TODD

Lola was born May 14, 1904, in New York. Her mother's maiden name was Wood, and at one time she was head of publicity at Tiffany Studios. Information on Lola's father is lacking. Lola was a Wampas Baby Star in 1925, but a bright cinematic future for her did not materialize. Following is a list of some of her features and her character's name in the film:

Dark Stairways ('24) — Stenographer; *The Iron Man* ('24) — Mimi; *The Demon* ('26) — Goldie Fleming; *The Tough Guy* ('26) — June Hardy; *The Count of Luxembourg* ('26) — Juliette; *The Fighting Peacemakers* ('26) — Jess Marshall; *The Bells* ('26) — Annette; *Remember* ('26) — Constance Pomeroy; *The Scarlet Streak* ('26) — Mary Crawford; *The War Horse* ('27) — Audrey Evans; *Red Clay* ('27) — Betty Morgan; *The Harvester* ('27) — Nurse; *Wallflowers* ('28) — Theodora; *Taking a Chance* ('28) — Jessie Smith

In the last listed film, *Taking a Chance*,

she had the female lead opposite cowboy Rex Bell.

Lola lived to be 91 years old, dying in Los Angeles on July 31, 1995.

Serials

1923

Ghost City. Univ., [15 Chapters] D: Jay Marchant; LP: Pete Morrison, Margaret Morris, Frank Rice, Al Wilson, Bud Osborne, Lola Todd, Alfred Allen, Princess Neela.

1924

The Iron Man. Univ., [15 Chapters] D: Jay Marchant; LP: Lucien Albertini, Margaret Morris, Joe Bonomo, Jack Daugherty, Lola Todd, Rose Dione, William Welsh, Jean DuBriac, Harry Mann.

1925

The Scarlet Streak. Univ., [10 Chapters] D: Henry MacRae; S: Leigh Jacobson; LP: Jack Daugherty, Lola Todd, John Elliott, Albert J. Smith, Al Prisco, Virginia Ainsworth.

1927

Return of the Riddle Rider. Univ., [10 Chapters] D: Robert Hill, Jay Marchant; SP/S: Arthur B. Reeve, Fred J. McConnell; LP: William Desmond, Lola Todd, Scotty Mattraw, Norbett Myles, Tom London, Grace Cunard.

ALINE TOWNE

Aline Towne was Republic's last serial queen, but unfortunately she never had a role the caliber of Jungle Girl, Nyoka, the Tiger Woman or Panther Girl. She was given the traditional subservient woman's role and had few chances of obtaining superior film footage, dialogue or wardrobe. Though competent enough, she did not have that special magnetism of such serial heroines as Frances Gifford, Phyllis Coates, Jean Rogers, Kay Aldridge, Lynne Roberts or Adrian Booth, though she made a larger number of serials. More fans probably remember Carol Forman as the Black Widow or Frances Gifford as Jungle Girl than remember any of Towne's five roles.

Aline was competent and professional enough but she came along in the dying days of cliffhangers when budgets were trimmed to the bone, stock footage used was increased and scripts were aimed at juveniles—*young* juveniles!

In *The Invisible Monster* ('50), she is

Ken Curtis and Aline Towne in *Don Daredevil Rides Again* (Republic, 1951).

an insurance investigator assigned to work with Richard Webb and track down the Phantom Ruler (Stanley Price), a power-mad genius with the secret of invisibility.

In *Don Daredevil Rides Again* ('51), she is a rancher opposite Ken Curtis. According to Jack Mathis in his book *Valley of the Cliffhangers*, this serial was made "to match the extensive library clips earmarked for recycling to maintain the serial's ecological viability in a regressive wasteland of theater attendance ... born out of a need to suppress inflationary production costs through the exploitation of stock footage from previous Zorro serials, but without the benefit of the Zorro name."

Radar Men from the Moon ('52) finds her as the assistant to Commando Cody (George Wallace), fighting to thwart the ruler of the moon (Roy Barcroft) in his plot to overthrow Earth.

In *Zombies of the Stratosphere* ('52), she is assistant to Judd Holdren, an executive in the Inter-Planetary Patrol. The story has to do with alien creatures attempting to displace Earth from its orbit through a gigantic atomic explosion, so that *their* planet can move into the void and enjoy a more favorable climate.

In her final episodic action thriller, *Trader Tom of the China Seas* ('54), she plays a nurse who, with Trader Tom (Harry Lauter) becomes involved in political intrigue and insurgency on a South Seas island after World War II. Aline never had the following or the stories to lift her out of the ordinary classification of heroines who always looked helpless and weak. The serials themselves were mundane affairs. Quality had slipped perceptibly.

Republic tried a Commando Cody TV series with Judd Holdren in the Cody role instead of Wallace and with Aline continuing as his aide. The series was short-lived.

Aline had been a beauty queen at the universities of Wisconsin and Iowa. She won a *Chicago Daily News* personality–beauty contest over hundreds of contestants, which brought her to the attention of MGM in 1948. She had bit roles in *A Date with Judy*,

The Kissing Bandit, Easter Parade and other films. Going to Republic in 1950, she essayed a supporting role in *Harbor of Missing Men* starring Richard Denning and was given the heroine role in Monte Hale's *The Vanishing Westerner*. She supported Steve Cochran and Virginia Grey in *Highway 301* ('50) and played opposite Allan Lane in *Rough Riders of Durango* ('51). Other features in which she appeared are *I Can Get That for You Wholesale* (Twentieth Century-Fox, '53), *Julie* (MGM, '56), *The Brass Bottle* (Univ., '64), *Send Me No Flowers* (Univ., '64), *A Guide for the Married Man* (Twentieth Century-Fox, 67) and *Song of Norway* (Cinerama, '70).

Aline was active in television and appeared on such shows as *The Lone Ranger*, *Hopalong Cassidy*, *Wyatt Earp*, *Maverick*, *Tales of Wells Fargo*, *Whispering Smith*, *Superman*, *Rough Riders*, *Colt .45*, *Gray Ghost* and *Man Without a Gun*.

Aline died February 2, 1996, at age 66.

Serials

1950

The Invisible Monster. Rep., [12 Chapters] D: Fred C. Brannon; SP: Ronald Davidson; AP: Franklyn Adreon; Cam: Ellis W. Carter; Mus: Stanley Wilson; LP: Richard Webb, Aline Towne, Lane Bradford, Stanley Price, Tom Steele.

1951

Don Daredevil Rides Again. Rep., [12 Chapters] D: Fred C. Brannon; AP: Franklyn Adreon; SP: Ronald Davidson; Cam: Ellis W. Carter; Mus: Stanley Wilson; LP: Ken Curtis, Aline Towne, Roy Barcroft, Lane Bradford.

1952

Radar Men from the Moon. Rep., [12 Chapters] D: Fred C. Brannon; SP: Ronald Davidson; AP: Franklyn Adreon; Cam: John MacBurnie; Mus: Stanley Wilson; LP: George Wallace, Aline Towne, Roy Barcroft, William Bakewell.

Zombies of the Stratosphere. Rep., [12 Chapters] D: Fred C. Brannon; SP: Ronald Davidson; AP: Franklyn Adreon; Cam: John Mac-Burnie; Mus: Stanley Wilson; LP: Judd Holdren, Aline Towne, Wilson Wood, Stanley Waxman, John Crawford, Leonard Nimoy.

1954

Trader Tom of the China Seas. Rep., [12 Chapters] P/D: Franklyn Adreon; SP: Ronald Davidson; Mus: R. Dale Butts; Cam: Bud Thackery; LP: Harry Lauter, Aline Towne, Lyle Talbot, Robert Shayne, Ramsay Hill, Tom Steele.

WILLIAM TRACY

William Tracy trained for the stage at the American Academy of Dramatic Arts and appeared in a number of Broadway plays and musicals. He went to Hollywood in 1938 to repeat his stage role in *Brother Rat*, playing a nervous young military school plebe; then he was browbeaten little messenger Pepi in *The Shop Around the Corner*, auto-crazy young hillbilly Dude Lester in *Tobacco Road* and Mac in Kay Harris' *Tillie the Toiler*.

Tracy got the starring role in *Terry and the Pirates* ('40), 15 thrill-packed episodes set in the Asian jungles, where Terry's dad disappeared while seeking the secrets of a lost civilization. His expedition has been captured by the jungle pirates of Fang (Dick Curtis), local warlord who is after a legendary treasure said to be hidden beneath the lost civilization's Temple of Mara. Terry and his friends battle Fang, his henchman Stanton (Jack Ingram) and Fang's Tiger Men.

Tracy later starred in the Hal Roach comedies *Tanks a Million* ('42), *About Face* ('42), *Fall In* ('43) and *Yanks Ahoy* ('43).

He was also in 1948's *Here Comes Trouble* and *The Walls of Jericho* and 1949's *Henry the Rainmaker*.

In the '50s, he was comic support in *On the Sunny Side of the Street*, *The Wings of Eagles*, *As You Were* and *Mr. Walkie Talkie*.

Tracy was born in Pittsburgh on December 1, 1917, and died in Los Angeles in 1967.

Serial

1940

Terry and the Pirates. Col., [15 Chapters] D: James W. Horne; SP: Mark Layton, George Morgan, Joseph Levering; P: Larry Darmour; Cam: James S. Brown, Jr.; Mus: Lee Zahler; LP: William Tracy, Granville Owen, Joyce Bryant, Allen Jung, Dick Curtis, Sheila Darcy, Charles King, Forrest Taylor.

GENE TUNNEY

James Joseph Tunny was born in New York City on March 27, 1897, of Irish

Catholic parents. A Greenwich Village longshoreman's son, Tunney overcame an assortment of physical handicaps and acquired a distaste for violence. He was a dropout at 16 and became a self-taught Shakespearean scholar. A steamship company employed him before World War I and he spent many hours in gyms.

By the time he joined the U.S. Marine Corps, he had taken part in 11 professional fights. In 1919, he won the light heavyweight championship of the American Expeditionary Forces in Paris. Tunney tried unsuccessfully to get back his $16.50-a-week shipping job when he left the Marines after the war. Then he began accepting professional fights.

He had done so well by 1922 that he was matched with Battling Levinsky for the light heavyweight title. Tunney outpointed his opponent in 12 rounds. He lost the title the same year to Harry Greb — the only defeat in his entire career of 76 fights. He then regained the title the following year in a rematch with Greb.

Tunney fought Georges Carpentier of France on July 27, 1924, and knocked his opponent out in the fifteenth round. This victory, plus subsequent wins over Tommy Gibbons and Bartley Madden, earned Tunney a shot at Jack Dempsey's World Heavyweight Title.

The fight took place on September 23, 1926, at the Sesquicentennial Stadium in Philadelphia. The world of sports was astounded when Tunney won the fight and the title on a ten-round decision.

The two fought again at Soldier Field in Chicago on September 22, 1927. There was a crowd of 104,943 people who paid $2,658,660. Dempsey, who was losing the fight, cornered Tunney in the seventh round and smashed him to the canvas with a series of blows to the jaw.

Tunney was stunned, and Dempsey stood over him — ready to finish him for good as soon as he rose to his feet. The referee ordered Dempsey to a neutral corner under new rules that had been established. But Dempsey continued to glower at the fallen champion. Finally, after about five seconds, Dempsey realized his mistake and went to a corner. Barry began to count and when he reached nine Tunney got up. Whether Dempsey's failure to obey the rule cost him the title has been a matter of dispute since.

Tunney worked out for the bout by running backwards for miles while zinging the left jab, and the practice served him well.

Tunney starred in the serial *The Fighting Marine* ('26), obviously made to capitalize on his name. He is a reporter seeking to protect an heiress (Marjorie Day) who, under the terms of a will, must reside in a Western mining town for six months. Naturally there are those who are determined that the conditions of the will not be met in order that they might gain the inheritance.

Tunney fought Tom Heeney in 1928 and, after winning by a TKO, retired from the ring undefeated. That same year he married Mary Josephine Lauder, a millionaire's daughter. They had three sons and a daughter. John, the eldest son, became U.S. Senator from California in 1971.

During World War II, Tunney served as Director of Athletics and Physical Fitness for the U.S. Navy. He authored the books *A Man Must Fight* (Boston, 1932) and *Arms for Living* (New York, 1941).

In 1970, Gene's daughter Joan Tunney Wilkinson, was committed to a mental institution after admitting she killed her husband with an ax as he lay asleep in bed. A psychiatrist testified that she suffered from schizophrenia and might kill again.

Gene Tunney, 80, World Heavyweight Champion from 1926 until he retired undefeated in 1928, died of a circulatory ailment in Greenwich, Connecticut, on November 8, 1978.

Serial

1926

The Fighting Marine. Pathé, [10 Chapters] D: Spencer G. Bennet; SP: Frank Leon Smith; LP: Gene Tunney, Marjorie Day, Walter Miller, Virginia Vance, Sherman Ross, Ann May Walthall, Wally Oettel, Jack Anthony, David Dunbar, Mike Donlin.

GEORGE TURNER

Historian William Russell endeavored to find out what happened to George Turner after he disappeared from the screen in 1948. He had no luck. And so the question remains, "Whatever happened to George Turner?"

Turner's one starring role was in Republic's *Son of Zorro* ('47). His other serial credits, in 1939 and 1945, were small supporting roles. In features his roles were seldom large but they were numerous: 1938's *I Am the Law*, 1941's *Among the Living, I Wanted Wings* and *Pacific Blackout*; 1942's *Dr. Broadway, The Fleet's In, The Forest Rangers, The Glass Key, My Favorite Blonde, Tramp, Tramp, Tramp, True to the Army* and *The Wife Takes a Flyer*; 1944's *The Contender, Here Come the Waves, I'll Be Seeing You, The Old Texas Trail* and *Practically Yours*; 1945's *Bring On the Girls, Duffy's Tavern* and *What Next, Corporal Hargrove*; 1946's *Cinderella Jones, Moon Over Montana, Rendezvous with Annie, The Return of Rusty* and *The Well-Groomed Bride*; 1947's *The Beginning of the End, Crossfire, Range Beyond the Blue* and *Vigilantes of Boomtown*; and 1948's *Call Northside 777* and *Race Street*.

Serials

1939

Daredevils of the Red Circle. Rep., [12 Chapters] D: William Witney, John English; LP: Charles Quigley, Herman Brix [Bruce Bennet], David Sharpe, Carole Landis, Charles Middleton, George Chesebro, Raymond Bailey.

Mandrake the Magician. Col., [12 Chapters] D: Sam Nelson, Norman Deming; LP: Warren Hull, Doris Weston, Al Kikume, Rex Downing, Edward Earle, Forbes Murray, George Chesebro.

Flying G-Men. Col., [15 Chapters] D: Ray Taylor, James W. Horne; LP: Robert Paige, Richard Fiske, James Craig, Lorna Gray [Adrian Booth], Don Beddoe, Dick Curtis, Ann Doran, George Chesebro.

1945

Jungle Raiders. Col., [15 Chapters] D: Lesley Selander; LP: Kane Richmond, Eddie Quillan, Veda Ann Borg, Carol Hughes, Janet Shaw, John Elliott, Jack Ingram, Charles King.

1947

Son of Zorro. Rep., [15 Chapters] D: Spencer Bennet, Fred C. Brannon; SP: Basil Dickey, Franklyn Adreon, Jesse Duffy, Sol Shor; AP: Ronald Davidson; Cam: Bud Thackery; Mus: Mort Glickman; LP: George Turner, Peggy Stewart, Roy Barcroft, Edward Cassidy, Ernie Adams, Stanley Price, Edmund Cobb, Charles King.

TOM TYLER

Tom was born Vincent Markowski on August 9, 1903, in Port Henry, New York, hardly a name or a desirable birthplace for a hero of the Old West. His childhood was spent mostly in Port Henry. Tom excelled in athletics and following his high school graduation perfected his skill as a weightlifter while working as a seaman on a merchant steamer, mining coal in Pennsylvania, lumbering in the Northwest, performing as a boxer and muscleman in a circus sideshow, and working a few other assorted jobs. He became a champion weightlifter and established records that stood for 14 years.

Arriving in Hollywood in 1924, young Markowski was determined to swap his weights for an acting career. After he took off his shirt to flex his muscles a few times, Vince had no difficulty in finding work as an extra. A casting director hired him for a small part in *Ben Hur* in 1924 which was followed by a bit in *Three Weeks* and a bit as an Indian in the serial *Leatherstocking*. He caught the attention of MGM executives who offered him a five-year contract, but he refused it. The young man who came to Hollywood penniless, who struggled from job to job missing many a meal, turned down one of Hollywood's leading studios. When asked why, he simply said he thought he could do better. And better he did. He signed for a Western series for R-C Pictures, released through FBO. Although he had never ridden a horse, he jumped at the chance to be a cowboy star and quickly learned the rudiments of horsemanship, eventually becoming an expert rider.

Tom's first Western was *Let's Go Gallagher* ('25), and go he did — galloping through smoke and bullets with six-shooters blazing in a red-hot action story. His billing was as Tom Tyler; never again would he be known as Vincent Markowski.

Twenty-eight more whirlwind thrillers followed for R-C/FBO, with fast, furious action, gunplay galore, and Tom himself in some of the most daring stunts ever filmed. He was only 23 and in the pink of condition. What he didn't have in thespian talents he more than made up for in red-blooded stories built around his athletic prowess. Little Frankie Darro was in most of the Tyler westerns, and the two worked well together. It was refreshing to see stories built around a talented youngster of Darro's caliber and not have to be subjected to ludicrousness of an all-thumbs, cornball acting sidekick with the brains of a cow.

Doris Hill, Peggy Montgomery, Jean Arthur and Nora Lane were among the bevy of heroines gracing the Tyler Westerns. Although romance was never really played up much in these action opuses, the actresses' talent and beauty added considerably to the overall enjoyment of the films, for they had above-average acting ability and succeeded in making a name for themselves as Western heroines.

When FBO temporarily ceased making Westerns in 1929, Tyler moved over to Syndicate, as did Bob Steele, Bob Custer, and some others. He made a total of eight silent Westerns, most of them directed by J.P. McGowan, who was notoriously inept as a filmmaker. While Syndicate was tooling up for the production of sound features, Mascot hired Tom for the lead in the sound serial *The Phantom of the West* ('30). His deep, commanding voice registered satisfactorily and was in keeping with his physical appearance; thus, his voice was an asset rather than, as in the cases of John Gilbert, Art Acord, and Tom Mix, a liability.

Tom was ideally suited to play a bigger-than-life hero and was enthusiastically accepted by Saturday matinee audiences. In fact, only Buster Crabbe exceeded him in popularity as a cliffhanger super hero in the sound era. In the next 13 years Tom was to star in six more serials: *Battling with Buffalo Bill* ('31), *Jungle Mystery* ('31), *Clancy of the Mounted* ('31), *The Phantom of the Air* ('31), *Adventures of Captain Marvel* ('41), and *The Phantom* ('43). These serials provided roughly 28 to 30 hours of escapist fare spread out over 85 weeks in 20 to 25-minute segments. Thus, the serials gave him a lot of exposure, which benefited his later features.

Tom's first sound Westerns were for Syndicate, beginning with *West of Cheyenne* ('31), followed by *God's Country and the Man* ('31) and *A Rider of the Plains* ('31). During the 1931-32 season he completed eight Westerns for the newly-formed Monogram Pictures, and then moved over to Freuler-Monarch for four of the better independent Westerns of 1933. *The Forty-Niners* ('32) was probably the best of the Monarch features.

Tom signed with Bernard B. Ray's Reliable Pictures (released through William Steiner) in 1934 and kicked up a lot of trail dust as he charged through eighteen slam-bang shoot 'em ups as a virtuous hero determined to see justice triumph and the heroine's virtue remain spotless. In a change of character, though, he played Sundown Saunders, a gunman with a conscience, in RKO's all-star Western, *Powdersmoke Range* ('35), and an unsympathetic gang leader in the same studio's *The Last Outlaw* ('36). Both films starred Harry Carey and Hoot Gibson.

In 1936-37 Tyler made eight programmers for Sam Katzman's Victory Pictures and then toured for a season with Wallace Brothers Circus as its stellar attraction.

After the circus tour Tom was unable to secure another series and so began to play villainous and character roles. His portrayal of Luke Plummer in John Ford's classic *Stagecoach* ('39) was convincing evidence that Tom was capable of more than simply "They went that-a-way" dramatics. *Frontier Marshal* ('39), *Gone with the Wind* ('39), *Brother Orchid* ('40), *Charokee Strip* ('40), *Texas Rangers Ride Again* ('40), *The Grapes of Wrath* ('40), and *The Mummy's Hand* ('40) gave him further opportunity to expand his dramatic boundaries.

Tyler was given the "Stony Brooke" role in the Three Mesquiteers series at Republic when Robert Livingston dropped out. Co-starring in 12 films with Tom was Bob Steele. Rufe Davis was in six, and Jimmie Dodd was in six. Several non-Westerns roles were taken by Tom during this period of time, most notably the lead in *The Adventures of Captain Marvel*. Probably he is best remembered for this Republic serial, although Columbia's *The Phantom* had its devotees. Republic turned out a glossy product that spelled quality in the low-budget field. The Three Mesquiteers series was a popular one, making the "top 10" list in 1941, '42, and '43.

Tyler freelanced alter 1943, appearing in *The Navy Way* ('44) with Jean Parker and Robert Lowery, *Boss of Boomtown* ('44) with Rod Cameron, *Ladies of Washington* ('44) with Trudy Marshall and Anthony Quinn, *The Princess and the Pirate* ('44) with Bob Hope and Virginia Mayo, *San Antonio* ('45) with Errol Flynn, *They Were Expendable* ('45), and *Sing Me A Song of Texas* ('45), in which he had one of the leads. Playing opposite him was Rosemary Lane; the Hoosier Hot Shots and Guinn (Big Boy) Williams were also featured.

After 1945 it was all downhill for Tom as crippling arthritis and other physical complications sapped away at his once great physique. His last several years on the screen were spent mostly playing heavies, at which he was very good. Few could play a bad gunman more convincingly than Tom.

His ill health forced his retirement from the screen after his role in *Cow Country* ('53) with Edmund O'Brien. Tom had to bow out of a proposed television series, while continuing to watch his once-muscular physique deteriorate.

And so the last sunset arrived for yet another great cowboy star. His last couple of years were spent in his sister's home in Detroit. There he died on May 1, 1950. He will be remembered for as long as there are those who can recall the days of the "B" Western when heroic saddle aces engaged in thrilling conflicts of wits, fists, knives, horsemanship, and guns, the *beau ideal* of open-air adventure entertainment. The Tyler sagas usually contained a punch in every minute of action without a lingering pause until the amazing cyclonic finish when Tom produced more dazzling gunplay, hard riding, and desperate fighting than one could find in any other two stories of the wide open spaces.

Serials

1924

Leatherstocking. Pathé. D: George B. Seitz; S: Robert Dillon; LP: Edna Murphy, James Pierce, Harold Miller, David Dunbar, Frank

Lackteen, Whitehorse, Vincent Markowski (Tom Tyler).

1930

The Phantom of the West. Mascot. D: Ross Lederman; S/SP: Wyndham Gittens, Ford Beebe, Bennett Cohen; P: Nat Levine; Camera: Benjamin Kline, Ernest Miller, Joe Novak; LP: Tom Tyler, William Desmond, Dorothy Gulliver, Tom Santschi, Joe Bonomo, Philo McCullough, Tom Dugan, Kermit Maynard, Frank Hagney, Dick Dickinson, Pee Wee Holmes, Ernie Adams, Halee Sullivan.

1931

Battling with Buffalo Bill. Univ. D: Ray Taylor; S: William Cody; SP: George Plympton, Ella O'Neill; P: Henry MacRae; LP: Tom Tyler, Rex Bell, Lucile Browne, William Desmond, Chief Thunderbird, Francis Ford, Bud Osborne, Yakima Canutt, Joe Bonomo, Franklyn Farnum, Jim Corey, Edmund Cobb.

1932

Jungle Mystery. Univ. D: Ray Taylor; SP: Ella O'Neill, George Plympton, Basil Dickey, George Morgan; S: Talbot Mundy — "The Ivory Trail" LP: Tom Tyler, Cecilia Parker, William Desmond, Philo McCullough, Noah Beery, Jr., Carmelita Geraghty, Sam Baker.

1933

Clancy of the Mounted. Univ. D: Ray Taylor; S: Based on the poem by Robert W. Service; SP: Basil Dickey, Harry O. Hoyt, Ella O'Neill; P: Henry MacRae; LP: Tom Tyler, Jacqueline Wells (Julie Bishop), William Desmond, Rosalie Roy, Francis Ford, Tom London, Fred Humes, Al Ferguson, Frank Lackteen, Earl McCarthy, William Thorne, Monte Montague, Steve Clemente.

The Phantom of the Air. Univ. D: Ray Taylor; S: Ella O'Neill; SP: Basil Dickey, George Plympton; LP: Tom Tyler, Gloria Shea, LeRoy Mason, Hugh Enfield, William Desmond, Sidney Bracey, Walter Brennan, Jennie Cramer, Cecil Kellogg.

1941

Adventures of Captain Marvel. Rep. D: William Witney, John English; SP: Ronald Davidson, Norman S. Hall, Arch B. Heath, Joseph Poland, Sol Shor; Assoc. P: Hiram S. Brown, Jr.; LP: Tom Tyler, Frank Coghlan, Jr., William Benedict, Louise Currie, Robert Strange, Harry Worth, Gerald Mohr, Bryant Washburn, John Davidson, Reed Hadley, Jack Mulhall, Eddie Dew, Edward Cassidy, Carleton Young, David Sharpe, Bud Geary, Ted Mapes, Nigel de Brulier.

1943

The Phantom. Col. D: B. Reeves Eason; SP: Morgan B. Cox, Victor McLeod, Sherman Lowe, Leslie J. Swabacker. LP: Tom Tyler, Jeanne Bates, Kenneth MacDonald, Frank Shannon, Ace (dog), Guy Kingsford, Joe Devlin, Ernie Adams, John S. Bagni.

RICK VALLIN

Rick Vallin began his movie career in 1941, and before it ended in the mid–60s he had appeared in 15 serials (but never as the main player) and a slew of features.

Desperate Cargo (PRC '41) with Ralph Byrd and Carol Hughes and *Escort Girl* (Continental '41) with Betty Compson and Margaret Marquis were his first screen credits. In 1942, he had a leading role in Monogram's *King of the Stallions*, which also featured Chief Thundercloud. Rick played Little Coyote. In *Secrets of a Co-Ed* (PRC '42), Vallin played a night club owner listed third in the cast behind Otto Kruger and Tina

Thayer. In *Panther's Claw* (PRC '42), he plays the assistant to Police Commissioner Sidney Blackmer. In *Lady from Chungking* (PRC '42), he plays a downed Flying Tigers pilot protected by Anna May Wong. Mae Clarke was also featured. Other 1942 credits are *Pardon My Stripes* (Rep., Sheila Ryan, Bill Henry), *Sleepytime Gal* (Rep., Judy Canova, Tom Brown) and *Youth on Parade* (Rep., Ruth Terry, John Hubbard).

Vallin's first of 15 serials was *Perils of the Royal Mounted* (Col., '42) playing Little Wolf in support of Nell O'Day and Robert Stevens (Kellard). His film credits for 1943 include *Nearly Eighteen* (Mon., Gale Storm, Bill Henry), in which Rick is a hustler and bookie who befriends Gale; *Riders of the Rio Grande* (Rep., Bob Steele, Tom Tyler, Jimmie Dodd), in which Vallin is the wayward son who is reunited with his father in the end; *Smart Guy* (Mon., Veda Ann Borg, Jack LaRue), with Vallin as a casino operator who kills a patron in his club; *Wagon Tracks West* (Rep., Bill Elliott, Gabby Hayes), co-starring Rick as a young medical school graduate who winds up in a lot of trouble but is aided by Wild Bill; *Clancy Street Boys* (Mon., The East Side Kids, Noah Beery, Sr.), with Rick as a kidnapper; *Corregidor* (PRC, Otto Kruger, Elissa Landi), in which Rick is Pinky, a tailgunner hero who dies defending nurses; *Ghosts on the Loose* (Mon., The East Side Kids, Ava Gardner), in which Rick marries Ava; *Isle of Forgotten Sins* (PRC, John Carradine, Sidney Toler), as Johnny Pacific, is killed in a fight over gold recovered from the sea. In the comedy *Army Wives* (Mon. '44), Elyse Knox and Rick have trouble getting married; he has only a bit in *The Desert Song* (WB, '44) starring Dennis Morgan and Irene Manning. With only two film appearances in '44 and none in '45, it is probable that he was in World War II service. In *Secrets of a Sorority Girl* (PRC, 1946) featuring Mary Ware, Rick was the head of a gambling organization who kills a motorcycle cop and later dies fleeing the police. *Dangerous Money* (Mon., 1946) features Sidney Toler, Gloria Warren and Vallin is a restaurant owner on Samoa.

In *Last of the Redmen* (Col., 1947) fea-

turing Jon Hall, Buster Crabbe and Julie Bishop, he is Uncas, a friend of the English forces; and in *Two Blondes and a Redhead* (Col., 1947) he is a millionaire who wants to marry Jean Porter. In the Columbia serial *The Sea Hound* ('47) starring Buster Crabbe, Vallin plays Manila Pete. *Brick Bradford* (Col. '47) features him as Sandy Sanderson, friend of Kane Richmond and second lead.

Jungle Jim (Col., 1948) finds Rick as a tribal friend of Jungle Jim (Johnny Weissmuller). In *The Story of Bob and Sally* ('48), an independent production, Rick is the alcoholic husband of Mildred Coles. In the fantasy film *Shamrock Hill* (Eagle-Lion, 1949), Vallin is a lawyer. *Tuna Clipper* (Mon., 1949) features Roddy McDowell, Elena Verdugo and Rick as Elena's brother. He had supporting roles in the 1949 Columbia cliffhangers *Adventures of Sir Galahad* featuring George Reeves and Charles King and *Batman and Robin* with Robert Lowery and Johnny Duncan features.

Captive Girl (Col., 1950) stars Johnny Weissmuller as Jungle Jim, with Rick playing Mahala, village chief and friend of Jungle Jim; in *Comanche Territory* (Univ., 1950) starring Maureen O'Hara and Macdonald Carey, Rick is Pakaneh, a chief's son; in *Killer Shark* (Mon., 1950), Vallin plays Agapito, member of a shark-hunting crew. His further credits include *State Penitentiary* ('50), *Snow Dog* ('50), *The Magic Carpet* ('51), *Jungle Manhunt* ('51), *When the Redskins Rode* ('51), *Hurricane Island* ('51), *Woman in the Dark* ('52), *Voodoo Tiger* ('52), *Aladdin and His Lamp* ('52), *Strange Fascination* ('52), *Bowery to Bagdad* ('53), *The Homesteaders* ('53), *The Marksman* ('53), *The Golden Idol* ('54), *Treasure of Ruby Hills* ('55), *Dial Red O* ('55), *Frontier Gambler* ('56), *The Tijuana Story* ('57), *Escape from Red Rock* ('58), *Pier 5 — Havana* ('59), *The Quick Gun* ('64) and *Cheyenne Autumn* ('64).

Vallin played in eight more serials for Columbia and one for Universal. He had the second lead in *Riding with Buffalo Bill* ('54) and *Adventures of Captain Africa* ('55), and was a major supporting player in the others. In the last serial ever made, *Perils of the Wil-*

derness ('56), Vallin is featured as Little Bear. It was his lot to always serve in the shadow of the hero. In addition to movies, he could be seen in TV shows.

    Vallin died in Los Angeles in 1977 at age 57.

Serials

1942

Perils of the Royal Mounted. Col., [15 Chapters] D: James W. Horne; LP: Nell O'Day, Robert Stevens [Kellard], Herbert Rawlinson, Kenneth MacDonald, Richard Fiske, John Elliott, Rick Vallin, George Chesebro.

1944

The Desert Hawk. Col., [15 Chapters] D: B. Reeves Eason; LP: Gilbert Roland, Mona Maris, Ben Welden, Kenneth MacDonald, Charles Middleton, Frank Lackteen, I. Stanford Jolley, Kermit Maynard, Forrest Taylor, Rick Vallin, Eddie Parker.

1947

The Sea Hound. Col., [15 Chapters] D: Walter B. Eason, Mack Wright; LP: Buster Crabbe, Pamela Blake, James Lloyd, Ralph Hodges, Hugh Prosser, Rick Vallin, Stanley Blystone, Robert Barron, Milton Kibbee.

Brick Bradford. Col., [15 Chapters] D: Spencer G. Bennet; LP: Kane Richmond, Rick Vallin, Linda Johnson, Pierre Watkin, Charles Quigley, Jack Ingram, John Merton, Charles King, Wheeler Oakman, Stanley Blystone, Nelson Leigh.

1949

Batman and Robin. Col., [15 Chapters] D: Spencer G. Bennet; LP: Robert Lowery, Johnny Duncan, Jane Adams, Lyle Talbot, Ralph Graves, Don C. Harvey, Rick Vallin, House Peters, Jr.

Adventures of Sir Galahad. Col., [15 Chapters] D: Spencer G. Bennet; LP: George Reeves, Charles King, William Fawcett, Pat Barton, Hugh Prosser, Lois Hall, Marjorie Stapp, Nelson Leigh, Pierce Lyden, Rick Vallin, Ray Corrigan.

1950

Cody of the Pony Express. Col., [15 Chapters] D: Spencer G. Bennet; LP: Jock Mahoney, Tom London, Jack Ingram, Pierce Lyden, Frank Ellis, Rick Vallin, Michael Whalen, Ben Corbett.

1951

Roar of the Iron Horse. Col., [15 Chapters] D: Spencer G. Bennet, Thomas Carr; LP: Jock Mahoney, Virginia Herrick, William Fawcett, Hal Landon, Jack Ingram, Pierce Lyden, Rick Vallin, Hugh Prosser.

1952

Blackhawk. Col., [15 Chapters] D: Spencer G. Bennet, Fred F. Sears; LP: Kirk Alyn, Carol Forman, John Crawford, Michael Fox, Don C. Harvey, Rick Vallin, Pierce Lyden, Terry Frost, Larry Stewart.

Son of Geronimo. Col., [15 Chapters] D: Spencer G. Bennet; LP: Clayton Moore, Tommy Farrell, Eileen Rowe, Lyle Talbot, John Crawford, Rick Vallin, Bud Osborne, Frank Ellis.

King of the Congo. Col., [15 Chapters] D: Spencer G. Bennet, Wallace Grissell; LP: Buster Crabbe, Gloria Dea, Leonard Penn, Jack Ingram, Rusty Wescoatt, Rick Vallin, William Fawcett, Lee Roberts, Frank Ellis.

1954

Riding with Buffalo Bill. Col., [15 Chapters] D: Spencer G. Bennet; LP: Marshall Reed, Rick Vallin, Joanne Rio, Shirley Whitney, Jack Ingram, Pierce Lyden, William Fawcett, Gregg Barton, Michael Fox.

1955

Adventures of Captain Africa. Col., [15 Chapters] D: Spencer G. Bennet; LP: John Hart, Rick Vallin, Ben Welden, June Howard, Bud Osborne, Terry Frost, Lee Roberts, Paul Marion, Michael Fox.

King of the Carnival. Rep., [12 Chapters] D: Franklyn Adreon; LP: Harry Lauter, Fran Bennett, Keith Richards, Robert Shayne, Rick Vallin, Gregory Gay, Robert Clarke.

1956

Perils of the Wilderness. Col., [15 Chapters] D: Spencer G. Bennet; LP: Dennis Moore, Richard Emory, Eve Anderson [Evelyn Finley], Kenneth MacDonald, Rick Vallin, John Elliott, Pierce Lyden, Bud Osborne, Kermit Maynard.

MARIE WALCAMP

Marie Walcamp, born in Denison, Ohio, on July 27, 1894, was one of the most admired serial queens of the '20s. A charming blonde, daring and resolute, she conquered a legion of fans.

Before entering movies she was a standout in musical comedy for four years with Wever & Fields, Kolb & Dill and De Wolf Hopper. With a remarkable personality, she was destined to become famous in the movies. Before being contracted to Universal, she starred in several two-reelers for 101 Bison in 1913.

She could be happy one moment and somberly reflective the next. She wasn't exactly beautiful, but her great individuality marked her as one having a beautiful soul. She was reserved and liked to spend odd moments in reading and study.

Marie supported Irene Castle and Milton Sills in their famous serial *Patria*, produced and released by Pathé in 15 episodes on January 14, 1917. Also in the cast was Warner Oland. She starred in several Universal serials, the first being *Liberty, A Daughter of the U.S.A.* ('16) in 20 episodes. This was the first all–Western serial, in which she was cast with Jack Holt, G. Raymond Nye, Roy Stewart and Neal Hart. Tom London, then billed as Leonard Clapham, appeared in a supporting role.

The next serial for Marie was the 16-episode *The Red Ace*, released on October 22, 1917. The plot was set in the wild mining country of Canada. A thrilling adventure story, it increased Walcamp's popularity. *The Lion's Claw*, released on April 6, 1918, in 18 episodes, was one of her most popular serials. During the filming, Marie was attacked by one of the lions and bore a scar for the rest of her life.

The Red Glove, released on March 17, 1919, in 18 episodes with Pat O'Malley co-starring, followed. In *The Dragon's Net*, released August 23, 1920, Harlan Tucker, her former partner in the Morosco Theatre of Los Angeles, was second in the cast. Some episodes were filmed in Tokyo, Japan. There Marie and Tucker were married and they returned from the Orient as wife and husband. The original title of *The Dragon's Net* was *The Petals of Lae Lee*, alluding to a flower with gold petals which had the gift of preserving youth forever.

Along with Pearl White, Ruth Roland and Helen Holmes, Marie became one of the popular serial stars prior to World War I. Known as "The daredevil of the movies," Marie won film stardom for fearless deeds such as jumping overboard in mid-ocean at a height of 40 feet and executing stunts with wild jungle animals. She did not hesitate to perform any hazardous stunt if she believed in her director. The daring stunts made her a popular star, but the fearless deeds limited her as to the type of roles she could play.

Marie was no stranger to jungle pictures, having previously starred in the two-reelers *From the Lion's Jaws* ('14), *The Jungle Master* ('14), *The Jungle Queen* ('15) and *A Daughter of the Jungle* ('15). For the most part, plots were negligible, mere threads of interest on which to hang the incidents featuring lions, leopards, chimpanzees and snakes.

In the next several years Marie starred in a number of short Westerns and action films and in a few features. It was as Tempest Cody that Marie gained her Western laurels in a series of two-reelers for Universal.

Marie was keeping her identification with Westerns intact in such outings as *A Railroad Bandit* ('16), a splendid two-reeler written by Wright Roberts. A bandit organization, a box of gold bullion and some attractive mountain scenic effects are among the ingredients. The action is good, including some stirring stunts of various kinds. *The Indian's Lament* ('17) was directed by Henry MacRae and starred Marie as Bess Conolly, loved by both good guy Lee Hill and bad guy E. N. Wallack, and respected by Noble Johnson in his role as Sleepy Horse, a redskin mistreated by Indian agent Wallack. An even meatier role was essayed by Marie in *Tongues of Flame* ('19), in which she plays Teresa, a dance hall girl who has killed her lover in a fit of jealousy. En Route to jail she escapes in the Carquinez Woods and is befriended by L'Eau Dormonte (Al Whitman), an educated half-breed who lives in the hollow trunk of one of the great redwoods. The sheriff (Alfred Allen) grows jealous of Dormonte, whom he thinks has stolen the love of Nellie Wynn (Lilly Clarke), and stumbles upon Teresa while waiting for his rival. Then Dormonte discovers that the sheriff is his own father. Events move fast, but the fates write the final chapter of the tangled romance: Fire sweeps the woods and the trio finds a pyre in the great redwoods that stood long before man.

After *The Dragon's Net*, Marie made only a few more pictures before retiring to devote herself to domestic and non-movie pursuits. In 1927 she came out of retirement to play a principal role in FBO's *In a Moment of Temptation*, then gave up moviemaking for good. She was found dead in a gas-filled room in her home in Los Angeles, November 17, 1936. Her body was discovered by her husband, Harlan Tucker.

Her passing was scarcely noticed by those who had once thrilled to her screen exploits. But true-blue serial buffs will always remember Marie as one of the heroines who molded the genre in its early years, and Western aficionados will not soon forget her Tempest Cody shoot-'em-ups when the roll of great Western heroines is prepared.

Serials

1916

Liberty (A Daughter of the U.S.A.). Univ., [20 Chapters] D: Jacques Jaccard, Henry MacRae; P/S: W. B. Pearson; SP: Jacques Jaccard; LP: Marie Walcamp, Jack Holt, Eddie Polo, Neal Hart, Roy Stewart, Leonard Clapham [Tom London].

1917

Patria. Pathé, [15 Chapters] D: Theodore and Leo Wharton, Jacques Jaccard; LP: Irene Castle, Milton Sills, Warner Oland, Dorothy Green, Wallace Beery, Marie Walcamp.

The Red Ace. Univ., [16 Chapters] D/SP: Jacques Jaccard; LP: Marie Walcamp, Larry Peyton, L. M. Wells, Bobby Mack, Charles Brinley.

1918

The Lion's Claw. Univ., [18 Chapters] D: Jacques Jaccard, Harry Harvey; SP: W. B. Pearson, Jacques Jaccard; S: W. B. Pearson; LP: Marie Walcamp, Roy Hanford, Neal Hart, Thomas Lingham, Gertrude Astor, Frank Lanning, Leonard Clapham [Tom London].

1919

The Red Glove. Univ., [18 Chapters] D: J. P. McGowan; SP: Hope Loring; S: Douglas Grant; LP: Marie Walcamp, Pat O'Malley, Trueman Van Dyke, Thomas Lingham, Leon De La Mothe.

1920

The Dragon's Net. Univ., [12 Chapters] P/D: Henry MacRae; SP: George Hively, Henry MacRae; S: J. Allen Dunn; LP: Marie Walcamp, Harlan Tucker, Otto Lederer, Wadsworth Harris.

JOHNNIE WALKER

Johnnie Walker was probably most effective in *Old Ironsides* ('26) as young Lt. Decatur, who conceived and carried out the daring scheme to sink the ship *Philadelphia*. The film starred Esther Ralston and Wallace Beery. In *The Third Alarm* ('23), Johnnie was cast opposite Ella Hall in a story about a fire station and Johnnie's horse. In *Children of Dust* ('23), he competes with Lloyd Hughes for the love of Pauline Garon. Both men join the military and Lloyd's life is saved by Walker, who marries Pauline upon his return home.

In the Western melodrama *The Scarlet West* ('25), Johnnie is Lt. Parkman, who loves Clara Bow and is demoted for fighting over her. Robert Frazer is the son of an Indian chief. He, too, loves Clara but gives up both her and his commission to return to the hills where his ancestors once lived and fought. *The Snarl of Hate* ('27) finds Johnnie playing brothers, one of whom is killed early by a human vulture (Jack Richardson) preying on luckless prospectors. In the city, the smooth-shaven twin tracks down the murderer through the discovery of a mating glove by the dog Silverstreak in the home of the heroine's guardian. There is a nightclub scrap with Wheeler Oakman, assistant villain.

In *Where Trails Begin* ('27), Johnnie shares the spotlight again with Silverstreak, who comes through the victor with the lech-

erous miscreant tucked under an avalanche. *The Matinee Idol* ('28) is a comedy-drama in which Johnnie, an actor, falls in love with Bessie Love, an amateur actress who mistakes an audience's laughter for ridicule. Thinking she has failed as a dramatic actress, she returns home. A few days later, Johnnie, burning with love for her, arrives to claim Bessie and explain her mistake.

Fantomas ('20) was Walker's first serial. Produced by Fox, it received wide distribution. In the story, Fantomas (Edward Roseman) is a super-criminal who is a specialist in disguises. When his offer to the police to give up his criminal career for amnesty is rejected, he vows revenge and begins a new crime wave. He kidnaps Prof. Harrington (Lionel Adams), much to the consternation of the professor's daughter, Ruth (Edna Murphy), her fiancé Jack (Walker) and Fantomas's nemesis, detective Dixon (John Willard).

Walker's second serial outing, *Galloping Hoofs* ('24), was made for Pathé. He was lucky to have Allene Ray as his co-star and George Seitz as his director. In the story by Frank Leon Smith, Carole Page (Allene Ray) has a box that her deceased father directed her to open at a specified time. Before she can do so, crooks steal it. Carole enlists the help of David Kirby (Walker) and together they undertake to recover the box and its contents. Carole is about to lose her horse farm because of debts, but in the end the box is recovered and the oil deed it contains solves her financial problems. Carole and David looked forward to a life together.

Vultures of the Sea ('28), an early Mascot serial, was a little bit out of the ordinary. It was produced more along the lines of a feature picture with each of the chapters almost a complete story in itself. The plot involves Walker's father, who is falsely accused of murder and sentenced to death. The crime was supposedly committed for the sake of a fortune hidden aboard the ship on which the father had been a crew member. Walker ships out on the vessel to learn the identity of the real culprit. Boris Karloff, Frank Hagney and Tom Santschi are among the suspects. Shirley Mason is the owner of the ship but she is held a virtual prisoner. It isn't until the final reel that both Walker and Mason evade death successfully for the last time and find both the hidden gold and the guilty party. The production is exceptional for a serial. There are many remarkable shots in the rigging of the ship and elsewhere. Richard Thorpe was to be commended for his good direction.

Johnnie was born in New York City in 1894. He attended Fordham University and briefly had a stage career before entering movies. He starred in many films through the '20s and early '30s, among them *Over the Hill to the Poor House* ('20), *Captain Fly-by-Night* ('22), *The Fourth Musketeer* ('23), *The Slanderers* ('24), *The Mad Dancer* ('25),

Transcontinental Limited ('26), *Wolves of the Air* ('27), *Rose of the Bowery* ('27), *Ladies of Leisure* ('30), *Up the River* ('30), and *Enemies of the Law* ('31).

In the early '30s, with his acting career in decline, he tried his hand at directing with only mediocre results.

Johnnie Walker died in 1949.

Serials

1920

Fantomas. Fox, [20 Chapters] D: Edward Sedgwick; SP: Edward Sedgwick, George Eshenfelder; LP: Edward Roseman, Edna Murphy, Johnnie Walker, Lionel Adams, John Willard, Eve Balfour, Rena Parker, Irving Brooks, Ben Walker, Henry Armetta.

1924

Galloping Hoofs. Pathé, [10 Chapters] D: George B. Seitz; S: Frank Leon Smith; LP: Alene Ray, Johnnie Walker, J. Barney Sherry, Ernest Hilliard, Armand Cortez, William Nally, George Nardelli, Albert Roccardi.

1928

Vultures of the Sea. Mascot, [10 Chapters] D: Richard Thorpe; P: Nat Levine; S/SP: Wyndham Gittens, William Burt; LP: Johnnie Walker, Shirley Mason, Boris Karloff, Tom Santschi, Frank Hagney, John Carpenter, George Magrill, Lafe McKee, Joe Bennett, Arthur Dewey, Joseph Mack, John P. Lockney.

LILLIAN WALKER

Grossman Pictures produced *The $1,000,000 Reward*, released in January 1920 on a states-rights basis. In the story, Betty Thorndyke (Lillian Walker) was the daughter of the richest diamond mine owner in

South Africa and the victim of two simultaneous plots against his person. When her father died, the stockholders offered a huge reward for the whereabouts of Betty. She had been carefully and secretly reared in California. Crooks read of the reward and decided to try for it, preferably by foul means. One of the stockholders (Charles Middleton) also wants to do away with her in the hope of gaining a larger share of the mines. Morgan Spencer (Coit Albertson) comes to the aid of Betty at every turn and in the conclusion the villains are disposed of and Betty gets her inheritance, plus a proposal from Spencer.

Grossman blanketed the nation with "wanted" posters offering a million dollars for information leading to the return of Lillian Walker. It was a clever advertising gimmick.

For several years Lillian was a popular actress, starring in *Hearts and the Highway* ('15), *The Blue Envelope Mystery* ('16), *The Dollar and the Law* ('16), *Green Stockings* ('16), *Hesper of the Mountains* ('16), *The Kid* ('16), *The Man Behind the Curtain* ('16), *Mrs. Dane's Danger* ('16), *The Ordeal of Elizabeth* ('16), *Indiscretion* ('17), *Kitty MacKay* ('17), *The Lust of the Ages* ('17), *National Association's All-Star Picture* ('17, with Walker as one of many stars), *Sally in a Hurry* ('17), *The Embarrassment of Riches* ('18), *The Grain of Dust* ('18), *The Love Hunger* ('19, produced by her own company) and *The Joyous Liar*

('19) and *A White Man's Chance* ('19), both as heroine to J. Warren Kerrigan. In *The Better Wife* ('19), she supported Clara Kimball Young. Also supporting were Kathlyn Williams, Ben Alexander, Irving Cummings and Edward Kimball.

She made no pictures in 1920. In '21, she supported Seena Owen and E. K. Lincoln in *The Woman That Changed* and in '22, she supported Ann Forrest and Bunty Fosse in *Love's Boomarang.*

In summary, Lillian starred in one serial and 18 features, and was a principal supporting player in three features, plus a cameo appearance in one.

Serial

1920

The $1,000,000 Reward. Grossman, [15 Chapters] D: George A. Lessey; S: Arthur B.Reeve, John W. Grey; P: Harry Grossman; LP: Lillian Walker, Coit Albertson, Charles Middleton, George A. Lessey, Joseph Marba, Leora Spellman, William Pike, Ray Allen, George Connors.

GEORGE D. WALLACE

George Wallace never gave acting a thought until it was thrust upon him. He joined the Navy in 1936 at age 19 for a four-year hitch. Discharged in 1940, he immediately re-enlisted after the attack on Pearl Harbor and served until 1946. He attained the rate of Chief Bosun's mate. (And, by the way, in 1939 he won the light-heavyweight boxing title of the Pacific fleet.)

After the war, Wallace worked a variety of jobs—cab driver, bartender, lumberman, etc. While working in a Los Angeles bar, he was heard singing along with the juke box by

columnist Jimmy Fidler. Jimmy introduced him to the father of Joel Grey, who taught George some Jewish songs and he sang at various Jewish events.

Wallace decided to use his G.I. Bill to study voice and dance. However, he never followed these as a career. Instead, he managed to get a part in *The Fat Man* ('51), followed by *Submarine Command* ('51). About this same time George appeared in a segment of TV's *Fireside Theatre.* Through his agent he learned that Republic was casting a new serial. He went out to audition for the role of

Graber, an Earthling who carries out the order of Retik (Roy Barcroft), ruler of the moon. He wound up instead with the leading role of Commando Cody in *Radar Men from the Moon* ('52). Retik and Cody crossed paths twice on the moon, but mostly Retik directed his minions on Earth to exterminate Cody and his crew. Over the course of 12 weeks Cody and members of his team faced an endless number of battles and hazards, narrowly escaping what seemed like certain death from molten lava, a couple of plane crashes, a collapsing bridge, an avalanche, etc.

Wallace was a mean and nasty pirate called Buller in the Columbia serial *The Great Adventures of Captain Kidd* ('53). He incites mutiny and, together with another notorious renegade, Capt. Culliford (Marshall Reed), leads the men through a succession of dastardly escapades.

Wallace continued working in movies and television for the next 50 years. In 1955, after finishing work in *Forbidden Planet*, he went to New York and auditioned for Oscar Hammerstein and Helen Trummel and won a part in *Pipe Dream*. Later he replaced John Raitt in *Pajama Game*, then did a musical called *New Girl in Town* with Gwen Verdon and Thelma Ritter.

A few of his other film credits are *The Lusty Men* ('52), *The Lawless Breed* ('53), *Star of Texas* ('53), *Arena* ('53), *Vigilante Terror* ('53), *Man Without a Star* ('55), *Destry* ('55), *Soldier of Fortune* ('55), *The Skin Game* ('71), *Punchline* ('88), *Defending Your Life* ('91), *Diggstown* ('92) and *Multiplicity* ('96).

Serials

1952

Radar Men from the Moon. Rep., [12 Chapters] D: Fred C. Brannon; SP: Ronald Davidson; AP: Franklyn Adreon; Cam: John MacBurnie; Mus: Stanley Wilson; LP: George Wallace, Aline Towne, Roy Barcroft, William Bakewell, Clayton Moore, Tom Steele.

1953

The Great Adventures of Captain Kidd. Col., [15 Chapters] D: Derwin Abbe, Charles S. Gould; SP: George H. Plympton, Arthur Hoerl; P: Sam Katzman; Cam: William Whitley; Mus: Mischa Bakaleinikoff; LP: Richard Crane, David Bruce, John Crawford, George Wallace, Lee Roberts, Ray Corrigan.

GEORGE WALSH

George Walsh's screen forte from the beginning in early silents had always been athletic heroics—he had one of the most perfect physiques in the movies. His success relied heavily on his muscular prowess and for a while he rivaled Douglas Fairbanks with his daring screen stunts. He was designated the star of the upcoming supercolossal Goldwyn production *Ben Hur.* But production delays and the merger of Goldwyn into MGM caused the dismissal in mid-production of the film's director, Charles Brabin, and the star and their replacement by Fred Niblo and Ramon Novarro, respectively.

George was born in New York City in 1892. The younger brother of Raoul Walsh, he studied law at Fordham and Georgetown Universities before deciding to enter films in 1914. After playing supporting roles in *The Fencing Master* ('15), *Don Quixote* ('15), *Intolerance* ('16) and other films, he became a star at Fox.

On January 23, 1922, Universal released *With Stanley in Africa*, starring George and Louise Lorraine and written by George H. Plympton, destined to become the foremost serial scenarist of the sound era. In the story, a young newspaper woman (Lorraine) aids Stanley (Walsh) in his search for Dr. Livingston in the wilds of Africa, with hero and heroine caught up in an attempt to revive the African slave trade. The plot adhered as closely as possible to historical facts, but in order to produce 18 chapters and give viewers the adventure and thrills which they expected from a serial, it was necessary to intersperse plenty of fiction with the truth.

Walsh married actress Seena Owen in 1916. They had a daughter, Patricia, and were divorced in 1924. By his second wife he had two sons. After retiring in 1936, he trained race horses for his brother and bought a lemon grove in Montclair. He also traveled extensively. His last film appearance was in *Klondike Annie* ('36). He died in 1981.

Walsh's films include *The Serpent, The Beast, Blue Blood and Red* (1916), *Melting Millions, This the Life, The Yankee Way, The Honor System* (1917), *The Pride of New York, I'll Say So, On the Jump, Brave and Bold, The Kid Is Clever* (1918), *The Winning Stroke, Luck and Pluck, Never Say Quit* (1919), *The Shark, From Now On, The Dead Line, A Manhattan Knight* (1920), *Serenade, Dynamite Allen* (1922), *Vanity Fair, Rosita, Slave of Desire, The Miracle Makers, Reno* (1923), *Blue Blood, American Pluck* (1924), *The Count of Luxembourg, The Prince of Broadway, The Kick-Off, A Man of Quality* (1926), *His Rise to Fame, The Broadway Drifter, The Winning*

Oar, Combat (1927), *Inspiration* (1928), *The Big Trail* (1930), *Me and My Gal* (1932), *The Bowery* (1933), *Belle of the Nineties* (1934), *Under Pressure* (1935) and *Klondike Annie* (1936).

Serial

1922

With Stanley in Africa. Univ., 1922 [18 Chapters] D: William Croft, Ed Kull; S/SP: George H. Plympton; LP: George Walsh, Louise Lorraine, Charles Mason, William Welsh, Jack Mower, Fred Kohler, Gordon Sackville.

LUANA WALTERS

Luana Walters was one of the writer's favorite Western heroines. In the ten years 1932–42 she appeared in 22 leather burners, lifting a few of them out of the horse trough. She was comely and capable. She was always clear-eyed and good-looking in proper outdoor style. She rode acceptably and was equal to the slight dramatic requirements of the hell-for-leather thrillers she graced. Importantly, she improved as she went along. Her Westerns are:

End of the Trail ('32)—Tim McCoy; *The Fighting Texans* ('33)—Rex Bell; *Aces and Eights* ('36)—Tim McCoy; *Ride 'Em Cowboy* ('36)—Buck Jones; *Under Strange Flags* ('37)—Tom Keene; *Where the West Begins* ('38)—Jack Randall; *Mexicali Rose* ('39)—Gene Autry; *Fangs of the Wild* ('39)—Dennis Moore; *The Return of Wild Bill* ('40)—Bill Elliott; *The Tulsa Kid* ('40)—Donald Barry; *The Range Busters* ('40)—Ray Corrigan, John King, Max Terhune; *The Durango Kid* ('40)—Charles Starrett; *The Kid's Last Ride* ('41)—Ray Corrigan, John King, Max Terhune; *Across the Sierras* ('41)—Bill Elliott; *Arizona Bound* ('41)—Buck Jones, Tim McCoy, Raymond Hatton; *Road Agent* ('41)—Dick Foran; *The Lone Star Vigilantes* ('42)—Bill Elliott, Tex Ritter; *Lawless Plainsmen* (42)—Charles Starrett, Russell Hayden; *Down Texas Way* ('42)—Buck Jones, Tim McCoy, Raymond Hatton; *Thundering Hoofs* ('42)—Tim Holt; *Bad Men of the Hills* ('42)—Charles Starrett, Russell Hayden

Luana was a California girl born in Los Angeles on July 22, 1912, and educated in Romona Convent, Alhambra. At 18, she was signed by United Artists. Her first film of record was *Reaching for the Moon* (1931) as a supporting player to Douglas Fairbanks. Shortly after completing this film, she appeared on stage in *The Shyster* in San Francisco; then an illness kept her inactive for over a year.

End of the Trail ('32) was the first film in which she had principal billing. She appeared occasionally in small roles in big pictures and big roles in small, non–Western pictures. Among her non–Westerns are *Miss Pinkerton* ('32), *The Merry Widow* ('34), *Broadway Melody of 1936* ('35), *Suzy* ('36), *Souls at Sea* ('37), *Algiers* ('38), *The Buccaneer* ('38), *Cafe Society* ('39), *Honeymoon in Bali* ('39), *Hotel Imperial* ('39), *Blondie Plays Cupid* ('40), *No Greater Sin* ('41), *The Corpse*

Vanishes ('42), *Arthur Takes Over* ('48) and *Mighty Joe Young* ('49).

In the serial *Shadows of Chinatown* ('36), European promoters want all West Coast Chinatowns closed to tourists and they hire Eurasian Sonya Rokoff (Luana) to accomplish the job. She enlists the aid of Victor Poten (Bela Lugosi), a madman who hates both the white and yellow races. Eventually she has a change of heart and, before she is killed, is instrumental in helping Herman Brix and Joan Barclay bring Lugosi to justice. Her role is reversed in *Drums of Fu Manchu* ('40), where she is the true-blue heroine fighting side by side with hero Robert Kellard to thwart the evil Fu Manchu (Henry Brandon) and his daughter (Gloria Franklin). But in *Captain Midnight* ('42), Luana plays Fury, daughter of the arch-villain Ivan Shark (James Craven), who is terrifying the nation as the tool of a foreign power.

Author Merrill T. McCord has written the most in-depth, entertaining article ever done on Luana, and he answers the question "Whatever happened to Luana Walters?" often asked by film buffs, especially Western addicts. He reports that her later years were unhappy ones. She had married actor Max Hoffman, Jr., in or about 1936. On May 31, 1945, Luana found him dead upon returning to their apartment. He had been appearing in the play *Good Night, Ladies*. His death was attributed to an accidental overdose of sleeping pills. Luana was back in Hollywood in 1946 but she had only limited success in attaining roles. She worked in *Shoot to Kill* ('46) and *Bells of San Angelo* ('47). After disappearing for several years, she resurfaced in *Girls in Prison* ('56) in a supporting role. She also had a very small role in *The She-Creature* ('56). McCord writes that she was working as a clerk in a Thrifty drug store at the time of her death in May 1965. She had not remarried, had few friends, and lived alone. Doctors gave alcoholism as the cause of her death. There was no one to claim the body and she was cremated as a pauper in Los Angeles. Merrill's article is found in the Fall 1999 issue of *Films of the Golden Age*. If you grew up loving Luana, this piece is a "must read."

Serials

1936

Shadow of Chinatown. Victory, [15 Chapters] D: Robert Hill; SP: Isador Bernstein, Basil Dickey; S: Rock Hawkey; Spv.: Sam Katzman; Cam: Bill Hyer; LP: Bela Lugosi, Herman Brix, Joan Barclay, Luana Walters, James Craven, Charles King, Maurice Liu, Forrest Taylor, James B. Leong, William Buchanan

1940

Drums of Fu Manchu. Rep., [15 Chapters] D: William Witney, John English; SP: Franklyn Adreon, Morgan Cox, Ronald Davidson, Norman Hall, Barney Sarecky, Sol Shor; AP: Hiram S. Brown, Jr.; Cam: William Nobles; Mus: Cy Feuer; LP: Henry Brandon, William Royle, Gloria Franklin, Robert Kellard, Luana Walters, Tom Chatterton, John Merton, Olaf Hytten, Dwight Frye, John Picorri.

1942

Captain Midnight. Col., [15 Chapters] D: James W. Horne; SP: George Plympton, Basil Dickey, Jack Stanley, Wyndham Gittens; P: Larry Darmour; Mus: Lee Zahler; Cam: James S. Brown, Jr.; LP: Dave O'Brien, Dorothy Short, James Craven, Sam Edwards, Luana Walters, Guy Wilkerson, Bryant Washburn, Joseph Girard, Ray Teal.

Luana Walters in *Blondie Plays Cupid* (Columbia, 1940).

1948

Superman. Col., [15 Chapters] D: Spencer G. Bennet, Thomas Carr; P: Sam Katzman; Cam: Ira H. Morgan; Mus: Mischa Bakaleinikoff; SP: Arthur Hoerl, Lewis Clay, Royal Cole; Adapt: George H. Plympton, Joseph F. Poland; LP: Kirk Alyn, Noel Neill, Tommy Bond, Pierre Watkin, Carol Forman, George Meeker, Charles Quigley, Herbert Rawlinson, Forrest Taylor, Charles King, Luana Walters.

ROBERT WARWICK

Robert Warwick was born Robert Taylor Bien on October 9, 1878, in Sacramento, California. In Paris he prepared himself for an operatic career, but instead he became a matinee idol on Broadway early in the century.

He entered films in 1914, appearing in *The Man of the Hour, The Dollar Mark* and *Across the Pacific.* In 1917, he was an army captain in World War I. He was the romantic star of many films through the early '20s.

He returned to the stage in the '20s but was back as a character actor with the advent of sound. He was one of Hollywood's truly sterling character actors in several dozen major films. His dark, brooding features and self-assured manner lent themselves equally well to the portrayal of kindly, benevolent patricians or scheming, grasping villains.

He worked in six serials, four for Mascot, one for Universal, and one for Columbia. His features of the sound era include *A Holy Terror* ('31), *I Am a Fugitive from a Chain Gang* ('32), *Cleopatra* ('34), *Night Life of the Gods* ('35), *A Tale of Two Cities* ('35), *Tough Guy* ('36), *Romeo and Juliet* ('36), *The Prince and the Pauper* ('37), *The Life of Emile Zola* ('37), *The Adventures of Robin Hood* ('38), *Devil's Island* ('39), *The Private Lives of Elizabeth and Essex* ('39), *The Sea Hawk* ('40), *Sullivan's Travels* ('41), *Tennessee Johnson* ('42), *Dixie* ('43), *The Princess and the Pirate* ('44), *Kismet* ('44), *Sudan* ('45), *Gentleman's Agreement* ('47), *In a Lonely Place* ('50), *Tarzan and the Slave Girl* ('50), *Salome* ('53), *Lady Godiva* ('55), *The Buccaneer* ('58) and *It Started with a Kiss* ('59).

In addition to the six serials, he could be seen in such outdoor adventures as *Hopalong Cassidy* ('35), *Bold Caballero* ('36), *Sutter's Gold* ('36), *Timber War* ('36), *Trigger Trio* ('37), *Law of the Plains* ('38), *In Old Monterey* ('39), *Konga — the Wild Stallion* ('40), *Deerslayer* ('43), *Fury at Furnace Creek* ('48), *Gun Smugglers* ('48), *Sugarfoot* ('51), *Chief Crazy Horse* ('55) and *Shoot-Out at Medicine Bend* ('57).

Warwick died in Hollywood from Pulmonary embolism in 1964 at age 85.

Serials

1933

Fighting with Kit Carson. Mascot, [12 Chapters] D: Armand Schaefer, Colbert Clark; P: Nat Levine; LP: Johnny Mack Brown, Betsy King Ross, Tully Marshall, Noah Beery, Sr., Noah Beery, Jr., Robert Warwick, Lafe McKee, Edward Hearn.

The Three Musketeers. Mascot, [12 Chapters] D: Armand Schaefer, Colbert Clark; P: Nat Levine; LP: Jack Mulhall, Raymond Hatton, Francis X. Bushman, Jr., Noah Beery, Jr., Robert Warwick, Creighton Chaney [Lon Chaney, Jr.], Al Ferguson.

The Whispering Shadow. Mascot, [12 Chapters] D: Albert Herman, Colbert Clark; P: Nat Levine; LP: Bela Lugosi, Henry B. Walthall, Viva Tattersall, Robert Warwick, Roy D'Arcy, George J. Lewis, Jack Perrin.

1935

The Fighting Marines. Mascot, [12 Chapters] D: B. Reeves Eason, Joseph Kane; P: Nat Levine; LP: Grant Withers, Adrian Morris, Ann Rutherford, George J. Lewis, Pat O'Malley, Robert Frazer, Frank Reicher, Jason Robards.

1936

Ace Drummond. Univ., [13 Chapters] D: Ford Beebe, Cliff Smith; LP: John King, Jean Rogers, Noah Beery, Jr., Guy Bates Post, Arthur Loft, Chester Gan, Lon Chaney, Jr., Robert Warwick, Al Bridge, Hooper Atchley, Edmund Cobb.

1937

Jungle Menace. Col., [15 Chapters] D: George Melford, Harry Fraser; LP: Frank Buck, Esther Ralston, John St. Polis, Reginald Denny, Charlotte Henry, William Bakewell, Duncan Renaldo, LeRoy Mason, Robert Warwick.

BRYANT WASHBURN

Bryant Washburn's baptismal name was Franklin Bryant Washburn and he was the third in as many generations to bear the name. His mother was Metha Catherine

Johnson, a native of Denmark. Bryant Washburn III was born in Chicago, April 28, 1889. When he was three years old, the family moved to Racine, Wisconsin, and, after seven years in that city, returned to Chicago. Washburn's education was completed at the Lake View High School there. He married Mabel Forrest Chidester in Chicago, July 3, 1914. They had two sons, Bryant and Dwight. The younger son has the distinction of being named for Washburn's great uncle, Dwight L. Moody, world's famous evangelist.

Washburn was truly a pioneer in the motion picture industry. His introduction to the silent drama dated back to those thankless days when an actor or actress who deserted the speaking stage for the screen was considered a rank heretic by those ingrained with legitimate stage ideals. Not only was the deserter ostracized on the screen, but his name was not revealed either by program or otherwise. The custom had at least one virtue in that it permitted the actor to hide his identity from the aspersions of his former fellow artists—the hiding made easy by the many disguises the film actor was forced to assume in his work.

Necessity really caused Washburn to seek his first motion picture engagement. Finding himself in New York, at the end of a not-too-prosperous theatrical engagement, he overheard a manager talk about the possibilities for a young man who would go to Chicago and work in pictures. The season of the year not being propitious for the securing of a theatrical engagement, he decided to investigate the new industry. He signed an agreement for the summer with Essanay. By the expiration of this contract he had developed a great aptitude for screen work, and the engagement that was entered into as "make work" resulted in his continuing with Essanay for seven years. During these years he played everything from dope fiends to kings. Just before leaving Essanay, he made what was considered to be one of the greatest comedies produced—*Skinner's Dress Suit.* It cost about $16,000 to make and returned $150,000. It was followed by *Skinner's Baby* and *Skinner Steps Out.*

Washburn and Mabel Forrest were divorced some time in the late 1920s. He then married actress Virginia Vance (a comedienne at Educational Studios). This marriage lasted until Virginia's death in 1942. Their daughter, Roberta, became a nun known as Sister Mary Luke of St. John's Convent in King City, California. His son, Bryant, who died in 1960, became a first lieutenant in the Army Air Force.

Washburn's salary was $200 weekly when he left Essanay to accept a contract with Famous Players in Hollywood at $1,000 a week. Though he had made the famed *Skinner's Dress Suit* and other hits for Essanay, George K. Spoor, its head, refused to meet the Hollywood offer, saying that a producer paying such a high salary would surely go broke. Washburn remained with Famous Players three years, then became a freelance player.

Prominent among his other screen hits of silent days were *It Pays to Advertise* ('19), *Mrs. Temple's Telegram* ('20), *Too Much Johnson* ('20), *The Road to London* ('21), *June Madness* ('22), *Hungry Hearts* ('23), *Try and Get It* ('24), *The Wizard of Oz* ('25), *Wet Paint* ('26), *Breakfast at Sunrise* ('27), *The*

Love Thrill ('27), *Beware of Widows* ('28), *Skinner's Big Idea* ('28) and *Jazzland* ('28).

Washburn appeared in many "B" programmers of the 1930s and 1940s as a supporting player. Among these films are *Mystery Train* ('31), *Arm of the Law* ('32), *Drifting Souls* ('32), *Devil's Mate* ('33), *Woman Who Dared* ('34), *The Throwback* ('35), *Sutter's Gold* ('36), *Gambling with Souls* ('36), *Sea Racketeers* ('37), *I Demand Payment* ('38), *Stagecoach* ('39), *Paper Bullets* ('41), *Carson City Cyclone* ('43), *The Law Rides Again* ('43), *Shadows on the Sage* ('43), *The Falcon in Mexico* ('44), *West of the Pecos* ('45) and *Sweet Genevieve* ('47).

It is the serials for which Washburn is remembered today. He appeared in 11 of them, and regardless of how big or small his parts, they contributed to the overall enjoyment of the cliffhangers.

After his wife died in 1942, Washburn remained a widower until his own death on April 30, 1963, at age 74 at the Motion Picture Country Home in Woodland Hills, California. A son and daughter survived.

Serials

1934

Tailspin Tommy. Univ., [12 Chapters] D: Louis Friedlander [Lew Landers]; LP: Maurice Murphy, Noah Beery, Jr., Patricia Farr, Walter Miller, Grant Withers, William Desmond, John Davidson.

The Return of Chandu. Principal, [12 Chapters] D: Ray Taylor; LP: Bela Lugosi, Maria Alba, Clara Kimball Young, Lucien Prival, Phyllis Ludwig, Bryant Washburn, Peggy Montgomery.

1935

Tailspin Tommy in the Great Air Mystery. Univ., [12 Chapters] D: Ray Taylor; LP: Clark Williams, Jean Rogers, Noah Beery, Jr., Grant Withers, Bryant Washburn.

The Adventures of Frank Merriwell. Univ., [12 Chapters] D: Cliff Smith; LP: Don Briggs, Jean Rogers, John King, Carla Laemmle, Sumner Getchell, House Peters, Jr., William Carleton, Alan Hersholt.

The Call of the Savage. Univ., [12 Chapters] D: Louis Friedlander [Lew Landers]; LP: Noah Beery, Jr., Dorothy Short, Harry Woods, Walter Miller, Bryant Washburn, Viva Tattersall, Frederic Mackaye.

1936

The Black Coin. S & S, [15 Chapters] D: Albert Herman; LP: Ralph Graves, Ruth Mix, Dave O'Brien, Constance Bergen, Clara Kimball Young, Matthew Betz, Robert Frazer, Bryant Washburn, Snub Pollard, Bob Walker.

The Clutching Hand. S & S, [15 Chapters] D: Albert Herman; LP: Jack Mulhall, Ruth Mix, Marion Shilling, Rex Lease, William Farnum, Reed Howes, Robert Frazer, Bob Kortman, Bryant Washburn, Tom London, Charles Whitaker, Yakima Canutt, Charles Locher [Jon Hall].

1937

Jungle Jim. Univ., [12 Chapters] D: Ford Beebe, Cliff Smith; LP: Grant Withers, Betty Jane Rhodes, Raymond Hatton, Henry Brandon, Evelyn Brent, Bryant Washburn, Paul Sutton, Frank Mayo, Al Bridge.

1941

The Spider Returns. Col., [15 Chapters] D: James W. Horne; LP: Warren Hull, Mary Ainslee, Dave O'Brien, Joe Girard, Keene Duncan, Alden Chase, Bryant Washburn, Corbet Harris.

Adventures of Captain Marvel. Rep., [12 Chapters] D: William Witney, John English; LP: Tom Tyler, Frank Coghlan, Jr., William Benedict, Louise Currie, Reed Hadley, Robert Strange, Harry Worth, Bryant Washburn, Kenne Duncan.

1942

Captain Midnight. Col., [15 Chapters] D: James W. Horne; LP: Dave O'Brien, Dorothy Short, James Craven, Sam Edwards, Guy Wilkerson, Bryant Washburn, Luana Walters, Joseph Girard, Al Ferguson, Ray Teal, Franklyn Farnum.

JOHN WAYNE

Most movie buffs are familiar with John Wayne's career. There have been books and hundreds of articles written about Wayne and his fabulous career; therefore, the author will only skim the surface in writing of this superstar.

Wayne's craggy and heroic profile is known worldwide. He was leathery, tough and masculine, a consummate master of timing, with personality nuances that have made his screen persona one of the most interesting in the cinema. He was the greatest moneymaker in movie history. It has been estimated that the gross revenue from his pictures exceeded $450 million. His personal income kept pace with his long and rising career.

In 1936, Wayne ranked seventh in the *Motion Picture Herald*'s pole of the most popular B-Western star. In '39, he ranked ninth. On five occasions ('50, '51, '54, '69, '71) he was the nation's most popular star. He ranked second as most popular star in '56, '57 and '63. After 1949 there was only one year ('58) when he was not in the top ten list of popular stars. No other actor or actress has been as successful as "The Duke." From 1928 to 1976 his popularity with the masses never waned.

Wayne was born Marion Michael Mor-

Lobby Card of *The Star Packer* (Lone Star, 1934).

rison on May 26, 1908, in Winterset, Iowa. Because of his father's poor health, the family moved to Lancaster, California, on the advice of his doctor. A year later, the elder Morrison opened a drugstore in Glendale and it was there that John grew up. He graduated from Glendale High and attended the University of Southern California on a football scholarship. He played tackle on the Trojan team, and as a member of the team he appeared in a small role in *Salute* ('29) starring George O'Brien. Rex Bell and Ward Bond also appeared in this football film.

It was Tom Mix who got Wayne into the Fox studio as a prop man in exchange for choice football tickets. While at Fox, Wayne was noticed by John Ford, who took a liking to him. He received bit parts in *Words and Music* ('29), *Men Without Women* ('30), *Rough Romance* ('30) and *Cheer Up and Smile* ('30). When Raoul Walsh was looking for a newcomer to star in *The Big Trail* ('30), Ford pointed out Wayne and said, "There's your man."

The Big Trail was a big picture, but it failed financially due to being filmed in 70mm. Most theaters were not equipped to handle the wide screen process. Marguerite Churchill was the leading lady and Fox again cast her with Wayne in a clinker titled *Girls Demand Excitement* ('31). Wayne later claimed it was the worst picture he ever made. Next the studio co-starred him with Loretta Young in *Three Girls Lost* ('31). Joan Marsh and Lew Cody supported. Wayne was ill-at-ease in a role obviously not suited to him.

Columbia picked up Wayne in 1931, casting him opposite Laura LaPlante in *Men Are Like That* ('31). Rumor had it that Harry Cohn, Columbia boss, thought Wayne and LaPlante were having an affair. Now Harry had an itch for LaPlante. Whether there was any truth to the rumor or not, Cohn punished Wayne by casting him in supporting roles in Buck Jones' *Range Feud* ('31), Jack Holt's *Maker of Men* ('31) and Tim McCoy's *Texas Cyclone* ('32) and *Two-Fisted Law* ('32).

Concurrent with and subsequent to Wayne's work at Columbia, he made three serials for Mascot. First was *Shadow of the Eagle* ('32). In the story, sky-writing messages from a pilot called "The Eagle" threatens the board of directors of an aircraft company. Nathan Gregory (Edward Hearn), known as the Eagle for his sensational flying in the war, is accused of being the culprit. He denies the charge although he admits a motive for revenge in the fact that the success of the corporation is due to an invention stolen from him.

Craig McCoy (John Wayne), stunt pilot, is in love with Gregory's daughter and struggles to prove Gregory's innocence and recover plans for an invention that the Eagle has stolen from Gregory. Craig himself becomes a suspect before the Eagle is unmasked to reveal a member of the board of directors of the aircraft firm. This serial certainly gave no indication that Wayne had much potential or that he would ultimately become the greatest moneymaker in movie history. He was still green but he was learning.

Yakima Canutt was stunt supervisor on the film as well as playing a character role. This was the first of many films on which Wayne and Canutt worked together. Shot in 21 days, the serial is fast-paced but shoddy in production values.

Wayne's second serial, *The Hurricane Express* ('32), is a railroad story of Larry Baker (Wayne), a young air transport pilot whose father is killed in one of a series of mysterious train wrecks, and the hair-raising situations which result when Larry tries to track down and demolish the Wrecker, who effectively disguises himself with masks of various principals in the story. Gloria (Shirley Grey), daughter of one of the suspects, helps Larry as he fights to bring the master criminal to justice.

Rivalry between the L&R railroad and the air transport line is keen and Gray (Lloyd Whitlock), head of the airline, is under suspicion. But so is Stratton (Edmund Breese), an escaped convict who had been falsely prosecuted by an official of the L&R for embezzlement. Then, too, there's Jordan (Matthew Betz), a discharged employee who vows to get even. And Gloria, Stratton's daughter, whom Larry loves, is, for reasons of her own, working under an assumed name as secretary to the railroad manager. In the last chapter, the Wrecker is unmasked. There are plenty of thrills and spills as the story is unfolded. Shirley Grey was a beautiful heroine and Wayne was adequate.

The Three Musketeers ('33), the last of Wayne's serials, had an exceptional cast. Wayne was still not a well-known player, so Jack Mulhall, Raymond Hatton, and Francis X. Bushman, Jr. were billed over him. Three legionnaires, Clancy (Mulhall), Renard (Hatton) and Schmidt (Bushman), are rescued by American aviator Tom Wayne (Wayne) from desert rebels. The four become involved in hunting down the mysterious El Shaitan, leader of the bandit cult who desires to wipe out the Foreign Legion. El Shaitan never shows his face until the last chapter when he is unmasked.

In *The Train Robbers* (Warner Bros., 1972).

Wayne always said that *Musketeers'* Ruth Hall was one of his favorite leading ladies. She also played with him in *The Man from Monterey* ('33).

When Columbia did not renew his contract in '32, Wayne signed with Warner Brothers to make six "B" Westerns that used footage from Ken Maynard silent Westerns where possible to reduce production costs and to make the films seem "bigger" than they were. His identity as a cowboy was born in these six oaters: *The Big Stampede* ('32), *Ride Him, Cowboy* ('32), *Haunted Gold* ('32), *The Man from Monterey* ('33), *The Telegraph Trail* ('33) and *Somewhere in Sonora* ('33).

In '33, Wayne had supporting roles in *Lady and Gent* with George Bancroft and Charles Starrett, *Central Airport* with Richard Barthelmess, *The Life of Jimmy Dolan* with Douglas Fairbanks, Jr., and Loretta Young and *Baby Face* with Barbara Stanwyck. He co-starred with Evalyn Knapp in *His Private Secretary*, a Showmen's picture.

Wayne moved over to Monogram in 1933 to star in 16 Lone Star productions. Though the budgets did not exceed $12,000 on these dusty oaters, they were well-re-ceived by Saturday-going theater crowds, especially in the rural areas of the South.

The "B" films, made from 1933 through 1939, that endeared John Wayne to horse opera addicts were *Riders of Destiny, Sagebrush Trail, West of the Divide, The Lucky Texan, Blue Steel, The Man from Utah, Randy Rides Alone, The Star Packer, The Trail Beyond, Neath Arizona Skies, Texas Terror, The Lawless Frontier, Rainbow Valley, Paradise Canyon, The Dawn Rider, Desert Trail, Westward Ho, The New Frontier, The Lawless Nineties, King of the Pecos, The Oregon Trail, Winds of the Wastelands, I Cover Chinatown, The Sea Spoilers, The Lonely Trail, Conflict, I Cover the War, Idol of the Crowds, California Straight Ahead, Adventure's End, Born to the West, Overland Stage Raiders, Pals of the Saddle, Santa Fe Stampede, Red River Range, The Night Riders, Three Texas Steers, Wyoming Outlaw* and *New Frontier.*

With the release of *Stagecoach* ('39), Wayne's career was revitalized; he was on the way to becoming a major star. For the next 30 years he would star in big-budget films, a preponderance of them Westerns. With John Wayne in the saddle, profits were assured, but then so were they with his non–Westerns.

His subsequent film credits are *Dark Command, Three Faces West, The Long Voyage Home, Seven Sinners* (1940), *A Man Betrayed, Lady from Louisiana, The Shepherd of the Hills, Lady for a Night* (1941), *Reap the Wild Wind, The Spoilers, In Old California, Flying Tigers, Reunion in France, Pittsburgh* (1942), *The Lady Takes a Chance, In Old Oklahoma* (1943), *The Fighting Seabees, Tall in the Saddle* (1944), *Flame of the Barbary Coast, Back to Bataan, Dakota, They Were Expendable* (1945), *Without Reservations, Angel and the Badman* (1946), *Tycoon* (1947), *Fort Apache, Red River, 3 Godfathers, Wake of the Red Witch* (1948), *She Wore a Yellow Ribbon, The Fighting Kentuckian, Sands of Iwo Jima* (1949), *Rio Grande* (1950), *Operation Pacific, Flying Leathernecks* (1951), *The Quiet Man, Big Jim McLain* (1952), *Trouble Along the Way, Island in the Sky, Hondo* (1953), *The High and the Mighty* (1954), *The Sea Chase, Blood Alley* (1955), *The Conqueror, The Searchers* (1956), *The Wings of Eagles, Jet Pilot, Legend of the Lost* (1957), *The Barbarian and the Geisha* (1958), *Rio Bravo, The Horse Soldiers* (1959), *The Alamo, North to Alaska* (1960), *The Comancheros* (1961), *The Man Who Shot Liberty Vance, Hatari, The Longest Day, How the West was Won* (1962), *Donovan's Reef, McLintock!* (1963), *Circus World* (1964), *The Greatest Story Ever Told, In Harm's Way, The Sons of Katie Elder* (1965), *Cast a Giant Shadow* (1966), *The War Wagon, Eldorado* (1967), *The Green Berets, Hellfighters* (1968), *True Grit, The Undefeated* (1969), *Chisum, Rio Lobo* (1970), *Big Jake* (1971), *The Cowboys* (1972), *The Train Robbers, Cahill U.S. Marshal* (1973), *McQ* (1974), *Brannigan* (1975), *The Shootist* (1976).

Hollywood might change, but John Wayne seems to go on forever. Though he has been dead 25 years, his films appear daily on television. He died from cancer at 5:35 P.M. on June 11, 1979, at UCLA Medical Center. The passing of the Duke was headline news around the world. With his passing, one of the greatest careers in films came to an end.

John Wayne courted Josephine Saenz quite a while before marrying her in 1933. She was a socially prominent, devout Catholic wife and he a hard-drinking, two-fisted, boisterous, non-religious, always-on-location actor. The marriage was rocky from the beginning, although they had four children together (two boys and two girls). They were divorced in 1945.

Duke's second wife was Esperanza Baur, a tempestuous Mexican actress whom he called "Chata." The marriage was hellish, childless and tormenting. They were divorced in 1953 and she died a year later from a heart attack.

In 1954, Wayne married Peruvian beauty Pilar Palette. They had three children, Aissa, John Ethan and Marisa. Twenty-four years later, Duke and Pilar separated with little chance of reconciliation.

The 72-year-old superstar agreed to see the Rev. Robert Curtis during the dwindling hours of his life. He was received into the Catholic Church hours before his death.

Serials

1932

Shadow of the Eagle. Mascot, [12 Chapters] D: Ford Beebe, Colbert Clark, Wyndham Gittens; Cam: Benjamin H. Kline, Victor Scheurich; Mus: Lee Zahler; Stunt Supv.: Yakima Canutt; LP: John Wayne, Dorothy Gulliver, Walter Miller, Kenneth Harlan, Edward Hearn, Richard Tucker, Ernie Adams, Roy D'Arcy, Bud Osborne.

The Hurricane Express. Mascot, [12 Chapters] D: Armand Schaefer, J. P. McGowan; S: Colbert Clark, Barney Sarecky, Wyndham Gittens; P: Nat Levine; Supv.: George Morgan, J. P. McGowan; Cam: Ernest Miller, Carl Wester; LP: John Wayne, Shirley Grey, Conway Tearle, Tully Marshall, Francis McDonald, Lloyd Whitlock, Al Bridge, Charles King, Glenn Strange.

1933

The Three Musketeers. Mascot, [12 Chapters] D: Armand Schaefer, Colbert Clark; SP: Norman Hall, Colbert Clark, Ben Cohn, Wyndham Gittens; P: Nat Levine; Cam: Ernest Miller, Tom Galligan; Mus: Lee Zahler; LP: Jack Mulhall, John Wayne, Raymond Hatton, Francis X. Bushman, Jr., Ruth Hall, Hooper Atchley, William Desmond, Robert Frazer, Robert Warwick, George Magrill.

MARJORIE WEAVER

Marjorie was a streamlined bundle of vibrant energy. She started life as the daughter of a livery stable owner in Crossville, Tennessee, on March 2, 1913. When she was a year old, her parents moved to Glasgow, Kentucky, and two years later to Gadsden, Alabama, where they remained for five years before finally settling in Louisville, Kentucky. Marjorie attended the J. M. Atherton High School in Louisville and then went to the University of Kentucky for one year. The final three years of her college life were spent at the University of Indiana. She became an honorary colonel of the R.O.T.C. at the University of Kentucky, and at the University of Indiana she participated in many extracurricular activities, notably swimming, volleyball and dramatics. She was no stranger to the stage, however, even before her college days. At the age of 14 she began taking lessons from a member of the McCawley Stock Company in Louisville and played in several productions with the company.

In the summer of 1936, Marjorie got a taste of life on the other side of the tracks by working as a social worker in the poorer district of Louisville.

Marjorie was the belle of the campus at Indiana and a prize scholar as well. Her ambition was to become a teacher. However, fate intervened in the form of Judy Parks, her roommate in the Kappa Kappa Gamma sorority. Judy, unknown to Marjorie, entered Marjorie's picture in a national beauty contest sponsored by one of the widely read film magazines. She won the contest and a dance scholarship in New York. Upon graduation she shuffled off to New York and, while pursuing the dancing course, worked part-time as a model for the John Robert Powers Agency. Among other things, she posed for cigarette, beer and soap ads and also figured in the illustrations in *Collier's* as the heroine of the Sax Rohmer series. Film scouts quickly descended upon her. Though reluctant at first, she finally took a screen test and accepted a film contract.

Sent post-haste to Hollywood, Marjorie went into the stock school for the final polishing touches. As usual, she was given bit parts in films while learning the finer points of cinematic drama, and she managed to attract a good deal of attention by her spontaneity, sparkle and bubbling enthusiasm.

Marjorie's big break finally came in *Second Honeymoon* ('37) when she had a good secondary role in this Tyrone Power-Loretta Young comedy. Several succeeding films established her as a vivacious, light comedienne and one of the most promising starlets in Hollywood. She won critical acclaim as Mary Todd in John Ford's *Young Mr. Lincoln* ('39), and she was eventually given leads. But like Lynn Bari, June Lang and several other actresses being groomed for stardom, it never really happened. Her dancing dark eyes and captivating smile adorned only a succession of "B" films. Disappointed, she left 20th Century-Fox in 1942 to freelance, with no spectacular results. She even wound up as the heroine in a Universal serial—which is certainly no disgrace, but in Hollywood it was like the kiss of death for one aspiring to stardom. But by this time Marjorie was content to enjoy her real-life role as wife and mother.

It is possibly not a unique experience, but certainly for a husband to return home after years in a Japanese prison camp to find his wife remarried and pregnant is not your everyday experience. It was just such an experience that involved Marjorie.

On October 22, 1937, Marjorie was married to Lt. Kenneth Schacht of the U.S. Navy at Goshen, Indiana, on the night before the Navy–Notre Dame football game in South Bend. The couple had known each other for several years. The couple spent only a short time together over the next several years as his Navy assignments kept him away from home, including two years in Manila just prior to the outbreak of the war. Their frequent long separations contributed greatly

to their inability to get along as well as they should have. They talked of divorce, but after Schacht's capture and imprisonment by the Japanese in March, 1942 he had no way of learning that Marjorie had obtained it. En route to Hollywood after his release in 1945, he had planned to woo her all over again. Marjorie had assumed him dead when he was reported missing in action. On August 6, 1942, she wed Lt. Donald J. Briggs and was, in October 1945, expecting a baby in January. It was quite a shock when Schacht walked in the door. Fortunately, Briggs was home at the time. The two men sat down to talk things over. Schacht understood perfectly and agreed to walk right out of their lives when he saw how much in love Marjorie and Briggs were (and her impending motherhood).

The marriage has been a lasting one, and the couple have two grown children. At one time the Briggs owned and operated a thriving liquor store in Brentwood.

Marjorie retired voluntarily. And though her career did not live up to its early promise, it nevertheless was a respectable one that left her a lot of loyal fans who remember her to this day.

Serial

1944

The Great Alaskan Mystery. Univ., [13 Chapters] D: Ray Taylor, Lewis D. Collins; SP: George H. Plympton, Maurice Tombragel; S: Jack Foley; LP: Milburn Stone, Marjorie Weaver, Edgar Kennedy, Martin Kosleck, Samuel S. Hinds, Joseph Crehan, Fuzzy Knight, Ralph Morgan, Harry Cording, Anthony Warde.

RICHARD WEBB

Richard Webb was on screen for nearly 30 years, but he is mostly remembered for his television roles in *Captain Midnight* and *L.S. Border Patrol* and perhaps for his serial *The Invisible Monster* ('50). He entered films in 1941 in *I Wanted Wings* and *Sullivan's Travels*.

His films include *American Empire* ('42), *O.S.S.* ('46), *Night Has a Thousand Eyes* ('48), *Sands of Iwo Jima* ('49), *I Was a Communist for the F.B.I.* ('51), *The Nebraskan* ('53), *The Black Dakotas* ('54), *Jubilee Trail* ('54), *The Phantom Stagecoach* ('57), *12 to the Moon* ('60) and *The Gay Deceivers* ('69).

Richard Webb committed suicide in Van Nuys, California, in 1993 by shooting himself. He was 77 and had been ill for a long time.

Following is a synopsis of Webb's *The Invisible Monster*: The Phantom Ruler is a big-time criminal organizer who secures his technical assistants by smuggling in aliens not eligible for immigration. He brings in four intelligent, well-educated Europeans— a locksmith, an attorney, an aircraft engineer and a chemist — and cows them into obedience by demonstrating his ability to make himself invisible through a combination of chemically treated clothing and a special type of light ray. He secures a position for the locksmith which enables him to get the combination of a bank vault, and then the Phantom Ruler, using his invisibility equipment, robs the vault.

Lane Carson, insurance company investigator, is assigned to the case and, with the help of his assistant Carole Richards, gets on the trail of the Phantom Ruler. Lane and Carol manage to disrupt and frustrate many of the Phantom's plans at the risk of their own lives in terrifying and dangerous experiences. Lane gets close to catching the Phantom Ruler when, after several contacts in which he barely escapes death, he recognizes the special type of light ray with which the Phantom effects invisibility. But the Phantom Ruler is eventually destroyed by his own evil doings when, in a terrific climax battle, he is accidentally electrocuted in a machine which he had built to execute his remaining foreign assistants.

Serial

1950

The Invisible Monster. Rep., [12 Chapters] D: Fred C. Brannon; SP: Ronald Davidson; AP: Franklyn Adreon; Cam: Ellis W. Carter; Mus: Stanley Wilson; LP: Richard Webb, Aline Towne, Lane Bradford, Stanley Price, Tom Steele.

JACQUELINE WELLS /
JULIE BISHOP

Born Jacqueline Brown in Denver, Colorado, on August 30, 1914, Jacqueline acted under three names—Jacqueline Wells, Diane Duval (once) and Julie Bishop.

She made her screen debut in Paramount's *Bluebeard's Eighth Wife* ('23) and followed with *Children of Jazz* ('23) and *Maytime* ('23). In 1924, she appeared in *Dorothy Vernon of Haddon Hall*; in '25, *Captain Blood* and *The Golden Bed*; in '26, *The Homemaker*, *Classified*, *The Family Upstairs* and the serial *The Bar-C Mystery*.

At this point, Jacqueline dropped out of films to concentrate on schooling and a normal childhood. She attended Westlake and Kenwood School for Girls in Los Angeles and studied dramatics at the Pasadena Community Playhouse. It was there she was re-discovered and signed to a contract by Hal Roach. She worked in two-reel comedies with Charley Chase (*Skip the Maloo*, *In Walked Charley*), Laurel and Hardy (*Any Old Port*) and Mickey Daniels (*The Knockout* and *You're Telling Me*). During this time she also studied ballet and dance under the tutelage of Theodore Kosloff.

In 1932, billed as Diane Duval, she appeared opposite Noah Beery, Jr., in *Heroes of the West*, a Universal serial. Billed as Jacqueline Wells, she made two more serials—*Clancy of the Mounted* ('33) starring Tom Tyler and *Tarzan the Fearless* ('33) starring Buster Crabbe. She used the name Jacqueline Wells until signing with Warner Brothers in 1941.

She was named a Wampas Baby Star in 1934 and received a lot of publicity. As a result, she went under contract to Paramount, but the studio did little for her except to loan her out to other filmmakers.

On May 16, 1936, Jacqueline was married to Walter Brooks III, scion of a wealthy Philadelphia family, but their romance lasted only two years. They separated on May 12, 1938, and in May 1939 a divorce was granted Jacqueline on grounds of cruelty.

From 1935 to 1941 Jacqueline played in a succession of "B" programmers: *Square Shooter* ('35, Tim McCoy), *Coronado* ('35, Johnny Downs), *The Bohemian Girl* ('36, Laurel and Hardy), *Night Cargo* ('36, Lloyd Hughes), *The Frame-up* ('37, Paul Kelly), *Girls Can Play* ('37, Charles Quigley), *Counsel for Crime* ('37, Otto Kruger), *Paid to Dance* ('37, Rita Hayworth), *Torture Ship* ('37, Lyle Talbot), *Flight Into Nowhere* ('38, Jack Holt), *Highway Patrol* ('38, Robert Paige), *Spring Madness* ('38, Maureen O'Sullivan), *My Son Is a Criminal* ('39, Alan Baxter), *Behind Prison Gates* ('39, Brian Donlevy), *The Kansas Terrors* ('39, Robert Livingston, Duncan Renaldo), *My Son Is Guilty* ('39, Harry Carey), *Girl in Room 313* ('40, Kent Taylor), *The Ranger and the Lady* ('40, Roy Rogers), *Young Bill Hickok* ('40, Roy Rogers), *Back in the Saddle* ('41, Gene Autry).

By 1941 she was tired of the filmfare she was being offered and took a vacation for several months. When she returned to Hollywood she signed with Warner Brothers and acquired the new name Julie Bishop, which she retained the rest of her career. For Warners, she made *The Nurse's Secret* ('41, Regis Toomey), *International Squadron* ('41, Ronald Reagan), *Wild Bill Hickok Rides* ('42, Constance Bennett), *I Was Framed* ('42, Michael Ames), *Lady Gangster* ('42, Faye Emerson), *Escape from Crime* ('42, Richard Travis), *Busses Roar* ('42, Richard Travis), *The Hidden Hand* ('42, Craig Stevens), *The Hard Way* ('42, Ida Lupino), *Action in the North Atlantic* ('43, Humphrey Bogart),

Princess O'Rourke ('43, Olivia de Havilland), *Northern Pursuit* ('43, Errol Flynn), *Hollywood Canteen* ('44, Joan Leslie), *Rhapsody in Blue* ('45, Robert Alda) and *Cinderella Jones* ('46, Joan Leslie).

After *Cinderella Jones* Julie became a freelancer, appearing in *Murder in the Music Hall* (Rep. '46, Vera Hruba Ralston), *Last of the Redmen* (Col. '47, Jon Hall), *High Tide* (Mon. '47, Lee Tracy), *Deputy Marshal* (Lippert '49, Jon Hall), *Sands of Iwo Jima* (Rep. '49, John Wayne), *Westward the Women* (MGM '52, Robert Taylor), *Sabre Jet* (UA '53, Robert Stack), *The High and the Mighty* (WB '54, John Wayne), *Headline Hunters* (Rep. '55, Rod Cameron) and *The Big Land* (WB '56, Virginia Mayo).

In July 1944, Julie married Lt. Col. (later Gen.) Clarence A. Shoop, who became an RKO executive. The marriage proved a good one and the couple had two children. Daughter Pamela became an actress and son Stephen an Air Force pilot. After Gen. Shoop's death in 1968, Julie married Dr. William Bergin, a well-to-do Beverly Hills surgeon.

Julie acted on stage as well as in the movies, and was lauded by the critics for much of her stage work, which included the role of Ophelia in *Hamlet* at the Pasadena Playhouse, *Rain*, *Sixth Floor*, *To Live Again*, *Dangerous Corner*, *Hotel Universe* and *The Isle*. She was a member of the Peninsula Players Repertory Company in Fish Creek, Wisconsin, at one time. During World War II, Julie gave much of her time to entertaining servicemen at the Hollywood Canteen. With her lustrous red hair, she was a favorite among the men.

Julie gave generously of her time and talent to numerous other charitable organizations. She was a member for many years of the National Charity League, Diadames and the League for Children. She also served as president of both the local and national chapters of ARCS (Achievement Rewards for College Scientists), a cause dear to her heart.

Julie was a woman of many talents, had an indomitable spirit and a great love for life. An accomplished artist, many of her paintings graced the walls of her home. She flew her own plane and earned her pilot's license. One of her great joys was flying co-pilot next to her husband.

Moving through the social circle of Beverly Hills, Julie was named one of the year's "ten best dressed women" in Los Angeles. But although her friends included presidents, artists, pilots, doctors, scientists and fellow thespians, it was on the headland cliffs of North California that Julie felt most at home.

In the arms of loved ones, actress Julie Bishop/Jacqueline Wells passed away in Mendocino, California, on August 30 (her birthday), 2001. At her side were her husband, retired general surgeon William F. Bergin, her daughter and son-in-law.

Serials

1926

The Bar-C Mystery. Pathé, [10 Chapters] D: Robert F. Hill; SP: William Sherwood; S: Raymond Spears; LP: Wallace MacDonald, Dorothy Phillips, Ethel Clayton, Philo McCullough, Johnny Fox, Violet Schram, Fred de Silva.

1932

Heroes of the West. Univ., [12 Chapters] D: Ray Taylor; SP: George Plympton, Basil Dickey, Joe Roach; S: Peter B. Kyne; LP: Noah Beery, Jr., Diana Duval [Wells/Bishop], Onslow Stevens, William Desmond, Martha Mattox, Philo McCullough.

1933

Clancy of the Mounted. Univ., [12 Chapters] D: Ray Taylor; SP: Basil Dickey, Ella O'Neill, Harry O. Hoyt; S: Robert W. Service; LP: Tom Tyler, William Desmond, Rosalie Roy, Francis Ford, Edmund Cobb, Tom London, Earl McCarthy.

Tarzan the Fearless. Principal, [12 Chapters] D: Robert F. Hill; SP: Basil Dickey, George Plympton, Walter Anthony; LP: Larry (Buster) Crabbe, Jacqueline Wells, E. Alyn Warren, Philo McCullough, Frank Lackteen, Mischa Auer, Matthew Betz, Edward Woods.

DORIS WESTON

Doris Weston was a pretty actress who had two femme leads at Warner Brothers— *The Singing Marine* ('37) and *Submarine D-1* ('37), then was at Republic for *Born to Be*

Doris Weston and Warren Hull in *Mandrake the Magician* (Columbia, 1937).

Wild ('38) and *Delinquent Parents*, and then over to Columbia for the serial *Mandrake the Magician* ('39). As Betty she endured dangers along with Mandrake as they fought "The Wasp" and his criminal band for control of the radium energy machine meant for medical treatment purposes. The Wasp knows it can be used as a lethal weapon of destruction. Doris had a pleasing screen personality and carried off her role like a pro. Two other films were made in '39 — *When Tomorrow Comes* and *Chip of the Flying U*. She left the screen after the Brown film. She had acting potential and probably could have had a good career had she continued.

Doris died in 1960 at age 42.

Serial

1939

Mandrake the Magician. Col., [12 Chapters] D: Sam Nelson, Norman Deming; SP: Joseph F. Poland, Basil Dickey, Ned Dandy; P: Jack Fier; Cam: Benjamin H. Kline; Mus: Lee Zahler; LP: Warren Hull, Doris Weston, Al Kikume, Rex Downing, Edward Earle, Forbes Murray, Kenneth MacDonald, Don Beddoe, Ernie Adams, George Chesebro.

Charles (Slim) Whitaker

Slim Whitaker was a familiar face to serial and Western audiences—"face" because most Saturday matinee attendees didn't even know his name, much less information about him. Yet he menaced saddle aces from Hoot Gibson to Lash LaRue, and he brought shivers to young buckaroos as he slugged or shot it out with serial stalwarts in such cliffhangers as *Rustlers of Red Dog*, *The Great Adventures of Wild Bill Hickok*, *The Miracle Rider*, *The Phantom Rider*, *The Clutching Hand* and *Winners of the West*. In fact, he appeared in 23 serials, nearly always as an uncouth badman.

During his career, Slim appeared with the following stars the indicated number of times, bearing in mind that sometimes he was unbilled and the author may have missed seeing him in a film.

Tom Tyler (23); Ken Maynard (18); Tim McCoy (16); Wally Wales (14); Johnny Mack Brown (13); John Wayne (13); Buck Jones (12); Gene Autry (12); Buster Crabbe (10); George O'Brien (8); Buffalo Bill, Jr. (8); Hoot Gibson (7); Lane Chandler (7); Robert Livingston (7); Dave O'Brien-Jim Newill (6); Bill Elliott (6); Tim Holt (6); Reb Russell (6); Bob Steele (5); Tom Keene (5); Charles Starrett (4); Bob Custer (4); Jack Luden (4); Jack Hoxie (4); Tex Ritter (4); Roy Rogers (4); George Houston (4); Harry Carey (3); Rex Lease (3); Yakima Canutt (3); Buddy Roosevelt (3); Jack Perrin (3); Bob Allen (3); Dick Foran (3); Lash LaRue (3); Kermit Maynard (2); Rex Bell (2); Ray Corrigan-John King (2); Al Hoxie (2); Jack Randall (2); Donald Barry (2); Eddie Dean (2); Lee Powell (2); Bob Baker (2); Fred Scott (2)

Slim was in at least one film each with Rod Cameron, Tom Mix, Fred Gilman, Pete Morrison, Fred Humes, Franklyn Farnum, Roy Stewart, William Desmond, William Farnum, "Big Boy" Williams, Monte Montana, Conway Tearle, William Boyd, Rin-Tin-Tin, Norman Kerry, Richard Dix, Sammy Baugh, Smith Ballew, Randolph

Charles Whitaker (left) and Hal Taliaferro (Wally Wales) in *Phantom Gold* (Columbia, 1938).

Scott, Bob Reeves, Kenneth Harlan and Robert Kellard.

Slim was born in Missouri on July 29, 1893. When the studios ceased production of "B" Westerns in the early '50s, things got tough for Slim. His last known film was *The Westward Trail* ('48) in which he played a bartender. What he did in the ensuing years is not known, except that he spent the last year of his life as a fry cook in a Los Angeles cafe. It was a sad comedown for a fine Western character actor who for 35 years worked in the studios at minimum pay. He died on July 27, 1963.

Good parts for Slim were found in *Twin Triggers* ('26), *Speedy Spurs* ('26), *The Bandit Buster* ('26), *Texas Tornado* ('32), *The Fiddlin' Buckaroo* ('33), *The Cactus Kid* ('34), *Arizona Bad Man* ('35), *Lawless Riders* ('35), *Pioneer Trail* ('38), *Phantom Gold* ('38), *Legion of the Lawless* ('40), *Prairie Law* ('40) and *Bullet Code* ('40).

Serials

1922

The Radio King. Univ., [10 Chapters] LP: Roy Stewart, Louise Lorraine, Sidney Bracey, Al Smith.

1926

The Range Fighter. Davis, [10 Chapters] LP: Ken Maynard, Dorothy Devore, George Nichols, Sheldon Lewis.

1933

Fighting with Kit Carson. Mascot, [12 Chapters] LP: Johnny Mack Brown, Betsy King Ross, Noah Beery, Sr., Noah Beery, Jr.

1934

Tailspin Tommy. Univ., [12 Chapters] LP: Maurice Murphy, Noah Beery, Jr., Patricia Farr, Walter Miller.

The Law of the Wild. Mascot, [12 Chapters] LP: Bob Custer, Rex, Rin-Tin-Tin, Jr., Ben Turpin, Lucile Browne.

The Lost Jungle. Mascot, [12 Chapters] LP: Clyde Beatty, Syd Saylor, Cecilia Parker, Wheeler Oakman, Warner Richmond, Wally Wales [Hal Taliaferro].

1935

Phantom Empire. Mascot, [12 Chapters] LP: Gene Autry, Frankie Darro, Betsy King Ross, Dorothy Christie, Wheeler Oakman.

Rustlers of Red Dog. Univ., [12 Chapters] LP: Johnny Mack Brown, Joyce Compton, Walter Miller, Raymond Hatton.

The Roaring West. Univ., [15 Chapters] LP: Buck Jones, Muriel Evans, Walter Miller, Frank McGlynn, Sr.

The Miracle Rider. Mascot, [15 Chapters] LP: Tom Mix, Joan Gale, Charles Middleton, Jason Robards, Sr., Robert Kortman, Charles King.

1936

The Clutching Hand. S & S, [15 Chapters] LP: Jack Mulhall, Ruth Mix, Marion Shilling, Rex Lease, William Farnum.

The Phantom Rider. Univ., [15 Chapters] LP: Buck Jones, Maria Shelton, Diana Gibson, George Cooper, Harry Woods, Charles King.

The Adventures of Frank Merriwell. Univ., [12 Chapters] LP: Don Briggs, Jean Rogers, John King, Carla Laemmle.

1938

The Great Adventures of Wild Bill Hickok. Col., [15 Chapters] LP: Gordon (Bill) Elliott, Carole Wayne, Frankie Darro, Monte Blue, Richard Cramer, Sammy McKim.

Flaming Frontiers. Univ., [15 Chapters] LP: Johnny Mack Brown, Eleanor Hansen, Ralph Bowman [John Archer], Charles Middleton, James Blaine, Horace Murphy, Charles Stevens.

The Lone Ranger. Rep., [15 Chapters] LP: Lee Powell, Chief Thundercloud, Lynne Roberts, Herman Brix, Lane Chandler, Stanley Andrews, George Letz [Montgomery], John Merton.

1939

The Lone Ranger Rides Again. Rep., [15 Chapters] LP: Robert Livingston, Chief Thundercloud, Jinx Falken, Duncan Renaldo, Ralph Dunn.

1940

Winners of the West. Univ., [13 Chapters] LP: Dick Foran, Anne Nagel, James Craig, Tom Fadden, Charles Stevens, Trevor Bardette, Harry Woods, Edmund Cobb.

1941

Riders of Death Valley. Univ., [15 Chapters] LP: Dick Foran, Buck Jones, Charles Bickford, Leo Carrillo, Jeane Kelly [Jean Brooks], Glenn Strange, Big Boy Williams, Monte Blue.

King of the Texas Rangers. Rep., [12 Chapters] LP: Slingin' Sammy Baugh, Pauline Moore, Duncan Renaldo, Neil Hamilton, Charles Trowbridge, Monte Blue.

1942

Captain Midnight. Col., [15 Chapters] LP: Dave O'Brien, Dorothy Short, James Craven, Luana Walters, Guy Wilkerson, Sam Edwards, Bryant Washburn, Joe Girard.

1948

Tex Granger. Col., [15 Chapters] LP: Robert Kellard, Peggy Stewart, Buzz Henry, Smith Ballew, Jack Ingram, I. Stanford Jolley, Terry Frost, Charles Whitaker.

PEARL WHITE

Iridescent, incomparable, fearless and peerless Pearl Fay White became the most famous of the silent serial queens. She was 5'6" tall, weighed about 120 lbs., had blue eyes and titian red hair. However, after *The Perils of Pauline* ('14) she began to use a blonde wig for better photographic effects. She was the ultimate expression of women's lib. Her screen adventures and uninhibited personal life fulfilled the dreams of both the sweatshop working girls and the small town belles whose dreams of emancipation were long dress balls and marcelled Charles Dana Gibson boyfriends.

Throughout her career, White gleefully lied her head off to interviewers about her past, her family and her career, even signing off on a highly dubious autobiography. Since her death, only one book has been published

Announcing
Pearl White
The nation's favorite
in the five part Gold Rooster Play
in Pathécolor
Mayblossom
Produced by Astra   Released April 8

In *Mayblossom* (Astra, 1912).

on her, but the 1969 *The Fearless, Peerless Girl* is not so much a biography as a collection of musings and questionable dialogues.

Pearl was born in the tiny hamlet of Greenridge, Missouri, near Sedalia, on March 4, 1889, and grew up in Springfield, Missouri. Her mother died when Pearl was about three years of age. Pearl was the last of nine children.

At 15, a child thrusting up from the filth, with no more design than a flower seeking the air that breeds beauty, she went to work in a print shop that turned out theater programs. She wanted a chance to play on the stage, and she created that chance for herself through contacts she made through her job. Fearing her father, who had forbidden her to do stage work, she continued to labor in the shop by day, while playing small parts at night for Diemer's Stock company in Springfield.

When Pearl reached 18 she left home and joined a stock company which travelled throughout Missouri, Kansas and Oklahoma. While in Oklahoma City on Columbus Day 1907, she married fellow actor Victor Sutherland. They separated after a few years and she was granted a divorce in April 1914.

While appearing in stock at South Norwalk, Connecticut, the strain of ranting in old-fashioned melodramas caused her voice to give out and she turned to the silent cinema. She kept the husky voice the rest of her life. She began her film career at Pathé. *The Life of Buffalo Bill* ('10) was released on August 2, 1910, and is reputed to be her first film. Paul Panzer did the villain honors. Other Pathé films included *The Girl from Arizona* ('10), *Tommy Gets His Sister Married* ('10), *Her Photograph* ('10), *Summer Flirtation* ('10), *Memories of the Past* ('11), *Through the Window* ('11) and *The Arrowmaker's Daughter* ('12).

For Powers she appeared in *The Missing Bridegroom* ('10), *The New Magdalene* ('10), *The Woman Hater* ('10), *Angel of the Slums* ('11), *For the Honor of the Name* ('11), *Home, Sweet, Home* ('11), *The Step Sisters* ('11) and others.

In 1912, Pearl went to work at Crystal and made at least 150 one-reel and split-reel comedies. The number could be closer to 200. Chester Barnett played opposite her in at least 140 of the films. Phillips Smalley directed most of them. A sampling of titles follows: 1912's *The Girl in the Next Room, The Chorus Girl, Bella's Beaus, Pearl's Admirers, The Gypsy Flirt* and *Her Dressmaker's Bills*; 1913's *The Other Girl, Lovers Three, Pearl as a Clairvoyant, Pearl as a Detective, Pearl's Mistake, What Papa Got* and *Who is in the Box?*; and 1914's *The Lifted Veil, The Shadow of a Crime, Get Out and Get Under, What Didn't Happen to Mary, The Hall Room Girls, The Paper Doll, The New Typist* and *His Awful Daughter.*

Pearl's last film for Crystal was *Some Collectors*, one-half reel, released on October 13, 1914, and co-starring Chester Barnett.

Pearl was induced back to Pathé by Louis Gasnier to star in his *The Perils of Pauline* ('14). The Hearst newspapers sponsored the serial as a device to increase circulation. Each installment appeared simultaneously in the press and on the screen.

Seen today, it's easy to understand all the fuss. *The Perils of Pauline* is still exciting and involving, and contains a lot of good-natured humor. She had great chemistry with her leading man, the curly-haired and charming Crane Wilbur. Pearl portrayed an

Crane Wilbur and Pearl White in *The Perils of Pauline* (Pathé, 1914).

orphaned heiress who is pursued by the murderous Koerner (Paul Panzer), next in line to her fortune. Her boyfriend, Harry Marvin (Wilbur), stands guard over Pearl.

But Pearl was terribly injured while filming *Pauline*, as was later confirmed by scenarist Charles Goddard. Paul Panzer was carrying an unconscious Pauline up a flight of stairs when Pearl shifted her weight, and the two went over backwards. "I struck on the top of my head, displacing several vertebrae," she recalled in 1920. "The pain was terrible. For two years I simply lived with osteopaths, and to this day I have some pretty bad times with my back." Indeed, Pearl's back injury — aggravated by years of active filming — eventually led to her retirement and early death.

By starring a heroine (lovely Pearl White) instead of a hero, the movies found a gold mine. Pearl went on to do a string of gooseflesh serials.

Nickelodeons were crowded to the

aisles for each reel of her thrillers. And the return of the fans the following week never was left to chance. Each episode ended with Pearl seemingly facing certain death. Bound to a railroad track ahead of an express train, perhaps, or suspended by her hair over a cliff. It was the latter ploy which gave the name to the whole serial genre — cliffhangers.

The serial enjoyed an enormous success and remains the best-known chapter play ever filmed. This and subsequent serials made Pearl the most popular star of her day, surpassing for several years the popularity of Mary Pickford and other leading stars of feature films. Her serials emphasized mystery and suspense more than action. She usually performed her own stunts, but because of her spinal injury required doubles for the more demanding acrobatics.

When she met Major Wallace Mc-Cutcheon, war hero and actor, that meeting seemed to bring the promise of true romance which she sought. McCutcheon was a man's man — and a woman's. He had the bearing and splendor of nature that signifies the knight. But the war had worked insidious and secret changes. One day he walked out of the Lambs Club and was never seen again. Again Pearl White's romance was shattered. In 1921, she obtained a divorce. Months later, McCutcheon was discovered in a sanitarium in Washington, D.C. The deadly gas of war and two bullet wounds has slowly worked grim vengeance.

In 1922, Pearl went to France, where she owned a country villa and a townhouse. She traveled extensively about the world after announcing that she had become tired of "being swung from cliffs and dropped from burning houses down into sewers." Her eyesight had also been impaired by the film studio lights. But her desire for retirement did not long survive the attractions and plaudits of Paris. There she drew crowds to the Montmarte Music Hall in a revue called "Tu Perds La Boule" and later, at a reputed $3,000 a week, to a London revue in which she co-starred with George Carney. She became a notable figure at the racetrack and gay nightlife places. Besides appearing in theatres in Eu-

rope, she made a tour in Asia Minor and Egypt. She made world headlines by spending time in an Alpine convent, "in search of her soul."

George Seitz lured her back to the States for one last serial, *Plunder* ('23), which she starred in as a favor to him more than for any other reason. The theme of the film dealt with a skyscraper in New York City and a hidden treasure beneath it which the villain sought to obtain any way possible. The serial was successful, as were all those made by Pearl, but it was not her best one. The back injury suffered in making *Perils of Pauline* was giving her more trouble than ever, and it was painful for her to subject her body to the rigors that were a normal ingredient of cliffhangers. Her last film was a feature titled *Terror* ('24), filmed in France and released in the U.S. as *The Perils of Paris.*

Surprisingly, none of Pearl's movies were made in California, nor is she known to have ever visited the state. But Hollywood profited by her pioneering efforts as the silent screen's most popular heroine, and every cliffhanger produced after 1915 — regardless of locale — was influenced by the example set by vivacious and daring Pearl White.

Mention should be made of the ten features she made for Fox in 1920–22. They are *The White Moll* ('20), *The Tiger's Club* ('20), *The Thief* ('20), *The Mountain Woman* ('21), *Know Your Men* ('21), *Beyond Price* ('21), *A Virgin Paradise* ('21), *Any Wife* ('22), *The Broadway Peacock* ('22) and *Without Fear* ('22).

Pearl died of a liver ailment on August 4, 1938, in the American Hospital in Neuilly, France, and is buried in the Passy Cemetery. Bertram Winthrop, an American lawyer, was in complete charge of the funeral arrangements. Thomas Cozzika, a Greek friend, was at her bedside when she quietly passed away.

Much of her estate was willed to charitable institutions. Part of her Rembouillet estate was given to a Catholic church. Other funds were left in trust for invalid performers. Her old father was left $150 per month for as long as he lived.

Whatever wealth Pearl White derived

from her cinematic acting was well-earned, but the greatest wealth was the happiness that Pearl imparted to the great world public with her thrilling, chilling and dauntless courage to win out over all odds.

Serials

1914

The Perils of Pauline. Pathé, [20 Chapters] D: Louis Gasnier, Donald McKenzie; SP: George B. Seitz; S: Charles Goddard; P: Leopold & Theodore Wharton; LP: Pearl White, Crane Wilbur, Paul Panzer, Edward Jose, Francis Carlyle, Donald McKenzie.

Exploits of Elaine. Pathé, [14 Chapters] D: Louis Gasnier, George B. Seitz; SP: C. W. Goddard, George B. Seitz; S: Arthur B. Reeve, Bertram Millhauser, Charles L. Goddard; P: Leopold & Theodore Wharton; Cam: Joseph Dubray; LP: Pearl White, Arnold Daly, Creighton Hale, Sheldon Lewis, Lionel Barrymore.

1915

The New Exploits of Elaine. Pathé, [10 Chapters] D: George B. Seitz, Bertram Millhauser; SP: charles W. Goddard, George B. Seitz, Bertram Millhauser; S: Arthur B. Reeve; P: Leopold & Theodore Wharton; Cam: Joseph Dubray; LP: Pearl White, Creighton Hale, Arnold Daly, Edwin Arden.

The Romance of Elaine. Pathé, [12 Chapters] D: George B. Seitz, Louis Gasnier, Joseph A. Golden; SP: Charles W. Goddard, George B. Seitz, Bertram Millhauser; S: Arthur B. Reeve; P: Leopold & Theodore Wharton; Cam: Joseph Dubray; LP: Pearl White, Creighton Hale, Arnold Daly, Lionel Barrymore, Bessie Wharton.

1916

Pearl of the Army. Pathé, [15 Chapters] D: Edward Jose; SP: George B. Seitz; S: G. M. McConnell; LP: Pearl White, Ralph Kellard, Marie Wayne, Floyd Buckley, W. T. Carleton, Theodore Friebus.

1917

The Fatal Ring. Pathé, [20 Chapters] D: George B. Seitz; SP: Bertram Millhauser; S: Fred Jackson; LP: Pearl White, Earle Fox, Warner Oland, Ruby Hoffman.

The Iron Claw. Pathé, [20 Chapters] D: Edward Jose, George B. Seitz; SP: George B. Seitz; S: Arthur Stringer; LP: Pearl White, Creighton Hale, Sheldon Lewis, Harry Fraser, J. E. Dunn, Henry G. Sell, Carey Lee.

1918

The House of Hate. Pathé, [20 Chapters] D: George B.Seitz; SP: Bertram Millhauser; S: Arthur B. Reeve, Charles A. Logue; LP: Pearl White, Antonio Moreno, Peggy Shanor, John Gilmour, John Webb Dillon.

1919

The Black Secret. Pathé, [15 Chapters] D: George B. Seitz; SP: Bertram Millhauser; S: Robert W. Chambers; LP: Pearl White, Walter McGrail, Wallace McCutcheon, George B. Seitz.

The Lightning Raider. Pathé, [15 Chapters] D: George B. Seitz; SP: Bertram Millhauser, George B. Seitz; LP: Pearl White, Warner Oland, Ruby Hoffman, William Burt.

1923

Plunder. Pathé, [15 Chapters] D: George B. Seitz; SP: Bertram Millhauser, George B. Seitz; S: Herbert Crooker; LP: Pearl White, Warren Krech [William], Harry Semels, Tom McIntyre, J. Elwood Pool, Wally Oettel, Charles Reveda.

LOIS WILDE

Lois Wilde played Diana Compton, newspaperwoman, in Republic's classic serial *Undersea Kingdom* ('36) starring Ray Corrigan (as "Crash" Corrigan). A series of earthquakes are originating from the bottom of the ocean where the continent of Atlantis was supposed to have vanished. Prof. Norton has invented a counteracting ray that will stop an impending quake. He enlists the help of naval officer Crash Corrigan and the two, along with the newspaperwoman, the professor's son and two sailors descend to the ocean floor in a special submarine, where they are drawn into an inland sea of the dome-covered Atlantis. They find two factions in deadly combat — the White Robes and the Black Robes.

Unga Khan, leader of the Black Robes, has harnessed the atom and is directing a disintegrating machine at North America as part of a plan to take over the upper world. Crash and his friends ally themselves with the White Robes and bring the downfall of Khan.

Wilde was a member of the Ziegfeld Follies and did modeling in the East. A major illness kept her inactive for a couple of years before moving to California about 1935.

In addition to *Undersea Kingdom*, she appeared as heroine in *Caryl of the Mountains* ('36) with Rin-Tin-Tin, Jr.; *Singing Cowboy* ('36) with Gene Autry; *Stormy Trails* ('36) with Rex Bell; *Wildcat Trooper* ('36) with Kermit Maynard; *Danger Valley* ('37) with Jack Randall; *Hopalong Rides Again* ('37) with William Boyd; and *Brothers of the West* ('37) with Tom Tyler. She was involved in an automobile accident in 1938 and left films to become a nurse until 1951 when she tried movies again in unbilled roles.

Lois Wilde died on February 16, 1995.

Serial

1936

Undersea Kingdom. Rep., [12 Chapters] D: B. Reeves Eason, Tracy Layne; SP: John Rathmell, Maurice Geraghty, Oliver Drake; Spv.: Barney Sarecky; P: Nat Levine; LP: Ray Corrigan, Lois Wilde, Monte Blue, William Farnum, Lee Van Atta, Raymond Hatton, C. Montague Shaw, Lon Chaney, Jr., Smiley Burnette, Lane Chandler, Frankie Marvin, Jack Mulhall, Tom Steele.

JAN WILEY

Jan Wiley, a slim, striking blonde, was a competent actress who got little recognition in movie reference books. It is almost as if she never existed. Far less accomplished actresses have garnered recognition for their efforts.

She was born in or about 1911, as her

reported age when she died from cancer in 1993 in Rancho Palos Verdes, California, was 82.

Tonto Basin Outlaws ('41), starring the Range Busters (Ray Corrigan, John King and Max Terhune), is the first credit the author can find for her. In the story she is a newspaper reporter romanced by Crash and Dusty while not busy breaking up an outlaw gang. Her second credit in 1941 was the Republic serial *Dick Tracy vs. Crime, Inc.*, in which she plays June Chandler. The serial is considered the best of the four Dick Tracys by most critics. Tracy's antagonist is a villain known as "The Ghost," who wears a rubber-like contour mask over his head and has the means of making himself invisible. His trademark, left at the scene of each of his crimes, was the thumbprint of an executed criminal named "Rackets" Reagan, who had been captured and executed through the efforts of detective Tracy. One of the Ghost's motives in carrying out his lawless campaign — aside from the wealth he accumulates— is to exact vengeance upon Tracy for the downfall of Reagan, his brother. Jan Wiley was adequate in her role.

In *Thunder River Feud* (Mon. '42), Jan plays Maybelle Pembroke, daughter of a rancher feuding with his neighbor rancher over a fence line. Again Crash and Dusty vie for her affection while settling the problem. In *The Strange Case of Doctor Rx* (Univ. '42) starring Patric Knowles and Anne Gwynne, she has a small part as Lily. Ray Corrigan is also present as "Bongo," the gorilla.

Jan plays a photographer in *Top Sergeant* (Univ. '42), featuring Leo Carrillo, Andy Devine and Anne Gwynne in the principal roles. And if one didn't blink his/her eyes, Jan could be seen as an announcer in *You're Telling Me* (Univ. '42) featuring Hugh Herbert and Anne Gwynne. Another brief bit was as a tenderfoot in *Parachute Nurse* (Col. '42) with Marguerite Chapman and William Wright. Her role as a member of a covered wagon train that Buck Jones is ramroding in *Dawn on the Great Divide* (Mon. '42) is a small one, overshadowed by Mona Barrie and Christine McIntyre.

Jan is billed third in PRC's *City of Silent Men* ('42) as a waitress killed by Dick Curtis, who tries to pin the crime on Frank Albertson. June Lang was co-featured. Jan is billed fourth in the cast of *Criminal Investigator* (Mon. '42) featuring Robert Lowery and Edith Fellows. As Miss Drake, she and a

confederate kidnap and murder a former showgirl before she can give incriminating evidence to Lowery. In *The Living Ghost* (Mon. '42), Jan plays Tina Craig, who stands to inherit a fortune from her brain-damaged father. James Dunn and Joan Woodbury star.

In the Ritz Brothers' *Never a Dull Moment* (Univ. '43), Jan is a cloakroom clerk, whereas in *So Proudly we Hail* ('43), she portrays Lt. Lynne Hopkins. It was an award-winning Paramount film starring Claudette Colbert, Paulette Goddard and Veronica Lake. She co-starred with Barton MacLane in *The Underdog* (PRC '43) as the wife who is proud of her job and contribution to the war effort and who resists her husband's desire to move back to the farm.

In *Gals, Inc.*, a comedy starring Leon Errol and Harriet Hilliard, she is a maitre d'. Grace McDonald is featured. And in *Jive Junction* (PRC '43) featuring Dickie Moore and Tiny Thayer, Jan plays Miss Forbes, music teacher.

Adventures of Kitty O'Day (Mon. '44) features beautiful Jean Parker in the title role; fifth in the cast, Jan portrays Carla Brant. She is a receptionist in *San Diego, I Love You* (Univ. '44), starring Jon Hall and Louise Allbritton.

In the Johnny Mack Brown Western *Law Men* (Mon. '44), Jan is the girlfriend of Kirby Grant, who gets mixed up in bank robberies. Johnny and Raymond Hatton save the day. In another prairie actioner, *The Cisco Kid Returns* (Mon. '45), Jan is a maid involved in a murder, but Duncan Renaldo comes to her rescue. In *Frontier Gal* (Univ. '45), Jan plays Rod Cameron's old girlfriend. She has only a small part as a young woman in *Patrick the Great* (Univ. '45) starring Donald O'Connor and Peggy Ryan; her part in *There Goes Kelly* (Mon. '45) is somewhat larger. She plays Rita Wilson, a radio singing star who is murdered as the story unfolds. Jackie Moran and Wanda McKay head the cast.

Jan has the feminine lead in Universal's chapterplay *The Master Key* ('45). A professor develops an Oraton machine that will extract gold from sea water. The Master Key was a diabolical enemy agent bent upon ruining the economy of the United States by flooding the world market with phony gold. F.B.I. agent Tom Brant (Milburn Stone), detective Jack Ryan (Dennis Moore) and reporter Janet Lowe (Jan Wiley) doggedly pursue the saboteurs.

Jan is the romantic interest in *Secret Agent X-9* (Univ. '45), a remake of the 1937

In *The Brute Man* (Universal, 1946).

serial, but with a different plot. Facing a shortage of aviation fuel, Japanese warlords order the beautiful Nabura (Victoria Horne), head of the feared Black Dragon Intelligence Service operating on neutral Shadow Island off the China coast, to smuggle an agent into America and secure a secret formula for synthetic fuel. Lynn Moore (Jan Wiley), an Australian agent posing as a quisling, learns of Nabura's plan and informs Secret Agent X-9 (Lloyd Bridges) of the plot. Ah Fong, a Chinese agent posing as a fan-tan dealer, joins X-9 and Moore in an attempt to thwart the evil scheme.

For some reason Jan was replaced by Joyce Compton and Christine McIntyre by Jean Carlin in *Behind the Mask* (Mon. '46), but Jan was third-billed in *Below the Deadline* (Mon. '46) featuring Warren Douglas and Ramsay Ames. Jan was Vivian Saunders, girlfriend of a gambling ring boss.

The Brute Man (Univ. '46) featured Rondo Hatton as "The Creeper" (it was his last film before his death), Tom Neal, Wiley and Jane Adams. In *Fig Leaf for Eve* (Cary Westen Corp. '46), a comedy-drama, Jan has the title role as Eve Lorraine, exotic dancer. Phil Warren is the male lead. In *She-Wolf of London* (Univ. '46), Jan is billed fourth behind Don Porter, June Lockhart and Sara Haden, playing the daughter of the latter. And in *Without Reservations* (RKO '46), starring Claudette Colbert and John Wayne, she has a small role as a manicurist. Ruth Roman and Dolores Moran also could be seen in bit roles.

There are no film credits beyond 1946 for Jan Wiley. A guess would be that she opted for marriage and retirement. At the time of her death, her name was Greene.

Serials

1941

Dick Tracy vs. Crime, Inc. Rep., [15 Chapters] D: William Witney, John English; SP: Ronald Davidson, Norman S. Hall, William Lively, Joseph Poland, Joseph O'Donnell; AP: W. J. O'Sullivan; Cam: Reggie Lanning; Mus: Cy Feuer; LP: Ralph Byrd, Jan Wiley, John Davidson, Ralph Morgan, Michael Owen, Kenneth Harlan, Robert Frazer, Robert Fiske, Anthony Warde.

1945

The Master Key. Univ., [13 Chapters] D: Ray Taylor, Lewis D. Collins; S: Jack Natteford, Dwight Babcock; SP: Joseph O'Donnell, George H. Plympton, Ande Lamb; LP: Milburn Stone, Jan Wiley, Dennis Moore, Sarah Padden, Russell Hicks, Addison Richards, Byron Foulger, Maris Wrixon, Lash LaRue, George Lynn, Jack Rockwell, Ed Cobb, John Merton, Al Ferguson, Ernie Adams, Ken Terrell.

Secret Agent X-9. Univ., [13 Chapters] D: Ray Taylor, Lewis D. Collins; SP: Joseph O'Donnell, Patricia Harper; S: Joseph O'Donnell, Harold C. Wire; LP: Lloyd Bridges, Keye Luke, Jan Wiley, Victoria Horne, Cy Kendall, Samuel S. Hinds, I. Stanford Jolley, John Merton, Jack Rockwell, Arno Frey, Edmund Cobb, Ann Codee.

ROBERT WILKE

Robert Wilke was a believable scoundrel — in build, voice and looks. There were other Western characters who had these same characteristics, but Wilke had something more, talent that enabled him to rise to the top as a heavy and to make the switch to "A" films and non-series Westerns once the dust had buried the "B" product.

Wilke entered films about 1938 and appeared in over 150 films. Most of his "B" Westerns were made by Republic. Other than Westerns and serials he appeared in *Earl Carroll Vanities, The Ghost Goes Wild, Passkey to Danger, Traffic in Crime, The Pilgrim Lady, Web of Danger, Daredevils of the Clouds, Blackmail, The Catman of Paris, Rendezvous with Annie, Homicide for Three, The Wreck of the Hesperus, The Blonde Bandit, The Traveling Saleswoman, The Las Vegas Story, Written on the Wind, Hot Summer Night, Never Steal Anything Small, The Tarnished Angel, Spartacus, Fate Is the Hunter, Tony Rome* and more.

Serials

1938

The Fighting Devil Dogs. Rep., [12 Chapters] LP: Lee Powell, Herman Brix, Eleanor Stewart, Montagu Love, Hugh Sothern, Sam Flint, Forrest Taylor, Carleton Young.

1939

Daredevils of the Red Circle. Rep., [12 Chapters] LP: Charles Quigley, Herman Brix, David Sharpe, Carole Landis, Miles Mander, Charles Middleton.

1940

Adventures of Red Ryder. Rep., [12 Chapters] LP: Donald Barry, Noah Beery, Sr., Tommy Cook, Maude Pierce Allen, Vivian Coe, Harry Worth, Hal Taliaferro, Robert Kortman, William Farnum.

1941

Dick Tracy vs. Crime, Inc. Rep. [15 Chapters] LP: Ralph Byrd, Jan Wiley, John Davidson, Ralph Morgan, Michael Owen, Kenneth Harlan, Jack Mulhall, Robert Fiske, Robert Frazer.

1942

Spy Smasher. Rep., [12 Chapters] LP: Kane Richmond, Marguerite Chapman, Sam Flint, Hans Schumm, Tristram Coffin, Tom London, Robert O. Davis, Robert Wilke.

1943

The Masked Marvel. Rep., [12 Chapters] LP: William Forrest, Tom Steele, Louise Currie, David Bacon, Rod Bacon, Anthony Warde, Nora Lane.

1944

Captain America. Rep., [15 Chapters] LP: Dick Purcell, Lorna Gray [Adrian Booth], Lionel Atwill, Charles Trowbridge, Russell Hicks, George J. Lewis, LeRoy Mason.

The Tiger Woman. Rep., [12 Chapters] LP: Linda Stirling, Allan Lane, Duncan Renaldo, George J. Lewis, LeRoy Mason, Tom Steele, Crane Whitley, Robert Wilke.

1945

The Purple Monster Strikes. Rep., [15 Chapters] LP: Linda Stirling, Dennis Moore, Roy Barcroft, James Craven, Bud Geary, Mary Moore, John Davidson.

1946

The Phantom Rider. Rep., [12 Chapters] LP: Robert Kent, Peggy Stewart, LeRoy Mason, George J. Lewis, Kenne Duncan, Hal Taliaferro, Robert Wilke, Chief Thundercloud, Tom London.

The Crimson Ghost. Rep., [12 Chapters] LP: Charles Quigley, Linda Stirling, Clayton Moore, I. Stanford Jolley, Kenne Duncan, Forrest Taylor, Virginia Carroll, Rex Lease, Tom Steele, Robert Wilke, Bud Wolfe.

King of the Forest Rangers. Rep., [12 Chapters] LP: Larry Thompson, Helen Talbot, Stuart Hamblem, LeRoy Mason, Tom London, Scott Elliott, Robert Wilke.

1947

The Black Widow. Rep., [13 Chapters] LP: Carol Forman, Bruce Edwards, Virginia Lindley, I. Stanford Jolley, Virginia Carroll, Anthony Warde, Robert Wilke.

G-Men Never Forget. Rep., [12 Chapters] LP: Clayton Moore, Ramsay Ames, Roy Barcroft, Drew Allen, Edmund Cobb, Tom Steele, Robert Wilke, Dale Van Sickel.

1948

Dangers of the Canadian Mounted. Rep., [12 Chapters] LP: Jim Bannon, Virginia Belmont, Anthony Warde, Dorothy Granger, I. Stanford Jolley, Dale Van Sickel, Robert Wilke, Ken Terrell, Tom Steele.

1949

Federal Agents vs. Underworld, Inc. Rep., [12 Chapters] LP: Kirk Alyn, Roy Barcroft, Rosemary LaPlanche, Bruce Edwards, Tristram Coffin, Jack O'Shea, Marshall Reed, Robert Wilke.

Ghost of Zorro. Rep., [12 Chapters] LP: Clayton Moore, Pamela Blake, Roy Barcroft, Gene Stutenroth, I. Stanford Jolley, Charles King, Robert Wilke.

1950

The James Brothers of Missouri. Rep., [12 Chapters] LP: Keith Richards, Noel Neill, Robert Bice, Roy Barcroft, Patricia Knox, Edmund Cobb, Lane Bradford, Robert Wilke, Tom Steele, John Hamilton.

EARLE WILLIAMS

Earle Williams was born on February 28, 1880, in Sacramento, California. For many years he was the top male star at Vitagraph and one of the leading personalities of the early silent screen. In 1914, he was the most popular man on the screen.

The Juggernaut ('15) was perhaps his greatest triumph, but there were others: *The Life of Moses* (1909–10), *Uncle Tom's Cabin* ('10), *A Tale of Two Cities* ('11), *Two Women and Two Men* ('12), *Happy-Go-Lucky* (one of many in which he co-starred with Clara Kimball Young) ('14), *Sins of the Mothers* ('15), *My Lady's Slipper* ('16), *Arsene Lupin* ('17), *The Soul Master* ('17), *A Diplomatic Mission* ('18), *Rogues of Romance* ('19), *Captain Swift* ('20), *Diamonds Adrift* ('21), *The Man from Downing Street* ('22), *Master of Men* ('23), *Borrowed Husbands* ('24), *The Adventurous Sex* ('25), *The Ancient Mariner* ('25), *Skyrocket* ('26), *Red Signals* ('27) and *Say It with Diamonds* ('27).

A rather quaint plot motivated *The Goddess* ('15) with Anita Stewart and Williams. They were the first-line heartthrob team which was keeping Vitagraph in the black. It was a popular serial. Good acting and skillful photography raised this film far and away above its plotline.

The Scarlet Runner ('16) derived its name from the high-powered automobile purchased by Williams. It was a means of earning his living when deprived of his allowance by his rich uncle, as he had made poor use of the money he had been given. Following his purchase of the car, he enters the service of a king traveling in disguise and helps to defeat a plot through which a friend is about to meet his death. Other adventures follow, each a separate and unrelated story. Each episode has a different cast except for the Williams' continuing role. Although he was a popular star, *The Scarlet Runner* was not nearly as popular with the serial clientele as was *The Goddess*.

Williams died from bronchial pneumonia in 1927 in Los Angeles. He was 47.

Serials

1915

The Goddess. Vit., [15 Chapters] D: Ralph W. Ince; SP: Gouverneur Morris, Charles W. Goddard; LP: Anita Stewart, Earle Williams, Paul Scardon, William Dangman, Ned Finley.

1916

The Scarlet Runner. Vit., [12 Chapters] D/P: Wally Van, P. S. Earle; SP: George H. Plympton; S: C. H. & A. M. Williamson; LP: Earle Williams, Marguerite Blake, L. Rogers Lytton, John Costello, Edith Storey, Adolphe Menjou, Zena Keefe, Charles Kent, Ethel Corcoran, Billie Billings.

KATHLYN WILLIAMS

Kathlyn Williams was a Western girl, supposedly having been born in Butte, Montana, on May 31, 1888. There has been doubt expressed about her birth year, some historians believing it was several years earlier because of her sudden "aging" in the early 1920s. Her father was a Norwegian, her mother Welsh. No doubt when she left Butte to conquer the world, she never dreamed that she would have to go through life pursued by a couple hundred assorted wild animals.

She began her stage career as a child, and soon became the protégé of Senator W. A. Clarke, a man ever ready to help talent in its development. She attended Wesleyan University, then studied at the Empire School of Acting in New York, later appearing in a number of well-known stageplays both in the city and on tour.

Coming to Los Angeles, Kathlyn became a member of the famous Belasco Stock Company and was also with Willard Mack in Salt Lake City for a time. Films came along about that time and she joined the Biograph Company under D. W. Griffith in 1909.

Her first film was *Lines of White on a Sullen Sea* ('09), a one-reeler with Linda Arvidson and Del Henderson. Her second was *Gold is Not All* ('10), also with the same two players.

In 1910, she shifted to Selig and quickly became the company's leading actress, scoring in *Two Orphans* ('11) and *The Adventures of Captain Kate* (a 1911 series). Her screen persona was that of a perfectly unspoiled girl as natural and genuine as a child, one keenly alive with a diversity of absorbing interests. Lovely blonde hair, deep blue eyes, exquisite coloring, a relaxed naturalness with both man and beast, polished acting ability — these were quite enough distinctive characteristics to give her the charisma that kept her working and the public excited about seeing her.

Kathlyn is vividly identified with her famous role of Cherry Malotte in *The Spoilers* ('14), having made this dance hall girl of the North so splendidly human, so superbly alive that it still stands out as one of the great roles of her career. But the reputation she gained for this film is nothing compared to *The Adventures of Kathlyn* ('13), the forerunner of all cliffhanger-type serials. In collaboration with *The Chicago Tribune*, Col. William Selig produced and released the serial concurrently with the *Tribune*'s publication of each episode's story.

For several years she worked in such animal films as *Lost in the Jungle* ('11), *Rescued by Her Lions* ('11), *Harbor Island* ('12), *A Wise Old Elephant* ('13), *Thor, Lord of the Jungles* ('13), *The Leopard's Foundling* ('14), *The Lady of the Tigers* ('14) and *In Tune with the Wild* ('14).

Her Westerns were few but good, and the stories were varied. *Chip of the Flying U* ('14) seems to be her best remembered and most-publicized Selig Western aside from *The Spoilers*. *The U. P. Trail* ('19) for Zane Grey Pictures was her most engaging one.

In 1915, Kathlyn made several hits — *The Ne'er Do Well*, *The Carpet from Bagdad*, *The Rosary*, *Sweet Alyssum* and *Thou Shalt Not Covet*, each feature-length and directed by Colin Campbell. It was her best year.

In March 1913, Kathlyn married actor Victor Kainer. The marriage collapsed but it did produce her only child, a son named after his father. In June 1916, she married Charles Eyton, an actor-producer later to be studio manager for Lasky's. This marriage last until 1931, after which she remained single. Her son Victor died in 1922 while on a trip to China with Kathlyn.

Kathlyn left Selig in late 1916 to join the Oliver Morosco Photoplay Company, where she reigned as a major dramatic actress until 1921. *Redeeming Love* ('16), directed by William D. Taylor, was her first hit. Twice she starred in Cecil B. DeMille epics—*The Whispering Chorus* ('18) and *We Can't Have Everything* ('18). For William DeMille she did *Tree of Knowledge* ('19), *The Prince Chap* ('20) and *Conrad in Quest of His Youth* ('20). Popular Wallace Reid was her co-star in *Big Timber* ('17) and *The Thing We Love* ('18); she played opposite Roy Stewart in *Just a Wife* ('20); and she brought vivid emotion to her dual portrayals of mother and daughter in *The Cost of Hatred* ('17).

After 1921, Kathlyn played major supporting roles through much of the '20s, since she was now too old to play ingenues with conviction. She was believable as an older woman and competent in each role she essayed. Making only a few talkies, Kathlyn retired in 1934 to travel, to enjoy a peaceful life pursuing her many hobbies, and to entertain socially now and then. A car accident in 1949 cost her a leg and she spent much of her remaining life in a wheelchair. Kathlyn died from a heart attack on September 24, 1960.

Throughout her career she had the respect and admiration of both the public and associates. Known as "The Selig Girl" and "The Bernhardt of the Screen," Kathlyn was also known as the diplomat of Hollywood. Her winsome smile and a nature devoid of any sign of temperament won her many friends. She had serenity and poise — not the artificial poise of the movies, but the poise of character.

Doubtless much of Kathlyn's success as an actress was due to her own charming womanliness, her beauty, her sincerity and her dignity — but her rare intelligence gave her the power of discerning the dramatic values of her roles no matter in what social realm they abided. She possessed the capacity to identify herself with her characters, and her work was always finely tempered,

subtle and well-balanced. The wholehearted manner in which she interpreted the woman who has made a mistake, the shallow society leader and the semi-moral of the early West, all displayed her splendid understanding of the feminine mind and heart.

Serial

1913

The Adventures of Kathlyn. Selig, [13 Chapters] D: F. J. Grandon; SP: Gilson Willets; S: Harold McGrath; LP: Kathlyn Williams, Charles Clary, Thomas Santschi, William Carpenter, Goldie Colwell, Lafe McKee, Franklyn Hall, C. J. Murphy, Edmund Cobb, Charles Courtright, Edwin L. Wallock, Guy Oliver.

BEN WILSON

Wilson was born in 1876 in Clinton, Iowa. As screen actor, director, producer and jack-of-all-trades, he had his hand in about every nook and cranny of the film industry in his long career and gave many an extra a chance at stardom. Jack Hoxie and Yakima Canutt are good examples. Wilson appeared in over 100 one- and two-reelers and 12 serials. As serial headliner, he was one of the most popular and successful of the silent era, though his serial laurels had to be shared with Neva Gerber. As co-stars, Wilson and Gerber reigned as king and queen of the serial genre in the late teens and early '20s. They teamed for eight serials and at least 13 features at a time when serials were held in high esteem and maintained a definite draw-

ing power at the box office. Wilson always performed effectively as the hero and Gerber was a pretty and active heroine.

Following up the success of *What Happened to Mary?* ('12), Edison decided to put out several serial pictures. Two of the first to appear were *Who Will Marry Mary?* ('13), again with Mary Fuller in the lead role, and *The Chronicles of Cleek*, a series of detective stories issued in collaboration with *Short Stories*, a well-known magazine. In this series, Benjamin F. Wilson appeared as Hamilton Cleek, a detective. As Cleek, Wilson solves a series of unrelated crimes in 13 episodes constructed along the lines of the two previous *Mary* films. The serial was yet to develop such characteristics as cliffhanger endings and a continuing story involving the same characters.

Wilson had been with the Edison players for several years, appearing in the films the company made in Bermuda and on a transcontinental trip across the Canadian Rockies. He was also with the company that spent the winter of 1912–13 in California and had been one of the principal players in both *What Happened to Mary?* and *Who Will Marry Mary?* Prior to joining Edison, Wilson gained a considerable reputation as a legitimate actor with the Spooner Stock Company and with the forces of Wagenhalls and Kemper.

The earliest credits the author finds for Wilson are *The Star Spangled Banner* ('11) and *The Battle of Bunker Hill* ('11). Beginning in January 1912, with *For the Cause of the South*, Wilson appeared in about 20 one-reelers with Laura Sawyer. His second most frequent co-star was Dorothy Phillips, who worked with him in about 35 one-, two- and three-reelers for Universal-Rex throughout 1915 and part of 1916.

After appearing in *Idle Wives* ('16) and *Society Hypocrites*, Wilson and Gerber began their astonishing serial careers together with the release of *The Voice on the Wire* ('17). They went on to make a total of nine serials together. Their serials moved fast with a lot of action, which endeared them to many serial fans. *The Mystery Ship* was released in 1917, and *Trail of the Octopus* came out in 1919. Both *The Screaming Shadow* and *The Branded Four* saw release in 1920. *The Mysterious Pearl* was released in 1921 with Western badman Charles King in a supporting role.

The team's last three serials were produced by Wilson and released by Davis Corporation on a states-rights arrangement. *The Mystery Box, The Power God* and *Officer 444*, all made in 1926, did not receive wide distribution. Wilson proceeded to produce and star in a series of independent Westerns, with Gerber often playing the heroine.

Wilson's inclinations gradually turned from acting to producing and directing, and he was responsible for directing and/or producing many of the films of Jack Hoxie, Yakima Canutt, Cliff Lyons, Dick Hatton, William Fairbanks, Cheyenne Bill and Roy Stewart. Small outfits such as Anchor, Rayart and Goodwill released the Wilson productions in the states-rights market; consequently, they were viewed only in the smaller theaters catering to cheaply made low-rental films.

Wilson's last film as an actor was *Shadow Ranch* ('30), starring Buck Jones. He died of a heart attack in Glendale, California, on August 25, 1930.

Serials

1912

What Happened to Mary? Edison, [12 Episodes] D: Walter Edwin et al.; SP: Bannister Merwin, James Oppenheim, Horace G. Plympton; LP: Mary Fuller, Bliss Milford, Marc MacDermott, Charles Ogle, Barry O'Moore, Bigelow Cooper, Ben Wilson, Miriam Nesbitt, Harold Shaw.

1913

Who Will Marry Mary? Edison, [6 Episodes] D: Walter Edwin; SP: Ida Damon; LP: Mary Fuller Ben Wilson, Richard Tucker, Harry Beaumont, Miriam Nesbitt.

1913–14

The Chronicles of Cleek. Edison, [13 Episodes] D: George A. Lessey, Ben Wilson; P: Thomas W. Hanshew; LP: Benjamin Wilson.

1917

The Voice on the Wire. Univ., [15 Chapters] D: Stuart Paton; SP: J. Grubb Alexander; S: Eustace Hale Ball; LP: Ben Wilson, Neva Gerber, Joseph W. Girard, Francis McDonald, Kingsley Benedict, Nigel De Bruiler, Howard Crampton, L. M. Wells, Frank MacQuarrie, Hoot Gibson, Ernest Shields, Frank Tokonaga.

The Mystery Ship. Univ., [18 Chapters] D: Harry Harvey, Francis Ford; SP: Milton Moore; LP: Ben Wilson, Neva Gerber, Duke Worne, Nigel De Bruiler, Neal Hart.

1919

The Trail of the Octopus. Hallmark, [15 Chapters] D: Duke Worne; S: J. Grubb Alexander; LP: Ben Wilson, Neva Gerber, Howard Crampton, Marie Pavis, William Carroll.

1920

The Screaming Shadow. Hallmark, [15 Chapters] D: Duke Worne, Ben Wilson; S: J. Grubb Alexander, Harvey Gates; P: Frank G. Hall; LP: Ben Wilson, Neva Gerber, Frances Terry, Howard Crampton, Joseph Girard, William Dyer.

The Branded Four. Select, [15 Chapters] D: Duke Worne; S/SP: Hope Loring, George W. Pyper; Spv.: Ben Wilson; LP: Ben Wilson, Neva Gerber, Joseph Girard, William Dyer, Ashton Dearholt.

1921

The Mysterious Pearl. Berwilla, [15 Chapters] D: Ben Wilson, Duke Worne; SP: J. Grubb Alexander, Harvey Gates; P: Ben Wilson; LP: Ben Wilson, Neva Gerber, Charles King, Ashton Dearholt, William Carroll, Duke Worne, Charles B. Mason.

1926

The Mystery Box. Davis, [10 Chapters] D/S: Alvin J. Neitz; P: Ben Wilson; LP: Ben Wilson, Neva Gerber, Lafe McKee, Robert Walker, Charles Brinley.

The Power God. Davis/Goodwell, [15 Chapters] D: Ben Wilson, Francis Ford; S: Rex Taylor, Harry Haven; P: Ben Wilson; LP: Ben Wilson, Neva Gerber, Lafe McKee, Allan Garcia, Ruth Royce.

Officer 444. Davis/Goodwell, [10 Chapters] D: Francis Ford; LP: Ben Wilson, Neva Gerber, Ruth Royce, Al Ferguson, Lafe McKee, Jack Mower.

LEWIS WILSON

Lewis Wilson came to Hollywood from the New York stage in 1943 as a contract player at Columbia. That year he was an extra in *Sahara* and had a bit in *Good Luck, Mr. Yates* starring Claire Trevor. Shirley Patterson, who would later play opposite him in *Batman*, also had a small part. Another bit role for Wilson was in *Klondike Kate* featuring Ann Savage and Tom Neal, who would team in *Detour* in 1945. In another film with Neal, *There's Something About a Soldier*, Wilson plays Bolivar Jefferson. Bruce Bennett and Evelyn Keyes were co-featured. In *First Comes Courage*, Wilson plays a young doctor in support of Merle Oberon and Brian Aherne; he is a reporter in the Charles Coburn–Marguerite Chapman comedy *My Kingdom for a Cook*; and in *Redhead from Manhattan*, starring Lupe Velez, he is an F.B.I. agent.

In 1944, Wilson was a bit player in the Cary Grant–Janet Blair film *Once Upon a Time*; in *Beautiful But Broke*, featuring Joan Davis and John Hubbard, he has a bit as a pilot; in *The Racket Man*, with Tom Neal and Hugh Beaumont, Wilson plays camp commander Capt. Anderson; and in *Sailor's Holiday*, with Arthur Lake, Wilson has a good role as "Iron Man" Collins.

Though he had a wife and child, Wilson, 23, was drafted in 1944 and served in Europe and in the front lines at the Battle of the Bulge. Upon his discharge, he returned to Hollywood but was unable to reactivate his career. After a return to New York for a spell, he resumed in Hollywood and was successful in getting second billing in the television series *Craig Kennedy, Criminologist* ('52) starring Donald Woods. Little work came his way and his last film role was in *Bwanga Bwanga* ('53). His son, Michael G. Wilson, co-wrote several of the James Bond films and was assistant to the producer and executive producer on others.

Wilson's claim to serial fame rests with *Batman* ('43), the Columbia chapterplay featuring J. Carrol Naish as Dr. Daka, Douglas Croft as Robin the Boy Wonder and Shirley Patterson as Linda, Bruce Wayne's girlfriend. Naish takes the acting honors. Batman and Robin battle an enemy undercover ring whose leader, Dr. Daka, maintains his power by transforming people into zombies. He is putting his evil genius to use to aid Hirohito and the Axis powers. Daka has a ray gun, kind of a miniature atom smasher. Requiring a small amount of radium to operate, however, the device's range is limited. With more radium, bigger and more powerful radium guns could be built. With such devices the Axis could defeat America and her allies with ease. When Daka attempts to steal the city's radium supply, Batman and Robin match wits and brawn with the agents of Japan.

In retaliation, Daka kidnaps Linda, only to have Batman rescue her. Daka tries

Lewis Wilson (Batman) and Douglas Croft (Robin) in *Batman* (Columbia, 1943).

several times to kill the crimefighter, but Batman narrowly escapes death. Finally he rounds up Daka's entire criminal organization, while Daka falls into his own alligator pit and is eaten alive. Probably the reptiles got indigestion from their meal.

Wilson died at age 80 in San Francisco from an aneurysm on August 9, 2000.

Serial

1943

Batman. Col., [15 Chapters] D: Lambert Hillyer; SP: Victor McLeod, Leslie Swabacker, Harry Fraser; P: Rudolph C. Flothow; Mus: Lee Zahler; Narrator: Knox Manning; LP: Lewis Wilson, Douglas Croft, J. Carrol Naish, Shirley Patterson, William C. Austin, Robert Fiske, George Chesebro, Charles Middleton, Charles Wilson, Tom London, Karl Hackett, Jack Ingram, Bud Osborne, Earle Hodgins.

GRANT WITHERS

Grant Withers came from a family of prominent publishers in Pueblo, Colorado, where he was born on January 17, 1904. His grandfather, Gus Withers, was founder of the Pueblo *Chieftain*, a newspaper. He was anxious for Grant to enter the Naval Academy, but Grant was movie struck and ran away to Hollywood. Failing to crash the gate of any studio, he was forced to look for work. He rustled freight at the Santa Fe railroad yards, worked briefly as a police reporter (he was fired when the editor learned that he was not familiar with a typewriter), became a fire watcher at Sierra Madre, drove Los Angeles police riot squad cars (and was hospitalized for three months when he hit another car at an intersection) and became a city fireman. During a factory fire, he was nearly killed when he plunged through a skylight and molten glass burned him. Again he spent three months in a hospital.

One day he received $15 for sitting on a suitcase in a hotel sequence as an extra at one of the studios and decided that he had been working too hard for both his adventure and money. So he became a screen actor. His rise to leading man was rapid.

His first credited role was in *The Gentle Cyclone* ('26) starring Buck Jones. Other silent films followed, including *In a Moment of Temptation* ('27) with Charlotte Stevens, *Bringing Up Father* ('27), a comedy with J. Farrell MacDonald, *Tillie's Punctured Romance* ('28) with W. C. Fields, *The Greyhound Limited* ('29) with Monte Blue and Edna Murphy, *Tiger Rose* ('29) with Lupe Velez and *The Time, the Place, and the Girl* ('29) with Betty Compson.

The '30s were good years for Withers. He worked steadily as either leading man or major supporting player. And it was in this decade that he made all six of his serials.

In *Tailspin Tommy* ('34), he plays Milt Howe, owner of Three Points Airline, who wins a mail contract thanks to Tailspin Tommy (Maurice Murphy). Tiger Taggart (John Davidson) would like nothing more than see Three Points fail and directs his confederate aerial pirates to attack Tommy, Milt and Three Points. In *The Red Rider* ('34), Withers plays Silent Slade, friend of Red Davidson (Buck Jones), who is attempting to clear him of murder charges. In *The Fighting Marines* ('35), Withers is Corp. Lawrence who, with Sgt. McGowan (Adrian Morris), endeavors to discover the identity of "The Tiger Shark," a mysterious scientific wizard who is sabotaging attempts by Marines to build a landing field on Halfway Island. Withers plays the title character in *Jungle Jim* ('37). Two safaris travel into the African jungles in search of a white girl (Betty Jane Rhodes) raised there and who has inherited a fortune in America. Jungle Jim leads one expedition; the other is headed by Bruce Redmond (Bryant Washburn), who wants the white girl killed so that the inheritance can become his. The Cobra (Henry Brandon) acts independently to keep the girl in the jungle for his own selfish reasons.

As an ordinary radio patrol cop, Pat O'Hara (Withers) undertakes, in *Radio Patrol* ('37), to protect a young boy and the secret formula for flexible bulletproof steel that has been left him by his late father, the victim of gangsters seeking the formula. In *The Secret of Treasure Island* ('38), Carter Collins, the Shark (Walter Miller), takes possession of an island reputed to contain hidden pirate treasure. He fortifies the island against outsiders. Reporter Larry Kent (Don Terry) and his girlfriend Toni Morrell (Gwen Gaze) decide to investigate the island and search for the treasure. The Shark is assisted in his nefarious schemes by Grindley (Withers).

Among Withers' features in the '30s were *Dancing Sweeties* ('30), *Swanee River* ('31), *Red Haired Alibi* ('32), *Gambling Six*

('32), *Secrets of Wu Sin* ('33), *Waterfront Lady* ('35), *Storm Over the Andes* ('35), *Lady Be Careful* ('36), *Skybound* ('36), *Bill Cracks Down* ('37), *Paradise Express* ('37), *Mr. Wong, Detective* ('39), *Mutiny in the Big House* ('39), *Mystery of Mr. Wong* ('39), *Mr. Wong in Chinatown* ('39), *Daughter of the Tong* ('39) and *Navy Secrets* ('39). Cinematically speaking, it was a good decade for Withers.

In the '40s, Withers usually played supporting roles but was in some fairly big films, such as *Billy the Kid* ('41), *The Bugle Sounds* ('41), *Northwest Rangers* ('42), *Tennessee Johnson* ('42), *In Old Oklahoma* ('43), *The Fighting Seabees* ('44), *In Old Sacramento* ('46), *Wyoming* ('47), *Wake of the Red Witch* ('48), *Fort Apache* ('48), *Old Los Angeles* ('48), *The Fighting Kentuckian* ('49) and *Hellfire* ('49).

Withers' films in the '50s included *Tripoli* ('50), *The Savage Horde* ('50), *The Sea Hornet* ('51), *Al Jennings of Oklahoma* ('51), *Springfield Rifle* ('52), *Hangman's Knot* ('52), *Fair Wind to Java* ('53), *Southwest Passage* ('54), *Lady Godiva* ('55), *The Last Stagecoach West* ('57) and his last, *I. Mobster* ('58).

Five times wed, Withers created a Hollywood sensation in 1930 when he eloped to Yuma, Arizona, with actress Loretta Young, then a 17-year-old Wampas Baby Star. Her mother met the plane when the couple returned and started annulment proceedings. Withers was later to marry actress Betty Vernon; Alice G. Walsh, a Cleveland aviatrix; and Inez Withers. All three marriages ended in divorce. On January 29, 1953, he married actress and singer Estelita Rodriguez, who had previously been married to Chu Chu Martinez, a nightclub singer. Wither was 49, Estelita 24. On September 24, 1954, Estelita found pajama-clad Withers unconscious in their Sherman Oaks home suffering from an overdose of ulcer medicine. Officers said the overdose was probably accidental. On November 9, 1955, Estelita was granted a divorce on testimony that he criticized her work until she became so upset that she could no longer sing and just cried all the time, and that he humiliated her in front of friends.

In the last three years of his life, Withers worked as a character actor in only seven movies and did some television work. Financial difficulties piled up on him and overdue bills dogged him right up to his death. Although he had been a leading man and had good roles in the '30s, stardom eluded him. He had good supporting roles in the '40s and early '50s, but film offers had about dried up.

Withers was one of John Ford's little band of character actors. A huge, hulking man, he was full of wild laughter and amusing escapades. As the years went by, the laughter died. He became a helpless victim of his compulsion to drink whiskey. He had gone through five disastrous marriages. His life was a record of arrests for drunken driving, car accidents and wife-beating. It was a painful existence.

On March 28, 1959, Withers was found dead in his North Hollywood apartment. Police attributed death to an intentional overdose of sleeping pills. He left two notes explaining his action. "It's better this way; thanks to my friends, sorry I let them down," read one of his notes. "I was so unhappy." Withers was only 55.

Serials

1934

Tailspin Tommy. Univ., [12 Chapters] D: Louis Friedlander [Lew Landers]; LP: Maurice Murphy, Noah Beery, Jr., Patricia Farr, Walter Miller, Grant Withers, John Davidson, Edmund Cobb.

The Red Rider. Univ., [15 Chapters] D: Louis Friedlander [Lew Landers]; LP: Buck Jones, Marion Shilling, Grant Withers, Walter Miller, Margaret LaMarr, J. P. McGowan, Dick Cramer, Edmund Cobb, Charles K. French, William Desmond.

1935

The Fighting Marines. Mascot, [12 Chapters] D: B. Reeves Eason, Joseph Kane; LP: Grant Withers, Adrian Morris, Ann Rutherford, George J. Lewis, Robert Warwick.

1937

Jungle Jim. Univ., [12 Chapters] D: Ford Beebe, Cliff Smith; LP: Grant Withers, Betty Jane Rhodes, Raymond Hatton, Henry Brandon.

Radio Patrol. Univ., [12 Chapters] D: Ford Beebe, Cliff Smith; LP: Grant Withers, Catherine (Kay) Hughes, Adrian Morris, Mickey Rentschier, Frank Lackteen.

1938

The Secret of Treasure Island. Col., [15 Chapters] D: Elmer Clifton; LP: Don Terry, Gwen Gaze, Grant Withers, Hobart Bosworth, Dave O'Brien, Yakima Canutt.

ANNA MAY WONG

The name Anna May Wong may not set off any recollections for today's movie patrons, but for those old enough to have frequented movies in the 1930s or who have studied that era of filmdom, hers is a familiar name. It may come as a surprise that she appeared in a serial, but that she did. The serial was Pathé's *The Fortieth Door* ('24) starring Allene Ray and Bruce Gordon with Anna and Frank Lackteen featured.

Born Wong Liu Tsang in the Chinatown section of Los Angeles on January 3, 1907, Anna entered films as an extra at the age of 12. After playing a number of featured parts, she attracted attention at age 16 in the plum role of a slave girl in Douglas Fairbanks' *The Thief of Bagdad* ('24). It brought Anna national recognition. Thereafter she went to the Canadian Rockies to play Keok in *The Alaskan* ('24) with Thomas Meighan and Estelle Taylor. And to round out a busy year, she presented a delightful Tiger Lily in *Peter Pan* ('24).

A vogue for Oriental mysteries elevated her to stardom in the late '20s. Her fame was international and she went to Europe, where she lectured and starred in British, French and German films. Her proficiency with language served her well. She starred in the German film *Song* ('28). On March 14, 1929, she made her stage debut in London in *The Circle of Chalk* playing the role of Chang Hi-Tan; Laurence Olivier was cast as Prince Po.

At Elstree Studios she was excellent in *Piccadilly* ('29) with Gilda Gray and Charles Laughton.

Elstree Studios produced *The Flame of Love* ('30) in three languages: English, French and German. Anna made all three versions, playing the leader of a Russian dance troupe. When the film opened in September 1930 in Paris, Anna was in Vienna making her German-speaking stage debut in the leading role of *Tschuin Tschi*. The Austrian critics were enraptured with her acting.

Anna's reason for going abroad to make films and star on the stage was because Hollywood filmmakers held to the tenet that players of particular ethnic backgrounds could not be stars in the accepted sense. In 1929–30, therefore, she remained abroad starring in *The City Butterfly* ('29 German), *Elstree Calling* ('30 Wardour) and *The Flame of Love* ('30 British International), plus 167 performances of the play *On the Spot*, a melodrama of Chicago racketeering. The play was followed by a road tour of the show.

Returning to Hollywood, Anna appeared in the following films: *Daughter of the Dragon* ('31), *Shanghai Express* ('32), *A Study in Scarlet* ('33), *Tiger Bay* ('33), *Chu Chin Chow* ('34), *Java Head* ('34), *Limehouse Blues* ('34), *Daughter of Shanghai* ('37), *Dangerous to Know* ('38), *When Were You Born?* ('38), *King of Chinatown* ('39), *Island of Lost Men* ('39), *Ellery Queen's Penthouse Mystery* ('41),

Bombs Over Burma ('42) and *Lady from Chungking* ('42). Then it was not until 1949 that she made another movie, *Impact* starring Brian Donlevy. It did nothing to boost her career. During the 1950s she made infrequent appearances on television. In 1960, she was lured back to the screen in *Portrait in Black* starring Lana Turner and Anthony Quinn. It was her last film.

Anna May had been considered for a lead role in *The Good Earth* ('37) but at the time studios were obligated to co-star an actor of the same race when starring a non-white performer. The studio had already decided to star Paul Muni.

Anna May Wong died from a heart attack on February 3, 1961, at age 54. She was a proud, aloof woman who never married.

During her lifetime she accomplished a stunning career against near impossible odds, becoming the first Chinese actress to become a major box office star.

Serial

1924

The Fortieth Door. Pathé, [10 Chapters] D: George B. Seitz; SP: Frank Leon Smith; S: Mary Hastings Bradley; Cam: Vernon Walker; P: C. W. Patton; LP: Allene Ray, Bruce Gordon, Frank Lackteen, Anna May Wong, Frankie Mann, Lillian Gale, White Horse, Bernard Siegel.

DOROTHY WOOD

Dorothy Wood's one serial was Universal's extremely popular *In the Days of Buffalo Bill* ('22) starring Art Acord. She had an especially strong part in this story of the building of the transcontinental Rail Road, told in 18 two-reel chapters.

But Dorothy also held the record of appearing with Hoot Gibson the most often — 13 times in 1920 in a series of two-reel Westerns. The two-reelers were popular with small town and rural audiences. They were like icing on the cake when packaged with a full-length feature, a chapter of a serial and maybe even a cartoon or comedy.

In the years 1920–26, Dorothy played opposite the following cowboys the indicated number of times: Pete Morrison (3), Franklyn Farnum (3), Yakima Canutt (3) and Buffalo Bill, Jr. (2). She had a few miscellaneous credits through 1925 and in 1936 sup-

ported Tom Tyler in *Santa Fe Bound*. In all probability she was working in the years 1926–36 in bit or extra roles. Except for the Universals, Dorothy worked only in low-budget, independent oaters and she never achieved much popularity. No biographical data on Dorothy can be found.

Serial

1922

In the Days of Buffalo Bill. Univ., [18 Chapters] D: Edward Laemmle; SP/S: Robert Dillon; LP: Art Acord, Dorothy Wood, Duke R. Lee, George A. Williams, Burton C. Law, Jay Morley, Otto Nelson, Ruth Royce, Pat Harmon, Joel Day.

JOAN WOODBURY

Joan Woodbury chalked up scores of film and stage credits during a long and highly successful acting career. She came into the world on December 17, 1915. Both her mother and grandmother were actresses. Her early education was received in a convent in San Francisco; she later graduated from Hollywood High School.

Joan studied dramatics and dancing and was able to get dancing jobs in cafes and night clubs prior to stage or film roles. But she finally got a bit in *Anthony Adverse* ('36). This led to a job with Francis Lederer in an Eastern vaudeville tour. Upon her return to Hollywood, she was signed by Paramount for *Eagle's Brood* ('35), a William Boyd Hopalong Cassidy Western. She later played in the oaters *Song of the Gringo* ('36) with Tex Ritter; *The Lion's Den* ('36) with Tim McCoy; *In Old Cheyenne* ('41) with Roy Rogers; *Northwest Trail* ('45) with Bob Steele; and *Flame of the West* ('45) with Johnny Mack Brown. These latter two films were especially good ones for her. She had a supporting role in *The Desperadoes* ('43) with Randolph Scott and Claire Trevor.

Joan could play a clinging vine when the role so dictated, but more often than not she eschewed soubrette roles in favor of playing prima donnas, as in *Brenda Starr, Reporter* ('45). A few of her non–Western credits are *They Gave Him a Gun* ('37), *Charlie Chan on Broadway* ('37), *Algiers* ('38), *Cipher Bureau* ('38), *Mystery of the White Room* ('39), *Paper Bullets* ('41), *Confessions of Boston Blackie* ('41), *Sweetheart of the Fleet* ('42), *The Whistler* ('44), *The Arnelo Affair* ('47), *Boston Blackie's Chinese Venture* ('49), *The Ten Commandments* ('56) and *The Time Travelers* ('64).

Producing and directing for the stage always appealed to this volatile leading lady more than moviemaking. So in 1949 after approximately 70 films in 15 years, she closed out her screen career except for a couple

films that she appeared in a few years down the road. For six years she ramrodded all grand and light operas for the Redlands (California) Bowl. She subsequently founded, with actor-husband Ray Mitchell, Palm Spring's Valley Players Guild Theatre. They celebrated their one-hundredth production in January 1980.

Over a period of several years, Joan wrote feature articles for magazines (*Palm Springs Life* and *Mexican World*) and newspapers, principally Riverside County's *Press-Enterprise*.

By her former marriage to actor Henry Wilcoxon, Woodbury had three grown daughters.

She made the one serial, *Brenda Starr, Reporter* with Kane Richmond playing opposite her. A gang of hoodlums believes that reporter Starr knows where a quarter of a million dollar payroll is hidden. She doesn't. A dying rogue has given her a coded message, which she is unable to decipher. The gang makes repeated efforts to force Brenda to talk but with the aid of Police Lt. Larry Farrell (Richmond) she is able to resist until the gang is captured, the message decoded and the money found.

Joan died from respiratory failure at age 73 in Desert Hot Springs, California, in 1989.

Serial

1945

Brenda Starr, Reporter. Col., [13 Chapters] D: Wallace Fox; SP: Ande Lamb, George H. Plympton; P: Sam Katzman; Cam: Ira H. Morgan; Mus: Edward Kay; LP: Joan Woodbury, Kane Richmond, Syd Saylor, Joe Devlin, Wheeler Oakman, George Meeker, Kay Forrester, Jack Ingram, Marion Burns, Ernie Adams, Anthony Warde, Billy Benedict, John Merton.

HARRY WOODS

Harry Lewis Woods certainly looked the part of the "Big Boss," a role he played in countless Westerns. He ranked right up there with Noah Beery, Sr., Walter Miller and Fred Kohler when it came to playing the head honcho of a gang of desperadoes. In fact, he was the epitome of the boss villain and the most imitated of all Western badmen. His suavity was uncontested; he has been called the "badman's badman."

Dressed in all black and sporting a black moustache, Woods looked every bit the part he played, invariably that of the boss whose minions carried out his devilish schemes. His delivery was always convincing and his timing perfect, a product of his stage training. He was a consummate actor, and that thin black mustache, black brows, piercing dark eyes, deep resonate voice and overall manly looks aided him in creating the characterization he portrayed in scores of films.

Woods was born in Cleveland, Ohio, on May 5, 1889. A good-sized man, he usually weighed around 210 pounds and stood six foot two. He had brown hair and greenish-hazel eyes.

Harry was earning a comfortable living as a millinery salesman, but at the insistence

Mary Brian and Harry Woods in *Shadows of Sing Sing* (Columbia, 1933).

of friends he gave it up and headed for Hollywood. He finally was able to get inside the Hal Roach Studio as a grip. There he was discovered by "Woody" Van Dyke, who hired him as a heavy in a Ruth Roland serial he was directing.

On October 28, 1911, Woods was married to Helen Hookenberry, and three children were born to this union: Maril Lee, Richard and Harrison. At one time Woods was a skating champion and a golf addict. His hobby was remodeling houses, and he made a lot of money doing so. He could build almost anything requiring carpentry or cement work. He died on December 28, 1968, at the age of 79.

His Western features include *The Bandit's Baby* (R-C/FBO, Fred Thomson), *A Man Four-Square* (Fox, Buck Jones), *30 Below Zero* (Fox, Buck Jones), *Cyclone of the Range* (FBO, Tom Tyler), *Jesse James* (Par., Fred Thomson), *The Candy Kid* (Dailey, Rex Lease), *The Desert Rider* (MGM, Tim McCoy), *The Lone Rider* (Col., Buck Jones), *Texas Gun Fighter* (Tif., Ken Maynard), *Haunted Gold* (WB, John Wayne), *Gallant Defender* (Col., Charles Starrett), *Robin Hood of El Dorado* (MGM, Warner Baxter), *When a Man's a Man* (Fox, George O'Brien), *Heroes of the Range* (Col., Ken Maynard), *The Unknown Ranger* (Col., Bob Allen), *Courage of the West* (Univ., Bob Baker), *Rolling Caravans* (Col., Jack Luden), *Panamint's Bad Man* (TCF, Smith Ballew), *The Ranger and the Lady* (Rep., Roy Rogers), *Sunset Pass* (RKO, James Warren), *Wild Horse Mesa* (RKO, Tim Holt), *Trail Street* (RKO, Randolph Scott), *West of the Pecos* (RKO, Robert Mitchum), *Westward Bound* (Mon., Hoot Gibson, Ken Maynard, Bob Steele), *Wyoming* (Rep., Bill Elliott), *The Ghost Rider* (Mon., Johnny Mack Brown) and *Marshal of Gunsmoke* (Univ., Russell Hayden, Tex Ritter).

Serials

1923

The Steel Trail. Univ., [15 Chapters] D: William Duncan; LP: William Duncan, Edith Johnson, Harry Carter, Ralph McCullough.

1924

Wolves of the North. Univ., [15 Chapters] D: William Duncan; LP: William Duncan, Edith Johnson, Joseph W. Girard, Esther Ralston.

The Fast Express. Univ., [15 Chapters] D: William Duncan; LP: William Duncan, Edith Johnson, Edward Cecil, Eva Gordon, Harry Woods.

Ten Scars Make a Man. Pathé, [10 Chapters] D: William Parke; LP: Allene Ray, Jack Mower, Rose Burdick, Frank Whitson, Harry Woods.

1935

The Adventures of Rex and Rinty. Mascot, [12 Chapters] D: B. Reeves Eason, Ford Beebe; LP: Rex, Rin-Tin-Tin, Jr., Kane Richmond, Norma Taylor, Mischa Auer, Harry Woods.

The Call of the Savage. Univ., [12 Chapters] D: Lewis Friedlander [Lew Landers]; LP: Noah Beery, Jr., Dorothy Short, Harry Woods, Walter Miller.

Rustlers of Red Dog. Univ., [12 Chapters] D: Louis Friedlander [Lew Landers]; LP: Johnny Mack Brown, Joyce Compton, Walter Miller, Raymond Hatton, Harry Woods, Charles K. French, Bud Osborne, Edmund Cobb, Wally Wales, Chief Thundercloud, Art Mix, William Desmond, Cliff Lyons.

1936

The Phantom Rider. Univ., [15 Chapters] D: Ray Taylor; LP: Buck Jones, Marla Shelton, Diana Gibson, Harry Woods, George Cooper, Charles King, Eddie Gribbon, Clem Bevans, Tom London, Wally Wales, Slim Whitaker, Helen Shipman.

1940

Winners of the West. Univ., [13 Chapters] D: Ford Beebe, Ray Taylor; LP: Dick Foran, Anne Nagel, James Craig, Tom Fadden, Harry Woods, Charles Stevens, Trevor Bardette, Edmund Cobb, William Desmond, Chief Yowlachie, Art Mix.

1943

The Masked Marvel. Rep., [12 Chapters] D: Spencer G. Bennet; LP: Tom Steele, William Forrest, Louise Currie, Johnny Arthur, David Bacon, Harry Woods.

CONSTANCE WORTH

Constance Worth, blonde, beautiful and gifted, was Australia's gift to American motion pictures. She was born Jacelyn Howarth on August 19, 1913. Her father, Moffat Howarth, was a prominent banker who also owned a large sheep station. Constance divided her girlhood years between schooling and riding the Australian range.

She was educated at St. Gabriel's School and Ascham College in Sydney. She also took a course in Miss Dupont's Finishing School for Ladies in Paris, France.

As a leader of the younger social set in Sydney, Constance became interested in amateur theatricals given in the interest of charity. Her performance in one such production, *Cynara*, attracted the attention of the directors of the Australian film company, Cinesound. She was induced to take a screen test and it resulted in her being cast in the leading role of the Cinesound production *The Squatter's Daughter*. Following that feature, a pronounced success in Australia, she played leads in three more Cinesound productions.

Stage producers in the meantime were attracted by the work of Constance and flooded her with footlight offers. Although under contract to Cinesound, she was permitted to appear in a number of stage plays. *The Wind and the Rain*, *Ten Minute Alibi*, *Michael and Mary* and *Tiger Rose* were among the dramas in which she appeared.

A success on both screen and stage, Constance came to the attention of English film scouts who persisted in efforts to sign her to contracts. It was with the intention of investigating these offers at their home source and visiting her parents who were in England at the time that she left Sydney in the early autumn of 1936.

She decided to make the trip by way of California and so disembarked at Los Angeles Harbor. News of her acting success had preceded her to Hollywood and what was to have been a brief social and sightseeing visit proved a round of business conferences, with RKO Radio the studio which secured her signature on a contract.

Constance was 5'3½" tall and weighed approximately 115 pounds. She had golden blonde hair, blue eyes and a "peaches and cream" complexion.

In Hollywood, she met George Brent and married him two months later. It was his third and her first. Unfortunately, the union did not last.

Constance will be remembered for her co-starring role in *G-Men vs. the Black Dragon* ('43). She played Vivian Marsh, a British secret service agent who faced deadly peril at the end of practically every chapter. In the first chapter she is locked inside a metal cabinet sprayed with inflammable paint and set ablaze as Cameron fights the heavies. As flames threaten to engulf her, she lets out a terrified scream as she writhes in an agony of fear.

The end of the second chapter found her in the classic cliffhanger peril of being tied before the teeth of a giant buzz saw as Cameron again fights the heavies. Only a timely bullet fired into the fuse box saves Constance from a messy death.

In another chapter she is tied to a chair facing a clock designed to eject a deadly spear at her when two figures on the clock come together. She just misses being impaled when Rod Cameron gets to her in time to cut the rope, allowing her to dodge death at the last moment.

Constance was the leading lady in numerous "B"s, among them *Windjammer* ('37), *Meet Boston Blackie* ('42), *The Dawn Express* ('42), *The Crime Doctor's Strangest Case* ('43), *Two Senoritas from Chicago* ('43), *Cyclone Prairie Rangers* ('44), *Dillinger* ('45), *Deadline at Dawn* ('46), *Western Renegades* ('49), etc.

Constance Worth, an unidentified actress, Roland Got and Rod Cameron in *G-Men vs. The Black Dragon* (Republic, 1943).

Constance died on October 18, 1963, in Los Angeles. She was 50 years old. The author has no details on her death or her personal life after 1949.

Serial

1943

G-Men vs. the Black Dragon. Rep., [15 Chapters] D: William Witney; SP: Ronald David-son, William Lively, Joseph O'Donnell, Joseph Poland; Cam: Bud Thackery; Mus: Mort Glickman; LP: Rod Cameron, Constance Worth, Roland Got, Nino Pipitone, George J. Lewis, Maxine Doyle, Donald Kirke, Ivan Miller.

LILLIAN WORTH

Lillian Worth played one important role in her screen career — that of Queen La of Opar in *The Adventures of Tarzan* ('23). It was produced by the Weiss brothers (Numa Pictures Corp.) and directed by Robert Hill, who was to make quite a name for himself in the serial field during the '20s. Elmo Lincoln had played Tarzan in the 1918 feature *Tarzan of the Apes* and was now portraying the jungle man in this 15-chapter serial. Louise Lorraine, who turned 16 during the filming, portrayed Jane.

Tarzan returns from civilization to his beloved jungle. There are enough wild animals introduced in each chapter to keep audiences on the edge of their seats. Much of the action concentrated on Tarzan's feud with Queen La (Worth), whose love he spurned, and his efforts to keep the Bolshevik Rokoff and Clayton, pretender to Tarzan's title as Lord Greystoke, from reaching Opar.

Gabe Essoe in his book *Tarzan of the Movies* (1968) says that *The Adventures of Tarzan* was one of the four most popular films of the year (and remember, it *is* a serial), equal to Rudolph Valentino's *The Four Horsemen of the Apocalypse*, Charlie Chaplin's *The Kid* and Pola Negri's *Passion*.

In late 1919, SLK Serial Corporation released *The Fatal Fortune*, produced by Sherman S. Krellberg. The serial starred Helen Holmes in a South Seas adventure in which a newspaperwoman leads a search for buried treasure on a desolate island, meeting many obstacles. Lillian had a supporting role but the nature of it is unknown.

Worth was quite active through the '20s and '30s, but most of her roles were small.

Some films in which she appeared are *The Girl with a Jazz Heart* ('20)— she plays Camille, who loves jazz and cabarets who befriends Madge Kennedy; *In Search of a Sin-*

ner ('20) supporting Constance Talmadge; *The Lady from Longacre* ('21)— she plays Lady Laura in support of William Russell and Mary Thurman; *The Foolish Age* ('21) as ex-chorus girl Flossie; *Wise Husbands* ('21) as the mother of Gladden James; *Rustlers' Ranch* ('26), supporting Art Acord and Olive Hasbrouck; *Upstream* ('27) as one-half of a sister act; *On the Stroke of Twelve* ('27), supporting June Marlowe and David Torrence; *The Docks of New York* ('28) as Clyde Cook's girl; *Stairs of Sand* ('29) as "Babe," a dance hall girl, in support of Jean Arthur and Wallace Beery; *Dangerous Paradise* ('30) in support of Nancy Carroll and Richard Arlen; *The Fighting Sheriff* ('31) as Florabel; Buck Jones stars; *Jealousy* ('34)— she has a bit in this Nancy Carroll film; *Case of the Lucky Legs* ('35), supporting Warren William as Perry Mason; *Carnival* ('35)— she plays half woman-half man; *Big City* ('37), supporting Louise Rainer and Spencer Tracy; etc.

Serials

1919

The Fatal Fortune. SLK, [15 Chapters] D: Donald McKenzie; LP: Helen Holmes, Jack Levering, Leslie King, Bill Black, Frank Wunderlee, Floyd Buckley, Lillian Worth, Nellie Lindruth, Sidney Delbrook.

1921

The Adventures of Tarzan. Numa, [15 Chapters] D: Robert F. Hill; LP: Elmo Lincoln, Louise Lorraine, Frank Whitson, George Momberg, Percy Pembroke, Charles Gay, Lillian Worth, Charles Inslee, Frank Merrill, Joe Martin (ape), Tantor (elephant), Regent (leopard), Numa (lion).

MARIS WRIXON

Maris Wrixon is remembered by serial followers for the 1945 serial *The Master Key*, in which for 12 chapters she is assumed to be on the right side of the law as Chief O'Brien's secretary, only to be revealed in the final chapter as "The Master Key," who directs foreign agents in attempts to steal and use an Orotran machine that will extract gold from sea water. Maris directed her agents through a microphone device which changed her voice, so it was a shock to serial audiences to find out that the chief villain was a woman.

Maris was born in Pasco, Washington, on December 28, 1916. She came to Hollywood with her aunt and soon landed a contract with Warner Brothers. There she met and married a young film editor, Rudi Fehr. They had four daughters. Maris appeared in small parts in *Nancy Drew, Detective* ('38), *Broadway Musketeers* ('38), *The Private Life of Elizabeth and Essex* ('39), *The Adventures of Jane Arden* ('39), *Code of the Secret Service* ('39), *No Place to Go* ('39), *Daughters Courageous* ('39), *Off the Record* ('39), *Private Detective* ('39), *Ride, Cowboy, Ride* ('39), *Dark Victory* ('39), *Each Dawn I Die* ('39), *Code of the Secret Service* ('39), *Calling Philo Vance* ('40), *A Child Is Born* ('40), *Flight Angels* ('40), *Knute Rockne, All American* ('40), *Santa Fe Trail* ('40), *Saturday's Children* ('40) and *Lady with Red Hair* ('40).

Maris is the object of Roy Rogers' wooing in the Weaver Brothers and Elvira comedy *Jeepers Creepers* (Mon. '39). The story concerns coal miners. Small fry cowpokes probably cringed to see Roy and Maris kiss.

In *The Ape* (Mon. '40), Boris Karloff is featured as a doctor who kills both human and simian to obtain spinal fluid with which he injects Maris to cure her crippled condition. In *Sunset in Wyoming* (Rep. '41), she has the soubrette part as a gal who owns timber land that is being cut, resulting in flooding of ranchers' homes. After being misled by crooks, she sees the light and aids Gene Autry to right things. In the Weaver Brothers and Elvira comedy *The Old Homestead* (Rep. '42), she plays Mary Jo Weaver, loved by Robert Conway. In *Sons of the Pioneers* (Rep. '42), she is an Eastern socialite who owns a ranch terrorized by Bradley Page and gang. Naturally, Roy Rogers brings to justice the dastardly villains.

Waterfront (PRC) stars John Carradine and J. Carrol Naish as agents of Germany on San Francisco docks. Wrixon is an innocent secretary whose mother, to protect family back home in the fatherland, allows homicidal Carradine to reside in her boarding house. Wrixon proved to be a talented and lovely leading lady.

Trail to Gunsight (Univ. '44) starred Eddie Dew as a lawman who trails bank robbers to Wrixon's ranch, where she lives with her adolescent son. Dew catches the badmen as they rustle Wrixon's cattle. She shows her grit in the showdown gunfight.

Wrixon as heroine and Richard Fraser as hero have their hands full in *White Pongo* (PRC) as they search for a white gorilla. Maris is the daughter of an English explorer. She gets kidnapped by villains looking for gold, but is rescued by the coveted simian, White Pongo. Pongo defeats a black gorilla and is captured and crated for study in London.

Maris went from the co-lead in *White Pongo* to an unimportant supporting role (sixteenth in the cast) in *This Love of Ours* (Univ.) starring Merle Oberon, Claude Rains and Charles Korvin. She makes an unsuccessful pitch for Korvin, who has a neurotic daughter and an only apparently deceased wife (Oberon).

Wrixon replaced ailing Vivian Austin in *The Glass Alibi* (Rep. '46). Douglas Fowley, her husband, devises a plan with Anne

Gwynne to murder Maris for her money. Anne is the mistress of Cy Kendall. Fowley shoots Maris in her bed, but actually she died of a heart attack earlier. Thus, Fowley can't be convicted of her murder. Anne is killed by jealous Kendall. Detective Paul Kelly manages to find Fowley's fingerprints in Anne's apartment and although he didn't do it, Fowley is convicted of the murder.

In *The Face of Marble* (Mon. '46), Maris is the fiancée of Robert Shayne, who is assisting John Carradine in experiments of revivification. In *Highway 13* (Lippert), she is a villainess again. She and Michael Whalen plot to kill investigator Robert Lowery and to enrich themselves by attacking trucks. Wrixon and Whalen die in a flaming highway accident.

Black Market Babies (Mon. '45) deals with the baby mill racket. Wrixon plays an unwed mother caught up in the illegitimate activities of Kane Richmond and Ralph Morgan.

Maris retired in 1948 to devote herself to her four daughters. However, she played in a couple of *Cisco Kid* TV Westerns with Duncan Renaldo in 1951. She accepted a small role in *As You Were* in 1952 and in 1967 played a bit in *The Graduate* because a director friend asked her to do it.

Maris Wrixon died at age 81 in Los Angeles.

Serial

1945

The Master Key. Univ., [13 Chapters] D: Ray Taylor, Lewis D. Collins; LP: Milburn Stone, Jan Wiley, Dennis Moore, Maris Wrixon, Sarah Padden, Addison Richards, Byron Foulger, Al LaRue.

CARLETON YOUNG

Carleton Young appeared in two 1936 films for which he is credited. He played Al, a foreign agent, in *Happy Go Lucky* (Phil Regan, Evelyn Venable), and he appeared in the crime drama *A Man Betrayed* (Kay Hughes, Eddie Nugent) as Smokey. But he is best remembered today for the role of Gordon Tracy in the Republic serial *Dick Tracy* ('37), the first of four popular Dick Tracy serials starring Ralph Byrd. Detective Tracy tenaciously seeks to discover the identity of "the Lame One," bring an end to terrorist activities of the Spider Gang and find his brother, Gordon, who has been kidnapped. Unknown to Tracy, his brother becomes a pawn to the Lame One through an operation performed by Moloch, the Lame One's lieutenant.

Young played minor villains and character parts in a half dozen of Republic's "Golden Age" serials, including a minor role as Dodds in *SOS Coast Guard* ('37). He played in a number of 1937 features: *Michael O'Hallaram* (Warren Hull) as a tough guy; *Dangerous Holiday* (Ra Hould, Guinn Williams) as Tango; *Round-Up Time in Texas* (Gene Autry, Smiley Burnette) as a henchman; *The Hit Parade* (Frances Langford, Phil Regan) as a radio announcer; *It Could Happen to You* (Alan Baxter, Andrea Leeds) as a thug; *Join the Marines* (Paul Kelly, June Travis) as a corporal; *Come On Cowboys* (Bob Livingston, Ray Corrigan, Max Terhune) in a minor bit; *Young Dynamite* (Frankie Darro, Kane Richmond) as Spike, a hoodlum; *Race Suicide* (Lona Andre) in a supporting role; *She Married an Artist* (John Boles), in support; *The Old Barn Dance* (Gene Autry, Smiley Burnette) in support; and *Navy Blues* (Dick Powell, Mary Brian) in a bit role.

In 1938, Young had the role of Johnson, a heavy, in Republic's *The Fighting Devil Dogs* with Lee Powell, Eleanor Stewart and Herman Brix. He supported Bob Baker in four Westerns: *Outlaw Express* as Ramon; *Prairie Justice* as Dry Gulch, an outlaw; *The Black Bandit* as Cash, a cowboy; and *Guilty Trails* as an outlaw. At Paramount, Young was the outlaw Jeff Caffrey, killed in the last reel of *Cassidy of Bar 20* starring William Boyd, Russell Hayden and Nora Lane. He supported Constance Worth and Blanche Mehaffey in *The Wages of Sin*; played the outlaw Connors in the Three Mesquiteers adventure *Heroes of the Hills*; was Hank Newell in support of Anne Nagel and Robert Kent in *Gang Bullets*; and had a bit in *Gunsmoke Trail* starring Jack Randall and Louise Stanley.

The year 1939 was a busy one for Young. At Republic he played Black, a heavy, in *The Lone Ranger Rides Again* starring Robert Livingston as the Lone Ranger, and Benito Juarez in *Zorro's Fighting Legion* starring Reed Hadley as Zorro. At Universal he was Scott in *Buck Rogers* starring Larry (Buster) Crabbe and Constance Moore.

Young played Sheriff Dade in *Adventures of Red Ryder* ('40) starring Donald Barry and played a bit part in Barry's *One Man Law* ('40). In Tex Ritter's *Cowboy from Sundown* ('40), he played Nick, a hot-headed son of the local banker, while in Ritter's *Pals of the Silver Sage* ('40), he is cast as Jeff, a cattle rustler. In another Ritter film, *Take Me Back to Oklahoma* ('40), Young is Ace Hutchison, foreman of the Pecos Stage Line. This was one of Ritter's better Monogram films, partially because Bob Wills and his Texas Playboys were featured. Other 1940 films were *Adventure in Diamonds* (George Brent) as a sailor; *Up in the Air* (Frankie Darro, Marjorie Reynolds) as Stevens; *Gun Code* (Tim McCoy, Inna Gest) as outlaw Slim Doyle; and *Pride of the Bowery* (Leo Gorcey, Bobby Jordan) as boxing promoter Norton.

In the serial *Adventures of Captain Marvel* ('41), Young is a heavy named Martin.

Carleton was featured in the Bob Steele "Billy the Kid" series at PRC as Bob's saddle pal along with Al St. John. In *Billy the Kid in Texas*, he was named Gil; in *Billy the Kid Outlawed*, he was Jeff Travis, whereas in *Billy the Kid's Gun Justice* his name was Jeff Blanxhard. The series continued in 1941 with *Billy the Kid's Range War* and *Billy the Kid's Fighting Pals* with Steele starred and Young playing Jeff. When Buster Crabbe took over the series, Young played Jeff in *Billy the Kid's Round-Up*. Rex Lease, Bud McTaggart and Dave O'Brien played the character in succeeding entries.

Young worked in four serials in 1942: *Gang Busters* as a motorcycle cop; *King of the Mounties* as Gus; *Overland Mail* as Lem; and *Spy Smasher* in a double role as the henchman Taylor and as a power clerk.

About the middle of the 1940s Young began appearing in higher-budgeted films and never again appeared in serials or quickie "B" Westerns.

Young appeared regularly on the *Wyatt Earp* and other television series. His son, Tony, followed him into films and television.

Serials

1937

SOS Coast Guard. Rep., [12 Chapters] D: William Witney, Alan James; LP: Ralph Byrd, Bela Lugosi, Maxine Doyle, Richard Alexander, Carleton Young, Herbert Rawlinson, George Chesebro.

Dick Tracy. Rep., [15 Chapters] D: Ray Taylor, Alan James; LP: Ralph Byrd, Kay Hughes, Smiley Burnette, Lee Van Atta, Carleton Young, John Picorri, Francis X. Bushman, Fred Hamilton, Edwin Stanley.

1938

The Fighting Devil Dogs. Rep., [12 Chapters] D: William Witney, John English; LP: Lee Powell, Herman Brix, Eleanor Stewart, Montagu Love, Hugh Sothern, Sam Flint, Forrest Taylor,

John Picorri Lester Dorr, Carleton Young, Edmund Cobb.

1939

The Lone Ranger Rides Again. Rep., [15 Chapters] D: William Witney, John English; LP: Robert Livingston, Chief Thundercloud, Jinx Falken, Duncan Renaldo, Ralph Dunn, Rex Lease, William Gould, Carleton Young, Stanley Blystone.

Zorro's Fighting Legion. Rep., [12 Chapters] D: William Witney, John English; LP: Reed Hadley, Sheila Darcy, William Corson, Leander de Cordova, Edmund Cobb, C. Montague Shaw, Charles King, Carleton Young, Bud Geary, Cactus Mack.

Buck Rogers. Univ., [12 Chapters] D: Ford Beebe, Saul A. Goodkind; LP: Larry (Buster) Crabbe, Constance Moore, Jackie Moran, Jack Mulhall, Anthony Warde, Henry Brandon, C. Montague Shaw, Wheeler Oakman, Reed Howes, Carleton Young, Kenneth Duncan.

1940

Adventures of Red Ryder. Rep., [12 Chapters] D: William Witney, John English; LP: Donald Barry, Noah Beery, Sr., Tommy Cook, Vivian Coe [Austin], Harry Worth, Hal Taliaferro, Jack Rockwell, Robert Kortman, Carleton Young.

1941

Adventures of Captain Marvel. Rep., [12 Chapters] D: William Witney, John English; LP: Tom Tyler, Frank Coghlan, Jr., William Benedict, Louise Currie, Robert Strange, Harry Worth, Bryant Washburn, John Davidson, Carleton Young.

1942

Spy Smasher. Rep., [12 Chapters] D: William Witney; LP: Kane Richmond, Marguerite Chapman, Sam Flint, Hans Schumm, Tristram Coffin, Franco Corsara, Tom London, John James, Buddy Roosevelt, Carleton Young, George J. Lewis.

Gang Busters. Univ., [13 Chapters] D: Ray Taylor, Noel Smith; LP: Kent Taylor, Irene Hervey, Ralph Morgan, Robert Armstrong, Richard Davies, Joseph Crehan, George J. Lewis, Stanley Blystone, George Watts, Carleton Young.

King of the Mounties. Rep., [12 Chapters] D: William Witney; LP: Allan Lane, Peggy Drake, Gilbert Emery, Russell Hicks, George Irving, Abner Biberman, Duncan Renaldo, Nestor Paiva, Bradley Page, William Bakewell, Carleton Young.

Overland Mail. Univ., [15 Chapters] D: Ford Beebe, John Rawlins; LP: Lon Chaney, Jr., Don Terry, Noah Beery, Jr., Noah Beery, Sr., Helen Parrish, Bob Baker, Robert Barron, Jack Rockwell, Chief Thundercloud, Carleton Young.

CLARA KIMBALL YOUNG

There was nothing of the poseur air about Clara Kimball Young in spite of her tremendous popularity. The quiet charm audiences involuntarily associated with her was even more evident in her off-screen personality. She was as refreshing as the soft purple twilight that comes at the end of a summer's day — and as beautiful! In spite of her touted beauty and success, she was as unspoiled as any girl whose name was not being acclaimed in every corner of the world. She was simple and direct and somewhat naive, especially in business matters, but interviewers found that an entente cordiale was easily established with her.

Some sources list Benton Harbor, Michigan, as her birthplace; others, Chicago, Illinois. The date was September 6, 1890.

Both of her parents were in show business. Her father, Edward Marshall Kimball, acted in a number of Clara's films, and her mother, Pauline Maddern Kimball, who died in 1919, lived to see her daughter established as one of the ten top money makers on the screen, a distinction Clara received in 1918 and held through 1921.

Considered one of the screen's greatest emotional actresses in her time, Clara was extremely popular in the 1912–22 era, after which her career nosedived into obscurity.

Making her stage bow at age three, Clara worked periodically on stage with her parents until the ripe old age of nine, at which time she "retired" to St. Xaviar Academy in Chicago. But by the age of 15 or 16, she was back on the stage making her mark in musical comedy and vaudeville.

It was while she was playing in the Orpheum Stock Company, in Philadelphia, that J. Stuart Blackton of the Vitagraph Company saw her and made her a screen offer. The salary offered her was small — one-fourth of that she was then making — but she optimistically accepted. In only a few short years, she was known from one end of the world to the other; her name flashed in electric lights on Broadway and from marquees of the great cinema palaces of the day. She was feted and made much over by an adoring public, and her personality and charm won for her many admirers and friends, as well as a salary that escalated to nearly $10,000 a week.

In 1912 or '13, Clara married actor-writer-director James Young, and before the marriage fizzled in 1919 the couple worked together on over 30 films, with Young alternating between acting, directing and writing. While they were at Vitagraph, James drew the same salary as his wife.

Maurice Costello was the leading male star at Vitagraph, and Clara made over 30 films with him. In 1912, when Vitagraph was organizing a company for a picture-making tour of the world, it was Clara who was chosen from the company's large number of actresses to play the feminine leads. The six-month jaunt produced a number of beautiful foreign pictures: *Jack's Chrysanthemum*

(Japan); *The Spirit of the Orient* (Egypt); *The Taming of Betty* (China); *A Faithful Servant* (Italy); *The Lonely Princess* (Italy); *A Maid of Mandalay* (Mandalay); *Cupid Versus Women's Rights* (Egypt); *On Their Wedding Night* (Japan, Egypt); and *Fellow-Voyagers* (on an ocean liner at sea).

Probably the film that projected Clara into fame's spotlight was the five-reel *My Official Wife* ('14), ranked as one of the notable achievements of the screen at that time. The story offered every requisite for a strongly dramatic film. Most of the scenes were laid in St. Petersburg, and the Russian atmosphere was created with convincing skill. The action unfolded in rapid-fire order leaving few dull moments. As the beautiful nihilist, Clara turned in a superb performance under the direction of husband James Young. By popular demand, the film was reissued in December 1916 by Vitagraph, which, however, had lost its star to World Films headed by Lewis J. Selznick.

Among the film Clara made for World were *Lola* ('14), a story of a woman whose soul has been claimed by death, but whose body still lives; *Hearts in Exile* ('15), the story of Hope Ivanovna, a veritable lily of the Russian snows, coveted by three men; *Trilby* ('15), based on the Paul Potterstage version of du Maurier's famous novel; *Heart of the Blue Ridge* (15), a story of a mountain girl and moonshiners; *Camille* ('16), the story of a courtesan doomed by a premature death; *The Feast of Life* ('16), a tale of aristocratic lineage in which a Cuban girl, to save the family estate, is forced into a loveless marriage with a wealthy landowner; *The Rise of Susan* ('16), depicting the rise of a young lady from menial work-room girl to model to impersonating a countess; *The Yellow Passport* ('16), in which Clara plays a Jewess who flees Russia and becomes a noted prima donna in America; and *The Deep Purple* ('16), the story of a clergyman's daughter who is lured to the city, where she falls among thieves and is rescued by a young hero.

When World Films went broke, Selznick formed his own company. Clara, too, soon formed her own producing company and contracted with Selznick to make pictures for him. It proved to be a profitable arrangement. For the next five years Clara was one of Hollywood's most popular actresses, counting among her successes *The Common Law* (1916), concerning the life of an artist's model who, because she believes she will ruin the career of the man she loves if she marries him, decides to be his common law wife; *The Foolish Virgin* (1916), from the novel of Thomas Dixon, brings out the chances young women take when they marry men without knowledge of their past history; *The Easiest Way* (1917), an adaptation of Eugene Walter's drama about an actress who sacrifices first, self-respect, and then love, and takes the "easiest way" to success; *Magda* (1917), an appealing dramatic picturization of Herman Sudermann's play; *Shirley Kaye* (1917), an adaptation of Hulbert Footner's play about a young lady whose quick wit defeats the plans of a powerful businessman who contemplated ousting her father from the presidency of a railroad; *The Marionettes* (1918), from the Pierre Wolff play about a demure convent girl and her transition into the butterfly of Paris; *The House of Glass* (1918), the story of a woman who marries a man unaware that he is a crook and then is sent to prison too when stolen goods are found in her possession; *The Reason Why* (1918), about a woman forced into a loveless marriage; *The Claw* (1918), a story of romance and adventure in the African veldt; *The Savage Woman* (1918), again set in Africa, with Clara parading in tiger skins in an adaptation of a French novel by Francois-Curel; *The Road Through the Dark* (1918), a story of World War I and a French girl who falls in love with an American but becomes the mistress of a German officer in order to save her village; *Cheating Cheaters* (1919), a high-class crook play, directed by Allan Dwan, in which the heroine is a famous detective; *Eyes of Youth* (1919), with a novel theme tying up a series of three separate and distinct plots; *Mid-Channel* (1920), a story of conjugal difficulties; *The Better Wife* (1920), a light society drama; and *For the Soul of Rafael* (1920), a tale of old California in the days of

Spanish missions with a theme based upon the redemption of a soul—the heroine, a convent-bred girl, promising her guardian to marry the latter's wayward son and give him spiritual uplift.

In 1920, Clara agreed to pay Selznick $25,000 a year for ten years to get out of her contract with him and turned the management of her career and her production company over to Harry Garson, whom she had met shortly after her divorce from James Young. The move proved disastrous for her. Garson directed her in nine films before her company floundered and she had to sell almost everything she had to pay her bills. Pride had kept her from accepting $7,000 a week plus 25 percent of profits from her pictures to work for Adolph Zukor. Selznick had agreed to work out something with her regarding her payments to him if she would dump Garson, but she refused. Consequently, he sued and obtained judgment against her for the money owed him. Following the demise of her company, she made a few more films of less than noteworthy quality and quit the screen in 1925, only four years after ranking near the top of Hollywood's money makers.

In order that the reader have a better appreciation of the reverence in which Miss Young was held by critics of the time, the following quotations are lifted from various trade publications of the era in which she worked.

Love's Sunset (1913)
"The play itself and the able way in which its course is directed are largely the results of Clara Kimball Young's refined interpretation of the leading part."
—*Moving Picture World*, December 6, 1913

Lola (1914)
"Clara Kimball Young plays with her usual discrimination and ease the rather difficult role of Lola."
—*Moving Picture World*, November 21, 1914

Hearts in Exile (1915)
"Beautiful Clara Kimball Young is at her best as the high principled Russian girl, who escapes the houndings of fate and arrives at ultimate happiness."
—*Motion Picture News*, April 17, 1915

Camille (1916)
"The vivid pulsating charm of her Camille is depicted with such an understanding faithfulness, that from the first, when she frisks into the scene a gay, flippant little Parisian courtesan, until the end, when she lies as silent and lovely and cold as her beloved Camelia flowers clasped in her dead hands, she holds the audience completely enthralled."
—*Motion Pixture Classic*, June, 1917

In 1928, Clara married Dr. Arthur S. Fauman, to whom she remained married until his death in 1937. Clara tried a comeback in 1931, but about all she could get were minor parts in mediocre films. The idolation she had once received was gone forever; she was mostly forgotten by the public. However, serial fans got to know and appreciate her and B-melodrama buffs probably appreciated *Women Go On Forever* ('31), *Mother and Son* ('31), *File 113* ('32) and *Probation*

('32). Producer Harry Sherman used her in three Hopalong Cassidy Westerns, and she appeared in a few other films in support of Gene Autry, Tom Kennedy, Jackie Cooper, the Three Stooges, Wallace Ford and Edward Everett Horton.

Death claimed Clara on October 15, 1960, in the Motion Picture Country Home at Woodland Hills, California. Of all her screen interpretations, Clara had been fondest of the Russian type (a raven-haired beauty) that she so often portrayed in the late teens and early twenties. Ironically, the small coterie of movie buffs who remembered her at all remembered her mostly for her supporting work in the serials of the '30s.

Serials

1915

The Fates and Flora Fourflush. Vit., [3 Episodes] D: Wally Van Nostrand; SP: James Young, Mark Swan; S: Charles Brown; LP: Clara Kimball Young, Charles Brown, L. Rogers Lyttan, Templer Saxe, George Stevens.

1934

The Return of Chandu. Principal, [12 Chapters] D: Ray Taylor; P: Sol Lesser; LP: Bela Lugosi, Maria Alba, Clara Kimball Young, Lucien Prival, Phyllis Ludwig, Bryant Washburn, Peggy Montgomery, Dick Botiller.

1936

The Black Coin. S & S, [15 Chapters] D: Albert Herman; S: George M. Merrick; Spv.: Louis Weiss; Cam: James Diamond; Mus: Lee Zahler; SP: Eddy Graneman, Dallas Fitzgerald, Bob Lively, Albert Herman; LP: Dave O'Brien, Ralph Graves, Ruth Mix, Constance Bergen, Matthew Betz, Josef Swickard, Snub Pollard, Clara Kimball Young, Richard Cramer, Juan Duval, Lane Chandler.

1937

The Mysterious Pilot. Col., [15 Chapters] D: Spencer G. Bennet; P: Jack Fier, Louis Weiss;

Cam: Edward Linden, Herman Schoop; Mus: Abe Meyer; S: William Byron Mowery; LP: Fred Hawks, Dorothy Sebastian, Rex Lease, Guy Bates Post, Yakima Canutt, Kenneth Harlan, George Rosener, Harry Harvey.

1938

The Secret of Treasure Island. Col., [15 Chapters] D: Elmer Clifton; SP: George Rosener, Elmer Clifton, George Merrick; Cam: Edward Linden, Herman Schoop; Mus: Abe Meyer; P: Jack Fier, Louis Weiss; LP: Don Terry, Gwen Gaze, Grant Withers, Hobart Bosworth, William Farnum, Clara Kimball Young, Walter Miller, Dave O'Brien, Yakima Canutt, Frank Lackteen, Sandra Karina.

Bibliography

This bibliography is divided into Books (page 809), Articles (page 811), Obituaries (page 821), and Serial Synopses (page 823).

Books

Autry, Gene. *Back in the Saddle Again.* New York: Doubleday, 1978.

Barbour, Alan G. *Cliffhanger.* Secaucus, NJ: Citadel Press, 1977.

_____. *Old Movies 2: The Serial.* Kew Gardens, NY: Screen Facts Press, 1969.

_____. *The Serials of Columbia.* Kew Gardens, NY: Screen Facts Press, 1967.

_____. *The Serials of Republic.* Kew Gardens, NY: Screen Facts Press, 1965.

Bifulco, Michael. *Heroes and Villains — Movie Serial Classics.* Bifulco Books, 1989.

Birchard, Robert S. *King Cowboy: Tom Mix and the Movies.* Burbank, CA: Riverwood Press, 1993.

Bojarski, Richard. *The Films of Bela Lugosi.* Secaucus, NJ: Carol Publishing Group, 1980.

_____ and Kenneth Beals. *The Films of Boris Karloff.* Secaucus, NJ: Carol Publishing Group, 1976.

Bonomo, Joe. *The Strongman.* New York: Bonomo Studios, 1968.

Broncho Billy and the Essanay Film Company. Berkeley, CA: Farwell Books, n.d.

Burke, Billie. *With a Feather on My Nose.* New York: Appleton-Century-Crofts, 1949. London: Peter Davies, 1951.

Carneau, Ernest N. *Hall of Fame of Western Film Stars.* North Quincy, MA: Christopher Pub. House, 1969.

Carroll, David. *The Matinee Idols (Francis X. Bushman).* New York: Arbor House, 1972.

Cary, Diana Serra. *The Hollywood Posse.* Boston: Houghton Mifflin, 1975.

Catalog of Copyright Entries, Motion Pictures 1912–1939. Washington, DC: Library of Congress, 1951.

Cinema of the Fantastic. New York: Galahad, 1972.

Cline, William C. *In the Nick of Time: Motion Picture Sound Serials.* Jefferson, NC: McFarland, 1984.

Copeland, Bobby J. *Bill Elliott, The Peaceable Man.* Madison, NC: Empire, n.d.

_____. *Charlie King — We Called Him "Blackie."* Madison, NC: Empire, 2003.

_____. *Roy Barcroft — King of the Badmen.* Madison, NC: Empire, 2002.

Crowley, Roger M. *John Wayne, An American Legend.* Madison, NC: Empire Pub.

Curtis, James, ed. *Featured Player: An Oral Biography of Mae Clarke.* Metuchen, NJ: Scarecrow, n.d.

DeMarco, Mario. *Buster Crabbe — King of the Serial Aces and Western Action.* West Boylston, MA: DeMarco Publications, 1984.

_____. *Colonel Tim McCoy — The Last Plainsman.* West Boylston, MA: DeMarco Publications, n.d.

_____. *Johnny Mack Brown — The All American Cowboy.* West Boylston, MA: DeMarco, 1982.

_____. *Ken Maynard: The Fiddling Buckaroo.* West Boylston, MA: DeMarco Publications, n.d.

_____. *The Photostory of Battling Bob Steele.* West Boylston, MA: DeMarco Publications, n.d.

_____. *The Photostory of the Dean of Cowboy Stars — Hoot Gibson.* West Boylston, MA: DeMarco Publications, n.d.

_____. *The Photostory of the Screen's Greatest Cowboy — Tom Mix.* West Boylston, MA: DeMarco Publications, n.d.

_____. *Serial Aces of the Silver Screen.* West Boylston, MA: DeMarco Publications, 1984.

_____. *Those Wonderful Movie Serial Heroes.* West Boylston, MA: DeMarco Publications, 1989.

Doyle, Billy. *The Ultimate Directory of the Silent Screen Performers: A Necrology of Births and Deaths.* Metuchen, NJ: Scarecrow Press, 1995.

Essoe, Gabe. *Tarzan of the Movies.* New York: Cadillac Publishing, 1968.

Everson, William K. *The Bad Guys.* Secaucus, NJ: Citadel Press, 1982.

Eyles, Allen. *John Wayne.* San Diego: A. S. Barnes, n.d.

Fenin, George N., and William K. Everson. *The Western: From Silents to Cinerama.* Rev. ed. New York: Grossman, 1973.

Feret, Bill. *Lure of the Tropix.* New York: Proteus Books, 1984.

Fitzgerald, Michael G., and Boyd Magers. *Ladies of the Western: Interviews with Fifty-one More Actresses from the Silent Era to the Television Westerns of the 1950s and 1960s.* Jefferson, NC: McFarland, 2002.

Halliwell, Leslie. *The Filmgoer's Companion.* Rev. ed. New York: Hill and Wang, 1967.

Harmon, Jim, and Donald F. Glut. *The Great Movie Serials.* Garden City, NY: Doubleday, 1972.

Harris, Charles W., and Buck Rainey, eds. *The Cowboy: Six-Shooters, Songs, and Sex.* Norman: University of Oklahoma Press, 1976.

809

Hoaglin, Jess L. *Wherever Is...?* Vol. II. Newell, IA: Bireline, 1983.

John Wayne & the Great Cowboy Heroes. Collector's Edition. New York: Starlog Press, n.d.

Katchmer, George A. *A Biographical Dictionary of Silent Film Western Actors and Actresses.* Jefferson, NC: McFarland, 2002.

_____. *Eighty Silent Film Stars: Biographies and Filmographies of the Obscure to the Well Known.* Jefferson, NC: McFarland, 1991.

Katz, Ephrain. *The Film Encyclopedia.* New York: Thomas Crowell, 1976.

Kinnard, Roy. *Fifty Years of Serial Thrills.* Metuchen, NJ: Scarecrow Press, 1983.

Kohl, Leonard. *Sinister Serials.* Baltimore: Midnight Marquee Press.

Lahue, Kalton C. *Bound and Gagged.* Cranbury, NJ: A.S. Barnes, 1968.

_____. *Continued Next Week.* Norman: University of Oklahoma Press, 1964.

_____. *Gentlemen to the Rescue.* New York: Castle Books, 1972.

_____. *Riders of the Range.* Cranbury, NJ: A.S. Barnes, 1973.

_____. *Winners of the West.* Cranbury, NJ: A.S. Barnes, 1970.

Lamparski, Richard. *Whatever Became of ...?* New York: Ace Books, 1970.

Leibfried, Philip, and Chei Mi Lane. *Anna May Wong: A Complete Guide to Her Films, Stage, Radio, and Television Work.* Jefferson, NC: McFarland, 2003.

Leonard, John W. *Wild Bill Elliott.* 1976.

Liebman, Roy. *The Wampas Baby Stars: A Biographical Dictionary, 1922–1934.* Jefferson, NC: McFarland, 2000.

McClure, Arthur F., and Ken D. Jones. *Heroes, Heavies, and Sagebrush.* New York: A. S. Barnes, 1972.

McCord, Merrill. *Brothers of the West.* Bethesda, MD: self-published, 2003.

_____. *Perils of Kay Aldridge: Life of the Serial Queen.* Washington, DC: Alhambra Publishers, n.d.

Magers, Boyd. *So You Wanna See Cowboy Stuff?* Madison, NC: Empire, 2003.

Mathis, Jack. *Valley of the Cliffhangers.* Northbrook, IL: Mathis, 1975.

Maturi, Richard, and Mary Buckingham Maturi. *Beverly Bayne, Queen of the Movies: A Biography; With a Filmography and a Listing of Stage, Radio, and Television Appearances.* Jefferson, NC: McFarland, 2001.

Miller, Don. *"B" Movies.* New York: Curtis Books, 1973.

_____. *Hollywood Corral.* New York: Popular Library, 1976.

Miller, Leo O. *The Great Cowboy Stars of Movies and Television.* New York: Arlington House, 1979.

Mix, Olive Stokes, and Eric Heath. *The Fabulous Tom Mix.* Upper Saddle River, NJ: Prentice-Hall, 1957.

Mix, Paul E. *The Life and Legend of Tom Mix.* New York: A.S. Barnes, 1972.

Nareau, Bob. *The "Real" Bob Steele and a Man Called "Brad."* Mesa, AZ: Da'Kine, 1991.

Parish, James Robert, and William T. Leonard. *Hollywood Players: The Thirties.* Highland City. FL: Rainbow Books, n.d.

Rainey, Buck. *The Fabulous Holts.* Nashville: Western Film Collectors Press, 1976. 215 pp.

_____. *Heroes of the Range.* Metuchen, NJ: Scarecrow Press, 1987.

_____. *The Life and Films of Buck Jones: The Sound Era.* Waynesville, NC: World of Yesterday Press, 1991.

_____. *The Reel Cowboy: Essays on the Myth in Movies and Literature.* Jefferson, NC: McFarland, 1996.

_____. *Saddle Aces of the Cinema.* New York: A.S. Barnes, 1982.

_____. *The Saga of Buck Jones.* Nashville: Western Film Collectors Press, 1975.

_____. *Serials and Series: A World Filmography, 1912–1956.* Jefferson, NC: McFarland, 1999.

_____. *The Strong, Silent Type: Over 100 Screen Cowboys, 1903–1930.* Jefferson, NC: McFarland, 2004.

_____. *Sweethearts of the Sage: Biographies and Filmographies of 258 Actresses Appearing in Western Movies.* Jefferson, NC: McFarland, 1992.

_____. *Those Fabulous Serial Heroines: Their Lives and Films.* Metuchen, NJ: Scarecrow Press, 1990.

Reeve, Arthur B. *The Exploits of Elaine.* New York: Harper & Brothers, 1915.

_____. *The Romance of Elaine.* New York: Harper & Brothers, 1916.

Ricci, Mark, and Boris and Steve Zmijewsky. *The Films of John Wayne.* New York: Citadel Press, 1970.

Rothel, David. *The Gene Autry Book.* Waynesville, NC: World of Yesterday Press, 1985.

_____. *Who Was That Masked Man? The Story of the Lone Ranger.* Cranbury, NJ: A.S. Barnes, 1981.

_____ and Chuck Thornton. *Allan "Rocky" Lane—Republic's Action Ace.*

Russell, William. *Legends of the West.* Western Review, 1998.

Rutherford, John A. *The Films of Johnny Mack Brown.* Waynesville, NC: World of Yesterday Press, n.d.

Schutz, Wayne. *The Motion Picture Serial: An Annotated Bibliography.* Metuchen, NJ: Scarecrow Press, 1992.

Seiverling, Richard F. *Tom Mix: Portrait of a Superstar.* Hershey, PA: Keystone Publishers, 1991.

Slide, Anthony. *Early American Cinema.* New York: Tantivy Press, 1970.

Steadman, Raymond William. *The Serials: Suspense and Drama by Installment.* Norman: University of Oklahoma Press, 1971.

Svehla, Gary, and Susan Svehla. *Bela Lugosi.* Baltimore: Midnight Marquee Press, 1995.

_____ and _____. *Lon Chaney, Jr.* Baltimore: Midnight Marque Press, 1997.

Thomas, Tony. *The West That Never Was.* Coral Communications, 1989.

Thomkies, Mike. *Duke: The Story of John Wayne.* Chicago: Henry Regnery, 1971.

Thornton, Chuck, and David Rothel. *The Great Show Business Animals.* New York: A.S. Barnes, 1980.

Tuska, Jon. *The Vanishing Legion: A History of Mascot Pictures, 1927–1935.* Jefferson, NC: McFarland, 1982.

Underwood, Peter. *Karloff.* New York: Crake, 1972.

Ward, Larry Thomas. *Truth, Justice and The American Way.* Nicholas-Lawrence Books.

Weiss, Ken and Ed Goodgold. *To Be Continued.* New York: Bonanza Books, 1972.

Weltman, Manuel and Raymond Lee. *Pearl White: the Peerless Fearless Girl.* New York: A.S. Barnes, 1969.

Witney, William. *In a Door, Into a Fight, Out a Door, Into a Chase: Moviemaking Remembered by the Guy at the Door.* Jefferson, NC: McFarland, 1995.

Wyatt, Edgar M. *More Than a Cowboy: The Life and Films of Fred Thomson and Silver King.* Raleigh, NC: Wyatt Classics, 1988.

_____. *The Hoxie Boys: The Lives and Films of Jack and Al Hoxie.* Raleigh, NC: Wyatt Classics, 1992.

Zolotow, Maurice. *Shooting Stars: A Biography of John Wayne.* New York: Pocket Books, 1975.

Magazine and Newspaper Articles

"Actor Foran [Dick] Wins Divorce." *Los Angeles Times*, December 20, 1940.

"Actor Frankie Darro Jailed on Ex-Wife Plea." *Los Angeles Times*, September 20, 1954.

"Actor Powell [Lee] with Marines Since 1942." *Chicago Herald American*, August 30, 1944.

"Actor's Split with Wife Held up by Judge." *Los Angeles Daily News*, July 11, 1953. [Dave O'Brien and Dorothy Short]

"Actress Divorces Man Who Laughs at Films." *Los Angeles Mirror*, November 15, 1961 [Lynn Roberts]

"Actress Ruled Not Wed Legally, Loses Alimony." *Los Angeles Times*, Friday, May 25, 1951, Part II, p. 3. [Lynn Roberts]

"Actress States Marriage with Gambler Costly." *Los Angeles Times*, April 22, 1943. [Claudia Dell]

Adams, Less. "An Interview with Slingin' Sammy Baugh." *TEMI*, Vol. 3, No. 26, 397–398.

_____. "Serials of Buck Jones." *Yesterday's Saturdays*, Vol. 1, No. 3, September 1974, 42–47.

"Adrian Booth." Publicity sheet, Library, Academy of Motion Picture Arts and Sciences, Hollywood, CA, undated.

Albert, Katherine. "She Eats and Tells." *Photoplay*, January 1931. [Evelyn Brent]

Anderson, Chuck. "The Saga of Kermit Maynard." *Favorite Westerns*, No. 4, 1982, 6–11.

Anderson, Chuck. "Remembering David Sharpe." *Favorite Westerns*, No. 6, 1982.

_____. "The Saga of Kermit Maynard." *Favorite Westerns*, 5 and 6, 6–11, 12–17.

Anherich, Michael G. "Reel Stars." *Classic Images*, No. 167, May 1989, 9–10. [Joyce Compton]

"Ann Doran." *Los Angeles Times* calendar, September 27, 1981.

"Anna Little." *Motion Picture Magazine*, March 1915, 108.

"Anna Little of the Mustang Company." *Motion Picture Magazine*, March 1916, 112–113.

"Anne Nagel Asks $350,000 for Alleged Sterilization." *Los Angeles Daily News*, December 23, 1947.

"Another Tunney in a Long-Count Story." *Los Angeles Examiner.* June 3, 1970.

Anthony, Edward. "Beatty Loves 'Cats' But a Cinch Mom Didn't Dig 'Em." *Variety*, January 5, 1966.

Bagwell, Jr., Lewis. "Allan Rocky Lane." *TV Western*, Vol. 1, No. 2, 1958.

Baker, Colgate. "The Girl on the Cover." *Photoplay*, June 1915. [Mary Fuller]

Barrett, E. E. "Ain't She Sweet." *Pictures and Picturegoer*, July 1927. [Laura LaPlante]

"Batman and Robin." *Screen Thrills Illustrated.* April 1963, 10–15 and July 1963, 12–16.

Bawden, J. E. A. "Why, If It Isn't Ann Rutherford!" *Filmography*, Vol. IV, No. 1 (3rd and 4th Quarters 1973) 12–21.

"Beatty Fights Off 7 Battling Lions." *Los Angeles Times*, February 6, 1952.

Beaumont, Charles. "Don't Miss the Next Thrilling Chapter!" *Show Business Illustrated*, Vol. 1 (March 1962) 52–56, 78–80.

Behlman, Rudy. "The Saga of Flash Gordon." *Screen Facts 2*, No. 4, 1965, 53–62.

Benvenuto, Tony. "Ruth Roman, A Tribute." *Classic Images*, October 2003, 75–78.

"Billie Burke, Movie Comedienne." *The New York Times*, Late City Edition, Saturday, May 16, 1970.

"Biography of Frances Gifford." Paramount Studio publicity release, June 1949.

"Biography of The Lone Ranger." Warner Bros. Publicity Dept. [Clayton Moore]

Blair, Earl W., Jr. "Rocketman Flies Again." *Film Collector's Registry*, No. 69 (October 1976) 11–13.

Bodeen, DeWitt. "Anita Stewart." *Films in Review*, March 1968.

_____. "Antonio Moreno." *Film in Review*, Vol. XVII, No. 6 (June–July 1967) 325–344.

_____. "Betty Compson." *Films in Review* (August–September 1966) 396–413.

_____. Evelyn Brent. *Film in Review*, Vol. XXXVII, No. 6 (June–July) 339–361.

_____. "Kathlyn Williams." *Films in Review*, Vol. XXXV (February 1984) 67–79.

Boone, Arabella. "Griffith's First Blond Hero." *Photoplay*, October 1919, 54–55. [Ralph Graves]

Bosch, Peter. "Unmasking the Masked Marvel." *Serial World*, No. 37 (Spring 1984) 11–22.

Braff, R. E. "An Index to the Films of Jack Hoxie." *Classic Images*, No. 170, 16, 27, 32.

_____. "The Films of Bryant Washburn." *Classic Images*, No. 151 (January 1988), Center 34, 35, 37; No. 152 (February 1988); Center 18–20.

Breeden, Al. "Ab Breeden in Hollywood: Dorothy Gulliver." *Wranglers Roost*, No. 69 (April 1984).

Brennan, Tom. "I Can't Forget Fred Thomson." *Classic Film Collector*, No. 30 (1971).

____. "The Oaters." *Classic Film Collector*, No. 38 (Spring 1973). [Duncan Renaldo]

Briggs, Colin. "Ann Rutherford." *Hollywood Studio Magazine*, Vol. 18, No. 6 (June–July 1985) 27–29.

____. "Julie Bishop: What's in a Name?" *Classic Images* (August 2001) 12+.

Brock, Allan. "Belated Oscar to Madge Bellamy: Her Talent, Her Beauty, Her Great Heart." *Classic Images*, No. 153 (March 1988) C35, 60.

____. "Tom Neal, Good Guy." *Classic Film Collector*, No. 38 (Spring 1973) 25.

____. "Unforgettable Priscilla Dean." *Classic Film Collector* (1971).

Brock, Patrick. "Mae Clark (sic)." *Hollywood Studio Magazine*, Vol. 19, No. 2 (January–February 1986) 28–29.

____. "I Once Knew Them: Mae Clarke." *Hollywood Studio Magazine*.

Brooker, John. "Charles The Menace King." *Screen Thrills*, No. 6 (1976) 1–2.

Brown, Gary E. "Tom Mix, King of the Cowboys, Remembered." *Hollywood Studio Magazine*, Vol. 17, No. 12 (January–February 1984) 5–7.

Browne, Betty. "The Mad Hatter of Hollywood." *Picture Play Magazine* (October 1919) 40–41, 100.

Bruner, Frank V. "Along Came Ruth." *Motion Picture Classic* (July 1919).

____. "The Real Pearl White." *Motion Picture Magazine* (July 1919) 32–33, 102.

Bryant, David and George Rehrauer. "Lionel Atwill." *Film Fan Monthly*, No. 139 (January 1973).

"Buck, Frank." *Current Biography* (June 1943).

"Buck Jones: Coconut Grove Night Club Fire Victim." *New York Times*, November 29, 1942, page 1, col. 1; November 30, 1942, page 13, col. 2.

"Buck Jones Dies as He Lived: In Harness and Before Public." *Hollywood Reporter*, December 1, 1942.

"Buck Jones, The King of the Cowboys." *Boys Cinema Annual* (Christmas 1936).

Buck, Jerry. "Masked Man Still Riding High." *Los Angeles Times*, June 2, 1970.

Burgess, Beth. "The Lady of the Lions Reconsiders [Kathlyn Williams]." *Photoplay* (January 1917).

Canote, Terry. "The B-Westerns of John Wayne." *The Old Picture Show*, Vol. 5, No. 7 (July 2001).

Capello, Bill. "Supporting Player Richard Fiske." *Three Stooges Journal* (Winter 1972) 6–7, 14.

Carroll, Harrison. "Helen Holmes." *Los Angeles Herald*, March 2, 1936.

____. "Luck of Tony Moreno." *The American Weekly*, February 27, 1949.

Carter, Aline. "Untouched by Ennui." *Motion Picture Magazine* (August 1921), 53–54, 99. [Kathlyn Williams]

Casaldi, Edgar. "Francis (sic). Waiting for the Morning." *Hollywood Studio Magazine*, Vol. XVI, No. 4 (March 1983) 31–32.

Cavanaugh, Irene. "Marriage Doesn't Kill Careers of Film Stars Now." *Los Angeles Daily News*, August 23, 1933. [Ruth Clifford]

Chaney, Warren. "Jim Bannon — His Story." *Western Film Collector*, Vol. 111, No. 1, 50–65.

Chatelain, Jim. "David Sharpe." *Western Revue*, Vol. 6, No. 1 (June 1980) 22.

"The Circus." *Time*, July 30, 1965. [Clyde Beatty].

"Claudia Dell to be Wed Again." *Los Angeles Times*, December 13, 1947.

"Clayton Moore Files $30 million 'Ranger' Suit." *Variety*, April 17, 1978.

"Clayton Moore: The Lone Ranger of the 1950s." *Classic Images* (January 2000) 16.

"Clayton Moore's Life." *Serial Report*, Chp. 32 (January–March, 2000) 1–12.

"Cleo Madison." *Motion Picture World*, April 14, 1914.

Cline, William C. "Jennifer Holt: A Lady who Made Westerns." *Under Western Skies*, No. 48, 39–40.

____. "Remembrance of Serial Idols Past." *TEMI*, Vol. 1, Chp. 10 (April–May 1971) 132–134.

Cocchi, John. "Don 'Red' Barry." *Classic Images*, No. 148 (October 1987) 19.

____. "Robert Livingston." *Classic Images*, No. 147 (September 1987) 19.

____. "Tom Keene." *Classic Images*, No. 147 (September 1987).

____. "Verna Hillie." *Cliffhanger*, No. 26, 31–32.

Cohn, Alfred A. "Harvesting the Serial." *Photoplay*, Vol. XI, No. 3 (February 1917) 19–26.

Collins, William S. "Lois Wilson." *Films in Review*, Vol. XXIV, No. 1 (January 1973) 18–35.

Collura, Joe. "Bob Livingston — Hollywood White Knight." *The Old Cowboy Picture Show*, 2001.

____. "Cecelia Parker: Her Serial Life and Beyond." *Cliffhanger*, No. 18, 53–59.

____. "Dialogue with Bob Livingston." *Under Western Skies*, No. 16 (November 1981) 25–32.

____. "Dick Purcell: Fighting the Good Fight." *Classic Images* (October 2000).

____. "Evelyn Finley: Perils of the Wilderness Serial and Much More." *Cliffhanger*, No. 12 (May 1990) 7–14.

____. "George J. Lewis: Foregoing the Fame." *Cliffhanger*, No. 12, 19–25.

____. "Harry Lauter: A Good Guy who Sometimes Donned a Black Hat." *Cliffhanger*, No. 11, 59–62.

____. "I. Stanford Jolley: Hollywood Heavy." *Classic Images* (January 2001) 63–65.

____. "John King: Give Me a Ship and a Song." *Cliffhanger*, No. 27, 17–26.

____. "Keye Luke Number One Son was a Serial Sidekick Too." *Cliffhanger*.

____. "Kirk Alyn: The Serial's Man of Steel." *Cliffhanger*, No. 18, 13–21.

____. "Lyle Talbot: An Actor's Actor and an all-around Nice Guy." *Cliffhanger*, No. 14, 29–35.

____. "Marion Shilling: Riding the Hollywood Trail." *Classic Images*, No. 129 (March 1986) 22–23, 58.

____. "Pauline Moore: Too Nice to be a Star." *Cliffhanger*, No. 26, 33–39.

_____ "Robert Armstrong Going the Distance." *Classic Images*, No. 337 (July 2003) 63–67.

_____. "Ruth Hall: The Three Musketeers' Desert Beauty." *Cliffhanger*, No. 22, 41–44.

_____. "Tommy Cook: One Little Indian." *Cliffhanger*, No. 22, 45–48.

_____. "Tom Steele: Before and After the Masked Marvel." *Cliffhanger*, No. 14, 19–24.

Compson, Betty. "When My Chance Came." *Picture and Picturegoer* (April 1921).

Condon, Mabel. "The Real Perils of Pauline." *Photoplay* (October 1914).

Connor, Edward. "The First Eight Serials of Republic." *Screen Facts*, Vol. 2, No. 1 (1964) 52–63.

_____. "The Geneology of Zorro." *Films in Review* (August–September 1957) 330.

_____. "The Serial Lovers" [Walter Miller-Allene Ray]. *Films in Review* (August–September 1955).

"Converging on Lucile Browne." *TEMI*, 1, Chp. 4 (April-May 1970) 39, 48.

Coons, Minard. "An Interview with Peggy Stewart." *The Film Collectors' Registry*, No. 57 (November 1975).

Coons, Robbin. "Don Barry Doing Film Based on Pacific Tour." *Hollywood Citizen-News*, Tuesday, June 27, 1944, 6.

Cooper, Texas Jim. "Battlin' Bob Steele." *Remember When*, No. 8 (September 1972).

Copeland, Bobby J. "Julia Thayer and the Painted Stallion." *Cliffhanger*, No. 11, 56–58.

_____. "On the Festival Trail with John Hart." *Cliffhanger*, No. 12, 5–6.

_____. "On the Festival Trail with Peggy Stewart." *Favorite Westerns and Serial World*, No. 28, 33–35.

_____. "Phyllis Coates— The Last Serial Queen." *Westerns and Serials*, No. 39, 50–51.

_____. "Remembering Nell O'Day." *Under Western Stars*, No. 6 (August 1989) 25–26.

Coriell, Vernell. "Elmo the Mighty." *Classic Film Collector*, No. 20–21 (1968).

"Corriganville Sold to Actor's Ex-Wife." *Hollywood Citizen-News*, June 9, 1964.

Cotterman, Dan. "The Saga of Johnny Mack Brown." *Horse and Rider*, Vol. XII, No. 9 (September 1973) 22–26.

Cotton, Robert. "Buck Jones: Hero in Films, Hero in Life." *Persimmon Hill*, Vol. 8, No. 2 (Spring 1978) 17–23.

"Couple Surprised Nude in Bedroom, Court Told" [Tom Keene]. *Los Angeles Times*, October 19, 1949.

Courtlandt, Roberta. "T. Chatterton — Rancher." *Motion Picture Classic* (August 1917).

"Courtot: Well, Who is She?" *Photoplay* (June 1915) 120–121.

Couto, Carlos de Paula. "Universal Serial Stars of the Silent Era." *Classic Film Collector*, No. 48 (Fall 1975) 24–28.

"Craig Reynolds." *Films of the Golden Age*, 1996, 87–88.

"Crash Corrigan Raid on Wife's Motel Reported." *Los Angeles Times*, (June 3, 1954).

"Crauford Kent." *The Moving Picture World* (January 2, 1915) 83.

"Cullen Landis Reaches Stardom Via FBO." *Motion Picture World*, August 26, 1922.

"Culture Begins at 40 for Mae Clark." *San Francisco Examiner* (September 1964) 28.

Davis, Henry R., Jr. "Clara Kimball Young was the Kind of a Woman who has Little Practical Sense." *Films in Review* (August–September 1961) 419–425.

Davies, Wallace E. "Truth About Pearl White." *Films in Review* (November 1959) 537–548.

Day, John. "The Incredible Credits of Mr. Hollywood" [Lyle Talbot]. *Los Angeles Times*, Calendar, February 19, 1984.

"Dead End Kid in Lost Weekend." [Billy Halop]. *Los Angeles Daily News*, June 2, 1954.

Dellinger, Paul. "Allan Rocky Lane." *The Old Cowboy Picture Show*, Vol. 6, No. 5 (May 2002).

_____. "Duncan Renaldo— The Cisco Kid." *The Old Picture Show*, Vol. 4, No. 11 (November 2000) 1, 4.

_____. "Kay Aldridge's Next Chapter." *Cliffhanger*, No. 1 (Winter 1983) 23–33.

_____. "Richard Simmons: Serial to Sergeant." *Cliffhanger*, No. 3 (1984) 48–50, 3.

_____. "Rod Cameron Serial Super-Hero." *Cliffhanger*, No. 4 (1983) 3–18.

_____. "Victor Jory: Tribute to a Bad Man." *Cliffhanger*, No. 2 (Spring 1983) 39–41.

DeMarco, Mario. "Charles 'Blackie' King." *Classic Images* (July 1991).

_____. "Dave Sharpe, Prince of Daredevils." *Classic Images*, No. 65 (September 1979).

_____. "Eddie Polo, the thrill Maker." *Movie Collector's World*, No. 311 (March 3, 1981).

_____. "Girls of the Golden West." *Movie and Film Collectors World*, Issue 190 (July 13, 1984) 25–26.

_____. "Kermit Maynard — The Star's Stuntman." *Hollywood Studio Magazine*, Vol. 18, No. 3 (March 1985) 18.

_____. "The Strong Silent Hero, Tom Tyler." *Classic Images*, No. 87 (September 1982).

_____. "Tom London, Ace of the Heavies." *The Big Reel*, No. 152 (January 15, 1987) 27.

_____. "William Desmond." *Classic Images*, No. 135 (September 1986).

_____. "Yakima Canutt." *Films of the Golden Age*, No. 3 (Winter 1995) 68–69.

Denny, Reginald. "Laura LaPlante." *Photoplay* (July 1924).

DeRoos, Robert. "Hollywood's Mother Hen [Helen Ferguson]." *TV Guide*, November 4, 1961, 28–30.

DeWitt, Bodeen. "Kathlyn Williams." Vol. XXXV (February 1984) 67–79.

"Dick Foran Fights Wife's Divorce Suit." *Los Angeles Herald*, November 5, 1940.

"The Dick Tracy Story." *Screen Thrills Illustrated* (June 1962) 52–59.

"Divorce Wins in Rift on America Versus Europe [Phyllis Coates]." *Herald Express*, Vol. LXXXIII (October 1, 1953).

"Divorce Won by Wife of Dick Foran." *Los Angeles Times*, May 19, 1945.

Dolven, Frank. "Remarkable Western Film Icon Tom London." *The Big Reel*, No. 262 (March 1996).

_____. "Tom Keene, The On and Off Again Cowboy Star." *Classic Images*, No. 224 (February 1994), 14, 16, 34.

Dowling, Gary. "Arline Pretty was Born that Way." *Photoplay* (June 1917).

Doyle, Billy H. "Lost Players: Allene Ray." *Classic Images*, No. 168 (May 1989) 45–46.

_____. "Lost Players: Vivian Rich." *Classic Images*, No. 152 (February 1988) C13.

Doyle, Neil. "George Brent: Emotional Support." *Classic Images* (December 2002) 6–14.

_____. "Lon Chaney, Jr." *Classic Images*, No. 329 (November 2002) 6–12.

Drew, William M. "Esther Ralston." *American Classic Screen*, Vol. 5, No. 4 (1981) 25–32.

"Edna Murphy." *New York American* (May 7, 1925).

Elliott, Malcolm. "The Youngest Grand Old Man!" [Jack Mulhall] *Photoplay* (November 1930).

"Estelita Tells Criticism, Divorces Grant Withers." *Los Angeles Times*, November 10, 1955.

Evans, Delight. "Br-r-r-r! The Villain!" *Photoplay* (February 1919) [William Desmond].

_____. "The Man Uncomfortable: Jack Holt Wrote His Own Title." *Photoplay* (November 1922) 30, 33, 111.

Everett, Eldon K. "Bertram Milhauser Remembers Pearl White." *Classic Images*, No. 83 (1982) 25.

_____. "Ford Beebe Recalls Helen Holmes and J. P. McGowan." *Classic Images*, No. 86 (August 1982) 34.

_____. "The Hollywood People…and Other Things [Pathé Serials]." *Classic Images*, No. 79, p. 24.

_____. "A Postscript to Pearl White." *Classic Film Collector* No. 55 (Summer 1977) 48–49.

_____. "Ruth Roland, Queen of the Cliffhangers." *Classic Film Collector* (circa 1974) 54–55.

Everson, William K. "Tom Mix." *Films in Review* (October 1957) 387–397.

Eyck, John. "Speaking of Pearls." *Photoplay* (September 1917).

Fagan, Herb. "The Distinguished Career of Walter Reed, From Lead to Character." *Classic Images*, No. 271 (January 1998) C–8, C–11.

"Fast Lane Lois." *People*, May 9, 1994. [Phyllis Coates]

Fernett, Gene. "Nat Levine: The Serial King." *Views and Reviews*, Vol. 1 (Summer 1969) 22–31.

"Film Actor Grant Withers Stricken by Drug Overdose." *Los Angeles Daily News*, September 23, 1954.

"Film Ranch Sale Stalled by Ex-Wife" [Ray Corrigan]. *Los Angeles Times*, May 12, 1964.

"Film Writer and Director and Betty Flournoy Leave Note on Doorstep of Girl's Home; Romance Began Several Months Ago." [Ralph Graves], *Los Angeles Examiner* (June 29, 1934).

"The Films of Madge Bellamy." *Classic Images*, No. 176 (February 1990) 26–27, 30.

Fleming, Sylvester. "Its Desmond and He's Irish." *Motion Picture Classic* (July 1918). [William Desmond]

Fletcher, Adele Whitely. "Brains-Beauty-or Luck?" [Betty Compson]. *Photoplay* (September 1930).

_____. "Reconsidering Pearl." *Motion Picture Magazine* (February 1921).

Foley, Karyn. "The Lone Ranger Still Rides." *Hollywood Studio Magazine* (February 1978).

"Frankie Darro Drank, Hit Her, Says Wife; Gets Divorce." *Harold Express*, November 26, 1954.

Franklin, Wallace. "That Snow-Cruze Lady." [Marguerite Snow]. *Photoplay* (October 1915).

Franchey, John. "What's in a Name?" [Donald Barry] *New York Times*, March 11, 1945.

"The Freaking Out of Jean Arthur." *Hollywood Studio Magazine*, Vol. 8, No. 10 (February 1974).

Fullbright, Tom. "Juanita Hansen, the Poppyseed Girl." *Classic Film Collector*, No. 23 (Spring 1969) 10.

_____. "Presenting Miss Beverly Bayne." *Classic Film Collector* (1971).

Fuller, Mary. "My Summer Vacation." *Photoplay* (November 1914) 111–114.

Gallagher, Tag. "Brother Feeney." [Francis Ford]. *Film Comment* (November–December 1976) 12–18.

Gallico, Paul. "Tunney Winds Up Unpopular Man" [Gene Tunney]. *Los Angeles Times*, February 2, 1964.

Gardiner, Gerry. "A Tribute to Bob Livingston." *Classic Images*, No. 83 (May 1982) 83.

Gassaway, Gordon. "Louise of the Lions" [Louise Lorraine]. *Motion Picture Classic* (July 1922) 36–37, 79.

Gebhart, Myrtle. "The Gold Girl" [Madge Bellamy]. *Motion Picture Magazine* (April 1922).

_____. "The Real Ruth Roland." *Picture Play Magazine* (December 1926).

Geltzer, George. "40 Years of Cliffhanging." *Films in Review* (February 1957) 60–67.

_____. "Ruth Roland." *Films in Review*, Vol. XI, No. 9 (November 1960) 539–548.

"Gene Tunney Daughter Admits Killing Spouse." *Los Angeles Times*, June 13, 1970.

"Gentleman Gene Helped Dempsey's Popularity." *Los Angeles Times*, November 8, 1978.

"Gertrude Olmstead." *Variety*, June 21, 1975.

Gibson, Helen. "In the Very Early Days." *Films in Review*, Vol. 19, No. 1 (January 1961) 28–34.

Gifford, Frances. "A Letter from Frances Gifford." *Hollywood Studio Magazine*, Vol. XVI, (August 1983) 4.

"The Girl Who Couldn't be Discouraged" [Lois Wilson] *Motion Picture Magazine* (May 1917).

"Gloria's Romance" [Billie Burke]. *New York Times*, May 23, 1916.

Goldbeck, Willis. "Early in the Morning" [Wallace MacDonald]. *Motion Picture Classic* (September 1921).

Golden, Eve. "Billie Burke: That Charming Mrs.

Ziegfeld." *Films of the Golden Age* (Spring 1996) 66–70.

Goldsworthy, James. "The Cullen Landis Story." *Classic Film Collector* (Spring/Summer 1970) 6–8.

"A Good Actor and He Knows It [Victor Jory]." *TV Guide*, September 3, 1960.

"Good Excuse Wins!" [Claudia Dell], *Los Angeles Examiner*, December 31, 1934.

Gross, Marge. "'Heavy' Actor Paints Himself Into the Sunset [Harry Lauter]." Ontario-Upland, *The Daily Report*, February 6, 1976, 11.

Groves, Gloria. "A Real Vaudeville Equilibrist" [Ruth Roland]. *Photoplay* (April 1919).

"Guide to Charlie Chan Films, A; Part One — Warner Oland and the First Chans." *Classic Images* No. 267 (September 1997) 28–32, C1.

Gussow, Mel. "Lyle Talbot, 94, Character Actor and TV Neighbor." *New York Times*, March 5, 1996.

Hall, Alice. "Roughing it With Ruth Roland." *Pictures and Picturegoer* (June 1921).

Hall, Alice. "The Ninety-Nine Lives of Pearl White." *Pictures and Picturegoer* (February 1921).

Hall, John. "Jay Tunney Recalls Dad's Ring Classic with Dempsey in 1927." *Los Angeles Times*, XXXX.

Hall, Prunella. "Buck Jones' Last Interview." *Boston Post*, December 1, 1942.

Hamilton, Sara. "He's No Romeo, But —-" [Jack Holt]. *Photoplay* (September 1932) 76, 99.

Handy, Truman B. "Differences and Priscilla." [Priscilla Dean]. *Motion Picture Classic* (October 1922) 36–37, 79, 85.

Hare, William. "The Outspoken Don 'Red' Barry." *American Classic Screen*, Vol. 1, No. 6 (July–August 1977) 33.

Hareison, Louis Reeves. "What Happened to Mary?" [Mary Fuller]. *Moving Picture World*, July 5, 1913.

Harvey, Steve. "Lone Ranger Rides to Court" [Clayton Moore]. *Los Angeles Times*, April 14, 1978.

"Hazards of Helen — Those Were the Days!" *Los Angeles Herald Examiner*, September 9, 1962, B-4.

Henderson, Sam. "Oklahoma Odyssey of Tom Mix." *The Sunday Oklahoman*, February 1, 1981.

"High Explosive Hero" [Joe Bonomo]. *Screen Thrills Illustrated* (June 1962) 10–15.

Hoagland, Jess. "Down Memory Lane: Dorothy Gulliver." *Hollywood Studio Magazine* (June 1982).

_____. "Nell O'Day." *Classic Images*, No. 102 (January 1984) 9.

_____. "Priscillla Dean." *Hollywood Studio Magazine* (June 1972).

_____. "Where Are They Now?" [Cecilia Parker]. *The Hollywood Reporter* (April 13, 1975).

_____. "Where Are They Today?" [Dorothy Gulliver]. *The Hollywood Reporter* (July 1972.)

Hoffman, Hugh. "As King Baggot Sees Himself." *Picture-Play Weekly*, Vol. 1, No. 21 (August 28, 1915).

Holland, Larry Lee. "Frances X. Bushman." *Films in Review* (March 1978) 157–173.

_____. "Warner Oland." *Films in Review* (June 1985) 355–360.

"Hollywood Business Woman" [Shirley Grey]. *New York Evening Post*, May 22, 1933.

"Hollywood Holts Are a Rare Threesome [Jack, Tim, Jennifer]." *Richmond (VA) Times-Dispatch*, December 6, 1942.

"Holt of the Secret Service." *Variety*, February 4, 1942.

Howe, Herbert. "His Last 50 Cents Earned Jack Holt a Million Dollars." *Photoplay* (July 1926) 91, 133.

Howes, Reed. "I Hit the Hollywood Skids." *Motion Picture Magazine* (September 1944).

Hunt, Jackson. "Play Ball" [Cullen Landis]. *Photoplay* (November 1919) 88–90.

"In Re the Fullers— Where Has Mary Been?" *Photoplay* (May 1917) 47.

Irvine, Clarke. "Helen Holmes." *Motion Picture World* January 16, 1916.

"Isn't Youth Just!" [Claudia Dell] *Photoplay* (November 1930).

"Jack Holt's Life Colorful." *Los Angeles Examiner*, January 19, 1951, Sec. 3, Col. 1, p. 25.

"Jack Mulhall, Actor in Earlier Films; First to Get $1,000 a Week." *New York Times*, June 8, 1979.

"Jack Mulhall Turns 90." *Classic Film Collector*, No. 57 (Winter 1977) 39.

Jackson, Gregg, Jr. "Serial World Interviews Louise Currie." *Serial World*, No. 7 (Summer 1976) 18–22.

_____. "Serial World Interviews Walter Reed." *Serial World*, No. 19 (Summer 1979) 19–22.

Jacobson, Laurie. "Bela Lugosi, the Curse of Dracula." *Hollywood Studio Magazine*, Vol. 21, No. 3 (March 1988) 10–13.

"Jacqueline Wells is Granted Divorce." *New York Herald*, May 12, 1939.

James, Joseph. "(Gene) Tunney." *Newsweek*, November 20, 1978.

"Jean Arthur Stars in an Animal Epic." *New York Post*, April 13, 1973; *Los Angeles Herald Examiner*, May 22, 1973.

"Jean Carmen Weds Sunday." *Los Angeles Examiner*, August 9, 1937.

Jennings, Dean. "The Woes of Box-Office King John Wayne." *The Saturday Evening Post* (1962).

"Joe Bonomo, Strongman, Stunter and Serial Actor, Recalls Old Hollywood." *Variety Weekly*, January 22, 1969.

"Joe Bonomo, Star of the Silent Films; Began as Stuntman." *New York Times*, April 1978.

"John Wayne: Still Bigger Than Life." *Scouting*, Vol. 67, No. 3 (May/June 1979).

Johnson, Ken. "Jack Ingram: A Nice 'Bad Man.'" *Western Film Collector*, Vol. 1, No. 3 (July 1973) 16–18, 30.

Jones, Ronnie. "Allan (Rocky) Lane, the Fightin'est Cowboy on the Screen." *Saturday's Heroes*, No. 1 (August 1977).

Jorday, Dan and Edward Connor. "Judge Hardy and Family." *Films in Review*, Vol. XXV, No. 1 (January 1974) 1–10. [Cecilia Parker]

Jorday, Joan. "Madge [Bellamy] Make-Believe." *Photoplay* (March 1921).

"Judge Orders Division of Oland Assets." [Warner Oland]. *Los Angeles Examiner*, April 2, 1938.

Katchmer, George. "Art Acord, the Holy Terror." *Classic Images*, No. 80, 1981, 32, 35, 55.

_____. "The Clean-Cut Hero Tom Tyler." *Classic Images*, No. 108 (January 1984) 23–24.

_____. "In Complete and Utter Admiration of Jack Hoxie." *Classic Images*, No. 85, 31–33.

_____. "Cowboy Edmund Cobb." *Classic Images*, No. 89, 20–22.

_____. "Forgotten Cowboys and Cowgirls" [Allene Ray]. *Classic Images*, No. 181 (July 1990) 56–57.

_____. "Forgotten? William Russell." *Classic Images*, No. 98, 52–53, 71.

_____. "The Idol of the Young — Fred Thomson." *Classic Images*, No. 110, p. 20.

_____. "Jack Mulhall." *Classic Images*, No. 117, 25–27.

_____. "Ken Maynard: Dr. Jekyll or Mr. Hyde?" *Classic Images*, No. 102 (December 1983) 49–51.

_____. "The Kids Loved Jack Perrin." *Classic Images*, No. 149 (November 1987) 13–15.

_____. "King of the Serials, Walter Miller." *Classic Images*, No. 116 (February 1985) 17–18, C8.

_____. "The Latin Lover Antonio Moreno." *Classic Images*, No. 79, 22–23.

_____. "The Man with the Smile — Herbert Rawlinson." *Classic Images*, No. 107, 38–40.

_____. The Old But Young Harry Carey." *Classic Images*, No. 112 (October 1984) 16–20.

_____. "The Riddle Rider William Desmond." *Classic Images*, No. 93 (March 1983).

_____. "Ruth Mix, A Chip Off the Old Block." *Classic Images*, No. 100 (October 1983) 34–35.

_____. "The Screen Girl of Action, Ruth Roland." *Classic Images*, No. 123 (October 1985) 23–26.

_____. "The Smiling Cowboy, Franklyn Farnum." *Classic Images*, No. 97 (July 1983) 38–39.

_____. "Wallace MacDonald." *Classic Images*, No. 99, 10–11.

Keene, Mary. "Romance Comes to Priscilla [Dean]." *Motion Picture Classic* (June 1920).

Kelley, Leo. "Hoxie and Accord 'Reel' Oklahoma Cowboys." *Chronicles of Oklahoma*, Vol. LXXIV, No. 1 (Spring 1996).

"Kenneth Harlan." *Photo Drama Magazine* (August 1921).

Kietzer, Patrice. "Holt of the Secret Service." *Favorite Westerns*, Nos. 23 & 24 [two parts] (1986).

King, Pamela J. "Don 'Red' Barry Keeps on Ryding High." *Los Angeles Herald Examiner*, March 4, 1978.

King, Paul. "On Two Sides of a Camera, One-and the Only-Duke." *Chicago Tribune*, Arts and Fun Section June 10, 1973.

Kinnard, Roy. "Interview: Jean Rogers." *Fifty Years of Special Thrills* (Scarecrow Press, 1983) 182–191.

"The Lone Ranger Rides Again." *Variety*, February 15, 1939.

"The Lone Ranger Rides Again." *Serial Quarterly*, Vol. 1, No. 3 (July-September 1966) 19 pp.

"The Lone Ranger Story." *Screen Thrills Illustrated* (April 1963) 6–13.

"Louise Lorraine." *Classic Images*, No. 75, 1981, 16.

"Louise Lorraine Personifies Youth." *Moving Picture World* (November 3, 1923).

"Lyle Tolbot: Breaking into Hollywood." *American Classic Screen*, Vol. 8, No. 2 (March/April 1984).

McClelland, Doug. "Maris Wrixon: Beauty and the B's." *Film of the Golden Age* (Spring/Summer

_____. "Nostalgic Nights with Constance Moore." *Film Fan Monthly*, No. 164 (February 1975) 19–28.

_____. "The Perils of Frances Gifford." *Cliffhanger*, No. 2 (Spring 1983) 20–23.

McCord, Merrill T. "Luana Walters: the Sexy Leading Lady of B-Westerns and More." *Films of the Golden Age*, No. 18 (Fall 1999) 58–73.

_____. "Robert Livingston." *The Big Reel* (April 1988) 12.

McCrea, Joel. "Hoot Gibson: Even the Heroine Blackened His Eye." *Western Stars*, Vol. 1, No. 5 (Spring 1950) 75.

McDowell, Bill. "Lane Chandler, Once on Same Level with Gary Cooper." *Western Revue* (Spring 1976) 8–12.

McElwee, John P. "John Wayne." *The Big Reel* (February 1988) 41–45.

McKelvic, Martha Groves. "Every Thing's Lovely." *Motion Picture Classic* (May 1918). [Marguerite Clayton]

Mace, James W. "John Wayne Rareties." *Classic Film Collector*, No. 38 (Spring 1973).

"Madge Bellamy Edition." *Fox Folks* (September 1925).

Magers, Boyd, ed. *Western Clippings* (Gene Autry Issue), No. 27 (January/February 1999).

"Mainly About Madge [Bellamy]." *Pictures and Picturegoer* (July 1926).

Maltin, Leonard. "Jackie Cooper Today." *Film Fan Monthly*, No. 156 (June 1974).

"Marguerite Courtot." *Motion Picture Magazine* (June 1915) 116.

"Marion Shilling: A Serial Sweetheart." *Cliffhanger*, No. 20, 4–10.

Maronie, Samuel James. "Ann Rutherford." *Films of the Golden Age* (Spring 1996) 22–24.

Martin, Pete. "The First King of Swoon." *The Saturday Evening Post* [Francis X. Bushman] (April 28, 1945) 14–15+.

Matheny, Frank. "An Interview with Duncan Renaldo." *Film Collectors Registry*, Vol. 7, No. 4 (April 1975) 15–16.

Matthews, John. "More on Rin-Tin-Tin." *Filmography*, Vol. II, No. 3 (Third Quarter 1971) 46–47.

Melchoir, L. C. "A Tribute to Kane Richmond." *TEMI*, Chp. 29, Vol. 3, No. 9, 438–441.

"Men of Action: Dave O'Brien." *TEMI*, Chp. 18, Vol. 2, No. 8 (August–September 1972).

"Miss Ruth Roland." *Moving Picture World* (March 7, 1914).

Mitchell, Charles P. and Paul Parla. "Reflections of George Wallace: 'Commando Cody.'" *Classic Images* (August 1999) 24–26.

Mitchell, George and William K. Everson. "Tom Mix." *Films in Review* (October 1957), 387–397.

Montanye, Lillian. "The Lone Star Girl [Allene Ray]." *Motion Picture Classic* (April 1921), 26, 68.

_____. "The Pretty Miss Pretty [Arline Pretty]." *Motion Picture Classic* (November 1919) 604.

_____. "A Reel Lover of the Ladies [Crauford Kent]." *Motion Picture Classic* (September 1921).

Moore, Doug. "Pauline Moore: Girl of the Golden West." *American Classic Screen*, Vol. 4, No. 2 (Winter 1980) 37–39.

Mullett, Mary B. "The Heroine of a Thousand Dangerous Stunts." *American Magazine* (May 1918).

Murphy, Jim. "Marguerite Chapman." *Films of the Golden Age*, No. 23 (Winter 2000).

Naureau, Bob. "Frankie Darro, the Forgotten Little Cowboy." *Westerns and Serials*, No. 32, 26–28.

_____. "The Real Steele [Bob]." *Westerns and Serials*, No. 38, 38–42.

_____. "The Twins [Bob Steele]." *Westerns and Serials*, No. 35.

Naylor, Hazel Simpson. "Cabbages and Kings." *Motion Picture Classic* (October 1921). [King Baggot]

"New Contract for Shirley Grey." *New York Harold Tribune*, February 22, 1933.

"A New Kalem Star" [Ruth Roland]. *Motion Picture World* (December 5, 1914).

Newton, Mike. "Jack and Al Hoxie — Brothers of the Saddle." *Classic Images*, No. 213 (March 1993).

O'Dowd, Brian. "Tarzans of the Silver Screen." *Hollywood Studio Magazine*, Vol. 17, No. 8 (August 1984) 26–28.

Oliver, Myrna. "Ruth Clifford; Early Movie Star, Character Actress." *Los Angeles Times*, December 31, 1998.

Osborne, Robin. "Serial Spotlight: Man of Menace — Trevor Bardette." *Wrangler's Roost*, No. 46 (June 1976).

Othman, Frederick C. "Face Her Fortune Again." *Hollywood Citizen-News*, March 14, 1941. [Veda Ann Borg]

"Pamela Blake Plans Divorce." *Los Angeles Examiner*, November 18, 1948.

Pando, Leo. "Dave Sharpe — a Stuntman and a Gentleman." *The Old Cowboy Picture Show*, Vol. 5, No. 6 (June 2001).

Panzer, Paul. "The Actor in the Early Days." *The Moving Picture World* (March 10, 1917) 1509–1510.

Parkhurst, C. M. "George J. Lewis/The Face is Familiar." *TEMI*, Chp. 19, Vol. 2, No. 9, (October/November 1972).

Parsons, Louella. "Foran [Dick] and Wife at Crossroads." *Los Angeles Examiner*, February 13, 1940.

_____. "Ralph Graves' Wife Will Sue for Divorce." *Los Angeles Examiner*, July 3, 1932.

"Paul Panzer Back from Lecture Trip." *The Moving Picture World* (May 1, 1915) 733.

Peltret, Elizabeth. "Betty Compson — Romance Girl." *Motion Picture Classic* (December 1919).

_____. "A Dreamer of Dreams [Cullen Landis]." *Motion Picture Classic* (July 1920).

_____. "When the Celluloid Clock Strikes Twelve." *Moving Picture Magazine* (June 1919) 69–70 [Carol Holloway].

Petersen, Elizabeth. "Comrad Ruth." *Motion Picture Classic* (April 1917).

_____. "The Serial Girl — Marie Walcamp." *Motion Picture Classic* (September 1919).

"Phyllis Coates of TV Divorces Band Pianist." *Los Angeles Times*, October 2, 1953.

Pilk, Robert. "Carol Forman Interview." *Cliffhanger*, No. 4. 51–56.

Pitts, Michael R. "Gilbert Roland, the Most Virile Actor in Movies." *Classic Film Collector* No. 32 (Fall 1971) 4–5.

_____. "Tom Keene, Man of Many Names." *Classic Images*, No. 87 (September 1982).

Pontes, Bob. "An Interview with Joan Woodburry." *Favorite Westerns*, (January 1983) 5, 18.

_____. "An Interview with Nell O'Day." *Favorite Westerns*, No. 12 (June 1983) 17–20.

_____. "An Interview with Sammy McKim." *Westerns and Serials*, No. 29, 17–19.

"Portraits of Popular Photoplayers [Marguerite Clayton]." *Photoplay* (March 1917) 11.

Powell, Larry. "Marion Shilling Remembering Buck Jones." *Under Western Skies*, No. 33, 45.

Pratt, George. "Mulhall [Jack] Still in Pic Biz with Sag." *Hollywood Citizen-News*, June 1, 1961.

Price, Bob. "Serial Queens." *Screen Thrills Illustrated* (January 1963) 12–18.

"Priscilla [Dean] in Name Only." *Photoplay* (November 1918).

Proctor, Kay. "Nobody Ever Heard of Her [Constance Worth]." *Photoplay* (August 1937).

"Quest of a Modern Prince Charming [Wallace MacDonald]." *Motion Picture Classic* (September 1921) 34–35, 71.

Rainey, Buck. "Anne Gwynne: Her Wholesomeness and Charm Made Her a Favorite on the 'B' Market." *Under Western Skies*, No. 30 (1984) 41–47.

_____. "Art Accord, an Enigma." *Western Revue*, Vol. 2, No. 2 (Summer 1975) 1–13.

_____. "Ben Wilson: Revered Serial King and Neglected Western Star." *Under Western Skies*. No. 34 (May 1988) 25–41.

_____. "Brothers Al and Jack Hoxie, Cinema Trailblazers." *Western Revue*, Vol. 3, No. 1 (March 1977).

_____. "Carol Forman Reminisces." *Serial World*, No. 37 (Spring 1984) 3–10.

_____. "Cinema Cowboys on the Sawdust Trail." *Classic Images*, No. 101 (November 1983) 12, 75.

_____. "Cleo Madison." *Classic Images*, No. 143 (May 1987) 17–20.

_____. A Conversation with Linda Stirling, Sensuous Siren of the Serials." *Film Collectors Registry*, No. 17 (December 1976) 3–7.

_____. "Dave O'Brien." *Classic Images*, Part I, No. 186 (December 1990); Part II, No. 187 (January 1991).

_____. "Dick Foran." *Classic Images*, No. 190 (April 1991) 38–41, 49.

_____. "Duncan Renaldo." *Classic Images*, No. 178 (April 1990) C–5, C–6, C–7.

_____. "Eileen Sedgwick." *Classic Images*, No. 129 (March 1986) 17–18.

_____. "Esther Ralston." *Classic Images*, No. 121 (September 1984) 23–24; Vol. 112 (October 1984) 31.

_____. "Evelyn Finley." *Under Western Skies*, No. 18 (May 1982) 34–64.

_____. "Everyone's Amigo Duncan Renaldo." *The Nostalgia Monthly*, No. 5 (May 1978) 39–41.

_____. "Film Career of Tom Keene." *Western Film Collector*, Vol. 1, No. 6 (January 1974) 21–33, 35.

_____. "The Film Career of Buster Crabbe." *Western Film Collector*, Vol. 2, No. 3 (July 1974) 2–17; *The Old Cowboy Picture Show* (January 2003) 1, 4–7.

_____. "The Film Career of William Duncan." *Classic Film Collector*, No. 55 (Summer 1977) 24–26.

_____. "Fred Thomson, Great but Forgotten Hero." *Western Film Collector*, Vol. 1, No. 3 (July 1973) 4–15.

_____. "A Gentleman: Harry Carey." *Under Western Skies*, No. 16 (November 1981) 5–19.

_____. "Hal Taliaferro, No Stranger to Horse Operas." *Western Revue* (Spring 1976) 3–7.

_____. "Herman Brix/Bruce Bennett." *Cliffhanger*, No. 10 (June 1989) 36–51.

_____. "Hi Yo Silver … Away!" *Under Western Skies*, No. 51. 4–14.

_____. "The Holts." *Views and Reviews* (Summer 1984) 11–18.

_____. "Hoot Gibson, Cowboy." *Films in Review*, Vol. XXIX, No. 8 (October 1978) 471–484.

_____. "Jack Mulhall: The Ever-Smiling Irishman with an Enviable Serial Career." *Cliffhanger*, No. 13 (1990) 5–40.

_____. "Jean Arthur." *Classic Images*, Nos. 105–106 (March–April 1984), 17–19; 42–43.

_____. "Jean Rogers—Talent, Versatility, Wholesomeness, Beauty, and Irrefragable Sexuality Combined to make her the Queen of the Serial World in the Late Thirties." *Cliffhanger*, No. 4, 37–50.

_____. "John 'Dusty' King." *Classic Images*, No. 157 (July 1988) C17–C18.

_____. "Johnny Mack Brown, Cowboy Immortal." *Blazing West*, Collectors Edition, Vol. 1, No. 1 (1984) 6–10.

_____. "Kane Richmond." *Classic Images*, No. 158 (August 1988) 22, C7.

_____. "Kathlyn Williams: A Mature Woman of Graphic, Poignant Charm, Exuding Courage and Poise in Every Conceivable Peril." *Cliffhanger*, No. 5 (1985) 19–26.

_____. "Leo Maloney, Range Rider of the Roaring 20's." *Under Western Skies*, No. 18 (August 1984) 47–57.

_____. "The Lone Ranger Rides Again." *The Nostalgia Monthly*, No. 8 (August 1978) 31–35.

_____. "Lorna Gray/Adrian Booth, a Beautiful Brunette Whose Endowments Won a Host of Fans." *Classic Images*, No. 119 (May 1985) 44–45.

_____. "Neva Gerber." *Blazing West and Serial Classics*, No. 2 (1986) 4–5.

_____. "Pearl White." *Serial World*, No. 34 (Spring 1983) 42–45.

_____. "The Pearl White Film List." *Serial World*, No. 36 (Winter 1984) 18.

_____. "Phyllis Coates: She Was Hollywood's Last Try at a Serial Queen." *Classic Images*, No. 138 (December 1986) 33–34.

_____. "Ralph Byrd." *Classic Images*, No. 155 (May 1988) C31–C34.

_____. "The 'Reel' Cowboy: Myth Versus Realism." *Red River Historical Review* (Spring 1975) 25–63.

_____. "Reminiscing with Nell O'Day." *Film Collectors Registry*, No. 65 (June 1976).

_____. "Reminiscences of Jack Holt." *Remember When*, Vol. 15.

_____. "Rex, King of the Wild Horses." *Film Collectors Registry*, No. 61 (February 1976) 9–11.

_____. "Rex Lease, a Pleasant and Competent Performer who Enhanced 15 Serials." *Cliffhanger*, No. 11. 19–50.

_____. "Roy Stewart, a Page From the Past." *Classic Film Collector*, No. 56 (Fall 1977) 30–32, 35, 51, 56.

_____. "Ruth Roland." *Serial World*, Part I, No. 35 (Summer 1983) 21; Part II, No. 36 (Winter 1984) 20–21; Part III, *Serial Classics*, No. 1 (1984) 18.

_____. "Tim McCoy: The Last Rough Rider." *Film Collectors Registry*, No. 77 (June 1977).

_____. "Tom Mix, a Page From the Past." *The Nostalgia Monthly*, No. 4 (April 1978) 43–47.

_____. "Trailin' Art Acord—Another View." *Favorite Westerns*, No. 12 (June 1983) 12–15.

_____. "A Tribute to Yakima Canutt." *The Big Reel*, No. 139 (December 1985) 67–69.

_____. "Virginia Brown Faire." *Classic Images*, No. 142 (April 1987) 13–16.

_____. "Yak." *Western Revue* (August 1977) 9 pp.

_____. "Zorro Rides Again…Again…and Again." *Western Film Collector*, Vol. III, No. 1 (Winter 1976) 2–24; *Cliffhanger*, No. 26, 5–24.

"The Rapid Rise of Ruth Roman." *Life*, Vol. 28, No. 18 (May 1, 1950) 51–52.

Reed, Warren. "Bill Desmond, Indestructible." *PicturePlay Magazine* (January 1920).

Reem, Craig. "Red Grange Raced Through Ventura." *Ventura County (CA) Star Free Press*, June 24, 1980.

Reinhart, Ted. "Lee Powell…Things Didn't Work Out Right." *Screen Thrills*, No. 4.

_____. "Saddle King Ken." *Under Western Skies*, No. 22 (January 1983) 19–21.

"Remember Antonio Moreno? He Hopes to be a Director." *Pittsburgh Press*, January 21, 1941.

Remont, Fritzi. "The Grave Mr. Graves [Ralph Graves]." *Motion Picture Classic* (November 1919).

_____. "A Twentieth Century Priscilla." *Motion Picture Classic* (February 1919) 30–31, 71.

_____. "Marie: The Mystic." *Motion Picture Classic* (January 1920). [Marie Walcamp]

Rense, Rip. "Look! Up on the Screen! It's…Lois Lane [Phyllis Coates]." *Los Angeles Times*, April 5, 1994.

"Revelations of Ruth Roland." *Pictures and Picture-goer* (January 1927).

"Richard Alexander; Best of the Badmen." *Western Revue*, Vol. 6, No. 1 (June 1980) 19–21.

Reimoldi, Oscar A. "The Amazing Gilbert Roland: Six Decades of Hollywood History." *Hollywood Studio Magazine*.

____. "Tom Mix, A Tormented Life Marked by Violence and Tragedy." *Hollywood Studio Magazine*.

Ringold, Gene. "Veda Ann Borg." *Films in Review*, Vol. XVI, No. 3 (March 1965) 188–190.

Roberts, John. "Buster Crabbe Saturday Matinee Hero." *Classic Images*, No. 328 (October 2002) 77–81.

____. "Dead End Kids in Films and Serials." *Serial World*, No. 36 (Winter 1984) 10–11.

Roberts, Stewart. "Tom Mix, the Tinsel Cowboy." *Westerner*, Vol. 4, No. 4 (July–August 1972).

Roman, Robert C. "Boris Karloff." *Films in Review* (August–September 1964).

Roos, Robert de. "Hollywood's Mother Hen." [Helen Ferguson], *TV Guide*, November 4, 1961, 28–30.

Rosa, Joseph G. "Buck Jones Bona Fide Hero." *True West* (July–August 1966) 20–21, 64.

Rosen, Sid. "Tom Mix, the Greatest Cowboy of the West." *Under Western Skies*, No. 9 (January 1980) 29–47.

Rubin, Jay. "Buster Crabbe." *Classic Film Collector*, No. 43, 1974, 9–10.

Rubin, Sam. "Kathlyn Williams." *Classic Film Collector*, Vol. XIV (Spring 1966) 9.

Russell, William C. "Alias Tom Keene." *Western Revue*, Vol. 6, No. 1 (June 1980) 1–12.

____. "Chief Thundercloud: Real 'Tonto' to Most Western Fans." *Western Revue*, (Spring 1976) 25–27.

____. "Johnny Mack Brown — The Flame of the West." *The Old Picture Show*, Vol. 6, No. 10 (October 2002).

____. "The Little Giant of Westerns." *Western Revue*, (May 1978).

____. "Trailing 'Crash' Corrigan." *Western Revue*, No. 1 (Summer 1975) 14–21.

"Ruth Clifford." *New York Morning Telegraph*, January 13, 1924.

"Ruth Clifford, Silent Film Star, Asks Divorce." *Los Angeles Examiner*, August 23, 1934.

"Ruth Roland Up-to-Date." *Picture and Picturegoer*, October 27, 1917.

"Ruth Roman: The Rise of a New Roman Empire." *Los Angeles Times Magazine*, January 1986) 19.

Rutherford, John A. "Lone Star Cowboy [John Wayne]." *Under Western Skies*, No. 40, 4–18.

St. Amant, Joe. "Daredevil Eddie Polo, Now 85, Plans Comeback." *Los Angeles Mirror*, March 3, 1961.

St. Johns, Adele Rogers. "An Interview with a Baby [William Desmond]." *Photoplay* (September 1920).

____. "Here Comes the Groom [William Desmond]." *Photoplay* (September 1919).

____. "Priscilla [Dean] Pins Her Hair Back." *Photoplay* (October 1919) 31–34, 113.

Sanford, Harry. "An Interview with William (Bill) Witney." *TEMI*, Chp. 13, Vol. 3, No. 1 (February–March 1973) 309–311.

____. "The Lone Ranger." *Classic Film Collector*, No. 25 (Fall 1968) 13–15.

Sansweet, Stephen J. "Under the Big Top: A Tent Circus Manages to Survive and Prosper [Clyde Beatty]." *The Wall Street Journal*, October 6, 1969.

Schaefer, Randall. "An Interview with Bill Kennedy." *Cliffhanger*, No. 20.

Schallert, Edwin. "Atmosphere Tingles as Volatile Ramsay Ames Reaches for Ice Bag." *Los Angeles Times*, August 20, 1944.

Schermerhorn, Jane. "One Thing or Another." *Detroit News Magazine*, January 3, 1967. [Cullen Landis]

____. "Cullen Landis: Now There Was a Silent Star." *Classic Film Collector*, No. 18 (Summer 1967).

Scheuer, Philip K. "Pioneer Film Actor [Antonio Moreno] Still Going Strong." *Los Angeles Times*, March 16, 1974.

____. "Earliest of Screen Villains Looks Back Over a Career of 40 Years." *Los Angeles Times*, June 18, 1944. [Paul Panzer]

Schmid, Peter Gridley. "An Animal Chat with Kathlyn Williams." *Motion Picture Classic* (January 1917) 33–34, 36.

"The Screen Girl of Action, Ruth Roland." *Classic Images*, No. 123 (October 1985) 23–26.

"Serials of Buck Jones." *Yesterday's Saturdays*, Vol. 1, No. 3 (September 1974) 42–47.

Sexton, Bill "Smoky." "A Tribute to Dennis Moore." *TEMI*, Chp. 28, Vol. 3, No. 8, 418–419.

Seymour, Alicia. "Slingin' Sammy Baugh; The Man Who Would be 'King.'" *Classic Images.*, No. 281 (November 1998) C–12 C13.

Seymour, Blackie. "George J. Lewis: Now That's a Star!" *Classic Images*, (August 2000) 65–66.

____. "Jack Ingram: They Couldn't Make a Serial Without Him." *Classic Images*, (December 2000) 70.

____. "Pentagram Profiles Roy Barcrift: Dean of the Heavies." *Classic Images*, No. 336 (June 2003) 72–77.

Shawell, Julia. "Clyde Beatty Says Women are Like Tigers." *Pictorial Review* (March 1934) 4, 26.

Shearer, Lloyd. "Heart Repairs and All, at 71 the Duke [John Wayne] is King." *Parade* October 22, 1978.

Sheppard, Gene. "Jennifer Jones Is a Many-Splendored Thing." *Hollywood Studio Magazine* (August 1984) 23–25.

Sheridan, Oscar M. "Pearl [White] in Paris." *Pictures and Picturegoer* (November 1923).

Sherman, Sam. "Republic Studios: Hollywood Thrill Factory." *Screen Thrills Illustrated* (January 1963) 24–31; (April 1963) 12–16.

____. "Buck Rogers." *Spacemen*, Vol. 6 (June 1963) 16–21.

Shipley, Glenn. "Allene Ray, Top Serial Star." *Classic Images*, No. 148 (October 1987) 43.

Shipley, Glenn. "Art Acord, Harry Carey, Buck Jones, Tom Tyler, Jack Hoxie, Fred Thomson." entire Special Issue, *True West*, No. 212, Vol. 52, No. 8.

Shirk, Adam Hull. "Ann Little and the Great Desire." *Motion Pictu4re Classic* (January 1919) 36–37.

Shoenberger, Jim. "Reminiscing with Frank Coghlan, Jr. and William Benedict." *TEMI*, Chp. 13, Vol. 3, No. 1 (Feb–March 1973) 304–306.

_____. "Reminiscing with Linda Stirling." *TEMI* Vol. 2, No. 3 (October–November 1971) 175–176.

_____. "Reminiscing with Reed Hadley." *TEMI*, Chp. 25, Vol. 3, No. 5, 366–368.

Slide, Anthony. "The Kalem Serial Queens." *Silent Picture*, No. 1 (Winter 1968–69) 7–10.

Sloan, Lloyd L. "Madge Bellamy Effective in 'Lady' Play." *Hollywood Citizen-News*, March 22, 1946.

Slobb, Kermit. "Resident Badman [Charles King]." *Classic Images*, No. 133, 16, 18–19.

Smith, Bertha H. "Nervy Movie Lady." *Sunset* (June 1914). [Kathlyn Williams]

Smith, David L. "Monte Blue: Regged Romantic Star." *Classic Images* (August 2000) 61–64.

Smith, Frank Leon. "The Man Who Made Serials." *Films in Review*, Vol. Vii (October 1956) 375.

_____. "Pearl White and Ruth Roland." *Films in Review* (December 1960).

Smith, Frederick James. "No Ice Today [Red Grange]." *Photoplay* (November 1926).

_____. "A Pearl in the Rough." *Motion Picture Classic* (January 1919) 16–19, 72.

_____. "Photoplay Finds Mary Fuller." *Photoplay* (August 1924) 58, 125.

Smith, Lewis. "Along Came Buck [Jones]." *Horse and Rider* (March 1973) 42–48.

Spears, Jack. "Comic Strips on the Screen." *Films in Review* (August–September 1956) 317–325, 333.

Spencer, Gary. "The Jesse James Serial Trilogy." *Favorite Westerns & Serials Plus*, No. 20 (n.d.) 31–33.

Squires, Harry. "Harry Carey." *Under Western Skies*, No. 16 (November 1981) 21–24.

Stanaway, John. "The Battle of the Serial Studios: Universal vs. Republic." *Serial Classics*, No. 1. 4–10.

Stanke, Don. "Ruth Roman." *Film Fan Monthly*, No. 142 (April 1973) 11–15.

Starling, Bart. "Jean Arthur." *Hollywood Studio Magazine*, Vol. 20, No. 9 (September 1987) 19–23.

Starr, Jimmy. "Starlet's Marriage [Pamela Blake] a Double-Feature." *Los Angeles Herald*, January 12, 1943.

Stephenson, Ron. "Concerning Serials & Trends." *TEMI*, Chp. 29, Vol. 3, No. 9.

Sterling, Ray. "Pearl White — Woman Wizard." *Photoplay World* (May 1919).

Stirling, Linda. "My Life As a Serial Queen." *Movie Digest* (May 1973) 44–49.

Stoginski, John. "Colonel Tim McCoy — Serially Speaking." *TEMI*, Chp. 28, Vol. 3, No. 8, 424–426.

Street, Chris. "Rocky [Allan Lane] — the Fighting Cowboy." *Wrangler's Roost*, No. 62 (Christmas 1981).

Stumpf, Charles K. "Eduardo Ciannelli — Master of Menace." *Cliffhanger*, No. 26. 27–29.

_____. "Fearless Clyde Beatty." *Cliffhanger*, No. 2 (Spring 1983) 33–39.

_____. "Marion Martin: The Blonde Menace." *Classic Images* (July 2000) 63–65.

_____. "Versatile Dick Foran: From Archaeologist to Singing Cowboy." *Under Western Skies*, No. 51 (circa 1998) 30–35.

_____. "Warren Hull — the Green Hornet, Mandrake the Magician, and the Spider — all rolled into One!" *Cliffhanger*, No. 26. 25–26.

Sulski, Jim. "The Girl Who was Dale Arden." *Fantastic Films*, Vol. II, No. 2 (June 1979) 56–62. [Jean Rogers]

Summers, Murray. "Laura LaPlante in 'Her Reel Life.'" *Filmograph*, Vol. II, No. 3 (3rd quarter 1971) 23–43.

"Super Idol [Francis X. Bushman] of the Screen Married — Five Children — Brutal to Wife." *Washington Times*, February 10, 1918.

Sutton, David. "A Post Interview with John Wayne: Image vs. Man." *The Saturday Evening Post* (March 1976) 55–57, 117, 120.

Talbot, Bob. "Kennedy [Bill] Ailing." *Detroit Free Press*, January 12, 1997. [Insiders Notebook.]

Talbot, Stephen. "My Father and Me — Our Lives on TV." *California* (July 1991). [Lyle Talbot]

"Tarzan of the Apes." *New York Times*, September 1, 1957.

Taylor, Frank. "John Wayne — America's Shooting Star." *Hollywood Studio Magazine*, Vol. II, No. 12 (n.d.) 10–15.

"TEMI talks with Larry 'Buster' Crabbe." TEMI, Chp. 14, Vol. 2, No. 4 (December 1971–January 1972) 193–194.

Thayer, Stuart. "Tom Mix Circus and Wild West." *Bandwagon*, March–April 1971, pp 18–23; May–June 1971, pp. 4–11.

"Theatrical Cliffhanger Serials of Yesteryear Still Sell 'Far Out.'" *Variety* February 12, 1964.

"The 13 Faces of Tarzan." *Screen Thrills Illustrated* (June 1962) 4–9.

Thomas, Anthony. "Tim McCoy." *Films in Review*, Vol. XIX, No. 4, 1968, 218–230.

Thomas, Bob. "Hollywood Changes But John Wayne Goes on Forever." *The Daily Ardmoreite*, September 27, 1978.

_____. "Hollywood's General of the Armies [Yakima Canutt]." *True, the Man's Magazine* (July 1966) 47–48, 86–89.

_____. "The Inscrutable Mr. Chan: A New Cult in the Offing?" *Los Angeles Harold Examiner*, February 9, 1968. [Warner Oland]

Thomas, Kevin. "Wampas Baby [Dorothy Gulliver] Gets New Career Start in 'Faces.'" *Los Angeles Times*, January 3, 1969.

Thomas, Ray G. "Here's to the Ladies/Louise Stanley." *TEMI*, Chp. 25, Vol. 3, No. 5, 374–375.

"Tom Keene Became Driftin' Cowboy, Says Actor's Wife." *Los Angeles Times*, March 6, 1941.

"Tom Mix." *American Classic Screen*, Vol. 4, No. 2 (Winter 1980).

"Tribute Paid to [Herbert] Rawlinson." *Los Angeles Examiner*, July 16, 1953.

"Tris Coffin; Acting Career Long, varied." *Los Angeles Times*, April 1, 1990.

Tully, Jim. "Laura LaPlante." *Vanity Fair* (January 1928).

Turner, George. "Making the Flash Gordon Serials." *American Cinematographer* (June 1983) 56–62.

Tuska, Jon. "In Retrospect: Ken Maynard." *Views and Reviews*, Vol. 1, Issue 1 (Summer 1969); Vol. 1, Issue 2 (Fall 1969).

_____. "Tim McCoy: In Retrospect." *Views and Reviews*, Vol. 2, Issues 1–4.

"$2,507,000 for Corrigan's Ranch." *Hollywood Reporter*, June 10, 1964.

Uselton, Roi A. "The Wampas Baby Stars." *Films in Review*, XXI (February 1970) 73–97.

Van Buren, Walter C. "Serial Queens of the Silent Screen." *Memory Lane*, Vol. 1, No. 7 (May 1980) 41–46.

Vaughn, Gerald F. "From Football to Western Movie Hero: Slingin' Sammy Baugh." *Cliffhanger*, No. 14, 41–42.

Vermilye, Jerry. "Jean Arthur." *Films in Review*, Vol. XXII, No. 6 (June-July 1966) 329–346.

Victorek, D. "Dave O'Brien." *Films in Review*, Vol. XXIII, No. 8, 449–464.

Virgines, George E. "Adios Amigo" [Jack Hoxie]. *Frontier Times* Vol. 39, No. 5 (September 1965).

Wagner, Laura. "Tom Neal: Breezing Along in the 'Bs.'" *Cliffhanger*, No. 27, 9–14.

"Wally Wales Has Ruth Mix, Daughter of Tom, for Lead." *The Brooklyn Daily Times*, July 19, 1931.

Ward, Jim. "The Buck Jones Story." *Wild West Stars*, Vol. 2, No. 5 (1970) 1–10.

Ward, Larry Thomas. "Noel Neill: Lois Lane Goes West." *Classic Images* No. 342 (December 2003).

"The Washburns [Bryant] Here." *The New York Morning Telegraph*, July 4, 1920.

Waterbury, Ruth. "Love and Esther Ralston." *Photoplay* (October 1926).

Watkins, Fred. "George Brent." *Film Fan Monthly*, No. 136 (October 1972) 3–14.

Weathers, Stormy. "The Kid [Bob Steele]." *Under Western Skies*, No. 28 (August 1984) 5–21.

Weaver, Tom. "Phyllis Coates, Superman's Girl Friend." *Starlog* Part I, No. 138 (January 1989) 49–52, 70; Part II, No. 139 (February 1989) 49–52, 57.

Weiner, Beth. "Ex-Actress [Eleanor Stewart] Is Content with Role as Author, Grandmother." *Rancho Bernardo (CA) Journal*, March 7, 1985, A10.

"Western Hall of Fame: Tom London." *Screen Thrills Illustrated*, No. 8 (May 1964).

"What a Wonderful Blonde! [Allene Ray]." *Photoplay* (February 1921).

"Whatever Became of Gene Tunney." *Coronet* (April 1968).

White, Pearl. "Putting It Over." *Motion Picture Magazine* (February 1917) 61–62.

"Why They Forsook Footlights for Filmdom [Marguerite Snow]." *Photoplay* (November 1914).

Wilkinson, Harry. "Looking Hollywood Way [Frank Buck]." *Good Old Days* (February 1971) 26–29, 32.

Williams, Nick. "Behind the Mask [Bob Livingston]." *Wild West Stars*, Vol. 1, No. 4.

_____. "Leo Maloney." *Western Film Collector*, Vol. 1, Nos. 4&5 (November 1973).

_____. "Peg of Our Hearts." *Western Film Collector*, Vol. 1, No. 6 (January 1974) 11–19, 35.

_____. "The Versatile Raymond Hatton." *Western Film Collector*, Vol. II, No. 3 (July 1974) 18–35.

Wilson, Bill. "The Hard-Boiled Gentleman [Jack Holt]." *Classic Images*, No. 73 (January 1981) 31.

Winship. Mary. "The Curly Kid [Cullen Landis]." *Photoplay* (April 1921).

_____. "A Little Domestic Drama [Priscilla Dean]. *Photoplay* (October 1920).

_____. "Oh, Why Did They Name You Priscilla? [Dean]." *Photoplay* (March 1924).

Wright, Mack V. "Serials, Stunts, and Six Guns." *Screen Thrills Illustrated* (February 1964) 26–31.

Obituaries

"Actor Oland [Warner] is Taken by Death." *Los Angeles Examiner*, August 6, 1938.

"Actor Who Played Heroes in Cowboy Films is Dead [Robert Livingston]." *Richmond News Leader*, March 8, 1988.

"Ann Nagel." *Variety*, July 8, 1966.

Anthony, Edward. "Clyde Beatty's Collaborator's Closeup on Great Animal Trainer." *Variety*, July 21, 1965.

Bacon, James. "Jack Mulhall Dead at 92 — Silent Era Leading Man." *Los Angeles Herald-Examiner*, June 6, 1979.

Berman, Art. "Clyde Beatty, Trainer of Wild Animals, Dies." *Los Angeles Times*, July 20, 1965.

"Big Boy Williams, Film Cowboy Dies." *Hollywood Citizen News*, June 6, 1962.

"Billie Burke Dead: Movie Comedienne." *New York Times*, Saturday, May 16, 1970 (Late City Edition).

"Billy Halop, Leader of Dead End Kids Gang, Dies at 56." *Los Angeles Times*, November 11, 1976.

"Bryant Washburn, Film Star, 79, Dies." *New York Times*, May 4, 1963.

"Buck Jones Dies as He Lived, In Harness and Before Public." *Hollywood Reporter*, December 1, 1942.

"Buck Jones is Dead of Injuries in Fire." *New York Times*, December 1, 1944.

"Carmelita Geraghty Wilson." *Variety*, July 11, 1966; *Variety Weekly*, July 13, 1966.

"Charles King Dies." *The Hollywood Reporter*, Thursday, May 9, 1957.

"Circus Hero Beatty Dies." *Hollywood Citizen News*, July 20, 1965.

"Clyde Beatty." *Variety*, July 20, 1965.

"Crauford Kent, Veteran Movie Actor, Dies at 72." *Los Angeles Times*, May 15, 1953.

Crivello, Kirk. "Passing Parade/Veda Ann Borg." *Hollywood Studio Magazine*, February 1978.

"Death Takes Noah Beery [Sr.]." *Los Angeles Times*, April 2, 1946.

"Dejected Actor Gulps Pills [Grant Withers], Dies." *Los Angeles Mirror News*, March 28, 1959.

DeMarco Mario. "The Passing of a Hero [Bob Steele]." *The Big Reel*, No. 177, February 15, 1989, B10.

"Desmond, Idol of Silent Films, Taken by Death." *Hollywood Citizen News*, November 3, 1949.

"Dick Foran." *Variety*, August 13, 1979.

"Donald (Red) Barry, 69, Film Actor is a Suicide." *New York Times*, July 19, 1980.

"Dorothy Fay Ritter, Western Leading Lady in the '30s and '40s." *Dallas Morning News*, November 13, 2003.

Drew, William M. "Esther Ralston." *American Classic Screen*, Vol. 5, No. 4, 1981, 25–32.

Dwyer, Timothy. "Red Grange, the Galloping Ghost, Dies at 87." *The Philadelphia Inquirer*, January 29, 1991.

"Eddy Polo, Silent Film Star, Dies." *Los Angeles Examiner*, June 15, 1961.

"Empty Saddles: Richard 'Dick' Simmons." *Western Clippings*, No. 52, March/April, 2003, 13–14.

"Film and TV Actress Helen Parrish Dies." *Hollywood Citizen-News*, February 23, 1959.

"Final Rites for Actress Ann Nagel." *Los Angeles Times*, July 8, 1966.

Flint, Peter B. "Irene Rich, Silent Screen Actress and Radio Personality Dies at 96." *New York Times*, April 25, 1988.

Folkart, Burt A. "Bob Steele, Prolific Star of Dozens of Western Films." *Los Angeles Times*, December 23, 1988.

"Francis X. Bushman of Silent Films Dies." *New York Times*, August 24, 1966, p. 1, Col. 3, p. 43, Col. 1.

"Francis Ford, Veteran Actor-Director Dies." *Los Angeles Examiner*, September 6, 1953.

"Frank Buck." *Variety*, March 29, 1950

"Frank Buck Dies at 66." *Los Angeles Examiner*, March 26, 1950.

"Franklin Farnum, Silent Star, Dies." *Hollywood Citizen-News*, July 5, 1961.

"Fred Kohler, Actor, Dies." *Los Angeles Examiner*, October 29, 1938.

"Friends Throng Church at Grant Withers Rites." *Los Angeles Times*, April 1, 1959.

"Funeral Rites Tomorrow for Crauford Kent, 72." *Hollywood Citizen-News*, May 15, 1953.

Furman, Bruce. "Trails End for a Legend [Ray Corrigan]." *Serial World*, No. 8, Fall 1976.

"George B. Seitz." *Variety*, July 10, 1964.

"George Seitz, 'Hardy' Films Director, Dies." *Los Angeles Times*, July 9, 1944.

"Gertrude Olmstead." *Variety*, January 21, 1975.

"Gloria Grey, Silent Film Star, Dies in Her Sleep." *Los Angeles Examiner*, November 23, 1947.

Goldstein, Richard. "Television's Lone Ranger and a Persistent Masked Man [Clayton Moore], Dies at 85." *New York Times*, December 29, 1999.

Goodman, Jr., George. "Dick Foran, Singing Actor, Dies; Was Veteran of Western Movies." *New York Times*, August 13, 1979.

"Grace Darmond." *Variety*, October 9, 1963.

"Grant Withers Ends Career with Suicide." *Hollywood Citizen-News*, March 28, 1959.

Haynes, Roy. "Movie Veteran Antonio Moreno Dies at 80." *Los Angeles Times*, date unknown.

"Helen Holmes. One of the Pioneer Cliffhanger Heroines, Dies at 58." *Variety*, July 10, 1950.

"Jack Holt, 62, Dies: Veteran Film Star." *New York Times*, January 20, 1951.

"Jack Holt Succumbs to Third Heart Attack." *Los Angeles Examiner*, January 19, 1951.

Jones, Jack. "Victor Jory, Veteran Stage, Film Character Actor, Dies." *Los Angeles Times*, February 13, 1982.

"Julie Bishop." *Classic Images*, October 2001, p. 56.

"King Baggot, Early Day Idol of Films, Dies." *Los Angeles Times*, July 12, 1948.

"King Baggot Gets Last Cue." *Los Angeles Examiner*, July 12, 1948.

"King Baggot, 68, Dies on Coast." *Motion Picture Herald*, July 17, 1948.

Lentz III, Harris. "Noah Beery, Jr.." *Classic Images*, No. 234, December 1994, 56+.

Leppard, Stan. "Film Star [Antonio Moreno] of Silent Era Dies." *Los Angeles Herald-Examiner*, February 15, 1967.

"Louise Lorraine." *Hollywood Reporter*, February 13, 1981.

"Louise Lorraine." *Variety*, February 11, 1981.

"Lyle Talbot." *Variety*, March 25, 1996.

Maxwell, Evan. "Dick Foran, Cowboy Star of '40s, Dies." *Los Angeles Times*, August 11, 1979.

Moore, Doug. "Pauline Moore: Girl of the Golden West." *American Classic Screen*, Vol. 4, No. 2 Winter 1980, 37–39.

"Leo Maloney." *New York Times*, November 3 and 4, 1929.

"Noah Beery, Jr." *Los Angeles Times*, November 2, 1994.

"No Services Planned in Actor's [Creighton Hale] Death." *Hollywood Citizen-News*, August 11, 1965.

Nordwin, Richard. "Character Actor Victor Jory Dead at 79." *Los Angeles Herald Examiner*, February 13, 1982.

"Oland [Warner], Film Chan, Dies in Sweden." *Los Angeles Times*, August 7, 1938.

"Oland and His Director Die Same Day." *Los Angeles Herald Examiner*, August 7, 1938.

Oliver, Myrna. "Pauline Moore, 87; Actress Made 25 B Movies in 1930s, Early '40s." *Los Angeles Times*, Monday, December 10, 2001.

Parsons, Louella O. "Helen Holmes Dies at 58." *Los Angeles Examiner*, July 10, 1950.

"Paul Hurst." *Variety*, March 3, 1953.

"Paul Panzer, Film Villain, Dies at 86." *Los Angeles Examiner*, August 17, 1958.

"Pearl White Dead: Ex-Star of Movies." *New York Times*, August 5, 1938.

"Peggy Snow, Ex-Star, Dies." *Los Angeles Examiner*, February 18, 1958.

"Ralph Graves." *Variety*, February 25, 1977.

"Rawlinson [Herbert], Film Actor, Dies at 67." *Hollywood Citizen-News*, July 13, 1953.

"Ray Corrigan." *Variety*, August 18, 1976.

"Rites Set for 'Hazards of Helen' Star." *Los Angeles Daily News*, July 10, 1950.

Salsinger, Harry, "Death Lifts Tom Tyler from Detroit Obscurity." *The Detroit News*, May 4, 1954.

"Services for Arline Pretty, 92, Star of Silent Movies, Slated." *Los Angeles Times*, April 19, 1978.

"Silent Film Star's [Ruth Stonehouse] Last Rites Awaited." *Hollywood Citizen-News*, May 14, 1941.

"Silent Film Actress [Rhea Mitchell] Slain." *Los Angeles Examiner*, September 17, 1957.

"Stage and Film Veteran William Desmond Dies." *Los Angeles Times*, April 1949.

Stewart, Bill. "Chapter 13 [obituary information on 26 serial performers]." *TEMI*, Chp. 9, Vol. 1 (February–March 1971), 116–117.

"Stunt Star Eddie Polo Dies at 86." *Los Angeles Mirror*, June 15, 1961.

Talbert, Bob. "Bill [Kennedy] is Gone, But if You Hear a Whistle…." *Detroit Free Press*, January 28, 1997.

"Tom Mix." *The New York Times*, October 13, 1940.

"Tom Tyler, Film Cowboy Made Famous by TV, Dies." *Hollywood Citizen-News*, May 3, 1954.

Townsend, Dorothy. "Jack Mulhall, 91, Movie, Stage, TV Actor, Dies." *Los Angeles Times*, June 7, 1979.

"20s Star Grange [Red], 87, Dies." *Los Angeles Times*, January 29, 1991.

"Veteran Film Actor Herbert Rawlinson Dies." *Los Angeles Times*, July 13, 1953.

"Victor Jory, 79, Found Dead; Veteran Bad Guy of the Films." *New York Times*, February 13, 1982.

Victorek, D. "Dave O'Brien." *Classic Film Collector*, No. 26, Winter 1970.

"Warren Hull, Vet of Radio-Pix-TV Dies." *Variety*, September 17, 1974.

"Wild Bill Elliott." *Variety*, December 1, 1965.

"William Desmond, Actor, Dies." *Los Angeles Examiner*, November 4, 1949.

"William Desmond Heart Victim at Age of 71." *Variety*, November 4, 1949.

Serial Synopses

Adams, Les. "The Lone Ranger — the Serial." *Memory Lane* (September 1980).

_____ and Rob Tucker. "Wild Bill Hickok." "Overland with Kit Carson." and "Valley of Vanishing Men." *Yesterday's Saturdays*, No. 18 (1982).

"Batman and Robin." *Screen Thrills Illustrated* (April 1983, pp. 10–15; July 1963, pp. 12–16.

Behlmer, Rudy. "The Saga of Flash Gordon." *Screen Facts*, Vol. 2, No. 4 (1965) 53–62.

Cline, William C. "Flash Gordon's Trip to Mars." *TEMI*, Chp. 14, Vol. 2, No. 4 (December 1971–January 1972) 189–192; and Chp. 15, Vol. 2, No. 5 (February–March 1972).

Dellinger, Paul. "The Adventures of Captain Marvel." *Cliffhanger*, No. 2 (Spring 1983) 5–21.

_____. "The Adventures of Red Ryder." *Cliffhanger*, No. 11, pp. 5–18.

_____. "Atom Man vs. Superman." *Cliffhanger*, No. 18, pp. 5–12.

_____. "Black Arrow." *Cliffhanger*, No. 3 1984.

_____. "Blackhawk." *Cliffhanger*, No. 6, pp. 5–23.

_____. "Daredevils of the Red Circle." *Cliffhanger*, No. 5, pp. 42–58.

_____. "Mysterious Doctor Satan." *Cliffhanger*, No. 14, pp. 4–18.

_____. "Radar Men from the Moon." *Cliffhanger*, No. 9, pp. 7–22.

_____. "Return of Captain America." *Cliffhanger*, No. 7, pp. 5–15.

_____. "Riders of Death Valley." *Under Western Skies*, No. 28 (August 1984) 58–74.

_____. "The Spider Returns." *Cliffhanger*, No. 5, pp. 5–17.

_____. "Spy Smasher." *Cliffhanger*, No. 7, pp. 29–44.

_____. "The Superman Saga." *Cliffhanger*, No. 12, pp. 27–44.

_____. "The Three Musketeers." *Cliffhanger*, No. 20, pp. 11–26.

_____. "Zorro Rides Again." *Cliffhanger*, No. 9, pp. 29–40.

"Dick Tracy Returns." *Variety*, August 10, 1938.

"Fighting Devil Dogs." *Variety*, May 18, 1938.

"Gordon of Ghost City." *Boys Cinema*, Nos. 735–745 (12 parts), January 6, 1934 through March 24, 1934.

Hise, Jim Van. "The Fighting Devil Dogs." *Film Collectors Registry*, Vol. 6, No. 11 (November 1974).

Hoffman, Eric. "Drums of Fu Manchu." *Serial World*, No. 28 (Fall 1981) 6–9.

_____. "Daredevils of the Red Circle." *Serial World*, No. 35 (Summer 1983) 3–8, 17.

_____ and Bob Malcomson. "Dick Tracy Returns." *TEMI*, Chp. 14, Vol. 2, No. 4 (December 1971–January 1972).

_____ and Bob Malcomson. "Dick Tracy's G-Men." *TEMI*, Chp. 18, Vol. 2, No. 8 (Aug–September 1972) 250–255.

_____ and Bob Malcomson. "Drums of Fu Manchu." *TEMI*, Chp. 20, Vol. 2, No. 10 (December 1972–January 1973) 284–290.

_____ and Bob Malcomson. "Hawk of the Wilderness." *TEMI*, Chp. 15, Vol. 2, No. 5 (February–March 1972) 206–210.

_____ and Bob Malcomson. "The Lone Ranger Rides Again." *TEMI*, Chp. 16, Vol. 2, No. 6 (April–May 1972) 218–220.

_____. "The Spider's Web." *Serial World*, No. 30, Vol. 4 (Spring 1982) 6–15; No. 31, Vol. 4 (Summer 1982) 9–12.

"Holt of the Secret Service." Serial Quarterly, Vol. 2, No. 3, pp 41–60.

Kelez, Steve. "Captain America." *Film Fan Monthly*, No. 61/62 (July/August 1966) 25–26.

Bob Malcomson. "Adventures of Captain Marvel." TEMI, Chp. 21, Vol. 3, No. 1 (February–March 1973) 298–304.

_____. "Dick Tracy vs. Crime, Inc." TEMI, Chp. 28, Vol. 3, No. 8, pp. 420–423.

_____. "The Fighting Devil Dogs." TEMI, Chp. 13, Vol. 2, No. 3 (Oct–Nov 1971) 170–174.

_____ and Eric Hoffman. "Spy Smasher." TEMI, Chp. 29, Vol. 3, No. 9, 434–437.

McCleary, Charles. "The Sea Hound." *Serial World*, No. 32 pp. 18–22.

Newton, Mike. "Riders of Death Valley." *Classic Images* (November 1999) 18.

Parkhurst, C. M. and Eric Hoffman. "The Fighting Devil Dogs." TEMI, Chp. 13, Vol. 2, No. 3 (October–November 1971) 170–174.

"Patria." *New York Times* December 4, 1918.

Price, Bob. "King of Jungleland." *Screen Thrills Illustrated* (September 1962) 20–25.

_____. "The Man Behind the Mask." *Screen Thrills Illustrated* (August 1964) 7–15.

_____. "Serial Queens." *Screen Thrills Illustrated* (January 1963) 12–18.

_____. "Shazam." *Screen Thrills Illustrated* (September 1962) 12–19.

Rainey, Buck. "The Ace of Scotland Yard." *Westerns and Serials*, No. 33, pp. 22–24.

_____. "The Black Book." *Serial World*, No. 33 (Winter 1983) 23–24.

_____. "Blake of Scotland Yard." *Westerns and Serials Combined Issue*, FW #31; SW #51 (1989) 18–19.

_____. "The Fast Express." *Serial World*, No. 34 (Spring 1983) 46–50.

_____. "A Final Reckoning." *Cliffhanger*, No. 14, pp. 43–45.

_____. "The Fire Fighters." *Serial World*, No. 32 (Fall 1982) 11–12.

_____. "Perils of the Wild." *Cliffhanger*, No. 12, pp. 15–18.

_____. "The Roaring West." *Cliffhanger*, No. 124, pp. 57–62.

_____. "Tarzan the Mighty." *Cliffhanger*, No. 12 (1990) 45–50.

_____. "Tarzan the Tiger." *Cliffhanger*, No. 12 (1990) 51–56.

"The Return of Chandu." *Screen World*, No. 21 (Winter 1980) 14–19.

Rutherford, John H. "The Adventures of Sir Galahad." *Cliffhanger*, No. 3 (1984) 5–22.

_____. "Undersea Kingdom: Sci-Fi in the Serials." *Cliffhanger*, No. 5, pp. 27–33.

Schaefer, Randall. "Ace Drummond." *Cliffhanger*, No. 20, pp. 29–46.

_____. "Daughter of Don Q." *Cliffhanger*, No. 16, pp. 45–57.

_____. "Dick Tracy." *Cliffhanger*, No. 22, pp. 5–40.

_____. "The Lost City." *Cliffhanger*, No. 18, pp. 23–31.

"The Secret Code." *Serial Quarterly*, Vol. 2, No. 1 (January–March 1967) 18 pp.

Serial Quarterly No. 1: "Daredevils of the Red Circle." "Overland with Kit Carson." "King of the Carnival." "Atom Man vs. Superman." "Trader Tom of the China Sea." "Adventures of Frank and Jesse James." and "Blake of Scotland Yard." (January–March 1966).

Serial Quarterly No. 2: "Son of Geronimo." "Terry and the Pirates." "Shadow of Chinatown." and "Brick Bradford" (April–June 1966).

Serial Quarterly No. 3: "The Lone Ranger Rides Again." "The Spider Returns." "King of the Royal Mounted." "Junior G-Men of the Air." and "Batman and Robin" (1966).

Serial Quarterly No. 4: "Haunted Harbor." "Blackhawk." "Perils of Thunder Mountain." and "The Sea Hound" (October–December 1966).

Serial Quarterly No. 5: "G-Men vs. the Black Dragon." "The Secret Code." "The Green Archer." and "Deadwood Dick" (January–March 1967).

Serial Quarterly No. 6: "Buck Rogers." "Congo Bill." "Mysterious Island." "Jungle Raiders." and "Captain Marvel." (April–June 1967).

Serial Quarterly No. 7: "Adventures of Red Ryder." "Jungle Queen." "The Vigilante." and "Holt of the Secret Service" (1967).

Spencer, Gary. "The Last Frontier." *Westerns and Serials*, No. 35.

Stringham, Jim. "Beasts of Paradise." *Westerns and Serials*, No. 29, pp. 34–38.

_____. "Blake of Scotland Yard." Serial World No. 32 (Fall 1983) 23–26; No. 33 (Winter 1983) 4–9.

_____. "Captain Video." *Westerns and Serials*, No. 37, 38.

_____. "Deadwood Dick." TEMI, Chp. 28, Vol. 3, No. 8, pp. 427–428.

_____. "A Fine Crop of Lemons." *Film Fan Monthly* (May 1967) 10–11.

_____. "The Ghost City." *Westerns and Serials*, No. 39, pp. H21–H25.

_____. "The Great Adventures of Wild Bill Hickok." *Serial World*, No. 9 (Winter 1977) 12–23.

_____. "Heroes of the West." *Favorite Westerns*, Nos. 2 and 3 (two parts).

_____. "Jungle Girl." TEMI, Chp. 25, Vol. 3, No. 5, pp. 362–365.

_____. "Jungle Goddess." *Westerns and Serials*, Nos. 34, 35, pp. 44–51.

_____. "Radio Patrol." *Serial World*, No.12 (Fall 1977) 4–10.

_____. "The Secret of Treasure Island." TEMI, Vol. 2, No. 3 (October–November 1971).

_____. "Tarzan the Tiger." *Favorite Westerns*, No. 25, pp. 7–11.

_____. "The Tiger Woman." *Serial Classics*, Vol. 1, No. 1 (collectors edition) 11–17.

_____. "The Whispering Shadow." TEMI, Chp.28, Vol. 3, No. 8, pp. 429–430.

"Superman." *Screen Thrills Illustrated* (June 1962,

30–37; September 1962, 42–48; January 1963, 52–57).

Thornton, Jimmy. "The Green Hornet." *TEMI*, Chp. 25, Vol. 3, No. 5, pp. 370–373.

"Tim Tyler's Luck." *TEMI*, Vol. 2, No. 3 (October–November 1971) 181–182.

Van Hise, James. "The Spider's Web." *Film Collector's Registry*, Vol. 7, No. 4 (April 1995).

Vivian, Ronald. "The Phantom Empire." *Serial World*, No. 19 (Summer 1979) 4–14.

Weathers, Stormy. "The Phantom." *Cliffhanger*, No. 4 (1983) 19–35.

Weaver, Tom. "The Crimson Ghost." *Serial World*, Part I, No. 24 (Fall 1980); Part II, No. 25 (Winter 1981).

"What Happened to Mary?" *The Ladies World* (August 1912 and following months).

Wyatt, Ed. "The Eagle's Talons." *Films of the Golden Age* (Winter 1996) 82–83.

"Zorro's Fighting Legion." *TEMI*, Chp. 19, Vol. 2, No. 9 (October–November 1972), 262–272.

Index